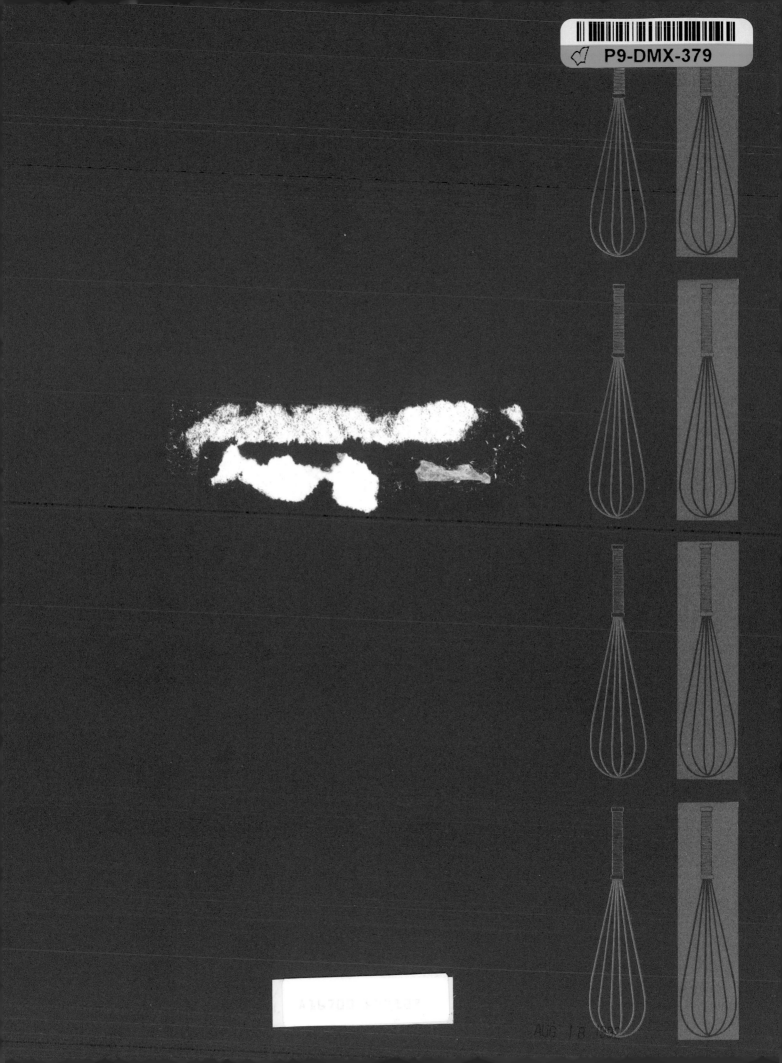

LAVARENNE
PRATIQUE

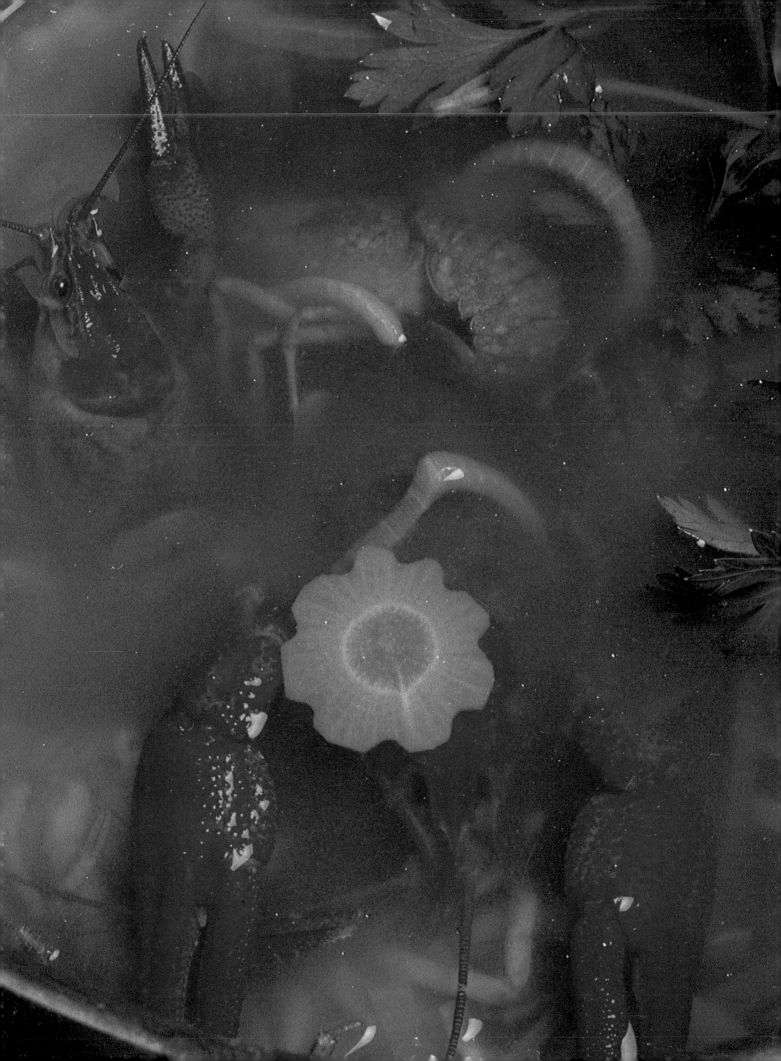

LaVarenne
PRATIQUE

The Complete Illustrated Cooking Course

techniques, ingredients, and tools
of classic modern cuisine

ANNE WILLAN

Crown Publishers, Inc., New York

Published in the United States by Crown Publishers, Inc., 201 East 50th Street, New York, New York 10022.

Published in Great Britain by Dorling Kindersley publishers Limited

CROWN is a trademark of Crown Publishers, Inc.
Printed and bound by Mondadori, Verona

Library of Congress Cataloging-in-Publication Data

Willan, Anne
La Varenne Pratique / by Anne Willan
p. cm.
1. Cookery. 1. Title
TX719.W5693 1989 89-1428
641.5944—dc20

ISBN 0-517-57383-0
First American Edition
10 9 8 7 6 5 4 3 2 1

Typeset by Tradespools Ltd.
Reproduced by Colourscan, Singapore

For the conception and planning of *La Varenne Pratique* Anne Willan would like to thank Jonathan Clowes and Jill Norman. For its production, she has been privileged to work with a wide range of talent. The contribution of those listed below is recorded with appreciation.
Chief editor: Amanda Phillips Manheim
Consultant editors: Mark Cherniavsky, Henry Grossi, Barbara Wheaton.
Contributing author: Barbara Kafka (Microwave Cooking)
Techniques demonstrated by: Chef Claude Vauguet, Director of cuisine at Ecole de Cuisine La Varenne, Paris and Burgundy, assisted by Pastry Chef Laurent Terrasson.
Assistant editors: Laura Garrett. Martha Holmberg.
Additional research and editorial help from Caroline Allen, Jane Bradley, Suzanne McLees, Eileen O'Hara, Margaret Smalec, and Laura Estrin Washburn
Nutritional consultant: Carol Gvozdich.
Recipe testing and development: Henry Grossi, Randall Price

Technique photography by Jerry Young
Recipe photography by Martin Brigdale
Dishes prepared by Jane Suthering
Stylists Gina Carminati, Andrea Lambton
Ingredients photography and research on mushrooms and herbs by Roger Phillips
Photographic research (New York) by Charles L. Pierce
Ingredients photography (New York) by Anthony Johnson
Illustrators: Fiona Bell Curry (pp.200–207), John Hutchinson (diagrams)
Art directed by Jacquie Gulliver
Project editor: Emma Johnson
Senior editor: Anderley Moore
Editors: Caroline Ollard, Deirdre McGarry, Linda Sonntag, Brigid Bell, Sarah Reid Pitcher
Designers: Ann Terrell, Ann Cannings, Sarah Ponder, Jane Taft, Peggy Sadler, Colin Walton, Hannah Moore
Managing editor: Victoria Davenport
Consultant editor: Jill Norman
American editor: Erica Marcus
Jacket design: Nancy Kenmore

For researching and drafting the following chapters Anne Willan owes a special debt to the following contributors:
Henry Grossi: *Soups and Stocks, Pasta, Herbs, Spices and Flavorings, Kitchen Equipment.*
Faye Levy: *Sugar and Chocolate, Fats and Oils.*
Amanda Phillips Manheim: *Vegetables, Fruit and Nuts, Grains and Legumes.*
Steve Raichlen: *Flour, Breads, and Batters.*
Lyn Stallworth and Martha Holmberg: *Preserving and Freezing.*

Anne Willan would also like to acknowledge expert review and guidance from Geoff Palmer (plant science) and Jon Rowley (fish) and further help on specific topics from Shirley Corriher, Elisabeth Evans, Judith Hill, Susan Stuck, and Nahum Waxman.

Sources of technical or commercial information consulted in the USA include: American Meat Institute; California Sunshine Fine Foods; Fisheries Development Foundations; Fleischmann's Yeast; Flying Food; Frieda's Finest; Lundberg Family Farms; National Meat and Livestock Board; Rodale Institute; South Mills Mushrooms Sales; The Sugar Institute; United Dairy Industry Association; United Fresh Fruit and Vegetables Association; United States Department of Commerce, Office of Fisheries; University of Maryland, Department of Horticulture; Paradise Bay Co., Washington for supplying fresh salmon. In Britain, special acknowledgements are due to Department of Zoology, British Museum (Natural History) for expert help and advice; Elizabeth David Cookshop, Covent Garden, for supplying kitchen equipment; The Mushroom Growers' Association.

Preface

In the past 30 years I have had the good fortune to work in food and in cooking in three different countries – France, Great Britain and the United States. This book is the distillation of that experience. It is also the fruit of almost continuous writing and research, much of it associated with La Varenne, the cooking school which I founded in Paris in 1975.

As its name implies, *La Varenne Pratique* is a book for the practicing cook. The point of departure is that mastery of ingredients is as important to success in the kitchen as mastery of technique. In each chapter, therefore, we consider carefully how to choose ingredients, how to store them, and indeed how to identify them in the first place. Modern technology has, in effect, transformed how we stock our kitchen and how we handle and prepare our food.

Allied with good ingredients must be a knowledge of technique, and it is here that French skill comes into play. The action photographs in this book were shot with French chefs in the heart of France, yet the techniques they demonstrate have universal application, covering such basics as chopping an onion, as well as the complexities of boning a rabbit and tempering chocolate. The principles of cooking apply equally to English roast beef and to a Texas barbecue.

With a knowledge of ingredients and technique, recipes follow naturally. You'll find a few of them here to illustrate possibilities, together with lists of many more ideas from around the world. *La Varenne Pratique* celebrates the pleasures of the table inside and outside the kitchen. It is dedicated to those who love to cook, and those who love to eat. To you all, bon appetit!

ANNE WILLAN   Paris, May 1989

Contents

PART *1*

HERBS, SPICES & FLAVORINGS 12

Choosing and handling herbs; alliums; fragile herbs; robust herbs; rare herbs; lemon-flavored herbs; herbs used as leaf and seed; choosing and handling spices; seeds as spices; fragrant spices; hot spices; salty flavorings; olives; capers; table sauces; essences and extracts; coffee and tea; cooking with wines and spirits; vinegar; marinades.

STOCKS & SOUPS 42

Making stocks and broths; white and brown stocks; fish stock; *court bouillon*; broth-based soups; consommé; bread-thickened soups; fish and shellfish soups; bisques; gumbos; puréed soups; enrichments to soup; cream soups; cold soups.

SAUCES 52

Whisking and straining sauces; mounting with butter, coating with sauce; white sauces; roux; brown sauces; last-minute thickeners; emulsified butter sauces; mayonnaise; vinaigrette and other salad dressings; bread-thickened sauces; tomato sauces; barbecue sauces; nut sauces; savory and sweet fruit sauces; custard and other sweet sauces.

MILK, CHEESE & EGGS 68

Milk and cream; sour cream, yogurt and buttermilk; cheese in cooking; goat, sheep and buffalo cheeses; fresh cheeses; soft cheeses; blue cheeses; hard cheeses; high-fat cheeses; whipping eggs; boiled eggs; exotic eggs; poached eggs; scrambled eggs; baked eggs; fried eggs; omelets; soufflés; savory and sweet baked custards; caramel custards.

FATS & OILS 96

Structure of fats and oils; saturation values; animal fats; rendering fat; butter; margarine; olive oil; general-purpose oils; flavoring oils; exotic oils; making infused oils; deep-frying; coating foods with flour, egg and breadcrumbs; batters; sautéed and pan-fried foods; savory croquettes and fritters.

PART *2*

FISH 110

Trimming, scaling, gutting, boning, filleting and skinning fish; cooking methods; small flat-fish; large flat-fish; ray and skate; caviar and other roes; shark and sturgeon; meaty fish; monkfish; firm white fish; flaky white fish; the cod family; thin-bodied fish; bony fish; salmon and trout; freshwater fish; rich oily fish; long-bodied fish.

SHELLFISH 152

Cooking methods; crustaceans: lobster, crab, shrimp, prawns and scampi, crayfish; mollusks: univalves – conch, abalone, snails; bivalves – oysters, scallops, clams and cockles, mussels; cephalopods: squid, octopus and cuttlefish; frogs; exotic sea-creatures.

Contents

POULTRY & GAME BIRDS 174

Singeing and drawing poultry; cutting a bird in half or in pieces; boning a whole bird; boning poultry breasts; trussing a bird; skinning a bird; spatchcocking a bird; cooking methods; chicken; turkey; duck; goose; game birds; barding and tying small birds; plucking a bird; exotic game birds.

MEAT & CHARCUTERIE 194

Meat preparation techniques; cooking methods; beef cuts; veal cuts; lamb cuts; pork cuts; variety meats; furred game; terrines and pâtés; raised meat pies; *pâtés en croûte*; sausages; bacon and cured pork; ham; other cured meats; aspic; *galantines* and *ballotines*.

PART 3

VEGETABLES 258

Preparing and cooking vegetables; salad greens; hearty greens; cabbage; broccoli and cauliflower; fruit vegetables; cucumber; okra; beans, peas and sweet corn; squashes; the onion family; roots and tubers; stalks and shoots; globe artichoke; exotic vegetables.

MUSHROOMS 304

Handling, preparing and cooking mushrooms; the common cultivated mushroom; other cultivated mushrooms; wild mushrooms; truffles.

GRAINS & LEGUMES 314

Cooking methods for grains; wild rice; rice; wheat and corn; couscous; buckwheat and millet; barley, oats and rye; unusual grains; cooking methods for legumes; soy beans; kidney beans; unusual legumes; lentils and peas; chickpeas; fava and lima beans; sprouts.

PASTA 328

Pasta shapes; eggless pasta; egg pasta; baked pasta; stuffed pasta; kneading, rolling and cutting dough; sandwich-stuffed pasta; pasta sauces; dumplings.

PART 4

FLOUR, BREADS & BATTERS 342

Wheat flour; non-wheat flours; ingredients for breads; using yeast; mixing and kneading dough; shaping loaves and rolls; baking bread; simple yeast breads; rich yeast breads; yeastless breads; fried bread and fritters; flatbreads; bread stuffings; bread puddings; crêpes; pancakes and batter puddings.

PASTRY & COOKIES 370

Pie pastry, *pâte brisée* and *pâte sucrée*; lining tart pans; baking blind; choux pastry; puff pastry; strudel and leaved pastries; sweet fillings; pastry cream; glazes for pastry; techniques with cookies; rolled and molded cookies; drop and wafer cookies; bar cookies; crackers.

Contents

CAKES & ICINGS 390

Cake-making techniques; lining cake pans; folding cake batter; unmolding cakes; slicing into horizontal layers; whisked cakes; creamed cakes; layer cakes; melted cakes; meringue cakes; cheesecakes; small cakes; butter cream; soft icings; royal icing; almond paste; whipped frostings.

SUGAR & CHOCOLATE 411

Types of sugar; sugar syrups; spun sugar; fondant; caramel; praline and nougatine; types of chocolate; tempering chocolate; chocolate decorations; chocolate sauces; boiled sugar candies; dipped and filled chocolates.

COLD DESSERTS & ICE CREAMS 430

Molded gelatin desserts; charlottes and creams; cold mousses and soufflés; meringue; other cold desserts; sorbet; ice cream; bombes, parfaits and frozen soufflés.

FRUIT & NUTS 446

Choosing and cooking fruit; apples; pears; rhubarb; citrus; grapes; berries; stone fruits; bananas; tropical fruits; avocado; pomegranate; persimmon; exotic fruits; figs; dates; frosting; candying; shelling and skinning nuts; nut butter; nut milk; toasting nuts; preparing coconut and chestnuts.

PART 5

PRESERVING & FREEZING 484

Drying; preserving in alcohol; preserving with fat; smoking; salting and brining; making gravad lax; pickles and chutneys; jams, jellies and marmalades; testing pectin; extracting juice for jelly; testing for jell point; fruit butters and cheeses; canning; freezing.

MICROWAVE COOKING 497

The possibilities of microwave cooking; cooking in a microwave oven; microwave cookware; adapting recipes for the microwave oven; seasoning food for the microwave oven.

COOKING EQUIPMENT 502

Materials for cookware; weighing and measuring tools; spoons, whisks and piercing tools; cutting tools; bowls; drainers, grinders and puréeing tools; pasta tools; wrappers; pastry tools; molds and baking pans; electric machines; ice cream machines; pots; oven cookware; special-purpose tools.

GLOSSARY OF CULINARY TERMS 512

INDEX 515

Weights and measures

LIQUID STANDARDS
1 ml = 0.035 fl oz
1 fl oz = 30 ml
1 US pint = 16 fl oz
1 UK pint = 20 fl oz
500 ml = 16 fl oz = 2 cups
1 tsp = 5 ml spoon
1 tbsp = 15 ml spoon
1 liter = 1 quart

SOLID WEIGHT STANDARDS
1 g = 0.35 oz
1 oz = 30 g
5 tbsp = ⅓ cup

SOLID WEIGHT CONVERSIONS

ingredients	US cups	metric	imperial
FLOUR	¼ cup	30 g	1 oz
	⅓ cup	45 g	1½ oz
	½ cup	60 g	2 oz
	⅔ cup	90 g	3 oz
	¾ cup	100 g	3¼ oz
	1 cup	125 g	4 oz (¼ lb)
	2 cups	250 g	8 oz (½ lb)
SUGAR	¼ cup	50 g	1¾ oz
	⅓ cup	60 g	2 oz
	½ cup	100 g	3¼ oz
	⅔ cup	135 g	4½ oz
	¾ cup	150 g	5 oz
	1 cup	200 g	6½ oz
BUTTER	¼ cup (4 tbsp)	60 g	2 oz
	⅓ cup	75 g	2½ oz
	½ cup (8 tbsp)	125 g	4 oz (¼ lb)
	⅔ cup	150 g	5 oz
	¾ cup	180 g	6 oz
	1 cup	250 g	8 oz (½ lb)
BREADCRUMBS (fresh)	1 cup	75 g	2½ oz
(dried)	1 cup	140 g	4½ oz
CHEESE (grated cheddar)	1 cup	75 g	2⅔ oz
(soft ricotta)	1 cup	160 g	5⅓ oz
RICE (uncooked)	1 cup	210 g	7 oz
(cooked)	1 cup	165 g	5½ oz
ALMONDS (whole)	1 cup	180 g	6 oz
(sliced)	1 cup	90 g	3 oz
(chopped)	1 cup	135 g	4½ oz
WALNUTS	1 cup	120 g	4 oz
HAZELNUTS	1 cup	130 g	4⅓ oz
RAISINS	1 cup	140 g	4½ oz

LIQUID CONVERSIONS

US cups	metric	imperial
2 tbsp	30 ml	1 fl oz
¼ cup	60 ml	2 fl oz
⅓ cup	70 ml	2½ fl oz
½ cup	125 ml	4 fl oz
⅔ cup	150 ml	5 fl oz
¾ cup	175 ml	6 fl oz
1 cup	250 ml	8 fl oz
1½ cups	375 ml	12 fl oz
2 cups (US pint)	500 ml	16 fl oz
2½ cups	600 ml	20 fl oz (UK pint)
3 cups	750 ml	25 fl oz
4 cups (US quart)	1 liter	33 fl oz

OVEN TEMPERATURE CONVERSIONS

°F	°C	gas
225	110	¼
250	120	½
275	140	1
300	150	2
325	160	3
350	175	4
375	190	5
400	200	6
425	220	7
450	230	8
475	240	9
500	260	10

LENGTH CONVERSIONS

1 cm = 0.394 inch
1 inch = 2.54 cm

1

page

HERBS SPICES & FLAVORINGS 12

STOCKS & SOUPS 42

SAUCES 52

MILK, CHEESE & EGGS 68

FATS & OILS 96

HERBS, SPICES & FLAVORINGS

HERBS, SPICES and flavorings are scarcely considered basic ingredients, yet we cannot cook successfully without them. Food would be dull indeed without the zest added by a sprinkling of herbs, a teaspoon of spice or a few drops of vanilla. Some flavorings are akin to salt and pepper, used as highly concentrated seasoning. They develop and heighten the flavor of other ingredients, rather than stand on their own. Other more perfumed additions such as saffron, wine and rose water flavor food with their own distinctive character. Significantly, the French word for flavoring is *parfum*. It is important that no flavoring should be overused; too many herbs or too much spice is worse than too little.

The distinguishing features of an herb are that it is green and leafy, may be eaten fresh or dried, and can be grown in temperate regions. A spice is the dried and sometimes ground seed, root, bark or stem of a plant grown in the tropics. Many herbs and spices, however, do not conform to these broad descriptions and some plants, such as coriander, serve as both herb and spice.

Flavoring principles

The expression "season to taste" appears in many recipes. It usually means that a dish should be tasted and the seasoning adjusted with salt and pepper. However, this narrow definition may be widened to include sugar where appropriate, and any herb, spice or flavoring already in the recipe. Since the taste of the ingredients can vary, as can the strength of the flavorings themselves, exact amounts cannot be specified. In the end, the amount of flavoring a dish will require is a matter of judgement, depending on individual preference and how the taste buds are stimulated. (Sour-sweet flavors are sensed at the front of the tongue, sour-saltiness on the side, and bitterness at the back.)

A careful cook tastes a dish not only when finished but throughout the cooking process. If seasoning is added only at the end of cooking, it may not have time to interact with the other ingredients and will be overpowering. On occasion, a flavoring may be deliberately added at the last moment in order to heighten its effect. Such is the case with Madeira added to a brown sauce just before serving. There are also some flavorings (notably ground pepper and certain fragile herbs such as mint and chervil) that lose their impact if heated for too long.

Some dishes always need more flavoring than others. Sauces and stuffings, which are typically paired with food that is bland, will need more seasoning than a soup that is served alone. Delicate steamed fish needs less seasoning than a robust beef stew. Remember that cold food requires more flavoring than hot, and iced dishes require most of all. If more intensity is desired in a dish, an extra pinch of salt is often the best way to draw out other flavors. Similarly, a teaspoon of sugar can enhance the flavor of fruits and sweet desserts. A pinch or two of sugar even enhances the flavor of savory salads, vegetables and meat stews.

In a menu, courses with more subtle flavors should be served ahead of more dominant ones. For this reason, meat traditionally follows fish, while cheese and sweet desserts with a lingering flavor are served at the end of the meal.

HERBS

Many herbs grow wild in the benign climate of southern Europe, and are cultivated in the less hospitable north. Colonial settlers brought their plants to the New World, growing them primarily for medicine, but also for dyeing clothes and for the kitchen. Despite this migration, many herbs are still firmly identified with the cuisines of particular countries. Rosemary tends to be associated with Italian roast and grilled meats, rigani (a type of oregano) with Greek lamb dishes, and dill with Scandinavian fish and vegetables. Nowadays, herbs are so widely available that only a few are restricted to a single country or area and some, like thyme, parsley and bay leaf, have become truly international. There are also herbs that complement certain foods – for example, the classic combination of mint sauce with roast lamb or chicken with tarragon. Herbs behave like all leafy plants. They sprout in spring, flourish through summer, flower, and then go to seed. Herbs such as thyme, mint and rosemary are perennials, returning every year from the same root. Others must be grown from seed each season as annuals: basil, summer savory and coriander are examples. A few herbs are biennials and have a two-year growth cycle. Parsley is an example, although it is better grown as an annual because its leaves are less flavorful in the second year.

Choosing fresh herbs

Most herbs are at their best just before flowering, and this is a critical time for herb gardeners, since the plant's energy is devoted to producing blossoms, to the detriment of the leaves. To overcome this problem, gardeners often nip off the buds before they bloom, forcing the plant to continue producing leaves. All herbs are best picked fresh during the summer, but the most popular varieties are now available from nurseries year-round, grown in greenhouses or imported from more temperate regions. For flavor, herbs grown outdoors always rank first, though many can be grown indoors, especially those that are short and bushy or trail easily from hanging baskets.

When shopping for fresh herbs, look for healthy sprigs that are strong in fragrance with no hint of mustiness. Avoid bouquets with dried ends, discolored leaves or wilted stems. Any leaves should stay firmly attached when the sprig is shaken, especially those with woody stems, like thyme and rosemary.

Storing fresh herbs

To store fresh herbs with short stems, put them in an unsealed plastic bag or wrap them in a moist paper towel and refrigerate them. They should keep for about a week. Herbs with longer stems can be treated like cut flowers: put them in a small container of water and leave them at room temperature, or refrigerate them, covered with a loose plastic bag. Herbs with their roots intact are best of all; wrap the roots in a damp paper towel, cover with a plastic bag, leaving the leaves outside, and then refrigerate.

Cooking with fresh herbs

The taste of any herb is most characteristic when it is uncooked. Puréed raw herbs form the base of various green sauces (p.64) and chopped raw herbs feature in other cold sauces. Whole leaves may be used in salads and as a decoration.

Not all herbs behave in the same way during cooking: fragile herbs such as parsley and tarragon, whose volatile oils dissipate rapidly when heated, are always added toward the end of cooking. More robust herbs (for example, thyme and rosemary) benefit from lengthy cooking since their flavors infuse a dish more slowly. The stems may be included for extra flavor in a cooked dish, and discarded before serving. As herbs vary in strength depending on the circumstances of their cultivation and method of packaging, always be prepared to adjust the quantities given in the recipe.

Whether the leaves of an herb are coarsely cut, chopped, or ground to a paste can significantly affect flavor. When they are lightly shredded in a chiffonade (p.259) the volatile oils are not extracted. Chopping bruises the leaves of more fragile herbs but has little effect on robust ones. However, when herbs are ground in a mortar and pestle or food processor, this releases the oils and intensifies their value as a flavoring. This is particularly noticeable when they are used uncooked, as in *pesto* sauce (p.17).

Preserving fresh herbs

Any herb to be preserved should be at the height of its flavor – for most varieties this is just before they flower. Choose the healthiest-looking growth and discard any damaged leaves. If you are gathering herbs from your garden, the best time to pick them is in the morning, after the dew has evaporated and when the essential oils are warmed, but before the drying sunlight of afternoon. Avoid washing the leaves unless absolutely necessary; simply wipe off any soil or grit that adheres.

The oldest method for preserving herbs is drying, while the most modern is freezing. Herbs can also be preserved as herb vinegar (p.41). Large-leaved herbs, like sage, can be stored in a jar covered with an all-purpose oil or layered and covered with coarse salt. They will keep for months and yield an added bonus of flavored oil or salt. See also Preserving and Freezing (p.484).

CHOPPING FRESH HERBS

There are several ways in which fresh herbs can be chopped. A food processor can be used, or a chef's knife (p.504), or a two-handled mincing knife (It. *mezzaluna*). For use as a garnish, herbs can also be shredded into a chiffonade (Vegetables, p.259).

Using a food processor Strip the leaves from the stems and put them in the food processor. Turn the machine on and off in short spurts, chopping the leaves to the desired consistency. Take care not to over-chop them as this will reduce the herbs to a purée.

Using a chef's knife

Strip the leaves from the stems and pile them on a cutting board. Cut the herbs into small pieces, holding the tip of the blade against the board and rocking the handle up and down. Chop the herbs coarsely or finely, as you wish. **Note** The knife must be sharp, otherwise you will bruise the herbs rather than cut them.

Using a two-handled mincing knife

1 Cut through the pile of herbs, rocking the knife to and fro without lifting it, and moving it gradually across the board.

2 Continue chopping until the herbs are the texture you want – either coarse or fine.

Choosing and storing dried herbs

Dried herbs should be vivid, not faded. Look for whole leaf herbs in preference to chopped herbs in glass bottles. Store them in sealed containers in a cool, dry place away from light. Dried herbs will gradually lose their aroma and should be used within a year.

The flavor of most herbs is about twice as strong when they are dried as when they are fresh. Fragile herbs like mint and basil, however, lose their intensity when dried and are best used fresh.

Drying herbs

Drying herbs is easy if you have a place, such as a shed or porch, that is well-ventilated, dry and warm. It should be light but shaded from direct sunlight, which bleaches the flavor and color of herbs. Herbs such as bay are almost always used dried; thyme, marjoram, and rose-mary are also well suited to drying. Fragile herbs do not dry well. Tie the herbs in bunches and hang them upside down. To prevent them getting dusty, the bunches may be tied inside paper bags cut with air holes. After about a week, the herbs should be completely dry; leave them in sprigs or store in airtight containers.

HERB MIXTURES

Often required in slowly cooked dishes, a bouquet garni always includes sprigs of thyme and parsley and a bay leaf, tied together with string or wrapped in cheesecloth. Sometimes a piece of leek green or a celery stalk is added for extra flavor, while bitter orange peel is a common addition in southern France. A bouquet garni can be made with dried herbs or bought pre-packaged, but is superior when made with fresh herbs. It is always removed before serving.

Three fresh herb combinations are commonly found in the kitchen. *Fines herbes* is a mixture of fresh chervil, chives and tarragon used raw, or added toward the end of cooking so it is scarcely heated. The herbs should always be fresh. Parsley may be added as well, or used alone instead of a dried *fines herbes* substitute. The second classic combination is a *persillade* of finely chopped parsley leaves and garlic or shallot, often added to sautéed meats and vegetables. It is only lightly cooked so that its fresh flavor is not lost. The Milanese *gremolata*, based on the acidic bite of lemon zest, used to include sage, rosemary and anchovy, but today it is most often limited to lemon, garlic and parsley. It is sprinkled over the braised veal shanks of *osso buco milanese* or other braised meat dishes just before serving so that the aroma of the citrus peel is retained.

Popular dried herb mixtures include *herbes de Provence*, a commercial mixture of thyme, savory and an anise-flavored herb such as fennel, perhaps with some sage, rosemary and bay leaf. Poultry seasoning is a commercial blend of ground rosemary, sage, ginger, oregano and black pepper intended to season roast poultry and stuffings. Salad seasoning is a similar dried product.

ALLIUMS

The onion family (*Allium*) provides some of our most familiar flavorings, including garlic, shallot and varieties of the onion itself. Chive, the only true herb of the family, is mild with a delicate "green" taste, while the others have a strong bite.

Some alliums can be used in small quantities as herbs. The green tops of scallions can take the place of chives, but they have a more pronounced onion flavor and should be used in smaller quantities. If young and tender, the pale-green inner leaves of leek can be chopped and eaten raw in salads, but are more often cooked like shallot. Rocambole, or giant garlic, develops mild-flavored edible bulbs and mauve flowers. It is seldom cultivated, however, and must be gathered in the wild. For the use of the onion family as vegetables, see Vegetables (p.289).

USEFUL INFORMATION

Season *Garlic and shallot:* summer to autumn. *Chives:* spring to autumn.
How to choose *Garlic and shallot:* compact bulbs, little dry skin. *Chives:* vivid green fresh leaves.
Problems *Garlic, shallot:* bitter if browned. *Chives:* snip with scissors to avoid bruising.

Processed forms *Garlic:* powder, minced, paste, preserved in oil. *Chives:* freeze-dried.
Storage *Garlic:* 2-3 months. *Shallot:* 1 month. *Chives, fresh:* refrigerate 5 days, freeze 6 months; *freeze-dried and bottled:* room temperature 1 year.

GARLIC

Renowned for its odor and mordant flavor, garlic is a staple in many cuisines, especially in Mediterranean and Asian countries. The three main types of garlic – white, violet and red-skinned – range from mild to strong. Elephant garlic, a giant variety, is the mildest of all and should be cooked as a vegetable.

The culinary value of garlic is as a seasoning and, when used moderately, it greatly enhances other flavors. It can also be used in larger quantities as a principal ingredient of Mediterranean sauces like *aïoli* (p.63) and *skordalia* (below). Raw garlic is most effective in a salad dressing or marinade. After long cooking, garlic mellows and sweetens. When frying, it must be cooked gently and quickly, as it burns easily and becomes acrid. For a mild garlic flavor, whole cloves can be lightly browned in butter or oil and removed from the pan before other ingredients are added.

Garlic sauce

Skordalia

This Greek garlic sauce is usually served with poached or fried fish, fried vegetables or fritters.

Makes 1½ cups/375 ml

2 slices white bread	¼ cup/22 g blanched sliced almonds
½ cup/125 ml red wine vinegar	2-3 tbsp/30-45 ml oil (optional)
6 cloves garlic	1 cup/250 ml olive oil

Cut the crusts from the bread and soak the slices in vinegar for 10 minutes. Squeeze the bread dry and work it in a blender or food processor with the garlic cloves and almonds. (If using a blender, add 2-3 tbsp/30-45 ml oil with the blades turning.) Gradually add the olive oil and work the mixture until smooth. Season to taste.

SHALLOT

The purple-hued shallot tastes like a combination of onion and garlic and is an essential ingredient in French cooking. Whole shallots can be treated as a vegetable (p.289), but they are more frequently chopped to use raw in vinaigrette-based dressings and marinades, or cooked to flavor dishes like mussels *marinière* and white butter sauce (p.62). Unlike onions, shallots should never be allowed to brown lest they become bitter.

CHIVE

The tubular leaf of the chive is the most useful part, although the pink-purple flowers can be used as edible decoration or in salads. Chives can be grown indoors and used as needed. More subtle in flavor than other alliums, chives may be used raw or simply added to a dish at the end of cooking. To avoid bruising, they are snipped with scissors, or sliced crosswise with a knife rather than chopped. When blanched, they can be used for tying small bundles of vegetables. Cut chives often garnish cream soups and may be added to salads, omelets and potato dishes.

Chinese chives, used like ordinary chives, have flat leaves and a mild garlic flavor. In Chinese cooking, the flower buds are stir-fried and the leaves blanched to serve with pork dumplings.

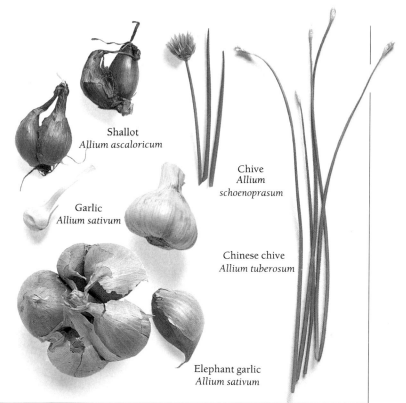

Shallot
Allium ascaloricum

Chive
Allium schoenoprasum

Garlic
Allium sativum

Chinese chive
Allium tuberosum

Elephant garlic
Allium sativum

PEELING & CHOPPING GARLIC

Garlic is best chopped, as crushing in a press can give too strong a taste. If it has started to germinate, discard the green heart.

1 To separate the garlic cloves, smash the bulb with your hands. Alternatively, pull a clove from the bulb with your hands.

2 To crush a clove, set the flat side of a chef's knife on top and strike it with your fist.

3 Discard the skin and finely chop the clove with the knife, moving the blade to and fro.

CHOPPING SHALLOT

Shallots, although they are smaller than onions, are chopped in exactly the same way.

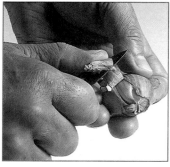

1 If necessary, separate the shallot into sections at the root. Peel each section and set it on a chopping board with the flat side down.

2 Hold the shallot section steady with your fingers. Using a large chef's knife, slice horizontally toward the root, leaving the slices attached at the root end.

3 Slice vertically through the shallot, again leaving the root end uncut.

4 Finally, cut across the shallot to make fine dice. The root end may be reserved for stock.

FRAGILE HERBS

There are five major herbs that are characterized by their soft, fragile leaves: parsley, chervil, tarragon, mint and basil. They are at their perfumed, pungent best when freshly picked and carefully handled so they do not bruise. The leaves, particularly of tarragon, basil and mint, bruise easily and are best coarsely chopped. Fragile herbs are often eaten raw and should be cooked only lightly. For longer cooking, their stems may be used to give flavor and the leaves can be added shortly before serving. Some fragile herbs are disappointing when dried, lacking the fresh perfume that is so much a part of their charm. The flavors of mint or parsley are potent and they are often used alone.

USEFUL INFORMATION

Season Spring to late autumn.
How to choose Bushy leaves with no bruises, good aroma, well-formed stems and leaves.
Problems Less flavor if immature or raised indoors; leaves wilt rapidly and bruise easily.
Processed forms *Parsley*: dried, chopped, frozen. *Chervil*: dried. *Tarragon*: dried, preserved in vinegar. *Mint*: dried, extract. *Basil*: dried, preserved in oil.
Storage *Fresh*: refrigerate 2-5 days; freeze 6 months; dry 1 year.

PARSLEY

The ubiquitous parsley, rich in vitamins and minerals, is used primarily as a garnish. It is usually chopped quite finely for sprinkling over sauces and gratins. Whole sprigs may accompany grilled and roasted meats, while deep-fried parsley adorns fried foods. Parsley stems or leaves are an integral part of a bouquet garni; the chopped leaves are combined with garlic or shallot to make both French *persillade* and Italian *gremolata* (p.14).

The more common curly parsley is preferred by many cooks because it keeps well when refrigerated, is attractive when left whole, and is easy to chop. Flat-leaf parsley, also called Italian or French parsley, is regarded as less bitter, with a fuller flavor. It is often used in combination with garlic and olive oil in braises, stews, and pan-fried or pasta dishes. Two other types of parsley – Neapolitan (p.298), grown for its stalk, and Hamburg (p.303) for its root – are used as vegetables.

CHERVIL

Chervil is one of the classic *fines herbes* (p.14), although parsley is sometimes substituted for it. The light green, feathery leaves differentiate it from parsley. Chervil is also used as a garnish, though it tends to wilt more rapidly. The tender leaves can be blanched and floated on consommé or cream soups, or chopped and sprinkled on butter sauces. Chervil is said to intensify the flavor of other accompanying herbs. Its own sweetish anise-like flavor is strongest when raw, so do not add it to hot dishes until just before serving.

TARRAGON

One of the classic *fines herbes* (p.14), tarragon is widely available fresh, dried or preserved. Fresh tarragon is the first choice because its sweet and spicy flavor is strongest. Dried tarragon has little flavor or aroma, so tarragon preserved in vinegar is the best substitute for fresh. The flavor of tarragon varies a good deal with soil and climate. The French variety is the best – an essential ingredient in béarnaise (p.61) and *rémoulade* sauces (p.63), well-suited to many egg and potato dishes, and good with chicken. Russian tarragon is easier to grow in cold climates but has no value as a flavoring.

Pennyroyal
Mentha pulegium

Chervil
Anthriscus cerefolium

Peppermint
Mentha piperita

Applemint
Mentha rotundifolia

Spearmint
Mentha spicata

Salad burnet
Sanguisorba minor

French tarragon
Artemisia dracunculus

Borage
Borago officinalis

Curled parsley
Carum petroselinum crispum

French parsley
Carum petroselinum

Purple basil
Ocimum basilicum purpureum

Green basil
Ocimum basilicum

MINT

Most of the mint grown for cooking is spearmint, named for its spear-shaped leaf. It is one of the most versatile herbs, used in a range of dishes from Middle Eastern salads to American mint julep cocktails. Peppermint leaf rarely features in cooking, but peppermint oil is used in making candies and as a medicinal flavoring. Fruit-flavored mints such as applemint are grown for use in beverages and fruit salads. Pennyroyal, a slightly bitter mint, has bright green leaves with a strong peppermint scent. It was once a favorite in British black puddings and herb teas.

BASIL

Basil, whose name derives from the Greek word *basilikon*, meaning "kingly", has an almost mystical reputation in some cultures. Sweet green basil is most familiar to our palates but other common varieties include purple basil and "minimum", or Greek basil, which has tiny green leaves. All three share the same rich, peppery flavor; other varieties include lemon-, anise- and cinnamon scented basils. Basil goes particularly well with tomatoes and is indispensable to many tomato-based dishes. One of the best uses for basil is in Italian *pesto* sauce. The leaves can be used in salads or as a garnish; crushed or chopped, it becomes the main seasoning in soups, grain and rice dishes.

BORAGE & SALAD BURNET

Also worthy of mention are borage and salad burnet. Both have a refreshing taste of cucumber that makes them a natural addition to summer punches. Borage leaves should be picked young, before the characteristic hairs of the plant are too thick. The leaves and blossoms are sometimes added to green salads in place of cucumber, and the attractive blue flowers may be lightly candied (see Candying fruit, p.475) to decorate frozen desserts. Borage pairs well with shellfish, and its stalks (especially when large) may be peeled and used like celery. Salad burnet introduces a nutty flavor to garnishes, herb butters and soft cheeses. Young leaves may be included in a salad or sprinkled on vegetables, but mature ones can be tough.

MAKING PESTO

This is a classic Italian sauce, originally from Genoa, that is used for hot pasta and pasta salads, or for flavoring. The southern French equivalent, *pistou* (made without pine nuts), is stirred into vegetable soups. To store *pesto*, put it in a glass jar and pour a thin layer of olive oil on top to seal it. Cover the jar tightly and refrigerate; it will keep for at least a week. *Pesto* also freezes particularly well, without loss of flavor or color.

Makes 1¾ cups/450 ml

1 cup/45 g basil leaves, washed and dried	⅓ cup /40 g pine nuts
6 cloves garlic, peeled	1 cup/125 g grated Parmesan cheese
	¾ cup/175 ml olive oil
	salt and pepper
	Food processor or mortar and pestle

If using a food processor: purée the basil, garlic, pine nuts and Parmesan cheese with 2-3 tbsp/30-45 ml olive oil. With the blade turning, slowly add the remaining oil so the sauce emulsifies. Season to taste with salt and pepper.

1 **If using a mortar and pestle:** chop the basil and add it to the mortar with the garlic, pine nuts and Parmesan cheese.

2 With the pestle, mix and pound the ingredients until they are thoroughly combined and form a smooth purée.

3 Gradually add the olive oil until the paste is well blended and smooth.

4 Season the sauce to taste with salt and pepper before serving.

ROBUST HERBS

Thyme, savory, bay leaf, rosemary, sage, oregano and marjoram can be considered together as robust herbs, with tough leaves that are resistant to winter cold, summer sun, and to the heat of the cooking pot. Their characteristics vary with growing conditions – the strongest-tasting varieties being common around the Mediterranean. Because they are ever-green in mild climates, bay trees and hedges of thyme and rosemary are decora-tive in the garden as well as providing culinary herbs. Strong in aroma and hearty in flavor, all these herbs are cooked because they tend to be harsh when raw. When they are dried, their flavor mellows and intensifies. Thyme and bay leaf are frequently used together in European cooking, often forming a triumvirate with parsley in bouquet garni (p.14). When a distinctive herbal flavor is desired, several of these herbs may be combined, as in *herbes de Provence* (p.14), one of the few instances where savory and rosemary are partnered with other herbs.

USEFUL INFORMATION

Season Late spring to autumn.
How to choose Moist, not withered leaves; pungent but not bitter smell.
Problems Unless very fresh, leaves are tough when served with food; strong flavors easily overpower delicate foods.
Processed forms *Thyme*: dried, whole or ground. *Savory*: dried, whole. *Bay leaf*: dried, whole or ground. *Rosemary*: dried, whole or ground. *Sage*: dried, whole, rubbed (crushed leaves) or ground. *Oregano and marjoram*: dried, whole or ground.
Storage *Fresh*: refrigerate 1 week, freeze; *dried*: 1 year.

THYME

Possibly the most popular of all the robust herbs, thyme is indispensable to many classic stocks, sauces, slow-cooked braises and stews. With a pungent taste that lingers on the palate, common thyme is used as fresh or dried sprigs that are removed before serving, or as tiny dried leaves that are crumbled into food while cooking. Common or garden thyme is a variable – and therefore much confused – species that has a number of cultivars. Other useful species for the cook are wild thyme, caraway thyme and lemon thyme. A North African substitute for thyme, *zatar*, has a much stronger taste.

Bay leaf
Laurus nobilis

Winter savory
Satureia montana

Summer savory
Satureia hortensis

Purple sage
Salvia officinalis purpurea

Golden sage
Salvia officinalis aurea

Common sage
Salvia officinalis

Clary sage
Salvia sclarea

Common thyme
Thymus vulgaris

Wild thyme
Thymus serpyllum

Lemon thyme
Thymus citriodorus

SAVORY

Savory has a larger leaf than thyme, but is similar in flavor, though rather more bitter. There are a number of varieties of savory, but the two most commonly used in the kitchen are summer savory, a hardy annual, and winter savory, a small shrubby perennial that can also be grown as a houseplant. Summer savory is sweeter and used more often than the winter variety. Both savories are more peppery in flavor than thyme and therefore stand up well to hearty vegetables such as cabbage and Brussels sprouts. Summer savory is the classic seasoning for fava beans in France, Switzerland and Germany, and both varieties may also flavor stuffings and sausages.

BAY LEAF

The status once given to bay, also called sweet bay or bay laurel, is reflected in its Latin name, *Laurus nobilis*, and its place in the Roman crown of victory.

In cooking, fresh bay leaf can be bitter and it is usually used dried. Most recipes call for a couple of leaves to be added early in the cooking process, then re-moved before serving. Ground bay leaf may be used in a stuffing but otherwise the whole leaf is the best choice, being easily retrieved from a finished dish.

Quick-cooking seafood or pork kebabs can have bay leaves threaded between the pieces on the skewer. The short cooking time allows just enough of the herb's flavor to be imparted to the final dish.

Bay leaf should not be confused with the cherry laurel (*Prunus laurocerasus*), which has a similar but darker leaf with no aroma and a bitter almond flavor.

Rosemary
Rosmarinus officinalis

Golden marjoram & Oregano
O. 'Aureum' & O. vulgare

Rosemary and lemon sorbet

This unusual and refreshing sorbet is so light it is best eaten within two days of making. More or less sugar and lemon may be added according to your taste, and depending on whether the sorbet is to be an appetizer or a dessert.

Serves 6

5 cups/1.25 L water

1¼ cups/250 g sugar (more if needed)

grated zest and juice of 2 lemons (more if needed)

½ oz/15 g fresh rosemary sprigs

Ice cream churn (p.509) or freezer tray

1 In a medium saucepan, heat the water and sugar until dissolved to a syrup. Boil steadily for 2-3 minutes. Divide the syrup in half. Add the lemon zest to one portion and simmer it over very low heat for about 10 minutes. Add the lemon juice and let the syrup cool.
2 Immerse the rosemary sprigs in the remaining syrup. Bring the syrup to a boil, turn down the heat and infuse for 10-15 minutes. Strain this syrup into the lemon syrup, adding more sugar or lemon to taste. Chill the mixture, then freeze it in an ice-cream churn until firm. Transfer to a chilled bowl and store for up to 2 days in the freezer. Alternatively, transfer the syrup to a freezer tray and freeze until it starts to set, 1-2 hours. Beat well and return the sorbet to the freezer until frozen. A half-hour before serving, move the sorbet to the refrigerator.

ROSEMARY

Rosemary grows best in those countries that have a mild climate, including southern Europe and parts of North America. It is found wild on hillsides in the Mediterranean region (its name means "dew of the sea"). An evergreen bush with lavender-blue flowers, rosemary is very aromatic; it should be used in moderation as it can have a strong camphor flavor. Fresh rosemary leaves are soft enough to chop and they combine well with other ingredients in many dishes. Once dried, however, rosemary can be brittle and tough: sturdy sprigs may be tied to pieces of meat for roasting or stuffed inside poultry, but they must be removed before serving. A fresh sprig may also serve as a basting brush to coat meat or fish with oil during grilling, thereby imparting a hint of rosemary flavor. Rosemary is particularly popular in Italian cooking, in dishes such as *pasta e fagioli* (soup with pasta and beans) and as a flavoring for roast lamb.

SAGE

Sage is traditional in stuffings and sausages. It is excellent with kebabs, and can be larded into meats or put under poultry skin for roasting, as well as cooked in stews and sautés. Fresh leaves have a more subtle, sweeter taste than dried, and in central Italy they are fried in butter to flavor pasta sauces. The leaves are also an important flavoring in the Italian veal dish *saltimbocca*. Dried leaves can be easily crumbled for recipes that call for ground sage. Apart from common sage, cultivated species suitable for the kitchen include pineapple sage, with a tart, fruity taste, and blue sage, named for the color of its flowers. Colored or variegated varieties are generally less aromatic. A possible substitute for ordinary sage is fresh or dried clary sage, whose large leaves are highly aromatic. Chia, a hairy plant of the sage family, was once popular in the United States. Clary and chia may still be found at health food or herbal stores.

OREGANO & MARJORAM

In the garden, these two herbs are difficult to tell apart; even in cooking they are interchangeable, although marjoram is often milder than peppery oregano. Oregano features strongly in Italian cooking, is used in pasta sauces, sprinkled on pizza, and included in southern Italian meat stews. Marjoram features in Scandinavian, German and Austrian dishes, and in the cuisine of the southwestern United States. In salads, both herbs are often used fresh; if dried, they should be added early on to stews and sauces. Rigani, characteristic of Greek cooking, is a general term for any of the wild species of oregano. Pot marjoram is a variety that grows well in colder climates, but it can be bitter. Mexican oregano and the wild oregano of the western United States are not related to true oregano but have a similar flavor.

Salad of mixed herbs

The herbs chosen for this salad are all traditional and have been combined in salads since the sixteenth century.

A selection of fresh herbs such as:

purslane
lovage leaves
tarragon
fennel flower
beet greens
chive flower
viola flower
curly endive
vinaigrette dressing (p.64)

1 Rinse and trim all the herbs.
2 Set the larger leaves in a dish and arrange the rest on top to make an attractive display.
3 Prepare the vinaigrette. Serve it separately or toss the salad in it.

RARE HERBS

In 1597, John Gerard included 1,800 woodcut illustrations of different herbs in *The Herball or Generall Historie of Plantes*; subsequent editions contained almost 3,000 entries. Like all old herbals, Gerard's book named many plants we now classify as vegetables or fruits. Herbals were important primarily because of the use of herbs in medicine and this belief in the healing or supposed magical qualities of herbs still survives, although many herbs have vanished from the modern kitchen. White horehound, which provides the menthol-like flavoring for throat lozenges and cough syrup, was once featured in sauces, stews and salads. Purslane with its vinegary flavor and crisp texture is still used in salads in continental Europe and is sometimes pickled (p.489). Herb bennet was used in Tudor times for its clove-flavored root, and is still appreciated by connoisseurs as a salad green. Costmary, a spicy herb used in ale, can flavor a variety of savory dishes, though it may be rather bitter. Comfrey has a cucumber flavor, like borage. It is good in drinks and salads and also makes excellent fritters. Melilot, or sweet clove, is one fragile herb whose leaves are better dried than fresh. It has the honey-sweetness of clover and hay, and is refreshing in country wines. Also evocative of hay is sweet woodruff, whose only contemporary use is in maywine and other punches. Bitter herbs such as gentian and rue are used rarely in the kitchen, but flavor certain spirits and liqueurs.

Note It is not advisable to pick wild herbs because of possible confusion with harmful look-alike plants.

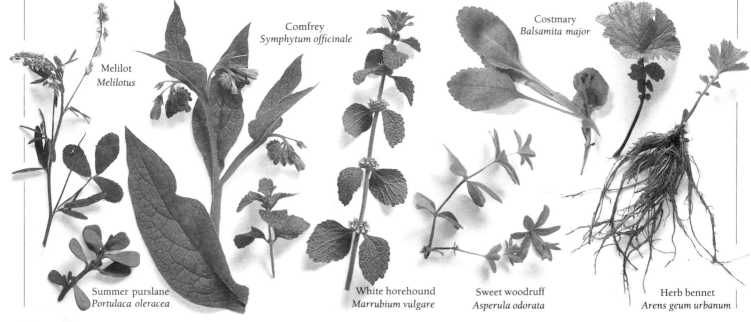

Melilot
Melilotus

Comfrey
Symphytum officinale

Costmary
Balsamita major

Summer purslane
Portulaca oleracea

White horehound
Marrubium vulgare

Sweet woodruff
Asperula odorata

Herb bennet
Arens geum urbanum

LEMON-FLAVORED HERBS

Several herbs are noted for their gentle citrus flavor, evocative of lemon. Apart from the herbs described below, some varieties of other herbs, for example thyme, basil and mint (pp.17 18) are lemon-scented. For all these herbs, lemon zest may be substituted in recipes, but the taste will be sharper.

Lemon balm (Fr. *citronelle*) is a member of the mint family, renowned in antiquity for its health-giving properties. The leaves may be chopped raw in salads and are also used to flavor white sauces for fish, mayonnaise and light meats such as veal and poultry. It was once common in the eel dishes of northern Europe, and still appears in stuffings, marinades and chutneys. It may be purchased dried at herbalist stores. Sorrel (see Vegetables, p.272) is similar in flavor, but more acidic. It can also be added to fruit salads, jellies, custards and fruit drinks.

Lemongrass, a member of the grass family, has a bulbous base. It contains *citral*, one of the essential oils present in lemon zest. It is a common ingredient in southeast Asian cooking, added to fish and braised meat soups and stews. It is sold worldwide in Asian food stores, fresh or dried in whole stalks. For cooking, it is usually cut in 1 in/2.5 cm pieces and removed from a dish before serving. The chopped stalks can be used in salads, and the leaves can be infused in hot water to make herbal tea (below).

Strongest of the lemon-scented herbs is lemon verbena, once a common fragrance in cosmetics. A native of South America, it is now cultivated in Europe and can be substituted for lemongrass in southeast Asian recipes. It is still used in sweet dishes and fruit salads, as well as in infusions, but only a modest amount is needed as it is highly perfumed.

Lemongrass
Cymbopogon citratus

Lemon balm
Melissa officinalis

Lemon verbena
Lippia citriodora

INFUSED TEAS

Long before tea reached Europe, people drank herbal infusions (Fr. *tisanes*) for health and pleasure. Indeed, the most common way to use herbs and spices as medicines was to steep them in boiling water as an infusion, or to make a "decoction" by boiling them for a few minutes before steeping. While most of us no longer rely on their curative properties, many herbs are enjoyed as infusions, notably sage, marjoram, borage, savory, thyme and rosemary. Mint is also popular, as is lemon balm. Dried leaves of lemon verbena, known in France as *verveine*, are used to make a soothing infusion, valued as a tonic for the liver. Linden tea, an infusion of dried lime leaves (Fr. *tilleul*), is regarded as a soporific.

Among the flower buds and blossoms, rose petals or hips, camomile and elderflower are often used as infusions. Aromatic teas can be made from spices such as ginger, clove, nutmeg and cinnamon.

To make any infused tea, steep two tablespoons of the fresh herb or one tablespoon dried in 1 cup/250 ml boiling water for a few minutes, then strain.

RIGHT: Infused teas made from borage, rosemary and cinnamon

HERBS USED AS LEAF & SEED

Some plants double as herb and spice, in the sense that both their leaves and their seeds or fruits are used in the kitchen. This is true of anise, fennel and sweet cicely (see Anise flavorings, p.24), as well as of the herbs shown here. In general, the leaves are quite fragile and are best eaten raw or used in dishes that require little cooking, while the seed takes longer to release its flavor. Coriander is unusual in that the taste of the leaf is quite different from that of the seed.

USEFUL INFORMATION

Season *Leaf and stem:* late spring to summer. *Seed:* late summer.
How to choose *Leaf and stem:* bushy, aromatic when crushed. *Seed:* aromatic.
Problems Flavors, particularly of seed, can be overwhelming.
Processed forms *Dill:* dried leaves, often as "dill weed"; dried seed, whole or ground. *Angelica:* candied stem. *Coriander:* dried leaves (no aroma or taste); dried seed, whole or ground. *Celery:* dried whole seed. *Fenugreek:* dried seed, whole or ground.
Storage *Leaf, stem and fresh seed:* refrigerate 2-5 days; freeze 6 months. *Dried seed:* 1 year.

DILL

The feathery sprigs of dill are common in Greek cooking, where they impart a spicy, anise-like flavor. Both sprigs and seeds are staples in Scandinavian cuisines. The leaves are left whole for decoration or added to marinades such as that used for Swedish *gravad lax* (p.488). They are also chopped raw into cold sauces, salads, and soups such as *borscht*. The seed is stronger, used in breads and pickles, potato salad, and to flavor spirits like *aquavit* (p.38). It may also be added to soups and stews that require long cooking, as it releases its flavor slowly.

ANGELICA

Angelica is appreciated for the sweet flavor of its toothed leaves, root and seed, though the celery-like stem is the part most widely available. The young stems are candied and make a bright green decoration for pastries and desserts. Angelica seed is used to flavor vermouth, various anise-based drinks, and gin. Its leaves may be boiled as a green vegetable, or chopped and added as a flavoring to salad or sweet custards.

Coriander seed

Celery leaf
Apium graveolens

Coriander leaf
Coriandrum sativum

Celery seed

Angelica leaf
Angelica archangelica

Fenugreek seed

Lovage
Levisticum officinale

Dill flower

Dill seed

Lovage seed

Dill leaf *Anethum graveolens*

CORIANDER

Coriander, sometimes called Chinese parsley, is often given its Mexican name, cilantro, in the United States. The seed, which has a gentle citrus-like perfume, is used in European pastries, cakes, and vegetable dishes, and Indian spice mixtures. It stands up well to long cooking. In sharp contrast, the leaves are bitter and musky. Like the fragile herbs (p.16), leaf coriander should be added at the end of cooking or sprinkled over a dish just before it is served, as its flavor dissipates when heated. Latin American, southwest American and southeast Asian cuisines make great use of leaf coriander in sauces, bean or meat dishes and salads, often in combination with chilies. In parts of Asia, the root is ground and added to long-simmered curries.

CELERY

Celery is a versatile plant. Its stalks appear on the table both as a salad and as a vegetable. Its leaves serve as an herb and its seeds as a spice. Celery leaves are tender but peppery and should be used sparingly in soups, stuffings and grain dishes. Celery seed is used in stuffings, pickles and salad dressing. Celery salt is a seasoning made from crushed celery seeds and refined salt.

LOVAGE

This herb has an unusual musky flavor that is similar to celery but with a hint of lemon. Since it is stronger than celery, it should be used more sparingly. The leaves are used raw in salads, or they can be cooked, particularly in soup. The stems are treated in the same way as celery, or may be candied like angelica. The seed is used in baking, especially with cheese. It is not often found in markets but is easy to grow.

FENUGREEK

Long a staple in Indian cookery, fenugreek has played only a minor role in Western cooking. Fenugreek seed is often toasted and ground to add to curry powders. It has a nutty, slightly bitter flavor. The leaf is eaten in India, where its bitter flavor complements curried dishes. Fenugreek grows easily and its seeds sprout well (Grains and Legumes, p.327).

SPICES

Since antiquity, spices have been among the most expensive and sought-after of ingredients. The most famous spices are native to the tropics – Sri Lanka, the East Indies, and other distant shores – though a few are indigenous to Europe and the Americas. Spices were originally valued in the kitchen for their role in enhancing the keeping qualities and taste of foods. Preserved meat could be overwhelmingly salty and was likely to be tainted after months of winter storage. Humble root vegetables could be camouflaged and improved with the coloring and flavoring of spices.

Today, spices are most often appreciated for their aroma. A particular spice or blend of spices defines many dishes such as *Risotto alla milanese* (p.25), and of course many Asian dishes. Some are used to provide color, from the bright yellow of saffron to red paprika. While spices are no longer significant as preservatives, they still feature in preserved foods such as sausages and pickles, partly for tradition, partly to give commercial products more character, but mostly for their distinctive flavor.

Choosing and storing spices

In contrast to herbs, most spices travel well and deteriorate slowly. Whenever possible, the cook should buy whole spices and grind them as needed. Buying spices in bulk is rarely economic, as once their color or aroma has faded the expense is wasted. Aroma is the best indicator of quality. Avoid packages that contain any stem or leaf; both dust and debris indicate careless handling or old age. Spices should be kept in sealed containers at room temperature, away from direct sunlight. Properly stored, most whole spices will keep at least a year and ground spices about six months.

Cooking with spices

Most spices are added near the start of cooking to allow their flavor to develop. Meats for roasting or braising can be rubbed with ground spice, as in German *sauerbraten* and American pot-roast. Whole spices are best for pickles, preserves, and for long-simmered dishes, as some ground spices can turn bitter after prolonged cooking. It is also easier to retrieve whole spices if they are tied in cheesecloth or enclosed in a teaball. Berries such as allspice or juniper can be bruised or crushed before cooking to release more of their flavor; others need to be toasted. In many Indian dishes, whole spices are often briefly fried before being added to other ingredients and western spiced dishes are improved by warming or toasting the spices first. However, toasting or frying must be done over low heat as spices scorch easily. When adding ground spices to dry ingredients, mix them well before adding any liquid to ensure even distribution.

Toasting spices

Indian cooks claim that raw spices are indigestible, so they make an early morning ritual of toasting and grinding fresh spices for the midday meal. Put the spices in a small skillet and set it over low heat. Toast the spices, stirring them or gently shaking the pan until they give off a light aroma and wisps of white smoke can be seen. Immediately remove the pan from the heat and transfer the spices to a mortar or grinder to cool before grinding (right).

Baked fennel with lamb and coriander

The musky, orange aroma of coriander seed complements the anise-flavored fennel. Serve with couscous (p.320) or boiled rice.

Serves 4

1½ lb/750 g fennel bulbs	salt and pepper
2 tsp oil	2 cups/500 ml French tomato sauce (p.65)
1 lb/500 g ground lamb	
3 cloves garlic, chopped	3-4 tbsp chopped parsley (more for serving)
1 tbsp ground coriander seed	

1 Trim the fennel, peeling off outer strings (p.299). Cut it in ¼ in/6 mm slices through the root. Cook the fennel in a large pan of boiling salted water until almost tender, 10-15 minutes, and drain. Heat the oven to 350°F/175°C.
2 Heat the oil in a frying pan and add the lamb, garlic, coriander seed, salt and pepper. Cook, stirring constantly, until the lamb is browned and broken up, about 5 minutes. Take from the heat. Stir in the tomato sauce and parsley and taste for seasoning.
3 Spoon half the lamb mixture into a buttered, shallow baking dish. Arrange the cooked fennel overlapping on top and cover with the remaining lamb. Cover with aluminum foil and bake in the preheated oven until the fennel is tender, 35-45 minutes. Serve hot or at room temperature, sprinkled with more parsley.

Grinding whole spices

Spices may be ground by hand in a mortar or small bowl. Coffee grinders or spice mills (p.506) save time, but they must be reserved for this purpose. For large quantities, a blender or food processor may be used. To coarsely grind or crack spices, seal them in a tough paper envelope and crush with a heavy saucepan.

SEEDS AS SPICES

A few plants are grown primarily for their seed, the other parts having little or no culinary value.

USEFUL INFORMATION
How to choose *Caraway, sesame, poppy:* firm but not too dry. *Cumin:* aromatic.
Problems Rancid if stored in warm area.
Processed forms *Caraway:* dried whole. *Cumin:* dried whole, ground. *Sesame:* dried, ground, paste, oil. *Poppy:* dried whole, oil.
Storage Airtight, in a cool, dry place, 1 year.

CARAWAY

Caraway is an important ingredient in many German and Austrian dishes, particularly in bread and cakes, where the seeds provide a contrasting texture as well as flavor. It is also used in meat and vegetable dishes, especially cabbage and sauerkraut and is one of the flavorings in *kümmel* liqueur. The seeds need long cooking to soften and release their flavor.

CUMIN

Although sometimes confused with caraway, cumin is quite distinctive, with an earthy, aromatic fragrance. White cumin is more common in Asia but it may be used as a substitute for the western brown cumin. Black cumin is more peppery than white or brown types. Cumin is usually ground, often in mixtures such as curry powder and chili powder (p.28). It is a prominent spice in North African dishes such as *couscous* (p.320) and Middle Eastern cooking, and now features in both southwest American and Creole cuisine.

SESAME

Sesame, valued for its oil (see Flavoring oils, p.103) has the nuttiest flavor of the spice-like seeds. Whole white sesame seed is sprinkled on top of breads, cookies and crackers, where it is browned during baking. Raw sesame seed is ground to make *tahini*, a Middle Eastern paste used to flavor *hummus* and other cold purées. Toasted seed is ground to make a darker paste used in cold dishes like Chinese *dan dan* noodles. Sesame also features in Armenian, Turkish and Greek cuisine, especially in baking, and in sweetmeats such as halvah. Black sesame seeds are sometimes used, but are inferior in taste.

Star anise

Ground star anise

Caraway

Fennel

Sweet cumin

Black cumin

Ground cumin

Sweet cicely

Licorice

Sesame

White poppy-seeds

Blue poppy seeds

POPPY

The only poppy with edible seeds is the opium poppy, but the seed itself is free of opium, which is extracted from the pod. The most common seed is blue-gray, but a pale yellow type (*khus-khus*) is native to India, where it is used mainly as a thickening for curry sauces. In Germany, Austria and other parts of Europe, milled poppy seeds are added to sweet cakes and pastries. For poppy seed oil, see p.103.

ANISE FLAVORINGS

The anise or licorice flavor found in so many cuisines can come from a variety of spices or herbs, notably anise, star anise, fennel and licorice.

Anise, also called sweet cumin; is sold most often as tiny, oval seeds (aniseeds) in molded cookies, pastries, candies, and breads such as German *springerle* and Swedish rye bread. The leaves, which sprout in fronds like dill, are used in salads or as decoration. In France, the leaves are often sprinkled over young vegetables just before serving.

The anise used in many liqueurs and anise-flavored drinks (*Fr. pastis*) is not true anise but star anise, a staple Asian spice also used whole or ground. This star-shaped spice has become popular with modern chefs for fish and shellfish stews and is an ingredient of five-spice powder (p.27). Stronger than anise, it can be bitter if used in excess.

Fennel seed, the progenitor of cultivated bulb fennel (Vegetables, p.298), is a convenient substitute for anise. Its flavor is similar to anise and star anise and it is used in much the same way, particularly with vegetables and in sausages or salamis such as Italian *finocchiona*. In the south of France, the seeds and dried stems are often cooked with fish. In Italy, fresh and dried fennel leaves are paired with pork or suckling pig. Fennel may also be used as a flavoring in stuffings and sauces.

Sweet licorice root is used in beverages or simply chewed to release the flavor. Dried slices of the root, or cakes made from the concentrated liquid are the most common forms. In China, licorice is much appreciated as a medicine and a flavoring for meat. In the West, its use is confined to confectionery and beverages.

With a taste that has a hint of both celery and anise, sweet cicely, also called anise chervil, must be cultivated or gathered wild as there are no processed forms on the market. All parts of the plant can be used: roots, leaves, the green fruit and seed. The mild fern-like leaves and the root may be boiled and dressed with oil and vinegar. The large green fruit may also be eaten in this way, while the dark-brown seed may be substituted for anise in baking and desserts, particularly fresh fruit salads.

COLORINGS

The stigma of the autumn-flowering saffron crocus is the most expensive of all spices. Over 250,000 blossoms are required to produce a mere pound of the dried threads that yield the characteristic yellow color. Fortunately, saffron is so strong it is added only by the pinch; when used in quantity its flowery, slightly bitter flavor is overpowering. It is best appreciated on its own and should not be combined with strong herbs or spices, although it marries well with fennel in fish soups and stews. The threads can withstand long cooking. Where an even color is important, add the saffron to the dish early. When adding it to any dish with plenty of liquid, crumble the thread lightly with your fingers and add it directly to the pot. For drier dishes, the thread or powder should first be steeped in a little hot water or other liquid. Saffron is obligatory in paella, *Risotto alla milanese* and the Provençal fish soup, *bouillabaisse*.

Several colorings may replace saffron but only turmeric has much flavor. It blends well in spice mixtures like curry powder and gives the bright ochre color that tints British piccalilli, chow chow pickles, American yellow mustard, and many Asian dishes. Turmeric may be added at any time during the cooking process or used raw in salad dressings and relishes. Other sources of yellow color are pot marigold, safflower ("Mexican saffron"), and annatto seed or achiote, a tasteless dye derived from a West Indian tree. Green can be extracted from spinach and other leafy greens, yellow-orange from carrots, purple from beets, brown from onion peel, and black from squid ink (p.170). Commercially produced colorings are almost always synthetic. However, grenadine, made from pomegranate, is still used in desserts and for tinting cocktails and candied citrus zest. Cochineal, made from an exotic insect, still provides a vibrant pink in icings for cakes and pastries.

Pot marigold

Annatto

Saffron

Saffron powder

Turmeric

ALLSPICE

The flavor of the allspice berry (the only spice, apart from chilies, native to the western hemisphere) was considered by Columbus to be a mixture of cloves, cinnamon and nutmeg – hence its name. The berry is picked green, aged, and then dried to its familiar reddish brown color; it is sold whole or (more commonly) ground. Most comes from Jamaica, leading to the nickname Jamaica pepper. Allspice is a latecomer to European cuisine, but is adaptable, featuring in meat mixtures and stews, as well as in preserving and pastry. it is often used with cinnamon and clove.

Risotto alla milanese

The color and flavor of saffron is essential to this dish. Risottos traditionally contain absorbent Italian short-grain rice.

Serves 6

6 cups/1.5 L veal stock (p.44), (more if needed)	2 cups/350 g *arborio* rice (p.317)
1 small onion, finely chopped	½ cup/125 ml dry white wine
¼ cup/60 g coarsely chopped beef marrow (p. 235)	large pinch of saffron threads
	salt and pepper
1 cup/250 g butter	1 cup/125 g coarsely grated Parmesan

1 Bring the stock to a boil, then reduce the heat and simmer. In a shallow saucepan, sauté the onion and marrow in 3 tbsp/45 ml of the butter until the onion is soft. Add the rice and sauté lightly for 1 minute, stirring with a wooden spoon.
2 Over medium heat, slowly add the wine and one third of the simmering stock. Lower the heat and simmer uncovered until the liquid is absorbed, about 5 minutes. Add another third of the stock and simmer, still stirring, 10-12 minutes. Meanwhile, add the saffron to the remaining stock and leave to infuse. When the rice has absorbed all the liquid, add the saffron-flavored stock and salt and pepper to taste. Continue simmering and stirring until the rice thickens, about 20 minutes. The grains of rice should be tender but firm and the mixture creamy but just stiff enough to hold a shape. If the rice thickens before it is cooked, add more hot stock and continue simmering.
3 Remove from the heat. With a fork, stir in the remaining butter and the Parmesan. Serve at once.

FRAGRANT SPICES

Fragrant spices, valued for their sweet flavor, are used extensively in Middle Eastern, north African and Indian cooking. In medieval Europe, spices symbolized prosperity, providing an economic incentive for exploration of the globe. Today, in the West, there are two levels of cooking with fragrant spices: the dishes that feature in northern Europe, which are mainly sweet or pickled, and the more fashionable savory dishes that look to modern Asian styles.

USEFUL INFORMATION

How to choose *Whole:* pungent when crushed or grated. *Ground:* strong aroma.
Problems *Ground:* lose strength if not sealed for storage; turn acrid if scorched.
Processed forms *Nutmeg:* dried whole; ground. *Mace:* dried blades; ground; mace oil. *Cinnamon:* dried sticks; ground. *Cardamom:* dried whole pods; seeds or ground. *Cloves:* dried whole; ground; clove oil. *Allspice:* dried whole; ground. *Juniper:* dried whole.
Storage Sealed in airtight container in dark, cool place. *Whole:* 1 year. *Ground:* 6 months.

NUTMEG & MACE

Nutmeg and mace come from the same fruit of a tropical tree native to southeast Asia: the two main commercial sources are now Indonesia and Grenada. The ripe fruit splits to reveal a walnut-sized seed enclosed in a lacy, bright red covering, or aril, which is dried into blades of mace. Nutmeg is the kernel of the seed, best bought whole and grated as needed (whole nutmeg will keep its flavor for years). While nutmeg and mace have a similar flavor, mace is sweeter and lighter than nutmeg. Nutmeg is often grated over milk-based sauces, custards and puddings. It is also used in terrines, ground meat dishes, and with spinach and pumpkin. Few spiced cakes or muffins taste right without nutmeg. When used in cooking, both spices should be added early so that their flavor mellows.

CINNAMON

The only bark used in the modern kitchen comes from the cinnamon tree, or the related cassia. In Europe, the true Ceylon cinnamon is more common, but in North America, cassia is often misleadingly sold as cinnamon, despite its harsher flavor.

Both form hard, tight scrolls, but cassia bark is thicker and coarser, and is also sold in flat pieces.

The sweet, nutty flavor of cinnamon remains distinctive even when ground and mixed with other spices. Ground cinnamon (or ground cassia) is used in baking. It may be sprinkled on top of baked custards or mixed with apples in apple pie. With butter, it is the traditional seasoning for baked squash; and in North Africa is added to beef and lamb stews. Germans use it in beer soup; it also appears in Greek dishes such as *pastitsio* meat pie. Whole cinnamon or cassia sticks are often infused in liquid for sweet sauces and spiced drinks, and they appear in pickles and chutneys. The sticks are usually removed before serving.

CARDAMOM

So-called "green" cardamom is the type known in the West, with a pod sometimes bleached white during the drying process. Scandinavian cuisine makes extensive use of it, notably for Danish pastry. Milder, black cardamom, with a much larger pod, is added to Indian meat and vegetable dishes and pickles. Although it is strong, cardamom marries well with cooked fruits and adds fragrance to Turkish coffee. The best cardamom is sold in the pod, since once opened, the seeds deteriorate rapidly.

CLOVE

More pungent than cinnamon, clove has many of the same uses. It is a tiny dried flower bud picked before it opens, and comes from a large tree that grows within 10 degrees of the equator. Clove is at its best near the ocean, and the island of Zanzibar is now the main center of clove growing, although the plant originates from southeast Asia. The nail-like shape of a clove has given rise to its name, which comes from the Latin *clavus*, or nail. It is well-suited to studding meat or fruit. Clove is used in savory dishes, especially stocks and stews, and often a clove is inserted into an onion so that it may be retrieved after cooking. Whole and ground cloves appear in desserts, particularly those with apple. Indian cooks use clove in pilafs, braised dishes, tomato sauce, and to flavor cooking oil. It should be used in moderation, as its flavor is intense. Clove oil contains a mild anesthetic, which is still commonly used to alleviate toothache.

JUNIPER

The juniper berry is a fragrant spice native to northern climates. It may be used fresh as well as dried. Juniper berries are blue when ripe. Best known as the distinctive flavor of gin and alcohols such as Dutch or Belgian *genever* or German *schinkenhagers*, juniper is also used to flavor game stews and hearty vegetables like cabbage and in curing ham. The flavor of the fresh berries is milder than the dried ones, and they are often used whole. Juniper is said to stimulate the appetite, but the berries, especially when fresh, are a diuretic and should not be over-used.

White cardamom

Black cardamom

Cloves

Juniper berries

Nutmeg

Ground nutmeg

Cinnamon scrolls

Cinnamon sticks

Cassia

Ground mace

Nutmeg (with mace)

Blades of mace

Flemish spiced cookies

Speculaas

These cookies are popular in the Netherlands. They are usually shaped before baking by chilling the dough in a block in the refrigerator and then slicing, but they can also be shaped into balls and flattened with a tumbler.

Makes 40-50 cookies

1¼ cups/150 g flour	½ tsp baking powder
½ tsp ground ginger	½ cup/125 g unsalted butter
½ tsp ground allspice	½ cup/100 g light brown sugar
¼ tsp ground cinnamon	3 tbsp/22 g sliced almonds

1 Sift the flour, spices, and baking powder together on to a sheet of paper. In a bowl, cream the butter with the sugar until light and soft. Add the flour in three batches, stirring until thoroughly mixed. If the dough seems very dry, add 1-2 tablespoons of water. Press the dough into a ball with your hands.
2 Turn the dough on to a lightly floured board and work it until smooth. Shape it into a block measuring 6 × 3 × 1 in/ 15 × 7.5 × 2.5 cm, wrap it and chill until firm, at least 2 hours.
3 Heat the oven to 400°F/200°C and line two baking sheets with aluminum foil, greasing the foil with butter. With a sharp knife, cut the thinnest possible slices of dough and set them on the foil. Alternatively, mold the cookies using a fork or a tumbler as shown on p.387. Sprinkle each cookie with a few sliced almonds, pressing them down lightly. Bake until golden, 5-7 minutes. While still warm, transfer the cookies to a rack to cool.

Gingerbread men On a lightly floured surface, roll the dough ¼ in/6 mm thick. With a gingerbread man cookie cutter, stamp out cookies. To decorate, replace almonds with currants or raisins.

SPICE MIXTURES

As with herbs, there are several traditional spice mixtures that may easily be bought pre-packaged. Curry powder was invented by the British in India in imitation of the many combinations of spices that Indian cooks make up themselves at home. Today, what distinguishes packaged curry powder from Indian compositions is the absence of cardamom and the presence of fenugreek, mustard seed and turmeric. Albeit unauthentic, packaged curry powder has given rise to a family of spicy stews and sauces that have become an established part of western cooking. There is no standard mix, however, and curry powder is sold in several strengths, depending on the amount of chili pepper used. It goes especially well with eggs, fish, chicken and lamb.

A much older Indian spice mixture is *garam masala*, which is toasted and ground, then added to a dish at the end of cooking. Traditionally, it includes cardamom, clove, cinnamon, black pepper, and perhaps nutmeg. The Punjabi version includes coriander and cumin and is closer to commercial combinations found in western stores. Indian cooks usually make their own mixture according to taste but *garam masala* is also available in the local bazaars.

Quatre épices, literally "four spices" in French, is a mixture of ground spices – cinnamon, clove, nutmeg and pepper. Its main use is in charcuterie. The proportion of each spice varies according to taste, and allspice (p.25) is a possible substitute. The Chinese have a five-spice powder that includes five to seven ground spices, among them cinnamon, clove, Sichuan pepper, ginger and star anise. This is used for marinating and braising meats, and has recently been introduced in the West for roasting and broiling.

American chili powder should not be confused with powdered or ground chilies of the cayenne pepper variety (p.28). The American version is a spice mix commonly used for meat stews and chilies. It relies heavily on cumin for its flavor, and often includes some oregano. Other American regional spice mixes include the peppery blends used in the Cajun cuisine of Louisiana, and the hot cayenne and bay leaf shellfish seasoning of the Chesapeake Bay.

There are a number of pickling spice mixtures for use in preserving or marinating vegetables. Although amounts vary, the mix is usually based on black pepper with various combinations of dried chilies, mustard seed, allspice, clove, dried ginger, mace and coriander seed. For preserving, spices are left whole so they do not cloud the liquid.

Chinese five spice   *Garam masala*

HOT SPICES

Every country uses some type of hot spice to excite the palate and sharpen the appetite, whether as a table condiment like pepper or prepared mustard, or as an ingredient in the cooking process itself. In hot countries, chili peppers add an intense heat that no amount of true pepper can achieve, while in temperate climates, spicy roots and seeds such as horseradish or mustard take their place.

USEFUL INFORMATION

How to choose *Fresh chilies:* firm, even color. *Dried whole chilies:* good color, unbroken. *Ground chilies, cayenne, paprika:* even color, good aroma.
Problems For all fresh, dried and ground chilies, heat and flavor vary enormously, so add small amount and adjust by tasting.
Processed forms *Chilies:* canned; blanched and frozen; pickled; preserved in oil; dried whole; crushed; ground; chili vinegar; chili oil. *Cayenne:* whole and ground. *Paprika:* ground.
Storage *Fresh chilies:* refrigerate 1 week. *Dried chilies, cayenne:* 1 year. *Paprika:* 6 months in an airtight container, longer if refrigerated.

CHILIES

The *Capsicum* family proliferates in dozens of pepper and chili varieties. Mild capsicums, or sweet peppers, are treated as vegetables (p.279). The hotter varieties are usually called chilies or chili peppers and are used mainly for flavoring. Both fresh and dried chilies range from piquant to burning hot, in colors from acid green to deep red. Afficionados claim hot chilies awaken the taste buds, making them more sensitive to subtle flavors.

Outside Latin America, where the capsicum originated, different varieties of chili are rarely distinguished. For cooking, they can be grouped into three categories: fresh green, fresh ripe, and dried. Fresh green chilies include the hot, rounded jalapeño and the thinner rajiao from Sichuan. Fresh ripe chilies in many colors, from yellow, orange and red to purple-black, range in heat from the sweet banana chili to the blistering hot tabasco. Fresh chilies may be chopped raw into sauces and marinades (p.41), or cooked so that their flavor mellows. Raw or cooked, their heat will permeate all the other ingredients. If too many chilies are added to a dish, little can be done to retrieve it. If scorched, they give off an acrid odor.

In general, the smaller the chili, the hotter it is. If in doubt, taste a tiny sliver of chili before adding it to a dish. If it is too hot, discard the seeds and ribs, as these parts are the hottest. A milder flavor can be achieved by browning a whole chili in hot oil then removing it, using the oil for cooking. An alternative method is to simmer a whole chili in liquid and remove it when the desired pungency has been reached. After handling a chili, fresh or dried, wash your hands and all surfaces in contact with it. The volatile oils can irritate and burn if they touch sensitive areas, especially the eyes. They can also contaminate uncovered food nearby.

Dried chilies are the most common group. One well-known example is the ancho chili, popular in American southwestern cooking. Dried to a deep reddish-brown, it is often soaked in liquid, then puréed as a base for *adobo* sauce. Anchos, usually mild and musty, can be pungent.

Crushed red pepper, also sold under the name "hot red pepper flakes", is somewhat milder than fresh chilies and made from dried crushed chilies. A common condiment in Italo-American cooking, it is an essential ingredient of hot Italian sausage and is used to make chili oil (p.103) and pickles. Chili powder has a different meaning on each side of the Atlantic. In the Americas, it is a mixture of ground herbs and spices (p.27) for *chili con carne*; in Britain, the name denotes dried ground chilies of a coarser texture than cayenne pepper.

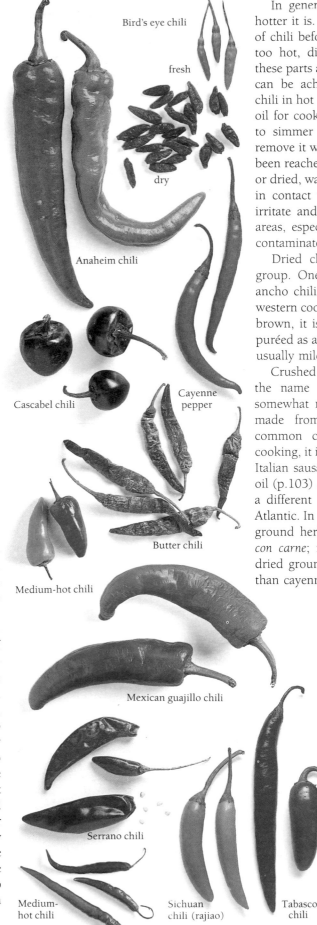

Bird's eye chili
fresh
dry
Anaheim chili
Cascabel chili
Cayenne pepper
Butter chili
Medium-hot chili
Mexican guajillo chili
Extra-hot chili
Serrano chili
Jalapeño
Medium-hot chili
Sichuan chili (rajiao)
Tabasco chili
Ancho chili

CAYENNE PEPPER

Cayenne pepper is a fiercely hot type of ground red chili, generally distinguished from other chili powders by its finer texture. Its name is derived either from Cayenne, the capital of French Guiana, which had a long association with the spice trade, or more probably from the South American *Tupi* word *cyinha*. The original method of preparing it was to grind the chilis, from which the core and seeds were removed, with a little flour and some salt to make a paste. This was dried in small blocks and then lightly baked before being ground to a fine powder. Cayenne is one of the basic spices in Western cooking and is sometimes provided as a table condiment. A pinch of cayenne pepper is often added to butter and cream sauces and to many egg dishes. Ground cayenne has a natural affinity for shellfish, giving a lift to bisques, and sauces such as *Nantua* (p.55).

PAPRIKA

Ground paprika is made from sweet European varieties of capsicum. It is an essential ingredient in many Hungarian dishes, and is also much used in Spain. Paprika is quite different from its fiery chili relations, for not only are the peppers themselves much milder, but the seeds and core are often removed before they are ground. Instantly recognizable by the glowing golden red it adds to a dish, the hallmark of paprika is a mild, sweet flavor rather than heat. The most flavorful paprika comes from Hungary, where it is produced in variations of pungency from mild to very hot. Paprika is often thought of as merely a bright red decoration sprinkled on soup, eggs, sauces and rice dishes, but when of high quality it is a key flavoring, for example in Hungarian goulash, and is often substituted for *ñora* pepper in Spanish Romesco sauce (right). Coating foods with paprika before browning must be done with care, as it scorches easily and becomes bitter.

PREPARING FRESH CHILIES

For a very hot dish, break off the stem and wash the pepper under cold water. For a milder, spicy flavor, remove the seeds.

1 To remove the seeds, halve the chilies lengthwise with a small, sharp knife.

2 Scrape or shake out the seeds and cut away the fleshy white "ribs" from each half.

To prepare dried chilies: cut off the stem end with scissors and shake the chili to empty it of seeds. If you are substituting dried chilies for fresh, put them in a bowl and cover them with warm water or milk. They should plump up in about 30 minutes. Drain the liquid unless the recipe states otherwise.

PIQUANT SAUCES

Sauces made with hot spices add piquancy to a dish. Shown below, clockwise from bottom left: horseradish, Caribbean hot pepper and Romesco sauces.

Caribbean hot pepper sauce Makes 1½ cups/375 ml sauce. Use sparingly, for fish and meat, especially pork. Mix 2 finely chopped onions, 3 tbsp chopped chives, 2 finely chopped cloves of garlic, and 1 finely chopped fresh green chili (more to taste). Pour over ½ cup/125 ml boiling water and let stand for 1 hour. Stir in 3 tbsp/45 ml lime juice; add salt and pepper to taste.

Horseradish sauce Makes 1 cup/250 ml sauce. For hot and cold roast beef, sausages, smoked fish. Mix together 3 tbsp grated fresh horseradish, 1 tbsp vinegar, salt and pepper. Fold in ½ cup/ 125 ml stiffly whipped heavy cream, and season to taste.

Romesco sauce Makes 2 cups/500 ml sauce. For fish, baked or deep-fried vegetables, grilled meat, and pasta. Often served alongside garlic mayonnaise (p.63). Soak 4 dried, seeded *ñora* peppers or ancho chilies for 30 minutes in cold water and drain. Heat 1 tbsp olive oil, take from heat and add peppers. After 2 seconds, pour off oil. Fry a slice of bread in 1 tbsp oil until golden. Put bread and peppers in a food processor with ¼ cup/22 g each of toasted almonds and toasted hazelnuts and 2 chopped cloves of garlic. Purée until very smooth. In a saucepan, cook ½ lb/250 g peeled, seeded and chopped tomatoes to a stiff purée, stirring often. Add to pepper mixture and purée again until smooth. With blades still turning, pour in ½ cup/125 ml olive oil. Add 2 tbsp red wine vinegar, and salt and pepper to taste.

PEPPER

Pepper can be sweet or pungent depending on its provenance, but the berries of one plant produce black, white and green peppercorns, the most familiar forms. Black pepper is the unripe berry that has been left to dry and darken. For white pepper, the berries are ripened, the outer casing is removed and the berries are dried, resulting in a less aromatic heat. Sometimes black peppercorns are polished to remove the hulls and are then sold as white pepper, but this is a deceptive practice and the taste is never the same as true white pepper.

Some dishes such as French *steak au poivre* and Italian *pollo alla diavola* depend on black pepper as an essential seasoning. White pepper is usually reserved for creamy recipes in which specks of black would be unattractive. The taste of pre-ground pepper fades with time, so it is always best to buy whole peppercorns, whether white or black, and grind them as needed. In a recipe that requires long cooking such as a stock or stew, whole peppercorns should be added because ground pepper loses its effect if cooked for more than a couple of hours.

Green peppercorns are the unripe pepper berries. While they share the basic taste of dried pepper, they also have a sharp, almost acidic taste that makes them useful as a foil to rich meats like duck, or a welcome addition to butter and cream sauces. In moderation they complement fish and shellfish salads. A pepper grinder is not necessary for green peppercorns. If they are preserved in brine, rinse the berries and add them directly to a sauce; if freeze-dried, crush them in a bowl or mortar before use.

Pink peppercorns are the berries of a small South American shrub. With a slightly piquant taste, pink peppercorns are a decorative alternative to green peppercorns, or the two may be used in combination. Sichuan pepper, also called *fagara* or anise-pepper, is the dried berry of an oriental shrub or small tree. More aromatic than peppery, it is used in a wide range of savory dishes in China and has become more prevalent in the West. To release its fragrance, Sichuan pepper is toasted in a dry skillet before crushing (see Toasting spices, p.23).

Black pepper

White pepper

Dry green pepper

Green pepper in brine

Sichuan pepper

Pink pepper

USEFUL INFORMATION
How to choose *Black and white, whole:* unbroken, good aroma. *Black and white, ground:* aromatic. *Green:* unbroken. *Sichuan:* unbroken, no stems or leaves.
Problems *Black and white, ground:* turns bitter after long cooking. *Green:* Too much gives sour taste.
Processed forms *Black and white:* dried whole; ground; crushed. *Green:* in vinegar and mustard; freeze dried. *Sichuan:* dried whole.
Storage *Black, white, pink, Sichuan peppercorns:* indefinitely if sealed. *Ground:* 3 months. *Green, unopened:* 1 year; *opened:* 1 week.

GINGER

Perhaps the most versatile of the hot spice plants is ginger, whose root-like rhizome is used fresh, dried and ground, pickled and candied. Ginger has long been essential in Asian and Middle Eastern cooking, and had reached southern Europe before Roman times. In the West, fresh ginger is a comparative newcomer in the kitchen, although in its dried or candied form it has been known for centuries, used in traditional recipes for gingerbread and gingersnaps. Modern cooks have begun to appreciate fresh ginger paired with fish and shellfish, and stronger poultry and meats. Finely grated fresh ginger or ginger juice is used in marinades and dipping sauces, or in the making of drinks such as ginger beer. Needle-thin julienne of whole ginger can be strewn over food as an attractive, zesty garnish.

For use in baking, the root of fresh ginger can be finely grated, although dried and ground ginger is more useful for this purpose. Pink pickled ginger is a traditional garnish for raw fish salads. Pungent and peppery, it is peeled and sliced to flavor a dish, and the pieces removed before serving. Crushed and chopped, it can be left in the dish but will have a stronger effect on the palate.

Preserved ginger, whether in syrup or candied, was once appreciated on its own as a sweetmeat but is now more common as a flavoring in baking and desserts such as ice cream. Since ginger in syrup is soft, and candied ginger is thickly coated with crystallized sugar, the two cannot be used interchangeably in a recipe. Stem ginger is the most superior kind, being made of the smallest, most tender shoots from the ginger root. Also available, but not so often used in the West, is dried ginger root (with or without skin) which requires bruising to release its flavor.

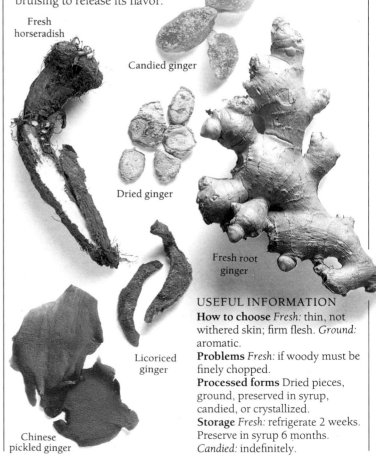

Fresh horseradish

Candied ginger

Dried ginger

Fresh root ginger

Licoriced ginger

Chinese pickled ginger

USEFUL INFORMATION
How to choose *Fresh:* thin, not withered skin; firm flesh. *Ground:* aromatic.
Problems *Fresh:* if woody must be finely chopped.
Processed forms Dried pieces, ground, preserved in syrup, candied, or crystallized.
Storage *Fresh:* refrigerate 2 weeks. Preserve in syrup 6 months. *Candied:* indefinitely.

PREPARING FRESH GINGER

Fresh ginger is peeled like a vegetable or thin-skinned fruit, then sliced, chopped or grated on a fine grater.

1 With a sharp knife, cut the skin from the ginger root.

2 For chopped ginger, first crush it under the flat of a knife.

3 Crushed ginger, its fibers separated, is easier to chop.

4 Chop the ginger as coarsely or finely as you wish.

Note Some recipes call for ginger juice. To extract it, squeeze the grated ginger in cheesecloth or use a garlic press.

HORSERADISH

Horseradish is a European root favored in northern countries. When freshly peeled and grated, it releases a flavor and aroma so pungent that it provokes tears. However, its strength fades quickly after grating, so it should be used promptly or preserved in vinegar (when it is known as "prepared" horseradish). Grated horseradish is most commonly used as a condiment to accompany meats, especially beef, but it is also served with smoked fish or strong-flavored vegetables. It may be added to sour cream or mayonnaise for a quick, cold sauce, or even to a warm sauce. It is also good in sauces that contain vinegar or cream, and in beet dishes. However, do not heat horseradish that has been cooked beyond the gentle simmer stage, as the heat will destroy its flavor.

Wasabi, the bright green Asian horseradish, is becoming more familiar in the West as an accompaniment to Japanese dishes. It is not, in fact, botanically related to Western horseradish, and is more aromatic. It is one of the strongest spices used in Japan, where the whole root is sold fresh. Elsewhere, it can be purchased as a powder or paste.

USEFUL INFORMATION

How to choose Clean, unbroken skin, flesh firm not dry.
Problems Flavor fades soon after horseradish is grated.

Processed forms Dried ground; preserved in vinegar ("prepared").
Storage Preserved in vinegar, about 6 months.

MUSTARD

Used worldwide, prepared mustard can be made with the seeds of any of three plants. Black mustard seed is considered the best, being the most pungent, and until World War II it was the basis for all European ground and prepared mustards. However, its unsuitability for mechanical harvesting led to its replacement by the milder brown mustard, from a plant of more manageable size. This is the species most commonly used in Europe today. A third type, yellow or white mustard seed, has the mildest character and is used in most American prepared mustards.

Whole mustard seed is used in pickles and relishes, and in marinades and chutneys, as well as in Indian cooking. Once ground into powder, it must be mixed with water to develop its pungent flavor. Salt and vinegar both inhibit this and should be added later. For this reason, dry mustard added to a sauce containing vinegar or lemon juice (such as mayonnaise) is weaker than when added already mixed.

One of the most famous prepared mustards is Dijon. To qualify for the name, it must follow a strict recipe of ground black mustard seed, salt and spices, with verjuice (see Vinegar, p.40), wine or vinegar. Others must be labeled "Dijon-style". Dijon mustard is particularly good with steak, hot and cold meats, poultry and stews, and in sauces or vinaigrette dressing (p.64). The darkest French mustard is the Bordeaux type with a mottled color that comes from unskinned seeds.

German mustards are usually smooth and may be dark or sweet. Bavarian is best with light meats and veal, while spicier Dusseldorf mustard pairs well with baked beans, fresh or dried sausage, sauerkraut and smoked meats. In Denmark, *fiskesennep* or fish mustard, made of coarsely ground seeds, is sold as a flavoring for the white sauce that is served with fish.

English or Chinese mustard is often stronger and sharper than other types. It is sold as a powder for mixing with small amounts of water to accompany roast beef, sausages, cheese and deep-fried Asian spring rolls. The two most popular American mustards are the dark deli-type that is similar to German mustard, and bright yellow "ballpark" mustard flavored with vinegar and colored with turmeric, to be eaten with hot dogs, hamburgers and hot pretzels. In addition to traditional mustards flavored with herbs, spices or green peppercorns, new combinations with flavorings such as whiskey, honey, and even varietal wines are becoming popular.

All prepared mustards may serve as condiments for cold meats, vegetable preparations like sauerkraut, and fried foods. If used in cooking, as in any recipe entitled "Dijonnaise", prepared mustard should be added at the end as it will turn bitter if allowed to boil.

Mustard powder

USEFUL INFORMATION

How to choose *Whole seed*: no trace of dust or stems. *Ground*: zesty taste.
Problems Mustard turns bitter if boiled.
Processed forms Dried whole and ground; prepared.
Storage *Dried seed*: sealed 1 year. *Dried powdered*: 6 months. *Prepared*: 1 year.

Yellow mustard seeds

Black mustard seeds

FLAVORINGS

Of all flavorings, salt is certainly the most elemental, and in much of the world soy-based sauces perform the same function. Anchovy paste and meat extracts add a salty touch, as do bottled hot sauces (p.35). Extracts and essences, wines, spirits, beer and cider, liqueurs and cordials, vinegar and marinades also play an important role in flavoring food.

SALT

The careful use of salt for seasoning is one sign of a good cook. Salt is usually added at the beginning of cooking, but with discretion; if too much is added at the end of cooking, the raw salt taste will be dominant. In soups or sauces that are boiled to concentrate the flavor, the salt will become stronger as the liquid reduces. Salty ingredients such as bacon or cheese can also be a trap since they will indirectly salt a dish. A dish that has been oversalted is hard to remedy. The effect may be balanced by adding a bland ingredient such as cream, milk, rice or potatoes. A soup or sauce can be diluted at the last minute with milk or water, then thickened with arrowroot or cornstarch (p.59). However, serious oversalting cannot be disguised or remedied.

Salt is almost indispensable in baking bread and pastry and can improve the flavor of cakes by highlighting their sweetness. Salt is sometimes used to draw out liquid, as when meats are soaked in brine to preserve them (p.488). Watery vegetables such as cucumber are sprinkled with salt to draw out liquid and soften them; others like eggplant are salted to remove bitter juices (p.261). The cut surfaces of meat, especially red meats, should never be salted in advance of cooking, or the surface of the meat will be too moist to brown.

Several forms of salt are available to the cook, whether mined or evaporated from natural brine from wells or springs, salt marshes or sea water. Table salt, the most common commercial type, is refined and ground into very fine grains appropriate for use as a seasoning. Most brands are purified to eliminate other minerals, but have iodine added as a dietary supplement, with magnesium carbonate to keep the salt dry.

Flat topping salt, perfect for pretzels and crackers, is generally used only by the food industry. Flaked or crystal salt, resembling snowflakes, is very fine and soft and dissolves instantly. It is used in the production of spice and herb mixtures and may be found on some super-market shelves. Kosher salt,

widely available in the United States, is refined into large, irregular crystals. It is considered less salty than ordinary table salt, and is free from additives and iodine. Many cooks prefer it, as the large grains are easy to pick up in the fingers.

Sea or bay salt evaporated from shallow salt water "pans", is widely considered superior to table salt, and is usually refined in a similar way. French *gros sel* is completely unprocessed. It is grayish, with a distinctive flavor.

Roughly crushed chunks of rock salt are commonly used to lower the temperature of ice for chilling ice cream in a hand churn freezer (p.509), or for displaying bivalves on the half-shell. Block salt is refined rock salt that is poured into molds, grated and used for pickling or curing meat. Pickling salt is generally preferred however, because it is superfine, fast-dissolving, and contains no additives that might cloud a brine.

Flavored salts, with the addition of celery seed, dehydrated onion or garlic, are popular with some cooks, but their flavor tends to deteriorate if stored for too long. Sesame salt is made with a high proportion of toasted seeds and is used as a flavoring and a topping. When home-made, in the food processor or in a mortar and pestle, these are usually superior to supermarket varieties.

Sour salt, or citric salt, is not salt at all but crystallized citric acid extracted from lemons or limes; it gives tartness to some Middle Eastern and Jewish foods. Salt substitutes and light salts, often containing potassium and sometimes sodium chloride, are available for those who have to restrict their salt intake for health reasons. Other ingredients that add sharpness, thus reducing the need for salt, are lemon and vinegar.

USEFUL INFORMATION

Problems Types vary in strength so must be tasted before use; lumps form if damp, so container must be airtight. A few grains of rice in the container will prevent salt from clogging.
Processed forms Granules; flakes; crystals; block.
Storage Indefinitely in an airtight container.

SOY SAUCE & OTHER SALTY FLAVORINGS

Soy sauce, used for centuries in Asia for its salty flavor, was first introduced to Europe 300 years ago as an ingredient in other bottled sauces, but is now sold on its own and is probably one of the most popular sauces in the world. Making soy sauce is usually left to manufacturers, as it involves fermenting cooked soybeans and wheat that have been salted and injected with an *aspergillus* mold. The taste depends on the proportion of soybeans to wheat. Good quality soy is aged from six months to two years so that the sauce matures and develops additional flavor. When the sauce is strained from the vats, a fairly light soy is produced. The residue may be pressed to extract a thicker liquid, usually called dark soy.

The many varieties of Japanese, Chinese and Indonesian soy sauces have subtly different effects. Japanese light soy is saltier than the dark, but, being thin and clear, does not darken marinades or tempura dips. Japanese dark soy is richer but can be used in greater quantities because it is less salty. It adds considerable color to a sauce and is the favorite accompaniment for *sushi* and *sashimi*. **Note** The name *shoyu*, Japanese for soy sauce, is also given to some soy sauces produced outside Asia.

Sea salt

Maldon salt

Salted black beans

Monosodium glutamate

Table salt

Rock salt

Chinese superior, pale or light soy looks like Japanese light soy but is slightly different, and best used if only a hint of soy flavor is required. Chinese dark or thick soy has a strong, rather salty flavor with caramel added for color and sweetness. It should be used for spicy dishes that require a more robust seasoning but little additional liquid. Molasses is added to Chinese black soy, the thickest and darkest of all the soy sauces. It is used for cold dishes and those that require maximum flavor with a minimum of liquid. Indonesian soy sauce is dark and very salty or rather sweet.

Another popular soy sauce is *tamari*, which is made from soy beans during the production of *miso* (below). *Tamari* contains little or no wheat and is therefore practically gluten-free. It can be very salty and is best used sparingly in marinades or dipping sauces. Artificial soy sauces are made with hydrolized soy protein, artificially colored and flavored with caramel and corn syrup.

Bean paste, known as *miso* in Japan and sometimes called bean sauce, is an Asian product used both in cooking and as a table condiment. Several varieties exist, produced by fermenting soy beans, flour, salt and water. Like soy sauce, bean paste is usually quite salty and should be used sparingly as a seasoning for stocks, soups and casseroles or as a base for salad dressings.

Salted black beans, also called fermented, Chinese or ginger black beans, appear as a seasoning in traditional Chinese cooking, and in some modern Western dishes. To make them, soy beans are fermented and combined with salt, ginger and spices. Salted black beans should be rinsed in water before use in sauces.

Monosodium glutamate, also called MSG, taste powder, gourmet powder, or by a brand name, is a controversial product as it can cause allergic reactions. It is a natural by-product in the manufacture of soy sauce and in China its use is widespread. Although tasteless itself, monosodium glutamate stimulates the taste buds to detect subtle flavors. It features in many processed foods and packaged spice mixtures.

USEFUL INFORMATION

Problems Use sparingly to avoid oversalting.
Processed forms Canned, bottled.
Storage *Soy sauce*: room temperature 6 months, or refrigerate indefinitely; will darken and become more concentrated over time. *Bean paste and salted beans*: refrigerate indefinitely.

Used in Marinades, soups, stews, basting sauces, stir-fried dishes, steamed dishes.
Also good with all ingredients needing salt, fish, shellfish, chicken, duck, beef, lamb, pork, mushrooms, tofu (soy). Scallops, shrimp, sole, salmon, chicken, beef, pork, broccoli, cauliflower (salted beans).

MEAT & YEAST EXTRACTS

Bottled meat and yeast extracts can also add a salty flavor to foods. Meat extracts are made commercially by a simple process invented more than a hundred years ago by Baron Justus von Liebig. Faced with a surplus of South American beef and no efficient means of distributing it, Liebig developed a method for extracting the flavor from beef. Yeast extracts are a mixture of salt and the brewer's yeast that is formed during the production of beers and spirits. Like meat glaze, meat and yeast extracts are used to reinforce the taste of soups and sauces. In Britain and Australia, they are often spread on bread and butter, and are valued for their nutritional benefits. Familiar brand names include Marmite, Vegemite, Maggi and Bovril.

ANCHOVY PASTE & ASIAN FISH SAUCES

Anchovy paste, made from mashed anchovy fillets, gives a salty flavor to robust tomato or fish sauces and salad dressings, is excellent with lamb roasts, and as the basis of British Patum Peperium or Gentleman's Relish. Anchovy paste is probably a descendant of the Roman *garum*, a sauce made by barrel fermentation of small fish such as sprats, mackerel and anchovies.

Asian fish sauces are produced by a similar fermentation process. The best known are Thai *nam pla*, Vietnamese *nuoc nam*, and Filipino *bagoong*. They are almost indispensable in Thai and Vietnamese cuisine, providing a salty bite to spicy seafood and coconut curries, fish stocks, and soups. With vinegar, they are good in sauces for deep-fried foods. Oyster sauce is a thick, pale brown sauce made from extracts of oysters, wheat and corn flours and rice. It appears in Chinese dishes and is predominantly salty with a slightly sweet, meaty taste.

Vietnamese shrimp kebabs

These baked kebabs combine succulent whole shrimp with a smooth shrimp purée enhanced with Asian fish sauce.

Makes 8

1 lb/500 g large raw shrimp, plus 32 whole shrimp for threading
1 tbsp flour
pinch of baking powder
1 egg, beaten
1 clove garlic, crushed
1½ tbsp soy sauce
1½ tsp fish sauce (*nuoc nam*)
½ tsp sugar or honey
3 tsp/45 ml vegetable oil
generous pinch salt and pepper
4 tbsp sesame seeds
2 tbsp dried white breadcrumbs
For serving
soy and chili sauces
8 long metal skewers, oiled

1 Peel the shrimp and remove the intestinal vein from each one (p.160). Wash them well then squeeze out the excess moisture on absorbent paper.
2 Put the peeled shrimp in a food processor with the flour, baking powder, egg, garlic, soy sauce, fish sauce, sugar and 1½ tsp oil. Season with salt and pepper. Work to a purée, then transfer to a plate, cover and chill for at least 1 hour until firm.
3 Combine the sesame seeds with the breadcrumbs on a baking sheet. Divide the shrimp mixture into 24 portions and toss each one in the sesame mixture, coating it and shaping it to a ball.
4 Carefully thread four whole shrimp and three shrimp balls on to each oiled skewer, alternating them.
5 Lay them on a lightly oiled baking sheet and brush carefully with oil. Bake in the oven at 400°F/200°C until the shrimps are pink and the shrimp balls are firm to the touch, 10-12 minutes. Serve at once with soy sauce and a hot chili sauce (p.35).

OLIVES

The olive tree is one of the most valuable oil-producing plants in the world, with a lifespan measured in centuries. Around the Mediterranean, owning olive groves is a sign of wealth, and throughout the world the olive branch is an emblem of peace.

Olives may be cured when black and ripe or when green and unripe. However, only ripe olives are crushed for oil (p.100). Even when ripe and freshly picked, the olive is bitter and inedible and needs to be cured for several months in oil, water, brine or salt, or for just a few days in lye, wood ash or caustic soda. The curing process varies enormously from place to place. In southern France, for example, black olives are cured in the sun, while in Calabria and Sicily green olives are lightly crushed and cured in oil. Most of the world's green olives come from Spain, often marketed without the pit and stuffed with anchovy, almond, capers, onion, celery or pimento (the classic addition to a martini cocktail). The Greeks, second to Italians as the largest olive producers in the world, export both green and black olives, the most popular being purplish-black *Kalamatas*, cured in brine. In France, olives are small and sold in many forms: the brownish *niçoise* is tiny, usually packed with the stem in an herbal brine, the *picholine* is larger, green and quite salty, and the wrinkled, slightly bitter, black olive from Nyons is dry-salt cured, then rubbed with oil or cured in brine.

Italy, celebrated for its olive oil, produces both large and small olives, usually black: the slightly acid *Liguria*, the salty *Lugano*, the mild *Ponentine*, and the dry, wrinkled *Gaeta* are just a few varieties. California's most popular olive is the crisp *Sevillano*, a green olive usually cured in salt, whole or with cracked skin that takes less time to cure. Other California olives include dry-salt cured Nyons-style, firm-fleshed Greek-style olives, and the common fleshy black olive, cured with lye and usually canned.

It is often important to use the exact type of olive specified in a recipe. The Provençal dip made with puréed black olives called *tapenade*, for instance, needs the piquancy of the *niçoise* cure. Niçoise olives are also important in the green bean and tuna salad of the same name. Italian olives are the most appropriate for topping pizza, while green olives contribute flavor to braised meat dishes. Olives are suitable accompaniments for fish and meats, and are also at home in light salads or in long-cooked stews. Olives in oil or vinegar may be stored at room temperature, but canned olives should be refrigerated after opening.

Large green olives

Large black olives

Small green olives

Dry salted black olives

Small green olives stuffed with peppers

Small black olives

Small green olives stuffed with almonds

CAPERS

Capers are the pickled buds of the *Capparis spinosa* plant. They are never consumed fresh, but always cured in salt or vinegar. Size varies, the largest capers having the strongest flavor, but the smallest, (*nonpareil*) are the most subtle. When buying capers, check that the liquid is clear, with little or no sediment. Marigold or nasturtium buds are sometimes pickled and sold as capers.

The acidic taste of capers makes them a good foil for rich meats and fish, particularly tongue, liver and tuna. They are indispensable to *sauce ravigote* (p.64) and *sauce rémoulade* (p.63), and caper sauce is a classic accompaniment to hot or cold meats, particularly lamb or mutton. Capers are added to shellfish salads and stuffed tomatoes and peppers. Heat intensifies their flavor, especially their saltiness, but they may be added to stews at the end of cooking.

Tapenade

Tapenade is a highly flavored purée from Provence, served with hard-boiled eggs, raw vegetables, or pasta.

Makes 1 cup/250 ml

¾ cup/150 g pitted black olives	5 cloves garlic, peeled
8 anchovy fillets	½ cup/125 ml olive oil
¼ cup/60 g capers, drained	black pepper

Put the olives, anchovy fillets, capers and garlic in a food processor. With the machine running, and using the pulse button, gradually add the olive oil to form a coarse or finely chopped mixture, as you prefer. Alternatively, pound the ingredients in a mortar and pestle, gradually working in the olive oil. Season to taste with pepper. *Tapenade* can be refrigerated, tightly covered, for up to three days.

TABLE SAUCES

While some bottled sauces are poor imitations of homemade sauces and chutneys, others are unique preparations impossible to imitate. British Worcestershire sauce, for example, contains an array of ingredients – mushroom ketchup, walnut ketchup, soy sauce, tamarind, sherry, brandy, vinegar, pork liver, cayenne pepper, black pepper, coriander, mace, anchovies, shallot, garlic and caramel. Many bottled sauces date from the late nineteenth century, which saw the dawn of the commercial food industry.

WORCESTERSHIRE, BROWN & BARBECUE SAUCE

Legend has it that Worcestershire sauce was formulated by the pharmacists Lea and Perrin at the behest of a retired army officer who had brought the recipe back with him from India. Unimpressed with the result, the client returned the sauce and it languished in storage. When discovered some time later, the sauce had matured and was pronounced excellent. The manufacturers perfected the recipe and developed it for commercial preparation. It soon became extremely popular as a table condiment.

Traditional Worcestershire sauce is thin, dark brown and pungent, with a visible sediment. It is soy- and vinegar-based but also contains an assortment of exotic ingredients, the proportions and precise details of which remain the manufacturer's secret. In addition to its use as a condiment, it is also used in cooking to add piquancy to sauces and some meat and fish dishes.

Brown sauce is another variety of bottled sauce that is commercially prepared. A wide selection of such sauces – London Club and HP are two examples – are manufactured in Britain and the United States and exported worldwide; the ingredients are numerous and varied, usually including a fruit such as apple, raisin or orange for sweetness, vinegar for sharpness, and spices ranging from cinnamon to cayenne pepper for piquancy. Exotic ingredients such as tamarind and mango may also contribute to the complex flavor. Brown sauces are excellent accompaniments to red meat, providing a contrasting sharp taste. They can be mixed with ground meats before cooking or poured on after broiling, or they can be added to soups, stews and other sauces, both hot and cold. Lighter versions of some brown sauces, made with white wine, are available for poultry, light meats, fish, and white stews.

Commercial barbecue sauces are similar to homemade ones (Sauces, p.65), but they usually have a higher concentration of salt, sugar and vinegar. Barbecue sauces may be used to coat foods before broiling, or they are brushed on to the meat while it is cooking. They must be applied in several coats during cooking so that they form a good, thick layer.

USEFUL INFORMATION

Problems Characteristic flavor easily overwhelms other ingredients.
Storage *Worcestershire, brown:* indefinitely if sealed. *Barbecue:* indefinitely in refrigerator.
Used in *Worcestershire, brown:* sauces, gravies, dressings, soups, stews, cocktails, dips. *Barbecue:* for basting and as a condiment.
Also good with cheese, mayonnaise, eggs, shellfish, fish, meats, tomato (Worcestershire, brown); broiled chicken, beef, pork (barbecue).

KETCHUP

While for many people, ketchup (or catsup) is simply a generic name for any tomato sauce made with vinegar, the word is probably derived from the Malay *ketjap*, the brine in which fish is pickled. Ketchups based on fish or shellfish are still common in Asia, but in the West, ketchups of fruit, vegetables, nuts or mushrooms are more popular. All ketchups include salt and spices, and often vinegar and sugar.

Tomato ketchup may be made at home quite easily, but for better or worse, the taste of the commercial product is often preferred. Commercial ketchup is akin to a smooth tomato sauce; it is highly seasoned and often spicy, with hints of clove, cinnamon, allspice and cayenne pepper.

A rarity in the United States, mushroom ketchup is still popular in Britain as a condiment as well as in cooking. Originally, it provided the most efficient way of preserving the vast quantities of field mushrooms that appeared in season. The tasty juice of the mushrooms was extracted by salting and boiling, then spices were added to flavor and preserve it.

USEFUL INFORMATION

Problems Dries and discolors if not sealed; darkens and loses flavor with age. *Tomato:* can be vinegary and watery. *Mushroom:* unattractive gray color.
Storage Refrigerate indefinitely; 3-4 months at room temperature.
Used in sauces, salads, stews, but most often as an accompaniment to foods.

HOT SAUCES & RELISHES

The chili or hot red pepper (p.28) is the principal ingredient of commercially prepared hot sauces and relishes. Some hot sauces are based on a thick purée of chilies, while others are thinner, the result of long fermentation. Both types are used as table condiments and may also be added to sauces, soups and stews during cooking. The best known thin chili sauce is American Tabasco, produced in Louisiana but named after a state in Mexico. To make it, fresh ground chilies are salted and left to mature for up to three years. The liquid is then extracted, mixed with distilled vinegar and bottled.

Other thin hot sauces are found elsewhere in the American South. They can enliven soups and stews, are invaluable for Creole dishes such as gumbo (p.49) and jambalaya (rice, p.317) and are useful in scrambled eggs, creamy dips and Mexican *guacamole*.

Thicker, puréed chili sauces that often include garlic, are found on the other side of the world, mostly in Asia. The *sambals* or hot pepper relishes of Indonesia, the hottest sauces in the world, are made from ground chilies and various spices and are used extensively in curries, meat stews and vegetables alike. In North Africa, *harissa* – a violently hot red pepper sauce – is a household staple. A purée of olive oil, chilies, garlic, coriander, caraway, and up to 20 other spices, *harissa* is used as a table condiment, and is an essential accompaniment to couscous (p.320).

USEFUL INFORMATION

Problems *Thin sauces:* color fades if stored in heat or light; strength fades and vinegar taste predominates as sauce gets older, after about 6 months.
Storage *Thin sauces:* at room temperature indefinitely. *Thick sauces:* refrigerate indefinitely.
Used in *Thin sauces:* soups, sauces, gumbos, shellfish stews. *Thick sauces:* Asian and Middle Eastern dishes or as a condiment.

ESSENCES & EXTRACTS

An essential oil, or essence, is an unstable but extremely aromatic product, distilled directly from a flavoring ingredient, be it fruit, plant or spice. In principle, an extract is weaker than an essence as it is made from an essential oil or essence that has been diluted, usually with alcohol. In practice, however, many commercial extracts are of comparable strength to essences, or may even be stronger. Extracts and essences therefore need to be used very carefully. A general rule of thumb is to add two or three drops of essence or one teaspoon of extract per 1 pt/500 ml of liquid or 1 lb/500 g of food, but more may be needed, depending on your final dish. Since much of an essence or extract evaporates when heated, it should be added when cooking is finished, preferably when the food is cold. Today, there are some 2,000 essences used as flavorings by the food industry, and most of them are manufactured chemically to ensure absolute uniformity of texture and a more concentrated taste.

By far the most common essence and extract is vanilla, followed by almond extract. Almond extract, distilled from the essential oil of bitter almonds, is frequently used in baking, when it reinforces the flavor of the nut itself. Almond extract combined with semolina may be used in inferior pastries instead of ground almonds. Other extracts widely used in the kitchen include cinnamon, clove, lemon oil and spearmint; synthetic examples include coconut, lemon, orange and rum. Extracts and essences are normally associated with sweet dishes, but they can appear in savory recipes too. Vanilla, for instance, is good with lobster, and coconut extract complements lamb curries.

USEFUL INFORMATION

Problems Overpowering if too much added; evaporate in heat and on keeping.
Storage Indefinitely at room temperature. *Flower waters:* in a dark place, 6 months.

Used in Baked goods, sweet sauces, syrups, ice creams, sorbets, mousses, icings and frostings, cordials, Asian curries, meat casseroles, candies, chocolates, creams and molded desserts.

FLOWER WATERS

Extracts made from flowers, or flower waters, are particularly popular in Mediterranean countries, India, and the Middle East. Their perfume can overwhelm a dish so they must be used sparingly.

In Egypt, violet flowers are pounded then boiled with sugar to make a syrup for flavoring sorbets. Orange flower water is used in pastries, creams and jams. Attar of roses, usually diluted as rose water, appears in sorbets, candies, and spicy chicken casseroles and curries. Since all flower waters are extremely volatile, they should be kept away from heat and light, and are often supplied in dark bottles.

Scented blancmange

Meaning literally "white food" in French, blancmange has been a popular dessert since medieval times.

Serves 6-8
2 cups/500 ml milk
1½ cups/150 g ground, blanched almonds
1½ tsp/10 g gelatin
½ cup/100 g sugar
2 tsp orange flower water
1½ cups/375 ml heavy cream, lightly whipped
Melba sauce (p.66) or apricot jam sauce (p.66) for serving
1¼ qt/1.25 L mold

1 In a medium saucepan, scald the milk with the ground almonds and leave to infuse in a warm place for 10 minutes. Strain, pressing to extract all the milk from the almonds.
2 Soften the gelatin (p.431) and stir it into the hot milk mixture with the sugar. Transfer to a bowl and let it cool, stirring occasionally. Stir in orange flower water to taste. Chill on ice until it begins to set.
3 Fold in the whipped cream. Pour the mixture into a mold and chill until set, at least 2 hours. Unmold the blancmange and serve with Melba or apricot jam sauce.

VANILLA

Vanilla is so indispensable to sweet cooking that its culinary role has been compared to salt in savory cooking. Vanilla is a bean, the pod of a tropical climbing orchid. The pods are picked while still yellow and unripe and then cured in the sun for up to a year until the vanillin is released and the pod turns a familiar black. Natural vanillin is also found in other foods, such as asparagus, to which it imparts its distinctive fragrance and taste. Most vanilla on the market originates in Madagascar, although it is grown in other parts of the world with a warm climate, such as the West Indies, Tahiti and Mexico. Tahitian vanilla beans are sweet and plump, but the Mexican type, despite its valued flavor, may be adulterated with a toxic substance called coumarin. It is essential, therefore, to make sure that you buy vanilla from a reliable source.

Whole vanilla bean has the most flavor, but is expensive because the plant must be pollinated by hand. Vanilla is therefore more familiar in the kitchen as an essence or extract. Vanilla essence, common in Europe, is so strong that only a few drops are needed. Vanilla extract, used in the United States, is milder, and should be added by the half-teaspoon. Both are distilled from whole vanilla beans and are bought ready-made, though extract can be made at home by soaking beans in alcohol.

Powdered vanilla, ground from the whole bean into a fine powder, is preferred to the extract or essence in baking because the flavor does not evaporate when heated. Vanilla sugar, which is made by leaving one or two vanilla beans in a jar of sugar, may be used in place of ordinary sugar to give a hint of its flavor. Artificial vanillin, a less expensive product, is often substituted for vanilla extract, but lacks its intense perfume and can be acrid.

USEFUL INFORMATION
Problems *Beans:* little flavor if dry.
Storage Indefinitely at room temperature.
Used in Baked goods; fillings; sweet sauces; custards; ice creams; beverages; syrups; charlottes; creams; liqueurs; fruit compotes; fruit salads.

USING A WHOLE VANILLA BEAN

Vanilla beans can be used to flavor any hot liquid such as milk, sugar syrup, or the juice from poaching fruit. After infusing, the vanilla bean may be rinsed, dried and used again.

1 Split the vanilla bean in half lengthwise with a sharp knife. Infuse it in a hot liquid such as milk, for 20-30 minutes depending on the desired strength of flavor.

2 To give a stronger flavor of vanilla, remove the pod from the milk and scrape the seeds out on to a board, then add them back to the liquid for a further 10 minutes.

COFFEE & TEA

Those most popular of beverages, coffee and tea, play a limited but important role as flavorings. Many coffee-flavored recipes bear the title "mocha", a term that once referred only to coffee grown around the Red Sea. Mocha can also mean a combination of coffee and chocolate, and in many recipes calling for chocolate, coffee makes a satisfactory substitute.

The flavor of coffee depends on how it is roasted; and for flavoring, a dark roast is best. Occasionally a dish is flavored by infusing ground coffee or coffee beans with liquid, particularly milk, but more often a very strong brew of coffee is used. To make a simple coffee extract, mix equal volumes of finely ground instant coffee and boiling water. Let the mixture cool and leave it to steep for a day. Strain and store for up to two weeks. Alternatively, boil freshly brewed coffee until reduced and thickened. Leave to cool and store for up to two weeks. The quality and strength of commercially prepared coffee extracts is variable.

Tea as a flavoring has a venerable history and enjoyed a certain popularity in creams and fillings in the eighteenth century. Today tea is a favorite in sorbets, often combined with lime or lemon. Green tea, with its grassy taste, is used in Japanese *soba* noodles (p.328), and is often featured in Asian desserts. Black fermented teas have deeper color and stronger taste, and are good in fruit breads such as barm brack, traditional in parts of Great Britain and Ireland. The smokey-flavored Earl Grey and Lapsang Souchong or delicate herb teas such as jasmine may be used in light desserts and ice cream. Tea even turns up in savory dishes, adding a bitter touch to beef stews or chicken fricassée.

USEFUL INFORMATION
Problems Strength of extracts varies, so add to taste.
Storage Homemade extract tightly sealed 2 weeks.
Used in *Coffee:* ice creams, pastries, cakes, desserts, fillings, frostings, creams, sauces. *Tea:* ices, cakes, desserts, fillings.

Coffee walnut spice cake

Serve this cake plain for afternoon tea, or topped with Chantilly cream (p.70) as a simple dessert.

Makes an 8-in/20 cm cake

1¾ cup/225 g flour	1¼ cups/250 g sugar
1 tbsp baking powder	2 eggs
½ tsp ground allspice	⅔ cup/150 ml strong coffee
½ tsp ground cinnamon	1¾ cups/175 g walnuts, finely chopped
pinch ground nutmeg	
pinch salt	
½ cup/125 g unsalted butter	**8 in/20 cm cake pan**

1 Grease the pan and line the base with paper. Grease the paper and coat it with flour. Heat the oven to 350°F/175°C. Sift the flour with the baking powder, allspice, cinnamon, nutmeg and salt.
2 Cream the butter and sugar (p.398). Beat in the eggs one by one, beating thoroughly after each addition. Fold the flour mixture into the batter in three batches alternating with the coffee. Finally, fold in the walnuts. Pour the batter into the prepared pan.
3 Bake the cake in the oven until lightly browned and a skewer inserted in the center comes out clean, 40-45 minutes. Transfer the cake to a rack to cool before serving.

COOKING WITH WINES & SPIRITS

Some wines and foods are natural partners: Madeira is perfect with tongue or ham, red wine with strawberries, cognac with chocolate. Marriages between alcohol and food have often been made as a result of common origins: kirsch is made from, and served with, cherries, just as Calvados, an apple brandy, is served with apples. The taste for a particular association may be regional, like the Alsatian custom of adding white Riesling to sauerkraut.

Red and white wines are employed in all areas of cooking. They add a richness to soups, stews and sauces, can enliven a stock, deglaze pan juices, and flavor desserts of all kinds. Brandies and spirits offer additional possibilities and most can be used in both savory and sweet recipes. Fortified wines provide a particularly elegant finish to sauces and soups as well as rich meats and desserts. As heartier alternatives, beer and hard cider are best suited to savory dishes – robust stews, braises, or batters for deep-frying which benefit from their effervescence. Liqueurs and cordials feature in dishes served at the end of the meal.

Flambéing food

When spirits or liqueurs are heated, alcohol boils off and can be ignited. As well as making a great show, the flame toasts the food and helps it to brown and, if it contains sugar, to caramelize it. Liqueurs can be flambéed alone, but for best effect they are mixed with a stronger spirit such as rum or brandy. If added directly to food, the alcohol is sometimes absorbed before it can be lit, so for best results the spirit should be heated separately beforehand.

For *crêpes Suzette* (recipe, p.367) Make sure the crêpes are very hot. Heat the spirit in a tiny saucepan or ladle until hot but not boiling. Stand back and light it with a taper or by tipping the pan toward a gas flame. Pour the flaming alcohol over the crêpes and baste the dish rapidly, if possible over the heat. If the dish is not hot enough, the flames will die at once. They should be left to go out naturally, indicating that all the alcohol has evaporated.

SPIRITS & BRANDIES

Distilled spirits are distinguished from wines by their high alcohol content and have many uses in the kitchen. If added at the beginning of cooking, even a few tablespoons of a spirit reduce to a concentrated flavor that adds body to a dish. Alternatively, a spirit may be added just before a dish is served, when only a spoonful or two will impart a full, punchy flavor. A spirit of any kind can act as a preservative, for example when used in terrines or Christmas cakes for long storage.

Distilled from wine, brandy has a confident yet adaptable taste that blends into many savory and sweet dishes, often combined with wine. The best known brandies are French cognac and its cousin armagnac. French *marc*, and its counterpart Italian *grappa*, are both distilled from the pressings of grapes or other fruits, and so have a harsher, pungent taste.

Fruit brandies, sometimes called *eaux de vie*, are not distilled from wine, but from fruit juices. Apple brandy, or applejack, comes from apple juice, and Calvados from apple cider; they have the pungency of *marc*, and are excellent with pork, kidneys and liver, as well as in typical Norman dishes like pork chops with Calvados, apples and cream (p.228).

Other fruit brandies are made from pears, raspberries, strawberries, mirabelle and quetsch plums, and even from oddities such as rosehips. Maraschino, made from marasco cherries, is sweet and perfumed, while kirsch, made from cherry pits as well as the fruit, has a hint of bitter almond and is indispensable to some desserts. Because they are strong, these fruit brandies are often flambéed; sometimes they are cooked further, as in duck or goose with mirabelle plums and plum brandy, and flambéed fruit desserts. These pungent "white" alcohols (in fact, they are colorless) should not be confused with fruit crèmes and liqueurs, which are sweeter, less strong, and often colored.

Whiskey, distilled from various combinations of grains, has the body of brandy with a smokey overtone. Less versatile in cooking than brandy, whiskey is suited to fish, beef and rich desserts. It can take the place of brandy for deglazing sautéed meats or for spiking a range of foods from venison sausage to Christmas cake.

Gin and its northern European relations such as *genever* are restricted because of their relative lack of flavor. They are the natural allies to juniper, which is their main flavoring. Vodka, distilled from grain or potatoes, is sometimes used in ices and sorbets to retard the formation of sugar crystals, and is used as a base for extracts. Other clear liquors such as Scandinavian *aquavit* (Ger. *schnapps*) and Mexican tequila are used occasionally in a sauce or marinade.

Rum is altogether more assertive with a slightly sweet taste. It is excellent with fruit and provides an unmistakable flavoring for desserts such as rum baba. The fuller flavor of dark rum is preferred for cooking and is excellent for flambéing fruit.

USEFUL INFORMATION
Problems Evaporates on standing; flavor harsh if too much added.
Used in braises, stews, sauces, pâtés and terrines, cakes, fillings, soufflés, mousses, charlottes, fruit compotes, flambés.

WINE

Wine can mellow to a remarkable richness when it is simmered in sauces, braises or stews. To avoid a raw taste, it must always be thoroughly reduced during cooking, red wine by half and white wine even more. First, the alcohol evaporates, then the wine concentrates so the finished dish is rich and mellow. This evaporation may be an integral part of the cooking process, as in the long cooking of a casserole or the simmering of a brown sauce. At other times the wine is reduced on its own, as when red wine is used to deglaze pan juices for a steak or when making the wine and vinegar base for a white butter sauce (p.62). Wine should be used in moderation to assure subtle flavoring.

If a wine is good enough to drink, you can also cook with it. While a great vintage wine is wasted in the pan, the basic characteristics of a wine will be passed on to the finished dish. A sparkling wine can contribute only its flavor – bubbles will be lost within a few minutes of cooking. Only in sorbets does some measure of the fizziness remain.

Red wines give a greater depth of flavor than white wines and go best with red meats and game, especially roasts and rich sauces, while both red and white wines suit veal and chicken. For fish, you need a delicate wine, and for creamy dishes and sauces use something light and dry. One school of thought favors red wine with almost everything, including fish and eggs. Sweet or fruity white wines are best in desserts or in sauces to accompany meats like pork, duck and kidneys which take kindly to a touch of sugar. Rosé wines are rarely used in cooking, because they lack the acidity of white wine and the depth of a good red.

By no means all ingredients are suited to wine. Salty food masks the flavor, and smoked foods will not benefit from wine unless it is very dry. Dishes with a high vinegar content tend to make wine taste flat, as do strong citrus flavors like grapefruit. Asparagus and artichokes do not go well with wine, either in cooking or when served with them. Chocolate is better with rum, fruit brandy or a liqueur than with a wine.

USEFUL INFORMATION

Problems If wine is acid, sauce will be sharp; if fruity, sauce may be heavy; if wine is not reduced, flavor is harsh ; if wine is cooked in aluminum, a metallic taste results.

Used in marinades, *court bouillon*, sauces, braises and stews, fruit compotes, gelatin molds, sorbets.

FORTIFIED WINES

Fortified wines are wines to which a spirit, usually grape brandy, has been added. While they may lack the versatility of wines, a dozen classic dishes would be lost without them. Good quality is important, as fortified wines are normally added at the end of cooking. Usually a few spoonfuls will suffice since the alcohol is not boiled off (as with wines) and therefore contributes a certain spike.

There are many types of sherry, ranging from very dry to sweet creams. Sweet sherries blend into desserts like trifle, while drier sherries such as *fino* feature in brown sauces and ragouts, particularly of game. A spoonful of sherry is the traditional crowning touch to turtle soup and consommé. Very dry sherry, however, can be too sharp to add to food.

Red port is available young and fruity (ruby), or aged (tawny or vintage) in a richer, nuttier, and more complex style. Port marries naturally with kidneys and sweetbreads and is an alternative to sweet sherry in many savory dishes. White port is a good substitute for sweet white wine.

In Italian cooking, Marsala, with its dark, rich flavor reminiscent of sweet aged sherry, is often used to deglaze the pan juices for veal or turkey escalopes, and as a flavoring for truffles and in game stews. It is the classic base for the dessert *zabaglione* (p.438), although outside Italy, Madeira is often substituted for marsala. Madeira has a smokey, caramel flavor and may be dry (Sercial) or sweet (Malmsey). It adds a finishing touch to red and white wine sauces, and goes well with pork, veal and variety meats. Malaga, from the Andalusian region of Spain, is a fortified wine that can be substituted for sweet sherries or Madeira.

USEFUL INFORMATION

Problems Too much is overpowering; can leave bitter aftertaste if boiled.

Used in braises, sauces, game stews, soups, desserts, cakes, and for deglazing pan juices.

LIQUEURS & CORDIALS

Liqueurs and cordials, sometimes called crèmes in the United States, are sweetened alcohols infused with fruit, nuts, or a mixture of herbs and spices. Their alcohol content tends to be moderate, although some, like anise liqueur, can be quite strong. Since most liqueurs are sweet, they feature in cream or fruit desserts and those made with chocolate. They are perfect for macerating fruits (p.451) and they flavor sweet fillings of all kinds. Liqueurs are often added to reinforce the fruit they are made with (for example, *crème de cassis* is often poured over a black currant sorbet), but liqueurs may also provide a contrast, as when orange liqueur sauce accompanies strawberries or raspberries. Most liqueurs are too sweet for savory dishes, but they appear occasionally in recipes like duck with orange and Grand Marnier, while anise flavors are important in dishes such as scallops with Pernod. Liqueurs with a moderate or low alcohol content are usually mixed with a spirit for flaming, but stronger anise liqueurs can be flamed alone, and are popular with barbecued fish in Mediterranean countries.

USEFUL INFORMATION

Problems Evaporate in heat or on standing; flavor can be excessively sweet if too much is added.

Used in dessert creams, fillings, mousses, soufflés, macerated fruits, some savory sauces.

BEER & HARD CIDER

Beer and hard cider are alternatives to wine, but in cooking they are less important. Even when reduced by long cooking, they do not produce the richness of wine. Beer often replaces stock or water in the hearty ethnic stews of central Europe and the carbonnades of Flanders. A light lager is best, as strongly flavored types can be overpowering. Some countries, notably Germany and Denmark, are fond of beer soup, usually thickened with bread or flour and often seasoned with cinnamon and brown sugar. Beer is popular used in the batter for deep-frying (p.105), as the bubbles produce a light, crisp coating.

Hard cider is robust and gives a light, dry finish with only a hint of apple. Since it is often produced locally, it appears in regional dishes such as the fish stews and sauces of Normandy and Brittany and in the famous fish in cider sauce of northern Spain. Cider is also good for basting baked hams, and sweeter varieties are often used for desserts.

USEFUL INFORMATION

Problems Flavor of heavy or sweet types can be overwhelming, so use in moderation.

Used in soups, stews, braises, sauces, batters, desserts.

ANGOSTURA BITTERS

Bitters have an alcoholic base and are flavored with orange or other citrus peel, aloe, mugwort, gentian, quinine, or other bitter plant products. Although bitters are widely used in liqueurs, aperitifs, *digestifs*, and cocktails, they can be added to fruit salads (especially where orange is included), sauces for fish, chicken and pork, and to dishes such as Caribbean crab soup. Common commercial bitters include Angostura from the West Indies and other brands from the Netherlands, Italy and France.

VINEGAR

The name vinegar comes from the French *vin aigre* or "sour wine". Like so many culinary discoveries, it was probably the result of a kitchen accident, as vinegar is produced naturally by acetic fermentation of alcoholic liquids such as wine and beer. Vinegar is one of the most versatile flavorings. It is indispensable for salads, sweet and sour combinations, and pickling and preserving, but is also an important addition to sauces, soups and stews, mayonnaises and marinades. In small amounts, it is good for deglazing and cooking juices of rich ingredients such as duck or foie gras. Vinegar is even found in some candies, pies and cakes.

Since there are so many different vinegars available, it is important to pair complementary flavors. Most adaptable is wine vinegar (right), made from red or white wine. Cider vinegar, with a mild, slightly sweet apple flavor, is made from apple pulp and can be cloudy unless filtered. Good for fruit salad dressings, it is also important in many preserves (p.489). Chinese or Japanese rice vinegars are generally mild, with a low acid content, ranging from the mildest white to a sweet red and the sweetest purple-black. Rice vinegars are well-suited to salads, especially those with raw vegetables such as cabbage and carrots, and are perfect for marinating fish and chicken. Malt vinegar is made from beer rather than wine and has a very distinctive taste. Malt barley is added to beer and fermented to produce a crude vinegar which is then left to mature. It is usually colored dark brown by the addition of caramel. Malt vinegar is a favorite condiment for British fried fish and chips, and is also used for preserving and in sauces for serving with cold meats.

White vinegar is colorless and is used in pickling, for which a clear brine is important. Distilled vinegar is stronger and more acid, and is often used for preserving watery vegetables. Most powerful of all is spirit vinegar, made by diluting acetic acid with water. Much too harsh for dressings, it is nevertheless a popular vinegar for homemade or commercial pickles (p.489).

Many flavored vinegars are enjoying a renewed popularity. Herb, fruit and flower vinegars feature in butter sauces and salad dressings, or are used for macerating fruits. Tarragon vinegar is probably the most familiar to cooks. It marries well with shellfish and chicken dishes and all kinds of salads, especially potato. Rosemary vinegar is good in lamb stew, blueberry vinegar suits green vegetable salads, and rose vinegar can add a subtle touch to the vinaigrette for a crisp green salad. All are easy to make at home (right), and good herb combinations include oregano with sweet marjoram or tarragon with rosemary.

Verjuice, made from the juice of tart fruits, usually apples or grapes, was a popular medieval flavoring in the days before lemon juice was common. Technically not a vinegar as it does not ferment, verjuice is still used today in the preparation of commercial mustard and in Middle Eastern cooking.

USEFUL INFORMATION

Common vinegars Red or white wine, balsamic, cider, rice, malt, distilled. *Herb:* basil, bay leaf, garlic, rosemary, tarragon, thyme, shallot, oregano, dill. *Fruit:* raspberry, lemon, strawberry, blueberry, kiwi; black currant.
Problems On standing, vinegar may cloud, which does not affect the flavor. Clarify vinegar by filtering through paper coffee filter; acid content of mild vinegars may be too low for pickling.
Used in fruit and vegetable salads; pickles and preserves; sauces; as a condiment.

RED OR WHITE WINE VINEGAR

Wine vinegar is produced from the acetic fermentation of red or white wine. The best is made by the Orléans method, in which wine is put into oak barrels and left for the culture, or "mother", to form. The "mother" (a layer of yeast cells and bacteria formed during fermentation) is the key to making wine vinegar. It can be obtained from a vinegar maker or winery, by pouring unpasteurized vinegar into new wine, or as a commercial preparation. As the vinegar develops, it is drawn off the bottom of the keg while fresh wine is added to maintain the level. Different wines, young or old, may be used, ranging from light Champagne (which has no bubbles) to varietal wines and fortified wine like sherry.

Balsamic vinegar (*aceto balsamico*) is an Italian red wine vinegar that is aged in barrels for between three and twelve years. It has a heavy, almost sweet flavor; indeed the best balsamic vinegar from Modena in Italy is so sweet, it is treated almost like a cordial, sprinkled on fresh berries or sipped after a rich dinner, and is very expensive to buy. Younger versions of the commercial type can add a hint of the real thing to a salad.

Making red or white wine vinegar

For red wine vinegar, pour a bottle of wine into a wide-mouthed half-gallon/two-liter jug, and add a "mother" or about ¾ cup/175 ml unpasteurized commercial red wine vinegar. Tie a double layer of cheesecloth over the jug and leave in a warm spot for about a month. For white wine vinegar, use half wine, half water and leave it at least three months. Taste to see if the wine has turned to vinegar and if so, strain it, reserving the "mother" to use again. (It must be kept moist with wine or it will die.)

White wine tarragon vinegar

Red wine vinegar

Making fruit vinegar

Flavored vinegar made with soft fruit or berries is excellent with vegetables such as beans, or with duck or liver. A little sugar added to sour fruits before heating them will counter their acidity.

To make 4-5 cups/1-1.25 L vinegar, soak 1 lb/500 g berries or soft ripe fruit in 3 cups/750 ml rice or white wine vinegar in a sterilized jar and seal (p.493). Leave it in a cool place for at least two weeks, shaking or stirring it occasionally. When the vinegar is well flavored, filter it through cheesecloth or paper coffee filters, pressing the berries to obtain as much juice as possible. Add 3-4 tbsp/45-60 g sugar and simmer the vinegar for 5-10 minutes. Strain into sterilized bottles (p.493) and either cap them or cork them, using a new cork. Store in a cool place (if kept in a warm environment, the vinegar may ferment and explode the cork).

Note If a new sediment forms, it is quite harmless, but may be strained out, if you like.

MAKING HERB-FLAVORED VINEGAR

White or red wine vinegars, and cider vinegar, are good for steeping herbs. Lightly bruise the herbs first.

1 Put about 1 cup/60 g fresh, lightly bruised herbs or ¼ cup/60 g crushed garlic or shallot into a sterilized, heatproof bottle (p.493). Bring 2 cups/500 ml of vinegar just to a boil. (Heating the vinegar helps to release the flavor of the herbs.) Pour the vinegar into the bottle and seal it. Let the herbs steep for at least 2 weeks, shaking the bottle occasionally.

2 Filter the vinegar through cheesecloth or paper coffee filters into a new, sterilized bottle. For an attractive presentation, add a fresh herb sprig to the bottle before pouring in the strained vinegar. Cork the bottle and store it in a cool, dark place.

MARINADES

A marinade is a highly flavored liquid in which food is soaked before cooking to give it flavor, prevent it from drying, and to tenderize it slightly. A marinade always contains an acid such as wine, vinegar, lime or lemon juice, as well as herbs and spices, and a little oil. Marinades for broiling must contain at least 25 percent oil.

There are two main types of marinade: raw and cooked. Raw marinades are used for relatively tender foods that need only short marination, such as fish or chicken. Sometimes a raw marinade can be used to "cook" the food, for example the lime juice marinade used with fish or shellfish in South American *seviche*. The ingredients are simply mixed together and poured over the food. They are generally composed of white wine, lime or lemon juice, oil, herbs, pepper and onion. Raw marinades containing red wine are sometimes used to marinate red meats before broiling. Flavoring liquids such as soy sauce and fruit juices may also be used. In Middle Eastern cuisines, plain yogurt is used as an uncooked marinade base; its active enzymes act as a tenderizer, as do the enzymes in papaya juice. Cooked marinades such as red wine marinade give a stronger flavor, best for beef and game.

The longer food is left in a marinade, the more flavor it absorbs. The food should be completely immersed, and turned from time to time in the marinade. Small pieces of meat require less marination than large ones. Flavors mature twice as fast if left at room temperature rather than in the refrigerator. **Note** As marinades often contain an acid, they should not be used in metal containers other than stainless steel.

Before cooking, drain the food and dry it thoroughly with paper towels, otherwise it will not brown but simply stew in excess moisture. After lengthy marinating, a good deal of juice will have been transferred to the marinade. This is often used in cooking the finished dish or to make an accompanying sauce.

Dry marinades are a third category. They are mixtures of herbs and spices rubbed directly on the food. Food marinated in this way may be pickled (Preserving, p.489), broiled after being brushed with oil or melted butter, simmered in a soup, or baked in a terrine.

USEFUL INFORMATION

Marinating times *Raw marinade:* half the time for cooked. *Cooked marinade:* whole game, meat or poultry 1-3 days; whole fish, game, meat, or poultry pieces 1-2 days. *Dry marinade:* game and red meats 1 day; white meats and poultry 6 hours; fish 2-3 hours.

Problems If cooked marinade is used warm, it will turn meat sour; lengthy marinating can overwhelm delicate ingredients and damage texture of food.

Used for *Red wine:* red meats, game, rich fish, poultry. *White wine:* white-fleshed fish, poultry, shellfish. *Soy-based:* barbecuing red meat, poultry and fish. *Fruit juice-based:* shellfish, fish, poultry.

Red wine marinade

This marinade makes enough for 5 lb/ 2.3 kg meat or poultry.

Makes 3 cups/750 ml

| 1 carrot, sliced |
| 2 onions, sliced |
| 1 stalk celery, sliced |
| ½ cup/125 ml olive oil |
| 1 bottle/725 ml red wine |
| ½ cup/125 ml red wine vinegar |
| bouquet garni |
| 12 juniper berries |
| 12 whole peppercorns |

1 In a saucepan, sauté the carrot, onion and celery slices in half the oil until soft but not browned.
2 Add the wine, wine vinegar, bouquet garni, juniper berries and peppercorns and bring to a boil. Simmer until the vegetables are tender, 15-20 minutes. Add the remaining oil and leave to cool.
3 Put the meat in a deep bowl and pour over the marinade so that the meat is covered completely. Refrigerate.

Marinade recipes

Raw marinade Mix all the ingredients for the cooked marinade (above) in a large bowl. Add the meat and turn it so it is completely covered. Marinate up to 2 days. A raw, concentrated marinade for the same quantity of veal may be made by substituting ⅔ cup/150 ml cognac and ⅔ cup/150 ml Madeira for the red wine and red wine vinegar.

Dry marinade Mix together 4 chopped cloves garlic, 1 tsp dried thyme, 1 crushed bay leaf, 6 crushed black peppercorns, and 2 tbsp coarse or kosher salt. Rub into the surface of 2 lb/1 kg pork, veal, duck or chicken and refrigerate 1 hour. Scrape the marinade off the meat before cooking.

STOCKS & SOUPS

STOCKS AND SOUPS are culinary siblings, but they are certainly not twins. Stocks are a means to an end, while soups are finished dishes appropriate as any course of a meal. A stock is the liquid left behind when water, bones, flavoring vegetables and seasonings have been slowly simmered. It is the base of many soups, sauces and stews; indeed, the French call it *fond*, which literally means "the foundation". Veal stock is the most versatile, then beef or chicken stock. Fish stock (Fr. *fumet*) comprises a separate category due to the nature of fish and its particular cooking properties.

The most common stock in home cooking is not, strictly speaking, a stock at all, but the broth made as a by-product of poaching meat or poultry. The French word for broth is *bouillon*, but in the United States the name "bouillon" is also associated with commercial stock cubes. (These must be used with care as they tend to be extremely salty.) *Court bouillon* is water boiled with seasonings, used for cooking delicate meats and fish. Vegetable stock is the lightest and least classic.

Soup has many forms: some soups are based on broth, which may be clarified (p.46), for example consommé; others are puréed soups, thickened with vegetables or a starch such as rice. Fish soups merit special consideration, while bisques, usually made with shellfish, are a kind of purée. Another group — cream or velouté — is thickened with flour. Most home-made and regional soups are broths, often reinforced with bread, as are many cold soups. Fruit soups (p.450), served as a first or last course, are common in eastern Europe, Germany and Scandinavia.

The characteristics of a well-made soup vary from one type to another, but a few general points apply to most: a soup should be true to its type; clear soup should be very clear, not muddy; a cream soup should be superbly smooth, and a bisque should display the essence of its principal ingredient. A soup is not a sauce but should stand on its own; the seasoning should be mild enough to allow the soup to be consumed in quantity and the flavor of the main ingredients must show through the most lavish additions of butter and cream. The consistency should not be so thick as to coat a spoon, even for starch-bound purées. For puréeing soup, see Vegetables (p.266).

One final consideration is the fat content of soup. A butter enrichment can be added at the last moment so that it melts without separating to leave a visible film of fat on the surface. In the case of hearty broth-based soups, however, it is correct to leave a little fat to form "eyes" on the surface of the soup to indicate its richness. For other enrichments see p.50.

Seasoning stocks and soups

For all stocks, moderate seasoning is the key, so that the flavors in the final dish are enhanced. Most cooks advise against adding salt since reduction of a liquid concentrates the stock, making it sufficiently salty. Whole peppercorns should be used rather than ground pepper which can turn bitter after prolonged cooking.

Soups, however, should be seasoned during cooking, always allowing for evaporation. Taste for seasoning again shortly before serving, bearing in mind that a soup should be less highly seasoned than a sauce. Cooked soups that are served cold should be tasted while hot, and again when cold, because the effect of the seasoning diminishes as the soup cools. For instructions on freezing soup, see Preserving, (p.496).

SKIMMING STOCKS & BROTHS

A hallmark of good stocks and broths is clarity, achieved by simmering rather than boiling the liquid. Never allow a stock or broth to boil for longer than a minute or two, otherwise the stock will cloud, and repeatedly skim off any scum that rises to the surface while it is simmering.

1 Using a small ladle or a large metal spoon, remove as much scum as possible and discard it. Do not worry about removing some of the liquid, as you can make up the lost volume with water.

2 Add cold water to the pot from time to time as the stock or broth is simmering. When the liquid returns to a boil, more scum will rise to the surface and should be removed with a ladle and discarded.

REMOVING FAT FROM STOCKS & BROTHS

Fat is the enemy of clear stock or broth. When using stock for consommé (p.46) or aspic (p.253) take special care to remove fat both with a ladle or metal spoon, and absorbent paper.

For cold stock or broth: allow the stock or broth to cool, then refrigerate it. As the liquid cools, the fat will form a crust on the surface; this may be removed with a large metal spoon or ladle.

For hot stock or soup: if time is short, skim off as much fat as possible with a small ladle, then draw a piece of absorbent paper over the surface of the liquid to absorb the remaining fat.

STRAINING STOCKS & SOUPS

A conical sieve (p.506) and a small ladle should be used to strain liquid, so that it flows in a stream from the point of the cone. A bowl strainer can be used, but the liquid tends to splash.

Hold the sieve over a large bowl or saucepan. Ladle in the liquid and solid ingredients. Tap the handle of the ladle on the edge of the strainer to speed the flow of the liquid. Press the solid ingredients with the back of the ladle to extract all the liquid, but do not attempt to purée them through the strainer.

Presenting soups

Ideally, there should be a similarity between the character of a soup and the type of bowl in which it is presented. The clarity of consommé calls for a simple, shallow porcelain soup plate to display the sparkling liquid. Broth-based soups are suited to pot-bellied terrines or rustic earthenware bowls, which double up as baking dishes for bread-thickened soups that are cooked partly in the oven. Opinions differ on whether creamy and puréed soups look more attractive in plain or colored bowls; it is a matter of personal taste.

Garnishes can transform a soup: a swirl of cream, a sprinkling of herbs or a single small ingredient such as a shrimp or a piece of tomato add extra color and flavor. Hot soup should be served very hot. Similarly, cold soup should be cold, though extreme chilling may dull the flavor.

Accompaniments to soups

Small pastries such as cheese straws can be served separately. Rice, noodles or *spätzle* (p.339) are added to the soup itself. Small choux puffs (p.376) may be added, but at the last possible moment so that they stay crisp. Perhaps the simplest accompaniment of all, and the most frequently abused, is the croûton. When properly made it is a welcome addition to a variety of soups, from rustic fish and broth-based soups to velvety bisques. Croûtons can be the traditional fried cubes of bread or simply cubes of toast. Alternatively, whole slices of French bread or rolls can be dried or toasted in the oven to make croûtes. These can be rubbed with a clove of garlic, in the style of Mediterranean cooking, for fish soups such as *bouillabaisse* or *Aigo saou* (p.48). Tiny cocktail crackers are a quick alternative. For almost any soup, crusty bread is an excellent accompaniment.

WHITE & BROWN STOCKS

Traditionally, and a little inaccurately, stocks are classified according to color. White stock is really pale golden, and brown stock only tends toward brown. The names probably derive from the treatment of the ingredients, which are browned for brown stock but left uncolored for white stock, resulting in quite distinct flavors. Furthermore, white stocks are made from meat and poultry, while brown stocks are based only on meat. In either case, neutrality is the key; a good stock reinforces and brings out other flavors but never calls attention to itself.

Veal, beef and chicken are excellent candidates for the stockpot, while lamb, pork and fatty poultry, such as duck and goose, have too distinctive a flavor. Bones from game make outstanding stock. Onion, leek, carrot and celery are standard aromatics, but they must be used in moderation. Good flavoring herbs are thyme, bay leaf and parsley, tied into a bouquet garni. A clove or two of garlic is an optional addition. Tomatoes or tomato paste are used to color and flavor brown stock.

Ingredients for stock need not be prime, but neither should the stockpot be used as a catch-all for leftovers. Fortunately, the less expensive and tougher cuts of meat, such as shank, also have the most flavor. Many modern cooks use little or no meat in their stock, relying on raw bones (Meat, p.235). Meat stocks are usually veal-based, sometimes with beef added for a brown stock. Chicken backs and necks can be used to make a poultry stock, or a whole bird may be simmered for its liquid and the meat used elsewhere. Broth can be substituted for stock in many dishes, but for finer sauces its flavor is too strong.

Good stock has a high level of gelatin, derived from heating collagen – the connective tissue found in all muscle and bone, especially that of young animals. Prolonged simmering extracts the collagen and converts it into gelatin. It is important to crack bones into pieces (p.235) before adding them to the stockpot so that they yield the maximum collagen and flavor during cooking.

USEFUL INFORMATION

When done Flavor is rich and concentrated; chicken bones should fall apart.
Problems Prolonged boiling before straining clouds stock; clarify with egg white (p.46).

Processed forms Cubes; granules; canned as broth; frozen.
Storage Refrigerate 2–3 days; after 3 days bring to a boil and simmer 10 minutes before returning to refrigerator.

White veal stock

Makes 2-3 qt/2-3 L stock

4-5 lb/1.8-2.3 kg veal bones, cracked by the butcher or cut in pieces
2 onions, quartered
2 carrots, quartered
2 stalks celery, cut into 2 in/5 cm pieces
large bouquet garni
10 peppercorns
1 clove garlic
3-4 qt/3-4 L water
Non-aluminum stockpot

1 Blanch the bones by bringing them to a boil in enough water to cover, then simmer for 5 minutes. Drain and rinse.
2 Put the bones and vegetables in a stockpot. Add the bouquet garni, peppercorns, garlic and water. Bring slowly to a boil, skimming often. Simmer for 4-5 hours, skimming occasionally. **Note** Stock should be reduced very slowly to avoid clouding.
3 Strain and taste the stock. If the flavor is not strong enough, boil until it is concentrated. Skim off any fat (p.42).

Chicken stock Substitute 3 lb/1.4 kg chicken backs and necks, or a whole fowl, for half the veal bones (above). Simmer stock for 3-4 hours. If using a fowl, remove it when thigh is tender when pierced with a skewer, 1¼-1½ hours.

Game stock Substitute 3 lb/1.4 kg game bones or tough game birds for half the veal bones. Finish as above.

Brown veal stock Put 4-5 lb/1.8-2.3 kg veal bones in a roasting pan and roast in the oven at 450°F/230°C for 30-40 minutes until well browned, stirring occasionally. Add the vegetables and brown them also, 15-20 minutes longer. Thorough browning gives stock flavor and color. For additional color, singe half an onion over an electric plate or gas burner. Transfer the bones, vegetables and singed onion to the stockpot. Discard the fat from the pan and deglaze (p.513) with 2 cups/500 ml water. Add the liquid to the pot, then make the stock. Add the garlic, 1 chopped tomato or 1 tbsp tomato paste, bouquet garni and peppercorns.

Brown stock Substitute 3 lb/1.4 kg beef bones for half the veal bones following the brown veal stock recipe above.

Beef stock Substitute 3 lb/1.4 kg beef bones for the veal bones in the brown veal stock recipe above.

FISH STOCK

Fish stock (Fr. *fumet*) needs careful handling. Prolonged cooking of fish bones can make the stock bitter, so maximum flavor is extracted by simmering the fish bones fast for no more than 20 minutes.

Bones, heads and tails of lean white fish, especially flat-fish, are recommended for stock. Sole, brill, plaice, lemon sole, flounder, whiting, hake, haddock and other mild-flavored fish all provide the necessary base. Avoid fatty fish such as mackerel which can make stock oily. Crustacean heads and shells, however, add a wonderful sweetness.

Onion or shallot is used to flavor fish stock but carrots are too sweet. To speed cooking, the onion can be sautéed briefly in butter before water is added. However, if the stock is intended for aspic or consommé, this is not a good idea as the fat may cloud it.

USEFUL INFORMATION
When done Perfumed, concentrated flavor.
Problems Bitter if overcooked; for clear, light color and good flavor, wash fish bones thoroughly, discarding gills.
Storage Refrigerate 2 days.

Fish stock

Makes about 1 qt/1 L stock

1 tbsp butter
4 shallots or 1 medium onion, finely chopped
1½ lb/750 g fish bones, cut in pieces
1 cup/250 ml white wine or juice of ½ lemon (optional)
1 qt/1 L water
10 peppercorns
large bouquet garni
Non-aluminum stockpot

1 In a large stockpot melt the butter and cook the onion slowly until it is soft but not brown, 7-10 minutes.
2 Add the fish bones, wine or lemon juice (if using), water, peppercorns and bouquet garni. Bring slowly to a boil, skimming often. Simmer, uncovered, for 20 minutes, then strain and leave to cool.

VEGETABLE STOCK

Although vegetable stock is a good base for many soups, it has never featured among the classic stocks because its flavor is often distinctive, even crude. For this reason, no classic recipe for vegetable stock exists. For good results, use a wide variety of ingredients, but do not allow one to overpower the rest. A good stock can be made with 1 lb/500 g chopped vegetables to 1 qt/1 L water. Strain the stock and discard the vegetables. Cabbage adds fuller flavor, while both carrot and parsnip have a sweetening effect. Leeks and garlic, in moderation, are useful additions. As plain vegetable stock can look unappetizing, singed onion halves and a little tomato can be added to give it color. This will turn the mixture into a brown vegetable stock, which can be used for a broth-based soup such as vegetarian minestrone. **Note** The liquid in which vegetables have been cooked is not a good substitute for stock since the vegetables, if correctly cooked, should retain their flavor, leaving a broth that is too weak to use as a stock.

COURT BOUILLON

Court bouillon is not a stock or broth in itself but aromatic cooking liquid used exclusively for blanching or poaching delicate meats, fish, variety meats such as brains or sweetbreads, and vegetables. It rarely features in the finished dish. For flavor, *court bouillon* must contain a substantial amount of lemon, wine or vinegar and seasoning. The French word *court*, meaning short, is an allusion to the relatively short cooking time needed to prepare *court bouillon* before adding the ingredient to be poached.

Basic court bouillon

Makes 1 qt/1 L court bouillon

1 qt/1 L water
1 carrot, sliced
1 small onion, sliced
bouquet garni
6 peppercorns
1 tsp salt
1 cup/250 ml dry white wine *or* ⅓ cup/75 ml vinegar *or* ¼ cup/60 ml lemon juice
Large non-aluminum saucepan

1 Combine all the ingredients in the pan, cover and bring to a boil. Simmer, uncovered, for 20-30 minutes.
2 The finished *court bouillon* need not necessarily be strained before using.

BROTH-BASED SOUPS

Broths are among the simplest soups to prepare. Typically, they derive their flavor from long simmering of all the ingredients together in one pot. Alternatively, an assortment of separately cooked foods may be added. Broth-based soups are wholesome rather than delicate, so they require ingredients such as potatoes, pasta or dried beans, pulses or grains. The Italian *zuppa pavese* (soup with eggs) which has a whole poached egg resting on slices of bread, or the large *leberknödeln* (liver dumplings) of Austrian cuisine, are characteristic. Italian *stracciatella* is broth-based soup at its simplest, made with merely a beaten egg, a grating of nutmeg and, occasionally, some grated lemon zest. Jewish chicken soup with matzoh balls or dumplings is equally basic, as is Chinese egg drop soup which is simply broth with egg. Other Asian broth soups are enlivened by the addition of such spices as chili pepper or the more exotic lemon grass (p.21).

Vegetable soups, with or without meat, are a little more complex: ingredients are cut into similar shapes, liquid is added and simmered until the solid ingredients are tender and the broth well flavored. Often the basic liquid is cold water since during long cooking, the ingredients contribute their flavor to the liquid.

In more sophisticated variations of broth-based soup, ingredients are added according to individual cooking requirements so that all finish cooking at the same time. This is especially important when delicate, quick-cooking ingredients such as green beans go into the pot with slow cookers such as dried beans.

A variety of different meats can be used in broths: cured meats – the original convenience food – improve flavor, and innards feature in many regional dishes. As in most soups less tender cuts of meat that require long cooking, like tripe, provide the best flavor.

Broth-based soups can become one-dish meals if the quantity and variety of ingredients are increased. Soups such as *Minestrone di verdura* have this potential, as do many other soups such as the egg-rich *waterzooi* of Flanders, the cock-a-leekie of Scotland, and the meat-laden borscht of eastern Europe, traditionally, a nutritional defense against the rigors of the winter climate.

USEFUL INFORMATION

Portion *Appetizer:* 1 cup/250 ml. *Main course:* 1-2 cups/250-500 ml.
Problems Pasta and rice may cloud broth, so cook separately.
Reheat In pan on top of stove; undercook tender ingredients slightly to allow for reheating and add fresh herbs just before serving.
Storage Refrigerate 2 days.
Additions Sherry or Madeira; lemon; hot pepper sauce (for clear soups); wine (red for veal and chicken, white for fish); beer (for cabbage and vegetable soups).
Accompaniments Baked or fried bread croûtes, sometimes rubbed with garlic; grated Parmesan or Gruyère cheese.
Garnishes Chopped fresh herbs.
Typical soups Avgolemono (rice, lemon and eggs, Greece); beer, sugar and egg yolks (Germany);
rabbit, ham, onion and tomato (Australia); oxtail, carrot and turnip (France); *harira* (chicken, vermicelli, chick peas, spices, Morocco); *barszcz* (dried boletus mushrooms, stock and beetroot, Poland); *caldo verde* (kale, sausage and potato, Portugal); *rassolnik* (sorrel, spinach, kidneys and sour cream, Russia); fava beans, ham, *chorizo* and saffron (Spain); Philadelphia pepper pot (tripe, veal, potatoes, green pepper and chili, USA); *busecca alla Ticinese* (tripe and white beans, Switzerland); *soupe au pistou* (beans, vegetables, pasta and *pistou*, France); *krupnik* (beef, vegetable and barley soup with sour cream, Poland); chicken with matzoh balls (Jewish); Scotch broth (mutton, carrots, turnips, leeks, barley, Scotland).

Minestrone di verdura

This famous Italian vegetable soup is also served in summer in northern Italy, where it is made in the morning and left to stand at room temperature until lunchtime.

Serves 8

⅔ cup/150 g white kidney beans	1 small cauliflower, divided into florets
¼ cup/60 ml olive oil	3 oz/90 g small macaroni
2 carrots, diced	2 zucchini, cut in ½ in/1.25 cm pieces
2 onions, diced	
4 stalks celery, sliced	3 tomatoes, peeled, seeded and chopped
3 qt/3 L chicken or vegetable stock	
1 bay leaf	2 tbsp/30 g chopped fresh basil or parsley
2 leeks, sliced	
12 green beans, cut in ½ in/1.25 cm pieces	**For serving**
	1 cup/250 g grated Parmesan cheese
1 clove garlic, crushed	
salt and pepper	

1 Soak the beans (p.322). Simmer them in enough water to cover until tender, about 2 hours. Take the beans from the heat and leave to stand in their liquid until needed.
2 In a large pot, heat the oil and sauté the carrots, onions and celery until lightly browned. Add the stock, bay leaf and kidney beans with their liquid and bring to a boil. Add the leeks, green beans, garlic, salt and pepper. Cover and simmer for 5 minutes, then add the cauliflower and macaroni and continue cooking until the pasta is *al dente* (p.333), about 10 minutes.
3 Add the zucchini and tomatoes and simmer until they are just tender, about 5 minutes. Remove the bay leaf. Stir in the basil or parsley and serve with Parmesan cheese.

Minestrone alla fiorentina
To make this variation of *Minestrone di verdura*, sauté 1 chopped onion, 1 crushed garlic clove and 1 slice raw ham, chopped, in 2 tbsp/30 ml olive oil. Add 1 sliced leek, 1 coarsely chopped small cabbage, 1½ cups/375 g dried white kidney beans, soaked (p.322) and enough broth to cover. Leave the broth to simmer until the vegetables are tender, about 20-30 minutes. Purée one quarter of the vegetables and add the purée back to the soup. Add 1 tsp chopped fresh rosemary and simmer for 5 minutes. Serve with toasted pumpernickel.

CONSOMME

Consommé is the most sophisticated of all stock-based soups. It is made by reducing veal, beef, chicken or, less frequently, game or fish stock and then clarifying it to produce a limpid, sparkling liquid. Its transparency is deceptive since good consommé has punch – a heady aroma and strong flavor that is neither bland nor salty, thin nor heavy.

The clarification process is simple. Well-flavored, fat-free stock is brought slowly to a boil while egg whites are whisked in. As the egg whites cook, they rise to the top of the stock in a gray froth that coagulates to form a filter. The consommé is left to simmer for about an hour so that the impurities percolate up through the filter leaving the liquid clean and sparkling.

While the egg whites clarify the liquid, they also absorb flavor, so ground or finely chopped vegetables are added to the stock, together with ground beef, fish or chicken. (The blood in red meat adds flavor, and also acts as a clarifying agent.) The term consommé double describes the process whereby meat or fish is used twice – first to make the stock, and then to clarify the consommé.

Madeira or sherry can be added just before serving or during clarification. Such flavorings should be merely an embellishment. Consommé should have a clear tint. Meat consommé should be darker than that of chicken or fish.

The gelatin content of consommé gives it a smooth texture when hot and sets it when chilled to just the right shivering jelly. Ideally, the original stock should be made with enough bones to set the consommé, but gelatin can be added during clarification to ensure that the consommé sets properly.

Consommé garnish is added just before serving so that it does not cloud the soup; a tablespoon per serving is sufficient. No ingredient should be larger than the size of a pea, although a few classic consommés call for whole poached eggs or *quenelles* (p.146). Chopped herbs, pasta and royales make good garnishes.

USEFUL INFORMATION

Portion ¾ cup/175 ml.
Problems If stock is tasteless, reduce it before clarifying; if pale, add tomato when clarifying; if cloudy after clarifying, pour through egg white filter and strain again or repeat clarification using 1-2 egg whites, simmer 5-10 minutes and strain.
Reheat In pan on top of stove without boiling.
Storage Refrigerate 2 days; loses clarity if frozen.

Accompaniments Cheese straws or wafers, small pastries.
Garnishes Tiny *quenelles*; crêpe strips; julienne of cured meat, vegetables; *pastine*; chopped herbs; vegetables *brunoise*. (p.259)
Typical soups *Dubarry* (garnished with cauliflower florets and royales); *Lucullus* (with sliced quail breast, chicken *quenelles* and truffle julienne); *madrilène* (flavored with celery and tomato with diced tomato garnish).

MAKING BEEF OR CHICKEN CONSOMME

Makes about 1qt/1L consommé

2 carrots, green tops of 2 leeks, 2 stalks celery, finely chopped

2 tomatoes, coarsely chopped

For beef consommé:
¾ lb/375 g boneless shin of beef, trimmed of fat and ground

For chicken consommé:
¾ lb/375 g chicken giblets or skinned chicken parts, chopped in pieces

3 egg whites, beaten until frothy (more if needed)

1½ qt/1.5 L flavored, fat-free stock (see p.42)

salt and pepper

Note Make sure the egg whites and flavorings are thoroughly mixed with the stock before heating or they will separate.

3 Let the consommé simmer gently for 30-40 minutes to extract flavor from the vegetables and meat, and to give the liquid time to clarify. At the end of cooking, the filter will form a solid crust and the consommé will be clear.

1 In a large bowl mix the vegetables into the chopped beef or chicken and egg whites. Heat the stock gently (it should be melted but not hot) and season to taste. Whisk the stock into the other ingredients and return the mixture to the pan. Bring slowly to a boil, whisking, for at least 10 minutes.

2 As soon as the liquid is frothy, stop whisking. When the stock boils, a solid clarification filter, or "raft", will form on top. Lower the heat then, with a ladle, make a hole (or vent) in the filter so the consommé can bubble without breaking up the clarification filter completely.

4 Place a damp dish towel in a strainer over a clean bowl or pan. Ladle the consommé into it, breaking the filter in pieces. Let the liquid drain through slowly. Once strained, leave the clarified consommé to cool.

Jellied consommé

To serve consommé cold as a jelly, you need the correct amount of gelatin to set it. Add some hot consommé to the gelatin to melt it, then add the dissolved gelatin back to the consommé. Too much gelatin will make the soup heavy so add it with caution (allow ¼ oz/7 g per 1 qt/1 L). To test, refrigerate one tablespoon of consommé on a saucer for about 15 minutes to see if it sets. Jellied consommé should melt on the tongue.

MAKING ROYALE GARNISH

Royales are tiny decorative shapes of egg custard made with fish, poultry or meat consommé. After baking in a ramekin, the custard is left to cool, then sliced and cut into tiny shapes with a knife or aspic cutter (p.505). Add the royale garnish to the hot consommé just before serving.

To make the custard: whisk 1 egg with 3 egg yolks and ⅔ cup/150 ml consommé until thoroughly mixed. Season and pour into a buttered mold or ramekin. Skim any foam from the surface. Set in a water bath and bake at 350°F/175°C until the custard is set, about 20 minutes, then chill. Cut the custard into ¼ in/ 6 mm slices. Using a knife or aspic cutters cut the slices into tiny shapes such as diamonds or crescents. Add them to the hot consommé just before serving.

BREAD-THICKENED SOUPS

Soups in which bread is a principal ingredient – as opposed to those served with bread as an accompaniment – can still be found in rural communities. Such soups are made by adding broth to dried bread or rolls and simmering until the bread is swollen and soft. Soups such as French onion and Spanish garlic follow this method but are distinguished by a single strong flavoring. As a slight refinement, dried bread may be stirred into a finished broth until the bread dissolves and binds the soup; the final texture is surprisingly light. Fresh breadcrumbs are often used to bind a bisque; they are added as it simmers.

Typical bread-thickened soups include gazpacho, with cucumber, peppers and tomato, and Tuscan *ribollita* with cabbage and other vegetables. Recipes are free-form, like French *garbure béarnaise*, with chopped or puréed vegetables. Some of the puréed vegetables are spread on garlic-flavored croûtes, which are immersed in the soup.

USEFUL INFORMATION

Portion *Appetizer:* ¾-1 cup/175-250 ml. *Main course:* 1-2 cups 250-500 ml.

Problems Lack of taste – always include a strong flavoring.
Reheat In pan on top of stove.

USEFUL INFORMATION/BREAD-THICKENED SOUPS

Storage Refrigerate 3 days
Accompaniments Grated cheese.
Garnish Chopped nuts; scallions; cracklings; crisp bacon.
Typical soups Garlic, eggs, bread (Spain); cabbage, cheese, bread (France); broth, bread (Italy); apples, bread, stock (Germany); black bread, stock (France); *à l'oignon* (France); *ago blanco* (garlic, almonds, bread, grapes, Spain), bread, butter, leeks, stock (France); Swiss chard, cabbage, potatoes and bread (Italy); cheese, broth, bread (Italy); peas, onion, broth, bread (Italy).

French onion soup

The key to good onion soup is to use well-flavored yellow onions. For variation, this soup can also be served covered with a layer of Parmesan cheese in place of Gruyère.

Serves 6

¼ cup/60 g butter	¾ cup/175 g grated Gruyère or Parmesan cheese
2 lb/1 kg yellow onions, thinly sliced	2 tbsp/30 g melted butter (to finish)
1½ qt/1.5 L brown stock (p.43)	
salt and pepper	
1 medium loaf French bread (p.353), cut in ½ in/1.25 cm slices	*6 individual ovenproof soup bowls*

1 In a large saucepan, melt the butter and cook the onions very gently until they are a deep golden brown, 15-20 minutes. Add the stock, salt and pepper, simmer for 10-15 minutes and taste.
2 Heat the oven to 300°F/150°C and bake the bread until dry and lightly browned, 15-20 minutes. Reheat the soup on top of the stove. Set two or three slices of bread in individual preheated soup bowls and pour the hot soup on top. Cover the soup with a thick layer of grated Gruyère or Parmesan cheese, sprinkle it with melted butter and broil until browned. Serve at once, as onion soup must be piping hot.

Aigo saou

This Provençal soup can be made with just one fish or several different types. (All fish should be weighed with their heads.) The fish and soup may be served as separate courses or in one bowl.

Serves 8

4-5 lb/1.8-2.3 kg white-fleshed fish (p.138), trimmed and cut into steaks, heads and trimmings reserved for stock	large bouquet garni
	1 strip orange zest
3 tbsp/45 ml olive oil	2 large sprigs fennel leaves or 1 tsp dried fennel seed
4 garlic cloves, chopped	salt and pepper
2 onions, sliced	*For serving*
fish stock (p.44)	2 tbsp/30 g chopped parsley
1 lb/500 g potatoes, thinly sliced	croûtes (p.352)
½ lb/250 g tomatoes, peeled, seeded and chopped	*rouille* (p.63)

1 Marinate the fish steaks in olive oil and garlic for 1 hour at room temperature. Remove the fish from the marinade and pour the marinade into a large saucepan.
2 Heat the reserved marinade, add the onions and cook them until soft but not brown. Add the stock, potatoes, tomatoes, bouquet garni, orange zest, fennel, salt and pepper. Bring to a boil and simmer, skimming occasionally, until all ingredients are tender, about 30 minutes. Taste the broth for seasoning and discard the orange zest and fennel leaves.

3 Add the fish steaks and cook until the flesh flakes easily, about 6-8 minutes. **Note** Liquid must continue to boil after the fish is added or the oil will separate from the broth.
4 Remove the fish with a slotted spoon and, if you prefer, discard the bones and skin. Arrange the fish on a preheated serving dish. Pour the soup into a tureen. Sprinkle both with chopped parsley and serve accompanied by croûtes and *rouille*.

FISH & SHELLFISH SOUPS

Seafood lends itself to visually appealing, hearty soups that can be a main course or a complete meal. A typical fish soup includes a selection of white fish such as cod, hake, haddock, halibut, red snapper, bream, perch, monkfish or gurnard, plus an oily fish such as eel or mackerel, and is often topped with mussels or clams. Within reason, the greater the variety, the better the soup, but the current vogue for adding expensive shellfish to traditional recipes can be overwhelming.

Many contemporary favorites, such as Tuscan *cacciucco*, which require a minimum of five types of fish, started out as a catch-all for whatever fish the fisherman didn't sell. The dish often provided his family with the most flavorful, if least select, remnants from the day's catch. The famous New England chowder follows the same principle; the name derives from the French *chaudière* or stewpot. Chowders are hearty, stew-like soups that can be based on a variety of ingredients and usually include milk. Simpler in spirit and preparation are soups that are called stews, a misnomer in this case. Most famous of these is Maryland oyster stew in which oysters (or steamed mussels) are poached in seasoned milk or cream.

Along most of the world's coasts, inventive cooks put various species of small crab to good use. Too small to provide much meat, they are full of flavor and can be used to make savory broths. Vegetables such as tomato, potato and zucchini, seasoned with a wide range of herbs and spices, are often added.

Given the delicate nature of fish, many soups call for carefully paced cooking, with firmer fish cooked first at the bottom of the pot. As a further refinement, rapidly cooked shellfish such as mussels or scallops can be poached separately and added with their liquid, just before serving, so that they heat through. Many people find fish bones cumbersome, but using filleted fish rather than chunks on the bone detracts from the characteristically hearty nature of fish soups. One compromise, used in making Provençal *bouillabaisse*, is to make a broth soup "bone first". This is when the bones and trimmings from the fish are used to make a broth in which to cook the vegetables and fish fillets.

As with poultry-based *Poule au pot* (p.182), soups such as *bouillabaisse* and *Aigo saou* (left) often make up a two course meal, with the broth as a first course and the fish as the main course. In the South of France, fish soups are frequently accompanied by sauces such as *aïoli* or *rouille* (p.63), which provide a piquant note that changes the character of the broth. A hallmark of these soups is to boil rather than simmer the broth so that it emulsifies and slightly thickens the soup.

USEFUL INFORMATION

Portion *Appetizer:* 1 cup/250 ml; *Main course:* 1-2 cups/250-500 ml.
Problems To avoid overcooking, layer fish in pot with firmest at the bottom. Always undercook the fish as it continues cooking in the hot broth.
Reheat In pan on top of stove; add delicate fish just before serving.
Storage Refrigerate 2 days.
Additions Dry white wine; hot pepper sauce; butter; chili oil.
Accompaniments Baked or fried croûtes, sometimes with garlic; oyster crackers; *aïoli* (garlic mayonnaise); *rouille* (hot red pepper sauce).
Garnish Small shellfish; lemon; chopped green pepper.
Typical soups Queensland crab (crab, cream, sherry, Australia); *sopa de camarones* (shrimp, potatoes, tomatoes, corn, Spain); New England chowder (clams, salt pork, potatoes, cream, USA); chick pea, salt cod, spinach, (Spain);

brodetto (broth with white fish, clams, eel, squid, Italy); conch chowder (conch, salt pork, tomatoes, potatoes, rice, milk, Caribbean, USA); Manhattan clam chowder (clams, tomatoes, potatoes, USA); scallop chowder (scallops, milk, potatoes, USA); *bouillabaisse* (fish, vegetables, *rouille*, France); *bourride* (fish, *aïoli*, France); partan bree (crabmeat, anchovies, rice, Scotland); cullen skink (smoked haddock, potato, Scotland); oysters, lemon, anchovies (Australia); cioppino (clams, shrimp, Dungeness crab, Burgundy wine, western USA); *shorbet el samak* (with mint and cinnamon, Turkey).

BISQUES

A bisque is a creamy purée that concentrates the essence of a single ingredient into a rich perfumed soup. Most popular are shellfish bisques but game, poultry and full-flavored vegetables such as tomato are also suitable, if less traditional.

Shellfish bisques follow a classic preparation; a complicated process calculated to bring out the maximum flavor. The principal ingredient is often sautéed and flamed, especially if live shellfish is used. Fish stock and aromatics are added, along with rice for thickening. When all the ingredients are cooked, the bisque is puréed, formerly with a mortar and pestle, but nowadays in a food processor. The bisque is then sieved before returning to the heat to simmer and marry the flavors. Scrupulous cooks then sieve it again, through the finest of conical sieves (p.506) before enriching it with cream, to achieve the characteristic velvety texture. The seasoning of a bisque is critical, often a hint of cayenne is added as a foil to the rich texture and flavor. Some recipes call for a final enrichment of shellfish butter (p.155). The name bisque is sometimes loosely applied to cream soups of shellfish or vegetables, such as crab or tomato, which do not follow the classic cooking procedure.

USEFUL INFORMATION

Portion ¾ cup/175 ml.
Problems If texture is granular, work in blender or through conical sieve; if watery, boil to reduce; if too thin, add arrowroot.
Reheat In pan on top of stove, then add cream.
Storage Refrigerate 2 days.
Accompaniments Fried croûtons.

Garnish Chopped shellfish or other main ingredient; tablespoonful of cream, whipped cream or *crème fraîche*; small whole shellfish such as shrimps.
Typical soups Lobster or spiny lobster (France); crayfish (France); artichoke and crab (USA); oyster and clam (USA); tomato (USA).

GUMBOS

Gumbo, the pride of Louisiana, takes its name from an African word for okra, the ingredient that gives the soup its characteristic gelatinous texture. Many gumbos are roux-based, but the term "roux" takes on new meaning in Louisiana's Créole and Cajun communities where the flour and fat are cooked for much longer, so the roux is just short of burned.

Gumbos are as much stew as soup; emphasis is on fully developed layers of flavor. Chicken may be paired with ham, green pepper and oysters; shrimp with oysters, okra, garlic and onion; duck with *andouille* sausage (p.247). Green gumbo is made with spinach, beet tops, turnip, mustard and collard greens.

Plain boiled or steamed rice is the usual accompaniment, with Southern biscuits (p.359) and hot pepper sauce or *rouille* (p.63).

Shrimp bisque

The best shrimp to use for bisques are the small gray shrimp, but any shrimp can be substituted, preferably with their heads.

Serves 6

⅓ cup/75 g butter	3 tbsp/45 ml heavy cream
2 tbsp/30 g diced carrot	**For serving**
2 tbsp/30 g diced onion	pinch of cayenne pepper
bouquet garni	12-18 cooked tiny shrimp, peeled
1½ lb/750 g raw shrimp	fried croûtons
½ cup/125 ml white wine	
2 tbsp/30 ml brandy	
5 cups/1.25 L veal stock	
2 tbsp/30 g rice	
salt and pepper	
shrimp butter (p.155)	
2 tbsp/30 ml sherry or Madeira	

1 Melt one tablespoon of the butter in a large saucepan. Add the vegetables and bouquet garni. Cover and cook over a low heat until they are soft, 5-7 minutes. Add the shrimp and cook, stirring, 2-3 minutes. Pour in the wine and brandy; boil for 2 minutes to reduce the liquid. Add 1 cup/250 ml stock and simmer until the shrimp are tender, 3-5 minutes. Let them cool slightly, then remove and peel them, reserving the shells. For large shrimp remove the intestinal vein (p.160).
2 Return the shrimp to the wine and vegetable mixture, add the remaining stock, rice, salt and pepper. Cover and simmer, 15-20 minutes. Make shrimp butter (p.155) with the remaining butter and shells.
3 Discard the bouquet garni and purée the bisque in a food processor or blender, then through a sieve or strainer. Alternatively, work soup through a drum sieve (p.506).
4 Bring the bisque to a boil, add the sherry or Madeira and cream and simmer for 2 minutes. Off the heat, stir in the shrimp butter piece by piece. Season to taste, add a pinch of cayenne, and a garnish of tiny shrimps. Pass croûtons separately.

PUREED SOUPS

The secret of a good puréed soup is thorough cooking so that the starchy ingredients which give it body – root vegetables and dried beans – are well blended. For some puréed soups, such as lentil or potato, the principal ingredient has enough starch of its own to bind the soup; others need additional potato or rice.

The consistency of a puréed soup varies according to the ingredients used and the way in which they are processed. A food mill gives the coarsest texture, then a food processor, while a blender or fine sieve gives the finest consistency (p.266).

Among the classic puréed soups are Vichyssoise (leek with potato), *potage Crécy* (carrots thickened with rice), and *potage Saint-Germain* (split pea flavored with ham). In Provence fish soups may be puréed, and in Italy some cooks work their minestrone through a food mill. There is also a range of half-puréed soups (often based on root vegetables or corn), in which some of the solid ingredients are puréed to thicken the broth, while the rest are left in pieces for texture. At one time poultry, meat and game purées were popular soups. Most familiar of these today is *potage à la reine*, a rich purée based on chicken stock.

USEFUL INFORMATION

Portion ¾ cup/175 ml.
Reheat In pan on top of stove, adding cream, egg yolk, fresh herbs just before serving.
Problems If too thick, thin with water or milk; if too thin, bind with arrowroot or cornstarch (p.59); if stringy or coarse, work through a sieve.
Storage Refrigerate 2 days.
Enrichments Cream; whipped cream; butter; herb butter.
Accompaniments Fried croûtons; diced, smoked meat; diced fried bacon; cracklings (p.229).
Garnishes Tablespoon *crème fraîche* or soured cream; chopped hard-boiled egg; sliced sausage;

thin slice of lemon; *chiffonnade* of herbs; toasted nuts; Mexican tomato sauce (p.65).
Typical soups *Crécy* (carrots, usually with rice); *Dubarry* (cauliflower); *Palestine* (Jerusalem artichokes); *Esau* (lentils and rice); *Parmentier* (potatoes); *Fréneuse* (turnips); *Saint-Germain* (split pea); *Soissonaise* (white beans, watercress, potato, milk): all from France; Vichyssoise (potato, leek, USA); *pasta e fagioli* (beans, salt pork, pasta, (Italy); pumpkin, nutmeg (USA, France); corn, salt pork, onions, potatoes, cream (USA); *puré de garbanzos* (chick pea, Spain); sweet potato (USA).

ENRICHMENTS TO SOUP

Last-minute additions can improve the character of a soup; add them just before serving or they will separate from the soup. Strong flavorings – herbs, wine and spices – are stirred into the soup itself (see Additions for broth-based, fish and cold soups).

Cream (for cream soups and bisques). Stir heavy cream or *crème fraîche* into the soup just before serving. An alternative is whipped cream with herbs, caviar or smoked fish folded into it.

Egg yolk and cream (for velouté soups) **or egg yolk** (for broth and bread-thickened soups). Combine egg yolks with heavy cream or *crème fraîche*, if using. Stir in a large ladleful of hot soup, then stir into the remaining soup. Heat gently, stirring, until the soup thickens. Do not allow soup to boil.

Whole egg (for broth soups). Whisk the egg until mixed. Stir into simmering soup from a height so that it forms strings.

Butter, herb and shellfish butters (for puréed soups and bisques). Add one to two tablespoons of firm butter at the last moment; it should melt but not separate.

Black bean soup

The classic accompaniment to black bean soup is moist white or yellow cornbread. Alternatively, serve with beaten biscuits.

Serves 4-6

1 lb/500 g black beans	salt and pepper
1 tbsp oil	4 tbsp/60 ml sherry or Madeira
2 carrots, chopped	1 tbsp dry mustard
1 onion, chopped	¼ tsp cayenne pepper
2 stalks celery, chopped	juice of ½ lemon
1½ qt/1.5 L water	*For garnish*
1 lb/500 g smoked ham hocks	lemon slices
bouquet garni	hard-boiled egg, sliced
2 cloves garlic, chopped	sour cream (optional)

1 Soak the black beans (p.322), then drain them.
2 Heat the oil in a large pot. Add the carrots, onion and celery and sauté over a medium heat, 5-7 minutes until lightly browned. Add the water, beans, ham hocks, bouquet garni, garlic, salt and pepper. Bring to a boil, cover, and simmer until the beans and ham hocks are tender, about 2 hours. Add more water if necessary.
3 Remove the ham hocks, cut the meat off the bones, dice it and set it aside. Remove the bouquet garni. Work the soup through a food mill, sieve, food processor or blender. If it is too thick, add a little water.
4 Just before serving, add the ham, sherry or Madeira, mustard, cayenne and lemon juice to the soup. Bring it back to a boil and season to taste with salt and pepper. Pour the soup into a tureen or individual bowls. Decorate it with the garnish.
White bean soup (*potage Soissonaise*) Substitute 1 lb/500 g dried white beans, soaked for the black beans. Omit the ham and garlic. Simmer for 1 hour, until the vegetables are tender, purée (p.266) and thin to desired consistency with white stock (p.44). Omit the lemon juice, sherry or Madeira.
Lentil soup Substitute lentils for the black beans. Simmer for 1 hour. Omit the lemon juice, sherry or Madeira.
Split pea soup (*potage Saint-Germain*) Substitute 1 lb/500 g split peas, soaked for black beans. Omit the onion, carrots and garlic. Simmer for 1 hour. Omit lemon juice, sherry or Madeira.

CREAM SOUPS

Cream soups use many of the same ingredients as puréed soups although they are richer, smoother and more refined in texture. Basic ingredients, such as lettuce or asparagus, tend to be lighter. Cream soups are thickened with flour, which may be added as a roux, as *beurre manié* (p.59) or, occasionally, as a simple flour and water paste. Whatever the method, the flour must be thoroughly cooked or the soup will taste of raw flour.

Vegetables such as onion may be softened in butter before adding the flour. More delicate vegetables like mushrooms are cooked directly in the soup stock. As cream soups are characterized by their smoothness, achieving the correct consistency is all-important; a blender or flat sieve gives the smoothest result because ingredients are emulsified and puréed.

USEFUL INFORMATION
Portion ¾ cup/175 ml.
Reheat In pan on top of stove, then add cream or *crème fraîche*.
Problems To prevent curdling, cook acid ingredients thoroughly and do not allow soup to boil.
Storage Refrigerate 2 days.
Enrichments Cream or *crème fraîche*; butter; egg yolk.
Accompaniments Fried croûtons; choux puffs; sesame crackers.
Garnish Chopped or shredded herbs; marbling of cream; chopped pieces of main ingredient.
Typical soups She-crab, sherry (southern USA); chicken, kohlrabi (Hungary); turkey, hazelnuts (USA); lobster (Australia); *potaje de col* (cabbage, Spain); smoked haddock (Scotland); Cheddar cheese (Canada); spring soup (carrots, leeks, spinach, radishes, Sweden); asparagus (UK); parsley (UK); chervil (France).

COLD SOUPS

Cold jellied consommé has long been a feature of the buffet table, and recently the repertoire of cold soups has broadened to include purées, cream soups and broths, particularly of vegetables. *Borscht* is a typical example of a soup that can be eaten hot or cold.

Chilling affects both the consistency and flavor of a soup. A cold soup should never be thin and is often more pleasant when it is almost too thick to pour. Most soups thicken naturally as they cool (egg yolk or butter enrichments can become too firm). Gazpacho, the Spanish combination of sliced cucumber, tomato, bell pepper and pounded garlic, is a good example of a cold soup. There are dozens of variations, many thinned with cold water or ice at the last minute.

Seasoning of a chilled soup is crucial. Taste repeatedly as the soup cools. If the soup has been made in advance, taste immediately before serving and adjust the seasoning again, perhaps adding herbs, seasoning or lemon juice. **Note** Allow a few minutes for salt to dissolve before tasting again.

USEFUL INFORMATION
Portion ¾ cup/175 ml.
Problems If too thin, add soaked breadcrumbs or puréed ingredient such as tomato.
Storage Refrigerate covered, 1-2 days.
Additions Hot pepper sauce (*rouille*); citrus juice.
Accompaniments Bread sticks; crackers; cheese straws.
Garnish Diced ingredients; herbs; cream; slice of lemon.
Typical soups *Tarator* (cucumber, walnut, yogurt, Bulgaria); buttermilk, egg yolks, sugar, lemon, cream (Denmark); breadfruit, onion, cream (Spain); *botrinya* (spinach, stock, sherry or champagne, Russia); *Tarhana çorbasi* (tomatoes, pepper, yogurt, Turkey); lentils, tomato, basil, radishes, scallions (USA); *Gazpacho* (sliced cucumber, tomatoes, bell pepper, garlic and bread, Spain).

Chilled spinach & avocado soup

A dash of lemon or lime juice added to this refreshing cold soup just before serving will perk up the flavor.

Serves 8

1 lb/500 g spinach	1 cup/250 ml *crème fraîche* or heavy cream
¼ cup/60 g butter	2 ripe avocados
salt and pepper	dash of Tabasco
pinch of nutmeg	juice of 2 limes or lemons
3 tbsp/45 g flour	**For garnish**
2 cups/500 ml milk	sprigs of parsley or coriander
2 cups/500 ml chicken stock	

1 Discard the stems from the spinach and wash it thoroughly in several changes of water. Place it in a large pan with a little water and cover tightly. Cook for about 5 minutes until wilted, stirring once. Drain the spinach well and let it cool. Squeeze out the liquid with your fist, then chop the spinach.
2 In a heavy saucepan melt the butter, then stir in the spinach, salt, pepper and nutmeg. Stir in the flour, then the milk and stock. Bring to a boil, cover and simmer for 10 minutes, stirring occasionally. Stir in half the *crème fraîche* or cream and season the soup to taste.
3 Let the soup cool, then purée it and pour it into a bowl. Peel the avocados and cut them in chunks, discarding the pits (p.470). Purée the avocados with one or two ladlefuls of soup and stir this mixture into the remaining soup. Cover the soup with plastic wrap to exclude air, and chill it in a refrigerator for at least 2 hours. **Note** Spinach and avocado soup should not be left to chill for longer than 24 hours as it will discolor.
4 Just before serving, add the Tabasco and lime or lemon juice, according to your taste. Ladle the soup into bowls and add a spoonful of the reserved *crème fraîche* or cream, stirring to marble it. Top with sprigs of parsley or coriander.

SAUCES

I T IS THE FRENCH who have written the grammar of sauces, defining a structure of "mother" sauces that have been absorbed into the international language of cooking. Conveniently, these can be divided into families according to their basic ingredients. Each family is governed by a basic mother sauce, or *mère* as it is known in France, for which there is a standard method. Variations are created by adding such ingredients as wine, shallots, mushrooms, cream, cheese, herbs or garlic. At the core of the system are the white and brown sauces made from a flour and butter roux or, as in basic brown sauce, another thickener such as arrowroot or potato starch. More complex, although just as fundamental, are the emulsified butter sauces, such as hollandaise and béarnaise, and that backbone of cold emulsified sauces, mayonnaise.

By no means all good sauces are French. According to the dictionary definition, a sauce is a thickened liquid that "adds zest or piquancy to other food", in which case gravies, barbecue sauces, and salad dressings also qualify, not to mention bread-thickened sauces, pasta, nut, piquant, tomato, and savory fruit sauces. This chapter covers all of these, omitting only those known as integral sauces, that is sauces that form part of a dish, such as a braise. Some sauces, for example ketchup and mustard, are now more commonly used as a condiment and are therefore to be found in the Chapter on Herbs, Spices and Flavorings (p.12).

Some dessert sauces are covered in this chapter, for example sabayon, custard and caramel; others can be found in Fruit (p.446), and Chocolate (p.411).

ESSENTIALS OF A GOOD SAUCE

Thick or thin, light or dark and irrespective of its origins, a well-made sauce should have the following characteristics. It should have a distinctive texture: unctuous for mayonnaise, frothy for sabayon, glossy for brown *demi-glace* sauce. It should have body, with flavors concentrated to just the right degree, mild or pungent, to complement the rest of the dish. Color, too, should accent the dish: pair white butter sauce with a salmon *mousseline*, or a yellow mustard sauce with kidneys.

Equally important to a sauce is consistency. Velouté sauces and white butter sauces should form a semi-transparent veil over the food, while brown sauces should be translucent, giving a light glaze to the meats beneath. Some sauces are as light as oil, with no added thickener at all. Only white sauces, hollandaise and béarnaise sauces, some pasta sauces and some sweet sauces are thick enough to coat ingredients. Even then, the shape and color of the food beneath should be discernible. A sauce should never be glutinous, even when designed to bind soufflés or to enrich gratins of vegetables that have a high water content. **Note** Sauces that are to be served cold need to be thicker than hot ones.

Seasoning sauces

The final, and most important, touch in perfecting a sauce is to adjust the seasoning. A well-balanced sauce aims for a subtle equilibrium of many ingredients with no single flavor dominating. The food it is to accompany must always be taken into account so that the sauce complements rather than overwhelms the dish.

The very origin of the word sauce, from the Latin *salsa* meaning salty, emphasizes its role in highlighting the flavor of a dish. For this reason a sauce should always taste too strong by itself; its flavor should be too concentrated to be palatable in quantity. If a sauce is to be reduced it should be lightly seasoned only, since it will become concentrated as the liquid reduces. As for specific instructions, Herman Senn best summed it up in his book, *The Book of Sauces* (1915): "It is most difficult to give any precise directions for seasoning ... Experience alone will teach a cook."

WHISKING A SAUCE

Rapid whisking of a sauce not only gives it a smooth consistency, but also allows it to be cooked over a higher heat so that it is less likely to form lumps. Rapid whisking also helps reduce the risk of sauce burning at the bottom of the pan.

For maximum effect and to avoid splashes on the sides of the pan, whisk in a figure eight motion, working round the sides of the pan and across the middle. From time to time, pass the whisk in a circle around the base of the pan to make sure no area has been missed.

Reducing sauces

The key to many sauces is reduction – cooking over a high heat to evaporate the liquid and concentrate the flavor, while at the same time achieving just the right consistency. Reduction is essential for many classic French sauces, particularly those such as velouté which are based on stock. As a general rule, the longer a sauce is simmered, the more subtle and mellow its taste. Leaving the pan uncovered speeds evaporation and concentration of the liquid.

To reduce a sauce, simmer it gently (do not boil hard or the sauce may cloud). Reduction may take anything from three minutes to an hour or more, depending on the ingredients used. Shortest cooking time is given to béchamel sauces, when three to five minutes will suffice. A velouté sauce should simmer for at least 15–30 minutes, while a good brown sauce needs an hour or more. For butter sauces, the wine, stock or cooking juices that form the base are reduced to a glaze.

STRAINING A SAUCE

A sauce is strained, preferably using a conical mesh sieve (p.506), to remove solid ingredients and to help emulsify liquid ingredients. By contrast, when a sauce is puréed all the ingredients are left in the finished sauce. When straining, the finer the mesh, the smoother and more glossy the sauce will be.

Ladle some sauce into a strainer that has been set over a saucepan. Push the ladle downward against the mesh in short, sharp strokes, pressing solid ingredients to extract maximum flavor.

MOUNTING A SAUCE WITH BUTTER

To "mount" a sauce is to add small pieces of cold, unsalted butter to it at the last moment, giving it gloss and a fresh butter flavor.

For a thickened sauce (velouté or brown):

Take the pan from the heat and add the butter. Shake and swirl the pan so that the butter melts and is incorporated with the sauce.

For a glaze base (butter sauce):

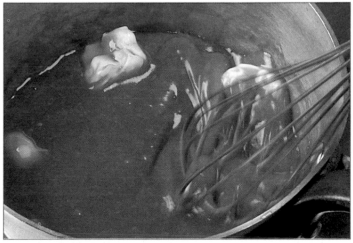

Let the pan cool until just hot to the touch. Add the butter a few pieces at a time, whisking thoroughly. Shift the pan on and off the heat so that the butter thickens and emulsifies, becoming creamy.

Serving sauces

There are three ways to serve a sauce: firstly, food may be coated with sauce (below); secondly, the sauce may be spooned on to a plate or dish, with the food carefully arranged on top; thirdly, sauces such as salad dressings and gravies can be served separately in a sauceboat or bowl. Modern chefs may use two sauces of a different color, sometimes swirling one on the other. Crisp ingredients such as puff pastry or croûtes should never be smothered in sauce as they will become soggy.

COATING WITH SAUCE

A sauce for coating should be sufficiently thick to stay on the food, but it should not be so thick as to mask completely the contours and color of the food beneath it.

To test for coating consistency, dip a wooden spoon into the sauce and lift it out. The sauce should cling lightly, leaving a clear trail when you draw your finger across it.

When coating food, fill a small ladle with sauce, tip it toward you and work away from you. **Note** Sabayon and rich white sauces are often browned under the broiler after coating, but butter sauces or egg custard would separate.

WHITE SAUCES

White sauces fall into two categories: milk-based, often called béchamel, and stock-based or velouté. Both are based on a butter and flour roux, and the velouté is made with fish, poultry or veal stock.

White sauces offer the widest range of possibilities in the whole sauce repertoire. They are used to bind soufflés, croquettes and fritters, as a base for gratins, and to thicken soups as well as their more usual function of coating foods (p.53). One reason for their versatility is the neutral background they offer to a wide range of flavorings, from wine and herbs to curry powder and capers.

USEFUL INFORMATION

Portion 3-4 tbsp/45-60 ml.
Problems If lumps form, work through sieve.
Reheat In pan on top of stove; thin with liquid if necessary.
Storage Refrigerate 2 days; freeze 1 year.

PREVENTING SKIN FORMING ON WHITE SAUCE

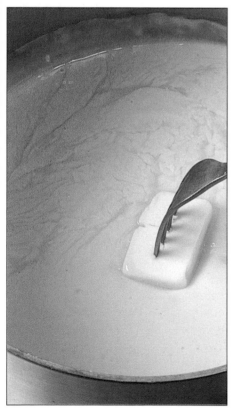

If leaving the sauce to stand for an hour or two, while it is still warm, rub the surface with a lump of butter so that it melts to form a thin coating.

BÉCHAMEL

Plain béchamel can be used with only salt, pepper and nutmeg for flavoring, but it is greatly improved if the milk is first infused with onion, bay leaf and peppercorns. Cooking is important if the sauce is not to taste of uncooked flour. Traditionally, béchamel was simmered for half an hour or more, but constant attention is needed to prevent the milk from scorching so most cooks now cook it for only two to three minutes. Béchamel is the only sauce deliberately made to different consistencies by varying the proportion of flour and butter to milk. Thin béchamel is used as a base for soups and other sauces, thick béchamel for binding, and medium béchamel for coating eggs, chicken, fish and vegetables.

Medium béchamel

Makes 1 cup/250 ml sauce

1 cup/250 ml milk
1½ tbsp butter
1½ tbsp flour
pinch grated nutmeg (more if needed)
salt and white pepper
Optional flavorings
slice of onion
small bay leaf
½ tsp peppercorns

1 If using flavorings, add these to the milk. Bring the milk to a boil in a saucepan, cover and leave to infuse for 10 minutes. For plain béchamel, simply bring the milk to a boil without adding any flavorings.
2 To make the roux, melt the butter in a heavy saucepan. Whisk in the flour and cook until foaming, about 1 minute. Remove the pan from the heat and let it cool slightly. Strain in the hot milk, whisking constantly.
3 Return the sauce to the heat and bring it back to a boil, whisking constantly until the sauce thickens. Season to taste with nutmeg, salt and pepper and simmer for a further 2 minutes.
Thin béchamel Substitute 1 tbsp butter and 1 tbsp flour for the quantity of butter and flour in the above recipe.
Thick béchamel Substitute 2 tbsp butter and 2 tbsp flour for the butter and flour in the above recipe.

Cheese sauce (*sauce Mornay*) To accompany eggs, fish, poultry, white meats, vegetables. Make 1 cup/250 ml thin béchamel. Off the heat beat in 1 egg yolk (optional) and ¼ cup/20 g grated Parmesan or Gruyère cheese. If you like, flavor the sauce with 1 tsp Dijon mustard. Do not reheat Mornay sauce or the cheese will become stringy. For gratins that are to be reheated, make the sauce without the egg yolk.
Cream sauce To accompany eggs, fish, vegetables, poultry. Add ¼ cup/60 ml *crème fraîche* or heavy cream to 1 cup/250ml béchamel sauce and simmer, whisking often, to the required consistency. Season to taste.
Mushroom sauce To accompany fish, poultry and veal. Heat 2 oz/60 g thinly sliced mushrooms in a small saucepan with 1-2 tbsp water, a squeeze of lemon juice, salt and pepper. Press a piece of parchment paper on top to absorb the fat, and sweat gently until the mushrooms are tender, 4-5 minutes. Add 1 cup/250 ml thick béchamel, bring to a boil and season.
Onion sauce (*sauce Soubise*) To accompany eggs, veal and lamb. Melt 1 tbsp butter in a heavy pan, add 2 chopped medium onions and salt and pepper. Dab a piece of parchment paper on top to remove excess fat, add the lid and cook gently for 15-20 minutes until soft but not brown. Stir the onions into 1 cup/250 ml thick béchamel and work through a fine strainer. Reheat and season.
Tomato sauce (*sauce aurore*) To accompany eggs, fish, veal, poultry. Whisk 2-3 tsp tomato paste into 1 cup/ 250 ml thin béchamel and season to taste.
Curry sauce (*sauce indienne*) To accompany eggs, fish and vegetables. Sauté 1 finely chopped onion in 2 tbsp butter. Stir in 1 tbsp curry powder and 1 peeled, seeded and chopped tomato and cook gently for 2-3 minutes, stirring. Add 2 cups/500 ml thin béchamel and simmer until reduced to 1½ cups/375 ml. Strain and season to taste.
Oyster sauce (*sauce Escoffier*) To accompany broiled steak. Whisk 2-3 tbsp oyster liquor with 2 egg yolks. Stir in 1 cup/250 ml medium béchamel sauce. Heat, stirring, until the sauce thickens slightly. Remove from the heat, stir in 4 poached and chopped oysters and season with cayenne pepper.

VELOUTE

A good velouté, which is a creamy, rich sauce, depends on the quality of the stock used to make it. Often this is the liquid in which the main ingredient of the dish has been cooked, as with poached fish or chicken *blanquette* (p.512). For other dishes the stock is made separately.

Although, like béchamel, velouté is based on a roux, it is cooked differently. More liquid is added at the beginning of cooking, so that the sauce is initially quite thin. Gentle simmering for up to an hour concentrates flavor, breaks down starch grains in the flour, and gives the sauce its characteristic velvety consistency.

The sauce should be stirred from time to time to prevent sticking. Skimming is also important, and more stock can be added to help clarify the sauce (below). If at the end of this time the sauce is too thin, it can be boiled to thicken and intensify the flavor. If cooked too quickly at the start, the sauce will be grainy. At the end of cooking, velouté sauce is often enriched with cream, and a few drops of lemon juice are added to heighten taste. To enrich and thicken the sauce, egg yolks and cream can also be added (See Last-minute thickeners, p.59).

As well as the classic velouté variations, free-form additions such as saffron or a purée of spinach, lead to some of the most innovative sauces in modern cooking. Velouté is most frequently used for eggs, fish, poultry, veal and vegetables.

CLARIFYING STOCK-BASED SAUCES

Long gentle simmering of stock-based sauces is important to bring impurities to the surface so that they can be skimmed off. At the end of cooking, the sauce should be almost translucent.

Remove the pan from the heat and add two to three tablespoons of cold stock or water from time to time during simmering to help bring the scum to the surface. Skim the surface of the sauce with a small metal ladle or spoon, removing as little as possible of the sauce itself (here velouté is shown).

Alternatively, set the pan half off the heat and skim off the impurities as they rise to the cooler side of the pan.

Velouté

Makes about 1 cup/250 ml sauce

1½ cups/375 ml white veal, chicken or fish stock (p.44)

1½ tbsp butter

1½ tbsp flour

salt and white pepper

Optional flavorings

an enrichment of ¼ cup/60 ml *crème fraîche* or heavy cream

squeeze of lemon juice

1 Bring the stock to a boil. Meanwhile, melt the butter in a heavy saucepan. Whisk in the flour and cook for 1-2 minutes until the roux is foaming and straw-colored.

2 Remove the pan from the heat, allow to cool slightly and whisk in three-quarters of the stock. Bring the sauce to a boil, whisking constantly until it thickens. Season lightly as the flavor will become more concentrated as it cooks.

3 Simmer the sauce for at least 15 minutes and up to an hour, stirring occasionally. Clarify the sauce (below) from time to time during simmering. For a very fine velouté, simmer over low heat for several hours. If the sauce is too thin, boil it over a high heat to reduce it to the required consistency.

4 Add the cream, if using, and boil again. To add gloss, work the sauce through a fine strainer. Season the sauce with lemon juice if you like.

Mushroom sauce (*sauce allemande*) To accompany veal and vegetables. Make 1 cup/250 ml veal velouté and add 2 oz/60 g chopped mushrooms during simmering. Strain the sauce and whisk in an egg yolk. Bring just to a boil, remove from the heat, and mount with 1 tbsp butter (p.53). Season to taste with lemon juice and grated nutmeg.

Lemon and parsley sauce (*sauce poulette*) To accompany sweetbreads, brains and vegetables. Make mushroom sauce, following the recipe above. Stir in 1 tbsp chopped parsley and season to taste.

Sauce suprême To accompany poultry. Make 1 cup/250 ml chicken velouté and add 2 oz/60 g chopped mushrooms during simmering. Strain sauce and whisk in ¼ cup/60 ml *crème fraîche* or heavy cream. Continue simmering until required consistency is reached and season with lemon juice, salt and pepper. Off the heat, mount the sauce with 1-2 tbsp cold butter cut into pieces; add the butter a piece at a time (p.53).

Tomato sauce (*sauce aurore*) To accompany eggs, fish, veal and poultry. Whisk 2-3 tsp/30-45 g tomato paste into 1 cup/250 ml velouté and season to taste.

Egg and lemon sauce (*avgolemono*) To accompany meat, fish and vegetables. Boil 1 cup/250 ml fish, chicken or veal stock. Whisk 3 egg yolks and the juice of 1 lemon until they are well mixed. Pour the boiling stock into the lemon mixture, whisking constantly. Return the sauce to the pan and cook gently, stirring constantly, until the sauce thickens slightly. **Note** Do not boil or the sauce will curdle.

Sauce cardinale To accompany white fish and fish mousses. The red lobster coral, evocative of a cardinal's robes, gives the sauce its name. Reduce 2 cups/500 ml fish velouté with 1 cup/250 ml fish stock to about 2 cups/500 ml. Add 1 cup/250 ml *crème fraîche* or heavy cream and reduce again to 2 cups/500 ml. Off the heat whisk in 5 tbsp/75 g shellfish butter (p.155) made with lobster shells, and season with cayenne, salt and pepper.

Crayfish sauce (*sauce Nantua*) Make 2 cups/500 ml fish stock using heads and shells from 1½ lb/750 g crayfish, then use the fish stock to make crayfish velouté (As an alternative, béchamel can be used instead of velouté.)

CHAUDFROID SAUCE

Chaudfroid sauce is based on sauces that are normally served hot (Fr. *chaud*), and it is used to coat cold (Fr. *froid*) meats, poultry and fish for the buffet table. To make chaudfroid sauce, the basic sauce (béchamel, velouté or brown) is mixed with aspic so that it sets to a creamy jelly when cold. The sauce adds flavor to food and, more importantly, provides a smooth pale background for decorations of tomato, truffle, hard-boiled egg white, leek or herb leaves. Usually a shiny coating of clear aspic is added to the layer of chaudfroid sauce.

Chaudfroid sauce can be refrigerated for up to a day, loosely covered with plastic wrap. Remove coated foods from the refrigerator just before serving.

White chaudfroid sauce To coat eggs, fish, veal and chicken. Simmer 2 cups/ 500 ml thin béchamel or velouté, made with veal, chicken or fish stock, with ½ cup/125 ml *crème fraîche* or heavy cream until reduced by half. Stir in 1 cup/250 ml aspic of the same flavor. Soften ½ tbsp gelatin (p.431), melt over low heat and stir into the sauce. Let the sauce cool, then use it for coating (see Aspic, p.253).

Tomato chaudfroid sauce To coat fish, eggs and chicken. Add 4-5 tbsp/60-75 g tomato paste to the béchamel or velouté in the above recipe.

Brown sauce To coat beef and game. Substitute brown sauce or espagnole made with brown veal stock (see recipe opposite) for béchamel in white chaudfroid sauce. Add 1–2 tsp meat glaze to the finished sauce.

MEURETTE

Meurette is a red wine sauce first made in Burgundy. Served with poached eggs, fish and brains, *meurette* breaks the tradition of white wine for light-colored ingredients. Often the wine is used to poach the food before making the sauce. To make *meurette*: sauté 1 tbsp each of diced onion, carrot and celery in 2 tbsp butter until soft. Add 1 bottle/750 ml red Burgundy wine with 2 cups/500 ml veal stock and simmer until reduced by half. Thicken the sauce with kneaded butter and garnish with bacon lardons, mushrooms and pearl onions.

ROUX

A roux (French for russet brown) is a mixture of equal volumes of flour, and fat (usually butter or oil) which is used to thicken béchamel, velouté and brown sauces. For béchamel, butter is heated in a heavy-based pan until foaming, then flour is whisked in and cooked, also until foaming, before the milk is added. For velouté the roux is cooked longer – some cooks like it to be straw-colored (Fr. *blond*) – before adding the stock. For espagnole, the roux is cooked a deep russet brown for extra color and flavor.

Cooking the roux before adding liquid breaks down carbohydrates so that the sauce is less likely to form lumps. Roux should be cooked over medium heat, and

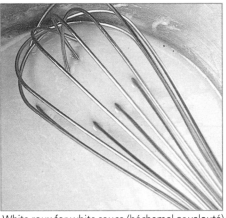

White roux for white sauce (béchamel or velouté) is cooked for only one minute.

must be watched constantly. Cooking time varies from about one minute for a white roux, and two to three minutes for a straw-colored roux, to five minutes needed to toast a brown roux thoroughly. The latter can also be toasted in a 450°F/ 230°C oven for 20 minutes or more, a method favored by Louisiana cooks for the deep brown roux they use in gumbos and other dishes.

Although opinions differ as to whether the liquid added to a roux should be cool or hot, for speed you can whisk in very hot liquid. If boiling liquid is added to a very hot roux, the sauce thickens so fast that the texture is grainy. On the other hand, if the liquid is too cold, time is lost whisking the sauce as it comes to a boil.

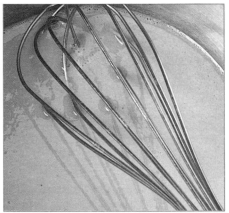

A blond or straw-colored roux is cooked for 2-3 minutes so the flour starts to brown lightly.

In a brown roux, flour is cooked very thoroughly until it is a deep brown and has the fullness of flavor needed for espagnole sauce (see opposite), rich ragouts and stews.

BROWN SAUCES

Espagnole, the original brown sauce, was once the glory of the French kitchen. The name dates from the eighteenth century, when the finest ham – an essential ingredient of espagnole – was said to come from Spain. Two or three days were required to make the sauce. First the roux was slowly browned to develop the flavor, then a rich brown stock – the preparation of which was a day's work in itself – was added, together with pieces of veal, ham, a stewing fowl or a game bird.

Today, most cooks have abandoned the roux thickening for basic brown sauce in favor of arrowroot or potato starch, both of which give a lighter sauce and bypass the long simmering required for traditional espagnole. However, the classic espagnole sauce, made by the traditional method, is still used to provide a more interesting alternative to basic brown sauce. The darker the stock used, the richer the flavor of the brown sauce will be. Veal stock is appropriate for poultry and white meats, while a dark veal or beef stock is more suitable for lamb, beef and game.

Basic brown sauce and espagnole are developed by mounting with butter (p.53) and adding flavorings such as wine, onion, mustard or herbs. Often these ingredients are reduced to a concentrated essence before being added.

USEFUL INFORMATION
Portion 3-4 tbsp/45-60 ml.
Problems If brown sauce is too concentrated and tastes slightly bitter, dilute with stock or water; if too acidic, add a pinch of shaved bitter chocolate to taste.
Reheat In pan on top of stove.
Storage Refrigerate 3 days; freeze 1 year.

ESPAGNOLE

For a fine espagnole sauce, the roux must be gently but thoroughly cooked so that it browns without scorching. The stock must have a full flavor with plenty of gelatin. The sauce must be skimmed while it simmers so that it clarifies (p.55), at the same time reducing to half its original volume. At first, the flavor of espagnole is harsh, but the sauce mellows and darkens during cooking "gradually taking on that brilliant glaze which delights the eye", as the great nineteenth-century chef, Antonin Carême, remarked.

Espagnole sauce

Makes about 2 cups/500 ml sauce

3 tbsp/45 ml oil
2 oz/60 g smoked bacon or raw ham, diced
½ onion, diced
½ carrot, diced
¼ cup/30 g flour
1 qt/1 L brown veal stock (p.44)
bouquet garni
1 tomato, quartered
2 tsp tomato paste
salt and pepper

1 Heat the oil in a heavy saucepan. Add the bacon and sauté until the fat runs, then add the diced onion and carrot and sauté until soft. Add the flour and cook gently, stirring, until the roux is a rich dark brown, about 5 minutes.
2 Bring the stock to a boil. Remove the roux from the heat, let it cool slightly and whisk in three-quarters of the stock. Bring to a boil, whisking constantly until the sauce thickens.
3 Add the bouquet garni, tomato and tomato paste. Leave the sauce to simmer very gently, uncovered, for 3–4 hours. Skim often, especially at the start of cooking, and stir occasionally. To clarify the sauce, add the remaining stock during cooking, and skim well.
4 When the sauce has reduced by half and become glossy and concentrated, strain it (p.53). Season to taste.

GRAVY

Gravy is made from meat juices which congeal and caramelize in the bottom of a roasting pan or heavy frying pan. For red meats, gravy should be dark brown and for lighter meats or poultry, a golden color. To add extra flavor to gravy made from roasts, cook a quartered onion and carrot, together with any bones, in the pan with the meat. If juices start to burn on the bottom of the pan, add a little stock or water. If juices are not dark enough at the end of cooking, reduce them beyond a glaze until caramelized. This also adds color and flavor.

Gravy can be thick or thin, flavored or plain. For unthickened gravy, all the fat is discarded from the pan. (When butter has been used for roasting, some cooks like to

GLAZE & MEAT COULIS

Meat glaze (Fr. *glace de viande*) Made by boiling white or brown veal stock until it is reduced to the characteristic syrupy consistency of a glaze. When cold, meat glaze sets and will keep, if refrigerated, for several months. Between 2-3 qt/2.3 L stock reduces to about 1 cup/250 ml glaze. One tablespoon of glaze is enough to intensify a *demi-glace* or Madeira sauce (p.58), or it can be diluted to make a nutty-tasting brown stock.
Chicken glaze and fish glaze Made in the same way as meat glaze, but with chicken and fish stock.
Meat *coulis* (Fr. *jus*) Lying midway between a stock and a glaze, meat *coulis* is made with meat bones, trimmed and chopped into pieces. The bones are browned in a little oil with onion and carrot and cooked thoroughly on top of the stove or in a very hot oven. Brown stock is stirred in to dissolve the pan juices and it is then boiled to a glaze. For maximum flavor, this process is repeated several times. Stock is added to cover the bones and the coulis is simmered until reduced by half, skimming often. Finally, it is strained. Use the *coulis* instead of stock for brown sauces, or as a base for butter sauces. It can be kept for a week in the refrigerator, or frozen for up to a year.

keep the flavored fat for further use.) Add stock, wine or water, or a mixture of wine and stock, and boil, stirring to deglaze the juices (p.513). Reduce the gravy until concentrated, strain and season to taste.

For thickened gravy, leave one or two tablespoons of fat in the pan, stir in one to two tablespoons of flour and cook thoroughly – browning is the key to good thickened gravy; perfectionists do not countenance the use of colorants such as gravy browning. Add stock, wine or water and reduce until the gravy thickens. Consistency is a matter of taste; the gravy may be too thin to coat a spoon, or it can be thick and rich. Cream or sour cream may be added, or even coffee, as used in America with ham or in Sweden with roast lamb.

BASIC BROWN SAUCE

Nothing could be simpler than basic brown sauce, made with stock and thickened at the last minute with arrowroot or potato starch (see Last-minute thickeners, opposite page). However, for a successful sauce, the stock must be very concentrated and rich with gelatin from meat bones. A brown sauce that is too strong can easily be diluted with water.

Usually, basic brown sauce is reduced before the thickening is added, rather than afterwards, as with espagnole and velouté. One advantage of this is that the stock is less likely to stick, so the sauce needs less attention than espagnole.

Basic brown sauce

Makes 1 cup/250 ml sauce

1 cup/250 ml brown veal or beef stock (p.44)
2 tsp arrowroot or potato starch
2 tbsp Madeira or cold water
1-2 tsp tomato paste (optional)
salt and pepper

1 Bring the stock to a boil in a saucepan and taste. If it lacks body, reduce it until concentrated. In a cup, mix the arrowroot or potato starch to a thin paste with the Madeira or water.

2 Whisk the paste into the boiling stock, which will thicken at once. Add only enough paste to thicken the sauce to the required consistency. Whisk in tomato paste, if using, adding enough to color the sauce slightly. Strain the sauce and taste for seasoning.

All of the following basic brown sauce variations can be made with espagnole sauce (p.57).

Demi-glace sauce A very rich brown sauce that accompanies meats and is used as a base for other sauces. Add 2 tbsp chopped mushrooms, 1 tsp tomato paste, 2 tbsp brown veal stock and 2 tbsp Madeira to 1 cup/250 ml espagnole sauce. Reduce to 1 cup/250 ml, skimming often. Strain and whisk in 1 tsp meat glaze (p.57). Mount the sauce with 1 tbsp butter (p.53) and taste.

Bitter orange sauce (*sauce bigarrade*) To accompany duck. Cut zest of 1 bitter orange in julienne strips and blanch for 2 minutes, then drain. Sauté 1 chopped shallot in 1 tbsp butter until soft. Add ¾ cup/175 ml red wine and juice from the orange and reduce to ½ cup/125 ml. Add 2 cups/500 ml brown sauce and 1 tbsp red currant jelly. Boil the sauce, strain, add the orange julienne and taste. If using a sweet orange, sharpen with lemon juice.

Devil sauce (*sauce diable*) To accompany roast and broiled meats and rabbit. Reduce ¼ cup/60 ml white wine, with ¼ cup/60 ml white wine vinegar, 1 finely chopped shallot and 1 tsp tomato paste to about 3 tbsp/45 ml liquid. Stir in 1 cup/250 ml brown sauce and bring to a boil. Remove from the heat, add a pinch of cayenne pepper and taste. Do not reboil the sauce.

Madeira sauce To accompany variety meats, beef fillet, veal and ham. Add 2 tbsp Madeira, or to taste, to 1 cup/250 ml brown sauce, with 1 tsp meat glaze (optional).

Mushroom, white wine and tomato sauce (*sauce chasseur*) To accompany meats, broiled or roast chicken and rabbit. Sauté 2 finely chopped shallots in 1 tbsp butter until soft but not brown. Add 4 oz/125 g thinly sliced mushrooms and cook until soft. Add 1 cup/250 ml white wine and reduce to about ⅓ cup/75 ml. Stir in 1 cup/250 ml brown sauce and 1 cup/250 ml tomato sauce, or 2 tbsp tomato paste, and bring just to a boil. Remove from the heat and mount with 2 tbsp butter. Stir in 1 tbsp chopped parsley and, if you like, 2 tsp chopped tarragon.

Red wine, shallot and bone marrow sauce (*sauce bordelaise*) To accompany steak, particularly entrecôte. Reduce ½ cup/125 ml red wine with 1 finely chopped shallot to about 2 tbsp liquid. Stir in 1 cup/250 ml brown sauce with a pinch of freshly ground black pepper. Bring to a boil and strain. Off the heat, mount the sauce with 1 tbsp cold butter. Scoop the marrow from a bone (p.235) with a hot knife. Slice and poach the marrow for 1-2 minutes. Drain, add the marrow to the sauce and season to taste.

Tomato brown sauce (*sauce bretonne*) To accompany roast lamb, particularly with dried white beans. Sauté half an onion, finely chopped, in 1 tbsp butter until soft but not brown. Add ½ cup/125 ml white wine and boil to reduce by half. Add 1 cup/250 ml brown sauce, 1 cup/250 ml French tomato sauce (p.65) or 2 tbsp tomato paste and 1 crushed garlic clove. Simmer for 8–10 minutes, then add 2 tsp chopped parsley and season the sauce to taste.

Mustard, vinegar and onion sauce (*sauce Robert*) A medieval sauce that accompanies pork. Sauté half a chopped onion in 1 tbsp butter until soft but not brown. Add ⅓ cup/75 ml white wine and 3 tbsp/45 ml white wine vinegar. Reduce to 2 tbsp liquid. Stir in 1 cup/250 ml

brown sauce and bring just to a boil. Remove from the heat and stir in 2 tsp Dijon mustard. Do not reboil.

Black pepper, red currant and cream sauce (*sauce poivrade*) To accompany duck, pork and game. Make 2 cups/500 ml brown sauce using braising liquid and/or marinade from game. Sauté 2 tbsp each of diced onion, carrot and celery in 2 tbsp oil. Add 1 cup/250 ml white wine and 1 bouquet garni and reduce to ½ cup/125 ml. Add 2 cups/500 ml brown sauce. Simmer for 10-15 minutes, skimming often. Strain, whisk in 1 tbsp red currant jelly and ¼ cup/60 ml heavy cream. Season to taste with freshly ground black pepper.

Truffle sauce (*sauce Périgueux*) To accompany beef fillet, steak tournedos, veal and eggs. Add the juice from 1 small can of truffles to 1 cup/250 ml brown sauce. Bring just to a boil, add the diced truffles and 1 tbsp Madeira. Mount the sauce with 2 tbsp butter (p.53) and season to taste.

Vinegar and pickle sauce (*sauce charcutière*) To accompany broiled or sautéed pork. Reduce ⅓ cup/75 ml white wine and 1 finely chopped shallot to about 1 tbsp liquid. Stir in 1 cup/250 ml brown sauce with 2 gherkin pickles, cut in julienne strips and season to taste.

LAST-MINUTE THICKENERS

By definition, a sauce recipe invariably contains an ingredient to thicken it. A variety of thickeners may be added at the last minute.

Arrowroot or potato starch

Used to thicken basic brown sauce and sauces made from liquid in which food has been cooked. The thickener is added at the end of cooking since it has no effect if simmered for more than two or three minutes. The result is a lighter sauce than that provided by a roux (p.56). A roux-based sauce that is too thin can be thickened at the last minute with a teaspoonful of arrowroot or potato starch.

For every 2 cups/500 ml liquid, mix 2-3 tsp arrowroot or potato starch with 2-3 tbsp/30-45 ml cold water or stock. Whisk enough of the starch mixture into the boiling liquid to thicken it slightly; the thickened sauce should be light and syrupy.

Cornstarch

Often used for binding sweet sauces and as a thickener in Asian cooking, cornstarch is added in the same way as arrowroot or potato starch (above). Sauces thickened with cornstarch will be stickier and can be cooked for longer without becoming thin.

Egg yolks and cream

To enrich and thicken velouté, and occasionally béchamel. Add the mixture just before serving as the sauce may curdle if heated for too long, or reheated. One egg yolk added to one to two tablespoons of cream will thicken 1-2 cups/250-500 ml, sauce.

1 Bring the sauce to a boil. In a separate bowl, whisk the yolks with cream. Stir in some of the hot sauce to cook the mixture partially.

2 Off the heat, whisk the mixture into the remaining sauce. Return to the heat and cook, whisking constantly, until the sauce thickens slightly. If the sauce contains no flour, do not boil it as it will curdle. If the sauce is roux-based, bring it just back to a boil after adding the egg yolks and cream. Serve the sauce as soon as possible.

Kneaded butter (*beurre manié*)

This is a paste of butter and flour, added in small pieces to a sauce at the end of cooking, rather than at the beginning, as in a roux. It gives a similarly rich consistency. The quantity of kneaded butter to sauce is 2 tablespoons to 1 cup/250 ml; 3 tablespoons to 2 cups/500 ml. A last-minute addition of kneaded butter can salvage a bland sauce, enriching both the texture and taste.

Cream the butter and, with a fork or whisk, work in an equal amount of flour. Drop chunks of kneaded butter into the boiling sauce, whisking rapidly. The butter will melt and distribute the flour evenly throughout the liquid, which will thicken at once. Continue adding pieces of kneaded butter until the sauce reaches the desired consistency.

Blood or liver

These ingredients add intense richness and color to brown sauces, especially when accompanying game. In Europe, a container of fresh blood may be sold with a game animal, but pig's blood is often substituted. If storing blood for a couple of days, mix it with one or two tablespoons of vinegar to prevent it from coagulating, and refrigerate in an airtight container. Finely chopped raw liver or foie gras can be substituted for blood. Sauce thickened with blood or liver cannot be reheated, otherwise it will curdle.

Bring the sauce to a boil. Chop the liver or work the foie gras through a sieve. Mix blood, liver or foie gras with a few tablespoons of hot sauce. Off the heat, whisk this mixture into the remaining sauce. Heat the sauce gently until it thickens slightly. Do not boil the sauce as it will curdle. Strain and serve.

EMULSIFIED BUTTER SAUCES

In search of lightness, more and more chefs have turned to the delicate emulsified sauces whose principal ingredient is butter. Chief among these are two sauces based on egg yolks – hollandaise, flavored with lemon juice, and béarnaise, flavored with vinegar, shallot and tarragon. The third basic butter sauce, white butter sauce, is not stabilized by the addition of egg yolks. It is thinner and separates more easily than hollandaise or béarnaise. The quality of all three sauces depends on using the best fresh unsalted butter. For a smoother hollandaise, use clarified butter.

Emulsified sauces are notorious for their tendency to separate and the key to making them is to create, and then maintain, the emulsion (suspension). At the start, the butter should be added very slowly until the sauce thickens, showing that the emulsion has begun. If the sauce is subjected to too high a temperature, or allowed to stand for too long, it will separate. When making emulsified sauces, the base of the pan should never be more than hand hot, otherwise the eggs will start to solidify and the sauce will curdle. Both hollandaise and béarnaise are served warm: hollandaise on its own or a small quantity added to a béchamel or velouté sauce for coating light meats or fish; white butter sauce should be scarcely more than tepid when it is served.

HOLLANDAISE

The most reliable method for hollandaise is to make a mousse by whisking egg yolks with water (a tablespoon per yolk), over heat, directly or in a double boiler. The process should take at least three minutes, by which time the mousse should be light but close-textured. The mousse acts as a stabilizer so that melted butter can be added without the sauce separating. Other methods of making hollandaise, for example by heating egg yolks and cold butter in a water bath, are slower and more difficult to master.

Formerly hollandaise was seasoned with a reduction of vinegar, but nowadays lemon juice is more common. Serve hollandaise plain or with flavorings, to accompany poached fish, eggs and vegetables. Leftover hollandaise or béarnaise can be kept, covered and refrigerated, for up to two days.

Mock hollandaise (*sauce bâtarde*), which is included as a hollandaise variation, is not really a hollandaise at all, but is based on a roux. It can be kept warm for longer than basic hollandaise and is more economical.

USEFUL INFORMATION

Portion 2-3 tbsp/30-45 ml.

Problems If the sauce curdles, add an ice cube, off the heat, and re-emulsify sauce by whisking briskly, then gradually draw in curdled sauce. If unsuccessful, start again, adding curdled mixture to a two-egg yolk and water mousse. If sauce has been cooked until egg is granular, it cannot be saved, although butter can be re-used by straining sauce to extract cooked egg.

Reheat Not advisable.

Storage Keep warm in tepid water (water bath p.510) for up to 30 minutes.

MAKING HOLLANDAISE

A heavy pan is important for hollandaise so heat is evenly distributed and the eggs cook to a close-textured mousse; copper is the ideal metal (p.510).

Makes 1 cup/250 ml sauce

¾ cup/175 g unsalted butter
3 tbsp/45 ml water
3 egg yolks
salt and white pepper
juice ½ lemon (or to taste)
Non-aluminum saucepan

1 Melt the butter, then skim the froth from the surface with a spoon. Let it cool until tepid.

2 In a small heavy saucepan, whisk the water and egg yolks with a little salt and pepper for 30 seconds until thoroughly combined and light in color.

EMULSIFIED SAUCES BY MACHINE

Machine-made sauces tend to be thinner and less creamy, but curdling can be dealt with by processing the sauce again.

Hollandaise Follow the basic recipe. Process the water, egg yolks, salt, pepper, and lemon juice for 10 seconds (blender: low speed). While the machine is running, add the hot butter in a slow, steady stream until the mixture emulsifies and becomes creamy.

Béarnaise Follow the basic recipe, steps 1 and 2. Strain the liquid into the work bowl or blender. Add the egg yolks, salt and pepper and process for 10 seconds (blender: low speed). While the machine is running, add the hot butter in a slow, steady stream until the sauce emulsifies. Add the tarragon leaves and parsley.

Mayonnaise Follow the basic recipe (p.63). Process the egg yolks, salt and pepper, vinegar or lemon juice, mustard (if using) and 3 tbsp/45 ml oil for 10 seconds (blender: low speed). While the machine is running, pour the remaining oil into a bowl or blender in a thin stream until the mixture emulsifies.

Variations

Orange hollandaise (*sauce maltaise*) To accompany vegetables, particularly asparagus. Blanch the zest of half a blood orange, cut in julienne strips, place in boiling water for 2 minutes and drain. Flavor 1 cup/250ml hollandaise to taste with juice from blood oranges. Stir in the julienne. If using a sweet orange, sharpen the sauce by adding lemon juice.

Chantilly hollandaise (*sauce mousseline*) To accompany fish, chicken, sweetbreads and vegetables. Fold ¼ cup/ 60 ml stiffly whipped *crème fraîche* or

3 Set the pan over a low heat and whisk for 3 minutes or until the mixture leaves a ribbon trail for 5 seconds. **Note** The base of the pan should not be too hot or the eggs will scramble.

4 Take from the heat and whisk in the tepid butter, a tablespoon at a time, until the sauce thickens, then pour in a steady stream. Leave the milky whey at the bottom of the pan.

5 Stir in the lemon juice and season. The consistency of hollandaise should be light enough to pour easily from a spoon. If it is too thick, add more water or lemon juice.

---

heavy cream into 1 cup/250ml hollandaise. Season to taste and serve.

Mustard hollandaise (*sauce moutarde*) To accompany eggs and fish. Stir 2 tsp Dijon mustard, or to taste, into 1 cup/ 250 ml hollandaise.

Brown butter hollandaise (*sauce noisette*) To accompany eggs, vegetables and savory soufflés. When making the hollandaise, use brown butter (p.98) instead of melted butter.

Mock hollandaise (*sauce bâtarde*) To accompany poached fish and vegetables. Makes 1¾ cups/430 ml sauce. Bring

1 cup/250 ml water to a boil. In a heavy saucepan heat 1½ tbsp butter until foaming. Off the heat, stir in 1½ tbsp flour until mixed. Whisk in boiling water; the sauce will thicken at once. Whisk in 1 egg yolk. Mount the sauce (p.53) with 6 tbsp/90 g cold butter, cut in pieces. Flavor the sauce to taste with lemon juice or vinegar, (or capers for poached fish), salt and pepper. Keep warm in water bath.

Tomato béarnaise (*sauce Choron*) To accompany steak, fish and eggs. Add 1½ tbsp tomato paste to 1 cup/250 ml sauce instead of tarragon leaves.

Bearnaise

Béarnaise is a thicker version of hollandaise, but it has a much more pungent flavor. Egg yolks are whisked with a reduction of tarragon vinegar, white wine, peppercorns and shallot, to form a thick, close-textured mousse. Melted butter is whisked in as for hollandaise. Béarnaise is suited to hearty foods such as broiled steak, lamb and salmon. For portion, problems, reheating and storage, see hollandaise.

Béarnaise sauce

Makes 1 cup/250 ml sauce

¾ cup/175 g unsalted butter
3 tbsp/45 ml white wine vinegar
3 tbsp/45 ml dry white wine
10 peppercorns, crushed
3 shallots, finely chopped
1 tbsp chopped fresh tarragon stems, or leaves that have been preserved in vinegar
3 egg yolks
salt and cayenne pepper
1 tbsp chopped fresh chervil or parsley
Non-aluminum saucepan

Follow the method for hollandaise. Melt and cool the butter; boil the vinegar, wine, peppercorns, shallots and tarragon stems until reduced to 1 tablespoon. Add 1 tablespoon of water to cool the mixture. Add the egg yolks and seasoning, whisk briefly, then continue whisking over low heat until light, about 4 minutes. Off the heat, whisk in the tepid butter until the sauce thickens. Strain the sauce and stir in the herbs. Serve the sauce warm.

WHITE BUTTER SAUCE

White butter sauce (Fr. *beurre blanc*), originally from the Loire valley, was made with the excellent local butter and white Muscadet wine. From its regional roots it has spread worldwide, and has developed an astonishing versatility. The four basic ingredients are white wine, vinegar, shallot and butter, of which the first three are reduced to a glaze and mounted with the butter (p.53).

Vigorous whisking is vital, particularly when the first batch of butter is added, and at no stage during whisking should the pan be more than warm. The butter should soften into a cream so that it forms an emulsion rather than melting to oil. The process takes only a couple of minutes, so the sauce can be made at the last moment. Keeping it warm, even for a few minutes, can cause it to separate.

The emulsion in white butter sauce is based on the whey – milk solids in the butter itself. Therefore the old trick of adding a tablespoon of cream to the glaze before mounting with the butter (thus adding milk solids), makes the sauce less likely to separate, although the addition of cream detracts slightly from the butter flavor. As a further precaution, the finished white butter sauce can be heated rapidly after adding the butter, whisking hard just to boiling point. The high heat helps set the emulsion. **Note** The emulsion must be complete before placing the sauce over high heat.

A few formal variations of white butter sauce exist, such as that made with red wine. The sauce is inspiration for many contemporary variations. Most are made from cooking juices, whether of fish, poultry or meat, which are reduced to a glaze and mounted with the butter. Wine may or may not be included in the reduction, and the glaze may be enriched with cream before the butter is added. White butter sauce is usually served with poached or broiled fish, and fish and vegetable terrines.

USEFUL INFORMATION
Portion 2–3 tbsp/30–45 ml.
Problems Cannot be re-emulsified if the sauce separates.
Reheat The sauce cannot be reheated.
Storage Keep warm on a rack over a pan of warm water, maximum 15 minutes.

White butter sauce

Makes 1 cup/250 ml sauce

3 tbsp/45 ml white wine vinegar
3 tbsp/45 ml dry white wine
2 shallots, finely chopped
1 tbsp *crème fraîche* or heavy cream (optional)
1 cup/250 g very cold butter, cubed
salt and white pepper

1 In a small heavy pan, boil the vinegar, wine and shallots to a glaze. Add the cream if using and re-boil to a glaze.
2 Mount the sauce with the butter (p.53). Over a high heat, bring the sauce just to a boil, whisking constantly.
3 Strain the sauce (p.53), or leave the shallots in, and season to taste.

Herb butter sauce (*beurre blanc aux herbes*) To accompany eggs, poached fish, vegetable mousses and savory soufflés. Stir 2 tbsp chopped herbs (tarragon, chives, basil, etc.) into 1 cup/250 ml white butter sauce.
Red butter sauce (*beurre rouge*) To accompany fish, sweetbreads and veal. Substitute 6 tbsp/90 ml red wine for white wine and vinegar in white butter sauce. If you like, add 1 tsp tomato paste to brighten the color of the finished sauce.
White wine butter sauce To accompany fish, poultry and white meats. Substitute ½ cup/125 ml white wine and ½ cup/125 ml white veal stock or cooking liquid from fish, poultry or meat for white wine and vinegar in white butter sauce.
Softened butter sauce (*beurre fondu*) To accompany fish and vegetables. Replace the white wine and vinegar in the basic recipe with 1 tbsp water. Do not boil after adding butter.

MAYONNAISE

Mayonnaise is a cold emulsified sauce based on egg yolks. If not carefully handled, it will separate into its constituent parts of oil, egg, and vinegar or lemon juice. The key is to keep the ingredients at room temperature or slightly warmer. A cold bowl, or eggs taken straight from the refrigerator, will prevent the mayonnaise from thickening.

An emulsion must be established right at the start by adding the oil, drop by drop, to the egg yolk mixture. Once this emulsion has been established, the rest of the oil can be added in a steady stream.

Mayonnaise should be thick enough to form peaks so that it can be used to bind salads such as potato, or vegetable *macédoine* (p.268), and to serve with cold food such as fish, chicken or hard-boiled eggs. For coating, mayonnaise must be thinned with one to two tablespoons of warm water, which also lightens the color.

Usual proportions for mayonnaise are about one egg yolk per ¾ cup/175 ml oil. If too little oil is added, the mayonnaise will be thin and taste of egg; if too much oil is added, it may start to separate. Flavors range from delicate, when vegetable oil is used, to nutty (with walnut or hazelnut oil), to the perfumed richness of virgin olive oil. Vinegar is the common seasoning (the amount depends on its sharpness) but lemon juice is a popular alternative.

Mayonnaise is the favorite thickened sauce for salads; it can also be served with fish, poultry, meat and vegetables. Variations other than the classics – garlic and green mayonnaise – are many. For example, Americans might add a purée of red and green peppers, and Israelis an avocado. Northern Europeans serve an apple sauce mayonnaise with boiled beef and with herring, and may even serve a banana mayonnaise with cold poultry.

USEFUL INFORMATION
Portion 2-3 tbsp/30-45 ml.
Problems If the sauce will not thicken, whisk in a few drops of boiling water; if it separates, whisk curdled mixture drop by drop into 1 tsp vinegar, 1 tsp Dijon mustard, or another egg yolk until it forms an emulsion, then continue as usual; if thinned too much, mayonnaise slides easily from smooth surfaces such as boiled eggs.
Storage Refrigerate for maximum 3-4 days because raw egg yolk will not keep longer; bring to room temperature before stirring.

MAKING MAYONNAISE

Seasoning for mayonnaise is determined by the type of oil and vinegar or lemon juice used. Mustard helps the emulsion.

Makes 1½ cups/375 ml mayonnaise
2 egg yolks
salt and white pepper
2 tbsp white wine vinegar or 1 tbsp lemon juice (more if needed)
1 tsp Dijon mustard (optional)
1¼ cups/300 ml peanut or olive oil

1 In a small bowl, beat the egg yolks until thick with a little salt, pepper, half the vinegar or lemon juice, and mustard if using. **Note** This will take a minute (or just under); all ingredients should be at room temperature. It helps to set the bowl on a cloth so that it does not move while you are whisking.

2 Add the oil, drop by drop, whisking constantly. After adding 2 tbsp oil, the mixture should be quite thick. Add the remaining oil more quickly, a tablespoon at a time, or pour from a jug in a very slow stream, whisking constantly. Stir in the remaining vinegar or lemon juice, and add more mustard, salt and pepper to taste.

3 Test the consistency of the mayonnaise: it should be thick and glossy, and should just hold its shape when dropped from the whisk.

Garlic mayonnaise (*aïoli*) To accompany fish soups, fish, eggs and vegetables. Pound 5-6 cloves of garlic to a paste with ½ tsp coarse salt. Add to basic recipe instead of mustard.

Chantilly mayonnaise To accompany vegetable salads. Fold ⅓ cup/75 ml stiffly whipped heavy cream into 1½ cups/ 375 ml mayonnaise and taste.

Green mayonnaise To accompany fish, eggs and vegetables. Blanch 4 oz/125 g spinach, watercress or parsley leaves (or a mixture of all three). Drain, rinse with cold water and squeeze dry with your hands. Chop the leaves finely and stir into 1½ cups/375 ml mayonnaise, or purée with mayonnaise and season to taste.

Piquant mayonnaise (*sauce gribiche*) To accompany cold fish, calf's head and pig's feet. Replace yolks in basic recipe with 3 hard-boiled egg yolks and add ¼ cup/60 ml additional oil. Add 3 hard-boiled egg whites, cut in julienne, and 1 tbsp chopped gherkin pickles, 1 tbsp chopped capers, 2 tbsp chopped mixed herbs. Season to taste with Dijon mustard, salt and pepper.

Russian dressing To accompany eggs, fish, shellfish, cold meats, vegetables and green salad. This dressing once included caviar, hence the name. To 1½ cups/ 375 ml mayonnaise add ¼ cup/60 ml tomato ketchup, ¼ cup/60 ml chopped gherkin pickles, 1 chopped shallot, 1 tsp grated horseradish and a few drops of Tabasco sauce. Season to taste. Louis dressing and Thousand Island dressing are similar zesty preparations.

Sauce rémoulade To accompany eggs, fried fish, vegetables and cold meats.

To 1½ cups/375 ml mayonnaise add 2 tsp Dijon mustard, 3 tbsp/45 g chopped capers, 3 tbsp/45 g chopped gherkin pickles, 3 tbsp/45 g chopped parsley, 1 tbsp chopped tarragon and 4 chopped anchovy fillets. Mix well and taste. (For celery root *rémoulade*, mayonnaise is flavored with mustard only).

Red chili pepper sauce (*sauce rouille*) To accompany fish soup, fish stew and eggs. In a mortar and pestle, pound ½ chopped red chili pepper with 5-6 cloves garlic, then mix with egg yolks, salt and pepper, omitting the vinegar and mustard. Finish with the olive oil. Whisk

in 2-3 tbsp/30-45 g tomato paste and season to taste; add cayenne pepper for a stronger flavor. The sauce can be served straight from the mortar.

Scandinavian mustard sauce To accompany *gravad lax* (p.488), salmon, baked ham and cold meats. Add 2 tbsp brown sugar and 3 tbsp/45 ml mustard to basic recipe (left). Stir in 3 tbsp/45 g chopped dill. Season to taste.

Tartare sauce To accompany deep-fried fish. Add 3 chopped hard-boiled egg whites, 1 tbsp chopped capers, 1 tbsp chopped gherkin pickles, 1 finely chopped shallot, 1 tbsp chopped parsley and 2 tsp chopped chervil or tarragon to 1½ cups/375 ml mayonnaise.

Tomato mayonnaise To accompany eggs, fish and vegetables. To 1½ cups/375 ml mayonnaise add 1-2 tbsp tomato paste and mix well.

Green goddess dressing To accompany fish and shellfish. Add 1 chopped clove garlic, 4 chopped anchovy fillets, 4 tbsp/60 g chopped parsley and ½ cup/125 ml soured cream to 1½ cups/375 ml mayonnaise. Season to taste with lemon juice, vinegar, salt and pepper.

VINAIGRETTE DRESSING

The flavor of vinaigrette depends on the careful balance of its few ingredients – oil, vinegar, Dijon mustard, salt and pepper. The classic proportions are three parts oil to one part vinegar. If lemon juice replaces vinegar, use one part lemon to four or five parts oil. The amount of mustard depends on its piquancy, but one teaspoon for every four tablespoons of dressing is typical.

Variations are created by using different oils, such as peanut oil or rich olive oil, and vinegars, such as full red wine vinegar or fruity raspberry. For more information on oils and vinegars, see Fats and oils (p.96), and Flavorings (p.40). The type of mustard used can make a great difference to the vinaigrette.

Chopped fresh herbs, whisked in at the last moment, improve vinaigrette, and finely chopped shallot is suitable for vinaigrette served with meat and root vegetables. Garlic should be used in small quantities – a cut clove rubbed around the bowl is enough to flavor a salad.

Note The name French dressing, often applied to vinaigrette in Europe, is given to a thickened, tomato-flavored commercial dressing in the United States. Italian dressing in the United States is the name given to a vinaigrette that is made with herbs and red peppers.

USEFUL INFORMATION
Portion 2-3 tbsp/30-45 ml, less for green salad.
Problems If oily, add vinegar and seasoning; if sharp, add salt and more oil.
Storage 1 week at room temperature; before use, whisk to re-emulsify and add flavorings.

Vinaigrette dressing

Makes ½ cup/125 ml dressing

2 tbsp vinegar or 1½ tbsp lemon juice
salt and pepper
2 tsp Dijon mustard (optional)
6 tbsp/90 ml oil

1 In a small bowl, whisk the vinegar or lemon juice with the salt, pepper, and mustard if using.
2 Gradually whisk in the oil in a steady stream until the vinaigrette is blended and thickened. Taste for seasoning.
Note If the emulsion separates, it can be reformed by rapid whisking.

Herb vinaigrette To accompany green salad, pasta salad or potato salad. Add 3 tbsp/45 g chopped fresh herbs to 1 cup/250 ml vinaigrette, made with balsamic vinegar (Herbs, Spices and Flavorings, p.40).
Sauce ravigote To accompany hot boiled beef, chicken, pig's feet, calf's head and cold root vegetables. Add 1 tbsp chopped capers, 1 tbsp chopped shallot and 2 tbsp chopped herbs (tarragon, mint, basil, dill) to 1 cup/250 ml vinaigrette.
Fruit vinaigrette To accompany cold chicken or variety meat salads and green salad. Add 2 tbsp each *crème fraîche* or sour cream and fruit vinegar (Herbs, Spices and Flavorings, p.40) to ½ cup/125 ml vinaigrette.

OTHER THICKENED SALAD DRESSINGS

From northern Europe and the United States come a group of salad dressings based on milk or cream, rather than oil. It is hard to make generalizations as these dressings vary from country to country; some are sharpened with vinegar or lemon, and often have a background of hot mustard, and many are sweetened with sugar. Cooked salad dressings are usually thickened with flour or egg yolk; some are uncooked emulsions, resembling an enriched vinaigrette in which the emulsion is helped by the actions of acid on milk. Typical examples of thickened salad dressings are American boiled dressing and English salad cream. These thickened salad dressings often replace mayonnaise.

Boiled dressing In a heavy pan mix 1½ tbsp flour, 1 tsp dry mustard, 1 tbsp sugar, pinch of cayenne and 2 egg yolks. Stir in 1½ tbsp melted butter, ¾ cup/175 ml milk and ¼ cup/60 ml wine or malt vinegar. Heat, whisking constantly, over low heat until thickened and smooth. Season to taste with salt and pepper and serve cold.
Salad cream Sieve 2 hard-boiled egg yolks into a bowl. Stir in 1 raw egg yolk, and 1 tsp water. Add ½ cup/125 ml heavy cream in a slow steady stream, stirring constantly. Season to taste with salt and pepper. Flavor with 1 tbsp lemon juice or flavored vinegar (Herbs, Spices and Flavorings, p.40).

BREAD-THICKENED SAUCES

Bread gives a light, soft texture to uncooked sauces. Fresh breadcrumbs can be added (dry crumbs produce a gritty texture), or slices may be soaked in liquid, squeezed dry and crushed to a paste. Puréeing the sauce in a blender or food processor is easier than using a mortar and pestle. Cooked bread-thickened sauces are delicate and surprisingly smooth; they can be reduced in the same way as roux-based sauces (p.56).

USEFUL INFORMATION
Portion 2-3 tbsp/30-45 ml.
Problems Overworking in a food processor may cause a gluey texture.
Storage Depends on other ingredients.

Italian green sauce (*salsa verde*) To accompany hot or cold boiled meats and fish. Makes 1½ cups/375 ml sauce. Discard the crusts from 2 slices white bread and soak for 10 minutes in ½ cup/

125 ml red wine vinegar. Squeeze bread dry and purée in a blender or food processor with a large bunch (1½ oz/45 g) parsley, 3 tbsp/45 g capers, 4 cloves garlic and 4 anchovy fillets. (If using a blender add 2-3 tbsp/30-45 ml olive oil). With the motor running, gradually add ⅔ cup/150 ml olive oil. Season to taste.
English bread sauce To accompany roast chicken, turkey and game birds. Makes 1 cup/250 ml sauce. Infuse 1 cup/250 ml milk with 1 slice onion, 2 cloves, 1 bay leaf, ½ tsp peppercorns and a piece of mace over low heat for 10 minutes. Strain, bring to a boil and stir in ½ cup/30 g fresh breadcrumbs. Cook, stirring constantly, for 2 minutes. Stir in 2 tbsp butter, in pieces. Season to taste.

TOMATO SAUCES

Tomato is a versatile base for a sauce, which is at home with a wide range of fish, poultry, meat and vegetable dishes. The quality of a tomato sauce depends on the availability of ripe fruit, which is, of course, variable. Deep red, vine-ripened tomatoes can stand on their own, but if tomatoes are pallid, they should be laced with a spoonful or two of canned tomato paste, or replaced by canned tomatoes. One or two chopped sun-dried tomatoes will add a concentrated flavor.

The essential character of tomato sauce is governed by how long it is cooked. Light cooking produces a fragrant coulis, while long simmering gives the sauce a dark, full-bodied flavor. There are also fresh tomato sauces in which the fruit is left raw.

USEFUL INFORMATION
Portion 3-5 tbsp/45-75 ml.
Problems If too pale, add tomato paste; if acid, add a pinch of sugar.
Reheat In pan on top of stove.
Storage *Fresh sauces:* serve at once if possible or refrigerate up to 8 hours. *Cooked sauces:* refrigerate for 3 days; freeze 2 months.

Uncooked tomato sauces

Uncooked tomato sauces are best served at once for, like all fruits, tomatoes are most fragrant when freshly cut.
Fresh tomato *coulis* To accompany vegetable and fish mousses. Makes 1 cup/250 ml *coulis*. Lightly season 1 lb/500 g peeled, seeded and finely chopped tomatoes. Leave to stand in a colander for 30 minutes to drain excess liquid. Mix the tomatoes with 2 tbsp chopped fresh herbs such as parsley or basil, juice ½ lemon, a pinch of sugar, and seasoning to taste. Serve the *coulis* chilled.
Italian tomato sauce (*sugo di pomodoro fresco*) To accompany hot pasta. Makes 1½ cups/375 ml sauce. Combine 1 lb/500 g peeled, seeded and chopped tomatoes, 2-3 chopped scallions, 1 crushed clove garlic, 2 tbsp chopped basil or oregano and 2-3 tbsp/30-45 ml olive oil. Season to taste.
Mexican tomato sauce (*salsa cruda*) To accompany Mexican dishes and for garnishing soups. Makes 1½ cups/375 ml sauce. Mix 1 lb/500 g peeled, seeded and chopped tomatoes, 1 finely chopped small onion, 1 fresh green chili, cored, seeded and chopped, 3 tbsp/45 g chopped fresh coriander, salt and pepper. Add more chilis and season the sauce to taste. A little lime or orange juice can be added, if you wish.

Cooked tomato sauces

Depending on the country of origin, the fat used may be butter or olive oil; the liquid may be stock or wine. A flavoring of onion and herbs is almost universal.
French tomato sauce To accompany vegetables and eggs, and to enrich other sauces. Makes 2 cups/500 ml sauce. Sauté 1 each finely chopped onion and carrot in 2 tbsp butter until soft. Stir in 2 tbsp flour and cook until foaming. Stir in 1½ cups/375 ml white veal stock (p.44) and bring to a boil. Add 2 lb/1 kg peeled, seeded and

chopped tomatoes, 1 crushed clove of garlic, bouquet garni and seasoning. Simmer uncovered, stirring often, for ¾-1 hour until the sauce is dark and thick. Strain the sauce (p.53). Season to taste. (Add tomato paste and sugar if necessary).
Italian tomato sauce (*salsa napoletana*) To accompany pasta and vegetables. Makes 1½ cups/375 ml sauce. Sauté 3 medium chopped onions, 1 finely chopped carrot, 2 stalks finely chopped celery and 2 oz/60 g bacon in 4-5 tbsp/60-75 ml olive oil until soft. Add ¾ cup/175 ml red or dry white wine and reduce by half. Add 2 lb/1 kg peeled, seeded and chopped tomatoes, ½ tsp dried thyme or oregano, salt and pepper. Simmer, stirring often, for 30-45 minutes until the sauce is thick and concentrated. Add 2-3 tbsp/30-45 g chopped herbs such as basil or oregano if you wish.

BARBECUE SAUCES

Barbecue sauces so often come from a bottle that the term has become synonymous in most people's minds with the commercial, highly-spiced tomato-based sauces. However, when home-made they are more versatile. A soy-sauce-based mixture with a touch of sugar goes well with ham and pork, particularly spare-ribs. Yogurt is the natural partner for lamb, while olive oil and lemon complement fish. A barbecue sauce is intended primarily for brushing meats, poultry and fish to flavor and moisten them during cooking. Pronounced flavors such as mustard, chili and lemon are appropriate ingredients for barbecue sauce and sweet-sour mixtures are also popular as sugar helps form a crust. Most importantly, a barbecue sauce must be thick enough to cling to food and not drip on to the coals.

USEFUL INFORMATION
Portion 2-3 tbsp/30-45 ml; allow ½-1 cup/125-250 ml sauce per 1 lb/500 g meat.
Problems Control barbecue heat to prevent scorching, particularly if the sauce contains sugar.
Storage Refrigerate 1 week.

American barbecue sauce To accompany beef, chicken and pork, and spareribs. Makes 2 cups/500 ml sauce. Sauté 1 chopped onion in 2 tbsp oil until soft. Add 2 lb/1 kg peeled, seeded and chopped tomatoes, 3 chopped cloves garlic, 4 tbsp/60 g brown sugar, ¼ cup/60 ml malt vinegar, 2 tbsp Worcestershire sauce, 1 tbsp tomato paste, 1 tbsp curry powder and 1 tsp celery seed. Simmer until sauce is thick, about 30 minutes, stirring occasionally. Season to taste.
Soy barbecue sauce To accompany pork chops, spareribs, ham steaks and chicken. Makes 1 cup/250 ml sauce. Heat 4 tbsp/60 g brown sugar, 4 tbsp/60 ml sherry, 4 tbsp/60 ml soy sauce, 4 tbsp/60 ml water, juice of 1 lemon and 1 tbsp finely chopped fresh ginger until the sugar has dissolved. Cook, stirring, until the sauce is thick, about 5 minutes. Remove from the heat and whisk in 4 tbsp/60 ml oil.
Mustard barbecue sauce To accompany fish and chicken. Makes ¾ cup/175 ml sauce. Whisk ¼ cup/60 ml white wine, 2 tbsp olive oil, 4 tbsp/60 g dry mustard with 2 tbsp honey, salt and pepper, until slightly thickened and emulsified.

NUT SAUCES

There are two ways in which nuts can be used in sauces: either as thickeners or infused to make nut milk (p.477). The effect of nuts as thickeners varies according to the way they are treated. No matter how finely chopped, nuts will always add a coarse, slightly crunchy texture to a sauce. For a smooth consistency, they must be pounded with a mortar and pestle (usually with other ingredients) or puréed in a blender or food processor.

Recipes are characteristic of particular regions of the world. Almond sauces are popular in parts of India and the Mediterranean; coconut sauces are typical of Asia and the Caribbean, while walnut sauces are popular in Southeast Asia, some parts of Africa and the southern United States.

USEFUL INFORMATION
Portion 3-4 tbsp/45-60 ml.
Problems If the sauce separates or is coarse-textured, re-emulsify it, pounding 1 tbsp until very smooth, then gradually working in the remaining ingredients.
Storage Refrigerate 1 week; freeze 6 months.

Walnut sauce (*salsa di noci*) To accompany pasta and roast chicken. Makes 1½ cups/375 ml sauce. Pound or purée 2 oz/60 g shelled walnuts, 3-4 tbsp/45-60 g parsley, stems removed, 3-4 tsp lemon zest, juice of ½ lemon, salt and black pepper. Gradually work in ½ cup/125 ml olive oil, adding the oil a little faster once the sauce begins to emulsify and thicken. Season to taste.

Asian peanut sauce (*bumbu satay*) To accompany meat and poultry kebabs. Makes 2 cups/500 ml sauce. Fry 1 cup/100 g raw shelled peanuts in 1½ tbsp peanut oil, stirring constantly, for 8-10 minutes until browned. Pound with ½ chopped onion, 1 clove of garlic, 1 tsp fennel seed and ½ tsp dried hot red pepper and work until smooth. Add 2 tsp ground ginger, 1 tsp each ground cumin and brown sugar, and 1½ tbsp lemon juice. Gradually beat in 1½ cups/375 ml coconut milk (p.477), or enough for the sauce to coat a spoon. Simmer for 2 minutes and season to taste.

Turkish tarator sauce To accompany boiled vegetables, cold chicken or seafood. Soak 2 slices of bread (crusts removed), in water and squeeze dry.

Crumble it and add ½ cup/125 g ground walnuts or hazelnuts and 2-3 crushed cloves of garlic. Gradually beat in ⅔ cup/150 ml olive oil and ¼ cup/60 ml wine vinegar. Season to taste.

SAVORY FRUIT SAUCES

Most fruit sauces consist of little more than fruit pulp with sweetener. It is the fruits themselves that lend character – apple sauce made with Golden Delicious apples is quite different from that made with the Granny Smith variety for example. More condiment than sauce, a savory fruit sauce is usually thicker than coating consistency and served cold. For chutneys, see Preserving (p.489).

Apple sauce To accompany pork, duck or goose, served warm or cold. Makes 1 cup/250 ml sauce. In a covered pan, cook to a pulp 1 lb/500 g cored, quartered, unpeeled apples with ½ cup/125 ml water, stirring occasionally. Sieve the pulp to remove lumps and skin and boil, stirring, until thick. Stir in 2-2½ tbsp sugar to taste, with ¼ cup/60 g butter.

Cranberry sauce To accompany turkey. Makes 1 cup/250 ml sauce. Boil 1 lb/500 g cranberries with 1 cup/250 ml water until the berries pop, 4-5 minutes. Remove from the heat and stir in 1 cup/200 g sugar, or to taste, and allow to cool.

Cumberland sauce To accompany cold ham, tongue, game, pork pie and meat terrines. Makes 2 cups/500 ml sauce. Blanch zest from 1 orange and 1 lemon cut in julienne strips, for 2 minutes and drain. Heat 1¼ cups/375 ml red currant jelly until melted. Stir in the juice from the orange and lemon, ¼ cup/60 ml port, ½ tsp each of ground ginger and dry mustard and simmer for 2-3 minutes. Stir in the fruit julienne, allow to cool and season to taste.

Plum sauce To accompany pork or ham. Makes 1 cup/250 ml sauce. Serve hot or warm. A spicier variation that is used in Asian poultry and meat dishes also includes soy and chili sauce. In a covered pan, simmer 1 lb/500 g halved, pitted purple plums with 1 cup/250 ml dry white wine and 1 tbsp cider vinegar until soft. Sieve, then boil until thickened with 2-3 tbsp/30-45 ml honey.

SWEET FRUIT SAUCES

Sweet fruit sauces are not just sweeter versions of the fruit sauces that accompany meat. They are generally thinner, and designed to fulfill the role of coating as well as accompanying desserts. Many are based on jelly or jam, while others are made from a simple fruit purée, strained and sometimes sweetened. They may also be enhanced with a fruit liqueur, and lemon juice (which prevents discoloration). Soft fruits such as berries, kiwi, persimmon and cooked rhubarb make particularly good sauces.
Note Some fruits – peach, for example – discolor quickly so the sauce should be served immediately.

Apricot or red jam sauce To accompany steamed puddings, cakes and charlottes, served hot or cold. Makes 1 cup/250 ml sauce. Heat ½ cup/150 g apricot or any red jam, 1 cup/250 ml water and 2 strips of lemon zest until the jam has melted. If it tastes bland, add more jam. Simmer for 5 minutes and strain. If the sauce is thin, whisk in 1 tsp arrowroot mixed to a paste with 1 tbsp water. Heat the sauce until it thickens, whisking constantly.

Melba sauce To accompany ice creams, mousses, charlottes and profiteroles. Serve cold. Makes 1 cup/250 ml sauce. Purée 1 pt/250 g fresh or drained frozen raspberries in a blender or food processor with 1-2 tbsp kirsch or raspberry liqueur. Work the sauce through a sieve to remove the seeds and add confectioners' sugar to taste. Refrigerate until well chilled before serving.

CUSTARD

Standard proportions for custard sauce are 5 egg yolks per 2 cups/500 ml milk, though more yolks may be added for richness. Classically, no starch is used, though the addition of a teaspoon of cornstarch is an economical way to obtain a thicker sauce; fewer eggs are needed and the custard is less likely to curdle. Variations do exist but remember that an acid ingredient such as orange juice will curdle the milk.

After initial whisking to thicken the egg yolks and sugar slightly, the sauce should be stirred over the heat with a wooden spatula or spoon so that it cooks to a creamy not frothy consistency. Gentle cooking is vital and some cooks prefer to use a double boiler. For more information about custards, see Eggs (p.94).

USEFUL INFORMATION

Portion 4-6 tbsp/60-90 ml.
Problems If the sauce curdles, strain it into a cold bowl. Working the sauce in a blender helps re-emulsify but cannot save it when overcooked.
Storage Refrigerate 2 days.

Vanilla custard
Crème anglaise

Serve the custard with fruit compote, cakes, hot soufflés and charlottes, or use it as a foundation for ice cream, bavarian creams and other sauces. Custard can be served hot or cold.

Makes 2 cups/500 ml sauce

2 cups/500 ml milk

vanilla bean, split or few drops vanilla extract

5 egg yolks

¼ cup/60 g sugar

---

1 Scald the milk; if using a vanilla bean, leave to infuse in the milk for 10 minutes.
2 Whisk the egg yolks and sugar until thick and light, 3-4 minutes, then stir in the hot milk.
3 Return the custard to the pan and heat gently, stirring constantly with a wooden spatula until the custard thickens slightly. If you draw a finger across the spatula it will leave a clear trail.

Note Do not overcook or boil custard as it will curdle.

4 Remove the custard from the heat at once and strain it into a cold bowl. Add vanilla extract. Cover tightly to prevent skin forming as it cools.

Chocolate custard Used for charlottes, as a base for bavarian cream and ice cream. Add 2-3 oz/60-90 g chopped semi-sweet chocolate to the milk after infusing it with a vanilla bean.
Coffee custard Used for cakes, as a base for bavarian cream and ice cream. Add 2-3 tsp dry instant coffee to the milk after infusing it with a vanilla bean.
Liqueur custard Used for poached fruit and fruit charlottes. Add 2-3 tbsp/30-45 ml liqueur, such as kirsch or rum, to finished custard.

Orange custard Used for bavarian cream and fruit charlottes. Omit the vanilla and infuse the milk with the grated zest of 1 orange. Flavor the custard with 1-2 tbsp orange liqueur.

OTHER SWEET SAUCES

Fruit sauces apart, the range of sweet sauces is generally limited to chocolate (p.425), the following sugar-based sauces, and English hard sauce (brandy butter).
Butterscotch sauce To accompany ice cream and puddings. Makes 1 cup/250 ml sauce. Melt 6 tbsp/90 g butter, add 1 cup/200 g dark brown sugar and 2 tbsp light corn syrup and cook gently until sugar dissolves. Stir in ⅓ cup/75 ml heavy cream and bring just to a boil.
Caramel sauce Serve cold with sliced oranges, mousses, and puddings. Makes 1 cup/250 ml sauce. Make the caramel (p.418) with ¾ cup/150 g sugar and ⅓ cup/75 ml water. Off the heat, add ¾ cup/175 ml warm water. **Note** Hot caramel tends to spit.
English hard sauce To accompany Christmas pudding. Cream 6 tbsp/90 g unsalted butter. Beat in 6 tbsp/75 g sugar until soft and light. Beat in the grated zest of 1 lemon and 2-3 tbsp/30-45 ml rum or brandy. Serve chilled.

SABAYON

Sweet sabayon sauce stems from the Italian dessert *zabaglione* made with whipped egg yolks, sugar and Marsala. It is the French who have transformed it into a sauce, often flavored with sweet white wine or Madeira. Sabayon is served separately with puddings and cakes, or may be poured over fruit and gratinéed.
Sweet sabayon For each egg yolk add 1 tbsp/15 g sugar and 2 tbsp liquid (sweet white wine, Madeira, Marsala, sherry, Grand Marnier, orange or lemon juice). Whisk in a large bowl, then set over a pan of hot water and whisk until light and thick enough to leave a ribbon trail (p.394), at least 5 minutes. (**Note** If sabayon gets too hot it will become grainy). Serve the sauce warm or whisk off the heat until it cools. If left to stand, the sauce will start to separate.

Savory sabayon This is made in the same way as hollandaise by whisking egg yolks and well-reduced fish or veal stock over the heat to form a mousse, then mounting the sauce with butter (p.53).

MILK, CHEESE & EGGS

DAIRY FOODS are fundamental to Western cuisine. Milk is the basis of many soups and sauces; it is the foundation of rice pudding and other popular puddings, of custards and thin batters like crêpes. It features in breads and pancakes, and desserts such as bavarian cream and ice cream. As well as drinking cold milk, we still consume generous quantities on breakfast cereal or in milk shakes and hot milk drinks.

Cream is only slightly less important. We take it for granted in our coffee; we use it to top fresh fruits and apple pie, and to enrich so many chilled desserts. Cultured dairy foods like yogurt are less versatile, but nonetheless useful to the cook in sauces, cold soups, salad dressings and vegetable dishes.

Cheese stands as a food in its own right. With bread and wine, it is one of the components of an ideal picnic. With other ingredients, it features as a seasoning, flavoring or topping, or as a rich creamy filling in recipes such as cheesecake.

Eggs, like milk, are a primary ingredient. Whipped whole eggs form the basis of many cakes, sweet mousses and other desserts. Egg yolks stabilize two of the most famous sauces – hollandaise and mayonnaise – and give silky body to vanilla custard sauce. Whipped egg whites are essential in meringues, *petits fours* and other creations of the pastry chef.

MILK & CREAM

Milk is one of the most basic of all foods. For infants, mother's milk constitutes a complete diet, and even for adults, cow's milk includes many essential nutrients, particularly calcium. Cream is made from the fat part of milk and contains a high proportion of butterfat (or milkfat), usually referred to simply as the "fat" content. Cream was formerly left to rise to the surface of the milk; in today's commercial process it is separated by centrifuge. Butter is produced from the fat that coalesces when milk or cream is churned; buttermilk is the residue.

Choosing and storing milk and cream
In many countries, the fat content, "sell-by" date, and any vitamin enrichment of milk or cream will be marked on the label. Check also for the presence of stabilizers and preservatives, which may affect certain processes such as whipping. The color is not an indication of the quality and may vary with the breed and diet of the cow. All milk and cream should be refrigerated in opaque containers, as light destroys the vitamin B content.

Milk and cream substitutes
The chief substitute for cow's milk is a liquid called soy milk, made from soybeans and water. It can directly substitute for milk in cooking but has a slightly nutty, obtrusive flavor. Other "vegetable milks" include emulsions made with oil-rich nuts such as almonds or coconut; coconut milk is used extensively in Indian cooking. "Non-dairy creamer" is available in both liquid and powdered form, and is made with corn syrup solids, emulsifiers and stabilizers as an alternative for light cream. The advantage of these substitutes is that they need no refrigeration, contain no fat, and are less likely to induce allergic reactions than cow's milk. Non-dairy substitutes may also be used with meat as part of a kosher meal. However, they do not have the pleasant flavor of milk or the rich thickness of cream.

Cooking with milk and cream
Most recipes require milk or cream to be fresh. They both scorch easily, so it is safest to use moderate temperatures. When bringing them to a boil, as a precaution first rinse the pan with water, and stir from time to time. Many cooks warn that cream will curdle if boiled, but very fresh cream contains little lactic acid so it can be boiled and reduced without danger. Heavy cream is less likely to curdle than light, as is cream containing stabilizers. To test for freshness, many recipes call for milk or cream to be scalded (p.514) before use since, if stale, they will curdle when heated.

Both milk and cream may be frozen (see Useful information) before being used in cooking, but thawed cream will not whip successfully.

The curdling or souring (sometimes called clabbering) of milk or cream cannot be rectified. It occurs when airborn bacteria convert the lactose (milk sugars) in cream or milk into lactic acid. Under normal refrigeration the process is slow, evidenced only by a slightly acid taste. However, when a sizeable amount of lactic acid has developed, or when an acid such as lemon juice is added, the milk or cream curdles and clots. The higher the temperature, the more rapidly curdling occurs. Rennin, an enzyme used to make cheese (p.73), may also be used to encourage the curdling action. It is contained in the coagulating agent rennet, which used to be extracted from the stomachs of unweaned calves, but is now synthesized commercially.

In some recipes the curdling of milk or cream is deliberate. For example, vinaigrette dressing (p.64) may be enriched by whisking in cream, which thickens in contact with the vinegar. Both milk and cream may be curdled with lemon juice for use in breads and cakes raised with baking soda: 1 cup/250 ml of milk or cream mixed with one tablespoon of lemon juice will begin to show signs of curdling within five minutes.

MILK

In the West, most cooks use cow's milk. Goat's and sheep's milks, rich in fat and protein, are sometimes drunk as a beverage, but the bulk is made into cheese. Water buffalo milk, highest of all in fat, is particularly good for cheese-making. Mare's milk is high in sugar and is popular in eastern Europe for fermented milk drinks.

Cow's milk contains about 87 percent water, with 3.5 percent protein (mostly caseine) and 5 percent carbohydrates (lactose). The fat content of milk, however, varies with the breed of cow and its feed, from around 3 percent to over 5 percent for Jersey cows. In most countries the sale of raw milk – milk straight from the cow, filtered but otherwise unprocessed – is illegal because it may contain dangerous organisms such as those that cause tuberculosis. To kill these bacteria and the enzymes that produce off-flavors, milk is pasteurized before sale by heating it to 144°F/62°C for 30 minutes, or 160°F/72°C for 15 seconds. Much pasteurized milk is then homogenized – processed so that the fat remains evenly dispersed within the milk. Some smaller American dairies and all British dairies also sell unhomogenized milk, offering cooks the option of pouring off the creamy "top".

In Europe and the United States, a good deal of ultra-pasteurized (sterilized) milk is also sold. Called longlife or UHT ("ultra-high temperature"), it is packaged in hermetically sealed boxes that allow it to be stored unrefrigerated for up to three months. The milk is heated in a sealed container to about 280°F/138°C for a few seconds. Ultra-pasteurization destroys much of the taste, which makes UHT milk less desirable for drinking, and best reserved for cooking, where it can be used like regular milk.

Given the concern about cholesterol levels in animal fats, low-fat milk is increasingly popular. Depending on the type, it may contain from 0.5 to 2 percent fat. Skim milk has even less fat; exact amounts vary from country to country but can be as low as zero. Because pasteurization also kills the fat-soluble vitamins A and D, milk is often sold "fortified" with these vitamins in compensation. Milk fortified with additional calcium is also available.

The lactose (milk sugar) in milk can cause severe indigestion in some adults. This reaction, more common in non-Caucasian populations, is due to a deficiency of the lactase enzyme that breaks down lactose in the human adult digestive tract. To counteract this, milk with added lactase enzyme has been developed, and has a slightly sweeter taste than regular milk. An alternative to high-lactase milk is acidophilus milk, which has lactose-consuming bacteria added. Low-sodium milk (available in the United States) is for those on a salt-free diet. These treated milks are similar in taste to regular milk and are used in the same way for drinking or cooking.

Two types of canned milk are common: evaporated milk (both whole and skim) and sweetened condensed milk. Evaporated milk has simply had its water content reduced, so it contains about double the solids of regular milk. The high heat required for canning adds a perceptible "cooked" taste. In some countries, evaporated milk is preferred with coffee; it may also be whipped like fresh heavy cream. Sweetened condensed milk is even more concentrated – reduced whole milk sweetened with so much sugar that any cooked taste is masked. Its consistency is thick and syrupy. Both types of canned milk are called for in certain recipes, such as Latin American flans.

Dry milk, sold as a powder or in granules, has had its water completely evaporated. Convenient in hot climates, it is usually made with low-fat or non-fat milk and is reconstituted by mixing with water, producing a result that is slightly thinner than fresh milk. Dry milk may be substituted for fresh in most recipes and is used in commercial baking to fortify bread doughs, giving a brown crust and extending shelf-life.

USEFUL INFORMATION

Storage *Pasteurized, unopened:* refrigerate 5 days; *opened:* refrigerate 3-4 days; freeze 3 months to use for cooking only. *Longlife (UHT), unopened:* at room temperature 2-3 months; *opened:* refrigerate 3-4 days. **Nutritive value** per 3½ oz/100 g. *Whole:* 61 calories; 3 g protein; 3 g fat; 5 g carbohydrates; 14 mg cholesterol; 49 mg sodium. *2% low-fat:* 50 calories; 3 g protein; 2 g fat; 5 g carbohydrates; 8 mg cholesterol; 50 mg sodium. *1% low-fat:* 42 calories; 3 g protein; 1 g fat; 5 g carbohydrates; 4 mg cholesterol; 50 mg sodium. *Skim:* 35 calories; 3 g protein; no fat; 5 g carbohydrates; 2 mg cholesterol; 52 mg sodium. *Longlife (UHT), whole:* 61 calories; 3 g protein; 3 g fat; 5 g carbohydrates; 13 mg cholesterol, 51 mg sodium. **Problems** *Unpasteurized and pasteurized:* sours quickly when not refrigerated; picks up flavors if left open in the refrigerator; curdles when mixed with acid ingredients. *Longlife (UHT):* flavor becomes stale with time; bland when drunk alone. **Processed forms** Canned evaporated; canned sweetened condensed; dry.

CREAM

Two characteristics of cream are important to the cook: its taste, whether sweet or nutty (as with *crème fraîche*), and its fat content. Most cream is sweet; it has been pasteurized or ultra-pasteurized (sterilized), thus destroying disease-causing bacteria and enzymes so the odor and flavor remain mild. In some countries, preservatives may be added that can further detract from the fresh flavor of sweet cream. Pasteurized or sterilized creams may also be homogenized to produce a smoother texture. *Crème fraîche*, on the other hand, has a stronger flavor.

The fat content of cream determines its richness and whipping characteristics. The richest cream, such as that from Jersey cows, may be as high as 60 percent fat. More standard is heavy cream, with about a 40 percent fat content, excellent for whipping and for adding richness to all manner of cooked dishes. In Britain, double cream with a fat content of 48 percent is the nearest equivalent. Whipping cream is slightly lighter; heavy whipping cream has a fat content of at least 36 percent, light whipping cream has 30-36 percent fat. Light or table cream (called single in Britain) is a good deal thinner, but with no less than 18 percent fat, while American "half-and-half" is lightest of all, with a fat content of 10-18 percent; it is used mainly for custards or in coffee. Half cream, the British equivalent, has 12 percent fat.

When unpasteurized cream is left to stand, it develops a full, slightly sour taste that mellows and intensifies over time. This is *crème fraîche*, the standard cream in France. Modern production methods use pasteurized cream that is recultured by adding bacteria to replace those destroyed by pasteurization. So important is *crème fraîche* in giving flavor to soups, sauces and savory dishes, particularly of fish, that local versions are now sold in many countries. The best contains as much as 60 percent fat.

As its name implies, clotted cream, often called Devonshire or Cornish cream, has a different texture from other creams. To make it, unpasteurized milk is left to stand until the cream rises to the surface, then heated so that the cream sets and can be skimmed off. The cream is pasteurized before sale. Creamy yellow, with a buttery texture and a fat content of over 55 percent, clotted cream is famous particularly in Britain, served with scones and strawberry jam, and it makes an excellent accompaniment to fresh or poached fruit.

USEFUL INFORMATION

Storage *Pasteurized sweet cream, unopened*: refrigerate 5 days; freeze 3 months but do not whip; *opened*: refrigerate 3-4 days. *High-fat crème fraîche*: refrigerate 3 weeks; freeze 3 months but do not whip. *Homemade or low-fat crème fraîche*: refrigerate 2 weeks.
Nutritive value per 3½ oz/100 g. *Heavy*: 345 calories; 2 g protein; 37 g fat; 3 g carbohydrates; 137 mg cholesterol; 38 mg sodium. *Light whipping*: 292 calories; 2 g protein; 31 g fat; 3 g carbohydrates; 111 mg cholesterol; 34 mg sodium. *Light or table*: 195 calories; 3 g protein; 19 g fat; 4 g carbohydrates; 66 mg cholesterol; 40 mg sodium. *Half-and-half*: 130 calories; 3 g protein; 12 g fat; 4 g carbohydrates; 37 mg cholesterol; 41 mg sodium.
Problems Curdles with acid ingredients; separates on whipping if too warm or overwhipped; if frozen, texture is affected, but not taste.

Making *crème fraîche*

Crème fraîche can be made at home by adding either buttermilk, sour cream or yogurt to cream, thereby replacing the bacteria destroyed during pasteurization. It can, therefore, be considered as a cultured dairy product but unlike other such products, it will not separate when boiled. The higher the fat content of the cream, the better; *crème fraîche* is best made with buttermilk rather than sour cream, and either is preferred over yogurt (for shelf-life, however, the order is reversed).

For every 2 cups/500 ml heavy cream (preferably pasteurized but not ultra-pasteurized), allow 1 cup/250 ml buttermilk, cultured sour cream or yogurt. Stir together in a saucepan and heat gently to 85°F/30°C until the mixture is no longer cold, but is cooler than body temperature. Pour into a container and partially cover. Leave at warm room temperature 6-8 hours or until thickened and slightly nutty in flavor. (On a hot day, the cream will thicken faster.) Stir the cream, cover and refrigerate. The flavor intensifies and the cream thickens on keeping. For a new batch, use 1 cup/250 ml of the *crème fraîche* as a starter instead of buttermilk, sour cream or yogurt.

WHIPPING CREAM

Heavy and whipping creams can be whipped to about double their volume and will stay stiff for several hours. The bowl, whisk and cream should be chilled before whipping and the cream must be refrigerated afterwards. Cream with less than 35 percent fat may become granular and form butter before it thickens. Very high-fat cream thickens much more quickly, reducing the likelihood that it will turn to butter. It can be heavy when whipped and may be diluted before whipping with iced water or milk.

1 Pour cream into a bowl and whisk until it starts to thicken. **For lightly whipped cream:** a soft peak should form when the whisk is lifted.

2 **For stiffly whipped cream:** continue whisking until a stiff peak forms and the whisk leaves clear marks in the cream. **Note** If overwhisked, the cream will separate and turn to butter. When this is about to happen, the cream looks granular and has a yellowish tinge.

CHANTILLY CREAM

Chantilly cream is whipped cream flavored with sugar, and vanilla or brandy. It is used in bavarian creams and charlottes (p.432), as a simple filling for *vacherins* (p.437) and other meringue desserts or for pastries such as cream horns or Chantilly swans (see Typical dishes, p.376). Chantilly cream may also accompany fresh and poached fruits. It is often piped in decorative rosettes and patterns using a star piping tube (p.507). When piping, always whip the cream just until stiff and use a large tube. The cream will be worked further when forced through the tube and may separate if it is already too stiff. Work quickly, as the heat of your hand on the pastry bag encourages separation.

For every 1 cup/250 ml cream, allow 1-2 tbsp granulated or confectioners' sugar and ½ tsp vanilla or 1 tsp brandy. Whip the cream until it starts to thicken, add sugar and flavorings and continue whisking until the cream stiffens again, about 1 minute. If you like, to further lighten the cream, fold in stiffly whipped egg white, allowing 1 egg white for every 1 cup/250 ml of cream.

Note Cream that has been lightened with egg white is less stable, and must be used within two hours.

Crème brûlée

Crème brûlée is topped with a layer of crisp caramel, while in contrast the creamy custard underneath is soft.

Serves 4

2 cups/500 ml heavy cream	½ cup/100 g sugar
1 vanilla bean, split or ½ tsp vanilla extract	*4 ramekins (¾ cup/175 ml capacity each)*
5 egg yolks	

1 Heat the oven to 400°F/200°C. Scald the cream (p.514); if using a vanilla bean, cover and leave to infuse for 10 minutes. Beat the egg yolks with 2 tbsp of the sugar in a bowl until slightly thickened. Stir in the hot cream and vanilla extract, if using. Strain the custard into the ramekins, dividing it equally between them. (Keep vanilla bean for another use.)
2 Set the ramekins in a cold water bath and cook in the oven until a skin forms on the surface, 15-18 minutes; the custard underneath will remain liquid. Chill the ramekins in the refrigerator at least 4 hours.
3 **To finish:** heat the broiler. Sprinkle each custard with 1½ tbsp sugar to form a thin layer. Broil as close as possible to the heat until the sugar melts and caramelizes, 2-3 minutes. **Note** Do not overcook the custard or it will bubble through the sugar. Allow to cool; the caramel will form a crisp layer on the custard. Serve within 2-3 hours, while the caramel remains crisp.

Variation

Raspberry crème brûlée Put 2-3 tsp fresh raspberries into each ramekin before adding the custard.

SOUR CREAM, YOGURT & BUTTERMILK

A number of dairy products are cultured by using bacteria to convert the lactose in milk or cream to lactic acid. Depending on the type of bacteria used and on the fat and acid content, the milk or cream converts to sour cream, yogurt or buttermilk. These cultured dairy products tend to separate when heated, so they should never be boiled and are usually added toward the end of cooking. In commercial products, not all the cultures remain active. When using them to make *crème fraîche*, yogurt or cheese, be sure to use "active" or "live-culture" types.

Cultured sour cream has a fat content of not less than 18 percent; it is made by adding lactic acid to pasteurized cream. Sour cream has the thickness of *crème fraîche* but cannot be substituted for it; the flavor is sharper and the texture less silky. Sour cream is particularly popular in eastern and central Europe, where it appears in cakes, toppings, dumplings and sauces, and as an accompaniment to soups such as *borscht* and hearty dishes such as Red cabbage rolls (p.276). The Russian-inspired *sauce smitane* (usually served with game) is also typical, made from brown sauce with sour cream whisked in just before serving. Sauces made with sour cream sweetened with sugar and vanilla are popular with fruit desserts. The acid in cultured dairy products helps lighten the crumb in bread and also softens cheesecakes, in which sour cream is often a major ingredient. (A lower-fat version of sour cream called sour half-and-half is available in the United States. *Smetana* is an alternative available in Britain, made from a mixture of skimmed milk and sour cream.)

Yogurt is fermented whole, low-fat or skim milk and can be thin or thick. The special bacteria in yogurt give it a characteristic flavor and texture. Most yogurt is labeled as containing "active cultures" since it contains live bacteria. However, some commercial fruit-flavored yogurts have been heated, rendering the bacteria inactive. Yogurt can be made from pasteurized whole milk (often called "plain"), although many commercial brands are made with low-fat or skim milk, often with milk solids added to give a smooth consistency, or the milk evaporated to produce a more concentrated yogurt. Yogurt is usually homogenized as well.

The flavor and texture of plain cow's milk yogurt varies depending on the culture used. Greek-style yogurt that is firm and creamy, sometimes made with sheep's milk, is popular in Britain. Standard in Greece and the Middle East and sold in European and North American health food stores, goat's milk yogurt is richer and more piquant than that produced from cow's milk. Apart from cheese, yogurt is the only dairy product commonly made from goat's milk. In cooking, it behaves like cow's milk yogurt.

A variety of hot and chilled soups are based on yogurt, such as Egyptian *labaneya* (spinach soup) and Armenian *tutmaj* (with pasta and noodles), while yogurt and sour cream are the basis of sauces like Indian *raita* and Austrian *schnittlauchsosse*, flavored with chives. In the Middle East and Asia, yogurt is often served plain as an accompaniment to hot curries and marinated salads. Because of its tenderizing properties, it also makes a good marinade for lamb or poultry.

Natural buttermilk is the liquid whey left behind when milk has been churned and the fat extracted as butter. Commercial buttermilk is made by adding a bacterial culture to low-fat or skim milk. Both buttermilks have a tart taste but the commercial version has a much smoother consistency. Dried buttermilk is also available. It must be reconstituted with water before use, and will be thinner than the fresh product. In soda breads, pancakes and biscuits, buttermilk not only gives flavor, but its acid reacts with the baking soda, releasing gas that raises the dough. Buttermilk features in Scandinavian soups, while salad dressings also benefit from its tart flavor.

Buttermilk and yogurt are the basis of several refreshing drinks, some of them alcoholic, popular in both Scandinavia and the Middle East. These include Norwegian *kaelder*, Indian *lassi*, Israeli *laban* and Middle Eastern *ayran* and *kefir*, the latter made from camel's milk. In Russia, *koumiss* is made from mare's milk. All of them share a reputation for aiding health and digestion, and promoting long life.

USEFUL INFORMATION

Storage *Sour cream*: refrigerate 3 weeks. *Yogurt, buttermilk*: refrigerate 2 weeks. Natural yogurt keeps better than fruit-flavored yogurt. *All*: freeze 6 weeks, but may separate on thawing.
Nutritive value per 3½ oz/100 g. *Sour cream*: 214 calories; 3 g protein; 21 g fat; 4 g carbohydrates; 44 mg cholesterol; 53 mg sodium. *Whole milk plain yogurt*: 61 calories; 3 g protein; 3 g fat; 5 g carbohydrates; 13 mg cholesterol; 46 mg sodium. *Low-fat plain yogurt*: 63 calories; 5 g protein; 2 g fat; 7 g carbohydrates; 6 mg cholesterol; 70 mg sodium. *Non-fat (skim) plain yogurt*: 56 calories; 6 g protein; no fat; 8 g carbohydrates; 2 mg cholesterol; 76 mg sodium. *Buttermilk*: 40 calories; 3 g protein; 1 g fat; 5 g carbohydrates; 4 mg cholesterol; 105 mg sodium (salted), 50 mg (unsalted).
Problems Curdles if overheated; becomes more tart with age.
Typical dishes *Sour cream: bef-*

stroganov (beef with onions and mushrooms, Russia); *köttbulloar* (meatballs in sauce, Sweden); *rommegrot* (porridge, Norway); baked potatoes (USA); *geschmorte rindszunge mit sauerrahm* (braised beef tongue with sour cream, Germany); chocolate sour cream poundcake (USA); *gefüllter kasbraten* (stuffed veal with sauce, Austria); *sos śmietankowy* with hard-boiled eggs, Poland). *Yogurt: armyansky borscht* (beef with yogurt, Armenia), chilled fruit soup (USA); *flensjes met yoghutt* (savory pancakes, Denmark); *yaourtopita* (cake with lemon, Greece); *yoğurtlu kebab* (with meat kebabs, Turkey). *Buttermilk: okroshka* (soup with cucumber, Russia); *buttermilch mit brombeeren* (with blackberries and honey, Germany); angel biscuits (USA); *appelepap* (apple soup, Denmark); ranch salad dressing (USA); *kartofi salata sas kiselo mleko* (potato salad, Bulgaria); *buñuelos* (dough fritters, Portugal/Spain).

Making yogurt

Yogurt made at home is fresher and therefore less tart than commercial types. The flavor and texture will vary depending on the fat content of the milk, the type of yogurt used as the starter, and the amount of time it takes to thicken. Pasteurized rather than ultra-pasteurized (sterilized) milk is preferable. To make 2 cups/500 ml yogurt, bring 2 cups/500 ml milk just to a boil and leave to cool to 100-115°F/38-46°C measured on a dairy thermometer (p.503). Outside this temperature range the bacteria are inactive. Whisk in 2 tbsp active-culture yogurt, pour into two 1 cup/250 ml jars and cover. Keep the mixture warm (about 75-85°F/24-29°C) by wrapping in a towel or leaving in an oven with a pilot light. **Note** Electric yogurt-makers maintain a constant temperature, which produces a more consistent texture than the above method. After 6-8 hours or when the yogurt has set, stir in any desired flavorings and refrigerate for 12 hours before use.

Broiled chicken in yogurt

In this Middle Eastern-style recipe, yogurt has a double advantage: first it tenderizes the chicken, then it helps thicken the sauce. This dish is delicious with couscous (p.320) or cracked wheat (p.319).

Serves 3-4

1 × 4 lb/1.8 kg chicken, cut in 8 pieces (p. 176)	2 cloves garlic, crushed
	2 tbsp ground coriander
2 cups/500 ml plain yogurt	½ cup/125 ml sour cream
1 onion, chopped	salt and pepper
2 tbsp/30 ml oil	2 tbsp chopped fresh coriander

1 Dip the chicken pieces in 1 cup/250 ml of the yogurt until well coated, cover and let them marinate in the refrigerator 3-4 hours.
2 Heat the broiler. Brush the yogurt from the chicken pieces and discard it. Dry the chicken pieces on paper towels, then broil them 3-4 in/7.5-10 cm from the heat until very brown and no pink juice runs out when they are pierced with a two-pronged fork. Allow 15-20 minutes, turning them once.
3 Meanwhile, fry the onion in the oil until soft and starting to brown. Add the garlic and ground coriander and continue cooking over medium heat 2-3 minutes, stirring constantly. Purée the onion mixture with the remaining cup/250 ml of yogurt in a food processor or blender, then add the sour cream. Season with salt and pepper. Stir in the fresh coriander, then heat the mixture gently in a small saucepan. Taste the sauce for seasoning and keep warm. **Note** Do not boil or the sauce will separate.
4 Pile the chicken on a serving dish and spoon over the sauce. The dish may be served hot or at room temperature.

CHEESE

To the gourmet, cheese is the most varied and tantalizing of foods. The cheeses of France are outstanding in their number and variety, but many other countries have a rich heritage. Thanks to different kinds of milk – whole or skim, from the cow, goat or sheep – plus a variety of preparation and aging methods, thousands of cheeses are produced around the world, most of them intended to be eaten plain with bread, crackers or fruit; some cheeses are also indispensable for cooking.

Cheese is made by curdling milk or cream (p.68). At its simplest, this happens naturally when milk (or cream) is soured by the natural production of lactic acid. To make cheese, milk is now most commonly curdled by adding rennet. (Vegetarian cheese is made with non-animal rennet.) Cheesemaking is a question of juggling moisture and acidity to achieve the desired result. The speed, timing and temperature of curd formation, how finely the curds are broken up, and how the cheese is shaped, all radically affect the finished product. Some cheeses (such as ricotta) are left to drain, while others are pressed. Still others are heated before pressing – Gruyère is a prime example.

Most important of all are the bacteria that give every cheese its character. Fresh cheese, which is not aged, has a mild flavor because the bacteria hardly have time to develop at all. In some cheeses, the bacteria work from the outside, forming a fluffy white mold, such as that on Brie. On others, a crust forms and it is interior organisms that give the flavor, often causing holes to form inside the cheese, as with Emmenthal or Samsoe. To make blue cheeses such as Roquefort, skewers are run into a cheese that has been innoculated with starter bacteria, thus creating an atmosphere for the bacterial growth that results in the blue veins.

Aging under carefully controlled conditions is also important to the quality of the finest cheese. The best fresh cheese is sold within a day or two of being made. Soft cheeses such as Camembert may age for only one to two weeks, but three to six weeks is needed for them to develop much individuality. Blue cheeses such as Roquefort and Stilton need three to six months, while it may be a year before a hard cheese like Gruyère or Parmesan develops its rich nutty taste. Often cheeses such as Gouda are sold at different stages of maturity, from mild and tender enough to slice, to crumbling and very salty when thoroughly aged. The older and more intense the taste of a cheese, the less of it is needed in cooking. To intensify flavor, the rind of some cheeses like French Munster and Belgian Limburger is washed with beer, wine and water, or brine during aging. Shape and size also affects the aging process. Miniature versions of traditionally large cheeses, such as Cheddar, will never ripen to the same full bouquet.

Originally all cheese was made from unpasteurized milk, but today pasteurized milk is often used, especially for softer cheeses that are more susceptible to harmful bacteria. Nonetheless, most top-quality table cheeses are made from unpasteurized milk, as are many hard cheeses; Emmenthal, for example, will not develop its characteristic holes if made from pasteurized milk.

Least interesting of all is processed cheese, made by grinding and melting cheese and combining it with stabilizers so that it keeps almost indefinitely. Many cheese spreads are also manufactured this way. Special diet cheeses are available with low salt or skim milk. Another popular commercial product is smoked cheese, either naturally wood-smoked, or with liquid smoke flavoring added.

Salt is the universal seasoning for cheese. Herbs such as sage or parsley provide color as well as additional taste – for example in English Sage Derby, a hard cheese, and Italian Torta Basilica, a soft cheese flavored with basil. Other possibilities include pepper, dill or caraway seeds, wine, and even white truffles.

Small goat and cow cheeses are often rolled in ashes; the dark streak in French Morbier is of similar origin. Other coatings that add flavor to cheese include vine leaves, paprika, grape pips, nuts and peppercorns.

Choosing cheese

Every cheese has individual characteristics, but some generalizations can be made. An unpasteurized milk cheese will always be superior to the pasteurized version. However, unpasteurized milk soft cheeses are scarce as many countries restrict their availability for health reasons. Cheeses from small-scale artisan producers will be superior to those manufactured on a large scale; processed cheeses, with their glutinous texture and undistinguished taste, are the least desirable of all.

To the connoisseur, odor is almost as helpful as appearance in selecting a cheese. Fresh cheeses should smell sweet, possibly slightly briny. High-fat cheeses such as Brillat-Savarin and most soft cheeses should be pleasantly aromatic, though some, like Pont l'Evêque, may be quite pungent. Hard, aged cheeses should smell as they taste, with an earthy savor. It is the washed-rind cheeses, such as Limburger, which announce their presence from afar – the French name for one of them is *vieux puant* or "old stinker". Nonetheless, no cheese should be acrid or so overripe that it smells of ammonia. Lack of aroma is also a bad sign: odorless cheese may have been overchilled or frozen and will taste insipid.

The rind of a cheese is another guide to its quality. As it ages, a cheese needs to breathe, so cheeses with synthetic rinds, often colored for effect, are unlikely to be good. On hard cheeses and most blue cheeses, the rind should be firm, even crusty, but a dry rind on soft cheeses indicates overaging. Worst of all is an orange tinge to the rind of a white-rinded soft cheese such as Brie: the flavor will be rank. Once sliced, the color of a cheese is not a guide to quality, as much depends on the richness of the original milk and on the method of production. Some cheeses also have coloring added, usually a natural product such as carotene.

A whole cheese is better than one that has been cut in pieces, particularly when the pieces have been sealed in plastic wrap. Dried edges on cheese are a bad sign, so are damp sweaty surfaces or mold growing on a cut surface. **Note** Moldy cheese is not harmful, though its taste may be affected. To remove any mold, slice ¼-½ in/1-2 cm below the moldy part of the cheese.

Storing cheese

Most cheese is sold ready to eat, so storage is a matter of maintaining ripeness at its peak rather than aging the cheese further. Once cut, a cheese should be eaten as soon as possible; keep it loosely wrapped, or more tightly for a moist cheese that will dry out quickly. Fresh cheese should be refrigerated in an airtight container. Whole hard cheeses should be wrapped in a slightly damp cloth; wrap individual pieces loosely in plastic.

Ideally, cheese should not be refrigerated but stored in a cool, moist place at around 50°F/10°C. However, in the refrigerator, hard and blue cheeses will alter little for about a week. Grated hard cheese can also be refrigerated for a week, but can mold quite quickly if moist. Delicate soft cheeses lose a good deal of their fragrance within 12 hours of cutting, though refrigerating them up to three days is acceptable. Cheese can be frozen for up to a month, but flavor will be lost; thawed cheese is best used for cooking.

Grating cheese

Cheese can be coarsely or finely grated on an upright grater, or finely grated in a rotary cheese mill. In the food processor, to assure an even texture, use the fine or coarse grating blade. To prevent crumbling, chill the cheese before grating.

Uncooked cheese dishes

Most cheese is eaten uncooked, whether in salads, sandwiches, or as part of a cheese tray. Uncooked cheese also features in salad dressings – blue cheese dressing is an American favorite with tomato or hearty greens like spinach. Caesar salad depends on grated Parmesan for its special flavor, while a julienne of cheese is essential in the American chef's salad and in many mixed salads featured on café or British pub lunch menus. Crumbled Roquefort pairs well with cabbage and vinaigrette dressing, while slivers of Gruyère mix agreeably with mushrooms, lemon and walnut oil.

CHEESE IN COOKING

Dishes that are cooked with cheese form an important part of the cook's repertoire. Cooked cheese has four basic uses: as a flavoring, as a filling, as a topping, and as the basis for some desserts. **Note** Many cheeses are quite salty. When combining them with other ingredients, taste before adding more salt.

Cheese has one disadvantage in cooking: if overheated, its protein coagulates and separates from the fat, forming strings. If adding grated cheese to a sauce, heat it just until melted. Never boil cheese sauce and do not reheat. If a cheese topping forms strings with globules of fat, it has been browned too fiercely. Hard, well-aged cheeses can tolerate higher temperatures than softer types, which is one reason why Parmesan, Gruyère, and their cousins are so valuable in the kitchen. Well-aged cheese must be used for the famous Swiss fondue, and the wine used when melting the cheese helps to prevent strings from forming.

Cheese for flavoring

Finest of all is aged Parmesan, valued for its concentrated flavor, nutty but not sharp. It is often grated to use as a condiment, particularly with pasta and *risotto* and with fish or vegetable soups. Parmesan and its cousin, Pecorino Romano, dissolve rather than melting over heat, so there is little danger of their forming strings unless cooked at a rolling boil. Gruyère is almost as useful for flavoring; it has a higher fat content, therefore it adds richness and melts more easily than Parmesan. It is the French favorite for sauces, soufflés and cheese pastries. Cheddars and other English-style cheeses are often substituted for Gruyère, but it is important that they be dry: if moist, the fat may separate when heated. Goat cheese lacks the depth of hard cheeses, but adds its own lively bite to cooked dishes, for instance the Norwegian Gjetost is added to sauces for game. Blue cheese is also used for flavoring, often in a white sauce or salad dressing.

Cheese for topping

Cheese used as a topping must melt satisfactorily and cook to an appetizing brown. Possibilities start with very soft creamy cheeses like mozzarella, a cheese used almost entirely for its texture. Less common as toppings, but also satisfactory are soft cheeses like Bel Paese, Saint Paulin, or Brie, which add flavor as well. (Some of these cheeses do not melt easily unless they are thinly sliced.) Hard cheeses like Gruyère behave somewhat differently. They must be grated, and often become crisp on the surface as they brown, typically on French onion soup or béchamel-coated gratins. Gruyère is classic for *croque monsieur*, the French open toasted sandwich with ham, while Cheddar or mature Caerphilly usually tops Welsh rarebit. Soft goat cheese melts and browns well, and is popular on croûtes of toasted bread to serve with a green salad or vegetable soup, or on a sophisticated pizza.

Cheese as a filling

Almost any cheese can feature in a filling. Soft cheeses are sliced to wrap in dough or to layer with vegetables such as eggplant or potato. They may provide the body for a filling: ricotta is mixed with spinach or basil to layer or fill pasta, phyllo pastries may be filled with feta cheese and chopped scallions. Combinations of one, two or even three cheeses are popular, for example, ravioli stuffed with ricotta and Parmesan in a Gorgonzola sauce. Cheese croquettes (p.107) are another option – thick cheese sauce or sticks of soft cheese such as mozzarella, coated in egg and breadcrumbs and deep-fried. Gruyère and Cheddar are favorite bases for quiches and other cheese tarts; blue cheeses add a piquant bite.

Cheese as a dessert

As a dessert, cheese is invariably combined with sugar, so the cheese itself must be mild, usually fresh. At its simplest, fresh cheese may be beaten with sugar and a flavoring such as vanilla to serve with fresh or poached fruits. Whipped cream or egg white may be added for lightness, particularly to commercial cream cheeses that contain stabilizers. Fresh cheese is used in a wide range of regional desserts; it can be molded into hearts and other decorative shapes, as in French *coeur à la crème* (p.76), and Italian *cassata Palermitana*, a sponge cake filled with ricotta, candied fruits and chocolate, or *tiramisu* made with fresh Mascarpone layered with ladyfingers and sprinkled with cocoa. Easter in Russia is celebrated with *pashka*, a tall pyramid of fresh cheese sweetened with sugar and candied orange peel. Cheese-cakes (p.403) and cheese tarts are another world in themselves.

Presenting a cheese tray

It goes without saying that the cheeses on a presentation tray should be at the peak of ripeness and not selected merely because of the label or name. A well-balanced selection of a few different cheeses in good condition is more important than a large variety. One simple approach is to include one hard, one blue, and one or two soft cheeses. Fresh cheeses (p.76) are not usually included as they are too moist to eat with bread. Color, texture and, most importantly, a contrast of flavor should be taken into account when choosing the cheese. Trays of several different types of goat cheese are also popular – one particular French restaurant offers a selection of identical little goat cheeses at every stage of ripeness.

A wooden board is practical for slicing cheese. There are also flat basket trays made especially for display. These should be lined with doilies, paper napkins, or best of all, vine leaves (substitutes from the garden should be flat and not bitter). All cheeses should be served at cool room temperature. Grapes may garnish the tray, while nuts or celery stalks can be served separately.

The indispensable accompaniment to cheese is fresh bread, crusty, light, dark or chewy according to your taste. Whole wheat bread flavored with walnuts is particularly good. Crackers are an alternative, often served in the United States and Britain, where slightly sweetened wholemeal cookies are also popular with cheese. Butter should be served only with hard or blue cheeses as soft types provide their own richness.

When serving cheese, the rind should be left on for the diner to remove if preferred. Whether or not to eat the rind is a matter of debate. On fresh or mild cheeses, and all goat cheeses, the rind can be pleasant, though some connoisseurs insist on discarding it. The older the cheese, the more rancid and less palatable the rind; on very strong cheeses, it is inedible.

Cheese on an assorted tray must be carefully cut so it does not become untidy. A wedge-shaped piece of cheese should be cut in slim wedges so each serving includes some rind and, for blue cheeses, a section of the ripe center. Small round or square cheeses are cut in wedges like a cake; logs are sliced like a loaf.

Whole large cheeses like Cheddar or Stilton are more tricky to serve. A round should be sliced off the top to act as a lid and shallow horizontal slices are cut, including some rind. Stilton and other blue cheeses may also be scooped with a spoon, leaving the rind as a protective wall around the remaining cheese.

GOAT, SHEEP & BUFFALO CHEESES

The greatest range of cheese is made with cow's milk, but several other animal milks provide some of our most famous cheeses. The zesty tart flavor of goat cheese (Fr. *chèvre*) is instantly recognizable. It ranges from fresh and soft to dry and crumbly, depending on age. In fact, unlike almost any other cheese, the same goat cheese may be eaten at four or five stages of ripeness. Soft enough to spread when young, it matures to become almost chalky, never showing the creamy, melting consistency of some cow's milk cheeses. Goat cheeses tend to be produced on a small scale, and are often distributed locally, so well-known names such as Chabichou and Crottin de Chavignol are few. Long a Norwegian, French and Mediterranean monopoly, goat cheese is now being produced in Britain, North America and Australia.

With a medium fat content, most sheep's cheese is pleasant but less distinguished than a cow's milk cheese, with the notable exceptions of Roquefort, certain cheeses from the French Pyrenees, and Scottish Lanark Blue. Genuine Roquefort is aged in the caves above the French village of the same name. Italian pecorinos are ewe's milk cheeses that resemble Parmesan and vary from soft to hard in texture. Greek feta can be made from sheep's as well as goat's milk. Fresh feta is crumbly and dripping with whey, but when mature it becomes dry with a salty bite.

Water buffalo milk is best known as the basis of the finest whey-drenched mozzarella, but it also provides us with Provola, Provolone and Scamorza. Unfortunately buffalo milk is so scarce that these traditional cheeses are now often made with cow's milk, lacking the richness and piquancy of the original.

USEFUL INFORMATION

Typical goat cheeses Cabrales (Spain); Bûche Cendrée (France); feta (Greece); Bouton de Culotte (France); Pyrenées (France); Ardi-gasna (France); Hawkstone (UK); Olivet (France); Gjetost (Scandinavia); Bûcheron (France); Satterleigh (UK); Crottin de Chavignol (France); Chabichou (France); Chevrotins (France); Valençay (France); Rocamadour (France); Cabécou (France). *Also made with cow's milk:* Mont d'Or (France); Saint-Marcellin (France).
Typical sheep cheeses Banon (France); Cardiga (Portugal); Canestrato (Italy); Brousses (France); Foggiano (Italy); Cincho (Spain); Kajmak (Yugoslavia); Cachat (France); Sheviock (UK); Cachcaval (Romania); Roquefort (France); Pecorino Romano (Italy); Manchego (Spain); Spenwood (UK).
Typical water buffalo cheeses Manteca (with fresh butter inside, Italy); Provatura (Italy); Mozzarella (Italy); Provola (Italy); Provolone (Italy); Scamorza (Italy).

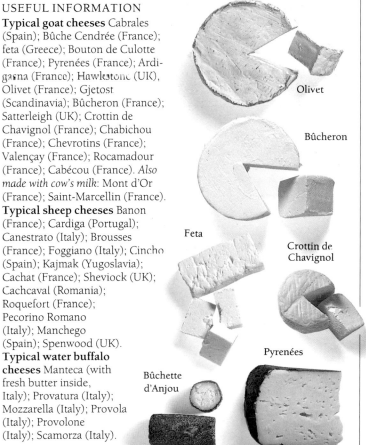

Olivet

Bûcheron

Feta

Crottin de Chavignol

Pyrenées

Bûchette d'Anjou

FRESH CHEESES

The vital elements of a fresh cheese are a refreshing taste and a light texture. Every country has its favorite, ranging from American cottage cheese to British cream cheese, Italian ricotta and French *fromage frais* (*fromage blanc* is similar and smoother). Many other fresh cheeses are almost as well known. Some are creamy and relatively high in fat like Italian Mascarpone and French Petit Suisse; while American creole cheese consists of a single large curd floating in heavy cream. Quark is a low-fat curd cheese made in Austria and Germany. Almost all are made with cow's milk, but they are surprisingly different in moisture and fat content, and cannot always be interchanged in recipes without appropriate adjustments. Yogurt may be drained in a cheesecloth to produce Labna, a white cheese popular in the Middle East.

The consistency of fresh cheese ranges from a smoothness similar to yogurt to the curds of cottage cheese and the creamy firmness of cream cheese. The fat content varies, and often whole or skim milk versions are available. Smaller dairies may produce local versions, using fewer of the stabilizers that are often added to commercial fresh cheeses. Most fresh cheeses are so soft they must be scooped with a spoon, but many stiffen as they age and their

moisture evaporates – a good example is American farmer cheese, which can be cut with a knife after a day or two.

Fresh cheese is rarely served alone. For a savory salad, it may be mixed with chopped scallion, tomato, nuts or herbs to serve with lettuce. The French often end a meal with fresh cheese sprinkled with chopped garlic and parsley – a homemade version of popular flavored cheeses such as Boursin. Similar fresh cheeses enhanced with pepper or cumin are also available. Fresh cheese is a prime ingredient in many spreads and cocktail dips like cream cheese with crab, or ricotta with spinach, while fresh fruit salads often include cottage or farmer cheese. A wide variety of desserts are also based on fresh cheese, for example poached pears with Mascarpone flavored with port wine.

Cottage cheese   *Fromage frais*   Cream cheese

USEFUL INFORMATION

Portion ⅓-½ cup/75-125 g.
How to choose Sweet aroma, light color; moist but not sloppy.
Storage Refrigerate tightly covered, 2-7 days depending on type. Do not freeze.
Nutritive value per 3½ oz/100 g. *Whole milk (creamed) cottage cheese:* 103 calories; 12 g protein; 5 g fat; 3 g carbohydrates; 15 mg cholesterol; 405 mg sodium. *Low-fat (2%) cottage cheese:* 90 calories; 14 g protein; 2 g fat; 4 g carbohydrates; 8 mg cholesterol;

406 mg sodium. *Cream cheese:* 349 calories; 8 g protein; 35 g fat; 3 g carbohydrates; 110 mg cholesterol; 296 mg sodium. *Ricotta (whole milk):* 174 calories; 11 g protein, 13 g fat; 3 g carbohydrates; 51 mg cholesterol; 84 mg sodium. *Ricotta (part skim milk):* 138 calories; 11 g protein; 8 g fat; 5 g carbohydrates; 31 mg cholesterol; 125 mg sodium.
Problems Acidic if poorly made or stored too long.
Typical fresh cheeses Scamorza (Italy); *fromage blanc* (France);

demi-sel (France); cottage cheese (USA), farmer cheese (USA); Villalon (Spain); cream cheese (UK); Cremina (Italy); Fromage de Fontainebleu (France); Crémet Nantais (France); pot cheese (USA); Burgos (Spain); curd cheese (UK); Paneer (India); Caboc (UK); baker's cheese (USA); Kajmak (Yugoslavia); Neufchâtel (USA).
Typical dishes *quarkauflauf* (curd cheese soufflé, Germany); *corniottes* (sweet or savory cheese puff pastries, France); *skyr* with

honey (curd cheese, Iceland); *pandorato alla crema di formaggio* (fried bread with cream cheese, Italy); *topfennockerl* (curd cheese dumplings, Germany); *frühlingskäse* (cream cheese spread, Austria); *empanadas de queso* (cheese-stuffed fried pastries, Mexico); cheese Danish (rich yeast dough with sweetened cream cheese, USA); *liptauer* (anchovy and paprika spread, Hungary); *cannoli* (sweetened ricotta stuffed in deep-fried pastry shells, Italy).

MAKING A FRESH CHEESE COEUR A LA CREME DESSERT

Any kind of smooth fresh cheese may be used to make *coeur à la crème*. Flavor will vary with the type of cheese used and also with the proportion of cream added. French *fromage frais*, English curd cheese, and American farmer cheese are all suitable for this dessert, which should be prepared two days before serving.

Serves 4

2 cups/500 ml fresh cheese	sugar or vanilla sugar (p.37)
1 cup/250 ml heavy cream	
3 egg whites	
For serving	
1 qt/500 g fresh strawberries or raspberries	*1 × 3 cup/750 ml heart-shaped perforated mold or 4 small molds*

2 Spoon the mixture into the mold or molds, set on a tray and cover. Leave to drain in the refrigerator for at least 8 hours and up to 36 hours.

3 An hour or two before serving, hull the strawberries, reserving 6-8 for decoration, or pick over the raspberries. Turn each mold on to a serving plate.

1 Line each mold with a piece of cheesecloth (this is not essential but it gives the dessert a neat patterned finish). In a large bowl, whisk the cheese and cream until smooth, adding a little more cream if necessary so the cheese falls easily from the spoon. In a separate bowl, whisk the egg whites until stiff. Gradually fold them into the cheese and cream.

4 Decorate with whole, unhulled strawberries or raspberries. Chill until serving. Sprinkle the remaining prepared berries with 1-2 tsp sugar and leave to macerate until serving.

MAKING FRESH RICOTTA

Fresh ricotta cheese is basic to many Italian dishes, serving as a useful binder for pasta fillings. When aged and pressed, it is also a popular table cheese. The quality of the finished cheese depends very much on the milk used to make it.

1 Mix 2 qts/2 L whole milk with 1 cup/250 ml live-culture buttermilk, yogurt or sour cream. Bring to a boil and simmer until the milk curdles, stirring constantly, 2-5 minutes.

2 Line a colander or large sieve with a piece of cheesecloth large enough to hang over the sides. Pour in the curdled milk to drain.

3 Gather together the edges of the cloth to make a bag, tie with string and suspend the bag over a bowl. Let drain until the curd is firm to the touch, about 1 hour.

4 Unwrap the cheese and use immediately, or store in the refrigerator for up to 3 days.

SOFT CHEESES

The best of all soft cheeses for cooking is fresh mozzarella, tender and moistened by its own whey. The increasingly scarce water-buffalo version and fresh cow's milk mozzarella have a higher fat content and are usually reserved for salads or as a table cheese. Older, commercial mozzarella is bland, but melts into a juicy, slightly stringy topping on pizza and baked pasta; mozzarella can also be cut in sticks to coat with breadcrumbs and deep-fry (*mozzarella impanata*), or crisply fried in a *carrozza* (Italian for carriage) of sliced bread. Another cheese designed to melt is Swiss raclette. When placed in front of a special grill, the cut surface softens to be scooped and served with boiled new potatoes.

There is a large group of soft cheeses which, like mozzarella, have a creamy texture sufficiently firm to slice and hold a shape after cutting. Typical are Italian Bel Paese, French Port Salut and Danish or Italian Fontina, but there are dozens of others. These are the pleasant, everyday cheeses that are often made with pasteurized milk and keep well. They are an agreeable part of a cheese tray and when cooked, melt easily in layers or as a topping.

Of all the table cheeses, creamy soft-paste types such as Brie, Coulommiers and Camembert are the most appreciated. Some washed-rind varieties like Vacherin and Epoisses can be quite pungent. They soften as they mature; at their peak they ooze gently when cut open, but they are hard to catch at the right moment. Much flavor is lost if they are heated, though they may be used in sauces or fritters such as Camembert croquettes (p.107).

USEFUL INFORMATION

Portion 3-4 oz/90-125 g.
How to choose Firm not dry rind, soft center. *Mozzarella:* white, soft and moist. *Brie and soft paste cheeses:* aromatic, no ammonia; rind white or creamy, not cracked or orange; soft to the touch; when cut, cheese should ooze gently.
Storage *Soft cheeses, pasteurized:* refrigerate 1 week; *unpasteurized:* refrigerate 3 days. *Mozzarella: Fresh pasteurized and unpasteurized:* refrigerate in brine 2-3 days. *Brie and soft paste cheeses, pasteurized:* refrigerate 3 days; *unpasteurized:* 24 hours in a cool place.
Nutritive value per 3½ oz/100 g. *Whole cow's milk mozzarella:* 281 calories; 19 g protein; 22 g fat; 2 g carbohydrates; 78 mg cholesterol; 373 mg sodium. *Skim mozzarella:* 254 calories; 24 g protein; 16 g fat; 3 g carbohydrates; 58 mg cholesterol; 466 mg sodium. *Brie:* 334 calories; 21 g protein; 28 g fat; no carbohydrates; 100 mg cholesterol; 629 mg sodium.

Problems Bland flavor, particularly in processed version. *Mozzarella:* tough if too old. *Brie and soft paste cheeses:* bland and firm if underripe; bitter if overripe.
Typical soft cheeses Esrom (Denmark); Munster (France); Brick (USA); Saint Florentin (France); Mahon (Spain); Brie (France); Camembert (France); Bel Paese (Italy); Monterey Jack (USA); Saint Paulin (France); Oka (Canada); Pont l'Evêque (France); Maroilles (France); Reblochon (France); Saint Nectaire (France); Gaperon (France); Liederkrantz (USA); Livarot (France); Port Salut (France); Milleens (Ireland); Herve (Belgium); Limeswold (UK).
Typical dishes *Lasagna al forno* (with Bel Paese and mozzarella, Italy); *zweibeln mit käse* (grilled onions with cheese topping, Germany); Brie baked in phyllo (USA).

Port Salut

Mozzarella

Vacherin

Pont l'Evêque

Brie

Monterey Jack

Wisconsin brick

Livarot

Camembert

Fontina

BLUE CHEESES

Blue cheeses are easy to enjoy. Their creamy, sometimes crumbly texture and piquant, often dominant flavors are as good with fresh bread as with celery sticks or a handful of walnuts. They may be crumbled in salads, on pizza, or blended with cream in a cocktail dip. Blue cheeses may be used to stuff pasta or to flavor a soufflé. The firmer blues – Stilton, Danish Blue, Roquefort, Fourme d'Ambert, Bleu d'Auvergne and blue versions of English hard cheeses like Wensleydale – all crumble easily for whisking into white sauces, or the celebrated American blue cheese dressing. The softer, creamier blues, such as Gorgonzola and Bleu de Bresse, are generally reserved for the cheese tray, but Gorgonzola is also used in creamy pasta sauces, often combined with other cheeses that melt easily to produce a smooth texture.

To say that all blue cheeses taste alike is heresy, but they do share a zesty flavor, produced in part by the veins of mold that run along the natural grain of the cheese. Some blue cheeses have tiny holes punched through them to encourage this desirable growth. The stronger types may be substituted one for another in recipes. Their taste should never degenerate into mere saltiness, a common fault of inferior blue cheese. Heating accents the salt, so taste before using large quantities in a hot dish.

USEFUL INFORMATION

Portion 2-3 oz/60-90 g.

How to choose Rind firm but not cracked, moist but not soggy; zesty but not sharp smell; creamy inside, not discolored, well marbled with blue.

Storage *Unpasteurized*: refrigerate 1 week; *pasteurized*: refrigerate 2 weeks.

Nutritive value per 3½ oz/100 g. *Roquefort*: 369 calories; 22 g protein; 31 g fat; 2 g carbohydrates; 90 mg cholesterol; 1,809 mg sodium. *Stilton*: 406 calories; 23 g protein; 35 g fat; 0.1 g carbohydrates; 120 mg cholesterol; 1,000 mg sodium.

Problems Poor-quality cheese may be salty; can be bitter or develop mites (maggots) if over-aged.

Typical blue cheeses Bluefort (Canada); Blue Dorset (UK); Roquefort (France); Stilton (UK); Gorgonzola (Italy); Castelmagno (Italy); Moncenisio (Italy); Vendôme Bleu (France); Castello Bianco (Portugal); Calabres (Spain); Mycella (Denmark); Cebrero (Spain); Ermite (Canada); Maytag (USA); Danish Blue (Denmark); Bleu d'Auvergne (France); Dunsyte Blue (UK); Cashel Blue (Ireland); Dolcelatte (Italy).

Typical dishes *Galettes au Roquefort* (cheese biscuits, France); *focaccia al Gorgonzola* (hot yeast flatbread topped with cheese, Italy); baked pears with watercress and Stilton (UK); *canapé de cabrales y pinones* (blue cheese and pine nut canapé, Spain).

Maytag

Bresse Bleu

Gorgonzola

Stilton

Roquefort

Danish Blue

Veal escalopes with Stilton

Plain sliced boiled potatoes and a moist chestnut purée are excellent accompaniments to these escalopes.

Serves 4

1½ lb/750 g veal escalopes	½ cup/100 g Stilton cheese, crumbled
½ cup/60 g flour seasoned with salt and pepper	salt and pepper
3 tbsp/45 g butter	chestnut purée (for serving)
½ cup/125 ml dry white wine	
1 cup/250 ml heavy cream	

1 Pound the veal escalopes to flatten them (see Tenderizing meat, p. 195). Coat with seasoned flour, patting to discard the excess.

2 Heat half of the butter in a frying pan and sauté half the escalopes until browned, allowing 2-3 minutes on each side. Remove them and fry the remaining escalopes in the remaining butter. Keep them warm.

3 Add the wine to the pan, stirring to dissolve the pan juices. Add the cream and boil 1-2 minutes, then add the cheese and whisk constantly over low heat until melted. Strain the sauce, taste it for seasoning and reheat it gently.

4 Arrange the escalopes on one side of four individual plates and spoon over the sauce. Add the chestnut purée and potatoes, or vegetables of your choice to the other side of the plate.

HARD CHEESES

Most countries have a common hard cheese, be it English or American Cheddar, Dutch Gouda, French Gruyère or Cantal, Italian Pecorino Romano, Spanish Roncal, or Swiss Emmenthal. Hard cheeses are diced for salads, grated to flavor sauces and omelets, melted on top of hamburgers or toasted in sandwiches. In the Netherlands and Scandinavia, hard cheese may be part of the standard breakfast with flatbreads, cured meats or fish Mild Edam is a particular favorite.

When it comes to grating cheese for flavoring a sauce or sprinkling as a topping for a gratin or soup, quality is important. The two outstanding cooking cheeses, Parmesan and Gruyère, are hard to match, partly because their concentrated flavors add so much depth, and partly because they are dry enough to take high temperature without forming strings (see Cheese in cooking, p.74). Both are "cooked" cheeses in that their curd is heated before being compressed and shaped. Gruyère refers to a specific cheese, but several regional versions are made in the same manner, notably Beaufort, Appenzell and Comté. Parmesan, one of a group of cheeses called *grana* in Italian, should come from the region around Parma, with the best stamped "*Parmigiano-Reggiano*" on the rind. Pecorino cheese is also a member of the *grana* family, and includes Pecorino Romano, which is sometimes substituted for Parmesan. Swiss, the name given to American-made Gruyère (with holes), tends to be high in fat and tastes quite different from true Gruyère. Cheddar and the other English-style hard cheeses may also be high in fat.

Hard cheeses are as indispensable on the table as in the kitchen. The field widens far beyond the half-dozen common cooking hard cheeses to include Italian Provolone and Caciocavallo and English cheeses such as Wensleydale and Double Gloucester. (The term "double" means that the cheese is made with morning and evening milk, as a longer-keeping cheese.) In France, a range of mountain cheeses, often called "*tommes*" (the name of the ring in which they are molded), have a lively flavor.

With hard cheeses, there is no ignoring the connection between age and quality. Even the finest hard cheese, made with meticulous care using unpasteurized milk, will be insipid unless given time to mature. But storage time costs money, hence the high price of aged cheeses such as Parmesan.

USEFUL INFORMATION

Portion 3-4 oz/90-125 g.

How to choose Dry rind (avoid rindless cheese or those with artificial rind); cut surface firm, moist but not damp; nutty aroma.

Storage In a cool place or refrigerate 2 weeks.

Nutritive value per 3½ oz/100 g. *Cheddar*: 403 calories; 25 g protein; 33 g fat; 1 g carbohydrates; 105 mg cholesterol; 620 mg sodium. *Edam (or Gouda)*: 356 calories; 25 g protein; 27 g fat; 2 g carbohydrates; 114 mg cholesterol; 819 mg sodium. *Gruyère*: 413 calories; 30 g protein; 32 g fat; no carbohydrates; 110 mg cholesterol; 336 mg sodium. *Parmesan*: 392 calories; 36 g protein; 26 g fat; 3 g carbohydrates; 68 mg cholesterol; 1,602 mg sodium.

Problems Soft and bland if not mature; turn rancid if stored at high temperature; stronger cheeses may overwhelm other ingredients.

Typical hard cheeses Cheddar (UK, Canada); Double Gloucester (UK); Gruyère (Switzerland); Parmesan (Italy); Edam (Holland); Wensleydale (UK); Gouda (Holland); Lancashire (UK); Bra (Italy); Bola (Portugal); Pellelay (Switzerland); Bagozzo (Italy); Colby (USA); Sage (USA); Elbo (Denmark); Cheshire (UK); Cantal (France); Jarlsberg (Norway); Derby (UK); Pannonia (Hungary); Tetilla (Spain); Sprinz (Switzerland); San Simon (Spain); Provolone (Italy); Caciocavallo (Italy); Samsoe (Denmark); Comté (France); Beaufort (France); Caerphilly (UK); Sage Derby (UK).

Typical dishes *Kaasbolletjes* (Edam and Gouda appetizers, Denmark); *caws pobi*/"Welsh rarebit" (toasted Caerphilly on toast, Wales); Cheddar cheese soup (UK); macaroni and cheese (with Cheddar sauce, USA); *fondue* (bread cubes dipped in melted Gruyère, Switzerland); *gougère* (cheese-flavored choux pastry, France); *gnocchi alla Romana* (baked polenta with Parmesan, Italy); *fettuccine Alfredo* (with Parmesan and cream, Italy); *el alino* (herb and cheese salad dressing, Spain); *pecorino con fave fresche* (fresh fava beans and cheese, Italy); *filetes de cerdo con pimentes y queso* (pimento and cheese-stuffed pork cutlets, Spain); Chester cakes (Cheshire cheese-filled cakes, UK); *waadtländer käseauflauf* (soufflé with Emmenthal and fried bread, Switzerland).

Pecorino

Parmesan

Jarlsberg

Gouda

Emmenthal

Gruyère

Traditional Cheddar

Double Gloucester

Provolone

HIGH-FAT CHEESES

High-fat cheeses are valued above all for their richness. They are rarely cooked, though they can be used sparingly in stuffings or spreads. Almost all are French, with double cream cheeses defined as having a fat content of over 60 percent, and triple creams more than 72 percent. In appearance they resemble Brie-type cheeses with a soft white rind, but inside, the texture is more like cream cheese, soft or firm and white or creamy yellow, depending on age and type. High-fat cheeses should be moist and light-colored with a sweet or piquant smell; if poorly made or stale, they can be chalky. They never age to the runny cream of a Brie; rather they are valued for their fragrant richness, which adds contrast to an assortment of table cheeses. Typical high-fat French cheeses are Fin de siècle, Explorateur, Gratte-Paille and Brillat-Savarin.

Brillat-Savarin

Explorateur

EGGS

Eggs from a variety of birds are edible, but nowadays in the kitchen, an egg basically means a hen's egg of reliable quality and graded size. The freshness of eggs, which once caused much concern, has lost importance in light of modern methods of production and distribution. A rotten egg is now a rarity. Regrettably, the rich flavor of a very fresh egg less than 48 hours old is equally rare, hard to find away from farming country.

Boiling an egg is the first lesson for the novice cook, closely followed by poached and scrambled eggs. Shallow- and deep-fried eggs can be a breakfast staple or a quick snack. Baked eggs, *en cocotte* in ramekins or *sur le plat* in gratin dishes, no longer retain the "invalid diet" image they once had, while omelets open a wealth of regional possibilities, both sweet and savory. Whole eggs are also the basis of savory and sweet custards, batters and crêpes, and without them one of the most famous culinary creations – the soufflé – could not exist.

As well as playing a role as an ingredient in dishes, eggs perform a dozen other subsidiary roles in cooking. When heated, egg whites stiffen a mixture, while egg yolks make it smooth, rich and slightly thickened. Eggs are important in enhancing soups and sauces, and in binding stuffings and purées. In baked custards, the egg white sets the milk or cream until firm, while the egg yolk enriches it. Egg whites are also used to clarify stock for consommé and aspic (Soups and Stocks, p.46). Whole eggs, or egg yolk mixed with a little water, form an excellent golden glaze for breads and pastries. Similarly, whole eggs, alone or mixed with a tablespoon or two of water or oil, act as a binder for coatings for foods to be deep-fried.

The place of eggs in a meal varies substantially from region to region. In northern Europe and North America, eggs appear on the breakfast table, usually boiled, baked or fried. Almost everywhere, more substantial egg dishes such as omelets or poached eggs with a sauce form the main course of a light lunch, supper or that American favorite, brunch. Soufflés, baked eggs *en cocotte*, and poached eggs in classic sauces like hollandaise (p.60) are standard French openings to a grand menu. American eggs Benedict comprises eggs garnished with hollandaise sauce, an English muffin and a slice of ham, while eggs in aspic is another popular appetizer. In country districts, a plain or filled omelet may start a hearty lunch, particularly in Spain and Portugal. Eggs also appear at the end of the meal in the guise of sweet soufflés, custards, dessert crêpes, or sabayon sauce.

Choosing eggs

The flavor of a very fresh egg is inimitable, but the difference in taste between an egg refrigerated for a few days and one refrigerated for several weeks is scarcely detectable. However, the moisture content does change over time as the egg dehydrates through its porous shell and the white becomes less viscous and more watery. The older the egg, the flatter and less spherical the yolk, while the white of a very fresh egg is cloudy and clings closely to the yolk. In many countries, egg cartons are dated at the time of packing. Freshness can also be tested by immersing an egg in water; the larger the air pocket, the older the egg is. If an egg floats on its side, it is very fresh, but if it floats vertically, rounded end up, it is two to three weeks old. An egg that floats right on the surface of the water could be several months old and should be discarded. Eggs are washed before sale, and are often lightly oiled to seal the shell and reduce dehydration. Cracked eggs – even those with hairline cracks – are normally detected by scanning equipment, then set aside, thus assuring uniform shelf-life.

Very fresh eggs are best for poaching (p.85), as they hold their shape, but when whisking egg whites, greater volume can be achieved with whites that are at least a few days old. A deep golden yolk is not necessarily superior in taste, though it helps add color to sauces and cakes; the color of the yolk depends on the diet of the chicken, just as the color of the shell varies with the breed of hen. Many American cooks prefer white shells that suggest purity; most Europeans opt for the country connotation of a brown egg. The shells of brown eggs are actually less porous than those of white eggs, so they may keep longer. The two threads, or *chalazae*, that run through the white are harmless and anchor the yolk to the shell. Any spots of blood in an egg yolk, or brown spots in the white are unsightly, but do not spoil the egg itself; pick out any spots using the cracked eggshell. Eggs can harbor bacteria, especially *salmonellae*, which penetrate the egg through cracks in the shell. A new cause for concern is that bacteria-carrying hens can lay infected eggs that are flawless in appearance. Reported cases are isolated but are receiving the attention of health authorities.

Storing eggs

Eggs should be stored in a very cool place or in the refrigerator, ideally with the pointed end down so the yolk is well centered within the egg. To minimize dehydration, cover them or leave them in their carton. Storage time depends on the freshness of the eggs when bought, but three weeks is a normal maximum. Out of the shell, eggs must be refrigerated and kept covered. Egg yolks dry out rapidly, so moisten them with a tablespoon or two of water, and cover them very tightly. Egg yolks can quickly develop bacteria out of the shell even when refrigerated. Dishes or sauces containing raw egg yolks, such as mayonnaise, should not be kept more than two days. Whole eggs out of the shell should be used within two days; whites will keep well for up to two weeks.

Eggs can be frozen (out of their shells), but must have small amounts of salt and sugar added before freezing to prevent the yolks becoming gelatinous (p.496). They may then be used in either sweet or savory dishes. Pasteurized and dehydrated eggs, convenient but inferior to fresh eggs in taste and texture, are used in many commercial preparations. Drying causes little or no loss to an egg's nutritional value.

Hen   Duck   Quail   Bantam   Goose

Nutrition and eggs

Eggs are an excellent source of protein and vitamins – the average egg contains six grams of protein, about 15 percent of an adult's daily requirement, along with significant amounts of iron and vitamins A, D, E and K. Eggs are low in calories, with an average of 80 calories per egg, but their high cholesterol content means that eggs are restricted in some diets for health reasons.

The structure of eggs

The molecular structure of eggs helps explain their valuable properties in cooking. The raw egg contains complex molecules of protein that lie in coils. When the coils are agitated, for example when the eggs are beaten, they unravel into long strands; these form a network of bubbles that stabilize as foam. Whole eggs can be beaten for a long time, but if egg whites are overwhipped, the protein coagulates so much that the whites start to separate.

When an egg is heated, its protein converts into a network of strands that stiffen during cooking. If overcooked, the strands of protein shrink, making the egg tough. In custards (p.94), where eggs are mixed with milk or cream, the same principle applies: at the right temperature, the egg cooks, thickening creamily if the custard is whisked, or firmly if it is left unstirred. However, if custard gets too hot, the egg protein starts to shrink, making the custard curdle. Egg whites start to coagulate at temperatures of 145°F/62°C and egg yolks at 155°F/70°C, or slightly higher when diluted with liquid. However, starch interferes with the shrinking action of protein, making it possible to boil custard containing even a small amount of flour or cornstarch.

Another important property of eggs is their emulsifying action, that is, their capacity to combine fat and water molecules smoothly, thanks to the presence in egg yolks of two emulsifying agents, cholesterol and lecithin. Successful emulsification is critical in lustrous sauces, rich butter creams, and even certain pastry doughs such as *pâte sucrée* (p.373).

Measuring eggs

In most Western countries, eggs are graded by quality and size/weight and some may also be marked "fresh" or "extra-fresh", though these are not clearly defined terms.

Egg sizes in the United States range from small (1½ oz/45 g) to jumbo (over 2 oz/60 g). In the European Economic Community, the scale ranges from size 7 (under 45 g) up to size 1 (70 g or over). The standard egg called for in a recipe weighs around 2 oz/60 g – the American large, or the European size 3 or 4. Just over half of the volume of an average egg is white, with 30 percent yolk and 12 percent shell. When measuring eggs in bulk, an 8 fl oz/250 ml cup holds four to five 2 oz/60 g whole eggs, six to seven whites, or 12-14 yolks.

Serving portions of eggs

The number of eggs served per person depends very much on how they are cooked and their place in the meal. As an appetizer, one boiled or poached egg can be sufficient if served with a copious garnish. For a main course, one or two eggs are standard when plainly boiled or baked *en cocotte*, though anything less than two eggs *sur le plat* looks mean. For an omelet or scrambled eggs, two eggs per person is minimum, three is preferred, while in a soufflé you should allow one egg yolk and one and a half whites.

Cooking with eggs

Eggs are very sensitive to temperature and in many cases should not be used straight from the refrigerator. For example, whole eggs and egg whites whip to greater volume if they are slightly warm. Very cold egg yolks will make mayonnaise curdle because the emulsion is less stable at low temperatures. Eggs, particularly egg yolks, should never be added directly to a hot mixture; instead a little hot mixture is beaten into the yolks to warm them first (see Enrichments to soup, p.50). Eggs overcook easily and just a second or two can make the difference between an egg that is tender and moist or one that is tough and dry. Eggs will continue to cook if left in a hot dish or transferred to very hot plates. If scorched, they acquire an unpleasant charred taste and tough texture. Always use gentle heat, except when making omelets, which are cooked briskly for a very short tme.

Salt and eggs

Salt "relaxes" the protein in egg white, making it easier to blend and to whip to a stiff foam. This is also useful in egg glaze, when a liquid mixture of white and yolk is needed. However, if salt is added more than a minute or two before cooking to scrambled eggs or an omelet, the eggs become thin. Poached eggs break up if cooked in salted water, and baked eggs look spotted if sprinkled with salt before cooking. To avoid this, seasoning should be added to the baking dish underneath the egg.

SEPARATING EGGS

Eggs are best separated with the help of the shell, which cuts easily through the white.

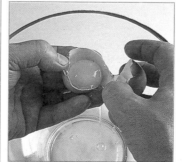

1 Crack the egg at its broadest point by tapping it against a bowl or a sharp edge. With your two thumbs, break open the egg, letting some of the white slip over the edge of the shell into the bowl.

2 Tip the yolk from one half of the shell to the other, detaching the remaining white from the yolk.
Note If the yolk breaks and some slips into the white, remove it with the eggshell.

3 To remove the white threads, nip them against the side of the eggshell with your fingertips.

WHIPPING WHOLE EGGS & EGG YOLKS

Whole eggs can be whipped with other ingredients over a water bath or very low heat. (If using an electric whisk, a water bath may not be needed.) Adding sugar stabilizes the mixture, forming the foundation of many cakes; citrus fruit juices and liqueurs are sometimes included for flavor, particularly in mousses. Egg yolks can also be whipped with other ingredients, for example with water as in hollandaise (p.60) and with sugar as in cakes (p.394).

In sweet recipes, whipping whole eggs with a little sugar helps the egg mixture to thicken and become creamy.

WHIPPING EGG WHITES

Egg whites can be whipped to as much as eight times their own volume, particularly if an unlined copper bowl (p.505) and balloon whisk are used. The whites interact with the copper to produce a dense texture, with maximum volume and a more stable foam: a balloon whisk is lifted easily in a high circular motion to incorporate more air. The next best alternative is an electric beater with a balloon whisk and a metal bowl. Glass and ceramic bowls are the least satisfactory as the whites tend to detach from the sides and separate; a plastic bowl is undesirable because it is difficult to remove traces of oil from the surface. To whip well, egg whites must be free of any trace of egg yolk, grease or water, as should the bowl and whisk. Egg whites that have been frozen will whip well. A small pinch of salt or cream of tartar added at the start of beating also helps egg whites stiffen. Sugar helps stabilize the foam, but must be added after the whites begin to stiffen, to make a firm glossy meringue.

Egg whites are ready as soon as the texture is fine enough to hold a shallow peak when the whisk is lifted. If whipped for too long, they separate and turn grainy; in this state they will be hard to fold smoothly into other mixtures and too weak to maintain their volume when combined with other ingredients. This rarely happens if whipping in a copper bowl, but is more common with an electric or hand beater. If egg whites separate and "grain", drop in one fresh unbeaten egg white for every four whites, and continue beating for about 30 seconds, until they are smooth. Plain whipped egg whites should be used within a few minutes, though unbaked meringue (p.435) can be kept 10-15 minutes without harm before shaping and baking.

Before using a copper bowl, the inside must be prepared by rubbing with one or two tablespoons of salt and a cut lemon (or one or two tablespoons of vinegar) to remove any accumulated film of toxic copper carbonate. The cleaned copper should be bright and have a pinkish cast. Rinse and dry the bowl before using; it can be cleaned one to two hours ahead, but not more.

2 As the whites break up and become frothy, increase the size of the circles until you are using the whole bowl area and whisking as fast as possible, still lifting the whisk high in a circle, out of the bowl. Do not stop whisking until the whites have become stiff.

3 When the whites are quite stiff, whisk in large circles as fast as possible with the whisk kept down in the egg whites, in contact with the bowl. This stiffens and "tightens" the whites rather than beating air into them.

4 Fully whipped egg whites are very smooth and hold a shallow peak when the whisk is lifted.
Note If overwhisked, they will become granular.
If beating egg whites in a machine: start beating slowly and gradually increase the speed.

1 **To whisk egg whites in a copper bowl:** start whisking slowly, working at first in the bottom of the bowl and then lifting the whisk up in a circle to beat in as much air as possible.

FOLDING EGG WHITES

Plain whisked egg whites are the lightest of all ingredients and are therefore the most difficult to combine with other mixtures; they should be folded in very carefully. Meringue is firmer than plain whipped whites, so in sweet recipes, some sugar should always be added to the whites to stiffen them. The lighter the basic mixture, the easier it is to fold in egg whites; heavy mixtures should first be lightened by stirring in a portion of the whipped whites before folding in the rest. To avoid a heavier mixture sinking to the bottom of the bowl, add it on top of the whites.

1 Stiffly whip the egg whites (if the recipe is sweet, sugar can be added to make meringue, p.435). Add about a quarter of the whites to the basic mixture (in this case spinach) and stir them together, scooping to the bottom of the bowl to mix thoroughly. Tip this mixture on to the remaining egg whites.

2 ABOVE: With a metal spoon or rubber spatula, cut down into the center of the bowl, scoop under the contents, and turn them over in a rolling motion. Turn the bowl in the opposite direction.

RIGHT: The finished mixture should be light and fluffy, with the egg whites and spinach combined evenly.

Presenting eggs

A plain boiled or poached egg cries out for a cosmetic touch of sauce, be it béchamel, cheese sauce, velouté, butter sauce, or even brown sauce. Mayonnaise is the top choice for salad eggs, often with a touch of tomato, herb, or a single slice of jet black truffle. Omelets can be garnished with a spoonful of their flavoring, or a ribbon of sauce around the dish. Many eggs benefit from an edible container such as a pastry tartlet shell, or a fried or toasted croûte of bread. Lighter alternatives include a bed of spinach, sliced tomatoes, or artichoke bottoms. When neatly sliced, hard-boiled eggs add colorful appeal to cold dishes like spinach salad or fish mousse, while fluffy sieved yolk forms a pretty garnish.

BOILED EGGS

The term "boiled egg" is a misnomer, for eggs should always be gently simmered, not boiled, partly to avoid cracking the shells, partly so the whites do not become rubbery. The water should generously cover the eggs and, to gauge the cooking time correctly, the eggs are best lowered into water that is already simmering. However, they can also be put in cold water and brought to a boil, or put in boiling water and left to cook off the heat. The latter method, called coddling, produces a soft-cooked egg with a particularly tender white. To deter cracking, eggs should be at room temperature: a tablespoon or two of vinegar in the water will help seal leaks of white from any cracks. Some cooks also advocate piercing the eggshell with a pin.

Eggs are boiled to three different stages: they may be soft-boiled (soft white and yolk), *mollet* (firm white and soft yolk), or hard-boiled until firm. Careful timing will produce a soft-boiled egg with the white runny or lightly set according to your taste. For eggs *mollet*, the white must be firm enough to hold in the soft yolk. **Note** Very fresh eggs take slightly longer to cook than eggs that are a week or more old.

Soft-boiled eggs are often eaten in the shell using an eggcup, or the contents can be scooped into a warm dish accompanied by slices of toast. Eggs *mollet*, which are still soft in the center, closely resemble poached eggs and are used in many of the same recipes. Their neat shape and smooth surface is preferred for molding in aspic, or for presenting on a rice salad, or on a bed of spinach as in eggs Florentine. Poached eggs lie flatter on croûtes, ham slices or veal escalopes.

Top: egg mollet (left), hard-boiled egg (right).
Bottom: halved egg mollet (left), halved hard-boiled egg (right).

A whole hard-boiled egg is invariably halved lengthwise or sliced, preferably with an egg slicer (p.505). Often the yolk is sieved to mix with a creamy "devil" stuffing that is piped back into the white. If hard-boiled eggs are to be served hot, they may be sliced to layer as a gratin with béchamel or cheese sauce and other savory ingredients.

USEFUL INFORMATION
Portion 1-2 eggs.
Storage *Soft*: always eat fresh. *Mollet, hard, unpeeled*: refrigerate 4 days; *peeled*: refrigerate in cold water 2 days.
Cooking times (for room temperature egg added to boiling water). *Soft*: 3-4 minutes. *Mollet*: 6-7 minutes. *Hard*: 10-12 minutes.
When done *Soft*: soft or set white, soft yolk. *Mollet*: firm white, soft yolk. *Hard*: firm white and yolk.
Problems *Hard*: if overcooked, yolk is black-edged and tastes of sulphur, white is tough; if refrigerated too long, white is tough; when coating eggs, sauce will run off if eggs are wet.

Reheat *Mollet, hard*: immerse 3-5 minutes in hot water, then drain.
Typical dishes *Soft*: oeufs cressonière (on toast with watercress purée and cream sauce, France); *oeufs Argenteuil* (on tartlet with asparagus purée and cream sauce, France). *Mollet*: eggs Cobb (with cornmeal pancakes, USA); *oeufs à la Bruxelloise* (with braised endive and cream sauce, Belgium). *Hard*: Tiroler eierspeise (gratinéed with anchovies, potatoes and spices, Austria); devilled eggs (stuffed with yolks mixed with mayonnaise and mustard, USA); stuffed eggs baked in sour cream pastry (Hungary).

PEELING BOILED EGGS

Hard-boiled and *mollet* eggs are sometimes hard to peel, depending on the freshness of the egg. In very fresh eggs, the outer membrane tends to cling to the albumen, making the egg harder to peel. Plunging the eggs into cold water as soon as they are cooked helps loosen the shell, as does peeling them under cold running water. Eggs *mollet* must be peeled very carefully.

Tap the egg all over to crack the shell in small pieces. Under running water, peel away skin and shell from the egg white. Dry the egg with absorbent paper.

EXOTIC EGGS

Some birds' eggs are valued on the gourmet table as much for their appearance as for their taste. Quail and gull eggs are often boiled (five minutes in simmering water will hard-boil them) and served as a garnish, unpeeled to display their speckled shells. Plain or seasoned salt is usually provided for dipping. Quail eggs may also be baked *sur le plat* (p.87) with tiny shrimps or wild mushrooms or added to soup. (Commercially available pigeon, partridge and pheasant eggs are also delicacies.) At the other end of the scale, the giant ostrich egg farmed in South Africa serves 10 people.

Duck, goose, and turkey eggs hardly seem exotic, though they are rarely seen away from the farmyard. They taste very like hen's eggs and can be directly substituted, though duck and goose eggs are richer. As their sizes do not conform to the 2 oz/60 g standard, they are used in dishes where measurement is unimportant, though the equivalence to hen's eggs can be obtained by weighing.

Eggs mimosa with curry mayonnaise

The yolks of hard-boiled eggs can be worked through a sieve to mix with other ingredients, or to form a crumbly decoration called mimosa, resembling the blossoms of the mimosa tree.

Serves 4-6

8 eggs
1 onion, finely chopped
1 tbsp oil
1 tbsp curry powder
1½ cups/375 ml mayonnaise (p.62)
For the rice salad:
1 cup/200 g uncooked rice
½ cup/125 ml vinaigrette dressing (p.64)
¼ cup/40 g raisins
¼ cup/40 g dried apricots, chopped
½ cup/75 g coarsely chopped walnuts
bunch of watercress (for decoration)

1 Hard-boil the eggs, peel them and leave in cold water until cool. For the curry mayonnaise: fry the onion in the oil until soft but not brown. Stir in the curry powder and cook gently, stirring, for 2 minutes. Let the mixture cool, then stir into the mayonnaise. Work it through a sieve; taste for seasoning.
2 For the rice salad: boil the rice in salted water (p.318) and drain it. While still warm, mix it with the vinaigrette, raisins, apricots and walnuts. When cool, season.
3 Pile the salad down one side of a long serving dish, or in the center of a round one. Reserve two eggs; arrange the rest on the rice, or cut them in half lengthwise

and place, cut side down. Coat them with the curry mayonnaise.
4 Sieve the yolks from the remaining eggs, scattering a little on top of each coated egg. Chop the whites and sprinkle between the eggs. Decorate with watercress; serve within a half hour.

Variations

Eggs mimosa with herb mayonnaise To the basic mayonnaise (p.62), add 3 tbsp chopped mixed fresh herbs (such as dill, parsley, basil or tarragon). Substitute lemon juice for the vinegar in the vinaigrette, and ¼ cup/30 g chopped scallions for the raisins and apricots.

Eggs mimosa with *orzo* pasta salad Use tomato mayonnaise (p.63). Instead of rice salad, make *orzo* salad: cook 1 cup/200 g orzo (Pasta, p.329), and use the vinaigrette from the main recipe. Add ½ cup/50 g toasted pine nuts and 3 tbsp chopped fresh basil instead of the dried fruits and walnuts.

POACHED EGGS

As their name implies, poached eggs are cooked in water that is barely simmering. When cooked, the white should be just firm enough to enclose a yolk that is still soft. At the start of cooking, the water should be at a rolling boil, trapping the egg in the turbulence and shaping it to an oval; up to six eggs may be added at a time. Then the heat is lowered and the egg is poached until firm. The fresher the egg, the closer the white clings and the neater it will be after poaching; stale eggs are instantly detectable as the white detaches almost completely from the yolk, swirling out into the poaching water. A little vinegar in the water will help the whites cling, producing a neater egg. Special molded pans to immerse in the water are also available for poaching eggs, but these are spurned by serious cooks, as the egg itself is not surrounded by water.

Poaching produces an egg that is soft and moist. A plain poached egg on buttered toast has long been a breakfast dish, sometimes complemented by smoked fish, or even steak. Poached eggs also appear in elaborate presentations such as eggs *à la reine* – poached eggs in a pastry shell with chicken, foie gras and truffles, cloaked in a velouté sauce. Occasionally eggs are poached in stock or wine, which is then used to make a sauce, a well-known example being eggs *meurette* (Sauces, p.56). Poached eggs with a slice of ham or a spoonful or two of diced vegetables are traditional components of gleaming eggs in aspic.

USEFUL INFORMATION

Portion 1-2 eggs.
Storage Refrigerate 2 days, covered in cold water.
Cooking times 3½-4½ minutes.
When done White is firm and yolk soft when pressed with a fingertip.
Problems Yolk breaks easily if white not well set.
Reheat Immerse 3-5 minutes in hot water, then drain.
Typical dishes *Velorene eier in senfsosse* (on toast with mustard sauce, Germany); *forlorade egg med selleri, smaltost och skinka* (with celery root, cheese and ham, Scandinavia); *oeufs Parmentier* (in a scooped-out baked potato with cream sauce, France); eggs Florentine (with creamed spinach and cheese sauce, USA); *oeufs noyés* (on buttered croûtons in onion and fennel soup, France); *huevos escalfados a l'española* (on a bed of sautéed onions, tomatoes, peppers and zucchini, Spain); poached in tomatoes, (Italy).

POACHING EGGS

A sauté pan or frying pan that is deep enough to hold a 3 in/ 7.5 cm layer of water is best for poaching. Vinegar added to the water in the proportion of 3 tbsp to every 1 qt/1 L helps seal the white. (Salt will break down the white and should not be used.)

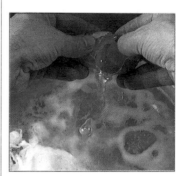

1 Bring water to a rolling boil. Break an egg into a bubbling area so the bubbles spin the egg and set the white around the yolk. Up to 6 eggs may be added, provided the pan is large enough.

2 Lower the heat to just below a simmer and poach the eggs about 4 minutes. To test, lift an egg with a slotted spoon and press with your fingertip; the white should be set with the yolk still soft. Transfer the eggs to a bowl of warm water if you are using them hot; use cold water for salad eggs.

3 Lift out the eggs and trim the ragged white with a knife or scissors. Keep the eggs in water and drain them on paper towels just before using.

Poached eggs Clamart

The town of Clamart, now a Paris suburb, was once famous for its green peas, which are a feature of this poached egg dish.

Serves 4

4 fresh eggs
1 cup/250 ml hollandaise sauce (p. 60)
4 cooked artichoke bottoms (p. 302)
2 tbsp/30 g butter
1 cup/150 g cooked green peas
2-3 stalks fresh mint

1 Poach the eggs and keep them in warm water. Make the hollandaise and keep it warm in a water bath. Wrap the artichoke bottoms in foil with half the butter. Warm them in a 350°F/175°C oven for 15 minutes or until very hot. Melt the remaining butter in a saucepan, add the peas and a stalk of mint, reserving 4 sprigs of leaves for garnish. Warm the peas over low heat until very hot.
2 Set the artichoke bottoms on 4 individual plates and fill them with peas. Drain the eggs on paper towels and set them on the peas. Coat the eggs with hollandaise, leaving some of the peas and artichoke showing. Top each egg with a mint sprig. Serve at once.

Variations

Eggs Sardou Use 2 cups/500 ml creamed spinach seasoned with nutmeg instead of peas and omit the mint.
Eggs Benedict Use toast or toasted English muffin instead of the artichoke, and ham or Canadian bacon instead of the peas. Omit the mint decoration.
Eggs New Orleans Substitute 1 lb/500 g lump crabmeat, sautéed in 6 tbsp/90 g butter, seasoned with salt, pepper, and brandy for artichokes and peas. Omit mint and sprinkle eggs with paprika.

SCRAMBLED EGGS

Good scrambled eggs are deceptively simple, for they actually require patient stirring over very low heat for at least five minutes to achieve the perfect creamy consistency. Some cooks use a double boiler or water bath to maintain a low, even heat. Usually the only seasoning is a sprinkling of salt and pepper added just before cooking. If the eggs are very fresh, a tablespoon of cream or water may be included for every two eggs, but this can make older eggs watery. Scrambled eggs may be cooked until very soft, or until fairly firm, but they should never be stiff. If they start to overcook, quickly stir in a tablespoon or two of butter or cream.

The flavor of scrambled eggs is subtle, an ideal background for small quantities of herbs, smoked salmon or other fish, asparagus or ham. Herbs are added directly to the raw eggs; more substantial ingredients are chopped and added when the eggs start to thicken. Scrambled eggs with fresh truffle or caviar and sour cream is the ultimate luxury. Whatever the flavoring, add only a little, as the eggs themselves should remain dominant. Like poached eggs, scrambled eggs benefit from a pastry tartlet or a fried bread croûte.

Variations on scrambled eggs include Basque *pipérade*, a mixture of sautéed bell peppers, tomato and onion cooked with egg to a thick purée. Scotch woodcock is a traditional British savory, served at the end of dinner, in which anchovy-flavored eggs are scrambled in a shallow pan so they cook into thick flakes, then served on toast.

USEFUL INFORMATION

Portion 2-3 eggs.
Storage Serve at once.
Cooking times 5-8 minutes.
When done Lightly thickened, creamy and just holding shape.
Problems If cooked too fast or too long, granular and lumpy; eggs continue to thicken in the heat of the pan so take from the heat before they are quite done.

Typical dishes *Kalbshirne mit eiern* (with calf's brains, Germany) *oeufs à la bonne femme* (with bacon on toast, France); with smoked salmon and dill (USA); with cream and curry powder (UK); *bacalhau e ovos* (with salt cod, potatoes and black olives, Portugal); *revuelto de langostino y espinacas* (with shrimp and spinach, Spain).

CURED EGGS

Pickled eggs gleaming through a marinade of vinegar, allspice, garlic and ginger are a tradition in New York delicatessens and English West Country pubs, offering a quick snack or a piquant accompaniment to cold meats and salad. In Asia, there are many possibilities: tea eggs are produced by simmering cracked eggs, boiled and still in their shell, with tea leaves and star anise, so that the whites turn a delicate marbled beige. For smoked eggs, boiled eggs are marinated and then smoked in a wok over burning tea leaves. When duck eggs are steeped in brine for a month to make salted eggs, their shells become bluish, the whites thin and salty, with a firm and deep yellow yolk. For gourmet cured eggs, however, the Chinese must take honors with their "1,000-year-old" variety. In reality, the eggs are cured for 100 days in lime, ashes and tea until they are stiff and dark and have acquired a pungent cheesy taste. 1,000-year-old eggs are served sliced to display their startling green and black ringed interior and served with fresh ginger as a banquet appetizer, or mixed with salted duck eggs and fresh eggs in the traditional "Three Egg Dish".

SCRAMBLING EGGS

Add cream or water, if using, and salt and pepper to the eggs just before cooking. Whisk the eggs for 1 minute until they are combined and frothy.

1 In a heavy pan, melt about 2 tsp butter per egg. If you like, set the pan in a water bath. Pour the eggs into the pan and cook very gently, stirring constantly with a wooden spoon. The eggs will start to cook first on the base of the pan.

2 As the eggs thicken underneath, scrape them with the wooden spoon so they mix back with the remaining uncooked eggs.

3 As the eggs continue cooking and begin to cook on the sides of the pan as well as the base, scrape them from the pan in the same way.

4 When the eggs are creamy, but somewhat thinner than the consistency you prefer, take the pan from the heat. Continue stirring until they are sufficiently thickened and serve them at once.

BAKED EGGS

One of the simplest ways of cooking eggs is to bake or "shirr" them in the attractive little dishes designed specifically for the purpose. An egg *en cocotte* is baked in a ramekin with sides high enough to protect the egg from direct heat. An egg *sur le plat* is baked on a flatter dish, traditionally a small gratin dish with eared handles, though any shallow baking dish can be used, providing it is not aluminum.

At their simplest, baked eggs are cooked in buttered dishes with only the addition of salt and pepper, sprinkled under the eggs so as not to spot their surface; at most a tablespoon or two of cream may be added for richness. However a tablespoon of garnish such as chopped herbs, ham, onion with fried croûtons, or smoked fish, added to the bottom of the ramekin, does not come amiss. Eggs *en cocotte* are cooked in a water bath on top of the stove, or in the oven. When left uncovered and without cream, a smooth shiny skin forms – hence the French name *en miroir*. For a skinless surface, they may be covered loosely with aluminum foil.

Eggs can also be left plain *sur le plat* but at the very least a slice of bacon or a few mushrooms sautéed in butter are generally included. The dish may also be sprinkled with cooked shrimps or chicken livers, or be lined with a colorful bed of spinach or bell peppers cooked *à la basquaise* with ham and garlic. With a copious garnish, eggs *sur le plat* become a meal in themselves. Since they are baked without a water bath, they are firmer than eggs *en cocotte*, and may be loosely covered to keep them moist.

USEFUL INFORMATION

Portion 1-2 eggs.
Storage Serve at once.
Cooking times *En cocotte*: bake at 375°F/190°C, 5-6 minutes or on top of stove. *Sur le plat*: bake at 375°F/190°C, 8-12 minutes.
When done White is set, while yolk is still soft.
Problems Eggs continue to cook in heat of the dish; remove them from heat before quite done.
Typical dishes *En cocotte*: with watercress (UK); *ovos à Portuguesa* (baked in a tomato shell with spices and breadcrumbs, Portugal); baked eggs Archduke (with onion and paprika, UK); *oeufs en cocotte au jus* (with roasted meat juices, France); *steka ägg i form med ansjovis* (with anchovy, Scandinavia). *Sur le plat*: *huevos en camisa* (yolk covered with beaten white, cheese and spices, Spain); *oeufs au diable* (with cream and cayenne pepper, France); Denver baked eggs (with cheddar, roasted peppers, bacon, tomatoes and cream, USA).

BAKING EGGS EN COCOTTE

Ramekins come in sizes to hold one or two eggs, depending on the desired size of the serving portion.

1 Butter the ramekins, sprinkle with salt and pepper and add any flavorings. Break in the eggs. Add a tablespoon of cream and cover the eggs loosely with foil if you like. Set the ramekins in a water bath and bring to a boil on top of the stove.

2 Continue cooking the eggs on top of the stove or bake them in a 375°F/190°C oven until the white is just set and the yolks are still very soft, 5-6 minutes. Test by shaking the ramekin. The eggs will continue cooking 1-2 minutes in the heat of the dish and will then be ready to serve.

BAKING EGGS SUR LE PLAT

Eggs may be baked *sur le plat* in individual dishes or in one large dish; porcelain or glass helps spread the heat so the eggs bake slowly and evenly, but enamelled cast iron dishes are popular too. In individual dishes, the garnish is spread around the dish with the eggs in the center. In one large dish, the garnish should be spread around the dish with the eggs spaced evenly on top. Cooking time varies very much with the type of dish and quantity of garnish used with the eggs.

1 RIGHT: Butter the baking dishes, sprinkle with salt and pepper and spread with garnish. Make a hollow in the garnish in each dish and drop an egg into it. Add cream and cover the eggs loosely with foil if you like.

2 Bake the eggs in a 375°F/190°C oven until the egg white is set but the yolk is still soft, 8-12 minutes.

FRIED EGGS

The pan-fried egg needs no introduction. One of the most popular snacks of all is an egg gently fried in butter, bacon fat or olive oil so that the white is firm and lightly browned on the underside, the yolk still moist. In the parlance of the American diner, the egg may be fried just on one side – "sunny side up" – or turned "over easy". A fried egg may be basted with hot fat during cooking so the white cooks more evenly, but this will also cook the yolk and dim its color. Seasoning is sprinkled on just before serving; with bacon fat none is needed. To prevent the eggs from sticking, use a well-seasoned frying pan (p.89) or one with a non-stick surface.

More rarely, eggs are cooked in hot deep fat. Although not actually deep-fried because a lesser amount of oil is used, this preparation is called deep-frying because the eggs remain oval in shape with a crisp brown surface and soft center. Presentation of the egg is neater than with pan-frying, provided the eggs are fresh so the white wraps neatly around the yolk, but some cooks find the texture of a deep-fried white to be rubbery. Also the technique can be risky, as the white must be folded around the egg with a wooden spoon, with the danger of hot fat splashing on the fire.

A fried egg is the natural partner of ham, sausages and bacon, not to mention French fries. A fried egg on steak makes the traditional rancher's breakfast of the American West. Like poached eggs, fried eggs are good with brown butter (p.98) spiked with capers and vinegar, while a fried egg achieves gourmet status as the crown on a sautéed escalope of veal Holstein with anchovy and capers, or overlapped with fried slices of eggplant à l'andalouse. Deep-fried eggs are part of the classic garnish for chicken Marengo, along with crayfish tails and fried croûtons.

USEFUL INFORMATION

Portion 1-2 eggs.
Storage Serve at once.
Cooking times 3-4 minutes.
When done White firm, yolk still soft.
Problems If overcooked, white is tough and scorched, with a metallic taste; if not very fresh, white spreads in pan and fails to cling round yolk, more crucial in deep-fried eggs.
Typical dishes *Pan-fried: huevos rancheros* (with beans and tomato salsa, USA); eggs in a nest (fried inside a slice of bread, USA); with corned beef hash (USA); *oeufs à cheval* ("on horseback" – with sausage on steak, France); *huevos fritos al ajillo* (with garlic and paprika, Spain); *wurstschusserl mit spinat und spiegelei* (with sausage and spinach, Germany); *asparagi alla Fiorentina* (with asparagus and cheese, Italy); *oeufs à la Provençale* (with tomatoes and fried eggplant, France); *huevos al plato con jamón* (with ham, Spain); *uova alla salsa di gambero* (with shrimp and pine-nut sauce, Italy). *Deep-fried: oeufs à l'Alsacienne* (on sauerkraut, France); *oeufs à l'Américaine* (with bacon and tomato sauce, France); *oeufs bamboche* (with grilled tomatoes, garnished with sweet peppers and onions, France); with Parmesan and herbs (Italy).

DEEP-FRYING EGGS

Eggs for deep-frying must be very fresh so the white clings round the yolk and does not disperse into the oil.

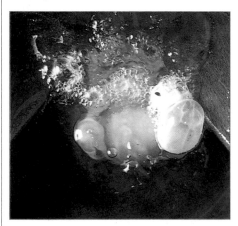

1 In a small frying pan, heat a ¾ in/2 cm layer of oil. Test heat with a cube of bread, which should brown in 30 seconds. Using a cup, slide an egg into the pan. At once use two wooden spoons or spatulas to fold the white over the egg yolk to cover it.

2 When the egg yolk is completely covered in cooked white, leave the egg to cook ½-1 minute until the white is firm and the yolk still soft.

3 When the white is crisp and brown on the outside, lift out the egg with two spatulas or a slotted spoon and drain it on paper towels.

PAN-FRYING EGGS

If the white of an egg spreads unevenly in the pan, it can be trimmed with a circular pastry cutter after cooking.

1 In a frying pan or skillet, for each egg, heat 1-2 tbsp fat until hot but not smoking. Add up to 3 eggs, sliding them from a cup or small bowl.

2 Fry the eggs over medium heat, basting with fat if you like, until the egg white is firm and the yolk still soft. The underside should be lightly browned and crisp.

3 If you like, flip the egg over in the pan and briefly brown it on the other side. Use a spatula to turn the egg carefully so as not to break the yolk. For a firmer yolk, continue cooking a few seconds longer.

OMELETS

There are three types of omelet: folded, flat and soufflé. Most familiar is the folded omelet, often made only with eggs and a seasoning of salt and pepper. A few finely chopped herbs or a sprinkling of grated cheese can be a welcome addition and other popular flavorings include ham, sautéed mushrooms or

seafood. A more substantial filling such as a spoonful of *ratatouille* (see Baking vegetables, p.264) or sautéed spinach may be added just before the omelet is folded, but the flavor of any filling should always be subordinate to the eggs themselves.

Flat omelets are altogether different. The eggs act as a binding agent for generous amounts of hearty ingredients such as onion, cubed potatoes or croûtons (p.352), ham, bell peppers and tomato. A sprinkling of garlic and aromatic herbs such as thyme or marjoram is sometimes added. While the folded omelet is typically French, the flat variety is more cosmopolitan, appearing in Spain and Mexico as *tortilla* and in Italy as *frittata*, albeit differently cooked (the eggs are cooked without stirring over very low heat so they gradually puff to form a light moist cake). Flat omelets (p.90) are usually cut in wedges for serving, but more

elaborate recipes may call for several flat omelets to be layered and sandwiched with a filling or sauce. As many as 10 differently flavored omelets may be stacked and baked in a mold.

Soufflé omelets, almost always sweet, lie midway between a flat omelet and a soufflé (p.92). The eggs are separated and both whites and yolks are beaten until stiff, then folded together. Usually both yolks and whites are whipped with sugar; a filling of jam or fruit may be added to the finished omelet, and it is often flamed with liqueur. The occasional savory soufflé omelet is made the same way, but has no sweet ingredients.

Asian omelets offer further variations: Japanese cooks use special rectangular pans to make omelets that are rolled into neat cylinders to slice for *sushi* or to shred and garnish soups. In Chinese cooking, thin omelets may serve as wrappers for other ingredients; thicker omelets may be filled with vegetables.

The first essential for making omelets is a well-seasoned pan (see below). Pans with non-stick coatings also work well. The size of pan is also important; a small 7 in/18 cm pan will hold 2-3 eggs for an omelet for one person, while a 9 in/23 cm pan is appropriate for a 4-5 egg omelet for two. Small omelets are best – attempting an omelet with more than 8 eggs (it will need an 11 in/ 28 cm pan) is impractical.

Most cooks like to whisk the eggs for folded or flat omelets until mixed and slightly frothy but in the famous *omelette Mère Poularde* from Mont St. Michel in Normandy, the whole eggs are whisked until they thicken, making a light, almost soufflé-like omelet. Seasoning, particularly salt, should be added just before cooking so the eggs are not watery.

Folded and flat omelets are one exception to the rule of using gentle heat for cooking eggs. They should be cooked over brisk, but not fierce, heat and should take only a minute or two, so the eggs are lightly cooked until agreeably brown on the underside and still runny or just set on top, depending on your taste. A folded omelet is then rolled in three with a quick twist that tips it onto the plate, while a flat one is turned over to brown the other side. **Note** A soufflé omelet is cooked more slowly because its high sugar content scorches easily.

Seasoning a pan

Cover the base with ½ in/1.5 cm oil and a generous handful of coarse salt, leave it overnight, then heat gently on the stove or in the oven until the oil is very hot and almost smoking. Leave the pan until almost tepid, then discard the oil and salt and wipe the pan dry. Once a pan has been seasoned it should never be washed, but wiped out with a cloth while still warm.

USEFUL INFORMATION

Portion 2-3 eggs.
Storage *Hot*: serve at once. *Cold*: 6 hours at room temperature.
When done *Folded*: runny or just firm. *Flat*: lightly browned and firm. *Soufflé*: puffed and brown.
Cooking times *Folded*: ½-1½ minutes; *Flat*: 3-4 minutes; *Soufflé*: 5-8 minutes.
Problems Tough if cooked too fast; sets without browning if cooked too slowly; dry if overdone; soufflé omelet shrinks.
Typical dishes *Folded*: aux fines herbes (France); with ham, potatoes and cheese (UK); *koniginomelett* (with creamed chicken and mushrooms, Germany); *fermière* (with ham, carrots and celery, France). *Flat*: *uova alla Romana* (with beans, onions and herbs, Italy); *tortilla asturiana* (with onion, tuna, tomato, Spain). *Soufflé*: flamed with rum (France); with cottage cheese, lemon and fruit compote (Czechoslovakia); *santé* (with mushrooms, chives, parsley and tomato sauce, France); *haselnuss-omelett* (with hazelnuts, Germany).

MAKING A FOLDED OMELET

Flavorings may be added when mixing the eggs, or a warm filling may be put inside the omelet just before it is folded.

1 Just before cooking, whisk the eggs until frothy with a little salt and pepper. Stir in any chopped flavoring ingredients.

2 For every 2 eggs, heat 2 tsp butter in the omelet pan until foaming and only just starting to brown. Add the eggs and stir briskly with the flat of a fork until they start to thicken, 8-10 seconds.

3 Quickly pull the egg that sets at the sides of the pan to the center, tipping the pan to pour uncooked egg to the sides. Continue until the omelet is lightly set, 15-30 seconds longer.

4 Stop stirring and let the omelet brown on the bottom. Cook until the top is still runny or lightly set, as you prefer. Add the filling to the omelet and have a warm plate ready.

5 To fold the omelet, hold the pan handle in one hand and tip the pan away from you. Give the handle a sharp tap with your other hand so the top edge of the omelet flips over, or fold the edge over with the help of a fork.

6 Half roll, half slide the omelet on to the plate so it lands folded in three with the seam underneath. Pull in the sides of the omelet with a fork to neaten it, brush the top with melted butter to give it a shine, and spoon any reserved filling on top. Serve the omelet at once, while it is still hot.

MAKING A FLAT OMELET

A flat omelet resembles a thick pancake. Serve it hot or at room temperature, cut into wedges.

1 Whisk the eggs and seasoning and add any flavorings as with a folded omelet (opposite). Pour the mixture into the buttered pan.

2 Stir the eggs gently until they start to thicken. With the fork, lift the edges of the omelet so the uncooked egg runs underneath.

3 Continue cooking the omelet until it is almost firm on top, 30-45 seconds, stirring occasionally. Leave without stirring, 20-30 seconds so the omelet browns on the bottom.

4 Take the pan from the heat, set a heatproof plate on top and turn the omelet on to it.

5 Slide the omelet back into the pan and brown the other side. Alternatively, brown the top of the omelet under the broiler.

Flavorings and fillings for folded omelets
For a 2-3 egg folded omelet made in a 7 in/18 cm pan:
Monterey omelet Add 2 tbsp peeled, seeded and chopped tomatoes, 1 oz/30 g grated Monterey Jack cheese and 1 tbsp chopped scallions.
Cheddar and bacon omelet Add 2 oz/60 g diced crispy cooked bacon and 1 oz/30 g grated Cheddar cheese.
Smoked salmon omelet Add 1 oz/30 g chopped smoked salmon, 2 tbsp sour cream and 1 tsp chopped fresh dill.
Omelet Waldorf Add 2 oz/60 g chicken livers, cut up and sautéed with 1 tbsp butter and 1 chopped shallot, with 3 large mushrooms, sliced and sautéed in 1 tbsp butter.
Creole omelet Fry 3 large mushrooms, sliced, 2 tbsp diced green pepper and 3 tbsp peeled, seeded and chopped tomato in 1 tbsp oil until peppers are soft and excess moisture has evaporated. Season with a dash each of Tabasco and Worcestershire sauce.

Flavorings for flat omelets
For a 4-5-egg flat omelet made in a 9 in/23 cm pan:
Peasant omelet Fry 4 oz/125 g diced bacon until brown. Add 2 diced medium potatoes and continue cooking until the potatoes are brown and crisp, stirring occasionally. Add pepper and 2 tbsp chopped parsley.
Spanish omelet Fry a thinly sliced onion in 2 tbsp olive oil until soft. Add ½ cup/75 g red or green bell pepper, cored and cut in strips with salt, pepper and 2 chopped garlic cloves. Cook, stirring, until the peppers are soft. Add 1 peeled, seeded and chopped tomato and cook until excess liquid has evaporated.
Shrimp and avocado omelet In 2 tbsp/30 g butter, sauté 4 oz/125 g peeled, deveined and coarsely chopped shrimp until they begin to turn opaque, 1-2 minutes. Add a quarter avocado, diced, stirring gently to warm. Season with salt, pepper and 1 tbsp chopped fresh coriander.

MAKING A SOUFFLE OMELET
A soufflé omelet may be cooked entirely on top of the stove, or partly in the oven. (**Note** A soufflé omelet overcooks and shrinks very quickly). If using the oven, heat it to 350°F/175°C. Separate the eggs and beat the yolks with sugar to the ribbon (p.394), allowing 1 tbsp sugar per yolk. Stiffly whip the egg whites, whisk in 1 tbsp sugar per egg white and continue whisking 30 seconds to make a light meringue. Fold the meringue into the egg yolk mixture as lightly as possible.

1 For every 2 eggs, heat 1 tbsp of butter in an omelet pan until foaming. Pour in the omelet mixture and cook over low heat without stirring until the edges start to puff.

2 If using the oven, bake the omelet in the heated oven until puffed and lightly brown, about 5 minutes; cooking can be continued on the stove top but the omelet will not brown on top.

3 Add a filling, such as melted jam, to the omelet, first spreading it along the center. The filling will be dispersed more evenly when the omelet is folded for serving.

4 ABOVE: Using a fork, fold the omelet in three. If you like, flambé it (p. 38) and sprinkle it with confectioners' sugar.

LEFT: Serve the soufflé omelet at once.

Fillings for soufflé omelets
For a 4-egg omelet made in a 9 in/23 cm pan:
Jam soufflé omelet Heat 3-4 tbsp strawberry or raspberry jam with 1 tbsp kirsch or lemon juice.
Soufflé omelet normande Sauté 1 sliced apple in 2 tsp butter and 2 tbsp sugar. Flambé with 2-3 tbsp Calvados. Stir in 2 tbsp cream.

SOUFFLES

A successful soufflé, puffy and golden brown, is a triumph of the cook's art, rising high above the rim of its dish in apparent disregard of gravity. A soufflé is made by mixing a highly flavored sauce or purée with stiffly whipped egg whites, which expand in a hot oven to give the mixture its dramatic height. Three points are crucial: a soufflé base of the right consistency, egg whites that are stiffly beaten, and careful folding of the two together so as to retain maximum volume and lightness (p.83). To ensure lightness, one- to two-thirds more egg whites than yolks are added to most soufflés; the volume of beaten whites should be at least double that of the basic mixture. The volume will decrease when the whites are folded into the basic mixture, but rise again when the soufflé puffs up in the oven. In the oven, a soufflé should increase by at least half, to as much as double its original volume.

For savory soufflés, the base is usually a béchamel or velouté sauce (p.54), although unthickened fish or vegetable purées are sometimes used alone. The soufflé base must be well-seasoned, and in fact over-seasoned, because of the quantity of bland egg whites that will later be folded in. Egg yolks are nearly always added to the base for richness and the finished consistency should be just soft enough to fall from the spoon. When the base is too thick, the soufflé won't rise properly, but if too thin, it knocks air out of the egg whites rather than combining smoothly with them.

Most dessert soufflés are based on pastry cream, again combined with one of a variety of flavorings or fruit purées. Only a very few soufflés can be made without flour, chocolate and lemon being the main examples. Even moist heavy ingredients like fish, vegetables and fruit purées need a starch to bind them.

For the greatest dramatic effect, the mixture should fill the dish to within ½ in/1.25 cm of the rim so it puffs to the greatest possible height. Some cooks like to wrap the dish with a paper collar so there is no danger of the soufflé mixture spilling down the sides of the dish, but this is not strictly necessary. Many concerns about a soufflé not rising in the oven are unfounded: provided the egg whites are carefully whipped and folded a soufflé puffs up in any temperature.

When baking a soufflé, set the dish low down in the oven so the soufflé has room to rise. If you open the oven door during baking to turn the dish so it cooks evenly, the soufflé will not sink, but do avoid drafts. It is the temperature at which a soufflé is baked that influences its final consistency. At high heat (at or above 400°F/200°C), a soufflé rises quickly to form a brown crust and a sauce-like center. Heavier fish and vegetable soufflés are usually baked for longer at 350°F/175°C, so that they cook through. After mixing, a soufflé can be kept for an hour or two in the refrigerator; once baked it should be served at once. In cool air it will start to shrink within three to five minutes.

Most soufflés need no accompaniment, but the firmer types of savory soufflé profit from a spoonful or two of appropriate sauce: curry velouté is good with fish, for instance, and hollandaise or tomato sauce with vegetable. To display their volume to the maximum, most soufflés are presented in their baking dish, but individual ones may be unmolded on to serving plates to serve with the sauce. Firmer fish and/or vegetable mixtures, often more mousse than soufflé, are the most suitable for unmolded soufflés, which can even be prepared ahead and reheated in sauce by baking in a hot oven, in the manner of *quenelles* (p.146).

MAKING A SOUFFLE

The classic straight-sided soufflé dish (p.511) is the key to a successful soufflé, though any tall, straight-sided, oven-proof mold can be used with good results. The dish should be thoroughly buttered, particularly around the rim, so the soufflé mixture can slip up the sides; sometimes a coating of breadcrumbs, cheese, or (for a sweet soufflé) sugar is added.

1 Make the sweet or savory base; it should be well seasoned to counter the blandness of the egg whites that will be folded in. For fish soufflé recipe, see opposite; for fresh orange soufflé, see p.460.

2 Mix the flavoring for the soufflé (in this case a spinach purée) into the basic sauce so that the two are combined evenly.

3 Add the egg yolks one by one and beat them into the soufflé base. At this stage, the consistency should be just soft enough to fall from the spoon.

4 Whisk the egg whites until stiff. Fold a quarter of the whites into the prepared mixture to lighten it.

Another delicious soufflé presentation is the roulade, for which the mixture is spread flat on a paper-lined baking sheet, just like a jelly roll. After brief baking, so that it remains moist, it is rolled with a sauce or filling to serve hot or at room temperature. A cold soufflé is not a true soufflé at all, but a creamy mixture lightened with egg white and molded in a soufflé dish with a high collar. When the collar is removed, the soufflé looks as if it has risen above the mold, like a hot soufflé. Most are sweet (Cold Desserts and Ice Creams, p.434); some savory mixtures are more substantial than soufflés and thus qualify as mousses (Fish, p.124).

USEFUL INFORMATION

Portion 6-egg white soufflé serves 4-6.
Storage Serve at once.
Cooking times (4-egg white soufflés). *Soft center:* bake at 375°F/190°C, 12-15 minutes. *Firm center:* bake at 350°F/175°C, 20-25 minutes.
When done Puffed and brown. *Soft center:* concave on top; center wobbles when shaken gently. *Firm center:* flat on top; center does not wobble when shaken gently.
Problems If egg whites overmixed, soufflé will not rise; if overcooked, it will shrink; if kept waiting before serving, it will fall.
Typical dishes *Savory:* with potatoes, ham and cream, Spain; *aux fruits de mer* (puréed shrimp and lobster, France); with corn, pimiento and green pepper (USA); *Bayrischer käsepudding* (Bavarian cheese pudding, Germany); *budino di ricotta* (with ricotta cheese and candied fruits, Italy); roulade with spinach (France); fish with chopped eggs in cream sauce (UK); mushrooms and Camembert (USA); *Emmenthaler* (Switzerland). *Sweet:* strawberry soufflé (UK); *kastanienkoch* (chestnut, Austria); *Brasil* (coffee, France); bitter chocolate with custard sauce (USA); *punschtorte* (lemon, Austria); raspberries and *crème fraîche* (USA). *Soufflé puddings:* hot vanilla soufflé (France); hot chocolate (USA); *flaméri aux bananes* (banana soufflé pudding, France); *à la normande* (with apples and Calvados, France).

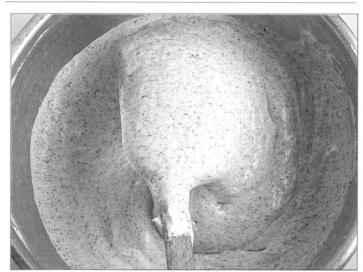

5 Fold the mixture into the remaining whipped egg whites. The consistency should be light and the mixture well blended.

6 Pour the mixture into the prepared dish. If you want the soufflé to rise with a high cap in the center, run your thumb around the edge to make a groove before putting it in the oven.

Fish soufflé

Smoked fish adds pleasant pungency to a soufflé, but any well-flavored cooked fish may be substituted.

Serves 4-6

1 cup/250 ml medium béchamel sauce (p.54)	2-3 tbsp light cream
4 egg yolks	6 egg whites
1½ cups/375 g cooked fresh or smoked fish, flaked	salt and pepper
	1½ qt/1½ L soufflé dish

1 Make the béchamel sauce and beat in the egg yolks one by one. Cook the mixture over low heat, stirring constantly, 1-2 minutes, until the egg yolks thicken it slightly. Take from the heat and stir in the fish. Beat until smooth, 1-2 minutes. Stir in 2-3 tbsp cream so the mixture falls easily from the spoon. Season the mixture well to compensate for the bland egg whites. Rub the surface of the mixture with a piece of butter to prevent a skin forming.
2 Heat the oven to 350°F/175°C and butter the soufflé dish. Whip the egg whites stiffly (p.82). Warm the fish mixture, stirring until hot to the touch. Stir a quarter of the egg whites into the fish mixture, then fold this mixture into the remaining whites.
3 Pour the mixture into the prepared dish and smooth the top with a metal spatula. Make a shallow groove around the edge (step 6, opposite) with your thumb so the center rises in a high cap.
4 Bake the soufflé in the pre-heated oven for 20-25 minutes until puffed and firm in the center. Serve at once.

Variations

Cheese soufflé Omit the fish and the cream. Add 1 tbsp Dijon mustard and ½ cup/60 g grated Gruyère or Parmesan cheese to the béchamel, reserving 1 tbsp for sprinkling over the soufflé as it goes into the oven. Bake at 400°F/200°C, 15-18 minutes until puffed but still soft in the center. Serve at once, giving each guest some crisp outside and soft center.

Mushroom soufflé Omit the fish and cream. Make a *duxelles* (p.306) with ¾ lb/375 g mushrooms, 1 tbsp butter, 1 finely chopped onion, salt, pepper and 2 tbsp chopped parsley and stir it into the béchamel. Bake at 400°F/200°C for 15-18 minutes until puffed but still soft in the center.

SAVORY & SWEET BAKED CUSTARDS

The smooth creamy texture of a well-prepared custard is half of its charm, no matter whether it is baked in the oven until set or stirred on the stove to make a custard sauce (Sauces, p.67). A simple flavoring of vanilla or nutmeg can be sufficient, or custard may act as a backdrop to the sweetness of caramel or to savory mixtures like the bacon and cheese of quiche Lorraine. It may also act as a binder in savory vegetable terrines such as spinach timbales (p.274), in desserts like bread and butter pudding, or as a topping – as in Alsatian fruit tarts, which are finished with a few spoonfuls of egg yolk and cream.

Standard proportions for custard are three eggs to 2 cups/ 500 ml of milk. For a richer mixture, a whole egg may be replaced by two egg yolks, and part or all of the milk by cream. Custard thickens at temperatures between 180°-190°F/82°-88°C and gentle steady heat is important. If cooked too quickly, a custard will lack some of the requisite creamy richness. Once overcooked, all custards curdle without remedy – custard sauce will thin and become granular, while a baked custard will form bubbles of liquid and collapse.

To maintain an even heat, plain custards are always cooked in a water bath. (When baked in a pastry case as for quiche, the pastry acts as a protection to the filling.) A custard should be taken from the heat as soon as it is cooked, or even a little before, as it will continue to cook in retained heat. Immersing the mold or pan in cold water will help stop cooking quickly. Tarts and savory custards may be served hot, but should be allowed to cool a little so they are less fragile. Baked custards are served cold and must be cooled until completely set if they are to be unmolded.

Custard comes to the fore in quiches and tarts with creamy fillings. In a true quiche (derived from the German word *kuchen* meaning cake), the custard is at least as important as the flavoring and assures an attractive golden-brown finish to the tart. Proportions may follow those of classic baked custard but often cream replaces some of the milk, and egg yolks take the place of whites, giving a softer, richer result. Full-flavored ingredients such as ham, cheese, herbs, anchovy or smoked fish are used in comparatively small amounts, though for vegetables and other mild ingredients, more substantial quantities are needed to give character. The Flemish tart *flamiche* uses bread dough instead of pastry, with custard as a moist topping.

Savory custards are also made without a crust, for example with vegetables, baked in little molds to unmold and serve with sauce or as an accompaniment to meats, poultry or fish (Vegetables, p.267). When fish or other ingredients are added, or the vegetables are coarsely chopped rather than puréed, the dish becomes a terrine (Vegetables, p.267).

Sweet custard pies are simple, smooth and satisfying, like the English custard tart with a hint of cinnamon and mace to accent the creaminess. The most famous of all custard desserts must be caramel custard, sometimes called flan, found in the cuisine of half a dozen countries. The term "flan" has several meanings, most commonly referring to plainly baked vanilla custard. In England, however, flan is a broader term, including sweet and savory pies not necessarily made with custard.

Another favorite custard dessert is the French *pots de crème*, consisting of vanilla, coffee, caramel or chocolate custards thickened only with egg yolk and baked in little porcelain pots with lids, so the contents come as a surprise. Richest of all is crème brûlée (p.71), classically flavored only with vanilla, though liqueurs and even fruit may be included, all sealed within a crunchy caramel topping.

Thin egg custard is often used to soak other ingredients for desserts. French toast is simply dry bread soaked in custard, fried in butter and sprinkled with sugar. In bread and butter pudding, the principle is the same: sliced bread is buttered, layered with fresh or dried fruits, then soaked with plain or flavored egg custard before baking (Flour, Breads and Batters, p.364).

USEFUL INFORMATION

Portion Plain quiche or custard made with 2 cups/500 ml milk serves 4.

Storage *Quiche*: refrigerate 1 day; reheat in low oven 10-15 minutes. *Plain custard*: refrigerate 2 days, unmold just before serving; reheat in low oven 10-15 minutes.

Cooking methods *Quiche*: bake at 375°F/190°C, 25-35 minutes. *Plain custard*: bake in water bath at 375°F/190°C, 40-50 minutes.

When done *Quiche*: just set in center and brown on top. *Plain custard*: set when lightly shaken and a skewer inserted in center comes out clean.

Problems *Plain custard*: curdles if cooked too fast or too long.

Typical dishes *Savory*: mushroom pudding (Czechoslovakia); double-crusted bacon and egg pie (UK); with puréed asparagus (France); *quiche au fromage* (with onion and cheese, Switzerland); veal timbales (France); *porrata* (pancetta and leeks in yeast dough crust, Italy). *Sweet*: lattaiolo (cinnamon custard, Italy); Norfolk pudding (with apples, UK); *flan à la Norvégienne* (with apricot jam, whipped cream and chocolate shavings, France); *flan de naranja* (with orange, Spain).

Quiches and savory tarts

Baking pastry crusts blind (p.375), or setting the pan on a preheated baking sheet can help keep the bottom crust crisp.

Cheese *flamiche* Serves 6. Fill a 10 in/25 cm pan lined with plain bread dough (p.353) with 8 oz/250 g sliced Maroilles or other strong, creamy cheese. Pour over custard made with 1 egg, 1 egg yolk and ½ cup/125 ml heavy cream seasoned with salt, pepper and grated nutmeg. Leave to rise 20-30 minutes, then bake at 400°F/200°C about 45-55 minutes, or until bread is browned and the filling is set.

Leek *flamiche* Trim, wash and thinly slice 1 lb/500 g leeks. Sweat them in 2 tbsp/30 g butter with salt and pepper (p.262) until very soft but not brown, 15-20 minutes. Substitute them for cheese in cheese *flamiche*.

Quiche Lorraine Serves 4-6. Blind bake (p.375) a 10 in/25 cm tart shell. In the base, spread 4 oz/125 g browned, diced bacon and 2 oz/60 g thinly sliced Gruyère cheese. Pour over a custard made with 2 eggs, 2 egg yolks, 1 cup/250 ml milk and ½ cup/ 125 ml heavy cream seasoned with pepper, grated nutmeg and a little salt. Bake at 375°F/190°C until filling is browned and just set, 25-30 minutes.

Alsatian onion quiche (*zewelwai*) Sweat (p.262) 1 lb/500 g thinly sliced onions in 2 tbsp/30 g goose fat or butter with salt and pepper until very soft but not brown, 20-30 minutes. Substitute the onions for the bacon and cheese in quiche Lorraine.

Spinach and feta pie Wash and stem 2 lb/1 kg fresh spinach. Boil and drain it, squeeze out excess moisture and finely chop it. Substitute spinach and ½ cup/50 g crumbled feta cheese for the onions in Alsatian onion quiche.

MAKING INDIVIDUAL CARAMEL CUSTARDS

Smaller versions of a large custard (see recipe) may be baked in ramekins. The quantities given in the recipe below make four individual custards.

As a variation on the basic recipe, omit the caramel and flavor the custard to taste with grated nutmeg, cinnamon or lemon zest. If flavoring with a spirit such as rum, use only 1¾ cups/425 ml milk. For a nut-flavored custard, infuse the milk with finely ground nuts (p.477) – almonds, pistachios or coconut are good – then strain before adding to the eggs.

1 Make the caramel, take it from the heat and let the bubbles subside. Pour the hot caramel into the ramekins and immediately turn them around to coat the base and sides evenly. The caramel will set at once.

2 Make the custard (see recipe) and pour it into the prepared ramekins. Put the ramekins in a water bath and bring it to a boil on top of the stove.

3 Bake the custards in the oven until they have just set and a skewer inserted in the center comes out clean, 20-25 minutes.

Caramel custard

(Crème caramel)

In this dessert, the baked custard is surrounded with a caramel sauce. When making caramel custard, be sure the caramel is thoroughly cooked and quite dark, so that the finished dessert is not too sweet.

Serves 4

| Caramel made with ¼ cup/60 ml water and ½ cup/100 g sugar (p.418) |
| 2 cups/500 ml milk |
| 1 vanilla bean, split lengthwise **or** 1½ tsp vanilla extract |
| ⅓ cup/60 g sugar |
| 2 eggs |
| 2 egg yolks |
| *1 qt/1 L soufflé dish or heatproof mold* |

1 Make the caramel, and line the mold with it. The caramel will set at once. Heat the oven to 350°F/175°C and prepare a water bath.
2 **For the custard:** bring the milk to a boil with the vanilla bean, if using; cover and leave to infuse off the heat 10-15 minutes. Add the sugar and stir until dissolved. Meanwhile, beat the eggs and egg yolks until mixed. Stir in the hot milk mixture and allow it to cool slightly. If using vanilla extract, add it at this point. Strain the custard and pour into the lined mold. Reserve the vanilla bean to use again.
3 Bake the custard in the oven in a water bath for 40-50 minutes until just set and a knife inserted in the center comes out clean.
4 Just before serving, run a knife around the edge of the custard and unmold it onto a deep dish: the caramel will have made a sauce for the custard.

FATS & OILS

FATS, TOGETHER with water, carbohydrates and proteins, make up the major components of food. Fats are extracted from animals as well as from certain fruits, nuts and plant seeds. Animal fats such as lard, suet and chicken fat are all derived from fatty tissue, while butter is made mostly from cow's milk. Margarine is usually made of vegetable oil, and so is shortening, although it can also contain some animal fat. Oils can be divided conveniently into general-purpose oils, which are good for frying and for salads, and flavoring oils, which are extracted from ingredients such as nuts, and have a strong characteristic taste. Olive oil is so versatile that it is covered separately. There are also infused oils flavored with herbs and spices, as well as exotic oils made from ingredients like avocado.

The choice of fat or oil used for cooking often gives an instant clue to the origins of a dish. Olive oil, for example, is associated with the Mediterranean and Middle East, and sesame oil with Asia. One of the identifying characteristics of the various provincial cuisines of France is the presence of butter, goose fat, lard or olive oil. In India, cooks may use ghee (p.98), coconut oil or sesame oil, depending on the region. Onions fried in lard typify the cooking of central Europe, and chicken fat features in the Jewish dishes of central Europe. Palm oil is used in dishes from Africa and African-settled regions of Latin America.

Structure of fats and oils
The term "fat" is used by cooks to refer to substances that are solid at room temperature, such as butter, margarine, shortening and lard. "Oil" refers to those that are liquid in normal conditions (exceptions are coconut and palm oil, which remain semi-solid). Food scientists, however, consider all oils to be fats and instead focus their attention on whether a fat is saturated, mono-unsaturated or polyunsaturated. In essence, these names describe different kinds of molecular structure, a saturated fat having the highest number of hydrogen molecules and a polyunsaturated fat the lowest, with mono-unsaturated in between the other two.

Saturated fats are normally solid at room temperature: butter is typical. They keep well since they oxidize less quickly than many unsaturated fats, which can rapidly acquire a rancid smell and taste. However, saturated fats are known to be a contributory factor in heart disease, because they can lead to increased cholesterol levels. Polyunsaturated fats are considered relatively healthy, mono-unsaturated fats are thought to be harmless.

In general, animal fats are composed of approximately half saturated fats and half unsaturated, while many vegetable oils are higher in polyunsaturated fats. However, refining of fats and oils to prolong their shelf-life or to change their viscosity tends to blur these distinctions. For example, in the making of margarine, oils are often artificially saturated – a process called hydrogenation. Also, many proprietary fats and oils are blended to make them healthier and more useful to the cook.

SATURATION VALUES FOR FATS & OILS

FATS (grams of fat per 3½ oz/100 g)	saturated	mono-unsaturated	poly-unsaturated
PORK	39.2	45.1	11.2
BEEF	49.8	41.8	4.0
BUTTER	50.5	23.4	3.0
DUCK	33.2	49.3	12.9
GOOSE	27.7	56.7	11.0
MARGARINE (containing coconut, safflower, hydrogenated palm and coconut oils)	56.9	8.3	11.7
MARGARINE (containing safflower, hydrogenated safflower oils)	9.2	23.2	44.5
OILS (grams of fat per 3½ fl oz/100 ml)			
COCONUT OIL	86.5	5.8	1.8
COLZA (rapeseed oil)	5.6	62.4	27.7
CORN OIL	12.7	24.2	58.7
COTTONSEED OIL	25.9	17.8	51.9
GRAPESEED OIL	9.6	16.1	69.9
HAZELNUT OIL	7.4	78.0	10.2
OLIVE OIL	13.5	73.7	8.4
PALM OIL	49.3	37.0	9.3
PEANUT OIL	16.9	46.2	32.0
SAFFLOWER OIL	9.1	12.1	74.5
SESAME OIL	14.2	39.7	41.7
SOYBEAN OIL	14.4	23.3	57.9
SUNFLOWER OIL	10.3	19.5	65.7
WALNUT OIL	9.1	22.8	63.3

MEASURING SOLID FAT
Solid fats are most accurately measured by weight. However, bulk fats, notably shortening, may be measured by displacement.

To measure 2 cups/500 g fat, first put 2 cups/500 ml cold water in a transparent measuring cup. Add fat until the water level rises to 1 qt/1 L, then discard the water.

ALTERNATIVELY, to avoid wetting the fat, pack it in a dry measuring cup.

Cooking with fats and oils

Fats and oils give variety, richness and smoothness to foods that might otherwise be too dry to eat. For the cook, the heating properties of fats and oils are as important as their flavors, and crucial to successful sautéing, deep- and shallow-frying, stir-frying, baking, and pastry and sauce-making. Since fats and oils can be heated to high temperatures, food is often fried very fast, producing a more intense flavor and a crisper texture than by any other cooking method.

Fats and oils are used in cake-making to moisten the batter and improve the keeping qualities of a cake. Flavored oils are key ingredients in salad dressings. Peanut oil, for instance, is agreeably light in a dressing, while olive oil is unmistakably rich and distinctive. All-purpose oils like corn and sunflower have no strong flavor to impart, but even small quantities of nut oils (notably walnut) or infused oils such as chili, add personality.

Oils are often used for basting broiled foods, and the effect may be unobtrusive or forceful, depending on the choice of oil. In hot dishes, a sprinkling of oil may be used in place of a sauce – for example, olive oil with chopped herbs is excellent on poached fish. Even fats that are more or less tasteless have their own particular consistency and individual effect in a sauce or pastry. For many dishes, using the correct fat is critical, for others, the cook has a choice.

ANIMAL FATS

Animal fats can be used for cooking in two ways: cut directly from the meat or rendered to remove non-fatty membrane. Unrendered pork fat has the most flavor and therefore features prominently in charcuterie, where it is often sliced for lining pâté and terrine molds or for barding roasts and poultry. Unrendered beef fat, called suet, is chopped for pies such as British steak and kidney pudding and some pastries. Lamb fat is also used in this way, but it can have a strong taste. In Britain, the drippings from roast meats are used for pan-fried potatoes, and in eastern Europe for sautéing onions.

Rendered pork fat, or lard, is perhaps the most familiar animal fat, and can easily be rendered at home (right). Both home-rendered and unrefined, store-bought lard have a soft, greasy texture and a pronounced taste, so some cooks prefer processed lard, which is firm, mild and longer-lasting. Relatively inexpensive, lard is used extensively in eastern Europe, northern and southwestern France, Spain and Mexico. Elsewhere it is used in sautéing and frying, in American biscuits, and in pie doughs, especially for savory meat pâtés and pies (p. 243), to which it adds crispness. Yorkshire and other lardy cakes take their name from bread dough mixed with lard, sugar and cinnamon.

Chicken fat, also called *schmaltz*, has a softer consistency than other animal fats. It is used a great deal in eastern European and in Jewish cooking, in recipes such as chopped chicken liver and matzoh balls. It can be heated to fairly high temperatures without burning and is therefore good for frying. Duck and goose fats, which are popular in southern France and Hungary, are regarded as superior alternatives to lard. When flavored with herbs and garlic, all these animal fats may be served instead of butter, for example on bread or in stews. Goose fat is also used in some leaved pastry doughs.

USEFUL INFORMATION

How to choose *Fresh:* white or clear color, fresh odor, no dried edges. *Rendered:* pale color, no sediment.
Nutritive value per 3½ oz/100 g. *All:* no protein; no carbohydrate; no sodium. *Lard:* 892 calories; 100 g fat; 92 mg cholesterol. *Suet:* 892 calories; 100 g fat; 107 mg cholesterol. *Goose:* 900 calories; 100 g fat; 100 mg cholesterol.
Problems Turns rancid if not properly stored or stored too long; strong flavor; can make fried foods greasy.
Storage *Fresh:* refrigerate 2 weeks, freeze 6 months. *Rendered:* refrigerate 1 month, freeze 1 year. *Processed:* at room temperature 1 month.

Lard

Ground beef suet

Chicken fat

Beef fat

Goose fat

RENDERING FAT

Fat should be rendered (melted) over low heat and may take as long as three hours. The crisp "cracklings" left behind after straining can be seasoned and eaten. To render about 1 cup/250 ml fat:

1 Coarsely chop 1 lb/500 g fat. Cut poultry fat into pieces and skin into 1 in/2.5 cm squares.

2 Cook the fat with ⅓ cup/75 ml water over low heat until melted and the water has evaporated.

3 Leave to cool slightly, then pour the melted fat through a conical strainer into glass storage jars. Keep in the refrigerator or a cool place.

BUTTER

Dairy butter consists of about 80 percent fat and 20 percent water and whey (milk solids left from the separating process). It is the milk protein in the whey that makes butter spoil quickly and, together with milk sugar (lactose), causes it to scorch when overheated. In the West most butter is made from cow's milk, but elsewhere butter from the milk of water buffalo, yak, goats and sheep is also available.

The quality of butter is affected by the cream used to make it, which in turn is influenced by the season and the feed of the animal. Color varies from very pale to deep yellow, but producers may add coloring (often annatto, p.25) to butter, particularly salted butter, so that it looks uniform throughout the year. Sometimes the cream is allowed to ripen, or a lactic yeast is added to give the butter a pleasant acidity and nutty aroma. For health reasons, most butter is pasteurized, which means that the milk used to make it has been sterilized by heating it briefly to destroy any harmful bacteria. In some countries, raw butter is also available; it has a better taste, but does not keep well. Butter is also graded according to quality in many countries.

Unsalted butter is made with fresh cream and hence is often called sweet cream butter in the United States. It is especially appropriate for delicate pastries, cakes and frostings, where even a pinch of salt would be detectable. In fact, many cooks like to use unsalted butter for all cooking, both for its flavor and because its whey content is usually lower, making it less likely to scorch. Salted butter is made from fresh or sour cream and has a salt content of between 1.5 and 3 percent. The salt acts as a preservative and therefore permits a higher whey content. In most European countries, most of the butter sold is unsalted and made from ripened cream, while in Britain and the United States, the reverse is true. However, both salted and unsalted kinds are usually available. Occasionally, "country" or "farmhouse" butter can be found. Highly salted with a strong, almost cheesy taste, it is produced on farms. American markets also stock whipped butter, which is lightened by air. It spreads evenly and melts quickly on warm foods, but it is very bland and rarely used for cooking because the extra volume makes it difficult to measure accurately.

Butter may be browned deliberately to make brown or hazelnut butter (Fr. *beurre noisette*), so called because of its nutty aroma. Black butter (Fr. *beurre noir*) is made like brown butter but is cooked until it is very dark brown.

Butter is the most valuable fat for baking as it adds substance and inimitable richness of flavor. Whether hard, soft or melted butter is required, it is important to the success of a recipe to use the consistency specified.

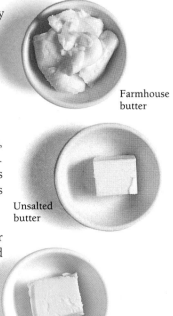

Farmhouse butter

Unsalted butter

Salted butter

Butter may be clarified to separate the fat from the water and milk solids, so that the remaining fat will not scorch or turn bitter. Clarified butter may be heated to a much higher temperature than regular butter and is good for sautéing. Creamed butter can be mixed with various flavorings to form compound butters (below, right). Savory butters are popular accompaniments to meats, fish and vegetables; sweet butters include sugar, and flavorings such as vanilla, grated citrus zest or liqueur.

USEFUL INFORMATION

How to choose Cool and firm with dry wrapping; when unwrapped, aroma should be fresh and untainted; intensity of color is no indication of quality, but color should be uniform.
Nutritive value per 3½ oz/100 g: 714 calories; no carbohydrates; no protein; 78 g fat; 828 mg sodium (*salted*); 11 mg sodium (*unsalted*); 221 mg cholesterol.
Problems Picks up flavors and aromas, so keep tightly covered; goes rancid if poorly stored.
Storage Refrigerate 2 weeks; salted butter keeps longer than unsalted; freeze 2 months. *Clarified:* refrigerate 2 months; freeze 3 months. *Compound:* refrigerate 2 days, freeze 1 month.

MAKING BROWN & BLACK BUTTERS

The caramelization of the milk proteins and sugars in the whey gives brown and black butters their particular color, aroma and flavor.

Brown butter (*beurre noisette*) Shown below. For fish and vegetables. Gently heat ½ cup/125 g butter in a pan until golden with a nutty aroma. At once take from heat, add 1–3 tbsp lemon juice and 2 tbsp chopped parsley (optional) and pour over the food while still foaming.

Black butter (*beurre noir*) For poached skate, brains, some egg dishes. Proceed as for brown butter, but cook a few seconds longer until the butter is brown. Remove from heat and add 2 tbsp drained capers. Pour the butter over the food. Deglaze (p.513) the pan with 3–4 tbsp red or white wine vinegar, pour over food and serve at once.

GHEE

Ghee is the primary cooking fat in India, and in many Arab countries where it is called *samna*. It is a type of clarified butter, but it is simmered until the moisture evaporates and the butter caramelizes, producing a strong, sweet flavor. It is made from buffalo's as well as cow's milk and can be bought in jars or made at home. Flavorings are often added: in India these might include bay leaves, cumin seeds, cloves, fresh ginger, turmeric, peppercorns or chili peppers; in Arab countries, herbs such as oregano or thyme are often used. Because butter is expensive, ghee is sometimes made with part butter and part margarine. In India, a vegetable ghee is also available.

CLARIFYING BUTTER

Clarified butter is used primarily for sautéing. Butter is melted until it gradually separates into three layers: a thin topping of foam, a thick yellow middle layer, which is pure butterfat, and a milky-white bottom layer. Both the upper and lower layers contain water, milk proteins and carbohydrates, and must be removed.

1 Melt the butter in a small saucepan over very low heat until it is liquid. Skim the froth from the surface of the butter.

2 Slowly pour the butter into a bowl, leaving behind the milky sediment. Alternatively, cover and refrigerate the melted butter until solid. Scrape off the thin top layer and pry away the clarified butter, leaving the sediment.

MAKING COMPOUND BUTTERS

Compound butters make delicious toppings for hot savory or sweet foods, and may also be melted to make a basting liquid or a last-minute enrichment for soups and sauces.

1 Cream the butter and mix with the flavoring (here chopped parsley and lemon juice).

2 Roll the butter in plastic wrap. Chill until firm then slice or use the soft butter to top hot food.

Sweet and savory butters

Seasoning amounts in these recipes are for unsalted butter.

Anchovy butter For broiled fish and meat, cold appetizers and canapés. Cream ½ cup/125 g butter with 2 tbsp mashed anchovy fillets, 1 tbsp lemon juice, and black pepper.

Mustard butter For broiled steaks, fish, kidneys, liver and sauces. Cream ½ cup/125 g butter with 2 tbsp Dijon-type mustard, salt and pepper, and 2 tbsp chopped parsley.

Parsley butter (*beurre maître d'hôtel*) For broiled meat and fish, breaded fried fish, vegetables. Cream ½ cup/125 g butter with 2 tbsp chopped parsley, 1 tbsp lemon juice, salt and pepper.

Herb butter (*beurre aux fines herbes*) For broiled meat, poultry and fish, vegetables, sauces and soups. As above, but substitute 1 tbsp each of chopped tarragon, chervil and chive for the parsley.

Orange butter For *crêpes Suzette* (p.367). Cream ½ cup/125 g butter with 1 tbsp confectioners' sugar, 1 tbsp strained orange juice, 1 tbsp grated orange zest and 1 tsp orange liqueur.

Honey butter For muffins, breads, pancakes, sweet crêpes. Cream ½ cup/125 g butter with 2 tbsp honey.

MARGARINE

When first developed in the nineteenth century, margarine was based on animal fats and sometimes whale oil, but it is now made almost exclusively from vegetable oils. Today, margarine is about 85 percent oil, with color and flavorings, salt and preservatives, and sometimes milk products added. While some margarines are high in polyunsaturated fats, others are relatively high in saturated fats because they have been hydrogenated to give them better keeping qualities and to make them firm enough to spread. The firmer the margarine is at room temperature, the more saturated fat it is likely to contain.

Margarine is the most widely used fat in the world. It is less expensive than butter and can be used in much the same way; like butter, it can also be clarified. However, cakes, pastries and cookies that depend on butter for their taste and texture will not be as good when made with margarine. In frying, margarine has a higher smoking temperature (p.104) than butter, but lacks the fine flavor. Soft margarines, or diet margarines (which have half the calories and saturated fat content of regular margarines), may give different results, particularly in baking, because they contain more water. Unlike margarines with a high proportion of saturated fat, these margarines cannot be used for frying.

USEFUL INFORMATION

How to choose Check label for content, especially when baking, as some types are very salty.
Nutritive value per 3½ oz/100 g.
Soybean: 721 calories; no protein; 78 g fat; no carbohydrates; 950 g sodium; no cholesterol.
Safflower, hydrogenated safflower: 716 calories; no protein; 80 g fat; 5 g carbohydrates; 1,079 mg sodium; no cholesterol. (Also see chart p. 96.)

Problems Absorbs odors, so keep away from strong ingredients.
Storage Refrigerate 4 weeks; freeze 9 months or shorter if it contains milk products.

Firm margarine

Soft margarine

Dutch butter cookies

Best quality butter should be used to flavor these cookies (Dutch *boterkoekjas*). As the dough stiffens quickly, cover the bowl with a damp cloth until you shape the cookies.

Makes 50 cookies

1 cup/250 g butter	
½ cup/100 g sugar	
½ tsp vanilla extract	
3 egg yolks	
3 cups/375 g flour (more if needed)	

For topping	
50 whole blanched almonds	
1 egg white, lightly beaten	
2-3 tbsp/30-45 g granulated sugar	
2 baking sheets	

1 Heat the oven to 350°F/175°C and grease two baking sheets. Cream the butter, add the sugar and beat until soft and light. Beat in the vanilla extract. Stir the egg yolks into the mixture one by one, alternating with the flour. The dough should be soft but not sticky; if necessary stir in more flour. Press the dough into a ball and leave it in the bowl.
2 With your fingers, pull off walnut-sized pieces of dough, quickly roll them into balls between the palms of your hands and set them 1 in/2.5 cm apart on the baking sheets. Press an almond into the center of each ball. Brush the cookies with beaten egg white and sprinkle lightly with sugar.
3 Bake the cookies in the preheated oven for 18-22 minutes or until lightly browned. Transfer them to a rack to cool. Store them up to one week in an airtight container layered with wax paper.

SHORTENING

Shortening has little or no flavor and may replace other fats for frying and baking; for example a pie crust made with shortening rather than lard produces a flakier pastry. Some brands have high smoking points and are good for deep-frying. Shortening is most commonly made from vegetable oils but sometimes animal fats are added. Both types are highly saturated (the degree of saturation should be listed on the label). Shortening can be stored unrefrigerated for up to one year.

OILS

Edible oils are most commonly made from nuts, grains and fruits. Oils vary considerably, each one having its own distinctive color, flavor, odor and cooking properties. The best quality pure oils are made from a single variety of nut, grain or fruit while inferior oils are a blend of several.

Oils are often labeled "salad" or "vegetable" oil and typically these contain mixtures of soy, safflower, sunflower, corn, or peanut oil. A blend labeled "for frying" may be less expensive and is likely to be based on cottonseed oil or some other highly refined oil. These have little or no taste, but they have a high smoking point. For details on smoking points, see Deep-frying (p.104).

Most edible oils are used for frying or flavoring, but a few mild oils are manufactured to be used as an ingredient in the commercial production of other foods, notably, palm kernel oil, palm oil (made from the pulp of the fruit of oil palms) and cottonseed oil. These are insipid on their own so they are often blended with other oils or used in the manufacture of margarine, shortening, bottled salad dressings and processed foods. Coconut oil is also used in this way, most commonly in the manufacture of vegetable margarines and cooking fats.

The best quality oil comes from the first pressing of the nuts, fruit or grains, carried out at a low temperature, a distinction that is particularly important with olive oil. Subsequent pressings, using higher and higher temperatures, yield an oil that requires extra refining to remove sediment and eliminate unpleasant odors and tastes. Ultimately, refining can eliminate so much flavor that the final product loses all its character. Refined oils do have the advantage that they keep for longer than unrefined ones.

Air, heat and light cause oils to oxidize and turn rancid, so more delicate oils should be stored in a cool place in an airtight container that is light-proof and tightly sealed. To help arrest oxidization, oil purchased in bulk can be poured into several small bottles. Refrigeration is essential in a hot environment, and although oil may turn cloudy and even solidify when chilled, it will clear again at room temperature. Many cooks refrigerate nut oils because they turn rancid quickly.

OLIVE OIL

One of the fascinations of olive oil is its variety, the result not only of the way in which the olives are harvested and pressed, but also of the type, and of the soil and climatic conditions in which they are grown. If extracted from fully ripe olives, the oil will be delicately sweet in taste and golden in color. When made from partially ripe olives, as is often the case in Italy, it has a sharper taste and a greenish tinge (although a few green olive oils are full and fruity).

Many connoisseurs feel the best olive oils come from Italy and Provence, but the robust aromatic oils of Greece, Portugal and Spain are also appreciated. Tunisia, Morocco, California and Turkey are other important producers.

The most common method for extracting oil has hardly changed over the centuries. It involves coarsely crushing the olives, including pits, placing them in heavy folded cloths and then pressing them; nowadays, this is usually done with a hydraulic press. The juice is pumped into settling tanks where the oil separates and is drawn off. The residual pulp from the first pressing, known as *sansa*, can then be reground and pressed again. These subsequent pressings extract substances that impart a harsh flavor to the oil, and further refining is usually necessary.

For cooking purposes, the best quality olive oil is the unrefined oil that comes from the first pressing performed at a low temperature using high grade fruit. This can be identified by the description "cold-drawn" or "cold-pressed" on the label. Unfortunately, the labeling of olive oil varies from country to country. It may also be marked "unfiltered and undecanted" and carry natural sediment, or it may have been clarified, thus lightening flavor and body and giving the oil a longer shelf-life. Most European producers grade these

Spanish extra virgin olive oil

Greek extra virgin olive oil

unrefined olive oils according to their acidity. "Extra virgin" has no more than 1 percent acid, middle quality oil is "extra fine" or "superfine", while "semi-fine" and "regular" oils may have an acid level of up to 3.3 percent. In the United States, "virgin" may be used to describe all first-pressed, unrefined oils. Unrefined and refined oils may also be blended together and labeled as "pure" or "sansa and olive oil".

When choosing olive oil, the most appropriate type depends on the style of cooking for which it is intended. The more assertive fragrance and flavor of the better quality unrefined oils shows to best advantage in zesty preparations such as Italian *pesto* sauce (p.17) or French *anchoiade*, a paste of anchovies, garlic and olive oil to spread on crusty toast or to use as a dip for vegetables. In Italy and many other Mediterranean countries, full-bodied olive oil often appears on the dining table as a condiment to add to soups, salads, vegetables and pasta. Marinades for meat benefit from a robust full-bodied oil, while fish and vegetables should be marinated in a lighter oil. Pasta and olive oil are natural partners, and the fuller the flavor the better it marries with any plain pasta. Occasionally, olive oil is used in cakes and pastries, such as the traditional Provençal olive oil cake, where a milder taste is more appropriate. A light oil is equally good for sautéing and pan-frying.

USEFUL INFORMATION

How to choose Fresh aroma; no rancid or acid taste; color indicates type of olive oil.

Nutritive value per 3½ oz/100 g: 884 calories; no protein; 100 g fat; no carbohydrates; no sodium; no cholesterol. Also see chart p.96.

Problems Turns rancid if exposed to too much air or light; clouds if refrigerated but clears at room temperature.

Storage In a cool, dark place; after opening, refrigerate or transfer to small containers for 6-12 months.

Olive oil, anchovy and garlic dip

Bagna cauda

Italian *bagna cauda* is traditionally made in a shallow earthenware casserole and kept hot on a table burner.

Serves 8

For dipping	
cardoon stalks	2 × 2 oz/60 g cans anchovy fillets in oil
sticks of celery, carrot, zucchini	4-6 cloves garlic, crushed
scallions	1 cup/250 ml olive oil
broccoli florets	black pepper
strips of green and red pepper	***Small flameproof earthenware casserole with burner** (p.510)*
radishes	

1 Wash the vegetables for dipping and trim if necessary (stalks may be left on, to make dipping easier). Arrange them on a tray or in a bowl. Rinse the anchovy fillets to remove excess salt. In a food processor or blender, or using a mortar and pestle, work the anchovies and garlic with a little olive oil until smooth. Work in the remaining oil and season with black pepper.

2 Heat the mixture very gently for 10 minutes but do not let it get too hot. Transfer it to the earthenware casserole and set it over a table burner. Serve the vegetables separately.

GENERAL-PURPOSE OILS

The ideal general-purpose oil is light in color and taste, and is good both for frying and for making salad dressings. Many such oils are sold by brand name and a close inspection of the ingredients label can be helpful to assess the nutritive value and level of saturation.

In North America, corn oil is widely available. It has a characteristic golden-yellow color, and is one of the few oils not extracted from a seed or nut. Instead, it is crushed from the germ of corn kernels. Some cooks do not like its slightly harsh taste and therefore reserve it for frying or baking. More widespread in Europe and much of Asia is colza oil (also called rapeseed oil). Colza oil has an unobtrusive flavor and is quite versatile in cooking, but the health effects of one of its ingredients, erucic acid, are in question. Golden-yellow safflower oil (extracted from the seed of a type of thistle) and pale blond sunflower oil are favorites among nutritionists because they are high in polyunsaturated fat. Safflower oil is so unsaturated that it will not cloud when refrigerated. Both are good for frying, and their mild taste makes them ideal for use in salad dressings.

Peanut or groundnut oil (sometimes called by its French name *huile d'arachide*) can be heated to very high temperatures and is therefore a good choice for all types of frying. Its slightly nutty taste is valued by many cooks. European peanut oil is mild and unobtrusive, but the American version has a distinct character that comes through clearly when used in dressings or for frying. Asian peanut oil is even darker, with a distinctive strong taste. Soybean or soy oil, the traditional oil in Asian cooking, is also becoming popular in the West, and in many countries is the cheapest all-purpose oil. It can be heated to high temperatures. The flavor is mild, though some varieties may have a slightly fishy aroma. It is high in polyunsaturated fats (p.96). Palm oil (also called palm-nut oil or *dende* oil) comes from the pulp of the fruit of oil palms. It has an orange-gold color and a pleasant nutty flavor, but turns rancid very rapidly.

Corn oil

Peanut oil

Sunflower oil

USEFUL INFORMATION

How to choose Mild taste; clear, bright color.
Nutritive value Typically, per 3½ oz/100 g: 884 calories; no protein; 100 g fat; no carbo-hydrates; no sodium; no cholesterol.
Problems Turns rancid; poor quality oils have acid flavor.
Storage In cool, dark place in sealed containers, 6-12 months.

Toasted walnut and Roquefort salad

Walnuts are a favorite crop of the Aveyron region of France, which is also the home of Roquefort cheese.

Serves 4

4 oz/125 g walnut halves	1 bunch watercress, washed, dried and stems discarded
1 tbsp walnut oil	
salt and pepper	2 oz/60 g Roquefort cheese, or other crumbly blue-veined cheese
croûtes (p.352) made with 12 thin slices French bread fried in 4-6 tbsp/60-80 ml all-purpose oil	vinaigrette dressing (p.64) made with 3 tbsp/45 ml cider vinegar, 2 tsp Dijon mustard, salt, freshly ground pepper, 6 tbsp/90 ml walnut oil
1 lettuce, washed and dried	

1 Heat the oven to 350°F/175°C. Toss the walnuts in the walnut oil and sprinkle with salt and pepper. Spread them on a baking sheet and bake for 5 minutes or until toasted. Leave to cool. Fry the croûtes.
2 Arrange the lettuce leaves on four large plates. Separate the watercress into four bunches and arrange on top of the lettuce. Crumble the Roquefort, toss with the walnuts and sprinkle on top of the greens. Spoon the vinaigrette dressing over the salad, arrange the croûtes around the edge and serve at once.

SPRAY OILS

For convenience, and to reduce calorie intake, some cooks use an aerosol spray product containing lecithin. Frying pans, utensils and even baking dishes can be coated with lecithin to prevent ingredients from sticking during cooking. Some brands also contain flour, eliminating the two-step process of preparing baking pans. Lecithin has no flavor or significant food value.

FLAVORING OILS

Oils with a distinct taste are used primarily for flavoring. They enhance a range of foods, from green salads to stir-fried vegetables and cooked meat dishes. A little goes a long way and they are sometimes diluted with blander oils.

Nut oils, outstanding for their aroma as well as their taste, are expensive. (Look closely at the label of a less expensive bottle as it is likely to be blended.) The perfumed flavor and aroma of walnut oil is popular for green salads, especially in France. Hazelnut oil, with its aroma of toasted nuts, is also costly; again it is best suited to delicate salads. American pecan oil is uncommon, but is prized for its light taste and color. Sweet and aromatic almond oil is traditionally used to coat molds for desserts and candy-making, and to oil the marble for sugar work. Some cooks like to add it to salad dressings and also use it for cakes and desserts. In India, almond oil may be added to ghee (p.98) or brushed on hot breads. Most nut oils turn rancid quickly and will last longer if refrigerated. Use them only at moderate temperatures, adding them toward the end of cooking.

Sesame oil is popular for flavoring and is made in several ways. Chinese or Japanese sesame oil is made from roasted sesame seeds, which give it an amber color and a rich pungent flavor and aroma. It is used in small amounts, as a seasoning, in salads and for stir-fry recipes. European sesame oil, made from unroasted seeds, is light yellow. It is less strongly flavored and can be used more generously both for cooking and in salads. Indian and Middle Eastern sesame oils are deep golden in color. Although lighter in flavor than the Chinese, they are still aromatic and can be heated to high temperatures. The Japanese combine sesame and vegetable oils to create a blend appropriate for deep-frying tempura (p.105). Chinese black sesame oil, made from black sesame seeds, is used in Chinese confectionery and as a flavoring in baking.

Tart, woody grapeseed oil, extracted from the residue of grapes, is often used for salads. It is also suitable for frying, but the flavor can be slightly harsh when used alone and some cooks prefer to mix grapeseed with other oils.

USEFUL INFORMATION

How to choose Clear bright color; no acrid smell.
Nutritive value Typically, per 3½ oz/100 g: 884 calories; no protein; 100 g fat; no carbohydrates; no sodium; no cholesterol.
Problems The oils turn rancid very quickly; flavor can be cloying or bitter.
Storage In warm climates, oils should be refrigerated.

EXOTIC OILS

Avocado oil is an oil pressed from the pulp of avocados. Its mild taste is best exploited in salads or used for sautéing vegetables, seafood and chicken. Mustard oil, pressed from mustard seed, features prominently in Indian cooking, especially in deep-fried dishes from northern and northwest regions. Raw mustard oil has a very harsh flavor and an odor that must be mellowed by heating the oil to its smoking point (p.104), then cooling it before use.

Poppy seed oil is pressed from either white or blue-gray poppy seeds. It is light in color with little flavor and appears in the cooking of northern France under the name *huile blanche*.

MAKING INFUSED OILS

Oils that have been infused with herbs or spices are intended for seasoning marinades and salad dressings rather than for cooking. Not only will their distinctive aroma fade when heated, but their flavor is often so strong that just a few drops will pervade a whole dish. The best oils to use are light varieties such as sunflower and safflower that will form an ideal background for a subtle blend of herbs. Popular herbs for making infused oils are tarragon, basil, garlic, fennel, mint, marjoram, thyme, rosemary and savory, and the most popular spices are ginger and chili pepper.

Distinctive Chinese or Japanese chili oil, also called hot oil, red pepper oil, and hot chili oil, is made from sesame or vegetable oil heated with spicy dried red chili peppers. It can be fiery hot, and is used sparingly, typically in dressings, and dipping and barbecue sauces. The Chinese make other infused oils, for example with ginger, scallions and Sichuan peppercorns. Less peppery but equally colorful, paprika oil is sprinkled over central European and Turkish dishes. Another type of paprika oil, used in Chile, is made by sautéing garlic cloves in vegetable oil before stirring in the paprika.

More infused oils are now being produced, both in the home and commercially. Garlic, along with a variety of herbs and spices is a popular addition to olive oil. Dried mushrooms such as *porcini* and white or black peppercorns are other good choices of seasonings.

To make herb-flavored oil: half fill a bottle with fresh herb leaves such as basil, or sprigs of thyme or rosemary. Fill the bottle with olive oil. Cover and steep for 1-2 weeks. (For a stronger flavor replace the herbs with fresh ones and store for a further 2 weeks). If using separate leaves, strain the oil. Sprigs may be left inside for decorative effect. Store the oil in a cool place.

DEEP-FRYING

Since fats and oils are used for high temperature cooking, their reaction when heated is vital. The most important temperature is the "smoking point", at which the fat begins to smoke and smell sharp. Beyond this point, the structure of the fat changes, giving it an unpleasant taste; it should not be used again, even at a reduced heat. The smoking point of animal fats is around 375°F/190°C, while some vegetable oils can withstand higher temperatures of 400°F/200°C or higher. Exact smoking points are extremely difficult to specify. For fats, the smoking point depends on how a fat has been refined and on its moisture content, particularly for butter. Pure oils can vary from harvest to harvest and from pressing to pressing, while the smoking point of general-purpose oils will differ according to blend and method of processing. Many such oils have unexpectedly low smoking points because they contain emulsifiers and preservatives.

Fats for deep-frying must have a smoking point well above the deep-frying temperature called for in the recipe; most popular are peanut and corn oils, since they are bland and have high smoking points of about 425°F/220°C; safflower and soybean oils are good alternatives. Traditionally, rendered beef fat was used for deep-frying. It can be heated to a very high temperature without burning but it is high in cholesterol. **Note** Fat can easily ignite when overheated. For safety precautions, see opposite.

The temperature of fat for deep-frying should never drop below 340°F/170°C, except for raw doughs, which are fried in a temperature range of 325-375°F/160-190°C. Raw fish, meat, poultry, croquettes and fritters are fried at 350-375°F/175-190°C. Most vegetables are deep-fried at 375°F/190°C. To determine the exact temperature of the oil use a deep-fat thermometer (p. 503), clipped to the side of the pan so that the bulb does not touch the bottom. Hot fat can also be tested with a cube of fresh bread. If the bread turns golden brown in one minute, the oil is at about 350°F/175°C; at 375°F/190°C it browns in about 40 seconds, and at 385°F/195°C, in less than 20 seconds.

COATING FOODS WITH FLOUR, EGG & BREADCRUMBS

Before being pan-fried or deep-fried, delicate foods such as fish fillets, veal escalopes, croquettes and soft vegetables should be protected by a coating of flour, egg, and crumbs such as dry white breadcrumbs, cracker crumbs or cornmeal, sometimes lightened with flour.

Preparation On one plate, mix ½ cup/60 g flour with ½ tsp salt, ¼ tsp pepper and other spices to taste. On a second plate, whisk 2 eggs with 1 tbsp oil or water and ½ tsp salt, using a fork.

1 Roll the food in the flour and seasoning, making sure it is thoroughly coated.

2 Dip the food in the egg, or brush it until it is coated. Drain off excess egg and transfer to the crumbs.

3 Turn the food in the crumbs until completely coated. Transfer to a plate or paper. If kept uncovered for 1-2 hours in the refrigerator, the coating dries and will be even crisper when fried.

Ingredients for deep-frying

The aim of deep-frying is to seal food by immersing it in hot oil so that all the flavor and the juices are retained in a crisp crust. Many ingredients may be deep-fried. If they have a soft, rich texture that contrasts with the crispy outside (for example, scallops and eggplant), so much the better. Deep-fried fish, chicken and vegetables – especially potatoes – are particularly successful. A whole range of deep-fried savory croquettes and fritters are very popular, while fruit fritters and deep-fried pastries are favorite desserts the world over.

The amount of oil in the pan is important; there should be enough to cover the food to be deep-fried by at least ¾ in/2 cm. The ingredients should not be too cold, and must be added in small batches so that they do not lower the temperature of the hot fat. Deep-frying is usually reserved for small pieces of food so that the outside does not brown before the inside is hot. However, there are some exceptions to this rule; the Chinese, for example, deep-fry whole fish. Some foods, such as French fries, are fried twice – once at a low temperature to cook them through, and then at a higher temperature for crispness.

Food with a high starch content, such as potatoes, can be deep-fried without a coating, but most others need protection from the hot fat. A coating also prevents oil from penetrating the food and stops the food from flavoring the oil, so that it can be used again. Coating with breadcrumbs (left) gives the best protection, while a batter (opposite, right) is good for less tender foods. Small items, such as strips of fish, can simply be coated with flour. Cornmeal and oatmeal are popular alternatives.

When used correctly, the fat for deep-frying should acquire little or no taste or odor from the foods that are deep-fried in it, and it can be re-used several times, although the smoking point will decrease each time. Hot fat should be cooled, strained through cheesecloth into a clean container and covered. If any sediment appears in the bottom of the container, use only the clean layer of fat. Raw potato slices, fried in the used oil, can help to clarify it. Oil that is dark, thick, or harsh-smelling should be discarded. Oil used for frying fish is most likely to retain odors.

DEEP-FRYING FOOD

Before deep-frying, read safety precautions (right) and make sure oil has reached the correct temperature (opposite, left). Use a wire basket in the pan so that the cooked food can be removed without delay. Keep finished food warm in a low oven while frying the rest. Do not cover or the food will become soggy.

1 Lower food into the oil gently so that it does not splash. Handle coated foods carefully to avoid damaging the surface.

2 Once the oil starts to bubble over the food, tip the basket slightly from time to time to see whether the coating has turned golden.

Pommes Dauphine

Left-over puréed potato works well in this recipe. You will need twice as much potato as choux pastry, by volume.

Serves 8

puréed potatoes made with 1½ lb/750 g potatoes, 3 tbsp/45 g butter, salt, pepper, nutmeg and ⅓ cup/75 ml warm milk	choux pastry made with ½ cup/ 60 g flour, ½ cup/125 ml water, ¼ tsp salt, ¼ cup/60 g butter, 3 eggs.
	fat for deep frying

1 Beat the puréed potatoes with a wooden spoon over low heat until fluffy. Make the choux pastry and beat it into the potatoes.
2 Heat the fat to 350°F/175°C. Using two teaspoons, drop six walnut-sized balls of mixture into the fat.
3 Cook the potatoes, turning them so that they brown evenly, until golden, about 4-5 minutes.
4 Drain the potatoes on paper towels. Keep warm in a 350°F/175°C oven with the door open while frying the remaining potato mixture. **Note** When keeping potatoes warm in the oven, make sure they do not touch, or they will lose their crispness.

Safety precautions

Fat easily catches fire when overheated and hot fat can inflict serious burns. To prevent flare-ups caused by spillage, use a pan that completely covers the heat source. The shape of the pan is also important in preventing splashing (Equipment, p.510). Never fill it more than one-third full and keep the handles out of the way so that there is no danger of the pan being knocked over. Hot fat explodes on contact with water, so food to be deep-fried should be as dry as possible. Always lower foods gently into the fat, using a basket that can be easily removed. Mop up any spills immediately and keep the outside of the pan free from fat.

Note If the pan catches fire, turn off the heat and cover the pan with a lid, baking sheet, or heavy blanket, to exclude air. Never move the pan or use water to extinguish the flames. Spreading flames can be quenched with baking soda or a fire extinguisher.

BATTERS FOR DEEP-FRYING

A batter is a thick but pourable mixture, usually bound with eggs and containing flour or another starch to give it body. Batters are used to coat food and protect it from the searing heat of deep fat. Water makes a batter light; milk gives it smoothness and makes it brown more quickly, while beer is popular in savory batters as it adds flavor as well as air. Some batters include raising agents; other, more robust batters for fish and vegetables, may be raised with yeast. A few spoons of oil or melted butter enrich batters and help prevent them from sticking to the pan. Salt and pepper are the most common seasonings, though flavorings such as chili pepper may be included, or liqueurs for sweet batters. Sugar should only be used in small quantities since it easily burns in the hot fat, as do delicate ingredients such as herbs.

Yeast or beer batters are appropriate for fish fillets, whole mushrooms and other raw ingredients that are fried for a relatively long time. For fragile foods like shrimp or vegetable sticks, or pre-cooked ingredients, the batter should be thinner. Japanese tempura batter (below) is the lightest of all. See also chapter on Flour, Breads and Batters (p.342).

USEFUL INFORMATION

Portion Batter made with 1 cup/ 125 g flour coats 1½ cups/375 g food.
Cooking methods Coat and deep-fry (p.106).

When done Crisp and brown.
Problems Heavy if too thick; runs off food if too thin; tough when cooked if overbeaten.
Storage Refrigerate 1 day.

Batter recipes

Onion rings Serves 4-6. Slice 4 large onions into ¼ in/6 mm rings (p.290) and soak in iced water, 1-2 hours. In a bowl, sift 1 cup/ 125 g flour and 1 tsp each salt and baking soda and make a well. Beat together 1 egg and 1 cup/250 ml buttermilk. Pour half the liquid into the well and whisk until smooth; gradually whisk in the rest. Drain and dry the onion rings. Dip them in batter and deep-fry at 370°F/188°C until golden. Drain on paper towels.
Shrimp tempura, Serves 4. Peel 1½ lb/750 g large shrimp, leaving on the tail fins. Whisk together 1 egg and 1 cup/250 ml water. Add 1¼ cups/150 g flour or rice flour and whisk very briefly; batter may be lumpy, but if overworked it will be heavy. Dip the shrimp in batter and deep-fry at 370°F/188°C until pale gold. Remove and drain on paper towels. Serve with soy sauce.

COATING FOOD WITH BATTER FOR DEEP-FRYING

Firm foods such as pieces of fruit, broccoli or cauliflower florets, or slices of zucchini, are best coated in batter before deep-frying. Shellfish, particularly shrimp, also work well.

1 Immerse a piece of food (here, apple rings) in batter so it is completely coated. Lift it out and drain for 1-2 seconds so excess batter drips into the bowl. Lower the food gently into the hot oil.

2 Coat and fry the food in small batches so that the pan is not crowded and the oil temperature remains steady. Cook fritters until crisp and brown, 3-4 minutes, then drain on paper towels.

Fruit fritters in beer batter

Beer makes a crisp, all-purpose batter for fruit and vegetables such as apple rings and sliced bananas.

Serves 4

1 lb/500 g peeled fruit such as apple or pineapple, cut in rings, pears or peaches, cut in wedges, or bananas, diagonally sliced	2 tbsp/30 g sugar
	1 tbsp oil
	oil for frying
1 cup/125 g flour	*For sprinkling*
pinch of salt	confectioners' sugar
½ cup/125 ml beer or ale (more if needed)	*For serving*
	apricot or red jam sauce (p.66) or honey
1 egg	
2 egg whites	

1 To make the batter: sift the flour and salt into a bowl and make a well in the center. Add half the beer with the whole egg and stir, gradually drawing in the flour to make a smooth paste. If too much liquid is added at this point, the batter will form lumps. Add the remaining beer, cover and leave ½ to 1 hour. It will thicken on standing.
2 If necessary, thin the batter with a little more beer. Stiffly whip the egg whites, add the sugar and continue whipping 30 seconds until glossy. Fold the egg whites into the batter. Heat the oil to 375°F/190°C.
3 Coat the fruit and fry the fritters. Keep warm on a baking sheet lined with paper towels in an oven with the door open while frying the rest. Sprinkle the fritters with confectioners' sugar and serve as soon as possible, accompanied by jam sauce or honey.

Vegetable fritters Omit the sugar and substitute onion rings, zucchini or eggplant sticks, small whole mushrooms, broccoli or cauliflower florets for the fruit. Serve with tomato sauce (p.65).

SAUTEED & PAN-FRIED FOODS

Food that is cooked by sautéing must be moistened with fat, but not soaked. A brisk heat is essential so that the food sautés (literally "jumps" in French) in the pan, until golden brown and slightly crisp. An open frying pan with low sloping sides should be used, so that ingredients can easily be tossed or stirred and are not too crowded. Unlike deep-fried foods, ingredients that are sautéed are not drained on paper towels but should remain moist and flavored with the fat.

Only butter gives the characteristic golden brown color and rich flavor of true sautéing, though margarine or an all-purpose oil can be used instead. For everyday sautéing, an inexpensive refined oil with a mild flavor and light body is best, provided it can be heated to a fairly high temperature – safflower oil and corn oil are particularly good. Animal fats such as lard, bacon, goose or chicken fat are valued for their flavor, especially for cooking bland ingredients like potatoes. Use just enough fat to circulate freely beneath the food; too much fat will give the effect of deep-frying.

If the fat is not hot enough, the food will not brown properly and the juices will not be retained. Test the temperature with a single ingredient before adding the rest: the fat should bubble briskly. Ingredients to be sautéed must also be completely dry or a layer of steam will develop between the food and the fat, and the food will not brown. To ensure a dry surface, food for sautéing can be coated in flour (p.104).

Similar to sautéing is pan-frying, with the difference that pan-fried food may be cooked briefly – often to reheat or brown it more thoroughly. Pan-frying is generally done over more vigorous heat than sautéing. Animal fat, butter or oil is used, depending on the food to be fried. Juices from pan-fried meat can be used to make sauce. Pan-broiling or dry-frying is used for fatty foods like fat bacon and sausages, and in cooking for low-fat diets. In this method, no fat is added at all; the cooking is started in a cold, often non-stick, pan and fat released by the food can be poured off. Yet another variant of sautéing is shallow-frying, done in fat of up to ½ in/1.25 cm deep; it is often used for coated fish, light meats, or patties or croquettes that should be browned at the sides as well as on the top and bottom. Unlike sautéed foods, shallow-fried foods may need to be drained on paper towels.

Sole fillets are floured and sautéed in butter for *sole meunière*.

SAVORY CROQUETTES & FRITTERS

A number of delectable snacks are made from savory mixtures that are wrapped in a coating to hold them together and then deep- or pan-fried. Fillings range from lobster to mushrooms, from chestnuts to cheese. Sometimes the raw ingredients are cut in pieces or sticks to fry in batter, but more commonly, they are cooked and chopped, then combined with a strongly flavored food like ham, anchovy, or chili pepper, perhaps with a thick sauce to bind them together.

The joy of a crumb-coated croquette is the contrast of crisp crust and a melting center. A rich brown or white sauce is used to bind the filling. The mixture is rolled into long finger shapes or round patties and breaded before being fried. The creamier the mixture, the more delectable the finished croquette but the harder it is to shape, so the cook must work carefully, chilling the mixture and handling it as lightly as possible. Meat or fish croquettes are usually served as a first course, while vegetable croquettes such as potato, chestnut or lentil are good accompaniments to beef and game. In France, a type of croquette called a *subric*, which is shallow-fried or sautéed rather than deep-fried, is popular as an appetizer.

Fritter is a more general term for any deep fried savory morsel with a crisp outside. Fritters can be made of mushroom-flavored choux pastry, for instance, or grated Parmesan cheese bound with eggs and a little flour, but usually they have a batter coating (previous page). Seafood or vegetables are popular as fillings, as in the Italian *fritto misto*. **Note** A chopped filling for fritters must be stiffer than for a croquette because a liquid batter will not hold the filling together as well as a breadcrumb coating.

Other coatings, notably pastry dough, can be used to make deep-fried parcels. A French rissole, or turnover, is shaped in a little triangle or semicircle and deep-fried. The filling should be sharply flavored: ground meat with Worcestershire or Tabasco sauce, or cheeses mixed with chives, are favorite fillings. Other tasty parcels include Indian *samosas* – spiced potato or ground meat wrapped in pastry – and Middle Eastern savory pastries.

Chinese cuisine has provided new appetizers for the Western table. Curly little wonton packages filled with crab and scallion are now familiar, as are spring rolls and egg rolls, with their stuffing of bean sprouts, seasoned pork and fresh coriander. Both are wrapped in wafer-thin doughs based on rice or wheat flour and deep-fried until golden and crunchy.

USEFUL INFORMATION

Portion *Croquettes, rissoles, spring rolls:* 1-3 per person. *Fritters, wontons:* 2-5 per person.
Cooking methods Deep-fry 2-4 minutes; shallow-fry 2-4 minutes each side.
When done Crisp and golden.
Problems Soggy if fried too slowly; hard to shape if filling is too soft; burst if wrapper is over-filled or if fried too long.
Storage Serve at once; *samosas* can be refrigerated.
Accompaniments Fresh or cooked tomato sauces (p.65); tartare sauce (p.63); sauce rémoulade (p.63); piquant sauces (p.29); hot mustard, duck sauce, soy sauce, fish sauce (for Asian dishes).
Typical dishes *Croquettes:* chicken and mushroom (USA); egg, with bacon (USA); *croquettes à la Dieppoise* (with mussels, shrimps and mushrooms, France). *Fritters: Genfer käsebeignets* (cheese, Switzerland); *fondue Bruxelloise* (fried cheese squares, Belgium); corn and green chili (USA). *Parcels:* fish rissoles (Portugal); *kohltäschen* (cabbage rissoles, Austria).

Camembert croquettes

French or Italian tomato sauce (p.65) and deep-fried parsley are excellent accompaniments to these cheese croquettes.

Makes 30 croquettes

1 lb/500 g Camembert cheese	**For the coating**
thick béchamel sauce made with ¼ cup/60 g butter, ⅓ cup/45 g flour, 2 cups/500 ml milk, salt, pepper	½ cup/60 g flour, seasoned with salt and pepper
3 egg yolks	2 eggs, beaten to mix with ½ tsp salt and 1 tbsp oil
1 tsp Dijon mustard	1 cup/100 g dry white breadcrumbs
pinch of cayenne pepper	vegetable oil for deep-frying
pinch of nutmeg	
salt and white pepper	**8-in/20-cm square cake pan**

1 Grease the cake pan with a little butter. Cut the rind from the cheese and discard it. Coarsely chop the cheese; it should weigh ½ lb/250 g.
2 Make the béchamel sauce and add the cheese and egg yolks. Simmer, stirring constantly, for 2 minutes, or until the mixture is smooth and thick but still soft enough to fall from the spoon. Do not boil the mixture, or the cheese will form strings. Take from the heat, stir in the mustard, cayenne and nutmeg and season to taste with salt and white pepper. Pour the cheese mixture into the cake pan and chill until set, at least 2 hours.
3 Warm the pan over heat for a moment or two to loosen the mixture. Unmold it on to a floured surface and cut into bars ¾ in/ 2 cm × 2½ in/6 cm. Coat each bar with the seasoned flour, egg and breadcrumbs.
4 Heat the vegetable oil to 375°F/190°C using a fat thermometer (p.503) as a guide to temperature. Fry the croquettes a few at a time until golden brown, 1-2 minutes. Remove them and drain on paper towels. Keep the first batch of croquettes warm by placing them in a moderate oven (350°F/175°C) with the door ajar, while you fry the rest.

2

page

FISH   110

SHELLFISH   152

POULTRY &
GAME BIRDS   174

MEAT &
CHARCUTERIE   194

FISH

FISH IS at once the most challenging and rewarding of all foods. The challenge is posed by the care with which it must be cooked. Different types of fish can be adapted happily to almost every imaginable cooking method, and a large number of creative techniques are involved in their preparation. Here lies the prize, in the vast array of fish dishes, simple and sophisticated, classic and contemporary.

In recent years, the increasing efficiency of refrigerated transport has revolutionized the availability of fresh fish and created a true world market in seafood. A superb Atlantic salmon on the slab in Hawaii may have been caught in Norway only 72 hours earlier. As consumers, we benefit not only from refrigerated air transport but also from major advances in processing technology on harvesting vessels. Although freezing does affect the texture of fish, in many cases it does less damage than would occur naturally through bacterial growth. If well-handled fish is frozen immediately, at its peak of quality and at the right temperature, then correctly stored and delivered to the point of sale, deterioration should be slight. Commercial canning is a successful alternative, especially for oily fish such as salmon, tuna, anchovy and sardine.

The other revolution in the industry is fish farming. World demand for fish cannot be met by harvesting at sea alone, particularly as in some ocean areas, stocks of wild fish are being depleted or are under threat from pollution. Trout farming is now taken for granted and a more recent innovation is the harvesting of most Atlantic salmon under controlled conditions. In the United States, catfish farming has been an enormous success – in just over a decade, the annual yield has increased thirty-fold to 300 million pounds. As consumers, the concession we have to make for more plentiful supplies of farmed fish is greater standardization. The flavor and texture of wild fish can vary enormously; the quality of farmed fish is much more consistent, but rarely attains the excellence of the finest wild specimens.

Most important for the cook is an understanding of the differences in taste, texture and bone structure among the various kinds of fish. A fish with an oily, rich flesh, such as mackerel or herring, is as different from a white-fleshed fish, such as hake, as duck is from chicken. Texture is another important characteristic: the coarse flesh of the cod differs from the fine texture of sole and neither could be confused with the firmness of shark or the softness of whiting. Tuna, swordfish and other very big fish invariably appear in the market as steaks, many looking more like meat than fish. Fish with a cartilaginous structure and no transverse bones, such as shark, require different methods of preparation from fish like shad, which seem to be all bone if they are carelessly dissected. Flatfish such as turbot and sole and fish with compressed bodies, such as bream, are better suited to filleting than cutting into steaks. Small fish such as herring and trout are often left on the bone to cook whole, while larger ones like salmon may be sold whole, filleted or cut in steaks.

In this chapter, fish are grouped into 14 categories according to their cooking affinities. First come sole, flounder and other small flatfish offering a wide choice of quality and price. Even more highly prized are halibut and other larger flatfish. Ray and skate are given separate coverage (as are monkfish, and shark and sturgeon), because of their unique cartilaginous structure. The next group of firm-fleshed fish, which includes tuna and swordfish, have firm, meaty flesh.

Firm white fish from the Atlantic and Pacific (snapper and grouper among others) follow; then come flaky white fish, including saltwater bass and mullet. Next is the cod family, which includes hake and pollack among others. Thin-bodied fish like bream and jack are another category for the cook, as are gurnard and other fish that have large heads and are very bony.

Salmon and trout are considered together, followed by the wide range of other freshwater fish. Last come two groups of oily fish: the first includes herring and mackerel (as well as small fish usually deep-fried) and the second includes long-bodied fish like eel. The chapter also covers specific preparations such as caviar and other fish roes, raw fish dishes such as *sushi*, and fish preserved by drying, salting and smoking are also discussed.

One last word about identifying fish. Not only do fish come in every conceivable shape and size, from one-ounce minnows to one- or two-ton tuna, but also the common vocabulary used to describe different kinds of fish is also loose to the extent that the same fish can have a variety of names. For example, one species of flatfish is called American plaice, Canadian plaice, sand-dab or long rough dab, depending on where it is sold. The reverse is true of redfish, popular in the Cajun cuisine of the southern United States. As the cuisine grew more popular, many inferior species of fish were listed as "redfish" by retailers. Similarly in Britain some inferior flatfish are marked as "sole", for example lemon sole or Torbay sole.

Handling fish

The quality of fish for eating greatly depends on how the fish was handled during the first three hours out of the water, and on whether it was caught by hook and line or in a net. If the fish was caught in a net, the amount of time it was kept there is critical – fish can become bruised and overheated if netted for long periods. Other conditions that influence quality depend on whether the fish was taken aboard the boat alive and how it was bled and eviscerated. Also, the fish should have been refrigerated before its body stiffened into rigor mortis. This point is important because a fish that is expertly refrigerated before rigor mortis sets in will resist bacteria for up to a week, while a fish that is already in rigor mortis when it is refrigerated will have a shorter shelf-life and poorer texture. Finally, to ensure that the fish remains at its peak of quality, it must be kept at the correct temperature during transportation from ship to market.

Choosing fish

The process of selecting fish in the market is not as straightforward as buying a cut of meat. The sea is unpredictable and in rough weather supplies fall and prices rise. Some fish migrate as water temperatures change, remaining seasonal despite modern transport, for example shad, herring and many other oily fish. The first rule when buying is to select fish that looks fresh, rather than choosing a variety that ought to be fresh. Luckily a fish in impeccable condition is easy to spot. When fresh, the flesh has a bright translucent clarity and a sweet smell, without trace of fishy odor. The scales should be intact and shiny, the eyes full, not sunken, and the gills a bright red. When poked, the flesh should feel firm and resilient. (In spawning season, which varies for different fish, the flesh softens and is inferior.) Fillets should not be dry or discolored, nor should they be surrounded by liquid (a sign of old or improperly frozen fish). Fish that has been treated chemically to extend shelf-life usually has an unnatural shininess and a slippery feel.

Note A fish that has been cut into steaks or fillets deteriorates more rapidly than a whole fish because the exposed flesh is more vulnerable to bacteria. For this reason, it is best to buy fish at a market that prepares portions on the spot rather than retailing them pre-cut. Alternatively, purchase a whole fish and cut it up yourself (see Trimming fish, right, and Filleting fish, p.114).

Storing fish

Fresh fish should be stored for as short a time as possible after purchase. Shelf-life depends on the type and quality of the fish. Well-handled fish can be kept for up to a week under ideal storage conditions. Use a reliable retailer and try to find out the history of the fish before deciding on how long it can be stored at home.

Temperature is the key to maintaining quality. Spoilage occurs twice as fast at 40°F/4°C (the usual temperature of a home refrigerator) than at 32°F/0°C, which is the ideal storage temperature. Whole fish will keep longer if they have been gutted; this eliminates the enzymes in the stomach that accelerate decay. Fish stored in a home refrigerator should be wrapped tightly in plastic and covered in ice. The melting ice should drain away from the fish. Cut fish should not be in direct contact with ice because this will discolor the flesh and draw out the juices.

Oily fish generally spoil most quickly. If not gutted and kept at the proper temperature, sardines and mackerel, for example, can start to smell and develop unpleasantly strong flavors within 48 hours of being caught.

Freezing fish

Freezing fish in a home freezer is recommended only in case of necessity. Home freezers chill more slowly than commercial machines, allowing the formation of ice crystals, which penetrate cell walls damaging flavor and texture. If freezing is unavoidable, make sure the freezer is set at the lowest possible temperature. Rich fish, such as salmon and firm-fleshed white fish, such as cod, freeze better than delicate ones such as whiting. For freezing methods, see Preserving and Freezing (p.496).

It is best to thaw frozen fish slowly in the refrigerator before cooking, to maintain texture and minimize moisture loss. However, some cooks like to cook fish fillets when they are still frozen; cooking times must be increased accordingly.

AVAILABLE FORMS OF FRESH FISH

The list below indicates the various forms of fresh fish available from fishmongers and the terms used to describe them. It is intended as a guide for selecting fish and following recipes.

Whole or round As it comes from the water.

Whole and dressed, drawn, cleaned, or gutted Gills and intestines removed.

Whole and pan-dressed Gutted, head removed with tail trimmed, fins and often scales removed.

Roast Large chunk or tail section of large, firm fish.

Steak Crosscut section of a large fish cut ¾-1½ in/2-4 cm thick. Depending on size of fish it may be whole, including the central backbone, or cut in half or quarters without bone.

Loin A longitudinal cut from fish such as tuna and halibut.

Fillet A side of fish removed from the central vertebrae. Fillets may come skinned or with skin.

Butterfly fillet, booked fillet Two fillets held together by the belly or the back skin of the fish.

Escalopes Diagonal slices ⅜ in/1 cm thick, cut from a large fillet. (They are sometimes called scallops in the United States.)

TRIMMING FISH

When a fish is to be served whole, the fins are trimmed so they do not interfere with serving. Here, bream is shown.

1 With a pair of heavy scissors, cut away the fins on either side of the fish. Then cut away the belly fins.

2 Cut away the fins along the back (dorsal fins).

3 Trim the tail by cutting a "V" shape into it.

SCALING FISH

Most fish need to be scaled before cooking, though a few, such as salmon, have tiny scales that do not need to be removed. A small number of fish, for example shark, have none at all. Scale fish outdoors or on a draining board. Here, bream is shown.

1 With a fish scaler (shown here), a curry comb or a serrated knife held at an angle, scrape off the scales, working from tail to head. Rinse the fish often under running water.

GUTTING FISH THROUGH THE GILLS

Small flatfish and fish to be poached keep their shape better when gutted through the gills. Also, fish to be cut in steaks maintain their natural round configuration. Here, bream is shown.

1 Hook your finger through the gills and pull them out (they can be quite sharp).

2 With your fingers, reach through the gill opening and pull out the stomach contents.

3 With scissors, make a small slit at the ventral (stomach) opening and pull out any remaining contents.

4 Run cold water into the gill opening and out through the ventral opening to clean the cavity.

GUTTING FISH THROUGH THE STOMACH

For most purposes fish are gutted (or dressed) through the stomach. Here, whiting is shown.

1 With a medium knife, slit the underside from gills to small ventral opening, taking care not to insert the knife too far.

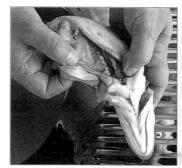

2 With your fingers, carefully loosen the stomach contents from the cavity and pull them out.

3 With your fingers pull out the gills. Clean the cavity by washing away any blood.

4 With a small spoon, scrape along the vertebrae in the cavity to remove the kidney.

SCORING FISH

Whole fish that are to be broiled, baked or steamed are scored along the sides so they cook more evenly. Here, bream is shown.

1 With a sharp knife, slash the fish diagonally 3-4 times on each side. The slashes should be about ½ in/1.25 cm deep to allow heat to penetrate.

BONING ROUNDFISH THROUGH THE STOMACH

Fish are usually boned through the stomach unless they are to be stuffed. The head and tail are left on to hold the fish together during cooking. Use a sharp knife with a flexible blade. Here, salmon trout is shown.

1 Gut the fish through the stomach (left). Continue the stomach slit on one side of the backbone as far as the tail.

2 Open the cavity and with the blade of the knife, cut loose the transverse bones lining the flesh.

3 Turn the fish over and slit the flesh at the base of the backbone on the other side.

5 With scissors, snip the backbone at the tail and head and, starting at the head, peel it away from the flesh with any attached transverse bones.

4 With the blade of the knife, cut loose the transverse bones lining the flesh as on the first side.

For cooking, boned fillets can be rolled in spirals, skin side inwards.

Alternatively, fold skin outwards, and tuck the tail inside.

BONING ROUNDFISH ALONG THE BACKBONE

Fish is often boned along the backbone in order to keep the stomach cavity intact for stuffing. The head and tail are left on. Use a sharp knife with a flexible blade. Here, mackerel is shown.

1 Slit the fish on either side of the backbone, cutting the flesh away from the bone until it is completely detached.

2 With scissors, snip the backbone once at the head and once at the tail.

3 Lift out the bone, together with the stomach contents and gills.

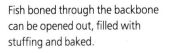

Fish boned through the backbone can be opened out, filled with stuffing and baked.

Alternatively, the tail can be tucked inside the head and through the mouth. The fish can be poached plain.

BONING FLATFISH

Flatfish are boned whole to be stuffed or breaded and deep-fried. The head, fins and stomach contents should be removed before boning. If possible, strip dark and white skin from the fish; if not, remove after cooking (p.117). Here, sole is shown.

1 Using a flexible knife, cut along the backbone and cut the flesh away from the bones, holding the knife almost parallel to the bones. Cut to the edge of the transverse bones but do not remove the fillet completely. Turn the fish and repeat for the opposite fillet.

2 With a pair of scissors, snip the spine at the head and at the tail end of the fish, taking care not to damage the flesh with the point of the scissors.

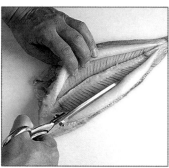

3 Fold back the flesh to the edge of the transverse bones and, with scissors, cut them away from the fin bones. Repeat on the opposite side of the fish.

4 Lift the backbone at the tail end and pull, stripping it from the flesh underneath.

5 For cooking, lay the fish flat and curl the top fillets back to expose the flesh underneath.

FILLETING ROUNDFISH

Two fillets are cut from most round fish, one from each side of the backbone. Here, salmon is shown.

1 Holding the knife horizontally, slit the skin from head to tail along one side of the backbone.

2 Cut down to the backbone just behind the fish head.

3 Holding the knife flat and keeping the blade in contact with the bone, cut away the flesh from head to tail in a continuous motion.

4 Cut back over the rib cage of the fish to free the flesh from the backbone, and remove the fillet completely.

5 Turn the fish over and remove the second fillet in the same way, working from head to tail.

FILLETING FLATFISH

For flatfish, the filleting technique depends on whether you want two wide, or four narrow, fillets. On larger flatfish, four fillets are usually cut. Here, turbot is shown.

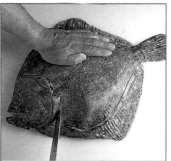

1 **To remove 4 fillets:** with the point of a sharp knife, cut round the edge of the fish to outline the shape of the fillets.

2 With the point of the knife, cut the fish to the bone in a semi-circle just behind the head.

3 Cut a straight line from tail to head along the spine, through to the bone. Keeping the knife almost flat, slip it between the flesh and the rib bones. Cut away the fillet, using a stroking motion and keeping the knife flat.

4 Continue cutting until the fillet and meat lying along the fins are detached with the skin in one piece.

5 Turn the fish round and slip the knife under the flesh of the second fillet. Detach the fillet from the bones beneath, following the same method as for the first fillet.

6 Turn the fish over and repeat steps 1-5 on the underside.

Note On many flatfish, fillets that are taken from the top side, which has darker flesh, will be thicker than those taken from the underside.

To remove two fillets: cut the fish to the bone behind the head. Working from the head along one side, slip the knife between the flesh and the rib bones, cutting as far as the backbone. Turn the fish round and repeat along the other side until the backbone is reached. Detach the fillet and repeat on the other side.

Using fish trimmings

The heads and bones left after filleting and boning fish can be made into fish stock (p.44). Fish bones and trimmings should be odorless and free of blood. Halibut and sole bones make the best stock, while bones from oily and strong-flavored fish should be avoided.

Skinning whole fish

The decision to skin or not is based on the flavor of the oils next to the skin and on whether the skin itself is tough or soft, thick or thin. For poaching, pan-frying, deep-frying and steaming, fish skin is often removed. For broiling and baking it may be left on, as it helps to keep the fish intact.

The skin of most fish must be cut away with a knife. However, the skin of monkfish, catfish, eel (p.151) and some flatfish (here, sole is shown) can be stripped off the fish before it is filleted, either from the tail end (flatfish), or from the neck end.

SKINNING FLATFISH

The easiest way to remove the skin of most flatfish is to strip it off the whole fish before boning or filleting. Here, sole is shown.

1 With the point of a knife, loosen the skin near the tail. Grasp the skin firmly with the help of a cloth or a sprinkling of salt. Pull the skin sharply, parallel with the flesh, to strip it away from the flesh.

SKINNING FISH FILLETS

Dark or tough skin is often removed from fish fillets before they are cooked. Use a sharp knife with a long flexible blade to remove the skin. Here, a turbot fillet is shown.

1 Place the fillet on the work surface, skin side down, tail end toward you. Make a small cut at the tail end to separate the skin from the flesh.

2 RIGHT Grasp the skin with the fingers of one hand (dipping them in salt or using a cloth if they slip). Hold the knife between the skin and the flesh, with the edge against the skin and the blade almost parallel to it. Work away from you with a sawing motion to remove the flesh, at the same time holding the skin beneath taut with your other hand.

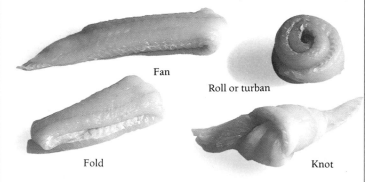

FLATTENING FISH FILLETS

When fish fillets are cooked, the thin membrane on the skinned side may shrink and cause them to buckle. To prevent this they are often flattened and scored. Here, a sole fillet is shown.

1 Place the fillet between two sheets of plastic wrap and pound it lightly with the flat side of a large knife blade.

2 With the tip of a knife, score the fillets lightly in parallel slanting lines on the side that has been skinned.

REMOVING PIN BONES FROM FILLETS

Depending on the structure of the fish, a line of tiny bones called pin bones may be left in the fillet after cutting it from the backbone. Here, a salmon fillet is shown.

1 With tweezers, or pinching between your thumb and the blade of a small knife, pull out the pin bones one by one.

FOLDING FISH FILLETS

For poaching or steaming, fish fillets can be folded in rolls, turbans, fans, folds and knots. Most decorative shapes are served plain, but when rolled or folded, they can also be stuffed. For flatfish, if the top and bottom fillets have been removed in one piece, cut them in half down the center. For a neat presentation, all fillets are folded with the skinned side inwards. Four methods of folding are shown below, using sole fillets.

Fan

Roll or turban

Fold

Knot

CUTTING FISH IN STEAKS

Most fish of 2 lb/1 kg or more are cut into ¾-1 in/2-2.5 cm thick slices for pan-frying, broiling, poaching and baking. The best come from the upper tail. Here, salmon is shown.

1 Cut the fish behind the head. Cut thick, even slices to within 6 in/15 cm of the tail. For large fish, a cleaver may be needed to sever the backbone and free the slices.

2 The tail section is usually cut horizontally in half to make two fillets rather than several small steaks.

PREPARING FISH STEAKS

When steaks are cut from the central body of the fish, the flaps of flesh around the stomach cavity can be tied in a round to make them look more presentable. Here, salmon is shown.

1 With a small knife, cut the bones lining the stomach cavity away from the flesh. Cut around the backbone with the point of the knife and remove it.

2 LEFT Curl the two flaps of flesh inward to form a heart shape and tie it with string, or secure it with toothpicks to hold the shape.

CUTTING FISH ESCALOPES

Large fish fillets can be cut into escalopes about ⅜ in/1 cm thick for steaming, baking and pan-frying. Here, salmon is shown.

1 With the tail facing away from you and working toward it, cut thin diagonal slices, keeping them as even as possible. Leave the skin behind.

Timing the cooking of whole fish

For a whole fish, or pieces of fish, less than 1 in/2.5 cm thick, cooking time depends on the method. However, when a whole large fish is baked, broiled, poached or steamed, the cooking time depends on the thickness of the flesh, measured at the thickest point. For every 1 in/2.5 cm of thickness, allow 10 minutes cooking time. When poaching whole fish, the time should be counted from the moment the liquid starts to bubble very gently in one corner of the pan.

TESTING FISH FOR COOKING

No other ingredient overcooks as easily as fish, so testing is vital. For fillets and escalopes, particularly of white fish, less than one minute can make the difference between fish being perfectly done and overcooked. Oily fish, however, can withstand overcooking slightly better than leaner fish. Just before it is done, the thickest part of the fish still clings to the bone and a thin layer (⅛ in/ 3 mm) of transparent, uncooked flesh is left in the center. When done, the fish flakes when tested with a fork and the transparent layer has just disappeared. When overdone, the fish is dry and falls apart at the touch of a fork. Here, bream is shown.

1 A transparent layer of flesh and clear eye show fish is uncooked.

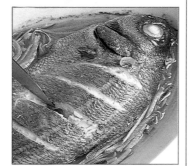

2 Flaking flesh and an opaque eye show fish is cooked.

BONING COOKED FISH STEAKS

Removing the bones from fish steaks makes them easier to eat, though the flesh divides in pieces. Here, cod is shown.

1 With a fork held upright, peel off skin surrounding the cooked fish by curling it round the back of the fork and turning the fork outward.

2 With the tip of a knife, pierce the central bone. Twist the knife and lift out the central bone with the surrounding spines attached.

3 Detach the small fin bones at the edge of the steak. On larger steaks, the flesh can be divided into four pieces after boning.

BONING COOKED SMALL FLATFISH

After steaming, broiling or pan-frying *à la meunière* (p.127), fish may be removed from the bone for serving. Here, sole is shown.

1 Lift the fish on to a plate. With a spoon and fork, ease the fin bones away from each side and push them to the side of the plate.

2 Cut along the backbone with the edge of the spoon and lift off each fillet, laying them on another plate or at either side of the fish.

3 Lift out the backbone, easing it away from the flesh.

4 For serving, replace the top fillets on the bottom ones.

TRIMMING & CUTTING UP LARGE COOKED WHOLE FISH

The flesh of all cooked fish is taken off the bone in the same way. Here, salmon is shown.

1 If poaching fish to serve cold, leave it to cool in the liquid until tepid to keep it moist. If serving hot, prepare it at once.

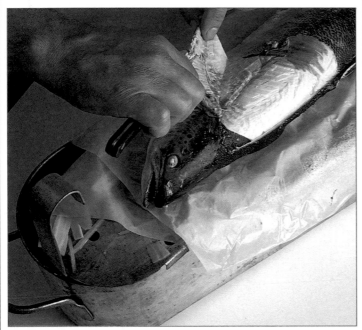

2 Cut the skin neatly at the head and tail. Carefully peel the skin away, taking care not to damage the flesh beneath with the knife.

3 Scrape away any remaining dark oily flesh with a knife.

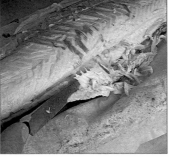

4 Scrape out bones lying along the back of the fish.

5 Use the paper from cooking or two large spatulas to lift and transfer the fish to a serving dish.

6 Cut down to the bone in a semi-circle around the head and at the tail end.

7 Divide the fish into two fillets by cutting a long line down the center. With a spoon and fork, ease one fillet toward the edge of the plate.

8 Remove the other top fillet in the same manner.

9 Snap the backbone at the head and pull it out at the tail.

10 Replace the top fillets neatly on the bottom ones to reshape the boned fish (reheat if necessary).

Sautéing and pan-frying fish

Good sautéed fish is colored to an even brown; it is slightly crisp on the outside and juicy inside. It should neither be dotted with black spots, which indicate too high a heat, nor pallid and falling apart, as when fried too slowly. To achieve the desired result, the fish is coated with flour that has been seasoned with salt and pepper (p.104). In the American South, a crunchy coating of cornmeal may replace the flour, and in Scotland oatmeal is used, particularly for herring. Sometimes the fish is first soaked in milk for an hour or two to improve the texture, then it is dried on paper towels.

Clarified butter (p.99) is an excellent fat in which to sauté fish, not only because of its flavor but also because it toasts to an agreeable gold at the medium temperature so well-suited to fish. Oil, or a mixture of oil and butter, are alternatives for frying. Many Mediterranean cuisines use olive oil, which adds flavor and browns nicely; other regional dishes call for lard. In all cases, the pan should be well-moistened with two to three tablespoons of fat, but the fish should not be swimming in it.

Some modern recipes call for cooking fish in a nonstick pan with hardly any fat at all – at most a quick brushing with butter. For this method, the fish must be cut in very thin fillets or escalopes; so the outside toasts lightly and the inside remains juicy. Firm-fleshed fish such as salmon, monkfish and sole are most suitable. Another variant of pan-frying uses a heavy ridged griddle pan (p.511). The fish cooks on the bars above the fat (usually oil), and acquires a brown, grilled or lattice pattern.

Almost any fish is good sautéed, whether left whole (if small), or cut in steaks or fillets. It is often served quite plain, with the juices from cooking and a wedge of lemon. Brown butter or butter from cooking fish *à la meunière* (p.127) may be made afterwards in the pan, but a more elaborate sauce would disguise the pure flavor of the fish. A few fried sliced almonds give texture to delicate fish like trout, while lardons of bacon and sliced mushrooms go with more robust fish such as bream.

Traditional accompaniments to sautéed or pan-fried fish include steamed potatoes, and boiled or steamed vegetables such as broccoli, zucchini, cucumber and peas. For luxury fish, a purée of vegetables is an alternative.

Deep-frying fish

Deep-frying is an excellent method for cooking fish, particularly white-fleshed types or tiny whole fish like smelts. The delicate flesh is protected by a breadcrumb or batter coating and cooked fast, so its elusive flavor is sealed at once. When well executed, using fresh oil and correct frying temperatures, deep-fried fish is outstanding. Unfortunately, inferior fried fish has given deep-frying a bad name.

Some cooks like to chill the coated fish before frying – the cold fish meeting the hot oil gives added crispness to the crust and the flesh stays moist. A flour, egg and breadcrumb coating protects fish thoroughly and is used for anything from fish fillets and sticks to fish balls and whole small fish like catfish.

A batter coating for fish may be delicately crisp, as in Japanese tempura, or form the robust jacket associated with British fish and chip shops. In one amusing presentation, the tail of a whole fish such as mackerel is tucked into its mouth (p.113). The French describe this presentation as *en colère*, meaning "in anger". The fish is then dipped in batter and deep-fried. British whitebait and French *goujons* (p.127) are deep-fried whole after tossing only in seasoned flour and served with a squeeze of lemon.

Deep-fried fish may form a first course, served alone or with a garnish of fried parsley. When fried fish is a main course, French fries are the universal accompaniment, with the possible addition of coleslaw. Given its richness, a sprinkling of lemon or vinegar would seem the most appropriate partner for deep-fried fish, or the spicy tomato sauce favored in the United States. However, rich piquant sauces such as tartare sauce (p.63) are also popular, with anchovy or savory butter (p.99) for fish in breadcrumbs.

Poaching fish

Most types of fish take kindly to poaching – a gentle method of cooking that adds flavor and keeps the fish moist. For whole fish, the head and bones contribute flavor to the poaching liquid, so *court bouillon* (p.44) or salted water are sufficient, sometimes with the addition of flavorings such as aniseed or fennel. The acid in *court bouillon* also helps firm up the flesh. For added flavor, fillets and pieces of fish are best poached in fish stock, which can then be used to make an accompanying sauce or coating of aspic (p.144). Fish may be poached in milk to remove strong flavors from salted or smoked varieties.

Fish for poaching are best gutted through the gills so the stomach vent does not curl open during cooking. If the stomach has been slit, a large fish will hold its shape better if wrapped in cheesecloth. It will also present a neater appearance if it is set with the belly down and flaps tucked underneath. Small fish can be poached in a shallow heatproof dish, but for large ones you will need to use a fish poacher (below, salmon is shown). For poaching, the fish should be just covered in cold liquid. Hot liquid makes the skin shrink and split.

Fish can be poached on top of the stove or in a 350°F/175°C oven. For small fish, steaks and fillets, time is counted from the moment cooking starts; timing for larger fish depends on the

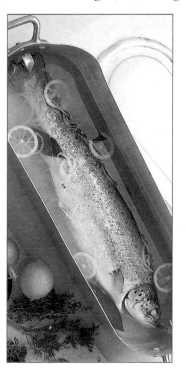

thickness of the fish (p.117) and starts when the water begins to bubble. After poaching, the fish must be drained on paper towels or a rack, otherwise it will "weep" liquid. To avoid patches of liquid on the plate, do not coat fish with sauce until just before serving.

Accompaniments to a whole poached fish tend to be simple. Hollandaise or white and red butter sauces (p.60) are popular. Steamed small potatoes and vegetables, particularly fresh peas, which coincide with the European wild salmon season, are common side dishes. Alternatively, whole cold fish may be coated in aspic and served with tomato or herb mayonnaise and cucumber salad or potato vinaigrette.

Poached fish steaks and fillets are served with a wide range of velouté and butter sauces, usually based on the cooking liquid. Shellfish often feature as a garnish. White sauces like Mornay, mushroom, anchovy, and British parsley sauce are alternatives. Such rich sauces are often served with rice or, more recently, pasta. Less classical accompaniments include all manner of vegetable *coulis*, nut sauces and even gooseberry purée.

Cold poached fish is often the basis of vinaigrette salads, enlivened by colorful vegetables like bell peppers and tomato, plus a flavoring of herbs and shallot. Fish salad in mayonnaise is another favorite, with tomato mayonnaise a pleasant contrast for white fish, or green mayonnaise for pink salmon.

Steaming fish

Steaming is a popular alternative to poaching fish. When surrounded by moisture, the flesh remains juicy. Plain water may be used, but the fish will acquire a more subtle savor from aromatic broths of vegetables. These may include assertive herbs such as fennel or dill and spices like anise. The fish may be laid on the steamer rack on a bed of herbs or even seaweed. Since fish cooks quickly by steaming, only a small amount of concentrated stock or broth is needed to provide the maximum flavor in a short time. Fillets, steaks and small whole fish can be steamed. They should be laid flat in the steamer (p.510) without overlapping, so that they cook evenly. So that the steam is in direct contact with the fish, the fish must be set over it on a perforated rack. The broth should already be at a brisk simmer when the rack is added, so its aromas have developed, then the pot should be tightly covered. Steaming fish takes about the same time as poaching. Be particularly careful not to overcook the fish, as steam is so hot.

Steaming displays the individual characteristics of a fish clearly, so *panachés*, or selections of contrasting types, are popular (p.130). An example is small fillets or escalopes of sole, salmon, red snapper or red mullet and monkfish, arranged in a fan against a background of red and white butter sauce.

Unlike poaching liquid, the broth from steaming is so strong that it can rarely be used as the basis for a sauce. Instead, the fish may be topped with a savory butter (see Fats and Oils, p.99). Often vegetables such as carrots, zucchini, cucumber, celery root and broccoli are steamed separately or together over the same broth as the fish.

Broiling and barbecuing fish

The intense heat of broiling best suits rich fish, though robust white-fleshed fish like bass and halibut are also suitable. Whole fish of up to 5 lb/2.3 kg can be broiled with great success, as their bones keep them moist and their skin protects them from the direct heat. They should be trimmed and scaled with the head and tail left on, and scored down the sides. Plump fish fillets with their skin, and steaks ¾ in/2 cm or more in thickness are good broiled, particularly when marinated for an hour or two in oil, lemon juice, and aromatic herbs like thyme and rosemary, and basted during cooking. Other basting sauces good with fish include soy and ginger mixtures (p.65).

Fish are best broiled 3-5 in/7.5-13 cm from the heat; the thinner the pieces, the nearer they must be. When broiling fillets with the skin, the cut side should be cooked first, and presented upwards on the plate. Leaving the skin on fillets helps hold them together. Note that thin fillets should be broiled only on the cut side, to avoid curling. Special fish-shaped racks can be used for barbecuing to help prevent whole fish from breaking up. Grill racks must be thoroughly oiled to prevent sticking, and the cooked fish must be handled gently.

Choose barbecue fuel with care. The energetic flavors of wood such as mesquite and hickory, for example, will overpower all but the most robust of oily fish unless used in moderation. In the south of France fish is sometimes barbecued over fennel twigs, then flamed with anise liqueur.

Savory butters (p.99) are the classic accompaniment to broiled or barbecued fish, but hollandaise and other butter sauces are also popular. Béarnaise is often served with salmon, and piquant Mexican tomato sauce is good with meaty fish such as tuna. Other partners include boiled or steamed peas, asparagus and broccoli, and stuffed vegetables for the finest of sole or turbot. For barbecued fish, vegetables such as tomato, eggplant and bell peppers may be broiled beside the fish. Simplest, and perhaps best of all, is a tossed green salad.

Baking fish

Baking is one of the easiest and most attractive methods of cooking fish. The fish, which may be large, small or in pieces, is laid in a shallow oiled or buttered dish, then seasoned. Moisture is provided by a sprinkling of oil, melted butter, lemon juice, wine, dry cider or fish stock. As with all whole fish dishes, a baked fish looks best with its head and tail intact and it should be scored (p.112) so it cooks evenly.

When fish is baked, flavorings such as chopped garlic, shallot or fresh ginger are often sprinkled on top, with breadcrumbs for a touch of brown on fillets. Vegetables such as tomatoes, bell peppers, mushrooms and eggplant may be layered beneath the fish. Baked fish often needs little accompaniment; the juice from baking forms a light sauce for both fish and vegetables. At most, a side dish of rice pilaf (p.315) or pasta is needed.

The abdominal cavity of a whole baked fish is ideal for a stuffing, even if only a bunch of herbs. Fish fillets, too, may be folded over a portion of stuffing. Herb and lemon breadcrumb mixtures are common, while around the Mediterranean olives and anchovies are popular. In the Pyrenees trout is stuffed with a ham mixture, and on the mid-Atlantic coast of the United States flounder is stuffed with crabmeat and baked.

No matter what the size, fish is usually baked at 350°F/175°C. To prevent the fish from drying, it can be loosely covered with aluminum foil, but most recipes state that fish should be baked uncovered so that it browns lightly. Baking counteracts the sometimes heavy flavor of oily fish and it also suits delicate fish that flake easily. Very firm fish like monkfish can become tough unless basted with plenty of liquid during baking.

Baking fish in aluminum foil

Aluminum foil is a convenient alternative to a parchment case (opposite) as it is easy to shape and retains all the juices of the fish and any garnish. Baking time, however, is harder to gauge as foil does not puff as easily as paper and does not brown. Foil can also be used to hold a fish in shape for poaching or steaming. By this method, as it is no longer in direct contact with the poaching liquid or steam, the fish stews in its own juices.

BAKING FISH IN A PARCHMENT PAPER CASE

Fish dries out easily, so it is often cooked in a protective case. Simplest is a case of parchment paper that encloses the fish with all manner of flavorings such as herbs, chopped garlic, shallot, ginger, sliced mushrooms, a julienne of mixed vegetables such as zucchini, carrots, celery or bell peppers, and a sprinkling of breadcrumbs. Shrimp and other shellfish are another possibility. Traditionally, the paper is cut into a heart shape and folded to form a package (Fr. *papillote*) around the fish. In the oven's heat, the ingredients steam and the flavors mingle. When the fish is cooked, the package browns and puffs to a balloon which is rushed to the table for the diner to open himself, releasing a rich aroma. Rice pilaf or precooked small vegetables may be added to the package, making it the ultimate one-dish individual serving. All but the most oily fish are good cooked in paper; usually fish fillets or steaks are used, but small whole fish can also be baked this way. Here, whole red mullet is shown.

1 Fold a large sheet of parchment paper in half and cut round it to make a heart shape when unfolded. It should be at least 2 in/5 cm larger than the fish. Brush the paper with butter. Set the fish on one half of the paper with salt, pepper and flavorings.

2 Fold the other side over it and make small pleats to seal the two edges, starting at the curve of the heart. Brush the outside of the package with butter so that it browns well.

3 Transfer the package to a baking sheet and bake in a preheated oven at 350°F/175°C until puffed and brown, 15-25 minutes depending on size of fish. Break or cut open the package at the table.

Pompano en papillote

The description *en papillote* is the French term for baking in paper. Canned crabmeat is good in this recipe, but be sure to pick it over to remove any membrane. Bream can be substituted for pompano.

Serves 4

2 pompano (about 1 lb/500 g each)	½ lb/250 g cooked crabmeat
2 cups/500 ml fish stock (p.44), made with bones and heads from pompano	½ lb/250 g cooked peeled shrimp, coarsely chopped
	pinch of dried thyme
¼ cup/60 g butter	2 tbsp/15 g flour
2 onions, finely chopped	2 egg yolks
1 cup/250 ml white wine	salt and pepper
2 shallots, chopped	4 bay leaves
1 clove garlic, chopped	
	Parchment paper

1 Fillet the pompano (p.115) and remove the skin. Rinse the fillets and dry them well. Use the bones and heads to make stock.
2 Melt half the butter and sauté the onion until soft but not brown. Add the fish stock, wine, shallots and garlic and boil until the liquid has reduced to 4 or 5 tablespoons. Stir in the crabmeat, shrimp and thyme, followed by the flour. Cook, stirring, for 2 minutes. Take from the heat and stir in the egg yolks. Season with salt and pepper and let the mixture cool.
3 Heat the oven to 375°F/190°C. Cut four large parchment paper cases (above left) and spread them with the remaining butter. Spoon the crab mixture on one side of the paper and set a fillet of pompano on top. Sprinkle the fish with salt and pepper and add a bay leaf. Seal the cases, set them on baking sheets and bake in the oven until brown and puffed, 15-25 minutes. Serve at once.

BAKING FISH IN A PASTRY CASE

Large and small whole fish or fish fillets can be baked in a case of puff pastry or brioche. Well-flavored fish with a firm texture such as snapper or sea bass are best suited to this method; salmon is another favorite. Soft-fleshed fish like hake produce too much liquid during cooking. Preparation can be as quick as a brushing of oil so the fish does not stick, as simple as a stuffing of herbs, or as elaborate as a stuffing such as *mousseline* (opposite) or *duxelles* (p.306). Trim, scale and gut the fish, leaving the head and tail on. Puff pastry or brioche made with 4 cups/500 g flour is enough to wrap a 5 lb/2.3 kg fish. Here, a whole salmon is shown wrapped in brioche dough (see Flour, Breads and Batters, p.355).

1 Divide the dough in half and roll out one portion to the length of the fish. Set the dough on an oiled baking sheet. Brush it with oil and set the fish, stuffed with herbs, on top. Trim the dough, leaving a 1 in/2.5 cm border round the fish and brush with egg glaze.

2 Roll out the remaining dough to the length of the fish. Loosely wrap the pastry round the rolling pin and unroll it on to the fish. Press the edges of the dough together and trim to a 1 in/2.5 cm border.

3 Mark "scales" with scissors or a piping tube and score the tail in lines with a knife. Add an eye, a mouth and a fin. Brush the dough again with egg glaze. Chill the fish for 30 minutes.

4 Bake the fish at 425°F/220°C until the dough starts to brown, 15-20 minutes. Lower heat to 375°F/190°C and continue baking until a skewer inserted in the center of the fish is hot to the touch when withdrawn. Cooking time depends on the thickness of the fish (p.117).

5 To serve, cut round the edge of the fish and lift off the crust. Each serving should consist of a piece of fish topped with a slice of the crust.

PUREEING FISH

Fish lends itself so well to puréeing that many special preparations based on fish purée exist, including *mousselines*, *quenelles*, *mousses*, *pâtés* and *terrines*. The basis of them all is puréed fish of a type with plenty of flavor. Classic choices are pike, whiting and sole. Salmon is valued for its color, particularly in terrines that are to be sliced; the puréed salmon mixture is usually placed in alternate layers with fish purées or strips of fish fillet of contrasting color.

The fish may be raw or cooked, depending on the recipe; it is most easily puréed in a food processor, though moist mixtures with some liquid can also be puréed in a blender. A drum sieve or food mill give the finest texture. Here, whiting fillets are puréed in a food processor and drum sieve.

1 Remove all skin and bones from the fish. Cut it in small fillets or medium-sized pieces and put them in a food processor.

2 Work the fish in the food processor, a little at a time, until smooth, scraping down the sides of the bowl as necessary. If you like, season the fish with salt and pepper. **Note** If overworked, raw fish will be tough when cooked. To avoid this, use the pulse button on the processor.

3 For the finest texture, after processing the fish purée, work it through a food mill or a drum sieve (p.506) to remove tiny bones, pieces of skin and fiber.

4 From time to time, use a flexible scraper to remove the puréed fish as it accumulates underneath the drum sieve or food mill, and transfer it to a mixing bowl.

MAKING MOUSSELINE

A *mousseline* consists of puréed raw fish, bound with egg whites and enriched with cream. The balance of ingredients is delicate: not enough fish means the *mousseline* will be tasteless; too much makes it heavy. Too much egg white gives a solid consistency; too little – or too much cream – makes the *mousseline* fall apart during cooking. Standard proportions are ½ lb/250 g raw fish to 1 egg white and ½ cup/125 ml heavy cream. Salt, white pepper and a grating of nutmeg are usually the only seasonings. *Mousselines* will not hold together if made with fish that has been incorrectly frozen.

Most commonly, *mousseline* mixture is molded in a ramekin or dariole mold (p.508). It can also be used to make *quenelles* (p.146), to fill seafood sausages and to layer fish terrines, though it will forfeit its lightness. A *mousseline* is usually served hot with a delicate sauce. If bones from the fish are available to make stock, velouté sauce variations (p.55), or a butter sauce based on fish glaze are appropriate accompaniments. Other popular choices include *sauce Nantua* (p.147) or a tomato *coulis*.

Mousselines can also be made with raw shellfish, veal or chicken. Here, whiting fillets are shown.

1 Work the puréed fish in a food processor or set it in a bowl, gradually beating in the egg whites. Work the mixture until smooth and firm. Chilling the mixture helps stiffen it. Beat in salt and white pepper; the salt also helps stiffen the mixture by increasing the coagulation of the egg whites.

2 RIGHT Set the mixture in a bowl over a larger bowl of crushed ice and gradually beat in the cream, a tablespoon at a time.

3 When all the cream has been worked in, taste the *mousseline* for seasoning adding more salt, pepper or nutmeg as necessary.

Note Cream can be combined with the purée in a food processor but it must be done with care as the *mousseline* will separate if overworked.

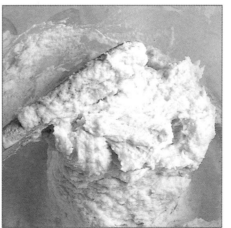

4 The mixture is the right consistency when thick and firm enough to hold a shape. Chill it over a bowl of ice or in the refrigerator for 15-30 minutes. If it seems too soft, chill the mixture for longer (up to an hour).

5 Fill individual buttered molds with the mixture. Put the molds in a water bath covered with parchment paper and bring the water to a boil. Transfer to a 350°F/175°C oven and bake until a skewer inserted in the center is hot to the touch, 20-30 minutes.

Hot fish mousses

Hot mousses made from raw fish are a much bigger family than *mousselines* since any light fish mixture qualifies as a mousse and almost any well-flavored fish can be used to make it. Often a mousse is nothing more than a *mousseline* mixture enriched with egg yolks. Sometimes it is a version of *quenelles* (p.146), bound with *choux* pastry, or held together with a thick white sauce. As the fish can easily be overwhelmed, careful seasoning with salt, pepper and mild spices, for example nutmeg, is important to highlight flavor. Hot fish mousses are usually molded and cooked in a water bath (p.510), then unmolded for serving with a sauce. *Sauce Nantua* (p.147) is a popular accompaniment.

Cold fish mousses

Cold mousses are made with cooked fish lightened with whipped cream rather than eggs. The flavor is highlighted by mixing cooked fish with béchamel, velouté or mayonnaise. Because the mousse is cold, seasoning must be brisk, with plenty of pepper, nutmeg, cayenne or capers to accent the flavor of the fish itself. Coarse-fleshed tasty fish like cod or grouper work well in a mousse but salmon, which has a mild flavor is also popular. Smoked fish, including the modest haddock, mackerel and kippered herring, are possibly best of all, often combined for color with chopped hard-boiled egg, olive or green or red pepper. The fish may be coarsely or finely flaked (removing bones and skin) to add texture, or puréed for smoothness. Mayonnaise or fish velouté is usually added, as well as whipped cream. Tomato paste and curry powder are favorite flavorings. Some fish mousses are deliberately left soft for serving with a spoon, but often the mixture is set with gelatin in individual ramekins or, best of all, molded in the shape of a swimming fish. A tart, refreshing sauce such as fresh tomato *coulis* or Mexican sauce (p.65) with a crisp cucumber salad are excellent accompaniments.

Fish pâtés, *rillettes* and terrines

The distinction between pâtés and terrines of fish is even more blurred than it is for meat (see Charcuterie, p.242). Unlike a traditional meat pâté, a fish pâté is rarely baked in pastry. Fish pâté is a wide term, covering rich mixtures that have been puréed until smooth, as well as rougher pâtés, piquant with horseradish or chili, or tart with lemon or vinegar. In general, a pâté is made with cooked fish and is soft and easy to spread, whereas a terrine is made from raw fish mixtures and is baked in a mold until firm enough to be sliced. A terrine can be served hot or cold, whereas a pâté is always cold.

Fish pâtés are rich enough to need little accompaniment apart from shredded lettuce, a wedge of lemon and perhaps some black olives, as well as toast or crusty bread.

Fish *rillettes* are becoming increasingly popular on restaurant menus. They are a type of pâté, based on rich-fleshed fish such as salmon or mackerel. The fish is cooked, flaked and beaten with softened butter to the coarse consistency that is characteristic of traditional pork *rillettes* (p.243). Fish *rillettes* often include a portion of smoked fish like eel or trout, and should be seasoned with plenty of lemon and black pepper.

Terrines closely resemble fish mousses, but whether hot or cold, they must be firm enough to cut. Slices provide an opportunity for displaying multi-colored layers, for example salmon and sea bass, or two white fish mixtures, one of them flavored with green herbs or spinach. A terrine may be dotted with bright ingredients like red or green bell peppers, or layered with fish strips. The mold itself may be lined with fish fillets, but fish that is likely to produce liquid during cooking should be avoided as too much moisture will cause the terrine to fall apart.

For serving, a generous slice of terrine is set on the plate against a contrasting background of sauce. For hot terrines, the choice is the same as for *mousselines*; a creamy white butter sauce enlivened with fresh chives is also popular. Fresh tomato *coulis* (p.65) and thin purées of herbs and cream go nicely with a cold terrine. An accompaniment of mayonnaise, plain or flavored, passed separately, is another possibility.

MAKING FISH PAUPIETTES

One of the finest and most delicate preparations for fish is a *paupiette*, a package made by wrapping a thin fish fillet or escalope around a *mousseline* or *quenelle* stuffing. The fish may simply be filled, folded and poached plain (p.119), or it may be filled, folded and poached wrapped in parchment paper to form a neat cylinder, which when sliced displays a spiral of fish and filling. With either method, the *paupiette* is served hot with a rich butter or velouté sauce (p.55). Here, salmon fillets are shown.

1 Cut thick fillets into escalopes (p.117), or cut thin ones horizontally almost in half to butterfly them. Put one fillet on a piece of parchment paper and spread it lengthwise with 1-2 tablespoons of filling. Roll the fillet into a cylinder with the aid of the paper. Wrap the cylinder tightly in the paper and twist the ends.

2 Heat a shallow pan of water until simmering. Add the *paupiettes* and poach them until firm to the touch, 12-15 minutes. (If making a large number of *paupiettes*, poach them in batches.)

3 Leave the *paupiettes* to cool slightly, then remove the paper and cut them in slices for serving.

Marinating fish for cooking

Fish is marinated before cooking primarily to enrich its flavor, as in the Japanese soy-based preparation, *teriyaki*, or in pungent mixtures of garlic, herbs and olive oil. A marinade with oil will help the fish remain moist during broiling or barbecuing, while a marinade containing an acid ingredient such as wine or citrus juice may be used to tenderize meatier fish such as tuna or shark. However, most fish are naturally tender when cooked, so marinating is of limited use and should be done for only a few hours if the fresh flavor of the fish is to be retained. If marinating mild fish, use lightly flavored oils and subtle herbs – the flavor of delicate fish can be overwhelmed by a strong marinade.

Whole fish (here, bream) is scored, steeped in white wine, oil and raw onion rings and left to marinate for 2-3 hours.

Raw fish dishes

Marinated raw fish is a preparation in its own right. The acid in a marinade "cooks" fish by acting on the albumen so the flesh is whitened and its texture stiffened while retaining a fresh clean flavor. Lemon or lime juice are prime marinade ingredients, sometimes replaced by fruit vinegar. A few tablespoons of olive or vegetable oil in the marinade keep the fish moist, while seasonings range from chopped shallot, scallions and fresh coriander leaf to peppercorns, cumin, cayenne, chili peppers and hot pepper sauce.

For all raw fish dishes, freshness of both the fish and the marinade is vital. Prime choices for marinating are full-flavored firm fish like salmon or sea bass, laid in wafer-thin slices on a plate, tightly covered and left for only 15 to 30 minutes before serving. In Latin American *seviche*, thin strips of fish are marinated in lime or lemon juice with strips of vegetables such as red onion, chili and bell peppers; often the vegetables are added to *seviche* after marinating to preserve their fresh crunch and bright color. *Seviche* may be marinated as long as 24 hours, though draining the marinade from the fish after six hours gives a firmer texture. In Scandinavian countries raw salmon is marinated with coarse salt and dill to make *gravad lax* (p.488), which is served as an appetizer with thin slices of bread and mustard sauce. Two Japanese raw fish dishes recently adopted by Westerners are *sushi* and *sashimi* (p.134).

Fish eaten raw must be fresh and come from an impeccable source, since freshwater varieties and some anadromous fish, which spend part of their lives in fresh water, may harbor parasites that cause disease. Always refrigerate raw fish preparations until just before serving.

MAKING RAW FISH SALAD

Salmon fillets (shown here) are particularly suitable for making raw fish salads, but firm fish such as sea bass may be substituted.

Cut slices as thinly as possible from a raw fish fillet. Spread the slices on a plate in a single thin layer. Sprinkle 1-2 tbsp olive oil and a few drops of lemon juice on to each serving, together with a little salt, pepper and chopped fresh herbs such as tarragon, chervil or chives. Leave to marinate for 15-30 minutes before serving. Serve chilled.

Cooked fish salads

A whole cold poached or steamed fish needs no more than mayonnaise or a herb vinaigrette to accent its flavor. Smaller pieces of baked or broiled fish are good topped with a piquant vinaigrette and left to marinate for half an hour. If the cooked fish is flaked or cut in strips, it may be mixed with shellfish like mussels, clams or shrimp, with vegetables of contrasting texture such as celery, fennel, or very mild onion, plus perhaps a Mediterranean-style addition of black olives or capers. One version, the famous *salade Niçoise*, combines green beans, tomatoes, potatoes and tuna with black olives in a vinaigrette dressing. Such dishes are at their best when served at room temperature. Further north, fish salads tend to be rich with mayonnaise or tart with vinegar. Herring comes into its own in half a dozen of the most popular salads of all. Central Europe is the home of *gefiltefish*, a Jewish preparation of puréed whitefish or pike mixed with egg, matzoh meal or breadcrumbs and seasonings, molded into balls or ovals, poached in broth and served cold with horseradish. It is most commonly served at Passover.

Other cooking methods for fish

Some cooking methods suit only certain fish. Tuna, for instance, is so meaty it can be treated like veal and braised with red wine and a *mirepoix* of vegetables (p.263). Monkfish, eel and other firm fish are good stewed with white wine, onions, tomato or artichoke.

Stir-frying is another method best suited to firm fish: fragile types crumble too quickly in the fierce heat. As always with stir-frying, Asian seasonings, such as fresh ginger, soy and oyster sauce come to mind; these are best with fish like grouper and shark. The fish should be cut in small, even pieces and cooked for only a short time with vegetables such as Chinese mushrooms, broccoli sprigs, snow peas, asparagus, bamboo shoots or a mixture of vegetables cut in julienne strips.

Fish is delicious deep-fried as croquettes as well as being outstanding in soups, whether in pieces, as in a hearty soup, or puréed, as in a bisque. It also does well in microwave ovens. Modern chefs sometimes make fish *pot-au-feu*: basically a stew in which a variety of fish are poached with vegetables in the manner of a beef *pot-au-feu*.

Currently popular in the United States is Cajun "blackened" fish, made by coating firm fish fillets with ground hot spices, then cooking them in a heavy frying pan over high heat, so the surface is literally blackened and the juices are sealed inside.

Presenting fish

Very often the presentation of fish is an integral part of the cooking method. A broiled or baked whole fish, for example, slashed along the sides with its skin toasted a crinkly brown, can look perfect on its own or adorned simply with wedges of lemon and sprigs of watercress. Vegetables such as tomatoes and bell peppers, broiled or baked with the fish, add extra color. For small whole fish served individually, the head should be left on and the tail and fins trimmed (p.111). Once again, little garnish is needed other than some lemon wedges and sprigs of greenery. Traditionally, the fish is set on the plate with its head facing left, so that the flesh is easy to remove for a right-handed person.

Whether hot or cold, a large poached fish should be served on the bone, trimmed and with the skin removed (p.118). Classically, hot fish is displayed on a white napkin on a silver platter, but nowadays, greens of some kind often replace the napkin. The sauce should be served separately so the fish is displayed in all its glory. Presentation of cold poached fish can be as elaborate as a coating of aspic with decorations of stuffed eggs, tomato baskets and cucumber boats.

Fillets and pieces of fish pose a greater presentation problem. Color should be exploited, for example the pink flesh of salmon or trout. Fish with brilliant skins like red snapper, red mullet or bluefish may be cooked with the skin on and presented skin side up. Fillets can be cut and folded in a variety of shapes, as can whole boned fish (p.113). **Note** Folding or cutting raw fish into evenly sized pieces makes a neat presentation as well as uniform cooking time.

A sauce is still the classic way to enliven a plain piece of fish. A complete coating is now out of fashion, the current style being to place the fish on top of a sauce so that the sauce serves as background. For poached and steamed fish, a colorful vegetable julienne or small vegetables turned in olive shapes (p.260), have replaced the ubiquitous white steamed potatoes. Pastry cases, *fleuron* decorations (p.378) of puff pastry and toppings of sliced truffle or olive can all contribute to a striking display.

The classic decoration for a fish platter includes semi-circles of sliced lemon, or a row of shrimp round the edge. Nowadays, the border is more likely to be plain, with fronds of chervil, chives or dill draped over the fish itself.

DRIED, SALTED & SMOKED FISH

Traditional ways of preserving fish have survived simply because they produce such good flavor. Most methods of preserving involve salt, the quality of which is crucial to the taste of the cure. A moderate cure is best so that the fish displays its characteristic slightly resinous taste, without being unpalatably dry.

Simplest is a dry-salt cure in which the fish, typically cod, is sprinkled with salt and then air-dried. For centuries, salt cod was less expensive than any form of meat except bacon, and therefore was an important part of many national cuisines. Before cooking, salt cod must be soaked in several changes of cold water for from six hours up to two days. Salt cod, known as *morue* in France and *bacalhau* in Portugal, is particularly successful in broth soups and stews with vegetables that need salt, such as potatoes or turnips. It can also be dipped in batter and deep-fried, or puréed with mashed potato, garlic and olive oil as in Provençal *brandade*.

Oily fish like herring also take well to a dry-salt cure, as of course does the anchovy (p.147), which flavors dishes as diverse as pizza, *Bagna cauda* (p.101) and Caesar salad. The saltiness of anchovies can be reduced by soaking them in milk or rinsing with water before use.

Fish that is salted in brine (often called pickled) is less intensely flavored, and is usually eaten straight from the pickle. Dutch *maatje* or "maiden" herrings are preserved in very light brine and traditionally eaten in spring with chopped onion and the first green beans. Herring fillets cured in salt and vinegar are called rollmops if rolled round a sweet pickle, and Bismarck or Baltic herring without the pickle. Soused herring is rolled, baked in vinegar and spices and served cold. In the United States, pickled herrings are preserved in vinegar with spices and bay leaf.

Stockfish is the name given to fish, usually cod or hake, that is dried by the oldest method of preserving – sun-drying. Stockfish requires long soaking and simmering to be edible and features in simple dishes such as a Dutch preparation of potatoes, rice, onions and mustard, *stokvis*. In Norway, stockfish is sometimes soaked in lye to make *lutefisk*, traditional at Christmas with yellow peas and boiled potatoes; *klippfish* is another variation that combines drying and salting. Scandinavian *gravad lax* (p.488) is made with dry-salt cured salmon.

Salmon is usually prepared by cold-smoking, a specialized process, varying from country to country, in which the fish undergoes salting and drying in smoke at 70-90°F/20-30°C for two to twenty days. European (especially Scottish) smoked salmon is regarded as best. In the United States, smoked salmon is sometimes called Nova Scotia salmon – a reference to the fact that most American smoked salmon used to come from there. Other cold-smoked fish include eel and sturgeon, eel being a favorite in northern Europe. Smoked salmon is different from American lox (usually served with bagels and cream cheese) since lox is unsmoked, salted salmon.

Hot-smoking is a quicker process that cooks as well as flavors fish, but does not preserve it for very long. On the west coast of America, hot smoked or kippered salmon is particularly popular. The name kipper, however, is usually associated with herring – an ordinary (herring) kipper is split, dipped in brine, dried and cold-smoked; a buckling is salted and hot-smoked, ready to eat; a bloater is a whole ungutted herring that has been salted and so lightly smoked that it keeps only a day or two. Other fish that are commonly smoked include trout, lake whitefish, Pacific black cod or sablefish, and flounder (a Norwegian specialty). Scotland produces a well-known smoked haddock called Finnan haddock.

Many smoked fish are sold ready to eat and need only a sprinkling of lemon, perhaps accompanied by buttered whole wheat bread and horseradish cream sauce. Freshly ground pepper is sufficient for smoked salmon, although capers, sliced onion and chopped hard-boiled egg often feature as well. Some smoked fish, such as kippered herring and smoked haddock, require further cooking, usually in water or milk. They may be eaten plain, flaked for a salad, or as the basis of a hot soufflé, a cold pâté or a fish mousse (p.124). For home smoking and salting, see pp.487-88.

SMALL FLATFISH
SOLE, FLOUNDER, PLAICE

When born, a flatfish swims upright like any other fish. However, early in life, it turns sideways and one eye moves to the other side, giving the fish a lopsided grimace. Depending on the species, the eye may move left or right, giving left- and right-faced fish.

To the fishmonger, a small flatfish is flounder or sole. (In the United States, winter flounder is often sold as lemon sole but should not be confused with European lemon sole.) Flatfish market names vary greatly from region to region. In this section we refer to flatfish by the most common name for their species, but it is important to bear in mind that around fishing ports, there are often local kinds of flatfish with names peculiar to the area. As one expert has declared, "whether you call it flounder or sole depends on your location, prejudices and habit". The truth is that few small flatfish are so distinctive as to be instantly recognizable. Plaice has large red spots, sand sole has brown freckles and yellowtail, as its name implies, has a yellow tail. All other flatfish are shades of gray, beige and brown.

It is a single species, the famous Dover sole, that gives an aura of repute to the name "sole". True Dover sole is widely found in European waters, but is not native to the waters around the coast of the United States. Its name is derived from a time when much of the catch was landed at Dover, rather than any preference of the fish for the English Channel. Complicating the matter is an eastern Pacific flounder that appears in the market place as Dover sole, and another Pacific flounder that is sold in the western United States as "English" sole. European lemon sole is not a true sole, but it bears a close resemblance to it.

With regard to flavor, winter flounder, gray sole (also called witch flounder, and in Britain, Torbay sole) and perhaps the Pacific petrale sole rank after Dover sole. All have fragrant, fine-textured flesh and make excellent fillets. European varieties of flounder are quite different from American flounder and inferior in taste. Dab, identifiable by its rough skin, also tastes good, while North American fluke, or summer flounder, has soft, bland flesh. Plaice is not found in American waters, but it is the most common flatfish eaten in Europe, where it is used as a substitute for sole and in a great variety of dishes in its own right. Freshness is vital for all flatfish; some varieties, such as Pacific sand-dab, need to get to the market within three or four days, though under ideal conditions superior fish like Dover or petrale sole can be stored for up to two weeks. The flavor of Dover sole is said to improve one or two days after it has been caught.

Many of these flatfish weigh a mere ¾-1lb/375-500 g, ideal as an individual serving on the bone; they can be pan-fried whole or simply scored and baked in the oven with parsley, a little butter and some white wine. Larger ones are usually filleted and rarely need cutting in smaller pieces. Fillets are usually folded into decorative shapes for cooking, for example a fan, knot or roll. Depending on size, two or three fillets make an average serving. A few species, notably the Dover sole, can be skinned by stripping the skin from the whole fish in one piece; others are skinned after the fillets have been cut from the bone. Special preparations include French *sole à la Colbert*, in which the backbone of the

fish is removed and the whole fish is then coated with bread-crumbs, deep-fried and served with seasoned butter. The finest sole or flounder is everything a cook could desire: firm-fleshed, nutty and sweet. Dover sole has inspired hundreds of classic French recipes, and is most often poached and served with a velouté or butter sauce. Typical are *sole Walewska* with lobster, truffles and cheese sauce, *sole bonne femme* with white wine, mushrooms and cream, or *sole Véronique* with white wine, cream and a garnish of white grapes. *Sole meunière*, which is floured and sautéed in butter, is universally appreciated. Sole or flounder is outstanding broiled, steamed or baked in a paper case (p.121) and served with vegetables and a butter sauce. It is also one of the best types of fish to use for fish terrines (p.124).

Any good quality flatfish can be substituted for sole. Simple preparations are wisest: for example, fillets sautéed and served with a few mushrooms or shrimp, fillets steamed and topped with a sprinkling of herbs and the finest olive oil or a whole fish broiled and served on the bone with a simple garnish of lemon wedges. Soft varieties are best broiled or baked so they do not break up. For sautéing they should be left on the bone, and for stuffing and baking they should be partially boned. Indeed, some cooks prefer all flatfish to be left on the bone, declaring that this is the only way to retain flavor and juices. In Britain, plaice is coated in batter and deep-fried for a traditional meal of fish and chips. Dried and salted lemon sole is regarded as a delicacy in Belgium. Scandinavians ingeniously add flavor by lightly brining and smoking whole flatfish, particularly plaice, to make *bakskuld*, which is then fried in butter.

To purée Dover sole for *mousselines* and *quenelles* would be a waste, but other firm flatfish such as the North American winter flounder and European sand sole are excellent choices. All but the most delicate flatfish can be stuffed and rolled for *paupiettes* (p.124). Firmer varieties may be cut in strips and tossed in flour or dipped in batter and deep-fried for *goujonettes*. The term *goujonette* comes from the French word *goujon* meaning gudgeon (a tiny freshwater fish). *Goujonettes* are not made with gudgeon but are so named because the strips of sole should be cut into fine strips resembling the size and shape of a gudgeon.

Plaice

European sole

Dover sole

Dab

SMALL FLATFISH

Portion *On bone with head:* ¾-1 lb/ 375-500 g. *Without head:* ½-¾ lb/ 250-375 g. *Fillets:* 6 oz/175 g.
Nutritive value per 3½ oz/100 g (raw). *Sole:* 88 calories; 18 g protein; 1 g fat; no carbohydrates; 80 mg sodium; 43 mg cholesterol. *Flounder:* 91 calories; 19 g protein; 1 g fat; no carbohydrates; 81 mg sodium; 48 mg cholesterol. *Plaice:* 91 calories; 18 g protein; 2.2 g fat; no carbohydrates; 120 mg sodium; no cholesterol.
Cooking methods *Whole:* bake at 350°F/175°C, 10-15 minutes; broil 3-5 minutes each side; deep-fry 4-5 minutes; sauté 3-5 minutes each side; poach 10-15 minutes; steam 10-15 minutes. *Fillets:* bake uncovered, or in parchment paper or aluminum foil at 350°F/175°C, 8-10 minutes; broil 4-6 minutes, without turning if thin; poach 8-10 minutes; sauté 2-3 minutes each side; steam 8-12 minutes. *Strips:* deep-fry 2-3 minutes; poach 3-5 minutes; sauté 2-3 minutes; steam 3-5 minutes; stir-fry 1-2 minutes.
Problems Lose flavor if stored; overcook easily.
Fresh forms Whole, fillets.
Processed forms Frozen.
Storage *Whole:* refrigerate 1-2 days. *Fillets:* refrigerate 1 day.
Typical dishes *Sole:* fillets baked in cheese sauce (Netherlands); poached in Marsala (Italy); poached in champagne with velouté sauce (France); *lenguado a la vasca* (baked with sliced potatoes in a mushroom, red pepper and tomato sauce, Spain); *paistettue kala* (fried in rye breadcrumbs, Finland); baked with shrimp and coriander (USA); fillets with piquant tomato sauce and capers (Italy); broiled Dover sole with lemon butter (UK); *florentine* (poached, with spinach and cheese sauce, France); *portugaise* (with white wine, tomatoes and bell peppers, France). *Flounder:* broiled, stuffed with crab (USA); baked with parsley and mustard sauce (UK); rolled, stuffed with bacon, onion and mushroom and poached in wine (Germany). *Plaice: rodspaette surprise* (fried, stuffed with creamed spinach, asparagus and shrimp, Denmark); fillets with celery root and herb sauce (France); fried, with a purée of potato and sorrel (Belgium); with smoked bacon (Germany); with cranberry sauce (Denmark); stuffed with breadcrumbs, parsley, shrimps, egg and nutmeg (USSR).

Fillets of sole with mushrooms and tomatoes

Traditionally in France poached fish is served in a sauce garnished with a border of piped *duchesse* potatoes. Lemon sole or flounder can be used in this recipe but Dover sole has the best flavor.

Serves 6 as an appetizer, 4 as a main course

Duchesse potatoes (p.296) made with 1½ lb/750 g potatoes, 3 tbsp/45 g butter, 3 egg yolks, salt, pepper and nutmeg	½ lb/250 g mushrooms, thinly sliced	kneaded butter (p.59) made with 3 tbsp/20 g flour and 3 tbsp/45 g butter
1½ lb/750g Dover sole, lemon sole, or firm flounder fillets	2 tomatoes, peeled, seeded and chopped (p.280)	1 tbsp chopped parsley
	salt and white pepper	**For the liaison**
1 tbsp butter	1 cup/250 ml fish stock (p.44)	2 egg yolks
2 shallots, finely chopped	½ cup/125 ml white wine	¼ cup/60 ml *crème fraîche* (p.70) or heavy cream
		Pastry bag and medium star tube

1 Make the *duchesse* potatoes and using a medium star tube (p.408), pipe them in a ring bordering a heatproof serving dish.
2 Rinse, dry and flatten the fish fillets. Fold them in fans, tuck in the ends, or roll them. Spread the butter in a shallow flameproof dish and add the shallots, mushrooms, tomatoes, salt and pepper. Lay the fish on top and pour over the stock and white wine.
3 Cover with buttered aluminum foil and poach on top of the stove until the fish just flakes easily, 8-12 minutes. Transfer it to drain on paper towels.
4 If necessary, boil the cooking liquid and vegetables until reduced to 1½ cups/375 ml. Make the kneaded butter. Whisk the butter into the boiling liquid, piece by piece, until it thickens enough to coat a spoon lightly. Taste the sauce and simmer it for 1 minute.
5 Whisk the egg yolks and the cream in a small bowl until mixed. Whisk in a little of the sauce and stir this liaison back into the hot sauce. Bring the sauce just back to a boil, whisking constantly. Take from the heat, stir in the parsley and taste again.
6 Heat the broiler. Arrange the drained fish fillets within the ring of potatoes on the serving dish. Coat the fish with sauce and broil until the fish and the potatoes are brown, 3-5 minutes.

LARGE FLATFISH
TURBOT, BRILL, HALIBUT, JOHN DORY

Large flatfish are few but famous. Top of the gastronomic list is turbot, a gustatory rival to Dover sole and considered by some to be the finest fish of all. The flavor is succulent, the flesh is white and firm and when cooked, it is tender and moist. Smaller, or "chicken" turbot weighing 2-3 lb/1-1.4 kg are preferred for their serving convenience, but the larger ones, which can weigh as much as 10 lb/4.5 kg, have a finer texture and taste. Their angular, almost square, shape is characteristic, and special pans exist for poaching them. Turbot is native to the North Atlantic, though in North America, Greenland halibut and arrowtooth flounder are sometimes marketed as turbot.

Brill is limited to European waters. It can reach 15 lb/7 kg in size, but the commonest size is 2-4 lb/1-1.8 kg. The flesh is similar to turbot, but slightly softer. The two fish can be distinguished by the turbot's warty skin and more angular shape, whereas the skin of brill has fine scales and the shape is oval.

Halibut is the largest of all flatfish, with specimens as large as 500 lb/230 kg and as long as 3 yd/2½ m, though the average is a tenth that size. It has olive green skin and firm white flesh, which may be somewhat drier than that of turbot, with a milder flavor. Species include the fine Atlantic halibut found in the North Atlantic from New York around to Scotland, and the equally tasty northern Pacific halibut. Both the Greenland halibut, which inhabits semi-Arctic waters on both sides of the North Pole, and the smaller California halibut are inferior, tending to be soft, with very little flavor.

John Dory is not strictly speaking a flatfish because it swims upright, but the body is so compressed that from the cook's viewpoint it should be considered as one. It has a nutty, sweet flavor with flaky meat. Found on both sides of the North Atlantic and the Mediterranean, John Dory is a picturesque fish, with huge spiny fins, a big head, and a big black "thumb" spot behind the eyes; this accounts for its French name of *St. Pierre* – St. Peter the fisherman is said to have grasped the fish between finger and thumb when searching for a silver piece to pay his tribute tax.

John Dory and smaller examples of large flatfish can be gutted and trimmed to poach whole, with the skin left on to add richness. All are high in gelatin, with prominent bones and so make excellent fish stock. Moist cooking particularly suits their succulent flesh, while the whole fish makes a spectacular presentation served with hollandaise or white butter sauce.

Larger turbot, halibut and brill are usually cut into thick steaks that are deliciously moist when steamed, sautéed or poached. Large halibut are generally cut into four fillets (p.115) that are sometimes called loins. A 3-5 lb/1.4-2.3 kg rectangular loin section is called a fletch. John Dory and larger species of flatfish may be filleted to cook like steaks.

More elaborate dishes include baking the fish in a paper case (p.121) with mushrooms, or a vegetable julienne, or poaching them as *paupiettes* with a *mousseline* stuffing. Turbot and brill are rarely puréed since their firm creamy texture would be lost, but halibut makes excellent *mousselines*.

John Dory

Turbot

Brill

Halibut

USEFUL INFORMATION

Portion *On bone with head:* 1 lb/ 500 g. *On bone without head:* ¾ lb/ 375 g. *Steaks and fillets:* 6 oz/175 g.
Nutritive value per 3½ oz/100 g (raw). *Turbot:* 95 calories; 16 g protein; 3 g fat; no carbohydrates; 150 mg sodium. *Brill:* 91 calories; 19 g protein; 1 g fat; no carbohydrates; 81 mg sodium; 48 mg cholesterol. *Halibut:* 110 calories; 21 g protein; 2 g fat; no carbohydrates; 34 mg sodium; 32 mg cholesterol. *John Dory:* 94 calories; 19 g protein; 2 g fat; no carbohydrates; 75 mg sodium; 42 mg cholesterol.
Cooking methods *Whole:* bake at 350°F/175°C; poach; time depends on thickness (p.117). *Steaks or fillets:* bake uncovered, in parchment paper or aluminum foil at 350°F/175°C, 15-25 minutes; broil 4-6 minutes each side; poach 12-18 minutes; sauté 3-5 minutes each side; steam 12-18 minutes.
Problems Large head and bones give low yield of edible flesh.
Fresh forms Whole, center cut, steaks, fillets.
Processed forms *All:* frozen. *Halibut:* dried, smoked, liver oil.

Storage: *Whole:* refrigerate 2-3 days. *Steaks or fillets:* refrigerate 2 days.
Typical dishes *Turbot: à l'Andalouse* (baked with onion, tomato, mushrooms and peppers, France); with lobster sauce (UK); poached with horseradish sauce (UK); roasted on a bed of vegetables (France); stuffed with fish mousse, in cream sauce (France); with hollandaise sauce (Netherlands). *Brill:* fillets with fresh saffron pasta and spinach (France); pan-fried with chanterelles (Sweden); with vermouth (UK). *Halibut:* fried steaks (Scandinavia); steamed fillets with fresh coriander and white wine (USA); baked with greens and clams (Spain); baked with vegetables (Germany); soup (Iceland). *John Dory: St. Pierre à la Parmentier* (baked with potatoes, France); sautéed fillets in Marsala (Italy); broiled with pecan butter (USA); with herbs, cider and cream (UK); with cheese sauce (Netherlands); *matelote de petits Saint-Pierres* (stewed in *court bouillon* with wine, shallots and garlic, France).

Panaché of steamed fish with dill butter sauce

A *panaché*, or selection, of contrasting fish is an ideal way of combining a variety of fish in one dish. Choose fish with skins of different colors and steam them skin upwards. Arrange them on individual plates to make an eye-catching presentation.

Serves 4

1 qt/1 L *court bouillon* (p.44)	10 oz/300 g fillet of bluefish, pompano or whiting	white butter sauce (p.62) made with 3 tbsp/45 ml white wine vinegar, 3 tbsp/45 ml dry white wine, 2 finely chopped shallots, 1 cup/250 g cold butter, salt and pepper
10 oz/300 g fillet of red snapper or mullet	bunch fresh dill	
10 oz/300 g fillet of turbot, halibut, brill or John Dory	salt and pepper	

1 Make a *court bouillon* in the bottom of a steamer. Trim and wash the fish fillets and cut each type in four. Strip the dill leaves and reserve the stems. Coarsely chop two tablespoons of leaves and reserve four sprigs for decoration.
2 Lay the fillets in the top of the steamer, sprinkle them with salt and pepper and cover. Add the dill stems to the boiling *court bouillon* and set the steamer with the fish on top. Steam it for 8-12 minutes, depending on the thickness of the fillets. If one fish cooks more quickly than the others, remove it.
3 Make the butter sauce, whisk in the chopped dill and taste. Keep it warm on a rack over a pan of hot water.
4 When the fish is cooked, spoon the sauce on to four warmed serving plates and arrange the fish upwards in a fan, on top. Alternatively, spoon the dill sauce over the fish and decorate with sprigs of dill. Serve at once.

RAY & SKATE

Ray and skate are among the most beautiful of fish. With their sail-like wings and vast size (manta, the largest, can weigh two tons) they resemble a flying saucer more than a fish, and can leap up to 6 ft/2 m out of the water. They are found almost worldwide.

Ray has a cartilaginous rather than bony skeleton, quite different from that of other fish. The wings, the part that is eaten, are made of semi-transparent bars of cartilage surrounded by long narrow strips of close-textured gelatinous flesh. The skin is thick; the underside has a gray or white tinge and the skin on top ranges from brown to gray and black, with mottled markings. The taste is said to resemble that of crabmeat or scallops, perhaps because of the shellfish diet preferred by ray and skate.

As so often with fish, the use of the names ray and skate is confusing: skate is in fact a species of ray. In the United States all edible ray are called skate, but in Britain the name is limited to larger species, and smaller varieties are still referred to as ray. The thornback and starry ray are the most commercially significant species. Others include flapper, flathead, longnose and smooth; their names give clues to their appearance.

The wings of a ray or skate are sold whole or in pieces, depending on size. The skin should be scrubbed with water and salt or vinegar to remove any slime, or cut away if the fish is to be sautéed. If there is any ammoniac smell, the meat should be soaked in water. To counteract a possibly glutinous texture, the meat is often poached in a vinegar *court bouillon*. After poaching, the skin can easily be peeled away and the flesh lifted from the cartilage. Black butter (p.98) is the classic finish. Ray or skate can also be floured to sauté in butter or olive oil. The British serve skate fricasséed with cream and wine. Unlike most fresh fish, the taste and texture of ray or skate improves with age. They will keep for up to three days if stored in a refrigerator.

USEFUL INFORMATION

Portion *On bone without head:* ¾-1 lb/375-500 g.

Nutritive value per 3½ oz/100 g (raw). 106 calories; 22 g protein; 2 g fat; no carbohydrates; 90 mg sodium; 45 mg cholesterol.

Storage Refrigerate 1-3 days.

Cooking methods Bake at 350°F/175°C, 15-25 minutes; poach 12-18 minutes; sauté 4-6 minutes on each side.

Problems Texture glutinous if undercooked.

Fresh forms Skinned or unskinned wings.

Processed forms Frozen; smoked.

Typical dishes *Raie en salade, sauce raifort* (cold poached ray with horseradish mayonnaise, France); pickled skate (Denmark); *raie au cidre et aux pommes* (with cider and apples, France); baked with chutney in a pastry case (UK); baked with tomatoes, saffron, garlic, onions and almonds (Spain); sautéed with capers and served with shrimp sauce (UK); *raie à la gelée* (in aspic made with fish stock and white wine, France).

Thornback ray

CAVIAR & OTHER ROES

Caviar consists of the eggs of fish, salted or pickled to preserve and flavor them. It is most commonly made with the roe, or eggs, of the sturgeon. Sturgeon is native to the northern hemisphere and, in principle, caviar can be produced wherever there are appropriate species. Until recently, caviar production was an Iranian and Russian monopoly based around the Caspian Sea and its river systems. However, a promising start has now been made in caviar production in the American northwest and in China. Making caviar is a slow process, since a female must be 15-20 years old before her roe can be converted into caviar. Furthermore, there is wide variation in roe quality from fish to fish and from species to species.

Caviar usually carries the description "malossol", which is simply Russian for "lightly salted", along with an indication of the type of sturgeon from which it comes. The largest eggs, gray in color, come from the beluga; darker and smaller, but of fine flavor, are those of the sevruga sturgeon, the most common caviar type. Sterlet, the "gold" caviar of the Czars, is very rare and should not be confused with the golden-brown *osietr* caviar. The cheaper but tasty *pausnaya*, or pressed caviar, comes from eggs too small or damaged to be packed whole-grain; it can be kept fresh longer than the whole-grain, unpasteurized caviars.

Part of the reason whole-grain caviar is so expensive is that it requires fast and extremely careful processing; once vacuum-sealed in a container, it will last at best six months, assuming tightly controlled temperature conditions. Shelf-life can be greatly extended by pasteurizing, but the taste is inferior. (Pasteurized caviar can be identified by the absence of a true vacuum seal on the container.) Fresh caviar should be kept refrigerated; once opened, it should be consumed within two to three days. Vacuum-packed pasteurized caviar may be kept unopened in a cool, dry place for up to six months, or refrigerated for up to one week after opening. Caviar must never be frozen, but because of its salt content it can be kept as cool as 26°F/−3°C.

Popular alternatives to caviar, prepared in the same way as sturgeon roe, include large red salmon caviar and golden steelhead caviar from the northwest Pacific. The cheapest and most common caviar substitute is lumpfish hard roe, processed with red or black vegetable dye (which has the disadvantage that it bleeds when mixed with other ingredients). The best (often Scandinavian) is only lightly salted. Many other fish are esteemed for their roe, whether the ovary of the female (hard roe) or the testes of the male (soft roe or milt). Fresh roe is often sautéed in butter to serve on toast. Hard roes are taken from shad and gray mullet, the latter being salted and pressed as the Mediterranean delicacy called *botargo*. It is served thinly sliced on toast with a squeeze of lemon juice, or in shreds to add piquancy to a bean salad. At one time it was beaten to a cream with olive oil to make the original Greek *taramasalata*, but its rarity makes it expensive these days, and smoked cod's roe is now used instead. Other widely appreciated hard roes are those from tuna and cod (also often smoked) and from carp and herring. Soft roes from the latter are also in demand, as well as those of mackerel and catfish.

SHARK & STURGEON

Shark and sturgeon are among the most primitive fish; both are cartilaginous, without a bony skeleton, and are therefore easy to cut up for cooking. Of the many species of shark found worldwide, only a dozen or so are commonly eaten. In Europe, the dogfish is popular; it is sometimes euphemistically referred to as rock salmon or rock eel. Most dogfish weigh under 10 lb/4.6 kg and make inexpensive thick slices which, fried in batter, are served in British fish and chip shops. Several species are found in both the Atlantic and the Pacific. Many much larger sharks are eaten, particularly in the Pacific, and commonly reach North American and European markets. All of them are light-fleshed and resemble swordfish in taste and texture. In Germany, the porbeagle or mackerel shark is hot-smoked as *kalbfisch*, as well as being eaten fresh. In the United States, this fish is sold as mako shark. Also popular in the United States is the blue shark, which differs from mako in that it has very white flesh.

In general, the color of shark meat varies from white or beige to pale pink, depending on the species and whether the fish was bled when caught. Meat that is a very deep red color is undesirable as it indicates poor handling. However, certain sharks such as mako and thresher have round dark red areas in their flesh that are part of their circulatory system. These red areas may be present even in properly handled fish; they are edible, but very strong tasting. Shark meat lightens in color as it cooks.

Sharks excrete through their skin and, a few days after being caught, may exude an ammoniac odor that can be reduced by soaking the meat in milk, or vinegar and water. Large species of shark are normally cut into steaks, and with all sharks the rough, scaleless skin should be removed before cooking, as otherwise it is likely to shrink considerably and tear the flesh.

The flavorful meat of shark is excellent braised or stewed with a piquant sauce such as Spanish *romesco* sauce (p.29) with chili pepper. Another alternative is to broil shark as a steak or in cubes as kebabs, brushed generously with oil and herbs, or an Asian wine, ginger and coconut milk mixture. It is one of the few fish to hold its shape when stir-fried. Some shark meat tends to be dry,

which can be countered by larding large steaks with bacon or anchovy fillets. The skin and other parts of some sharks are valuable: the skin is tanned for shagreen leather and the fins are pickled, salted or dried and used in soup. Although one species of shark has been used so much for soups that it earned the name soupfin, any shark fins can be made into a lightly-flavored but highly gelatinous stock. It serves as a base for soup to which chicken, pork and other ingredients are added.

With its curious prehistoric-looking armored back and its fabulous load of caviar (p.131), sturgeon excites universal curiosity. Sturgeon was once commonly available as a food fish, and in the Pacific supplies are slowly increasing again as a result of energetic conservation measures. There is now a great demand for sturgeon to be marketed fresh as well as smoked. The freshwater paddlefish found in the American Mississippi river resembles sturgeon, but its roe is unremarkable.

Like salmon, some sturgeon are anadromous, dividing their life between fresh and salt water, while other sturgeon live permanently in fresh water or in brackish estuaries. From the cooking viewpoint, the firm white meat of sturgeon places it beside shark, tuna and swordfish. Sturgeon was the original inspiration for the great Russian culinary classic *coulibiac*, in which layers of sturgeon, mushroom *duxelles* (p.306), buckwheat and hard-boiled eggs are wrapped in brioche or puff pastry to make a giant raised fish pie. In Russia, the gelatinous central cartilage is dried, ground up and used to bind the ingredients together – a product called *vesiga*. Nowadays, salmon often takes the place of sturgeon in *coulibiac*. Small sturgeon can be poached whole but larger fish are usually cut into steaks and pan-fried or broiled on a barbecue.

Dogfish

Mackerel shark

USEFUL INFORMATION

Portion *On bone without head:* ½-¾ lb/250-375 g. *Steaks and fillets:* ½ lb/250 g.

Nutritive value per 3½ oz/100 g (raw). *Shark:* 130 calories; 21 g protein; 5 g fat; no carbohydrates; 79 mg sodium; 51 mg cholesterol. *Sturgeon:* 105 calories; 16 g protein; 4 g fat; no carbohydrates.

Cooking methods *Steaks and fillets:* bake uncovered or in parchment paper or aluminum foil at 350°F/175°C, 15-25 minutes; braise or stew 20-30 minutes; broil 4-6 minutes each side; deep-fry 3-5 minutes; poach 12-18 minutes; sauté 4-6 minutes each side; stir-fry 1-2 minutes.

Problems Gristly texture if undercooked.

Fresh forms *Shark:* whole (small), steaks, fillets. *Sturgeon:* steaks, fillets.

Processed forms *Shark:* frozen. *Sturgeon:* frozen; smoked; canned in brine, tomato sauce; canned smoked. *Sturgeon roe:* caviar.

Storage *Whole:* refrigerate 2-3 days. *Steaks and fillets:* refrigerate 1-2 days.

Typical dishes *Shark:* broiled brochettes (USA); pie with tomatoes and garlic (USA); stir-fried mako shark (USA);

barbecued (USA); shark's fin soup with crabmeat (China). *Sturgeon:* marinated and stewed, (France); fish sausage (Hungary); baked in cherry sauce (Russia); fried with plum compote (Russia); broiled escalopes with brown butter (USA); broiled with olive oil and lemon (Romania); *zukuska* (cooked in tomato and vodka, served cold, Romania).

MEATY FISH
TUNA, SWORDFISH, MARLIN

Tuna is found in warm seas worldwide and half a dozen species of varying size appear in the markets. Large tuna are caught by longline, harpoon or nets. The bluefin is a vast blue-backed creature weighing well over a ton. Such a fish would provide firm, dark red steaks for at least 1,000 people. At the other end of the scale and weighing around 10 lb/4.5 kg is the little skipjack, whose meat is almost as dark. It is often known as ocean bonito or by its Hawaiian name of *aku*.

Albacore, the only white-fleshed tuna (sometimes marketed as "chicken of the sea"), is preferred above all others for canning. In the United States, only albacore is entitled to the label "white-meat tuna", while anything else must be called "light" tuna. Among the tunas supplying this lighter meat is the 400 lb/180 kg big-eye, especially favored for Japanese *sashimi*. For eating fresh, the smaller yellowfin (Hawaiian *ahi*) is considered the finest; with the skipjack, it forms most of the commercial catch, though some other tunas may be available fresh in local markets.

With air freight now operating so efficiently, fresh tuna is more and more widely available. Like all oily fish, tuna, particularly the darker types, should be eaten as fresh as possible. Tuna is a warm-blooded fish and requires expert handling at sea; excessive struggle during capture will cause its body temperature to rise and "burn" the meat. The dismemberment of large species like the bluefin and yellowfin is a specialized skill: the flesh must be thoroughly chilled and bruises so easily that it can be marked by the pressure of a hand. Tuna is so large that the quality of meat can vary depending on what part of the fish it comes from: belly, the oiliest section of the bluefin, is prized by the Japanese for a type of *sashimi* called *toro*, while the red meat along the backbone is leanest. With the exception of tuna steaks, the skin of tuna is generally removed before cooking.

Like tuna, swordfish has tantalized fishermen since antiquity: its long, sword-like nose features in several Roman mosaics. This sword is a real weapon, and not long ago wooden boats were insured against its depredations. The same species of swordfish is found throughout the world, with any minor differences (mainly in size) being a function of habitat. The swordfish is subject to a large wormlike parasite which is unattractive but harmless. More seriously, meat from large swordfish can contain relatively high amounts of mercury, and is therefore toxic if eaten in large quantities. Mercury levels are monitored in several countries, including Italy, the United States and Japan.

Marlin (sometimes called spearfish), with its short spiked nose, is similar in appearance to swordfish, but is plumper and more muscled. It is becoming an increasingly important food fish. There are four species: the white and the blue marlin are native to the Atlantic; the striped and the black, particularly valued in Japan for *sashimi* (p.134) and fish sausages, are native to the Pacific. Like tuna, the flesh varies from beige to reddish brown, depending on the species. Rarer and even more striking than swordfish and marlin is the sailfish, which has a high dorsal fin for a "sail". Fresh sailfish is not as good as marlin, but in Florida it is smoked successfully in small quantities.

The flesh of fresh tuna and swordfish is often compared to veal. Just occasionally small whole tuna will appear in the market, but by far their most common form, as with swordfish, is as thick, juicy steaks. Dark-fleshed types such as bluefin and skipjack can taste strong, even when fresh, and many cooks favor soaking them overnight in lightly salted water before cooking – this approach is also suitable for white-fleshed tunas.

Broiling with olive oil and herbs, whether as steaks or kebabs, is unbeatable for all these fish. Their firm, meaty texture also makes them good choices for barbecuing, perhaps first marinated with garlic and soy sauce. All are good steamed to serve with braised vegetables and a butter sauce. Equally tempting is the Turkish manner of baking swordfish with olives, scallions and dill. Braised tuna is a classic dish, some cooks even going so far as to lard the fish with bacon in the manner of braised beef. Greeks might bake their tuna with tomato sauce, parsley and bread-crumbs; in Provence, they add lettuce, tomato and garlic; while in the Caribbean, tuna is often stewed with coconut and spices. The texture of raw tuna, tender with no trace of pulpiness, is perfect for slicing very fresh to marinate with lemon or lime, olive oil and a touch of chili pepper. For raw dishes, however, it is the Japanese who take the prize with their vivid displays of raw tuna in *sushi* and *sashimi* (p.134).

Bluefin tuna

USEFUL INFORMATION

Portion *On bone without head:* ¾ lb/375 g. *Steaks, fillets:* ½ lb/ 250 g.

Nutritive value per 3½ oz/100 g (raw). *Tuna:* 144 calories; 23 g protein; 5 g fat; no carbohydrates; 39 mg sodium; 38 mg cholesterol. *Swordfish, marlin:* 121 calories; 20 g protein; 4 g fat; no carbohydrates; 90 mg sodium; 39 mg cholesterol.

Cooking methods *Whole or large pieces:* bake or braise at 350°F/ 175°C, time depends on thickness (p.117). *Steaks or fillets:* bake or braise at 350°F/175°C, 20-30 minutes; broil 5-7 minutes each side; marinate 1-2 hours to serve raw; poach 15-20 minutes; sauté 4-6 minutes each side; steam 15-20 minutes; stew 20-30 minutes; stir-fry 1-2 minutes.

Problems *Tuna:* strong-flavored if stale; tough if overcooked. *Swordfish:* dry if overcooked.

Fresh forms *Tuna:* whole (small), steaks, fillets. *Swordfish, marlin:* steaks.

Processed forms *Tuna:* frozen; salted; dried; spice-cured (Japan); canned in oil, brine, tomato sauce. *Swordfish:* frozen; liver oil; smoked. *Marlin:* frozen; smoked.

Storage *Whole:* refrigerate 2-3 days. *Steaks or fillets:* refrigerate 1-2 days.

Typical dishes *Tuna:* raw with fennel in vinaigrette (France); baked in beer (Brazil); *tonno alla livornese* (fried in slices then stewed in tomato and garlic, Italy); marinated, sautéed steaks (Portugal); tuna tartare (raw with onion, capers, cornichons, USA); broiled kebabs with fresh sage (Italy); larded with anchovy and braised (France); stewed with potatoes, peppers and tomatoes (Spain); pan-fried with tomatoes, olives and garlic (France). *Swordfish:* baked with tomatoes (Turkey); marinated in soy and broiled (USA); rolled fillets stuffed with cheese, herbs and onions (Italy); baked in pastry with zucchini and capers (Sicily); baked with scallions (Mexico). *Marlin:* broiled with ginger sauce (USA); smoked with scrambled eggs and chives (Cuba).

SUSHI & SASHIMI

The terms *sushi* and *sashimi* denote the traditional Japanese styles of preparing raw fish. Both are now very popular in the West, especially North America. *Sushi* refers to delicacies made with fish or shellfish molded on top of rice "fingers", seasoned with vinegar and accompanied by a dab of *wasabi* (Japanese horseradish, p.31). Another popular variation, *chirashi-sushi*, is a dish of sliced raw fish laid on top of rice; cold pickled ginger is always served on the side as a decorative pale pink garnish and to refresh the palate between bites; soy sauce and *wasabi* are served for dipping. *Sashimi* is a more generic term for thinly sliced raw fish. It is often accompanied by seasoned rice and an assortment of pickled vegetables and may also be served with thin slices of Japanese omelet.

All these preparations demand precise skill: there is nothing quite like watching a *sushi* chef at work with his sharp knives. The rice must be sticky but not too soft, the fish sliced correctly and molded tightly around the rice. Certain types of *sushi*, however, such as finger rolls of fish, rice and *nori* seaweed can be duplicated quite well at home.

Whatever the approach, the fish for *sashimi* or *sushi* must be extremely fresh, preferably no more than 24 hours out of the water. Fish that has been frozen is not appropriate for these preparations because the texture tends to soften and the natural juices leach out during thawing. Some fish do not have the right texture for slicing: for example shark and swordfish are too gristly, while others such as weakfish or white sea bass are very fragile and may disintegrate. Others are bland when raw, like cod, or too strong, such as bluefish. Fish that are easy to fillet, and free of small bones are the best choice; tuna (*maguro*), flounder (*hirame*), yellowtail (*hamachi* or *buri*), squid (*ika*), sea bream (*tai*), sea bass (*suzuki*), salmon (*sake*) and salmon roe (*ikura*) are favorites. Some *sushi* presentations also use cooked or cured fish, including cooked shrimp (*ebi*), pickled mackerel (*saba*) and broiled or smoked eel (*unagi*). It is unwise to venture outside this narrow range as many freshwater fish and ocean fish may harbor harmful parasites.

Baked tuna with fennel and mushrooms

Dark or light tuna is equally good in this Italian recipe, which is excellent with an accompaniment of shell pasta as well as fennel and mushrooms.

Serves 4

3 tbsp/45 ml olive oil	2 lb/1 kg tuna steaks (cut ¾ in/2 cm thick)
1 tbsp butter	salt and pepper
1 onion, finely diced	½ cup/125 ml veal stock (p.44)
1 carrot, finely diced	1 tbsp anise-flavored liqueur
1 clove garlic, finely chopped	**For the mushrooms**
2 anchovy fillets, finely chopped	3 tbsp/olive oil
3 fennel bulbs, trimmed and sliced (p.299)	1 clove garlic, finely chopped
1 tbsp chopped parsley	½ lb/250 g mushrooms, very thinly sliced
1 bay leaf	1 tbsp chopped parsley
¼ cup/60 ml dry vermouth	

1 In a sauté pan, heat the oil and butter. Add the onion and carrot and cook gently until soft but not brown, 2-3 minutes. Add the garlic and anchovy and cook, stirring, 1 minute. Add the fennel slices, parsley, bay leaf and vermouth and simmer until fennel is soft, 8-10 minutes.
2 Sprinkle the tuna on both sides with salt and pepper. Lay it on top of the vegetables and pour over the stock. Cover and cook over medium heat 5-7 minutes. Turn the fish and continue cooking about 5 minutes longer, until it almost flakes.

3 Meanwhile, heat the olive oil and fry the garlic for 30 seconds. Add the mushrooms and cook over high heat until the moisture has evaporated, 3-5 minutes. Add the parsley.
4 When the tuna is almost cooked, spoon the mushrooms on top and continue cooking until the fish flakes easily, 1-2 minutes. Discard the bay leaf, pour over the anise liqueur and season the fennel to taste. Serve the tuna in the cooking dish, or transfer it to a serving dish and spoon the fennel around it.

MONKFISH

Monkfish, also called anglerfish, is an ugly fish, with a huge head and gaping mouth, but its excellent flesh more than compensates for its disconcerting appearance. Slightly chewy, mild and sweet, monkfish has long been appreciated in southern Europe and is gaining more recognition in Britain and North America. It is native to the Mediterranean and both sides of the Atlantic. The average weight is 10 lb/4.5 kg. The tail section, the most important to the cook, consists of one central cartilaginous bone and two fillets.

Monkfish is easy to prepare, with no spine bones and firm flesh that does not overcook easily. Known as "poor man's lobster", it can be substituted for the real thing in dishes that call for pieces of lobster. Monkfish is traditional in the fish soup *bouillabaisse* and in Spanish paella, but it has also inspired modern dishes, such as monkfish and shrimp ravioli in saffron cream sauce.

USEFUL INFORMATION

Portion *On the bone:* ½ lb/250 g. *Fillets:* 6 oz/175 g.
Nutritive value per 3½ oz/100 g (raw). 76 calories; 14 g protein; 2 g fat; no carbohydrates; 18 mg sodium; 46 mg cholesterol.
Cooking methods bake at 350°F/175°C, 8-10 minutes; poach 5-10 minutes; sauté 4-6 minutes.
Problems Only tender when thoroughly cooked; shrinks more than most fish.

Fresh forms Fillets; steaks; on backbone.
Storage refrigerate 1-2 days.
Typical dishes *Lotte à l'américaine* (in a garlic and tomato sauce, France); *cotriade* (fish soup, Brittany, France); with scallops and pasta (USA); sautéed in basil and fennel, USA).

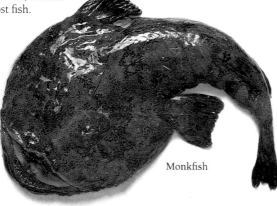

Monkfish

FILLETING MONKFISH

Monkfish tail can easily be filleted to yield two thick boneless pieces of meat. Its dark, tough skin is usually removed before sale, leaving a thin membrane to be cut off by the cook.

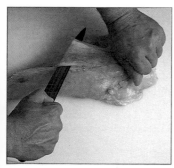

1 With a filleting knife, cut away the thin membrane covering the outside of the fish.

2 Cut along one side of the central bone to remove the fillet. Repeat on the other side.

Escalopes of monkfish with lime and ginger

The delicate seasoning of lime and ginger in a butter sauce is also excellent with other kinds of white fish, notably sole and pompano.

Serves 4

2 lb/1 kg monkfish, on the bone	½ cup/125 ml white wine
2 cups/500 ml fish stock (p.44) made with bone from the monkfish	1 lb/500 g fresh green *fettucine*, cooked (for serving)
salt and pepper	***For the sauce***
pinch of dried thyme	¼ cup/60 ml heavy cream
juice of 1 lemon	1 cup/250 g cold butter, cut into pieces
1 tbsp olive or vegetable oil	
pared zest of 2 lemons, cut in julienne (p.460)	juice of 3 limes
	1 tbsp grated fresh ginger
1 tbsp butter	2 tbsp chopped parsley
4 scallions, thinly sliced, including some green	

1 Fillet the monkfish and use the bone to make stock. Cut the monkfish fillets in escalopes (p.117). Marinate the fish in salt, pepper, thyme, lemon juice and oil for 1 hour.
2 Blanch the lemon julienne by boiling in water for 3-4 minutes, then drain and rinse with cold water.
3 In a sauté pan, melt the butter, add the onions and cook gently until soft. Add the fish, fish stock and wine. Simmer until the fish just loses its transparency, 1-2 minutes.
4 Remove the fish, cover and keep warm. Cook the *fettucine* and keep warm. Meanwhile, make the sauce: boil the cooking liquid until reduced to a glaze (p.52). Add the cream and reduce to about 2 tablespoons. Mount the sauce with the butter (p.53). Stir in the lemon julienne, lime juice, ginger and parsley. Season.
5 Arrange the monkfish escalopes with the *fettucine* on individual plates and spoon the sauce over the fish.

FIRM WHITE FISH
SNAPPER, GROUPER, ORANGE ROUGHY, MAHI MAHI

This varied group of fish offers juicy, firm flesh with excellent flavor. Size varies enormously, many species being small enough to cook whole, while larger fish are sold in fillets and steaks.

Snapper is plump and bright-eyed with big fins and colorful skin; the combined effects of these make an alluring picture on the market slab. It has a large head and prominent bones, so the yield of flesh from a whole fish is low. Red snapper and its look-alike silk snapper are generally acknowledged as the best for eating, with firm savory white flesh. Other good snappers include the gray or mangrove snapper, yellowtail, muttonfish and the little red lane snapper. These species swim in subtropical Atlantic waters and the Gulf of Mexico, but there are also Hawaiian and South Pacific snappers. Sizes range from 2-10 lb/1-4.5 kg, with an average snapper weighing about 5 lb/2.3 kg. The name snapper can be given to other little fish that shut their mouths with an energetic snap – bluefish is an example. Red snapper is so sought-after that other fish with red skin are commonly passed off as snapper, including the reddish Atlantic ocean perch – sometimes called "redfish" – as well as various Pacific rockfish (p.142), which are sold as skinned fillets. Always buy red snapper with its skin still on to be certain that it is the real thing.

For the cook, grouper closely resembles snapper. A dozen species are scattered throughout the world's warmer waters, but they have little of the brilliant color of snapper, tending more to gray and brown. Many varieties of grouper range in size from 2-4 lb/1-1.8 kg, but others run into hundreds of pounds. The larger the fish, the coarser the texture, so most of the commercial catch is of a more modest size, around 50 lb/23 kg. Common groupers include Nassau grouper, black grouper and red grouper, which is one of the best. The jewfish, found in the warm waters of the Gulf of Mexico and along the coast of South America as far as Brazil, is a giant grouper, weighing as much as 700 lb/320 kg. To exploit their impressive appearance, snapper and grouper are often trimmed (p.111) and baked whole on the bone on a bed of vegetables, such as sliced onion, fennel, tomato, bell pepper, eggplant or avocado. Whole red snapper may be steamed so that the intense color is retained, then served classically with a butter sauce or in Asian fashion with a piquant sauce for dipping. Small whole fish are often broiled or sautéed in butter and sprinkled with lime juice – a traditional Florida breakfast dish. Even when they are filleted, the skin of the red varieties of snapper is generally left on for broiling or steaming, while grouper is likely to be found deep-fried in batter or barbecued with robust herbs such as rosemary. The cheaper, less eye-catching species of snapper are good in stew with lively seasonings of saffron or chili pepper. Bluefish are more oily than other varieties of snapper and are therefore most suitable for barbecuing or broiling.

Orange roughy, a Pacific deep-sea fish which takes its name from its bright orange skin, resembles snapper in taste and texture. Although relatively new to most Western markets, it is well known in New Zealand. First sold as snapper, its full-bodied slightly yellow flesh has now earned it independent repute.

Another fish that has grown in popularity is Hawaiian mahi mahi, or dolphin fish, found in warm waters in the Pacific and western Atlantic. The mahi mahi is not related to the true dolphin, which is a mammal and a protected species. Also called dorado because of its magnificent gold and jewel colored skin, it ranges from 5-40 lb/2.3-18 kg. Specimens larger than 15 lb/7 kg taste best. Once the fish is caught, the brilliant colors fade rapidly. It is advisable to marinate the fish before cooking (lemon or lime with oil and garlic work well), as the flesh cooks quickly and has a tendency to become dry. Moist cooking methods such as braising or baking in sauce work best, although quickly deep-fried mahi mahi is another possibility. When cooked, the pink, flaky flesh has a mild, almost sweet flavor.

Red snapper   Grouper

USEFUL INFORMATION

Portion On bone with head: 1 lb/ 500 g. On bone without head: ¾ lb/ 375 g. Steaks and fillets: 6 oz/175 g.
Nutritive value per 3½ oz/100 g (raw). Snapper: 100 calories; 21 g protein; 1 g fat; no carbohydrates; 64 mg sodium; 37 mg cholesterol. Grouper: 92 calories; 19 g protein; 1 g fat; no carbohydrates; 53 mg sodium; 37 mg cholesterol. Orange roughy: 126 calories; 15 g protein; 7 g fat; no carbohydrates; 63 mg sodium; 20 mg cholesterol. Mahi mahi: 85 calories; 19 g protein; 1 g fat; no carbohydrates; 88 mg sodium; 73 mg cholesterol.

Cooking methods Whole, large: bake, poach or steam, time depends on the thickness of the fish (p.117). Whole, small: bake at 350°F/175°C, 15-25 minutes; broil 5-7 minutes each side; poach 15-25 minutes; sauté 5-7 minutes each side; steam 15-25 minutes. Steaks and fillets: bake uncovered or in parchment paper or aluminum foil at 350°F/175°C, 12-18 minutes; broil 3-5 minutes on each side; deep-fry 3-5 minutes; poach 10-15 minutes; sauté 3-5 minutes each side; steam 10-15 minutes.

Problems Softer types break up easily.
Fresh forms Grouper: whole, steak, fillet. Snapper: whole, fillet. Mahi mahi: steak, fillet. Orange roughy: fillet (frozen).
Processed forms Frozen.
Storage Whole: refrigerate 1-2 days. Steaks and fillets: refrigerate 1 day.
Typical dishes Snapper: baked with wine and herbs (USA); baked with coriander and chilis (Mexico); fried with butter and lemon juice (Australia); baked in a paper case with carrots and cheese (USA); sautéed with olives and bacon (USA); adoba de pescado (in a casserole with tomatoes and ancho chilies, Mexico). Grouper: broiled with oregano, garlic and orange (Mexico); baked with oyster stuffing (USA). Mahi mahi: broiled with lime juice and olive oil (USA); broiled with lemon and vermouth (Hawaii); stewed with sherry and mushrooms (Hawaii) capone. apparecchiato (fried with tomatoes, capers and olives, Sicily). Orange roughy: baked with lemon juice and black pepper (USA).

Marinated red snapper

Escabèche

This Caribbean dish is derived from the Spanish method of pickling meat and fish.

Serves 8

4 lb/1.8 kg snapper fillets	¼ cup/15 g parsley sprigs
1 cup/250 ml plus 1 tbsp olive oil	1 tbsp paprika
⅓ cup/80 ml red wine vinegar	¼ tsp cayenne pepper
1 medium onion, chopped	salt and pepper
2 cloves garlic, chopped	4 bay leaves
pared zest of 1 orange and 1 lemon	

1 Cut the fish fillets into 3 in/7.5 cm pieces about 1 in/2.5 cm thick. Brush a frying pan with one tablespoon of olive oil and warm over very low heat. Arrange the fillets in the pan in a single layer, so they do not touch the sides. **Note** If the pieces do not fit, cook the fish in two batches and leave the first batch to cool while cooking the second.
2 Cover with a tight-fitting lid and cook over low heat until the flesh on the underside becomes opaque, about 10 minutes. Turn the fish, cover and continue cooking until firm, 8-10 minutes more. Remove the fish from the pan and allow to cool.
3 For the marinade: combine the remaining oil, red wine vinegar, onion, garlic, orange and lemon zest, parsley, paprika and cayenne pepper in a blender or food processor. Chop all the ingredients very finely and combine them with the oil and vinegar. Alternatively blend until smooth and creamy. Season to taste with salt and pepper.
4 Pour half the marinade into a serving dish. Arrange the fish in the marinade in a single layer and top with the bay leaves. Pour the remaining marinade over the fish. Cover tightly and refrigerate for at least 8, and up to 24 hours. Discard the bay leaves.

FLAKY WHITE FISH
BASS, MULLET, DRUM, CROAKER

Bass is a very general name used for many quite different and unrelated salt- and freshwater fish on both sides of the Atlantic and Pacific. The common denominator of the saltwater bass is a fine, firm flesh and a color that varies from blue-gray to black. Sea bass live off or close to shore, depending on the species, and many are migratory, moving to warmer deep waters in winter.

With regard to culinary merit, Europeans would probably claim highest honors for common (sea) bass but Americans would undoubtedly choose their East Coast striped bass. One of the most colorful of all fish is the species of sea bass called tilefish, with hues varying from a blue-green back with yellow spots down to a bright rose belly. It is native to the northwest Atlantic.

Mullet resembles trout, with a mild eye and amiable expression. In color they are closer to a bass, ranging through shades of gray, mottled, striped and plain, sometimes with a yellowish tint. The flesh of all the mullets is pleasant, fine-textured with a mild flavor that is sometimes slightly oily.

Red mullet is very different from common mullet, both in family and reputation. It is small and savory with brilliant red skin. It is usually found in the Mediterranean but is related to the North American goatfish, which is almost as delicious. Red mullet has earned the nickname "woodcock of the sea", partly for its gamey flavor, partly because it shares with woodcock the distinction of often being cooked with its entrails. It is usually cooked whole and the skin is always left on.

Resembling sea bass in size and appearance are the drum and croaker, found all along the northwestern Atlantic coast. These fish get their names from a muscle attached to their air bladders that makes a resonating sound. There are only a few gastronomically notable drums, as their flesh tends to be coarse and rather tasteless. However small drums of up to 10 lb/4.5 kg,

Gray mullet

Red mullet

such as spot and black drum, can be agreeable. As with so many mild-flavored fish, freshness and careful handling are important.

One drum that has achieved fame is the redfish – red drum or channel bass – star of the highly spiced Cajun dish from Louisiana called blackened redfish. Alternative cooking methods are baking or poaching. So popular has the redfish become that supplies have been greatly diminished and black drum is often passed off in its place. Weakfish, despite its unpromising name, is one of the better drums. The family also includes Pacific white sea bass and Atlantic spotted, speckled or gray sea trout; confusingly these are unrelated to true bass and trout. The French qualify their opinion of the only eastern Atlantic drum by calling it *maigre*, meaning meagre fish. The name kingfish (not to be confused with king mackerel, p.148) is given to another species of drum that makes fair eating. Silver perch, despite its name, is a small drum, found in the Atlantic. It is usually pan-fried whole.

Tilefish

Weakfish

Striped bass

Common bass

Black drum

Portion *On bone with head:* 1 lb/ 500 g. *On bone without head:* 3/4 lb/ 375 g. *Steaks or fillets:* 6 oz/175 g.

Nutritive value per 3½ oz/100 g (raw). *Bass:* 97 calories; 18 g protein; 2 g fat; no carbohydrates; 69 mg sodium; 80 mg cholesterol. *Mullet:* 117 calories; 19 g protein; 4 g fat; no carbohydrates; 65 mg sodium; 49 mg cholesterol. *Red drum:* 90 calories; 19 g protein; 1 g fat; no carbohydrates; 75 mg sodium; 50 mg cholesterol. *Croaker:* 104 calories; 18 g protein; 3 g fat; no carbohydrates; 56 mg sodium; 61 mg cholesterol.

Cooking methods *Whole, large:* bake at 350°F/175°C, broil, poach, steam, time depends on thickness (p.117). *Whole, small:* bake at 350°F/175°C, 15-25 minutes; broil 5-7 minutes each side; poach 15-25 minutes; sauté 5-7 minutes each side; steam 15-25 minutes. *Steaks or fillets:* bake open or in parchment paper or aluminum foil at 350°F/175°C, 12-18 minutes; broil 3-5 minutes each side; deep-fry 3-5 minutes; poach 10-15 minutes; sauté 3-5 minutes each side; steam 10-15 minutes.

Problems Flavor of bass is easily tainted by polluted waters; drum and croaker fillets lose flavor when stored and break up easily when cooked.

Fresh forms *Bass:* whole, steak, fillet. *Mullet:* whole, fillet. *Drum, croaker:* whole.

Processed forms Frozen.

Storage *Whole:* refrigerate 2-3 days. *Steaks or fillets:* 1 day.

Typical dishes *Bass:* stewed with scampi and artichokes (France); marinated with basil and fresh coriander (USA); *lubina "albufera"* (baked in almond sauce, Spain); *bar aux herbes en chemise* (stuffed with spinach and herbs, wrapped in lettuce leaves and poached in white wine, France). *Mullet:* marinated and broiled with fennel (France); baked with mushrooms (UK); grilled with oranges (Portugal); baked with potatoes and saffron (France); with bacon and sage (UK); stuffed with currants, pine nuts and spices and baked in tomato sauce (Armenia); *setúbalense* (broiled red mullet, Portugal). *Redfish:* creole (with piquant sauce, hard-boiled eggs and bacon, USA); fried, with pecan butter sauce (USA).

Croaker is a common western Atlantic group of fish belonging to the same family as the drum, but unfortunately in the kitchen it is even less remarkable than the drum. Most croakers are small with soft flesh; they are best left on the bone to pan-fry. In an effort to upgrade them, they are sometimes named "golden" croaker. Spot is a similar small drum. Drum and croaker are susceptible to trematode parasites; these are killed by cooking, but none of the family should be eaten raw.

Sea bass, striped bass and red mullet are to be found in the finest restaurants, lovingly broiled or steamed on a bed of seaweed. Their fillets can be served with delicate butter sauces and young vegetables. Other species of bass are more than worthy of similar handling. A whole poached bass, served hot or cold with appropriate accompaniments, is a princely treat.

When fresh, gray mullet and the best species of drum and croaker also merit such attention. Broiling a small fish on the bone is particularly successful, preferably after marinating to add flavor. Little fish are also good fried in bacon fat, or sautéed in butter to serve with lemon. The "blackened" approach popular in the Cajun cooking of the American South, where the fish fillets are coated with spices then baked in a literally red-hot pan, is yet another way to add piquancy. Otherwise, mullet, drum and croaker are best baked on the bone, or in fillets or steaks with plenty of herbs and seasoning and served against a background of vegetables. Alternatively, they may be simmered in stews or chowder, which in traditional American Cajun cooking would be spiced with a generous sprinkling of red hot pepper sauce to bring out the flavors of the fish.

THE COD FAMILY
COD, HADDOCK, HAKE, POLLACK

Cod, haddock, hake and pollack, along with other members of the cod family, form almost half the world's commercial catch of fish. In many respects they resemble one another, being mild-flavored, firm-fleshed and somewhat flaky. Since medieval times cod has been a staple in the kitchen and it remains the most important food fish in Europe and North America. The astonishing abundance of cod was one reason for the rapid colonization of New England. Gradually supplies have dwindled, and now most cod is fished in the northern Atlantic off Greenland and Newfoundland, and in the northern Pacific. Ships come from all directions and competition for the catch is fierce.

In North American and European markets, much the most important species is the sandy-brown Atlantic cod. Pacific cod, indistinguishable from Atlantic for the cook, is exported to Russia and Japan and is now being caught in the Bering Sea, primarily for the United States market. Big Atlantic cod weighing over 100 lb/ 45 kg were once landed, but now anything over 25 lb/12 kg is officially graded as jumbo or "whale" and left. In the United States, any small member of the cod family from 1½-2½ lb/750 g-1.2 kg is classed as "scrod".

Abundance is only one reason for the success of cod. Full-flavored, with a good yield of thick, slightly flaky white fillets, cod is adaptable in the kitchen. Everyone must have encountered the anonymous deep-fried pieces or "fingers" of cod offered by fast food outlets. Don't let prejudice stand in the way of what can be a real feast when carefully cooked at home and served with French fries, home-made tartare sauce (p.63) and a sprinkling of lemon. This hearty, down-to-earth approach exactly suits the robust juiciness of cod. It is excellent broiled, sautéed or steamed to serve with a rich or piquant sauce like anchovy or Mexican tomato sauce (p.65); it can be baked whole or in pieces, with the Mediterranean touch of olives and garlic, or the Portuguese flavor of tomato, anchovy, garlic and coriander. Scandinavian recipes often pair cod with dill, as in the classic Swedish dish *stuvad östersjö-torsk*, in which whole, small cod are baked with chopped dill, parsley and lemon juice and served with boiled potatoes. Sophisticated wine-based sauces are wasted on cod, which is at its best with a simple cream or cheese sauce. Mushrooms, particularly shiitake (p.308) and boletes (p.311), give a wonderful lift to cod. It also makes a full-bodied and slightly flaky chowder. Poaching can make its already moist texture soggy.

Salt- and dried cod are also popular (p.126). Cod liver oil is an important source of vitamins. Cod roe is eaten fresh, smoked or salted (p.131). In a traditional Belgian dish, the translated name of which is, aptly, "a pocketful of roe", fresh cod roe is wrapped in cheesecloth to keep its shape, blanched, then sliced and fried to serve on toast. The cheeks of cod are sweet and are sold separately, as is cod's tongue, excellent sautéed in butter.

Cod has several important relatives. Firstly haddock, which is identifiable by a black "thumbprint" behind the gills. Smaller and less abundant than cod, it is found in the North Atlantic and Arctic from the Bay of Biscay to New England. Some cooks maintain that haddock is slightly softer in texture than cod.

From the culinary viewpoint, hake and whiting are inferior to cod, with soft flesh and a pleasant, innocuous flavor. Color shades from slate gray to dark blue and silver, depending on the species. Strictly speaking, whiting and hake are separate species, but terminology is confusing since two or three species of hake are often sold as whiting in the United States because the name sounds more appetizing. Hake is generally larger than whiting, which is usually sold under 1 lb/500 g; hake can be as large as 25 lb/12 kg, though on average it is closer to 2 lb/1 kg. Common species include red or squirrel hake, silver hake or Atlantic whiting, white hake and Pacific whiting.

Hake and whiting are best steamed or poached gently so they do not break up. Given their soft flesh which purées easily, they often form the basis of *quenelles* (p.146) and *mousselines* (p.123) though they need to be paired with lively ingredients, such as full-flavored fish and shellfish or assertive vegetables such as sorrel.

Atlantic pollack is currently being re-evaluated. It is also called saithe, coalfish and coley, and is found in both the North Atlantic and the Pacific. The flavor is similar to hake, with a coarser-textured, gray flesh which whitens on cooking.

Other fish associated with the cod family include cusk, native to the North Atlantic, and the rockling of the northwest Atlantic and Mediterranean. Both resemble hake, as does ling, which is native to the northeastern Atlantic, and its northwestern relative, cobia. There is also a freshwater member of the cod family found on both sides of the Atlantic, the burbot. It is usually found in deep waters, particularly lakes. It has firm white flesh but is slightly oilier than freshwater cod. For cooking, it is best cut into steaks and prepared in the same way as cod steaks.

USEFUL INFORMATION/COD FAMILY

Portion On bone with head: ¾-1 lb/ 375-500 g. *On bone without head:* ½ lb/250 g. *Steaks or fillets:* 6 oz/ 175 g.

Nutritive value per 3½ oz/100 g (raw). *Cod:* 82 calories; 18 g protein; 1 g fat; no carbohydrates; 54 mg sodium; 43 mg cholesterol. *Haddock:* 87 calories; 19 g protein; 1 g fat; no carbohydrates; 68 mg sodium; 57 mg cholesterol. *Hake:* 90 calories; 18 g protein; 1 g fat; no carbohydrates; 72 mg sodium; 67 mg cholesterol. *Pollack:* 92 calories; 19 g protein; 1 g fat; no carbohydrates; 86 mg sodium; 71 mg cholesterol.

Cooking methods *Whole, large:* bake at 350°F/175°C, broil, poach, steam, time depends on thickness (p.117). *Small, whole:* bake at 350°F/175°C, 15-25 minutes; broil 5-7 minutes each side; deep-fry 5-7 minutes; poach 15-25 minutes; sauté 5-7 minutes each side; steam 15-25 minutes. *Steaks or fillets:* bake uncovered, in parchment paper or aluminum foil at 350°F/175°C, 12-18 minutes; broil 3-5 minutes each side; deep-minutes; sauté 3-5 minutes each side; steam 10-15 minutes.

Problems May become too flaky if carelessly handled or overcooked.

Fresh forms Whole, steaks, fillets.

Processed forms *Cod:* frozen; smoked; canned (plain and smoked); salted; dried; liver oil. *Haddock:* frozen; smoked; salted; pickled; canned; liver oil. *Hake, pollack:* frozen; smoked; salted; pickled.

Storage *Whole:* refrigerate 2-3 days. *Steaks and fillets:* refrigerate 1 day.

Typical dishes *Cod:* with puréed potatoes and Mornay sauce, (France); *fiskepudding* (baked pudding, Norway); poached in parsley sauce (UK); New England fried cod cakes (USA). *Haddock:* baked with noodles and cheese (USA); baked with mushrooms in piquant sauce (Germany). *Pollack:* deep-fried fillets with chili butter (USA); gratinéed with cheese (Norway). *Whiting:* cabbage stuffed with whiting *mousseline* (France); baked with potatoes in cream sauce (Portugal).

Haddock

Hake

Rockling

Whiting

Cod

Cod, shrimp and samphire pie

If the sea vegetable samphire (p.283) is unobtainable, green beans or asparagus may be substituted in this recipe.

Serves 8

puff pastry or quick puff pastry (p.381) made with 2 cups/250 g flour	¼ cup/60 g butter
	¼ cup/30 g flour
2 cups/500 ml light cream	2 lb/1 kg skinned cod fillets
pared zest of 1 lemon	½ lb/250 g peeled cooked shrimp
½ lb/250 g samphire	salt, pepper and nutmeg
1 small onion, finely chopped	1 egg, beaten to mix (for glaze)

1 Make the puff pastry and chill it 30 minutes. Put the cream and lemon zest in a small saucepan. Scald, remove from the heat and leave to infuse, 10-15 minutes. Trim roots and wash the samphire. Blanch it in boiling salted water 2 minutes and drain.
2 Cook the onion in the butter until soft but not brown. Add the flour and cook 2-3 minutes. Strain in the cream, off the heat, then bring the sauce to a boil, whisking until it thickens. Season to taste with salt, pepper and nutmeg, simmer 1-2 minutes and leave the sauce to cool.
3 Divide the puff pastry in half. Roll out one portion and cut a 12 in/30 cm round. Roll out the remaining pastry dough and cut another, slightly larger round, about 14 in/36 cm. Reserve the pastry trimmings to use as decoration.
4 Cut the cod fillets into chunks. Add the cod and the shrimp to the sauce and taste for seasoning. Transfer the smaller round to a baking sheet lightly sprinkled with water. Arrange the samphire in the center of the dough. Spoon the fish mixture on top. Brush the pastry border with egg glaze and top with the other round. Seal the edges and scallop them. Make strips from the pastry trimmings. Brush the surface of the pie with egg glaze and lay the strips on top in a lattice, then glaze the pie again. Cut slashes in the top to allow steam to escape. Heat the oven to 450°F/230°C. Chill the pie 15 minutes.
5 Bake the pie in the preheated oven until beginning to brown, about 15 minutes. Lower the heat to 350°F/175°C and continue

cooking until pastry is crisp and golden brown and a skewer inserted in the center of the pie is hot to the touch, 20-25 minutes. Serve the pie hot and cut into wedges.

THIN-BODIED FISH
POMPANO & OTHER JACKS, SEA BREAM

Jack and sea bream have a similar body line – oval with prominent fins and a wide Y-shaped tail. Most of them live in tropical or warm waters worldwide. The meat is generally firm, with widely varying flavor, from the light fragrance of the best sea bream to the richness of some species of jack. At first glance, opah or moonfish might also be a bream, but it is quite a different fish, growing up to 100 lb/45 kg. The meat is excellent, pink and full of flavor, and species are found worldwide.

Species of jack vary a great deal. Most have the heavy bones and soft flesh typical of warm water fish, but a few of them, such as the pompano, are very desirable, with sweet, white meat. Pompano's silky, smooth silver skin is instantly recognizable. Permit is a very similar fish, though it is much heavier – up to 50 lb/23 kg, in contrast to the pompano's usual 2 lb/1 kg – with

a somewhat coarser, drier flesh. A third look-alike is called palometa or longfin pompano. As true pompano commands a higher price, all these fish are often sold as pompano.

Despite its name, the horse mackerel or scad is also a jack. Superficially its dark green back does resemble mackerel, but it has less flavor. Most other jacks, notably the blue runner and the crevalle, are undistinguished. The shape of a runner is more

Horse mackerel

Pomfret

Dentex

Pompano

torpedo-like than the plump oval of most jacks. Yellowtail (not to be confused with yellowtail snapper, p.136) and amberjack are other members of the jack group. Smaller fish are preferred as the large ones may be strong-flavored. Runners and yellowtails smoke well and because of their rich meat are valued for *sashimi* (p.134). Amberjack should not be eaten raw.

More than 20 species of sea bream have been identified in the Mediterranean alone, with dozens more elsewhere. Noted for their sweet flavor are the Japanese red sea bream and yellow bream, and the Mediterranean gilt-head and dentex. Also worth looking for are the European red bream and black bream, together with the only bream found on both sides of the Atlantic, called the sea bream in Europe and the red porgy in the United States.

Bream sold under other names in the United States include scup, and the excellent black-striped "sheepshead." Linked to the bream family by virtue of its compressed body shape is pomfret or Ray's bream, which has slightly pink flesh resembling that of skate. In Europe, the name pomfret often refers to the butterfish. Both are plump and rather tasteless and found worldwide.

Sea bream and jack commonly weigh under 2 lb/1 kg, and at this size they are usually left whole and cooked on the bone as an individual serving. For richer jacks, such as yellowtail, broiling is ideal, but baking is traditional for whiter-fleshed varieties, particularly gilt-head bream and pompano. A simple treatment would be to frame the fish with a colorful Mediterranean blend of tomatoes, red and green bell peppers and eggplant, or to stuff it with breadcrumbs or kasha (p.320) and onions, then smother it in sour cream and bake it in the oven.

Given the delicacy of the flesh, large bream or jack are excellent filleted to broil or sauté in butter. In the American South, a coating of cornmeal or cracker crumbs is customary. Many popular dishes for baked fillets feature a bed of vegetables, either open to the heat of the oven or in a parchment case (p.121). The package may be stuffed with a rich mixture of crabmeat and shrimp or perhaps oysters or mushrooms, with a generous thick fillet of fish on top.

USEFUL INFORMATION

Portion *On bone with head:* 1 lb/ 500 g. *On bone without head:* ½ lb/ 250 g. *Fillets:* 6 oz/175 g.
Nutritive value per 3½ oz/100 g (raw). *Pompano:* 164 calories; 18 g protein; 9 g fat; no carbohydrates; 65 mg sodium; 50 g cholesterol. *Jack:* 159 calories; 19 g protein; 9 g fat; no carbohydrates; 52 mg sodium. *Bream:* 105 calories; 19 g protein; 3 g fat; no carbohydrates.
Cooking methods *Whole, large:* bake at 350°F/175°C, or steam, time depends on thickness (p.117). *Whole, small:* bake at 350°F/175°C, 15-25 minutes; broil 5-7 minutes each side, steam 20 minutes.

Fillets: bake uncovered at 350°F/ 175°C, 12-18 minutes; broil 3-5 minutes each side; poach 10-15 minutes; sauté 3-5 minutes each side; steam 10-15 minutes.
Problems Strong if stored too long; flesh flakes if overcooked.
Fresh forms Whole, fillets.
Processed forms Frozen; smoked.
Storage *Whole:* 2 days. *Fillets:* 1 day.
Typical dishes *Pompano:* fillets baked in red wine (USA); broiled with anchovy butter (USA). *Jack:* stuffed with apples, raisins and suet and baked with mustard sauce (UK); broiled over mesquite, with smoked vegetable *salsa* (USA). *Bream:* stuffed with leeks and fennel (France); with horseradish and apples (Russia); baked with garlic (Yugoslavia); baked with lemon and capers (USA).

Red sea bream

Mediterranean baked bream

As a variation, other vegetables such as zucchini, eggplant or mushrooms, can be added to the peppers. The fish may be served hot or at room temperature.

Serves 6-8

4 lb/1.8 kg whole bream, or two smaller fish	1 lb/500 g tomatoes, peeled, seeded and chopped
½ cup/125 ml olive oil	½ cup/80 g small black olives
2 onions, sliced	8 anchovy fillets, chopped
2 red bell peppers, cored, seeded and sliced	2 cloves garlic, crushed
2 green bell peppers, cored, seeded and sliced	salt and pepper
	6-8 sprigs fresh thyme
2 yellow bell peppers, cored, seeded and sliced	juice of 1 lemon

1 Trim, scale and gut the fish (pp.111,112). Rinse and dry it, then score both sides (p.112). Heat the oven to 350°F/175°C.
2 In a large flameproof baking dish or roasting pan, heat 2 tablespoons of the oil and fry the onions until browned. Stir in the peppers, tomatoes, olives, anchovy fillets, garlic, salt and pepper and take from the heat.
3 Set the fish on the vegetables and tuck a sprig of thyme in each slash. Spoon the remaining oil over the fish and sprinkle with salt, pepper and the juice of 1 lemon.
4 Bake the fish uncovered in the oven, basting occasionally, just until it flakes easily, 30-35 minutes for the large fish or 20-25 minutes for the smaller ones.
5 Transfer the fish to a serving dish and keep warm. Continue cooking the vegetables on top of the stove until all the liquid has evaporated and they are tender. Season to taste and spoon them around the fish.

BONY FISH
GURNARD, SCORPION FISH, ROCKFISH

Fish that offer little in the way of meat often come into their own in soups or stews. In such dishes, their large heads and prominent bones are a positive advantage, as the bones hold the flesh together during long simmering and the heads are used to make stock.

Typical examples are the eye-catching gurnards, a group of fish with bulky bones and well-developed, frond-like fins. Much of the flavor is concentrated in the bones. The gurnard family clusters around the northeastern Atlantic and Mediterranean. Names like gray, shining, armed, and streaked gurnard give an indication of their varied appearance; the rose-red piper is also a gurnard. Most important is the red gurnard, which spreads over to the North American coast, where it is often called the sea robin. It is also good broiled on the bone, or filleted to sauté or deep-fry. **Note** Its French name of *rouget grondin* causes some confusion with the red mullet or *rouget*, a greatly superior fish (p.137). Nonetheless, the flesh of gurnard is firm-fleshed and palatable, if a little dry. It is best served with a sauce.

Sculpin are also common, found throughout the North Atlantic and also in the Pacific, while a couple of species live in fresh water. Unfortunately for the cook, the meat is disappointingly mild. Unattractive as it looks, scorpion fish is a better bet. This is the famous French red rascasse, indispensable in *bouillabaisse*, though its cousin, black rascasse, is sometimes substituted. Both have firm white flesh, which bakes well in the manner of bream (p.141). Blue-mouth, found on both coasts of the North Atlantic is closely related.

Other prime ingredients of *bouillabaisse* are weever, one of several species of fish with poisonous spines, and its relative the spider; both are eastern Atlantic and Mediterranean fish. *Bouillabaisse* also offers an honorable end for the wrasse, found throughout the North Atlantic and Pacific under the names of sheepshead, cunner, hogfish and tautog. All wrasse are white and delicate, good broiled on the bone as well as in soup.

Rockfish are a large and varied family, found mainly along the American coasts. Some members, including the Pacific Ocean perch and the Atlantic Ocean perch, look similar to red snapper and are often sold as such, although they are inferior. The flesh of rockfish varies from fairly firm to very soft and difficult to handle. For this reason soup is the most advisable cooking method for it. Other notable rockfish include bolina and goldeneye, which approach the mild firm flesh of snapper. The yellowtail rockfish has less taste and the boccaccio is softer; other common varieties are disappointing. The name rockfish is also sometimes given in the United States to the striped bass (p.137) and the scorpion fish family.

Flying fish now share their Latin name of *exocetus* with a missile. Found in both Atlantic and Pacific tropical waters, flying fish are more stunning to watch than to eat. Lumpfish does not even look attractive, its real asset being its roe, which is used to make a "poor man's" caviar (p.131).

Equally curious in appearance is the little puffer, or blowfish, found in warm water along the northeast Atlantic. When frightened, it puffs up like a bullfrog and is about the same size. The tail yields two small fillets of tender meat. The puffer's skin is armed with prickly scales, so protective gloves are advisable when skinning and dressing it. When preparing blowfish for cooking, it is important to gut, trim and wash the fish thoroughly; its liver and intestines contain toxins, which although not fatal, taste unpleasant. (**Note** In Japanese species the toxins are harmful.) The skin should also be removed. The triggerfish or leatherjacket has a sharp, triggerlike spine on its head. Found in warm waters on both sides of the Atlantic, with a Pacific cousin, its meat is excellent, but the thick skin must be removed before cooking.

All these fish need the support of flavorings like herbs, tomato, saffron, fennel, garlic and other members of the onion family. For most fish soups, the fish is prepared in similar fashion: after gutting, the fins and tail are trimmed and the fish is scaled, then thoroughly washed. Depending on the recipe, the body is cut in large pieces or steaks, including the bones for shape and flavor; the flesh may also be filleted. Marinating the fish for an hour or two before cooking adds flavor and the acid touch of lemon or white wine is helpful too, possibly with a dash of hot pepper sauce or Worcestershire sauce. For many fish soups (p.48), the head and bones are simmered to make stock in which the fish itself is then cooked, thus further concentrating the flavor.

Yellowtail rockfish

Scorpion fish

Gurnard

USEFUL INFORMATION

Portion *On bone with head:* 1-1¼ lb/500-625 g. *On bone without head:* ¾ lb/375 g. *Fillets:* 6 oz/175 g.

Nutritive value per 3½ oz/100 g (raw). *Scorpion fish:* 94 calories; 19 g protein; 2 g fat; no carbohydrates; 60 mg sodium; 35 mg cholesterol. *Rockfish:* 94 calories; 19 g protein; 2 g fat; no carbohydrates; 60 mg sodium; 35 mg cholesterol.

Cooking times *Whole:* bake at 350°F/175°C, broil, time depends on thickness (p.117). *Fillets:* broil 3-5 minutes each side; sauté 3-5 minutes each side; simmer in soup 7-12 minutes.

Problems Bland, so need plenty of seasoning; fall apart easily.

Fresh forms Whole, fillets.

Processed forms Frozen; smoked.

Storage *Whole:* refrigerate 1-2 days. *Fillets:* refrigerate 1 day.

Typical dishes *Gurnard:* stewed with garlic and onions (France); with almond sauce (Turkey); fried and pickled (Italy); baked in cider with mushroom and sausage meat stuffing (France). *Scorpion fish:* fried with tomatoes and almonds (Spain); with onions, tomatoes and anchovies (France). *Rockfish:* baked with tomatoes, olives, capers and chilies (Mexico); broiled with saffron butter sauce (USA). For information on fish soups see Stocks and Soups (p.48).

SALMON & TROUT
PACIFIC SALMON, ATLANTIC SALMON, SALMON TROUT, RAINBOW TROUT

At first sight, salmon and trout might seem quite different, but for the cook they demand similar preparations. The two fish have a similar bone structure, small fins, and thin skin with tiny scales. Both salmon and trout are now farmed with great success, ensuring a steady supply of reliable fish in standard sizes for filleting and for cooking as large whole fish.

The unique qualities of the salmon family need little introduction. Its imposing size, deep pink flesh and delectable flavor have earned salmon the accolade "king of fish". Salmon are anadromous, in other words, they are born in rivers in fresh water, then journey far into the ocean, where they live for one to six years before returning to their birthplace to spawn and in the case of Pacific salmon, to die. Wild salmon once were native to most northern temperate rivers, but pollution and the dams that frustrate their run upstream have reduced their numbers. However, conservation measures and farming have helped stabilize the supply.

There are two groups of salmon: firstly the Pacific salmon, of which there are six very different species, and secondly the Atlantic salmon (the Baltic salmon is of the same species but its flesh is paler and slightly fattier). All are similar in appearance – handsome fish, with sleek silver skin and a small head. Their color ranges from gray to brown or dark blue, sometimes with speckled markings of red or black, and the largest can weigh up to 100 lb/ 45 kg, though most are much smaller. The best of the Pacific species, king or chinook salmon, is larger and richer, with a heavier flavor than the Atlantic salmon.

Other Pacific salmon include the sockeye or red salmon, which has rich deep red meat that was once much used for canning, but is now in demand fresh as well. The coho or silver salmon has light, well-flavored meat, while pink salmon is fine-textured and mild; it spoils rapidly so it is generally used for canning. Coarse-textured chum or dog salmon has the lowest fat content; its orange roe is valued for red caviar. One species, the cherry salmon, is found only on the Asian side of the Pacific.

The best wild salmon are caught by hook and line either in the ocean or after entering the river to spawn. Large-scale farming of several salmon varieties is being conducted in Canada, Norway, Scotland, Ireland, the United States, Chile and New Zealand. Farmed salmon has the advantage of consistent quality and availability, but the challenge for the industry is to duplicate the flavor and texture of wild salmon.

The salmon trout is a family of several species: the sea trout, the brown trout found in rivers, and the lake trout. Salmon trout migrates throughout the North Atlantic, as well as being found in some larger inland freshwater areas. The normally pink flesh is firm like trout with a mild flavor evocative of salmon, and some people regard it as superior to both. Salmon trout commonly average 4-5 lb/2-2.3 kg, with the smaller fish being the more flavorful. In some regions of the United States, the term sea trout confusingly denotes a species of croaker. A relative of the salmon trout is the Arctic char, native to Atlantic and Pacific Arctic water

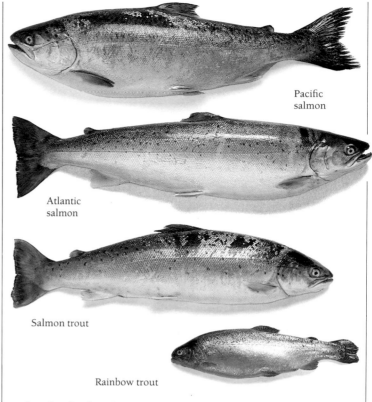

Pacific salmon

Atlantic salmon

Salmon trout

Rainbow trout

and to landlocked lakes in areas further south, such as England's Lake Windermere and France's Lake Annecy. Most varieties weigh only a couple of pounds, and their flesh varies from white to pink.

Other species of trout can live in both fresh and sea water. The most familiar is the rainbow trout, which takes its name from its multi-hued skin, liberally spotted with brown. Freshwater rainbow trout weighs more than 2 lb/1 kg. However, on the Pacific east coast, rainbow trout also travels to the sea and becomes a "steelhead". Such trout, with tasty pink flesh, can grow up to 50 lb/23 kg. Both fresh and smoked steelhead are excellent, and its caviar (p.131) is of good repute.

Among the many trout fished for sport is the pink-spotted Dolly Varden, found in the northern Pacific. The brook or speckled trout, which has rusty red spots, lives only inland. Lake or gray trout, native to the northern American and Canadian lakes, is a large fish, fattier than most trout. It is often smoked, but also makes good eating when fresh. Related to trout, but with only an echo of its flavor, is the grayling, a freshwater fish found in Europe and North America.

Because they are such excellent fish for sport, trout have been transplanted from one continent to another; for example the rainbow trout was once only native to the east Pacific but is now found throughout Europe and North America.

Habitat and feeding affect the taste and color of salmon, trout and salmon trout. Pinkness in fresh or farmed trout or salmon is caused by a pigmentation reaction between the fish and the pigment contained in certain crustaceans. These crustaceans are found in fresh or salt water that has a high level of chalk or limestone in it. The degree of pinkness in the fish depends on how long it has been in these waters and on its feeding habits. For example, a trout that has only had insect larvae to feed on will have white flesh. With farmed fish, the color of the fish can be influenced by a controlled diet.

The cooking possibilities for salmon and trout are almost endless. Their succulent meat invites poaching or steaming to serve with a butter sauce; the pronounced flavor of salmon easily holds its own with béarnaise, while white butter sauce goes best with trout. The famous French *truite au bleu* or blue trout, is simply a freshly killed rainbow trout dipped quickly in vinegar so the skin turns blue, then simmered in *court bouillon*.

Small fresh trout fried outdoors with a slice of bacon are the fisherman's dream, equalled only by trout sautéed in butter and topped with sliced almonds or a sprinkling of herbs and lemon. Salmon steaks broil well, while whole salmon or trout can be split and "planked" to roast in front of an open fire in American Indian style. Both fish may be baked in parchment paper or aluminum foil, perhaps on a bed of vegetables. Large salmon fillets are often cut into escalopes (p.117) to pan-fry or steam.

A whole poached salmon is a royal treat, whether served hot with hollandaise, or cold in a robe of aspic (below). If a fish poacher is not available, the fish can be wrapped tightly in aluminum foil to bake whole in the oven. Salmon is one of the few fish that braises well in fish stock with red or white wine. The cooking liquid makes a delectable sauce when bound with kneaded butter (p.59).

Salmon and trout, often mixed with a portion of smoked fish, make excellent pâtés, terrines and *mousselines* and, in the case of salmon, add an attractive pink color. Salmon is ideal for marinating to serve raw (p.125). One reason for its popularity is the excellence with which it can be preserved by dry-salting and smoking (see Preserving and Freezing, p.488). The roe of several species of salmon can be substituted for sturgeon roe to make a more than acceptable caviar (p.131).

USEFUL INFORMATION/SALMON & TROUT

Portion *On bone with head:* ¾ lb/ 375 g. *On bone without head:* ½ lb/ 250 g. *Steaks or fillets:* 6 oz/175 g.
Nutritive value per 3½ oz/100 g (raw). *Pacific salmon:* 180 calories; 20 g protein; 10 g fat; no carbohydrates; 47 mg sodium; 66 mg cholesterol. *Atlantic salmon:* 142 calories; 20 g protein; 6 g fat; no carbohydrates; 44 mg sodium; 55 mg cholesterol. *Rainbow trout:* 118 calories; 21 g protein; 3 g fat; no carbohydrates; 27 mg sodium; 57 mg cholesterol. *Salmon trout:* 148 calories; 21 g protein; 7 g fat; no carbohydrates; 52 mg sodium; 58 mg cholesterol.
Cooking methods *Whole, large:* bake or braise at 350°F/175°C, poach, steam, time depends on thickness (p.117). *Whole, small:* bake at 350°F/175°C, 12-18 minutes; broil 5-7 minutes each side; pan-fry or sauté 5-7 minutes each side; poach 12-18 minutes; steam 12-18 minutes. *Steaks or fillets:* bake uncovered or in parchment paper or aluminum foil at 350°F/175°C, 12-18 minutes; broil 3-5 minutes each side; marinate sliced to serve raw 1-2 hours; poach 10-15 minutes; sauté 3-5 minutes each side; steam 10-15 minutes.
Problems Trout lose flavor rapidly when stored; in some salmon, dark flesh under skin can be strong, so scrape it off after cooking.
Fresh forms *Salmon:* whole, steaks, fillets. *Trout:* whole, fillets.
Processed forms *Salmon:* frozen; canned fresh and smoked; cold and hot smoked (kippered); salted (lox); cured (*gravad lax*); dried (Pacific). *Trout:* frozen; smoked; canned.
Storage *Whole salmon:* refrigerate 2-3 days. *Salmon steaks or fillets:* refrigerate 2 days. *Whole trout or fillets:* refrigerate 1-2 days.
Typical dishes *Salmon:* steaks with hollandaise (France); broiled (Scandinavia); warm salad with ginger-soy dressing (USA); raw, marinated in fresh ginger and herbs (France); sautéed with white wine and shallots (France); fillets baked in paper with fresh dill (USA); barbecued with lemon juice (USA). *Trout: truite du Gave* (with mushrooms, garlic, cream and *pastis*, France); pan-fried, stuffed with bacon (USA); marinated and fried (Norway); poached in beer, white wine, herbs and horseradish (UK); cold in orange marinade (Italy); stuffed with wild mushrooms (France); *forelle blau* (poached in vinegar and water, served with butter, Germany).

Poached salmon in aspic

Any plump round fish such as sea bass, cod or hake can be served in aspic, but none makes quite the impact of pink-fleshed salmon.

Serves 8-10

A 6-7 lb/3 kg salmon, trimmed, scaled and gutted (p.111)	8-10 medium shrimp, cooked and peeled
4-5 qt/4-5 L fish stock (p.44)	tomato, green and Chantilly mayonnaise (p.63)
2 qt/2 L aspic (p.253) made from salmon stock	salt
2 medium cucumbers	*Fish poacher (p.510)*

1 Poach the salmon (p.119) in the fish stock and leave to cool in the stock until tepid. Drain the salmon, reserving the stock, and peel off the skin (p.118). Transfer the salmon to a rack set over a tray and chill until very cold. Make aspic with the fish stock.
2 Peel the cucumbers, leaving stripes of skin, and slice very thinly. Sprinkle them with salt and let stand 30 minutes.
3 Rinse the cucumber with water to wash away the salt and drain thoroughly. Arrange sliced cucumber over the salmon to resemble the scales of a fish and set the shrimp upright in the groove along the back of the fish. Chill the fish again.
4 Pour a thin layer of aspic on to a large tray and chill it until set. Coat the salmon with 2-3 layers of aspic (see Charcuterie, p.253), chilling between each coating. Chill any remaining aspic and chop it into decorative shapes (p.253).
5 Transfer the fish on to a tray and decorate with chopped aspic. Serve the three kinds of mayonnaise separately.

FRESHWATER FISH
Carp, pike, catfish, whitefish, perch

Unfortunately, supplies of freshwater fish have dropped dramatically owing to overfishing and pollution. Conservation measures are now being taken, but farmed freshwater fish, with its relatively standard, handy size and reliable if unremarkable quality, will continue to occupy the lion's share of the market.

Many and varied as they are, freshwater fish have in common a mild, delicate flavor. The flesh is sometimes coarse, sometimes fine. Simple treatment is the best, top choices being poaching, steaming and sautéing in butter. Freshwater fish are more likely than other fish to be contaminated by pollution; the toxins tend to collect in the skin and the thin layer of fat just below it. Therefore it is a sensible precaution to remove the skin and fat from freshwater fish before cooking them.

Carp (one variety of which is the goldfish) has long been raised for food the world over. The common carp, which is big-boned and plump, often reaching 5 lb/2.3 kg, is the most common type found in Europe and North America. The texture of carp can be described in culinary terms as "coarse", but if you are lucky, the flesh is sweet; its quality, however, depends more on habitat than almost any other fish. If a carp has been living in mud, for example, it will taste poor. This is one reason why carp farmed in clean water can be better than some wild types.

A group of fish resembling the carp is the North American sucker family. Best is the buffalofish, which usually weighs 3-4 lb/1.4-1.8 kg, and the smaller white sucker (also called freshwater mullet) which, despite its name, has an olive skin and fine scales. The freshwater sheepshead is pearly-gray, somewhat egg-shaped and, like carp and sucker, usually coarse-fleshed. Confusingly, the name sheepshead also describes a sea bream (p.140) and a species of wrasse.

Baking on the bone or simmering in sauce are good choices for cooking these fish, which tend to be bland and flaky. The mild flavor of carp marries well with sweet ingredients, as in French *carpe à la juive*, simmered in fish stock with raisins and almonds.

A predatory and wily game fish, pike is easy to recognize by its sharp, saw-like teeth and blue-black, mottled body. It is found throughout Europe and North America, with substantial supplies being exported from Canada to Europe. Belonging to the same family as pike are North American grass pickerel and muskellunge, together with the European pike-perch or zander, the American blue and wall-eye pikes, and the Canadian sauger. "Pickerel" is not a separate fish, but a name given in some places to small pike and pike-perch.

The meat of all the pike family is sweet and fine-textured, the best of all freshwater fish. Their only problem is a network of fine hair-like bones, especially in smaller fish, which are almost impossible to remove by hand. The classic solution is to purée and sieve pike and its cousins for fish dumplings, whether as French *quenelles* (p.146) or Jewish *gefiltefish* (p.125).

Distinguished by its bewhiskered face, the freshwater catfish is sweet and white-fleshed like pike; it averages in size from 1 lb/ 500 g to 20 lb/9 kg, though some species may attain 600 lb/ 270 kg. Catfish is a favorite in the American South, where it is often coated with cornmeal and pan-fried in butter.

Whitefish is a large and varied family, which also has some saltwater relatives. Most famous is the lake whitefish from the Great Lakes, with the largest catch coming from the rivers and lakes of Canada. Lake herring is a close, dark-fleshed relative. Europe has its own species of whitefish and they are particularly abundant in Russia. Whitefish is pleasant, slightly flaky and richer than most white-fleshed fish, so it smokes well. A whole fish is good poached, while fillets are particularly succesful when lightly sautéed in butter and served with a sprinkling of fresh herbs.

Perch is a label applied to a variety of fish, both freshwater and seawater. The freshwater yellow perch is found in the Great Lakes and all its tributaries. The yellow and the European perch are both good little fish for pan-frying and are often sold as boneless butterflied fillets.

North American sunfish, unlike British sunfish which is another name for the seawater opah or moonfish, is very similar to perch, though the names of the different species – flier, pumpkinseed, redbreast – seem designed to lend them individuality. Best known of all are the black and white crappies, and the rock and calico basses. Good eaten when very fresh, their main attraction is for weekend fishermen. The delicate sweetness of these freshwater fish pairs well with *beurre blanc* (p.62) and light

Pike

Carp

Perch

Catfish

toppings of herbs, butter and citrus. A dusting of flour or cornmeal and a quick sauté in butter is an equal guarantee of success, perhaps with a sprinkling of slivered almonds and a squeeze of lemon or lime.

USEFUL INFORMATION

Portion *On bone with head:* 1 lb/500 g. *On bone without head:* ½ lb-¾ lb/250-375 g. *Fillets:* 6 oz/175 g.

Nutritive value per 3½ oz/100 g (raw). *Carp:* 127 calories; 18 g protein; 6 g fat; no carbohydrates; 49 mg sodium; 66 mg cholesterol. *Catfish:* 116 calories; 18 g protein; 4 g fat; no carbohydrates; 63 mg sodium; 58 mg cholesterol. *Whitefish:* 134 calories; 19 g protein; 6 g fat; no carbohydrates; 51 mg sodium; 60 mg cholesterol. *Pike:* 88 calories; 19 g protein; 1 g fat; no carbohydrates; 39 mg sodium; 39 mg cholesterol. *Perch:* 86 calories; 18 g protein; 1 g fat; no carbohydrates; 61 mg sodium; 90 mg cholesterol.

Cooking methods *Whole, large:* bake at 350°F/175°C; poach or steam, time depends on thickness (p.117).

Cooking methods *Whole, small:* bake at 350°F/175°C, 15-25 minutes; broil 5-7 minutes each side; poach or steam 15-25 minutes; sauté 5-7 minutes each side. *Fillets:* broil 3-5 minutes each side; deep-fry 2-3 minutes; poach or steam 8-12 minutes; sauté 2-3 minutes each side.

Fresh forms Whole, fillets.
Processed forms Frozen.
Whitefish: smoked.
Storage *Whole:* 1-2 days. *Fillets:* 1 day.
Typical dishes *Carp:* in *meurette* sauce with grapes and bacon lardons (France); *schwarzfisch* (poached with almonds and

prunes, Germany); baked with soft roe stuffing (UK); baked in beer (Germany); baked with paprika and sour cream (Hungary). *Pike:* stewed with white wine, cream and mushrooms (France); stuffed with mushrooms, breadcrumbs, anchovies and bacon (UK); poached in horseradish cream

(Hungary); wall-eyed pike broiled with chili butter (USA). *Catfish:* poached, with hollandaise (USA). *Whitefish:* sautéed with morels (UK). *Perch:* sautéed and baked with white wine and prunes (France); *waterzootje* (fish soup, Netherlands); baked in sour cream (Scandinavia).

MAKING QUENELLES

Quenelles are made with puréed raw fish (or white meat or poultry), whole eggs or egg whites, and cream, but they are not to be confused with *mousselines* (p.123). *Quenelles* always have a binding agent, whether a *panade* (p.513) of butter, water and flour, or choux pastry, which has a high egg content to puff and lighten the mixture during cooking. Sometimes butter or extra egg yolks are added to the *quenelles* mixture for richness.

Unlike *mousselines*, *quenelles* are never cooked in a mold, but are poached directly in water, or occasionally baked in the oven. After cooking, *quenelles* are traditionally coated with sauce and baked in the oven to serve hot. Favorite sauces are crayfish-flavored *sauce Nantua* (opposite) and lobster *sauce Cardinal* (p.55). However, following a more modern style, *quenelles* are poached at the last minute and presented on top of a layer of butter sauce. Small *quenelles* can also garnish soup. The fish should be puréed, using a food processor if you like. For finest texture, it should then be worked through a drum sieve particularly if a bony fish such as pike is used.

3 Gradually beat in cream, then season the mixture to taste with salt, pepper and nutmeg. The salt helps stiffen the mixture. Meanwhile bring a large, shallow pan of fish stock or salted water to a boil.

1 Set the fish purée in a bowl over ice (chilling the mixture helps to stiffen it). Whisk the egg whites until frothy and gradually beat them into the fish, a little at a time. (This may be done in a food processor.)

4 Dip 2 tablespoons in the stock, then scoop out a generous spoonful of mixture.

5 Shape the mixture into a neat, three-sided oval by turning the spoons one against the other.

2 Make the choux pastry (p.376) or prepare a *panade*, depending on the recipe. Spread it on a plate to cool. Gradually beat it into the fish mixture.
Note The beating of egg whites and choux pastry into the fish can be done in the food processor, but the mixture must then be thoroughly chilled before the cream is added to it.

6 Drop the *quenelle* into the pan. Poach it 2-3 minutes to be sure it does not break up. If it does, beat another egg white into the mixture and chill thoroughly. Add enough *quenelles* to the pan to fill it without crowding and poach until firm when pressed with a finger, 8-15 minutes depending on size. Drain quickly on paper towels and serve while still hot with a sauce (opposite).

Quenelles sauce Nantua

The streams and lakes of the Alpine foothills around Nantua are famous for their crayfish, which inspired this classic sauce.

Serves 6-8 as a main dish

4 lb/1.8 kg pike, trimmed (p. 111)	1 carrot, finely chopped
choux pastry (p.376) made with ½ cup/125 ml water, ½ tsp salt, 3 tbsp/45 g butter, 9 tbsp/60 g flour and 2 eggs	2 lb/1 kg crayfish
	2 tbsp brandy
	½ cup/125 ml white wine
6-7 egg whites	1 qt/1 L fish stock made with pike heads and bones (p.44)
2 cups/500 ml *crème fraîche* or heavy cream (p.70)	bouquet garni
	⅓ cup/45 g flour
pinch of grated nutmeg	2 cups/500 ml *crème fraîche* or heavy cream
salt and pepper	
For Nantua sauce	1 tsp tomato paste (optional)
¾ cup/175 g butter	pinch cayenne pepper
1 onion, finely chopped	

1 Fillet the fish (p.114) and remove the skin. Rinse the fillets and dry them. Use the pike heads and bones to make stock. Make the choux pastry.
2 Make the *quenelles* (left) using the pike flesh, egg whites, choux pastry and *crème fraîche* or heavy cream and season with nutmeg, salt and pepper. Shape and poach them. Set them on a buttered baking sheet and cover them with buttered foil.
3 **For the Nantua sauce:** melt a quarter of the butter in a large shallow pan and sauté the onion and carrot until soft. Add the crayfish and sauté, tossing over high heat until they turn red, about 2 minutes. Add the brandy and flame (p.38). Add the white wine, fish stock, bouquet garni, salt and pepper and simmer 8-10 minutes until the crayfish turn bright red. Remove them and shell them (p.162), discarding the intestinal vein. Work the shells in a food processor with a little liquid from the pan until finely

chopped, or work them a little at a time in a blender. Return them to the pan and simmer 10 minutes longer. Strain the mixture, pressing hard on the shells and vegetables to extract all the liquid. Melt all but 3 tablespoons of the remaining butter in a saucepan, whisk in the flour and cook until foaming but not browned. Whisk in the shellfish liquid and bring the sauce to a boil, whisking constantly until the sauce thickens. Simmer 10-15 minutes or until the sauce just coats a spoon. Add the heavy cream or *crème fraîche* and bring just back to a boil. If the sauce is pale, stir in a little tomato paste, add a pinch of cayenne pepper and taste it for seasoning.
4 Meanwhile warm the *quenelles* in a 400°F/200°C oven 8-12 minutes. Arrange them on 6-8 individual plates, spoon the sauce on top and sprinkle them with crayfish tails for decoration. Serve immediately; *quenelles* should be hot.

RICH OILY FISH
HERRING, SARDINE, SHAD, MACKEREL, BLUEFISH

The flavors of different types of oily fish are very characteristic – no one would mistake the taste of herring for that of mackerel. Their flesh is soft and flaky and most weigh under 5 lb/2.3 kg, with a few bigger fish weighing 10 lb/4.5 kg. They are found worldwide; some are richer and oilier than others – one or two species of mackerel, for instance, can be quite firm and white. Despite these differences, the cook can take a consistent approach to cooking them.

Most common is the herring, a fish that for centuries supported the economy of the entire seafaring communities of countries such as Norway and Denmark. Today, just as in former times, more herring is eaten pickled or cured than fresh. Herring roe, sautéed or baked in butter, is as popular as the flesh.

Sea herring is limited to two very similar species, the Atlantic herring and the Pacific herring, both found throughout the two oceans. The fat content of the fish varies with the season. The flesh of a plump, full-grown herring caught in the fall or early winter will be much richer than in spring, after spawning.

Close relatives are pilchards, most of which end up in cans. Small pilchards are sold as sardines. Sardines are young pilchards but the name is also applied to baby Atlantic or Pacific herring, and to sprats, silvery little fish so small that their name has become synonymous with insignificance. Another small oily fish, the smelt, can grow to the size of a little herring and is cooked in the same way. They are found worldwide in both salt- and freshwater. The anchovy, another oily little fish, has a characteristic flavor at its best when salted and used as a seasoning, though fresh anchovies are quite good fried or baked. On the market slab, these fish vary in color from blue to green or black, always with a strong shading of silver.

The coloring of the shad, however, is closer to gold – an appropriate color for the most prestigious member of the herring family. The fine-textured flesh is delicate, and appreciated all the more because the season is short: shad is caught as it runs upriver to spawn. Native to the northwest Atlantic, the shad has been transplanted successfully to the northeast Pacific. The European species of shad are less tasty than their American relatives. The North American alewife, or branch herring, and the blueback herring also belong to the shad family, though they resemble an insipid herring. Shad roe is a particular delicacy, often more popular than the bony fish that bears it.

The prolific mackerel family is found in a dozen species, typically with rich, fine-textured flesh. The Atlantic mackerel is one of the smaller species, weighing under 5 lb/2.3 kg, though big king mackerel can weigh as much as 100 lb/45 kg. In Europe Spanish mackerel denotes a small fatty fish, while the American Spanish mackerel is leaner and larger, commonly 2-3 lb/1-1.4 kg. The flesh of cero is whiter, but the frigate mackerel's flesh is so dark it is often compared with tuna. Note that horse mackerel is a member of the jack family (p.140). Mackerel are easy to identify, with iridescent skin in shades from blue-green to gold, marked in mottled lateral lines. Only the American Spanish mackerel is different, with spots instead of lines. The king mackerel is often called kingfish, a confusing name also applied to the king whiting and to the renowned game fish, wahoo.

The wahoo (also known as *ono*, meaning "sweet" in Hawaiian) is distinguished at the table, with white flesh and outstanding flavor. It is native to the Gulf of Mexico and the Pacific, with an average weight of 30 lb/14 kg or more. The bluefish is smaller, rarely more than 15 lb/6.8 kg. Found commonly on the west Atlantic coast, its flesh is soft and dark like mackerel with a pleasant flavor that gets stronger when the fish is large. Similar to wahoo in taste and texture is the barracuda.

Elegant, steely-blue bonito looks like tuna, but its flesh is less meaty, closely resembling mackerel. One species or another is found in warm waters worldwide, and they usually weigh under 10 lb/4.5 kg. Note that the striped bonito, however, is a real tuna, called the skipjack (p.133).

The intricate network of fine bones in many oily fish causes problems in preparation. At their worst, as in shad, they must be removed by a professional. For this reason, shad is generally sold off the bone as fillets. The delicate bones of herring, and, to a lesser extent, those of mackerel, are also tiresome, though with care they can be cut out from raw fish, or pulled with the backbone from the cooked meat. Small soft fish can be boned by hand, pulling out the backbone with your fingers (Boning small oily fish, opposite). The skin of oily fish is usually left on during cooking to hold the flesh together, but it can have a strong taste and is not necessarily eaten.

Absolute freshness and careful handling, including immediate gutting and chilling or icing, are prerequisites for all oily fish. The high oil content oxidizes and turns rancid rapidly, causing an acrid taste and a strong smell even when frozen. Yellow patches, particularly on the belly, are a bad sign. Furthermore, lack of refrigeration of certain oily fish can produce histamines in the flesh, which may cause an allergic reaction. However, with careful handling, these fish can be outstanding. Think of crisply broiled sardines as found in cafés on the Mediterranean, to be crunched whole with a glass of cold wine. They are favorites with the Portuguese, who often broil them and sandwich them in corn bread called *broa*. Try the first baby herring offered on the streets of Holland in May, brined and then boned to eat raw with just a touch of onion and salt and a glass of schnapps. Sample shad, roasted on a plank of wood in front of an open fire, or a line-caught mackerel, broiled briefly on the barbecue.

Despite their richness, many oily fish are good pan-fried, since this seals in flavor and helps dissolve fat under the skin. Boiled rather than fried potatoes are the best accompaniment, plus a wedge of lemon or a hot mustard sauce. Deep-frying is reserved for the smallest of rich fish (p. 119).

Broiling can also perfectly balance rich fish, with nothing more than a sprinkling of salt, pepper and perhaps an aromatic herb like thyme; quite big fish can be cooked this way, as their fatty skins baste the meat inside. Appropriate accompaniments include baked potatoes, broiled tomatoes, and a topping of herb or anchovy butter for the fish itself. Both large or serving-sized whole fish can be baked in the oven, again with simple flavorings. A topping of thinly sliced bacon is traditional with shad and with herring.

Another approach to oily fish is to counteract their richness with some acid ingredient – a favorite Scandinavian tactic. Herring and mackerel are baked with vegetables and plenty of vinegar, forming a mild pickle; fish may be lightly salted before frying to

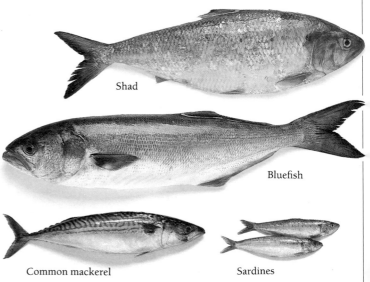

Shad

Bluefish

Herring

American Spanish mackerel

Bonito

Common mackerel

Sardines

serve with lingonberries in Scandinavian style, or fried and then marinated with vinegar and herbs. Herring with sour cream is an international classic.

Texture is not a problem when cooking rich fish, for their flesh is tender, yet holds its shape well. Their main disadvantage is strong or cloying flavor, so methods like steaming and poaching, designed to enhance delicate flavors, should be avoided. Nor are they suitable for soup, though a mixture of white and oily fish may be called for in stews like Breton *cotriade* with mussels, and smoked oily fish have a place in creamy chowders.

USEFUL INFORMATION

Portion *On bone with head: ¾ lb/ 375 g. On bone without head: ½ lb/ 250 g. Steaks or fillets: 6 oz/175 g.*
Nutritive value *per 3½ oz/100 g (raw). Herring:* 158 calories; 18 g protein; 9 g fat; no carbohydrates; 90 mg sodium; 60 mg cholesterol. *Sardine:* 142 calories; 19 g protein; 7 g fat; no carbohydrates; 100 mg sodium; 52 mg cholesterol. *Shad:* 197 calories; 17 g protein; 14 g fat; no carbohydrates; 52 mg sodium; 80 mg cholesterol. *Mackerel:* 139 calories; 19 g protein; 6 g fat; no carbohydrates; 59 mg sodium; 76 mg cholesterol. *Bluefish:* 124 calories; 20 g protein; 4 g fat; no carbohydrates; 60 mg sodium; 59 mg cholesterol.
Cooking times *Whole, large:* bake at 350°F/175°C; broil, time depends on thickness (p.117). *Whole, small:* bake at 350°F/175°C, 15-25 minutes; broil or pan-fry 5-7 minutes each side. *Steaks or fillets:* bake at 350°F/175°C, 12-20 minutes; broil or pan-fry 3-5 minutes each side; poach with vinegar 12-20 minutes; simmer in stew 8-12 minutes.
Problems Flavor is strong if stored; dark meat just under the skin is also strong.

Fresh forms *Herring, sprat, smelt, sardine, anchovy:* whole. *Mackerel:* whole, fillets. *Shad:* whole, boneless fillets. *Wahoo:* steak, fillet. *Barracuda:* whole, fillet. *Bonito:* whole, fillet.
Processed forms *Herring:* frozen; smoked (kipper, red herring, bloater, buckling); salted; dried; pickled; canned in oil, tomato, spiced sauce. *Sardine:* frozen; salted; dried (Japan); pickled; canned in oil, tomato. *Mackerel:* smoked; salted; dried; pickled; canned in oil or tomato sauce.
Storage *Whole, steaks or fillets:* refrigerate 1 day.
Typical dishes *Herring:* baked with potatoes, sage and onions (Wales); Yorkshire herring pie (UK); pickled (Finland); in salad with dill sauce (USA). *Sardines:* in salad with potatoes, tomatoes, anchovies and herbs in vinaigrette (France). *Mackerel:* poached with gooseberry sauce (UK); soup (with potatoes, dill and pepper, Sweden); caveach (fried and pickled, Scotland). *Shad:* with its roe in cream sauce (USA); dried and pressed with bay leaves and broiled (Italy). *Bluefish:* broiled with capers and onions (USA).

BONING SMALL OILY FISH

Small oily fish such as sardines or sprats are so soft they can be boned with your fingers. Here, sardine is shown.

1 Pinch off the head of the fish between your finger and thumb and discard it, together with the gills.

2 Press open the belly with your finger and scoop out the intestines.

3 Open the fish flat along the belly and pull out the backbone, starting at the head end and loosening it with your fingers. Snap the backbone at the tail, then rinse the fish fillets and leave them to dry before baking or frying.

Pickled fried herring

Small mackerel can be substituted for herring in this Scandinavian dish. It can be served hot or cold.

Serves 4

4 herring, ¾ lb/375 g each, trimmed, scaled and gutted (p.112)	**For the pickle**
	1½ cups/375 ml white vinegar
salt and pepper	½ cup/100 g sugar
2 eggs, beaten to mix	2 tbsp/25 g allspice berries
1½ cups/175 g dry white breadcrumbs	3 bay leaves
	1 small onion, thinly sliced
¼ cup/60 g butter	¼ cup/15 g dill or parsley sprigs
¼ cup/60 ml oil	

1 **For the pickle:** heat the vinegar, sugar, allspice, bay leaves and onion until sugar dissolves. Simmer 5 minutes and leave to cool.
2 Bone the herring through the stomach, leaving the head and tail on. Rinse the fish, dry them on paper towels and sprinkle with salt and pepper. Fold them in a fan, tucking the tail through the mouth (p.113). Coat the fish in egg, then roll them in the breadcrumbs.
3 Heat the butter and oil in a frying pan until foaming, add the fish, tail-side upwards and fry briskly until browned, 3-5 minutes. Turn and brown the other side.
4 Drain the fish on paper towels and arrange them in a flat shallow serving dish. Add the dill to the pickle and pour over the fish. Cover and refrigerate at least 3 hours, or overnight. Serve chilled, with potato salad or as part of a *smörgåsbord* – a Scandinavian-style cold buffet.

LONG-BODIED FISH
EEL, GARFISH, LAMPREY

Eels have been fished for centuries but until recently their life cycle was a mystery. Baby elvers (called glass eels because they are almost transparent), 2-3 in/5-7 cm long appear in spring at the mouths of rivers, bunched together by the million in long shoals that make their way upstream. There the elvers grow, first turning a yellowish color, then silver. After several years they return to sea to spawn. Their spawning grounds were unknown until early this century, when it was proved that Atlantic eels return from Europe and America all the way to the Sargasso Sea.

Eels are caught commercially at two stages: as elvers, and fully-grown when returning to the sea to spawn. Half-grown eels, caught in rivers in eel traps or with rod and line, are good to eat only if they have matured enough to be fatty. Eels are best sold live so they are very fresh. They are killed by piercing the spinal cord before being skinned.

The common eel grows to about a yard (less in North America), and Japanese and Australian eels look and taste very similar. The meat is outstandingly firm, rich and slightly oily, with a clear, yet subtle flavor much appreciated by connoisseurs. In Japan, a popular dish is broiled eel that has first been marinated and steamed. However, eel is by no means a universal favorite, as some people are repelled by its serpentine shape. Consequently, much of the North American catch is exported to the Netherlands and Scandinavia, where eel features in traditional cooking.

Conger eel is sold in Europe but not in North America. Conger eels are much larger than the common eel, and the meat, which is very different from and inferior to that of common eel, is best when cut from the middle and upper section. The vicious moray, native to warm waters, and the muddy-tasting sand-eel are less commonly eaten, although baby sand-eels are good for whitebait. Other edible long-bodied fish include the American eel pout and ocean pout.

Garfish belong to the needlefish family, with long, eel-like bodies and a characteristic pointed nose. The garfish has earned the name green bone because of the color of its bones. The flesh, however, is white, firm and well-flavored, though it may be dry and benefits from moist cooking methods such as poaching. The flesh is white, firm and well-flavored when cooked. Similar species are found in the northeastern Atlantic, the Mediterranean and Australian waters, with a soft-fleshed freshwater look-alike in North America, called gar. A smaller relation is the needlefish or skipper, native to the northern Atlantic. The names of the cutlassfish found in the western Atlantic and Pacific, and the eastern Atlantic scabbardfish are even more evocative. Their flesh resembles that of the garfish.

Most curious of all is the sea lamprey, which looks like an eel but is cartilaginous without bones. Lampreys are not usually eaten nowadays, though they are still favored in Portugal, Spain, the Bordeaux region of France, Latvia and Estonia.

All these long-bodied fish are easy to bone and the long meaty fillets are often broiled, while whiter types like the garfish are excellent poached or sautéed. Another approach is to slice them crosswise into thick steaks for soups and stews, like the Flemish herb-laden *anguille au vert*, or *matelote* from the French Loire Valley, made with baby onions, mushrooms, white wine and plenty of cream. Eels are gelatinous fish. When poached in a vinegar *court bouillon* (p.44) then left to cool, they produce a liquid which sets to a fragrant jelly. Eel is often part of a mixture of fish in soup, and the bones make excellent fish stock. Much of the eel catch, however, goes to the smokehouse for smoked eel which, when served with a sprinkling of lemon juice or a spoonful of horseradish sauce, is perhaps the greatest treat of all.

Elvers are so tiny they should be cooked only a minute or two. They can be deep-fried like whitebait (below), quickly sautéed in olive oil with a little garlic and chili pepper, or lightly pan-fried then cooked with eggs in an omelet.

USEFUL INFORMATION

Portion *On bone with head*: ¾ lb/ 375 g. *On bone without head*: ½ lb/ 250 g. *Steaks or fillets*: 4-6 oz/125-175 g.
Nutritive value per 3½ oz/100 g (raw). *Eel*: 184 calories; 18 g protein; 12 g fat; no carbohydrates; 51 mg sodium; 126 mg cholesterol. *Garfish*: 105 calories; 19 g protein; 14 g fat; no carbohydrates; 90 mg sodium; 70 mg cholesterol.
Cooking methods *Steaks*: broil 2-4 minutes each side; poach 8-12 minutes. *Fillets*: broil 2-3 minutes each side; poach 5-7 minutes; sauté 2-3 minutes each side.
Problems Strong flavor if stored.
Fresh forms Whole, steaks, fillets. *Eel*: live, steaks, fillets.
Processed forms Frozen smoked; canned; jellied; pickled.
Storage *Whole*: buy live if possible.

Fillets: refrigerate 1 day.
Typical dishes Eel pie (UK); fried eels with creamed potatoes (Denmark); spit-roasted (Italy); fried with capers and pickled beets (Scandinavia); *gestoofde paling met appeltjes* (baked, with spiced apples, Netherlands); *anguille Médocaire* (stewed with red wine, France); *anguille à l'oseille* (broiled, with sorrel sauce, France).

Eel

WHITEBAIT

Contrary to popular belief, the English term "whitebait" refers not to a single species of fish, but rather to a dish that may consist of several kinds of young fish, deep-fried until crisp and golden brown. The most common today are immature herrings and sprats, preferably no bigger than 2½ in/6 cm long, but any combination of tiny fish may be used, provided that they are small enough to have very delicate, edible bones. Baby eels, called glass eels or elvers, are good, as are anchovies, smelts and even tiny sole. Fish for whitebait is often sold frozen and should be thawed before coating and frying.

The dish seems to have originated in England in the late eighteenth century, and at that time at least a half dozen varieties of fish were standard for the mixture. Today many national cuisines have their own version of whitebait: the French deep-fry *nonnat* and *goujons* (p.127); the Dutch have a version with freshwater fish called *witvis*.

To fry whitebait Rinse and dry the fish, but do not head or gut them. Dust them with flour and shake to remove excess. In a deep frying pan, heat oil to about 375°F/190°C and deep-fry the fish until golden brown and very crisp, 1-2 minutes. Season with salt and pepper, and serve immediately with deep-fried parsley and wedges of lemon.

SKINNING EEL

Eel should be cooked as soon as possible after skinning. It is often sold live, as the tough skin is easier to remove immediately after the eel is killed.

1 Grasp the eel just behind the head, using a cloth to get a good grip. Pierce the spinal cord through the back of the head with the point of a knife. (Alternatively pierce the eel with a strong hook.)

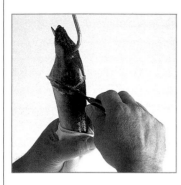

2 Thread the hook through the gills of the eel and suspend it from a securely balanced pole or tie it with string. Slit around the skin just behind the head.

3 Cut the edge of the skin loose, and with the help of a knife start peeling away, working from the head to the tail.

4 Holding the skin with a rough cloth, or with the help of pliers, continue to strip it downwards to skin the eel completely.
Note Even though it is dead, the eel's nerves may continue to twitch.

FILLETING EEL

Unlike many fish, eel should be skinned before being filleted because its tough skin is difficult to cut from the filleted flesh.

1 Lay the skinned eel flat on its side on a cutting board. With a sharp knife, cut across the flesh to the backbone just below the head. Alternatively, cut off the head and discard it.

2 Starting at the head, run a flexible knife along the center of the back and cut away the fillet. Repeat on the other side of the backbone to remove the second eel fillet in the same way.

Broiled marinated eel or mackerel

An Asian-style recipe to suit any oily fish. Softer fish like herring or mackerel should be filleted with the skin left on.

Serves 4

1½ lb/750 g skinned eel fillets or mackerel fillets with skin on	½ cup/100 g dark brown sugar
	1 red chili pepper, cored and sliced into thin rings
salt	
For the marinade	2 scallions, sliced
¾ cup/175 ml rice wine or sherry	
¼ cup/60 ml dark soy sauce	

1 Bring a steamer pan of salted water to a boil. Lay the eel or mackerel fillets on the steamer rack, cover with the lid and set the rack over the boiling water. Steam the fish until flaky on the outside but still transparent in the center, 4-5 minutes for eel, 2-3 minutes for mackerel. Leave the fish to cool.
2 For the marinade: heat the rice wine (or sherry if using), soy sauce and brown sugar until the sugar dissolves. Leave the marinade to cool, then add the chili peppers and scallions. Lay the fish fillets in a shallow dish and pour over the marinade. Cover and leave for 1-2 hours at room temperature.
3 To finish: heat the barbecue or broiler. Drain the fish and pat dry with paper towels. Barbecue or broil the fish 2-3 in/5-7.5 cm from the heat until brown, 3-5 minutes, basting occasionally. For eel, turn and brown the other side; for herring or mackerel, brown only the skinless side.

SHELLFISH

FOR THE COOK'S purposes, shellfish can be divided conveniently into three categories: crustaceans, mollusks, and cephalopods. For the cook, they share at least one characteristic in common: freshness is so important that they are often sold alive.

Technically, crustaceans are animals with external skeletons; their bony outer shells, jointed for movement, are shed periodically as their owners grow larger. Lobster is most prized of all, closely followed by crab, various kinds of shrimp and prawns, and freshwater crayfish.

Mollusks are univalved or bivalved, meaning that they have one or two shells (or valves) that expand as the animal grows. They can be hard to extract from their shells, leading to expressions such as "winkle out" and "clam up". Apart from the snail, univalves such as abalone, conch and whelk tend to be neglected in the kitchen. Bivalves are another story, for they include the more popular oysters, mussels, scallops and clams.

Cephalopods – namely, squid, cuttlefish and octopus – are classed as mollusks. They have a reduced internal shell (a "pen" or, in the case of cuttlefish, a cuttlebone), and share many of the cooking characteristics of shellfish. So do an ill-assorted band of exotic sea and land creatures, such as turtles and frogs, all of which are covered in this chapter.

Sautéing shellfish

Usually, shellfish is extracted from its shell before sautéing (cephalopods are cleaned first). The meat may be raw or cooked and is cut into even pieces so that they cook at the same speed. Sautéing takes very little time – two to three minutes on each side for all but the plumpest of scallops or largest of shrimps. Oysters are cooked in two to three minutes (see information on individual species for how to test when they are done). If the meat is already cooked, sautéing should be even more brief, simply sufficient to warm the pieces through and brown them lightly.

With flavor in mind as well as browning, butter is preferred for sautéing in all but the most robust ethnic shellfish dishes. The shellfish may be lightly coated with seasoned flour, but usually it is left plain and cooked with minimum seasoning so the full, sweet flavor of the meat itself can be appreciated. Common additions are shallots, garlic, herbs, tomato, ham, mushroom, bell pepper and cream. For crustaceans, a pinch of cayenne or chili pepper heightens the flavor.

Other cooking methods for shellfish

Shellfish differ so much from one another that the cooking methods which suit them tend to be distinct to each species. They are often mixed together after cooking, for example in sauce as a gratin, or as a filling for crêpes. They are outstanding in bisques and chowders (Stocks and Soups, p.48) and in *quenelles, mousselines* and terrines (Fish, p.146).

CRUSTACEANS

Crustaceans provide some of the finest eating in the world. Most turn pale or vivid pink when cooked and their flesh is notably firm and sweet. The females, particularly crab and lobster, are sought-after for their coral (eggs), which not only tastes delicious but adds brilliant color to a dish.

Storing crustaceans

Crustaceans should be very fresh. If sold ready-boiled they may be overcooked and of questionable freshness. They are best bought alive, preferably from salt water tanks, and the more vigorously they move the better. At home they can be refrigerated in a plastic bag of dry ice, or in an insulated box filled with damp seaweed. For storage time, see notes on individual species.

Boiling crustaceans

Crustaceans should be cooked in a large, deep pot with sufficient salted water to cover them. Allow at least 1 quart/1 liter water and one tablespoon of salt per 1 lb/500 g shellfish (with minimum 2 quarts/2 liters water); a classic *court bouillon* (p.44) can be substituted. Optional flavorings added to taste are wine, vinegar, lemon, bay leaf, dill stems, parsley stems, sliced onion, peppercorns, cayenne, hot red pepper or Tabasco, and powdered shellfish seasoning, available off the shelf for crab and crayfish.

Bring the water and seasonings to a boil and simmer for five minutes. Turn up the heat again and when the water is at a rolling boil, add the shellfish (live crustaceans will die in a few seconds). Simmer, counting the cooking time from the moment the shellfish is added to the water. Drain at once and let cool. Small lobster, scampi and crayfish may be served *à la nage* – that is, moistened with cooking liquid that has been boiled down until reduced by half. For this method of cooking, reduce the quantity of salt by one-half or one-third.

Steaming crustaceans

Steaming is a reliable method of cooking small crustaceans because it helps to keep them moist. In a wide shallow pan, bring to a boil ½ in/1.25 cm water (lobsters may need 1 in/2.5 cm) with wine, vinegar, and aromatics such as peppercorns, dill, bay leaf, fennel, star anise, and saffron. Simmer for five minutes, then place a few shellfish at a time on a steamer rack, evenly spaced so that steam reaches each item. Set the rack over the simmering liquid, cover and steam. Large shellfish such as lobster and crab are cooked when they turn red (five to ten minutes), small shellfish after three to five minutes, and bivalves should be steamed until they open. Serve the shellfish with butter sauce (p.62) or simply with melted butter.

Broiling crustaceans

Since crustaceans dry out easily during broiling, they must be basted often with marinade, oil or melted butter. Once cleaned, they also benefit from marinating for an hour or two before cooking. For broiling, split the lobster, thread scampi or crayfish tails and prawns, peeled or unpeeled, on to skewers. Sprinkle them with melted butter or oil, seasoning and chopped herbs, or brush with marinade (p.41). Broil them 2-3 in/5-7 cm from the heat, turning once. When done, the flesh is firm and loses its transparency. Serve the shellfish with a butter sauce (p.62), or sprinkled with olive oil.

Other cooking methods for crustaceans

Crustaceans lend themselves extremely well to soups, especially bisques (p.48). Maximum flavor can be extracted by simmering the shells or by making shellfish butter (p.155). Certain preparations suit individual crustaceans. Scampi and prawns, for instance, are often deep-fried in batter or sautéed; crabmeat may be baked with butter and seasonings, in a sauce, shaped into patties or used as seafood stuffing; lobster may be roasted in the oven instead of broiled. The greatest variety of lobster dishes can be made with the meat – notably gratins, stir-fried dishes, and classic French preparations such as lobster Thermidor, or the American creation, lobster Newburg, with cream and wine sauce.

On the eastern shore of the United States, blue crab feasts are a traditional summer event. Boiled crabs, steamed clams and sweetcorn are accompanied by melted butter and vinegar for dipping and served with small wooden mallets for cracking the crabs. A spectacular cold salad of crab with Louis dressing (see Russian dressing, p.63) and mixed greens is an American favorite and a dish that can be made with any of the crustaceans.

Presenting crustaceans

Shellfish are highly decorative items in their own right: the color of a lobster, let alone its complex structure, would be hard to dream up, and even the humble shrimp is made handsome by its whiskers and curly tail. Whether they are served hot or cold, lobster shells, split lengthwise, form a natural container for stuffing. Smaller crustaceans such as prawns, shrimp and crayfish, preferably with their heads left on, adorn the edge of fish dishes and peep temptingly over the rim of a bowl of soup. In salads, shellfish add to the appearance as well as to the taste of the dish.

LOBSTER

The acknowledged king of shellfish is the clawed lobster, which is blue-black until cooked when it turns a brilliant red. There are two closely related varieties of clawed lobster that are found in the North Atlantic and Mediterranean. The Northern lobster has larger, fleshier claws and a wider tail. Elsewhere in the world, the less colorful, brownish-pink, spiny lobster prevails, also called rock lobster, crawfish, or *langouste* (not to be confused with *langoustine*, p.160). In European waters the common spiny lobster is fished locally. Flat, slipper, or locust lobsters have a broad flat body and less meat than the spiny lobster. They are found in the Mediterranean and along the Atlantic coasts of Europe and North America and are related to the Australian flathead locust lobster, locally known as the Moreton Bay bug.

The flesh of clawed lobster is slightly sweeter and more tender than that of the spiny lobster. Both can weigh 10 lb/4.5 kg or more, but commercial sizes average 1-3 lb/500 g-1.4 kg; the flat lobster is smaller, weighing approximately ½ lb/250 g. Many countries impose a minimum fishing limit of ¾ lb-1 lb/375 g-500 g on small or "chicken" lobsters, no matter what species.

USEFUL INFORMATION

Season *Farmed:* year-round. *Wild:* supplies, particularly of clawed lobster, drop during winter months.

How to choose *Uncooked:* should be alive and moving strongly. *Cooked:* should be heavy, with tail bent under, showing lobster was alive when boiled (some cooks insist on tying the tail so that it stays straight during cooking). Female has wider tail and two soft feelers at joint between body and tail; in male these are stiff.

Portion *Whole in shell:* 1-1½ lb/ 500-750 g (if served with rich sauce, portion may be halved). *Raw or cooked meat:* 6 oz/180 g.

Nutritive value per 3½ oz/100 g: 90 calories; 17 g protein; 2 g fat; 1 g carbohydrates; 260 mg sodium, 100 mg cholesterol.

Cooking methods *In shell:* boil 5 minutes first 1 lb/500 g, 3 minutes each extra 1 lb/500 g; split and broil 6-10 minutes depending on size; steam 8 minutes first 1 lb/500 g, 4 minutes each extra 1 lb/500 g.

When done Color changes to bright red.

Processed forms *In shell:* frozen raw (best); frozen cooked. *Meat:* canned; frozen.

Storage *Live:* 12-18 hours in cool place. *Cooked in shell:* refrigerate 2 days; freeze 6 months. *Cooked, shelled:* refrigerate 2 days; freeze 2 months.

Typical dishes Bisque (France); salad with pineapple (Australia); broiled with melted butter (USA); fritters (UK); *Fra Diavolo* (with brandy and mustard, Italy); Newburg (with cream sauce, USA); stew (New England); Thermidor (cream sauce, mustard, Parmesan, France); *navarin d'homard* (with vegetables and white wine, France); *bordelaise* (with white wine sauce, France); *americaine* (with tomatoes, garlic, brandy, France), with tomatoes and coconut milk (Brazil); clambake (lobsters, green maize and clams baked on a barbecue, USA); *langosta con pollo* (with chicken, tomatoes, hazelnuts and chocolate, Spain). *Also good with* citrus fruits, hot red pepper and tarragon.

Spiny/rock lobster

Clawed lobster

153

KILLING & CUTTING UP LIVE LOBSTER

A whole lobster is killed in a few seconds if plunged into boiling water. However, where the recipe calls for a live lobster to be cut up before cooking, proceed as follows:

1 Set the lobster on a board and cover the tail with a cloth. Hold the lobster firmly with one hand and, with the point of a large knife, pierce down to the board through the cross mark at the center of the head. **Note** Although the lobster is killed when the knife is inserted, it may continue to twitch because of cut nerve endings.

2 Turn the lobster round. Holding it by the head, continue cutting down the middle, until you reach the crosswise tail joint.

3 ABOVE Chop off the claws and legs with a single blow of the knife on each side of the body.

4 RIGHT Gripping the head firmly, slice the tail section across, into medallions (p.157). Cut the head in half.

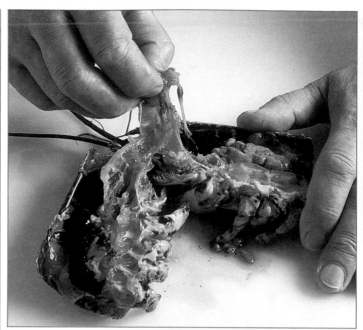

5 ABOVE Discard the head sac. Scoop out the tomalley (greenish liver) and any coral (black when uncooked) and reserve for soup or sauce. Save the liquid that runs from the lobster also.

6 RIGHT Crack the claws with the back of a knife, but don't shell them. The body and legs may be cooked to add flavor, but they are not normally served. **Note** Discard the intestinal vein after cooking.

ALTERNATIVELY, the lobster can be split in half lengthwise. Discard the intestinal vein, then clean the body and crack the claws as shown above.

UNCOOKED LOBSTER

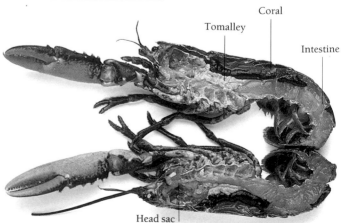

Coral

Tomalley

Intestine

Head sac

CUTTING UP COOKED SPINY LOBSTER

Once cooked, lobster can be tightly covered and refrigerated for 24 hours. Whole spiny lobster, or rock lobster tails, which are often sold without the body, are prepared in this way.

1 Holding the lobster with both hands, twist and pull the body and tail apart, leaving the tail meat in one piece.

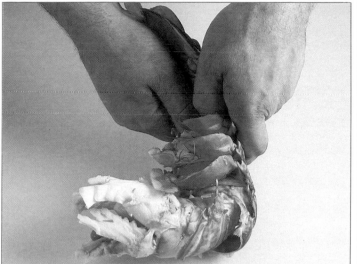

ALTERNATIVELY, cut off the tail fins and push the meat out of the shell.

5 Cut off the intestinal meat at the end of the tail.

6 RIGHT Cut the tail meat in medallions or leave it whole, depending on size. Finally, extract the meat from the claws and legs, and clean the body.

2 ABOVE With kitchen scissors, cut along the underside of the tail on each side.

3 RIGHT With your fingers, press the shell on both sides to loosen the tail meat.

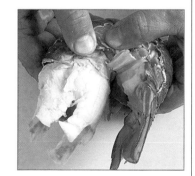

4 LEFT Peel back the shell with your hands and extract the tail meat in one piece.

Making shellfish butter

Shellfish butter is important in adding flavor to classic bisques and sauces such as *Nantua* (p.55). In a mortar, pound ½ lb/250 g crab shells, lobster shells, or shrimp, prawn or crayfish heads and shells with ⅓ cup/75 g butter. If the hard shells of crab or lobster are omitted, the mixture can be worked in a food processor. There are two methods: one produces a delicate butter that can be served as an accompaniment, the other makes a more strongly flavored butter that can be added to soups and sauces.

For the first method, press the mixture through a sieve to extract all the butter and juices. For the second method, heat the mixture with 1 cup/250 ml water in a saucepan. Continue to heat gently for 15 minutes, stirring occasionally. Strain the mixture into a bowl and chill. The butter will set to a firm cake and the water can be discarded.

REMOVING LOBSTER MEAT

For serving, lobster meat is replaced in its shell, with the pincer meat set on top of the body meat. The meat is usually mixed with a sauce if served hot, or with mayonnaise or dressing if served cold.

1 Follow the same method for all types of lobster: pierce the end of the tail with a large knife and lift the carcass to drain the cooking liquid. If the lobster has been boiled, it is likely to contain a great deal of surplus liquid.

4 Remove and discard the head sac. The remaining meat is edible. This includes the tomalley (greenish liver) and, in the female, red coral.

5 Detach the intestinal vein from the tail and discard it. Twist off the claws and legs.

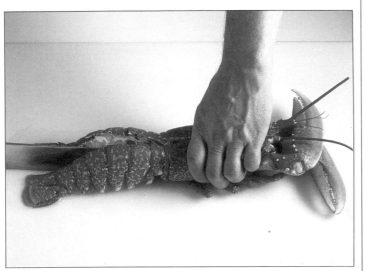

2 Set the lobster on a board, back upwards. Holding it firmly with one hand, pierce down through the cross at the center of the head with the point of a large knife. Continue cutting the tail in half.

6 RIGHT Crack the claws in two or three places with the back of a knife or with nutcrackers, without crushing the meat inside.

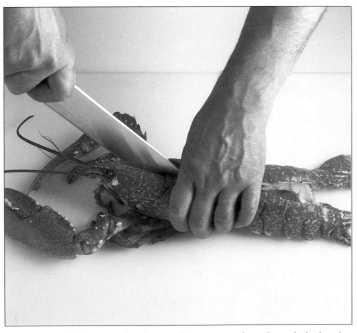

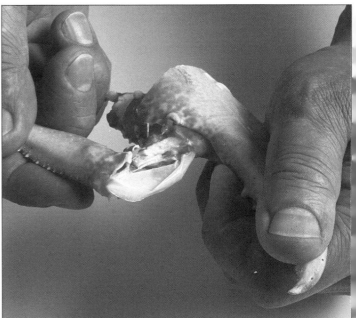

3 Turn the lobster around so that it is facing you and cut through the head. The lobster will fall apart down the middle.

7 ABOVE Pull the flat membrane, which is attached to the small pincer, from the claw meat.

8 RIGHT Carefully remove the claw meat from the remaining shell in one piece.

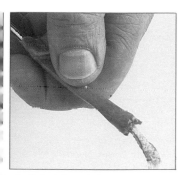

9 If the lobster is large, use a skewer to push the meat from the legs; if it is small, simply use the legs to decorate the finished dish (see Lobster salad Green Goddess).

10 Lift the tail meat from the shell, pulling it out neatly and in one piece. Discard the shell.

11 With a sharp knife, cut the tail meat into slices and set them aside until needed for the finished dish.

12 ABOVE Discard the gills (called "dead men's fingers" because of their shape and color) from the underside of the body shell.

13 For serving, place the slices of lobster meat in the shell with the claw meat on top.

Dressing cooked lobster

Split and clean the lobster as shown on the previous page. Mix the claw meat, coral and tomalley (greenish liver) with a little sauce and pile it onto the body meat in the shell, placing the pincer meat on top. Remove the tail meat and spoon a little sauce into the tail shell. Set the meat, rounded side up, on top and add more sauce.

Lobster salad Green Goddess

Green Goddess dressing was created at the Palace Hotel, San Francisco in the 1920s to celebrate a play of that name.

Serves 4

4 lobsters, ¾ lb/375 g each	
1½ cups/375 ml Green Goddess dressing (p.63)	***For garnish (optional)***
	4 tomato roses (p.283)
¾ lb/375 g mixed salad greens (arugula, leaf lettuce, curly endive)	2 lemons, halved

1 Make the dressing. Cook the lobster by plunging it into boiling water (p.152), then extract the meat (Removing lobster meat, steps 1–12), cutting the tail meat into medallions. Reserve the claw and tail meat, with the legs, then coarsely chop the remaining meat and mix with 3-4 tablespoons of the dressing.

2 Arrange the salad on four plates, pile the lobster meat in the center and lay the medallions on top, overlapping into a tail pattern. Decorate with the claw meat and arrange the legs in a zigzag pattern around each plate.

3 Spoon some dressing over the salad so that the lobster can still be seen. If garnishing, put a tomato rose and a lemon half on each plate. Serve the remaining dressing separately.

CRAB

Found worldwide, this large family has at least 12 edible members. In the kitchen, crabs fall into two categories: large-bodied crabs with plenty of body meat, and long-legged crabs with meat mostly in the legs and claws. Large-bodied crabs, which resemble the zodiac symbol, are most familiar in the kitchen. Their body size, which varies enormously with age and species, can be as large as 10 in/25 cm. The larger they are, the easier the meat is to extract from the shell and inner membrane enclosing it. Most crabs are pink or brown, so the delicate North American blue crab is easily recognizable, as is the green shore crab of the United States and Europe. Like other crabs, both turn red when cooked. With certain species of crab, such as the Florida stone crab and the Australian mud crab, only the claws are eaten. Because of this, the claws are broken off and the creature is thrown back in the ocean, where eventually it grows new claws.

The Japanese giant spider crab can measure 6 ft/2 m from claw to claw. The long-legged snow crab, found in the North Pacific, is about half the size. Its legs are delicious steamed or broiled with butter. However, most long-legged crabs weigh less than 2 lb/1 kg, and are best served in soup since they yield little meat.

One small treat that is edible but not sold commercially is the hermit crab, a curious creature that inhabits abandoned shells. Equally odd is the land crab, which lives in holes on sandy beaches. While the blue and red land crabs are edible, other varieties are not. The tiny oyster or pea crab lives in mussel shells, offering a crunchy contrast to the softness of the mussel flesh.

USEFUL INFORMATION

Common large-bodied crabs
Blue (Atlantic, Mediterranean); Dungeness (Pacific); common European (Atlantic); green shore (Atlantic, Mediterranean); Jonah (Atlantic); land/white/mulatto (Atlantic, Caribbean); mud/mangrove (Pacific); common rock (Atlantic); stone (North America); sand/lady/calico (Atlantic).

Common long-legged crabs
Queen (Atlantic, Pacific); tanner (N. Pacific); spider/thornback (Atlantic, Mediterranean); king or Alaskan king (N. Pacific); red (Atlantic); Snow (N. Pacific).

Season *Warm waters*: year-round. *Elsewhere*: late spring through autumn.

How to choose *Live*: should be kicking. *Cooked*: heavy in the hand. Female crab has broader "apron" flap of shell under body that contains coral.

Portion ½ cup/125 g crabmeat (the meat yield from whole crabs varies enormously with the type and size of crab).

Nutritive value per 3½ oz/100 g: 93 calories; 17 g protein; 2 g fat; 1 g carbohydrates; 260 mg sodium; 76 mg cholesterol.

PICKING MEAT OUT OF COOKED CRAB

The structure of meaty crabs varies from species to species, but the essential parts of claws, legs and large body remain the same.

1 Set the crab, back down, on a board. Twist and break the claws and legs from the body.

2 To extract the leg meat: snip along each side of the shell with shears and lift out the meat with a crab pick or skewer.

3 Crack the claws with the back of a knife, taking care not to crush the meat. Remove the flat membrane; extract the meat with a pick.

4 To open the body: first lift up the apron flap (tail), then twist it off and discard it.

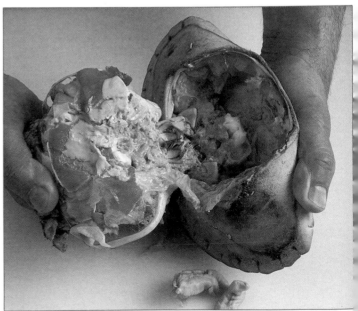

5 With the point of a knife, or with your hands, crack the central section of the shell under the tail and pry it apart. (Some crabs, for example the Atlantic blue variety, have a tail that can be used to pull away the under shell from the meat). Pull the meat from the shell.

Cooking methods *Large-bodied crabs in shell:* boil 5-6 minutes per 1 lb/500 g; steam 8-10 minutes per 1 lb/500 g. *Large crab legs in shell:* bake in oven at 350°F/175°C 15-25 minutes; broil 4-6 minutes; boil in shell 4-6 minutes. *Medium or small long-legged crabs in shell:* simmer 15-30 minutes in soup.
When done Shells change to bright red.
Processed forms *In shell:* frozen (best). *Crabmeat:* vacuum-packed; pasteurized; canned; frozen.
Storage *Live:* 1-2 days in a cool place. *Cooked in shell:* refrigerate 1-2 days; freeze 3 months. *Crabmeat:* refrigerate 3 days; freeze 1 month; pasteurized (less flavor than fresh) 2 weeks; vacuum-packed 1 month.
Typical dishes Deviled (USA, UK); *Soupe de Pélous* (soup with tomatoes, saffron and bread, France); Louis (cold salad with chili sauce, horseradish and

mayonnaise, USA); cioppino (stew with mussels and clams, USA); bisque (USA); *centollos* (spider crab in tomato sauce, sherry and brandy, Spain); *riz aux favouilles* (with rice, tomatoes and saffron, France); stuffed with sole and breadcrumbs (Austria); curried mousse (UK); partan bree (with anchovy, cream, rice and chicken stock, Scotland); baked claws or legs with butter (USA, Australia);

crab cakes (USA); imperial (with cream sauce, USA); crabmeat soufflé (France); with Marsala (USA). *Also good with* citrus fruit, tomato, green pepper, basil.

Spider crab

Common European crab

Blue crab

Killing and cutting up live crab

Unlike lobster, crab is rarely cut up live in Western cuisine. Usually, a live crab is killed by steaming or boiling (p.152).

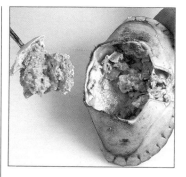

9 LEFT With a spoon, scoop out the soft brown meat (some species have only white meat) from the shell, discarding the head sac. In females, extract the coral-colored roe also.

10 If serving crab in the shell, cut around the line marking the edge of the shell to form a neat container. Wash the shell thoroughly.

6 Discard the soft gills ("dead men's fingers") from the sides of the central body section.

7 Crack the central body section with your hands or cut it in pieces with a knife.

Preparing and dressing cooked crabmeat

Whether fresh, canned or frozen, cooked crabmeat should be picked over with your fingers or a knife to extract any membrane or shell. For cold cooked crab, arrange the white meat in one half of the crab shell. Mix any brown meat with a little mayonnaise and pile it into the other half. Decorate the top with chopped parsley, chopped egg white and sieved egg yolk and add the shelled crab claws. Serve mayonnaise separately.

SOFT-SHELL CRAB

A specialty of the East Coast of the United States and of the Venice area of Italy, the soft-shell crab is the blue crab or shore crab caught when shedding its shell. Soft and translucent, it is trimmed of the tail, gills and eyes and eaten whole. At its best sautéed in ample butter, soft-shell crab can also be deep-fried or broiled.

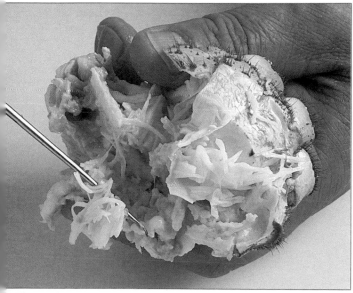

8 Pry out the meat with a pick or skewer, discarding any small pieces of membrane.

SHRIMP, PRAWNS & SCAMPI

Distinctions between these three – the most popular of all shellfish – are somewhat hazy. Everyone agrees that the smallest are shrimp, which are scarcely more than 1 in/2.5 cm long. Tiny pink shrimp are a specialty of areas as far apart as Scandinavia and San Francisco Bay, and are familiar worldwide. Highly prized are the pungent, almost spicy, tiny gray shrimp from Britain and northern France. The effort involved in catching and shelling such small morsels means that they are expensive to buy. They are at their best in salads, with plain buttered bread or in a smooth bisque.

Medium-sized shrimp are called shrimp in North America, but prawns elsewhere. Species vary around the world and, although they are found in a wide range of colors, all have firm sweet flesh. What matters most is freshness; unfortunately, after poor handling or long storage they can deteriorate badly, so suspect seafood should not be eaten. Medium-sized shrimp form the foundation of a seafood menu, and are found in shrimp cocktail, speared as kebabs, deep-fried, or baked in sauce. Usually, you get between 25 and 50 shrimp per 1 lb/500 g, depending on size. Less fragile than tiny shrimp, they need careful cooking and seasoning if they are not to be overwhelmed.

Jumbo shrimp or jumbo prawns, also known by the Spanish name, *gambas*, yield less than 10 per 1 lb/500 g (depending on whether the heads are included). At this size, the shrimp or prawns develop a special character, and some varieties have an impressively salty tang. The huge tiger prawn is a favorite on the barbecue and buffet table.

Scampi are often confused with jumbo prawns, although they are in fact small members of the lobster family with long claws. They are known by many names including Dublin Bay prawns, Norway lobsters and, in France, *langoustines*. Similar in size to large prawns, they have a more fragile texture and taste.

USEFUL INFORMATION

Common medium shrimp/ prawns White shrimp (Atlantic); common/sand (European waters); triple-groove shrimp (Atlantic, Mediterranean); greentail prawn (Pacific, Australian waters); royal red shrimp (US Atlantic); sand (US Atlantic); US brown (US Atlantic, Gulf of Mexico).
Common jumbo shrimp Coon-stripe (American Pacific); giant tiger (Pacific); kuruma (Pacific); side-stripe (American Pacific).
Season Year-round.
How to choose *Raw or cooked, with or without shell:* moist and sweet-smelling; smell of chlorine if stale.

Portion *Shelled, raw or cooked:* 4 oz/125 g. *In shell with heads:* 6 oz/ 180 g. *Whole scampi:* 6-12.
Nutritive value per 3½ oz/100 g: 90 calories; 19 g protein; 1 g fat; 1 g carbohydrate; 64 mg sodium; 166 mg cholesterol.

Jumbo prawn

Scampi/Dublin Bay prawn/*langoustine*   Pink shrimp/common prawn   Gray shrimp

Cooking methods *Tiny shrimp in shell:* boil 1-2 minutes; steam 3-4 minutes. *Medium shrimp/prawns:* bake at 350°F/175°C, 15-20 minutes; boil 3-5 minutes; barbecue or broil 2-3 minutes each side; deep-fry 2-3 minutes; marinate up to 6 hours; pan-fry or sauté when peeled 3-5 minutes; steam 5-7 minutes; stir-fry when peeled 2-4 minutes. *Jumbo shrimp/ prawns:* bake at 350°F/175°C, 15-25 minutes; boil 5-8 minutes; barbecue or broil 3-5 minutes each side; marinate up to 12 hours before cooking; pan-fry or sauté, peeled, 5-7 minutes; steam 6-8 minutes.
When done *Tiny shrimp:* firm when pinched. *Medium shrimp/ prawns:* firm when pinched; color dark pink. *Scampi:* bright pink.
Processed forms Canned (usually tiny shrimp); frozen raw and cooked, with or without shell.
Storage *Raw in shell:* refrigerate 2 days; freeze 6 months. *Cooked in shell or shelled:* refrigerate 2 days; freeze 1 month.
Typical dishes Prawns with cocktail sauce (UK); potted shrimps (UK); tempura (Japan); shrimp gumbo (okra stew, southern USA); deep-fried scampi (UK); *risotto con gamberetti in bianco* (with rice and white wine, Italy); shrimp with peas and dill (Finland); prawns with piparrada sauce (Portugal); scampi Provençale (France); shrimp Creole (tomato, celery, wine, cayenne and chili pepper sauce, southern USA); *gambas al ajillo* (with garlic and green chilis, Spain); paella (Spain). *Also good with* sesame oil, almonds and cashews, garlic, brandy, saffron, coconut, lime.

PEELING SHRIMP & PRAWNS

For tiny shrimp: discard the heads and remove the shell with your fingers. **For jumbo shrimp or prawns:** use scissors to cut each side of the undershell, then peel back the shell to reach the meat. Shells, especially heads, are used for shrimp butter (p.155).

1 **For large shrimp:** pull the head (if still attached) from the body, leaving the tail meat intact.

2 Peel off the shell with your fingers, leaving the tail flange on if you like.

3 Make a shallow cut along the back of the shrimp or prawn.

4 Remove the dark intestinal vein that runs along the back.

Peeling scampi

The tail meat is extracted as for prawns. Large scampi also contain claw meat, revealed by cracking, and some edible body meat.

Shrimp & scallop brochettes

Vegetables such as mushroom caps, baby tomatoes and chunks of onion or green pepper may be included on the skewers.

Serves 4

¾ lb/375 g large raw shrimp	⅓ cup/75 g melted butter
¾ lb/375 g medium scallops	freshly ground black pepper
1 cup/250 ml white wine	paprika
2 tbsp/30 ml oil	rice pilaf (p.315)
1 tbsp chopped fresh tarragon	lemon wedges
1 tbsp chopped mixed fresh herbs (thyme, oregano, parsley)	**4 skewers**

1 Peel the shrimp and remove the vein. Discard the small membrane from the side of each scallop. In a bowl, combine the wine, oil and herbs, add the shrimp and scallops and toss well. Cover the bowl and marinate in the refrigerator for 2-4 hours.
2 Heat the broiler. Drain the marinade from the shrimp and scallops and thread them on to the skewers, then brush them with melted butter and sprinkle with black pepper and paprika.
3 Broil the brochettes about 3 in/7.5 cm from the heat, turning once, until the seafood loses its transparency, 6-8 minutes. Baste often during cooking.
4 Serve the brochettes on a bed of rice pilaf and decorate with lemon wedges.

Butterflying large shrimp, prawns and scampi

When slit and cooked, the flesh of shrimp, prawns and scampi will curl into an attractive butterfly shape. First peel them, then make a full-length cut along the backs, about halfway through the flesh. Remove the dark intestinal vein that runs along the back and open out the shrimp, prawns or scampi for cooking.

CRAYFISH

The crayfish is the odd man out among crustaceans because it lives in fresh water. It looks like a tiny clawed lobster and is found worldwide except in Africa. Crayfish are particularly prized in Scandinavia, eastern Europe, France, Louisiana, the Pacific Northwest, and in Australia where they are nicknamed "yabbies". Most crayfish weigh 1-3 oz/30-90 g, but in Australia, giant species can run to the size of lobster. The red-clawed crayfish is preferred to the paler white-clawed variety. Both are commonly farmed since wild crayfish, though abundant in some rivers, are devils to catch. The swamp crayfish is often called "crawfish" in the USA.

USEFUL INFORMATION

Common freshwater crayfish Swamp (southern USA); signal (N. America); grey foot/marsh (eastern Europe); red foot (western Europe); "yabbies" (Australia); marron (Australia).
Season *Farmed:* year-round. *Wild:* peak spring to early autumn.
How to choose *Live:* buy when moving strongly. *Frozen and thawed:* should smell sweet.
Portion *In shell:* 8 oz/250 g or 6-8 crayfish. *Shelled:* 4 oz/125 g
Nutritive value per 3½ oz/ 100 g: 76 calories; 16 g protein; 1 g fat; 1 g carbohydrates; 53 mg sodium; 158 mg cholesterol.
Cooking methods *In shell:* boil 6-8 minutes. *Tails:* broil 3-5 minutes; steam 10-14 minutes.
When done Shells turn red, flesh is opaque.
Processed forms Canned; frozen in shell (best); cooked and shelled.
Storage *Live:* 12 hours in refrigerator. *Cooked in shell:* refrigerate 24 hours; freeze 2 months. *Cooked and shelled:* refrigerate 2 days; freeze 1 month.

Typical dishes Bisque (France), *étouffé* (garlic, parsley and shallot stew, Louisiana, USA); *havskräftor* (in dill *court bouillon*, Scandinavia); *cardinale* (cream sauce with cognac, white wine and spices, France); *écrevisses au gratin* (with cream and white wine or Cognac, France); with saffron, peppers, tomatoes and wine (Romania). *Also good with* cream, thyme.

Freshwater crayfish uncooked and cooked (below)

Cleaning live crayfish

With farmed crayfish, cleaning is unnecessary as they are purged before being sold. Wild crayfish are cleaned by removing the bitter-tasting intestine from the tail. This can be done while the crayfish are still alive.

Wearing a glove as protection from the claws, hold the body of the crayfish firmly in one hand. With the other hand, grasp the central flange at one end of the tail and twist, pulling gently. The dark intestine can be drawn out easily.

EXTRACTING MEAT FROM CRAYFISH

If the crayfish are to be eaten whole, peel the meat as below. The juices and coral may be extracted by sucking them out of the body. Often the crayfish are served *à la nage*, that is moistened with *court bouillon*, or the reduced cooking liquid (p.102).

3 Turn the crayfish and nip the end of the tail to loosen the meat.

4 Gently pull out the tail meat in one piece.

5 Remove the intestine from along the back of the meat.

6 If using all the meat for cooking, pull open the body and scrape out the yellow fat, with the red coral if any, to use for sauce.

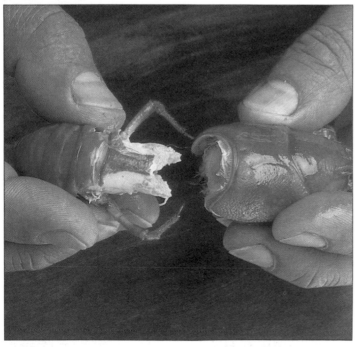

1 Pull apart the body and tail of the crayfish in such a way that the tail meat remains intact.

2 With your fingers, peel the top flange from the body.

BALMAIN BUGS & MANTIS SHRIMP

On opposite sides of the world are two curious crustaceans. The Australian Balmain bug found in Sydney Harbour is a tiny flat lobster, with a similar flavor and delicate texture. Its broad shell is large in proportion to the meat. The European mantis shrimp, popular in Italy and Spain, has distinctive mouthparts and legs like a praying mantis. Both creatures can be cooked like prawns. Often, Balmain bugs are sold pre-cooked.

MOLLUSKS

Mollusks come in many shapes and sizes. They include univalves, which have single, often spiral shells, bivalves like oysters with a double shell, and cephalopods (p.170) such as squid and octopus. Whether they are being prepared to eat raw or cooked, mollusks in the shell must be alive. Univalves should retreat into their shell when poked and bivalve shells should be tightly closed (although scallops and soft-shell clams never close completely, even when alive). In the shell or out, all mollusks should have a sweet sea-salt smell. They are often sold according to size and the grading for sought-after kinds such as oysters is complicated (p.166).

Never gather mollusks in the wild if you are in doubt about whether the area is safe; they are susceptible to pollution and can carry diseases such as hepatitis. Natural phenomena, for example red tides, may also cause diseased shellfish; check for area warnings. Purging by soaking in water will not rid mollusks of disease.

Storing and cleaning mollusks

When refrigerated and covered with a wet cloth, freshly caught mollusks stay alive for 24 hours or more, depending on the species. To prepare them, scrub the shells under cold, running water, detaching any weed and scraping off barnacles. Discard broken shells and any that do not close when tapped. If the shells are covered with sand, the mollusks can be purged by soaking in a bucket of seawater, or water salted with a handful of salt per 1 quart/1 liter of water, for two to three hours. If you leave them for longer, change the water, otherwise the mollusks will die from lack of oxygen. Some cooks add one to two tablespoons of flour or bran to the cleaning water to plump up the meat before cooking.

Oysters

Mussel

Cockle

Clam

Clams

Scallop

Clam

Presenting mollusks

The obvious choice for serving mollusks such as oysters and clams, is on the half shells. Scallops are so pretty that their shells have become a seafood trademark, used to present any fish or shellfish dish. As for univalves such as conch, abalone and the snail tribe, the appeal of their resilient meat would certainly diminish if they came in a plainer wrapper.

UNIVALVES

Univalves are as much a gastronomic curiosity as a delicacy. Because they are hard to extract from the shells while alive, all but the largest abalone and conch must be cooked before shelling. The smallest – shiny black winkles or periwinkles – have an agreeable iodine taste but require patience to eat.

Whelks are more generous, growing as large as 6 in/15 cm long, with a good portion of rich meat in the larger shells. Top shells, which resemble a toy spinning top, are edible too, as are hornshells, which contain meat that can be extracted easily from the long pointed shell. The southern European spike-shelled murex appears on the table, but is more famous as the source of Tyrian purple, the royal dye of antiquity. Conical limpet shells are a familiar sight on rocky beaches. Both can be eaten raw, but they tend to be tough and neither is worth marketing.

There are greater culinary possibilities with the two largest univalves – conch, and abalone or ormer, which are found mainly in the South Pacific, Mediterranean and both coasts of North and South America. As with all mollusks, the main problem is toughness, so the meat must be tenderized by pounding once it has been extracted from the shell. The meat must be cooked either very lightly, or long and slowly. The flavor, particularly of abalone, is delicate, resembling that of the clam. Large whelks may be prepared and cooked in the same way as conch and abalone. (See Cooking methods, below.)

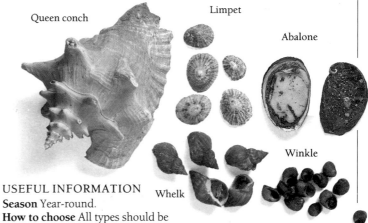

Queen conch

Limpet

Abalone

Winkle

Whelk

USEFUL INFORMATION
Season Year-round.
How to choose All types should be sweet-smelling. *Periwinkle, whelk, conch:* operculum (lid) firmly shut, or animal retracts into shell when poked. *Abalone:* dark fringe around edge of shell retracts when poked.
Portion *Small univalves:* 1 pt/500 g yields about ⅓ cup/90 g meat to serve 1. *Abalone and conch:* 1-2 per person.
Nutritive value per 3½ oz/100 g: 98 calories; 17 g protein; 1 g fat; 5 g carbohydrates; 206 mg sodium; 111 mg cholesterol.
Cooking methods *Small univalves:* boil 10-30 minutes depending on size; shelled in salad; simmer in soup 5-10 minutes. *Abalone and conch:* chop and simmer 2-3 hours to make soup; deep-fry 1-2 minutes; marinate before cooking 1-2 hours; pan-fry or sauté 2

minutes each side; stew 1-1½ hours.
When done Resilient but tender.
Problems Abalone and conch overcook very easily.
Processed forms *Abalone and conch:* shelled, canned. *Abalone:* smoked, dried (Asian stores).
Storage *Raw in shell:* 24-36 hours, depending on size. *Raw shelled:* 24 hours. *Cooked:* 2 days.
Typical dishes Conch chowder (USA); broiled conch or abalone (Portugal); conch fritters (Bahamas); conch salad (Martinique); abalone and onion turnovers (Chile); rice and conch stew (French West Indies); conch with tomato sauce (Italy); braised abalone in oyster sauce (China); winkles in wine sauce (Ireland).

EXTRACTING & CLEANING RAW ABALONE MEAT

Abalone meat must be pounded with a mallet before cooking to tenderize it.

1 Free the abalone meat from the shell by sliding a metal spoon around the edge of the flesh and between the flesh and the shell.

2 With a swift, sharp movement, push the spoon, rounded side up, under the stem muscle, cutting it from the shell.

3 Clean the flesh with a small knife by cutting away the viscera attached to it.

4 Discard the viscera and remove the dark fringe around the meat. Wash the meat, scrubbing off the black mucus with a brush.

5 Cut the meat into 2 or 3 rounds. Put the slices between 2 sheets of plastic wrap and pound with a cleaver to tenderize.
ALTERNATIVELY, butterfly the meat by slitting it lengthwise, opening it out and pounding it flat.

Extracting and cleaning raw conch meat

With a hammer, tap a hole in the third spiral down from the top of the shell. Insert a thin knife, angled towards the top, and cut the muscle that attaches the meat to the shell. Pull out the meat by grasping the hard lip attached to the claw-shaped "foot"; discard the operculum (lid) from the foot. Cut away the soft intestines and eyes, then peel the skin from the meat with your fingers. Cut the meat in ½ in/1.25 cm slices across the grain and pound the slices for 30-60 seconds with a mallet to tenderize. Alternatively, slit the meat lengthwise and pound it flat.

Poaching and shelling small univalves

Small univalves, such as whelks and winkles can be poached in liquid, usually water with one tablespoon of salt added per 1 quart/1 liter. Flavorings such as onion, aromatic herbs, peppercorns, allspice, coriander and dried chili pepper may be added; *court bouillon* (p.44) may be used also. Place the shellfish in a pan and cover them completely with liquid. Cover the pan and bring the liquid to a boil. Poach the univalves, counting the cooking time, which depends on the individual mollusk, from boiling point. Let the shells cool in the liquid and, if storing, leave them in the liquid. To remove the meat from the shells, discard the operculum (lid), impale the meat with a pin, skewer or small fork and pull gently, twisting the shell so the meat emerges in one piece.

Small univalves are often served in the shell, alone or as part of a cold shellfish platter. Pile the shells into a bowl or on to a serving dish. Pins, impaled in a cork, are needed to extract the meat and small forks to eat it. Serve mayonnaise separately, and a bowl of vinegar mixed with chopped shallot as an accompaniment.

Other cooking methods for univalves

Shelled univalves make good soup or chowder, but take care not to overcook the meat. The cooked meat is good in vinaigrette dressing with additions such as chopped onion, bell pepper, walnuts or celery. Raw abalone and conch can be marinated, like scallops, in a citrus marinade, broiled, sautéed in oil or butter as steaks, or chopped or ground for fritters. Best of all, perhaps, are the many conch and abalone stews that are cooked for one to two hours, some of Caribbean inspiration, others from California or Australia.

SNAILS

The best known univalve of all – the snail – is actually a land animal. Snail parks have existed since Roman times and modern farms can pack as many as a million snails into 200 square meters. Today, snails are fattened on a diet of cabbage, wheat or oats. The most commonly cultivated are the Burgundian or Roman snail, the giant African Achatina snail and the tasty little *petit gris* or garden snail. Many other varieties are edible and in Europe, particularly near the Mediterranean, gathering snails after a shower of rain is a favorite pastime. Preparing wild snails is laborious, so most cooks opt for ready-prepared snails that have been cleaned and simmered in *court bouillon* (p.44). These are usually processed in France after being raised in Eastern Europe, China or Taiwan. Recently the United States has entered the market, offering garden snails in several sizes. The latest taste in France is for snail's eggs, more expensive than sturgeon caviar.

USEFUL INFORMATION

Season *Wild:* spring to winter. *Farmed:* year-round.

How to choose Unless hibernating, snails should retreat when poked; hibernating snails are sealed with chalky secretion.

Portion 6 very large snails or up to 12 small ones.

Nutritive value per 3½ oz/100 g: 90 calories; 9.9 g protein; 4.4 g fat; 4.4 g carbohydrates.

Cooking methods *In shell:* after poaching bake at 450°F/230°C, 5-7 minutes; broil with butter 5-7 minutes; roast or barbecue 8-12 minutes. *Without shells:* simmer in soup or sauce 10-15 minutes.

When done Firm but tender.

Storage *Live:* 1-2 weeks. *Cooked:* 3 days.

Processed forms Canned without shells (shells sold separately); frozen in shell or shelled.

Typical dishes *À la Bourguignonne* (with garlic and herb butter, France); roasted (France); *caracoles en salsa* (with tomato and garlic sauce, Spain); hot pepper and anise stew (Tunisia); *lumache alla milanese* (with anchovy, fennel and wine sauce, Italy), *fricassée* (Caribbean). *Also good with* shallots, anchovy, lemon, parsley.

Burgundian/ Roman snail

Petit gris/ garden snail

Cleaning and preparing wild snails

To purge snails of poisonous herbs or pesticides, leave them outside in a ventilated box for a week, moistening them regularly with water. For the last two days, feed them on lettuce leaves or a few spoonfuls of flour or cornmeal. Hibernating snails, however, need not be purged. They bury themselves in the ground, particularly in vinestocks, and should be dug up two to three weeks after hibernation starts. The chalky deposit sealing the snails must be chipped away. Soak the purged snails in water to draw them from their shells, discard any that do not move, then drain and toss the snails with coarse salt, allowing two table-spoons per 12 snails. Leave them for 10-15 minutes so that they froth, drawing out the slime. Rinse them thoroughly with cold water and drain.

Poaching and shelling wild snails

Cover the snails in *court bouillon* (p.44) and simmer for two to three hours until tender. (Alternatively, blanch the snails for 10-15 minutes, remove them from their shells and continue to cook for two to three hours until tender.) To shell the snails, drain them and extract them with a pin or small fork, giving a twist to the shell. Discard the operculum (lid) and trim away the soft stomach at the tip of the meat. Wash the shells to use as containers for the prepared snails.

Cooking methods for snails

Given their unique container, snails are often put back into their shells with aromatic butter then baked or broiled and served on snail plates (p.511). Snails can be roasted in their shells on a barbecue, or served in a large pot after poaching, still in the shell, accompanied by garlic mayonnaise or a piquant sauce – both are favorite methods at vineyard feasts in Languedoc and Provence. Out of their shells, snails go well with rich wine sauces and warm salads, or they may be mixed with pasta. They may also be served in a puff pastry shell with garlic butter. Given their dark color, they look best on a bed of lettuce with tomatoes or herbs.

Making aromatic snail butter

For 24 large snails, cream 1 cup/250 g butter. Beat in one finely chopped shallot, one finely chopped garlic clove, two tablespoons of finely chopped parsley, two tablespoons of white wine, with salt and pepper to taste. Alternatively, use a food processor. Spoon a little butter into the snail shells, add the snails; top with the remaining butter. Set the shells on snail dishes or on dishes filled with rock salt or slices of bread with holes cut in them, broil or bake in the oven at 450°F/230°C for five to seven minutes.

BIVALVES

Of all types of shellfish, bivalves offer the widest cooking possibilities. The most highly prized of them all is the oyster, which is so outstanding fresh that some people say to cook it at all is sacrilege. In fact there are more than 12 species that reach tables around the world and some are excellent when cooked. The sweet meat of scallops is a universal favorite, whether marinated raw in South American *seviche* or cooked in one of half a dozen ways. Mussels and clams arouse partisan feelings, with northern Europeans preferring the mussel and North Americans the clam.

Broiling bivalves

Open bivalves on the half shell are ideal for broiling with a topping. Pry the shells open and remove the meat from the shells, then drain and scrub the shells clean. Place a spoonful of flavoring or sauce in each shell, add the meat and set the shells on heatproof snail dishes (p.511) or plates filled with rock salt. Add more sauce or flavoring (often butter-based) to the meat and broil the bivalves so that the topping browns before the meat is overcooked. (Some recipes suggest baking the bivalves in a very hot oven rather than broiling.) Serve the bivalves piping hot. Popular flavorings are snail and herb butter for mussels and clams, champagne sauce for oysters (p.167) and white or red butter sauce for scallops (p.62)

Deep-frying bivalves

The more tender mollusks such as oysters, scallops and clams are excellent deep-fried. Shuck and drain them thoroughly, dry them on absorbent paper if necessary, then dip them in a batter or in flour, egg and breadcrumbs (p.104). In the American South, cornmeal is popular, giving a crisp coating. Deep-fry the mollusks with the oil at 375°F/190°C until golden brown, for two to four minutes. Drain and serve with tartare sauce (p.63) or lemon.

Other cooking methods

All bivalves are good simmered in soups or stews to which their juices add so much flavor. The chowders of New England and the mixed fish soups of Brittany, Portugal and Italy at once spring to mind. If left in their shells, mussels and clams add to the appearance as well as to the taste of dishes such as paella or fish soup. Scallops are good sautéed or baked in butter with garlic or a pungent herb such as tarragon. Overcooking, the great danger with all mollusks, is less likely when they are steamed and served in a sauce based on the juices. Large clams, like long-necked geoducks, can be skinned and used raw for Japanese *sushi* or *sashimi*. Mussels have a vivid taste as well as color: together with their juice they add a characteristically salty bite to other seafood.

OYSTERS

The habitat of an oyster is crucial, for unlike other shellfish the flavor depends less on the species than on where they are grown. Of the two main types of oyster now grown in Europe, the more highly regarded is the round, flat European or common oyster. This fine "native", usually eaten raw, is differentiated by the names of the places where it flourishes – Colchester and Whitstable (England), belon, gravette d'Arcachon, bouzigue (France). Different names for the same oyster may seem confusing, but there is sense in the system since the habitat is what gives flavor. Some "natives" are not as fine as the less regarded Pacific oyster – for instance, the French Marennes – if it comes from favored waters.

The second type is the Portuguese, originally from the Pacific. It is longer and craggier than the common oyster. The lower shell is deeper – hence such names as the cupped oyster (Britain) and *huître creuse* (France). Because it is reproduced in laboratories, European waters being too cold, it is on sale year round. This cheaper, more commonly available oyster is considered to be a better choice for cooking.

In the United States, the Eastern or American oyster's regional names include Virginia, Apalachicola, Blue Point, Cape Cod, Chinoteague and Indian River oyster. In the Chesapeake Bay and the Gulf of Mexico, wild oysters are still dredged by the bushel. Native Northwest oysters include the Pacific or Japanese oyster (the second kind cultivated in Europe) and the tiny Olympia.

Oysters are farmed throughout Europe, the United States and Australia. Methods include stake, umbrella, tray, raft and longline, which allow oysters to grow above muddy estuarine flats; the result is a clean, fresh-tasting oyster that is also easier to market.

Because they are the most highly-prized mollusk, oysters are carefully graded according to size. For example, American East coast oysters are sold as count (extra large), extra select (large), select (medium), standard (small) and very small. In France, sizes range from 000 to 4. In Britain, oysters are graded from 1 to 4, with grade 1 the largest and 4 the smallest; tiny ones are known as "buttons". When oysters are served raw, subtle differences of flavor become apparent. When cooking them, the main consideration is size and, if they are to be baked, the shell, which should be hollow.

USEFUL INFORMATION

Season Traditionally, cooler months with an "r" (reversed in southern hemisphere). Now often sold year-round but in summer oysters are breeding and may be watery.

Portuguese oyster

How to choose Shells should be tightly closed; habitat is most important; size governs price.

Portion 6-12 on the half shell; 24 medium shucked oysters measure about 1½ cups/375 ml, serve 3-4.

Nutritive value *per 3½ oz/100 g:* 68 calories; 8 g protein; 2 g fat; 2 g carbohydrates; 112 mg sodium; 50 mg cholesterol.

Cooking methods *On half shell:* serve raw; stuff and bake at

Common oyster

425°F/220°C or broil 4-5 minutes. *Shucked:* bake in casserole at 350°F/175°C, 10-15 minutes; deep-fry 1-2 minutes; simmer 1-2 minutes in soup.

OPENING OYSTERS

Pick over the oysters, discarding any seaweed. Rinse any mud from the shells, but do not scrub them or soak them in water.

1 Take a short, pointed oyster knife in one hand, cover the other hand with a thick glove or cloth and grip the shell in your palm. Keeping the oyster level with the knife, insert the point of the blade next to the hinge and twist to pry the shell open.

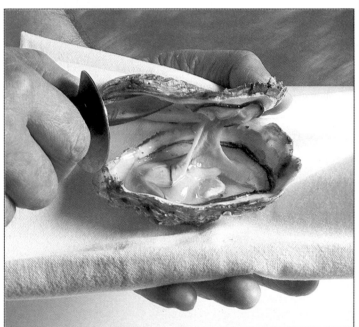

2 Cut the muscle of the animal from the shell and discard the top shell. With the knife, loosen the muscle in the lower hollow shell. If shucking the meat, tip it, with the juice, into a bowl. If serving on the half shell, leave the oysters on the bottom shell and serve on ice.

When done Edges curl up, center remains soft.

Storage *Live in shell:* in a cool place, 1-2 weeks. *Raw shucked with juice:* refrigerate 3 days. *Cooked:* refrigerate 2 days.

Processed forms Cooked canned (whole and chopped); smoked; shucked pasteurized; frozen.

Typical dishes Bisque (France); Rockefeller (baked with greens, herbs, cheese sauce, USA); angels on horseback (skewered with bacon, UK); deep-fried oysters with devil sauce (UK); deviled (Australia); stew (UK, USA); carpetbag steak (stuffed with oysters, Australia, New Zealand); steak, kidney and oyster pie (UK); scalloped (USA); creamed with hearts of palm (Brazil); croquettes (South America); marinated in lime juice (Guatemala); baked with blue cheese (USA). *Raw oysters also good with* lemon, hot sauce, cocktail sauce, wholewheat bread and butter. *Cooked oysters also good with* caviar, crayfish, white wine, artichoke, mushrooms.

Pacific

Eastern (USA)

Oysters in champagne sauce

In this variation on hollandaise sauce (p.60), oyster liquid is whisked in with the egg yolks, adding extra flavor to the luxurious, buttery sauce.

Serves 4

24 oysters	salt and pepper
¾ cup/180 g butter	few drops lemon juice
1½ cups/375 ml champagne	
4 shallots, very finely chopped	
4 egg yolks	**Heavy saucepan (not aluminum)**

1 Open the oysters and shuck them into a bowl (see Opening oysters) with their juice. Scrub the shells clean and set them flat on four individual ovenproof plates filled with rock salt to stop them from tilting. Drain the oysters, reserving the juice, and set them on the shells.

2 For the sauce: melt the butter and skim the froth from the surface, then allow it to cool until hand-hot. Meanwhile, boil all but ¼ cup/60 ml champagne with the shallots in a heavy pan, until reduced to 2-3 tablespoons. Cool slightly, then whisk in the egg yolks and reserved oyster juice. Continue whisking to a mousse, working on and off the heat for 3-4 minutes until it is thick enough to leave a ribbon trail when the whisk is lifted.

3 Remove the pan from the heat and whisk in the hot butter, first a teaspoon at a time, then in a steady stream, leaving the whey at the bottom of the pan. **Note** If the butter is too hot or added too quickly, the sauce will separate.

4 Flavor the sauce to taste with salt, pepper and lemon juice. It can be kept warm in a water bath (p.510) for up to 30 minutes.

5 Heat the broiler. Just before serving, stir the rest of the champagne into the sauce and spoon it over the oysters. Broil until brown, 3-5 minutes, and serve at once.

SCALLOPS

The scallop shell is associated with the birth of Venus, who rode in one, and also with St. James, whose pilgrims wore a shell badge in their hats. This was probably a European great scallop shell, striped in beige and cream, but the shells of other species can be tinged with yellow, orange, pink and even purple. The fluted lower shell of the scallop acts as an attractive container for the meat. Scallops are gathered wild by trawling or dredging, and are often shucked and cleaned at sea as they die quickly out of water. In the United States, usually only the round white muscle is sold but elsewhere the crescent-shaped orange coral is also eaten.

Small scallops have mild little nuggets of meat about ⅜ in/1 cm across. Giant ones can be as large as 3 in/7.5 cm, but most species are of medium size, with three to four serving one person. Small scallops should be left whole but large ones are usually sliced in ⅜ in/1 cm thick rounds. The meat is sweet and tender, lending itself to numerous cooking methods, often with butter or cream.

USEFUL INFORMATION

Common small scallops Bay (Atlantic, Pacific); calico (Atlantic); Iceland (Atlantic, N.W. Pacific); queen princess (Atlantic); tipa/queen (Pacific, Australia/NZ).

Common medium and large scallops Great (Mediterranean, Atlantic); pilgrim/St. James's scallops (W. Europe); *Coquille St. Jacques* (Mediterranean); giant rock scallop (Pacific Coast, Canada, Mexico); rock (Atlantic); sea (Atlantic).

Season Autumn to spring. Western Europe, peaks in winter; peak varies elsewhere depending on species.

How to choose Unlike other mollusks, scallops do not have to be alive when cooked. *Live:* shells grip if pinched sideways. *In the shell or cleaned:* sweet smell is indication of freshness.

Portion *Medium scallops:* 5-6. *Scallop meat:* 4-6 oz/125-180 g.

Nutritive value per 3½ oz/100 g: 87 calories; 16 g protein; 1 g fat; 3 g carbohydrates; 87 mg sodium; 36 mg cholesterol.

Cooking methods *Whole medium scallops:* bake at 425°F/220°C, 6-8 minutes; broil 1-2 minutes each side; deep-fry 1-2 minutes; marinate to serve raw

2-6 hours; poach 1-2 minutes; sauté 2 minutes. *Tiny scallops and slices:* halve all cooking times.

When done Opaque but slightly transparent in center.

Problems Tough when over-cooked.

Processed forms Frozen; smoked; vacuum-packed; dried (Asian).

Storage *Shucked raw:* 24 hours. *Cooked:* 2 days.

Typical dishes Soup with cream (Australia); *parisienne* (with mushrooms in wine sauce, France); deep-fried bay scallops with tartare sauce (USA); *provençale* (with tomato and garlic, France); brochettes with bacon (UK); with garlic and cream sauce (France); *seviche* (marinated, South America); with shallots and cranberries (USA); in puff pastry with ginger sauce (USA); *mousseline de coquilles* (France); with tart fruit sauce (UK); *terrine de coquilles St. Jacques aux légumes* (with vegetables, France).

Queen scallop

Great/common scallop

Marinating scallops

Small and medium scallops are tender enough to marinate and serve raw. Cut medium or large ones in horizontal slices and leave small ones whole; the coral may be marinated also. Sprinkle with one tablespoon of lemon or lime juice per 2 oz/60 g scallops and toss them well. The juice will "cook" the scallops slightly. Other flavorings can be added: grated lemon or lime zest, finely chopped shallot, spring onion, garlic, ginger, bell or chili pepper. Leave to marinate for at least two hours and up to six hours. Add herbs or seasoning just before serving. Arrange the scallops on plates, sprinkle with a little oil and decorate with herbs or citrus wedges.

OPENING & PREPARING RAW SCALLOPS

To use the hollow undershells of scallops as containers, first scrub them thoroughly, then boil them for five minutes in water.

1 Pick over and rinse any mud from the shells. Take a medium-sized pointed oyster or clam knife in one hand, and hold the scallop shell level in your palm, flat shell upwards. Insert the knife between the top and bottom shell, and slide it around the flat shell.

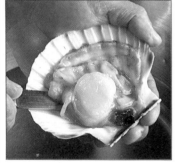

2 Sever the muscle and discard the top shell. Loosen the muscle from the bottom shell and tip the meat into a bowl of water.

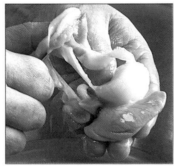

3 Extract the white muscle and red coral, discarding the fringe-like membrane and dark organs. Wash the meat and coral thoroughly.

4 Cut the small crescent-shaped muscle from the white meat and discard it as it is inedibly tough.

5 If the recipe calls for sliced scallops, cut the scallop meat into rounds.

CLAMS & COCKLES

Although they are found and eaten worldwide, clams are particularly popular in the United States. For the cook, one variety is distinctive – the American soft-shell clam, also called steamer, "long-neck" or sand-gaper. It has a thick, protruding neck so the shell is never tightly shut. Soft-shell clams are found on the northwest Atlantic coast from North Carolina and in the northeast Atlantic, from the White Sea to France. A dozen or more make a good serving. Clams with hard shells are many and various in shape and size. There are elegant clams, stubby ovals and long razors. The flesh is usually beige or cream, sometimes spiked with red coral, with shells ranging from white and purple to yellow and red. The flavor tends to be saltier and more intense than that of soft-shell clams, and they will overcook more easily. Smaller hard-shell clams are often eaten raw on the half shell (p.169). The large razor or horse clams, which weigh 1 lb/500 g or more, are best chopped for soups, sauces, or to make fritters. One of the largest, the Pacific geoduck (pronounced goey-duck) provides seaside sport as it must be caught by digging under mud to catch its muscular neck, which can be as long as 4 ft/1.5 m when fully grown. In the eastern United States the hard shell or quahog clam is graded according to size: chowder (medium and large), cherrystone (small) and littleneck (very small). Soft-shell clams are graded as large, and steamers (medium).

Cockle is a popular name for a group of plump bivalves of various species, which are characterized by their rough or ridged shells, deeply hollowed into a heart shape. For cooking, they should be treated like clams. Commercially, clams and cockles are gathered by dredging deep into mud, and purging in salt water.

USEFUL INFORMATION

Common hard-shell clams Bean/coquina (Mediterranean, Atlantic, Pacific); butter (Atlantic, Pacific); carpet shell/palourde (Atlantic, Pacific, Mediterranean); geoduck (Pacific); caper/horse clam (Pacific); littleneck (Pacific); quahog (Atlantic, Pacific); *tartufi marini* (Mediterranean).
Common cockles Giant Atlantic (Atlantic); common (Atlantic, Mediteranean); dog (tropics); heartshell (Atlantic, Mediterranean).
Season Regionally and locally variable depending on species.

How to choose Smell sweet when shucked. *Hard-shells*: tightly closed. *Soft-shells*: slightly open; neck between shells retracts if poked.
Portion 1 qt/1 L small to medium clams serves one; shucked they yield ¾ cup/175 g meat and juice, enough for 2 portions soup.
Nutritive value per 3½ oz/100 g: 60 calories; 9 g protein; 1 g fat; 3 g carbohydrates; 56 mg sodium; 60 mg cholesterol.
Cooking methods *In shell*: steam 5-7 minutes, more if large or shell is very thick. *Raw on shell*: stuff and

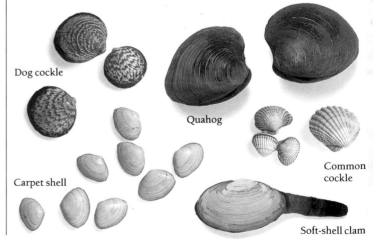

Dog cockle

Quahog

Common cockle

Carpet shell

Soft-shell clam

USEFUL INFORMATION/CLAMS & COCKLES

bake at 450°F/230°C, 4–6 minutes; broil 3-4 minutes. *Whole:* deep-fry 1-2 minutes. *Chopped:* fry 1-2 minutes in fritters; simmer 1-2 minutes in soups, sauces.
When done Edges firm, center soft.
Storage *Live in shell:* 24-36 hours in a cool place. *Raw, shucked with juice:* refrigerate 3 days. *Cooked:* refrigerate 2 days.
Processed forms Canned whole and chopped; smoked whole; frozen in shell and shucked; bottled juice.

Typical dishes *Soft-shell:* with melted butter (USA); deep-fried in cornmeal batter (USA). *Hard-shell:* New England clam chowder (USA); spaghetti *alle vongole* (Italy); cockles with vinegar (UK); *amêijoas à Bulhão Pato* (with garlic and coriander, Portugal); raw with green pepper and onion (USA); stuffed palourde clams (France); steamed or fried with bread (Netherlands); Casino (broiled with bacon, garlic and green peppers, USA). *Also good with* white wine, thyme, bacon, tomato.

OPENING RAW CLAMS

Before opening the clams, pick them over and rinse any mud clinging to the outside of the shells.

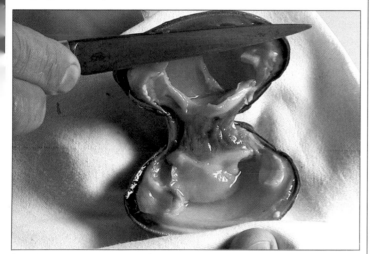

1 Hold the clam in a cloth in the palm of one hand and insert the knife blade between the shells. Twist the knife to pry the shells apart, then sever the hinge muscle and discard the top shell.

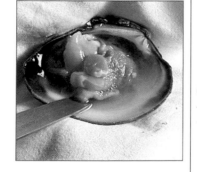

2 With the knife, loosen the muscle in the lower shell. If shucking the meat, tip it, with the juice, into a bowl.

Serving raw clams on the half shell

Follow the method above for opening clams, discarding the top shell. Set the bottom shell on rock salt or ice. Serve the clams with vinegar and chopped onion or with lemon, Tabasco or tomato cocktail sauce.

Cooking clams

Small clams are prepared and cooked like other bivalves (p.165), large ones are generally sold without the shell. Steam them open in boiling water (p.170), drain and strip off the neck skin. Slit the neck to butterfly it, pound it flat and sauté, or chop the meat for making soup or fritters. When preparing horse clams, discard the dark stomach meat before cooking.

MUSSELS

Found worldwide, mussels come in a variety of colors, although most have blue-black, pointed shells and cream or orange meat. Often farmed by growing on poles or ropes which are exposed at low tide, mussels cling by a stringy "beard" that must be pulled away when the shells are cleaned. **Note** Mussels are susceptible to pollution so gathering them wild is not recommended (p.163)

Mussels are usually cooked, although certain species, such as the date-shell, can be eaten raw. Small mussels are steamed (empty shells form handy pincers for removing meat) or made into soup, while plump mussels are broiled or stuffed and baked.

USEFUL INFORMATION

Common small mussels Atlantic blue/edible (Atlantic); date-shell (Mediterranean); green (Asia).
Common large mussels Horse/bearded (Atlantic, Pacific).
Season Regionally and locally variable, depending on species.
How to choose Shells should be tightly closed; halves should not slide across each other when pinched; open mussels should close when tapped. They should smell sweet and not be sandy.
Portion 1 qt/1 L medium mussels yields ¾ cup/175 g mussels when shelled and serves one.
Nutritive value per 3½ oz/100 g: 89 calories; 12 g protein; 2 g fat; 5 g carbohydrates; 270 mg sodium; 63 mg cholesterol.
Cooking methods *In shell:* steam 5-7 minutes. *Steamed on half shell:* bake at 425°F/220°C, 3-5 minutes; broil 2-3 minutes. *Shelled:* reheat gently in liquid.
When done Edges curl; center remains soft.
Processed forms Canned whole, chopped and in shell; smoked whole; frozen in shell.
Storage *Raw in the shell:* 1 day. *Cooked with juice:* 2 days.
Typical dishes Billi-bi (saffron soup with cream, USA); marinated (Spain); deep-fried (Italy); with cream (Belgium); pilaf (France); *mouclade* (with saffron or curry sauce, France); cheese gratin (Scandinavia); with red pepper mayonnaise (USA); stuffing (USA). *Also good with* shallot, rice, white wine, parsley, paprika.

Blue mussel

CLEANING & OPENING RAW MUSSELS

Before opening the mussels, follow the instructions for cleaning and purging under mollusks (p.163).

1 Just before cooking, pull the stringy "beard" from the shell with a small knife.

2 Pry open the shell. Since this often kills the mussel, it must be eaten or cooked at once.

Steaming open mussels and clams

After cleaning, mussels and clams are often steamed to open the shells and cook the meat at the same time. Place 4 quarts/4 liters mussels or clams in a very large pot to allow room for the shells to open. Add about 1 cup/250 ml liquid, such as white wine, fish stock, *court bouillon* or water, with flavorings such as finely chopped onion, garlic, celery, aromatic herbs and saffron, but no salt. Cover the pan tightly and cook over a high heat for about five minutes, shaking or stirring occasionally, just until the shells open; discard any that are still closed. Sprinkle the mussels or clams with chopped parsley and stir. Taste the liquid for seasoning and strain it to get rid of sand. Cooked mussels and clams can be served in the shells with their liquid.

SERVING MUSSELS ON THE HALF SHELL

Once the mussels have been steamed open, the shells can be used as containers for stuffing. Serve the prepared mussels in their shells on a large dish.

Steam large mussels until they open. Discard one shell, remove the mussel from the remaining shell and pull off the rubbery ring surrounding it. Replace the mussel in the shell for serving.

SQUID, OCTOPUS & CUTTLEFISH

Squid is the most widely available edible member of the cephalopod family, which includes other tentacled marine animals such as cuttlefish and octopus. There are hundreds of species found worldwide in tropical and warm waters, but only a few are commonly eaten.

Buried in the flesh of some cephalopods (literally, "head with foot") is the vestige of a skeleton – a long "pen" (squid), an oval "cuttlebone" (cuttlefish) or a hard "beak" (octopus). Squid are considered to be sweeter and more tender than cuttlefish while on the Mediterranean and in Asia, octopus is more highly regarded.

Young squid with tentacles only 1 in/2.5 cm long are delicious cooked whole. Most grow larger, with the head forming an ideal pouch for stuffing, while the tentacles are sliced. The body sac can also be sliced into rings. Octopus or very large squid must be tenderized and in some countries fishermen beat freshly caught octopus on the rocks.

Quick cooking over high heat or long, slow cooking is the rule for cephalopods. The ink (which is squirted to confuse predators) may be used to darken and enrich a sauce. The famous sepia ink of Roman times was derived from the ink of cuttlefish. Care must be taken not to break the ink sac while cleaning the meat, but frozen or cleaned squid does not contain ink. Most recipes are interchangeable, but allow more time for cooking octopus.

USEFUL INFORMATION

Common squid California/San Pedro/Monterey (Pacific); common (Mediterranean and Atlantic); flying/calamar (Eastern Atlantic, Mediterranean); long-finned/bone (Atlantic); short-finned/summer (Atlantic); small (Atlantic).
Common cuttlefish Mediterranean; Atlantic.
Common octopus: *Octopus macropus* (Atlantic, Pacific, Indian Ocean, Mediterranean, Gulf of Mexico); giant/Pacific (Pacific); white/curled (Mediterranean).
Season Year-round.
How to choose Sweet-smelling, moist meat.
Portion 6 oz/180 g cleaned meat or 2-3 small squid.
Nutritive value per 3½ oz/100 g: 87 calories; 13 g protein; 1 g fat; 6 mg carbohydrates; 238 mg sodium; 200 mg cholesterol.
Cooking methods *Tiny squid* and *cuttlefish*: deep-fry 3-4 minutes; poach 5-7 minutes. *Squid or cuttlefish pieces*: bake at 350°F/175°C or stew ½-1 hour; barbecue 2 minutes each side; deep-fry 2-3 minutes; poach 2-3 minutes; sauté 1-2 minutes each side. *Octopus pieces*: poach up to 45 minutes; stew up to 2 hours.

When done Fairly tender.
Processed forms Pickled; canned, canned smoked; dried (Mediterranean and Japan); frozen raw.
Storage *Cleaned, raw or cooked*: refrigerate 2 days; freeze 3 months.
Typical dishes Sautéed squid (USA); deep-fried squid (Italy); *calamares en su tinta* (squid stewed in their ink and wine, Spain); *octapodi maratho krasato* (with fennel in wine, Greece); *riso con le seppie* (cuttlefish risotto, Italy); *Also good with* citrus fruits, onion, olive oil, dark soy sauce.

Cuttlefish

PREPARING SQUID & CUTTLEFISH

Once cleaned, the pouch, fins and tentacles can be chopped, sliced or left whole.

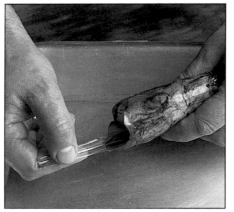

3 **To clean the squid pouch:** discard the semi-transparent "pen" that emerges from it.

4 **To clean the cuttlefish pouch:** push or cut the cuttlebone from the pouch.

1 Holding the fish over a dish to catch the ink, pull the body from the head and tentacles, gently but firmly. If the ink sac is unbroken, pierce it so that the ink drains into a dish. **Note** The ink of squid or cuttlefish can be used in the finished dish (p.173).

2 Open the tentacles to reveal the "beak" (mouth) in the center. Squeeze out the beak, cut it off and discard it. Cut the tentacles from the head and intestines, discarding them too.

5 Pull off the purplish skin covering the pouch and fins. Wash the meat thoroughly, turning it inside out to reach the inside.

Octopus

Squid

6 Cut the fins from the pouch. The pouch, fins and tentacles are now ready to cook and can be chopped, sliced or left whole according to the recipe.

PREPARING OCTOPUS

After cleaning, octopus and large squid must be tenderized by pounding, or parboiling for 30-40 minutes in *court bouillon*.

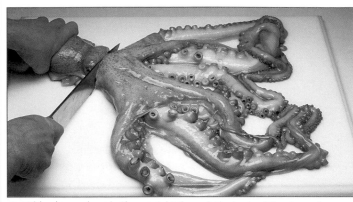

1 With a large, sharp knife, cut right through the body of the cleaned octopus to separate it from the tentacles.

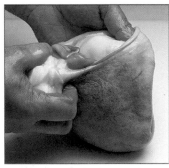

2 Pull open the body sac and locate the innards.

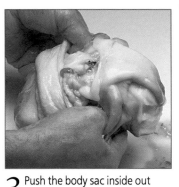

3 Push the body sac inside out through the orifice in the head.

4 Cut away the eyes and innards; then locate the hard "beak".

5 Push the "beak" through to the other side and cut it away.

6 With your hands, peel the skin from the body pouch and tentacles of the octopus.

7 RIGHT If necessary, loosen the skin by parboiling the octopus for 2 minutes, then peel it away with your hands. To tenderize the flesh, pound it with a mallet for a couple of minutes on each side.

FROGS

As amphibians, frogs can be viewed as either fish or meat. Wild frogs are not generally eaten now that frogs are reared commercially on a large scale. Stuffed, whole frog was once an Italian specialty, but now only the back legs are eaten, sold in pairs attached by a short strip of backbone. Females are larger than males, though size has little bearing on the quality of commercial frog's legs, as all are raised to be tender. Since they taste rather like chicken, they are suited to many of the same recipes. Alternatively, the meat can be combined with shellfish, or with sauces based on fish stock. They may also be deep-fried to serve with a piquant sauce. As frog's legs dry out easily, they must be stored covered, and may be soaked in milk before cooking.

USEFUL INFORMATION

Common frogs American bullfrog; green (Europe); leopard (N. America).
Season *Farmed:* year-round. *Wild:* best in spring.
How to choose Moist, plump and light pink.
Portion 2 large or 6 small pairs frog's legs, weighing 6 oz/180 g.
Nutritive value per 3½ oz/100 g: 73 calories; 16 g protein; no fat, no carbohydrates; 87 mg sodium; 50 mg cholesterol.
Cooking methods Bake at 375°F/190°C, 5-8 minutes ; broil on skewers 2-3 minutes; deep-fry 2-3 minutes; poach to serve in sauce 3-5 minutes; sauté 1-2 minutes each side; stew 10-15 minutes.
When done Tender.
Processed forms Frozen raw; canned smoked.

Frog's legs

Storage *Fresh or cooked:* 2 days.
Typical dishes *Poulette* (with chicken stock and parsley sauce (France); *provençale* (sautéed with garlic, France); pan-fried (USA); fricassée (France).

STUFFING SQUID & CUTTLEFISH

Clean and prepare the squid or cuttlefish, leaving the pouch in one piece. The rest of the cleaned flesh can be chopped and used as part of the stuffing mixture.

1 Use a pastry bag or small spoon to stuff the mixture loosely into the pouch (see recipe opposite).
Note The stuffing will swell when cooked to fill out the pouch.

2 Secure the pouch with a trussing needle and string, or with toothpicks, and cook as directed in the recipe.

Stuffed squid in its ink

If the squid has been cleaned and the ink sac removed by the fishmonger, the ink can be omitted from this recipe. Capers, fennel, celery or bell peppers can be added to the sauce.

Serves 4

3 lb/1.4 kg squid (about 2 lb/1 kg if cleaned)	**For the stuffing**
2 tbsp/30 ml olive oil	1 onion, chopped
2 lb/1 kg tomatoes, peeled, seeded and chopped	2 cloves garlic, chopped
	2 tbsp/30 ml olive oil
2 cloves garlic, crushed	2 tbsp chopped fresh parsley
bouquet garni	6 ripe olives, pitted and chopped
2-3 tbsp shredded fresh oregano or basil	½ cup/30 g fresh breadcrumbs
	salt and pepper

1 Prepare the squid (p.171), reserving the ink sac.
2 **To make the stuffing:** chop the tentacles and fins. Fry the onion and garlic in the olive oil until soft, but not brown. Stir into the chopped squid with the parsley, olives and breadcrumbs. Season with salt and pepper. Fill the squid pouches with stuffing (see Stuffing squid and cuttlefish, left).
3 In a sauté pan or shallow casserole heat the olive oil. Stir in the tomatoes, garlic, bouquet garni, salt and pepper and simmer for 2-3 minutes, stirring.
4 Add the stuffed squid to the pan, spoon the sauce over them and cover with a lid. Simmer very gently, stirring occasionally, for 30-40 minutes or until the squid is very tender. Add a little water during cooking if the pan starts to get dry.
5 Remove the pouches and set them aside. Mix the ink with a little water and add 2 or 3 tablespoons of sauce. Stir this mixture back into the remaining sauce, adding basil or oregano, and simmer for 10 minutes. Discard the bouquet garni and taste for seasoning. Slice the stuffed pouches. Spoon the sauce into a dish (or on to individual plates) and set the squid on top.

Barbecuing squid or cuttlefish

Cut the skinned meat into strips about 1½ in/3.7 cm wide and 5 in/12.5 cm long. With a sharp knife, score both sides of the flesh in a diagonal pattern and thread on to skewers, working in and out so that the meat lies flat. Sprinkle the meat with oil, lemon juice, salt, pepper and seasonings such as dried red pepper, thyme or ground aniseed. Leave to marinate for 30 minutes to two hours, turning occasionally. Barbecue the meat over a high heat or broil it for two minutes on each side, until tender.

Other cooking methods

The squid family is much appreciated in southern Europe and the Mediterranean, where highly flavored soups and stews are popular. In the Caribbean, octopus stew spiced with red pepper sauce is a favorite. Often the squid pouch is stuffed with the chopped tentacles, or the pouch can be split open, pounded flat to tenderize it and broiled or sautéed. Members of the cephalopod family are often poached in *court bouillon* (p.44), then sliced in strips to serve in a salad with olive oil, lemon juice and herbs. Squid or cuttlefish slices can be deep-fried; whole tiny squid or cuttlefish are a special treat.

EXOTIC SEA CREATURES

Looking like black, spiny pincushions, sea urchins are an unexpected delicacy, particularly appreciated in France and Japan. The bright orange coral is served raw in the shell or in *sushi* (p.134), or can add a salty richness to fish sauces and soufflés. Although there are over 500 species of sea urchin, table varieties are scarce and expensive. They are gathered along North American and European coasts, during a season lasting from late summer through to spring. To prepare sea urchins; hold them with a thick cloth and cut around the underside with scissors. Shake out the dark intestines (the coral clings to the sides of the shell). Eat the urchin with a squeeze of lemon juice as part of a raw shellfish platter. Serve with a teaspoon, or scoop out the meat and use as a filling for omelets or flavoring for soups and sauces.

There are three kinds of edible barnacle: Mediterranean violet barnacles are eaten raw in the manner of a sea urchin; gooseneck barnacles, popular in Portugal and Spain, have a long neck and are generally steamed like a soft-shell clam; the giant barnacle of the Pacific is popular in South America, where it is steamed and eaten with butter. Common on the ocean floor, if not on the table, are sea anemones, which grow worldwide in a multitude of colors, shapes and sizes. Many are edible, and only need thorough washing before being slowly simmered for soup. The sea cucumber is often sold dried in Asian stores. It needs to be extremely well cleaned or it will not swell properly and soak up the cooking sauce. After cooking for several hours, a sea cucumber develops a special gelatinous texture, not unlike the jellyfish, which is also sold dried, and cooked in similar Asian dishes.

Turtle meat is rarely eaten in Europe, though in the United States some freshwater turtles occasionally appear on the table. Terrapin is a freshwater turtle used for soup or stew, or served in a cream sauce. Diamond-back is the finest variety, long regarded as a great delicacy. The mock turtle soup seen on menus is usually made with calf's head.

POULTRY & GAME BIRDS

STRICTLY SPEAKING, the term poultry covers all birds that can be domesticated for the farmyard – chickens, ducks, geese, turkeys and guinea fowl. However, given modern methods of raising birds commercially, several others creep in "under the wire", including the cross-bred Rock Cornish hen and game birds such as pheasant, pigeon, partridge and quail. Also covered in this chapter are the true wild game birds such as grouse, woodcock and snipe, and wild duck and wild goose.

So popular are birds on the table that they are sold in many forms – whole, cut into pieces, with bones and boneless – often leaving little preparatory work for the cook. However, free-range and wild game birds are still found in many areas, and this chapter gives details of preparing them, from plucking and drawing to cutting in pieces, boning and carving.

Choosing poultry

The way poultry is reared is of great importance. A good diet (preferably grain) and freedom to roam in the open air are vital to the flavor of a bird. Unfortunately, such free-range birds are now few. They can be identified by a generous layer of fat under the skin, firm meat, and callouses on the feet, as well as by their high price. With a young bird, the point of the breastbone is flexible.

Supermarket birds offer little variety, but a few rules hold: the bird's skin should be light colored and moist (the yellowish color of some chickens shows only that they have been fed yellow foodstuffs), and the breast meat should be plump, particularly on turkey and goose. Fresh meat is preferable to frozen, but when frozen quickly and handled correctly, poultry suffers little.

Storing poultry

Freshly killed poultry should be drawn before storing. Remove plastic packaging from oven-ready birds. Store loosely covered in the refrigerator for up to two days for small birds, and four days for goose and turkey. Frozen poultry should be kept no more than two days. For information on freezing and defrosting poultry. see Preserving (p.495)

Poultry is particularly susceptible to contamination by salmonella bacteria, which cause food poisoning. It must be chilled properly during storage, and equipment and hands should be washed after handling the raw flesh. Frozen birds must be completely thawed before cooking. All birds should be brought to room temperature before cooking and the cavity should be only loosely stuffed, or not stuffed at all, to ensure that heat penetrates thoroughly to kill the salmonella.

Cleaning poultry

Raw poultry should not be rinsed before cooking. Simply wipe the inside of the bird with a damp towel and, if necessary, wipe the skin. Supermarket birds, particularly if frozen, should be wiped with a paper towel to absorb as much moisture as possible.

SINGEING & DRAWING POULTRY

You may need to remove down and pin feathers from undrawn poultry. Remove them with tweezers, or tug with a knife.

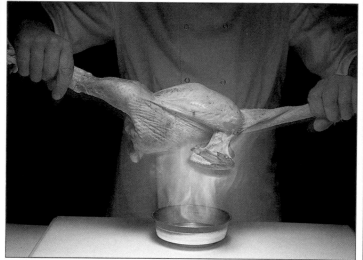

1 Holding the bird in both hands, stretch it over an open flame (gas or alcohol) and singe the down, turning the bird so that the skin does not scorch and split in the heat.

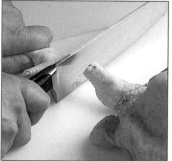

2 Set the bird on a board and chop off the feet with a large knife or cleaver, about 1in/2.5cm below the first joint. (The feet can be cleaned and used for stock.)

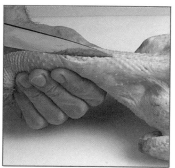

3 Turn the bird over, stretch the neck skin against the vertebrae, and slit the neck skin lengthwise.

4 Holding the neck in one hand, with the other, pull the skin away from the flesh.

5 Turn the bird over and cut off the neck, as close to the body as possible, leaving the skin intact. With a large knife, chop off the head and discard it. Turn the bird so that it is breast down, then pull the tubes from the neck skin, and cut them off.

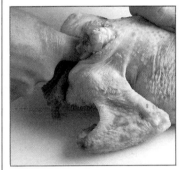 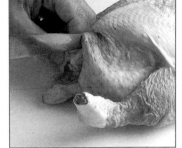

6 Insert a forefinger into the neck end of the bird and turn it against the bone to loosen the lungs and other innards.

7 Turn the bird over. Make a vertical slit in the tail cavity to enlarge it. Insert your finger and turn to loosen the innards.

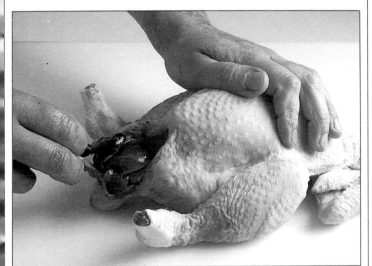

8 Gently pull out the innards in one piece, taking care not to break the gall bladder (the green sac attached to the liver) as the bitter juice will taint the meat. Wipe the inside of the bird with a damp cloth. The innards consist of the lungs, heart, liver, gall bladder and gizzard. (In game birds they include the intestines.) Discard the lungs and intestines, cut the gall bladder from the liver and discard it.

Note The giblets, which comprise the heart, liver, gizzard and neck of the poultry, can be sliced, cooked and used as ingredients for stuffing or stock. Before being used they should be washed in cold water and trimmed. The gizzard is first split and the crop, or hard membrane, is cut away and discarded. For additional ideas on how to cook giblets, see Poultry trimmings (p.189).

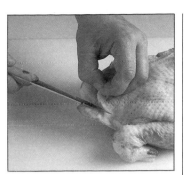

9 Turn the bird breast down and cut the oiling gland from behind the tail cavity.

10 Using a carving steel, remove the tough sinews from the legs (p.190). Trim the wing pinions. If necessary, wipe the bird with a cloth.

CUTTING A BIRD IN HALF

When cutting up birds, the number of pieces depends very much on the weight of the bird. A small bird, such as a *coquelet* (shown here), can be cut in half before or after cooking. This method is for raw or cooked birds, weighing 1-3lb/500g-1.4kg.

1 Set the bird, back down, on a board. Slit closely along the breastbone with a knife to loosen the meat.

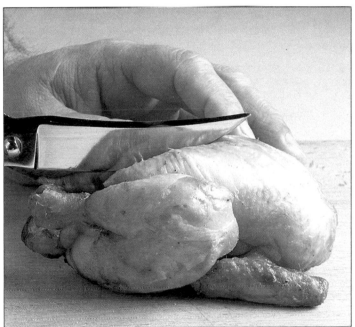

2 ABOVE Cut along one side of the breastbone with poultry shears.

3 Turn the bird over, cut along each side of the backbone and discard it. If the bird is cooked, trim the leg knuckles and wing pinions; otherwise, do so after cooking.

CUTTING A BIRD IN PIECES

Large birds can be cut into four, six or eight pieces, depending on their size. Dark meat cooks more slowly than light, so legs should be cut into smaller pieces than the breast.

Cutting into four pieces

For raw or cooked birds weighing 2½-3½ lb/1.2-1.6 kg.

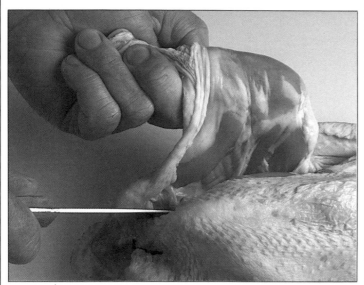

1 **To remove the legs:** use a knife or a pair of poultry shears to cut the skin between the leg and the breast.

2 With the tip of the knife, locate the oyster meat lying against the backbone and cut round it so that it is attached to the thigh joint.

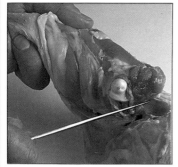

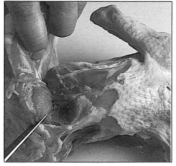

3 Twist the leg sharply outward to break the thigh joint, severing the leg with oyster meat attached.

4 Turn the bird round and remove the other leg, leaving the oyster meat attached to it.

5 Cut off the wing pinions and discard them. Cut forward to remove the meat that lies along the backbone.

6 **To separate the whole breast:** set the bird back down. Slit closely along the breastbone to loosen the meat, then split the breastbone with a knife or shears.

7 Turn the bird over, and with a knife or shears, cut the rib bones and backbone from the breast in one piece, leaving the wing joints attached to the breast. If the bird is cooked, discard the backbone.

8 Cut the breast in half with poultry shears or a knife.

9 Trim excess bone from the breast, and from knuckles and wings after cooking.

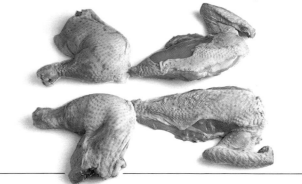

Cutting into six or eight pieces

For raw or cooked birds weighing 3-5 lb/1.4-2.3 kg.

10 **For 6 pieces:** cut the bird into 4 pieces and trim as above. Cut the legs in half through the joint, between the thigh and the drumstick, using the line of white fat on the underside as a guide.

11 **For 8 pieces:** divide each breast in half diagonally with poultry shears or a knife, cutting through the breast and rib bones so that a portion of breast meat is cut off with the wing.

BONING A WHOLE BIRD

Choose a bird with the skin intact so that you can keep it whole for wrapping (duck is shown here). Birds may be partially boned, leaving the leg and wing bones in to give shape for stuffing, and to make carving easier. This is common practice for small birds and for presentations such as chaudfroid (Sauces, p.56).

Partially boning

1 With a boning knife, cut off the wing tip and middle section, leaving the largest wing bone. With the breast of the bird down, slit the skin along the backbone from neck to tail. Cut out the wishbone.

2 Carefully cut and pull the flesh and skin away from the carcass, working evenly with short sharp strokes of the knife. After each cut, ease the flesh and skin away from the carcass with your fingers.

3 Cut the flesh from the saber-shaped bone near the wing, and remove the bone.

4 When you reach the ball-and-socket joints connecting the wing and thigh bones to the carcass, sever them so that they are separated from the carcass but still attached to the skin.

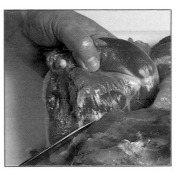

5 Continue cutting the breast meat away from the bone until you reach the ridge of the breastbone, where the skin and bones meet. Turn the bird round and repeat on the other side. At the end, the meat will be detached from the carcass and the skin will cling only along the ridge of the breastbone.

6 ABOVE Pull gently to separate the breastbone and carcass from the flesh (the skin tears easily). The carcass and other bones can be used to make stock.

7 The partially boned bird (above), with leg and wing bones left in, is now ready for stuffing.

Completely boning

A bird is often completely boned to stuff and roll. Follow the directions for partially boning a bird, then proceed as follows:

8 Holding the outside of the wing bone in one hand, cut through the tendons and scrape the meat from the bone. Pull out the bone, using the knife to free it.

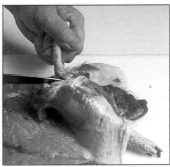

9 Holding the inside end of the leg bone, cut through the tendons attaching the flesh to the bone. Use the knife to scrape the meat from the bone, pushing it away from the end of the bone as if sharpening a pencil. Cut the bone free of the skin. If any sinews still remain in the leg, cut them out.

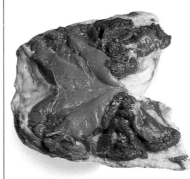

10 Repeat on the other side, then push the leg and wing skin side out. Place the completely boned bird on a board; most of the skin will have meat attached to it.

BONING POULTRY BREASTS

Sometimes double poultry breasts are sold jointed along the breastbone in one piece, or they may be single breasts, split along the breastbone:

If using a double breast

1 Place the breast, skin side up, on the board. Crack down sharply with the heel of your hand to snap the breastbone. Remove the skin, if you wish.

2 Cut out the wishbone, then continue cutting and scraping the meat from the breastbone until it is free.

3 Turn the breast, bone side up. Scrape the meat from the ribs and cut out the rib bones.

4 RIGHT Strip the tendon from the center of each breast, stroking it with a knife to remove it cleanly. If the inner fillet becomes detached from the meat, replace it. Finally, trim the meat.

If using a single breast

Strip off the skin, if you wish. Turn the pieces bone side up and cut and scrape out the bones. Remove the tendon and trim as above.

BONING A BIRD BY THE GLOVE METHOD

This method, which leaves the skin and meat of a bird in one piece, like a pouch, is convenient for stuffing (the bird need not be cleaned first). Boning by the glove method is suitable for large birds, such as turkey, and duck (shown here), but it is difficult with small birds.

1 RIGHT Pull back the neck skin and cut out the wishbone. Find the wing joint. Using short sharp strokes of the knife, and your fingers, half cut, half ease the breast meat and skin away from one side of the carcass. Keep the knife in close contact with the carcass so that the skin is not damaged.

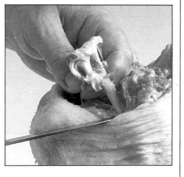

2 LEFT Locate the saber-shaped bone and pull it out. Continue cutting until you reach the wing joint, then sever it; repeat on the other side. Turn the bird over, backbone upward. The skin now lies on the backbone and will tear easily.

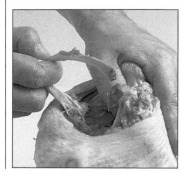

3 Pull the meat and skin back from the carcass.

4 Continue cutting, pulling the flesh from the bone and turning the carcass from one side to the other, working toward the tail end.

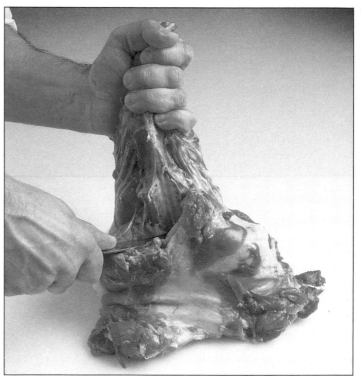

5 When you reach the leg joints, sever them, leaving the bones attached to the meat and skin.

6 Continue cutting until the carcass is separated from the meat and attached to the skin only at the breastbone.

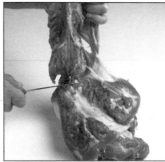

7 Pull the breastbone and carcass from the flesh. The leg bones may be left attached, or removed (see Completely boning, p.177).

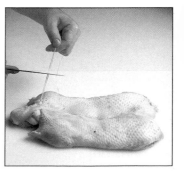

8 Turn the pouch inside out so the skin is on the outside. Cut off the tail skin and tie at the tail end, ready for stuffing.

Stuffing poultry

A seasoned stuffing (p.364) not only adds flavor, but it helps plump the bird into an appealing shape. Birds with white meat are preferred, since birds such as duck and goose need careful cooking to ensure that the stuffing is not too fatty. The basis of the stuffing mixture is often a carbohydrate or grain, for example breadcrumbs or rice. Chestnut stuffings are popular with turkey and game, while little birds such as quail or squab are best with a veal or pork-based mixture; oyster stuffing for goose and turkey is popular in the eastern United States. Flavorings should complement the bird: fruits such as apple, dried prune or apricot go well with duck and goose, lemon and herbs with white-fleshed birds, while onion enhances most mixtures, and nuts add texture.

Small birds are often boned to make stuffing easier, leaving in the leg and wing bones (p.177). Larger birds weighing 3 lb/1.4 kg or more may be left on the bone, or boned and stuffed. The stuffing is usually a fine-textured veal, ham or pork mixture. Allow about 1 cup/175 g stuffing per 1 lb/500 g bird and fill the tail cavity loosely; it must have room to swell a little during cooking. Large birds may have a second stuffing added at the neck (p.186). Contrasting mixtures can be used, such as a sage and onion stuffing, with a second one of pork and chestnut, or wild rice stuffing with another of celery, apricot and walnut. Truss the bird to hold the neck skin in place and cook it, allowing half an hour extra cooking time for small stuffed birds and up to an hour extra for larger ones. **Note** Do not stuff a bird more than three hours before cooking; if the stuffing is warm, the bird must be cooked at once.

TRUSSING A BIRD

Trussing not only keeps in the stuffing, it also holds the bird together so that a sprawling leg or wing does not overcook, and the cooked bird sits neatly for carving. When trussing ducks and geese, tuck the legs well back under the breast so that the bird rests flat in the pan. Birds under 1 lb/500 g are simply tied (p.193).

1 Draw the bird (p.174). If already drawn, remove the giblets. Thread the trussing needle.

2 Pull out any pieces of fat located around the tail cavity.

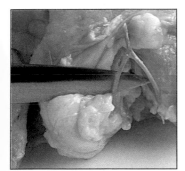

3 Remove the wishbone, as it prevents the breast from being carved in neat slices. Fold back the neck skin and remove the wishbone using the point of a sharp knife to cut it out. Remove any fat.

4 Set the bird breast up, and push the legs well back and down so that the ends sit straight up in the air. Insert the trussing needle into the flesh at the knee joint, push it through the bird and out through the other knee joint.

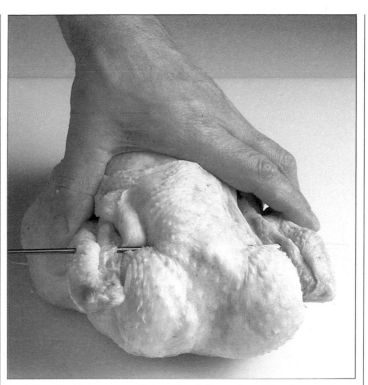

5 Turn the bird over on to its breast and, if the wing pinions have not been trimmed, tuck them under the second joint. Pull the neck skin over the neck cavity, and push the needle through both sections of one wing and into the neck skin. Continue under the backbone of the bird to the other side. Now catch the second wing in the same way as the first, pushing the needle through both wing bones and pulling it out the other side.

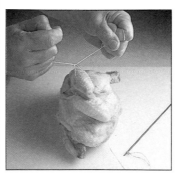

6 Turn the bird on to its side, pull the ends of the string (from the leg and wing) firmly together and tie them securely.

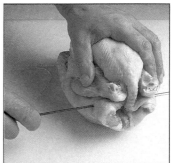

7 Turn the bird breast side up. Tuck the tail into the cavity of the bird and fold the top skin over it. Push the needle through the skin.

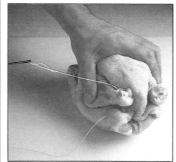

8 Loop the string round one drumstick, under the breastbone and over the other drumstick.

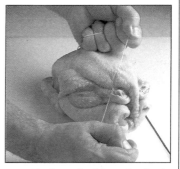

9 Tie the ends of the string firmly together. The bird should sit level on the board.

SKINNING A BIRD

The skin of a bird, removed in one piece, can be used as a container for stuffing. The meat is used separately.

1 Cut off the wing pinions and trim the leg knuckles. Slit the skin along the backbone from the head to the tail.

2 Cut and peel the skin from one side of the bird, using short sharp strokes of the knife.

3 Turn the leg and wing skin inside out as it is reached.

4 Continue peeling away the skin, up to the breastbone. Repeat on the other side. Gently pull the skin from the carcass. Then go on to cut the meat from the carcass. The skin can be used instead of barding fat to line a terrine mold, or to wrap stuffing for a *galantine* (p.255).

ALTERNATIVELY, some cooks prefer to bone the bird along the backbone removing skin and meat together, then cutting the meat from the skin.

Marinating poultry and game birds

Given the tenderness of poultry, marinating might seem unnecessary, but marinades also add flavor to a dish. Light marinades, based on white wine with plenty of spices, are perfect for white meats, while more traditional red wine marinades can be used for duck and goose. Barbecue sauces (p.65) are sometimes used to marinate poultry before cooking, and even a short soaking in olive oil, lemon juice and herbs can be beneficial. The bird should be turned often in the marinade.

Marinades come into their own with game birds. Braises and ragouts of dark birds such as grouse and quail are incomparable when thoroughly imbued with a concentrated cooked marinade of red wine and herbs. There should be sufficient marinade to cover the poultry pieces, or small birds, when they are put into a deep bowl. The marinade is used later to baste the bird during cooking or to make a sauce.

SPATCHCOCKING A BIRD

Small birds are spatchcocked – split and flattened, often on skewers – as an attractive presentation for baking or broiling. The French call it *en crapaudine*, since, with a stretch of the imagination, the bird resembles a flat toad or *crapaud*.

1 Cut off the wing pinions at the joint with a pair of poultry shears or with a knife.

2 Hold the bird in your hand, breast down. Cut along each side of the backbone with poultry shears and remove it.

3 Clean the inside of the bird by wiping it with paper towels. Trim the skin. Open the bird out and snip the wishbone in half or remove it.

4 Set the bird, breast side up, with the legs turned in. Using the heel of your hand, push down sharply on the breast to break the breastbone and so flatten the bird.

5 Make a small cut in the skin between the leg and breastbone and tuck in the leg knuckles.

6 Thread two skewers through the birds, to hold the wings and legs in a flat, splayed position.

ROASTING TEMPERATURES AND TIMES

Poussin/Cornish hen	400°F/200°C	25-40 mins total
Guinea fowl	400°F/200°C	15 mins per 1lb/500 g +15 minutes
Chicken	400°F/200°C	18 mins per 1lb/500 g +18 minutes
Capon	375°F/190°C	25 mins per 1lb/500g
Turkey under 10 lb/4.5 kg 10-14 lb/4.5-6.5 kg over 14 lb/6.5 kg	350°F/175°C	20 mins per 1 lb/500 g +20 minutes 18 mins per 1 lb/500 g 16 mins per 1 lb/500 g

Roasting poultry

The French method of roasting poultry in a fairly high heat is the most successful. Some cooks prefer a lower heat, but with this method the bird tends to stew in its juices. When cooking large birds, foil can be draped loosely over the bird half-way through roasting to keep it moist and to prevent the skin from scorching.

Truss the bird, with or without stuffing, season it and spread the skin with a little butter, if you like. Spreading the flesh with softened butter enriches the meat and gives it a characteristic golden color. Alternatively, to prepare a self-basting bird, lift the breast skin, ease it away from the meat with your fingers, then spread the flesh with softened butter.

Game birds with little natural fat are often draped with barding fat or strips of bacon (p.193). Herbs such as rosemary, thyme or tarragon, or spices such as juniper (for game) may be added to the inside of a bird, but essentially poultry should be roasted plainly to bring out the fullest flavor.

Set the bird on its side in a roasting pan in which it just fits, and roast, basting every 10-15 minutes. Turn the bird on to the other side about a quarter of the way through the total cooking time and, finally, turn it on to its back so that it cooks evenly. For small birds, high heat is maintained throughout cooking, but larger birds are first browned at high heat, then cooked more slowly at a lower heat. (Very large birds are too heavy to turn.)

For fatty breeds of duck and goose, long cooking is needed to extract as much fat as possible and produce crisp skin. High heat is advisable, and the skin should be pricked lightly so that the fat can escape while the juices are retained.

If fat or juices in the pan start to scorch during long cooking, add a few tablespoons of water or stock. Once cooked, discard trussing strings, cover the bird loosely with foil and let it stand for 10-15 minutes, depending on size, so that the juices are redistributed before carving. Meanwhile, make the gravy (p.57).

Roast poultry accompaniments vary enormously from one country to another. With chicken or turkey most cooks choose sautéed or puréed potatoes (although in Britain oven-roast potatoes are traditional), and green vegetables such as zucchini. Game birds are often served with fried potato cake or straw potatoes. Oranges, peaches, cherries and apples are traditional with duck, and in winter, dried fruits take their place; duckling arrives with green peas in spring, apple sauce and turnips in the autumn. In Sweden, goose is often served with apples and prunes; in Germany it appears with sausages and sauerkraut. The American custom of serving cranberry compote with festive turkey is spreading to Europe, while all the autumn roast birds – turkey, goose and game – go well with chestnuts, purée of turnip and root celery, or red cabbage.

Spit-roasting poultry

When birds are roasted on a turning spit, the principles are the same as for oven-roasting, but the smaller the bird, the closer it should be to the heat. Make sure the bird is balanced evenly so that it does not tear itself away from the spit. Little or no basting is needed since the bird cooks in its own juice as it turns, but it can be brushed with butter or a barbecue sauce (p.65). Spit-roasting is particularly suitable for fatty birds such as duck, where the fat must be rendered from under the skin and there is very little juice for making gravy.

Pot-roasting poultry

Pot-roasting (Fr. *en cocotte*), as applied to poultry, is not at all precise. It means to cook in the oven in a covered casserole, but with what, and how, is open to the cook's imagination. Often the bird is left whole and browned in butter, then cooked in its own juices with vegetables such as onions, small potatoes and carrots.

An important point to remember is the size of the pot, which should contain the ingredients without crowding them. Cooked in this way, the bird tastes like a succulent roast, and it reheats well, unlike a plain roast bird. One variation of pot-roasting is to bake the poultry in a clay pot or chicken brick, shaped to fit it. The pot needs to be soaked in water first so that the contents stay moist during cooking.

Simple seasonings such as herbs, lemon and olive oil can be added to mingle with the bird's juices. A similar effect can be obtained by wrapping the bird (together with the seasonings) tightly in foil and cooking it in the oven. The time-honored brown paper bag or special plastic roasting bag can also be used, but because they are slightly porous, the bird tends to dry and brown more thoroughly than if cooked in foil.

Braising poultry

Designed for tough well-flavored meat, braising is ideal for boiling fowl, mature geese or turkey, and old game such as pheasant. Birds are usually left whole but if very large they may be cut into pieces. With old birds, marinating is critical for tenderizing and adding flavor. The bird is browned before being moistened with a complex mixture of wine, stock, garlic, shallot, herbs and a *mirepoix* (p.263) of diced vegetables. After straining, other ingredients are added to the sauce to give the braise its individual character. These vary from the standard onions and mushrooms with bacon, to turnips (classic with duck), artichokes and onions (good with turkey), and garlic (with duck or goose).

In Normandy, apples, Calvados and cream are used to flavor and thicken the sauce of braised chicken, and in Flanders, beer may be added. From Germany come braises with bacon and sauerkraut; a Norwegian variation includes soft cheese and cream. For white-fleshed poultry, the stock should be light and often white wine is used. Instead of browning the bird, it may be braised *à blanc* – cooked gently in butter until whitened and simmered with vegetables to make a delicate cream sauce. Because so many ingredients are included in a braise, accompaniments should be simple – plain, starchy foods, such as pasta, boiled rice or rice pilaf (p.315), boiled or creamed potatoes are the most suitable.

Stewing poultry

Poultry stew (Fr. *ragoût*) is a free-form braise that can be cooked on top of the stove or in the oven. The bird is cut into pieces so that the liquid covers it completely. It is ideal for mature birds, as in *coq au vin*, but tender birds can be used too. A stew has no *mirepoix* (p.263), and instead slow-cooking vegetables such as turnips and carrots, or fruits such as dried apricots or prunes, may be included. Quick-cooking examples such as bell peppers or mushrooms, are added midway through cooking. Unusual ingredients such as samphire, or salty shellfish like mussels and shrimps, can also be used. A poultry fricassée is a white stew with white wine and cream, and richest of all is *poulet au sang*, a stew thickened and darkened to a velvety black with blood.

Making a poultry sauté

Poultry is the ideal main ingredient for a sauté. Cut into pieces, the moist, tender meat of young birds cooks perfectly in its own juice with added butter or olive oil, thus developing and concentrating the often elusive flavor. Aromatic vegetables such as shallot, garlic or leek added early on will permeate the meat, and little or no liquid should be added until near the end of cooking. When birds such as duck are cooked as a sauté, the fat is extracted from under the skin by thorough cooking, and should be discarded. Once this has been done, the variety of additional ingredients and garnishes is almost limitless – vegetables, herbs, spices, fruits, and shellfish, red or white wine, stock, and sometimes cream to add body. The sauce for a poultry sauté should always be light and concentrated, very much in the modern style; often, it is not necessary to add a thickening of any kind.

Given the small quantity of sauce, accompaniments to a poultry sauté can be extended beyond the usual pasta and rice, although the choice depends on the ingredients already in the dish. Small fried potatoes or a potato cake are delicious, as are chestnuts and root vegetables such as carrots and root celery.

Poaching poultry

Poaching is a good method of cooking mature birds, particularly white-fleshed ones, as it tenderizes the meat and the juices yield a superior sauce. If you are adding a stuffing, the cavity must be closed properly when trussing to prevent leakage. Old birds should be blanched first to clean and whiten them, but younger birds and those with dark flesh need no preparation.

With poached poultry, it is common for the vegetables to be cooked with the bird, and all poaching recipes are related to the classic *Poule au pot*. Other vegetables such as mushrooms, cabbage or turnips may be added and the dish made more substantial by adding bacon or sausages. Flavorings such as wine or vinegar, and aromatics such as saffron or star anise (for duck), can be added during cooking. When a sauce is made, a dish such as Rice pilaf (p.315) or pasta is the classic accompaniment.

Poultry pieces, usually chicken or turkey breasts, can also be poached in stock in the oven, but the flavor will be milder than that of a whole bird. Meat from the poached bird may be used for sandwiches or salad and the liquid saved for sauces such as velouté, soup or stock.

Poule au pot

Poached chicken in the pot is a complete meal. The cooking broth is served as soup, followed by stuffed chicken with vegetables.

Serves 8

6-9lb/3-4kg boiling fowl	1 clove garlic, chopped
1 onion, studded with 2 cloves	4 tbsp chopped parsley
large bouquet garni	pinch grated nutmeg
1 tsp black peppercorns	salt and pepper
1 stalk celery, cut in pieces	1 egg, beaten to mix
1 cinnamon stick	**Vegetable garnish**
1 tbsp salt	1½lb/750g medium carrots, trimmed
5 qt/5L water (more if necessary)	2lb/1kg leeks, trimmed and split
For the stuffing	1lb/500g small turnips
4 slices dry white bread	**For serving**
1 cup/250ml milk	¼lb/125g very fine noodles **or** French bread, sliced diagonally
1 tbsp/15g butter	
½ onion, chopped	
chicken liver and heart	
½lb/250g raw or cooked smoked ham, ground	**Trussing needle and string (p.503)**

1 To make the stuffing: soak the bread in the milk for 10 minutes, then squeeze it dry and crumble it. Melt the butter and fry the onion until soft. Add the chicken liver and heart and sauté for 1-2 minutes until brown but still pink in the center. Cool slightly, then chop the mixture and stir into the breadcrumbs with the ham, garlic, parsley, nutmeg, salt and pepper to taste. Stir in the egg to bind the stuffing.
2 Stuff the chicken and truss it (p.179). Tie the onion, bouquet garni, peppercorns, celery, and cinnamon in cheesecloth. Put the chicken in a pot with the cheesecloth bag, salt and water to cover, and bring slowly to a boil, skimming often. Simmer uncovered for 1 hour, skimming occasionally.
3 For the garnish: tie the carrots and leeks in bundles and add them with the turnips. Simmer for another hour or until both chicken and vegetables are very tender. Add more water if necessary so that the bird is always covered.
4 Transfer the chicken to a board and discard the trussing strings. Reduce the broth until it is well flavored. Carve the chicken (p.185) and arrange the pieces on a dish. Pile the stuffing on top and the vegetables around the chicken, then cover the dish with foil and keep warm until ready to serve.
5 If serving the broth with noodles: a short time before serving, spoon about 1 qt/1L broth into a pan and simmer the noodles for 5 minutes or until tender. If serving with bread, toast the slices in the oven at 350°F/175°C for 10-15 minutes, until golden brown.
6 Discard the cheesecloth bag, and skim off as much fat as possible (p.42). If serving with noodles, add them to the broth. If serving with bread, add it to soup bowls and pour the broth over.

Broiling or barbecuing poultry

Broiling poultry is a mixed blessing. Although it is an unrivalled way of drawing out the flavor, the intense heat tends to dry the delicate meat rapidly, and chicken breasts are particularly vulnerable to this. Poultry should be cut in quite large pieces with plenty of bone left to disperse the heat – small birds, split or spatchcocked (p.180), do particularly well. Marinating the meat beforehand helps, as does brushing with melted butter, oil and flavorings, or an American-style Barbecue sauce (p.65). A Greek marinade of yogurt and oregano, or an Asian one of soy sauce, rice wine and hot peppers is also delicious.

Accompaniments such as mushrooms, tomatoes, sliced eggplant or squash are often broiled with the bird. Potatoes can be baked on a barbecue, and fried matchstick potatoes accompany broiled poultry. In France, poultry is often cooked with herb butter or piquant brown sauce.

Sautéing and pan-frying poultry

Most pieces of poultry are too large to sauté or pan-fry successfully, but boned chicken breasts, duck *magrets* (p.188), and escalopes cut from breast of turkey are conspicuous exceptions. With or without a coating of seasoned flour, chicken and turkey retain moisture and taste when browned in butter and the result recalls a veal escalope; duck *magrets* need no flour and can be pan-fried in just a tablespoon of fat. Be sure to cook the skin side very thoroughly to render the fat.

Stir-frying poultry

The key to stir-frying poultry is cutting the boneless meat neatly. The pieces, whether sliced, diced, or cut in small cubes or strips, must be the same size so that they cook evenly and remain juicy.

The seasonings dictate the character of a stir-fry and with poultry there is plenty of choice. Start with scallion, garlic, fresh ginger and shallot, adding a touch of vinegar, lemon or soy sauce, star anise which is so good with duck, or the Sichuan pepper which is the ideal match for chicken. The type of oil you use – sesame, peanut or corn – adds individuality too, as does a handful of crunchy nuts or coconut. Root vegetables such as carrot and celery, and green vegetables such as beans, broccoli, cabbage, bell peppers, zucchini and squash are all good additions. Bamboo shoots, bean sprouts, and cloud ear mushrooms are among the Asian ideas for an authentic stir-fry dish.

Other cooking methods

With its dark and light meat, rich or delicate according to choice, there's scarcely a cooking method that doesn't suit poultry. Breast of chicken or turkey can be baked *en papillote* – in a case of parchment paper or foil with herbs and garlic, quick cooking vegetables such as scallions, shallots, or leeks, a spoonful or two of wine, a knob of butter, and a slice of lemon. Steamed poultry is even simpler and produces little fat, but without generous seasoning it can be bland. At the other end of the calorie scale is the characteristic deep-fried chicken of the southern United States, now found as fast food practically worldwide.

The uncooked white meat of poultry can be made into *quenelles* and *mousselines* (Fish, p.146), dumplings to serve in a soup or sauce, or into sausages such as *boudin blanc* (p.246). Duck, goose and game are outstanding in a terrine, together with all poultry livers (best of all is the legendary foie gras). Cooked poultry can be used in a wide range of classic dishes such as creamed poultry croquettes, or in a sauce encased in edible wrappings. For example, the French fill crêpes with creamed poultry, while the Italians use it to stuff cannelloni and ravioli; in Mexico, spicy mixtures are wrapped in corn or flour tortillas and served as enchiladas and burritos, and in Asia all types of poultry mixtures are hidden within deep-fried wrappers.

Cooked poultry is also popular in salads such as the American chicken with celery, grapes and walnuts bound with mayonnaise, and triple-decker club sandwiches with turkey, tomato, lettuce, bacon and mayonnaise. The French prefer cold poultry plain, with mayonnaise on the side, while the British may serve it with chutney and pickles. As for pastry, nearly every country has a tradition of baking poultry inside a crust. In France chicken is baked *en croûte*, in vol-au-vents and *bouchées* (p.380); in Britain it is served in game pie, farmer's chicken pie and Christmas turkey pie. Eastern Europe is famous for *piroshki* (p.374), Morocco for pigeon *bstilla*, and Latin America for *empanadas*, while chicken pot pie can be found all over the United States. Whole chicken is sometimes buried in a deep pot of salt and baked, a method that seals in the juices and leaves a crusty golden skin.

Finally, explore the notes in this chapter on giblets, the chapter on Preserving (p.484) for smoking or preserving *en confit*, and the chapter on Stocks and soups (p.42).

Presenting poultry

A bunch of fresh watercress or a few potatoes is sufficient decoration for a whole bird that has been trussed (p.179) and is golden brown from roasting. Often a bird, braised or pot-roasted with vegetables, needs no embellishment other than a sprinkling of chopped parsley. The plump breast of a chicken or capon, perhaps in "half-mourning" with slices of black truffle under the skin, is enhanced by a creamy velouté sauce (p.55).

A cold buffet is hardly complete without poultry, the boned turkeys or chickens sliced to reveal a stuffing of veal, mushroom or ham, the duck breasts layered with orange slices before being coated with aspic. For a grander display, the birds can be carved, reshaped on the bone and displayed in chaudfroid (p.56) with a rich white or brown sauce for flavoring, surrounded by a panoply of stuffed vegetables and decorated with checkerboards or garlands of flowers cut from egg white, truffle, tomato and leek.

More challenging is the presentation of poultry when cut into pieces. During cooking the meat shrinks, often exposing pieces of the joint and rib that should be trimmed for serving. The poultry can be served on individual plates, with vegetable garnish neatly placed on one side or, if presented on a serving dish, the bird should be arranged in a fan shape, starting with the legs and leading inward to the breast pieces. A formal arrangement is important for aspic dishes, but in more rustic recipes, the pieces can be piled up, with sauce and garnish spooned on top.

When breast meat is off the bone, it is often carved in neat diagonal slices that are arranged in a fan shape on the plate, making an attractive frame for a fruit or vegetable garnish; the sauce is spooned under rather than over the meat. Some poultry recipes dictate their own presentation – deep-fried chicken should come in a basket, American pot pie in a deep dish, while poultry stuffed in pasta or tortillas rarely needs decoration.

CHICKEN

No bird is available in so many different sizes as a chicken. Baby birds, weighing as little as 1 lb/500 g for one serving, may be specially fattened *poussins*, but more commonly they are *coquelets* or small cock birds. The middle range of somewhat skinny chickens, which serve two to four people, are good for some purposes (they are often classed as spring chickens, broilers and fryers), but they lack flavor because of their youth (nine to twelve weeks). At three to five months, chickens are usually classed as roasters and weigh upward of 3½ lb/1.6 kg. As well as being sold whole, chickens of more than 3 lb/1.5 kg are commonly cut into pieces, and individual parts such as legs or wings are also available, together with chicken breasts, with or without the bone.

Traditionally, the larger the bird, the better the flavor (though this rule does not always apply to mass-produced birds). Fat develops both under the skin and in the meat, making it more tender when cooked. In France, the importance of a chicken's maturity is marked by the change of name from *poulet* to *poularde*. When buying a large chicken of 5 lb/2.3 kg or more to roast, be sure it is not too old. Aptly called a boiling fowl, a hen has lived for at least 10 months, long enough for the meat to toughen. The full flavor of a hen is perfect for making a rich sauce, but the meat needs simmering or braising to tenderize it.

Particularly large is the capon, a neutered male of less than eight months, weighing up to 10 lb/4.5 kg, and specially fattened to yield impressive quantities of white breast meat. Capon is a delicacy, but it can be bland if not seasoned carefully. Also rare (except in country markets) is the connoisseur's treat, an old cock bird. The meat is tough and needs to be marinated as well as simmered for hours. The flavor resembles that of a wild bird.

Of all meats, chicken is the triumph of mass-production, but this can also mean mediocrity. Blandness can be countered by marinating the meat, by seasoning with care and adding plenty of spices and flavorings. Quality may depend on how the birds are processed before sale: certain cleaning processes use scalding water which affects the bird's skin, and thus the flavor. Most countries have inspection procedures and voluntary grading systems set by the government, but these do not necessarily ensure top quality. When free-range chickens are available, the extra expense is worth considering. In many European countries such prime birds can be found (the chickens of Bresse in France are particularly famous), and gradually the United States is following suit.

Other white-fleshed poultry, cooked like chicken, includes the small North American cross-bred Rock Cornish hen (developed from the Plymouth Rock hen and Cornish game cock). At five to seven weeks old, it has more flavor than a battery chicken and is sold in sizes that will serve one or two people. Popular in Europe is the guinea fowl – a lean, golden-fleshed bird weighing 2-4 lb/1-1.8 kg – which is often barded (p.193) before cooking.

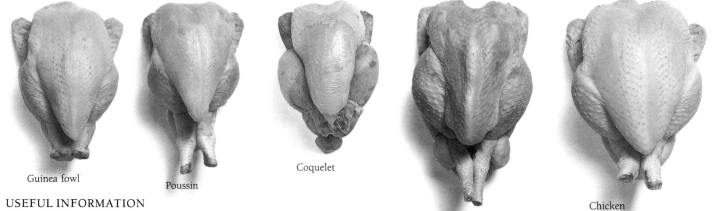

Guinea fowl
Poussin
Coquelet
Boiling fowl
Chicken

USEFUL INFORMATION

Season Year-round.

How to choose *Whole birds:* little moisture, unbroken skin with no dark patches, plump breast, pliable tip of breastbone, fresh smell. *Pieces:* little moisture, fresh smell.

Portion *Whole dressed bird on bone:* ¾-1 lb/375-500 g. *Pieces:* ¾ lb/ 375 g. *Boneless meat:* 4 oz/125 g.

Nutritive value per 3½ oz/100 g (raw skinless meat): *Chicken:* 119 calories; 21 g protein; 3 g fat; no carbohydrates; 77 mg sodium; 70 mg cholesterol. *Guinea fowl:* 110 calories; 21 g protein; 3 g fat; no carbohydrates; 69 mg sodium; 63 mg cholesterol.

Cooking methods *Whole birds:* braise or pot-roast at 350°F/ 175°C, 15-20 minutes per 1 lb/ 500 g, depending on age; poach 12-20 minutes per 1 lb/500 g, depending on age; roast (p.181)

Pieces: bake at 350°F/175°C, 25-35 minutes; barbecue 15-20 minutes; braise or stew 350°F/175°C, ½-1½ hours, depending on age; broil 20-25 minutes; deep-fry 8-10 minutes; poach 20-45 minutes, depending on age; roast (p.181); cook as sauté 25-40 minutes. *Breast:* sauté 5-7 minutes; steam 12-15 minutes; stir-fry 1-2 minutes.

When done *Whole birds:* juice from cavity runs clear when bird is lifted with a two-pronged fork; if poached, juice runs clear when thigh is pricked. *Pieces:* tender enough to fall easily from a two-pronged fork.

Processed forms Frozen whole and pieces, raw and cooked; canned whole and pieces; smoked whole and breast; vacuum-packed.

Typical dishes Broth with rice and lemon (Greece); *waterzooi* (with root vegetables, Belgium); cock-a-leekie (with leeks, Scotland); Buffalo wings (with hot sauce and blue cheese dressing, USA); *coq au vin* (with onion, mushroom, bacon, wine sauce, France); *chasseur* (with mushroom, tomato and white wine, France); with green almond sauce, (Mexico); *cacciatore* (with tomatoes and green peppers, Italy); with eggplant purée (Turkey); in anchovy sauce (Germany); with preserved lemons and olives (Morocco); hindle wakes (with fruit, lemon and vinegar stuffing and mustard sauce, UK); in chorizo and wine sauce (Spain); Marengo (with mushrooms, tomatoes, crayfish and deep-fried egg, France); Kiev (deep-fried

Capon

suprêmes stuffed with herb/garlic butter, Russia); Tettrazini (pasta, cheese, cream and brandy, USA).

CUTTING CHICKEN SUPREMES

The suprême of a chicken is the skinless breast, including the wing bone. It is often served with a velouté sauce *suprême* (p.55), or it can be sautéed or breaded and fried to serve with a garnish of asparagus, foie gras or truffles.

1 Remove the legs from the bird with a knife. Pull the skin from the breast meat, using a knife to cut gently where necessary. Locate the wishbone, then cut round it and remove it.

2 Cut along one side of the breastbone, easing the meat away from the bone.

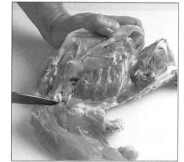

3 Continue cutting, until the meat is eased free and you have reached the wing joint.

4 Cut through the wing joint, freeing the meat and wing bone from the carcass. Trim the wing bone at the first joint. Repeat on the other side. Trim the breast meat and cut out the tendon (p.178).

5 RIGHT Scrape the wing bone clean with a knife and trim the end (below).

Deep-frying chicken

Chicken is the only bird that is commonly deep-fried. For frying, the chicken pieces should be small and of equal size – often, only the wings or drumsticks are used. Batter, or a coating of egg and breadcrumbs, may be used. In the southern United States milk replaces egg, with a mixture of flour and cornmeal instead of breadcrumbs giving a particularly dry, crunchy surface. The fat for frying may be oil (for lightness) or lard (for flavor). Creamed corn, broiled tomatoes, dumplings or biscuits are classic accompaniments, with thickened gravy (p.57) served as well.

CARVING CHICKEN

When carving chicken, give each person some white and dark meat, if necessary slicing meat from the thigh to serve everyone. Small cooked chickens should be halved or quartered according to size. For large birds over 5 lb/2.3 kg:

1 Let the bird stand for 10 minutes in a warm place, then discard the trussing strings. Set it, back down, on a carving board. Cut the skin between the leg and breast (right). With a carving fork, turn the bird on its side. Cut round the oyster meat (p.513) very carefully so that it remains attached to the thigh.

2 With the two-pronged fork, spear the leg at the thigh and twist it up and forward to break the joint.

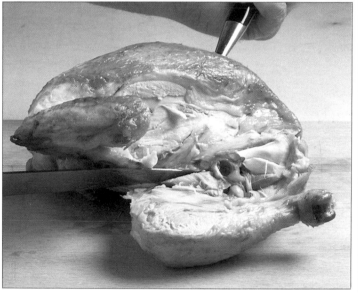

3 ABOVE Finish cutting away the leg joint and pull the leg from the carcass with the oyster meat still attached.

4 Halve the leg by cutting through the joint, using the line of white fat as a guide.

5 If the wishbone was not removed before cooking, cut it out.

6 Cut horizontally above the wing joint, through the breastbone, so you can carve a complete slice.

7 Carve the breast in slices parallel to the rib cage. Cut off the wing and carve the other side.

TURKEY

Turkey offers little of the variety of chicken. Sizes range from 7 lb/ 3.2 kg to huge birds weighing 40 lb/18 kg, but all are tender enough to roast. Although it is hard to detect their age, most supermarket birds will be about nine months old. An older bird will be much too tough to roast and must be simmered slowly instead. Hen turkeys are rarely more than 16 lb/7.2 kg, and in Europe they are appreciated for their plump breast. In the United States the male is king: the bigger the turkey, the more it is admired, especially on the Thanksgiving table.

Once limited to festivals, turkey is now available year-round, both whole and as a boneless roast, rolled and tied ready for cooking. Boneless turkey breasts can be cooked whole or sliced as an inexpensive substitute for veal escalope. Also readily available are packaged thighs, legs and wings, which should be treated like chicken pieces and are equally versatile. Usually larger than chicken pieces, they take longer to cook. Free-range turkey is a notable improvement on the average supermarket bird, so it is well worth the effort if you can find one. Like free-range chickens, they are raised partly in the open air and fed on grain.

USEFUL INFORMATION

Season Year-round, peaking late autumn.

How to choose *Whole birds*: little moisture, unbroken skin with no dark patches, plump breast. *Pieces*: little moisture, no smell.

Portion *Whole dressed bird on the bone*: 1 lb/500 g (if turkey is over 12 lb/5.5 kg, allow ¾ lb/375 kg). *Boneless meat*: 4 oz/125 g.

Nutritive value per 3½ oz/100 g (raw, skinless meat): 119 calories; 22 g protein; 3 g fat; no carbohydrates; 70 mg sodium; 65 mg cholesterol.

Cooking methods *Whole birds* (use shorter cooking time per 1 lb/ 500 g for large birds). *Rolled roast*: braise at 350°F/175°C, 12-15 minutes per 1 lb/500 g; poach 10-12 minutes per 1 lb/500 g; pot-roast at 350°F/175°C, 12-15 minutes per 1 lb/500 g; roast (p.181). *Pieces*: bake at 350°F/ 175°C, 25-35 minutes; braise or stew at 350°F/175°C, 1-2 hours; broil 20-25 minutes; poach 20-30 minutes; cook as sauté 25-35 minutes. *Slices*: poach 10-15 minutes; sauté 5-8 minutes; steam 10-15 minutes; stir-fry 5-8 minutes.

When done *Whole birds*: juice runs clear when thigh is pricked. *Pieces*: tender enough to fall easily from two-pronged fork; internal temperature 185°F/85°C. *Slices*: juice forms drops on surface.

Processed forms Frozen whole and pieces, raw and cooked; canned pieces; smoked.

Typical dishes Soup (USA); roast with parsley and lemon stuffing (UK); turkey neck pudding (UK); marinated with garlic, pepper, onion and vinegar and roasted Brazil); stewed with red wine, vinegar, olives, capers, potatoes and peas (Caribbean);

in *mole poblano* sauce (with chocolate, nuts and chili peppers, Mexico); with chestnut stuffing (France); baked with yams and apples (USA); roast with fruit stuffing (UK); honey-glazed (USA); with pomegranates (Italy); with beans and celery (Germany); with mixed nuts and sweet spices (Middle East).

Boning turkey breasts

Turkey breasts are usually divided along the breastbone into two single pieces. For instructions on how to bone them, see Boning poultry breasts (p.178).

CUTTING TURKEY ESCALOPES

First bone the turkey breast (p.178) and remove the skin. Cut escalopes from the breast and cook like veal escalopes.

1 Remove the fillet and cook separately.

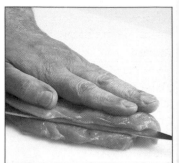

2 With one hand on the meat to steady it, start cutting diagonally.

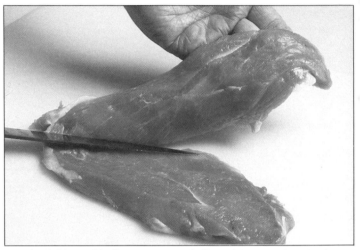

3 Cut 3-5 large thin slices. Remove each slice as it is cut, and set the slices one at a time between sheets of wax paper or plastic.

4 With a rolling pin, lightly pound each slice to flatten to about ⅜ in/1 cm thick, as for veal escalopes (p.218).

STUFFING THE NECK END OF A BIRD

Two stuffings are often used for large birds, one to fill the carcass cavity, the other mounded under the neck skin.

1 Cut out and discard the wishbone. Pull back the neck skin and mound the stuffing inside.

2 Turn the bird on to its breast and pull the neck skin over the stuffing before trussing (p.179).

Turkey escalopes with julienne of vegetables

Other vegetables, such as mushrooms or scallions may be substituted for the vegetables used here, and puréed chestnuts or spinach may be served instead of potatoes.

Serves 4

1½ lb/750 g boned turkey breast	
2 leeks, white part only, cut in julienne strips	
2 carrots, 1 turnip, 1 zucchini, 3 stalks celery cut into julienne	
salt and pepper	
1 tbsp oil	
2 tbsp/30 g butter	

For the sauce

1 cup/250 ml white wine
2 cups/500 ml *crème fraîche* or heavy cream
1 tbsp Dijon mustard, or to taste

For serving

1 lb/500 g sweet potatoes or puréed potatoes (p.296)

1 Cut the turkey breast into escalopes.
2 Bring a steamer of salted water to a boil. Season the vegetables and put them on a steamer rack. Cover the pan and steam for about 4-6 minutes until the vegetables are just tender but still slightly crisp.
3 Heat the oil and half of the butter in a frying pan. Sprinkle the escalopes with salt and pepper. Add half to the pan and sauté until lightly browned, 2-3 minutes. Turn and brown on the other side. Remove the escalopes and keep them warm. Sauté the remaining escalopes in the rest of the butter.
4 **To make the sauce:** remove the fat from the pan. Add the wine and boil, stirring to dissolve the pan juices, until reduced to a glaze (p.513). Add the *crème fraîche* or cream and boil until slightly thickened, 3-5 minutes. Remove from the heat and stir in the mustard. Taste for seasoning, adding more mustard if necessary, then stir in the vegetable julienne.
5 Arrange the escalopes, overlapping, on one side of a serving dish or on individual plates. Spoon over the sauce and vegetables and arrange the potato purée down the other side.

CARVING TURKEY

Roast turkey can be carved in the kitchen and the breast meat replaced on the carcass for serving. A small turkey should be carved like a chicken (p.185). For a large bird over 10 lb/4.5 kg:

1 Leave the turkey for 10-15 minutes in a warm place, then discard the strings. Hold the bird steady with a carving fork.

2 Remove the wing, severing it at the joint. Cut the skin between the leg and the breast. With a sharp knife, cut diagonal slices from the breast, working toward the cavity.

3 RIGHT At the wing joint, make a horizontal cut to facilitate carving and give good sized slices.

4 Carve the breast in slanting slices parallel to the rib cage (and including the stuffing), starting at the leg end and working toward the cavity. Repeat the procedure on the other side.

5 To remove the leg, force it outward with a fork, then locate the joint with a knife and cut through it.

6 Holding the leg firmly, carve slices from the thigh, working parallel to the bone. Cut the leg in half through the joint.

7 Carve slices of meat from the drumstick, working parallel to the bone. Repeat with the other leg.

DUCK

The meat of a duck varies greatly from one breed to another, and so does the best method of cooking it. Some varieties, notably the American Long Island or Pekin and the British Aylesbury, have rich meat with a good deal of fat secreted under the skin. This fat must be dissolved, so thorough cooking is important.

Barbary or Muscovy ducks, and the Nantais breed popular in France, are less fatty. The Barbary is large, with generous amounts of firm breast meat; Nantais are smaller, more tender and delicately flavored. In the United States, smaller varieties of duck can be found in Chinese markets. A new *Mulard* crossbreed is one of several offering leaner meat than the common Long Island duck. Unique to France is the Rouen duck, which resembles a game bird in taste and texture, and is killed by smothering so that its meat is dark from the blood.

Opinions differ on how well-done a duck should be. Many connoisseurs insist that the breast meat should remain pink, though the legs should always be thoroughly cooked, but this is hard to achieve with fattier breeds such as the Long Island duck. For a roast bird, one common solution is to serve the breast first, while rare, then continue to roast or broil the legs.

Duck is not an economical bird as the weight of bone is high in proportion to the meat. A duckling of around 4 lb/1.8 kg serves only two people, while a 5-6 lb/2.5 kg bird is needed for four. Only the Barbary at 10 lb/4.5 kg serves six to eight people, although other breeds sometimes reach that size. A duckling or *canette/caneton* is under two months old, while a duck or *canard* may be up to three months. As ducks are rarely kept to lay eggs, there is no large supply of older birds. Only where they are bred for foie gras are you likely to come across them. However, foie gras producers are on the increase; there are even some in the United States. Tougher, fatty birds can be stewed, but it is better to preserve the legs *en confit* (p.486), the companion product to foie gras. The leftover fat makes wonderful fried potatoes. The breasts are boned as *magrets* and cooked rare like steak, with green peppercorns, blackcurrants or roast garlic.

USEFUL INFORMATION

Season *Duckling*: spring. *Older birds*: year-round.

How to choose Light-skinned, plump but not too fat, little moisture.

Portion *Whole bird on bone*: 1¼-1½ lb/625-750 g; 2-3 pieces (about 1 lb/500 g). *Boneless meat*: 4 oz/125 g.

Nutritive value per 3½ oz/100 g (raw skinless meat): 132 calories, 18 g protein; 6 g fat; no carbohydrates; 74 mg sodium; 77 mg cholesterol.

Cooking methods *Whole birds*: braise or pot-roast at 350°F/175°C, 20-25 minutes per 1 lb/500 g; roast (p.181). *Pieces*: braise or stew at 350°F/175°C, 1-1½ hours; broil 25-35 minutes; cook as sauté 45-60 minutes. *Breast*: broil or sauté 4-7 minutes; stir-fry 2-3 minutes.

When done *Whole birds*: for rare

roast meat, juice runs pink when breast is pricked with a skewer; for well-done roast meat, juice from cavity runs clear when bird is lifted with a two-pronged fork. *Pieces*: tender enough to fall easily from a fork when pierced.

Processed forms Frozen whole and pieces; canned pieces; canned preserved (*confit*) pieces; vacuum-packed raw breasts (*magrets*); smoked whole and pieces.

Typical dishes sweet and sour soup (Germany); warm salad (USA); sweet and sour with cherries (France); with orange juice, dates, pears, prunes and grapes (Brazil); with olives (Italy); duckling with wine (Latin America); with rum (Caribbean); Long Island duck stew (USA); with cranberry, pear and pistachio dressing (USA); *pasticcio* (layered with prosciutto in a crust, Italy); with marmalade (Australia); with sauerkraut (Yugoslavia); with turnips (France); with wild plums (USA); stewed in beer (Germany); with cucumbers (Romania); cassoulet (stewed with white beans and sausage, France); with bananas (Portugal); with olives in sherry sauce (Spain); with pomegranate sauce and walnuts (Middle East); braised with rice (Portugal); *Also good with* peaches, onions, apples, beans, green peas, green peppercorns.

Boning duck breasts (*magrets*)

Cut the legs from the duck, then follow instructions for boning poultry breasts (p.178). Often the skin is left on the breasts for added richness, but it should be trimmed neatly.

CARVING DUCK

A small duck of up to 5 lb/2.3 kg can be halved or quartered. If the bird is larger, it is often served in two stages with the breast meat rare and the legs well-done. However, if well-done meat is preferred, both breast and leg meat can be cooked and served together. Use a sharp pliable knife with a long blade.

1 Pierce the bird with a fork and cut the skin between the legs and body, forcing the legs outward with the flat of the knife so breast meat is revealed. Do not remove the leg.

2 Cut horizontally just above the wing joint, through the breast meat to the bone. If the wishbone has not been removed, cut it out.

3 Cut long needle-shaped strips of breast meat (Fr. *aiguillettes*) working the full length of the carcass, parallel to the rib cage.

4 Replace the meat on the carcass, for the first serving. Duck wings have no meat and are not normally served.

5 To remove the legs, tip the bird sideways and insert the fork into the thigh. Force the leg outward to break the joint located well under the bird. Sever the leg, then repeat with the other leg. If the legs are still rare, continue cooking them according to the recipe, and when well done, cut them in half through the joint (p.176).

POULTRY TRIMMINGS

Birds are generous in providing not just meat, but several extra pieces for the pot. The carcass makes excellent stock, particularly when raw, though soup made from cooked bones should not be overlooked. The fat that accumulates in mature birds can be rendered for cooking (p.97); chicken fat is valued in Jewish cooking, while the French, particularly in the southwest around Gascony, rely on goose fat for frying and for making pastry.

When buying a prepared bird, be sure the giblets are included: poultry giblets provide necks for the stockpot, gizzards and hearts can be smoked or preserved *en confit* for salads or traditional casseroles, and the feet can be added to stock for gelatin. Cockscombs – once considered an aphrodisiac – are part of such luxury garnishes as the Renaissance *béattiles* or tidbits, which consisted of a collection of small delicacies such as sweetbreads, artichokes, mushrooms, truffles and cock's kidneys. Cockscombs must be simmered for two to three hours until tender.

Poultry livers, trimmed of tubes and membranes, are the best of all the trimmings. The liver should not be dark or strong smelling, nor tinged with green from the gall bladder. Poultry livers add richness to terrines and can be used to make pâté, but if overcooked they become dry and grainy. The liver from game birds can be sautéed in butter, chopped and spread on croûtes. Large livers, especially of duck and goose, can be broiled or sautéed in butter and served on toast. Livers can also be included in a stuffing for the bird, or chopped and simmered in sauce.

Duck ragout with pears & orange

A nutty grain such as brown rice, wild rice, or bulghur is a good accompaniment to this duck dish.

Serves 4

1 large duck, about 6lb/2.7kg	3 tbsp Grand Marnier or orange liqueur
1 tbsp oil	
1 tbsp butter	***For stock***
salt and pepper	1 tbsp oil
1 orange, sliced	backbone of duck, wing pinions, giblets
3 pears, peeled, quartered and rubbed with cut lemon	
	1 onion, sliced
2 tbsp/30g brown sugar	bouquet garni
¼ cup/60ml white wine vinegar	1 tsp tomato paste
1 cup/250ml basic brown sauce (p.58)	2 cups/500ml water

1 Cut the duck into 6 pieces (p.176). **To make the stock:** chop up the backbone, wings and giblets, heat the oil and brown them for 10-15 minutes. Add, and brown, the onion. Discard the fat, add the remaining ingredients and season. Simmer, for ¾-1 hour until reduced to 1 cup/250 ml, then strain.
2 Meanwhile, heat the oil and butter in a sauté pan, and season the duck pieces. Add the leg and thigh pieces to the pan, skin-side down and sauté for 5 minutes. Add the breast and sauté for 10-15 minutes on each side until brown.
3 Lower the heat, cover the pan and continue cooking, for 15-25 minutes, turning occasionally.
4 Meanwhile, pare the orange zest, cut in julienne strips (p.259) and blanch for 2 minutes. Drain and rinse in cold water. Pare the white pith from the orange and slice the flesh.
5 When the duck is almost tender when pierced with a fork, discard the fat. Add the pears, cover and sauté gently over a low heat until the duck is tender and the pears are cooked but firm.
6 Remove the duck and pears and pour off any fat. Add the sugar and vinegar to the pan and simmer until reduced by half. Stir in the brown sauce, stock and Grand Marnier. Bring to a boil.
7 Return the duck to the pan and simmer for 10-15 minutes, remove and keep warm. Return the pears to the pan and reheat gently. To serve, spoon the sauce over and garnish with oranges and julienne.

GOOSE

Geese are an extravagance in the farmyard, eating more food to produce the same weight of meat than any other bird. Size varies according to breed and sex – the female bird reaches only two-thirds the weight of a gander. A mature bird for roasting averages 8-12 lb/3.6-5 kg, and serves six to eight people. Although they are raised commercially, many geese are still free-range, maturing to eight or nine months just in time for the winter holidays. The quality varies more than with any other domestic bird and pale fatty skin and a plump breast are important signs of excellence; old birds get very tough. Be sure to remove fat deposits inside the cavity of a goose before cooking. Goose fat is a delicacy; so too is the liver, especially when the geese are fattened on corn to produce the famous foie gras.

Goose is almost always roasted whole, though it braises and pot-roasts well. It is even richer, more gamey and fattier than duck, so needs very thorough cooking to render all the fat from under the skin. When cut in pieces, goose takes to stewing with onions, garlic, sauerkraut and the same fruits that go so well with duck. Finest of all is goose *confit* (p.486), traditionally made from the meat of birds that have been fattened for foie gras. Long slow cooking tenderizes the meat and matures its flavor to a splendid richness. Goose *confit* can be baked or pan-fried until the skin is crisp, then served with potatoes fried in goose fat. Alternatively, it can flavor soups, baked vegetable dishes and the famous French baked bean cassoulet (p.322).

USEFUL INFORMATION

Season Year-round, peaking late autumn.
How to choose Light-skinned, plump breast, little moisture, backbone pliable.
Portion *Whole bird:* 1½ lb/750 g. *Pieces:* ½ lb/250 g.
Nutritive value per 3½ oz/100 g (raw, skinless meat): 161 calories; 23 g protein; 7 g fat; no carbohydrates; 87 mg sodium; 84 mg cholesterol.
Cooking methods *Whole birds:* braise or pot-roast at 350°F/175°C, 15 minutes per 1 lb/500 g; roast (p.000). *Pieces:* braise or stew at 350°F/175°C, 1-2 hours, depending on age.
When done *Whole bird:* juice runs clear when thigh is pricked with a fork; internal temperature 370°F/185°C. *Pieces:* fall easily from a two-pronged fork.
Processed forms Frozen whole; *confit* in pieces; smoked whole and breast; vacuum-packed raw breast.
Typical dishes Soup (Austria); roast with sour cream sauce (Yugoslavia); with sage and onion stuffing (UK); stuffed with wild rice and cranberries (USA); tagliatelle with preserved goose sauce (Italy); garlicked (with chestnut and apple stuffing, USA); pickled (Germany); with pears (Spain); stew with sausage and chestnuts (Italy); with walnut stuffing (Russia); with currants (Germany); in beans (Hungary). *Also good with* garlic, fennel, turnips, onion, red cabbage, apple sauce, gooseberry sauce.

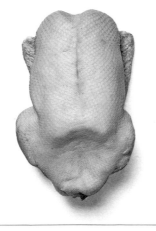

Carving a goose

Carve goose in the same way as duck (p.188). The breast meat is much more tender than the leg, which can be very tough, even when cooked thoroughly.

FOIE GRAS

Foie gras, the enlarged liver of a force-fed goose or duck, is an ancient delicacy. The Romans are known to have force-fed geese with figs to fatten their livers to three or four times the original size; nowadays the same effect is achieved using corn. The art of foie gras is said to have been fostered in Alsace by the Jews, who developed a charcuterie of the goose – since pork was a forbidden meat. Now Israel, as well as central Europe, supplies many of the livers that go into making the canned terrines and pâtés that France exports. The latest foie gras producer is the United States.

Opinions are divided as to whether duck foie gras, with its winey flavor, or goose foie gras, slightly richer and more mellow, is to be preferred. In either case, a perfectly fattened foie gras will be firm, but may vary in color from pink to yellow ochre, with color no indication of quality. Raw foie gras comes in two lobes. To prepare them, cut out all traces of green gall bladder from the liver, then pull the lobes apart with your hands. Slit each lobe lengthwise and pull out the veins.

For cooking in a terrine, the livers may first be marinated in port wine, salt, pepper, spices and a little brandy. Subtle seasoning and slow cooking of foie gras is crucial. When baked in a terrine or wrapped in a cloth and poached in a cylinder, the liver quite literally melts away if the cooking temperature rises above 195°F/90°C. In fact, because of the risk of failure, most foie gras enthusiasts leave the task of cooking the liver to professionals.

If you begin with cooked foie gras, you can choose between fresh (always pink in the center) or canned and vacuum-packed varieties. The latter will have been sterilized at high temperatures and, unlike fresh foie gras, will be of uniform color and texture. For baking cooked foie gras in a brioche, or whisking into a sauce, a solid block of liver is needed. To make it go further, the liver may be puréed to a mousse (available in cans). It is less expensive than *bloc* cans of solid liver, but it melts if heated.

The greatest luxury of all is fresh foie gras, thinly sliced and sautéed for a few seconds in butter. Fruits such as grapes or currants complement the richness, and the pan is often deglazed with cognac, Madeira or fruit vinegar. Serve on green beans or salad, with wild mushrooms or crayfish and a glass of Sauternes.

REMOVING SINEWS FROM GAME & POULTRY

Turkey, goose, mature duck, chicken and game birds have large sinews that must be removed from the leg before drawing. Locate the sinews lying along the bone and pull them out with pliers.

Slit the leg skin with a knife and locate the sinews. Insert a sharpening steel underneath the sinews and twist it round to break them. Continue turning until the sinews are pulled completely from the leg meat. Trim the leg.

GAME BIRDS

In the kitchen, game birds are not what they used to be. The hunting season for wild birds is increasingly short, the supply small and the price correspondingly high. As the sale of wild game is prohibited in the United States, it tends to be eaten only by those who hunt their own (wild turkey hunts are still traditional). However, game birds are now being raised commercially in large numbers and ever-increasing variety. Some, such as pheasant, partridge, quail, and pigeon (often called squab when young), can be found all year round in specialty stores.

The king of game birds, the British red grouse, is too shy to raise successfully. Other members of the grouse family, regarded as gastronomically inferior, include ptarmigan, capercaillie, hazelhen, and blackcock in Europe, with sage grouse, spruce grouse and Sierra grouse in North America. All are northern birds that thrive in the mountains.

Pheasant, which usually serves two people, is a pleasing table bird, with a mild flavor, but partridge (Fr. *perdreau*, meaning young partridge or *perdrix* if older) which is smaller, is usually considered superior. Confusingly, in the United States the name partridge is often applied to quail or ruffed grouse.

Raised pigeon is another delicacy, with rich dark meat that lends itself well to roasting and preparations in which the breast is served rare, thinly sliced on the plate with a sauce. Wild pigeon or dove, however, is often tough and strong, and better-suited to a pie. Quail is a tasty, less expensive alternative to pigeon. It can be roasted or braised whole and is delicious barbecued. Other small wild birds are rare and also difficult to shoot. They can be spatchcocked (p.180) and broiled, barbecued or roasted (p.181). For gamey flavor, some cooks roast these little birds with their innards (excluding the crop).

Wild ducks and geese, which range in size from less than 1 lb/ 500 g to 10 lb/4.5 kg, can vary enormously in taste. As always in the kitchen, size and age are much more important than species. Richer than land birds, wild ducks and geese roast particularly well, but those living on the seashore may taste unpleasantly fishy.

Game birds are often served with fried straw potatoes or a fried potato cake, and in England with fried breadcrumbs, game chips and bread sauce (p.64). In France, the bird is sometimes set on a croute spread with liver pâté. The gravy for game birds may be made into a sauce, sweetened with fruit, while in Scandinavian countries, a fruit compote of bilberries or cranberries is often served separately.

USEFUL INFORMATION

Season *Raised:* year-round. *Wild:* late summer through to spring, depending on bird and country of origin.

Portion *Whole bird:* ¾-1 lb/375- 500 g. *Pieces:* ½-¾ lb/250-375 g.

Nutritive value per 3½ oz/100 g (raw, skinless meat): *Pheasant:* 133 calories; 24 g protein; 4 g fat; no carbohydrates; 37 mg sodium; 66 mg cholesterol. *Quail:* 134 calories; 22 g protein; 5 g fat; no carbohydrates; 51 mg sodium; 70 mg cholesterol.

Cooking methods All times depend on age and size of bird. *Whole birds:* braise or pot-roast at 350°F/175°C, ½-3 hours; spatchcock (p.180) and barbecue or broil, 8-15 minutes; roast (p.192), cook in a sauté 15-45 minutes. *Pieces:* barbecue or broil 8-15 minutes; braise or stew ½-2 hours; cook as a sauté 15-45 minutes.

When done *Rare game:* juice runs pink when meat is pricked. *Whole birds:* juice runs pink when lifted with a two-pronged fork. *Well- done game:* when pierced with a two-pronged fork, meat is tender and pieces fall easily from the fork.

Processed forms Frozen whole; canned whole and pieces; smoked whole and breast.

Typical dishes *Partridge:* with chestnuts and cabbage (UK); pot- roast (Denmark); with sausage, truffles, Marsala and lemon (Italy); marinated in port and stuffed with duck liver pâté (Portugal); *Chartreuse* (gelatin mold with vegetables, France). *Pheasant:* with beans (USA); with corn dressing (USA); baked in phyllo (Greece); sautéed with lemon (France). *Grouse:* pâté (UK); roast with grapes (UK); pie (UK).

Male pheasant

Grouse

English partridge

Mallard

US Pheasant

Woodcock

French partridge

Wild duck

Pigeon

Quail

USEFUL INFORMATION/GAME BIRDS

Common large game birds
(6-10 lb/2.7-4.5 kg). Wild turkey (USA, Central America); capercaillie/wood grouse (Europe); sage grouse (USA). *Geese:* graylag, Canada, pink-footed, snow, brant/black (Northern Hemisphere).

Common medium game birds
(1-6 lb/500 g-2.7 kg). *Grouse:* red, hazel/hazelhen (Europe); ruffed, Sierra, spruce (USA); black/blackcock (USA, N. Europe). *Pheasant:* common (Europe, USA); silver, golden (Europe); Chinese ringneck, English ringneck (USA). *Duck:* black/black mallard, canvasback, redhead (USA); pintail (Europe); blue winged (Americas, Europe); Carolina/wood; scaup;

shoveler (Europe, USA); widgeon (Europe).

Common small game birds
(1 lb/500 g and under). Green or blue winged teal (Americas, Europe); common woodcock, gray plover, green plover (Europe); North American woodcock, white-tailed ptarmigan (USA); common snipe, willow ptarmigan, golden plover (USA, N. Europe). *Partridge:* chukar (Europe, USA); grey (Europe); red-legged (UK, France). *Pigeon/dove:* wood, rock, stockdove, turtledove (Europe); white-winged, band-tailed (Europe, USA). *Quail:* common (Europe, raised in USA); messana (USA, Mexico).

Choosing game birds

The age of a wild bird is vital for the cook. Old birds (six months or older for most species) need long cooking in plenty of liquid. Unfortunately, judging the age of a wild bird is not easy: look for soft plump breast meat and feet that are not too scarred and calloused. Lift the bird by its lower beak, which will snap if the bird is young. Short spurs on a cock bird indicate youth, so does a flexible point on the breastbone of a male or female bird. With young pheasant and partridge, the last large feather is pointed while in older birds it is rounded. With wild ducks and geese, the webs between the toes of young birds can be torn easily. Avoid any bird that has been badly damaged by shot.

The flavor of raised game cannot match the intensity of wild game, but the great advantage is that raised game is guaranteed to be plump and tender.

Hanging game birds

Wild birds are hung before plucking and cleaning. They are suspended by the neck in a cool, airy place, to tenderize the meat and develop the flavor. Opinions vary on how long to hang a bird, or indeed whether to hang game at all. Above all, hanging time depends on the weather and to some extent, the type of bird. In cool, dry weather, wild duck can be hung for two to three days, grouse for up to 10 days, partridge for up to two weeks, and pheasant three weeks. Wild geese need at least three weeks, but pigeon does not need hanging. However, when it is warm and humid, two to three days is sufficient for any bird.

Cooking methods for game birds

The flavor of game birds varies from the delicate pheasant to the pungent grouse. They should be served rare with the breast pink and juicy; the legs are always chewy. If in any doubt about a bird's age, braising or stewing is advisable. For roasting, birds should be barded. Marinating also helps tenderize tough game, although some cooks feel that it masks the true flavor.

A distinguished end for an old bird is game pie. Often this is simply a version of a stew, with the meat, flavorings and sauce sealed under a crust and baked as long as necessary to tenderize the meat. The meat may be boned and mixed with a meat stuffing for *pâté en croûte* or an English raised pie with a pastry crust.

ROASTING TEMPERATURES AND TIMES

Small game birds	450°F/230°C	15-30 mins total
Duck and medium game birds	400°F/200°C (rare) (well-done)	15 mins per 1 lb/500 g 20 mins per 1 lb/500 g
Large game birds	425°F/220°C (rare) (well-done)	12 mins per 1 lb/500 g 15 mins per 1 lb/500 g

Barbecued quail with pepper marinade

This recipe can be prepared with squab (baby pigeon), which is also delicious when barbecued.

Serves 8 as a first course, 4 as a main dish

8 quail, giblets removed	½-1 tsp crushed dried red pepper (optional)
½ cup/125ml olive oil	salt
3 tbsp/45 ml lemon juice	
1 tsp crushed peppercorns	**16 long skewers**

1 Spatchcock the quail (p.180) and thread each one on to two skewers, inserting the skewers through the wings and legs to hold the birds flat.
2 Whisk together the olive oil, lemon juice, peppercorns, and red pepper if using. Put the quail on a tray, pour over the marinade and brush the birds to coat thoroughly. Cover and leave to marinate at room temperature for up to 3 hours, turning occasionally.
3 Light the barbecue or broiler. Sprinkle the quail with a little salt and barbecue or broil the birds 2-3 in/5-7 cm from the heat for 5-6 minutes, until brown and slightly charred. Turn and brown on the other side. The quail should be pink and juicy in the center.
4 Remove the skewers and, if serving as a first course, cut the quail in half. Serve them very hot.

BARDING & TYING SMALL BIRDS

Small birds can simply be tied with string rather than trussed. Barding with fat or bacon keeps them moist during cooking.

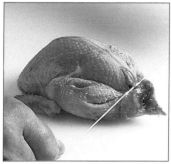

1 Tuck neck skin and wings underneath. Pass string under tail and knot over the leg joints.

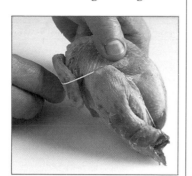

2 Take the strings along the sides of the body, and loop them around the legs.

3 Bring the strings under the bird and tie them under the body to catch the wing bones.

4 Drape barding fat on top. Tie two strings around the bird to hold the fat in place.

EXOTIC GAME BIRDS

Throughout history, exotic birds have captured the cook's imagination. Menus of medieval banquets in Europe list many birds that are now protected by law. The star dish was often a peacock, or swan, in its plumage, brought on in procession by a lady of outstanding beauty and high rank. To achieve this sensational presentation, the cook stripped off the feathers and skin together, cooked the edible part, and then put the bird together again with wire supports for a life-like effect.

Songbirds, such as larks, thrushes and warblers, are still gourmet items on the southern European table, particularly in Italy, Spain and the south of France. The garden bunting (ortolan) is a particular prize, once netted in thousands, but now increasingly rare. Such small birds are usually barded with fat and vine leaves and roasted, often with their innards to add flavor. They should "fly through the oven" so that the meat remains rare, or they may be roasted on a spit. The head, with beak, is presented to the diner. Small birds can be boned and stuffed, luxuriously, with foie gras and truffles, or combined with forcemeat in a terrine. Lark pâtés were once the speciality of Pithiviers and Chartres, towns in the vast, wheat-growing plain west of Paris. Now that larks are protected by law, ducks are often used instead.

PLUCKING A BIRD

To make plucking easier, first dip your hands in water. To avoid the labor of home plucking, the bird can be skinned with the feathers, though it will lose juice during cooking. Without its skin, the meat can be stewed or braised, but not roasted.

1 Start plucking feathers from the breast and work toward the neck. Tug the feathers, firmly but not sharply in the direction they grow so that the skin is not broken.
Note If the feathers are hard to remove, immerse the bird for 30 seconds in boiling water, off the heat. Cook the bird as soon as it has been plucked.

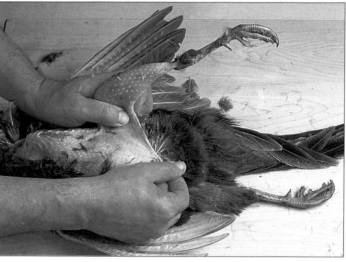

2 Turn the bird round and start plucking away from you, toward the tail feathers.

3 LEFT Turn the bird breast down, and remove the feathers from the back. Stretch out the wings and pluck the wing feathers.

4 Cut through the wing pinions to remove the quills.

5 Finally, tug out the tail feathers and pull out pin feathers along the backbone with tweezers.

MEAT & CHARCUTERIE

ONLY THREE animals are commonly domesticated for their meat – the ox, the sheep and the pig. The meat they yield varies greatly from country to country, and even region to region, particularly in the case of beef. For one thing, carcass characteristics depend on the breed of animal: contrast the richness of cuts from the sturdy Scottish Aberdeen Angus with the leanness of the vast French Charolais cattle. Diet plays a large part, affecting both the speed at which an animal matures and the quality of the meat. Corn-, grain- and grass-fed animals each taste different, and the use of growth stimulants is another factor that can affect flavor.

Just as important for the cook is the butcher. For example, a side of beef is divided in several different ways around the world. It is even more confusing when you consider that the terms "porterhouse" and "rump" refer to quite different pieces of meat in Britain and the United States. Fortunately, veal, lamb and pork terminology is less confusing because butchers everywhere handle them in a similar fashion. The number of ribs may vary, the knife may be angled differently, but generally this does not affect how the cook treats an individual cut. In the illustrations in this chapter, lamb is used for many of the techniques because the cuts are compact, and are commonly butchered in the home kitchen.

What we refer to as meat is red fleshy muscle. The harder the muscle works, the tougher it is. Thus, tender meat comes from young animals, and from less active parts of the animal, such as the hindquarters, the loin, and particularly the tenderloin or fillet (which is protected by the ribs and hardly moves at all). However, youth and idleness are not in themselves decisive indicators of quality – immature meat can be bland, while the tenderloin and other inactive muscles tend to have less flavor than tougher meat.

In Europe, butchers divide meat along the muscles and bones following the configuration of the carcass. The use of electrical saws leads to straighter dismemberment but the saws cut across the fiber. Meat cut this way shrinks and divides along the natural joints when cooked and more juice may be lost.

National cooking styles also influence the meat trade. To the French, a braise or stew, slowly simmered in a rich sauce, is the equal of any roast or broiled meat. Since braises and stews call for mature, firm meats whose flavor is developed by long cooking, French animals are deliberately handled to provide lean, close-textured meat with none of the streaks of fat that give tenderness to Scottish or Texan beef. This explains why the British consider French roasts far too lean, and the French think English stews lack body. Sizes of portions also vary according to the country. In Asian dishes, a small amount of meat serves to accent an array of vegetables, while in America, a giant 12 oz/375 g steak may be served surrounded only by its steaming juices.

Aging meat

Meat is left to age so that flavor develops and enzymes break down tough tissues, making the meat firmer, drier and more tender. The traditional aging method is to hang meat in an airy, moist atmosphere at a temperature between 34-38°F/1-3°C. Beef and pork are usually aged for up to ten days and lamb for up to a week. Veal, tender by nature, does not benefit from aging. **Note** According to Jewish dietary laws the aging of meat is forbidden, so it cannot be sold as kosher.

A quicker, moist method of aging, whereby the meat is first wrapped in plastic, has been developed. This improves tenderness, but may compromise taste. In many countries, particularly the United States where economic pressures often result in meat being rushed from field to table, only specialty butchers supply well-aged meat. Unfortunately, storing meat in a home refrigerator does not improve quality.

Storing meat

At home, meat should be stored, loosely wrapped in plastic, in the coldest part of the refrigerator. Variety meats, ground meat, and cuts such as veal escalope are best eaten within a day; chops, steak and small pieces can be left for two to three days; large roasts for up to five days. Red meats keep better than white meats, and lean cuts better than fat, as fat turns rancid first.

An unpleasant smell, slimy surface and greenish tinge are all danger signs that meat has been stored at too high a temperature or for too long and that bacteria have developed. Problems caused by rapid commercial chilling of the carcass, which toughens fibers, are less easily detected, although pallid color and a wet package are an indication. For freezing details, see Preserving (p.495).

Choosing meat

There are a few general rules for selecting all meat. Look for good butchering (a skilled meat cutter follows the contours of muscle and bone), with small cuts sliced evenly or in uniform pieces so that they cook at the same speed. Cuts should be trimmed of sinew, leaving enough fat to keep the flesh moist. Except in France, it is rare to see boned and tied roasts at the butcher's.

Marbling (p.208) is the key to the flavor and tenderness of meat. Veal and baby lamb have little marbling, but older lamb, mutton, and to a lesser extent, pork, should be streaked with fat. With beef, marbling is a clear indication of quality. Its ultimate form is Japanese *Kobe* beef, specially fattened for the table.

Meat should have a clear but not bright color; a grayish tinge is a bad sign. Yellow fat signals old age (except in beef from certain breeds such as British Jersey and Guernsey cattle that are reared exclusively on grass), and dried edges betray dehydration.

Meat grades

Many countries have developed grading systems for retail meat, but these are often voluntary, unlike hygiene inspections which are usually mandatory. Grades are based on two factors: the age and the plumpness of the carcass. Although grading systems exist for veal, lamb and pork, they are less important as the quality of their meat is more uniform than that of beef.

A useful benchmark are the categories established by the United States Department of Agriculture (USDA). For beef these are: prime, choice, select, standard, commercial, utility, cutter and canner. The consumer usually sees only the first three grades. Prime, forming only about seven percent of production, is rich, well-marbled meat, usually destined for restaurants and specialty butchers. Choice is the everyday grade, forming over 60 percent of production. Quality varies very little, though a sharp eye may pick out the plumper roast or the more marbled steak. Select has less fat and is tougher than prime or choice. A new word – "light" – has entered the American meat trade vocabulary, reflecting concern about cholesterol in animal fats. Light meat contains 25 percent less fat than the standard product and calls for slow, moist cooking. In the European Economic Community (EEC), no mandatory standards have been developed for beef, but wholesalers have devised their own grading systems to help the retailer estimate the yield of a carcass.

TENDERIZING MEAT

Meat can be tenderized in various ways, including pounding, or scoring (below). Commercially, meat is tenderized by the injection of an enzyme, such as that found in papaya juice, into the carcass. At home, the use of commercial preparations is not advisable as the effect is often excessive, leaving meat flabby and flavorless. Marinating is merely a way of tenderizing the surface of the meat, especially in thicker cuts. In order to break down the fibers, pound thin cuts such as flank steak and veal escalope or lightly score them with a knife.

1 Lay the meat between two sheets of plastic wrap or wax paper and pound with a mallet, cutlet bat, or the flat of a heavy knife.

ALTERNATIVELY, score the meat lightly in a lattice pattern with the blade of a sharp knife (butchers have a special tool for this).

TRIMMING & CUTTING MEAT

Despite extensive trimming by the butcher, a cook invariably has to trim meat further before cooking it.

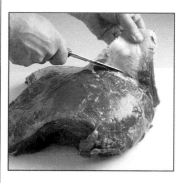

1 **For sautéing and stewing:** meat should be as lean as possible. Using a sharp knife, cut the fat from the surface of the meat.

2 Cut out the sinew, sliding the point of the knife underneath to loosen it then cutting it away.

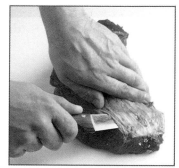

3 Cut out the tough connective tissue (silverskin). If stewing meat, this can be left as it will dissolve during cooking.

4 To prepare the meat, first pull apart muscles that are loosely connected with tissue, then cut the meat, across the grain, into 1½ in/ 4 cm cubes.

For broiling: cut away most of the fat, leaving a ¼ in/6 mm layer.

For roasting: remove all the fat and bard (p.196) with pork fat.

MARINATING MEAT

Marinating heightens the flavor of meat. Marinades may be wine-based or simply a mixture of oil, herbs and vinegar (p.41). During long marinating, juice is drawn from the meat, so the marinade may be used in the cooking.

Beef and game, the darkest and toughest meats, need to be soaked in a robust cooked marinade for one to three days. The marinade for lamb depends on the age of the animal: herby and light for lamb, strongly flavored for mutton. Pork is suited to more exotic sweet, sour, and spicy flavorings. For ribs, a barbecue sauce (p.65) is sometimes used both as a marinade and basting sauce. Meats such as veal and variety meats should only be marinated for one to two hours or natural juices may be lost.

BARDING & TYING MEAT

In Europe, veal, beef tenderloin, cuts of beef for braising, and other meats lacking natural fat are often barded with a thin layer of pork fat that melts during cooking and thus moistens the meat. (In medieval times, the word "barde" referred to a horse's protective armor.) Herbs and spices may be sprinkled under the fat, but salt should be spread on top as it draws out juices if added directly to the surface of the meat. Thinly sliced bacon may be used in place of pork fat, but will add saltiness. Any barding fat that remains after cooking should be discarded before serving. Barded meat will never brown to a crust.

Meat is tied to keep it in shape, often after boning. For a roll, one long string is used, twisted with one hand in a series of loops. They should be pulled tightly where there is more flesh, and more loosely where it is narrow, so the meat forms an even cylinder. Long rolls of meat, such as beef tenderloin, should have a piece of string tied lengthwise also, to prevent the meat from curling out of shape while it is cooking.

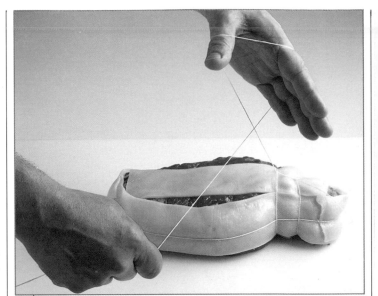

1 **To bard meat:** sprinkle it with pepper and herbs; wrap strips of thinly sliced fat around the circumference and along the length of the meat.

2 **To tie meat:** wrap a string lengthwise around the meat to hold the barding fat in place.

3 ABOVE Tie one end of a length of string around the meat. Loop the string around your hand and slip the loop around the meat, pulling to secure the fat. Repeat along the length of the meat.

4 Turn the meat over and tie the string around each loop along the length of the meat. Finish with a knot at the end.

LARDING MEAT

Meat is larded by inserting strips of pork fat (lardons) into lean meat – usually braising or stewing cuts – with a channeled larding needle (Fr. *lardoire*, p.503) to moisten it and add flavor. The fat may first be soaked in a mixture of brandy, chopped garlic, shallot and herbs. Pickled tongue may be used instead of fat. When the meat is sliced, an attractive checkered pattern of fat running through the meat is revealed. Larding can also be done with a hinged larding needle (Fr. *piqué*, p.503) by sewing short strips of fat under the surface of the meat (bacon lardons, p.249, are too soft and short for this). Such larding is less common now that selective breeding guarantees more tender meat.

1 **To lard inside the meat:** first push the larding needle through the meat, then insert the fat into the channel of the needle and pull the needle right through the meat, taking the fat back with it.

2 **To lard the surface of the meat:** thread the *piqué* needle and sew neat stitches 1-2 in/3-5 cm apart and about ½ in/1 cm deep.

Boning meat

When boning meat, study the anatomy of the cut first. Use your fingers to locate bones as you work. Try to picture the final stage: is the aim to make a pocket for stuffing, to prepare a rolled roast, or simply to take out bones before cutting the meat in pieces? A butcher's boning knife is a useful piece of equipment (p.504), whether it has the narrow blade favored in the United States, or the broader French blade.

Boning often opens a pocket in the meat for stuffing. If the pocket has to be enlarged, try to keep an even layer of meat on each side of the knife as you cut. After boning, cut away gristle, sinews and excess fat. (See also individual cuts of meat.)

Blanching meat

Meats are blanched by putting them in a large pan of cold water, bringing the water slowly to a boil and simmering for five to ten minutes, depending on the size of the pieces. Blanching effectively firms up soft variety meats, such as sweetbreads and brains, and is also an efficient method of cleaning sweetbreads, veal, and veal bones. Meats for such delicate dishes as *blanquettes* and fricassées are blanched to whiten them. Blanching also reduces strong flavors, especially of salt (for example, in ham and bacon), so the water for blanching should not be salted.

While the meat is being blanched, any scum that rises to the surface of the water must be skimmed off with a metal spoon. When the meat has been sufficiently blanched, it should be drained in a colander and rinsed with cold water.

Stewing meat

The cooking method for a meat stew (Fr. *ragoût*) is very similar to a braise. For a brown stew, the meat is browned, then simmered with liquid and a variety of flavorings. Unlike a braise, the liquid must cover the meat. Meat for a stew must be well trimmed, with fat and sinew removed, before it is cut into evenly sized cubes, as large as 2 in/5 cm for meats such as beef that require lengthy cooking. Veal, and more tender cuts of pork and lamb, cook more quickly and are usually cut into smaller pieces.

For white stews like veal *blanquette* and fricassée of pork, the meat is simmered, without browning, in light ingredients – white wine, light veal stock, or water. Flavorings are also light in color, for example, onions, mushrooms and leeks. White stews need careful reduction to avoid blandness (Sauces, p.52).

A stew is usually thickened with flour at the start of cooking when the meat is browned, but kneaded butter (Fr. *beurre manié*) or arrowroot (p.59) may be added at the end of cooking, with cream or egg yolk, particularly in a white stew. Sometimes puréed vegetables such as tomato or potato are used to give a stew extra body. For all stews, a rich, full-bodied consistency is important.

Every country has its own version of stew: the French *navarin* is made with lamb with baby vegetables, English haricot of mutton with dried beans, Hungarian beef goulash (*Gulyás*, p.212) with onion, paprika and caraway, and the ubiquitous American chili with venison, beef or pork and always cayenne pepper. Often the stew is complete in itself, needing at most an accompaniment of boiled potatoes, pasta or rice.

Poaching meat

Meats are rarely poached, yet the exceptions – Spanish *olla podrida*, Italian *bollito misto*, French *pot-au-feu*, and many other national variations – take their place on the grandest tables. The broth produced during poaching is served as a first course, with the meat and vegetables as the main dish.

In principle, a variety of cuts should be used when poaching, some with bone for flavor, others with plenty of gristle to add gelatin to the broth. Veal bones, calf's or pig's feet and head can be included and at least one piece of meat should be lean enough to slice for serving. In the famous French *petite marmite* – half soup, half stew – a boiling fowl is included with the meat, while in Lancashire hotpot, mutton is combined with kidneys.

In poached meat dishes, it is critical to add the main ingredients one by one to the broth at the right time so the flavors blend and develop, but nothing overcooks. The poaching liquid may be water – salted or unsalted – or stock, together with herbs and spices like peppercorns and cloves. Vegetables such as carrot, onion, celery and leek flavor the broth, and for easy handling they are often tied with string or put into cheesecloth bags. Poaching in unsalted water is a favorite way to cook meats that are already salted and pickled, and it gives them a characteristic softness. The broth, however, is often too salty to be used.

The term "boiled", sometimes used in the United States and Great Britain (as in New England boiled dinner and British boiled mutton), is strictly speaking inaccurate, since the ingredients should be simmered not boiled so that the meats cook without toughening and vegetables do not break up. Poached meats are often served in a marinade of oil, vinegar and herbs and used as the centerpiece of a cold salad.

Broiling and barbecuing meat

Only the most tender meat cuts, liberally marbled with fat, are suitable for broiling. A layer of fat helps to keep the meat moist, but all connective tissue must be trimmed as it will toughen in high heat. Beef steak and lamb chops or cutlets are the best cuts for broiling. Pork chops or ribs need regular basting and veal will dry out if not continually basted with butter or oil. Meat should be cut no more than 2 in/5 cm thick, though thicker cuts like Châteaubriand may be broiled, then finished in the oven.

Broiling should be done quickly: beef and lamb must be seared on both sides. If further cooking is needed, move the rack further away from the heat. Pork and veal are cooked more slowly to be easily digestible, but they need to brown well for flavor. Use a pair of tongs rather than a fork to turn meat, to avoid pricking it and losing valuable juices.

Careful seasoning is necessary for broiled meats. They can be marinated (p.195) beforehand or brushed with clarified butter (p.99) or oil and sprinkled with herbs and pepper. Add salt only at the last moment otherwise it will draw out juices and prevent the meat from browning properly. Some cooks prefer to salt the meat after cooking.

Drier meats benefit from brushing with a barbecue sauce (p.65) during broiling, but at the very least, constant basting with oil and lemon juice helps keep meat moist. Cubed meat can be interspersed with slices of bacon, onion, bell pepper and cherry tomatoes on a skewer to make kebabs. Even lean pieces of pork loin or leg of lamb take well to broiling in this fashion.

Unless basted with a full-bodied barbecue sauce, broiled meats need an accompanying slice of seasoned butter (p.99) or a spoonful of sauce. Traditional with beef and lamb are truffle, Madeira and béarnaise sauces, or Devil sauce (Fr. *sauce diable*, p.58). Mustard, vinegar and onion sauce (*sauce Robert*, p.58) accompany pork, and anchovy sauce goes well with veal. Classic garnishes and accompaniments include sprigs of watercress, broiled vegetables such as tomatoes, mushrooms, eggplant and peppers, and matchstick or straw potatoes (p.296). Other more unusual possibilities are grain dishes such as kasha, bulghur wheat and couscous (p.320). Mexican tortillas and beans are particularly popular accompaniments in the United States.

BROILING AND BARBECUEING

All times are calculated in minutes per 1 lb/500 g for 1 in/2.5 cm thick steaks that have been brought to room temperature.

cut	rare	medium	well-done
tenderloin/fillet	4	5-7	
porterhouse, rib, rib-eye, T-bone	6-7	9-12	12-15
sirloin	6-7	12-14	16-20
boneless rib, top loin, sirloin minute	5-6	7-10	10-12
flank	4-5	6-7	8-9
brisket	best cooked over very low flame until well-done, about one hour per 1lb/500g		
veal or pork cutlets	best cooked until well-done but juicy	10-12	

TESTING BROILED OR PAN-FRIED MEATS

Cooking time obviously depends on the temperature of a broiler or barbecue and the distance between the heat source and meat. To test, press the meat with your finger:

Very rare (Fr. *bleu*) Cook until seared on both sides. Meat offers no resistance when pressed. When cut, it is rare to almost blue. For steak and some game.

Rare (Fr. *saignant*) When drops of blood come to the surface, turn the meat and brown on the other side. Meat should be spongy when pressed and pink when cut. For steak, game, kidneys and lamb.

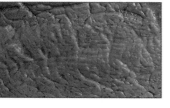

Medium (Fr. *à point*) Turn meat when drops of juice are visible on surface. Meat will resist when pressed. When cut it is pink in the center. For steak, lamb, veal, kidneys and liver.

Well-done (Fr. *bien cuit*) Turn meat when drops of juice are clearly visible. Cook until firm to the touch, showing that heat has reached the center. When cut, there is no trace of pink. For pork.

Making meat sautés

Since a sauté cooks mainly in its own juices, meat cuts are limited to those such as veal escalope, veal and pork chops, pork tenderloin, rabbit, and many variety meats that are already tender and do not need additional liquid. Some of the more tender stewing cuts of veal and lamb are also suitable for sautés.

Whichever meat you choose, it must be cut into even-sized pieces and rolled in salt and pepper, often dusted with a little flour, perhaps with allspice as well. The meat is then gently browned, usually in butter. The degree of browning governs flavor: dark meats should be well caramelized, pale meats can be golden or cooked in butter until white and firm.

During sautéing, each piece of meat should be in contact with the bottom of the pan and the pan should be covered. The meat may render a lot of fat, which should be drained before vegetables and other ingredients are added.

Vegetables like mushrooms, pearl onions, tomatoes, carrots or zucchini are first choices as garnishes. Alternatives include ham or bacon (lightly browned to remove fat), olives and dried fruits. A flaming of brandy, *marc* or Calvados adds pep, then the pan is moistened with a liquid such as stock or wine. Robust ingredients like red wine and brown stock go with dark meat sautés, lighter ones with a white sauté, but the meat should never swim in liquid.

At the end of cooking, ingredients for garnish should be cooked and the meat tender enough to fall easily from a two-pronged fork.

Classic combinations for a meat sauté include veal chops *Dijonnaise* with mustard, lamb chops with garlic and shallot, pork tenderloin with apple, and Rabbit with prunes (p.239). However, a sauté can be what you want to make it, using whatever is to hand. A simple accompaniment such as boiled rice or small fried potatoes is usually sufficient.

Pan-frying and sautéing meat

In general, pan-frying is an alternative to broiling. The same cuts are suitable and similar accompaniments are appropriate. Use a heavy-bottomed pan and only a tablespoon or two of fat, just enough to prevent sticking. Oil is the usual choice as it burns less easily, but butter can be added for flavor and color. Ridged pans allow meat to toast above the fat and give it a diamond pattern.

Sautéing implies less vigorous heat than pan-frying. Meats such as veal escalope or round *noisettes* of lamb, which dry out when broiled or pan-fried, can be sautéed successfully, most often in butter. Do not confuse this cooking method with that for making a meat sauté (above).

The advantage of pan-fried or sautéed meat is that a simple gravy (p.57) or sauce can be made by dissolving pan juices in wine or stock, with a flavoring of garlic, shallot or herbs. A tablespoon or two of flour gives a thick gravy. Cream or butter can be added to the juices to make a richer sauce.

Roasting meat

Meat for roasting should be the best, both in quality and cut. Let meat come to room temperature so that it cooks evenly. Small roasts should be cooked at a higher temperature than large ones, and red meats at a higher temperature than white meats.

There are reasons for and against boning a roast. Bones retain juices and reduce shrinkage, but boned meat cooks more evenly, slices well with little waste and can also be stuffed. Meat that does not have a layer of natural fat can be barded (p.196). The French often stud lamb with a few slivers of garlic before roasting, while many Americans favor a coating of mustard for roast beef. Herb or spiced breadcrumb toppings are sometimes added, and sweet basting mixtures, such as apple juice and honey, are often used for pork and ham. Frequent basting is important to keep the meat moist, even when barded or covered with fat. The meat must fit the pan: if it is too large, juices will burn during cooking; if too small or too deep, the meat steams.

The meat is often browned on the stove in a little oil. To flavor the gravy and prevent meat stewing in the fat and juices at the bottom of the pan, place any bones and a quartered onion and carrot under the meat. Alternatively, set the roast on a rack. If juices at the bottom of the pan start to scorch, add a cup or two of stock or water, replenishing it as it evaporates. However, do this only toward the end of cooking, so the meat does not steam.

Some cooks prefer to roast meat in the oven at 450°F/230°C for 10-12 minutes to produce a crisp crust, and then lower the heat to 350°F/175°C to finish. This is the method generally followed in this chapter. Others roast their meat at a constant lower temperature so that the meat shrinks less and is evenly cooked throughout. However, this method can be dangerous, if carried too far, since very low heat encourages the growth of bacteria.

Purists insist that true roasting can be done only on a spit before an open fire as the meat never stews in its own juice and develops an agreeably crisp crust. But temperature and cooking time are hard to control and lean meats may dry out.

Horseradish sauce, mustard, and boiled and roast root vegetables are the traditional Anglo-Saxon partners for beef. The British make a particular specialty of serving mint sauce or red currant jelly with lamb. In Paris, roast lamb is often accompanied by white kidney beans, green *flageolet* beans, or *haricots verts*. The British taste for apple sauce with pork is paralleled by the French and Scandinavian fondness for serving fresh or dried fruits such as plums or prunes with pork and ham. American or British oven-roast potatoes, potatoes fried French-style in butter or baked with cream are appreciated with any roast meat.

Testing when roasted meat is done

Approximate roasting times can be calculated from the type of meat and its weight. In the roasting chart opposite, estimates only are given since time varies with the shape of the cut. The most reliable test is with a meat thermometer inserted into the center of the meat, away from bones. A skewer can perform the same function: insert it into the thickest part of the meat and wait 30 seconds. If the skewer is cold when withdrawn, the meat is not done; if it is warm, the meat is rare; if hot, it is thoroughly cooked.

Connoisseurs like their beef rare or medium-done and their lamb to be pink. Veal is normally roasted until well-done, but still juicy, while pork must always be cooked thoroughly. **Note** Large roasts will continue to cook from retained heat as long as ten minutes after removal from the oven.

Carving roasted meat

Depending on the size of the cut, a resting period of 5-15 minutes before carving roasted meat is essential, as juices are reabsorbed during standing and the meat presents an even surface when sliced. Use a short- or long-bladed knife, and a two-pronged carving fork with a guard (p.503). To prevent the meat from losing juice, steady it with the flat of the fork, rather than piercing.

Procedures for carving meat vary by country and by cut. However, the general principle is to cut across the grain of the meat in even slices so that the meat is easy to chew. The more tender the meat, the thicker the slices can be. For instructions on carving particular cuts, see individual meats.

Braising or pot-roasting meat

Meat, particularly beef, is the ideal foundation for a braise, offering maximum opportunity to develop complex flavors during long cooking. Tougher cuts with plenty of flavor but little fat remain moist, while gristle dissolves to give a syrupy texture to the sauce. In general, whole cuts are used. Gentle heat is vital to dissolve tough tissue; if allowed to boil, a braise will be unpleasantly tough. To prevent a sauce from sticking, always use a heavy casserole and a tight-fitting lid.

A cut for braising is often larded (p.196) if very lean, and then tied so that it cooks evenly. If the meat has been marinated first, dry it well so it will brown thoroughly. Slow browning caramelizes juices deep into the surface of the meat, adding flavor to the sauce. Brown a *mirepoix* (see Basic vegetables mixtures, p.263) of onion, carrot and celery, cutting the vegetables in large chunks if the

meat is large, as cooking may last three hours or more; a few bacon lardons (p.249) are often added at this stage. Red or white wine is added next and should be boiled a few minutes to mellow the flavor before stock and seasonings are added. Do not submerge the meat in liquid.

It is at this stage that flavorings, ranging from aromatic herbs to tomato paste, are added. In a true braise, all these ingredients will be strained out of the sauce with the *mirepoix*, three-quarters of the way through cooking. The sauce should be skimmed of fat and well reduced to a concentrated essence of meat and vegetables (see Glaze and meat *coulis*, p.57). Then, more ingredients can be added to the braise. Final cooking time will depend on the recipe. When done, braised meat should be very tender when pierced with a two-pronged fork.

In America, braised meat often appears as a pot-roast, without the *mirepoix*, and is spiced with mustard, nutmeg or cinnamon. All braises mellow when reheated; the best accompaniments are potatoes, pasta, beans or rice that absorb the sauce, or chestnuts, root vegetables and cabbage.

GENERAL ROASTING TIMES FOR MEATS

type	mins per 1 lb/500 g	internal temperature when done	
BEEF	12-15	(125°F/51°C)	rare
and	15-18	(140°F/60°C)	medium
LAMB	18-20	(160°F/70°C)	well-done
WHOLE BEEF	4-6	(125°F/51°C)	rare
TENDERLOIN	7-10	(140°F/60°C)	medium
Note Whole tenderloin is cooked entirely at high heat, 450°F/230°C.			
VEAL	15-20	(160°F/70°C)	best served well-done
PORK	20-25	(170°F/75°C)	best served well-done
GAME	10-15	(125°F/51°C)	best served rare

Times are calculated for meats at room temperature, roasted for 15 minutes at 450°F/230°C and finished at 350°F/175°C. Roasts that are larger than 8 lb/3.6 kg benefit from slow roasting at 325°F/160°C after the initial high heat. Remove the meat when a meat thermometer reaches the correct reading. The meat may continue to rise a few degrees as it rests.

Stuffing meat

Many meat dishes call for hearty stuffings (p.364) with plenty of body and contrasting taste. The mixture is often meat-based: ground pork or sausagemeat adds richness, while veal makes a more delicate stuffing. If boning a cut such as veal breast, trimmings may be ground to add to the stuffing. These can also be made into a firm mousse, bound with egg whites and breadcrumbs and then added to the meat.

Stuffings for meat need plenty of pepper and spice, as well as flavorings such as onion and garlic, and aromatic herbs such as thyme and sage. Chopped vegetables like red peppers or carrots can provide color or texture, breadcrumbs give lightness, and cooked grains like rice or bulghur wheat add substance. Dried fruits and nuts complement pork; veal and lamb go well with ham, anchovy, eggplant, and spinach stuffing, flavored with onion, carrot and celery. Even seafood can be used with meat; in Australia and New Zealand, for example, the classic "carpetbag" steak is stuffed with oysters.

BEEF (US)

The common divisions of an American beef carcass are shown in the box below. Smaller retail cuts are numbered correspondingly.

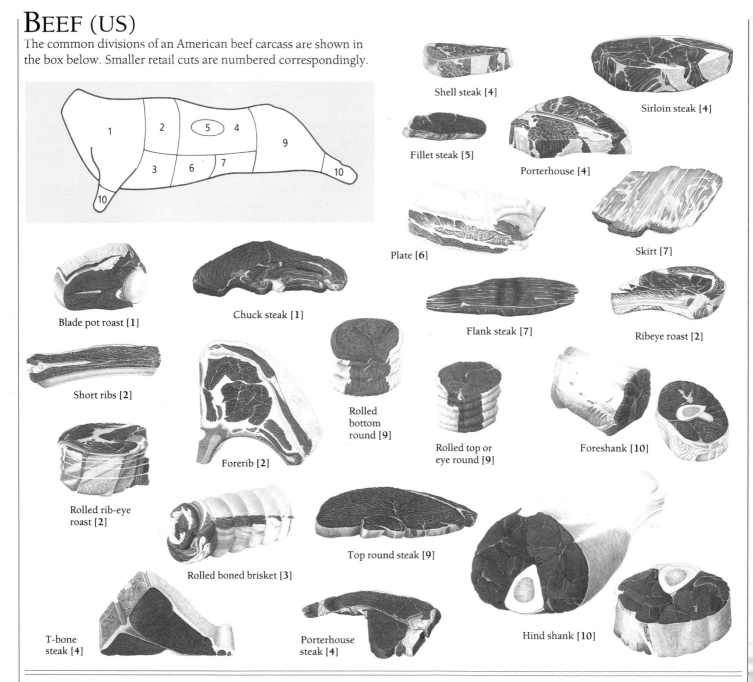

Shell steak [4]

Sirloin steak [4]

Fillet steak [5]

Porterhouse [4]

Plate [6]

Skirt [7]

Blade pot roast [1]

Chuck steak [1]

Flank steak [7]

Ribeye roast [2]

Short ribs [2]

Rolled bottom round [9]

Rolled top or eye round [9]

Foreshank [10]

Forerib [2]

Rolled rib-eye roast [2]

Top round steak [9]

Rolled boned brisket [3]

Hind shank [10]

T-bone steak [4]

Porterhouse steak [4]

NUTRITIVE VALUES OF BEEF (based on a 3½ oz / 100 g portion)

cut	calories	protein (g)	fat (g)	carbohydrates (g)	cholesterol (mg)	sodium (mg)
Tenderloin (fillet)	150	21	7	0	62	54
Shoulder (chuck), brisket	153	20	7	0	63	72
Rib, Flank	169	20	9	0	55	73
Loin	152	21	7	0	60	57
Leg (round)	139	22	5	0	58	56
Plate, skirt	164	21	8	0	60	65
Shank	128	22	4	0	39	63
Lean ground	264	18	21	0	75	69
Regular ground	310	17	26	0	85	68

BEEF (French)

The common divisions of a French beef carcass are shown in the box below. Smaller retail cuts are numbered correspondingly.

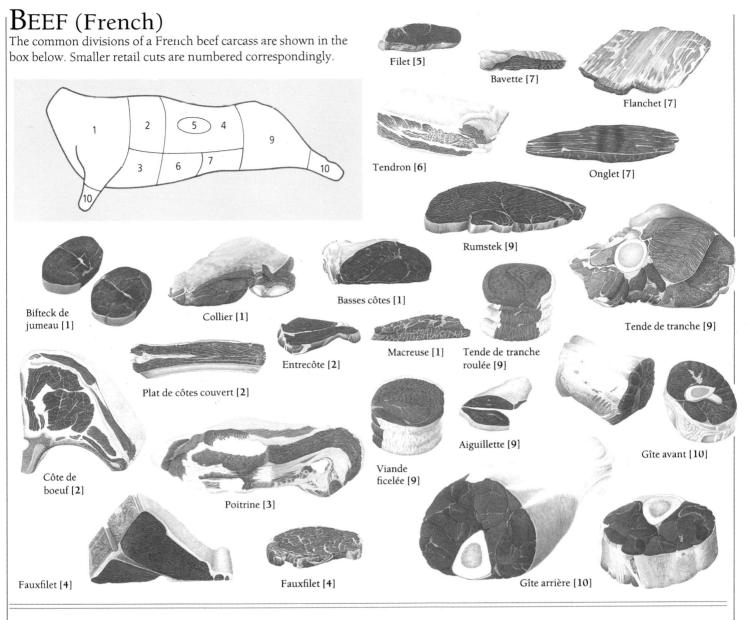

Filet [5]

Bavette [7]

Flanchet [7]

Tendron [6]

Onglet [7]

Rumstek [9]

Basses côtes [1]

Bifteck de jumeau [1]

Collier [1]

Tende de tranche [9]

Entrecôte [2]

Macreuse [1]

Tende de tranche roulée [9]

Plat de côtes couvert [2]

Côte de boeuf [2]

Poitrine [3]

Aiguillette [9]

Viande ficelée [9]

Gîte avant [10]

Fauxfilet [4]

Fauxfilet [4]

Gîte arrière [10]

COOKING METHODS FOR BEEF

Braise/pot roast chuck roast; top blade roast; under blade roast; neck; shoulder roast; arm roast; cross rib; shank; knuckle; chuck steak; blade steak; arm steak; short ribs; shank steak; top sirloin; tip; top round; eye round; bottom round or rump; heel of round; flank or skirt; plate flanken; brisket; shank bone; shank steak.

Roast tenderloin or fillet; rib roast; rib eye roast; sirloin; shell roast; top round; rump; steamship.

Broil steaks: rib, rib eye, top loin (club, delmonico, shell, sirloin strip, strip), T-bone, porterhouse, sirloin, minute, flank; steak; London broil; hanging tenderloin; sirloin tip; top sirloin; top round; eye round; bottom round; rump; heel of round; steamship; flank or skirt.

Sauté/pan-fry steaks: top loin (club, delmonico, shell, sirloin strip, strip), T-bone, porterhouse, sirloin, minute; ground chuck and shoulder cuts; top sirloin; sirloin tip; top round; eye round; bottom round; rump; heel of round; flank; skirt.

Barbecue steaks: rib, rib eye, top loin (club, delmonico, shell, sirloin strip, strip), T-bone, porterhouse, sirloin, minute. Also brisket, flank.

Marinate roasts: chuck, top blade, under blade, neck, cross rib, shoulder, arm, top sirloin, sirloin tip, top round, eye round, bottom round or rump, heel of round; steaks: chuck, blade, arm shank, top loin (club, delmonico, shell, sirloin strip, strip), T-bone, porterhouse, sirloin, minute. Also, brisket; hanging tenderloin; flank or skirt; London broil; shank; short ribs.

Stir-fry (thinly sliced pieces or cubes) chuck; blade steak; arm; short ribs; shank steak; chain; also thin slices from meaty cuts suitable for roasting, barbecueing or broiling.

Stew top round; plate; short ribs; plate flanken; brisket; steaks: chuck, blade, arm, shank, flank, skirt.

Stuff chuck; top blade; under blade; neck; cross rib; shoulder; top sirloin; sirloin tip; top round; eye round; bottom round; rump; heel of round; flank.

Simmer in water brisket; heel of round; short ribs; plate; knuckle; flank; shank.

201

VEAL (US)

The common divisions of an American veal carcass are shown in the box below. Smaller retail cuts are numbered correspondingly.

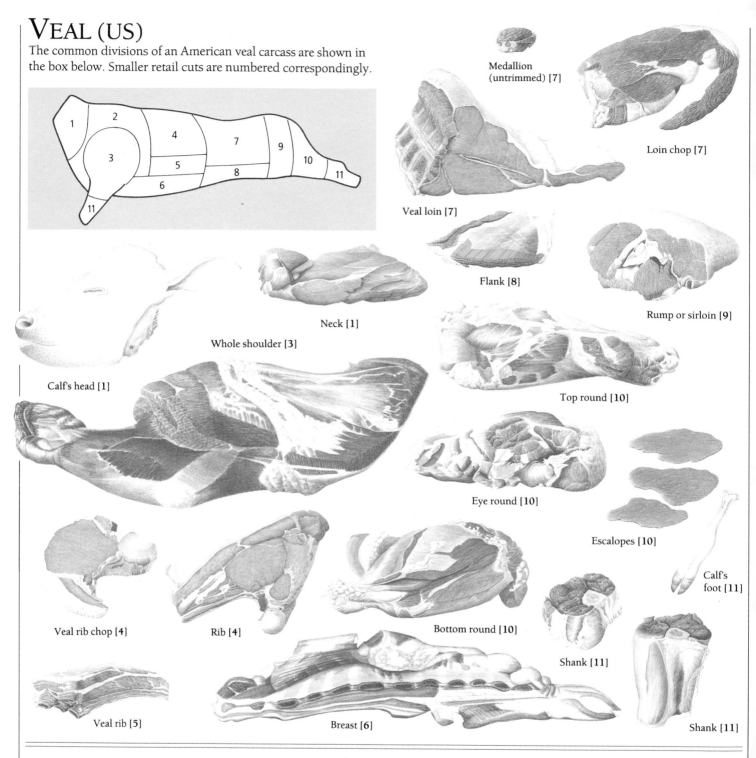

Medallion (untrimmed) [7]

Loin chop [7]

Veal loin [7]

Flank [8]

Rump or sirloin [9]

Neck [1]

Whole shoulder [3]

Calf's head [1]

Top round [10]

Eye round [10]

Escalopes [10]

Calf's foot [11]

Veal rib chop [4]

Rib [4]

Bottom round [10]

Shank [11]

Veal rib [5]

Breast [6]

Shank [11]

COOKING METHODS FOR VEAL

Braise/pot roast shoulder; blade roast; shoulder chops; shoulder steaks; center rib chops; loin; saddle; rump or sirloin chops; eye.
Roast crown roast; center rib; loin; saddle; rump; sirloin.
Broil/barbecue center rib chops; loin medallions; loin chops.
Sauté/pan-fry shoulder chops; shoulder steaks; center rib chops; loin chops; loin medallions; rump or sirloin chops; tenderloin.
Stir-fry thinly sliced loin; tenderloin; sirloin; rump.
Stew cubed shoulder chops and steaks; neck; cubed rump or sirloin.
Stuff breast; crown roast; scaloppine.

Osso buco

In Italy, the name *osso buco* refers both to a specific cut of meat – the veal shank – and a finished dish of stewed veal shanks. The shank is always cut up into circular pieces, called *osso buchi*, of about 3½ in/9 cm in diameter and 1½-2 in/4-5 cm thick, always including a bone that contains the marrow. The best *osso buchi* come from the leg. Each piece is tied with string to keep its shape before being cooked slowly for up to two hours. *Osso buco* is always finished with a liberal sprinkling of *gremolata* seasoning (p.14) and the cooked marrow is extracted at the table by the diner. *Risotto alla milanese* (p.25) is a popular accompaniment.

VEAL (French)

The common divisions of a French veal carcass are shown in the box below. Smaller retail cuts are numbered correspondingly.

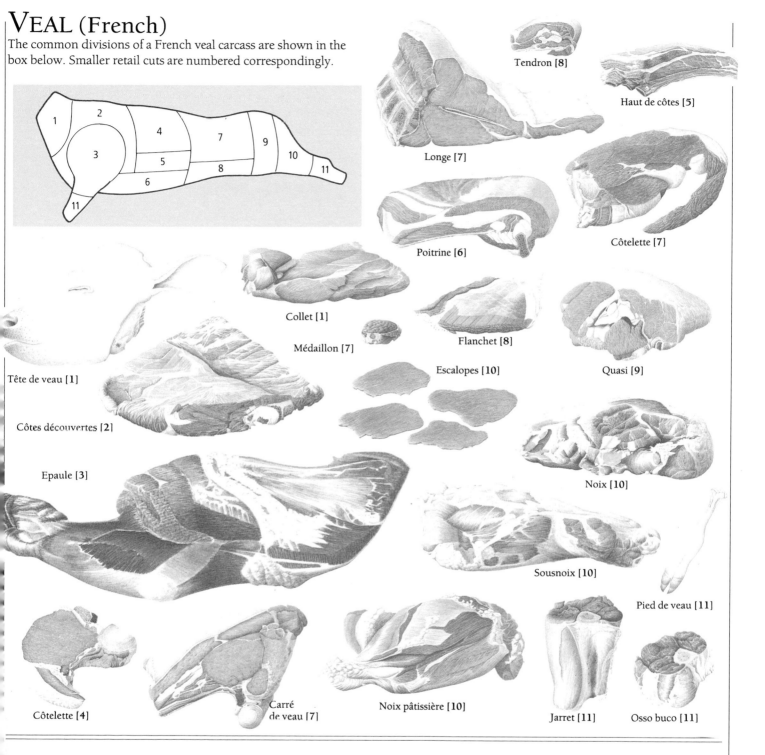

Tendron [8]

Haut de côtes [5]

Longe [7]

Côtelette [7]

Poitrine [6]

Collet [1]

Médaillon [7]

Flanchet [8]

Escalopes [10]

Quasi [9]

Tête de veau [1]

Côtes découvertes [2]

Epaule [3]

Noix [10]

Sousnoix [10]

Pied de veau [11]

Côtelette [4]

Carré de veau [7]

Noix pâtissière [10]

Jarret [11]

Osso buco [11]

NUTRITIVE VALUES OF VEAL (based on a 3½ oz/100 g raw portion)

cut	calories	protein (g)	fat (g)	carbohydrates (g)	cholesterol (mg)	sodium (mg)
Shoulder	112	20	3	0	85	89
Neck	116	20	4	0	88	94
Loin	119	20	4	0	76	86
Flank, Shank, Rump	111	20	3	0	76	77
Leg	109	21	2	0	76	90
Ribs, Breast	123	20	4	0	80	91

LAMB (US)

The common divisions of an American lamb carcass are shown in the box below. Smaller retail cuts are numbered correspondingly.

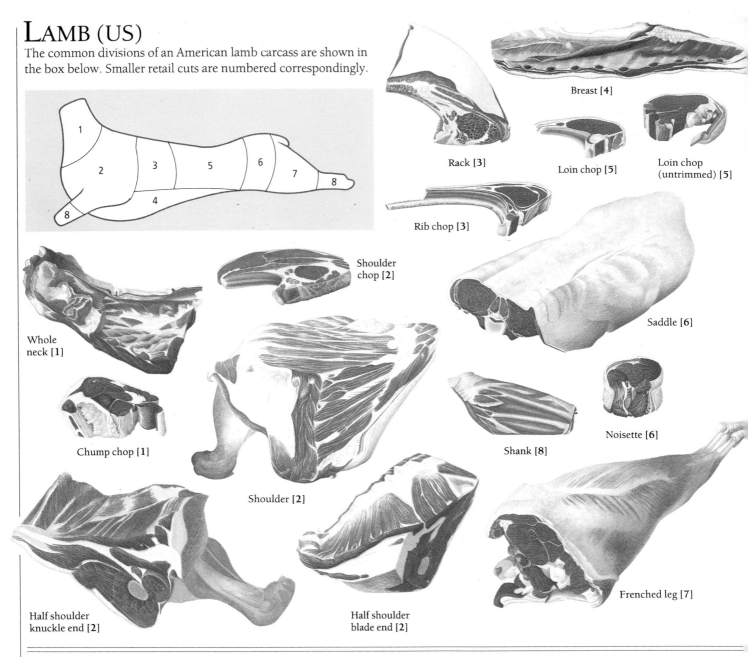

Rack [3]

Breast [4]

Loin chop [5]

Loin chop (untrimmed) [5]

Rib chop [3]

Shoulder chop [2]

Saddle [6]

Whole neck [1]

Noisette [6]

Chump chop [1]

Shank [8]

Shoulder [2]

Frenched leg [7]

Half shoulder knuckle end [2]

Half shoulder blade end [2]

COOKING METHODS FOR LAMB

Braise/pot roast shoulder; blade, arm and loin chops; neck; loin; leg; cubed leg; breast; riblets; boneless breast strips; shank.

Roast shoulder; rack; loin; saddle; leg; breast.

Broil blade, arm, rib and loin chops; noisettes; leg steaks or escalopes.

Sauté/pan-fry blade, arm, rib and loin chops; noisettes; leg steaks or escalopes.

Barbecue blade, rib and loin chops; boned and butterflied leg; leg steaks or escalopes; cubed leg (as kebabs); breast riblets.

Stir-fry thinly sliced loin; shoulder; leg; breast; tenderloin.

Stew cubed shoulder; neck; cubed leg; boneless breast strips; breast riblets; shank.

Stuff crown roast; shoulder; breast; leg.

Boil neck; shank.

Middle Eastern lamb dishes

Middle Eastern cuisine is characterized by the use of lamb or mutton. Two Turkish lamb dishes are now popular worldwide. The *doner kebab* is a marinated, boned leg of lamb, roasted on a vertical spit. Slices are cut to order and often served on *pita* bread, perhaps with tomatoes, onions and yogurt sauce. *Shish kebab* is made from chunks of lamb, tomatoes, onion and bell pepper threaded on skewers and barbecued. The lamb is often marinated first in olive oil or yogurt.

Each Middle Eastern country has a favorite version of *kofta* – ground meat combined with onion and perfumed with allspice, coriander or cumin. The meat is ground to a paste and shaped on skewers or molded into balls or patties. The Syrians and Lebanese take pride in their national dish, *kibbeh*. Ground lamb is mixed with cracked wheat or bulghur, pounded to a paste and eaten raw, deep-fried or broiled, sometimes with a filling. Small *kibbeh* may be added to tomato- or yogurt-based stews.

LAMB (French)

The common divisions of a French lamb carcass are shown in the box below. Smaller retail cuts are numbered correspondingly.

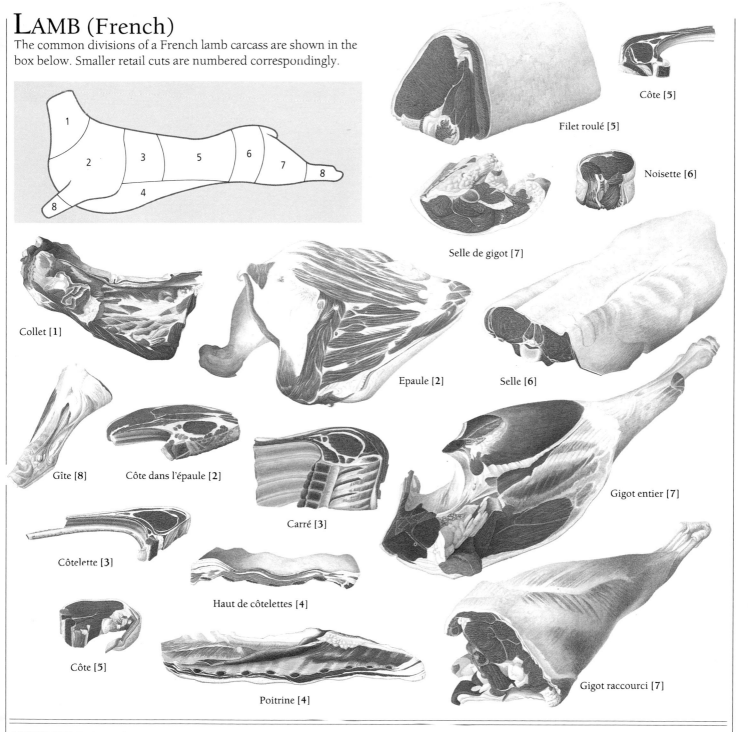

Côte [5]

Filet roulé [5]

Noisette [6]

Selle de gigot [7]

Collet [1]

Epaule [2]

Selle [6]

Gîte [8]

Côte dans l'épaule [2]

Carré [3]

Gigot entier [7]

Côtelette [3]

Haut de côtelettes [4]

Côte [5]

Poitrine [4]

Gigot raccourci [7]

NUTRITIVE VALUES OF LAMB (based on a 3½ oz/100 g raw portion)

cut	calories	protein (g)	fat (g)	carbohydrates (g)	cholesterol (mg)	sodium (mg)
Shoulder	125	20	5	0	67	81
Neck	139	19	7	0	67	72
Rack	152	20	8	0	66	78
Loin	138	21	6	0	67	72
Sirloin (chump)	129	21	5	0	66	68
Leg	120	21	4	0	65	67
Breast/Shank	111	21	3	0	69	94

PORK (US)

The common divisions of an American pork carcass are shown in the box below. Smaller retail cuts are numbered correspondingly.

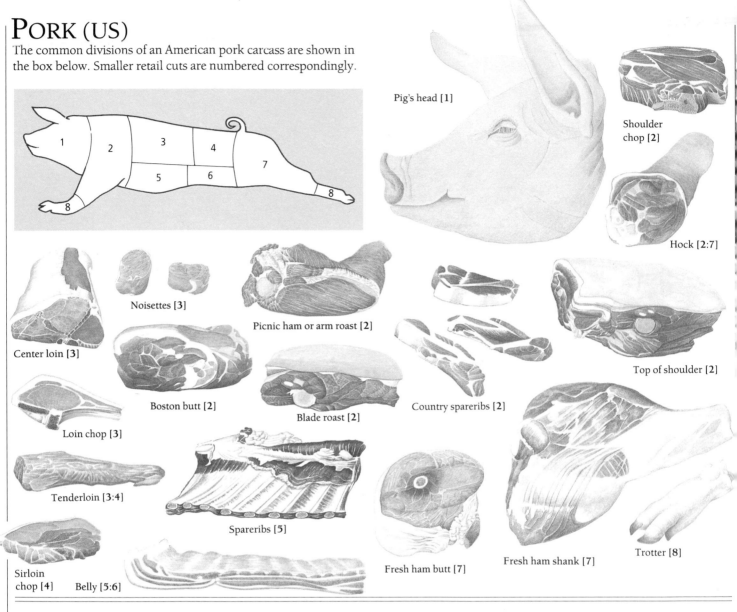

Pig's head [1]

Shoulder chop [2]

Hock [2:7]

Noisettes [3]

Picnic ham or arm roast [2]

Center loin [3]

Boston butt [2]

Blade roast [2]

Country spareribs [2]

Top of shoulder [2]

Loin chop [3]

Tenderloin [3:4]

Spareribs [5]

Fresh ham butt [7]

Fresh ham shank [7]

Trotter [8]

Sirloin chop [4]   Belly [5:6]

COOKING METHODS FOR PORK

Braise/pot roast shoulder; Boston arm roast; hocks; feet; blade steaks; arm or picnic steaks; tenderloin; sirloin chops; country style ribs; leg or fresh ham; butt; shank.

Roast shoulder; picnic ham; arm roast; Boston butt; hocks; loin; sirloin; crown roast; tenderloin; leg or fresh ham; butt; shank.

Broil country-style spareribs; sirloin chops; filets mignons; spareribs; leg or fresh ham steaks.

Sauté/pan-fry blade steaks; arm or picnic steaks; filets mignons
Barbecue spareribs; country-style ribs; leg or fresh ham steaks.
Marinate country-style spareribs; sirloin chops; leg steaks (butt or shank).
Stir-fry leg or fresh ham steaks (butt or shank), also thin slices from meaty cuts suitable for roasting or broiling.
Stew hocks; neck.
Stuff crown roast; spareribs; chops.
Simmer belly.

NUTRITIVE VALUES OF PORK (based on a 3½ oz/100 g raw portion)

cut	calories	protein (g)	fat (g)	carbohydrates (g)	cholesterol (mg)	sodium (mg)
Shoulder	154	19	8	0	67	76
Loin	156	21	8	0	60	64
Leg (fresh ham)	136	20	5	0	68	55
Belly	518	9	53	0	72	32
Spareribs	286	17	24	0	78	76

PORK (French)

The common divisions of a French pork carcass are shown in the box below. Smaller retail cuts are numbered correspondingly.

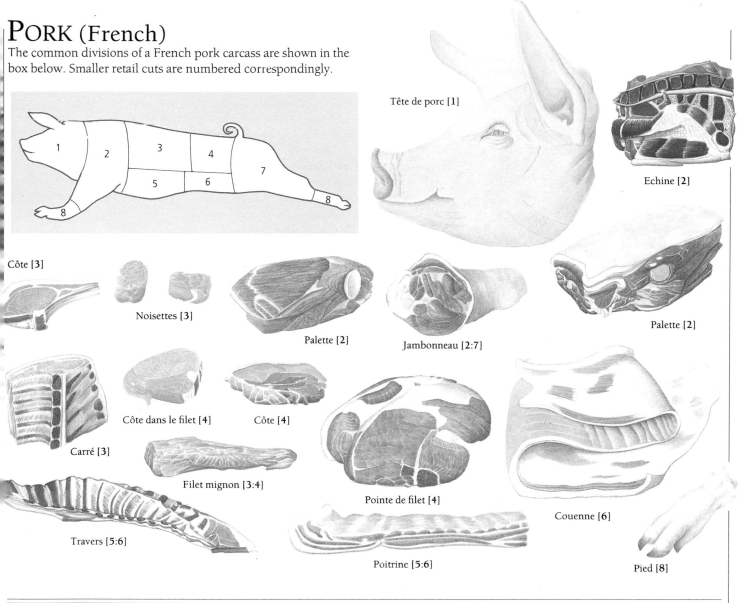

Tête de porc [1]

Echine [2]

Côte [3]

Noisettes [3]

Palette [2]

Jambonneau [2:7]

Palette [2]

Côte dans le filet [4]

Côte [4]

Carré [3]

Filet mignon [3:4]

Pointe de filet [4]

Couenne [6]

Travers [5:6]

Poitrine [5:6]

Pied [8]

MEAT CUTS & BONES

Aitchbone Part of the pelvic bone joining backbone to hip. As a transverse bone, it causes problems when boning and carving and so should be removed.

Chine Section of lower backbone which interlocks ribs and vertebrae. To facilitate boning or carving, the chine bone should be removed or partially severed from the ribs by the butcher.

Chuck The largest of the forequarter cuts, usually refers to beef. Divided differently, depending on butcher.

Escalope A thin boneless slice generally from the leg, but also from the rib, loin and shoulder.

Eye Any long muscle which slices into neat rounds; "eye" often refers to meat lying above the ribs, and to a muscle in the leg.

Filet mignon Another name for fillet, particularly in smaller animals. Both fillet and *filet mignon* are often sliced as steaks.

Loin Cut lying along the backbone including ribs and sometimes the vertebrae.

Medallion or noisette A neat round slice, without bone, usually ½-1 in/6 mm-1.25 cm thick ("noisette" means nut).

Sirloin Cut from the lower backbone, where ribs end.

KNIFE SHARPENING

Keeping knives sharp involves two processes: occasional honing and regular sharpening. A dull blade should be honed or ground against a carborundum stone. A long sharpening steel is used to smooth the blade after honing, and to sharpen the knife each time you use it.

1 To hone a blade Holding the knife at a slight angle to the stone, rub the blade against it on one side and then the other.

2 To sharpen a blade Holding the knife against the steel at an angle of 20°, draw one side and then the other rapidly along it.

Other cooking methods for meat

In Western cuisine, deep-fried meats tend to be ground and breaded first (for example Scotch eggs or German meatballs) as the searing heat instantly toughens even tender cuts. Deep-frying in batter is more characteristic of Japanese tempura and Chinese sweet-sour dishes. Asian cuisine has also spread West in the form of stir-fried meat dishes. The meticulous, wafer-thin slicing needed for stir-fried dishes suits cuts such as chuck steak, or pork or lamb shoulder, which otherwise would toughen over such high heat. Often the thin layers of meat used for stir-frying are first marinated in soy sauce, rice wine, or rice wine vinegar, together with seasonings like chopped fresh ginger, spring onion or Sichuan peppercorns. Sometimes the meat is partially pre-cooked by poaching or briefly deep-frying.

A bonus in the kitchen is leftover pieces of meat that may be formed into croquettes (p.107), topped with potatoes as in British shepherd's pie, or diced for the numerous varieties of hash served on both sides of the Atlantic. When served cold, meat leftovers are enlivened by marinating an hour or two in vinaigrette dressing spiked with chopped pickles, capers and herbs, before being piled on top of fresh greens or a salad of cooked root vegetables. Boiled beef makes an excellent salad, served with hot red pepper sauce (*rouille*) or *sauce gribiche* (p.63) and lettuce and tomato.

Presenting meat

The presentation of meat depends very much on the way it is cooked. Traditionally, grand roasts such as sirloins of beef, barons of lamb and suckling pigs are displayed brown and crisp on the bone. Here, as with smaller roasts like leg of lamb, the meat is often carved, before being reshaped on the bone for guests to help themselves. The garnish – stuffed tomatoes, oven-roast potatoes, Brussels sprouts – is clustered around the meat. A bouquet of glazed vegetables such as carrots, green beans, onions and peas, is a universal favorite with veal. However, when a roast is to be carved at the table, a copious garnish can interfere so the decoration is best limited to bunches of watercress with vegetables served separately. Raw meat dishes should not be forgotten, for example, wafer-thin carpaccio sprinkled with vinaigrette, or steak tartare which is accompanied by chopped onion, an egg yolk, anchovies and capers, or the Middle Eastern *kibbi naybe*.

For boned roasts, pot-roasts and *pot-au-feu*, the meat is sliced in the kitchen and arranged down the center of the dish, with vegetables on either side. Smaller pieces of meat such as steaks and chops may be arranged overlapping on a serving dish, bones on top pointing outwards. Watercress is a popular garnish for broiled or pan-fried meats; chopped parsley is used when the meat is moist with sauce. As with roasts, vegetables that complement the meat should be added to the plate as a garnish. Individual plate presentations of meat and accompaniments are more and more popular, particularly for meats like kidneys, and for kebabs or chops that form their own decoration. Presenting meat dishes on individual plates simplifies service and looks attractive but lacks the splendor of a great platter.

Cold meats destined for the buffet table are a *tour de force*. Spectacles hard to match are roast beef, ham in gleaming white chaudfroid sauce (p.56), pâtés and terrines in shimmering aspic coats, all flanked by banquet trappings of tomato baskets and stuffed cucumber and artichoke bottoms.

Glossary of meat terms

Since meat terminology can be confusing, the following list gives some standard definitions used in this chapter.

Connective tissue holds muscles together. There are different kinds of connective tissue but each contains collagen and elastin. Connective tissue is semi-transparent, and is often referred to as silverskin or sinew. The more connective tissue meat contains, the less tender it will be.

Collagen is a nutritious protein found in bones, skin, tendons, muscles and connective tissue, which is released during moist cooking. When meat is cooked in hot liquid, the collagen dissolves and converts to gelatin. An acid ingredient such as wine also helps this conversion.

Elastin is a tough elastic substance found in blood vessel walls and ligaments. In older animals, collagen converts to elastin, which is not dissolved or made tender by heat.

Cartilage/gristle is a type of connective tissue that surrounds veins, arteries, and bones and is seen in lower-quality cuts.

Fat is found in almost all muscular tissue. See Animal fats, p.97.

Muscle is a mass of long fibrous cells bound together by connective tissue. The cells grow larger and toughen the muscle as the animal grows and exercises. Muscles that are little used are more tender than those that work hard.

Grain The structure of muscle fibers and the way in which they are grouped together determines whether the grain of the meat is fine or coarse. It is easier to cut along the grain than across it.

Marbling refers to muscle that contains striations of fat. Extensive marbling is easy to recognize, although all meat is marbled to some extent. The more marbling meat has, the more tender it will be.

FESTIVE & UNUSUAL MEAT

Whole roast pig, lamb and goat are traditional spring treats in many countries. Roast suckling pig is one of the world's most festive dishes: the succulent flesh has a crisp coating of crackling and fat, and like all small animals, it may be roasted on a spit or in a large roasting pan in the oven, stuffed with the same mixtures that are used for mature pork. Suckling lambs are particularly popular in Italy, Greece and the Middle East, where they are spit-roasted with garlic, cumin, cardamom and black pepper or stewed with sauces of rosemary and vinegar or mint and tomatoes; the chops can be breaded and deep-fried. Young goat or kid is another treat, served at spring feasts since medieval times, when it was prepared with sage, sweet wine and allspice. It is still cooked for spring festivals in France, roasted over an open fire with herbs, or cooked in a white stew. In the Middle East, kid roasted on or off the bone is served on a platter with perfumed rice and hard-boiled eggs.

To many people, the idea of eating horsemeat is distasteful. In the United States, for example, it is used only as pet food, and the British have never taken to it. In France and Belgium, where even small towns have a horse butcher, it is considered tasty, and demand is high considering it is as costly as beef. Butchered like beef, and similar in texture, horsemeat is less fatty with a low cholesterol content and a tell-tale sweetness. Horsemeat gained popularity in Napoleon's time; later in the century it became the rage at banquets, where it was served *à la mode*, or as fillet accompanied by a salad dressed with horsemeat oil.

BEEF

Of all meats, beef offers the greatest variety and challenge to the cook. The old English vicarage ditty "hot on Sunday, cold on Monday, hashed on Tuesday, minced on Wednesday, curried on Thursday, broth on Friday" is just the start of the story. There are cuts of beef that lend themselves to every cooking process imaginable, not to mention beef that is preserved by pickling and salting (p.488).

More than any other meat, the quality of beef varies with age, breed and feeding. Most beef comes from steers (young castrated males) fattened for the table. Typically they are 18 months old, with a carcass weight of 500-600 lb/225-270 kg, of which about 30 percent is fat and 16 percent bone. Some European breeds are raised exclusively for meat, but most are cross-bred to produce both milk and beef. In Europe, beef from heifers (young cows) and older cows and bulls is also sold, although it is inferior to that of the steer.

Breed affects both the size of the carcass and the meat itself, whether fat or lean, close-grained or coarse. Some of the best beef is marketed according to breed – for instance Scottish Aberdeen Angus, Italian Chianina and Texan Santa Gertrudis. As for feeding, American beef comes from corn-fed steers, but European farmers often feed their cattle grain or grass.

Basically, the least esteemed and toughest cuts of beef come from those parts of the animal that move the most – that is the lower legs (shanks), shoulders, flanks, neck and tail. The best, most tender cuts come from the hindquarter and from the prime ribs in the forequarter. Providing it is correctly handled, commercial freezing does little harm to beef.

Wholesale and retail nomenclature for the different cuts is very confusing, not only because the same terms denote different parts of the animal in different countries (or even regions) but also because carcasses are not dismembered according to a common standard. Nevertheless, in the mind's eye, a steer can be divided into eight main segments, and here we consider individual retail cuts within each segment.

SEGMENTS OF THE CARCASS

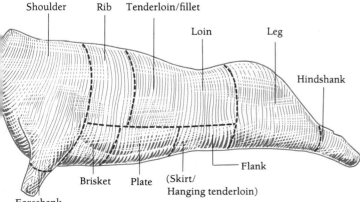

A steer can be divided into eight main segments, each with certain cooking characteristics. These segments do not correspond to retail cuts. See also Beef cuts (p.200).

USEFUL INFORMATION

Season Year-round.

How to choose Deep red, moist meat generously marbled with white fat; yellow fat betrays old age but can also indicate grass feeding; beef is purple after cutting but the meat quickly "blooms" to bright red on exposure to the air; well-aged beef is dark and dry; to avoid paying for waste, be sure meat is thoroughly trimmed by a butcher.

Nutritive value See Beef cuts, p.200.

Processed forms Salted; pickled (corned); smoked; dried; canned; extract and essence.

Bistecca cacciatora (steak with tomato, fennel and Marsala, Italy)

Cooking methods Cooking times for tougher cuts depend very much on the cut. *Whole cut:* braise or pot-roast at 350°F/175°C, 25-35 minutes per 1 lb/500 g; marinate 2-3 days; roast (p.199). *Steaks and ribs:* bake at 350°F/175°C, 1-2 hours; barbecue or broil (p.197); braise or stew at 350°F/175°C, 1½-2½ hours; cook as a sauté ¾-1 hour; marinate 1-2 days; pan-fry or sauté (p.198); simmer 1½-2½ hours; stir-fry 1-2 minutes. *Cubed:* braise or stew at 350°F/175°C, 1½-2 hours; cook as a sauté ¾-1 hour; simmer 1½-2½ hours. *Ground:* see Ground meat, p.214, and Hamburgers, p.213.

When done *Whole cut:* braise, pot-roast, or simmer until tender when pierced with two-pronged fork; roast to 125°F/51°C on meat thermometer for rare meat, 140°F/60°C for medium-done meat, 160°F/70°C for well-done meat. *Steaks:* broiled or pan-fried (p.198); braise, simmer or stew until meat falls easily from two-pronged fork. *Cubed:* falls easily from fork.

Storage *Whole cut or pieces:* Wrap well to refrigerate 3-5 days; freeze 1 year. *Ground:* refrigerate 2 days; freeze 2 months.

Typical dishes Beef Wellington (whole tenderloin with liver pâté, baked in pastry, UK); *tournedos Henri IV* (with artichoke bottoms and béarnaise sauce, France); *tournedos Rossini* (with foie gras, truffles and Madeira sauce, France); *sauerbraten* (marinated pot-roast, Germany); *estofado Catalan* (pot-roast with red wine, white beans and vegetables, Spain); *carne claveteada* (pot-roast studded with almonds and bacon, Mexico); pot-roast with prunes, olives and mushrooms (USA); roast beef, roast potatoes and Yorkshire pudding (UK); *rôti de bœuf flamande* (roast with mustard and pepper, France); *pieczeń huzarska* (boneless rump or round with onion, egg, vodka and bread stuffing, Poland); rib roast in red wine simmered with vegetables, (France); New England boiled dinner (corned beef, beans, potatoes, rutabagas, cabbage, USA); *matambre* (flank steak marinated, stuffed and rolled, Latin America, Mexico); Sussex stewed steak (with mushroom ketchup, stout and port, UK); *finken* (casserole with mashed potatoes, apples and nutmeg, Finland); *tzimmes* (beef stew with carrots, sweet potatoes, honey and prunes or dried fruit, Jewish); *bœuf à la bourguignonne* (stewed with red wine, mushrooms, onions, garlic and bacon, France); *stroganoff* (stewed with sour cream, onions and mushrooms, Russia); steak Diane (with Worcestershire sauce and onions, USA); steak tartare (raw minced fillet with egg, capers and parsley, France); *steak au poivre* (steak with cracked black pepper, France); deviled short ribs (with mustard sauce, USA); *sukiyaki* (fried with noodles, bean curd and soy sauce, Japan).

Rib roast braised in red wine with vegetables (Australia)

TENDERLOIN OR FILLET

By common consent, tenderloin or fillet (Fr. *filet*) is the finest cut of beef. It is the only one that varies very little from country to country, except in size. The tenderloin lies under the lower backbone, where it does not move, so it is splendidly tender though it can lack the rich flavor of more active muscles. Tenderloin can be roasted whole or cut into tournedos and smaller *filet mignon* steaks. From the center of the tenderloin comes the Châteaubriand, a small roast that serves two people.

Tenderloin calls for luxury accompaniments in the cook's repertoire: a brown sauce finished with foie gras or truffles, or more modestly, with Madeira sauce (p.58). Ever-popular is *filet en croûte*, or beef Wellington, in which the meat is wrapped in puff pastry or brioche with pâté, foie gras, or *duxelles* purée (p.306). Stuffed artichoke bottoms, baby vegetables, small fried potatoes, or a fried potato cake are further embellishments.

TRIMMING BEEF TENDERLOIN

Untrimmed, tenderloin weighs from 7-9 lb/3.2-4 kg, but it loses about one-third of its weight when trimmed.

1 Cut and pull away surrounding fat to expose the meat.

2 RIGHT Cut away the chain muscle that lies to the side of the main fillet. The chain muscle is tough but can be used, after trimming, for stewing or grinding.

3 ABOVE Stretch and pull out the white membrane (a tough, tight coat of tissue or "silverskin") that surrounds the meat and, using a small knife, slit it and cut it away from the meat, leaving the red tender meat lying beneath it.

4 For roasting a whole tenderloin, fold under the tapered end to make a neat shape for even roasting, or cut away 4-5 in/10-13 cm of the tapered end. These trimmings may be used for kebabs, or for dishes such as beef stroganoff. Alternatively, cut the tenderloin into steaks (see right, top).

Tail end / Châteaubriand / Tournedos or *filet mignon* steaks / Fillet steaks / Trimmings

For roasting: sprinkle the meat with pepper and seasonings, bard and tie the tenderloin (p.196).

For tournedos: cut 3-4 slices, 1½ in/4 cm thick, from the thick head end and bard them.

For Châteaubriand: cut a 5 in/12.5 cm section from the center of the fillet. (The head muscle is sometimes substituted but it is inferior.)

For fillet steaks: cut the rest of the meat into ¾-1 in/2-2.5 cm slices. Châteaubriand sections can also be cut into fillet steaks.

Roasting whole beef tenderloin

In a roasting pan heat a tablespoon of oil and brown the meat. Roast it at 500°F/260°C for 25-35 minutes, turning it over every eight to ten minutes. For rare meat, the thermometer should register 125°F/51°C, and for medium-done, 140°F/60°C. Let it stand before carving.

Cooking a Châteaubriand

Sprinkle the meat with salt and pepper. Brush it with melted butter and broil for eight to ten minutes on each side until well browned, basting occasionally. Transfer to a 500°F/260°C oven and roast for about 10 minutes until the meat is still tender to the touch for rare meat (125°F/51°C on a meat thermometer), or springy for medium-done meat (140°F/60°C on a thermometer). Let it stand for five minutes. Carve it in ⅜ in/1 cm diagonal slices giving each person a crisp end slice and some rare slices.

SHOULDER

The shoulder is a large section of the animal, often called chuck, which includes the neck, four to five ribs lying behind the shoulder, the shoulder, and foreleg; it can weigh 100 lb/45 kg or more. All this meat is tough, with scanty marbling of fat and a good deal of connective tissue. Half a dozen cuts are made from the shoulder, all producing meat for pot-roasting or braising if left whole. The shoulder bone structure tends to complicate carving, so the meat is best boned and tied. Good cuts for simmering (as for boiled beef or *pot-au-feu*) also come from the shoulder.

The shoulder is a great source of ground beef, particularly in the United States where there is a high demand for hamburger meat. Indeed, the one compensation for the toughness of shoulder meat is its full-bodied flavor. Some cuts, for example the upper shank, can be sliced conveniently to leave on the bone as steaks, and a few meaty tips of rib are also trimmed from the shoulder. As with most tough meats, marinating of shoulder cuts improves texture and flavor before braising or stewing.

USEFUL INFORMATION

Portion *With bone:* ¾ lb/375 g. *Without bone:* ½ lb/250 g.
US cuts *Whole:* arm pot-roast; cross rib pot-roast; shoulder pot-roast; flat ribs; short ribs; neck pot-roast; blade pot-roast; top blade pot-roast; under blade pot-roast. *Pieces or cubed:* chuck steak; blade steak; arm steak; short ribs; shank steak.
UK cuts *Whole:* blade roast; chuck roast; back rib roast; thick rib roast; shin; knuckle. *Pieces/ cubed:* neck or sticking; clod; chuck steak; blade steak; short ribs; shin steak.
French cuts *Whole:* jumeaux; plat de côtes découvertes; paleron; macreuse; gîte or jarret; crosse. *Pieces or cubed:* collier; plat de côtes découvertes; macreuse; gîte or jarret.

RIB

Considered by many cooks to be the finest beef cut for roasting, the rib cut includes from four to seven ribs and can be cooked whole or divided into two or three smaller parts. The lower ribs, containing the large eye muscle, are superior to the upper ribs nearer the neck where the muscle is divided, but all the meat is top quality. Rib is best cooked on the bone so the meat stays moist. It looks good and makes excellent large lean steaks. Boned rib roast is also known as rib eye, while rib steaks are known as rib, rib eye, or most commonly by their French name *entrecôte*. When the ribs are trimmed, a braising cut of short ribs (Fr. *plat de côtes couvertes*) is formed. Because of the rib bones, carving a rib roast requires a special technique (see right).

USEFUL INFORMATION

Portion *With bone:* ¾ lb/375 g. *Without bone:* ½ lb/250 g.
US cuts *Whole:* rib roast; rib eye roast; short ribs; back ribs. *Pieces:* rib steak; rib eye steak.
UK cuts *Whole:* rib roast; short ribs. *Pieces:* rib steak.
French cuts *Whole:* côte. *Pieces:* entrecôte.

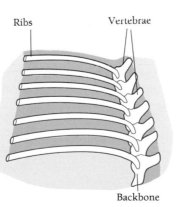

Ribs   Vertebrae

Backbone

CARVING A RIB ROAST

To simplify carving, the chine bone (part of the backbone) at the base of the ribs should be removed by the butcher.

For a 2-3 rib roast:

1 Set the meat upright and, holding it steady with a two-pronged fork, cut away the rib bones at the base.

2 Turn the meat on to its side and carve it into diagonal slices across the grain. The slices may be thin or thick, whichever you prefer.

For a 4-7 rib roast:

1 Hold the meat steady with a two-pronged fork and cut along the rib bones to remove them completely.

2 Set the meat on a board, boned side down, and cut vertically to form thick or thin slices, whichever you prefer.

Hungarian beef stew

Gulyás

This stew includes potatoes so no accompaniment is needed, though small dumplings or *spätzle* (p.339) may be added.

Serves 4

1 tbsp oil	2 tomatoes, peeled, seeded and chopped
2 oz/60 g piece smoked bacon, cut in lardons (p.249)	1 green bell pepper, cored, seeded and sliced
1½ lb/750 g onions, chopped	
2 tbsp paprika	1 lb/500 g potatoes, peeled and cut in 1 in/2.5 cm dice
1½ lb/750 g lean beef for stewing	
2 cloves garlic	4-6 small hot red cherry peppers, trimmed (optional)
¼ tsp caraway seeds	
2 cups/500 ml water	salt and pepper

1 Heat the oven to 350°F/175°C. In a casserole, heat the oil and fry the bacon lardons until lightly browned and their fat is rendered. Stir in the onions, cover and cook over very low heat, stirring often, until very soft and transparent, at least 20 minutes. Stir in the paprika and cook for 2 minutes longer.
2 Meanwhile, trim the beef and cut it in 1½ in/4 cm cubes. Finely chop the garlic with the caraway seeds. Stir the beef and garlic into the onions with the water. No seasoning is needed at this stage.
3 Cover and cook in the oven until the beef is tender, for 1½-2 hours. If the onions start to stick, add more water.
4 Add the tomatoes, green pepper and potatoes, with cherry peppers, if using. Season to taste with salt, adding black pepper if you like. Cover and continue cooking until the potatoes are tender and the meat is very soft, 20-30 minutes. Taste the stew again; it should be thick and rich. If adding small dumplings or *spätzle*, drop them into the stew a few minutes before serving, keeping the lid on to let them cook through properly.

LOIN

The loin, stretching from the ribs almost to the end of the backbone, is the source of many delicious cuts. Underneath it lies the tenderloin or fillet (p.210).

In the United States loin is used almost exclusively for steaks, starting at the rib end with top loin, leading to the T-bone which contains a small nugget of tenderloin, to porterhouse, which has more tenderloin, and finally to sirloin. Sirloin is a large steak (when cut 1 in/2.5 cm thick it will serve two to three people). The muscles in sirloin change shape as slices approach the rear of the animal, but sirloin always includes a small amount of bone. When the tenderloin is removed, the meat lying on top of the backbone can be boned as a long, meaty shell roast, or cut into boneless shell steaks.

In Britain, the whole loin section is called sirloin and is most commonly divided into roasts; the best sirloin roasts include part of the tenderloin. Alternatively, the sirloin may be cut into porterhouse steak (unlike American porterhouse, this is cut near the rib and contains no tenderloin), or made into T-bone and sirloin steaks (these approximate to the American cuts). In France, where boned roasts are preferred, the loin is often boned as *contre-filet*; the same meat can also be cut in steaks.

USEFUL INFORMATION

Portion *With bone:* ¾-1 lb/375-500 g. *Without bone:* ½ lb/250 g.
US cuts *Whole:* sirloin; shell. *Steaks:* top loin (also called club, Delmonico, Kansas City strip, New York strip, shell, sirloin strip, or strip); T-bone; porterhouse; sirloin; minute.
UK cuts *Whole:* sirloin. *Steaks:* porterhouse; sirloin; T-bone.
French cuts *Whole:* contre-filet or faux-filet. *Steaks:* contre-filet or faux-filet.

LEG

Leg or round (USA) of beef is an outstanding source of lean meat with little bone or connective tissue, full flavored and tender, provided it is cooked slowly in moist heat. The meat consists of five muscles that may be cut across or divided along their connective tissue. The way they are cut makes little difference to how they should be cooked. Some cuts, notably the American top round (also called sirloin tip or silver tip), the British top rump, and the French *gîte à la noix* can be roasted at high temperature providing the meat is top quality. As steaks for broiling, however, they will always be chewy. Marinating helps, as does slashing in a shallow lattice pattern to cut across the grain as cube steak (p.195). London broil is also often cut from the leg. Roasts from leg cuts are excellent cold, when they can be very thinly sliced. A steamship roast (USA) encompasses the whole round of the leg and weighs about 80 lb/36 kg. It is usually served at banquets and hotel restaurants.

Leg meat is consistently at its best when braised, pot-roasted, or stewed slowly with plenty of flavorings to make a rich sauce. Alternatively, the meat may be sliced thinly, stuffed and braised as beef rolls, and used for top-quality ground beef. The tougher leg cuts such as the American bottom round and the British silverside are often salted or pickled. Rump, a relatively tender cut in Britain, is a tougher cut in the United States, corresponding to British silverside. The shank (Fr. *jarret* or *gîte*) is always cut off the leg and treated separately. Shank may be braised with the bone, or without for flavoring stocks or consommé.

USEFUL INFORMATION/LEG

Portion *With bone:* ¾-1 lb/375-500 g. *Without bone:* ½ lb/250 g.
US cuts *Whole:* top round; eye round; bottom round or rump; heel of round. *Tip steaks:* top round; bottom round, eye round London broil; minute.

UK cuts *Whole:* silverside; topside; top rump or thick flank. *Aitchbone steaks:* top rump or thick flank; topside.
French cuts *Whole:* aiguillette; aiguillette baronne; tranche grasse; gîte à la noix. *Steaks:* rumsteck.

PLATE

Plate is cut from the lower part of the rib cage. At the brisket end it includes some ribs, but most of it is fatty meat streaked with connective tissue aptly called skirt. Plate must be thoroughly trimmed. It is best simmered or stewed, though the ribs can also be braised. The lower part of the skirt, near the brisket, may be used for pastrami (smoked beef cured with pepper and other spices and garlic) or for corned beef (Preserving, p.489).

USEFUL INFORMATION

Portion *With bone:* ¾-1 lb/375-500 g. *Without bone:* ½ lb/250 g.
US cuts *Whole and pieces:* plate short ribs; plate flank; skirt steak.

UK cuts *Whole and pieces:* flank or skirt.
French cuts Tendron.

FLANK

The flank of beef, running down from the loin, contains tough fibrous meat with a good deal of fat and connective tissue. Most of this meat must be thoroughly trimmed and is good for stewing or grinding. One exception is the small flank steak muscle.

USEFUL INFORMATION

Portion ½ lb/250 g.
US cuts *Cubed or ground:* flank or skirt.

UK cuts *Cubed or ground:* thin flank; skirt.
French cuts *Cubed or ground:* flanchet; bavette.

LONDON BROIL, FLANK STEAK & HANGING TENDERLOIN

Inside the beef flank is hidden flank steak or London broil (USA) (Fr. *onglet*), a stringy muscle with excellent flavor, which benefits from marinating. The whole steak weighs only 2 lb/1 kg, so it can be broiled whole as well as sliced diagonally into steaks or very thin slices for stuffing as rolls. So popular is London broil that imitations are often cut from the tail, the fillet, or the first cut of the top round. They tend to be tougher with less flavor than flank itself. Hanging tenderloin is a little-known cut from the bottom of the flank; it is outstandingly tender, but there is only one from each carcass.

To cook these cuts whole, trim off tough outer skin. Marinate steak for a couple of days if you like. Pat the steak dry with a paper towel and season with salt and pepper. Brush with oil and broil for six to eight minutes on each side so the surface is well-browned. The meat should still be soft when pressed with a fingertip and is always served rare. Mushroom sauce is the traditional accompaniment, together with a baked potato, but in the United States and Mexico, slices of London broil can be wrapped inside a flour tortilla and served with tomatoes.

BRISKET

Brisket is the name given to the front section of beef breast. The ribs and breastbone are always removed, leaving meat that tends to be tough and stringy. It is good boiled, especially with a spicy sauce, and is a useful inexpensive cut for simple dishes such as *pot-au-feu*. The section nearer the plate is more meaty and can be braised or pot-roasted. Brisket requires long, moist cooking to tenderize it and is often salted or cured for corned beef (p.488). In the United States it is the top choice for pastrami.

USEFUL INFORMATION

Portion ½ lb/250 g.
US cut Brisket.
UK cut Brisket.

French cuts Milieu de poitrine; gros bout de poitrine.

SHANK

The shanks of beef near the feet contain the toughest meat in the animal, though they are lean with plenty of taste. On the bone, shank is used to flavor soup, while boned meat is shredded to simmer for clarifying consommé and aspic. Shank or knuckle bones (Fr. *crosse*) are used in beef stock because they contain a great deal of collagen. Some butchers trim further up the shank, cutting meaty steaks with a central bone for braising. The fore-shank is more fleshy than the hind-shank.

USEFUL INFORMATION

Portion *With bone:* ¾ lb/375 g. *Without bone:* 6-8 oz/175-250 g.
US cuts Knuckle; shank bone; shank steak.

UK cuts Knuckle; shin bone; shin steak.
French cuts Crosse; jarret or gîte.

HAMBURGERS

The popularity of hamburgers has become international. To make a good hamburger is simplicity itself: all you need is 6-8 oz/175-250 g coarsely ground beef, more or less lean as you prefer. Leave the meat plain or add finely chopped flavorings such as herbs, capers and onion. Some gourmets add a spoonful of Worcestershire or brown sauce (p.35), but "stretchers" such as breadcrumbs are, strictly speaking, forbidden. Gently form the beef into a ball without crushing it and flatten to a patty 1-1½ in/2.5-4 cm thick. Sprinkle the hamburger with salt and pepper and broil or pan-fry it 4-12 minutes turning it over once, until done to your taste, using high heat to give a crispy, well-browned crust.

Some people prefer their hamburgers seasoned only with salt and pepper, perhaps with a sprinkling of dried herbs. However, for many hamburger devotees, the most important and varied additions come at the end: thickly sliced tomato and sweet onion, dill pickles, and a leaf or two of lettuce. A topping of broiled cheese and a slice of bacon to crown the hamburger are other possibilities, as are chili, avocado slices, mushrooms, and various sauces. You will find up-market hamburgers served with béarnaise sauce (p.61) and broiled hamburgers basted with barbecue sauce. Condiments served with hamburgers include mustard, ketchup, mayonnaise, piccalilli and other relishes. The bun in which the hamburger is served may vary from plain white to wholewheat, sometimes topped with sesame or poppy seeds or onion flakes. Buns should be lightly toasted on the cut side.

VEAL

Veal comes from calves up to six months old, which weigh no more than 200-250 lb/90-110 kg. For good veal, the animal is fed on milk rather than grain to ensure tender, pink meat. Most milk-fed veal comes from three- to four-month-old calves, as older animals have usually started to eat grass, on their way to becoming young cows. The meat of grass-fed veal is darker and coarser, with neither the full-flavored richness of beef nor the delicacy of milk-fed veal. Veal from calves inhumanely reared and doctored with growth stimulants (illegal in some countries) is hard to detect, so a reliable supplier is important.

Because the meat is young and the carcass small, cuts of veal are less distinctive than in other animals. Most cuts are tender and can be cooked in many ways as their connective tissue has not yet toughened. However, given its low fat and high moisture content, freezing may toughen veal. Note, too, that the tissues of cut veal shrink easily, although good butchering will ensure that they are severed as little as possible.

Veal should not be considered as just a youthful version of beef; the character of the two meats is totally different. In cooking, veal, like chicken, absorbs and highlights flavors as diverse as capers, tuna and wild mushrooms. Many veal and chicken recipes are interchangeable. Both meats can be used as the basis of *quenelles* and silky smooth *mousselines* (see Puréeing fish, p.122).

Despite its tenderness, veal is not ideal for cooking over high heat as it has little natural fat. Roasting and broiling must be done with care, and at lower heat than for other meats (see roasting chart, p.199). Braising, pot-roasting or simmering over gentle heat with plenty of moisture, is often a better approach. Larding or barding veal with fat (p.196) is helpful, but marinating (p.195) is usually restricted to an hour or two.

Veal stock sets to a firm jelly, and is the basis for many fine, glossy sauces. Calf's feet are often added to other meat casseroles to enrich the sauce. This is because the collagen in the connective tissue and bones of the veal dissolves to gelatin in moist heat.

VEAL: SEGMENTS OF THE CARCASS

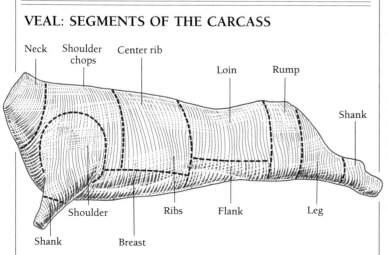

A calf can be divided into eleven segments, each with certain cooking characteristics. These segments do not always correspond to retail cuts. See also Veal cuts (p.202).

USEFUL INFORMATION

Season Year-round, best in summer months.

How to choose Clear, light pink meat with a fine grain; fat will be sparse, but look for shiny membrane and connective tissue; bones should be white or pink; avoid dry or brown spots, reddish or gray meat; wet packaging shows the meat was frozen.

Storage *Whole cut:* refrigerate 2-3 days; freeze 6 months. *Escalopes, ground:* refrigerate 2 days; freeze 3 months.

Cooking methods *Whole cut:* braise or pot-roast at 350°F/175°C, 25 minutes per 1 lb/500 g; roast (p.199). *Chops and ribs:* bake at 350°F/175°C, ¾-1 hour; braise or stew at 350°F/175°C, 1-1½ hours; broil (p.197); marinate 1-2 hours; pan-fry or sauté (p.198); simmer 1-1½ hours. *Cubed:* braise or stew at 350°F/175°C, 1-1½ hours; cook as sauté ¾-1 hour; simmer 1-1½ hours.

Scaloppine ai carciofi (escalopes with artichoke bottoms, Italy)

When done *Whole cut:* braise or pot-roast until tender when pierced with two-pronged fork; roast to 160°F/70°C on meat thermometer. *Pieces:* broiled or pan-fried, meat resists when pressed and juices form drops on surface; baked, braised, simmered, steamed or stewed, falls easily from two-pronged fork. *Cubed:* falls easily from two-pronged fork.

GROUND MEAT

Given their versatility and low cost, it is no wonder that ground beef, lamb, pork and veal are so popular, appearing in staples such as British mince, American hamburgers, Italian Bolognese sauce, Texas chili and Mexican tacos. Ground meat is also used in stuffings for vegetables, in fillings with herbs, eggs and bread-crumbs, and for meatloaf. In the Middle East, ground meat is mixed with grains to make stuffings and deep-fried dishes such as lamb *kibbeh*, in which spiced mincemeat is wrapped around a mixture of cooked mincemeat, onions and pine nuts. Meatballs come in many guises: in Italy as *polpettine*, served with a white wine and caper sauce; and in Germany and Austria as *klopsen* with sour cream and sauerkraut.

Different cuts of meat yield different qualities of ground meat. For beef, cuts from the leg, such as round, are lean and may dry out on high heat. Chuck and other cuts from the beef shoulder are fattier and have a richer flavor. Less expensive ground meat from the neck or flank is likely to include more connective tissue which, even when ground, toughens the meat. For other meats, the cut used for grinding is less important. The more freshly ground meat is, the better; if possible buy a whole piece and have it ground by the butcher or do it yourself at home. Ground meat begins to deteriorate within a few hours and should not be stored in the refrigerator for more than two days. Tightly wrapped and frozen it can be kept for up to two months.

Quick coarse grinding is best for most dishes since the process tends to heat and bruise the meat. However, a finer texture may be needed for forcemeats or smooth pâtés. A hand or electric grinder cuts meats satisfactorily, and coarseness may be varied according to the disk used. On an electric grinder, the pulse button helps to control the speed. For the best results, chop the meat by hand using a large chef's knife. First cut the meat into cubes, then continue to chop until you reach the consistency you want.

USEFUL INFORMATION/VEAL

Typical dishes *Holsteiner schnitzel* (escalopes breaded and sautéed with eggs and anchovies, Germany); *parmigiana* (breaded escalopes with mozzarella cheese and tomato sauce, Italy); *wiener schnitzel* (breaded escalopes, Austria); *paprikaschnitzel* (breaded escalopes with paprika, Austria); *escalopes a la zíngara* (escalopes in sherry, Spain); *jägarschnitzel* (minced escalopes with mushroom sauce, Sweden); *scaloppine al Marsala* (escalopes with Marsala, Italy); *saltimbocca* (escalopes with prosciutto, Italy); *ternera con Coñac* (escalopes sautéed with olives and brandy, Spain); Clementine (breaded escalopes with bacon, lemon, capers and wine, Australia); escalopes with cream, Calvados and apple (France); Orloff (sliced roast with cheese and onion sauce, France); roast shoulder with bread stuffing (UK); *bocconcini* (morsels rolled with ham and cheese, Italy); breast stuffed with rice, peas, and mushrooms (Netherlands); breast stuffed with sausages and vegetables (Wales); *osso buco* (braised veal knuckles and shanks with tomatoes, Italy); braised shanks with hominy grits (USA); steak with ham and sweet potatoes (southern USA); *paupiettes de veau Valentino* (veal birds stuffed with asparagus served with tomato sauce, France); *zraziki w sosie* (steaks fried in caper sauce with cream and lemon juice, Poland); *budin de ternera* (ground veal pudding with béchamel or tomato sauce, Spain); *alla valdostana* (thin cutlets stuffed with Fontina and truffles, Italy); *blanquette de veau* (stew with mushrooms and onions in cream sauce, France). *Also good with* butter, cream, shallots, mushrooms, tarragon, rosemary, sage, lemon, ham, Marsala, port, Madeira, white wine, rice pilaf.

SHOULDER (USA, UK), *épaule* (France)

Veal shoulder is less recognizable than that of lamb (p.221) as the shank bone has been removed. The shoulder cut is severed at the shoulder joint and it is often boned to form a rolled roast or cushion roast for stuffing. The whole shoulder is large, weighing 20 lb/9 kg with the bone, so it is usually divided into blade and arm roasts, or into shoulder chops or steaks.

Portion *With bone:* ¾ lb/375 g. *Without bone:* ½ lb/250 g.

SHOULDER CHOPS (USA), middle neck (UK), *côtelettes découvertes* (France)

The French name "uncovered ribs" aptly describes the ribs that are exposed when the shoulder is removed. French butchers usually bone this cut, but it can also be sliced for chops. The meat is of average quality, better braised rather than roasted or broiled.

Portion *With bone:* ¾ lb/375 g. *Without bone:* ½ lb/250 g.

Boning shoulder chops

Shoulder chops are boned in the same way as veal loin (p.216), but they have no fillet meat. A knife must be worked around the neck bones at the upper end of the cut.

Braised, stuffed veal breast

The veal may be served hot or cold. If hot, the cooking juices form a gravy that goes well with glazed carrots and onions. If cold, the juices should be chilled until set, then chopped as decoration. Vinaigrette salad with potato is a good accompaniment.

Serves 6-8

3-4 lb/1.4-1.8 kg veal breast	**For the stuffing**
2 hard-boiled eggs, sliced	1 onion, finely chopped
2 oz/60 g cooked ham, cut in julienne strips	2 tbsp/30 g butter
	1 lb/500 g ground lean veal
1 tbsp oil	1 cup/60 g fresh white breadcrumbs
2 tbsp/30 g butter	
1 onion, quartered	2 cloves garlic, finely chopped
1 carrot, quartered	grated zest of 1 lemon
1 stalk celery, cut in large pieces	2 tbsp chopped parsley
1 cup/250 ml white wine	pinch grated nutmeg
1 qt/1 L veal stock (more if needed)	salt and pepper
	2 eggs, beaten to mix
1 clove garlic, crushed	
bouquet garni	

1 For the stuffing: fry the onion in butter until soft. Stir it into the ground veal, with the breadcrumbs, garlic, lemon zest, parsley, nutmeg, salt and pepper. Stir in the beaten eggs and beat the stuffing for 1-2 minutes until it comes away from the sides of a bowl. Fry a small piece in the pan and taste for seasoning. Heat the oven to 350°F/175°C.
2 Bone the veal breast and butterfly it (see for rolled roast, p.217), reserving the bones. Set the meat, fat side down, season it and spread with the stuffing, leaving a 1 in/2.5 cm border. Top with the sliced eggs, scatter strips of ham over the eggs, roll the veal and tie it in a cylinder (p.196).
3 In a casserole brown the veal in the oil and butter, then remove it and discard all but 2 tablespoons of fat from the pan. Add the vegetables and cook gently until soft, for 5-7 minutes. Add the veal bones and set the meat on top. Add the wine, stock, garlic, bouquet garni, and more salt and pepper.
4 Cover the pan and bring to a boil on top of the stove. Braise in the oven until the meat is tender, 2-2½ hours. Add more stock during cooking if the pan gets dry. Remove the meat, strain the cooking liquid into a saucepan and skim off the fat. If necessary, boil the liquid until well reduced and concentrated. Season to taste. The veal will slice more easily if left, covered, for 15 minutes. Carefully remove the string before slicing.

NECK (USA), scrag end (UK), *collet* (France)

A triangular cut containing neck bones and sinewy meat. Neck must be trimmed well and is usually sold in slices. The meat can also be boned and cut up for stew.

Portion *With bone: 1 lb/500 g. Without bone: 6-8 oz/175-250 g.*

CENTER RIB (USA), best end of neck (UK), *carré* (France)

A prime cut of eye meat lying along the backbone, which makes an outstanding roast, on or off the bone. The cut also provides the best veal chops, with the chine bone and tips of the rib bones trimmed off by the butcher. The exposed bone ends are scraped thoroughly before cooking. Crown roast consists of seven to eight ribs from the center and loin. It is prepared in a similar way to a crown roast of lamb (p.223), but only one set of ribs is used. Crown roast benefits from a moist pork stuffing.

Portion *With bone: ¾ lb/375 g. Without bone: ½ lb/250 g.*

Boning center rib

Center ribs are boned in the same way as veal loin (see below), but they have no fillet meat lying under the bone.

LOIN (USA, UK), *longe* (France)

Loin is a choice cut consisting of eye meat above the backbone and tenderloin, or fillet, below. Often the tenderloin is removed and cut into medallions – rounds of lean meat cut ½-¾ in/1.25-2 cm thick. Loin may be left on the bone but is tricky to carve, so more often it is boned. It may also be cut into chops, before or after boning. Veal saddle is the double loin, which is usually left on the bone and carved in the same way as lamb saddle (p.219).

Portion *With bone: ¾ lb/375 g. Without bone: ½ lb/250 g.*

BONING VEAL LOIN

A whole boned veal loin makes an excellent roast. Alternatively it can be cut into boneless chops.

1 Set the meat, fat side down, on a board. Using a boning knife, strip out the long rib bones.

2 Free the meaty tenderloin lying along the backbone and remove it to slice as medallions.

3 With the tip of the knife, outline the vertebrae. Angle the knife horizontally and continue cutting away the meat from between the bones, scraping them to free the meat in one piece.

4 Insert the knife under the bones so the backbone can be cut away in one piece.

5 Cut away the backbone and trim the fat from the meat.

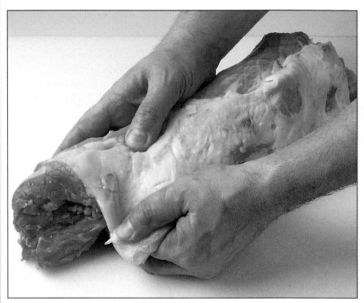

6 ABOVE Trim the flank meat, leaving a 3 in/7.5 cm piece and roll the meat neatly, with the fat on the outside.

7 RIGHT Tie the flank flap in place using separate pieces of string at 1 in/2.5 cm intervals. For boneless chops, cut between the strings.

Preparing veal saddle

See Preparing a lamb saddle (p.219).

RUMP sirloin (USA), fillet (UK), *quasi, culotte* (France)

Names for this portion of the hindquarter vary depending how it is divided up by the butcher. In Britain, and sometimes in the United States, a diagonal cut is made to separate the rump – a plump meaty cut for roasting. Alternatively, the carcass may be cut straight down to the belly as rump or sirloin (USA), fillet (UK), and *quasi* (France). In France a small cut, the *culotte*, is taken from the tip of the backbone, including part of the leg meat. All these cuts are best rolled for roasting or pot-roasting, or cut into chops.

Portion *With bone: ¾ lb/375 g. Without bone: ½ lb/250 g.*

LEG (USA, UK), *cuisseau* (France)

Excellent roasts come from the leg of veal, which divides into three main muscles. The eye round (USA), cushion or topside (UK), or *noix* (France) comes from the inside leg. On the outside of the carcass is the top round (USA), silverside (UK), or *sousnoix* (France), a tougher, coarser cut. Lastly, under the lower leg lies the bottom round (USA), thick flank (UK), or *noix pâtissière* (France) – the choicest cut, together with the eye. All these cuts are boneless and should be barded and tied for roasting.

The leg is also the source for escalopes (p.218). From the bottom round or the top round come *grenadins*, neat rounds formed by slitting the muscle lengthwise, then cutting it into ¾ in/ 2 cm slices. In the United States, veal leg may also be butchered by slicing across to include bone as shank roast, plus round and rump roasts and steaks, but this method of cutting veal leg is less satisfactory as the meat tends to shrink badly

Portion *With bone: ¾-1 lb/375-500 g. Without bone: ½ lb/250 g.*

FLANK (USA, UK), *flanchet* (France)

This is the flap of belly meat running down from the sirloin. It is a thin, meaty cut with much connective tissue but no bone and should be thoroughly trimmed. The flank can be rolled and tied, sometimes with a filling, to braise, or cubed for stewing. The flank is also good for ground veal.

Portion *Without bone: ½ lb/250 g.*

BREAST (USA, UK), *poitrine* (France)

This cut contains the breastbone, together with ribs, some of them cartilagenous rather than bony. The breast has a generous amount of fat as well as connective tissue so it is a rich cut for braising or simmering, especially in white stews such as *blanquette*. The meat can be stuffed, with or without bones, or cut in strips.

Portion *With bone: 1 lb/500 g. Without bone: ½ lb/250 g.*

BONING VEAL BREAST

Breast may be partially boned, leaving the rib bones, then stuffed as a cushion roast, or cut in strips. Alternatively, the rib bones are removed, and the meat rolled and stuffed, or cut in cubes.

5 **For cushion roast:** starting from the cavity left by the breastbone, cut deep pockets into the meat on either side. Fill each pocket with stuffing, pressing it in so the meat is plump.

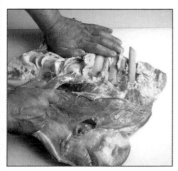

1 To remove the ribs, set the meat bone side up. Outline the bones using the point of a sharp knife.

2 With the back edge of a heavy knife or cleaver, pound sharply between each rib bone to separate the meat from the bones.

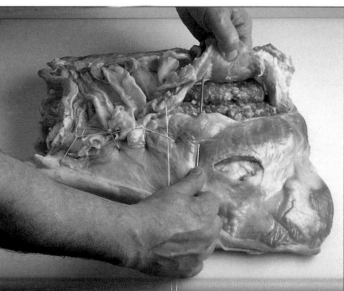

6 With a trussing needle and string, sew the edges of the breast meat together to make a cushion roast.

3 Cut the cartilage joining the rib bones to the breastbone and remove the bones, one by one.

4 Cut around the breastbone, keeping the knife close to the bone; then cut and pull the bone free and remove it.

For rolled roast: butterfly the breast by slitting each end of the cavities and opening out the meat. Spread the stuffing lengthwise on the meat, then roll and tie (p.196) to form a long thin roll for roasting.

RIBS (USA, UK), *haut de côtes* (France)

A narrow section cut from the rib cage, lined with bones containing a great deal of connective tissue. The bones are easy to strip out. The meat that is left after boning resembles breast meat and is cooked in the same way. Often this cut is included with the breast, almost doubling its size.

Portion *With bone:* 1 lb/500 g. *Without bone:* ½ lb/250 g.

SHANK (USA), shin (UK), *jarret* (France)

The upper portion of the shank is surrounded by a good deal of meat, particularly on the hind legs. It makes a neat tasty cut for braising, and is used thickly sliced in the Italian dish *osso buco*, when the marrow inside the bone is revealed. Thinner 1 in/2.5 cm slices are called steaks. The knuckle end of shanks (Fr. *crosse*) are usually cut off to make stock or soup.

Portion *With bone:* ¾-1 lb/375-500 g. *Without bone:* ½ lb/250 g.

VEAL ESCALOPE

The most popular of all veal cuts, a good veal escalope or paillard (It. *scaloppine*, Ger. *schnitzel*) is milk-fed, pearly pink, and cut across the meat grain so it is tender. The best veal escalope comes from the eye round and bottom round flank muscles of the leg, but demand is such that escalopes are also cut from the top round, and even from the shoulder. Such escalopes are often seamed with connective tissue and can be tough if not cut across the meat grain. They should be lightly pounded to tenderize (p.195). Escalopes deteriorate rapidly and are best eaten within a day.

Good veal escalope is extraordinarily versatile. It can be floured or breaded and fried in butter. It is well-suited to stuffing, whether flat as in veal cordon bleu, or rolled as veal birds (Fr. *paupiettes*). Less tender escalopes are best cooked briefly in a sauce, or as a sauté. Escalopes can be steamed, baked *en papillote*, or cut in slivers to stir-fry. Whatever the method, cooking should be brief so the meat does not become dry.

Escalope goes a long way – a portion of 4-6 oz/125-175 g serves one person and there is no waste, though the cut is costly. Given all these advantages, it is no wonder that imitation veal escalopes are cut from chicken and turkey breasts. Pork tenderloin is sometimes used for smaller and thinner *scaloppine*, and can be a pleasant substitute for the real thing.

CUTTING VEAL ESCALOPES

The thickness of an escalope can vary from ⅛-⅜ in/3 mm-1 cm, but it should be at least 5 in/12.5 cm at its widest. Trim the meat of all fat and sinew (the thin connective tissue). Cut diagonally across the muscle to give the largest possible slices, cutting across the grain of the meat. Put the escalope between two sheets of plastic or wax paper. With a rolling pin or cleaver, lightly pound to flatten and tenderize it (see Cutting turkey escalopes, p.186).

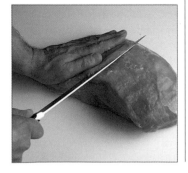

LAMB

Smaller than beef and pork, a full-grown lamb of about eight months old rarely weighs more than 115 lb/52 kg. The meat is so tender that almost all cuts may be roasted, even when the animal is mature. Lamb is eaten at many stages of growth, starting with milk-fed baby lamb under three months old. They are often roasted whole, or cut into large pieces such as baron of lamb. Most of the meat on the international market is spring lamb, sold when three to nine months old. After this time it is known as a yearling, plain lamb, or winter lamb. Mutton from older animals, over two years, is quite rare in retail markets; it should be braised or stewed to keep the meat tender.

The flavor of the meat depends on pasturage, so that salt marsh lamb and mountain lamb (grazed on herbal ground cover) are particular delicacies. The older the animal, the stronger the taste: baby lamb is mild and subtly piquant, spring lamb is sweet, while mutton has a gamey taste. If reheated, or if the outer skin (fell) is not completely removed, lamb can have an unpleasantly strong flavor. Lamb and mutton can be commercially frozen incurring little harm; in fact a great deal of lamb is produced in New Zealand and frozen for export. The size of lamb cuts varies enormously; a leg of milk-fed lamb obviously serves fewer than that of a six-month-old animal. Portions given with the following cuts are therefore approximate.

SEGMENTS OF THE CARCASS

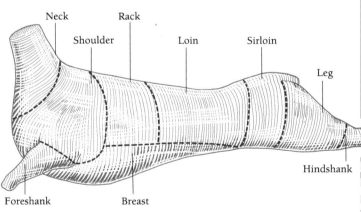

A lamb can be divided into eight segments that do not always correspond to retail cuts. See Lamb cuts (p.204). Each has certain cooking characteristics.

USEFUL INFORMATION

Season *Baby lamb:* early winter to spring. *Spring lamb:* spring to autumn. *Yearling, Mutton:* year-round.

How to choose *Baby lamb:* bones tiny, meat light pink and moist, resembling veal. *Spring lamb:* white fat, generous marbling, meat deep pink not red. *Yearling, mutton:* fat creamy, not dry, meat dark and firm-grained, generously marbled.

Nutritive value See Lamb cuts, p.204.

Cooking methods *Whole cut:* braise or pot-roast at 350°F/175°C, 20 minutes per 1 lb/500 g; marinate 2-3 days; roast (p.199). *Chops, ribs, steaks:* bake at 350°F/175°C, ¾-1 hour for well-done meat; barbecue or broil (p.197); braise or stew at 350°F/175°C, 1¼/1¾ hours; marinate 12-24 hours; pan-fry or sauté (p.198); stir-fry 1-2 minutes. *Cubed:* braise or stew at 350°F/175°C, 1¼-1¾ hours; cook as sauté ¾-1 hour.

When done *Whole cut:* roast to 125°F/51°C on meat thermometer for rare, 140°F/60°C for medium-done, 160°F/70°C for well-done; braise or pot-roast until tender when pierced with two-pronged fork; boil until very tender when pierced with fork. *Chops, ribs, steaks:* broil or pan-fry until springy when pressed with finger for medium-done lamb, firm for well-done; bake, braise, or stew until meat falls easily from two-pronged fork. *Cubed:* falls easily from fork.
Processed forms Smoked (Scandinavia); frozen.

Storage *Whole cut or pieces:* refrigerate 2-4 days, freeze 9 months. *Ground:* refrigerate 2 days, freeze 3 months.
Typical dishes *Gigot bretonne* (roast leg with dried beans, France); roast leg with mint sauce (UK); shoulder with sour cream sauce (Scandinavia); Northumbrian duck (shoulder boned and stuffed to resemble duck, UK); *printanier* (with spring vegetables, France); *braise d'agneau à la chicorée* (stew with Belgian endives, Belgium); Lancashire hot pot (casserole with kidneys and oysters, UK).

2 Run the knife along the backbone, cutting and scraping to release the tenderloin but leaving it attached to the skin.

3 Slide the knife under the ends of the vertebrae and cut around to sever them from the meat. When the tip of the backbone is reached, do not cut any further.

LOIN (USA, UK), *côte*, *filet* (France)

The loin, which is often divided into chops, lies along the back of the lamb. It consists of the eye muscle and, at the hindquarters, the tenderloin lying under the characteristic T-shaped bone. The kidneys are sometimes included in English chump chops. In France, the loin includes up to 13 vertebrae and is divided into *côte*, and *filet* (including the *filet-mignon* under the bone). Loin can be left on the bone, or boned as a roast. The saddle of lamb is the double loin joined along the backbone; a short saddle, without chops, forms the best roast. In the United States and Britain, the saddle is sometimes sliced as butterfly chops. A baron, the traditional grand roast, consists of the entire hindquarters, meaning the double loin and both legs. For how to bone a lamb loin, see Boning veal loin (p.216).

Portion With bone: 3/4-1 lb/375-500 g. *Without bone:* 1/2 lb/250 g.

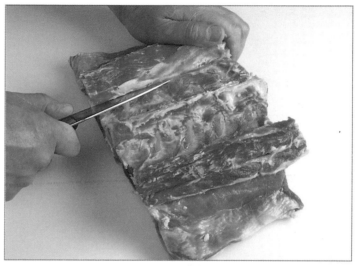

4 Repeat on the other side to expose all the vertebrae. Scrape the meat from under the backbone to loosen it, without piercing the skin.

SIRLOIN (USA), fillet or chump (UK), *selle* (France)

A narrow cut from the lower back, found mainly in France. In the United States and Britain, this cut is often divided between loin and leg. In France the *selle* forms the classic saddle roast, one of the most luxurious of all cuts. Noisettes (or medallions) are sliced from the meat after boning and tying. For boning lamb sirloin, see Boning a pork sirloin (p.227).

Portion With bone: 3/4 lb/375 g. *Without bone:* 1/2 lb/250 g.

5 Press down with your hand and pull out the backbone.

6 Roll the flank flaps over the tenderloin and eye meat.

PREPARING A LAMB SADDLE

For boning use a fillet or short saddle, sometimes sold with kidneys. Saddle can also be roasted on the bone.

1 Set the lamb on a board, skin side up, with flank flaps spread out. Trim the flank flaps to 6 in/15 cm and all but a thin layer of fat.

7 RIGHT Finally, tie the saddle in shape with string.

Note The technique for carving lamb saddle on the bone is the same as for carving saddle of venison on the bone (p.238). Serve diners with slices of eye and fillet meat, as well as a piece of crisp fat from the flank.

PREPARING LAMB NOISETTES

Noisettes are ¾ in/2 cm slices cut from a boned rolled sirloin, tenderloin, or short saddle (below). Six to eight noisettes can be cut to serve three to four people. There are two methods for preparing noisettes: the first is to cut the boned saddle meat in half with the flank flap and roll it; the second is to cut out the eye muscle and slice it.

Method 1

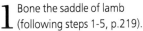

1 Bone the saddle of lamb (following steps 1-5, p.219).

2 RIGHT Cut the meat in half and roll each flank flap around the tenderloin and eye meat.

3 To secure the roll, tie the meat at ¾ in/2 cm intervals with string. For noisettes, cut between the strings. Flatten each noisette slightly with the flat of a heavy knife before cooking.

Method 2

1 This gives smaller, leaner noisettes. Bone the saddle of lamb (following steps 1-5, p.219). Remove the tenderloin.

2 RIGHT Cut off the flank flap, leaving only the eye meat. Trim the fat around the eye meat and cut away the sinew from the edge of the meat. **Note** Some cooks prefer to remove all the fat.

3 Cut the eye meat at 1 in/2.5 cm intervals, into noisettes.

4 Flatten the noisettes lightly with the flat of a heavy knife.

BREAST (USA, UK), *poitrine* (France)

This is one half of the belly of lamb, running down from the rack. The breast is a flat, triangular cut tender enough to roast. It is spiked with a dozen or so ribs, some cartilagenous rather than bony. The bones may be removed and the meat should be well trimmed of fat and cartilage. Often a pocket is cut in the breast for stuffing. With or without bone, the breast may be cut in riblets (each containing a piece of breastbone) or strips for stewing. An *épigramme* is a piece of the breast together with a boned chop, breaded and pan-fried in butter or broiled. Created in eighteenth-century France, it is rarely seen on menus today. For roasting or stewing, breast of lamb needs thorough cooking so that the connective tissue breaks down, making the meat tender.

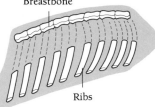

Breastbone

Ribs

Portion *With bone: ¾-1 lb/375-500 g. Without bone: ½ lb/250 g.*

BONING A LAMB BREAST

Lamb breast may be boned and a pocket cut to stuff and sew as a cushion roast. Alternatively, the boned meat may be rolled in a cylinder and tied, or cut in strips for stewing.

1 Set the meat on a board, fat side up. Cut off the skin and trim all but a thin layer of fat.

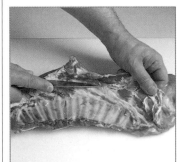

2 Turn the meat over. Lift the flap of meat lying along the bones and with a knife loosen the meat, without severing it.

3 Run the knife along the end of the rib bones to loosen the meat. Cut until the bones are separated, scraping the bones so the meat stays in one piece.

4 RIGHT Remove and discard the bones. Trim the meat, cutting away the thin layer of connective tissue and any excess fat.

Note Cut a pocket for stuffing by slitting the meat along the breastbone side, holding your hand flat on the meat to guide the knife.

SHOULDER (USA, UK); *épaule* (France)

The meat is sweet and streaked with fat. In France, the cut contains only the shoulder blade and foreleg; in Britain and the United States, rib bones may be included. It always contains the blade and two arm bones. For roasting, at least two bones should be removed. If completely boned it can be rolled or stuffed. Mock duck is made from boned shoulder, leaving the shank bone.

Portion *With bone: ¾ lb/375 g. Without bone: ½ lb/250 g.*

BONING LAMB SHOULDER

Boning leaves a convenient pocket for stuffing as a cushion roast. Alternatively, after boning, the shoulder can be rolled, with or without stuffing, into a cylinder. The position of the three shoulder bones depends on which side of the carcass they come from. In some countries, part of the shank is removed already.

1 Set shoulder on a board, meat side up. If some rib bones and backbone are included (UK and US cuts), cut around them until the shoulder joint is located. Sever it, detaching the bones.

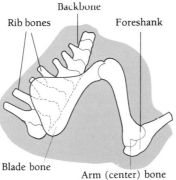

Backbone
Rib bones   Foreshank
Blade bone   Arm (center) bone

2 Turn the shoulder fat side up and pull off any skin, cutting away with a knife where necessary. Trim most of the fat, leaving a ¼ in/6 mm layer.

3 Turn the shoulder, meat-side up. With a sharp knife, make a slit on the far side of the shoulder from the shank bone. With the point of the knife, trace around the triangular blade bone.

4 Cut and scrape the meat from the surface of the blade bone to expose it, until you reach the joint.

5 Sever the joint by pulling it apart with your hands so that the blade bone can be removed.

6 Strip out the blade bone by holding the end and pulling it sharply toward you.

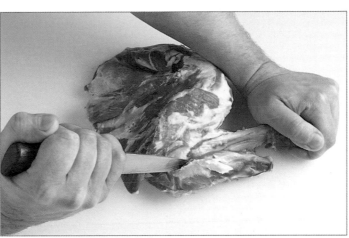

7 Turn the shoulder around and cut along the shank bone to expose it. Scrape the meat free from the bone.

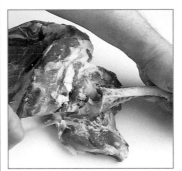

8 With the point of the knife, find the joint connecting the shank bone to the center (arm) bone, and cut through it. Remove the shank bone and discard it.

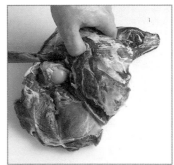

9 Remove the center bone "tunnel" style: cut the tendons around each end of the bone to expose the ends. Carefully scrape the bone clean, working from each end until it can be pulled out.

10 Pull out the center bone by grasping it at the large end. A pocket will be left inside the meat that may be enlarged with a knife for stuffing. The trimmed meat may be cut up for stew.

NECK (US, UK), collet (France)

This cut is similar in all three countries. In Britain, neck is divided into middle neck and the aptly named scrag end. Neck is full-flavored but tough, consisting of vertebrae surrounded by lean meat and connective tissue. Usually sliced, neck is occasionally boned to stuff, and is a splendid cut for stews and soups.

Portion *With bone:* ¾ lb/375 g. *Without bone:* ½ lb/250 g.

RACK (USA), best end of neck (UK), carré (France)

The upper ribs, which in French cuts run as far as the neck, include seven to nine ribs. Roasted whole, the rack forms a small roast containing lean meat. The spiked line of ribs is decorative and is often shaped into a crown roast, or a "guard of honor", which is two racks interlinked (opposite page). For chops, cut between the rib bones. The best chops, one rib thick, are cut from here, also in the United States single or double rib chops.

Portion *With bone:* ¾-1 lb/375-500 g.

CARVING RACK OF LAMB

A single rack, or rib roast, can be cut into chops and served simply, with accompanying vegetables.

1 Set the rack on a carving board, ribs upward. Cut down between each rib, or between every two ribs.

2 Arrange the cutlets on a plate with the ribs fanning upward. Add a cutlet frill if you like.

PREPARING RACK

Whether for roasting or slicing as chops, rack must be thoroughly trimmed. In some countries, the butcher will remove the chine bone (backbone) holding the rib bones together. If it has not been removed, chop it off before starting to prepare the rack. After cooking, bones may be crowned with a cutlet frill. A single rack serves two to three people with a generous portion of three ribs each. For roasting, leave the rack whole and for a more spectacular presentation, use two racks to form a guard of honor or a crown. For chops, cut down between the bones in even slices.

5 Turn the rack over. Place it over the edge of the board and, with a sharp knife, score down to the bone about 2 in/5 cm from the tips of the rib bones.

1 Holding meat vertically, cut off the chine bone with a cleaver, using short sharp strokes.

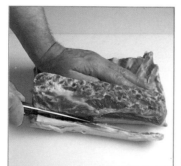

2 Set the meat on a board, ribs upward, and cut out the sinew lying under the ribs.

3 Cut away the small crescent of cartilage at one end; pull off the thin layer of skin over the fat.

4 Score the fat and meat down to the rib bones, about 2 in/5 cm from the end of the bones.

6 Cut out the meat between the bones and scrape the bones very clean with a knife.

7 RIGHT Turn the rack over and cut away the layer of meat and fat. Scrape the meat from the bones removing all traces of skin. If necessary, trim bone ends with a cleaver (p.504).

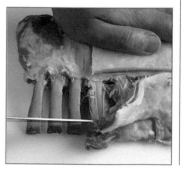

SHAPING RACK OF LAMB

Two racks of lamb can be shaped into either a guard of honor roast or a crown roast. Both usually serve six people.

A guard of honor (below) is shaped from two racks tied back to back with the fat on the outside. Set the racks on a board, bones interlinked, tie and knot a piece of string around the rack, between each set of bones, to hold the roast together. Cover the rib bone ends with aluminum foil during roasting to prevent them from charring. To carve the roast, discard the trussing strings and cut down between each rib on either side.

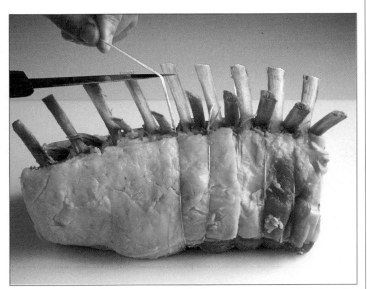

A crown roast (below), shaped from two racks, is ideal for stuffing. However, this prevents the meat from roasting evenly, so it is best to cook meat and stuffing separately and to add the stuffing after cooking.

1 Prepare two racks. Slit the membrane between the ribs so that the racks can be bent round into the crown shape.

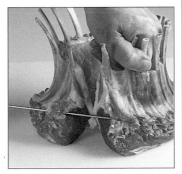

2 Set the pieces end to end. Sew the ends together loosely on the rib side with a stitch, using a trussing needle and string. Curve the bones in a circle, rib outwards, then sew the ends together.

3 LEFT Loop a piece of string around the meat to hold it in shape. To carve the meat, discard the trussing strings and cut down between the rib bones.

Stuffed crown roast of lamb

An alternative to filling the crown with rice pilaf would be a bulghur wheat pilaf or glazed baby vegetables (p.263).

Serves 6

2 trimmed racks of lamb, 1½-2 lb/ 750 g-1 kg each	75 g raisins, ½ cup/75 g pine nuts (follow method for Currant and pistachio pilaf, p.315)
2 cloves garlic, cut in slivers	
1-2 tbsp olive oil	**For the gravy**
salt and pepper	1 cup/250 ml white wine
1 tbsp dried rosemary	1 cup/250 ml veal stock
rice pilaf, made with 1½ cups/ 300 g rice, 2 tbsp oil, 1 onion, 3 cups/750 ml light veal stock or water, salt and pepper, ½ cup/	**For the garnish**
	14-16 paper cutlet frills (optional)
	1 bunch watercress

1 Heat the oven to 400°F/200°C. Shape and tie the lamb as a crown roast. Slit the meat and stud it with garlic; set it in a roasting pan. Spoon over the oil and sprinkle with salt, pepper, and rosemary. Roast the meat in the oven for 30-35 minutes to 125°F/51°C on a meat thermometer for rare lamb, and for 40-45 minutes, to 140°F/60°C, for medium-cooked lamb. Meanwhile, cook the rice pilaf and keep it warm.

2 Transfer the cooked roast to a serving dish and keep it warm while you make the gravy. Remove as much fat as possible from the pan, then add the wine and boil until reduced by half, stirring to deglaze the juices (p.513). Add the stock, bring to a boil and strain. Season to taste.

3 Remove the strings from the lamb and pile the rice pilaf in the center of the crown. Decorate the bones with cutlet frills and the platter with watercress if you wish. Serve the gravy separately.

LEG (USA, UK), *gigot* (France)

Possibly the most popular cut, leg of lamb offers plenty of lean meat. There are differences worldwide: in the United States and Britain, part of the backbone from the sirloin is often included, adding more lean meat. In the United States, the shank bone may be removed and the surrounding meat tucked under to give a cushion appearance. Another alternative is to divide the leg in half as shank, and sirloin or fillet end, forming two small roasts. The sirloin end can also be sliced crosswise into steaks (with bone) or escalopes (boneless), and the firmer shank end cut up for stewing.

Portion *With bone: ¾-1 lb/375-500 g. Without bone: ½ lb/250 g.*

BONING LEG OF LAMB

Leg of lamb is boned to tie as a boneless roast, with or without stuffing, or to slit open and butterfly. The partial boning of a leg, removing the pelvic bone, will make carving easier. The knobbly end of the shank bone can also be trimmed, leaving enough bone to hold the roast steady for carving.

Tarsal Aitchbone bone

Hindshank

Leg (center) bone

Hip bone

1 Steady the joint with your hand. Tear off the skin (you may get a better grip with a cloth), cutting where necessary with a knife. Trim any fat from the meat.

2 The pelvic bone is made up of the aitchbone and hip bone. It is an irregular-shaped bone running at an angle to the leg bone, and attached to it by a ball and socket joint. To loosen it, place the leg on a board, pelvic bone upward. With a sharp knife outline the edges of the bone that are exposed at the sirloin end.

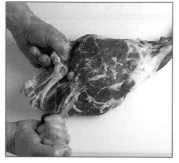 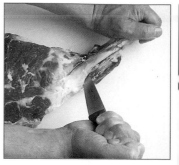

3 Cut deeper around the pelvic bone, freeing it at the joint and cutting through the tendons connecting it to the leg bone. Remove the bone.

4 Grasp the shank bone at the tip of the leg and cut all tendons at the base of the bone. Cut the meat away from the bone, keeping the meat on the other side in one piece.

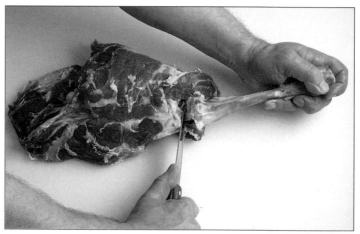

5 When the bone is clean, locate the knee joint at the point where the shank bone is connected to the leg bone. Cut the tendons at the joint and remove the shank bone.

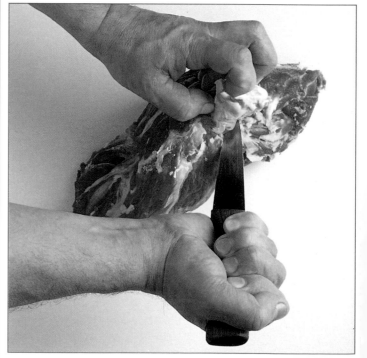

6 Now only the leg bone remains in the center of the meat and is removed "tunnel" fashion, by gently releasing each end from the meat.

7 Cut and scrape to clean the bone, easing it out as you work.

8 Twist the bone and pull it out. With a small knife scrape the tendons one by one from the meat.

BUTTERFLYING LEG OF LAMB

Leg of lamb, particularly when small, is butterflied, boned, and spread flat for barbecueing or broiling. First bone the leg, following the instructions on the opposite page.

1 Keeping the blade of the knife horizontal, partially slit open the cavity left by the leg bone. Turn the flap outward, like the page of a book and spread the meat flat.

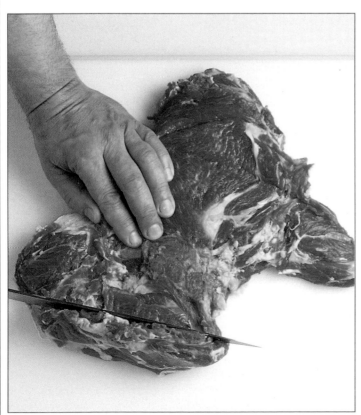

2 Working from the center, make a similar horizontal cut in the thick muscle opposite, so that it can be opened out flat.

CARVING LEG OF LAMB ON THE BONE

There are several ways in which to carve a leg of lamb. If the pelvic bone is included with the leg, cut it out before cooking (steps 2-3, opposite). For all methods, slices should be about ¼ in/6 mm thick.

Method 1 This will give large slices of meat that are progressively rare near the bone.

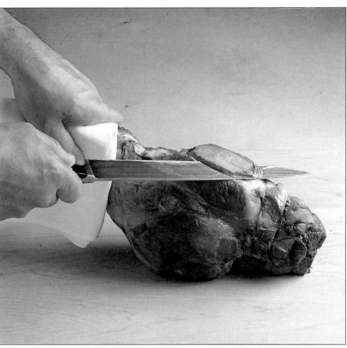

1 Hold the leg by the shank, rounded muscle upward. Cut horizontal slices lengthwise, until you reach the thigh bone.

2 Turn the leg over and set the cut side flat on the board. Carve horizontal slices on this side of the bone. Finally, carve slices from the meat that is left next to the bone.

Method 2 Leg of lamb can also be carved like ham (p.252). With this method, there is a more even distribution of well-done and rare meat, with crisp outside and center meat in each slice.

SHANK (USA, UK), *gîte* (France)

Shank is a popular cheap cut for country stews. The hind or fore shank is the piece left when the shoulder or leg is cut up for chops and steaks. The foreshank, particularly, is well-flavored, even though full of stringy connective tissue. Shank can be boned out to use for stew or ground meat, or braised like veal shank (p.218). The best shank is from a young, lean animal.

Portion *With bone:* 1 lb/500 g.

PORK

Of all the animals we eat, the pig is the one that has stimulated the ingenuity of man. Primarily, it is economical, producing more edible meat in relation to feeding costs than any other domestic animal. Virtually every bit of the carcass is edible. On a "baconer", an animal that is commercially bred for its fat flanks, more than half of the meat is converted into ham, bacon, sausages, and other charcuterie items.

Pigs are generally killed at about eight months old, when the carcass weighs from 150-160 lb/68-73 kg. It is heartening that despite the advent of freezing, the preservation of pork by salting, smoking and drying is still unassailed. Leg of pork, one of the finest cuts for roasting, is often cured as ham. The fattier bits of belly, the hocks, even the cheeks, which in most animals are low-grade cuts, also cure well.

All the cuts are relatively tender, so there is no need for a formal, detailed grading system such as that for beef. However, pork can harbor the worms that cause the disease trichinosis. Contamination is now less common, but nonetheless, pork should always be cooked until its juices run clear and are no longer pink. The internal temperature of a roast must reach 170°F/75°C on a meat thermometer.

Despite its layers of fat, pork dries out easily since the fat encircles the flesh rather than marbling it. Pork therefore is well suited to braising or simmering; if roasted or broiled it should be cooked relatively slowly and basted often.

SEGMENTS OF THE CARCASS

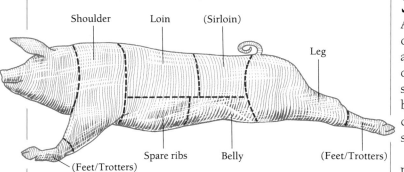

A pig can be divided into five segments that do not always correspond to retail cuts. See Pork cuts (p.206).

USEFUL INFORMATION

Season *Full grown:* year-round, peaking autumn. *Suckling pig:* spring.

How to choose Moist meat, deep pink not gray or red in color; white or creamy fat; avoid dry or discolored surfaces and wet packages, which indicate poor handling.

Nutritive value See Pork cuts, p.206.

Cooking methods *Whole cut:* braise or pot-roast at 350°F/175°C, 25 minutes per 1 lb/500 g; roast (p.199); *Chops:* bake at 350°F/ 175°C, 1-1½ hours; barbecue or broil (p.197); marinate 1 day; pan-fry or sauté (p.198); cook as a sauté ¾-1 hour; simmer 1-1½ hours. *Steaks, cubed:* braise or stew at 350°F/175°C, 1-1½ hours; simmer 1-1½ hours; stir-fry 2-3 minutes.

When done *Whole cut:* tender when pierced with two-pronged fork, at least 170°F/75°C on meat thermometer. *Chops, steaks, cubed:* meat falls easily from fork.

Processed forms Salted; pickled; smoked; canned.

USEFUL INFORMATION/PORK

Storage *Whole or pieces:* refrigerate 2-4 days; freeze 9 months. *Ground:* refrigerate 2 days; freeze 3 months.

Typical dishes Roast shoulder with crackling and baked apples (UK); *épaule braisée aux marrons* (braised shoulder stuffed with chestnuts, France); *puerco en naranja* (loin with mustard and orange sauce, Mexico); pork olives (rolled pork fillet with sage and onion stuffing, UK); *carré braisé Niçoise* (braised loin with vermouth and lemon peel, France); roast loin with sage and onion stuffing (USA); loin with cornbread stuffing (USA); *lombo di maiale al forno* (garlic-roasted loin, Italy); *lombo di maiale al prosciutto* (grilled loin with prosciutto, Italy); *lomo de cerdo al Jerez* (roast loin with sherry, Spain); loin roast with bitter marmalade, brandy, lemon, and ginger (Australia); *schlesisches himmelreich* (salted belly, stewed with dried fruit, Germany); *kasseler rippchen mit rosinenpudding* (pickled smoked chops with sauerkraut and onions, Germany); *costolette di maiale al finocchio* (braised chops with white wine and fennel seed, Italy); *jungfernbraten mit rahmsauce* (chops in dill and paprika sauce, Austria); chops with apricot sauce (Australia); *goo lo yuk* (sweet and sour pork, China); *guiso de puerco* (pork stewed with onions, chilies, cloves, cinnamon, pepper, cumin, garlic, and vinegar, Mexico); *daube de porc aux bélangères* (stewed with eggplant and allspice, Caribbean); *arista alla fiorentina* (roast with garlic, rosemary, and cloves, Italy); pork and apple stew (Ireland); *pökelrippchen mit dicken bohnen* (with white beans, Germany); spareribs layered with apples, prunes, and brown sugar (USA); maple barbecued spareribs (mustard, tomato, and maple syrup sauce, USA); *székelygulyás* (goulash with sour cabbage, Hungary); *schweinfrikassee* (stewed with onions, pig's blood, and cream, Switzerland); *noisettes de porc aux pruneaux* (pork fillet with prunes and cream, France); *veřova pecěře* (roasted with caraway seeds, Czechoslovakia).

Also good with rosemary; thyme; sage; honey; dried fruits; plums; red currants; cranberries; pickles; chutney; mustard, red and white cabbage; boiled potatoes; braised endive; carrots; beer.

SHOULDER (USA, UK), *épaule* (France)

A large cut containing the blade bone and two leg bones, shoulder of pork is usually cut in at least two pieces. The upper part lying along the backbone (US Boston butt, UK neck end) is meaty and often cut into chops. In Britain and France, this cut may be further split into sparerib (Fr. *échine*) containing backbone and ribs, and blade (Fr. *palette*) with blade bone. (**Note** Sparerib is not the same cut as ribs.) Sometimes pieces of pork neck (Fr. *gorge*) are sold separately for stewing.

The lower part of the shoulder that runs down the leg (USA picnic ham or arm roast, UK hand or spring, Fr. *jambonneau*) is coarser grained. In the United States and Britain, butchers make a second cut to form hocks, though in France these form part of the *jambonneau*. Last of all come feet (Fr. *pieds*).

Meat on pork shoulder is juicy, streaked with fat and a thin layer of connective tissue. Shoulder makes an economical roast, though it is too fatty for some tastes. The upper section can be oven-roasted, but cuts near the leg tend to be tough, so pot-roasting or braising is wiser. To simplify carving, the meat is best boned and rolled.

Of the smaller cuts, hocks are rarely available fresh. If they are, they should be braised or simmered. Blade steaks (UK sparerib or blade chops) are cut from the upper section, while tougher arm (or picnic steaks in the United States) come from the leg. Shoulder chops are best baked or sautéed in fat. Leg meat may be boned and cut for stew or ground for sausage meat.

Portion *With bone:* ¾-1 lb/375-500 g. *Without bone:* ½ lb/250 g.

LOIN (USA, UK), *carré* (France)

The loin in pork is proportionately longer than any other domestic animal as the pig has one or two extra ribs. It is divided into two parts: loin and sirloin (US); fore-loin and chump end (UK); and *carré* and *filet* (France). Both are prime cuts for roasting, on or off the bone, needing only to be thoroughly trimmed. Loin is the only cut of pork that is not usually salted or pickled, though chops can be bought salted or smoked to use in dishes such as braised sauerkraut.

Meat on the fore-part of the loin consists of a single eye muscle, often boned for easy carving. Follow the method for boning veal loin (p.216). Crown roast of pork, made from two loins with the chine bone removed, offers a spectacular presentation. It is shaped and tied like crown of lamb (p.223).

Meat at the sirloin end is sweeter than loin, but the cut is best boned as the pelvic bone complicates carving. Under the lower backbone lies the tenderloin or fillet, a lean tender cut weighing up to 1 lb/500 g. Ideal for roasting or braising whole, tenderloin is also cut in ½ in/1.25 cm slices as tiny *filets mignons* to broil or pan-fry, or into thin slices as a substitute for veal escalopes.

Both the fore- and hind-loin are frequently cut into chops, excellent for broiling and cooking over high heat as well as braising more slowly. Loin chops may be boned and butterflied (opened out flat), and American butchers sometimes slit the fore-loin lengthwise, dividing the muscle in half between backbone and rib bones to form country-style spareribs. The sirloin or chump chops (Fr. *côtes de filet*) may contain a nugget of tenderloin under the bone and sometimes they include a slice of kidney.

Portion *With bone: ¾-1 lb/375-500 g. Without bone: ½ lb/250 g.*

CUTTING LOIN CHOPS

With a cleaver, chop between the rib bones and through the chine bone (backbone) to separate the chops.

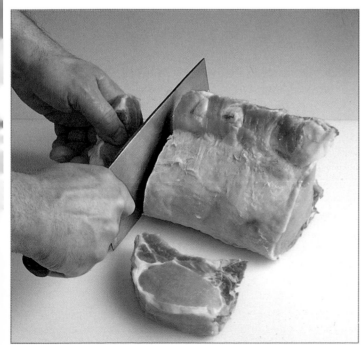

Trim excess fat from the chops, leaving a border of fat up to ½ in/1.25 cm wide to prevent the meat drying out during cooking.

BONING A PORK SIRLOIN

When boning a pork sirloin, the aitchbone and hip (that make up the pelvic bone) bone need to be removed as well as the backbone. The tenderloin, which is the tenderest cut of pork, lies under the backbone. Once it has been removed, it can be used for another purpose, for example it can be roasted, sliced into scallops or cubed and threaded on skewers for broiling. The bones that have been removed may be used to make pork stock.

1 Cut along the backbone to free the tenderloin.

2 With a knife, outline the pelvic bone to expose it.

3 Cut around the pelvic bone, loosening it without removing it.

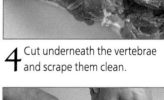

4 Cut underneath the vertebrae and scrape them clean.

5 Lift off the pelvic bone, using a knife or cleaver to remove it.

6 Lift off the backbone and rib bones together.

7 Trim the excess fat, leaving a ¼ in/6 mm layer. Roll the meat and tie it for roasting, or cut in ½ in/1.25 cm slices for chops.

BELLY (USA, UK), *poitrine* (France)

Pork belly is almost always cured as bacon. However, the fresh meat can be trimmed and rolled to simmer as boiled pork. In Britain, it is roasted, while in France it is sometimes added to stews of leaner meat to provide a contrast of flavor and texture.

Portion *Without bone: 4-6 oz/125-175 g.*

FRESH HAM (USA); leg (UK), *jambon* (France)

The leg meat of a pig is fleshy and lean, with little connective tissue and an outer layer of fat that may be thick or thin, depending on the breed. It is an ideal cut for roasting. In France, leg of pork is invariably cured, and is known as the *jambon*, meaning ham.

A whole leg can weigh anything from 10-20 lb/5-10 kg, so in the United States and Britain it is usually divided into butt or fillet and shank or knuckle, with the hocks removed. The butt or fillet is more economical, consisting almost entirely of meat, but the shank is often easier to carve. The meat of both cuts is tender and juicy. Leg of pork is also cut into thick ham steaks that can be either baked or boiled.

Portion With bone: ¾-1 lb/375-500 g. *Without bone:* ½ lb/250 g.

Carving leg of pork

Sometimes part of the aitchbone remains attached to the leg, and it should be cut out before cooking. Follow the directions for carving a cooked ham (p.252).

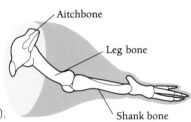

Aitchbone

Leg bone

Shank bone

SPARERIBS (USA, UK), *plat de côtes* (France)

Pork spareribs are a treat everywhere, though no other nation holds them in quite the same esteem as the United States. They should be cut from the breast of the pig, but so great is the demand in the United States, that spareribs are also cut from the shoulder and loin. However, these lack the nutty richness of breast ribs. The breast cut is triangular, with the broad end and longer bones being more meaty. When buying spareribs, allow about 1 lb/500 g of ribs per person.

Ribs are traditionally cooked on a barbecue, but this must be done slowly, with frequent basting, so that fat is thoroughly drained and meat is tender. A safer approach is to parboil ribs just until tender, about 30 minutes, or to bake them in a 350°F/175°C oven for about 45 minutes. They are then cut into pieces to barbecue or broil.

Barbecued spareribs are traditionally served with a special barbecue sauce. Every region of the United States has a recipe: most are tomato-based (Sauces, p.65) but some are spicy and others hot. Asian sweet-sour combinations with soy sauce, honey, ginger and hot mustard are also popular. In country districts of Europe spareribs may be roasted or broiled as a rustic curiosity, but they are generally regarded as an inferior cut to be stewed.

Pork chops with apples and cream

This dish from Normandy combines all the ingredients for which the region's cuisine is famous – apples, cream and Calvados.

Serves 4

4 thick loin pork chops (2½-3 lb/1.2-1.4 kg)
salt and pepper
1 tbsp oil
1 tbsp butter
2 onions, sliced
2 tart apples, peeled, cored and sliced
3 tbsp/45 ml Calvados or brandy
1 tbsp flour
1½ cups/375 ml veal stock, more if needed
pinch grated nutmeg
¾ cup/175 ml *crème fraîche* or heavy cream
For the garnish
2 tbsp/30 g butter
2 firm dessert apples, unpeeled, cored, and cut in ⅜ in/1 cm slices
2 tbsp/30 g sugar

1 Sprinkle the chops with salt and pepper. Heat the oil and butter in a large frying pan or sauté pan and fry the chops over a medium heat until brown on both sides. Remove them, add the onions and cook until soft but not brown. Add the peeled apples and continue cooking over a fairly high heat until the onions and apples are golden brown.

2 Replace the chops, pour over the Calvados and flambé (p.38). Stir the flour into the juices, add the stock and nutmeg and bring to a boil. Cover and simmer on top of the stove, or bake in a 350°F/175°C oven for 1-1½ hours until done. If the sauce thickens too much during cooking, stir in more stock.

3 For the garnish: heat the butter in a frying pan. Dip one side of each apple slice in sugar. Cook the slices, sugar side down, in butter over a high heat for 4-5 minutes or until the sugar caramelizes. Sprinkle the rest of the sugar on the apples, turn and brown the other side.

4 Remove the chops, arrange them overlapping on a serving dish or individual plates and keep warm. Work the sauce through a sieve, pressing to extract the apple and onion pulp. Add the *crème fraîche* or cream and bring the sauce back to a boil. If necessary reduce it until it is thick enough to coat the back of a spoon and season it to taste.

5 Spoon the sauce over the chops and use the slices of apple to garnish them.

VARIETY MEATS

Variety meats include the edible internal parts of an animal, such as the liver and kidneys, as well as the head, tail and feet. The term also covers delicacies such as sweetbreads, brains and testicles (also called fries and mountain oysters), and more robust food like tongue and tripe, as well as oddities that are more rarely eaten, such as ears, cheeks and stomach.

Liver is generally accepted, but a taste for kidneys and sweetbreads varies from country to country. Interest in other types of variety meats is even more limited in the United States and Britain, where dishes such as Lancashire tripe and onions, and Texas mountain oysters (calf's testicles) are regarded as regional eccentricities.

Choosing and storing variety meats

Variety meats need careful handling, and freshness is crucial. They spoil more quickly than other meats and for most types, two to three days is the maximum storage time after slaughter. Fresh variety meats are moist and shiny with no dry patches; a greenish color, slimy surface or strong smell are all danger signs. Tripe, testicles, cheeks and ears freeze well and sweetbreads can be frozen after blanching. However, red meats like liver and kidneys do not improve when frozen.

Blanching variety meats

Delicate variety meats, such as sweetbreads, brains and tripe, must be blanched before cooking to clean them and strengthen the texture (see Preparing sweetbreads, p.232). Rinse variety meats thoroughly in cold water and put them in a large pan of cold water. Bring slowly to a boil, skimming froth as it rises to the surface. Simmer for a few minutes, then drain them and rinse well.

Poaching variety meats

Poaching suits many variety meats, particularly tongue, head and parts of the stomach, which become tender after slow moist cooking. Brains, however, are gently poached to keep them firm. Poaching may be done in salted water, but *court bouillon* (p.44) is generally preferred as the vinegar, lemon juice or wine contained in it helps tenderize tough meats. Herbs and pepper in the bouillon add flavor.

Provided the original *court bouillon* was not too strongly flavored, liquid from poaching variety meats can be strained, then reduced and spooned over the meat, a method popular with calf's head. Meats such as tongue may be poached and then baked with a little liquid, basting often to produce a shiny glaze, or the liquid may be used in a velouté sauce (p.55) to accompany the meat.

Alternatively, variety meats are drained after poaching and the liquid is discarded. Calf's head and brains may be served plain with a tart *sauce ravigote* (p.64) to counter the richness. Pig's feet are sprinkled with breadcrumbs for broiling after poaching, and lamb's or calf's feet may be served in a rich *sauce poulette* (p.55) with lemon and parsley. Poached tongue is drained and served hot with Madeira sauce, a piquant Devil sauce (*sauce diable*) or *sauce charcutière* (p.58), or it may be pressed in a mold and sliced to serve cold.

ANIMAL EXTREMITIES

Although their appeal may be limited, the extremities of animals provide an abundance of interesting dishes. Calf's, pig's, or lamb's heads can be simmered in *court bouillon*, then boned, chopped, and made into "head cheese", or poached or roasted and eaten whole. A whole pig's head sometimes appears as a showpiece on banquet tables in place of the boar's head of the past.

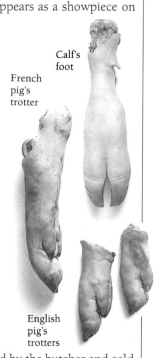

Calf's foot

French pig's trotter

English pig's trotters

Parts of the head are considered delicacies in their own right. Calf's or pig's ears benefit from long poaching or braising after initial blanching. They can then be coated with breadcrumbs and broiled or baked until crisp, making a container for stuffing with mushrooms or sausagemeat.

After long cooking to tenderize them, ox cheeks are often used in brawn, or savory pies. Pig's cheeks, in England called Bath chaps, are sometimes cured and simmered to eat cold like ham, or cured and added to French country soups. In the American South, they are added to cooked greens.

Although rarely eaten in the United States, lamb's and cow's udder is eaten in France and the north of England, where it is generally prepared and cooked by the butcher and sold by the slice. The sliced udder resembles pale liver. It can be lightly fried until golden and served with vegetables.

Pig's skin (Fr. *couenne*), which is full of gelatin, is useful in stocks and braised dishes when it may be diced after cooking to add to the sauce. An alternative is to cut the skin in strips and deep-fry it as cracklings. The British prefer to roast their pork to a crisp crunchy surface with the skin in place.

Feet (Fr. *pieds*) are part of the culinary mainstream. They are an excellent source of rich-flavored gelatin for setting and enhancing stocks and stews. Pig's feet, often called "trotters", can also be split and simmered in *court bouillon*, then coated in breadcrumbs and fried or broiled. A tangy sauce such as mustard or vinaigrette is a frequent accompaniment. Calf's feet are usually added to other dishes, but lamb's feet are excellent in a sauce.

Perhaps the most popular of these animal extremities is the oxtail, meaty and ideal for hearty stews and the well-known oxtail soup. Oxtails can also be boned, stuffed, and braised. Pig's tails contribute to stews and soups, but lamb's tails are generally quite small and are more likely to be found in a meat pie. All animals' tails should be trimmed of fat, and boned or cut into pieces through the joints. The tip of the tail can be used for stock.

Oxtail

Braising and other cooking methods

Braising concentrates and heightens flavors and is appropriate for more robust variety meats such as tongue, heart, liver and kidneys. A low, even temperature is important during cooking, and meats are generally left whole so that they retain their juices. Tender meats such as kidneys and liver are cooked until just pink and moist in the center; others need to be thoroughly braised to tenderize. Red wine, Madeira, Marsala or port is added to intensify the flavor of a braise. Toward the end of cooking a garnish of small onions, mushrooms, truffles and bacon may be added. Fruit such as orange, raspberry, red currant or raisin can give the sauce an agreeable tang, but meats like sweetbreads are better suited to a lighter addition, such as white wine.

Rich, tender variety meats such as kidneys and liver are excellent sliced and sautéd in butter, with or without a coating of flour for crispness. Broiling is outstanding for kidneys, but other variety meats tend to dry out. A classic favorite is brains or sweetbreads coated in breadcrumbs, deep-fried and served with tartare (p.63) or tomato sauce (p.65).

Presenting variety meats

Variety meats are usually cut up for presentation: sweetbreads, tongue and liver are cut on the diagonal into escalopes; brains are thickly sliced. A rich, glossy brown sauce (p.57), or a butter sauce (p.62) with fresh herbs for color and vegetables such as carrots or zucchini are usual accompaniments. Alternatively, a whole tongue can be molded and enrobed in aspic (p.254).

Kidneys with Madeira

Prepare the kidneys (see opposite page). Crispy fried potatoes are the perfect accompaniment.

Serves 4

2-3 calf's kidneys or 8-10 lamb's kidneys (1½-2 lb/750 g-1 kg)	6 tbsp/90 ml Madeira
2 tbsp/30 g butter	1 cup/250 ml brown veal stock (p.43)
½ lb/250 g mushrooms, thinly sliced	½ cup/125 g cold butter, cut in pieces (for sauce)
salt and pepper	*For garnish*
1 tbsp oil	1 tbsp chopped parsley

1 Prepare the kidneys, leaving lamb's kidneys whole and cutting calf's kidneys in half.
2 Melt half the butter in a frying pan, add the mushrooms with salt and pepper and sauté until they are tender and the liquid has evaporated, 5-7 minutes. Keep the mushrooms warm.
3 Heat the oil and remaining butter in a large frying pan until foaming. Add the kidneys and sauté them over medium heat until brown, 2-3 minutes for lamb's, 5-6 minutes for calf's. Turn and brown the other side, allowing a total of 5-6 minutes for lamb's or 10-12 minutes for calf's kidneys. Add half the Madeira and flambé (p.38). Transfer the kidneys to a board.
4 Add the stock to the pan and boil until reduced to a glaze. Add the remaining Madeira and simmer for 30 seconds. Take the pan from the heat and mount the sauce with the cold butter (p.53). Season to taste.
5 Slice the calf's kidneys or cut the lamb's kidneys in half and arrange them, cut sides up, on four individual plates. Pile the mushrooms beside them. Spoon the sauce over the kidneys, sprinkle with chopped parsley and serve at once.

LIVER

Liver from young animals is mild and tender, with calf's liver the top choice for broiling, sautéing and pan-frying. A whole calf's liver weighs around 3 lb/1.4 kg and comes in one large piece with a smaller lobe attached; livers from other animals may have several lobes. Lamb's liver is drier and less delicate, but can also be sautéed. A large piece weighing 1 lb/500 g or more of calf's or lamb's liver is excellent braised. The flavor of pig's liver is strong, and so best in pâtés and terrines, faggots and *gayettes*, while beef liver, which is the least expensive, should be braised with full-flavored ingredients to counterbalance its pronounced taste.

USEFUL INFORMATION

How to choose Fresh, sweet smell; liver from young animals brownish pink, darker when mature.
Portion 4-6 oz/125-175 g.
Nutritive value per 3½ oz/100 g: 138 calories; 20 g protein; 4 g fat; 4 g carbohydrates; 320 mg cholesterol; 68 mg sodium.
Cooking methods *Whole:* bake or braise at 350°F/175°C, 12-15 minutes per 1lb/500g. *Sliced:* broil 5-8 minutes; pan-fry or sauté 5-8 minutes.
When done Pink in center. *Whole:* 140°F/60°C on meat thermometer. *Slices:* resistant when pressed with finger; drops of juice on surface.
Problems Tough when overcooked.
Processed forms Commercially frozen.
Storage *Whole:* refrigerate 2 days. *Sliced:* refrigerate 1 day.
Typical dishes *Foie de veau grillée à la moûtarde* (broiled calf's liver with mustard and breadcrumbs, France); broiled with Marsala (UK); with bacon and onions (UK);

fegato alla salvia (with tomatoes, garlic and sage, Italy); *foie m'chermel en sauce* (marinated with pickled lemons and green olives, Morocco); braised with pear and bacon (Scandinavia); roasted and stuffed with parsley and eggs (France). *Also good with* onions, mushrooms, Madeira, mustard, white wine, cream, sour cream, coriander, nutmeg, thyme.

Calf's liver

PREPARING LIVER

To tone down its strong flavor, liver may be soaked in milk, but it should not be blanched as this will toughen it.

1 If preparing a whole liver, divide the lobes. Cut off any exposed ducts or connective tissue.

2 Using your fingers, peel off the opaque outer membrane.

3 If slicing liver, cut diagonally into slices. Remove any internal ducts from the slices.

KIDNEYS

Calf's (or veal) kidney is the top choice for broiling or cooking as a sauté in a dark wine sauce. Bean-shaped lamb's kidney is the next best thing; it tastes just a little less rich. Pig's and beef kidneys, often mixed with other ingredients, as in British steak and kidney pie, are well suited to braising and stewing, when they yield a wonderfully rich sauce.

USEFUL INFORMATION

How to choose Fresh, no ammoniac smell. *Calf's:* deep pink or beige color, not red. *Lamb's:* deep pink color, not red. *Pig's or beef:* red color, not black.
Portion *Calf's:* one kidney. *Lamb's:* 1½-2 kidneys. *Pig's or beef:* 4-6 oz/125-175 g.
Nutritive value per 3½ oz/100 g: 108 calories; 17 g protein; 4 g fat; 1 g carbohydrate; 350 mg cholesterol; 183 mg sodium.
Cooking methods *Whole calf's or lamb's:* braise at 350°F/175°C, 30-45 minutes; roast in fat at 450°F/230°C, 30-40 minutes per 1lb/500 g; cook as a sauté 15-20 minutes. *Sliced calf's or lamb's:* broil 6-8 minutes; sauté 6-8 minutes. *Sliced pig's or beef:* braise or stew at 350°F/175°C, 1½-2½ hours.
When done *Whole:* juice runs pink when pierced. *Sliced:* calf's and lamb's kidney should be pink in center; pig's and beef, very tender.
Problems Ammoniac taste if stale or poorly handled.
Processed forms Frozen.

Storage Refrigerate 1 day.
Typical dishes *rognoncini trifolati* (sautéed with Marsala, Italy); with tomatoes, olives and hot peppers (USA); sautéed with hard-boiled eggs (Spain); dumplings (UK); in lemon and white wine sauce (Germany); with tomatoes and boletes (France); with mustard and Madeira sauce (France); with pork (Ireland). *Also good with* ham, mushrooms, red wine, sherry, herbs.

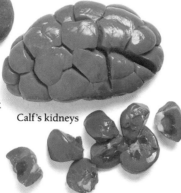

Lamb's kidney

Calf's kidneys

PREPARING CALF'S KIDNEYS

Kidneys are sometimes sold with a thick layer of fat left on them. Calf's and lamb's kidneys are sometimes roasted whole with the fat.

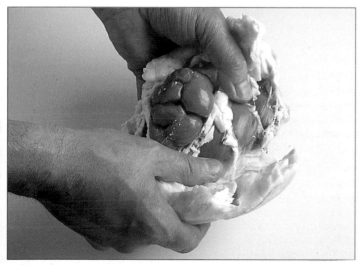

1 If the kidney is encased in fat, snip the fat where it is attached to the core of the kidney and pull it away with your hands.

2 Peel off the covering skin (membrane) and discard it.

3 Cut the ducts from the center, without damaging the kidney.

4 Calf's, pig's or beef kidneys are cut into cubes for cooking. (First make sure the ducts have been removed completely from the center.)

PREPARING LAMB'S KIDNEYS

When preparing lamb's kidneys, remove the outer layer of fat following the method described for calf's kidneys.

1 Partially slit the kidney lengthwise, with the rounded side upward.

2 Peel off the outer membrane with your hands, cutting where it is attached to the core. Leave the small fatty core intact.

3 LEFT Open out the kidneys butterfly-fashion, ready for broiling.

Note You may need to skewer the kidneys to keep them flat during cooking.

SWEETBREADS

These are usually the thymus glands of young animals, but occasionally the pancreatic glands are sold instead. The sweetbreads tend to shrink and toughen once the animal's diet changes from milk. Sweetbreads come in pairs, joined by a duct. The compact "heart" sweetbread slices evenly and is preferred to the looser, elongated "throat" sweetbread. Calf's sweetbreads are best.

Sweetbreads are cooked in several stages: first they are blanched, then braised or poached in *court bouillon* or, occasionally, in milk. After blanching, they are pressed and may be sliced or divided into small lobes to reheat in sauce, sauté in butter, deep-fry, or serve in a salad.

USEFUL INFORMATION

How to choose Compact texture; white or pale pink color, no dark discoloration.
Portion 4-6 oz/125-175 g, one calf sweetbread.
Nutritive value per 3½ oz/100 g (calf's): 94 calories; 18 g protein; 2 g fat; no carbohydrates; 466 mg cholesterol; 98 mg sodium.
Cooking methods *Whole*: braise at 350°F/175°C, 30-40 minutes; poach 20-30 minutes. *Slices or pieces*: broil 6-8 minutes; deep-fry 3-4 minutes; sauté 3-5 minutes.
When done Tender; connective tissue dissolved.

Problems Chewy if undercooked; pieces break up if too much membrane is removed.
Processed forms Frozen.
Storage *Fresh*: refrigerate 1 day. *Blanched*: refrigerate 2 days.
Typical dishes *Mollejas a la pollensina* (with bacon and onions Spain); *ris de veau forestière* (calf's sweetbreads with shallots, white wine and *cèpes*, France); *animelle di vitello* (calf's sweetbread fried in butter and Marsala, Italy). *Also good with* white wine, Madeira, mushrooms, truffles, celery.

Throat and heart sweetbreads

PREPARING SWEETBREADS

Sweetbreads are very perishable and should be soaked and precooked in advance, particularly if not used immediately.

1 Soak the sweetbreads in cold water for 2 hours to clean them. Cut away any discolored parts. Blanch sweetbreads by putting them in cold water, bringing to a boil and simmering for 5 minutes (calf's) or 3 minutes (lamb's), then drain them.

2 Pull away the ducts. Remove the skin and outer pieces of membrane from the sweetbreads.

Note Some connective tissue will dissolve during cooking, so do not remove so much that the sweetbread starts to break up.

Sautéed sweetbreads with vegetables

Any root vegetable, such as Jerusalem artichoke or salsify, can be used instead of celery root.

Serves 4

1½ lb/750 g (2-3 pairs) calf's sweetbreads	1 lb/500 g celery root
1 qt/1 L *court bouillon* (p.44)	1 lb/500 g pearl onions, peeled
½ cup/60 g flour seasoned with ½ tsp salt and ¼ tsp pepper	½ lb/250 g bacon, cut into lardons
¼ cup/60 g butter	2 tsp sugar
For the glazed vegetables	pinch of nutmeg
1 lb/500 g carrots	salt and pepper
¾ lb/375 g turnips	2 tbsp/30 g butter

1 Soak, blanch and trim the sweetbreads (see preparing, left). Put them in the *court bouillon* and poach them for 20-25 minutes. Drain the sweetbreads and press them between two plates with a 2lb/1kg weight on top and chill them.
2 Turn the carrots, turnips and celery root (p.260) so that they are the same size as the onions. In a sauté pan or frying pan, cook the lardons until they begin to brown, about 5 minutes. Remove them, add the carrots, turnips, celery root and onions. Pour in enough water to cover, add the sugar, nutmeg, salt and pepper, and bring to a boil, uncovered. Cook over high heat until tender and the liquid is reduced to a thick, syrupy glaze, about 15 minutes. Stir and toss the vegetables occasionally. Replace the lardons and taste for seasoning.
3 Using a small, sharp knife, cut the sweetbreads into ⅜ in/1 cm diagonal slices or escalopes (see pressing and slicing sweetbreads, opposite) and coat them on either side with the seasoned flour. In a large sauté pan or skillet, heat the butter over medium heat and sauté the sweetbreads until they are golden brown, about 2 minutes on each side. Arrange portions of sweetbreads, overlapping, on individual warmed plates.
4 Reheat the vegetables in the pan and add the remaining butter, tossing to glaze them. Serve the glazed vegetables as an accompaniment to the sweetbreads.

PRESSING & SLICING SWEETBREADS

After blanching, sweetbreads should be pressed and chilled before being sliced so that the slices are compact.

Set the sweetbreads between two plates with a weight on top and chill for 2 hours or until firm. Cut the sweetbreads in ⅜ in/1 cm diagonal slices (escalopes) before cooking.

BRAINS

Brains have a more creamy texture and fragile structure than sweetbreads. Calf's brains are the best, then lamb's, pig's, and beef. The richness of brains can be overwhelming, so they are usually simply poached in *court bouillon* (p.44) laced with vinegar. They can also be braised or simmered in red wine, which is then made into a *sauce meurette* (p.56).

Brains are valued for their texture more than their taste, and are thus suited to recipes such as poached brains in brown butter with capers, or to poaching, coating and deep-frying. Cooked brains can be used to enrich stuffings, puréed to thicken sauces, or braised with vegetables for flavor.

USEFUL INFORMATION

How to choose Compact; white color with little blood or discoloration, fresh smell.
Portion 1-2 halves; 3-4 oz/90-125 g.
Nutritive value per 3½ oz/100 g: 125 calories; 10 g protein; 9 g fat; 1 g carbohydrates; 1750 mg cholesterol; 120 mg sodium.
Cooking methods *Whole*: braise at 350°F/175°C, 15-20 minutes; poach 15-20 minutes. *Slices or pieces*: deep-fry 2-3 minutes; sauté 3-4 minutes.
When done Firm with no transparent center.
Problems Tendency to break up if cooked too fast.
Storage Refrigerate 1 day.
Processed forms Frozen.
Typical dishes *Fritte alla fiorentina* (marinated, breadcrumbed, fried, and served with spinach, Italy); *al*

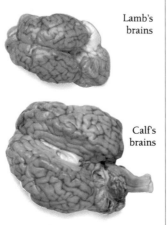

Lamb's brains

Calf's brains

burro nero (with black butter, Italy); *à la genoise* (fried, with Parmesan and tomato sauce, France); with parsley and cream (UK). *Also good with* mashed potatoes, eggs, tomatoes, white wine, cream, olives, anchovies.

PREPARING BRAINS

Brains need not be blanched, but they must be thoroughly cleaned. They have two lobes and can be left whole or sliced.

Rinse the brains thoroughly 2-3 times in cold water to remove blood and discolored tissue. Soak the brains in cold water for 1-2 hours to whiten them.

HEART

Since the heart of an animal is a well-used and hard-working muscle, it tends to be tough and is therefore best braised or stewed with plenty of vegetables. In fact the heart makes a natural container for a breadcrumb and herb, or sausagemeat, mixture. It can be roasted, plain or stuffed.

Veal and lamb hearts are the best; beef heart is larger, can take three to four hours to become tender, and should be cooked in plenty of liquid. Heart from younger animals takes two to three hours.

Ox heart

USEFUL INFORMATION

How to choose Deep-colored, not bright red or brown; fresh smell.
Portion 6 oz/175 g or 1 lamb heart.
Nutritive value per 3½ oz/100 g: 131 calories; 17 g protein; 6 g fat; 1 mg carbohydrates; 136 mg cholesterol, 59 mg sodium.
Cooking methods *Whole pork, lamb, veal heart*: stuff and braise 2-3 hours. *Sliced pork, lamb, veal heart*: sauté 5-7 minutes. *Beef*: braise 4-6 hours.
Problems Tough if undercooked or cooked too fast.

Storage Refrigerate 1-2 days; freeze 3 months.
Typical dishes *Coeur de boeuf bourgeois* (casserole with other offal, herbs and white wine, France); *Coeur de veau farci braisé* (veal heart stuffed with sausage-meat wrapped in caul fat and braised, France); *gefühltes kalbsherz* (veal heart stuffed with chopped veal and ham, marinated in white wine, Germany); *coeur de veau en casserole à la bonne femme* (veal heart sautéed with baby onions, potatoes and bacon, France).

PREPARING HEART

Lamb's heart serves one person, pig's or veal heart two people, and beef heart four.

1 With a sharp knife, trim the fat surrounding the heart and wash the meat thoroughly.

2 Cut out the arteries and fibrous tissue. Heart may be left whole or sliced to cook.

TONGUE

The tongue of all large domestic animals tastes good, but the flavor of beef tongue is outstanding. Beef tongue can weigh up to 5 lb/2.3 kg, calf's tongue is about half that weight, while pig's and lamb's tongue can weigh about 6 oz/180 g. Beef tongue is often pickled or smoked for added flavor, and it freezes well. The tongue of some animals is quite rough and the skin may have black markings, but this is not a bad sign.

Most tongue is cooked by poaching in *court bouillon* (p.44); calf's, pig's, and lamb's tongue may be blanched then braised until tender. The richness of hot tongue may be emphasized by a full-bodied brown sauce, or by a strong-tasting fruit sauce or vegetable such as spinach or sauerkraut. Cold pressed tongue is sliced to present in aspic garnished with chopped parsley and hard-boiled egg, or simply served with pickles or chutney.

USEFUL INFORMATION

How to choose Moist with clear pink or reddish color.
Portion 5-6 oz/150-175 g.
Nutritive value per 3½ oz/100 g: 195 calories; 16 g protein; 13 g fat; 3 g carbohydrates; 94 mg cholesterol; 90 mg sodium.
Cooking methods *Whole:* poach 45-60 minutes per 1 lb/500 g; braise at 350°F/175°C, 45-60 minutes per 1 lb/500 g. *Whole or sliced after poaching:* bake at 350°F/ 175°C, 20-30 minutes.
When done Tender; bones at root pull away from meat.
Problems Chewy if not very thoroughly cooked.
Storage Refrigerate 2-3 days; freeze 6 months.
Processed forms Smoked; pickled; frozen.
Typical dishes Salad with diced cooked vegetables (Germany); with mushroom sauce (Finland); pickled in almond sauce (Spain); *au gratin* (Scandinavia); with apple

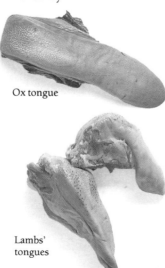

Ox tongue

Lambs' tongues

cider (UK); sweet and sour (USA); with red wine, lemon and almond sauce (Poland); with brandy and currants (Italy); grilled in *sauce diable* (cayenne, shallots, pepper, France). *Also good with* bacon, lentils, rosemary, thyme, garlic, fennel, anchovies, mustard.

Pressing a cooked tongue

Beef tongues are pressed singly, but smaller tongues can be curled one around the other. Curl the tip of the tongue around its root and pack it into a tongue press (p.511) or pack tongue into the smallest possible saucepan, adding a plate with a weight on top.

PREPARING & SLICING COOKED TONGUE

Tongue may be poached in *court bouillon* until very tender, or blanched for 10 minutes then drained and braised.

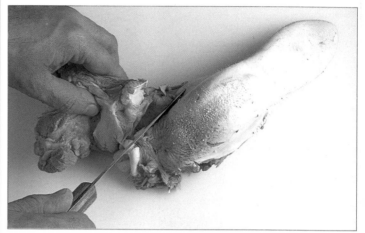

1 After cooking, let the tongue cool until tepid. First drain the tongue, then cut away the bones from the root end with a knife.

2 Holding the tongue in one hand, make a small incision at the tip and peel away the skin with your hands. Use a small knife if it is easier.

3 Set the tongue on a board. Starting at the tip, cut large diagonal slices. Each portion should include some slices from the tender root and some from the firmer tip.

4 Continue cutting, angling the knife so that each slice is as large as possible. After slicing, the tongue may be served cold, or it can be reheated by baking or warming in a suitable sauce (See Typical dishes for tongue, left).

TRIPE

Tripe is the stomach tissue of ruminant (cud-chewing) animals, usually beef. The first stomach yields "blanket" or ridged tripe, and the second "honeycomb" tripe, which is more tender. Tripe is sold parboiled and should be clean and white. First it should be soaked for 5-10 minutes in cold water, then rinsed thoroughly and cut into strips or 2 in/5 cm squares. Tripe is cooked further by poaching for an hour or two until tender, then it is drained and sautéed with onions or coated with breadcrumbs and deep-fried; Devil sauce (*sauce diable*, p.58) is a good accompaniment. Alternatively, tripe may be braised as in *tripes à la mode de Caen* with vegetables and Calvados.

Blanket tripe

Honeycomb tripe

USEFUL INFORMATION
How to choose White color; moist; fresh smell.
Portion 6 8 oz/175-250 g.
Nutritive value per 3½ oz/100 g: 98 calories; 15 g protein; 4 g fat; no carbohydrates; 95 mg cholesterol; 46 mg sodium.
Cooking methods Blanch 10-15 minutes, refresh then bake at 350°F/175°C; braise or stew 3-4 hours; blanch and deep-fry or sauté 10-12 minutes.
Problems Tough if undercooked, strong flavor if stale.
Processed forms Pre-blanched; pre-cooked (parboiled).
Storage Refrigerate 1-2 days; blanch and freeze 3 months.

Typical dishes *Trippa verde* (in green sauce, Italy); Philadelphia pepperpot soup (with veal knuckles, USA); *callos a la andaluza* (stew with sausage, Spain).

OTHER INNARDS

Another valuable part of the stomach is the caul fat (Fr. *crépinette*), the lacy fat that lines an animal's stomach. Pig's caul is the most commonly available, often used to line terrine molds and to wrap patties and sausages. Intestines, particularly of the pig, are often used as sausage casings (p.248). American chitterlings are pig's intestines, parboiled like tripe and then braised, sautéed, or deep-fried.

Other tough but edible animal innards include the lights (lungs), melt (spleen), and mesentery (abdominal membrane) that is sometimes prepared like tripe.

Pig's caul

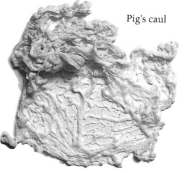

BONES

Meat cooked on the bone is juicier and less likely to shrink. The bones of young animals, particularly calves, contain a good deal of collagen which dissolves during cooking to form gelatin, enriching stews and soups (see Veal and chicken stocks, p.44). The bones of older animals contain less collagen, but contribute more taste. Veal bones are the basis of white stock, which has a mild flavor suited to all meats, as well as poultry. Beef bones are valued for consommé and for the brown stock used with red meats and game. The flavor of lamb bones is more obtrusive, suited only to lamb dishes and soups such as Scotch broth, while pork bones, low in collagen, are cooked only with pork or for sauces. Cooked ham bones flavor hearty dishes, especially those with beans. When roasting or braising, chop any bone trimmings and cook them with the meat to add flavor to gravy or sauce.

Knuckle bones yield the most gelatin and should be cracked in two to three pieces by the butcher. Shank bones have a hollow center containing marrow that provides rich flavor for stocks and soups. Although marrow contains fat, it is also high in nutrients. In dishes such as Italian *osso buco*, the marrow is left in the bone to eat with the meat. Marrow can also be extracted from cleaned bones (below). A large beef marrowbone is a traditional treat, poached until tender, then served on a white napkin with a special long spoon to scoop out the marrow.

EXTRACTING MARROW

Ask the butcher for bones cut in 3 in/7.5 cm sections. Poach them in salted water for one or two minutes, scoop out the marrow and slice it for sauces and dishes such as *Risotto milanese* (p.25). Alternatively, split the bones and extract the marrow (below).

1 ABOVE Using a cleaver or broad knife to steady the bone, strike it forcefully with the back of a heavy cleaver until it cracks.

2 Separate the cracked bone and push out the marrow with your fingers. Cut the marrow into slices and poach it gently in salted water for 1-2 minutes. (Do not allow the water to boil.)

FURRED GAME

Once a staple food, the meat of most large wild animals is now rarely eaten, and is found only in high-priced restaurants. Large game that does reach retail markets is usually venison, the meat of deer or, more rarely, wild boar. Other large animals such as bear, elk and buffalo can be eaten but you are unlikely to find their meat in a retail store.

Small game is another matter: in Europe, rabbit is standard fare, offered in supermarkets alongside poultry. These days, however, rabbits are usually bred in the backyard and are seldom tracked down by the hunter. Hare and other small animals are alternatives, depending less on local supply than on local taste.

The hunting of game is mostly limited by law to certain seasons. In the United States, the sale of wild game is illegal, so all game meat sold in markets is either farmed or imported frozen.

Note Few countries inspect fresh wild game for hygiene, so avoid carcasses that show signs of injury or disease, or that have been clumsily shot.

Hanging furred game

Like game birds, game animals are often aged by hanging in a cool airy place to develop flavor and tenderize the meat. After gutting, the unskinned animal should be suspended by the feet. The darker the flesh of the animal, the more it matures. Hare, for instance, develops a full, ripe flavor, while domestic rabbit changes very little. In cold dry weather, large animals such as deer may be left two to three weeks; a week is sufficient for smaller ones. In warm or damp weather, hang the animal for half the length of time and watch for warning signs of green tinges and strong smell.

Marinating furred game

Marinating helps tenderize the meat of older animals and also tones down the strong flavor of game. Taste for furred game varies: current trends favor mild game that is hardly marinated at all, but more traditional recipes call for soaking the meat for several days. The classic marinade for dark game is a cooked red wine mixture (p.41), while meats such as baby wild boar and rabbit may be soaked in a lighter, uncooked marinade.

Roasting furred game

All the cook's resources for dealing with tough meat are called into play when roasting game. After marinating, cuts should be larded or barded (p.196) and cooked with complementary seasonings such as juniper berries with venison, or thyme and rosemary with rabbit. Musty spices such as coriander and allspice go well with hare and other strong game. Roast the meat at 400°F/200°C for the first half hour, then lower the heat to 350°F/175°C. Baste the meat often and cover it with foil if it shows any sign of dryness. For the rare meat preferred by most game lovers, allow 10-15 minutes per 1 lb/500 g, or two to three minutes more for medium-done meat. For a rare roast: juices run pink when the meat is pricked with a two-pronged fork (125°F/51°C on a meat thermometer); for medium-done meat, the temperature on a meat thermometer should be 140°F/60°C. If you prefer your game well-done, or if the animal is not in its first youth, always braise rather than roast it. Wild boar and bear are served well-done like pork.

The roast can be served with a simple pan gravy, or one of the classic brown game sauces such as *poivrade* (p.58). Other accompaniments to roast game include braised red cabbage, purée of chestnuts, celery root or lentils, with *spätzle* (p.339), noodles, boiled or straw potatoes. A touch of sweetness is rarely amiss, whether it is in the form of red currant jelly in the sauce itself, apples in the cabbage, a garnish of sautéed fruit slices, or a side dish of bilberry or cranberry relish.

Other cooking methods for furred game

There are several other ways to cook game animals. One is to pan-fry tender cuts, such as fillet or tenderloin steaks from the loin, or escalopes cut from the leg of venison or wild boar, and serve them in a light wine sauce based on the cooking juices.

For all other cuts, and for any cut from an older animal, braising or stewing is the wisest course. These are the age-old ways of dealing with tough game, but they are by no means second best. They include winter casseroles of rabbit and lentils, jugged hare or full-flavored ragouts in which the meat is marinated for several days, then simmered in a sauce, perhaps with orange peel, raisins or prunes. The traditional *civet* is a stew of game with baby onions, bacon lardons, and mushrooms in red wine thickened with the blood of the animal.

A compromise between roasting and braising is to cook the game as a sauté, thus ensuring moist rather than dry heat. Older game can be used in a terrine (p.242), or a classic game pie laced with brandy or port. Inexpensive cuts of game, especially venison, can be ground to make unusual hamburgers or Texas game chili.

VENISON

Common species of European deer include the plump, tender little roe deer, the robust red deer – excellent for sport but less good for eating – and the fallow deer, which is of average quality. In the United States, at least 12 species of white-tailed deer are found, together with the heavier, stockier mule deer. The flavor of venison varies from mild to pungent, depending on whether the animal has been hung and if so, for how long. It resembles very lean lamb. Farm-raised venison may lack the pungency of meat from wild animals, but its tenderness compensates for this. Much of the venison eaten in Europe and the United States today comes from Scottish red deer bred in New Zealand.

As with all game, the quality of venison varies according to its age: the meat is at its best in mature animals of 18-24 months. Very young animals may lack flavor, while the meat from older animals is very tough. Since farmed venison is leaner than all other red meat and surprisingly low in cholesterol, it is likely to become a valuable commercial product in the future.

Cuts of venison are similar to those of lamb. Loin is best for roasting and is usually divided in two as rack and loin (USA), or loin and sirloin (UK). Often the loin is left attached along the backbone as saddle. Tenderloin chops or steaks for sautéing are cut from the boned loin. Leg or haunch of venison is leaner and more likely to become dry. If so, braising is a good option. Shoulder, neck and breast should be ground or cut up for stew.

USEFUL INFORMATION

Season Autumn or winter.
How to choose Young meat is clear red in color, fine-grained with white fat; scars and worn feet on carcass betray old age.
Portion *With bone:* ¾-1 lb/375-500 g. *Without bone:* ½ lb/250 g.
Nutritive value per 3½ oz/100 g: 126 calories; 21 g protein; 4 g fat; no carbohydrates; 86 mg cholesterol; 51 mg sodium.
Cooking methods All times depend on age. *Whole:* braise or pot-roast 20 minutes per 1 lb/500 g; marinate 2-3 days; roast (p.199). *Steaks:* pan-fry or sauté 6-10 minutes; cook as sauté ½-1 hour. *Pieces:* Stew 1½-3 hours. *Ground:* barbecue or broil 6-10 minutes.
When done *Braise:* tender when pierced with a fork. *Roast:* best rare (125°F/51°C on meat thermometer). *Steaks, ground:* pan-fry, slightly resistant when pressed; in a sauté, falls easily from fork. *Pieces:* fall easily from fork.

Processed forms Frozen; dried (biltong); canned; smoked, especially hams (hind legs).
Storage *Whole, pieces:* refrigerate 1-2 days; freeze 6-9 months.
Typical dishes *Radjurssler* (roast loin with cranberries, Norway); roast with cherries (UK); *braserad radjursstek* (braised steaks, Finland); *ragoût de chevreuil chasseur* (stew with onions, mushrooms and white wine, France); chili (USA); cutlets with mushrooms and dried fruit (France); *épaule de chevreuil farcie* (stuffed shoulder, France); meatloaf with morels (Sweden); *gebratener rehrucken* (roast saddle with sour cream, juniper and red currant jelly, Germany); escalopes in mushroom sauce (Germany); *braserad kalystek* (braised loin, Scandinavia). *Also good with* fruit, (especially berries), and juniper, aromatic herbs, cumin, allspice, cinnamon, black pepper, chestnuts, celery root, port.

Boning shoulder or preparing a loin of venison
Follow instructions for lamb (p.221), taking care to cut away the fat and tough bluish membrane covering the meat.

CARVING LEG OF VENISON
Venison is usually served pink in large thin slices. The meat will be progressively rare near the bone.

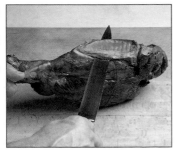

1 Hold the leg by the shank in one hand, rounded muscle upward. Cut one or two slices lengthwise so the meat has a base to sit on.

2 Turn the meat over and set it firmly on the board. Cut horizontal slices of muscle on the other side until you reach the bone.

3 Turn the meat and cut slices from the first side.

4 Finally, cut short slices from the meat remaining at the sides.

Venison with wild mushrooms

The older the venison and the stronger you like the flavor, the longer it should marinate (for a maximum of three days). *Spätzle* (p.339) are a good accompaniment to this festive roast.

Serves 10-12

red wine marinade (double quantity, p.41)	1 tbsp chopped parsley
7-8 lb/3.2-3.6 kg haunch or saddle of venison	1 lb/500 g fresh wild mushrooms, trimmed, *or* 2 oz/60 g dry wild mushrooms, soaked and drained
¼ lb/125 g piece of bacon, cut in lardons	¼ lb/125 g common mushrooms, quartered
3 tbsp/45 g lard or oil	3 tbsp/45 g butter
1 cup/250 ml veal stock (p.44)	3 cups cranberry sauce (p.66) (for serving)
1 cup/250 ml sour cream	
salt and pepper	***Larding needle***

1 Make the marinade and let it cool. Lard the venison with the bacon lardons
2 Set the venison in a deep bowl and pour over the marinade to half cover the meat. Cover and refrigerate for one to three days.
3 Heat the oven to 400°F/200°C. Drain the venison and pat it dry with paper towels; strain and reserve the marinade. In a roasting pan, heat the lard, add the venison, and baste with the hot fat. Add 1 cup/250 ml strained marinade and half the stock. Roast in the oven for 1¼-1½ hours for rare meat and 1¾-2 hours for well-done meat. Baste the meat often, adding more marinade if the pan gets dry. Reduce remaining marinade to 1 cup/250 ml.
4 Transfer the venison to a serving dish and keep warm. Discard any fat from the pan and reduce the pan juices to a glaze (p.57). Add the reduced marinade and remaining stock and reduce to about 1 cup/250 ml. Stir in the sour cream and heat gently, then season to taste. Sprinkle with parsley.
5 Sauté the mushrooms in the butter, season and spoon around the meat. Serve the sour cream and cranberry sauces separately.

CARVING A SADDLE OF VENISON ON THE BONE

Saddle of venison is prepared like saddle of lamb (p.219), but does not include any flank fat.

1 Cut lengthwise along the backbone, holding the knife against the bone, and sever the meat from the bone.

2 Angle the knife slightly and cut the first slice. Continue cutting slices from the loin, each time angling the knife a little more, until the last slice is cut horizontally and parallel to the vertebrae.

3 Loosen the slices and lift them off the bone. Turn the saddle round and repeat on the other side of the backbone.

4 Turn the saddle over, cut out the two fillets lying along the backbone and slice them .

5 Serve each person several slices of saddle meat and a small slice of the tender fillet.

WILD BOAR

The meat of wild boar (Fr. *sanglier*) is a richer, leaner, full-bodied version of pork. These fierce, wily game animals are still found throughout Europe, Asia, North Africa and North America; the smaller peccary is native to South America and the southwestern United States.

Baby wild boar under six months old (Fr. *marcassin*) is a particular delicacy. Mature animals are best when one to two years old, after which they develop tell-tale black skin. However, boar is edible until at least ten years old and can live until treble that age. Wild boar is divided up like venison with the same cuts. However, since the meat is juicier, the leg and cuts from the loin make excellent roasts. Boar's head was traditionally boned, cooked, and stuffed to serve as a Christmas trophy, garlanded with holly.

USEFUL INFORMATION

Season Autumn (may vary according to country).
How to choose *Baby:* moist pink meat, small bones. *Mature:* deep red meat with some fat.
Portion *With bone:* ¾-1 lb/375-500 g. *Without bone:* ½ lb/250 g.
Nutritive value per 3½ oz/100 g: 113 calories; 21 g protein; 8 g fat; no carbohydrates; others n/a.
Cooking methods See venison, p.237.
When done *Braise:* tender when pierced with fork. *Roast:* served well-done (170°F/75°C on meat thermometer). *Pieces:* fall easily from fork.
Processed forms Frozen.
Storage See venison, p.237.
Typical dishes Stuffed roast with chestnuts (UK); leg with artichoke and asparagus tips (Italy); barbecued ribs with honey and vinegar (USA); *filet de marcassin au cidre* (fillet in cider, France); *marcassin Ardennaise* (roast leg with celery root, France); breast braised with vegetables (Hungary); braised shoulder with juniper (France).

Other large game animals

Game animals that resemble deer – Arctic reindeer, caribou, and the American elk or wapiti – are treated in the same way as venison in the kitchen. European elk is closest to North American moose, which is the largest deer in the world, and chamois still inhabits a few European mountains. Antelope, particularly gazelle, makes good eating. Buffalo (European bison) is protected from hunters, though it is now farmed and sold as steaks. The meat resembles gamey beef, as does the American crossbreed, beefalo, available only in the United States. Water buffalo, valued as a work animal, is eaten in Asia. Similar to beef, but less tender, it can be cooked in the same way. Bear meat has a musky taste and needs lengthy marinating. In Russia, however, bear paw is considered a delicacy. The meat of the huge North American big-horn sheep and the smaller European moufflon are akin to mutton.

EXOTIC REPTILES

Eccentric gourmets are developing a taste for farm-raised reptiles such as alligator, crocodile and snake. The tail meat of alligator and crocodile is relished in the southern United States, South America, and Africa where it is cooked in stews or sautéed in butter. Farm-raised alligator, sometimes compared to lobster, is usually braised or sliced and deep-fried. Snake meat (or prairie eel), thought by some to be an aphrodisiac, is found on menus in Africa, South America and Asia. The French occasionally eat grass snake, which is prepared in the same way as eel.

RABBIT & HARE

Like other game, wild rabbit is lean and must be kept moist during cooking. It may be marinated and simmered in the rich dark sauces appropriate to other game and is well suited to cooking in a terrine. Roasting is only appropriate if the rabbit has been boned and barded.

The meat of domestic rabbit, on the other hand, is light and delicate, closely resembling chicken. It is excellent cut in pieces on the bone to be baked with herbs, or sautéed like chicken with light combinations such as paprika, tomatoes, and sour cream.

Hare is a European animal, the North American equivalent being the jack rabbit, sometimes loosely called hare, which it resembles. In contrast to domestic rabbit, true hare has dark gamey flesh and cannot be raised in captivity. Hare suits all the classic game marinades and blood-thickened sauces. The greatest delicacy is the saddle cut, roasted on the bone or boned as fillets.

USEFUL INFORMATION

Season Year-round.
How to choose *Rabbit:* light moist flesh, white bones. *Hare:* young animals have soft ears and a narrow cleft in the lip.
Portion Whole rabbit weighs 2½ to 4½ lb/1.2-2 kg, serving 2-3; hare weighs 6-8 lb/2.7-3.6 kg, serving 6-8.
Nutritive value per 3½ oz/100 g: *All:* No carbohydrates. *Domestic rabbit and hare:* 162 calories; 21 g protein; 8 g fat; 61 g cholesterol, 41 mg sodium. *Wild rabbit:* 135 calories; 21 g protein; 5 g fat; 89 mg cholesterol; 50 mg sodium.

Domestic rabbit

Wild rabbit

Hare

Storage Refrigerate 1-2 days, freeze 6-9 months.
Cooking methods *Whole boned rabbit:* braise or pot-roast at 350°F/175°C, 1½ hours. *Pieces:* bake, braise or stew at 350°F/175°C, 1-1½ hours; marinate 1-2 days; cook as sauté ¾-1 hour. *Whole hare:* braise or pot-roast at 350°/175°C, 1½-2 hours depending on age; roast at 400°F/200°C, 20-30 minutes for saddle, on the bone. *Pieces:* braise or stew at 350°F/175°C, 2-3 hours depending on age; marinate 2-3 days.
When done *Whole rabbit:* very tender. *Pieces:* fall easily from two-pronged fork. *Whole roasted hare:* juice runs pink when pricked, served rare (125°C/51°C on meat thermometer). *Braised whole hare or pieces:* very tender.
Processed forms Frozen.
Typical dishes *Rabbit:* roast with herbs (France); with mustard sauce (France); *conejo en pepitoria* (in egg and lemon sauce, Spain); saddle with Marsala (Italy); deep-fried with sour sauce (yogurt, sour cream, herbs, Australia). *Hare:* jugged (stewed with wine, onions, blood sauce, UK); *gulasz Przodka* (goulash, Poland); *lepre in agrodolce* (with pine kernels, yellow raisins, and chocolate, Italy); *rable de lièvre à la Piron* (saddle with grapes, France); *lasen-braten* (marinated, Germany). *Also good with* raisins, red bell peppers, zucchini, tomatoes, apples, beans, brandy, cider, cabbage, shallots, wild mushrooms, mustard.

Rabbit with prunes

Rabbit and prunes are a classic combination, appearing in many recipes. Boiled new potatoes or noodles go well with this dish.

Serves 4

1 rabbit (2-2½ lb/1 kg), cut in pieces (p.240)	1 tbsp chopped parsley (for sprinkling)
6 oz/175 g prunes	***For the red wine marinade***
1 tbsp oil	1 onion, coarsely chopped
1 tbsp butter	1 carrot, coarsely chopped
2 tbsp/15 g flour	large bouquet garni
1 cup/250 ml red wine	6 peppercorns, lightly crushed
1 cup/250 ml veal stock	½ cup/125 ml red wine
1 clove garlic, crushed	1 tbsp oil
salt and pepper	

1 To marinate the rabbit: pack the pieces in a deep bowl, layering them with onion, carrot and bouquet garni. Sprinkle with peppercorns and pour over the wine and oil. Cover and refrigerate for 12-24 hours, turning the rabbit pieces occasionally.
2 Pour boiling water over the prunes and leave them to soak until cool. Drain the rabbit and pat dry with paper towels, reserving the marinade ingredients. In a sauté pan or shallow casserole, heat the oil and butter and brown the rabbit pieces on all sides. Remove from the pan, add the onion and carrot from the marinade and sauté lightly until soft. Sprinkle flour over the vegetables and cook, stirring, until the flour browns. Stir in the marinade, bouquet garni, and wine and bring to a boil. Stir in the stock, garlic, salt and pepper and replace the rabbit in the pan.
3 Cover and simmer for 25 minutes on top of the stove or in the oven at 350°F/175°C. Transfer the rabbit to another shallow casserole and strain the sauce over it, pressing hard on the vegetables to extract the liquid. Drain the prunes, add them to the rabbit and cover the pan. Simmer for 10-15 minutes or until the rabbit and prunes are tender.
4 Arrange the rabbit on a serving dish with the prunes on top. If necessary, boil to reduce the sauce until it just coats a spoon. Season the sauce to taste and pour it over the rabbit. Sprinkle with parsley before serving.

BONING RABBIT OR HARE

Removing the bones leaves a carcass suitable for stuffing and roasting. The hind legs may be left to give shape to the roast.

1 Cut off and discard the head. Set the carcass on its back, hind legs toward you and split the chest.

2 Cut along the rib bones on one side, lifting each rib and scraping it to free the meat.

3 Cut and ease the meat away from the backbone, stopping when you reach the thin skin under the backbone. Work along the backbone, scraping the meat from it.

4 Using both hands split the pelvic bone so the legs lie flat. **Note** In most cases this bone is split during cleaning.

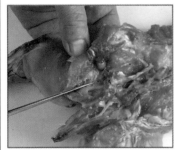

5 Cut under the tail bone and pull up the pelvic bone to loosen it.

6 Separate the thigh bone from the hip joint, expose the leg bone and lift it out.

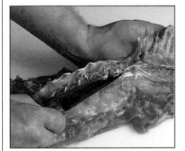

7 Cut round and loosen the backbone from the meat but do not remove it. Repeat steps 2-7 on the other side.

8 Sever shoulder joints. Remove the shoulder and forelegs.

9 Cut and pull the rib cage and backbone from the meat in one piece. Use the bones for stock.

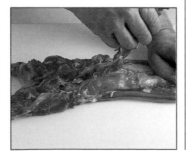

CUTTING UP RABBIT OR HARE

The toughest part of the rabbit is the hind legs, which are often removed to cook apart from the saddle and the forelegs. The legs are usually simmered in a stew, while the saddle may be roasted on the bone, or cut in pieces to stew with the legs. Whole rabbit or hare that has been roasted, can be divided into pieces when cooked. The head may be cooked with other pieces, or discarded. Trim and discard the flaps of skin, tips of forelegs, and any excess bone. With a heavy knife, divide the carcass crosswise into three sections: hind legs, back, and forelegs including the rib cage. Cut between the hind legs to separate them; trim the backbone.

Chop the front carcass into two pieces to separate the forelegs. **For six to seven pieces:** cut the saddle crosswise into two or three pieces, depending on the size. **For eight to nine pieces:** divide the hind legs through the knee joint.

EXOTIC SMALL GAME ANIMALS

Only a few game animals are eaten throughout the world, but a surprising number have regional appeal. Rodents, including the gray squirrel, are traditional ingredients in the American Colonial dish Brunswick stew, which also contains tomatoes, okra, corn kernels, lima beans and bell peppers. Both the muskrat, found in the eastern United States, and the South American guinea pig are raised for food, and cooked on the barbecue or fricasséed. The hefty marmot (USA woodchuck or ground hog) can weigh 25 lb/ 12 kg and has rich meat. All of these animals closely resemble rabbit and are roasted and stewed in a similar fashion. Small carnivorous animals such as the badger were once spit-roasted as a rural treat. Nowadays badgers are rarely eaten, and in many European countries they are a protected species. In the United States, the raccoon – half pet, half pest – may be stuffed with herbs, onions, dried fruit and nuts. In the southern United States, opossum is sometimes roasted and stuffed.

Armadillo, known as "poor man's pig" during the Depression, may be baked in its armor with herb stuffing or made into spicy sausages, from Texas down to South America. Spined animals such as the hedgehog and the porcupine are disarmed in the kitchen by rolling in clay and baking so that the quills peel away when the clay jacket is removed.

Note One of the reasons that small game animals are rarely eaten is that they can carry diseases. A reliable source of supply is therefore crucial for home cooking.

CHARCUTERIE

In French, the word charcuterie literally means *chair cuite*, cooked meat. A charcuterie is a standard store in most European towns, while in other countries charcuterie is found at the delicatessen counter of large food stores. It usually centers around pork products, including some of the prides of French cuisine: pâtés and terrines ranging from simple puréed liver to fine-textured veal pâtés or rustic country mixtures studded with hazelnuts or peppercorns and a selection of stuffed *galantines* and *ballotines* coated with aspic.

Ham, bacon, sausages and cured meats are the staples of charcuterie, found worldwide in innumerable guises. Traditionally, charcuterie consisted only of completely or partially prepared pork dishes, but the repertoire now includes game or veal and ham pies, as well as pork pies and *pâtés en croûte*. Fish and vegetable terrines and *mousselines*, as well as the famous *pâté de foie gras* (p.190) and even prepared salads are also included in the range.

TERRINES & PATES

Strictly speaking, a pâté is distinguished from a terrine by the way in which it is cooked: a pâté is baked in pastry and a terrine (Fr. *terre*, meaning earth) is cooked in a special earthenware terrine mold (p.511). However, over the years these distinctions have been less rigorously observed and the definitions have acquired a much looser meaning. Fine-textured, rich mixtures that used to be baked in pastry are still known as pâtés, even though the pastry has been replaced by a terrine mold or loaf pan; liver pâté is a good example. The name pâté is also applied to mixtures that have been baked in the oven or sautéed in a frying pan, then puréed to a smooth consistency.

Pâtés and terrines are based on a stuffing, sometimes called forcemeat (Fr. *farce*), which varies in texture from velvety smooth to coarsely chopped. It is seasoned and baked in the oven, usually until it is firm enough to unmold for serving. The stuffing can be plain or layered with strips of meat such as veal, ham or game, which are often marinated first in wine and brandy; it can be dotted with liver for richness, or with pistachios, truffles or pieces of blanched red and green pepper for color. Egg may be added to bind the mixture and breadcrumbs for lightness.

Pork, valued for its flavor and rich fat, is the primary ingredient of pâtés and terrines. Classic proportions for a stuffing are 1 lb/ 500 g lean pork (or a pork and veal mixture), 2 lb/1 kg veal, game or poultry meat, and 1½ lb/750 g ground pork fat. This high proportion of fat is necessary to prevent a dry stuffing, while the gelatin in veal provides body. Chicken and turkey may be substituted for veal, but are too dry to replace pork in a recipe.

The meat for pâtés and terrines is usually worked once or twice through the coarse or fine blade of a grinder, according to the desired texture. A food processor tends to crush the meat and give an elastic consistency, but a grinder also has a disadvantage – its friction tends to heat the meat, so for finest flavor, a perfectionist will chop the meat by hand. For further information, see Cooking Equipment (p.502).

Standard proportions for seasoning a pâté or terrine mixture are 2½ teaspoons of salt and a scant teaspoon of pepper per 2 lb/ 1 kg meat, but this can vary according to the type of meat used. Spices such as nutmeg, allspice, ginger and cloves provide additional flavor, as does a spoonful of alcohol such as brandy or Madeira. Herbs, finely chopped garlic, sautéed onion or shallot are other possible additions. Seasoning must be tested by tasting: fry a small ball of the mixture or bake it in the oven, and taste, bearing in mind that food to be served cold requires more seasoning than when served hot. Seasonings chosen should balance one another; no single herb should predominate.

USEFUL INFORMATION

Portion *Appetizer*: 2-4 oz/60-125 g, depending on richness.
Cooking methods *In terrine mold*: bake in a water bath at 350°F/175°C, 25-35 minutes per 1 lb/500 g (metal molds need less cooking time than earthenware). *In pastry*: bake at 425°F/220°C, 15 minutes, lower heat to 350°F/175°C and bake a further 20-30 minutes per 1 lb/500 g.
When done Skewer inserted in center of mixture for 30 seconds is hot to the touch when withdrawn; 170°F/75°C on meat thermometer; liquid around mixture should be bubbling and clear, showing meat juices are cooked; (pink color in commercial pâtés or mixtures comes from use of preservatives).
Problems Bland if underseasoned; dry if too little fat is used; mixture shrinks and loses juices if overcooked.
Storage Flavors mellow with time. *Meat*: up to 4 days. To store whole meat terrines up to 10 days, cover surface with a layer of lard; once cut, use within a day; slices of meat terrine discolor within an hour if not kept tightly covered; mixtures with a high fat content like meat *rillettes* freeze well. *Fish and vegetable*: refrigerate at least 1 day, up to 2 days.

Accompaniments *Meat*: gherkin pickles, olives, pickled onions. *Game*: Cumberland sauce (p.66), lingonberries.
Typical dishes *Pâtés*: *kalfspâté* (veal with sour cream, Madeira and bacon, Belgium); liver with bacon, truffles, oregano and cloves (Netherlands); liver with sherry, lemon and bacon (Austria); liver with brandy and parsley (Italy); partridge with truffles and sherry (Spain); *leberkäse* (hot liver pâté with bacon, Germany); *de vendange* (rabbit with wine and brandy, France); liver with anchovies (Sweden); liver with bacon and anchovies (Denmark); hot calves' liver pâté with veal and pork (France); duck liver mousse (France); *pâté de foie gras* (goose liver pâté, France); *pâté de gibier* (game meat with herbs, France). *Terrines*: venison with juniper (Germany); spiced hare (with lemon, parsnip, vinegar and capers, Hungary); rabbit with prunes (France); goose with wild mushrooms (Poland); veal and ham with cinnamon and bacon (Spain); Whitby polony (lean beef with ham, mace and cayenne, UK); foie gras with truffles (France); *torta manfreda* (liver with Marsala and Parmesan, Italy); potted goose (UK).

Presenting terrines and pâtés

Soft pâtés, *rillettes* and potted meats are often served in the crock in which they were cooked; an alternative is to transfer the mixture to individual ramekins, or to scoop or pipe it in rosettes directly on to plates decorated with a lettuce leaf. Firmer pâtés and terrines can be unmolded and arranged in overlapping slices for serving. Chilling dulls flavor so most mixtures are best served at room temperature.

The layers of many terrines are decorative, particularly when they contain multi-colored ingredients such as pistachios or bell peppers. Luxury pâtés like foie gras may be decorated with aspic (p.253), while more earthy terrines call for olives and pickles. Rich pâtés should be served with dry crackers or toast, while meaty terrines go best with French or whole wheat bread.

Terrines

There are many types of terrine mold; all should have a tight-fitting lid, which is often sealed with a luting paste of flour and water during cooking.

To keep a terrine mixture moist, the mold is always lined with fat, usually barding fat. Caul fat (p.235) may be used instead; it cooks to an attractive lacy pattern on top. Fat bacon, the most common substitute for barding fat, adds attractive stripes but has a pronounced taste that may overwhelm delicate mixtures; if using bacon, add less salt to the stuffing. The fatty skin of duck or goose is a good lining for poultry mixtures.

A terrine mixture may simply be baked in the mold, particularly if the texture is very coarse. Alternatively, it is layered with strips of pork fat, ham, or meat such as veal escalope or game, that reinforce the main flavoring theme. A band of chicken liver, wrapped in barding fat, may be bedded down in the center. When sliced, these additions form a pretty mosaic pattern.

Molded terrines are usually cooked in a water bath (p.510) to diffuse heat evenly; exceptions are rough country terrines, which are baked uncovered. After baking, the terrine is left to cool, then pressed so the texture is compact and easy to slice.

PREPARING & COOKING A TERRINE

If you do not have a terrine mold, the bottom of a loaf pan may be lined with one long strip of fat, and the sides left bare.

1 **To line a terrine mold:** cut barding fat to fit the sides of the mold and line the mold with it. If serving the terrine unmolded, for attractive effect put a bay leaf and herbs at the bottom of the mold then cut strips of fat and arrange them in a lattice pattern on top of them.

2 Add the terrine mixture. **Note** Fill the mold to the brim, as the mixture will shrink during cooking. Cut a single piece of fat and arrange it over the terrine to keep the top moist.

To make the luting paste: stir 1-1½ cups/250-375 ml water into 1½ cups/200 g flour and mix to a rough paste.

3 RIGHT Seal the gap between the lid and rim of the mold with luting paste to keep in most of the steam. Roll the paste into a rope and insert it into the gap around the lid.

4 Cook in a water bath (see recipe). Cool until the terrine is tepid. Remove the lid and set a 1 lb/500 g weight on top so the mixture is compressed and slices well. Refrigerate until cold and unmold for serving.

242

Country terrine

Terrine de campagne

The classic accompaniment to a country terrine is gherkin pickles, but a tart fruit chutney (p.489) is also delicious.

Serves 8

½ lb/250 g barding fat	2 eggs, beaten to mix
1 tbsp butter	2 tbsp/30 ml brandy
1 onion, chopped	1 tbsp each salt and pepper
1 lb/500 g pork, half fat, half lean, ground	½ lb/250 g thickly sliced cooked ham, cut in strips
½ lb/250 g veal, ground	1 bay leaf
½ lb/250 g chicken livers, ground	sprig of thyme
2 cloves garlic, finely chopped	luting paste (below left), optional
¼ tsp ground allspice	
pinch ground cloves	2 qt/2 L terrine mold
pinch ground nutmeg	or loaf pan

1 Line the mold with the barding fat, reserving some for the top. Heat the oven to 350°F/175°C.
2 To make the stuffing: melt the butter in a small pan and fry the onion slowly until soft but not brown. Mix the onion with the remaining ingredients except the ham, herbs and luting paste. Beat with a wooden spoon to blend in the seasoning. Sauté a small piece and taste – it should be quite spicy. Beat the mixture for 2-3 minutes so it holds together.
3 Spread one-third of the stuffing in the lined terrine, add a layer of half the ham strips and top with another third of pork stuffing. Add the remaining ham and cover with the last third of the stuffing. Cover with the remaining barding fat, set the bay leaf and thyme on top, cover with the lid, and seal with luting paste. If using a loaf pan, cut the barding fat into strips, place it on top of the stuffing in a lattice and do not cover.
4 Bake the terrine in a water bath (p.510) in the oven for 1¼-1½ hours, until cooked. **Note** Keep the water simmering and if too much evaporates, add more.
5 Cool and press the terrine (left). Store for three days or up to a week so the flavor mellows. Serve in the mold, or in slices.

Pâtés

Rich, smooth pâtés are often liver-based, with ingredients like veal added for body. Unusual flavorings distinguish a pâté: wild mushrooms with pork, barberries with game, or apple with chicken livers. However, moist ingredients must be used sparingly, or pâtés become too soft and do not keep well.

Classic pâtés are not the end of the story. *Rillettes* are made by baking a fatty meat in a pottery crock with a little water, salt and pepper until the meat falls apart. When cool, the meat is shredded with forks and mixed with the rendered fat to give a characteristic coarse texture. (For fish *rillettes*, see p.124.)

Potted meats are a British specialty made with robust meats such as ham or tongue that are baked slowly with butter or lard and spices, ground to a purée and packed in a crock. Shellfish and rich fish such as salmon may also be potted.

For smooth pâtés, mixtures need to be puréed; softer meats like liver purée well in a food processor, as do cooked meats, but most pâté mixtures are too stiff to work in a blender. A drum sieve (Fr. *tamis*, p.506) and pestle gives the finest texture for liver pâtés and *mousselines*. A food mill also works well.

RAISED MEAT PIES & PATES EN CROUTE

To bake food in a crust is a traditional way to seal in juices and protect rich or delicate meats from direct heat. British raised pies, usually of meat or game, are shaped with a hot water pastry dough (p.244). For grander occasions, Europeans wrap meat or fish mixtures in puff pastry, brioche dough or *pâte à pâté* (p.373) to make elegant meat or fish *pâtés en croûte*. Dough must be robust to retain juices and withstand long cooking.

USEFUL INFORMATION

Portion 4 × 10 in/10 × 25 cm pie or pâté serves 8-10.
Typical pan Hinged oval or rectangular mold.
Preparation of pan Greased.
Cooking methods *Large pies or pâtés*: bake at 400°F/200°C, 30 minutes, then reduce heat to 350°F/175°C and continue cooking 1-2 hours depending on recipe. *Small pies or pâtés*: bake at 400°F/200°C, 30 minutes, then reduce heat to 375°F/190°C and continue cooking 15-35 minutes.
When done Crust brown; meat thermometer inserted in center of pie or pâté reads 170°F/75°C.
Problems Ingredients shrink

during cooking so should be packed tightly inside dough; juice leaks if dough is not carefully sealed; if dough starts to brown too much, cover loosely with foil.
Storage *Uncooked*: refrigerate 12 hours. *Cooked*: refrigerate 3 days; freeze 1 month.
Typical dishes *Raised pies*: game (UK); pheasant (UK); pork (UK); chicken and ham (UK). *Pâtés en croûte*: salmon with rice and *duxelles* (Russia); *pâté d'Alsace* (with wine, Madeira and shallots, Alsace, France); *hasenpastete* (hare pâté, Austria); duck pâté with olives (France); *croûte d'anguilles* (eel pâté, France).

Raised meat pies

The classic casing for a raised meat pie is British hot water pastry, which can be molded like potter's clay and sets to form a firm, freestanding case; the most common example of its use is in British pork pie. Softer doughs are rolled out to line a hinged pie mold: the French generally use *pâte à pâté* (p.373), while the British also make a soft suet dough with ground suet and self-rising flour and use it for steak and kidney pudding.

LINING A RAISED PIE MOLD

In Europe, particularly England, hot water pastry (p.244), which can be molded to shape as it cools, is the traditional pie casing.

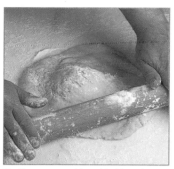

1 Grease a mold and baking sheet. On a floured surface, roll three-quarters of the dough to a circle thicker in the center than at the sides.

2 Sprinkle the dough generously with flour and fold it in half to form a semi-circle thicker in the center than at the sides.

3 Roll the thicker part so the dough flattens to form a pouch.

4 Gently open out the pouch by slipping your hands inside it.

5 Lower the dough pouch into the mold, overhanging it at the rim. Press the dough well into the bottom and against the sides, taking care not to make pleats. Fill the pie (see recipe, p.244).

6 Trim the pastry, leaving about ½ in/1.25 cm over the edge, then fold it over the filling and brush the edges with egg glaze. Roll out the remaining dough as a lid, lift it on to the filling and press the edges of the dough together to seal them.

7 Trim off excess dough and, using a small knife, crimp the edges to decorate. Brush with glaze.

8 Poke a hole for steam to escape and insert a piping tube or cylinder of foil. Decorate the pie with pastry decorations (p.373).

Raised veal & ham pie

Cumberland sauce (p.66) and potato salad are excellent accompaniments for veal and ham pie. As a variation, a game pie can be made by substituting venison or pheasant for the ham.

Serves 8–10

1½ lb/750 g boneless veal shoulder, ground	2 tsp salt
	¾ cup/175 g lard
¾ lb/375 g uncooked lean ham or unsmoked bacon, ground	1 cup/250 ml water (more if needed)
grated zest of ½ lemon	***4 × 10 in/10 × 25 cm oval or rectangular raised pie mold***
1 tsp dried thyme	
1 tsp dried sage	
¼ tsp ground nutmeg	
salt and pepper	
4 hard-boiled eggs	
egg glaze (p.385)	
1 cup/250 ml jellied veal stock, p.44 (more if needed)	
For the hot water dough	
4 cups/500 g flour	

1 For the filling: toss the meats with the lemon zest, thyme, sage, nutmeg, salt and pepper. Sauté a spoonful of the mixture and taste for seasoning; it should be quite spicy.
2 **For the hot water dough:** sift the flour into a bowl with the salt and make a well in the center. In a pan over high heat melt the lard in the water until completely melted and very hot. Pour the melted lard and water mixture into the well in the flour, stirring rapidly with a wooden spoon and drawing in flour to make a smooth dough. If the dough seems dry add a few more spoonfuls of hot water. Press it into a ball. Set the bowl over a pan of hot water and cover the dough with a wet cloth. Leave to rest for 5 minutes until cool enough to handle.
3 Preheat the oven to 400°F/200°C. Grease the mold (and, if it is a bottomless mold, a baking sheet as well). Reserve a quarter of the dough for a lid and roll out the remainder to form a pouch with which to line the mold. (See Lining a raised meat pie mold, p.243.) Try to avoid making creases in the pastry when lining the mold or tearing it when adding the filling, as this will spoil the appearance of the finished pie. Pack half the filling into the pastry case. Lay the eggs along the middle and cover with the remaining veal and ham filling.
4 To make the lid, turn in the edges of the dough lining the mold and brush them with egg glaze. Roll out the remaining dough and cover the filling with it. Trim the edges with a knife or scissors. Crimp the edges (p.243) to seal and brush the lid with glaze. Poke two holes in the lid and insert rolls of foil to form chimneys through which steam can escape. Roll out the dough trimmings, shape a rose (p.373) and decorate the pie with it. Chill the pie for 15 minutes or until firm.
5 Bake the pie for 30 minutes. Lower the heat to 350°F/175°C and continue baking 1-1½ hours or until the pie is cooked (When done, p.243). If the pie browns too quickly during cooking, cover it loosely with aluminum foil.
6 Let the pie cool for 5-10 minutes, then loosen the mold and remove it. Leave to cool then chill for 6-8 hours or overnight before serving. When the pie is thoroughly chilled, melt the jellied veal stock and pour it into the pie through the holes in the top to fill the gap between the filling and the lid. Chill the pie and serve when the stock has set to a gel.

Pâtés en croûte

Fillings for *pâtés en croûte* differ little from those used for terrines, though the elegant pastry coating is better matched by veal, ham or game rather than plain pork. The stuffing is often layered with strips of meat, which help to hold the pâté in shape.

Doughs for *pâtés en croûte* must be pliable and firm enough to hold their shape. Richest of all is puff pastry, reserved for luxury fillings, while brioche is ideal for particularly moist mixtures. *Pâte à pâté* (p.373), a version of *pâte brisée* made with whole egg instead of egg yolk, is easy to use and often lard is substituted for butter when the filling contains pork.

Like raised meat pies, *pâtés en croûte* may be served cold, but they are also delicious hot, particularly the small individual pâtés (*petits pantins*) of France.

WRAPPING LARGE PATES EN CROUTE

This technique can be used for wrapping fillings for beef Wellington and fish mixtures such as *coulibiac* (p.132). The pâté may be decorated with strips of pastry, as here, or with other decorations such as pastry leaves or a pastry rose (p.373).

1 Roll the dough to a ¼ in/6 mm thickness. Cut two strips 14 in/35 cm long, one 4 in/10 cm wide, the other about 8 in/20 cm wide. Transfer the narrower strip to a greased baking sheet.

2 Shape the filling neatly on top of the narrower strip, leaving a ½ in/1.25 cm border. Turn up the edges of the dough and brush them with egg glaze. Loosely wrap the larger strip of dough around a rolling pin and unroll it over the filling. Press the edges of the two pieces of dough together with your fingers to seal them. Using a small, sharp knife, trim any excess dough from around the edges.

3 On a floured surface, roll out the dough trimmings and cut long strips ⅜ in/1 cm wide. Lay the strips diagonally across the top and sides of the pâté and wrap one long strip around the base to neaten it.

4 With a sharp knife, cut two holes on top of the pâté and insert a roll of foil into each to form chimneys through which steam can escape. Cover and refrigerate the *pâté en croûte* until firm, ½-1 hour.

WRAPPING SMALL PATES EN CROUTE

Small pâtés with fillings of fish or meat are wrapped in a single piece of dough like a parcel.

1 Roll the dough about ¼ in/6 mm thick and cut into 6 in/15 cm squares. Put a large spoonful of filling in the middle of each square. Cut a small square from each corner of the dough. Brush the dough with egg glaze.

2 Fold the sides over to enclose the filling.

3 Turn the pâté over so that the seam is underneath. Brush the top with egg glaze and decorate it.

Game pâté en croûte

Serve this pâté hot with glazed chestnuts and a *sauce poivrade* (p.58). Alternatively, it can be served cold with celery root *rémoulade* and Onion confit (p.291).

Serves 10-12 as a main course

sour cream dough (p.373)	¼ lb/125 g chicken liver, finely chopped
½ lb/250 g cooked ham	2 eggs, beaten to mix
1½ lb/750 g boneless venison, pheasant or other game meat	2 tsp ground allspice
2 tbsp/30 ml white wine	1 tsp ground nutmeg
3 tbsp/45 ml brandy	1 tsp salt (more if needed)
egg glaze (p.385)	1 tsp ground pepper (more if needed)
For the stuffing	
2 lb/1 kg ground pork, equal parts fat and lean	

1 Make the sour cream dough and chill it for 30 minutes.
2 Cut the ham and half the game meat in ½ in/1.25 cm strips and the remainder in small pieces. Put the strips in a shallow dish, pour over the white wine and half the brandy. Cover and marinate for 30 minutes.
3 **For the stuffing:** work the pork and the remaining game meat through the fine plate of a meat grinder into a bowl. Add the rest of the brandy and remaining stuffing ingredients. Drain the marinade from the ham and game strips and add it to the stuffing. Beat the mixture well with a wooden spoon until it comes away from the sides of the bowl, 2-3 minutes. Sauté a small piece of stuffing and taste for seasoning; it should be quite spicy.
4 To shape the pâté: divide the dough in two and roll each piece into rectangles. Divide the stuffing into three. Spread one portion lengthwise on one of the pastry rectangles. Top with half the strips of game. Repeat with another layer of stuffing. Cover this with the remaining game strips followed by the remaining stuffing. Mold the filling with your hands to a thick rectangle. Wrap the filling in the rest of the pastry, decorate it and brush it with egg glaze. Cover and refrigerate the pâté for ½-1 hour until firm. Heat the oven to 400°F/200°C.
5 Bake the pâté until the pastry starts to brown, 15-20 minutes. Lower temperature to 350°F/175°C and continue baking until the pâté tests done (p.243), about 1¼ hours. Allow the pâté to cool on a baking sheet for 5 minutes before serving.

SAUSAGES

Sausages are any mixture stuffed into a casing (traditionally the large or small intestines of domestic animals). In practice most sausages are pork-based, though beef and veal feature in a few types, and game can add a ripe flavor. White sausages are sometimes made with chicken or veal, while fish or shellfish sausages are a gastronomic conceit often based on luxury ingredients such as lobster or sea scallops. They usually take the form of fish *mousselines* (p.123) stuffed in a casing.

Sausages are indigenous to many nations because they often provide a way of preserving meat for short or long periods without refrigeration. As with curing ham, new commercial preservatives have replaced the saltpeter (potassium nitrate) traditionally used. In theory all sausages can be made at home, but in practice few households have the equipment for smoking or the cool, dry climate needed to smoke and dry sausages successfully. However, some kinds of fresh sausage are excellent home-made.

Additions to sausages fall into two categories: fillers like breadcrumbs and oatmeal that lighten the meat and make it go further, as in the British "banger", and seasonings, commonly herbs such as sage and thyme, spices such as the hot red peppers in Spanish *chorizo*, and the indispensable salt. Small casings are used for fresh sausages so heat penetrates easily to the center. French *crépinettes*, which are rolled in caul fat, are not, strictly speaking, sausages although they are treated in the same way.

As fresh sausages may contain raw ingredients, they have a short shelf-life, although this may be extended by additional cooking processes such as smoking, drying, blanching or boiling. Both the delicate *boudin blanc* of France, made from pork, chicken or veal and sometimes eggs and cream, and the heartier *boudin noir* or German *blutwurst* made of blood, spices and onions, are examples of semi-cooked sausages that have been blanched to firm their texture and extend their shelf-life by a few days. Seasoned with spices and garlic, the famous Polish *kielbasa* and German *knackwurst* are both slightly smoked. More local in their appeal are French *andouillettes*, made of fresh pig's intestines and stomach, and Scottish haggis, made of the lungs, liver and heart of sheep stuffed into the stomach lining.

Like all pork, fresh and semi-cooked sausages must be thoroughly cooked before eating to avoid any danger of trichinosis infection. They are often poached so they remain moist, but sausages with a generous fat content may be fried, broiled or baked in the oven.

Distinct from fresh and semi-cooked sausages are those that are sold ready to eat. These may be fully cooked, sometimes by hot-smoking (p.487), or completely cured by drying. Included in this wide category are the familiar *mortadella, bologna* and liver sausage. Casings are often large and the sausages may be studded with pieces of fat or meat to make a decorative slice. Some liver-based sausages are soft enough to spread; they may be flavored with onion, herbs, garlic, anchovies or spices and resemble pâté packed in a casing. The distinctive French *andouille*, made of pig's intestines stuffed one inside the other, combines smoking, drying and cooking in its fabrication.

The third general category is sausages that are uncooked but are totally preserved by drying. They are eaten without further cooking, often thinly sliced and served cold with cheese, vegetable salads and other cold meats. Although these sausages do not require cooking, some varieties, notably Italian *peperoni* and a dried version of *chorizo*, appear in cooked dishes such as pizza and hearty stews. Besides *chorizo* and *peperoni* two types of dried sausage dominate this field: *cervelat* (UK or USA *saveloy*) is an international term for mild semi-dry beef and pork sausages that are sometimes lightly smoked. Most countries have a version flavored with herbs, aromatic spices like coriander seed and perhaps garlic. The second type, salami-style sausages, are drier and more highly spiced; since they may be dried for up to six months, they have a harder texture. Pork and beef are often combined in salami, and frequently wine is added to the mixture, giving the sausage a characteristic tangy flavor.

Polish *kaszanka*

Morcilla

Andouillette

Frankfurter

Bockwurst

Cervelat

Haggis

Boudin noir

English black pudding

Knackwurst

Boudin blanc

USEFUL INFORMATION

Common fresh and semi-cooked sausages Andouillette (tripe and chitterlings stuffed into themselves, sometimes fully cooked, France); black pudding (UK); blood pudding (Wales); blood sausage (Sweden); *blutwurst* (blood sausage, Germany); *morcilla* (blood sausage, Spain); *boudin blanc* (mixture of pork, veal, chicken or rabbit, France); *rostbratwurst* (country-style, flavored with lemon, nutmeg and caraway, Germany, Switzerland); *bockwurst* (spicy mixture of veal and pork or beef flavored with pepper, nutmeg, coriander, ginger and garlic, Germany, USA); Cambridge (mixture of pork, rice and meat flavored with sage, cayenne, mace, nutmeg and pepper, UK); chipolata (small pork sausage with pork fat and rice mixture seasoned with coriander, pimento, nutmeg, thyme, cayenne, white pepper, France, UK); *kaszanka* (pig's liver, lungs and blood bound with buckwheat, Poland); *luganeghe* (fresh pork sold by the length, Italy); *chorizo* (pork, pimento, with various seasonings, Spain, Mexico); *cotechino* (pork, pork fat with white wine and garlic, Italy); *crépinettes* (meat wrapped in caul fat with seasonings, France); Cumberland (pork with black pepper and herbs, formed into one continuous coil, UK); frankfurters/*wiener* (pork and fat mixed to a smooth paste and smoked, Germany, USA, Austria); *kielbasa* (flavored with spices and garlic, Poland); *salciccie* (small sausage, country-style pork mixture, Italy); *weisswurst* (small veal sausage with cream and eggs, Germany); *zampone* (pork mixture in a boned pig's foot, Italy).

Common cooked sausages Andouille (large pork sausage with tripe or chitterlings, sometimes smoked, France); *bologna* (mild, smooth, lightly smoked, usually of pork and beef but can be made with veal, chicken or turkey, Italy, USA); *boule de Basle* (beechwood-smoked mixture of pork, beef and pork fat, Switzerland); *knackwurst* (cold-smoked mixture of pork, beef and pork fat with cumin and garlic, Germany); liver (flavored with onion, eastern and central Europe).

Common semi-dry or dry sausages Alpenkluber (air-dried, pork, beef, and pork fat, Switzerland); *bierwurst* (spicy pork with hard back fat usually flavored with garlic, Germany); *butifarra* (pork with wine and spices, Spain); *landjäger* (smoked beef with caraway and garlic, Switzerland, Germany); *linguica* (garlic flavored, Portugal); *pepperone* (coarsely chopped pork and beef flavored with hot peppers, fennel and spices, Italy); salami (spiced sausages made with uncooked beef or pork often flavored with garlic and pepper, Italy); *spegelpolse* (mixture of pork, beef and pork fat seasoned with spices and garlic, Denmark).

How to choose *Fresh*: moist, pink not gray, sweet-smelling, no dry edges. *Cooked*: if large, sausage should be uncut or cut to order, moist and fresh-smelling. *Dry*: firm but not too dry.

Portion *Fresh*: 6-8 oz/175-250 g. *Cooked, dry*: 3-4 oz/90-125 g.

Cooking methods Times depend on diameter and type of sausage: bake at 350°F/175°C, 10-20 minutes; barbecue, broil, pan-fry or sauté 6-10 minutes; simmer 10-15 minutes; stew 30-45 minutes.

When done Tender, no longer pink in center and a skewer inserted in center for 30 seconds is hot to the touch when withdrawn.

Problems Fresh sausages burst if cooked too fast, are dry if not basted well; if stale, taste harsh and vinegary; turn rancid if stored too long or in too warm a place.

Storage Type of sausage will determine exact storage time. *Fresh*: refrigerate up to 2 days, or freeze no longer than 3 months. *Semi-cooked*: refrigerate 1-2 weeks. *Cooked*: refrigerate up to 2 weeks. *Dry*: hang in cool, airy place indefinitely.

Typical dishes With warm potato salad (France); *bollito misto* (with other boiled meats, Italy); *himmel und erde* (apples and potatoes with blood sausage, Germany); *bratwurst* with apples in currant sauce (Germany); *saucisses à la Languedocienne* (Toulouse sausages with garlic and tomato, France); *lecso* (simmered with tomatoes, green peppers and paprika, Hungary); *choucroute garni* (with sausage, smoked pork, bacon, sauerkraut, France); *varzà cu porc* (pork sausage with sauerkraut, eastern Europe); *fabada asturiana* (stew with sausages and white beans, Spain); with beans and basil (France); *kielbasa* and cabbage (Poland); *bigos polski* (hunter's stew with mushrooms, sauerkraut, cabbage and pork, Poland); *stracotto* (stew with sausages, beef and vegetables in white wine, Italy); rice, liver and raisin sausages (Finland); toad in the hole (in batter, UK); baked sausage pancakes (Scandinavia); with kale and potato (Netherlands); mixed grill (broiled sausages with kidney, mushrooms, lamb chop, fillet steak and tomato, UK); Scotch eggs (pork sausagemeat wrapped around hard-boiled eggs, coated with breadcrumbs and fried, Scotland); *zuppa alla senese* (with lentils, Italy); with leeks (Switzerland). *Also good with* red cabbage, mustard, onions, red and green bell peppers, bacon, shellfish, chicken, eggplant, game birds, dried fruits.

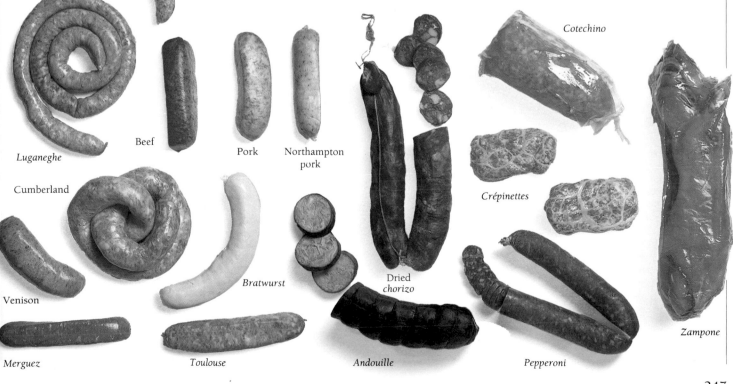

Pork chipolata

Luganeghe

Beef

Pork

Northampton pork

Cumberland

Bratwurst

Dried chorizo

Cotechino

Crépinettes

Venison

Merguez

Toulouse

Andouille

Pepperoni

Zampone

Sausage casings

Casings vary in size from the ½ in/1.25 cm diameter of small pig's intestines, to the 3-4 in/7.5-10 cm of large beef intestines, and each sausage calls for a specific type. The French distinguish between small sausages or *saucisses*, and *saucissons*, which are large. After thorough cleaning, casings are sold fresh or salted and can also be found frozen. Synthetic casings are commonly used for fresh sausages. Bladder or stomach lining may also be used.

Spanish spiced sausages

As well as being served alone, these spiced sausages (in Spanish, *chorizo*) often give soups extra spice and also add flavor to dishes like Paella (p.317).

Makes 12 4 in/10 cm medium sausages

3 lb/1.4 kg fatty boneless pork	2 tsp salt
½ lb/250 g fatback, without rind	1 tsp ground coriander
6 cloves garlic, crushed	½ tsp ground cumin
½ cup/125 ml red wine	½ tsp ground black pepper
4 tbsp/60 g sweet paprika	*Medium sausage casings*
2 tsp crushed, dried red pepper	

1 Work the pork through the coarse blade of a meat grinder into a large bowl. Cut fatback into ¼ in/6 mm cubes and add to the pork. Add the garlic, wine, spices and salt, then beat for 1-2 minutes so the mixture holds together. Sauté a small ball and taste, adding more spices and seasoning if necessary.
2 Stuff the casings and tie into 4 in/10 cm lengths (right). Wrap and refrigerate, 1-2 days.
3 Prick the sausages so they do not burst. Broil or fry them in a little butter or oil until they are brown and not pink in the center, 5-7 minutes on each side.

STUFFING SAUSAGE CASINGS

Before use, soak the casings for 1-2 hours in cold water to remove salt and make them pliable. Drain but do not dry them.

1 Clean and open each casing by attaching one end to a tap and running cold water through it. Tie each casing with string at one end. Attach the open end to the base of a funnel. Slide the casing up the funnel until the closed end of the casing is reached.

2 Work the sausage filling through the funnel into the casing. Do not pack the filling too tightly or the sausages will burst as they cook. Twist the casing at intervals as you go, to make a string of sausages. Tie the casing with string at the end.

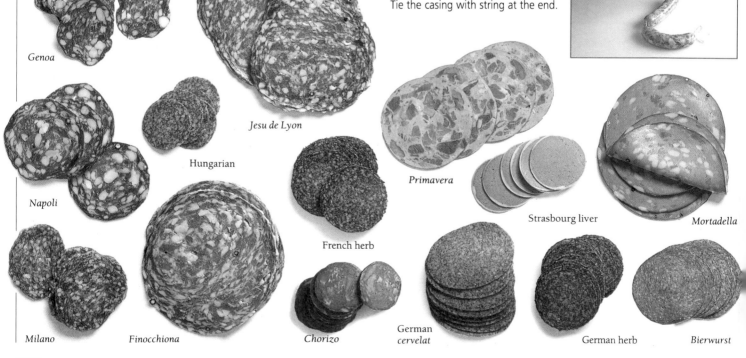

Genoa

Jesu de Lyon

Hungarian

Napoli

French herb

Primavera

Strasbourg liver

Mortadella

Milano *Finocchiona*

Chorizo

German cervelat

German herb *Bierwurst*

BACON & CURED PORK

There are three methods of curing bacon and salt pork: with dry, coarse salt, with brine, or with a mixture of salt, sugar, seasonings and preservatives. After salting, the meat may be smoked. Results vary depending on the cure and breed of pig.

Most bacon is made from the fatty chest meat that runs under the pig. This is called streaky bacon in Great Britain, bacon in the United States, and *lard* in France; the meat may be salted or both salted and smoked. Unsmoked salt bacon in Britain is described as "green"; in the United States most bacon is smoked. In much of Europe, the rind (Fr. *couenne*) is usually included with the bacon, then it is cut off before cooking and used to add gelatin to stocks and stews.

French bacon is the meatiest, suitable for flavoring braises and stews in the form of lardons (right) rather than being served as a separate ingredient; if fried it is tough. In Britain, bacon cut in slices or rashers can be fried until it is tender and fairly crisp, while in the United States, fried bacon is usually served very crisp. Any type of lightly cured fatty bacon may be used instead of pork fat for barding.

Other cuts of pork are commonly cured as bacon. In Britain gammon denotes the hind leg of a pig cured in one piece, that is with the ham and bacon together. In North America, the lean eye muscle from the loin appears separately as Canadian bacon (Fr. *bacon*), or occasionally on the bone as smoked pork chops. In Britain the loin is included in back bacon.

Salt pork varies from country to country. In France, cuts such as pork belly and hock are cured in brine for up to a month as *petit salé*. This is used for hearty soups, and baked with cabbage, lentils or dried beans. British salt pork is similar, but in the United States salt pork normally refers to pork back fat that has been dry-salted, often braised with collard greens as a side dish.

USEFUL INFORMATION

How to choose *Bacon:* white fat, clear pink meat, little moisture. *Lean salt pork:* pale fat, no dry edges. *Fat salt pork:* pale color, firm texture.
Portion *Fat bacon or pork:* 3-4 oz/ 90-125 g. *Lean bacon or pork:* 4-6 oz/125-175 g.
Nutritive value per 3½ oz/100 g raw bacon (fat or lean): 665 calories; 8 g protein; 69 g fat; 1 g carbohydrate; 685 mg sodium; 53 mg cholesterol.
Cooking methods *Whole lean bacon:* bake or simmer like ham (p.251). *Lean salt pork:* simmer like ham. *Sliced bacon:* bake at 350°F/ 175°C, 8-12 minutes; broil or pan-fry, 4-8 minutes.
When done *Whole lean bacon or salt pork:* tender; skewer inserted in center for 30 seconds is hot to touch when withdrawn. *Sliced bacon:* meat is dark pink and fat is tender or crisp according to taste.
Storage *Strongly cured:* 1-2 months in cool dry place. *Mild cure:* refrigerate 1 week.
Processed forms Canned.

Typical dishes Bacon cake (France); pancakes with egg (Denmark); pie with potatoes (UK); bacon tart (Germany); with mackerel (Germany); stewed with pears (Switzerland); fidget pie (layers of bacon, onion and apples, UK); bacon stuffing with prunes (Australia); *galette* with cheese and potato (France); baked with sweet peppers or broad beans (Italy); bacon soup (Belgium, Netherlands); pancakes (Sweden, Belgium, Netherlands); sautéed with kidneys (UK); with liver and onions (UK, Austria); *omelette bonne femme* (with potatoes, France); with red cabbage and apples (Spain).

CUTTING BACON LARDONS

Lardons are small cubes of bacon used to flavor a variety of dishes. Bacon may be smoked or unsmoked depending on the recipe.

Score a line underneath the skin. Holding the bacon down with one hand, cut underneath the skin to remove the rind. Cut the bacon into ¼ in/6 mm slices. Stack two bacon slices and cut them crosswise into strips, then dice them.

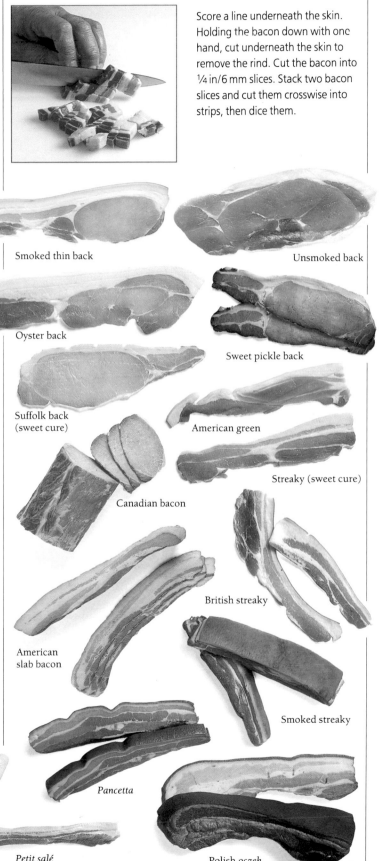

Smoked thin back

Unsmoked back

Oyster back

Sweet pickle back

Suffolk back (sweet cure)

American green

Streaky (sweet cure)

Canadian bacon

American slab bacon

British streaky

Smoked streaky

Pancetta

Salt pork

Petit salé

Polish *oczek*

HAM

Ham is the cured hind leg of a pig, smoked, or salted and smoked to preserve it. Hams that are dry-salted have the best flavor and are the most tender, but other hams are plunged straight into brine, or cured in a way that combines both methods. Curing time can be as long as two months, so commercially produced hams are often injected with brine to accelerate the process (with predictably inferior results). Salt used for curing is usually mixed with sugar, an assortment of spices, particularly pepper, and with nitrite preservatives that add pink color and protect the meat from botulism toxins. For health reasons, the traditional curing agent, saltpeter (potassium nitrate) together with sodium nitrate, is no longer used.

The feed given to the pig affects the taste of ham: the peanuts of Virginia, the peaches of Georgia and the acorns of Andalucia all contribute to flavor and texture. After salting, the ham may be smoked over fragrant woods such as apple, beech and hickory. Then it is left to age for three months to two years. The atmosphere must be cool and dry; many famous hams are cured in mountain regions.

A cured ham (often called a country or home-cured ham) may weigh as much as 20 lb/9 kg, but small or medium hams up to 15 lb/6.8 kg are less likely to be fatty. When buying ham, look at the label to see if it is raw or cooked. Some hams, like the famous Parma ham, are intended to be eaten raw in thin slices (see Carving a raw ham, opposite) and are often accompanied by fresh fruit such as melon or figs or delicate vegetables like asparagus. Many hams bought raw, however, need to be simmered before being served. If dry-cured and salty (shown by a firm skin and salty crust), whole hams should be soaked in cold water for

several hours if necessary, before simmering. Once cut, ham slices may need to be blanched in boiling water to remove the salt.

Some hams are sold pre-cooked. These may be served plain or cooked further and are eaten either hot or cold. The saltiness of a plain cooked ham is complemented by sweet accompaniments such as fruit chutney and apple sauce. The French often braise a cooked ham in cider with cream and apples, while the central Europeans favor ham baked in a dough or bread crust; sometimes the ham is pre-sliced and layered back on the bone with an herb or spinach stuffing. In the southern United States, ham steaks are often pan-fried to serve with red-eye gravy made with coffee or even Coca-Cola, but in Britain, cheese sauce is considered the better partner. Ham is as much a flavoring as a separate ingredient, appearing in omelets and in hearty stews and soups, especially those of beans or cabbage. **Note** Raw or cooked hams may be sold whole, divided in half into shank and butt (USA) or knuckle and fillet (UK), or sliced. If a ham has been boned, carving is easy, but the meat will lack flavor. Many countries insist that the quantity of water injected into cooked ham to increase weight must be stated on the label.

In view of the popularity of ham, several commercial look-alikes have been produced. Although they lack the authentic sweet, nutty flavor of real ham, picnic shoulder and hocks (Fr. *jambonneau*) are both cured by the same method. English gammon is leg of pork, sometimes shoulder (hand), cured on the side like bacon. All should be cooked in the same way as ham.

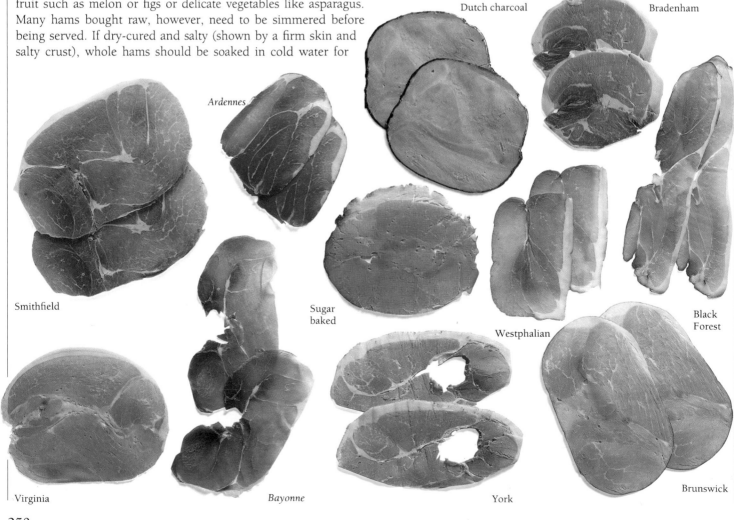

Dutch charcoal · Bradenham · Ardennes · Smithfield · Sugar baked · Westphalian · Black Forest · Virginia · Bayonne · York · Brunswick

250

USEFUL INFORMATION

Common types of ham eaten raw
Ardennes (cured, Belgium); *Bayonne* (golden, lightly smoked, France); *capocollo* (pork shoulder cured in wine and nutmeg, Italy); *culatello* (cured in wine, Italy); Irish (dry-salted, smoked over peat, Ireland); *jambon de campagne* (locally cured, France); Kentucky (smoked over apple, sassafras or hickory and aged 10-24 months, USA); *prosciutto crudo/prosciutto di Parma* (sweet, aged for a minimum 9 months, Italy); *prosciutto San Daniele* (stronger and redder than Parma, Italy); *Serrano* (cured in wine, air-dried in oil and paprika, Italy); *presunto* (smoked, Portugal); Westphalian (acorn-fed, smoked over juniper twigs and berries, Germany); *prosciutto Veneto* (delicate aroma and sweet taste, Italy); Cumbria (air-dried, UK).

Common types of ham eaten cooked Bradenham (sweet, mild cure, black skin, UK); Danish (cured like bacon, Denmark); *jambon de campagne* (locally cured, France); Paris/*glacé* (unsmoked or lightly smoked, France); Pennsylvania Dutch (cured in spiced vinegar, smoked over apple and hickory, USA); Prague (cured in brine, smoked over beech, Czechoslovakia); Smithfield (nut-fed, covered with pepper and hickory smoked, USA); Suffolk (sweet cure, delicate flavor, UK); Virginia (smoked over apple and hickory, USA); Wiltshire (cured like bacon, mild, UK); York (mild, classic ham, UK).

How to choose Firm flesh, not too dry (depending on cure); some, but not too much, fat; a skewer inserted near bone should smell sweet; moisture in commercial hams betrays injection with water.
Portion *With bone:* ½-¾ lb/250-375 g. *Without bone:* 6-8 oz/175-250 g.
Nutritive value per 3½ oz/100 g. *Boneless raw cured ham:* 162 calories; 2 g carbohydrates; 18 g protein; 8 g fat; 53 mg cholesterol; 685 mg sodium.
Cooking methods *Whole raw ham, 3-5 lb:* simmer ½ hour per lb/500 g; *5-10 lb:* simmer 20 minutes per 1 lb/500 g plus 20 minutes; *over 10 lb:* simmer 15-18 minutes per 1 lb/500 g, allowing less time for larger hams. *Cooked whole ham:* bake or braise at 350°F/175°C, 10 minutes per 1 lb/500 g. *Slices:* bake or braise at 350°F/175°C, 30-45 minutes; broil, pan-fry or sauté 6-10 minutes.
When done Tender when pierced; 170°F/75°C on a meat thermometer
Problems If too salty, remove the salt by soaking or blanching; meat can be dry if cut too thick; trim excess fat after cooking.
Storage *Whole raw country ham:* hang in cool dry place, time depends on cure. *Cooked whole ham:* refrigerate 10 days. *Slices:* refrigerate 3 days; freeze 1 month.
Processed forms Pre-packaged fresh, smoked, canned.
Typical dishes Glazed with brown sugar, apple juice, ginger syrup, preserved ginger and mustard (Australia); glazed with maple syrup in raisin sauce (USA); stuffed with almonds, onions, rye bread and foie gras (Austria); in cider (UK); *à la crème de Saulieu* (in mushroom cream sauce, France); *sformatoi prosciutto* (molded soufflé, Italy); *labskovs* (hashed with onions and potatoes, Denmark); *bouchées aux jambon* (stuffed puff pastry shells, France); baked in a rye crust (Germany); gratin with endive (Belgium); *holsteiner schinkenklösse* (ham dumplings, Austria); steaks with almonds (Switzerland); baked in mustard sauce (France); fruity gammon (with mincemeat and oranges, UK, Australia); vine leaves stuffed with ham (Spain). *Also good with* melon, fig, apple, mustard, pineapple, cloves, dried fruits, Madeira, spinach, dried peas, sauerkraut.

Serrano

San Daniele

Coppa

Parma

CARVING A RAW HAM

Once a ham has been cut, keep the cut surface covered, preferably with cheesecloth, so that the meat does not dry out.

If the ham has a thigh bone it should be held in a clamp. The meat is sliced horizontally until the bone is reached. For boneless ham, place the ham flat on the board. Trim skin and dried edges from the ham. Cut most of the fat from underneath. With a long thin knife, carve the ham in the thinnest possible slices.

Boiling a raw ham

Whether it is to be served plain, or cooked further by braising or baking with a topping to serve hot or cold, a raw ham is soaked and then simmered in water. If it is salty, soak the ham for 12-24 hours in cold water, changing the water often. Drain the ham and put it in a large pan with enough fresh water to cover, bring to a boil and simmer for 30 minutes, skimming occasionally. Taste the water – if it is very salty, discard it and start cooking again in cold water, subtracting 30 minutes from the total cooking time. Add seasonings such as onion, apple, wine, cider, bay leaf, pepper-corns, allspice berries and cloves. Cover and simmer until done. Let the ham cool to tepid in the liquid, then drain it. Peel off the skin and trim all but a ½ in/1.25 cm layer of fat. If serving plain, press browned breadcrumbs into the surface of the fat to form a coating, then slash the fat with a knife in a shallow lattice pattern.

Baking a ham with glaze

A fully cooked ham is often baked further in the oven with a glaze to heat it and to add flavor. Toppings for ham fall into two categories. The most common are melted, syrupy glazes; typical examples are maple syrup, apple juice with honey, and soy sauce with brown sugar and sherry. Baste the ham constantly, taking care that the glaze does not scorch on the bottom of the pan. Toward the end of cooking, fat melts from the ham, enriching the glaze. Often the surface of the ham is scored so that the glaze penetrates the fat, and it may be studded with cloves for flavor.

The second type of topping for ham is a crisp coating, for example, breadcrumbs mixed with parsley and mustard, or sliced pineapple with brown sugar; the latter fall off easily, so careful basting is important. After baking, the ham may be served hot or cold. A sweet relish such as spiced fruit or a chutney is a good accompaniment to a cold ham. A pungent ingredient like mustard complements ham served hot or cold.

CARVING A COOKED HAM

For carving, a knife with a long flexible blade is needed. Trim the ham of excess fat and any dried-out or discolored patches. Alternatively, it may be carved like leg of lamb (p.225).

1 Cut around the pelvic and hip bones with a boning knife until the hip joint is reached. Sever the joint and remove the bones.

2 Set the ham on a board, knuckle down, grasping the shank bone. Holding the ham with the rounded muscle down, cut 3-4 slices from the other side so that the ham will rest flat on the board.

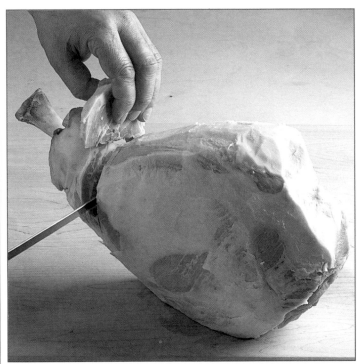

3 With a long thin knife, make a vertical cut in the ham close to the shank end, cutting down to the bone. Slice the ham in wedge-shaped slices about ¼ in/6 mm thick, cutting right down to the bone.

4 After the first few slices, start angling the knife a little more with each slice to carve larger and larger thin slices. Meat left under the bone is usually kept to slice later. For serving, you can replace the ham slices on the bone or arrange overlapping slices on a plate.

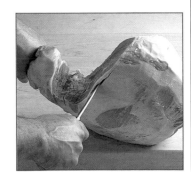

OTHER CURED MEATS

In the days before refrigeration when meat was a luxury, preservation methods needed to be as varied as possible. A family's entire meat supply for a season might come from a single animal. Today we continue to cure meats partly for variety and partly because we value their special flavors. Some cured meats are a legacy from times when meat was survival food, for example African *biltong*, which consists of air-dried and smoked strips of beef, buffalo, venison, antelope or even ostrich. The American Indians made pemmican by powdering air-dried venison and making it into little cakes with melted fat and bitter berries. Similar examples are southeast Asian air-dried *dendang* and South American *tassajo* and *chalona*. The Spanish enjoy air-dried *cecina* and *jamón de toro*. In the United States strips of sun-dried beef called beef jerky (from the Spanish-American word *charqui*) are still popular as a snack food. Humid climates often necessitate initial salting or soaking in brine to absorb the juices before the meat is dried. Germany's *speck* and Norway's *spekemat* are typical; these can be made of beef, game or even mutton smoked over fragrant woods.

Beef jerky

Beef biltong

Cured meats are often described as "pickled", which may mean either salted or corned (a reference to the coarse kernels or "corns" of salt used in the process) or cured in brine and vinegar. In the former category, corned beef (the British equivalent is salt beef) is probably the most popular: beef brisket is rubbed with salt, chopped vegetables, spices and herbs over a period of several weeks, then soaked and boiled or barbecued. Often piled high on American sandwiches is pastrami, lean beef that has been dry-cured, well-peppered and smoked. Chipped beef receives similar treatment, after which it is smoked lightly and air-dried. Although smoking is more common for pork or game, salt beef is sometimes cured this way (frequently the meat is treated with molasses or sugar to counteract the toughening effect of the salt). Meat can also be brine-cured, for example British pickled tripe, a dish of boiled, scraped beef stomach pickled in a vinegar and salt brine and flavored with cloves, allspice, mace, cinnamon, hot chilies and pepper.

Salt beef

Bresaola

Pastrami

American corned beef

In the Alps of Italy and Switzerland, cured meats are delicacies. Italian *bresaola* is dried beef tenderloin, aged for two months to a rich, deep red, then thinly sliced and served raw with olive oil, lemon juice and parsley as an appetizer. The Swiss version is *bundnerfleisch*, which is treated with white wine then salted; both are a far cry from simple air-dried meats!

ASPIC

Aspic (Fr. *gelée*) is the savory jelly made from clarified stock (p.55), used to coat meats, poultry, fish and vegetables. It first comes to mind as part of grand banquets and buffets, but it is also an important part of charcuterie. Clarified aspic may be used to add a shiny and protective coating to a cold roast bird or to *galantines* and *ballotines* (p.255). It can also be layered in a mold, as in the popular poached eggs set in aspic with a slice of ham and a piece of truffle. For more elaborate aspic molds cooked vegetables are arranged in complex designs, sometimes with ham and chicken. Each layer is allowed to set firmly before another is added. Sliced aspic can be cut in pretty shapes to decorate canapés and salad platters. Many country specialties that do not require the shimmering transparency of clarified aspic are simply made with boiled-down cooking liquid. Aspic can also be used instead of plain gelatin in savory mousses.

Clarified aspic is made in the same way as consommé, by clarifying veal, chicken or fish stock. The consistency is important as the finished aspic must set firmly at room temperature. Before clarifying the basic stock, its gelatin content must be tested to determine whether extra gelatin is needed, and if so, how much. The flavor of the stock is boosted by simmering ground lean beef or poultry and chopped vegetables with the egg whites used for clarifying the consommé. Light, crystal-clear aspic is the ideal, but the darker the color, the less it will show any remaining cloudiness – an escape route that leads wily cooks to use red wine-based aspic, secure in the knowledge that the color will conceal any impurities.

Working with clarified aspic to create buffet dishes is an art in itself. The main ingredient – an impressive salmon, a ham or perhaps a roast turkey – is often left whole as a background for bouquets of flowers or geometric patterns of vegetable garnishes as well as truffles and hard-boiled egg white. Thin slices of cucumber may mimic the scales of a fish, while poultry is often clad in chaudfroid sauce (p.56). A classic arrangement is a tray lined with aspic and bordered with crescents and triangles.

USEFUL INFORMATION

Portion 3-4 tbsp/45-60 ml per person.
Storage *Coated poultry and meat*: refrigerate 2 days. *Coated fish*: refrigerate 1 day. *Molded poultry and meat*: refrigerate 5 days. *Molded fish and eggs*: refrigerate 2 days. Do not freeze or aspic will crystallize.
Problems Fatty stock clouds aspic; if aspic has too little gelatin, coating melts and mold will not set; if too much gelatin, texture is

unpleasantly thick and rubbery.
Processed forms Crystals (a poor substitute).
Typical dishes Chicken in jelly (UK); turkey breast glazed with sherry aspic (USA); Marsala aspic layered with marinated meats (Italy); jellied eel (UK); wild rabbit in jelly (France); *oeufs en gelée* (eggs in aspic, France); game birds in aspic (Sweden); aspic of pork (Hungary); game jellies (Scotland); duck pâté in sherry aspic (USA).

Presenting aspic

To capitalize on aspic's luster, the finished dish should be presented on a flat stainless steel or silver platter that reflects light. Pour a layer of aspic into the base and chill to set before adding the food. Decorate the border with tiny crescents or triangles (called wolves' teeth) cut from aspic slices. Leftover aspic is finely chopped to pipe around the edge or coarsely chopped to pile on to the platter. Remove the dish from the refrigerator just before serving so that the aspic softens slightly.

Adding gelatin to stock

Few clarified aspics are certain to stay set without the addition of packaged gelatin to the stock. It is important to add only just enough to avoid a rubbery texture. To test how much gelatin you need, pour a spoonful of stock on to a plate and refrigerate it until cold. If it sets only lightly, soften gelatin in cold water (p.431), using 1 tbsp/7 g gelatin per 2 cups/500 ml stock. If the stock does not set, double the amount of gelatin. Clarify the stock as for consommé (p.46); let it simmer for 30-40 minutes, then add the gelatin through the hole in the filter. Proceed with clarification.

COATING FOODS WITH ASPIC

All food and decorations to be coated with aspic should be dry and thoroughly chilled in advance. Allow time for several thin coatings; the aspic will cling better and more evenly than with one thick coating.

1 Set about 1 cup/250 ml melted aspic in a metal bowl over ice. Stir gently until the aspic is very cold, turns syrupy and starts to set.
Note Do not stir too fast or bubbles will form.

2 Set the food on a rack over a tray (to catch the drips). Working quickly, brush or spoon a coating of aspic over the cold food. Chill. Melt more aspic, chill it until it is on the point of setting, and coat the food again. Repeat the process once or twice as needed.

CUTTING ASPIC INTO DECORATIVE SHAPES

Aspic decorations such as wolves' teeth or crescents are cut from chilled aspic to adorn the border of cold platters.

Turn a thick layer of chilled aspic on to a damp sheet of wax paper. With a large knife cut the aspic into ⅜ in/1 cm slices, then cut out shapes with an aspic cutter, cookie cutter or small knife. Shown above are crescents and daisies (top), and wolves' teeth (bottom).

CHOPPING ASPIC

Chopped aspic is one of the simplest decorations to make. It is important to use a damp knife.

1 Pour the aspic into a well-dampened shallow pan and refrigerate until set. Turn it out on to a piece of damp wax paper.

2 With a large dampened knife, cut the aspic into strips and then across into small cubes. Finally, chop it coarsely. To avoid crushing the aspic, do not hold the point of the knife on the board. Do not chop it too much as it will sparkle more if coarse.
Note Avoid touching aspic with your hands, otherwise they will cloud it.

Clarified aspic molds

Lining and filling a mold with clarified aspic is similar to the process of coating. Choose a mold that is not too deep or too complicated to unmold easily, preferably one with sloping sides, for example a charlotte mold (p.508). A metal mold is ideal as it is a good heat conductor and allows aspic to set quickly and unmold cleanly. For an attractive appearance, it is important to start with a generous layer of aspic, coating the base and sides.

Once the first layer of aspic has set, various ingredients can be added for decoration: circles of colorful vegetables such as unpeeled zucchini, radish or carrot are popular. Sometimes the sides are also decorated: favorites are egg whites, truffles, tomatoes, asparagus or sticks of carrot, set vertically. Once in place, these are set with another layer of aspic.

The rest of the mold is then filled with alternate layers of cooked ingredients and aspic (layers should be no more than 1 in/ 2.5 cm thick). Ham and tongue are effective, but watery foods such as tomato cause the aspic to collapse, and beets are not suitable since the color bleeds. Foods that are untidy or lack color such as sliced chicken breast, boiled beef, or liver pâté should be set well inside other ingredients. Heavy ingredients should be positioned in the upper layers of the mold so that when it is unmolded they will be at the bottom. A final layer of aspic to fill the mold should completely cover all the ingredients. When filling a mold with aspic and ingredients, it is important to achieve the right balance – too much aspic can be cloying.

MAKING AN ASPIC MOLD

1 Set the charlotte mold on a bed of ice. Add 1 cup/250 ml aspic and chill until on the point of setting. Rotate the mold to coat it on all sides and pour out any aspic that does not adhere. For a good appearance, the whole mold should be coated with an even layer at least ¼ in/6 mm thick, especially at the bottom. Chill over ice until firmly set.

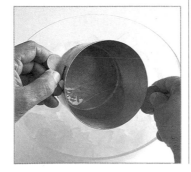

2 LEFT When the layer of aspic has set, arrange neatly cut decorations on top and cover with a second thin layer of aspic. Leave in a cool place to set.

3 When the aspic has set, pipe or spoon a layer of the filling (here, a ham mousse) into the mold in a spiral.

4 Using a ladle, pour cold aspic down the sides of the mold to fill any gaps and chill again until set.

5 Repeat steps 3 and 4 until the mold is filled; finally add enough aspic to cover the mousse. Chill for 2 hours or until completely set.

6 To unmold the aspic, turn the mold in your hands so that their warmth loosens the aspic. Gently ease the contents away from the mold with your fingertips. Set a serving plate on top of the mold, turn both upside down and detach the aspic with a sharp sideways jerk.

UNCLARIFIED ASPICS

By no means all aspics are made with clarified stock. Many rustic preparations are made with meats full of gelatin, like beef shank or pig's and calf's head; often a pig's or calf's foot and a bit of pork rind is added to the pot. After cooking, the liquid is simply boiled down until it sets to a firm gel, then it is mixed with the chopped or shredded meat. Typical is brawn (Fr. *fromage de tête*) made with pig's (or sometimes calf's) head and feet, including the cheek and tongue. More elaborate dishes are created by layering meat and liquid, as in *boeuf à la mode en gelée*, in which braised beef is sliced and layered with carrots, onions, green beans and cooking liquid.

The term aspic is sometimes applied to molded gelatin salads that may or may not contain stock. Popular in the United States as an appetizer or the main course of a light lunch, these salads contain a range of flavors – from a delicate combination of green grapes with fresh mint to a robust blend of tomatoes, garlic and wine. Aspic salads are often set into decorative molds and garnished with watercress or cooked vegetables. Serve them with vinaigrette dressing or a cream-based dressing or mayonnaise.

GALANTINES & BALLOTINES

Galantines and *ballotines* are rolls made from birds or cuts of meat that have been boned and stuffed. A *galantine* is shaped in a cylinder (so that it is easy to slice), then wrapped in a cloth and poached in stock. It is always served cold, usually in aspic. Chicken and turkey *galantines* often have a veal or ham stuffing, while a pork stuffing is more common for richer meats.

A *ballotine* may be rolled or sewn in a cushion shape (Fr. *ballot*, bundle); it is poached or braised to serve hot in a sauce made from the cooking liquid, or presented cold in aspic. Individual *ballotines* may be made from boned poultry legs. *Dodine* (Fr. *dodu*, meaning plump) is another word for *ballotine*; it also refers to a medieval poultry dish in spiced sauce.

USEFUL INFORMATION

Portion *Appetizer:* 2-4 oz/60-120 g. *Main course:* 6-8 oz/175-250 g.
Cooking methods Poach 20 minutes per 1 lb/500 g; braise at 350°F/175°C, 30 minutes per 1 lb/500 g.
When done A skewer inserted in center for 30 seconds is hot to the touch when withdrawn; 170°F/75°C on a meat thermometer.
Problems If cooked too fast, bursts; if overdone, dry.
Storage Refrigerate 3 days.
Typical dishes *Galantines:* duck with apricots (Belgium); fish and asparagus (France); tuna fish roll (Spain); turkey with sherry and truffles (Spain); capon and mushrooms (France); pheasant or pigeon (France); pork (Italy); ham and bacon (UK). *Ballotines:* duckling (France); *matambre* (stuffed rolled flank steak, Argentina); *à la Régence* (chicken stuffed with chicken mousse and artichokes, France); with pork stuffing (France); *de dinde Clamart* (turkey stuffed with *mousseline* and garnished with peas, artichokes and parisienne potatoes, France).

Presenting galantines and ballotines

When sliced, a *galantine* or cold *ballotine* displays an attractive mosaic of meat and stuffing dotted with nuts, olives, chunks of ham or pork fat, and sometimes truffles. Slices are arranged flat on the dish so that they scarcely overlap. The classic decoration is a shiny coating of aspic and sometimes part of the *galantine* is left unsliced to coat with chaudfroid sauce (p.56). A garnish such as stuffed tomatoes adds color but is not obligatory given the colorful appearance of the dish itself.

When a *ballotine* is served hot, it is essentially a boned stuffed roast. A generous garnish of vegetables is usually cooked with it and the braising liquid makes a rich sauce.

Turkey galantine

Decoration for a *galantine* should be simple so that the patterned slices can be seen clearly. A layer of aspic will help prevent drying and give the galantine an attractive shine.

Serves 16-18 as an appetizer or light main course

A 6-7 lb/approx 3 kg turkey	***For the stuffing***
½ lb/250 g thickly sliced cooked ham, cut in strips	½ lb/250 g ground pork
½ lb/250 g thickly sliced cooked tongue, cut in strips	½ lb/250 g ground veal
½ cup/125 ml sherry	4 oz/125 g ground pork fat
salt and pepper	1 onion, chopped
½ lb/250 g chicken livers, including liver from bird	1 tbsp butter
calf's or pig's foot, split and blanched (p.229)	¼ cup/60 g pistachios, blanched
2 qt/2 L veal or chicken stock (p.44)	1 tsp ground allspice
2 qt/2 L aspic made from turkey cooking liquid (p.253)	1 clove garlic, crushed
	½ cup/125 ml white wine
	1 egg, beaten

1 Bone the turkey, reserving the bones. Carefully remove the flesh from the skin, keeping the skin in one piece (see Boning by the glove method, Poultry p.178.) Cut the breast into strips. Toss them with the ham and tongue, half the sherry, salt and pepper. Leave to marinate ½-1 hour.
2 To make the stuffing: work the remaining turkey meat, pork, veal and pork fat through the fine blade of a grinder. Cook the onion in butter until soft but not brown and add to the meat with the pistachios, allspice, garlic, white wine, egg, and the sherry drained from the meat strips. Season with salt and pepper and beat with a wooden spoon until well mixed. Sauté a ball of stuffing and taste – it should be highly seasoned. Weigh the stuffing and the strips of meat. Add or subtract strips until the meat and stuffing are of equal weight.
3 Spread the turkey skin, cut side up, on a board and fold the leg and wing skin over the openings to make a neat parcel. Divide the stuffing into three. Spread one-third of the stuffing over the skin in a rectangle about 3 in/7.5 cm wide and 10 in/25 cm long. Arrange half the strips of meat lengthwise on top.
4 Spread half the remaining stuffing on the meat. Top with the chicken livers and remaining meat strips. Cover with the last portion of stuffing, shaping it to form a neat cylinder. Wrap the cylinder in the turkey skin.
5 Wrap the *galantine* tightly in a dish towel. **Note** It is important to stretch the towel to avoid creases – creases in the towel will make wrinkles on the galantine. Tie both ends with string, pressing the mixture so it is tightly packed.
6 Place the *galantine* in a large pan with the turkey bones, calf's or pig's foot, remaining sherry and enough veal or chicken stock to cover. Poach it for 1½-2 hours or until done. Leave the *galantine* to cool, then drain it, reserving the stock. During poaching the cloth around the *galantine* will have become quite loose, untie the string and rewrap the *galantine* as tightly as possible, tie it with fresh string, top with a board and a weight and chill it overnight. Use the reserved stock to make aspic.
7 Unwrap the *galantine* and cut it into ⅜ in/1 cm slices. Set the slices on a rack over a tray to catch drips and chill them thoroughly, then coat them with aspic using a spoon or brush Repeat coating once or twice as necessary.
8 Set the slices on a serving dish lined with aspic and decorate it with aspic cutouts. Cover the *galantine* loosely with plastic wrap and refrigerate for up to 24 hours until ready to serve. A *galantine* should be served cold.

3

page

VEGETABLES   258

MUSHROOMS   304

GRAINS
& LEGUMES   314

PASTA   328

VEGETABLES

TODAY, VEGETABLES play a major role at almost every meal. Yet it was not until the 1950s that our current fascination with fresh, high quality produce began. In recent years, the abundance and diversity of vegetables in local markets has resulted in a far larger repertoire of dishes that complement meat and fish or stand on their own.

Just a few generations ago, the seasons strictly defined which vegetables were available: few people could afford young vegetables or pay the market price for scarce, imported produce. Today's bounty is the product of modern cultivation, genetic engineering and improved transportation. New varieties and hybrids are constantly being selected and developed, and the consumer is now offered a great variety of produce of a uniform size, color and shelf-life, although often at the expense of flavor.

At the peak of their season, fresh vegetables come to life with a minimum of seasoning, perhaps salt and pepper or a dash of lemon juice or herbs. As well as being served alone or in combination, some vegetables, such as onions and tomatoes, become an integral part of the flavoring of certain dishes, lending richness as they cook. Vegetables are naturally high in vitamins and nutrients, contain little fat and no cholesterol. However, nutritive content, like quality, varies according to factors such as weather, soil conditions and variety.

Choosing vegetables
Refrigerated transportation of vegetables ensures a steady supply of fresh produce at the supermarket. In the depth of a northern winter, fresh vegetables are shipped from warmer regions, often in the southern hemisphere. Owing to modern methods of preserving and shelf-life extension of perishable vegetables, the cook is provided year-round with an astonishing array of both familiar and unusual types.

Each individual vegetable has its own indicator of quality, but generally crispness and bright color are the key to freshness. Vegetables past their prime are betrayed by brown patches, wilted leaves and limp flesh. Avoid any vegetables that are damaged, bruised or frostbitten. The younger and smaller the vegetable, the more tender and sweet it will be, although vegetables that are actually immature often lack juiciness and may be bitter. Some markets now sell "baby" vegetables, including tiny zucchini, cherry-sized squash and finger-length corn; many are dwarf varieties, others are regular varieties picked at an early stage, without the flavor or sweetness of the fully mature vegetable. Small squashes, however, are always sweet, with more flavor than larger specimens.

Certain varieties of tomato, lettuce and cucumber are grown hydroponically, that is, with their roots in nutrient-rich water instead of soil. These vegetables are pretty to look at, but their flavor is usually more bland than those grown in soil. For further details on choosing vegetables, see individual entries.

Storing vegetables
Root vegetables and hardy winter squashes keep well at cool room temperature around 60°F/16°C. Cut the tops off root vegetables to prevent juices flowing to the leaves. Store greens and soft vegetables, such as cucumbers, in the refrigerator, on the lower shelves or in the crisper compartment, loosely folded in plastic wrap or a cloth (airtight wrapping encourages bacteria). Do not wash vegetables until just before you use them, as moisture encourages rot and leaches vitamins. Different vegetables are best stored separately and away from fruits, which emit a gas that makes carrots bitter, for example. Onions cause potatoes to spoil more quickly, and taint dairy products, such as milk.

Peeling vegetables
Vegetables that absorb water easily, such as potatoes, are often boiled or steamed with the skin left on so that they retain vitamins and absorb less moisture. Beets will not bleed if cooked with their skin. Vegetables that are waxed, such as cucumbers and peppers, should be peeled before using; a vegetable peeler or small paring knife (p.504) is the best utensil. Peppers are usually charred to loosen their skins (p.281), while tomatoes are blanched. Some vegetables, such as eggplant and squash, may be baked first and the cooked flesh scooped out of the skin.

Note Many modern pesticides concentrate in vegetable skin and cannot be removed simply by washing in water. Peeling vegetables therefore reduces the likelihood of contamination.

Cutting vegetables by hand
Carefully cut vegetables not only cook evenly, but contribute to the appearance of a dish. Good sharp knives are essential for cutting; use a large or small chopping knife, depending on the vegetable. It is important that you handle the knife correctly. Grasp the knife firmly with all four fingers wrapped around the handle. Use your free hand to steady the vegetable as you cut, with your fingertips curled under and your knuckles guiding the knife.

A machine can make cutting vegetables much easier. The two most efficient and widely used are the hand-operated mandoline (p.505), good at producing perfectly formed slices, and the food processor, where speed and ease of operation compensate for lack of precision. Using a variety of blades and disks, a food processor can grate zucchini, chop onions or cut carrots into julienne with ease. With the cutting blade, however, vegetables can easily be overworked to a pulp.

Slicing vegetables
First peel the vegetable. If it does not sit flat on a cutting board, cut a slice from the base or cut it in half. Slice in even, vertical slices. With each cut, move the hand holding the vegetable so as to guide the knife. Alternatively, cut the vegetable diagonally for larger, more attractive slices. See also individual vegetables.

CUTTING INTO JULIENNE STRIPS

Julienne strips – fine strips of vegetable the size of a matchstick – cook quickly and make a garnish for many dishes. Juliennes of different colored vegetables, such as carrot, leek and turnip, are often mixed for decorative effect.

1 Peel the vegetable and cut a thin strip from one side so that the vegetable lies flat on the board.

2 Cut the vegetable crosswise into 2 in/5 cm lengths, then lengthwise into thin vertical slices.

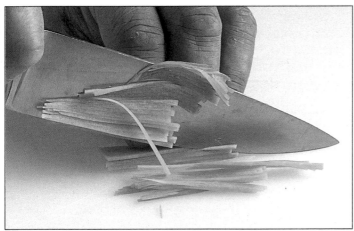

3 Stack the slices and cut them lengthwise again into strips. For very fine strips, continue cutting, keeping the tip of the knife on the board.

SLICING INTO A CHIFFONADE

Vegetable leaves such as cabbage, spinach, and lettuce may be cut into coarse shreds, known as a *chiffonade*. Large-leaved herbs such as basil may also be cut this way.

1 Stack the leaves (here romaine lettuce is used) and roll the pile tightly.

2 Slice across the roll to make fine or coarse strips, depending on the leaf you are using.

DICING VEGETABLES

Cubed or diced vegetables may be used as the foundation of braises and casseroles, as a flavoring mixture (*mirepoix* p.263), raw or cooked in vegetable salads or soups, or as a garnish for consommé (*brunoise*, below).

1 Peel the vegetable. Square off the sides, reserving trimmings for soups or purées. Slice the vegetable vertically, cutting thickly for large dice, thinly for small dice.

2 Stack the slices and cut even strips of uniform thickness.

3 Gather the strips together into a pile and slice them evenly crosswise to produce dice of the required size.

Large dice

Medium dice

Small dice (*brunoise*)

TURNING VEGETABLES

Vegetables may be "turned" or whittled into a classic olive shape, usually the size of an elongated walnut, traditionally with seven sides. Turned vegetables cook evenly, look attractive and are a hallmark of classic French dishes. Use the parings for soups.

1 **For round vegetables (here turnip):** cut the vegetables in quarters or eighths, depending on size. If necessary, halve each piece lengthwise.

2 **For long vegetables (here zucchini):** cut the vegetables into 2 in/5 cm lengths. If necessary, halve each piece lengthwise.

3 Hold the vegetable steady with your fingertips and, with a small paring knife, trim all the sharp edges.

4 Work from the top to the bottom of the vegetable in a quick curving movement, turning the vegetable slightly between each cut.

5 The finished vegetables should be of uniform size and shape. For zucchini and summer squash, some of the skin may be left on for decorative effect.

ROLL-CUTTING VEGETABLES

This Asian technique, adapted by many Western cooks, produces pieces of uniform shape, each with the maximum amount of surface area, perfect for quick-cooking sautés and stir-fried dishes. Long vegetables such as carrots and parsnips work best.

Holding the peeled vegetable in one hand, cut a diagonal slice near the end. Turn the vegetable a quarter turn and make another diagonal slice. Continue to turn and cut until all the vegetable is used.

Cutting vegetables in balls

Root vegetables and squashes may be scooped into decorative balls or ovals with a melon baller (p.505). They cook and brown very evenly. Sizes vary from pea-size for soups to small walnut-size for *parisienne* of potato balls sautéed in butter. First, peel or cut open the vegetable. Then, with a scooping movement, press the cutter firmly into the vegetable to form a round ball.

Blanching and parboiling vegetables

Vegetables are often blanched in boiling water before further cooking. Some, like cabbage, are blanched to remove a strong flavor; vegetables with a sharp taste such as onion, or with bitter juices, such as eggplant, also benefit. Blanching softens root vegetables, prevents pale vegetables such as Jerusalem artichokes from discoloring, sets the color of greens and loosens the skin of vegetables like tomatoes to facilitate peeling. The method depends on how the vegetable is cooked; green vegetables and tomatoes are blanched in boiling water, while roots are started in cold water and the blanching time counted from the moment the water comes to a boil. Different vegetables should be blanched separately, though similar types used in the same dish can be blanched together.

To blanch vegetables, fill a large pan with water, adding salt only if called for in the recipe. Depending on the vegetable, add it to cold water, or first bring water to a boil. Bring the water back to a boil as fast as possible, counting blanching time from when the water reboils. Time may be as short as one minute for delicate greens such as lettuce, or as long as five minutes for carrots.

Parboiling (partly boiling) vegetables goes a step further than blanching but is done the same way. Tough vegetables, such as celery root, are often parboiled so that further cooking is easier to control. Vegetables that are to be deep-fried are parboiled so that they will be fully cooked by the time they are golden and crisp on the outside. Blanching and parboiling may often be done ahead and the vegetables kept up to 24 hours in the refrigerator.

DRAWING OUT BITTER JUICES WITH SALT

The French term *dégorger* is often used for this process, which draws out the sometimes bitter juices from ingredients, usually vegetables such as eggplant, cucumber or bitter melon (a type of gourd, p.288).

1 Cut the vegetable in slices or chunks with a large sharp knife. Spread the pieces in a shallow dish and sprinkle evenly with salt.

Note Drawing out the juices also helps firm up the texture of the vegetable so that it holds its shape.

2 After 15-30 minutes, the salt will have drawn out the juices. Transfer the vegetable pieces to a colander and rinse thoroughly. Dry on paper towels.

Preventing discoloration

Vegetables that discolor easily, such as celery root, salsify and artichoke bottoms, may be cooked in a *blanc* (below) or with acid to keep them white. They should also be cut with a stainless steel knife to prevent discoloration from carbon steel, and the pieces should be dropped into acidulated water until all the vegetables are prepared and ready for cooking.

1 To make a *blanc*: bring a pan of salted water to a boil. Make a soft paste by stirring water into flour, allowing 3 tbsp/45 ml water and 1 tbsp flour for every 1 qt/1 L of water. Stir this into the boiling water and add the juice of half a lemon for every 1 qt/1 L. Add the vegetables and boil for the usual time.

2 Acidulated water: add the juice of two lemons to 1 qt/1 L cold water. Immerse the vegetables until ready to cook them.

Testing when vegetables are cooked

In some countries, notably China and the United States, vegetables are cooked until crisp and crunchy (*al dente*). In Europe, they are often cooked until tender with a fuller flavor but less texture. Test for tenderness with a fork or the point of a knife. Greens will wilt as soon as they are tender. When in doubt, test vegetables by tasting them, as they can overcook rapidly.

Boiling vegetables

Boiled vegetables, always versatile, may be served plain, sautéed in butter, or with a sauce; they may be puréed (p.266) or added warm or cold to a salad. Boiled vegetables turn up in crêpes and terrines as well as in savory pies. They are the basis for many soufflés, soups and stews, and are an integral part of French *pot au feu* and American boiled dinner. They also make excellent salads on their own, such as potato, green beans or beet with vinaigrette or mayonnaise.

The method and speed of boiling vegetables are all-important: green vegetables are cooked quickly, while roots must be simmered slowly. Plunging green vegetables into a large quantity of boiling salted water keeps cooking time to a minimum, and allows the vegetables to retain their color, texture and taste. Always boil green vegetables uncovered, so that volatile acids from the vegetables will not get trapped in the pan and cause discoloration. For root vegetables, heat must penetrate slowly to cook them through. Immerse the vegetables in plenty of cold water, then bring it to a gentle simmer. **Note** Asparagus and artichokes should not be boiled in an aluminum pan as they will discolor and acquire a metallic taste.

There is no equal to tiny boiled new vegetables, tossed at the last minute with a knob of butter and fresh chopped herbs. More mature vegetables can be enlivened with garlic or chopped nuts, or coated with cream or cheese sauce and browned in the oven as a gratin (p.264). The British favor boiled new potatoes and peas with mint, the Italians often sauté boiled broccoli and cauliflower in olive oil, garlic and herbs with a little chopped chili, while in Germany, bacon-flavored brown sauce is a favorite topping for boiled turnips, potatoes or carrots.

Refreshing vegetables

After boiling, green vegetables are often drained and refreshed under cold water to set their color, texture and flavor. To avoid running a strong stream of water over delicate vegetables, immerse them in a bowl of cold water and drain them again. The vegetables can then be reheated in butter or oil, or cooked further, for example in a gratin. Root vegetables that are to be stored after cooking or used in cold salads may also be chilled with cold water.

Steaming vegetables

An alternative to boiling vegetables is to steam them above boiling water, leaving them intact, yet moist and tender. Almost any vegetable can be steamed; if done correctly, more of the nutrients and flavor are preserved than when the vegetable is boiled. However, steam is so hot that vegetables can easily overcook, and the color of greens fades fast. Steaming is not good for assertive vegetables such as cauliflower and turnip, which need to be boiled to tone down their flavor.

The best equipment for steaming is a metal or bamboo steamer or a collapsible steamer that can be inserted in a large saucepan (p.511). The vegetables should not be added until the water is at a rolling boil and they should be spread out in a single layer so that they cook evenly. Set the rack about 1 in/2.5 cm above the boiling water and cover the steamer with a lid. Since the vegetables are not tenderized by contact with water, steaming often takes longer than boiling. Steamed vegetables should be cooked to the same tenderness as boiled vegetables, and are used in the same way.

Sautéing and pan-frying vegetables

Almost all vegetables do well sautéed in a little fat, whether plain or with flavorings like chopped shallot, garlic, bacon or herbs. Season them with salt and pepper, hot pepper, spices, or even a touch of anchovy. The fat used for sautéing and pan-frying is important: butter adds a touch of distinction to a wide range of vegetables, while olive oil brings a fuller flavor to eggplant, beans, zucchini and vegetable mixtures with tomato. Bacon fat or lard is more regional, an appropriate choice for sautéing hearty greens, cabbage and, of course, potatoes.

A sautéed or pan-fried vegetable should be golden and slightly crisp on the outside, moist and juicy within. When cooking a mixture of vegetables, those that take longer to cook, such as potatoes and roots, should be put in first. Watery vegetables like summer squash require fairly high heat and just a little fat so that the moisture evaporates quickly, while firm vegetables such as cauliflower and celery root should be parboiled to soften them before sautéing. Completely cooked vegetables, often left over from some other dish, can be sautéed successfully. British "bubble and squeak", made with coarsely crushed potato and cabbage fried to form a crisp brown crust, is one example of using leftover vegetables to good effect.

Sweating vegetables

"Sweated" vegetables are cooked covered, with a little fat, over very low heat so that they cook in their own juices without browning. A little salt and pepper is usually added, and a piece of parchment paper is pressed down on the vegetables before the pan is covered with its lid. Vegetables are often sweated for soup and for flavoring stuffings and dishes like quiche.

A similar technique, known as "stoving" in Scotland, is very successful with new potatoes and evenly cut pieces of Jerusalem artichoke. A light patching of golden brown is desirable.

Stir-frying vegetables

When vegetables are cooked by this method (a Chinese culinary tradition) the texture remains crisp and the color vivid. Stir-frying requires speed and control, so vegetables should be prepared in advance. They must be cut into small uniform pieces so that they can be tossed easily and cooked quickly in the high heat produced by a wok: slice long vegetables diagonally or in a roll-cut (p.260) and short, round ones in small, thin slices. Roll-cutting exposes as many surfaces to the heat as possible, and is useful when stir-frying. It is particularly suitable for vegetables such as carrots and white radishes that take longer to cook than softer vegetables.

A light peanut or all-purpose oil is best for stir-frying, while stronger oils such as sesame may be sprinkled on just before serving. Use just enough fat to coat the pan. Garlic, hot pepper, ginger or scallions are often added to flavor the oil and may be removed before adding the vegetables. Watery vegetables such as zucchini and spinach may be stir-fried without adding oil (this is called "dry-frying"). Good stir-fry combinations include cabbage with tiny ears of corn and snow peas, and asparagus with carrots and broccoli. Paper-thin slices of meat, or shellfish, may be added. Another option is to add liquid – a little wine or sherry, or a Chinese sauce such as soy, black bean or oyster, and a last-minute thickening of cornstarch.

Stir-fried vegetables

Almost any crisp vegetable is excellent stir-fried to serve with broiled foods. This recipe uses broccoli and cauliflower.

Serves 4

½ lb/250 g cauliflower, divided in florets	2 medium carrots, cut in ⅛ in/3 mm diagonal slices
½ lb/250 g broccoli, divided in florets	salt and pepper
3-4 tbsp/45-60 ml peanut oil	1 tbsp white wine vinegar
2-3 thin slices fresh ginger	1 teaspoon sesame oil
1 scallion, thinly sliced	*Wok and metal spatula*

1 Cut the cauliflower and broccoli florets in ¼ in/6 mm slices. In a wok, heat the peanut oil until very hot, add the ginger and fry for ½-1 minute over high heat. Stir until the ginger browns, then discard it. Add the scallion and carrots and fry, stirring constantly, about 1 minute. Add the cauliflower and continue stirring for 1 minute. Finally add the broccoli, season with salt and pepper, and stir-fry the vegetables until almost tender, 1-2 minutes.
2 Add the vinegar, cover the vegetables with a lid, lower the heat and continue cooking until tender, 3-5 minutes. Add the sesame oil, season to taste and serve at once.

Deep-frying vegetables

Deep-fried potatoes (p.296) must be the most popular of all vegetables – think of thin and crispy French *pommes frites*, American French fries that are just as crisp but more substantial, and the British chip that goes so well with fried fish. Many other vegetables deep-fry well, even if they do not have the same versatility: sharp onions, matchsticks of zucchini, eggplant sticks, broccoli florets, sliced parsnips and sweet potatoes all add crunchiness as well as taste to a dish, while a mixed platter makes a perfect appetizer, as in Italian *fritto misto* or the more delicate Japanese batter, *tempura*.

Croquettes made from chopped or puréed vegetables may also be deep-fried. The softer the vegetable, the thicker the binding agent should be. Mashed potato is good for holding together vegetables like carrots, mushrooms, broccoli and spinach, and is also popular fried on its own in croquettes. Cheese, and even chopped meat or chicken, may be included.

As with all deep-frying (Fats and Oils, p.104), a crisp, non-greasy coating and a succulent center are essential. Most vegetables need protection from the hot oil: fritter batter provides a crunchy covering, while a breadcrumb or cornmeal coating gives a crisp bite. Herbs or grated lemon zest in the batter are particularly good with mushrooms, young artichokes or okra. Make sure the coating completely covers the vegetable. A few vegetables, such as starchy roots and tubers, may be deep-fried without a coating. Vegetables that discolor should be rubbed with lemon before coating, and any marinated vegetables must be dried thoroughly before frying.

A golden color and a tender center show that deep-fried vegetables are done. Serve them at once, while still crisp, with tomato sauce (p.65), tartare sauce (p.63) or spicy fruit chutney.

Braising vegetables

Braising is an ideal way of cooking heartier vegetables such as fennel, cardoon, cabbage and celery, which benefit from slow, even heat that mingles the flavors. Left whole or cut in pieces, the vegetables are cooked with a little butter or oil, usually with a *mirepoix* of diced vegetables (right) or a layer of sliced onions or leeks on the bottom of the pan. (In less classic versions, these vegetables may be left out altogether.) Liquid may be added – water, stock, wine or even tomato sauce – but vegetables such as Belgian endive that release juice as they cook may not need any at all. Covering the vegetables with aluminum foil or parchment paper retains moisture and gives them a brighter color. After simmering for half an hour or more on the stove or in the oven, the liquid reduces to a few spoonfuls of concentrated syrupy glaze.

Aromatic herbs, garlic or bacon add extra character to a braise, while a little sugar cuts the acidity of vegetables such as tomatoes or artichokes. The French enjoy simple combinations such as lettuce braised in chicken stock or cabbage braised with apples and cider, *à la normande*. The Portuguese enjoy whole onions braised in beef stock with bay leaf and parsley, while Italians often braise artichokes in water, olive oil, garlic and mint and use tomato-based sauces for braising celery. Braised vegetables provide a good balance to rich meats. Braised red cabbage, for example, is an excellent partner to game, braised white cabbage counters the confident flavor of sausage, while milder braised fennel, cardoon and celery pair well with chicken and veal.

GLAZING VEGETABLES

Ordinary root vegetables with a slightly sweet flavor, such as carrots, turnips and onions, can be transformed by glazing. Sometimes a touch of sugar is added. Tiny vegetables are left whole, and large ones should be turned (p. 260), scooped into balls or cut into even shapes. Classically, the vegetables are completely cooked in the liquid that makes the glaze, but they may also be blanched and drained before being cooked with the glazing ingredients.

1 Put the raw vegetables in a pan. For every 1 lb/500 g vegetables, add 2-3 tablespoons of butter with 1 tablespoon of sugar if you like. Add salt, pepper and enough water or light stock to barely cover the vegetables.

2 Bring to a boil and simmer until the liquid has almost evaporated. If the vegetables are not tender, add a little more water and continue cooking. When the liquid has almost evaporated, shake the pan to coat the vegetables evenly with the glaze. **Note** Different vegetables should be glazed separately, then tossed together.

3 Take from the heat, taste the vegetables for seasoning and add any chopped herbs such as parsley or mint, with an extra tablespoon of butter if you like for added flavor.

MIREPOIX & BATTUTO

Many braises, sauces and stews acquire additional flavor from a base of vegetables. The French *mirepoix* is a mixture of two parts each diced carrots and onions to one part celery, and sometimes a small amount of leek, cooked in butter in a saucepan. It forms an essential part of braises and some brown sauces, and may be used when roasting to give flavor to gravy. It is added at the beginning of cooking so that there is time for the vegetables to contribute their flavor. It is always strained out of the liquid before serving. The size of the cut vegetables depends on the cooking time of the main ingredients, and varies from small dice for *sauce espagnole* (p.57) to larger pieces for meat that can take three hours or more to braise in the oven.

In Italy the flavor base is often provided by a *battuto*, a similar combination of onion, carrot and celery, usually with parsley and garlic. Traditionally lard is combined with the vegetables, but nowadays olive oil is often used. When a *battuto* is sautéed before other ingredients are added, it is called a *soffrito* Both a *battuto* and a *soffrito* form an integral part of the dish and are not strained out before serving.

Baking vegetables

Baked vegetables cooked in the oven come in a variety of forms: they may be baked whole in their skins, layered in a casserole with or without sauce, stuffed with meat or other vegetables or, perhaps the most popular method of all, cooked *au gratin*. Vegetables with a high moisture content, such as potatoes and eggplant, are well-suited to baking because they keep their shape during long cooking and need no additional liquid. Less moist vegetables such as cabbage may also be baked, but they will cook faster and be more tender if blanched first.

Surely the most famous baked vegetable is the baked potato – crisp-skinned with a fluffy interior that begs for butter, sour cream or gravy. For baking, potatoes and whole unpeeled root vegetables should be pricked so that during cooking steam escapes from their interior. (However, beet is left with the skin intact so that it does not bleed.) Other large vegetables – for example, winter squash – need minimal treatment and may be baked whole, in halves or in pieces, topped with butter, herbs and a sprinkling of breadcrumbs or brown sugar. The more tender small root and fruit vegetables, such as tomatoes, may be baked with or without their skin, in just a little butter, herbs and seasoning.

Fruit vegetables such as eggplant, tomatoes and peppers, and members of the squash family such as zucchini, are often baked together. Sometimes they are flavored with herbs and garlic, as in the ratatouille of Provence. In Greece, okra and potatoes are baked as *briam*, while from central Spain comes *pisto manchego* of zucchini, green peppers and tomato, sometimes with bacon or potatoes added. No matter what the nationality of the recipe, the vegetables should be cut into evenly sized pieces and baked with a cover to retain moisture.

Simple baked vegetables may appear as a first course or main dish accompaniment, but heartier recipes can make a main course in themselves. In this category come German puddings made from purées bound with eggs, the French *tians* bound with eggs and cheese, and the baked dishes of Italy, such as pasta layered with eggplant and tomato sauce, topped with mozzarella and Parmesan. Other baked appetizers and main dishes include vegetable soufflés, custard quiches and savory tarts filled with vegetables and cheese.

Vegetables au gratin

The French verb *gratiner* means to bake au gratin (with a cheese topping). Gratins are so popular that shallow baking dishes, which give the maximum amount of crisp, brown crust, are often called gratin dishes. Typical vegetable gratins are made with cauliflower or root vegetables such as turnips or carrots. The cooked vegetables are coated with a cheese or béchamel sauce (although a tomato sauce may be substituted), and sprinkled with a topping of grated cheese, breadcrumbs or chopped nuts, or a combination of these. The gratin is browned in the oven until golden, or it can be browned under the broiler. The sauce may be left plain without a topping, for a smooth, melting crust.

Slow-cooking vegetables, such as potatoes and pumpkin, can also be gratinéed successfully in the oven. Here the key is to cook the vegetables gently and thoroughly without burning the topping, and for this a deeper baking dish is needed. The most famous example of such gratins is perhaps *gratin dauphinois* – potatoes baked in cream with a touch of garlic and a topping of cheese. American scalloped potatoes are very similar. **Note** Root vegetables take longer to cook in a sauce containing any acidic ingredient, and in such cases parboiling may be advisable. Tomatoes, particularly, can have a hardening effect on vegetables because of the acid they contain.

Sometimes an already baked or stuffed vegetable is browned in the oven or under the broiler as a finishing touch. Gratins often stand alone as a main course or appetizer, like other baked vegetable dishes such as the Flemish favorite of Belgian endive wrapped in ham and baked in béchamel sauce with a cheese topping. When prepared more simply, gratins pair well with roasted or broiled meats and poultry.

Vegetables that release their juices easily, for example summer squash and spinach, may not need sauce at all and may simply be covered with a layer of dry breadcrumbs, which are then sprinkled with melted butter or olive oil to produce a golden crust when baked in the oven.

Broiling vegetables

Vegetables cooked under the broiler must be basted so that they retain their juices and do not dry out under the direct heat. Most vegetables can be basted with oil, although mushrooms are best dotted with butter. An assortment of broiled or barbecued vegetables, basted with oil and flavored with fragrant herbs, makes an excellent appetizer when served with a spicy tomato or rich nut sauce such as *tarator* (p.66). However, vegetables are more often broiled to accompany other foods – steak or sausages for instance. Most popular of all are the broiled accompaniments to a barbecue, cooked over the coals with meats such as chicken or spare ribs. Aromatic woods like apple and hickory impart more flavor than plain charcoal, and robust herbs like rosemary and thyme add fragrance. Brush the vegetables liberally with oil so they do not stick; olive and sesame oil impart their own special flavor. Marinating vegetables beforehand with oil and seasonings such as lemon juice, soy sauce or hot spices is another possibility. Never broil vegetables too close to the heat and always baste them frequently during cooking.

Large vegetables such as eggplant should be evenly sliced or halved and scored for broiling. To barbecue, first place them cut-side down on the grill to sear them, then turn them over and raise the grill a little higher over the heat source, Cook the vegetables until they are soft. One neat solution is to pack a selection of evenly cut vegetables on to a skewer so that they moisten each other. Usually, the skin is left on for protection, but vegetables such as bell peppers and tomatoes may be peeled after broiling. Halved tomato, bell pepper, onion and eggplant all broil well and can be placed directly on the broiler, with a simple basting of oil and seasoning. Slow-cooking vegetables such as potatoes should be blanched first so that they cook through without charring and drying out. Further insulation may be provided by wrapping vegetables in aluminum foil packages, though this will steam rather than broil them. Foil-wrapped vegetables may be buried in the embers of a fire to cook. The American summer standby – sweet corn on the cob, often served with a knob of butter – provides its own package: the silk is discarded, but the husk is left on to provide protection against the heat and to hold a basting of oil and seasoning.

Stuffing vegetables

Many vegetables, for example, green and red bell peppers, tomatoes and squash, make natural containers. These stuffed vegetables appear in recipes around the world. Other less obvious vegetables may also be stuffed: roots like potato, kohlrabi and turnip can be hollowed out to hold a filling, the leaves of robust greens such as cabbage are perfect wrappings for a stuffing mixture; while globe artichoke bottoms and mushroom caps offer a convenient small cup shape. In the Middle East, where stuffed vegetables are a specialty, eggplants and onions are also popular. Usually the stuffing is baked or broiled inside the vegetable, but occasionally young vegetables or a vegetable purée are cooked separately and spooned or piped in just before serving.

The scooped-out flesh of vegetables such as eggplant, potatoes and squash may form the base of the stuffing. Brisk flavorings are added (fried onion, garlic, olive, celery, anchovy, capers, lemon peel or chopped chili peppers) with béchamel or breadcrumbs to bind. The Turkish *imam bayaldi* – eggplant stuffed with onion, tomato, garlic and generous amounts of olive oil – is a popular example of a vegetable stuffed in this way.

Stuffed vegetables can make elegant appetizers or accompaniments, for example artichoke hearts filled with green peas, mushrooms (Stuffed shiitake, p.309), or the hollowed out turnips with carrot purée that traditionally adorn roasted veal. More substantial dishes are made with meat stuffings, such as English vegetable marrow with ham and breadcrumbs or French and central European cabbage with pork. Other recipes that extend to a main course include peppers or baked potatoes stuffed with fish or meat in a sauce or with other vegetables. Green bell peppers filled with *prosciutto*, Parmesan cheese and rice, then baked in broth, are an Italian inspiration, while American cooks might fill acorn squash with creamed onions and spicy meat.

When a vegetable is stuffed for baking, it is important to fill it completely without packing it so tightly that it bursts during cooking. Vegetables such as bell peppers may be left *al dente* (p.261), while others, for example eggplant, are best when tender. Allow for differences in the cooking times for stuffing and container by precooking the container or stuffing as necessary. This is important when dealing with large winter squashes.

STUFFING VINE LEAVES

Leaves that are to be stuffed are always blanched first. Cook the stuffed leaves in a mixture of olive oil, lemon juice and water until tender, about two hours. Drain and serve warm or cold.

1 Put a tablespoon of filling (here a mixture of rice, toasted pine nuts, onion, raisins and spices) in the center of the blanched or washed vine leaf.

2 Fold the sides and near end of the leaf over the filling. Roll it away from you to form a cylinder.

The small rolls (above) can be served as an appetizer or a vegetable accompaniment to a main dish.

COOKING WITH LEAVES

Grapevine leaves play a conspicuous role in the cuisines of the eastern Mediterranean. Sold fresh in summer months, they are available year-round canned, vacuum-packed or bottled in brine. Many are produced in Greece, though California leaves are said to be more tender. Fresh leaves should be washed and steamed or blanched until tender; those in brine should be rinsed.

For Greek *dolmades*, vine leaves are filled with rice seasoned with dill and lemon and served cold with lemon juice or warm with *avgolemono* sauce (p.55). Turkish *dolmas* may be filled with rice and meat mixed with raisins and nuts, while Lebanese *mashi* are flavored with mint and served with a yogurt sauce. In parts of France, odds and ends of cheese are baked in vine leaves for a fresh-tasting snack on country bread. Vine leaves are also wrapped around small game birds and fish to keep them moist, cut into strips to add to salads, or used to line a platter of fruit or cheese.

Other large leaves act as a wrapper for foods to keep them moist and protect them from heat, rather than to eat with the finished dish. Banana leaves are popular in Latin America and southeast Asia, wrapped around fish or chicken or as an accompaniment to sweet and sour meat dishes. The shiny leaves of the *ti* plant – used for hula skirts in Hawaii and the South Pacific – impart a unique flavor to fish, often served with coconut or sweet sauce. Chestnut leaves are the classic covering for the soft French Banon cheese, but nowadays leaf-shaped paper is often used instead. In China, lotus leaves are a favorite wrapping.

In Latin America, the papery husk of corn is used as a wrapper. Dried tan-colored husks must be soaked in hot water for one to two hours before wrapping around foods to be steamed or broiled. Typical are *tamales* filled with a mixture of *masa harina* (Flour, Breads and Batters p.343) and meat, poultry or cheese flavored with chilies.

Puréeing vegetables

Vegetable purées are extremely versatile, forming the base of molds, mousses, terrines and soufflés, of sauces and soups, even of sweet recipes like American pumpkin pie and German carrot cake. Alone they make a colorful side dish, especially if several purées of contrasting colors are served together on one plate. They may provide a bed for a main ingredient such as fish, sliced meat or a poached egg, a filling for a pastry case or a stuffing for other vegetables.

Vegetable purées have recently enjoyed a resurgence in popularity – one reason may be that machines can now do the work that previously took so long by hand. Most purées are made of boiled, steamed or baked vegetables that have been finely mashed or sieved and then enriched with butter and cream. The vegetables should be cooked a little longer than usual so that they are soft. Vegetables that absorb a lot of moisture, such as eggplant, should be baked rather than boiled to prevent the purée from becoming too watery. White vegetables are sometimes simmered in milk or a flour and lemon *blanc* (p.261) to preserve their color. For serving alone, a vegetable purée should be the consistency of soft ice cream, falling easily from the spoon. Vegetables that contain little starch, such as green beans or turnips, may be mixed with potatoes, dried beans or rice to thicken them in a purée.

Another method of thickening is to beat whipped egg white into the hot purée. This also lightens the purée, as in a hot vegetable mousse, which is nothing more than a purée with whipped egg white or cream, or both. The cream should be folded in at the last possible minute. Tomato, lettuce and spinach purées are particularly successful when finished this way.

A purée or mousse must be highly seasoned – with salt and pepper, and perhaps fresh herbs, spices, or a touch of cayenne. Nutmeg is a classic addition, particularly to spinach and cauliflower; other combinations include cinnamon with carrots and sweet potatoes, mint with peas and allspice with beets. Lemon or orange juice is sometimes used, or a spoonful or two of liqueur, such as an anise-flavored one with fennel. Even whole fruits can be cooked and puréed with a vegetable. Apple, for example, is excellent with cabbage.

Cream dilutes flavor as well as thickness, blunting the sharpness of acid vegetables like sorrel, while the flavor of fresh butter, melted by stirring into the hot purée, lends an unrivalled richness. These additions are best when made at the last minute, as purées easily lose their flavor.

When puréeing soups and sauces with a good deal of liquid, the solid ingredients should be strained and puréed separately. The liquid is then stirred back into the purée until it is smooth.

Note Purées containing potato, chestnut or dried beans deteriorate within half an hour if kept hot and may be heavy when reheated. Purées of less starchy vegetables, such as spinach, can be kept hot an hour or two in a water bath (p.510).

MAKING A VEGETABLE PURÉE

The food processor is now the favorite tool for puréeing most vegetables; the texture it produces is excellent for many purées, terrines and timbales. However, it must not be used for starchy vegetables, notably potato, as they quickly turn to a gluey pulp. A blender produces a fine purée, good for vegetable fruits like eggplant, but it will not break down firmer vegetables. Neither machine will cut fiber, so stringy vegetables like celery must be sieved after puréeing. **Note** Acidic vegetables such as tomatoes will discolor if in contact with an aluminum mesh sieve.

1 **A food mill** may be substituted for a drum sieve and is useful for firm vegetables like roots, and peppers (used here). Turn the handle to force the vegetables through.

2 With a pastry scraper or a spatula, scrape the puréed vegetable from the bottom of the food mill into a bowl.

A drum sieve is useful for vegetables that have fibers, strings or skin, such as celery, or peas (shown here). Using a large wooden pestle, work the vegetables through the mesh, then scrape the purée into a bowl. A bowl strainer and wooden spoon may be used instead. **Note** To save time, it helps to purée the vegetables a little in a food processor first.

A food processor produces a fine purée with even consistency for vegetables without starch, such as carrots or spinach. Push the vegetables down in the bowl.

A masher may be used for starchier vegetables, such as potatoes, that have very little fiber. Mash a small amount at a time until smooth.

Hot vegetable molds

Vegetable molds are usually made from a purée, whether plain, layered with another purée or mixed with other diced, grated or sliced vegetables. The purée is often bound with eggs or béchamel sauce, or occasionally with breadcrumbs. Some vegetable molds are bound with a *mousseline* of meat or fish. The final dishes are often named for the containers in which they are molded, for example a timbale, which is a small cylindrical mold (p.511), while vegetable terrines or loaves are much larger and usually more elaborate, producing many slices, each patterned with color. Small vegetable molds, too, may hide a "surprise" such as a mushroom or artichoke heart in the middle.

Almost any puréed vegetable with plenty of flavor can be molded, though starchy vegetables such as potatoes or beans may be a little heavy. Coarsely chopped vegetables or ingredients such as ham and anchovy may be added to the purée for texture and additional flavor. For molding purées into layers, combine vegetables of contrasting colors – spinach, carrots or sweet potatoes with celery root or turnip. More elaborate terrines can be made with mixtures of varying textures and an array of cooked vegetables. For a special presentation, a mold may be lined with blanched spinach, lettuce or cabbage leaves, displaying its vivid color only when sliced. A lining can also help when unmolding the dish.

Vegetable molds are baked in a water bath (p.510) to set and bind the ingredients. Larger terrines are tricky, as many vegetables render liquid as they cook, threatening the stability of the mixture and making it harder to slice. Watery vegetables such as zucchini should be baked or sautéed before adding to a terrine, so that moisture content is minimized. Hot vegetable terrines are baked in the same way as those made with meat (p.241). To bake small vegetable molds such as timbales, see page 274.

A slice or two of terrine, or small molds served singly or together, make popular appetizers, perhaps with tomato sauce (p.65) or a white butter sauce (p.62). Individual carrot, parsnip or sweet potato molds make a good side dish for beef or pork, while more delicate molds such as asparagus go well with fish. Corn molds are good with game; spinach molds or timbales (p.274), are more versatile and can accompany most dishes.

Cold vegetable molds

Most cooked vegetable molds may be served cold as well as hot, and a few cold molds are made from the raw vegetable, for example cucumber. Cold layered terrines are most popular, presented on a bed of lettuce with mayonnaise, or a fresh tomato *coulis*. A cold vegetable mousse or purée may also be folded with whipped cream or layered with a *mousseline* of meat or fish. Gelatin diluted in water or chicken stock may be added to stabilize the mousse and give it a little body. Molds of savory or unclarified vegetable aspic with layered vegetables are also popular. Clarified aspic may be used to provide a shimmering background for a more elegant presentation, or simply a thin topping for a vegetable mousse.

Like other cold mousses, vegetable mixtures are often set in ring or fluted molds, then unmolded and decorated with hard-boiled egg, tomato roses, watercress or piped mayonnaise. The mousse mixture itself may be piped into rosettes to serve alone, or into hollowed tomatoes, zucchini cups or cucumber boats.

Cold vegetable terrine

Almost any cooked vegetables can be used in a terrine, providing they are not too moist.

Serves 10-12

1 lb/500 g carrots, sliced lengthwise	3 cups/750 ml heavy cream
½ lb/250 g green beans	9 egg yolks
2 red bell peppers, peeled, cored and cut in strips	½ tsp grated nutmeg
	salt and pepper
1 lb/500 g leeks, white part only, chopped	1 tbsp/7 g gelatin, softened in cold water (p.431)
¾ lb/375 g small mushrooms, sliced	fresh tomato *coulis* (for serving) (p.65)
2 tbsp/30 g butter	
2½ cups/250 g grated Gruyère	*2½ qt/2.5 L terrine (p.511)*

1 Heat oven to 325°F/160°C and prepare a water bath (p.510).
2 In separate batches, cook the carrots, green beans and peppers in salted boiling water until tender, 3-5 minutes each. Drain and pat them dry with paper towels. Boil leeks in salted water 8-10 minutes until tender, drain and dry them.
3 Sauté the mushrooms in the butter until tender and their moisture has evaporated, 2-3 minutes. Season to taste, drain and dry on paper towels.
4 Butter the terrine mold. Arrange layers of red pepper, leek, carrot, beans and mushrooms in the mold, sprinkling cheese between each layer. **Note** Do not pack the vegetables down.
5 In a bowl, whisk the cream, egg yolks, nutmeg, salt and pepper until mixed. Gently heat the gelatin until melted and stir it into the cream mixture. Pour the mixture over the vegetables, making sure it seeps between the layers.
6 Cover the terrine with the lid. Set it in the water bath and bring the water to a simmer. Transfer to the oven and bake until it is set at the sides, but the center is still soft, 1¾-2 hours. Remove from the heat and allow to cool. Refrigerate at least 4 hours, or up to 1 day.
7 Unmold the terrine on to a serving dish and cut into ½ in/ 1.25 cm slices. Serve with fresh tomato *coulis* (p.65).

COOKING WITH FLOWERS

Many flowers are edible as well as decorative. Large-petaled blossoms, such as zucchini or squash, may be stuffed with delicate meats or cheeses, baked or deep-fried in a light batter, or pickled, all methods favored for nasturtiums too. Delicate petals such as a rose or elderflower are often added to jams and jellies, while rose petals and violets are a well-known candied decoration for special pastries. Heavily scented flowers, such as lavender and orange flowers, are traditional flavorings, especially in the Middle East, while lilies feature in Asian cooking. Some flowers may be sprinkled on top of foods, pressed into fresh cheese or tossed in a green salad. Larger flowers such as lilies may be set afloat in a tureen of clear soup or a bowl of punch, or used to garnish a roast. Certain flavors are well suited to flowers: seafood and light poultry salads blend well with dandelions (p.272); sage, nasturtium and pot marigolds (calendula) go well with cheese; chives and marjoram are often sprinkled on egg dishes.

Zucchini flower

Nasturtium

Note Many flowers are poisonous, so do not use them in the kitchen unless you are certain they are edible.

Other cooking methods for vegetables

As well as the cooking methods described above, vegetables can be used in many different ways that are described in other chapters: they are the main ingredient in innumerable soups, such as Italian minestrone or Spanish gazpacho, and of some interesting sauces, like onion *sauce Soubise* and mushroom and tomato *sauce chasseur*. They are important in many egg dishes – as fillings for quiches and in mixtures for soufflés and custards, particularly spinach, zucchini, mushrooms and asparagus. Flat omelets generously flavored with chopped bell peppers, zucchini, spinach or onion appear on tables from Spain to Scandinavia or the Middle East, while elegant crêpes are folded around simple combinations of cheese with leeks, onions or spinach, as well as more complex vegetable mixtures such as ratatouille or vegetable curry.

Savory pastries filled or flavored with vegetables, such as Russian *pelmeni* filled with cabbage, Greek spinach *spanokopitas* and Spanish potato *empanadas*, make popular snacks. The dumplings of central Europe may be filled with vegetables like mushrooms and are frequently made from potatoes. Cooked vegetable mixtures flavored with garlic and olive oil top Italian pasta and pizza alike, while spicy Asian-style combinations pair well with noodles and rice dishes.

Nor should the role of vegetables in other dishes be forgotten. They add depth to braises or stews of meat and poultry. Garlic, shallot, scallion and leek as well as the humble onion are vital to all western cuisines. Together with carrots and tomatoes they are indispensable as basic flavoring ingredients, while potatoes and root vegetables act as thickeners and provide body to integral sauces. Sweet and chili peppers are also important as flavorings.

VEGETABLE SALADS

Salads can be made with a variety of raw vegetables: crudités fashioned from fresh, peeled seasonal produce and served with a red chili pepper sauce (p.63) or *Bagna cauda* dip (p.101), ripe tomatoes moistened with olive oil and lemon; julienne of celery root *rémoulade* with mustard mayonnaise. Cooked vegetables are even more versatile, tossed in a vinaigrette dressing or mixed with mayonnaise. They are also the basis of hearty salads like French *salade niçoise* with tuna and olives.

Texture is important for vegetable salads. Uncooked vegetables should be crunchy; if they seem tough, they should be blanched. Cooked vegetables should be cooked until just tender but firm, and then refreshed and thoroughly drained. Whether raw or cooked, marinating for an hour or two benefits robust vegetables such as onions, but after 12 hours they may start to lose flavor and become acidic. Dressings and mayonnaise should be added just before serving, except for potato vinaigrette (below), where the dressing is added to the warm vegetables. Vegetable salads should be stored covered in the refrigerator. However, most taste better at room temperature, so take them out half an hour before serving.

Vinaigrette salad Serves 4. Boil 1 lb/500 g vegetables such as leek, asparagus, green beans, potatoes or root vegetables until tender. Drain the vegetables and while still warm and absorbent mix with ½ cup/125 ml of vinaigrette dressing.

Macédoine of cooked vegetables/Russian salad Serves 6. Cut 2 medium carrots and 1 medium turnip in ⅜ in/1 cm dice. Simmer them in salted water 5-7 minutes until tender, and drain. Cook 1 cup/250 g shelled fresh peas in boiling salted water until tender, 7-12 minutes. Drain and refresh them. Cut ¾ cup/175 g green beans in short sticks, cook 3-5 minutes in boiling salted water, drain and refresh also. Mix the vegetables with ¼ cup/60 ml vinaigrette dressing. Stir in ½ cup/125 ml mayonnaise and taste for seasoning.

Coleslaw Serves 8. Shred 1 lb/500 g white cabbage and 3 medium carrots. Combine with dressing made from 1 cup/250 ml mayonnaise, 1 tsp red wine vinegar, 1 tsp Dijon mustard, 1 tsp celery seed and salt and pepper to taste. Chill 1-2 hours.

Presenting vegetables

The agreeable shapes and vibrant colors of vegetables make them a good choice for eye-catching presentations. A dull-looking dish that lacks life can often be saved by the addition of a garnish of shiny glazed carrots or a bundle of neatly arranged green beans tied with a string of leek. Modern plate presentations set great emphasis on displays of assorted vegetables at the peak of freshness, all carefully cut to shape.

A more traditional garnish for great platters of roast meats and poultry is an assortment of stuffed vegetables. The fillings may be smaller vegetables such as peas, a vegetable purée or a zesty filling flavored with herbs and lemon – a vivid, eye-catching contrast is the key. Some puréed vegetables can be piped into rosettes. Potatoes are most often used for this, but carrots, sweet potatoes, turnips and even green beans also pipe well.

In vegetable salads, appearance plays an even more important role, for the crispness of the leaves of a fresh green salad, or the nicely balanced color of a cooked vegetable salad are half the appeal of the dish.

SALAD GREENS
LETTUCE, CHICORY FAMILY, ARUGULA, LAMB'S LETTUCE

Lettuce has been cultivated the world over for centuries. Today only a few main varieties find their way to market, but many more varietal seeds are sold for the garden. The most common is head lettuce, of which there are two types: crisphead and butterhead. Crisphead, also called iceberg and Webb's Wonder, is common in the United States and becoming better known in Europe. It has a tightly packed, firm head with little taste but an agreeably crunchy texture that makes it useful in sandwiches and dishes such as Mexican tacos. The yellowish core may have a slightly bitter tang. Crisphead lettuce leaves are quite stiff, making pretty cups for salads and sauces as well as wrappings for Asian stir-fried mixtures.

Lamb's lettuce

Water-cress

Garden cress

The term "butterhead" covers a more varied group of lettuces, all with a soft delicate leaf and a richer, almost buttery flavor. This type – Boston and Bibb are two examples – has a small head that is much more loosely packed than crisphead lettuce. Some butterheads have quite a crunch, particularly at the pale heart, while the darker outer leaves have more flavor. When grown hydroponically (in water with nutrients), the roots are usually left attached to a clean, crisp head. Butterhead lettuce combines well in green salads with bitter greens.

Long-leaved lettuce, usually known as romaine or cos, was originally grown on the Greek island of Kos. Romaine lettuce combines a crisp texture with a mild taste, and stands up well to strong flavors such as anchovy and Parmesan cheese in Caesar salad. Loose-leaf, also called leaf, oak leaf or salad bowl lettuce, is a fairly recent type. It has no heart but the leaves grow in a loose bunch, the advantage being that you can cut what you require without damaging the plant. Red-leaved varieties add color to mixed leaf salads. Leaf lettuce is often preferred to crisphead types, and it stands up quite well to cooking.

Green salad may be made with lettuce alone, so perfectly do the leaves go with a simple vinaigrette dressing. However, lettuce also makes an excellent cooked summer vegetable, adding consistency without being sticky, and giving a smooth texture to soup or when cooked with peas *à la française*. Lettuce braises well with a little onion and bacon, and the blanched leaves may be used to wrap fish or other light fillings, retaining moisture and providing a splash of color.

Chicory nomenclature is very confusing. What the British call chicory is Belgian endive in the United States, while the vegetable that both British and Americans know as curly endive is called *chicorée frisée* in France. What the French and Italians call escarole may also be identified as flat or broad chicory in the United States, and as Batavian endive in Britain. **Note** The chicory used as a bitter additive to ground coffee comes from the toasted root of a Belgian endive variety that is not eaten as a vegetable.

Belgian endive (Fr. *endive*), has a compact plump white head, the result of forcing (when the leaves are cut off and the roots banked up in the dark to produce long, oval *chicons*). Belgian endive is often wrapped for sale in dark blue paper to keep it white and mild. Most is still exported from Belgium, hence its name and high price. When raw, Belgian endive is crisp and sweet-tasting with a slight bite, a favorite for mixing in salads with contrasting watercress or avocado. The leaves are sliced diagonally or broken individually from the head, when they may also be used for dipping. Belgian endive is delicious braised to accompany meats or poultry, or to serve in a gratin in cheese sauce. However, the vegetable can be bitter (removing the core may help eliminate this). On account of this slight bitterness it is a wonderful accompaniment to game.

The other members of the chicory family pack a peppery punch into colorful, resilient leaves, good for salads or in cooked vegetable dishes. Curly endive (Fr. *chicorée frisée*) is perhaps the prettiest, with an almost lacy head of green, white and yellow leaves. Escarole or flat chicory is equally bushy but has flat, rather broad dark green leaves and a stronger bite. Curly endive and escarole can be similarly prepared.

Red-leaved chicory, usually found as the tight-headed Verona-type radicchio or looser, long-leaved Treviso (the British red Treviso chicory or French *trevise*) is grown primarily in Italy but is gaining recognition elsewhere, thanks to its eye-catching purple and white stripes, and sharp taste. The leaves often curl to resemble a small cabbage, providing a striking cup-shaped container. They keep their color when cooked and are delicious as part of a broiled vegetable platter. In Europe, especially Italy, at least a dozen other chicory varieties can be found in regional markets. Leafy Italian *punterelle*, or asparagus chicory, and sweet French *pain de sucre* are particularly well-liked.

Similar to dandelion (p.272) in taste, but with the texture of lettuce, is arugula or rocket. Common in the Mediterranean region, arugula is also becoming popular in the United States as a salad green. The long spear-shaped leaves have a spicy bitterness that makes them as addictive as coriander leaf; they are good mixed with other greens or tossed with a hot bacon dressing. When puréed with ingredients such as Parmesan cheese and pine nuts they make an excellent sauce resembling basil-flavored *pesto* (p.17) for meats, fish or pasta.

Although not strictly speaking a lettuce, lamb's lettuce is the perfect name for the plant also known as *mâche* or corn salad, as this most delicate of greens appears at the same time as baby lamb, sprouting through winter frost. The soft, rather bland leaves melt in the mouth like butter; for serving they should be left attached above the root like dandelions. Lamb's lettuce can be used to balance stronger greens, or served alone in a light vinaigrette. Its classic partner is beetroot.

Belgian endive

Arugula

Boston lettuce

Romaine lettuce

Batavian endive

Iceberg lettuce

Butterhead

Frisée de Ruffée

Salad bowl Red lollo

Curly endive

Oak leaf lettuce

Radicchio

Red oak leaf

USEFUL INFORMATION/SALAD GREENS

Peak season *Lettuce*: spring to winter. *Belgian endive*: winter to summer. *Chicory family*: early summer.

How to choose Fresh smell, crisp green leaves. *Crisphead*: light green heads give slightly when squeezed. *Butterhead*: soft leaves; well-formed heart. *Romaine*: dark green leaves, full and closely bunched. *Belgian endive*: crisp pale heads. *Chicory family*: heavy heads; pale heart. *Radicchio*: well-formed heart. *Arugula*: long leaves. *Lamb's lettuce*: soft green leaves.

Preparation Remove discolored leaves. Rinse thoroughly, if necessary in several changes of water; drain well.

Portion: 1 lb/500 g raw greens serves 4-5. One large endive per person if cooked, one half if raw.

Nutritive value per 3½ oz/100 g (raw). *All*: no fat, no cholesterol. *Lettuce (romaine)*: 16 calories; 2 g protein; 2 g carbohydrates; 8 mg sodium. *Belgian endive*: 17 calories; 1 g protein; 3 g carbohydrates; 22 mg sodium. *Chicory family (escarole)*: 20 calories; 2 g protein; 4 g carbohydrates; 14 mg sodium. *Arugula*: 23 calories; 3 g protein; 3 g carbohydrates; trace sodium. *Lamb's lettuce*: 43 calories; 4 g protein; 7 g carbohydrates; trace sodium.

Cooking methods *Lettuce*: blanch 1-2 minutes; braise at 350°F/ 175°C, 30-45 minutes; steam 4-7 minutes. *Belgian endive*: bake at 350°F/175°C, 20-30 minutes; braise 15-20 minutes; broil 15-20 minutes. *Chicory family*: blanch 2-3 minutes; braise 30-45 minutes; steam 8-10 minutes. *Radicchio*: blanch 1 minute; braise 30-45 minutes; broil 5-7 minutes; chop

and sauté or stir-fry 3-5 minutes; steam 5-8 minutes.

When done Crisp when sautéed or stir-fried, tender for other methods.

Problems *Lettuce*: browns if in contact with ripening fruits. *Belgian endive*: wilts if humid, can be crisped in ice water. *Arugula, lamb's lettuce*: wash well to remove sand in crevices.

Processed forms *Belgian endive*: canned.

Storage The softer the green, the sooner it should be used; refrigerate loosely wrapped in a damp cloth; do not freeze. *Crisphead, Belgian endive*: 1-2 weeks. *Romaine*: 3-5 days. *Chicory family*: 5-7 days. *Butterhead, leaf, radicchio, arugula*: 2-3 days. *Lamb's lettuce*: 2 days.

Typical dishes *Lettuce*: Caesar salad (romaine lettuce dressed with eggs, garlic, lemon, oil, anchovy and Parmesan, USA); braised with bone marrow (France). *Belgian endive*: gestoofde andijvie (with cream sauce, Netherlands); (lamb stew with endive, (Belgium); *Mornay* (braised in cheese sauce, France); *à la milanaise* (with Parmesan and noisette butter, France). *Chicory family*: sautéed radicchio with mushrooms and fennel (UK); escarole and rice soup (Italy); deep-fried red radicchio (Italy). *Arugula*: salad with lobster (USA). *Lamb's lettuce: salade d'hiver* (with beets and walnuts, France); *salade de vignerons* (with bacon, dandelion and walnut oil, France). *Also good with* pears, citrus fruits, mustard, goat cheese, chicken, avocado, nuts, potatoes, walnuts, lemon, beets.

CRESSES

Cresses appear as decoration on all kinds of cold and hot dishes, and the stems and leaves may be added to soups, salads and sauces, or prepared like spinach. Mustard-flavored watercress is plentiful in most temperate countries. It grows wild in river streams, but since they may be polluted it is wiser to use commercially grown watercress, which has just as much taste. Watercress is highly perishable, rapidly turning yellow, so it should be stored on ice. Other cresses for the kitchen include field and land cress, which grow wild in winter and have curly, deep-green leaves. They may be substituted for watercress and mix well with other bitter greens in a salad. Garden cress is usually sold in combination with mustard seed and can be grown from seed on damp blotting paper. It is lighter and sweeter in taste than watercress, but is similarly used, in salad and as a garnish.

CORING CRISPHEAD LETTUCE

Removing the core from a head of crisphead lettuce makes it easier to then unfold and separate the leaves.

1 Hold the head of lettuce, core down, and strike it hard on the work surface to loosen. Twist out the core, detaching it with a knife, if necessary.

2 To separate the leaves easily, hold the head of lettuce under cold running water.

GREEN SALAD

The cook's principle of balancing color, texture and taste applies particularly to green salads. Whether made of lettuce alone or a mixture of greens, a green salad should be dressed suitably and never overwhelmed by other ingredients. Each salad combination will provide its own taste and texture. For hot dressings, firm greens like dandelion or chicory are best, as they wilt only slightly. Other vegetables may be added to cold salads, while herbs like parsley, basil or chives contribute their own perfume.

When preparing lettuce, large leaves should be torn away from the stem, or pulled into smaller pieces by hand, as a knife bruises them. Wash the leaves thoroughly in lukewarm or cold water and either spin them in a salad spinner or pat them dry with paper towels or a dish towel. Wet leaves dilute the dressing and reduce the crispness of a good salad. Vegetables that are juicy, like tomatoes, or those that bleed color, like beets, should be added just before tossing to serve.

It is the dressing that gives a salad individuality, and for green salad a light vinaigrette is the best choice. Variations may be made with flavored mustard, some chopped shallot or scallion and a particular vinegar or oil. Always toss a green salad at the last minute so that there is no time for the dressing to wilt the leaves (especially if it is a hot dressing).

For garlic flavor, rub a wooden salad bowl with a cut clove, or add a piece of crushed clove to the dressing. The French make a *chapon* by rubbing garlic over a crust of bread and burying the crust in the lettuce. Keep the crust in the bowl when tossing the salad, but discard it before serving. In France, plain green salads are served after the main course, to clear the palate for cheese and dessert. In the United States, green salad usually opens the meal, or may be eaten between the appetizer and main course; in Britain it often accompanies a cold main dish, while in Italy it may accompany fish or meat. Green salads that include other vegetables or seafood are usually served as a first course.

New variations on the simple green salad include American chef's salad with julienne of ham, turkey and cheese; dandelion greens (p.272) in hot bacon dressing; toasted goat cheese *croûtes* on a bed of curly endive; salad greens with fresh foie gras; sweetbreads, or thinly sliced smoked duck breast tossed with walnut oil and raspberry vinegar, and arugula with pears and walnuts and a balsamic vinegar dressing.

Hot salad of chicken livers

This recipe is typical of the first-course salads that enjoyed such popularity during the 1920s and 1930s. Many of them have recently been adopted and featured in restaurants by modern chefs.

Serves 4

½ lb/250 g head of curly endive or escarole	4 thick slices French bread, cubed
½ lb/250 g chicken livers	3 shallots, finely chopped
salt and pepper	1 clove garlic, finely chopped
⅓ cup/75 ml oil (more if needed)	1 tbsp raspberry vinegar or other fruit vinegar
4 oz/125 g piece of bacon, cut in lardons (p.249)	1 tbsp chopped fresh chives

1 Wash the salad greens, drain and dry them well. Put them in a salad bowl. Trim the chicken livers of any membrane, and cut each one in two or three pieces. Season them with salt and pepper.
2 Heat 1 tbsp of oil in a frying pan and brown the lardons. Remove them with a draining spoon and add to the salad greens. There should be about ¼ cup/60 ml fat left in the pan; add more oil if needed. Fry the bread cubes, stirring until brown; add to the salad.
3 Add remaining oil to the pan and fry the livers briskly until browned on the outside but still pink in the center, 2-3 minutes. Add them to the salad with the fat, tossing the salad lightly.
4 Add the shallots and garlic to the pan and cook for 1 minute. Add vinegar to deglaze the pan juices and cook, stirring, until reduced by half. Pour this over the salad with the fat, tossing so the leaves wilt. Sprinkle with chives and serve at once.

HEARTY GREENS
Spinach, collards, kale, dandelion, sorrel

The flavor of hearty greens ranges from the gentle piquancy of beet greens to the acidity of sorrel, but most are prepared in the same way and used in similar dishes. When young and tender many hearty greens are agreeably sharp-tasting, and they can be eaten raw, or at most lightly cooked. However, mature leaves, particularly of species such as turnip greens, can be tough and almost inedibly peppery.

The acidity or bitterness of any hearty green can be muted by blanching (p.260) or by cooking with cream. Most greens need plenty of butter, though some cooks prefer to use lard, bacon fat or olive oil. Try greens in broth-based soups, winter stews or mixed with grains or rice for a savory stuffing. Measure them by weight rather than by bulk, for all of them lose at least half their volume during cooking.

Spinach is the most adaptable of all greens, with dark, arrow-shaped leaves, flat or curly. Commercially grown spinach is cultivated to travel and store well, but it tends to be more assertive in flavor and tougher than homegrown varieties. Spinach is known to be rich in vitamins and minerals although part of its reputation is undeserved, as by the time the leaves are cooked all but a trace of iron is eliminated.

Unlike most of its leafy cousins, spinach is popular raw as well as cooked, especially in the United States, where it is made into a robust salad, often paired with blue cheese or bacon. In Europe, spinach is usually boiled or steamed, its presence in a wide variety of dishes signaled by the French term *florentine*. Spinach pairs equally well with spicy and delicate foods and with fish, meat and eggs alike; in fact there are few foods it does not suit. Cooked spinach flavored with nutmeg or lemon makes an excellent filling for crêpes, soufflés, omelets and pasta, especially when combined with soft cheese or a creamy sauce.

Mountain spinach, also called orache, is a rather crinkly green, red or yellow relative of ordinary spinach and may be used in its place in most dishes. Two Asian varieties now found in some Western markets are Ceylon spinach and sweet-leaved Chinese spinach. New Zealand spinach belongs to another family: with its small, very thick leaves and bland taste, it is best served cooked. Milder and more tender than spinach, beet greens are often sold still attached to the beet. Best when young and tender, they are often cooked separately to serve with the beets themselves, or with lentils and pork.

American collard greens are a type of cabbage, possibly one of the oldest forms, with broad leaves, no heart, and a strong taste. Collards are particularly popular in the southern states, where they are boiled in soups, added to stews and braised as a side dish for boiled meats such as salt pork or ham. The dark green paddle-shaped leaves are much sturdier than those of cabbage and stand up well to long cooking. Actually a young cabbage, British spring greens are cooked like hearty greens.

Kale is another ancient relative of the common cabbage. The curly-leaved Scottish variety is the most familiar. Stronger and coarser than collards, kale needs even longer cooking. In Scotland, it is chopped and served with potatoes or grains, but it is largely ignored in the rest of Europe. In the United States, kale is popular as a partner to hearty southern foods such as dried beans, cornbread and smoked ham.

The term mustard green or leaf mustard refers to a number of different vegetable leaves, all with a strong, peppery taste. Most mustard greens in the market are quite soft with rough green leaves and long stems. The smaller the leaf, the less pungent the green. Popular in Asia, Italy and the American South, mustard greens are often interchangeable with collards, and when mature are best eaten stewed or braised. Tender raw leaves can be added sparingly to salads or chopped as a garnish for broth soups.

Turnip greens are another member of the mustard family, with a strong, peppery taste. Unlike beet greens, which often come attached to their root, turnip greens must be gathered before the turnip root has fully developed. The "bite" of turnip greens can be diminished by blanching, and they are best in baked dishes or vegetable stuffings.

The dandelion is a weed to most gardeners, but is also cultivated or picked wild for the kitchen. To be tender, wild dandelion leaves must be gathered before the first bright yellow flowers bloom (they too are edible). The plant is picked whole and only the root should be trimmed, leaving the leaves in a clump. At their best slightly wilted by a dressing of hot bacon lardons (p.249), dandelion greens may also be added raw to a mixed green salad, particularly with a creamy mustard dressing.

The most acidic green is sorrel. Its sour bite comes from the oxalic acid in its pointed, spinach-like leaves. In the United States, sorrel is usually considered an herb, to be added sparingly to salads, or to add flavor to a dish. In Europe, where sorrel is more appreciated, it is considered too acidic to eat raw, and so is cooked as a base for purées, soups, stuffings and sauces. When heated, even without liquid, the leaves soften rapidly to a purée that needs a generous addition of butter or cream if it is to be eaten alone. Sorrel leaves combine well with spinach.

Flat spinach

Sorrel

Turnip greens

Kale

Spring greens (UK)

Dandelion

272

USEFUL INFORMATION

Peak season *Spinach*: late spring. *Beet greens*: summer. *Collards, kale*: autumn to spring. *Dandelion, mustard, turnip greens, spring greens*: winter to early spring. *Sorrel*: spring to summer.

How to choose Young, with small tender leaves; fresh, springy to the touch; avoid limp, dry or yellowed leaves; woody stalks show old age.

Preparation Wash thoroughly in several changes of water and drain.

Portion *Spinach, sorrel*: 2-3 lb/ 1-1.4 kg yields 2 cups/500 ml cooked to serve 3, but variable. *Beet, collards, mustard, turnip, dandelion, spring greens*: 2 lb/1 kg yields 3 cups/750 ml cooked to serve 4. *Kale*: 1 lb/500 g yields about 2½ cups/625 ml cooked to serve 4.

Nutritive value per 3½ oz/100 g (raw). *All*: no fat; no cholesterol. *Spinach*: 22 calories; 3 g protein; 4 g carbohydrates; 70 mg sodium. *Beet greens*: 19 calories; 2 g protein; 4 g carbohydrates; 201 mg sodium. *Collards*: 19 calories; 2 g protein; 4 g carbohydrates; 28 mg sodium. *Kale*: 50 calories; 3 g protein; 10 g carbohydates; 43 mg sodium. *Dandelion*: 45 calories; 3 g protein; 9 g carbohydrates; 76 mg sodium. *Mustard*: 26 calories; 3 g protein; 5 g carbohydrates; 25 mg sodium. *Turnip greens*: 27 calories; 2 g protein; 6 g carbohydrates; 40 mg sodium. *Sorrel*: 28 calories; 2 g protein; 6 g carbohydrates; 5 mg sodium.

Mustard greens

Beet greens

Collard greens

Cooking methods *Spinach, sorrel, young* or *chopped hearty greens*: depends on type of leaf. Bake in sauce at 350°F/175°C, 20-30 minutes; blanch 2-3 minutes; sauté or steam 3-5 minutes; stir-fry 1-2 minutes. *Other greens*: blanch 5-8 minutes; boil 5-7 minutes; braise or stew 30-45 minutes; sauté 5-10 minutes; steam 10-12 minutes.

When done *Young leaves*: wilted. *Tough leaves*: tender.

Problems Gritty and sandy if not thoroughly washed; color and taste deteriorate if not drained thoroughly after boiling, or if braised with too much liquid; can develop bitter aftertaste when steamed; slimy and tasteless if cooked too long.

Processed forms *Spinach*: canned; frozen chopped and leaf. *Sorrel*: canned purée.

Storage Refrigerate, loosely covered, up to 5 days; tender leaves wilt more quickly; blanch and freeze 6 months.

Typical dishes *Spinach*: sautéed in olive oil with pine nuts (Italy); *à la crème* (with cream, France); *papriot* (hearty spinach soup, Italy); *spanakopitta* (spinach pie, Greece); *tian d'épinards* (gratin of spinach with cheese custard, France); *espinacas con anchoas* (sautéed with anchovies, S. America); casserole with mushrooms (USA); *spinazie* (spinach with eggs, Netherlands); spinach and prune *khoresh* (Morocco); spinach soup with yogurt (Turkey); spinach and walnut pastries (Egypt). *Beet greens*: boiled and buttered (USA); *bai gup kao* (sautéed with fish sauce, Thailand). *Collards*: pot likker (with cooking juices and ham, USA); stuffing with cornbread (USA). *Kale*: *couve à Mineira* (sautéed in bacon fat and garlic, Brazil); Holy Ghost soup (with beef, sausage and potatoes, USA); *caldo verde* (soup, Mexico). *Dandelion*: fresh salad with green onions (USA); *salade de pissenlits aux champignons et à l'œuf poché* (salad with mushrooms and poached eggs, France). *Mustard greens*: with potatoes (USA); boiled with ham hocks (USA); gumbo (with cloves, allspice and ham, USA). *Turnip greens*: simmered with hog jowl (USA); *navets verts à l'anglaise* (blanched with butter, France); cream soup (USA). *Also good with* nuts, cheese, bacon, dried beans, grains, cream, pork, ham, fish, chicken, salad greens, variety meats, spices, lemon juice and vinegar.

REMOVING STEMS

Many greens, but especially beet tops, spinach and kale, should be stripped of their stems before cooking.

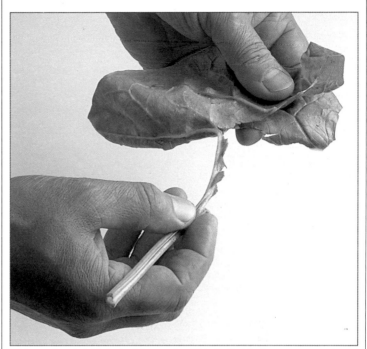

With one hand, fold the leaf (here spinach) in half with the stem upwards and the ridge outwards. With the other hand, tear the stem from the leaf.

COOKING SPINACH

Spinach can be cooked two ways: either in a generous quantity of boiling salted water, or with a small amount of water so the leaves wilt rather than boil. With both methods, thorough draining of all moisture after cooking is essential.

1 **To boil spinach:** bring a large pan of salted water to a boil. Add the cleaned, stemmed spinach in handfuls, pushing it under the water with a spoon so that it is submerged. Bring back to a boil and cook until the leaves are tender, 1-2 minutes.

2 **To wilt spinach:** pack the spinach into a pan with ½ in/1.25 cm water. Cover the pan and cook the spinach over high heat until the leaves start to wilt. Stir, cover, and continue cooking until the spinach is completely wilted and tender, 1–2 minutes.

3 **To squeeze spinach dry:** drain boiled or wilted spinach in a colander. (Do not refresh with cold water.) When cool enough to handle, squeeze the spinach in your fist to remove excess moisture.

MAKING SPINACH TIMBALES

These make a colorful first course or accompaniment to broiled fish and roast meats.

Serves 10

white butter sauce (p.62)	salt and pepper
3 lb/1.4 kg fresh spinach	pinch of grated nutmeg
¼ cup/60 g butter	pinch of cayenne
1 cup/250 ml heavy cream	
4 eggs	**10 ⅓ cup/75 ml timbale molds or**
2 egg yolks	**ramekins (p.511)**

1 Make the butter sauce and set aside. Heat the oven to 375°F/190°C. Butter the molds.

2 Wash the spinach thoroughly, removing the stems. Blanch about 30 large leaves in boiling salted water for 30 seconds. Remove the leaves with a slotted spoon and dip them in iced water to stop them cooking. Spread them out carefully on paper towels. Use the leaves to line the molds, letting them hang over the rims (left).

3 Cook the remaining spinach (p.273). Purée it with any leftover leaves in a food processor or chop it finely with a large knife. In a saucepan, melt the butter and cook the spinach until the moisture has evaporated, 2-3 minutes. Stir in the cream and cook for 1 minute. Leave to cool.

4 Stir the eggs and egg yolks into the spinach mixture and season with salt, pepper, nutmeg and cayenne.

5 Spoon the mixture into the molds and fold the overhanging leaves over to cover the mixture. Cover all the molds with a piece of buttered aluminum foil. Put the molds in a water bath (p.510) and bring the water to a boil on top of the stove. Transfer the bath to the heated oven and bake until the timbales are firm to the touch and a skewer inserted in the center comes out clean, about 12-15 minutes.

6 Reheat the sauce. Meanwhile, run a knife around the timbales and unmold them on to a dish or plates. Spoon the sauce around them.

CABBAGE
CABBAGE, BRUSSELS SPROUTS

One of the oldest of all vegetables, the cabbage is both versatile and hardy, appearing in such regional dishes as Scottish colcannon, German sauerkraut, Irish corned beef and cabbage, French *potée* stews, and the many European cabbage soups. Whole cabbage stuffed with ground pork, ham and breadcrumbs or rice has long been a country favorite, while individual leaves may also be rolled around stuffing.

All cabbages are part of the *Brassica* genus. The leaves of some are loose, but other varieties have compact, dense heads that may be round, flat, pointed or elongated, smooth or curly, with a range of color from yellow-green to magenta red. When some varieties of cabbage are cut, they release a strong mustard oil; this will dissipate during cooking or may be reduced by blanching. Cabbage steam can also have an unpleasant odor, but adding a piece of bread, a walnut or a sprig of parsley to the cooking water may help. Cabbage should be cooked until it is *al dente* or just tender; when overcooked it becomes soggy and may taste unpleasantly strong.

The most common European cabbage, often called white or Dutch, is sometimes sold trimmed of its darker, tough outer leaves, leaving a firm, pale-green head and a solid core with a rather strong taste. For milder flavor, it is often blanched before further cooking; lemon juice or vinegar in the cooking water will help keep it pale. A multi-purpose vegetable, the common cabbage may be shredded raw for salads, simmered in soups and stews, or sautéed. When quartered and cored, it may be braised, as well as boiled and steamed. The common cabbage is used for making sauerkraut – the leaves are shredded, layered with salt and left to ferment, originally a necessary preserving method. Opinions differ as to whether sauerkraut should be rinsed before cooking, but most cooks agree that it is at its best after long braising as in the pork-garnished *choucroute* of Alsace or the many German sauerkraut dishes.

Red cabbage, whose color is such a decorative advantage, is similar to the common cabbage in texture, but with a sweeter taste. It is tougher, takes longer to cook than white cabbage, and is a favorite for the long, slow cooking of soups and stews. To set the vibrant color of red cabbage for salads, toss it with two to three tablespoons of vinegar after shredding, or rinse the cabbage leaves with boiling water and vinegar. For the same reason, red cabbage must always be cooked with an acidic ingredient such as apple or wine. Braised red cabbage, especially when seasoned with the German sweet and sour combination of vinegar and brown sugar, is a well-known complement to sausages, game and rich meats like duck and pork.

The crinkly Savoy or curly cabbage has a pale-green head, loosely wrapped in deep blue-green outer leaves. Less sturdy than white cabbage, its delicate flavor and crisp texture are perfect raw, or for braising and stuffing. Savoy cabbages also make picturesque containers for party dips and salads. Becoming popular in the West are Asian cabbages, including Chinese or celery cabbage, an elongated specimen with long flat ribs that must be pulled away from the stalk. With a crunchy texture and light flavor of mustard, it is similar to the shorter, stubbier Nappa cabbage. All are excellent in soups, stir-fries, pickles and salads.

Brussels sprouts, which originated in Belgium (hence their name), are a miniature cousin of the cabbage with similar compact green leaves forming a firm head. Brussels sprouts shoot out from a tall, thick stem topped by shady leaves that protect the sprouts beneath. Unlike cabbage, Brussels sprouts are rarely eaten raw, and are usually boiled or steamed or cut into halves or quarters and then sautéed or stir-fried. Serve them plain with a knob of butter or in a brown sauce flavored with bacon or onion as in Germany. They are good with grated cheese and nutmeg, Belgian style, and may be mixed with glazed chestnuts or chopped walnuts.

USEFUL INFORMATION

Peak season *Cabbage*: several white and red varieties available year-round. *Savoy*: better autumn to spring. *Brussels sprouts*: autumn to spring.

How to choose *Cabbage*: crisp leaves, bright color, no brown or damaged patches or discolored veins; tight-leaved and -headed cabbages should be firm and heavy, not puffy; after long storage, leaves curl back from stem. *Brussels sprouts*: small, tightly closed heads; bright green color with no wilted leaves; smell strong if old or stale.

Preparation *Cabbage*: cut off stalk and discard outer leaves; rinse in cold, salted water. *Brussels sprouts*: trim base and discard outer leaves; cross-hatch core in order to reduce cooking time.

Portion *Cabbage*: depends on variety; 2 lb/1 kg white cabbage serves 6-8. *Brussels sprouts*: 1 lb/ 500 g trimmed serves 4-6.

Nutritive value per 3½ oz/100 g (raw). *All*: no fat; no cholesterol. *White cabbage*: 24 calories; 1 g protein; 5 g carbohydrates; 18 mg sodium. *Red*: 27 calories; 1 g protein; 6 g carbohydrates; 11 mg sodium. *Savoy*: 27 calories; 2 g protein; 6 g carbohydrates; 28 mg sodium. *Asian*: 16 calories; 1 g protein; 3 g carbohydrates; 9 mg sodium. *Brussels sprouts*: 43 calories; 3 g protein; 9 g carbohydrates; 25 mg sodium.

Cooking methods *Cabbage, shredded*: bake or braise at 350°F/ 175°C, 20-40 minutes; boil, sauté or pan-fry 5-7 minutes; steam 5-10 minutes; stir-fry 3-5 minutes. *Cabbage, quartered*: bake or braise at 350°F/175°C, 45-60 minutes; boil 10-15 minutes; steam 6-9 minutes. *Cabbage, whole, stuffed*: simmer 45-60 minutes. *Cabbage leaves, stuffed and rolled*: simmer 25-45 minutes; steam 20-40 minutes. *Brussels sprouts*: blanch and braise or bake in sauce at 350°F/175°C, 30-40 minutes; boil 5-10 minutes; steam

10-15 minutes.

When done *Cabbage*: *al dente* or just tender. *Brussels sprouts*: tender when pierced with a knife.

Problems *Cabbage*: if reheated becomes strong and slightly sour. *Red*: leaves discolor easily so chop with stainless steel knives. *Asian*: mature stalks may be bitter.

Processed forms *Cabbage*: pickled; canned; canned as sauerkraut. *Brussels sprouts*: frozen; canned.

Storage *Cabbage*: tight-leaved varieties keep better than loose-leaved; refrigerate 5-10 days; do not freeze. *Brussels sprouts*: refrigerate 3-4 days, flavor gets stronger with age; blanch and freeze 1 year.

Typical dishes *Cabbage*: *ratza* (with braised duck, Romania); *pirog s kapustoi* (baked in pastry, USSR); coleslaw (USA); *chou rouge flamande* (braised with apple, honey and bacon, Belgium); *stamppot met spek* (boiled with potato and bacon, Netherlands); *kohltäschen* (cabbage parcels, Germany); *cervene zeli* (sautéed with caraway seeds and cream, Czechoslovakia); *kelkaposztafasirt* (pancake, Hungary); sautéed red cabbage with sugar, cider, vinegar and red currant jelly (Netherlands); *rotkohl mit äpfeln* (red cabbage with apples, Germany); *col con tomate* (with tomato sauce, Italy). *Brussels sprouts*: *choux de Bruxelles gratinés* (gratin with cheese, béchamel and breadcrumbs, France); *bayrisches weisskraut* (with caraway and dumplings, Germany); *pikanter kohl* (sweet and sour, Germany); savory cabbage pudding (Balkans); *kelbimbo vajasmorzsaval* (with butter and breadcrumbs, Hungary); with chestnuts (UK). *Also good with* carrot, sour cream, onion, chickpeas, bay leaf, potato, bacon, pork (cabbage); game, butter, pepper, squash, tomato, beef, mushrooms, garlic (Brussels sprouts).

Savoy cabbage

Chinese cabbage

Nappa cabbage

Round cabbage (UK)

Red cabbage

European green cabbage

Brussels sprouts

White cabbage

SHREDDING CABBAGE

The inner stem (or core) of cabbage must be removed so that the leaves cook evenly.

1 Cut the cabbage in half. Cut a wedge around the core and remove it, working from the top to the stem of the cabbage. ALTERNATIVELY, quarter the cabbage and slice away the core.

2 **To shred the cabbage:** set it cut-side down on a board and cut crosswise in very fine slices. After shredding, discard any thick ribs. Roll loose leaves and cut crosswise into shreds (p.259).

STUFFING A WHOLE CABBAGE

The leaves of white or loose-leaf red cabbages may be separated, blanched and reassembled with a ground meat, herb and vegetable stuffing for cooking, then simmered in a cloth until firm.

1 Immerse the cabbage in a large pan of boiling, salted water. With 2 tablespoons, peel off outer layers of leaves as they soften. Refresh the leaves with water (p.261) and cut out the thick rib running up the center of each. Core and shred the remaining cabbage if it is to be incorporated with the stuffing ingredients.

2 Drape a scalded dish towel in a colander. Line the towel with an overlapping layer of the prepared cabbage leaves.

3 Fill the center with stuffing and wrap the leaf ends over to form a parcel that encloses the stuffing completely.

4 RIGHT Gather the cloth over and tie it with string to make a tight ball. Simmer the cabbage in boiling water for 45-60 minutes, or until a skewer inserted in the center is hot to the touch when removed.

5 Drain and unwrap the cabbage. Turn it out on to a serving plate, core end down. Slice and serve.

Red cabbage rolls

Cabbage rolls are an excellent accompaniment to pork or game, or as a first course topped with sour cream and chopped chives.

Makes 12 rolls

2 lb/1 kg whole red cabbage	6 pitted prunes, chopped
½ cup/125 ml red wine vinegar	⅛ tsp ground cinnamon
salt and pepper	¼ tsp ground cloves
½ lb/250 g piece of fat bacon, cut in lardons (p.249)	3 tbsp red currant jelly
1 medium onion, chopped	½ cup/30 g fresh white breadcrumbs
1½ lb/750 g cooking apples, peeled, cored and chopped	2 eggs, beaten to mix
	1 cup/250 ml veal stock (p.44)

1 Immerse the cabbage in boiling, salted water to loosen the leaves. Add 2 tbsp of the vinegar to set the color. Drain the cabbage and remove 12 outer leaves. Let the cabbage cool.
2 Core, quarter and finely shred the remaining cabbage and toss with all but 2 tbsp of the remaining vinegar, salt and pepper. Sauté the bacon lardons in a large casserole until the fat runs. Add the onion and cook until soft but not brown. Stir in the shredded cabbage, apples, prunes, cinnamon, cloves and red currant jelly. Cover and simmer over medium heat, stirring occasionally, until the cabbage is tender but firm, 35-45 minutes.
3 Heat the oven to 350°F/175°C. Lift out the cabbage mixture with a slotted spoon and leave to cool. Mix it with the breadcrumbs and egg to make a stuffing, and taste for seasoning.
4 Spread 2-3 spoonfuls of stuffing on each cabbage leaf, turn in the sides and roll in a parcel (see Stuffing vine leaves, p.265). Pack the rolls tightly in a baking dish, pour over the stock and remaining vinegar, and cover with aluminum foil.
5 Bake for 25-30 minutes or until a skewer inserted in the center of a roll is hot to the touch when withdrawn. Drain the rolls and serve hot with a few spoonfuls of the cooking liquid.

Variations

Other sturdy leaves, such as Swiss chard and spinach may be stuffed and rolled; a rice pilaf stuffing (p.315) is also popular. White cabbage is excellent when stuffed with apple and onion mixed with ground pork.

BROCCOLI & CAULIFLOWER

Broccoli and cauliflower, both members of the cabbage family, have attractive, tightly budded tops that give them a distinctive air. Broccoli comes from Italy, where a sprouting species with long, leafy stems and small purple, white or green florets is commonly cultivated. Popular in the United States is another variety, called Italian green broccoli or Calabrese, which looks like a small cauliflower with a dark green, compact head. Chinese broccoli, sometimes called Chinese kale, has a long thin stem and few buds, and is very different from European varieties. In Asia, it is seasoned with hot spices and paired with bland foods which act as a good foil for the peppery broccoli taste.

Broccoli de rape, also called rape or broccoli rape (It. *cime di rapa*) is an Italian favorite, especially when sautéed with good olive oil and a little garlic. The small, thin leaves usually have a nice bite (though they can be bitter), and even the stem is edible when peeled. *Broccoli de rape* is bitter if overcooked: like spinach, it is cooked as soon as it wilts.

Native to the eastern Mediterranean countries, cauliflower has been common in the West longer than broccoli. The most familiar type has a white creamy head, or curd, prized by gardeners, but sometimes sea green, lime green or purple cauliflowers can be found. (Disappointingly, the purple ones turn green as they cook.) In certain climates, cauliflowers can be hard to grow and are therefore relatively expensive. The larger green leaves that surround a cauliflower head on the plant are often removed before it reaches the market.

Cauliflower is generally cut into short-stemmed florets to remove the hard central core, and broccoli receives the same treatment but leaving more stem. Both vegetables overcook easily and should be boiled or steamed only until *al dente*. They are interchangeable in recipes and are sometimes mixed together. Often served plain, puréed or topped with a sauce, cauliflower and broccoli also make a good base for soups and soufflés, and are well suited to gratins, quiches and other baked dishes.

USEFUL INFORMATION

Peak season *Sprouting broccoli:* mid-winter to late spring. *Tight-headed broccoli:* autumn to winter. *Rape:* late spring. *Cauliflower:* autumn.

How to choose Size of heads does not indicate quality. *Sprouting broccoli:* strong, firm stems and fresh leaves; avoid yellow flowers. *Tight-headed broccoli:* firm stems, closely packed deep green heads. *Rape:* dark green leaves and strong stalk; avoid wilted leaves or droopy florets. *Cauliflower:* fresh smell and firm head; avoid brown spots, loose florets or limp leaves.
Preparation Wash in warm, salted water.
Portion *Broccoli, cauliflower:* 1 lb/ 500 g serves 3-4. *Rape:* 1 lb/500 g serves 4-6.
Nutritive value per 3½ oz/100 g (raw). *All:* no fat; no cholesterol. *Broccoli:* 28 calories; 3 g protein; 5 g carbohydrates; 27 mg sodium.

Cauliflower: 24 calories; 2 g protein; 5 g carbohydrates; 15 mg sodium.
Cooking methods *Broccoli and cauliflower, florets and stems:* bake in sauce at 375°F/190°C, 30-35 minutes; blanch 3-5 minutes; boil 7-10 minutes; chop and sauté 4-5 minutes; steam 15-20 minutes. *Florets only:* blanch 3-5 minutes; boil 5-8 minutes; deep-fry in batter 3-5 minutes; steam 5-8 minutes; stir-fry 5-6 minutes. *Rape:* blanch 3-5 minutes; braise 5-10 minutes; sauté 2-3 minutes; steam 4-7 minutes; stew 10-20 minutes. *Cauliflower, whole:* blanch 8-10 minutes; boil or steam 12-20 minutes.
When done *Broccoli, cauliflower:* tender but firm when pierced with knife. *Rape:* leaves wilted.
Problems *Broccoli:* florets cook more quickly than stems, so peel stems or trim thinly. *Cauliflower:*

adding a bay leaf to boiling or steaming water helps diminish strong odor.
Processed forms *Broccoli:* frozen florets. *Cauliflower:* pickled; frozen florets.
Storage *Broccoli, rape:* refrigerate, loosely wrapped 2-5 days; blanch and freeze 6-12 months. *Cauliflower:* refrigerate, loosely wrapped, 2-4 days; watery if frozen.
Typical dishes *Broccoli: alla romana* (sautéed in olive oil and braised in wine, Italy); *à la crème* (with cream sauce, France); *polonaise* (with hard-boiled eggs and brown butter, France); *al burro e formaggio* (with butter and cheese, Italy); *gwaytio rad nar* (stir-fried with rice noodles, Thailand). *Cauliflower: cavolfiore stracciato* (boiled and fried in olive oil and garlic, Italy); *blom kal med agg* (boiled with egg sauce, Sweden); *gefüllte blumenkohl* (stuffed with meat, Germany); *rakott karfiol* (baked with ham and sour cream, Hungary). *Also good with* nutmeg, dill, olives, lemon, bacon, anchovies, white wine (broccoli); dried beans, chickpeas, pasta,

Broccoli

Cauliflower

pork, game, squash, chicken (rape); tomato, beef, onions, black or brown butter (cauliflower).

PREPARING BROCCOLI

Peeled broccoli stems may be combined with florets for soup, or cut into julienne for garnish. Peeling or splitting the raw stems ensures even cooking.

1 **If leaving stems:** trim the base of each stem and discard any tough leaves.

2 With a small paring knife, strip the tough outer skin from the base of the stalk up to the heads.

3 LEFT Split each stalk lengthwise 2-3 times to divide the broccoli.

4 **If separating into florets:** lay stems on a board and cut off florets where they start to branch. Break apart any additional stems.

PREPARING CAULIFLOWER

Cauliflower can be cooked whole or separated into florets, which may be molded back into a cauliflower shape for serving.

1 Cut off all the outer leaves from the cauliflower and trim the stem near the base of the head.

2 With a paring knife, cut around the core to remove it.

3 If separating into florets: break the cauliflower into pieces, then cut into florets.

4 To reshape cauliflower florets: pack the cooked florets into a buttered bowl, stems inward. Fill the center with more florets, press lightly with a plate and leave for 5 minutes in a warm place.

5 RIGHT Carefully unmold the cauliflower on to a serving plate. ALTERNATIVELY, both cauliflower and broccoli florets can be used.

FRUIT VEGETABLES
TOMATO, EGGPLANT, PEPPERS

The botanist considers tomatoes, eggplants and peppers to be fruits, but for the cook they are treated like vegetables in every respect. All three feature prominently in Mediterranean dishes, contributing exuberant color and flavor. They share similar cooking characteristics: all can serve as the principal ingredient in a dish, or act as a background for other more assertive flavors such as anchovy and garlic. They also form natural containers for stuffing with a variety of ingredients.

Today, the tomato seems indispensable. Yet for centuries after its introduction from the New World the tomato was thought to be toxic, and it was not widely accepted in the Western kitchen until the nineteenth century. There are now many varieties, ranging in shape from round to long, in color from green or yellow to the familiar red, and in size from the hefty American beefsteak down to the aptly named cherry tomato.

The sweetness or acidity of a tomato depends greatly on the type. Long or plum tomatoes (the classic varieties are San Marzano and Roma) have particularly meaty flesh, good for soups and sauces. The round common or European tomato has a moderate amount of juice and thicker skin, good for slicing, stuffing and cooking. In Italy, salad tomatoes are often sold while still immature and crisp, with little juice. Juice tomatoes, on the other hand, are mainly grown for commercial use in canning and are rarely seen in markets.

Green tomatoes are not a separate variety but unripe red tomatoes usually picked at the end of the season. (They are not to be confused with tomatillos, p.303.) They are excellent when pickled, made into a spicy sauce or sliced, coated in breadcrumbs and fried. Yellow tomatoes are a distinct variety, cultivated for their color as well as their sweetness and lower acid content. They are popular for salads and preserves.

A ripe tomato is fragile and perishable, therefore much of the supply that reaches the market is picked while still green and resilient. The green tomatoes are kept in cold storage, then ripened in special warming rooms until they are bright red – but unfortunately lack the flavor of those ripened on the vine. Hydroponic tomatoes (grown in water) are colorful, with a pleasing shape, but their taste may also be disappointing. The flavor of tomatoes also depends on how long they are cooked. When fresh or cooked lightly, as for fresh tomato *coulis* (p.65), they retain a delicate flavor. When baked for about an hour until very soft, they become sweet and rich, while if cooked for two or more hours, they develop a marked piquancy.

The eggplant belongs to the same botanical family as the tomato. Common throughout Europe and North America, it probably originated in tropical Asia. Most eggplants are deep purple, some as large as a cantaloupe melon, others smaller and elongated. There are also white, green, lavender and tan varieties, some with thicker skin and a firmer flesh. What makes the eggplant appealing is the melting richness of its flesh and the vivid color of its skin, usually left on for cooking. If the skin is tough, it may be peeled for dishes in which color is not important. Raw eggplant is only eaten when pickled.

Eggplant may contain bitter juices, particularly when mature – shown by well-developed seeds when the vegetable is sliced.

Salting (p.261) is not mandatory, but it draws out the juices, which helps to reduce bitterness and also the amount of fat the vegetable absorbs when fried. **Note** Traditional Asian varieties are the least likely to be bitter.

Sweet peppers are relatives of the hot chili pepper (p.28), being the milder members of the *capsicum* family. The bell pepper is the most familiar sweet variety, named for its shape and grown in shades of green, red, yellow, orange and purple. All bell peppers are green before they are ripe and, not surprisingly, unripe peppers are less sweet than mature ones. Some sweet peppers are elongated in shape, resembling chili peppers. They include the European *corno di toro*, or bull's horn, which is often used for the Italian *peperoni* of red peppers roasted and layered with olive oil, and the American cubanelle, a green-yellow or red type with meaty flesh. The pimiento (*pimiento* is the Spanish word for pepper), or pimento, is widely cultivated on both sides of the Atlantic for roasting or packing whole in cans; it too, is sweet, with a bright orange color. Other varieties of red pepper are also sometimes canned under the name of pimiento. Sweet peppers do more than add color to a dish: their flavor is assertive, sharp and somewhat grassy for green pepper, sweeter for mature red, yellow and orange peppers. Sweet peppers are particularly popular in the Balkans and Hungary, where they are eaten, fresh as well as pickled, and appear in many traditional dishes.

A few chili peppers that are used dried as spices are also mild enough to eat fresh as a vegetable. Examples are the American Anaheim, the yellow banana pepper and the Mexican poblano, often stuffed with cheese and deep-fried as *chiles rellenos*. Pasilla peppers are still hotter, but also occasionally eaten as a vegetable. All can be used in place of sweet peppers, particularly in casseroles and sauces or added to eggs, but should be treated with care and tasted for their level of heat before using. Other hot peppers such as the jalapeño may also be roasted, peeled and stuffed to make a fiery accompaniment to meats, but they should not be used as a substitute for sweet peppers.

The range of recipes for tomato, eggplant and peppers is notably international. They marry well with onion, garlic, robust herbs like thyme, and above all with olive oil, summed up in ratatouille. A melange of peppers and eggplant is good when sautéed or stir-fried. When broiled or roasted and peeled, red peppers acquire a particularly sweet flavor, and are excellent marinated with garlic and olive oil, perhaps with some anchovy, dried tomatoes and capers. The Italians often cook thinly sliced eggplant in a similar fashion, while thicker slices are baked in recipes like Greek moussaka with ground lamb, and Neapolitan eggplant Parmesan, now so popular in America and elsewhere, layered with tomato sauce and cheese.

Baking suits all three vegetables, though they must be watched with care so that they do not overcook. Baked eggplant is puréed with garlic and spices in recipes such as *baba ghanoush* ("poor man's caviar"), popular in the Middle East. Often a large eggplant is halved after baking and the flesh scooped out to mix with onions, tomatoes and garlic, or with the anchovies and bread-crumbs appreciated in southern France. Similar seasonings suit stuffed bell peppers, filled with a mixture of boiled rice, tomato and cooked ground meat. Large tomatoes can be served in a similar fashion, seeded and stuffed, to be eaten raw, or baked and eaten hot or cold.

USEFUL INFORMATION

Peak season *Tomato*: summer. *Eggplant*: spring. *Peppers*: mid to late summer.

How to choose *Tomato*: deep color, firm not soft, smooth with no splits. *Eggplant*: shiny; no brown or soft spots; firm and weighty not soft and light. *Peppers*: bright color, firm with no soft patches.

Preparation Rinse and remove or trim stem; peel if called for in recipe or if waxed.

Portion *Tomato*, raw: 1½ lb/750 g serves 4; *cooked*: 4 lb/1.8 kg serves 4. *Eggplant*: 1½ lb/750 g serves 4. *Peppers*: 1 lb/500 g serves 4.

Nutritive value per 3½ oz/100 g (raw). *All*: no fat; no cholesterol. *Tomato*: 19 calories; 1 g protein; 4 g carbohydrates; 8 mg sodium. *Eggplant*: 26 calories; 1 g protein; 6 g carbohydrates; 4 mg sodium. *Peppers*: 25 calories; 1 g protein; 5 g carbohydrates; 3 mg sodium.

Cooking methods *Tomato, whole*: bake with or without stuffing at 350°F/175°C, 10-20 minutes; blanch 10-25 seconds. *Halves*: bake at 350°F/175°C, 10-15 minutes; broil cut side up 5-8 minutes; sauté cut side down 5-7 minutes. *Chopped*: sauté 5-10 minutes; simmer 5-45 minutes, depending on use; *Eggplant, whole*: bake at 350°F/175°C, 10-25 minutes. *Halves*: bake with or without stuffing at 350°F/175°C, 15-35 minutes; broil cut side up 7-12 minutes; sauté cut side down 5-8 minutes. *Slices or pieces*: bake at 350°F/175°C, 15-20 minutes; stew 10-15 minutes; stir-fry 3-5 minutes. *Peppers, whole*: bake stuffed at 350°F/175°C, 20-30 minutes. *Halves*: bake at 400°F/200°C, 10-15 minutes; broil 3-6 minutes each side; steam 5-8 minutes. *Slices*: blanch 1-2 minutes; deep-fry in batter 3-5 minutes; sauté 3-6 minutes; stew 10-15 minutes; stir-fry 3-5 minutes.

When done Tender; for some dishes, tomatoes should cook to a purée.

Problems *Tomato*: can be acidic if not vine-ripened; acquires a metallic taste if cooked in aluminum. *Eggplant*: discolors when cut or exposed to air, so cook quickly or sprinkle with lemon juice; bitter if too mature. *Peppers*: some sweet varieties can be bitter; chili peppers may be hot and sting skin and eyes, so try to avoid touching the seeds when preparing them.

Purple pepper

Cubanelle pepper

Eggplant

White pepper

Green pepper

Red and yellow peppers

Beefsteak tomato

Green tomato

Yellow tomato

Common tomato

Cherry tomato

Plum tomato

USEFUL INFORMATION/ FRUIT VEGETABLES

Processed forms *Tomato*: canned as purée, paste, stewed, crushed, whole, quartered, sauce, juice; sun-dried whole or in pieces in oil or dry; frozen. *Eggplant*: pickled. *Peppers*: chopped frozen.

Storage *Tomato*: ripens at room temperature; refrigerate when ripe 2-3 days; serve at room temperature; freeze raw to use in cooking 3 months; freeze when cooked 6 months. *Eggplant*: refrigerate loosely wrapped 2-3 days; blanch or steam and freeze 6-8 months. *Peppers*: refrigerate loosely wrapped 2-3 days; watery if frozen.

Typical dishes *Tomato*: with fresh mozzarella and basil (Italy); *farcies à la provençale* (stuffed with onions and anchovies, France); *gestegten tomaten* (fried with breadcrumbs, Netherlands); conserve (UK); *e capperi* (salad with capers, Italy); *soupe à la tomate fraîche aux feuilles de basilic* (fresh tomato soup with basil, France); fritters (pan-fried in batter, USA); cream of tomato soup (USA); chutney (UK). *Eggplant*: *baba ghanoush* (puréed with spices, Middle East); *escalivada* (roasted and marinated, Italy) *ikra iz baklazhan* (cold, baked, crushed with tomato, USSR); *kiopoolu* (purée with peppers, Bulgaria); *aubergine farci* (stuffed with anchovies, tomatoes and olives, France); *zeilook* (salad, Morocco); stuffed with brains (Morocco); *kahrmus* (purée, Morocco); *moussaka* (layers of sliced eggplant alternating with spiced ground lamb, Greece). *Peppers*: *lesco* (stewed vegetables with paprika, Hungary); *poivrons farcis à la bordelaise* (stuffed and baked with rice, garlic, onion and pine nuts, France); *ardei cu untdelemn* (roasted and marinated, Romania); *piments à la diable* (devilled pepper salad, France); *yesil buberli salca* (sauce with mustard and lemon, Turkey); *peperonata* (sautéed with tomato and onion, Italy); western omelet (USA); *purzheni chushki s sirene* (fried and stuffed with cheese, Bulgaria); *pisto* (stewed sliced red peppers, tomatoes and zucchini, Spain). *Also good with* garlic, bay, thyme, oregano, cheese, beef, chicken, veal, fish (tomato); mushroom, cheese, ham, cream, mint, caraway, oregano, pasta (eggplant); garlic, rosemary, marjoram, sausages (pepper).

PEELING, SEEDING & CHOPPING TOMATOES

Tomatoes are peeled, seeded and chopped for many soups, stews and sauces that are not strained. If the mixture is to be strained, the tomatoes may simply be chopped. For baking and stuffing, the skins are left on, a slice is cut from the top of the tomato and the seeds are gently squeezed out.

1 **To peel a tomato:** bring a large pan of water to a boil. With a paring knife, cut the core out of the tomato.

2 Turn the tomato over and lightly cross-hatch the bottom.

3 Immerse the tomato in boiling water for 8-15 seconds, depending on ripeness, until the skin curls away from the cross-hatch. This shows that the skin will peel easily.

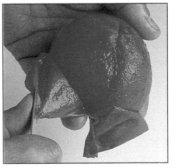

4 Lift the tomato out, let it cool slightly, and peel it.

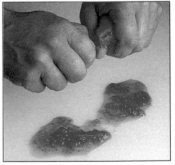

5 **To seed a tomato:** halve the tomato crosswise and squeeze. Scrape away the rest with a knife.

6 **To chop a tomato:** with a large knife, cut the tomato halves in slices, then roughly chop them.

Fresh tomato substitutes

Reflecting their popularity, tomatoes are sold prepared in at least a half-dozen ways. In winter months, canned whole or crushed tomatoes often have more flavor than fresh ones and may be substituted, weight for weight, in any cooked dish. Slightly more concentrated is tomato sauce, followed by canned purée, with the most concentrated tomato product being tomato paste. Tomato paste may be substituted for purée by stirring in an equal amount of water, but it is darker and more salty. Sun-dried tomatoes are just as they sound: plum tomatoes dried in the sun until leathery. They are sold dry or packed in olive oil and have an extremely concentrated flavor. Just one or two sun-dried tomatoes lend richness to a dish; the flavor of dry-packed ones is improved if they are rehydrated in warm water for half an hour before using.

HALVING & SCORING EGGPLANT

Before salting (p.261) and baking, eggplant should be scored with a knife so that it cooks evenly.

1 With a large knife, cut the eggplant in half lengthwise and discard the stem.

2 With the tip of a paring knife, cut a ⅜ in/1 cm rim round the edge. Score the flesh deeply, in a crisscross pattern.

BROILING & PEELING PEPPERS

Green peppers may be peeled, but as their skin is thin it is often left on. This technique is most often used for red, yellow and purple peppers, which have thicker skins.

1 Roast the pepper under a broiler, turning as needed until the skin is black and blistered, 10-12 minutes.
ALTERNATIVELY, hold the pepper with a two-pronged fork over a gas flame until the skin is charred.

2 Cover the pepper with a wet cloth or wrap it in a plastic bag and leave until cool. The steam helps loosen the skin.

3 RIGHT With a paring knife, peel off the skin and rinse the pepper under running water.

CORING, SEEDING & SLICING PEPPERS

Peppers may be peeled before coring, or they may be cored, halved and then broiled to char the skin.

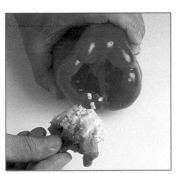

1 Cut around the core, twist and pull it out.

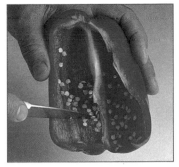

2 Halve the pepper and scrape out the seeds.

3 On the inside of the pepper, cut away the protruding ribs.

4 Set the pepper cut-side down on the board and press down with the heel of your hand to flatten it. With a large knife, slice it lengthwise into strips.

5 **For stuffing a whole pepper:** cut off core end and scrape out seeds and ribs with a teaspoon.

6 **For rings:** cut the pepper crosswise with a large knife.

Stuffing peppers

Bell peppers are ideal for stuffing, and are just the right size for a single serving. Pilafs of rice, cracked wheat or couscous (p.315) are favorite fillings, the mild flavor providing a contrast to the sweetness of the pepper itself. To bake peppers, add stuffing loosely, and set the peppers in an oiled baking dish, packing them closely so they remain upright. Cover with buttered aluminum foil and bake in the oven at 350°F/175°C for 25-35 minutes, until the peppers are tender but still hold their shape.

CUCUMBER

Cucumbers come in many sizes, from long, thin European types to stubby American, and prickly Asian varieties. The skin may be smooth or ridged, the color varies from deep green to the palest yellow. For the cook, they are usually divided into eating and pickling cucumbers. Those for eating are often dark green, with tapering ends and pale flesh, but some are lemon-colored and round, with yellowish flesh that is delicious dressed in vinegar. European eating cucumbers are regarded as superior, with crisp flesh and few seeds; the Armenian or Turkish variety is botanically a melon, but it looks and tastes like a cucumber.

Pickling, or Kirby, cucumbers are smaller than eating varieties and are characterized by their tiny white or black spines. Most common are the French *cornichon*, the American dill, and the English or West Indian gherkin, all with a specific pickle named after them. Pickling cucumbers are paler in color than eating ones and can be bitter when raw. Since they are not usually waxed before sale, they dehydrate rapidly. (For how to pickle cucumbers, see Sour gherkins in vinegar, p.490.)

The cool, refreshing taste of raw cucumber is exploited in recipes as diverse as Spain's most famous cold soup, gazpacho, Middle Eastern yogurt salad and English teatime sandwiches. Cucumbers may be lightly marinated in vinegar with perhaps a few sliced sweet onions added. Some cooked dishes also make use of cucumber – for example, a *doria* garnish of sautéed cucumbers tossed with mint for roast lamb or salmon, or Flemish cucumbers baked with ham and cream. Raw cucumber can be used as a container for food too. Halved lengthwise and hollowed out, it can be stuffed with meat and herbs and baked in central European style, or peeled and hollowed out to make decorative cucumber cups (opposite).

USEFUL INFORMATION

Peak season Summer.
How to choose Firm with no soft spots or blemishes; if puffy, can be too mature with bitter taste and large seeds.
Preparation Rinse, completely peel any waxed skin, detectable by shiny surface; unwaxed skin may be peeled completely, or for decorative effect, peeled in strips with a small knife, channel knife or garnishing tool (p.505).
Portion 1 lb/500 g sliced raw serves 4.
Nutritive value per 3½oz/100 g (raw): 13 calories; 1 g protein; no fat; 3 g carbohydrates; 2 mg sodium; no cholesterol.
Cooking methods Blanch 1-2 minutes. *Halves:* boil 7-10 minutes; steam 15-20 minutes. *Quarters:* boil 5-6 minutes; steam 10-15 minutes. *Pieces:* boil 3-5 minutes; steam 10-15 minutes; sauté 3-5 minutes; stir-fry 2-3 minutes.
When done Tender but with a firm bite (p.261).
Problems Can be bitter (detected by tasting); wilts if too cold.

Processed forms Pickled, salted.
Storage *Whole:* refrigerate loosely wrapped 3-5 days. *Cut:* immerse cut end in water. Do not freeze.
Typical dishes *Malosol'nye ogurtsy* (salted cucumbers, Russia); *augurkesalat* (with vinegar and dill, Netherlands); cream of cucumber soup (USA); *tzatziki* (finely chopped with garlic and yogurt, Greece); *concombre en daube* (sautéed with onion and tomato, Caribbean); deep-fried in batter with ginger (Australia); *toureto* (salad with bread, Israel); *à la Poulette* (creamed, France). *Also good with* onion, tomato, feta cheese, coriander, olives, mint, sour cream, sweet pepper, shellfish, fish, lemon.

Pickled gherkin

CUTTING CUCUMBER STICKS & CRESCENTS

After halving lengthwise and seeding, cucumbers may be sliced into crescents, or cut into strips, then crosswise into sticks.

1 For sticks: peel the cucumber, cut it in half lengthwise and, if you like, scoop out the seeds with a teaspoon. Cut halves in several lengthwise strips, then cut across.

2 For crescents: peel the cucumber in strips as for cups (opposite), halve it, and, if you like, scoop out the seeds. Cut the cucumber in thin crosswise slices.

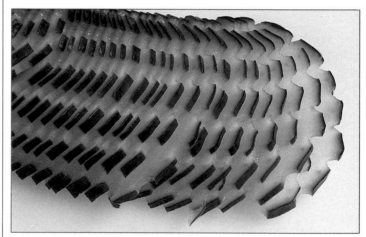

For a decorative garnish, fan out the cucumber crescents with your hand.

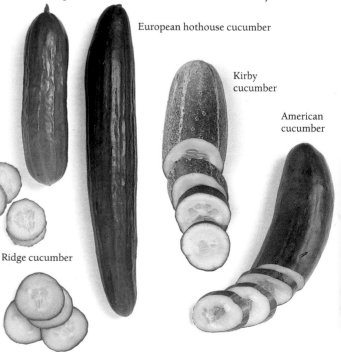

European hothouse cucumber

Kirby cucumber

American cucumber

Ridge cucumber

PEELING & HOLLOWING CUCUMBER CUPS

When the seeds are scooped from cucumber, cups can be cut for stuffing, to serve raw or baked. A shellfish or mushroom filling is particularly good.

1 Peel the cucumber in strips with a channel knife (p.505). If the skin is waxed, peel it completely.

2 Cut the cucumber in 1½ in/4 cm lengths. Scoop out the seeds to form a deep cup.

OKRA

Okra, or lady's finger, is a pretty vegetable with a five-sided, elongated pod. When steamed, pickled or deep-fried in a crisp cornmeal coating (a specialty of the American South), okra pods stay slightly crunchy with an earthy flavor that pairs well with spicy sauces. In India, okra is curried with other vegetables, in the Caribbean it is stewed in coconut sauce, and in Greece it may be baked with lemon and tomato. Okra is also popular in Turkey, where piles of it are found in every summer market, to be strung up and dried for the winter.

Okra contains a sticky juice that is released when the pod is cut. When sliced and thoroughly cooked, this gelatinous quality helps to thicken dishes, such as gumbo. To prevent the pod becoming slippery when cooked, be sure not to pierce it. Adding tomatoes and other acid ingredients to the dish also helps.

USEFUL INFORMATION

Peak season Summer.
How to choose Small, not more than 4 in/10 cm long; bright green; punctures crisply when pressed with a fingernail.
Portion 1 lb/500 g serves 4.
Preparation Rinse, and trim cap close to stem.
Nutritive value per 3½ oz/100 g

Okra

(raw): 38 calories; 2 g protein; no fat; 8 g carbohydrates; 8 mg sodium; no cholesterol.
Cooking methods Bake in sauce at 350°F/175°C, 40-50 minutes; blanch 1-2 minutes; sauté or deep-fry 3-5 minutes; simmer or stew 30-60 minutes; steam 8-15 minutes.
When done Just tender.
Problems Gummy if overcooked.
Processed forms Frozen, pickled, canned.
Storage Refrigerate tightly wrapped 2-3 days; freeze 6 months.
Typical dishes Braised with tomato (Greece); gumbo (stewed chicken or ham with vegetables, USA); *yahni* (lamb stew, Greece); *ila* (stew with shrimp, bananas and onion, Africa); deep-fried (USA). *Also good with* sausage, rice, corn, onion, chili pepper.

VEGETABLE DECORATIONS

Fresh vegetables provide not only good eating, but also a number of eye-catching decorations. Simple ideas are often the most effective: for example, a crisp bouquet of dark green watercress or a scattering of multi-colored julienne strips.

Clockwise, from center: tomato rose, cucumber and carrot flowers, radish flowers, scallion brush, cucumber twists, carrot bundles tied with a blanched leek strip.

SEA VEGETABLES

The land may provide us with most of the vegetables we eat, but plants that grow in or around the sea are becoming more popular. Most are high in minerals and vitamins, one reason for their appearance in health-food stores.

The sea plant, samphire, is native to both Atlantic and Pacific coasts and is well known locally in England and France. There are two types: rock samphire, also called sea fennel or *herbe de St. Pierre* is found on rocks and cliffs; marsh samphire, or glasswort, grows on salt marshes close to the sea. Both types of samphire may be eaten as a vegetable: it is best boiled or steamed and simply served with butter, like asparagus, or as an accompaniment to fish, shellfish and poultry. It may be blanched and pickled or included in a salad.

There are many types of edible seaweed. Carragheen moss, native to Ireland, is a particularly concentrated gelatin substitute, used to set puddings and jellies. Before use, it is simmered in liquid, usually milk, then left to cool. Dark, leafy dulse is very similar and used in Iceland, New England and Canada. Asian agar-agar seaweed is another very effective gelatin substitute.

Laver is a bright green, strandlike seaweed, popular in Japan and Britain, especially Wales, where it is stewed in water to make a spinach-like purée, traditionally mixed with oatmeal and fried into cakes called laverbread. Japanese laver is used as an edible wrapper, while in China, purple laver is dried and used to flavor vegetable soups. Japanese seaweeds such as the giant-leaved *konbu*, sweet *arame* and tissue-thin *nori* are popular for soups, for wrapping *sushi* (p.134), or for crumbling over foods to flavor them.

Marsh samphire

BEANS, PEAS & SWEET CORN

Beans and peas belong to the legume family, a group of vegetables with double-seamed pods containing a single row of seeds. Every continent has its own varieties and, while a few are common to all, such as green peas, others are still regional. Conveniently for the cook, most peas and beans are prepared in a similar way, no matter what the variety. There are three types: those cultivated to eat young in the pod before the seed is ripe; shelling peas and beans that are left to mature and eat fresh without the pod; and dried beans and peas (see Grains and Legumes pp.323-6). In the kitchen, sweet corn is treated in the same way as beans and peas, though botanically it is not a legume.

The green, string or snap bean is aptly named – picked when young to eat with the pod, it should snap in half. Often the strings need stripping, though newer varieties may be stringless. The family includes the ordinary American green bean, valued for its juicy crunchiness, and the sweet yellow or pale green and shiny wax bean. Britain's runner bean, also called scarlet runner, has a thin-skinned flat pod with pink seeds. The flat, rather tough Italian or Romano bean is similar, with an assertive flavor.

The French bean, or *haricot vert*, is sought-after for its slender little pod and intense taste. The tender pod does not snap like other green beans and has no strings: only the ends need trimming. The skinny Chinese bean is a giant that sometimes grows up to a yard long. Botanically a pea rather than a bean, it is related to the snow pea and black-eyed pea. It holds its texture well when cut and deep-fried or stir-fried, and is occasionally left to mature as a dried bean. The winged bean (also called an asparagus pea or *dimbala*) has deep ruffled ridges that stand out like wings. It is a stronger substitute for the green bean.

Green beans are usually boiled or steamed and then finished with butter or olive oil. Lemon, parsley, nuts, sautéed onions or grated cheese may be added. In Greece green beans are stewed with tomato and cumin, in Asia they are simmered in coconut milk, and in Germany they may be paired with bacon or fruit. In the United States, beans are pan-fried with ham, while in France they may be puréed. Green beans are excellent in salads or when pickled.

Mature shelling beans are almost always dried; only a few varieties, such as the tender green American lima, are eaten fresh. Lima beans may be served with hot spices, sausages or ham. Popular in Europe and the Middle East is the fava or broad bean. One of the earliest cultivated species, its slightly cheesy flavor is good in soups and purées; young favas are delicious steamed or sautéed in butter for serving with rich poultry like duck and goose. (Some people are very allergic to the lining of fava bean pods, a condition known as favism). Also commonly marketed both fresh and dried, are the European red and white coco beans, and the pale green French *flageolet*.

Less heavy than when dried, fresh shelling beans complement rich ingredients such as sausage, bacon, duck and game birds. They are easily transformed into purées, soups and stews, and may be marinated in vinaigrette for a summer salad. In Europe, the combination of *haricots verts*, fresh *flageolet* beans simmered with cream and savory, and roast leg of lamb is famous.

In the southern United States, the cowpea or black-eyed pea, a white pea with a black speckle, is a favorite ingredient in dishes such as Hopping John, with rice and ham or bacon. In South America and the West Indies, it is the small yellow pigeon pea that is the most popular, used for soups and rice dishes.

A harbinger of summer is the first crop of young green peas, some with red or purple pods. The best are French *petits pois*, a tiny variety especially cultivated to remain sweet after picking; most are canned. Americans prefer larger varieties, but peas are always at their best when small and young. Unfortunately, most shelling peas lose flavor soon after picking. Fresh peas bought from the market are inevitably a disappointment, hence the attraction of frozen and canned peas.

Fresh peas need only to be boiled or steamed until just tender. Strong tastes will overpower their sweetness, so use them with herbs and delicate ingredients like mushrooms, lettuce or pearl onions. Cooked fresh peas are good in salads like cooked vegetable salad (p.268), and added to vegetable garnishes for color. Mature green peas are best braised with ham, bacon or garlic, puréed or used for soup.

Unlike beans, most fresh peas are eaten shelled, but two fashionable peas with edible pods are the snow pea and the sugar snap. Snow peas are also known as *mangetouts*, French for "eat everything". Popular in Asia, snow peas are harvested when the pods are very tender and the peas still immature, barely showing through the flat, translucent skin. They are excellent raw, or quickly stir-fried, sautéed or steamed until only just tender. Light seasonings are best, such as a sprinkling of lemon, a knob of butter or a spoonful of creamy sauce.

American sugar snap peas are fully mature peas with a crisp, stringless pod that remains tender, so the peas can be cooked and served unshelled. They are best cooked quickly and simply,

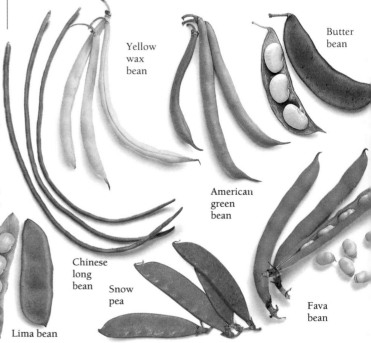

Yellow wax bean

Butter bean

American green bean

Chinese long bean

Snow pea

Lima bean

Fava bean

making an excellent accompaniment to light meats. Raw snow peas or sugar snap peas make a crunchy addition to a salad.

Long before the discovery of the New World, bright yellow and creamy white strains of sweet corn were cultivated in Mexico. White corn is the older type, although yellow corn, with a higher vitamin A content, is more widespread. The kernels cling to a thick core or cob and are enclosed in a papery husk rather than a pod. Nowadays, over 200 varieties are grown in the United States alone, ranging in size from tiny young corn to large, multi-colored ornamental corn. Like peas, most varieties of corn contain sugars that begin converting to starch as soon as the cob, or ear, is picked. Freshness is thus a priority, although some new breeds convert more slowly.

Traditionally, shucked corn (with the husk removed) is boiled and served still on the cob with butter. It may also be blanched, rewrapped in the husk with butter and broiled on the barbecue; spicy chili pepper and herb butters are a favorite topping. Most corn recipes are American in inspiration: the raw kernels may be cut from the cob and simmered in cream until tender, or the cooked kernels may be scraped or cut off and added to salads, mixed with rice, or puréed as a base for fritters, timbales or fresh corn chowder. Mature kernels do well baked in a cream or tomato-based sauce, and are often made into sweet relishes or pickles. See also the chapter on Grains and Legumes, p.319.

USEFUL INFORMATION

Peak season *Green bean, shelling bean, pea*: early summer. *Corn*: summer.

How to choose *Green bean*: bright color, snappy pod, no soft spots; if seeds are large, pod is tough. *Shelling bean*: plump, moist pods with no brown streaks; beans small and moist. *Green pea*: plump pods, small, deep-green peas, no wrinkles. *Snow and sugar snap pea*: crisp moist pods. *Corn*: moist, bright green husk with fresh tassel; no sign of worms or infestation; kernels unformed at tip, but small and tightly packed elsewhere.

Preparation *Green bean, snow and sugar snap pea*: rinse, trim ends and strings (p.286). *Shelling bean, pea*: rinse after shelling (p.286). *Corn*: shuck (p.286).

Portion *Green bean, snow and sugar snap pea*: 1 lb/500 g serves 4. *Shelling bean, pea*: 1 lb/500 g serves 2. *Corn*: 1-2 ears per person; 2 ears yield 1 cup/200 g kernels.

Nutritive value per 3½ oz/100 g (raw). *All*: no fat; no cholesterol. *Green bean*: 31 calories; 2 g protein; 7 g carbohydrates; 6 mg sodium. *Pea*: 81 calories; 5 g protein; 14 g carbohydrates; 5 mg sodium. *Snow and sugar snap pea*: 42 calories; 3 g protein; 8 g carbohydrates; 4 mg sodium. *Shelling bean (fava)*: 72 calories; 6 g protein; 12 g carbohydrates; 50 mg sodium. *Corn*: 86 calories; 3 g protein; 19 g carbohydrates; 80 mg sodium.

Cooking methods Times depend very much on age. *All*: blanch 2-3 minutes. *Green bean, snow and sugar snap pea*: bake or braise at 350°F/175°C, 20-40 minutes; boil or steam 5-12 minutes; sauté 3-6 minutes; stir-fry 2-4 minutes. *Pea*: boil 5-10 minutes. *Shelling bean*: braise or simmer at 350°F/175°C, 25-45 minutes. *Corn, ear*: boil 4-7 minutes; roast in husk or aluminum foil at 375°F/190°C, 20-30 minutes; steam 6-10 minutes. *Corn kernels*: bake or braise at 350°F/175°C, 30-40 minutes; sauté 3-5 minutes; simmer 8-15 minutes.

When done *Green bean, snow and sugar snap pea*: tender but *al dente* (p.261). *Shelling bean, pea, corn*: tender.

Problems *All*: tough and starchy if too mature or stored too long. *Green bean*: tough once seeds start to form. *Snow and sugar snap pea*: slimy if overcooked. *Corn*: kernels will be tough if cooked too fast or boiled with salt.

Processed forms *Green bean*: canned, pickled, frozen. *Shelling bean, pea*: canned, frozen. *Corn, ear*: canned and pickled (baby), frozen; *kernels*: canned, frozen.

Storage *Green bean*: refrigerate in plastic bag or tightly wrapped 2-3 days; blanch and freeze 6-12 months. *Snow and sugar snap pea*: refrigerate 4-5 days; blanch and freeze 9-12 months. *Shelling bean, pea*: refrigerate 4-5 days in plastic; blanch and freeze 6 months. *Corn*: best if eaten within 24 hours; *ear*: refrigerate overnight in husks; blanch and freeze 1 year; *kernels*: blanch and freeze 3 months.

Typical dishes *Green bean: judias verdes barcena* (with cured ham, Spain); *fasoulia* (braised in tomato sauce, Greece); *zoldbab leves* (soup with lemon and dill, Hungary). *Shelling bean: habas con jamón* (limas sautéed with ham, Spain); *mojhettes à la crème* (creamed *haricots verts*, France); *piyazi* (salad with vegetables and lemon, Turkey). *Snow pea*: with carrot and mint (USA). *Pea: risi e bisi* (with rice, Italy); *erwtensoep* (soup, Belgium); *petits pois au jambon* (with ham, France); *erbenspuree* (puréed with egg and cream, Austria); with water chestnuts and mushrooms (USA); with creamed new potatoes (USA); *menestra de quisantes* (pea stew, Spain); with parsley sauce (UK). *Corn*: corn Creole (relish with green pepper and tomato, USA); *fiatal tejszines kukorica* (in cream, Hungary); corn chowder (creamy corn and potato soup, USA); *sopa d'elote* (soup, Mexico).

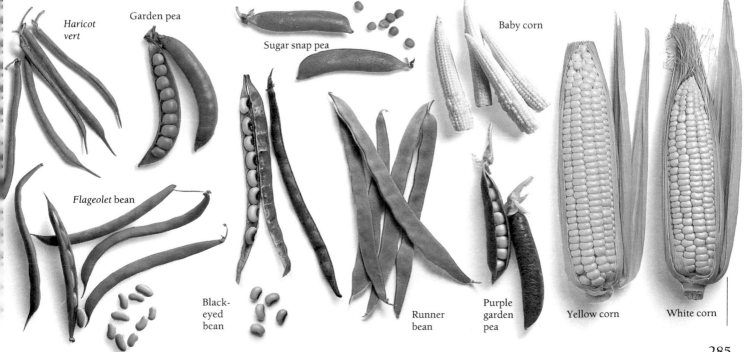

Haricot vert

Garden pea

Sugar snap pea

Baby corn

Flageolet bean

Black-eyed bean

Runner bean

Purple garden pea

Yellow corn

White corn

Stringing green beans, snow and sugar snap peas

Snow peas and some varieties of green bean must have the strings removed. Nip off the top and pull the string down the pod. Repeat at the other end, pulling the string from the other side.

SLICING RUNNER BEANS

Runner beans must have their tough strings removed before they are sliced for cooking.

1 Hold the bean between your forefinger and thumb and make a thin diagonal slice.

2 Continue slicing the bean in thin slivers of equal length.

SHELLING BEANS & PEAS

Peas and beans should be shelled just before cooking so that they do not dry out; if necessary, keep in cold water before cooking.

Squeeze the pod between two fingers to split it open. With your thumb, scoop out the contents.

SKINNING FAVA BEANS

The skin of young fava beans is soft and can be left on for cooking. However, larger beans have a tough skin that must be removed.

Make a lengthwise slit in the skin of the bean. Pinch the opposite end of the skin to squeeze out the inside flesh of the bean.

SHUCKING CORN

Whether it is to be served on the cob or as kernels, an ear of corn must be shucked before cooking. Remove the husk and the silky threads known as the tassel or corn silk.

Pull the papery husk down the ear to the base. Snap or trim off the husk and stem. Strip away the corn silk.

REMOVING CORN KERNELS FROM THE COB

Kernels can be cut whole from the cob. Alternatively, the juicy pulp can be extracted, leaving the skin behind.

1 **To cut kernels:** hold the ear of corn vertically on the board and cut from the tip down to the board with a sharp knife, removing as many whole kernels as possible. A thin layer of pulp will be left.

2 **To extract pulp from the kernels:** with a small knife, cut down each row of kernels to split them.

3 Holding the ear vertically on the board, scrape the pulp from the cob with the back of a knife. The flesh and milk will spurt out, and can be scooped up to use in chowder.

SQUASHES
ZUCCHINI, VEGETABLE MARROW, PUMPKIN, ACORN SQUASH

Squashes, which are members of the gourd family, are native to the Americas. They take their name from a Narragansett Indian word meaning "something green". Many different colors, shapes and sizes of squash are grown, mostly in North America, but for the cook the important division is between summer (or soft-skinned) and winter (or hard-skinned) varieties.

Soft-skinned summer squash are green in the sense that they are picked before they are fully mature. The archetype is the little zucchini with its mild flesh, tender enough to be eaten raw. Zucchini is grown worldwide, and is at its best when less than 6 in/15 cm long. In Italy and France the flowers are often stuffed or deep-fried in batter. American summer squash include the yellow or green crookneck and straightneck, the pale pattypan, and the fatter scalloped squash.

Common in Britain is the vegetable marrow. The pear-shaped chayote (also known as vegetable pear, christophene or mirliton) is well known in Central America and the Pacific; it needs longer cooking than other summer squashes. Like zucchini, these squashes are at their sweetest when small.

In the kitchen, there is little to choose between varieties of summer squash. Pleasantly mild, they reduce to mush when overcooked, so the skin is often left on to add taste and texture. Large varieties like scalloped squash or vegetable marrow provide a perfect container for stuffing and baking, often with an herb or meat mixture. Small squash may be boiled or steamed to serve with butter, or sautéed with other soft vegetables such as tomato. They are easy to grate for fritters but should be salted first to draw out moisture (p.261). Firm summer squash is excellent in cooked vegetable salads (p.268), or pickled in vinegar, while raw zucchini and straightneck squash may be cut into sticks for dipping.

The best-known winter squash is pumpkin, with its thick skin, fragrant, slightly fibrous flesh and large seeds. Pumpkins may be round or more cube-shaped, with pale or bright orange skin and white to deep orange flesh. Pumpkin is puréed for rich soups and to serve as a vegetable, and sweet pumpkin pie is a North American tradition in the autumn, particularly at Thanksgiving.

North America is home to a great range of other winter squash, including the tan club-shaped butternut, the acorn, the warty hubbard, turban or buttercup, the sweet-fleshed dumpling squash, and the oval delicata. Bright yellow spaghetti squash has stringy flesh that separates into spaghetti-like strands when baked.

Winter squash are picked when fully mature: the skin is thick and hard, often ribbed, and the flesh is compact and unsuited to eating raw. The seeds are fully developed and must be scooped out before cooking; the skin cannot be eaten, so winter squash is always peeled before or after cooking. Smaller squash may be halved to bake in their skins with a topping of butter and seasoning, often with brown sugar and spices. Slices of squash with the skin removed are good steamed, sautéed or added to stews and soups. Most winter squash also purée well, making a good foundation for soups as well as sweet pie fillings.

USEFUL INFORMATION

Peak season *Summer*: late spring to early autumn. *Winter*: autumn to winter.

How to choose *Summer*: thin, unbroken skin, firm with no soft or brown patches; flavor decreases as size increases. *Winter*: hard skin with no softness, heavy for its size.

Preparation *Summer*: wash, trim stem, peel only if specifically required. *Winter*: halve or slice, scrape out seeds and peel (p.288).

Portion *Summer, winter*: 1 lb/500 g cooked serves 4.

Nutritive value per 3½ oz/100 g (raw). *All*: no fat; no cholesterol. *Summer*: 20 calories; 1 g protein; 4 g carbohydrates; 2 mg sodium. *Winter*: 37 calories; 1 g protein; 9 g carbohydrates; 4 mg sodium.

Cooking methods *Summer, whole or halved stuffed*: bake at 350°F/ 175°C, 20-30 minutes. *Pieces or slices*: bake at 350°F/175°C, 10-15 minutes; blanch 1-2 minutes; boil or steam 5-10 minutes; deep-fry 2-3 minutes; sauté 3-5 minutes; simmer or stew 8-15 minutes; stir-fry 2-3 minutes. *Winter, halved*: bake at 350°F/175°C, 30-45 minutes. *Pieces or slices*: bake at 350°F/175°C, 25-35 minutes; blanch 2-3 minutes; boil or steam 8-15 minutes; deep-fry 2-3 minutes; sauté 3-5 minutes.

When done Tender but still firm.

Problems *Summer*: soft and tasteless if too mature; soft and watery if overcooked. *Winter*: dry and fibrous if too mature.

Processed forms *Summer*: pickled; frozen. *Winter*: canned; frozen.

Storage *Summer*: refrigerate loosely covered 2-3 days; does not freeze well. *Winter*: 1-2 weeks in a cool, dry place; blanch and freeze 1 year.

Typical dishes *Summer*: *tortino di zucchine* (with white sauce, Italy); *tokpaprikas* (shredded with beef, sour cream and paprika, Hungary); sautéed with onions (USA); stuffed with pork, ginger and mint (UK); *christophene au gratin* (Caribbean); zucchini bread (USA). *Winter*: sautéed with cloves, tomatoes, garlic, bacon and curry (Caribbean); pumpkin soup (with onion, nutmeg and cream, Australia); cooked pumpkin and apple with onion and lemon (Germany); pumpkin pie (USA).

Chayote

Butternut

Acorn

Small patty pan

Hubbard

Spaghetti

Scalloped squash

Vegetable marrow (UK)

Pumpkin (UK)

PREPARING SUMMER SQUASH

This technique works well for large summer squash with tough seeds, such as vegetable marrow (shown here).

1 Trim the end and cut the squash into thick rings.

2 Scoop out the seeds with a teaspoon before cooking.

MAKING A ZUCCHINI BOAT

Zucchini boats make a perfect container for a savory stuffing such as breadcrumbs with onions and anchovies, or pork with onion, parsley and bacon.

1 Cut a lengthwise slice to remove about one third of the zucchini. Alternatively, slice the zucchini in half lengthwise.

2 ABOVE Insert the tip of a small knife and cut a ¼ in/6 mm border around the flesh.

3 Using a teaspoon or melon baller, scoop out the flesh and seeds, leaving ¼ in/6 mm of flesh on the bottom. The scooped-out flesh may be reserved for stuffing the zucchini boat.

PREPARING WINTER SQUASH

Before peeling and seeding, cut large squash (here pumpkin is shown) into manageable pieces.

1 First cut the squash in half and scoop out the seeds with a large spoon. Discard the seeds and the bitter fibers surrounding them.

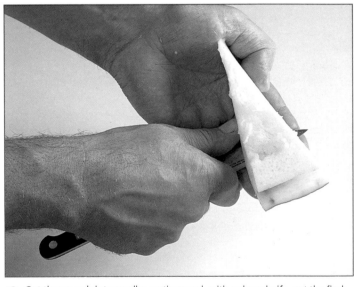

2 Cut the squash into smaller sections and, with a sharp knife, cut the flesh away from the skin.

GOURDS

Edible members of the gourd family are by no means limited to squash. Bitter melon, also called balsam pear or bitter gourd, is native to tropical India and cultivated in other warm regions, including the United States. Resembling its relative the cucumber, bitter melon has light green, warty skin and pale pearly flesh with large brown seeds that are similar to eggplant. It must be salted and sometimes blanched as well, to draw out the bitter juices (p.261). Bitter melon is often sautéed or stir-fried in oil with hot spices, or braised in a spicy sauce. Spiny bitter melon, smaller and spikier, is prepared in the same way. Winter melon – an Asian specialty – has smoother skin and a more swollen shape. The flesh is bland, but when seeded and hollowed out the vegetable makes a spectacular container for soup or stew.

All gourds are best when small and immature, before the flavor becomes too bitter. Other varieties include the snake or serpent gourd (long and convoluted), the ivy gourd or *tindori*, the bottle gourd, and the loofah gourd, shaped like an angled cucumber. Their squash-like flesh absorbs other flavors, suiting them to sautés and stews, particularly when other squash, eggplant or tomato are included. All may be stuffed, and those with less watery flesh may be steamed to serve with meats.

THE ONION FAMILY

The onion and its relatives – leek, scallion, shallot and garlic – come in a huge number of wild and cultivated varieties and are indispensable both as seasonings (p.14) and vegetables. Their color, size, texture and intensity of flavor depend as much on environment and growing conditions as on botanical variety; generally the milder the climate, the sweeter the onion.

Blanching onions reduces their acidity, mellows their flavor and makes milk or cream mixtures containing onions less likely to curdle. Onions should be sautéed carefully in butter or oil; when soft and transparent the flavor is sweet and mild, but they quickly turn brown if cooked too rapidly, and at too high a temperature will turn black and bitter. Onions and leeks are often sweated (p.262) so they soften until almost melted. Garlic and shallots should never be browned as they become bitter.

After harvesting, onion bulbs are left to dry, when they form a papery outer skin. Most familiar are mature bronze-skinned globular or elongated yellow onions, also known as globe, common or storage onions. They store well and, as they are often stronger than other types, are best for flavoring hearty dishes such as Flemish *carbonnade* stew and French onion soup. A slowly cooked *confit* of yellow onions, caramelized until brown and sweet, is a perfect way to mellow their taste. Large white onions are milder than yellow types, and do not develop the same caramel taste.

Larger and milder are yellow or white sweet onions, often named for their place of origin, such as Bermuda, Valencia (Spain), Maui (Hawaii), Vidalia and Walla Walla (USA). When grown elsewhere, these sweet onions tend to become as strong and sharp as ordinary yellow varieties. Sweet onions are often eaten raw in hamburgers, sandwiches and salads, and are good for stuffing or grilling on the barbecue and in dishes like onion pie. Red onions, sweet or strong depending on the variety, are a different family. Often called Spanish (round) or Italian (long) onions, they are valued raw for their color, and in cooking are interchangeable with mild yellow or white onions.

Pearl onions, also called small, silverskin or pickling onions, are cherry-shaped and harvested when less than 1 in/2.5 cm in diameter. "Boiling" onions are similar but a little larger. When very fresh, pearl onions taste similar to scallions, but their flavor intensifies when dried. They are often included in garnishes for meat stews and braises, or in marinated salads and pickles. British pickled onions, however, are usually made with small yellows, while pickled "cocktail" onions are white onions planted close together so that they remain small.

The long slender scallion, also called spring onion or green onion, is the immature bulb of the yellow onion, cultivated in a number of sizes for its grassy flavor. Long cooking does not suit scallions, but they provide a pleasing contrast to softer, sweeter vegetables in a quick dish such as a stir-fry. Tree onions, also called Egyptian onions, form tiny bulbs on top of tall green stalks. They may be used like scallions but have a much stronger bite and are delicious pickled. Better suited to stews is the Welsh onion (U.S. Japanese bunching onion, Fr. *ciboule*), with a flavor between scallion and chives, much used in Asian cooking.

Leek is the mildest of the onion family, a popular European vegetable. The white part of young leeks may be sliced thinly for salad, but leeks are usually boiled to serve in vinaigrette dressing (p.64) or béchamel sauce (p.54), or they may be braised with veal stock. Leek is commonly combined with other vegetables to flavor soups and stocks, and cut in julienne as a garnish. Broiled baby leeks, basted with olive oil, are excellent with broiled meats and fish. Ramp is wild leek, popular in the eastern and southern United States.

Shallots and garlic play a double role in the kitchen – as vegetables, and seasonings (p.14). Shallots are very different from onions despite their similar appearance and papery skin. A shallot grows in heads rather than singly; individual cloves or bulbs resemble a large, misshapen pickling onion and the flavor is as pervasive although much less acid. Shallots are sometimes roasted whole or substituted for pearl onions.

Like shallot, garlic (Fr. *ail*) grows in a head that divides into individual cloves. It is pungent and most often used as a flavoring. Roasted whole garlic is surprisingly mild with a sweet nutty flavor, excellent puréed or in a sauce. Whole heads may be served with roast meats and poultry, and the soft flesh scooped from the skin. Garlic soup is renowned in Mexico and the Mediterranean, while in Asia whole garlic cloves are pickled.

USEFUL INFORMATION

Peak season *Yellow, sweet, red, pearl onion*: summer. *Scallion*: spring. *Shallot, garlic*: summer to winter. *Leek*: summer.

How to choose *Onion, shallot*: firm with no sign of sprouting; dry skins, no black or powdery spots. *Scallion, leek*: bright green tops, firm texture, no dry or slimy leaves.

Preparation *Onion*: (pp.290-1). *Shallot, garlic*: peel, trimming tops and root (p.15). *Leek*: (p290).

Portion *Onion*: 1 lb/500 g yields 1 cup/250 ml chopped to serve 3-4. *Pearl onion*: 1 lb/500 g yields about 20 onions to serve 3-4. *Scallion, shallot*: 2-3 per person. *Leek*: 2 lb/ 1 kg yields 2 cups cooked to serve 4.

Nutritive value per 3½ oz/100 g (raw). *All*: no fat; no cholesterol. *Yellow, red, pearl onion*: 34 calories; 1 g protein; 7 g carbohydrates; 2 mg sodium. *Leek*: 61 calories; 2 g protein; 14 g carbohydrates; 20 mg sodium.

Cooking methods *Yellow, sweet, red onion, whole*: varies with size of onion. Bake or braise at 375°F/ 190°C, 60-90 minutes; blanch 2-3 minutes; boil 10-20 minutes. *Sliced*: blanch 1-2 minutes; broil each side 3-5 minutes; deep-fry 2-3 minutes; sauté 3-5 minutes; stir-fry 2-3 minutes; sweat 20-25 minutes. *Pearl onion, shallot*: bake, braise at 350°F/175°C, 20-30 minutes; blanch 1-2 minutes; boil 10-15 minutes; sauté (glaze) 10-15 minutes. *Scallion*: steam 8-12 minutes; stir-fry 1-2 minutes. *Leek, whole and split*: braise at 350°F/ 175°C, 20-30 minutes; blanch 2-3 minutes; boil 10-15 minutes; broil 5-7 minutes; steam 12-15

Yellow onion

Red onion

Pickling onion (UK)

Common white onion

Scallion

minutes. *Sliced*: blanch 1-2 minutes; sauté 3-5 minutes; simmer 10-15 minutes; steam 10-12 minutes; stir-fry 2-3 minutes; sweat 20-25 minutes.

When done *All except scallion, whole*: tender when pierced with a knife but still holding shape. *Sliced or chopped*: very tender. *Scallion, sliced or chopped*: (depends on use) softened and slightly wilted.

Problems Store separately as strong flavors are picked up easily by other foods; taste is bitter if allowed to sprout during storage; sweet onions become more pungent with age. *Onion*: rub hands with vinegar, lemon juice or salt to remove smell; volatile oils sting the eyes so peel under cold water; chop with care in a food processor as it bruises easily. *Leek*: slimy if overcooked; gritty if not well washed, yellow center may be hard or shriveled if too mature.

Processed forms *Yellow onion*: frozen, chopped, paste, powder, salt, juice, dried, pickled, canned. *Scallions*: frozen. *Pearl onion*: frozen, canned.

Storage *Yellow, pearl onion, shallot, garlic (after drying)*: 1-2 months in cool dry place with circulating air; *chopped*: refrigerate 1 day or freeze 3 months to use in cooked dishes. *Sweet, red onion*: 1-2 weeks in cool, dry place; *chopped*: refrigerate 1 day; flavor diminished if frozen. *Scallion*: refrigerate loosely wrapped 2-3 days; do not freeze. *Leek*: 1-2 weeks in cool, dry place; freeze 3 months.

Typical dishes *Yellow onion*: *cebollas con garbanzos* (braised with tomato sauce and chickpeas, Spain); creamed (with nutmeg and wine, Australia); calf's liver, apples

and onions (Germany); onion tart (France); *sciule pieune* (stuffed with macaroons, breadcrumbs, cheese, spices, sultanas, Italy); *marmelade d'oignons* (marmalade, France); stuffing with sage, for poultry (UK); stuffed with meat, rice, cinnamon and vinegar (Saudi Arabia); Cornish onion pie (with apples and sage, UK); *soupe à l'oignon* (soup with cheese and croûtes, France); *zweibelwahe* (onion and cheese tart, Switzerland); *oignons farcis* (stuffed and braised, France); *gevulde wien* (stuffed with mushrooms and cheese, Netherlands); sour onion soup (Romania). *Sweet, red onion*: tobacco (deep-fried with paprika and cayenne, USA); rings deep-fried in batter (USA); *cebollas encurtidas* (pickled rings, Mexico); salad with tuna (Italy); with vinegar and mint (Iran). *Pearl onion*: baked onions with pecans and pepper (USA); stewed pork with onion sauce (USA). *Scallion*: stelk (with mashed potato, Ireland); stir-fried shrimp and scallions (USA); sautéed with green tomatoes (USA). *Leek*: vinaigrette (France); pie with bacon (Wales); *prasa con tomate* (boiled in tomato sauce, Spain); *frittata de prasa* (with potatoes and cheese, Italy); *Vichyssoise* (cold creamy potato soup, USA); herb pie (with spinach and cress, UK); braised (USA); mousse (with fish, France); *cawl manigu* (broth with mutton, Wales); cock-a-leekie (stew with chicken and prunes, Scotland). *Shallot*: vinaigrette (France). *Garlic*: soup (Spain); roasted whole (France); *poulet aux cinquante gousses d'ail* (chicken roasted with fifty cloves of garlic, France); *skordalia* (sauce, Greece). *Also good with* thyme, vinegar, rice, grains, hearty greens, pasta, chili pepper, cumin, meats (yellow onion); tomato, fish, chilies, avocado, cucumber, herring (sweet, red onion); sweet pickles, carrots, potatoes, gravy, beef, stewed fruit, peas (pearl onion); butter, pork, snow peas, summer squash, ginger, green pepper, soy sauce, sausage (scallion); veal, lemon, ham, cheese, basil, sage, thyme, mustard (leek).

Boiling onion

Leek

CLEANING LEEKS

Leeks are notorious for harboring grit within their layers; they should be cleaned thoroughly before cooking.

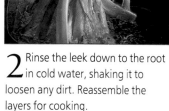

1 Trim the top of the leek, leaving some green, or removing it altogether depending on the recipe. Discard the outer leaves and trim the root. Split the leek in quarters or halves almost through the root, depending on size.

2 Rinse the leek down to the root in cold water, shaking it to loosen any dirt. Reassemble the layers for cooking.

Note If the leek is to be sliced or chopped, it may be fully quartered or halved before cleaning.

SLICING ONION

Onions may be cut in thick or thin slices to use in a variety of dishes, particularly soups and stews. Sliced onions feature in many salads and can be sprinkled for a fresh garnish. Some recipes may call for onions to be finely diced or chopped.

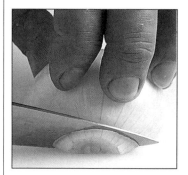

1 Peel the onion, trimming the top. Cut it in half, set it cut side down on a board and trim the root.

2 Hold the onion firmly and cut it in vertical slices, guiding the knife with your bent fingers.

SLICING ONION INTO RINGS

Onions are sliced into rings for broiling, baking or to eat raw in hamburgers and sandwiches.

Peel a large onion, trimming the stem and root. Turn the onion on its side, hold it securely on the board with one hand and cut thick or thin slices in downward strokes. Leave the slices whole or push them apart into rings.

DICING & CHOPPING ONION

An onion can be sliced, then cut into even dice, then chopped more finely if called for in the recipe. The thickness of the initial slices will determine the size of the dice.

1 Peel the onion, leaving the root on to hold the onion together. Cut the onion in half and lay one half, cut side down, on a chopping board.

2 With a chopping knife, make a series of horizontal cuts from the stem toward the root. Cut just to the root, but not through it.

3 Make a series of lengthwise vertical cuts, cutting almost but not quite through the root.

4 Finally, cut the onion crosswise so that it falls into dice. Guide the blade of the knife with your bent fingers.

5 To chop the onion into smaller pieces, continue chopping, bouncing the knife up and down on the board and holding the point down with one hand. Continue until the onion is chopped as finely as you like.

Onion confit with raisins

Onion *confit* is excellent hot with roast pork and game, or served at room temperature with pâtés and terrines.

Serves 4-6

1 lb/500 g pearl onions, peeled and trimmed (below)	¼ cup/50 g sugar (more if needed)
1¼ cups/310 ml water	3 tbsp/45 ml tomato paste
¼ cup/60 ml wine vinegar (more if needed)	½ cup/70 g raisins
3 tbsp/45 ml olive oil	bouquet garni
	salt and pepper

1 Put all the ingredients, except the salt and pepper, into a saucepan and bring to a boil. Reduce the heat and simmer, uncovered, until the onions are very tender, about 45 minutes. Most of the water should evaporate so that the mixture is moist but not swimming in liquid.

2 Add salt and pepper and taste for seasoning. Discard the bouquet garni and remove from the heat. Serve the *confit* hot or at room temperature.

Peeling pearl onion

A good method when peeling large amounts of pearl onions or shallots is to blanch them in a large pan of boiling water for 5-10 seconds. Drain the onions, and rinse them with cold water. Trim the stem and root, and with your fingers slip off the skin.

ROOTS & TUBERS
CARROT, TURNIP, PARSNIP, BEET, SALSIFY, RADISH

The broader family of vegetables that grow underground includes roots such as carrot, turnip, parsnip, beet, salsify and radish, and tubers such as Jerusalem artichokes and, the most universal of all, the potato which is dealt with separately (p.294). More exotic examples include taro root. Most roots and tubers can be substituted for each other and they store well without refrigeration. There is a marked difference between those newly harvested, often when small and young, and those intended for storage, which are larger and more mature.

Roots and tubers need to be cooked until just tender but not breaking up, so cooking is started in cold water and continued at a gentle simmer, in contrast to the rolling boil appropriate for green vegetables. Steaming is an alternative, but the vegetables must be cut in equal sizes to ensure they cook evenly. Some roots and tubers, notably Jerusalem artichoke, celery root and salsify, discolor when cut, so they must be kept in acidulated water (p.512) and are not suitable for steaming.

Roots and tubers purée outstandingly well to serve as a side dish or to use as the base for soups, soufflés and vegetable molds. They must be cooked until very soft, then thoroughly drained. All except carrot should include half as much potato to add starch and body. Roots and tubers may be baked as a gratin or simmered slowly in braises or stews. They may be sautéed, stir-fried or grated for fritters, and appear in many soups. Plump roots like turnips are scooped out for stuffing, while a few, such as parsnips, are deep-fried with a light coating of breadcrumbs or batter. However, they dry too easily in the intense heat of broiling. Young roots and tubers are best cooked simply by steaming or glazing to highlight their sweet taste; they do not purée well. Some roots, notably carrots and radishes, are served raw in salads, and sometimes form the basis of moist cakes and breads, many of central European origin.

The original carrot varieties were red, purple and black; it was not until the seventeenth century that the familiar orange carrot was developed in Holland. Today, white carrots are also cultivated in the United States. Carrots can be short, round and stubby, or more pointed, like the "Mediterranean" type commonly found in the United States. Flavor is fairly consistent between varieties, though tiny new carrots are generally sweeter than the large, mature ones. The sweetness of carrot complements almost any ingredient. It has the advantage of not breaking up during lengthy cooking, making it a favorite addition in soups and stews, in which it is valued for both its color and sweetness. Carrot invariably appears in a julienne garnish of mixed vegetables and in mixed cooked salads (p.268). To cook as a side-dish, tiny carrots should be left whole with a stub of their green stems for color, but larger ones cook best when sliced on the bias with a roll cut, or when turned (p.260). Carrots may be boiled, steamed, or wrapped in aluminum foil to bake. Tossing in butter at the last minute gives them an attractive gloss; the British might add chopped mint or parsley, and the Americans brown sugar and cinnamon.

Closely related to the carrot, and even sweeter and nuttier in taste, is the parsnip; one type is long like a carrot, the other round and squat. The parsnip has an assertive taste that pairs well with salty and smoked foods, a combination particularly enjoyed in Germany and Scandinavia. Parsnips are cooked in soups and stews, fried in butter or oil or puréed with cream and butter.

Turnip is a member of the cabbage family, though dissimilar in appearance. Domestic varieties that vary in shape and color are cultivated worldwide, but flavor differs little. The peppery taste of raw turnip mellows when they are glazed (p.263) or boiled, then puréed with cream, butter and a pinch of sugar. Raw turnip may be grated and salted also, as a variation of sauerkraut. Turnip complements ingredients such as game birds and turkey, as well as rich meats like duck. Tender young spring turnips are also highly regarded, especially in France.

Rutabaga is often confused with the turnip but it is in fact a different species, part wild cabbage, part wild turnip and with a

Jicama

White radish

Red radish

Long white radish

New carrot

Rutabaga

Turnip

distinctive, cabbage-like flavor. Rutabaga (called swede in Britain) is larger, with a broader top and coarse, yellow-purple or yellow-white skin. It is prepared like turnip, but takes longer to cook. Rutabaga purées well and is often made into savory puddings and pies.

The taste of kohlrabi is similar to that of turnip. Rather than a root, the edible part of kohlrabi is the stem of the plant which swells above the ground with protruding leaves. The leaves may be cooked like spinach but are often discarded before sale. Pale green, purple or white kohlrabi is best steamed in its skin, then peeled and finished with lemon, butter and parsley. Kohlrabi is good in a gratin or cheese sauce and can be substituted for turnip in most recipes.

Beets are popular in central and eastern Europe – where the soup *borscht* is prepared in dozens of ways – and they are slowly gaining favor elsewhere. Most beets are small and round with thin red-brown skin and a notably sweet flavor; recently a golden beet has been developed. Red beets have the peculiarity of bleeding a crimson dye called betanin if their skin is pierced before cooking, so they are usually baked, steamed or boiled whole, with some of the greens left intact. Even when sliced after cooking they have a tendency to stain other ingredients, an effect which is sought for some soups and salads. Cooked beets are paired with dark meats like beef and game, and with spicy sausage. Pickled beets appear in Scandinavia and as a side dish, while sweet-sour "Harvard beets" are popular in the United States.

Celery root, also called celeriac or root celery, is a large knobbly root with a thick skin that must be peeled before cooking. Its ugly exterior is misleading, for the flesh is sweet and peppery, reminiscent of the stalk celery to which it is related. Raw celery root is cut in fine julienne for salads, often mixed with mustard-flavored dressings, as in French *céleri remoulade*, or it may be simmered in soup or braised in a brown sauce to mellow its flavor. Celery root may be used as an alternative to turnip in braises and mixed vegetable garnishes, but its taste is strong and can be overwhelming.

Jicama is a tuber from a plant that also produces beans, hence its other name of yam bean. Mexicans distinguish between milky and watery varieties, but in the kitchen they behave identically. Jicama should be juicy and crisp with a thin, pale brown skin; a thick skin shows it is too old. Often eaten raw with lime juice and chili pepper, it may also replace water chestnuts in a stir-fry.

The Jerusalem artichoke, also called root artichoke or sunchoke, is a curious little tuber. It is a member of the sunflower family – the English name Jerusalem comes from the Italian *girasole*, meaning sunflower – but is native to North America. Root artichokes are knobby and can be tiresome to peel whether raw or cooked; they also discolor quickly once cut. In the eastern Mediterranean, root artichokes are treated like potatoes – they make excellent deep-fried chips. The nutty taste of root artichoke, resembling that of the globe artichoke, is most obvious when boiled or steamed, but it can be sliced to bake in sauce or to sauté in butter with herbs such as dill or thyme. It is particularly sweet when roasted with meat or puréed for soup.

The roots of salsify and scorzonera are closely related; they are long and thin, always earthy and hard to clean. Salsify is white-skinned, dubbed the "oyster plant" because of its taste; scorzonera has a darker skin. Both discolor quickly when cut open, but have an excellent flavor. They are native to southern Europe, and boiled salsify or scorzonera is a popular dish in Italy, dressed with lemon juice and olive oil.

Smallest and most peppery of all the roots is the bright red or white spring or summer radish, harvested young and usually eaten raw in salads. Radishes can be round or long, and some varieties are candy-striped red and white, while others are all white, lavender or pale green. Black-skinned radishes have a stronger flavor than their more colorful counterparts. Winter radishes include the pale-skinned Asian daikon, now familiar in Western markets, which can grow to over a foot. Daikon radish may be steamed, and it is excellent pickled or thinly sliced to eat raw. With their peppery bite, radishes make an excellent salad and often accompany Japanese *sushi* (p.134). They may be cooked like turnip, and Scandinavians like to add them to springtime vegetable soups. Radishes can be fashioned into flower shapes for garnishing food (p.283).

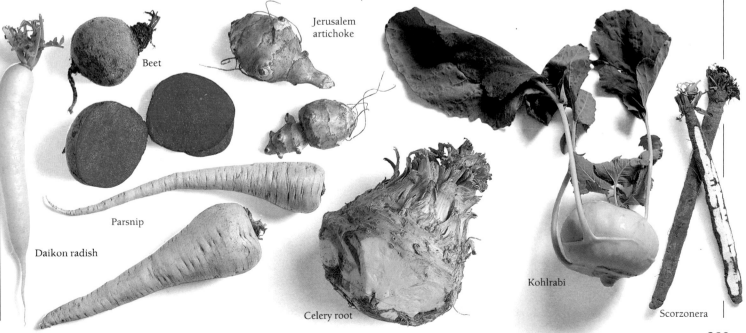

Beet

Jerusalem artichoke

Parsnip

Daikon radish

Celery root

Kohlrabi

Scorzonera

VEGETABLES

Peak season Carrot, kohlrabi, beet: summer. Turnip, parsnip, rutabaga: autumn. Celery root: late summer. Jerusalem artichoke, salsify: autumn. Red, black, daikon radish: late spring. Jicama: year-round.

How to choose Loose roots are better than packaged; firm and heavy in the hand; avoid flabby, damaged flesh and dry patches; leaves should be fresh, not wilted if tops are still attached.

Preparation Brush off dirt, wash and drain, trim tops and roots; peel thin skins with a vegetable peeler, thicker skins with a small knife; remove skin from young vegetables by scrubbing. After peeling, keep roots in cold water, adding lemon or vinegar. *Beet*: do not peel before cooking. *Jerusalem artichoke*: easier to peel after cooking. *Carrot, parsnip*: if large, cut into quarters and remove core.

Portion 1 lb/500 g serves 3-4. *Radish*: 1 lb/500 g serves 6.

Nutritive value per 3½ oz/100 g (raw). *All*: no fat; no cholesterol. *Carrot*: 43 calories; 1 g protein; 10 g carbohydrates; 35 mg sodium. *Turnip*: 27 calories; 1 g protein; 6 g carbohydrates; 67 mg sodium. *Parsnip*: 75 calories; 1 g protein; 18 g carbohydrates; 10 mg sodium. *Rutabaga*: 36 calories; 1 g protein;

8 g carbohydrates; 20 mg sodium. *Kohlrabi*: 27 calories; 2 g protein; 6 g carbohydrates; 20 mg sodium. *Beet*: 44 calories; 1 g protein; 10 g carbohydrates; 72 mg sodium. *Celery root*: 39 calories; 2 g protein; 9 g carbohydrates; 100 mg sodium. *Jicama*: 41 calories; 1 g protein; 9 g carbohydrates; 6 mg sodium. *Jerusalem artichoke*: 76 calories; 2 g protein; 17 g carbohydrates; 4 mg sodium. *Salsify*: 82 calories; 3 g protein; 19 g carbohydrates; 20 mg sodium. *Radish*: 17 calories; 1 g protein; 4 g carbohydrates; 24 mg sodium.

Cooking methods Vary with size. For 1 in/2.5 cm pieces or thick slices. *Carrot, parsnip, celery root*: bake or braise at 350°F/175°C, 45-60 minutes; blanch 4-5 minutes; boil 10-15 minutes; deep-fry 2-3 minutes (not carrot); sauté 5-7 minutes; steam 12-18 minutes; stew 45-60 minutes; stir-fry 2-3 minutes. *Turnip, rutabaga, kohlrabi, Jerusalem artichoke, salsify*: bake or braise at 350°F/175°C, 30-45 minutes; blanch 4-5 minutes; boil 8-12 minutes; sauté 5-7 minutes; steam 10-15 minutes; stew 45-60 minutes; stir-fry 2-3 minutes. *Jerusalem artichoke only*: deep-fry 2-3 minutes. *Beet, whole*: bake at 300°F/150°C, 60-90 minutes; boil or steam 30-60 minutes.

Radish, whole: glaze (p.263), or steam 5-15 minutes; sauté or stir-fry 5-10 minutes.

When done Tender when pierced with point of knife. *Beet*: tender to touch, skin rubs off easily.

Problems *Carrot, parsnip*: have tough core when mature. *Rutabaga, celery root, salsify*: fibrous if mature. *Turnip, radish*: bitter if mature. *Beet*: bleeds when cut, so handle carefully and do not pierce until cooked.

Processed forms *Carrot*: canned, frozen, juice. *Celery root, Jerusalem artichoke, salsify*: canned. *Beet*: canned whole or sliced, pickled. *Radish*: pickled.

Storage *All*: cut off leafy tops before storing; store covered in cool dark, dry place or refrigerate 1-3 weeks; do not freeze. *Carrot*: turns bitter if stored near apples.

Typical dishes *Carrot*: soup with chervil (USA); with apple (UK); cake with almonds (Italy); with raspberry vinegar (France); carrot and raisin salad (USA); candied (with brown sugar and cinnamon, USA); *carottes à la Vichy* (glazed, France); carrot cake (with pineapple and fragrant spices, USA); Ohio pudding (gratin with sweet potatoes, USA). *Parsnip*: curried soup (UK); roast parsnips (UK); *timbales de panais* (France).

Celery root: purée von sellerie (purée, Austria); *céleri-rave sauté* (chips with melted cheese, France). *Turnip*: mashed with nutmeg and butter (USA); *torshi* (relish with lime juice, Tunisia); *broccoletti strascinati* (tops braised with garlic, Italy); boiled and buttered (USA); cream of turnip soup (France, UK). *Rutabaga*: bashed neeps (with haggis, Scotland); baked with honey (USA). *Kohlrabi*: à l'aneth (blanched, with dill and cream sauce, France); *gefüllte kohlrabi* (stuffed, Germany); *kalarabeleves* (soup, Hungary). *Beet*: salat iz suyokly (grated salad with walnut, USSR); red flannel hash (with pork, potatoes and corned beef, USA); *rødbedesalat* (diced with apple and horseradish, Denmark); *borscht* (soup with onion and sour cream, USSR); *chlodnik* (cold soup with shrimp, Poland); *betteraves au four à la crème de citron* (baked, with lemon cream, France). *Jerusalem artichoke*: relish (with green pepper and onion, USA); *topinambours en daube* (braised, France). *Salsify*: sautéed with herbs (France); braised in butter (Germany); *salsifis à la crème* (with Parmesan cheese, butter and garlic, France). *Radish*: shlada dyal fejjel (salad with orange, Morocco).

POTATO

The potato (Fr. *pomme de terre*, meaning "earth apple") is a staple ingredient so international that it is impossible to catalog all its forms. Although the potato tuber is hardy in almost any climate, it has a checkered history. Imported from the New World in the late sixteenth century, it took 200 years to achieve widespread acceptance in Europe. Even today, of the dozens of varieties of potato that exist, only a few are widely cultivated outside South America, and even fewer are marketed. It is up to the home gardener to grow better varieties with good flavor. However, these are too low in yield to be of commercial value.

Botanically, a potato is a swelling, or tuber, of the underground root of the potato plant, this being the site where energy is stored in the form of starch. At low temperatures (below 45°F/11°C) the starch converts to sugar and the potato blackens, which is why it should not be stored in the refrigerator. In cooking, the starch is helpful as a binder for pancakes and croquettes, or as a thickening agent for vegetable purées or stews. When deep-fried, however, the starch prevents crispness, so cut potatoes should first be soaked in water to remove starch, and dried before frying.

In the kitchen, potatoes divide into two types: waxy and mealy. The firm, waxy type, sometimes called all-purpose, has a high moisture content, with low starch and thin skin. It is best for boiling as it does not fall apart easily, and is well suited for sautéing and salads. A mealy or floury potato, sometimes called a

baker, has more starch; it is light and fluffy when cooked, best for baking, puréeing, and cooking in liquid or in sauce as a gratin. When cooked by other methods, a mealy potato often dries and falls apart, while waxy potatoes take longer to cook than floury types. Both types may be used for deep-frying.

The cooking properties of a potato vary according to the time of year. Starch content increases with maturity and storage time. The growing season, wet or dry, early or late, has a marked effect on the potato crop. In early summer, so-called new or baby potatoes appear, freshly dug and still immature. Flavor is sweet and texture waxy, so they are best plainly boiled and served often with the skins left on, with butter and an herb such as mint or parsley. New potatoes are generally expensive and very perishable.

Each country has its favorite potato. In Britain, the red Desirée has made headway, but the most widely available all-purpose potato is the white King Edward. The small, waxy Channel Island potato, called the Jersey Royal, is valued for boiling. In the United States, the mealy Idaho potato is preferred for baking. The yellow Finnish potato, with sweet golden flesh, is also becoming popular. The French favor the *Belle de Fontenay*, with its waxy flesh that steams so well; for puréeing they prefer red-skinned varieties. In some northern European countries the potato is so highly valued that it often appears in at least two different ways as an accompaniment to both lunch and dinner.

Potatoes can be adapted to almost any method of cooking.

They may be used whole, simply baked in the oven or in hot ashes, or quartered, chopped, grated or sliced in various ways. They can be peeled, or left with the skin on as it contains flavor and nutrients. Potato skins do, however, detract from the crisp surface desired in frying, and from the melting texture sought in a gratin. Boiled or steamed potatoes are generally preferred for absorbing rich sauces and stews. Deep- or shallow-fried potatoes, usually peeled, accompany plainer roasts and broiled meats, and the British oven-roast them in dripping, with the meat.

More complex potato dishes such as gratins and potato pancakes may feature as a first course, particularly when mixed with other roots such as turnip, or with members of the onion family. Potato soup is often named *Parmentier* in France, after the scientist who finally converted the French to eating potatoes; there are many versions of potato soup, although it is the combination of leek and potato in *Vichyssoise*, often served cold, that appears most often on restaurant menus. When puréed (p.296) potato is used as a base for soufflés and even some breads, not to mention purées of other vegetables such as celery root.

The sweet potato, often wrongly identified as the yam, comes from a different botanical family than the ordinary potato, though it, too, is a native American tuber. In appearance it is quite similar, with rather thick skin and crisp flesh that cooks to a soft pulp. Sweet potatoes may be orange, white or yellow-fleshed and have a sweet, chestnut flavor; some have a dry, mealy flesh and a tan skin, while other varieties are moist and reddish brown in color. Boiling, baking and puréeing suit sweet potatoes better than pan-frying; when deep-fried they are an unusual alternative to French fries. To emphasize the vegetable's natural sweetness, sugar or honey and sweet spices are often added; standard American Thanksgiving fare is sweet potato "candied" with orange juice and brown sugar. Its sweet flesh also provides a delicious purée for sweet or savory pies, puddings and breads.

The true yam is another tuber that can grow much larger than the sweet potato (some have been recorded at over 6 ft/1.8 m), but may be used interchangeably. The flesh ranges from white to deep orange, red and even purple, and is less sweet than the sweet potato. In the Pacific and Caribbean, where they are also plentiful, yams are often used as a foil for spicy meat or fish stews. The yam is Asian in origin, but is now common in the southern United States, as well as Africa, South America and parts of Europe.

USEFUL INFORMATION

Peak season *New potato*: spring. *Mature potato*: summer, autumn. *Sweet potato, yam*: autumn, winter.
How to choose *Potato*: firm, heavy in the hand with no soft spots, green or black discoloration; no sprouted eyes; already-washed potatoes store badly. *New potato*: skin should rub away easily with your fingers. *Sweet potato, yam*: firm, no decaying spots.
Preparation Scrub off soil, wash and drain; scoop out eyes; peel with a vegetable peeler, cutting off any discolored patches; after peeling, keep immersed in cold water, or peel after cooking.
Portion 2 lb/1 kg serves 4-6.

Nutritive value per 3½ oz/100 g (raw). *All*: no fat; no cholesterol. *Potato*: 79 calories, 2 g protein; 18 g carbohydrates; 6 mg sodium. *Sweet potato*: 105 calories; 2 g protein; 24 g carbohydrates; 13 mg sodium. *Yam*: 118 calories; 2 g protein; 28 g carbohydrates; 9 mg sodium.
Cooking methods *Waxy potato, small whole (1 in/2.5 cm), pieces or thick slices*: blanch 3-5 minutes; boil or steam 12-18 minutes; braise or stew 20-30 minutes; sauté 8-15 minutes. *Mealy potato, sweet potato, yam, whole*: bake at 375°F/190°C, 45-60 minutes; boil 20-30 minutes; *pieces*: bake at 375°F/190°C, 20-30 minutes; boil or steam 10-15 minutes; braise or stew 20-30 minutes; deep-fry (p.296); sauté 5-10 minutes.
When done Tender when pierced with point of a knife.
Problems *Potato*: discolors if exposed to air; loses starch if soaked more than 1-2 hours.
Processed forms *Potato*: canned; frozen, peeled whole and cut in slices or French fries, dehydrated. *Sweet potato, yam*: canned whole, sliced and purée.
Storage *Potato*: 2-3 weeks in cool, dark, dry place; do not refrigerate or freeze; if exposed to bright light may turn green and become toxic; if stored near onions will rot. *Sweet potato, yam*: in a cool, dark, dry place 7-10 days; do not refrigerate or freeze.
Typical dishes *Potato*: *latkes* (pancakes, Jewish); *kartoffelklösse* (dumplings, Germany); fried with apples (Germany); *Tiroler grostl* (fried with onion and beef, Austria); *rosti* (shredded and fried as a cake, Switzerland); *kailkenny* (mashed with creamed cabbage, Scotland); *paprikas burgonya* (with paprika, Hungary); mutton stew (Ireland); corned beef hash (USA); twice-baked potatoes (puréed and stuffed back into skins, USA); *pommes Anna* (sliced and baked, France); bread (Ireland); *gratin dauphinois* (sliced and baked with cream, cheese and garlic, France); *kartoffelsalat* (hot or cold salad, Germany); *gnocchi alla Romana* (dumplings with tomato sauce and cheese, Italy). *Sweet potato, yam*: sweet potato pie (USA); yam salad (boiled and diced with green pepper, celery and egg, West Africa); *dulce de camote* (puréed with nuts and dried fruit, Mexico); candied (boiled and baked with brown sugar and spices, USA); *yam foo foo* (boiled and puréed, Africa); *pastel de mapueyes* (yam pie, Dominican Republic). *Also good with* parsley, mint, dill, tarragon, fennel, chives, paprika, sour cream, *crème fraîche*, corn, cheese, beef, dried beans, hearty greens (potato); pork, ham, poultry, turnip, bacon, cinnamon, honey, coconut, citrus juices, nutmeg, sherry (sweet potato).

Yam

White potato

Sweet potato

Baking potato

New potato

Red potato

Puréeing potato

Puréed or mashed potato can be used plain with meat or fish, as a topping for open savory pies, or piped around a dish as *duchesse* potato garnish. Puréed potato can also be used to bind croquettes and fish and vegetable cakes. The consistency of the potato can vary from stiff, with a few lumps for texture, to an ultra-smooth cream, beaten with generous amounts of butter and hot milk or heavy cream until light and satiny.

To purée potatoes, first peel and boil them and drain them thoroughly. Leave them in the pan over very low heat for two minutes to dry any remaining moisture. Alternatively, they may be steamed. For coarse-textured potatoes, crush them with a potato masher, or for finer texture work them through a drum sieve or vegetable mill. (**Note** Do not purée potatoes in a food processor or electric mixer as this develops starch and makes them gluey). Over low heat, gradually beat hot milk into the potato, allowing up to 1 cup/250 ml milk to every 1½ lb/750 g potato. Heat expands the starch grains in the potato and makes it light. Beat in at least 2 tbsp/30 g and up to 6 tbsp/90 g butter, with salt and pepper to taste. The texture of the purée may be stiff, or almost soft enough to pour, according to the recipe, or simply how you like it.

***Duchesse* potatoes** After beating in the butter, take the potato from the heat and beat in three egg yolks. Do not add milk. The potato may be piped in a decorative border, or shaped as rosettes, brushed with egg-yolk glaze and browned in the oven.

Deep-frying potatoes

Potatoes may be shaped in a dozen different ways for deep-frying. For successful deep-fried potatoes, the pieces should be of uniform size and thickness. Keep the cut potatoes in water to prevent discoloration and to soak out some of the starch; drain and dry them thoroughly before frying. For best results, French fries and any thickly-cut potatoes are cooked in two stages: first they are fried at a low temperature until tender, then they are fried again in very hot fat until they are crisp and brown. Finely-cut potatoes, such as matchstick or *gaufrette* potatoes, are fried only once at high heat. Drain them on paper towels after frying.

If too many potatoes are added to the pan at once the temperature is lowered, making the potatoes greasy rather than crisp. Stir or shake the pan from time to time to separate the potatoes during cooking. Larger shapes that have been fried twice lose their crispness more quickly and should be served as soon as possible, but thinner types that are fried only once can be kept an hour or two. Season fried potatoes with a light sprinkling of salt only just before serving, as salt makes them soggy. In Belgium, French fries are served with thin mayonnaise, the British might sprinkle malt vinegar, while in the United States tomato ketchup is the favorite accompaniment.

Straw potatoes (Fr. *pommes pailles*): Trim the ends and sides of the potato and cut into the finest possible slices, then into fine strips about 3 in/7.5 cm long. Fry once at 375°F/190°C, 2-3 minutes until light golden. American shoestring potatoes are similar to straw potatoes, but longer.

Matchstick potatoes (Fr. *pommes allumettes*): Trim the ends and sides of the potato and cut into ⅛ in/3 mm julienne strips about 2½ in/6 cm long. Fry the strips once at 375°F/190°C, 3-4 minutes until golden.

French fries (Fr. *pommes frites* or *pommes mignonettes*): Trim the ends and sides of the potato and cut ¼ in/6 mm sticks about 3 in/7.5 cm long. Fry once at 325°F/160°C, 5-6 minutes until tender and just starting to brown. Drain and let cool. Fry again at 375°F/190°C, 1-2 minutes until crisp and brown.

Straight-cut potatoes (Fr. *pommes Pont Neuf*): Trim the ends and sides of the potato and cut into ½ in/1.25 cm sticks, 3 in/7.5 cm long. Fry as for French fries.

Waffled potatoes (Fr. *pommes gaufrettes*): With a mandoline slicer (see below), cut horizontal fluted slices, rotating the potato 90 degrees between each cut so the slices are latticed. Fry at 375°F/190°C, 2-3 minutes until golden.

Chips: With a mandoline slicer or a large sharp knife, cut paper-thin slices of potato. Fry them as for waffled potatoes.

Soufflé potatoes (Fr. *pommes soufflées*): Trim the potato to a 1¼ × 2 in/3 × 5 cm rectangle, and slice very evenly 1/16 in/3 mm thick, preferably with a mandoline slicer. Fry at 350°F/175°C until tender and just beginning to brown, 4-5 minutes, stirring often. Drain and let cool. Fry a few potatoes a second time at 380°F/195°C – they will puff up at once. Continue frying until crisp and brown, 1-2 minutes.

USING A MANDOLINE

The mandoline (Cooking Equipment, p.505) has an adjustable blade for shredding or slicing wafer-thin rounds of vegetables, and is useful for obtaining different shapes of potato.

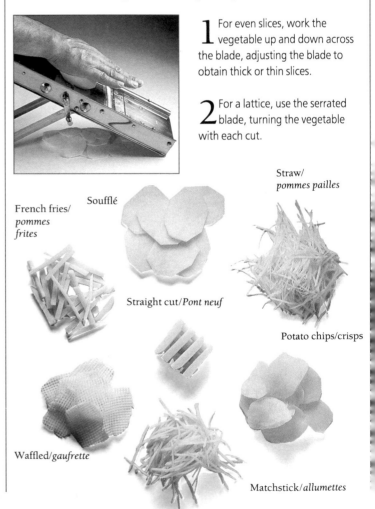

1 For even slices, work the vegetable up and down across the blade, adjusting the blade to obtain thick or thin slices.

2 For a lattice, use the serrated blade, turning the vegetable with each cut.

Straw/ *pommes pailles*

Soufflé

French fries/ *pommes frites*

Straight cut/*Pont neuf*

Potato chips/crisps

Waffled/*gaufrette*

Matchstick/*allumettes*

MAKING POTATO BASKETS

Potato baskets can be made from raw potato chips, while nests (Fr. *nids d'oiseau*) may be fashioned from straw potatoes. Do not soak the raw potatoes in water as their starch is needed to hold the nest together. Other root vegetables such as celery root can also be made into baskets or nests.

1 Peel and slice potatoes, preferably using a mandoline slicer (left). Dry them thoroughly on paper towels.

2 Using a metal potato basket, line the larger basket with potato rounds, overlapping them thickly at the bottom.

3 Clamp the smaller basket on top. Immerse the basket in fat at 350°F/175°C. Fry until the potato starts to brown, 3-4 minutes.

4 Lift out the basket, open it and gently pry out the potatoes, if necessary using a knife.

5 Drop potatoes back into the fat and continue to fry until golden, 1-2 minutes. Drain on paper towels.

6 The finished baskets are often used as a garnish to hold straw potatoes, other deep-fried potatoes or small vegetables.

Peruvian mashed potatoes

This potato dish (Sp. *papas con limone*) is an excellent accompaniment to a pot-roast of beef, or it can be a complete course served with cooked shrimp or hard-boiled eggs.

Serves 4

2 medium-sized sweet potatoes, peeled and cut in ½-¾ in/1.25-2 cm slices	¼ cup/60 ml lemon juice (or to taste)
2 lb/1 kg baking potatoes, peeled and cut in pieces	¼ cup/60 ml olive oil
1 onion, chopped	½ tsp red pepper flakes (or to taste)
1 jalapeño or other fresh hot chili pepper, cored, seeded and finely chopped	salt and pepper
	¼ cup/75 g black olives
	4 oz/125 g Monterey Jack or other mild cheese, cut in small cubes.

1 Put the sweet potatoes and baking potatoes in separate pans of cold salted water, cover them and bring to a boil. Boil until they are just tender, 15-20 minutes. Drain both pans and keep the sweet potatoes warm.
2 Return the baking potatoes to the pan and crush them with a potato masher. Add the onion, chili pepper, lemon juice, olive oil and red pepper flakes. Season to taste. Pile the potatoes on a dish and sprinkle with the olives and cheese. Put the cooked sweet potatoes around the edge. Serve hot or at room temperature.

STALKS & SHOOTS
ASPARAGUS, CELERY, FENNEL, SWISS CHARD, CARDOON

Vegetable stalks share a juicy crispness when raw and a perfumed aroma when cooked. The category includes asparagus, exotic seakale and common celery. All have been eaten for centuries and have bitter-tasting wild cousins. Some stalks discolor easily and should be stored or cooked in acidulated water.

Asparagus is the herald of spring: the part we eat is the immature sprout that ranges in color from white to green and purple depending on variety and how it is grown. The Germans, Belgians and French admire fat pale yellow or white stalks – colorless because they are picked before they sprout above ground. The British, Italians and Americans generally prefer fresh-tasting bright green or purple asparagus, which has acquired its color from sunlight. Finer stems, sometimes called sprue in Britain, are often preferred for their piquant flavor. Green asparagus is cheaper in the United States because it is easier to harvest; all varieties are prepared by boiling or steaming. Since asparagus tips are fragile, the stalks are often tied in a bunch to cook upright, the stems immersed in the boiling water and the tips kept above it; other cooks prefer to steam the whole stalk. Whatever the method, quick cooking is essential so that texture and sweet flavor are retained.

Asparagus is often served warm with melted butter or a rich butter sauce (p.62); sauce Maltaise, a hollandaise (p.60) flavored with blood oranges, was created specifically for asparagus. In Germany, where asparagus cultivation is a popular pastime, fried breadcrumbs are a favored topping. Cold asparagus may be served simply with olive oil and lemon, or in vinaigrette with chopped hard-boiled egg and parsley. It is often eaten with the fingers, discarding the tougher stem ends. Puréed asparagus provides delicate flavor for creamy soup, soufflés or timbales. Spears are a popular garnish for sautéed meats or poultry. For stir-frying or sautéing, asparagus should be sliced on the diagonal.

Celery doubles as a vegetable served alone and as a flavoring ingredient in soups, *mirepoix* (p.263), and garnishes like the classic *Demidoff*, in which carrots and mushrooms are sliced in crescents to echo the shape of the sliced celery. Common white celery is mild and sweet; northern European varieties have a golden tinge and are often canned. Asian *kintsai* celery is more pungent, and used for its flavorful leaves; it is closely related to thin wild celery. Cooked in the same way as celery is Neapolitan parsley, grown for its stalk rather than its leaf.

Celery is best cooked by braising with a little liquid or baking in sauce as a gratin; steamed or boiled celery is tasteless. The outer stalks have long stringy fibers that must be removed before cooking, but the celery heart is tender and needs only to be trimmed. Celery stalks are the most popular vegetable to munch raw or dip in a savory sauce; they may be filled with fresh cheese, or chopped as a crisp addition to salads and sandwich fillings.

Sweet or Florence fennel looks like a bulbous celery heart and is distinguished by its anise flavor, although its airy leaves resemble the herb dill. Before cooking, the strings are usually removed. Raw fennel may be cut in slices, wedges or sticks for salad, or to serve with Parmesan or goat cheese and dry Marsala

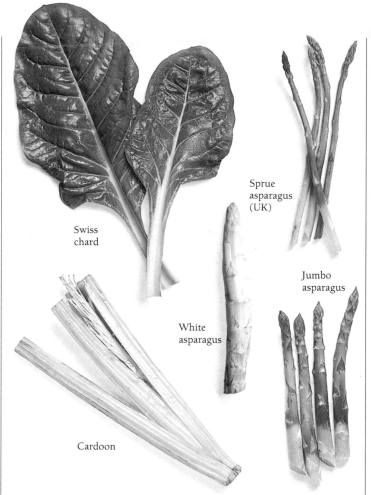

Swiss chard

Sprue asparagus (UK)

Jumbo asparagus

White asparagus

Cardoon

wine. Fennel is sliced and blanched to marinate in vinaigrette; it may be coated with breadcrumbs and fried, or sautéed with spring vegetables. Fennel also provides a fragrant base for soups and stews, especially in combination with fish or braised veal.

A relative of the beet, Swiss chard is two vegetables in one, cultivated for both its leaves and its thick white or bright red stalk (called ruby chard). Despite its name, Swiss chard (Fr. *blette*) is native to the Mediterranean. It can be eaten whole only when very young and tender. The stalk recalls the flavor of beet and may be combined with fruit or sugar. More often it is cooked in dishes with olive oil, garlic and orange. The leaves taste like strong spinach and are prepared like any other hearty green (p.272). White-stemmed cabbage, also called *bok choy* or *pak choy*, looks rather like Swiss chard and has succulent white ribs and delicate green leaves. Seakale beet is a cousin of Swiss chard, with similarly prominent stalks and leaves, and is cooked the same way. True seakale, on the other hand, has the look of unruly celery, with juicy stems and a nutty texture. Both are good lightly blanched and served with melted butter, or eaten raw in salads. All are good in soups, stir-fries, pickles and salad.

Another Mediterranean favorite is the cardoon, an edible thistle and close relation of the globe artichoke. Flavor is comparably delicate. The cardoon has prickly outer leaves that are stripped before sale, leaving the silver ribs. The outer stems must first be peeled to remove strings, and are then treated like celery or fennel. Cardoon is best braised or sautéed in butter or cream to go with meats, especially beef. Tender stems may also be eaten raw, served with Italian *Bagna cauda* (p.101).

Celery

Fennel

carbohydrates 88 mg sodium. *Swiss chard*: 19 calories; 2 g protein; 4 g carbohydrates; 213 mg sodium. *Cardoon*: 20 calories; 1 g protein; 5 g carbohydrates; 170 mg sodium.

Cooking methods *Asparagus, green*: blanch 2-3 minutes; boil 7-12 minutes; deep-fry in batter 4-5 minutes; sauté 3-4 minutes; simmer in soup 10-15 minutes; steam 4-5 minutes; stir-fry 2-3 minutes. *White*: double times for green. *Celery, fennel, Swiss chard stalks*: braise at 350°F/175°C, 20-30 minutes; blanch 2-3 minutes; sauté 3-5 minutes; simmer in soup 15-20 minutes; steam 8-15 minutes; stir-fry 3-5 minutes. *Swiss chard leaves*: boil or steam 5-8 minutes. *Cardoon*: blanch 8-10 minutes; boil 12-15 minutes; braise 20-30 minutes; steam 15-20 minutes.

When done Tender with slight bite.

Problems *Asparagus*: tips cook faster than stem. *Celery, fennel*: wilt in humid atmosphere, so crisp in ice water. *Swiss chard, cardoon*: stalks darken when cooked, so blanch in water with lemon or vinegar; discolor if cooked in aluminum.

Processed forms *Asparagus*: frozen, canned. *Celery*: canned. *Fennel*: canned.

Storage *All*: wrap in a damp cloth, or immerse cut stems in water; do not freeze. *Asparagus*: refrigerate 1-2 days; blanch and freeze 9 months. *Celery, fennel, cardoon*: refrigerate 1-2 weeks; blanch and freeze 6 months. *Swiss chard, seakale*: refrigerate 2-3 days; blanch and freeze 1 year.

Typical dishes *Asparagus*: served cold with olive oil (France); with Parmesan cheese (Italy); with ham (USA). *Celery*: braised with juices (France); boiled with potato and almonds (Spain); *minestra di sedano e riso* (celery and rice soup, Italy). *Fennel*: fennel, potato and leek soup (USA); salad with radish and orange (Italy); with cheese sauce (France); *fritti* (batter-fried, Italy); braised (UK). *Swiss chard*: *acelgas en crema* (sautéed with onion, carrot and potato, Argentina); *all'agro* (boiled with olive oil and lemon, Italy); stuffed leaves with saffron rice, raisins and walnuts (UK). *Cardoon*: in onion cream sauce (UK); *sformato di cardoni* (sautéed and topped with béchamel, Italy); *cardons aux anchois* (braised with anchovies, France).

USEFUL INFORMATION

Peak season *Asparagus*: spring. *Celery*: late autumn. *Fennel*: autumn, winter. *Swiss chard*: spring. *Cardoon*: winter, spring. *Seakale*: spring, summer.

How to choose Cut stem dry but not withered. *Asparagus*: straight plump, even-sized stalks with tightly budded tips; thick stalks more tender than thin. *Celery*: crisp, brittle stalks of light color with no brown patches. *Fennel*: crisp, fully-formed white or pale-green bulbs with no brown patches. *Swiss chard, seakale*: firm white stalks, fresh unwilted dark-green leaves. *Cardoon*: dark green leaves, silver-gray supple stalks with small root.

Preparation Rinse under running water, scrub stalks.

Portion *Asparagus, Swiss chard, seakale, cardoon*: 2 lb/1 kg serves 4. *Celery, fennel*: 1 lb/500 g serves 4.

Nutritive value per 3½ oz/100 g (raw). *All*: no fat; no cholesterol. *Asparagus*: 22 calories; 3 g protein; 4 g carbohydrates; 2 mg sodium. *Celery*: 16 calories; 1 g protein; 4 g carbohydrates; 88 mg sodium. *Fennel*: 16 calories; 1 g protein; 4 g

PREPARING ASPARAGUS

White asparagus has a thick woody skin that must be peeled. The lower stem of plump green asparagus should also be lightly peeled, but thin asparagus may simply be trimmed. Prepare asparagus only shortly before cooking, as it dries out quickly.

1 With a vegetable peeler or small knife, scrape the length of each stalk, starting below the tip and cutting almost to the stem end.

2 Break off the woody end of the stem, together with the peel.

3 Bunch the asparagus spears together and trim them with a knife to about the same length.

4 Tie with string in a serving-sized bundle. This makes them easy to handle for cooking.

PREPARING STALKS

The outer stalks of celery, fennel, Swiss chard and cardoon have strings running lengthwise, which must be removed.

1 Break off any tough outer stalks or leaves and discard. Cut off and discard upper stem and trim the root.

2 For leafy stalks, cut off green tops and reserve for another use.

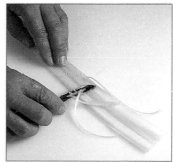

3 Peel any strings from the outer sides of the stalks.

ALTERNATIVELY, cut off the upper stem, outer layers and leaves. Cut part-way through the stalk and gently pull away the strings toward the root.

Asparagus with breadcrumb sauce

When asparagus is coated with a topping or sauce the tips should
be left uncovered. The sauce in this recipe also works well with
cooked cauliflower (florets or whole).

Serves 4

1½ lb/750 g asparagus	⅓ cup/45 g fresh, coarse white breadcrumbs
1 hard-boiled egg, chopped	2 tbsp chopped fresh parsley
½ cup/125 g butter	1 tbsp chopped fresh chives

1 Trim asparagus and tie it in 4 equal bundles (p.299). Immerse
the bundles in boiling salted water and cook until tender but still
firm, 6-8 minutes. Drain them, set on a serving dish and discard
the strings. Sprinkle with chopped eggs, cover with aluminum foil
and keep warm.

2 Melt the butter in a frying pan, add the breadcrumbs and cook,
stirring constantly, until the foam has subsided and the
breadcrumbs are golden brown, 5-7 minutes. (**Note** They must be
cooked thoroughly to be crisp.) Take from the heat and add the
parsley and chives, standing back as the butter will splatter.
Quickly stir the sauce to mix and pour it over the asparagus stalks,
leaving the tips uncovered. Serve at once.

GLOBE ARTICHOKE

The bud of an edible thistle, the globe or French artichoke has
been cultivated for hundreds of years. The daunting cluster of
outer leaves, which may include prickles, conceals an edible
bottom. An artichoke is usually boiled or steamed whole until
tender so that its leaves can be pulled off one by one to nibble.
Finally, a hairy "choke" is revealed, in reality the flower, which
blooms a bright blue if the artichoke is left to mature. When the
choke is scraped away, the cup-shaped bottom is left free of fiber
and ready to eat. Melted herb butter or butter sauce are favorite
accompaniments for hot artichokes, as are vinaigrette or mayonnaise when the artichoke is served cold. The raw artichoke bottom
may also be trimmed of leaves, leaving a handy cup shape that can
be boiled, trimmed of the choke, then stuffed to form an elegant
garnish for roast and broiled meats. It may also be quartered to
simmer *à la grecque* (Mushrooms, p.307).

The Italians, who developed the modern artichoke, make great
use of the young vegetables, picked while the leaves and choke are
still soft and completely edible. They may be eaten raw, sliced and
dipped in a sauce of salt and olive oil, or deep-fried to make the
Roman dish *carciofi alla giudea*. Young artichokes may also be
baked in tomato sauce, and they are canned as artichoke hearts.

USEFUL INFORMATION

Peak season Spring, autumn.
How to choose Compact green
heads with no dark patches or dry
streaks; on most varieties, leaves
spread when too mature; diameter
of base, not size of artichoke,
indicates size of bottom. *Young*:
small, soft leaves and stem.
Preparation Soak in warm salted
water for an hour to draw out
insects or grit.
Portion *Whole or stuffed bottom*:
serves 1. *Young, bottom*: 2-3 per
person.
Nutritive value per 3½ oz/100 g
(raw). 51 calories; 3 g protein; no
fat; 12 g carbohydrates; 80 mg
sodium; no cholesterol.
Cooking methods *Whole*:
depending on size, blanch and
braise at 350°F/175°C, 45-60
minutes; boil 20-40 minutes;
steam upside down 25-35
minutes. *Baby*: blanch 5-10
minutes; boil 20-35 minutes;
braise or stew at 350°F/175°C, 30-
45 minutes; deep-fry 5-7 minutes.
Bottoms: braise or stew at 350°F/
175°C, 20-30 minutes; poach 20-
30 minutes; steam 15-20 minutes.
When done *Whole*: a leaf pulls out
easily. *Bottoms*: tender.
Problems *Bottoms*: discolor when
cut and exposed to air: rub with
lemon and store in acidulated
water, then cook in a *blanc*. *Whole*:
blacken when boiled if not
completely submerged in water, so
weigh down with heatproof plate
or put wet cloth on surface of
water during cooking.

Globe

Young
globe

Processed forms *Young*:
canned, marinated or in brine.
Bottoms: canned; frozen.
Storage Refrigerate loosely
wrapped 4-5 days; freeze cooked
bottoms 6-8 months.
Typical dishes *à la vinaigrette*
(France); bottoms stuffed with
mushrooms and cheese (France);
pudding with cheese (UK);
artichauts à la Barigoule (stuffed
with *duxelles* and bacon, France);
purée with cream (France); *carciofi
alla romana* (steamed with garlic
and mint, Italy); stuffed with
mortadella, cheese and
breadcrumbs, (Italy); fricassée,
(Italy); with shrimp (UK); with
fava beans (Greece); stew with pine
nuts (Spain). *Also good with* bay
leaf, garlic, dill, tomato.

PREPARING & COOKING WHOLE ARTICHOKES

Artichoke may be served with a sauce on the side, or with the sauce spooned into the center of the upturned cone of leaves.

1 Break the stem of the artichoke so that any fibers are pulled out. Trim the base with a knife so the artichoke sits flat, and rub the cut surface with lemon juice to prevent discoloration.

2 Trim the leaves with scissors to remove spines.

3 With a large knife, cut off the pointed top of the artichoke, parallel to the base.

4 Bring a large pan of salted water to a boil and add the artichokes. Weigh them down with a heatproof plate or lay a wet cloth on top of them so that they are submerged.

5 Simmer for 35-45 minutes until a central leaf can be pulled out easily. Drain the artichokes upside down so water is not trapped by the leaves. Let the artichokes cool slightly.

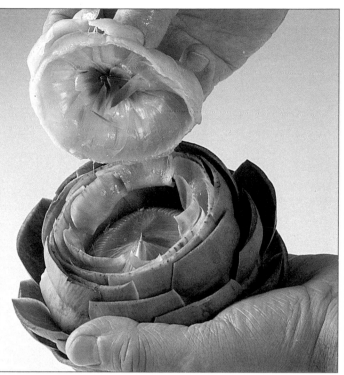

6 ABOVE Grasp the central cone of leaves and with a quick twist, lift it out. Reserve it.

7 LEFT Carefully scoop out the choke with a teaspoon or melon baller and discard it.

8 Set the cone of leaves upside down in the center of the artichoke. If you like you can fill the cup in the center of the leaves with vinaigrette or another sauce for serving.

Artichokes and pine nuts

Spanish *alcachojas con piñones* makes an excellent appetizer or side dish for lamb.

Serves 8

8 large fresh artichoke bottoms, quartered
¼ cup/60 ml olive oil
½ lb/250 g smoked bacon lardons (p.249)
4 large onions, thinly sliced
6 cloves garlic, chopped
2½ cups/625 ml veal or chicken stock (more if needed) (p.44)
½ cup/125 ml white wine
salt and pepper
juice ½ lemon (or to taste)
¼ cup/60 g pine nuts, toasted

1 Blanch the artichoke quarters by boiling them in salted water for 5-8 minutes, then drain. Heat olive oil in a deep frying pan, add the lardons and cook over low heat, stirring until the fat runs, 6-7 minutes. Add the onions and cook over low heat until very soft and starting to brown, 8-12 minutes. Stir in the garlic and stock, wine, salt and pepper, and add the artichoke quarters.

2 Bring the liquid to a boil, then reduce the heat and simmer, covered, for 20-30 minutes or until the artichokes are tender and the stock is almost absorbed. If the pan becomes dry, add more stock during cooking. Let the mixture cool to tepid, stir in the lemon juice and pine nuts and taste for seasoning. Serve at room temperature.

PREPARING & COOKING ARTICHOKE BOTTOMS

Artichoke bottoms vary greatly in size and only the largest are good for stuffing; small ones should be cut up to simmer in sauce.

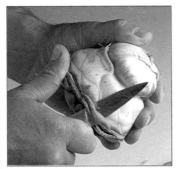

1 Break off the stem of the artichoke. Using a very sharp knife, cut off all large bottom leaves, leaving a cone of soft small leaves in the center. Alternatively, snap off bottom leaves with your hands.

2 Trim the base of any remaining green parts. Cut off the soft cone, leaving only the choke behind. Rub the base well with a cut lemon to prevent discoloration.

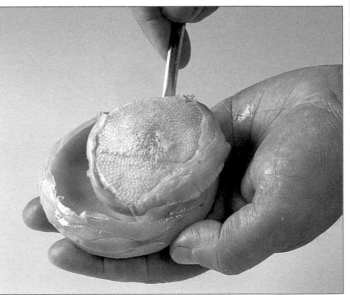

3 LEFT Trim the base to an even round shape, slightly flattened at the base, and bevel the top edge. Rub again with lemon and drop into a bowl of cold water with lemon.

4 **If leaving bottoms whole:** prepare a *blanc* (p.261). Add bottoms to the boiling water; weigh them down with a heatproof plate.

5 ABOVE Simmer the artichokes for 15-20 minutes until tender when pierced with a knife, then drain. Scoop out the choke with a teaspoon.

If cutting bottoms in pieces: cut them in quarters and cut the choke from each piece with a knife. Cook according to recipe.

EXOTIC VEGETABLES

More and more unfamiliar vegetables are appearing in our markets, brought in from regions far afield where they may be everyday fare. Taro, for example, also known as dasheen or colocassi, is an Asian staple valued for its carbohydrates. It is also grown in the Caribbean, where it is called the eddo. The root may be as large as a rutabaga or small as a new potato, with a brown shaggy skin circled with rings and smooth white flesh. Serve it boiled, deep-fried or puréed for fritters; it must be very hot as it becomes dense and waxy on cooling. Taro has a flavor evocative of chestnut and potato, complementing rich meats as well as hot chilies and sweet coconut. The leaves are cooked like hearty greens (p.272). Often mistaken for the taro is the malanga, possibly the world's oldest cultivated tuber, with juicy crisp flesh that is particularly good when deep-fried.

The tropical yuca or cassava root is the basis of tapioca (a starchy paste). Yuca root grows mostly in Latin America, though it is now cultivated in Africa and the Far East. Bitter varieties are poisonous when raw, so yuca must always be cooked. It is a good thickener for stews, breads and dumplings as it has a high starch content and is often dried and ground to meal. Yuca is different from the southwest American yucca plant, also eaten as a vegetable. The Pacific lotus root is a member of the water lily family and produces the sacred lotus flower. The skin looks disagreeably decayed, but inside, the flesh is juicy and crisp, with characteristic star-patterned seeds. Slice lotus root thinly to stir-fry or serve in salads.

Cultivated primarily in Japan but found growing wild in Europe and North America is burdock or gobo, a long thin root with prickly burrs. The pale gray flesh is slightly bitter and, like so many roots, discolors when exposed to air. Slivers or large pieces may be used in soups and stews. Hamburg, or root parsley, is a variety of parsley grown in Europe for its carrot-shaped, grayish root. Usually served alone as a vegetable, or in soups or stews, it is often compared to celery root. Resembling the Jerusalem artichoke, but more delicate in flavor, is the Chinese or Japanese artichoke (Fr. *crosne*), a spiral tuber that is best known in Europe and Asia. It may be cooked unpeeled, or rubbed with coarse salt to remove the skin. The Asian water chestnut is a nutty-crisp tuber that grows on the bottom of lakes and ponds. It has a tough brown skin and in Asia is eaten fresh, though in western markets it is generally canned. Water chestnuts may be eaten raw in salads and when cooked they retain a rich taste and slight crunch. In Asia, water chestnut flour is used much like cornstarch in the West. The breadfruit grows on a tree commonly cultivated in the West Indies and Latin America. It is cooked like a potato and good in thick soups or cut into French fries or crisps. When ripe it has creamy yellow flesh and a green skin which should be peeled off.

Mexico and the American southwest have brought tomatillos and nopales to the international table. The tomatillo, also called the Mexican green tomato or ground tomato, ranges from cherry to plum size and is often sold when pale green and acid, though the fruit ripens to bright yellow, even shading to purple. It is a main ingredient in Mexican *mole verde*, which accompanies many Mexican dishes, and may also be used raw in salads or simmered in robust soups and stews. Closely related (and surrounded by a similar parchment-like husk) is the ground cherry or husk tomato, found in the Americas and some parts of Europe. Its flavor is somewhere between a tomato and a strawberry, and it is excellent for sauces, relishes and savory jams.

The fruit-bearing prickly pear cactus also provides an edible pad or nopale – the succulent new growth of the cactus, which has slippery flesh akin to that of okra. To prepare a pad, trim the edge, scraping off the eyes and prickles with the point of a small knife. Pads may be boiled, steamed or sautéed in butter or olive oil. Steamed strips, which remain crunchy on the outside, are good in salads or chopped for stews and soups.

Fresh hearts of palm are rarer; they are found fresh in the Caribbean where the tropical palm tree grows, but they are commonly canned for export. Hearts of palm may be chopped for fritters, or marinated for salad. The bamboo plant yields similarly edible shoots, gathered soon after they break the surface of the soil. When mature, they are covered with a sheath that is tough unless boiled and they should be treated like asparagus. Familiar in stir-fries, bamboo shoots are commonly available outside Asia, either fresh or in cans.

Two ordinary edible greens are rarely seen in markets. Fiddleheads, the tightly coiled fronds of the ostrich fern, grow in North America beside streams, from early spring to late July. When boiled or steamed while still bright green and small they have an earthy flavor that needs only butter, cream or a light sauce to complement it. (Some ferns are poisonous, so be sure of your source). The young green leaves of the stinging nettle, tasting rather like sorrel, are another surprise. They should be cooked like spinach, and can be used to good effect in soup. A third spring vegetable, popular in northern Europe, is the shoot from the hop plant that is used to flavor beer.

Yuca

Tomatillo

Bamboo shoots

Nettle

Water chestnut

Taro root

Lotus root/ burdock

Breadfruit

MUSHROOMS

THE WORLD OVER, mushrooms excite passionate devotion. It is said that while on his deathbed, King Louis XIII strung the season's first morels for drying, and in nineteenth-century Japan, the Empress-Dowager journeyed for hours to the pine woods in search of matsutake. In many central European countries, wild mushroom hunting has been a national pastime, and often a financial necessity, for centuries.

The first breakthrough in mushroom cultivation came in the seventeenth century in France, but it took much experiment before scientists at the Pasteur Institute managed to germinate spores and produce sterilized mushroom spawn in the 1890s. Even today many farmers ban visitors from the beds where the pasteurized compost has been planted with mushroom mycelium under carefully controlled conditions.

There are an estimated 40,000 species of mushroom worldwide. All belong to the fungi family, which also includes molds and yeasts. Mushrooms are the fruit of fungi, which grow underground in the form of cottony strands of mycelia. The fact that they can spring up mysteriously overnight is simply the result of particular moisture and temperature conditions which prompt fungi to bear fruit above ground. Since they are unable to convert sugars, fungi extract them from other plants – hence the symbiotic relationship of some species with trees such as the oak or elm.

Nutritionally low in almost everything but protein (although a very few varieties are high in vitamins A or D), mushrooms are valued for the rich earthy flavor and chewy texture they contribute to a dish. The sought-after varieties are expensive, but usually they have such a strong flavor that a few go a long way. In fact, so pervasive is the aroma of a single truffle that it can perfume a basket of eggs in a few hours simply by permeating the shells.

Cultivated and wild mushrooms

The distinction between cultivated and wild mushrooms is increasingly blurred, but for cooking purposes the three-part classification followed in this chapter is useful. Firstly, there is the common cultivated mushroom, which is cheap and universally available. Secondly, there are a small but growing number of wild varieties that are now quite widely cultivated and are to be found fresh or dried in specialty stores. Thirdly, there are the almost legendary mushrooms, such as morels, chanterelles and boletes, which still defy successful cultivation and must be gathered in the wild. For all three groups of mushroom, preparation and cooking techniques are broadly similar.

Since edible mushrooms have look-alikes that can cause death or serious illness, in no circumstances should any non-cultivated mushroom be eaten unless it has been expertly authenticated. Because wild mushrooms differ from one terrain to another, it is not sufficient to select edible species simply by using mycological charts and reference books.

Choosing and storing mushrooms

Freshly picked mushrooms should be firm but moist with no damp patches. Dryness, particularly at the end of the stem, betrays that they have been stored for several days. If mushrooms impress by a heady smell, it is a guarantee of freshness, though by no means all species have much aroma.

Mushrooms picked in the wild come in many different sizes and stages of maturity, with leaves, earth and fragments of wood sticking to them; cultivated versions of the same variety are likely to be cleaner and more uniform. To detect worms, break the stems from the caps or cut one or two mushrooms open; a few worms are not harmful and can be cut away easily with a knife.

Cultivated common mushrooms should have white or light tan caps and no discoloration. As the common mushroom matures, it flares open to expose the pinkish to brown gills on the underside.

If too moist, mushrooms deteriorate rapidly so do not wrap them in plastic. Store them in the refrigerator, covered with a damp cloth, or in a paper bag with holes poked in it for ventilation. They will keep for three to four days; clean them just before using.

Cleaning mushrooms

Pick over mushrooms to remove earth and trim the stems; in some wild species the stem is woody and must be cut off. Wipe the mushrooms clean with a soft brush or damp cloth. However, if they are sandy, plunge them into a bowl of cold water and shake them to loosen the sand. Lift the mushrooms out, and drain in a colander. Mushrooms quickly absorb moisture so avoid bloating them – the common variety needs only 30-60 seconds washing. Species with deep gills or indentations, notably morels, must be soaked for up to five minutes to loosen grit. Some species, such as wild horse mushrooms, have a thick skin that should be peeled from the cap.

Cooking mushrooms

Only the common mushroom can safely be eaten raw. Do not eat other varieties uncooked without first checking them.

Most mushrooms, including the common mushroom, produce a good deal of liquid which evaporates as they cook, leaving them tender and considerably shrunk in size. A few species, notably boletes, chanterelles and oyster mushrooms, produce so much liquid during cooking that they can turn slimy. Often they must be sautéed first in a little oil to draw out the juice, then drained before cooking a second time. Other mushrooms, such as the hedgehog and chicken of the woods, tend to be dry and should be cooked gently, covered if they seem likely to scorch.

Mushrooms are great communicators, adding their distinctive flavor to other ingredients and quickly absorbing a sauce. Some cooks advise against cooking them in aluminum because they can discolor and acquire a metallic taste.

CHOPPING MUSHROOMS

Mushrooms vary in size, so in order to cook evenly they should be cut into equal pieces. For speed when chopping by hand, use the largest knife you are comfortable with. There are two methods of chopping mushrooms – by hand or food processor.

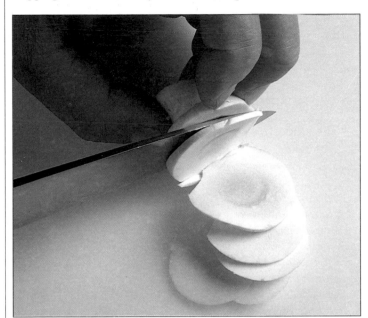

1 When chopping by hand, hold the cap steady and cut the mushroom in slices.

2 Pile the slices one on top of the other and cut them crosswise in rough sticks.

3 Finally, chop the sticks. Holding the point of the knife down with the flat of your hand, bounce the blade up and down, working to and fro across the board.

ALTERNATIVELY, some cooks like to hold 2 knives in one hand like a double-bladed knife, bouncing them up and down across the board. The chopped mushrooms should be very fine and crumbly with no coarse pieces.

Much time can be saved by chopping common and firm wild mushrooms in a food processor. A pulse switch on the machine can help prevent overworking, although the mixture will never be as dry as when chopped by hand. Shown above are mushrooms chopped by hand (left) and by food processor (right).

SLICING MUSHROOMS

Some recipes call for caps only to be sliced, with stems used for stuffing or soup. However, for an attractive presentation, slice the mushrooms through the stem and cap to make a "tree" shape.

Trim the stem just level with the cap. Hold the mushroom, stem down, and slice vertically through the stem and cap.

ALTERNATIVELY, slice common mushrooms in a food processor. Layer them sideways in the tube and use the slicing blade. Other mushroom varieties tend to be too firm or delicate to slice by machine.

Sautéing mushrooms

Butter would be most cooks' first choice for sautéing mushrooms, but vegetable or olive oil is an alternative. Some regional recipes call for walnut or hazelnut oil. Bacon fat (rendered from lardons p.249) is good with meaty wild mushrooms such as shiitake. The lardons can be served with the mushrooms. As a rule, 1 lb/500 g sautéed mushrooms will serve four or five people.

In a shallow frying pan, heat two to three tablespoons of butter until foaming, or oil until hot. If you like, add a little chopped onion or shallot and sauté until soft. Add 1 lb/500 g mushrooms, sliced or cut in large pieces, with salt and suitable flavorings such as a chopped garlic clove, a sprig of thyme, a pinch of nutmeg or coriander. A classic accompaniment to almost any type of mushroom is a *persillade* (see parsley, p.16), finely chopped.

Sauté briskly, stirring constantly, until the liquid has evaporated and the mushrooms are tender (cooking time depends very much on the type and age of the mushroom). Firm dry mushrooms need to be cooked more slowly, covered with a lid. When cooked, add one tablespoon of fresh herbs, such as tarragon or chives, and season.

Stewing mushrooms

Follow the directions for sautéing and when the mushrooms are almost cooked add two to three tablespoons of Madeira or wine with 1 cup/250 ml or more of stock or cream. Cover and simmer for 10-15 minutes so that the flavors blend and the mushrooms are very tender. If the sauce is thin, thicken it with one teaspoon of arrowroot dissolved in one tablespoon of cold water. Serve the mushrooms on toast or as an accompaniment to meat and game.

Making *duxelles*

Chopped cultivated or wild mushrooms are often made into a *duxelles* (dry purée) to flavor stuffings and soups. Finely chop 1 lb/500 g mushrooms. In a sauté pan or deep frying pan, melt one tablespoon of butter and fry two to three tablespoons of chopped onion or shallot until soft. Add the mushrooms, seasoning and, if you like, a chopped clove of garlic. Cook over a high heat, stirring occasionally, until all the liquid has evaporated and the *duxelles* is quite dry (cooking time depends on how moist the mushrooms are; common mushrooms need 15-20 minutes). Stir in one tablespoon of chopped parsley and taste.

Using dried mushrooms

Much the best way of preserving mushrooms is to dry them. Some cooks even prefer dried morels, boletes, shiitake and matsutake because of their intense flavor. Cloud ear mushrooms are almost always dried and added to a dish for texture rather than taste. The flavor of dried Chinese winter or black mushrooms is outstanding, and often these turn out to be shiitake.

To reconstitute dried mushrooms, soak them in warm water to cover for 30-60 minutes, depending on the size of the pieces, tossing them occasionally to loosen sand. Drain and trim them (the liquid can be strained through cheesecloth or filter paper for soups or sauces). Once reconstituted, the mushrooms are used like fresh ones, although they may need cooking for longer to become tender. About 1 oz/30 g dried mushrooms is the equivalent of ½ lb/250 g fresh. To dry mushrooms at home, see Preserving (p.485).

THE COMMON CULTIVATED MUSHROOM

Juicy enough to withstand the high heat of broiling, deep-frying and stir-frying, yet firm enough to be simmered and stewed without losing its identity, the common white mushroom appears with a huge variety of other ingredients in a wide range of dishes. Left whole, it provides an agreeably chewy texture; sliced it makes an attractive shape; chopped and cooked down as *duxelles* it gives an impressively musky flavor to stuffings and soups. It can be pickled, and when made into ketchup or powder it becomes a seasoning. Simplest of all is a salad of raw mushrooms marinated in a vinaigrette dressing with herbs. The one disadvantage of the common mushroom is its muted grayish brown color, which can be counteracted by cooking with lemon juice (*à blanc*, p.308), or rubbing a cut lemon over the mushroom cap.

The common white mushroom is sold at three stages of growth: caps when young (often called buttons), the standard size which opens to a cup for stuffing, and the older, open flat mushroom. A mature mushroom has more taste than a young one with a closed cap. A cousin of the common mushroom, the Italian Cremini has a tan cap and holds its shape well when cooked.

USEFUL INFORMATION
Agaricus bisporus
Found Worldwide.
Season Year-round.
How to choose Moist, white or light tan with no discoloration.
Portion 3-4 oz/90-125g.
Nutritive value per 3½ oz/100 g: 28 calories; 2.7 g protein; 5 g fat; 4.4 g carbohydrate; 15 mg sodium; no cholesterol.
Cooking methods Bake 10-15 minutes at 350°F/175°C; broil 3-4 minutes; deep-fry whole 3-4 minutes; marinate raw 1-2 hours; sauté 3-5 minutes; stew whole 10-15 minutes; simmer for soup or sauce 10-15 minutes; stir-fry 1-2 minutes; stuff, and broil about 5 minutes, or bake 15-20 minutes at 350°F/175°C.
When done Tender.
Processed forms Canned in water or marinated; dried.
Typical dishes Puff pastry filled with mushrooms (France); cream of mushroom soup (UK); stuffed and baked (UK, USA); fritters (Scandinavia); mushroom cabbage cutlets (Russia); sautéed with garlic and parsley (Italy); broiled (Pennsylvania, USA); poacher's pie (with rabbit, UK); *funghi alla parmigiana* (stuffed with breadcrumbs, parmesan, garlic, herbs, Italy); pudding (Hungary,

Czechoslovakia); tamales (S. America); casserole (USA); *sauce forestière* (France); dumplings (Vienna); bisque (Switzerland); mushroom and shallot sauce (Belgium); preserved (Germany); mushroom and beef pockets (in sour cream dough, Poland); vine leaves stuffed with mushrooms (Bulgaria). *Also good with* eggs, cheese, artichokes, zucchini, potatoes, spinach, veal, chicken, beef, duck, game, Madeira, wine, garlic, thyme, oregano, basil, paprika.

DICING A COMMON MUSHROOM

If possible, use a large mushroom as it makes dicing easier. A medium or large kitchen knife is best.

1 Trim the mushroom stem level with the cap. Cut the cap into thick (for large dice) or medium (for medium-sized dice) horizontal slices.

2 Stack the slices and cut them crosswise into thick or medium-sized sticks.

3 RIGHT Gather the sticks and cut across to make dice.

CUTTING COMMON MUSHROOM JULIENNE

Mushroom julienne are generally mixed with colorful vegetables such as carrot and leek. As for dicing, use a medium or large kitchen knife for cutting.

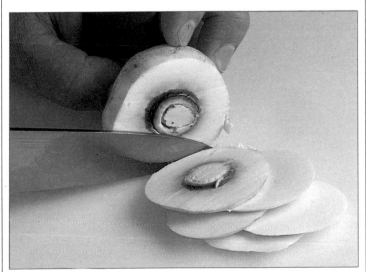

1 ABOVE Hold the mushroom by the stem and cut the cap into thin horizontal slices, discarding the bottom slice as soon as the gills can be seen.

2 RIGHT Stack the slices and cut them lengthwise into thin strips. Unlike vegetable julienne, the strips will not be of even length.

Mushrooms à la grecque

This popular appetizer is often served with other vegetables, such as pearl onions and artichokes, cooked in the same way.

Serves 4

1½ lb/750 g small mushrooms
3 tbsp/45 ml olive oil
18-20 pearl onions, peeled
½ cup/125 ml white wine
1¼ cups/300 ml veal stock (p.44) or water
½ lb/250 g tomatoes, peeled, seeded and coarsely chopped
1 tbsp tomato paste
juice of ½ lemon (more if needed)
1 tbsp peppercorns
2 tbsp coriander seeds
large bouquet garni
salt and pepper

1 Wash the mushrooms if necessary and trim. Quarter them if large. In a sauté pan or shallow saucepan heat the oil, add the onions and sauté for 2-3 minutes until lightly browned. Add the rest of the ingredients (except the mushrooms) and bring to a boil.
2 Add the mushrooms, pushing them under the liquid. Boil over a high heat for 15-20 minutes until the mushrooms are tender and the liquid has evaporated to form a light sauce. **Note** Boiling emulsifies the oil and stock so that the sauce thickens slightly.
3 Let the mushrooms cool until tepid, then discard the bouquet garni. Taste, adding more lemon juice, salt and pepper as needed. Chill in the liquid for at least 12 hours before serving.

FLUTING A COMMON MUSHROOM

Very fresh white mushrooms, and a small kitchen knife, are needed for fluting. The technique requires a certain skill: rotating the mushroom against the knife blade, at the same time turning the knife against the mushroom, is the key.

1 Use a small paring knife and hold the blade at a slight angle to the center of the mushroom. Cut a thin curved strip from the center to the edge of the cap.

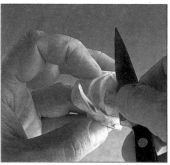

2 Continue cutting strips, turning the mushroom at the same time as the knife but in the opposite direction. Trim the stem.

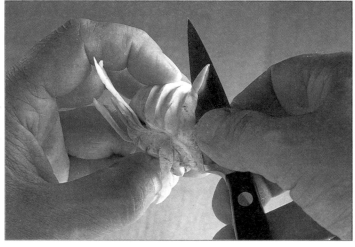

3 Using a rhythmic twisting motion, continue until the cap is evenly fluted all the way around, then discard the parings.

4 With the point of the knife, impress a five- or six-point star in the center of the cap. To display their pattern, fluted mushrooms are often cooked *à blanc*, or rubbed with a cut lemon.

Cooking common mushrooms *à blanc*

To keep them white, common mushrooms are cooked with lemon. Clean 1 lb/500 g mushrooms and slice, quarter or leave them whole as needed. Put them in a saucepan with the juice of half a lemon, salt and pepper and just cover with water. Cook over a high heat for three to five minutes until the water foams to the top of the pan and the mushrooms are tender. Reserve the cooking liquid to use as flavoring for sauces and stocks.

CULTIVATED MUSHROOMS

With modern technology it is now possible to cultivate several species of mushroom which used to be available only in the wild. No sooner does a wild variety become sought after – the oyster mushroom in the United States for example – than it seems some enterprising grower starts reproducing it commercially. Such mushrooms can be spotted by their clean appearance and relatively uniform size. Unfortunately, like so many farmed ingredients, they tend to be an emasculated version of the wild original, with a milder flavor and paler color.

SHIITAKE

The shiitake mushroom, best when grown on hardwood logs (*shiia* is an oriental chestnut), is a relative newcomer to the West. The flavor is meaty and the resilient texture and impressive, earthy flavor make shiitake a substantial treat. Their flat shape is ideal for stuffing, and they are wonderful in stews, sautéed in butter, or with meat or poultry, particularly game. Given their Asian origin, some recipes call for them to be stir-fried, or broiled with plenty of oil to keep them moist; they also make excellent soup. Shiitake are cultivated in the United States, and are now available fresh in some European countries, although they are more often found dried (p.306) as Chinese or Japanese black mushrooms.

USEFUL INFORMATION

Lentinus edodes
Other names Chinese or Japanese black, black forest, golden oak.
Found Asia, USA, Netherlands.
Season *Cultivated:* better in spring and autumn. *Wild:* spring and autumn.
How to choose Moist and fleshy.

Portion 3-4 oz/85-125 g.
Nutritive value Low in calories, high in vitamin B and fiber.
Cooking methods Bake 15-20 minutes at 350°F/175°C; broil 5-7 minutes; sauté 5-7 minutes; stir-fry 3-5 minutes; simmer for soup or stew 15-20 minutes.
When done Tender but resilient.
Processed forms Canned; dried.
Typical dishes Broiled with olive oil (USA); stuffed with shrimp paste (China); with *fettuccine* and cream (California, USA); steamed with fish in parchment (USA); with chicken (Japan); relish (with *sake* and dark soy sauce, Japan); shiitake rice (Japan). *Also good with* ham, bacon, garlic and sesame oil.

OYSTER MUSHROOM

Wild oyster mushrooms grow in abundance on rotting tree stumps and logs and are also easy to cultivate. Known as "shellfish of the woods", they are thought to resemble pale oyster shells and have a mild flavor reminiscent of shellfish. Their flesh is moist and can produce a good deal of liquid during cooking, so they are best baked, broiled or stewed. They can also be left whole, coated with egg and breadcrumbs and deep-fried like real oysters. Even when thoroughly cooked, the texture of oyster mushrooms is chewy.

Pleurotus ostreatus
Found Asia, N. America, Europe, Australia.

Season *Cultivated:* year-round. *Wild:* spring and late autumn.
How to choose Soft silky caps with no dark wet patches.
Portion 2-3 oz/50-85 g.
Nutritive value High in vitamin B.
Cooking methods Bake 10-15 minutes at 350°F/175°C; broil 3-5 minutes; deep-fry 2-3 minutes; sauté 3-5 minutes; stew 10-15 minutes.
When done Tender but still very firm.
Processed forms Dried.
Typical dishes Deep-fried with tartare sauce (USA); marinated (UK); broiled (Japan); in cream sauce (UK); warm oyster mushroom and pasta salad (California, USA). *Also good with* chicken, cabbage, dill.

CLOUD EAR

The cloud ear mushroom has little flavor and is valued, particularly in Asian cooking, for its dramatic dark shape and crinkly texture suggestive of seaweed. As a bonus, it is said to lead to long life and even to reduce heart disease. Most commonly available dried, it is a type of bracket fungus, protruding shelf-like from trees. Cloud ears are popular in China, best mixed as a contrast to other ingredients, usually in a stir-fried dish. The American and European Jew's ear (*Auricularia auricula-judae*), which is commonly found on elder trees, is a similar species.

USEFUL INFORMATION

Auricularia polytricha
Other names Wood ear, tree ear.
Found Asia, USA.

Dried and reconstituted

Season Year-round.
How to choose Glossy and moist, but not limp.
Portion 2-3 oz/50-85 g.
Nutritive value Low in sodium and calories.
Cooking methods Steam 10-15 minutes; stew 10-15 minutes; stir-fry 3-5 minutes.
When done Soft, slightly crunchy.
Processed forms Dried.
Typical dishes Sweet soup with litchis (Malaya); stir-fried with pork and noodles (China); with lemon chicken (USA). *Also good with* snow peas, shellfish, chicken, bamboo shoots.

ENOKITAKE

More of a garnish than a cooking mushroom, enokitake are crisper than their frail appearance suggests. With their sweet lemony flavor, they are excellent raw in salads and should be cooked only briefly, as when added to soup or broth just before serving. When found in the wild, enokitake are known as velvet shank or velvet foot and they look very different from the cultivated form. They have slippery caps, colored reddish orange instead of the cream of the cultivated variety. They grow in clusters and the base may need trimming if it is woody.

Flammulina velutipes
Other names Snow, snow-puff, pin-head.
Found *Cultivated:* Japan, Malaysia,

USA (California). *Wild:* Europe, N. America.
Season *Cultivated:* available all year. *Wild:* autumn and winter.
How to choose Firm and crisp.
Portion 1-2 oz/25-50 g.
Nutritive value High in vitamin D and fiber.
Cooking methods Simmer 1 minute in soup; bake 5 minutes at 350°F/175°C; steam 3-5 minutes; use raw in salads and as a garnish.
When done Tender but still firm.
Processed forms Canned.
Typical dishes Foil-cooked (Japan); with mixed greens (USA). *Also good with* lemon, walnuts.

Stuffed shiitake

Any large mushroom can be used for stuffing; field mushrooms with their dark, flat gills are also ideal.

Serves 4

¾ lb/350 g medium or large (8-10) shiitake	4 oz/125 g chopped cooked ham
¼ cup/60 g butter	1 cup/60 g fresh white breadcrumbs
1 onion, finely chopped	2 tbsp chopped fresh parsley
1 tbsp lemon juice	pepper, and salt (optional)

1 Heat the oven to 350°F/175°C. Cut the shiitake stems from the caps. Chop the stems (discarding any tough ends) and two mushroom caps. Melt the butter and fry the onion until soft. Stir in the chopped mushrooms, with the lemon juice, and cook for 3-5 minutes, stirring occasionally, until the moisture has evaporated.
2 Remove from the heat, stir in the ham, breadcrumbs, parsley and pepper and taste. Pile the stuffing into the shiitake caps and set the mushrooms in the buttered baking dish.
3 Bake the shiitake in the oven until tender, 10-15 minutes.

WILD MUSHROOMS

The wild relative of the common cultivated mushroom is the European and North American field mushroom (*Agaricus campestris*), which pops up in pastureland in late summer and autumn. The gills are bright pink at first, then darker, and the flavor more intense than that of the common mushroom. Relatives of the field mushroom include the horse mushroom, which looks similar but grows larger, and the wood agaric, which has a trick of staining red when cut.

Today, "wild mushroom" on a menu means one of the more unusual cultivated varieties. Given their high price, it is fortunate that they mix well with the ordinary cultivated mushroom, adding body and flavor. No doubt in time some of the more valuable species such as morels and chanterelles will be cultivated commercially, but they will not be the equal of those in the wild.

Note Many edible mushrooms have poisonous or deadly look-alikes, so never gather any field or woodland varieties without expert authentication.

MOREL

The morel, the only serious rival to truffles, has a sweet intensity of flavor which some gourmets prefer to the musky heaviness of the truffle. The places where morels grow are the jealously guarded secret of a few gatherers who return year after year. The dusky head of a morel makes it hard to spot and the season is short, often lasting less than a month. Luckily, it dries extremely well (p.485). The morel, with its tall pitted cap and hollow stem, looks quite different from almost all other mushrooms. The cap varies from beige to chocolate brown, depending on the species.

Morels have an affinity for cream, which they absorb like sponges until plump and juicy. Alternatively, they can be cooked with light stock to moisten them. A few morels are enough to perfume egg and pasta dishes, stuffings and stews generously; they are excellent in sauces for veal and chicken, and the hollow caps can be stuffed.

USEFUL INFORMATION
Morchella esculenta (common morel)
Morchella elata (black morel)
Found N. America, Europe.
Season 3-4 weeks in spring or summer, depending on location.
How to choose Fragrant smell; caps clean and not dry.
Portion 2-3 oz/50-85 g.
Nutritive value High in vitamin D and fiber.
Cooking methods Bake in sauce 15-20 minutes; sauté gently 5-7 minutes; simmer for soup, stew or sauce 15-20 minutes.
When done Tender.
Processed forms Canned; bottled; dried.
Typical dishes Warm salad (USA); with chicken and Jura wine/*vin jaune* (France), with wild rice (USA); creamed (Scandinavia); with fillet of beef (UK); in pastry (France); quiche (USA, France); with scrambled eggs (France). *Also good with* onions, duck, venison.

Dried morel

Cleaning morels
Because the cavities of fresh morels tend to be full of sand, they must be soaked carefully in a bowl of water for up to five minutes before draining (see Cleaning mushrooms, p.304).

Morels with cream

This rich mushroom dish can be served as a first course or accompaniment to roast chicken or veal.

Serves 4

¾ lb/350 g fresh morels or 1½ oz/45 g dried morels	1 cup/250 ml *crème fraîche* (p.70), or heavy cream
3 tbsp/45 g butter	2 tsp arrowroot, dissolved in 2-3 tbsp/30-45 ml cold water (optional)
salt and pepper	
1 tbsp Madeira or sherry	toasted white bread, for serving
1 cup/250 ml heavy cream	

1 Clean the fresh morels or soak and clean the dried ones. Strain and reserve the soaking liquid.
2 Melt the butter in a sauté pan or frying pan and add the morels with salt and pepper. Sauté gently for 2-3 minutes, stirring.
3 Add the Madeira or sherry, the soaking liquid from the dried morels and the cream, or cream and *crème fraîche*. Bring to a boil, cover and simmer until the morels are plump and tender and the liquid has reduced and thickened, 8-12 minutes for fresh morels, 15-20 minutes for dried ones.
4 Taste the sauce for seasoning. If it is thin, whisk in the arrowroot, dissolved in water, and cook for 1 minute. Serve the morels on toast, or with toast served separately.

BOLETE

The king bolete, or cep, is a monarch indeed, third only to the truffle and morel in the gastronomic hierarchy. It is part of a large family of chubby mushrooms with bulbous stems and fleshy caps (the Italian name for cep is *porcini*, meaning little pigs). Boletes have a spongy mass of tiny tubes under the cap instead of gills. Their flavor is at once perfumed and pungent, vividly evocative of the hardwood and coniferous woods where they grow. Unless picked young, they easily become soggy.

Boletes come in earthy colors – terracotta, orange, olive green and, in king boletes, rusty brown with a white stem. Many types of bolete are edible, some agreeable, some rather tasteless, a few are unpalatably bitter. Their soft texture leads some cooks to prefer dried ones to fresh, especially since fresh boletes also have a tendency to attract worms.

In the kitchen, all boletes (except those with a sticky cap, which must be peeled, dried and used as powder for flavoring) should be treated alike. If the sponge seems very soft, scrape it off with a teaspoon and use only the cap and the firm stem. King boletes are outstanding sautéed with garlic and shallots, or simmered in a wine stew; when stuffed they are natural partners for game. They are famous in soup, with scrambled eggs, risotto and pasta. In the pan, boletes often produce large quantities of liquid, which should be drained and reserved for stock or soup, or evaporated over high heat as rapidly as possible.

USEFUL INFORMATION

Boletus edulis (king bolete)
Other names Cep, *cèpe, porcini.*
Found N. America, Europe, N. Africa, Australia.
Season Summer and autumn.
How to choose Fleshy but firm; check cap for worms.
Portion 3-4 oz/85-125 g.
Nutritive value High in vitamin D.
Cooking methods Bake 15-20 minutes at 350°F/175°C; broil or sauté 5-7 minutes; simmer 20-30 minutes in soup or stew; stir-fry 3-4 minutes.
When done Tender.
Processed forms Canned; bottled; dried.
Typical dishes Wild mushroom soup (Italy); with entrecôte (France); with veal escalope (France); with lamb's kidneys (Italy); béarnaise (with garlic, breadcrumbs and parsley, France).

Also good with meat, goat cheese, snails, tomato, Madeira, sherry, oregano.

PARASOL MUSHROOM

The parasol mushroom is unusual in that it thrives in both pastures and woods, though it prefers sandy soil, and can be found by the sea, on sandy edges and cliff tops. It sprouts tall and conspicuous, sometimes with a cap as wide as 8 in/20 cm in the United States and Europe. Although the smaller, younger parasols are best to eat, the large caps are spectacular when stuffed. Fragrant but delicate, parasols are excellent sautéed or broiled with a little butter and shallots, or with fresh herbs. They are also suitable for drying (p.485).

USEFUL INFORMATION/PARASOL

Lepiota procera
Found N. America, Europe.
Season Late summer and autumn.
How to choose Firm but not leathery.
Portion 3-4 oz/85-125 g.
Cooking methods Broil or sauté 3-5 minutes; stuff and bake at 350°F/175°C, 20-30 minutes.
When done Tender.
Processed forms None.
Typical dishes Sautéed with Madeira sauce (USA); fried (Scandinavia). *Also good with* ham, poultry liver, artichoke, Cheddar cheese, walnuts, Marsala.

HEDGEHOG MUSHROOM

A toothed mushroom, the gnarled hedgehog has tiny white spines on its underside instead of gills. According to one mycologist, it resembles a drunken gnome with a floppy hat! Mild and sweet, but also very dry and brittle, hedgehog mushrooms can be cooked like common mushrooms and are good broiled with olive oil, sautéed or stewed with cream and herbs, or aromatic spices.

USEFUL INFORMATION

Hydnum repandum
Other names Rubber brush, sweet tooth, *pied de mouton.*
Found N. America, Europe.
Season Summer and autumn.
How to choose Moist, no dried stems.
Portion 3-4 oz/85-125 g.
Cooking methods Broil or sauté 3-5 minutes; stew 10-15 minutes.
When done Tender.
Processed forms Canned; dried.
Typical dish Sautéed with butter and baby vegetables (USA).

Also good with broccoli, cauliflower, zucchini, carrots, onions.

SHAGGY MANE

The shaggy mane is a tall mushroom with a characteristic ragged cap which dissolves to black inky fluid as it matures. It must be picked when small and white, before the edge of the cap has started to flare and darken, and should be cooked within a few hours of picking. Mild-flavored shaggy manes are best split and broiled, baked or simmered with cream and seasoning.

Note Severe poisoning can be caused by drinking alcohol when eating the closely related ink cap (*Coprinus atramentarius*).

USEFUL INFORMATION

Coprinus comatus
Found N. America, Europe.
Season Spring to winter.
How to choose Fresh, small, white.
Portion 2-3 oz/50-85 g.
Cooking methods Broil 2-3 minutes; bake at 350°F/175°C; simmer 8-12 minutes.
When done Tender but not mushy.
Processed forms None.
Typical dish Shaggy manes baked with cream and brandy (USA). *Also good with* eggs, ham, bacon, lemon.

MATSUTAKE & WOOD BLEWIT

The matsutake (pine mushroom) is the most prized of Japanese fungi. It also flourishes in northwest North America. With its powerful flavor and meaty texture, the matsutake is as valued as the best boletes though some cooks tone down the flavor with milder species. It can be steamed, marinated in soy sauce and broiled, used in broth soups (p.45) and stews, or to flavor eggs and stuffing. The wood blewit is a milder cousin that grows in Europe and North America and can be used in place of matsutake.

USEFUL INFORMATION

Wood blewit

Armillaria ponderosa (matsutake); *Lepista nuda* (wood blewit).
Found Japan, N.W. America (matsutake); Europe, N. America (wood blewit).
Season Late summer, autumn, winter.
How to choose Firm, fleshy, aromatic.
Portion 3-4 oz/90-125 g.
Cooking methods Bake at 350°F/ 175°C; broil 3-5 minutes; steam 8-10 minutes; stew 15-20 minutes.
When done Tender but resilient.
Processed forms Canned; dried.
Typical dishes Barbecued in foil (Japan); broiled with soy sauce and wine (Japan); creamed (USA). *Also good with* eggs, rice, beef broth, goat cheese, sour cream.

CHICKEN OF THE WOODS & HEN OF THE WOODS

The chicken of the woods is a bright yellow and orange mushroom. It grows in great clusters on tree trunks and stumps. A single fungus can weigh up to 20 lb/9 kg. The mature caps can be simmered to flavor soup; the succulent young ones are said to resemble chicken. They can be deep-fried in batter, sautéed, stir-fried or stewed in a rich sauce.

Another polypore that grows on the trunks of deciduous trees is the hen of the woods. The reason for its name is clear: the curling clusters resemble tail feathers. Milder and more fragile than the chicken of the woods, with a touch of bitterness, it can be cooked in the same way.

USEFUL INFORMATION

Chicken of the woods

Polyporus sulphureus (chicken of the woods); *Grifola frondosa* (hen of the woods).
Found Chicken of the woods: USA; *hen of the woods*: Europe.
Season Late spring and autumn.
How to choose Moist, resilient caps which are not woody.
Portion 3-4 oz/85-125 g.
Cooking methods Deep-fry 2-3 minutes; sauté 7-10 minutes; simmer in soup 20-30 minutes; stir-fry 3-4 minutes.
When done Moist and fairly tender.
Processed forms None.
Typical dishes Sautéed with turkey (UK); crisp-fried (USA); creamy soup (Japan); sauce with cream and herbs (USA). *Also good with* poultry, veal, cheese, sherry, ginger.

CHANTERELLE

Golden-trumpeted chanterelles are easily recognized and are prized for their aroma and perfumed taste. Firmer than many types of mushroom, they keep well since they dry out slowly and are usually free of worms. Those found in North America are often much larger than their European counterparts, but they have just as much texture and flavor. Colors range from cream through yellow, to reddish gold. A related species is the dark purplish-black variety called horn of plenty or *trompette de la mort* (trumpet of death) in France. This edible mushroom is sometimes used as a color substitute for truffles.

Since they are particularly susceptible to becoming water-logged, chanterelles should be kept dry and cleaned only with a cloth or dry brush. Like oyster mushrooms and boletes, they often exude large amounts of juice while cooking, and they may need to be drained once during the cooking process.

Chanterelles are versatile, lending themselves well to baking, broiling and stir-frying as well as to stews and soups. Simple preparations are the best: a dish of mixed black and gold chanterelles, baked or sautéed in butter or stewed with cream is a visual as well as gustatory delight.

USEFUL INFORMATION

Horn of plenty

Cantharellus cibarius (golden); *Craterellus cornucopioides* (horn of plenty).
Found N. America, Asia, Europe, Australia.
Season Summer and autumn.
How to choose Large, moist trumpets of deep color; stem ends should not be dry.
Portion 2-3 oz/50-85 g.
Nutritive value High in vitamins A and D.
Cooking methods Bake 10-15 minutes at 350°F/175°C; broil 3-5 minutes; sauté 3-5 minutes; simmer 15-20 minutes for soup.
When done Tender but resilient.
Processed forms Canned; preserved in oil; dried; powdered (black).
Typical dishes Sautéed in butter with garlic and parsley (France); pickled (Scandinavia); *à la crème* (France); with scrambled eggs (France); with bacon (France); baked with fish (USA); marinated with seafood salad (USA).

Golden chanterelle

Also good with smoked ham, poultry, poultry liver, potatoes, cream, ginger, hot chili peppers.

PUFFBALL

One mushroom family that has many members is the puffball family, which is found throughout North America and Europe. Puffballs are round or pear-shaped and range in size from a walnut to a large melon, with a smooth or warty whitish skin.

Puffballs must be eaten young and firm, when the flesh inside is smooth and white; when mature they disintegrate easily to brown powder, hence the name. Mild flavored, they are excellent thickly sliced, coated with egg and breadcrumbs and fried, or brushed with a little oil and broiled until brown and just tender.

USEFUL INFORMATION/PUFFBALL

Found N. America, Europe.
Season Spring, late summer, autumn.
How to choose White or light gray, smooth and firm.
Portion 3-4 oz/85-125 g.
Cooking methods Broil or sauté 2-3 minutes each side; deep-fry sliced 2-3 minutes.
When done Tender.
Processed forms Fresh only.
Typical dishes Casserole with cheese (USA); steaks (coated with egg and breadcrumbs, Scandinavia). *Also good with* other mushrooms, tomatoes, cream, dark soy sauce, sesame oil, oregano.

Other edible mushrooms

Found in pine and hardwood forests, the **saffron milk-cap**, together with its cream and bluish cousins, is best sautéed or stewed until tender. The **beefsteak mushroom**, which grows on tree trunks, looks like a broad red beef tongue, with fibrous flesh that should be sliced across the grain then soaked in salt water before cooking like boletes (p.311). The bright **lobster mushroom**, which resembles the color of cooked lobster, is meaty enough to withstand a long-simmered sauce. By contrast, **fairy ring mushrooms**, which grow in a circle, are delicate and are best sautéed or added to pasta or eggs (the woody stem must be trimmed before cooking). These tiny mushrooms are particularly good for drying (p.485). The perfumed fleshy **Caesar's mushroom** and the commonly found **honey mushroom** can be confused with poisonous varieties (see warning, p.310). They must never be eaten raw, but should be cooked like chanterelles, and go particularly well with pasta.

USEFUL INFORMATION

SAFFRON MILK-CAP (*Lactarius deliciosus*) **Found** N. America, Europe. **Season** summer to autumn.
BEEFSTEAK MUSHROOM (*Fistulina hepatica*) **Found** N. America, Europe. **Season** Summer to autumn.
LOBSTER MUSHROOM (*Agaricus silvaticus*) **Found** N. America, Europe. **Season** Summer to autumn.
FAIRY RING (*Marasmius oreades*) **Found** N. America, Europe. **Season** Summer.
CAESAR'S MUSHROOM (*Amanita caesarea*) **Found** Southern Europe, Asia, Africa, USA. **Season** Summer to autumn.
HONEY MUSHROOM (*Armillara mellea*) **Found** N. America, Europe. **Season** Midsummer to autumn.

Honey mushroom

Beefsteak mushroom

Fairy ring

Saffron milk-cap

TRUFFLES

For centuries truffles have maintained an aura of mystery. The strangeness of their rough appearance is heightened by the jet-black interior of the French truffle, a color matched by no other food. As for the flavor – one small fresh truffle will pervade a whole dish. Most truffles are the size of a walnut, although 5 in/ 12 cm giants can weigh 1 lb/500 g or more. The greatest truffle puzzle is how they are propagated. They grow underground on the roots of certain oak species, but the places they choose seem arbitrary, for they will appear in one field but not in another, under one tree but not the next. Clearing the ground of other plants seems to help them spread. Each year, however, the wild crop gets smaller and the price higher.

Truffle-hunting is carried out in age-old tradition by a man with a pig or dog trained to sniff out the treasure hidden a few inches underground; some experts say they follow a tell-tale truffle fly. There are many varieties of truffle, but the black truffle of Périgord is acknowledged supreme. Italian white truffles from Piedmont are esteemed for their sharp, distinctive peppery flavor, much appreciated when shaved or grated raw on salads or pasta. Indeed all truffles are perhaps best eaten raw, thinly sliced and dressed with walnut oil or scattered over cheese fondue.

Poultry stuffed with slices of black truffle inserted under the skin, is imbued with their delicious flavor. To make them go further, truffles can be added to a stuffing or *demi-glace* sauce (p.58), but the greatest treat is a whole truffle (or truffles) braised in Madeira or baked with foie gras, and wrapped in puff pastry.

When canned, truffles shrink to half their original size and lose much of their perfume. Nevertheless, they add a luxurious touch to pâtés or the aspics of a grand buffet. Once opened, canned truffles should be kept in a closed jar in light olive oil or Madeira and used within a month as they will lighten.

Fresh truffles lose their aroma and taste in less than a week, but they can be preserved. Scrub them to remove sand, then pare off the rough skin, reserving it to chop. Put the truffles in a small pan and cover with brandy or Madeira. Simmer, covered, for 30-60 minutes, until tender. Pack in a jar, add the cooking liquid and refrigerate for up to two months. Alternatively, submerge a fresh truffle in dry rice and refrigerate for up to two weeks. Use the liquid or rice for its flavor. Truffles can also be frozen (p.495).

USEFUL INFORMATION

Tuber melanosporum (black, Périgord); *Tuber magnatum* (white, Piedmont)
Found *Black:* France. *White:* northern Italy.
Season Autumn to winter.
How to choose Firm, overwhelming aroma. *Black:* very dark. *White:* no discolored patches.
Portion 1-2 oz/25-50 g.
Cooking methods Bake in pastry 30-40 minutes at 400°F/200°C; braise ¾-1 hour; sauté 2-3 minutes; simmer 10-15 minutes.
When done Resilient, almost crunchy.
Processed forms Canned whole, pieces, purée, juice; frozen.
Typical dishes Soup (France); white truffle and celery salad

(Italy); baked in pastry (France); cheese fondue with truffles (Italy); spaghetti with fish and black truffles (Italy); pheasant stuffed with truffles (Italy); *sauce Périgueux* (France); in wine (Germany); white truffle risotto (Italy). *Also good with* eggs, artichokes, boiled potatoes, champagne, Madeira, thyme.

GRAINS & LEGUMES

GRAINS AND LEGUMES have been staple foods for thousands of years, sustaining human life in temperate, arctic and tropical conditions. Wheat, corn and rice are among the world's most important cereal crops, offering an alternative to animal protein for those with limited access to meat. Legumes – essentially dried peas and beans – offer similar nutritional benefits. Grains and legumes are also vital because, when fully ripe and dried, they can be stored for months without spoiling, providing reliable winter food.

In recent decades, intensive agricultural research has revolutionized grain and legume yields. Thousands of hybrid varieties have been developed with better storage and cooking characteristics, and most importantly, improved nutritional quality.

In many parts of the world, grains make up a large part of every meal. Their use is often associated with a particular part of the world, for example, rice with Asia, cornmeal with Italy and the American South, and buckwheat with eastern Europe. National tastes in legumes are equally varied: one kind of white kidney bean is customary for American baked beans, another for Italian minestrone. Yet local cooking styles now move across frontiers so easily that many grain- and legume-based dishes are acquiring an international standing, particularly given increasing understanding of the links between diet and health. Once familiar only in hearty European dishes such as bean cassoulet and cornmeal polenta, many grains and legumes are now found tossed in salads with fresh vegetables or as side dishes for meat and fish. Dishes such as Mexican refried beans and rice, and Iranian perfumed rice *pullaos* are now well known beyond their countries of origin.

GRAINS

Botanically, grains are the fruits of cereal plants of the grass family (*Gramineae*): the fruit (ovary) wall being the outermost layer of the husked grain. There are about 8,000 species of grain, but only a few, from less than a dozen grasses, are commonly prepared in the kitchen. Most kernels are covered in a tough, thin husk that must be removed when harvested to make the grain edible. The kernel itself has three parts: a multi-layered, high-fiber, protective outer coat (the bran), a rich oil-containing embryo or seed (the germ) for a new plant, and an endosperm that is high in protein and nourishes the plant. Often only the endosperm is used, as in the production of white wheat flours (p.342).

By the time it is harvested, a cereal grain has dehydrated significantly; it only becomes palatable after it is cooked and reabsorbs water. Water is the usual cooking medium, but meat or chicken stock may be used for savory dishes such as pilaf and risotto, while grains that are simmered gently in milk become much creamier; this method is used for hot breakfast cereals such as British porridge and dessert puddings.

Choosing grain

Grain should always be as fresh as possible, so buy it from a source that has a relatively fast turnover. Fresh grain is dry, plump rather than shriveled or crumbly and of bright, even color. The odor will vary, depending on the specific grain, but should not be sour or musty. Despite proper handling, whole grain is susceptible to infestation from weevils (mealworms), which lay their eggs while the grain is still in the field, and may begin to breed within what seems to be an airtight container. Though undesirable, weevil eggs are harmless and disease-free.

Storing grain

Grain should be stored in a cool, dry place in airtight containers to keep out both moisture and insects. Whole grain, whether processed or not, contains the oily germ so quickly turns rancid from exposure to heat, light and moisture. It should be refrigerated, for up to four months depending on the type. Polished grain (p.316) may be stored for up to a year at room temperature. Storage time for cracked, rolled and other processed grains depends on how they have been treated and whether or not the germ has been removed, since any residual oil from the germ will affect shelf-life.

Before cooking, many grains, particularly whole kernels, should be rinsed in cold water to remove dirt particles or dust.

Boiling grain

Grain is usually boiled in water, although a light stock may be used for extra flavor. Generous amounts of liquid are needed so that the starch that is produced during cooking (particularly by pearled or cracked grains) is washed off. Use approximately four times the amount of water to grain. Cooking times depend on the type of grain, its age and how it has been processed (see individual grains). Adding a tablespoon of butter or oil helps prevent the water from boiling over, while a slice of lemon in the water helps keep the color of white rice.

Bring the water to a boil. Add the grain slowly so that boiling continues uninterrupted, stir once, then boil uncovered as fast as possible, so the movement of the water separates the grains. Stir only occasionally, otherwise the grains will become sticky. Whole grain should be boiled until *al dente* (p.316). When cooked, drain it in a colander, rinse with hot water to wash away starch, and leave to drain at least five minutes so that the grain is fluffy.

To reheat boiled grain: spread the cooked grain in a buttered shallow baking dish and cover with buttered foil. Bake at 350°F/175°C until the grain is very hot.

Steaming grain

To steam grain, bring a wide, shallow pan of water or other liquid to a boil. Spread the grain on a drum sieve (p.506), the rack of a couscous pot (p.511), or a coarse steamer rack lined with cheesecloth, set over the pan. Cover and steam without stirring until *al dente* (p.316). Leave for five minutes before stirring.

SIMMERING GRAIN BY THE PILAF METHOD

The pilaf method, in which grain is simmered without stirring until the liquid is totally absorbed, is a popular method for whole or cracked grains. When cooked, the grain should be fluffy but separate. Risotto (p.25) is a variation of this method.

1 Measure double the volume of stock or water to grain. If you like, sauté the grain in 1-2 tbsp oil or butter per cup of grain for 2-3 minutes until it becomes opaque, lightly toasted and coated in fat. Add the measured liquid, salt and pepper. If not sautéing, bring stock or water directly to a boil and slowly stir in the grain.

2 Cover the pan with wax paper or a lid and bring to a boil. Lower the heat and simmer without stirring, or bake at 350°F/175°C. When the liquid is absorbed, test the grain: it should be *al dente*. If moist, continue cooking; if too firm, add more liquid. When done, let the grain stand 5 minutes, fluff with a fork, and season.

Pilaf recipes

Mushroom brown rice pilaf Serves 6 as a side dish. To accompany meat or poultry. Melt 2 tbsp butter in a frying pan and sauté 4 oz/125 g sliced fresh mushrooms for 2-3 minutes. In a heavy casserole, melt 3 tbsp/45 g butter and sauté 2 chopped medium onions and 4 oz/125 g chopped lean bacon until the onions are soft but not brown. Add 1½ cups/300 g long-grain brown rice and cook about 2 minutes, stirring until all the butter is absorbed and the grains look transparent. Add the mushrooms and 2¼ cups/550 ml hot veal or beef stock with salt and pepper. Bring to a boil, cover, and turn down the heat. Simmer until the rice is tender, about 45 minutes. Let the pilaf stand 10 minutes. Fluff with a fork, taste for seasoning and serve.

Currant and pistachio pilaf Serves 6 as a side dish. To accompany meat, poultry or fish. Blanch ¾ cup/85 g shelled pistachios for 1 minute, drain and halve them. In a heavy casserole, melt 2 tbsp butter and sauté 1 finely chopped small onion until golden brown. Stir in 1½ cups/300 g long-grain white rice and cook about 2 minutes, stirring until all the butter is absorbed and the grains look transparent. Pour over 2¼ cups/ 550 ml chicken stock, and season with salt and pepper. Bring to a boil, cover the pot and turn down the heat. Simmer until all the liquid is absorbed and rice is tender, about 20 minutes. Let stand 10 minutes, then stir in the pistachios, ¾ cup/100 g currants and 2 tbsp butter. Fluff with a fork, taste for seasoning and serve.

SIMMERING GRAIN BY THE STIRRING METHOD

Many dishes are made by adding grain to simmering liquid, then stirring constantly until the consistency is tender and creamy. This is the method used for making Italian polenta (p.319) and some types of *gnocchi* (p.338), as well as for American grits and Scottish oatmeal porridge. Water, milk and light stock are the most common cooking liquids.

Grain is added to the boiling water, milk or stock a little at a time; allow approximately four times the amount of liquid to grain. Cooking is continued at a steady simmer until the grain is *al dente* (p.316) or, if preferred, thick, creamy, and soft enough to fall from the spoon. For sweet puddings, sugar is added at this stage as it tends to scorch if added earlier.

A variation of this method includes using only a part of the liquid at the beginning. More is added as it is absorbed during cooking, making the right amount of liquid easier to judge. Another approach is to cook the grain very slowly in a water bath, stirring only occasionally, a method used for smooth mixtures such as cream or rice. Oatmeal porridge may also be made this way.

1 Add the grain or meal (here, cornmeal is shown) to the boiling water a little at a time so the temperature is maintained.

2 Continue cooking, stirring steadily, until the mixture is thick but still soft and creamy enough to fall from the spoon.

GRAIN PUDDINGS

Grain puddings, usually moistened with milk or cream, are baked in a very low oven so that the grains swell and absorb the maximum amount of liquid. Up to 6 cups/1.5 L liquid may be absorbed per cup of grain. Some grain puddings are savory, but more often they are sweetened and flavored with vanilla, spices or dried fruits: British rice pudding with raisins and New England Indian pudding with cornmeal and molasses are typical. Rice puddings such as Portuguese *arroz doce* with lemon and cinnamon, and Moroccan *roz bil hleeb* with almond milk, follow the same basic method, but are cooked on top of the stove.

For a grain pudding, mix the grain with a quarter to half of the liquid in a greased baking dish. Cover and bake at 300°F/150°C until the liquid is absorbed, stirring occasionally. Stir in more liquid with any flavorings and sugar and continue baking. A third or fourth portion of liquid may be added and baking continues until the grain is very creamy and soft. For a brown crust on milk puddings, remove the cover during the last part of cooking. Serve hot or warm, with cream if you like.

Testing when grain is done

Cooking time and the extent to which a grain swells, vary not only with the type of grain but with its age and dryness. Most whole grains should be cooked until *al dente*, tender on the outside but with a slight bite. Whole grains retain a more chewy texture when completely cooked than polished grains. With the pilaf method (p.315), cooking can be judged by eye as the grain is usually done when all the liquid is absorbed. Some grains burst when completely cooked – wild rice is an example – but most should hold their shape and bursting is a sign of overcooking.

To test for tenderness, bite into a couple of grains or press a grain between your finger and thumb. Dishes such as pilaf or risotto should be soft, but the grains should still hold their shape. Only in desserts such as rice pudding is the grain cooked until so soft that it falls apart.

Fluffing grain

After simmering, steaming or baking, grain should be left to stand in the pan, still covered, to cool for five minutes. This allows the kernels to contract slightly. To separate them without crushing, gently toss the grain with a fork.

Cooked grain dishes

The soft texture and bland flavor of grains is their strength, for they pair equally well with delicate or spicy foods: the perfume of saffron, the earthy flavor of cumin and coriander seed, lively flavorings such as lemon or soy sauce, herbs such as mint and basil, and even with molasses. Grains may be plainly boiled, steamed or simmered as pilaf to serve as a side dish or combined in hearty salads with vegetables or sweet ingredients such as dried fruits. Cooked grains also form the basis of many savory casseroles, cooked with complementary vegetables: millet with tomatoes and cheese, or barley with mushrooms, olives and sour cream are examples.

Grains are particularly suited to stuffings: millet goes well with pork and bulghur with lamb, while rice is often the base of poultry stuffings. Cracked grains may be molded into croquettes bound with egg, nuts or cheese (p.107). Traditional in northern Italy is cornmeal polenta (p.319), often topped with a rich tomato, cheese or wine sauce, while in the United States cornmeal breads and cakes are popular. A few grains, such as wild rice and buckwheat, are more limited in scope, best on their own or as a complement to rich game birds or meats.

Grain processing

Most grains are difficult to digest if left unprocessed. In some cases, processing is needed to remove the tough husk, in others processing simply makes the grain cook faster. Whole grain is the least processed form; if there is a husk, it is removed but otherwise the grain is untreated and retains its full nutty flavor. Whole grain (also called whole berries, kernels or groats) is commonly found in health food stores, gourmet shops, or at mills, and is considered to be more nutritious than processed grain. It often takes longer to cook. Cracked grain, also called grits, is the whole grain cut with steel blades or stones; some grains such as bulghur wheat are cooked and then cracked. When ground more finely, flours and meals are produced (see Flour, Breads and Batters, p.342).

When scraped of its germ and bran with only the endosperm remaining, grain is labeled as pearled or polished. Pearl barley and polished white rice are the most common examples. Rolled grain or flakes are flattened between rollers so that they are easier to cook and more digestible. Sometimes flakes are also toasted or steamed to shorten their cooking time. They may contain as many nutrients as whole grain; however, many commercial types are not made from the whole grain but are refined, that is, processed to remove the bran and germ, resulting in a lower nutritive value.

Puffed grains, usually sold as breakfast cereals or snacks, are made of whole grain that is cooked, dried, then heated under pressure until the endosperm expands to be light and dry.

In malted grain, the starch is converted to sugar by fermentation. Malted grains, particularly barley and rye, are often used for beers and spirits or for malt syrup, made from malted barley or barley and corn. Grain syrup is made by a similar process. Both syrups are used like other liquid sugars (p.413).

WILD RICE

Wild rice is not, strictly speaking, a rice at all, but the seed of an aquatic grass native to the Minnesota Lakes of the United States. A slightly different species is also found in Asia. Traditionally, wild rice was harvested by the American Indians, and although it still grows wild, it is now often cultivated, especially in California. The kernel, which is surrounded by a tough husk, is long and dark brown; when cooked the husk bursts open and displays its pale interior. True wild rice is chewy with an outstandingly earthy flavor; cultivated types have less taste but are usually less expensive. Cultivated grains are often plumper and lighter in color than wild grains.

Wild rice pairs well with poultry, particularly game birds like duck, and with shellfish. In addition to being served plain, wild rice is often mixed with nuts, bacon, hearty greens, wild mushrooms, colorful vegetables, dried fruits, or fresh fruits. Wild rice may also be ground into flour to enrich simple breads or to be made into dishes such as pancakes or waffles.

A little wild rice goes a long way, with about 1 cup/150 g raw wild rice providing 3-4 cups/750 ml-1 L cooked rice to serve 5 or 6. It may be boiled for 40 minutes, steamed 45-50 minutes, or simmered by the pilaf method for 3/4-1 hour. If overcooked, wild rice loses its fragrance and characteristic robust texture, and may coagulate due to the starch released.

Wild rice

Wild rice pilaf Serves 6 as a side dish. To accompany roast turkey or game. Melt 1/4 cup/60 g butter in a heavy casserole and sauté 2 chopped medium onions until soft. Add 1 1/4 cups/225 g wild rice, stirring to coat it with the butter. Pour over 3 1/2 cups/875 ml beef or veal stock, bring to a boil and cover the pot. Simmer the rice for 30 minutes. Add 1 seeded and diced red bell pepper and 2 cups/300 g yellow corn kernels (p.285) and continue cooking until the liquid is absorbed and the rice and corn are tender, 15-30 minutes more. Fluff with a fork, taste for seasoning and serve.

Seafood paella

The Spanish dish paella is traditionally made with plump short-grain rice, although long-grain varieties may be substituted. A wide shallow pan ensures that the cooking liquid in paella evaporates rapidly.

Serves 8-10

¼ cup/60 ml olive oil	1 lb/500 g raw smoked ham, cut into strips
3 onions, chopped	1 lb/500 g *chorizo* sausage, sliced
1 green and 1 red bell pepper, cored, seeded and cut into strips	1½ lb/750 g tomatoes, peeled, seeded and chopped (p.280)
3¾ cups/650 g short-grain rice	2 cups/500 g cooked green peas
1½ qt/1.5 L veal or chicken stock or water (more if needed)	1 lb/500 g cod or haddock fillets, cut into strips
large pinch of saffron threads, soaked in 1 cup/250 ml boiling water	1½ lb/750 g raw, unpeeled shrimp
3 cloves garlic, crushed	3 lb/1.4 kg mussels or clams in their shells, washed and cleaned (p.169)
salt and pepper	**20 in/45 cm paella pan or shallow flameproof casserole**
1 lb/500 g cleaned squid (p.171), sliced	

1 Heat the oil and cook the onions and peppers until soft but not brown. Add the rice and cook, stirring, until the grains are transparent and the oil is absorbed. Add the stock or water, saffron, garlic, salt and pepper. Add the following ingredients in layers: squid, smoked ham, *chorizo*, tomatoes, peas, and fish.
2 Bring the liquid to a boil and boil fairly rapidly on top of the stove or on an outdoor barbecue until all the liquid has been absorbed and the rice is tender, 25-30 minutes. Stir from time to time, especially when the paella starts cooking, and add more stock or water if the liquid evaporates before the rice is cooked.
3 Ten minutes before the end of cooking, set the shrimp and mussels or clams on top of the paella and do not continue to stir it. Keep the paella warm over a very low heat for 5-10 minutes before serving so that the flavors mellow.

RICE

Rice is native to Asia and the staple crop of more than half the world's population, competing with wheat as our most important food. Newly harvested, or rough, rice is processed first by cleaning the whole kernels. It may then be "converted", that is, soaked and pressure-steamed to reduce surface starch that would cause the grains to cling together during cooking. The inedible husk is removed, leaving brown rice, which still contains the bran layer. Finally, the rice may be polished to remove the bran and the germ, producing white rice. After milling, rice may also be cooked and then flash-frozen to produce instant (minute) rice. Rice appears in many American regional dishes such as the jambalayas of Louisiana with smoked ham or sausage and peppers, and the perloo of Carolina, baked with bacon fat, vegetables and shrimp.

Rice, which may be brown or white, is classified into long-grain, medium-grain, and short-grain types. Long-grain rice is distinguished by its narrow kernel, which is four to five times as long as it is wide. When cooked, it becomes tender and fluffy, with separated grains.

Aromatic varieties of long-grain rice are valued for their nutty flavor; highly prized is basmati, a thin rice grown in the foothills of the Himalayas that is essential to the traditional Indian pullaos and biriyani pilafs. It is often aged to improve its flavor and should be washed before using; in traditional Asian dishes it is often soaked so that the grains expand and are flexible enough to withstand long cooking. Iranian *domsia* is a similar rice used in traditional *polos* or *chilaus* (rice cakes). American aromatic rice includes brown or white texmati, pecan rice (a new brown rice strain with a taste evocative of pecan nuts) and wehani (a recent brownish-red California strain developed from Indian basmati) which has an exceptionally strong aroma and earthy taste.

Medium-grain rice is plumper, and often moister and stickier than long-grain rice, but the two are almost interchangeable. Some new medium-grain varieties have a distinctive flavor. In the United States, black japonica is an ancient Japanese variety, with a distinctive bitter taste.

Short-grain rice, often called pearl, round, or pudding rice, is almost as wide as it is long. It contains more starch than long- or medium-grain and becomes quite sticky as it cooks, making it a perfect choice for molds, puddings (p.315) and Italian risottos. In fact, Italian short-grain rice is excellent, the most popular being *arborio*, an especially plump variety that absorbs a sauce without turning too soft during long cooking. *Arborio* rice has a distinctive white spot on each kernel. Other Italian favorites include stubby *vialome nano*, which cooks quickly but stays firm, and scarce *carnaroli*, a variety that cooks to be perfectly tender.

The Japanese use short-grain rice in many dishes, including *sushi*, where it is mixed with rice vinegar (p.40). Spanish paella (left) is also traditionally made with short-grain rice. Glutinous rice, also called sticky rice, is another Asian short-grain variety that is molded into decorative shapes and used for breakfast and dessert dishes; it is a favorite for baby food.

Within each type, the substitution of one variety of rice for another generally causes no problems, but long- or medium-grain rice should never be substituted for short-grain in a recipe. Certain regional recipes require a specific rice variety.

All rice expands to at least twice its size when cooked, although volume will depend on the variety and age of the rice. Aged rice, which is especially appreciated in India, absorbs more liquid than freshly harvested grain. With the exception of basmati, rice need not be soaked unless stipulated for a particular cooking method. All methods of cooking rice release starch, which can cause grains to coagulate. Therefore, when a fluffy, rather than creamy, texture is sought, some recipes may call for rinsing and draining the rice thoroughly after cooking.

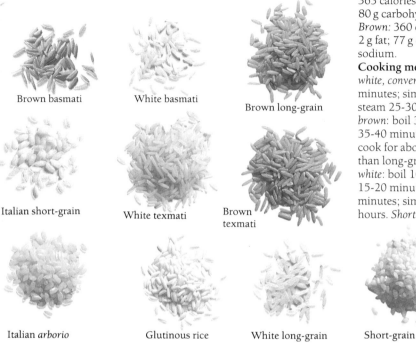

Brown basmati   White basmati   Brown long-grain

Italian short-grain   White texmati   Brown texmati

Italian *arborio*   Glutinous rice   White long-grain   Short-grain

USEFUL INFORMATION

Portion *Long- and medium-grain, brown, white, and converted:* 1 cup/200 g makes 3½ cups/875 ml cooked to serve 4. *Short-grain:* 1 cup/200 g makes 3 cups/750 ml cooked to serve 3-4.

Nutritive value per 3½ oz/100 g (raw). *All:* no cholesterol. *White:* 363 calories; 7 g protein; no fat; 80 g carbohydrates; 5 mg sodium. *Brown:* 360 calories; 8 g protein; 2 g fat; 77 g carboydrates; 9 mg sodium.

Cooking methods *Long-grain white, converted:* boil 15-18 minutes; simmer 15-20 minutes; steam 25-30 minutes. *Long-grain brown:* boil 30-40 minutes; simmer 35-40 minutes. *Medium-grain:* cook for about 5 minutes longer than long-grain rice. *Short-grain white:* boil 10-15 minutes; simmer 15-20 minutes; steam 25-30 minutes; simmer as porridge 2-3 hours. *Short-grain brown:* double the cooking times for short-grain white. *Sweet:* boil 12 minutes; steam 20-45 minutes, depending on type.

When done *Al dente* (p.316), creamy or very soft.

Problems White rice overcooks quickly; medium- and short-grain is sticky unless thoroughly rinsed after cooking.

Processed forms Flour; pre-cooked cereal flour; paper; puffed; crackers; flakes; nuggets; cakes; breakfast cereal.

Storage In an airtight container, 1 year at room temperature.

Typical dishes *Long- and medium-grain, white or brown:* kedgeree (baked with haddock and eggs, UK); dirty rice (with chicken livers, southern USA); *khichhari* (with lentils, India); *spanakorizo* (with spinach, Greece); *nasi goreng* (fried rice, Indonesia); pancakes with raisins and cinnamon (Germany). *Short-grain, white or brown:* risotto with Parmesan cheese (Italy); *plov* (with chicken and dried fruits, Russia); *kefta* (with meat balls, Middle East); *risgrynsgrot* (Christmas porridge, Sweden); *zarda* (sweet pudding with saffron and nuts, India); *flan de arroz al limon* (lemon caramel custard, Spain). *Sweet:* red rice (with adzuki beans, Japan); *mochi* (cakes, Japan); *fritelle di riso* (rice fritters, Italy).

Indian creamed rice

Kheer

For special occasions, Indian creamed rice is often decorated with edible silver leaf as well as nuts.

Serves 6

1½ qt/1.5 L milk, more if needed	½ cup/40 g sliced almonds, toasted
6 tbsp/75 g short-grain rice	2 tbsp rosewater
4 cardamom seeds, crushed	***For decoration***
1 in/2.5 cm piece cinnamon stick	chopped pistachios
2 whole cloves	toasted sliced almonds
6 tbsp/75 g sugar	silver leaf (optional)
⅓ cup/50 g raisins	

1 Bring the milk to a boil in a large saucepan, reserving ½ cup/125 ml. Wash the rice thoroughly in a sieve and stir into the milk. Cook over very low heat, stirring constantly, for 15 minutes. Add the spices and continue cooking for 1 hour, stirring occasionally.
2 Add the sugar and raisins and simmer for another hour, until the raisins are plump and the mixture thickens, stirring from time to time. If the rice starts to stick, add more milk. At the end of cooking, it should be very creamy and fall easily from the spoon. Add more milk if the sauce is too thick.
3 Remove from the heat and transfer to a bowl. Remove the cinnamon stick and cloves and stir in the almonds and rosewater. Chill before serving in individual dishes sprinkled with chopped pistachios, toasted almonds and silver leaf.

WHEAT & CORN

Wheat is grown over more of the earth's surface than any other grain, by far the most important crop being common or bread wheat. In the United States, corn rivals wheat in importance. Both wheat and corn are commonly processed into flour or meal as well as various types of breakfast cereal. Corn is also processed into cornstarch (p.344), oil (p.102) and syrup (p.413).

Commercial wheat is planted in early winter or spring; the grains range in color from white to reddish or bluish and may be hard (rich in the gluten protein needed for bread-making) or soft (low in gluten). Hard wheats have a glossy appearance. The type is of great importance for milling and making different flours, but matters much less when cooking.

Wheat berries or kernels are the husked whole grain. They may be cooked for a long time by the stirring method, or simmered as pilaf for a shorter time until *al dente* (p.316). Cooked wheat berries pair well with meats and they are good mixed with other grains in salads and pilafs. Wheat berries are also easily sprouted.

Cracked wheat is split from the whole berry and cooks much faster than the whole grain. Fine- and medium-cracked wheat is best for bread or for adding to batters, while a coarse grind is better suited to salads, pilafs, and breakfast cereal. Both cracked wheat and whole wheat berries cook faster if they are first soaked overnight.

Bulghur (also bulgur or burghul) is a type of cracked wheat with a deeper gold color and nuttier flavor. To make bulghur, wheat berries are parboiled, then dried and some of the bran removed before being cracked. Bulghur expands and becomes tender when simply soaked in water, or it may be steamed or simmered as pilaf, cooking more quickly than rice. A staple in the Middle East, bulghur is the basis for *tabbouleh* salad with tomatoes, parsley, lemon and mint. In Turkey, bulghur with ground lamb and pine nuts is a favorite filling for vine leaves. Bulghur may also take the place of rice in soups, casseroles and desserts.

Semolina is made from hard durum wheat (Flour, p.343) milled to varying degrees of coarseness. Most is made from hard wheat as the yield is higher but soft wheat semolina is also available. Semolina is used for milk puddings, for Italian *gnocchi* and for sprinkling on fresh pasta to prevent sticking. For semolina flour see Flour (p.343)

Farina is a fine meal, halfway between semolina and flour in texture. It is usually made from wheat and used for thickening puddings and also as a breakfast cereal.

Other wheat products include rolled wheat, or wheat flakes, which may be used in bread, cookies and oatmeal. Sprouted wheat berries, whether whole or ground, add a particularly sweet flavor to breads. Wheat germ, separated from the kernel during milling, has a pleasant nutty flavor that is developed even further by toasting. It is often sprinkled over yogurt and fresh fruit, or it may be added to breads, muffins and scones. Wheat bran is valued as fiber, added for texture to breads and cookies. It may also be included in stews and baked dishes.

There are two basic types of corn: sweet corn (p.285), usually eaten as a vegetable, and field corn. Certain varieties of sweet corn, with small ears and pointed grains, "pop" when the dried kernels are heated in hot oil or in a microwave oven. Usually flavored with butter or oil, popcorn may also be sweetened, for example with caramel. Blue corn is another sweet corn, grown in the southwestern United States. It has a particularly earthy taste and is most often ground for flour, particularly for bread or corn chips.

Field corn is harder and starchier than the sweet varieties and is used for animal fodder and for processing into cornmeal and cornstarch (p.344), oils, and hominy. Cornmeal is a popular ingredient in quick breads, pancakes and batter breads. In Britain it is also cooked in boiling water or milk as a porridge, called polenta in Italy and cornmeal mush in the United States. Polenta may be made into a soft, thick purée or topped with all manner of sauces and stews. Cooked polenta is often spread in a buttered baking dish, left to set, and then sliced to toast or fry. Cornmeal mush is spooned out of the dish like a pudding, or it may be sliced like polenta; sweet accompaniments such as maple syrup are popular. In Romania, a similar cornmeal preparation called *mamaliga* is almost a bread, served with stews, sauces, made into dumplings, or fried like polenta. In the West Indies, cornmeal puddings and porridge are popular. Cornmeal may also be added to bind other ingredients, as in the Pennsylvania Dutch breakfast dish, scrapple, made with cornmeal and ground pork.

Hominy, sometimes called pearl hominy, is truly American, made from polished white or yellow corn that is soaked in a lye solution until it swells and acquires its distinctive taste. It must be soaked overnight before cooking. Hominy grits or ground hominy is served in the South at breakfast.

Popcorn

Hominy grits

Cracked wheat

Whole wheat berries

Coarse bulghur

White cornmeal

Blue cornmeal

Yellow cornmeal

USEFUL INFORMATION

Portion *Wheat berries:* 1 cup/180 g yields 2 cups/500 ml cooked to serve 4. *Cracked wheat, bulghur:* 1 cup/175 g yields about 2½ cups/ 625 ml cooked to serve 3-4. *Cornmeal:* 1 cup/125 g yields 3½ cups/875 g to serve 5-6. *Whole hominy:* 1 cup/180 g makes 3 cups/ 750 g to serve 3-4. *Grits:* 1 cup/ 160 g makes 3½ cups/875 g to serve 4-6.

Nutritive value per 3½ oz/100 g (raw). *All:* no cholesterol. *Berries and flakes:* 340 calories; 10 g protein; 2 g fat; 76 g carbohydrates; 2 mg sodium. *Germ:* 363 calories; 27 g protein; 11 g fat; 47 g carbohydrates; 3 mg sodium. *Bran:* 213 calories; 16 g protein; 11 g fat; 47 g carbohydrates; 9 mg sodium. *Bulghur:* 354 calories; 11 g protein;

USEFUL INFORMATION/WHEAT & CORN

2 g fat; 76 g carbohydrates; 7 mg sodium. *Cornmeal with germ:* 355 calories; 9 g protein; 4 g fat; 74 g carbohydrates; 1 mg sodium. *Degerminated cornmeal:* 364 calories; 8 g protein; no fat; 78 g carbohydrates; 1 mg sodium. *Hominy grits:* 362 calories; 9 g protein; 1 g fat; 78 g carbohydrates; 1 mg sodium.
Cooking methods Times vary with age of grain and texture preferred. *Wheat berries:* soak overnight, simmer 50-60 minutes. *Cracked wheat:* simmer as pilaf 15-25 minutes; steam 20-30 minutes. *Bulghur:* half as long as cracked wheat. *Wheat flakes:* simmer 15-20 minutes. *Cornmeal:* simmer 15-20 minutes, stirring constantly; bake at 325°F/160°C, 1½-2 hours. *Hominy:* soak overnight, boil 50-60 minutes. *Grits:* simmer over hot water 30 minutes.
When done *Wheat berries:* al dente (p.316) or creamy. *Cracked wheat, bulghur:* tender and fluffy. *Cornmeal grits:* soft but still pourable. *Wheat flakes:* creamy.
Problems *Wheat berries:* acids in the bran can make whole berries difficult to digest. *Cracked wheat, bulghur:* overcook quickly and

become gluey. *Wheat germ, cornmeal:* turn rancid if not refrigerated. *Polenta:* must be stirred constantly. *Grits:* must not be stirred.
Processed forms *Cornmeal:* processed or degerminated. *Polenta:* instant (pre-cooked). *Hominy:* canned, frozen.
Storage *All:* freeze in airtight container up to 2 years. *Wheat berries, cracked wheat, bulghur, wheat flakes, hominy, grits:* airtight container in cool, dry place for 1 year. *Wheat germ, cornmeal with germ:* refrigerate 1 month. *Degerminated cornmeal:* room temperature 6 months.
Typical dishes *Wheat berries: kutia* (pudding with poppy seeds and honey, Poland); steamed with chicken and hard-boiled eggs (Egypt). *Cracked wheat, bulghur: khiyar dolma* (cucumber stuffed with meat and tomato, Jewish). *Cornmeal: milhassou* (sweet cornmeal pudding, France). *Polenta: alla piemontese* (layered with meat, Italy); cooked and fried with feta cheese (Bulgaria); cooked with okra (West Indies). *Hominy:* with salt pork and beans (USA). *Grits:* buttery garlic grits (USA).

COUSCOUS

Contrary to popular belief, couscous is not a type of grain, but a pasta made from durum wheat (p.328). However, couscous is cooked like grain and plays a similar role in a menu. The name applies both to the pasta granules and to the finished dish, a specialty of

Couscous

Morocco. The traditional preparation of couscous is laborious: the grain is moistened with water, rubbed between the hands to separate the lumps, then passed through a fine sieve to separate each granule. It is then steamed in a *couscousière*, or couscous pot (p.511), above the bubbling vegetable or meat *tagine* (stew) it typically accompanies. The *tagine* is highly spiced, often redolent with spices such as cinnamon and flavorings such as orange or apricot. Specific recipes vary according to region and family tradition. Finally the couscous is fluffed and steamed again before serving with *harissa* (p.35), a spicy sauce. Although associated with North African cuisine, variations on the traditional dish are also found in Sicily, France, Senegal, and even Brazil, where it is spelled *cuscuz* rather than couscous.

Today, a quicker-cooking (though less tasty) form of couscous is readily available. To prepare it, the pasta is simply soaked in boiling water, then fluffed with a fork, a method similar to that for bulghur (p.319). It is served plain, mixed with butter to accompany meats or fish, or accompanied by a mild or spicy stew. Cold couscous offers a pleasantly bland background for vegetable and fish salads, dressed with a tart lemon or lime dressing.

BUCKWHEAT & MILLET

Buckwheat is not a cereal grain but a fruit native to parts of the Soviet Union and closely related to rhubarb. The name derives from the Dutch *bockweit* meaning "beech wheat" because of its resemblance to the beechnut. Bees make an excellent honey from the fragrant flowers of buckwheat. In the kitchen it is used like a grain, as an alternative to rice. The three-sided buckwheat kernel is surrounded by a tough husk that must be removed to reveal the edible berry or groat.

Many cooks know buckwheat as kasha, the roasted groats or kernels that are sold whole, or coarse, medium or finely ground. With a nuttier flavor than unroasted groats, kasha is popular in eastern and central Europe where it often appears as a side dish, as a stuffing for meats and game, and in stews. To keep the kasha kernels separate during cooking, they should be mixed with a whole egg, then toasted in a heavy pan before cooking by the pilaf method (p.315). Popular in Jewish cooking is kasha *varnishkes*, a dish of kasha mixed with bow-tie noodles. Unroasted buckwheat groats may be simmered as a hot breakfast cereal, or to use in stuffings, or milled into grits that are also used for stuffings and sausage fillings. Buckwheat flour is famous in Breton crêpes and Russian *blinis*.

The millet family of cereal grains is native to the tropics, but it also grows well in cold climates. It is a staple food grain in undeveloped countries where wheat and rice crops are less successful. It is boiled or simmered like other grains, and although it becomes tender, it retains a slight crunch, barely doubling in bulk. The bland flavor is good with spicy stews, curries, and in stuffings. It makes a welcome addition to hearty salads and serves as a side dish for broiled or highly spiced barbecued meats. In Africa and Asia, millet is milled as flour for flatbreads and for smooth porridge.

Sorghum, best known for its sweet syrup, is related to millet and grows in similar parts of the world, where it is important as a staple grain. Some varieties are still used in eastern Europe and Italy to make black bread.

USEFUL INFORMATION

Portion *Buckwheat groats, kasha:* 1 cup/165 g makes 3 cups/700 ml to serve 3-4. *Millet:* 1 cup/200 g makes 3 cups/750 ml to serve 4-6.
Storage *All:* 1 year in a cool place.
Nutritive value per 3½ oz/100 g (raw). *All:* no cholesterol. *Buckwheat groats, kasha:* 335 calories; 12 g protein; 2 g fat; 73 g carbohydrates; *Millet:* 327 calories; 10 g protein; 3 g fat; 73 g carbohydrates; 5 mg sodium.
Cooking methods *Buckwheat groats:* simmer as pilaf 15-30 minutes, depending on granulation. *Kasha, buckwheat grits:* simmer as pilaf 10-15 minutes. *Millet:* boil 8-10 minutes.
When done Al dente or tender.
Problems *Kasha:* overcooks fast.
Processed forms *Buckwheat:* flour, pancake mix, grits. *Millet:* flour.
Typical dishes *Buckwheat: vareniki*

dumplings, Russia); *kig-ha-farz* ("meat in pudding", Brittany); porridge (Austria); stuffed into sausages (Germany); with mushrooms and cream (Russia). *Millet:* dumplings (Africa); *ragi dosas* (stuffed batter, India).

Buckwheat groats

Millet

Kasha

BARLEY, OATS & RYE

Once cultivated out of necessity in areas where wheat could not be grown, barley, oats and rye are still of importance in some regional cuisines. The dark breads of Russia and central Europe are often made with rye, and barley bread is also traditional. Barley appears in the comforting winter soups of northern Europe and America, and is still a staple grain in the Middle East, used in dishes such as *belila*, a hot pudding with nuts and orange water. Oatmeal and rolled oats feature prominently in Scottish dishes, especially porridge and oatcakes. Barley is also used as malt for brewing beer and distilling spirits.

Hulled barley, with the husk removed, is usually found in health food stores; a faster-cooking variety is labeled as hull-less. Scotch, or pot barley is husked and stripped of the outer layers of the kernel; it must be soaked overnight and cooked for at least an hour to be tender. Pearl barley, by far the most common, only takes about half an hour to cook and needs no soaking, but it is the least nutritious. Barley grits, the cracked form, is available in a range of grinds from fine to coarse. Malted barley, made from the toasted and ground sprouted grain, flavors American milkshakes and some commercial baked goods. Oats are usually rolled or flaked and are suitable for quick breads and cookies, while Scottish- or Irish-style oats, often produced by local mills, are favorite for oatcakes. Steel-cut oats are made from the whole berry, thinly sliced with sharp blades. They are often used for hot cereal and cook to a thick, rich consistency.

Rye is cultivated primarily to make flour, and for distilling whiskey. The grain is particularly subject to *ergot* fungus, a source of the drug LSD. Whole rye berries may be cooked as a hearty side dish or with other grains as a pilaf; they expand much less than barley. Cracked rye, or rye cereal, is commonly available as a hot breakfast dish, while rye flakes, also called rolled rye, are good in soups, casseroles, and as a binder for robust meat stuffings.

USEFUL INFORMATION

Portion *Barley, hulled, pot, pearl:* 1 cup/160 g makes 3 cups/750 ml cooked, to serve 4-6. *Whole oats, rye:* 1 cup/180 g makes 2 cups/500 ml to serve 4. *Oats, rolled:* 1 cup/100 g makes 1⅔cups/350 ml to serve 2. *Oats, steel-cut:* 1 cup/160 g makes 2 cups/500 ml to serve 2-3. *Rye flakes:* 1 cup/100 g makes 2½ cups/625 ml to serve 2-3.
Storage *All:* 1 year in a cool, dry place. *Pearl barley:* indefinitely.
Nutritive value per 3½ oz/100 g (raw). *All:* no cholesterol. *Pearl barley:* 348 calories; 9 g protein; 1 g fat; 78 g carbohydrates; 3 mg sodium. *Whole and rolled oats:* 390 calories; 14 g protein; 7 g fat; 68 g carbohydrates; 2 mg sodium. *Whole rye:* 334 calories; 12 g protein; 2 g fat; 73 g carbohydrates; 1 mg sodium.
Cooking methods *Barley, hulled, pot, pearl:* simmer 25-30 minutes. *Whole oats, rye:* soak overnight, simmer 45-60 minutes. *Oatmeal:* simmer by stirring 5-10 minutes;

cook as pudding. *Quick-cooking oat porridge:* 3-5 minutes.
When done *Al dente*, creamy, or very soft (p.316).
Problems *All:* whole grain cooks slowly and is hard to digest.
Processed forms *Barley:* water, sugar (candy), malted, malted flour, malt syrup. *Oats:* instant oatmeal, quick-cooking, puffed.
Typical dishes *Barley:* krupnik (soup with meat and mushrooms, Poland); flatbread (Scandinavia); in mutton and leek broth (Wales); with beans and smoked pork (Yugoslavia); Scotch broth (soup with vegetables and mutton, Scotland); with oats (Scotland); salad with celery, avocado, and red onion (USA); baked casserole (Germany); porridge (Finland); cold salad with chicken and avocado (Italy); cereal with raisins and currants (Germany); cereal with cinnamon, cranberry juice and raisins (Netherlands). *Oats:* cream crowdie (toasted and served with cream and brown sugar,

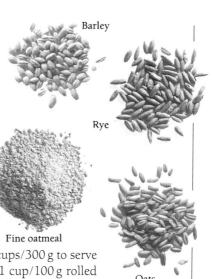

Barley

Rye

Fine oatmeal

Oats

Scotland); bannocks (griddle bread, Scotland); *parevalling* (porridge with pears, Denmark); oatmeal and raisin cookies (USA); apple crumble (UK); oatmeal jelly (Scotland, Wales); *potage à l'avoine* (soup, France); herrings coated with oatmeal (UK); dumplings (Finland); parkin (cake with treacle, UK). *Rye:* cookies (Sweden); Mecklenburg baked ham (in rye crust, Germany); raisin rye (with raisins and chopped ham, USA); Boston brown bread (USA).

Homemade granola Makes 4 cups/300 g to serve 8-10 people. Thoroughly mix 1 cup/100 g rolled oats, ½ cup/30 g wheat bran, ¼ cup/30 g sunflower seeds, 1 cup/85 g sliced almonds, ¼ cup/40 g sesame seeds. Toast in a 400°F/200°C oven 15 minutes. Add 1 tbsp oil, ½ cup/70 g raisins, 10 chopped, pitted dates, 6 chopped, dried figs, and 1 tbsp honey. Pack in an airtight container and refrigerate up to 3 weeks. Serve as a breakfast cereal with milk or yogurt, topped with fresh fruit or more honey.

UNUSUAL GRAINS

Several grains now being cultivated commercially are likely to be of increasing importance. Triticale was the first man-made grain, developed in Sweden in the late 1950s. It is a hybrid of wheat (botanical name *Triticum*) and rye (*Secale*). Triticale berries are longer and more shriveled than wheat, with a pleasant taste, a high protein content and generous amounts of lysine, an essential amino acid. The berries may be cooked like wheat and when flaked, they can substitute for rolled oats. The gluten (Flour, Breads and Batters, p.342) in triticale flour is delicate, so for yeast breads, triticale must be mixed with wheat.

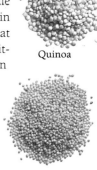

Quinoa

Amaranth

The quinoa plant, native to the South American Andes and now cultivated in the United States and China, is billed as a "supergrain", with a high content of essential nutrients. Unfortunately, quinoa has one disadvantage: the outer layer of seeds (like buckwheat, quinoa is not a true cereal grain) is filled with bitter, soapy resin that must be removed before the grain is palatable. Quinoa has a unique, grassy flavor and is used in meat substitutes, breads and pasta. The tiny, round grains may also be cooked whole as a substitute for rice.

Amaranth is a similar "supergrain", native to Mexico. When cooked, the tiny amaranth grains turn quite sticky with a strong flavor. Too robust as a side-dish pilaf or salad base, amaranth is better suited to hearty vegetable or meat casseroles. It may also be cooked like polenta (p.319), or chilled and sliced for frying to serve with syrup and butter.

Job's Tears, named for its shape, is an ancient Asian grain that is new to Western markets. It is also called river grain, or *yobe*.

LEGUMES

Plants that yield edible seeds in a pod, often consumed after drying, are known as legumes and include beans, lentils and dried peas. As a source of food, they are second only to cereal grains in importance. Rich in proteins, fats, carbohydrates and minerals, they often take the place of meat in a vegetarian diet.

Choosing and storing legumes

Legumes should have a clear, bright color and a plump appearance; if they are dusty or broken, it is a sign of age, while pinprick holes may betray insect infestation. Legumes should be of even size, so that they cook at the same speed. They become drier with age, and will need longer cooking. The older and drier the legume, the more it tends to fall apart during cooking – good for purées, but not appropriate for dishes such as baked beans, for which the legume should remain whole even when tender. They are resistant to disease and are rarely treated with chemicals, but should be picked over before cooking to remove grit and husks. Once moistened, legumes begin to sour and ferment.

Soaking legumes

Most dried legumes must be soaked in water before cooking, as this shortens cooking time and helps prevent splitting. However, lentils and split peas are often tender enough to need little or no soaking, and some beans are now processed so that they will not need soaking. Cold water can be used, or the process may be speeded by using boiling water, or by bringing the legumes to a boil, then leaving them to stand. They are likely to double in volume, so use a large pot. Some cooks soak legumes with baking soda to soften the skins, but this gives them a slightly soapy taste, and makes them more difficult to digest. Allow at least 1 qt/1 L water to 1 lb/500 g legumes. Soak for 6-8 hours or overnight, discarding any legumes that float to the surface. **Note** When hot water is used, the legumes may ferment more quickly. Alternatively, bring 1 lb/500 g beans to a boil in 1 qt/1 L water, then reduce the heat and simmer about 2 minutes. Let the legumes stand, covered, for one hour off the heat.

Simmering legumes

All dried legumes are cooked by slow simmering in a covered pan, stirring from time to time until they are tender. When baking in the oven, the liquid may be added gradually until the right amount is absorbed. Legumes should remain moist, becoming soupy. Always use a large pot to allow for expansion. Aromatic herbs, garlic, chili pepper, onions and carrots are popular additions. Acid ingredients such as tomatoes toughen legume skins and should be added when the legumes are cooked.

Legumes must first be boiled fast to eliminate toxins on the skin. Lentils and peas need only to be brought to a boil; other beans must be boiled for 10 minutes.

Testing when legumes are done

The simplest test is to taste a sample: for serving whole, the skin may be slightly chewy but the interior should be soft. For puréeing, the whole legume should be soft.

Cooked legume dishes

The most popular approach to many legumes, particularly beans, is to bake them, as in American Boston baked beans (p.324), Mexican *frijoles de olla* with garlic, lard and salt, or the celebrated French cassoulet with layers of duck or goose *confit* (p.190), garlic sausage and tomato. Beans also feature in stews that have other ingredients added to the tender beans, for example Greek white bean stew with tomato and mint, and the grand Brazilian *feijoada* of black beans with fresh and cured meats.

All legumes are well-suited to puréeing: in the Mediterranean, a lentil purée might be seasoned with lemon and garlic, while in India, split pea *dals* regularly appear as an accompaniment to curry. In the Middle East *hummus bi tahina* of chickpeas puréed with sesame paste, garlic, lemon juice and olive oil is a favorite light snack, served with pita bread, alone or with other salads. In Venezuela, black beans are served with cornbread, while Mexican refried beans are reheated in fat or with a small amount of their cooking liquid until reduced to a thick paste.

Legume-based soups include Italian white bean *zuppa di cannellini*, British split pea soup, Mexican pinto bean *tarasco* and southern American black bean soup (p.50). Legume and grain combinations include the hopping John (black-eyed peas and rice) of the American South, Mexican tortillas and refried beans, and Jamaican red beans and rice. A few legumes (like soybeans for example) can be roasted to make a crisp snack – a popular practice in Asia.

SOYBEANS

The popular Asian soybean or soya bean is small, round, and usually black or yellow, though a few varieties are red and green. Unlike most beans, it contains a good deal of oil as well as carbohydrates. The soybean may be dried and ground into flour, cracked in quick-cooking granules or grits, or processed to produce cooking oil. Fermented soybeans and miso are flavoring ingredients (p.33), while soy sauce (p.32) is a favorite condiment. Soy milk (p.68) is a popular beverage. Whole soybeans are available fresh or dried and, although they take longer to cook, may be used like white kidney beans.

Soybeans are also the basis of many health food products adopted from traditional Asian cuisine. Tofu (bean curd or soy cheese) is made by puréeing soaked soybeans with water, straining them to extract the soy "milk", cooking the milk, and adding a solidifying agent. The resulting curds are pressed to be slightly soft or very firm. Fresh tofu has very little taste when uncooked but soaks up other flavors, making it popular in stir-fries and for creamy desserts. It must be refrigerated in water and will remain fresh up to a week if the water is changed daily. Fried and baked tofu are also available.

Tempeh is made from cooked soybeans cultured with a special bacteria to form a white, distinctively flavored "cheese". It is often used as a meat substitute as it holds its shape well when cooked. Like tofu, it absorbs other flavors. Textured vegetable protein is compressed soy flour, often colored to resemble a variety of meat products. Granules may be added directly to other ingredients or in chunks that must be reconstituted by soaking in liquid.

KIDNEY BEANS

Hundreds of beans are sold dried, many of them related to the common kidney bean (*Phaseolus vulgaris*), which they resemble. Different varieties are cultivated in almost every country, but the main types can be conveniently categorized by their shape, color and cooking time.

White beans are the mature, dried seeds of the green bean (p.284) and the most common kind of kidney bean. They feature worldwide in casseroles, soups, or puréed with garlic or lemon, spices such as black pepper or fragrant herbs. Most have a mild flavor and slightly mealy texture. They also have a rather tough skin and so hold their shape well when cooked. The Boston bean, also called navy bean, pearl haricot, or pea bean, is one of the smallest varieties, as traditional in France for cassoulet as in the United States for baked beans (p.324) and Senate bean soup, favored by politicians and served on Capitol Hill every day. The Great Northern bean, also known as the haricot or white haricot bean, is slightly larger, but otherwise barely distinguishable from the Boston bean. The *cannellini* or *fazolia* bean is also small and white; first cultivated in Argentina, and now grown extensively in Italy for dishes such as minestrone soup (p.45) and *tonno e fagioli* (tuna and beans).

Not a true kidney bean, but with a similar shape, ivory color and a distinguishable black "belly", is the black-eyed bean, also called the black-eyed pea or the cowpea. It has a pleasant, smooth flavor that adapts well to almost any white bean recipe. Although native to Asia, black-eyed beans are often linked with the "soul food" of the American deep South, usually served with salt pork and hearty greens. In Africa, the same beans are mashed to make *akara* or *koose* balls, served with rice as a side dish. Unlike most other kidney beans, black-eyed beans contain vitamin A. Equally recognizable are the mild-flavored, pale-green *flageolet* beans, grown principally in France and Italy. *Flageolets* are immature beans, removed from the pod when very young. They are the most delicate of all beans. Traditionally served with roast lamb, they are also delicious in salads with a dressing of lemon juice and olive oil, or an enrichment of *crème fraîche*. Their mild flavor is easily overpowered by heavy seasoning.

Red beans are valued for their color and the robust, almost sweet flavor they develop in long-cooking stews and marinated salads. Most common is the plain red kidney bean, ranging from dark pink to deep burgundy in color, used in Mexican *chili con carne*. In the American southwest, it is baked with chili, cheese and cilantro, and in Guadaloupe may be stewed with conch

The pretty beige speckled pinto (meaning "painted" in Spanish), also called the pink bean, is native to Mexico but now grown mostly in the United States; slightly smaller than the red kidney bean, it may be substituted for it. Another speckled group are the rosecoco beans: the Italian *borlotti* has a pink background with tan markings and is often paired in salads with bitter greens such as *radicchio*; the American cranberry bean is another look-alike with a deep-red background and creamy speckles. Rosecoco beans may be substituted for pinto beans. When they are cooked, the speckled markings on all these beans disappear and they become soft and creamy in texture.

Two beans less common in the West are the red or yellow rice bean, so-called because of its taste, and the sweet adzuki or aduki, enjoyed in Asia as a side dish and in sweet confections such as

bean jam. Known in Japan as the "king of beans", the adzuki is available in many forms, including paste and flour.

The striking color of the black kidney bean conceals a creamy white interior. Smaller varieties are often referred to as turtle beans. The black bean, which is very hard when dry, cooks relatively quickly and is popular for soups and stews. It keeps its shape when cooked, so is also well suited to salads, to coarse purées, and to the bean cakes and spicy modern pâtés of American southwestern cuisine. The rust-colored Swedish or Dutch brown bean is related to the black bean, though its mild flavor more closely resembles white beans. In Central and South America the black bean turns up as *frijoles negros*, a common side dish with fried plantains. This black bean is not the same as the Asian black bean, which is actually a type of soybean that is fermented with salt and used as a flavoring (p.33).

USEFUL INFORMATION

Portion *White*: 1 cup/190 g makes 2½ cups/600 ml cooked to serve 3-4. *Red*: 1 cup/200 g makes 2½ cups/600 ml cooked to serve 3-4. *Black (turtle)*: 1 cup/180 g makes 2 cups/500 ml cooked to serve 3-4.
Nutritive value per 3½ oz/100 g (raw). *All*: no cholesterol. *White*: 340 calories; 22 g protein; 2 g fat; 61 g carbohydrates; 19 mg sodium. *Red*: 343 calories; 23 g protein; 2 g fat; 62 g carbohydrates; 10 mg sodium.
Soaking times *All*: overnight.
Cooking times *All*: vary with age. *White*: simmer 1-3 hours. *Black-eyed bean*: simmer 1-2 hours. *Red*: simmer 1-1½ hours. *Pinto, black (turtle)*: simmer 1-1½ hours.
When done Tender, or soft enough to purée.
Problems *All*: older beans may cook more slowly; if overcooked, beans become soggy; they ferment quickly on standing.
Processed forms *All*: canned, frozen.
Typical dishes *White*: spiced (Morocco); with pork, garlic sausage and tomato (France); with sour cream and bacon (Hungary); stewed with veal and cherries (Russia); *caldo gallego* (soup, Spain); casserole with bacon and pears (Germany); cowboy beans (in spicy sauce, USA); *fassolada* (vegetable soup, Greece); *garbure béarnaise* (soup with pork, vegetables, *confit*, France). *Red*: with spareribs, sauerkraut, tomatoes and sour cream (Hungary); winter succotash (pintos and corn, USA); with cheese (Mexico); *baghla polo* (with lamb and rice, Iran); with pumpkin, corn and tomatoes (Chile); stew with blood sausage and salt meat (Spain). *Black*: casserole with tomato and rice (Cuba); mashed with pork, eggs, and sausage (Brazil); with pork (Mexico). *Other*: brown beans with bacon (Netherland); *flageolet* purée (France).

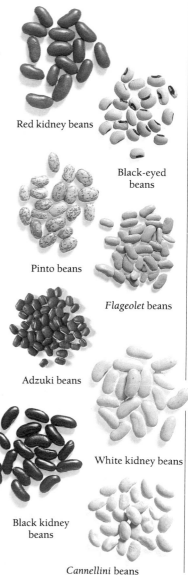

Red kidney beans

Black-eyed beans

Pinto beans

Flageolet beans

Adzuki beans

White kidney beans

Black kidney beans

Cannellini beans

Baked beans with red wine

Savory baked beans are simmered in the oven until meltingly tender. Use a large pot to allow for expansion.

Serves 8

1 lb/500 g piece of salt pork or slab of bacon, skin scored	2 cups/500 ml red wine
	1 tbsp salt, or to taste
2½ cups/500 g red kidney beans, soaked (p.322) and drained	
boiling water	*Bean pot or heavy casserole*

1 Heat the oven to 250°F/120°C. Cut a slice of salt pork or bacon and lay it in the casserole. Add the beans and remaining salt pork or bacon and boiling water to cover. Bake the beans, covered, until tender, 3-4 hours, adding more water as it is absorbed.
2 When the beans are tender, stir in the red wine. Cover and continue to cook for half an hour. At the end of cooking, the baked beans should be soupy. Remove the salt pork, dice it and replace it; taste the beans for seasoning before serving.

Variations

White beans with port wine Replace the red beans with white kidney beans in the above recipe and substitute 1 cup/250 ml port wine for the red wine. Bake as above, until beans are tender.
Boston baked beans Replace the red beans with Boston beans and add ¼ cup/60 ml molasses plus 2 tbsp sugar, or ½ cup/125 ml maple syrup and ½ tbsp dry mustard instead of the red wine. Bake the beans for 8 hours, adding more water as it is absorbed. To form a crust, as soon as the beans are tender, remove the salt pork, dice it and replace it in the beans. Bake the beans uncovered for the last half hour.

UNUSUAL LEGUMES

Mung beans are best known in the West as bean sprouts, though the bean itself is consumed worldwide. Actually a dried pea that may be green, brown or black with yellow flesh, mung beans are sweet and creamy in texture, making them popular in purées such as Indian *dal*. Whole mung beans need soaking before simmering, but often they are sold split; these do not need soaking. Asian cellophane noodles are made with mung bean flour.

The urd or black gram, another tropical Asian bean with a black coat and creamy interior, is closely related to the mung bean. Often it is skinless and split, used for spicy purées, perhaps flavored with ginger and onions. In India, the whole cooked bean is mashed and shaped into balls or pancakes. The lab lab or hyacinth bean originated in India but is now popular in the rest of Asia and the Middle East; it is sometimes called the kidney bean of Egypt. It is the seed of a type of hyacinth, and may be black or white with a hard skin that must be removed before cooking.

The red, white or speckled tepari bean also resembles a kidney bean in shape and is found in the southwestern United States and northern Mexico. The tepari can be cooked like red kidney beans, and is well suited to stews and casseroles. Its skin is thick so thorough soaking is needed before cooking. Similar in looks and taste is the American Indian anastasi bean, a legume that is enjoying renewed popularity.

The African and Caribbean pigeon pea, also known as the congo pea, or by its Indian name of *toor dal*, is slowly making its way into Western markets. It is a distinctive legume: each purple-blotched pea grows in a separate pod, and has a ridge along one side like the lab lab bean. Pigeon peas are occasionally sold fresh, but the skin of the dried peas is so thick that they are more likely to be found skinned and split. Indian savory samosa pastries are often filled with pigeon pea purée. In Africa, they are the basis of a pungent sauce, while in Jamaica pigeon peas are used in a popular stew with tomato, orange and hot spices.

A few unusual beans with particularly appealing names are now sold in the United States soon after harvesting. They do not need soaking and will cook in less than an hour. Less starchy than many other beans, these newcomers are especially well-suited to salads and purées. Examples include the brown-speckled rattle-snake bean, the purple-speckled tongues of fire and the multi-colored appaloosa bean. These kidney-shaped beans are often combined with hot spices such as chili peppers, cayenne pepper, hot sauce or mustard. More delicate in taste are brown and white speckled Christmas lima beans (named for their winter season) and the snowcap bean, which resembles a cranberry bean. The season for these fresh legumes is much shorter than the season for varieties that are sold dried.

LENTILS & PEAS

Dried peas are not easily distinguished from lentils as the terminology differs around the world. In principle, all lentils have a hard nutritious seed that must be cooked to be edible, while peas are relatively soft when young and are left to harden by drying. Different varieties of the two legumes vary little in flavor.

Large green lentils

Red lentils

Brown lentils

Marrowfat peas

Green split peas

The distinguishing characteristics of most lentils are their color and shape. They range from green to brown or orange on the outside, with a cream to russet golden flesh. The smaller the lentil, the better it tastes. Most familiar is the brownish-green continental type, and the brown lentil, both of European origin but also grown in the United States. Usually sold whole, they have a barely perceptible seed coat. In France, lentils grown on volcanic soil around Le Puy are renowned for their flavor and color, a deep green, marbled with turquoise. In the Middle East, red (often called Egyptian) and yellow lentils are more common, often referred to by their local name of *dal*. (This name is applied to many legumes, including some beans, and also to the spiced purées made from them.) *Dal* lentils are often peeled or "washed" to reveal their bright color and are usually split in two. Another popular Indian lentil is the pink or *masoor dal* lentil, a red variety that may or may not have the skin removed and that turns a yellowish color when cooked.

Always pick over lentils before cooking, as they easily camouflage small stones. Lentils rarely need soaking and if peeled they cook in a relatively short time; they quickly turn to purée as soon as they are tender. Lentils that still have their seed coat, notably the continental variety, take a little longer but keep their shape in high heat. They are excellent in soups or simply boiled to serve with meats and poultry, particularly game. In France, they are baked with lightly salted pork as *petit salé aux lentilles*, while in Asia they are often puréed to varying degrees to serve as a side dish with curries and rice.

The source of dried whole peas and split peas is the field pea, less sweet than the garden pea (Vegetables, p.284). Like lentils, dried peas have long been a staple around the Mediterranean and are now widely cultivated in northern Europe. Common varieties include the blue or gray pea, the brownish-black British carlin, the Bavarian winter pea, the brown raisin pea and the marrowfat pea, which is also sold fresh. Dried whole peas must be soaked before cooking and often need simmering to be tender.

Split peas are varieties of field pea that split in half when dried because their seed coat peels away; yellow varieties are milder than green ones. Split peas tend to be sweeter and less starchy than whole dried peas; they seldom need soaking and cook rather more quickly. The Indian *chana dal* resembles the yellow split pea, but is smaller, with a nutty taste.

USEFUL INFORMATION

Portion *Lentils, dried peas, split peas*: 1 cup/200 g makes about 2½ cups/600 ml cooked to serve 4-6.
Nutritive value per 3½ oz/100 g (raw). *All*: no cholesterol. *Lentils*: 338 calories; 28 g protein; 1 g fat; 57 g carbohydrates, 10 mg sodium. *Split peas*: 348 calories, 24 g protein; 1 g fat; 63 g carbohydrates; 40 mg sodium.
Soaking times *Lentils, split peas*: do not soak. *Whole peas*: soak overnight.
Cooking methods Vary with type and age. *Lentils, split peas*: simmer 1-1½ hours. *Whole peas*: simmer 1-2 hours.
When done Very tender.
Problems *Lentils, split peas*: fall apart when overcooked.
Processed forms Canned.
Typical dishes *Lentils*: soup with vegetables and caraway (Austria); with bacon (France); cakes with rice (India); *kichhari* (boiled with rice and ginger, India); *cotecchino con le lenticchie* (with boiled sausage, Italy); tropical lentil salad (USA); *khatti dal* (with ginger, tamarind, and turmeric, India); with dried apricots and walnuts (Germany); braised partridge (France); soup with chicken and spices (Egypt); savory pudding (Brazil); with rice and pasta (Turkey). *Whole peas*: soup with pig's knuckles (Austria). *Split peas*: *potage picard aux pois* (soup, France); *phulouri* (fritters, Trinidad); bacon and pea hot pot (UK); Maine pea soup (USA); soup with ham hocks (USA); pease pudding (UK); *grochowka* (puréed, with smoked ham, Poland); *erwtensoep* (soup with leeks, celery, potato and sausage, Netherlands).

Spiced lentil purée Serves 4-6. To accompany spiced sausages, curries, and marinated roast meats. In a saucepan combine 1¼ cups/250 g lentils with 1 onion stuck with a clove, and 1 carrot, quartered. Add 3 cups/750 ml water, cover and simmer over low heat until tender, 1-1½ hours, adding more water as necessary. Half-way through cooking add salt and pepper. At the end of cooking, the lentils should be soupy. Purée them in a food processor or work them through a food mill. In a saucepan fry a sliced onion in 2 tbsp butter until soft. Stir in 1 finely chopped clove garlic, 1 tsp each ground allspice and coriander, and ½ tsp each ground cumin and nutmeg. Sauté over low heat, stirring constantly, 2-3 minutes. Stir in the lentil purée and cook 1-2 minutes until very hot.

CHICKPEAS

For the cook, the chickpea lies somewhere between a pea and a bean, though botanically it is yet another species. Also known as garbanzo beans, and by their Italian name of *ceci*, chickpeas are a Mediterranean favorite, though they are grown worldwide. They are wrinkled and irregular in shape, somewhat larger than a pea, and colored in shades from yellow to red or black. They can be bought in cans, already cooked, and ground as flour for making traditional savory Indian pancakes and breads. When bought dried, chickpeas need soaking for several hours, before simmering for one to two hours until tender. Unlike most beans and peas, chickpeas keep their shape well and do not dissolve into a purée if overcooked. Chickpeas are best known as a key ingredient in the Middle Eastern purée *hummus bi tahina* in which they are puréed with sesame paste, garlic, lemon juice and olive oil. They also lend their rich nutty flavor to dishes ranging from the Spanish stew, *cocido*, with meat and sausage to Turkish *falafel* – deep-fried balls of chickpeas with spices – or French chickpea fritters, called *panisse*.

FAVA & LIMA BEANS

Two distinctive beans are the fava, called a broad bean in Britain, and the lima bean. Both are large, with a thick skin and a particularly meaty taste and texture. For more delicate dishes, the skin can be slipped off after cooking (p.286), rather like peeling a nut. The fava, also called the horse, Windsor, and field bean, may be eaten fresh when young but is more familiar dried or canned. This was the common European bean before the influx of New World varieties and is still popular. Round and plump with light brown skin and creamy flesh, its taste is slightly starchy. Fava beans are good in purées or served Middle Eastern-style with yogurt, and they take well to ingredients such as bacon and sausage. *Ful medames* (Egyptian brown beans) are a small variety of fava found in the Middle East; in Egypt *ful medames* is served in a dish with garlic, lemon, parsley and hard-boiled eggs.

The lima bean resembles the fava, but has a pale green skin and a more floury taste. It is eaten fresh as well as dried, in dishes such as American succotash with corn kernels. A butter bean is a large lima bean, with a similar taste but tougher skin. Like the fava, it is good with robust herbs, garlic and rich meats such as pork and duck. **Note** Favism, an anemic condition, affects certain people susceptible to the fava bean toxin, present in the beans when undercooked, or in the pollen of the plant.

USEFUL INFORMATION

Portion *Fava*: 1 cup/180 g makes 2½ cups/625 ml cooked to serve 5-6. *Lima*: 1 cup/180 g makes 2 cups/500 ml cooked to serve 3-4.
Nutritive value per 3½ oz/100 g (raw). *All*: no cholesterol. *Fava*: 341 calories; 26 g protein; 2 g fat; 58 g carbohydrates; 13 g sodium. *Lima*: 123 calories; 8 g protein; 1 g fat; 22 g carbohydrates; 2 mg sodium.
Cooking methods *Fava*: simmer 1-2 hours. *Lima*: simmer ½-1 hour.
When done Tender or soft enough to purée.
Problems Thick skin when very mature. *Fava*: long cooking reduces the chances of favism.
Processed forms *Fava*: canned. *Lima*: canned, frozen.
Typical dishes *Fava*: *ful nabed* (purée with spices, Middle East, Italy); *tamiya* (fritters, Middle East); sautéed with dill (USA); *à la tourangelle* (with ham, France); in parsley sauce (UK); risotto with sage (Italy); purée with marjoram and black pepper (USA); *alla romana* (with onion and *pancetta*, Italy); *bissara* (purée with spices, Egypt) *ful imdamis* (salad with mint and tomatoes, Middle East). *Lima*: *crema de Lima* (soup, South America); succotash (casserole with corn kernels, USA); stewed with garlic and tomatoes (France); barbecued (USA); savory loaf with green pepper and onion (USA); *gigantes plaki* (in tomato sauce, Greece); *cholent* (with onion, potato, beef, Jewish); *tzimmes* (with honey and meat, Jewish).

Lima beans

Ragout of lamb and fava beans

The globe artichoke bottoms in this Mediterranean stew may be replaced by sliced Jerusalem artichokes or carrots. Alternatively, the stew can be made without meat and served hot as a vegetable side dish or cold as a salad.

Serves 6-8

4½ lb/2 kg boneless breast or shoulder of lamb or mutton	bouquet garni
2 tbsp olive oil	2 large tomatoes, peeled, seeded and chopped
1½ lb/750 g onions, sliced	salt and pepper
¾ cup/175 ml white wine	1½ lb/750 g dried fava beans, cooked (p.322)
2½ cups/625 ml veal stock (p.44) or water (more if needed)	12 small or 6 medium artichoke bottoms (p.302)
4-5 garlic cloves, chopped	3-4 tbsp chopped parsley

1 Trim any excess fat from the meat (p.195). If using breast, cut it in sections or, if using shoulder, cut it in 2 in/5 cm chunks. Heat the oil in a heavy casserole, add the meat and brown it well on all sides over a fairly high heat.
2 Remove the meat from the casserole, add the onions and cook gently, stirring often, for 10 minutes or until they are soft but not brown. Stir in the white wine and veal stock (or water, if using), return the meat to the pan and add the garlic, bouquet garni, chopped tomatoes, salt and pepper. Bring to a boil, cover and leave to simmer 1 hour for lamb or 2 hours for mutton.
3 Gently stir in the pre-cooked fava beans. Cover and continue cooking for ¾-1 hour. Blanch the artichoke bottoms by simmering them in salted water for 5 minutes, then drain them. Add the artichokes to the meat and simmer for another 30 minutes or until the meat and artichokes are tender. Discard the bouquet garni from the ragout, stir in the parsley and taste for seasoning.
Note Add more stock or water to the beans during cooking so they remain moist but not soupy.

Bean salads

Cooked beans may be used to good effect in salads. They provide a substantial base for other flavorings, both delicate and mild, and can serve as a piquant side dish or a hearty main course. Almost any bean may be used in a salad, although those with tougher skins, such as fava beans, are less satisfactory. Beans marinate well and will soak up a dressing. Almost every country has a bean salad or, at least, one that is associated with the national cuisine. In France, lentils are a popular salad ingredient, dressed lightly with lemon juice, Dijon mustard and good quality olive oil. Seasonings such as black pepper and garlic are additional options. In Spain, pimentos and sausage are favorite partners for lentils. A combination of different colored beans – red and white kidney beans and chopped, cooked haricot beans, for example, looks attractive.

White bean salads are usually simple: in Germany, cooked bacon and tomato may be added; in Italy, tuna is a common addition, and around the Mediterranean, especially in Greece and the Middle East, white beans are often simmered in a tomato sauce with cumin, then cooled and served at room temperature with handfuls of parsley. Black beans are a favorite in American salads, often tossed in a spicy lemon or lime dressing with crunchy vegetables such as bell pepper and red onion.

Mexican bean salad Serves 8 as a side dish. Gently mix 1 lb/500 g cooked pinto beans (p.323) with one seeded and sliced cucumber, one thinly sliced medium red onion, one seeded and chopped jalapeño or other green chili pepper, and 1 tsp dried oregano leaves. Whisk together ¼ cup/60 ml cider or malt vinegar and ⅓ cup/75 ml vegetable oil. Season with salt and pepper and pour over the beans. Toss well before serving at room temperature.

Mexican bean salad can be served with sausages or cured beef.

SPROUTS

Almost any seed, grain or legume can be sprouted (that is, germinated so that it begins to grow as a plant) – a technique long applied in Asia. Grains or legumes that have been sprouted are even more nutritious than their whole counterparts as their reserves of protein and starch are converted to more soluble products that are more easily digested.

In order to sprout, the grains, beans or seeds must be whole, unhusked and unprocessed. Wheat, corn and rye all sprout well, as do most beans. The most popular commercial sprouts are those grown from mung beans (sold as "bean sprouts"), and spicy alfalfa. Soybean sprouts mold easily; they must be rinsed often and should always be cooked before eating. Commercial sprouting also extends to black-eyed beans, lentils, and to seeds such as fenugreek, pumpkin and mustard.

Sprouts may be used as both garnish and flavoring in salads, added to sandwiches for a healthy crunch, or mixed into soft cheese or eggs to make a filling. In Asia, sprouts are usually lightly cooked in stir-fried dishes or combined with other ingredients. Sprouts, especially those from wheat berries, are a good addition to hearty breads, for which they should grow to only ¼ in/6 cm. The berries may be made into flour or left whole.

Note Sorghum grains, fava and lima beans, as well as certain vegetable seeds like tomato, should not be sprouted as they may develop toxins. Also, seeds sold for planting may be treated with fungicides and should not be used for sprouting.

SPROUTING MUNG BEANS

Most sprouts are ready in 2-3 days, though some legumes and seeds, such as alfalfa and lentils, may take up to a week. Pick over the seeds carefully first, removing any stems or stones.

1 Soak about 1 tbsp seeds or ¼ cup/60 g grain or beans in 1 qt/1 L lukewarm water overnight (here, mung beans are shown). This encourages germination. **Note** Many expand to 5 or 6 times their original size, so be sure they have room to expand.

2 Drain the beans and put them in a large sterilized jar or crock, at least 1 qt/1 L capacity. Cover it with a dampened piece of cheesecloth, fasten with a rubber band, and put in a warm place around 70°F/21°C, away from direct sunlight. Rinse the beans 2-3 times a day (soybeans and chickpeas should be rinsed 4 times), filling the jar with water and then draining it before adding fresh water to cover the beans again. Keep the jar covered with cheesecloth.

3 When the sprouts have grown to the size you wish, rinse them and discard any seeds that have not germinated. Sprouts can be refrigerated up to 2 days after draining.

PASTA

PASTA IS a food that has universal appeal. While noodles, macaroni and spaghetti have long been popular both at home and in restaurants, more elaborate forms of pasta have become a symbol of the modern cuisine.

All pasta (meaning paste in Italian) is based on starchy dough. There are two kinds of dough, one containing egg, the other eggless. They are more or less interchangeable. The simpler and probably the original form is eggless pasta, made from a variety of flours, including whole wheat and rice flour. Dried commercial pasta, the most familiar type of eggless pasta, is made with hard wheat (durum) flour and water and makes a resilient dough that can withstand rolling and shaping by machine.

In the opinion of most cooks egg pasta is superior. It is best fresh, if possible made shortly before cooking. Soft flour is best for egg pastas, though durum flour, or a mix of wheat and non-wheat flours such as buckwheat and rye may be used. See also Flour, Breads and Batters, p.342.

Both eggless and egg pastas are most commonly cooked by boiling in water. Cooked pasta (*pasta asciutta*) is almost always finished with a sauce, albeit a simple one of melted butter, olive oil or a beaten egg. If served in meat or vegetable broth, it becomes *pasta in brodo*. *Tortellini*, *vermicelli* and *capellini* often feature in *brodo* recipes. Cooked pasta may also be baked in a sauce, as in lasagne. Raw pasta dough is sometimes stuffed before being boiled, as in, for example, ravioli or *tortellini*. Fruit-filled ravioli or lasagne, or noodles tossed with butter and sugar, qualify as dessert pasta, which is currently enjoying a revival on international menus. Occasionally, fresh pasta is deep-fried, as in Asian wontons.

The Italian influence has been felt in so many countries that most pasta dishes are known by their Italian names and are served in the traditional Italian way. However, the practice of serving pasta as a main dish did not originate in Italy. In a typical Italian meal, a relatively light serving of pasta is wedged between the *antipasti* – a light first course – and the main course.

Asian pasta is characterized by a wide variety of noodles. Many are made with wheat flour, with or without the addition of egg, and sold fresh or dried; others are based on vegetable starches such as mung bean starch, which is used for thread noodles and cellophane noodles, or on rice flour, for example rice sticks or *vermicelli*. **Note** Most Asian pastas can be boiled like European pastas, but rice sticks and cellophane noodles must be soaked first to soften them.

Of the many varieties of Chinese and Japanese pasta, examples now familiar in the West include Chinese wontons and egg rolls and Japanese wheat noodles such as *udon*, a flour and water noodle that can be made at home and *somen*, fine white noodles made from flour and oil that come tied in attractive little bundles. *Soba*, or buckwheat noodles, and *harusame*, made from potato starch, are two other Japanese examples.

FLOURS FOR PASTA

For details about different types of flour and their protein content see the chapter on Flour, Breads and Batters, p.342.

Semolina flour or **durum wheat flour** yields a resilient dough that is more difficult to roll and stretch at home, but easy to boil to the *al dente* stage (p.333). Used for eggless pasta doughs.

All-purpose unbleached flour results in a light dough that is easier to handle and stretch. Excellent for egg pasta doughs.

Whole wheat pasta flour should be mixed with an equal amount of all-purpose flour and may be used in egg pasta dough.

Rye flour must be mixed with wheat flour. It is not suitable for stuffed pasta.

Buckwheat flour must be mixed with wheat flour. The dough will be soft with a slightly musty taste. Use for egg pasta doughs.

Italian pasta names

Within the Italian language there are a number of adjectives that describe particular pasta shapes. *Corta* or *mezza* means short; *festonata* or *riccia*, ruffled; *fina*, thin or fine; *grande*, big; *grossa*, thick or fat; *liscia*, smooth; *lunga*, long, and *rigata*, ridged. Kitchen Italian is also rich in suffixes. For example, thin spaghetti is *spaghettini*. Other diminutives to describe small pasta are *-cino*, *-ello* and *-etto*. The suffix *-oni* means the opposite; thus *spaghettoni* are thick strands of spaghetti.

Casareccia

Conchiglie (conch shells)

Pastina (alphabet)

Orecchiette (ears

Ruoti (wheels)

Fusilli (twists)

Stellini (stars)

Farfalle (butterflies

EGGLESS PASTA

Eggless pasta is one of the great convenience foods. Sold dried in countless forms, it has an indefinite shelf-life. Unfortunately, not all dried, eggless pastas are the same: the best comes from southern Italy and is made with durum wheat (p.343). The main point to bear in mind is that good quality pasta is labeled "100% pure durum wheat" or "pure semolina". Inferior brands are apt to become mushy when cooked. Although commercial eggless pasta is widely available in stores, some cooks still take the trouble to make fresh eggless pasta at home.

The most famous eggless pasta shape is spaghetti, the easiest for manufacturers to mass-produce. Although there are other shapes that are prettier (shells or spirals), and certainly easier to eat, spaghetti holds and distributes sauce so well that it has become almost a generic name for all dried pasta. Other common eggless pasta shapes include small conceits such as *lumache* (snails) and *radiatori* (radiators). In practice, if a recipe calls for one shape, another with similar characteristics may be substituted.

Among the most attractive small shapes are *orecchiette*, tiny ear-like cups and *cavatieddi* (sea shells), perfect for capturing the olive oil and vegetable sauce with which they are commonly served. *Pastina* includes a wide variety of miniature pasta, cut into stars, letters of the alphabet or any other tiny shape. These are used in broths or tossed in butter and served with meat.

USEFUL INFORMATION

How to choose Pale gold color; slightly rough texture; good wheat flavor.

Portion (raw pasta) *Soup:* 1 oz/30 g. *Appetizer:* 2-4 oz/60-125 g, depending on sauce and use. *Main course:* 6-8 oz/180-250 g.

Cooking methods *Raw:* boiling times vary enormously with shape and thickness of pasta. *Cooked:* bake in sauce at 350°F/175°C, 20-30 minutes; deep-fry 2-5 minutes; pan-fry 3-5 minutes.

When done Bake as p.334; boil or steam until *al dente* (p.333); deep-fry until brown and crisp; pan-fry until golden brown.

Problems Raw pasta sticks if not stirred; tastes raw if underboiled.

Processed forms Dried; frozen or canned in sauce.

Storage *Dried at home:* at room temperature, up to 1 month in dry place. *Dried commercially:* indefinitely.

Typical dishes (all from Italy): *spaghetti alla puttanesca* (with tomatoes, olives, capers and garlic); *spaghetti alla rustica* (with garlic, anchovies and oregano); *spaghetti all'Amatriciana* (with pancetta, tomatoes and hot pepper); *spaghetti con briciolata* (with toasted breadcrumbs); *bucatini con le sarde alla Palermitana* (with fresh sardines); *bucatini alla boscaiola* (with eggplant, mushrooms and tomato sauce); *linguine al tonno* (with tuna); *linguine con le lumache* (with snails and parsley); *linguine con le vongole* (with clams); *vermicelli con il sugo di melanze e peperoni* (with peppers and eggplant); *zuppa di bue con spaghettini* (in beef soup); *maccheroni con cavalfiore* (with cauliflower); *perciatelli alla carrettiera* ("cart driver style" with hot peppers and pork); *penne alla Giovannino* (with sausage sauce); *rigatoni al forno con le polpettine* (with tiny meatballs); *lumache con patate* (with potatoes and cheese); *conchiglie con il sugo di salsicce, panna e pomodoro* (with sausage, cream and tomato).

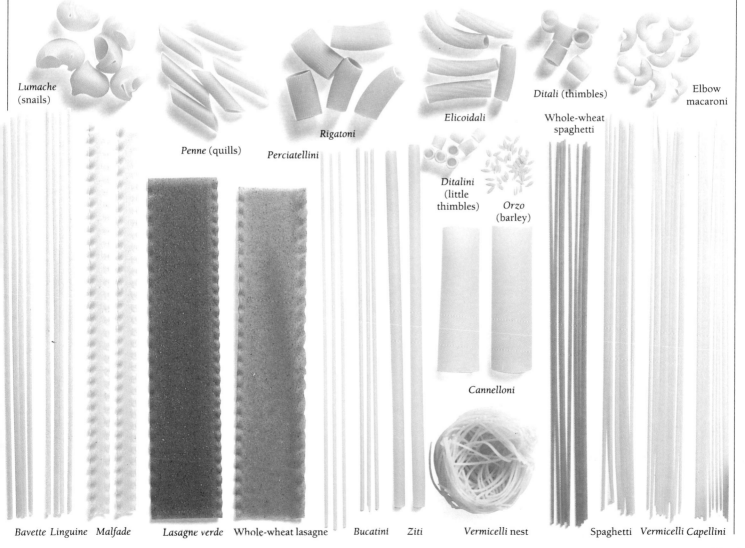

Lumache (snails)

Penne (quills)

Perciatellini

Rigatoni

Elicoidali

Ditali (thimbles)

Whole-wheat spaghetti

Elbow macaroni

Ditalini (little thimbles)

Orzo (barley)

Cannelloni

Bavette Linguine Malfade Lasagne verde Whole-wheat lasagne Bucatini Ziti Vermicelli nest Spaghetti Vermicelli Capellini

Basic eggless pasta

Eggless pasta may be made and used fresh or it can be dried (p.333). It is particularly suited to rich sauces.

Makes 1 lb/500 g

1 cup/180 g semolina flour
1 cup/125 g all-purpose flour
pinch of salt
¾ cup/175 ml water (more if needed)

1 Mix the semolina flour, all-purpose flour and salt on a work surface and make a large well in the center. Pour the water into the well and, with your fingertips, gradually stir in flour from the sides. If the dough seems dry when almost all the flour has been blended in, add more water. It should be firm not sticky, so do not add too much. Knead the dough until elastic (p.332), cover it with an upturned bowl and leave it to rest for ½-1 hour.
2 Divide the dough into two or three pieces, roll it, and cut it into the shape you want. Dry the pasta for at least 1 hour before using. Cook it in boiling salted water.

Plain eggless pasta tossed with butter.

EGG PASTA

Egg pasta (It. *pasta all'uovo*) is usually eaten fresh, although it does appear dried and packaged as egg noodles or occasionally in the United States as "Pennsylvania Dutch" noodles. Some cooks claim that the only correct way to make egg pasta is with flour and egg alone. Adding oil and salt makes a dough that is easier to roll, but the final texture is not quite as resilient. All-purpose unbleached wheat flour is normally used for egg pasta, as egg pasta made with durum wheat flour (p.343) is almost impossible to roll to the ideal thickness – a mere 1/16 in/1.5 mm. For stuffing, the pasta should be thinner still. A manual or electric pasta machine can be used to knead, roll and cut the dough to the correct shape and thickness. Common egg pasta shapes include flat, wide and narrow ribbons, stuffed shapes such as ravioli, *agnolotti*, *tortellini* and *cappelletti*, and small shapes such as bows, which are the American equivalent of *farfalle*.

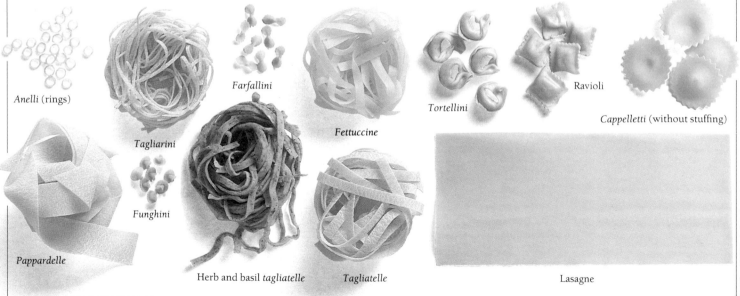

Anelli (rings)

Farfallini

Tortellini

Ravioli

Cappelletti (without stuffing)

Tagliarini

Fettuccine

Funghini

Pappardelle

Herb and basil *tagliatelle*

Tagliatelle

Lasagne

USEFUL INFORMATION

Portion *Appetizer:* 4-6 oz/125-180 g. *Main course:* ½ lb/250 g.
Cooking methods Boiling times vary with thickness and dryness of pasta. *Fresh:* 30 seconds-5 minutes. *Dried:* 3-10 minutes. *Cooked:* bake in sauce at 350°F/175°C, 20-30 minutes; deep-fry 1-2 minutes; pan-fry 5 minutes.
When done Boil until *al dente* (p.333); bake until sauce bubbles and a skewer inserted in center is hot to touch; pan-fry or deep-fry until golden brown.
Problems If dough is too soft, it sticks or tears easily; if too dry, it will crumble; rapidly overcooks when fresh.
Processed forms Dried; refrigerated; frozen.
Storage *Fresh, unfilled:* if not using within 2-3 hours, dry (p.333) and store in cool place 3-4 days; freeze 2 months. *Fresh, filled:* refrigerate 1 day; freeze 2 months.
Typical dishes *Trenette al pesto* (with *pesto* sauce, garlic and Pecorino, Italy); *kashka varnishkas* (with buckwheat groats, Jewish); *nüssnudeln* (with nuts and butter, Austria); *fettuccine* with goat cheese (USA); black pepper *fettuccine* with red pepper sauce (USA); *tagliatelle* *ai quattro formaggi* (with Parmesan, Romano, Gorgonzola and Fontina, Italy); *tagliatelle con salsa di noci* (with walnut sauce, Italy); *pappardelle con la lepre* (with hare, herbs and wine, Italy); *lasagnette del lucchese* (with sauce of spinach, ricotta, chicken livers, Italy); *garides yahni* (with braised shrimp, Greece); noodles with Roquefort (France).

MAKING FRESH EGG PASTA

Egg pasta may be eaten very fresh, within two to three hours of rolling, or it may be dried and stored (p.333). To achieve the right consistency use all-purpose unbleached wheat flour (p.342).

Makes about ¾ lb/375 g

1½ cups/180 g all-purpose unbleached flour (more if needed)	**For green pasta (pasta verde)** ½ lb/250 g spinach, Swiss chard leaves or other greens, cooked, squeezed dry and finely chopped or puréed
3 eggs, lightly beaten	
1 tbsp oil (optional)	
½ tsp salt (optional)	

1 Put the flour on the work surface and make a well in the center. Add the eggs to the well with the oil and salt (if using). The oil will make the dough softer and easier to handle. If making *pasta verde*, or another colored pasta, add the spinach or other coloring.

2 With your fingertips, gradually mix in the flour from the sides, drawing in more flour as the dough thickens. (Add more flour if the dough is too moist.)

3 Knead the dough until it is elastic and you can gather it into a ball. Cover it and leave to rest for ½-1 hour.

4 Divide the dough into 2-3 pieces, roll and cut into desired shape. Just before serving, cook in boiling salted water until *al dente* (p.333).

Variation

Buckwheat pasta Substitute ¾ cup/100 g buckwheat flour and ¾ cup/100 g all-purpose flour for the flour in the recipe.

Coloring egg pasta

Tinting pasta by adding a coloring ingredient is a popular trend, perfected by the Italians. However, though it may please the eye, colored pasta does not necessarily have more taste. For most colored pasta, the basic egg dough will need extra flour to absorb the moisture in the coloring.

Red pasta Add 1 tbsp tomato paste or 2-3 tbsp puréed cooked carrot or red pepper to the eggs.

Beet pasta Add 1 tbsp puréed cooked beet to the eggs.

Chocolate pasta Add 1 tbsp unsweetened cocoa powder to the eggs (such a small amount will not sweeten the pasta).

Saffron pasta Add a large pinch powdered saffron to the eggs.

Herb pasta Add 2 tbsp chopped fresh parsley, basil or another herb to the eggs.

Note Other, more unusual, colorants for pasta include squid ink, and chopped chili peppers which impart a spicy bite.

Making pasta by machine

Pasta dough can be made in a food processor: combine all ingredients except ½ cup/60 g flour in the work bowl. Process until the dough forms a ball. Continue working for three to five minutes until the dough is smooth and elastic, adding more flour if necessary. Cover the dough and leave it to rest as when making by hand. Very often a manual pasta machine (p.332) is used for rolling. There are also small-scale extrusion machines that knead the dough, extrude it and cut it into shapes. Extrusion machines make the task of kneading and rolling pasta dough less laborious, but be careful not to overwork it or it will yield pasta that is too soft to give the right *al dente* bite when cooked.

PASTA SALADS

Versatile and easy to make, pasta salads are now recognized as part of the cook's repertoire. The range of possibilities for pasta salads extends from simple side salads with dressings and vegetables to more substantial salads made with fish or meat. Alternatively, a selection of different pasta salads can be served as an accompaniment to various salamis and cold meats. Eggless pasta works best as it holds its shape well after cooking; short pasta such as macaroni, *rigatoni* and *lumache*, or thin ones like *linguine*, are ideal shapes for distributing the dressing. The texture of the pasta used in a salad is important too; take care not to overcook it and always rinse it after cooking to wash away the starch. The ingredients and dressing should be tossed while the pasta is still warm so that it absorbs the flavorings.

The Italians may toss pasta with a simple dressing of olive oil and freshly squeezed lemon juice, then mix it with piquant ingredients such as capers and anchovies. Plain raw or cooked vegetables, cold fish, meat or poultry are possible additions. Americans are even more creative, mixing the pasta (often colored), with combinations ranging from mayonnaise with vegetables and herbs, or spicy peanut and honey dressings, to peppery southwestern chili sauce with chicken and avocado. Stuffed pastas are also popular in salads, tossed in vinaigrette (p.64) or in a fragrant sauce such as *pesto* (p.17), to make a pleasant summer lunch. Pasta salads should be stored in the refrigerator and served slightly chilled or at room temperature.

KNEADING & ROLLING PASTA DOUGH BY MACHINE

The dough may crumble slightly at the start but will hold together after two to three rollings. It does not have to rest before rolling.

1 **To knead by machine:** set the rollers on their widest setting. Feed the dough through.

2 Fold the strip in thirds or quarters to make a square.

3 Feed the pasta dough through the machine again, starting with one of the open ends. Repeat this folding and rolling until the dough is satiny smooth and elastic, about 7-10 times. If the dough starts to stick in the machine, or rough ridges appear on the surface, dust it with a little flour before continuing.

4 **To roll by machine:** lower the rollers one notch and feed through the dough strip. From this stage on, do not fold the pasta. Continue rolling, decreasing the spacing of the rollers one notch each time until you reach the required thickness. By the end of rolling, the dough will be about 1 yd/1 m long.

CUTTING PASTA BY MACHINE

Let the dough hang over the edge of the table or work surface to dry for 5-10 minutes before cutting. When it has a leathery look, it is ready to cut. The machine can be set for a variety of widths.

1 Fit handle next to appropriate roller and run dough through.

2 As the strips of dough emerge, catch them on your hand.

KNEADING & ROLLING PASTA DOUGH BY HAND

Pasta dough can be kneaded and rolled by hand, or simply kneaded by hand, then rolled in a machine. Before kneading, the dough should be pliable, but firmer than bread dough. During kneading, more flour should be worked in if necessary so that the dough remains firm and supple.

1 **To knead by hand:** flour a work surface and knead the dough by pushing it away with the heel of your hand.

2 Peel the dough from the work surface, compress it to a ball, and repeat the pushing and peeling action several times.

3 After 10 minutes' kneading, the dough should be satiny smooth and elastic. Press your finger into the center of the dough. If it is moist, knead in a little more flour.

4 LEFT Shape the dough into a ball, cover it with an inverted bowl and leave to rest at room temperature for ½-1 hour.

5 **To roll by hand:** pat the dough into a circle. Roll it out, maintaining a roughly circular shape.

6 At the end of rolling, the dough should be a large thin sheet that is almost translucent.

7 If the dough is to be cut by hand after rolling, let it dry over a broom handle (opposite page), on a pasta rack (p.506) or on a kitchen towel, until the surface is dry but the dough is still soft and pliable, ½-1 hour. If cutting by machine (see left), dry for only 5-10 minutes. If the dough is to be filled and shaped, use it at once while it is still malleable.

CUTTING PASTA BY HAND

When you have rolled the pasta dough by machine or by hand and it has dried a little, cut it into pieces of manageable length and lay it on a floured board.

For cannelloni: with a large knife, trim the edges of the dough and cut it into 3 × 6 in/7.5 × 15 cm rectangles. (**For lasagne,** the dough is cut into strips about 2 in/5 cm wide.)

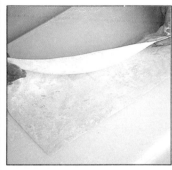

1 **For fettuccine:** generously flour the dough and shape it to a loose roll by folding it several times.

2 With a large knife, cut the rolled dough into ¼ in/6 mm strips.

3 Carefully unravel the strips of fettuccine with your hands and leave them to dry on a clean floured cloth or dish towel.

Drying and storing fresh pasta

The pasta should be dried thoroughly or mold will develop; dry it over a broom handle (below, right) propped between two chairs, or on a pasta rack (p.506), for at least two to three hours. String-shapes such as *linguine* and *fettuccine* may be left to dry between two clean dish towels (they can be curled into nests while still pliable). Lay dried unfilled pasta in a box or plastic bag, sprinkle with cornmeal so that pieces do not stick together and store at room temperature – three to four days for egg pasta, one month for eggless pasta. Stuffed pasta should be placed, without the sides touching, on a baking sheet dusted with cornmeal and refrigerated for up to a day.

Boiling pasta

To boil pasta, allow 4 qt/1 L of water for 1 lb/500 g pasta, increasing the quantity of water by 1 qt/1 L for each additional ½ lb/250 g pasta. Bring the water to a boil, add one tablespoon of salt for each 1 lb/500 g of pasta and return the water to a boil. Some cooks add a tablespoon of oil to the water in the belief that it helps to prevent sticking, but this is not necessary. Add the pasta, stirring from time to time as it cooks so that the pasta does not stick together. Long pasta, such as spaghetti, must be bent into the water as it softens, until it is completely covered. Test fresh pasta, which cooks very quickly, as soon as the water comes to a boil. Thin, dried pasta should be tested after three minutes boiling; larger dried pasta shapes may take as long as 12 minutes to cook.

Testing and draining pasta

Pasta should be boiled until it is *al dente* – firm when bitten, but cooked through with no hard center or raw taste. It is the taste more than anything else which tells you when the pasta is done. If it is to be baked after boiling, take care not to overcook it. As soon as the pasta is cooked, either drain it into a colander or, using tongs or pasta forks, lift it from the water. If serving pasta hot, transfer it to a warmed serving bowl and toss it at once with butter or sauce as appropriate. Uncoated cooked pasta will stick together as it cools. **Note** Pasta should be rinsed in cold water only if it is to be served cold, as in a salad, or cooked again as in baked or fried pastas. Rinsing prevents further cooking and washes away the surface starch.

Pan-frying and deep-frying pasta

Uncooked fresh egg pasta, particularly the string shapes, may be pan-fried in hot oil to make a crisp, brown cake to serve with sauce. Another method is to pan-fry cooked pasta in plenty of oil or butter. This ensures that the strands remain separate while the pasta browns – a favorite method for *spätzle* (p.339). Cooked pasta may also be mixed with egg, then pan-fried as a flat pancake. In Italy, filled pasta such as ravioli, and tube shapes like cannelloni are sometimes deep-fried, as in cheese-filled *focaccette fritte*. It is the Chinese who have provided our most popular fried pastas, in the form of wontons and egg rolls.

BAKED PASTA

Several different shapes of pasta are ideal for baking and many commercial eggless pastas are made specifically for this purpose. The most common in Italy is lasagne, but other favorites for baking are the tube-shaped *ziti* (little bridegrooms) and *penne* and large pasta such as *rigatoni* and *cannelloni* for stuffing. Before baking, pasta is usually boiled until just *al dente* (p.333), since it will cook further in the oven. **Note** Some baked pasta recipes call for fresh, uncooked dough.

Many sauces can be used in baked pasta dishes. Italian meat sauce (*ragù bolognese*, p.338) and French béchamel (p.54) are traditional for lasagne, where they are used in the layers to coat the pasta and provide a topping. In other baked dishes, pasta and sauce are tossed to mix before spreading in the baking dish with meat or vegetables.

More elaborate baked pasta includes the Italian *timballo*, a drum-shaped mold of pasta, *gnocchi* or rice, baked as a pie with other ingredients. There is also *pasticcio*, traditionally a sweet pastry pie filled with *tagliatelle*, macaroni or *tortellini* and sauce. However, the word *pasticcio* has come to mean any composite baked dish made with pasta and other ingredients.

USEFUL INFORMATION

Portion *Appetizer:* 4 oz/125 g. *Main course:* 6 oz/180 g.
Cooking methods Bake at 350°F/175°C, ½-¾ hour.
When done Sauce bubbles; skewer inserted into center is hot to the touch.
Problems To prevent pasta sticking, butter baking dish, or coat it with sauce; to prevent a crust, coat surface of pasta generously with sauce, or cover dish with aluminum foil.
Storage Refrigerate 2 days; freeze 3 months.
Typical dishes *Timballo con le sarde* (macaroni, sardines, pine nuts, raisins, fennel, Italy); lasagne with *pesto* and ricotta (USA); *lokshen kugel* (*vermicelli* in custard with apples and raisins, Jewish); tuna noodle casserole (USA); macaroni and cheese (USA); *pasticcio* (macaroni, white sauce, meat and tomato, Italy); chicken *tettrazini* (with cheese sauce and noodles, USA); *turos csusza* (with curd cheese, Hungary); *lasagne con anitra* (with duck, Italy); *lasagne con le verdure* (with vegetables, Italy); *schinkenfleckerln* (noodle squares with ham, Austria); *timballo di maccheroni e melanzane* (with eggplant and *pesto*, Italy).

PASTA AND CHEESE

Pasta lovers are often surprised that many Italian pasta and sauce combinations do not call for cheese. In Italy, cheese accompanies pasta in broth (*pasta in brodo*) more often than dry pasta (*pasta asciutta*) and is considered to be out of place in a pasta dish that includes delicate or distinctive flavors such as fish or olives.

If cheese is added to a finished pasta dish, use a good quality, aged variety such as a mellow Parmesan (the best is *Parmigiano-Reggiano – grana*), a slightly salty Pecorino Romano, or a nuttier cheese such as *Asiago da allevo*. Fresh mozzarella, made from either buffalo's milk (the most fragrant) or cow's milk, is the perfect choice for baking with pasta, although Bel Paese and Fontina, both rich and creamy, melt equally well. Ricotta cheese, when mixed with herbs and spinach or other cooked vegetables, is excellent for baked pasta. In a sauce, any good quality cheeses may be used. Blue-veined, tangy Gorgonzola and sharp Caciocavallo are popular, but should be used in moderation. See also Milk, Cheese and Eggs (p.73).

Spinach & ricotta lasagne

Pasta tends to absorb sauce as it bakes, so add sufficient sauce to moisten the lasagne thoroughly.

Serves 8-10 as a first course or 6-8 as a main course

fresh lasagne made with double the quantity of *pasta verde* egg pasta dough, p.331 *or* dried *lasagne verde*	pinch of ground nutmeg
	salt and pepper (to taste)
For the filling	4 cups/1 L medium béchamel sauce (p.54)
2 lb/1 kg spinach, cooked, squeezed dry and chopped	1½ cups/175 g Parmesan cheese, freshly grated
¼ cup/60 g butter	2 tbsp/30 g butter
½ lb/250 g ricotta cheese	***9 × 13 in/23 × 33 cm baking dish***

1 Heat the oven to 350°F/175°C and butter the baking dish. Cook the pasta in boiling salted water until barely *al dente* (p.333). Transfer the cooked pasta to a bowl of cold water to stop it cooking, then drain on a kitchen towel.
2 **To make the filling:** sauté the cooked spinach in the butter. Allow to cool slightly then mix with the ricotta, nutmeg and salt and pepper to taste.
3 Spread 3-4 tablespoons of the filling in the baking dish and arrange a layer of pasta on top. Spread more ricotta filling, top with another layer of pasta, cover with a thin layer of béchamel and sprinkle with grated cheese.
4 Continue layering in this manner (pasta, ricotta filling, lasagne, béchamel and cheese) until the dish is nearly full, then finish with a layer of ricotta topped with béchamel and cheese. Dot the top with the butter.
5 Bake the lasagne until very hot and the top is golden brown, 30-40 minutes. Let it rest for 5 minutes before serving.

Variation

Lasagne bolognese Substitute 5 cups/1.25 L Italian meat sauce (p.338) for the spinach and ricotta filling. Layer the lasagne with béchamel sauce, Parmesan cheese, and Italian meat sauce.

STUFFED PASTA

Both egg and eggless pasta doughs can be used for fresh stuffed pasta, the simplest of which are sandwiches with the filling contained between two layers of dough, as in the popular ravioli or *tortelli*. The sandwiches, cut in circles or squares, come in many sizes. Small parcels are another option, folded over and sealed to form triangles or half-moons. Other forms of stuffed pasta involve further folding into eccentric shapes to resemble little hats (*cappelletti*) or even "courtesans' navels" (*tortellini*). Two popular Chinese filled pastas are spring rolls and wontons (meaning "swallow a cloud"), tiny dough parcels enclosing a filling of meat, poultry, fish or vegetables that are deep-fried and served with a dipping sauce such as soy sauce.

The third category is pasta rolls – the most common being *cannelloni* – in which a large square of cooked pasta is rolled around a filling and baked. A more impressive form is a *rotolo di pasta*, in which a sheet of pasta is spread with filling, perhaps of spinach, pine nuts and ricotta cheese, and rolled, jelly-roll fashion, into a large log. The filled pasta is wrapped in a cloth, poached in water, sliced and coated with sauce to bake.

Commercially dried pasta is often sold pre-shaped for stuffing. After boiling until barely *al dente* (p.333), it can be filled with a ricotta cheese mixture or a similar stuffing. The dried version is heavier than fresh stuffed pasta, so the serving can be smaller.

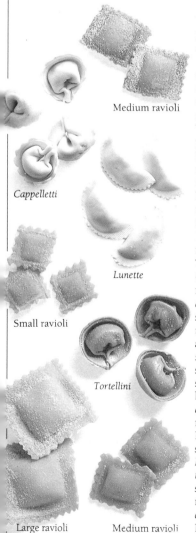

Medium ravioli

Cappelletti

Lunette

Small ravioli

Tortellini

Large ravioli   Medium ravioli

USEFUL INFORMATION

Portion *Soup or appetizer:* 4 oz/125 g. *Main course:* 6 oz/180 g.
Cooking methods Boil 5-7 minutes. *Rotolo:* poach 20 minutes, then bake at 400°F/200°C, 15 minutes.
When done Filling is tender and pasta *al dente* (p.333).
Problems Dough bursts if too much filling or pot too crowded; filling leaks if dough too soft.
Processed forms Dried; refrigerated; frozen.
Storage *Uncooked:* refrigerate up to 1 day; freeze 1 month. *Cooked:* refrigerate 2 days; freeze 3 months.
Typical dishes Cappelletti con pollo (with chicken, Italy): wild mushroom ravioli (USA); *agnolotti alla Romana* (with ground beef, salami, and Parmesan, Italy); *ravioli alla piemontese* (with beef and vegetables, Italy); *pansoti con salsa di noci alla ligure* (triangles stuffed with greens in walnut sauce, Italy); *bocconotti* (ravioli baked with sweet custard, Italy); *cannelloni alla partenopea* (with ricotta, mozzarella, and ham, Italy); *tortellini di piccioncello* (with squab stuffing, Italy); *cappelletti di Romagna* (with cheese, Italy); *tortelli di zucca* (with pumpkin stuffing, Italy); roasted sweet onion ravioli (USA); *tortellini alla panna con tartufi* (with cream and truffles, Italy).

MAKING FOLDED STUFFED PASTA

Any of the fillings given below can be used. The pasta should be rolled as thinly as possible, not more than ¹⁄₁₆ in/1.5 mm thick.

1 With a pastry cutter, cut circles or squares, about 2-3 in/5-7.5 cm squares for ravioli and 3 in/7.5 cm circles for *tortellini* and *cappelletti*.

2 Add a little filling and, with a pastry brush, paint the edge of half the dough with water.

3 Holding the dough in the palm of your hand, fold one side of pasta over the other to enclose the filling. Seal by pinching the edges together with your fingers.

4 For *tortellini* and *cappelletti*: curve the dough round your forefinger, at the same time turning the sealed edge up to make a curved upward pleat. Pinch the pointed ends together to form a ring.

Note Leave the pasta on a towel to dry, spaced well apart so that it does not stick together.

Fillings for stuffed pasta

All these recipes make about 2 cups/500 ml filling, enough to fill about 30 ravioli. Cool any cooked fillings before using.

Meat filling In a frying pan, sauté 1 small onion, 2 carrots and 1 celery stalk, all finely chopped, in 3 tbsp/45 g butter. When soft, add ½ oz/15 g dried mushrooms, soaked and chopped, and 1 lb/500 g ground lean beef. Cook, stirring, until the meat is brown, 4-5 minutes. Add ½ cup/125 ml Marsala and boil to evaporate the liquid. Add 2 tbsp tomato paste and enough of the mushroom soaking liquid to dissolve the paste. Cover the pan and simmer for 1 hour, stirring occasionally. Add more water if the mixture sticks.

Meat and spinach filling Sauté 2 oz/60 g finely chopped bacon in 1 tbsp of olive oil until the fat runs. Add 1 small finely chopped onion and cook until soft. Add 5 oz/150 g ground veal and cook until tender, about 20 minutes. Stir in 1 cup/250 g cooked spinach, finely chopped. Cool, then beat in 1 beaten egg, ¼ cup/30 g grated Parmesan, a pinch of nutmeg, salt and pepper.

Spinach and ricotta filling (See previous page.)

Pumpkin or squash filling Mix 1 cup/125 g puréed cooked pumpkin or acorn squash, 2 oz/60 g crushed *amaretti* cookies, 1 egg, 1 cup/125 g grated Parmesan cheese, ¼ cup/30 g breadcrumbs, grated nutmeg, salt and pepper to taste.

MAKING SANDWICH-STUFFED PASTA

Any of the fillings given for stuffed pasta on the previous page can be used. Here, spinach and ricotta is used.

1 Roll out a sheet of pasta as thinly as possible, not more than 1/16 in/1.5 mm thick. Trim to a neat shape and paint the surface with water.

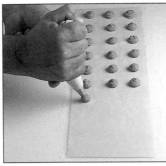 

2 With a teaspoon or pastry bag, place small mounds of filling on the dough, spacing them evenly, about 1½ in/4 cm apart.

3 Lay a second layer of pasta over the top, either by folding over part of the pasta that has no filling, or using a second piece of dough.

4 Press a floured pastry tube over the mounds to seal the layers without cutting them. Or press between them with your fingers.

5 With a pastry wheel or large knife, cut between the mounds to separate the pieces. Ravioli cutters or molds (p.506) can also be used.

Fresh stuffed pasta should be cooked within a day of being made.

Shrimp ravioli with goat cheese

Adding oil to the basic egg pasta recipe ensures that the dough is soft enough to seal the ravioli.

Makes about 30 3 in/7.5 cm square or round ravioli to serve 4-6

fresh egg pasta dough (p.331)	2 tsp lemon juice
1 lb/500 g cooked and peeled tiny shrimp, chopped	salt and pepper
	For the sauce
2 oz/60 g fresh goat cheese or cream cheese	3 cups/750 ml heavy cream
4 tbsp chopped fresh basil	4 oz/125 g fresh goat cheese or cream cheese, crumbled
2 tbsp chopped fresh parsley	6 tbsp chopped fresh basil
1 tsp chopped fresh thyme or ½ tsp dried thyme	

1 Make the pasta dough; cover and let it rest.
2 Mix together the chopped shrimp, goat cheese or cream cheese, basil, parsley, thyme, and lemon juice and season to taste with salt and pepper.
3 **For the sauce:** in a saucepan, bring the heavy cream to a boil, reduce the heat and simmer until reduced to about 2 cups/500 ml. Remove from the heat and stir in the goat cheese or cream cheese, whisking until smooth. Stir in the chopped basil, season to taste and set aside.
4 Roll out the pasta dough as thinly as possible. Set spoonfuls of filling on the dough, 1½ in/4 cm apart. Lay a second thin sheet of dough on top. With a fluted pastry cutter, cut the pasta into ravioli (left).
5 Boil the ravioli until *al dente* (p.333) and drain. Reheat the sauce and toss the ravioli with it.

PASTA SAUCES

A pasta sauce may simply be spooned on top of cooked pasta, it may be tossed with the pasta, baked with it (p.334) or served separately. The hallmark of any good pasta sauce is a full, concentrated flavor. For boiled pasta, the sauce should be used sparingly (a couple of tablespoons is usually sufficient for a portion) and ideally there should be enough to coat the pasta without leaving excess sauce in the bowl.

A few key ingredients distinguish the different categories of pasta sauce. Sauces based on olive oil include *briciolata*, in which breadcrumbs are sautéed in a generous quantity of oil until crisp, then seasoned with salt and plenty of black pepper. There are also sauces that combine olive oil with garlic and anchovy, or with puréed raw ingredients such as herbs and nuts. *Pesto* sauce (p.17), flavored with basil, oil and garlic is the best-known example. Even these simple ingredients are an unnecessary addition, as plain pasta with melted butter, or a bubbling high-quality olive oil is hard to beat.

Dairy sauces include *Alfredo*, and the popular *paglia e fieno* (so named because the combination of spinach and egg noodles recalls straw and hay) is often served with a cream, *prosciutto* and pea sauce. *Carbonara*, the egg and bacon sauce so familiar to tourists in Rome, is usually served with spaghetti.

Another family of pasta sauces is associated with the tomato, the most simple being *napoletana* (Sauces, p.65). The best-known sauce is surely *ragù bolognese*, a rich meat sauce with a generous background of tomato. Here long, slow simmering is essential to meld the many ingredients. There are also pasta sauces based on simmered wine or broth to which shellfish or vegetables are added.

Pasta sauces based on shellfish can fall into any of the main categories. Sometimes the shellfish is left in the shell, steamed open, and a *battuto* (p.263) of diced vegetables is added, along with olive oil and tomato. Alternatively, the shellfish may be shucked or peeled and sautéed in olive oil with garlic, red pepper and white wine, with or without tomato. Butter and cream are thought by Italian cooks to mask the true flavor of a shellfish sauce, and are rarely added. However, in other countries, particularly the United States, shellfish sauces often include cream and are very popular.

The following are typical sauce recipes for cooked hot pasta. Quantities are rarely followed exactly, since pasta sauces are simply a melange of flavors. (See also chapter on Sauces, p.65).

Olive oil and garlic (*aglio e olio*) For 1 lb/500 g thin pasta such as *cappellini* or *spaghettini*. Makes about ½ cup/125 ml sauce. Heat 4 finely chopped garlic cloves in ½ cup/125 ml olive oil until golden brown. Season with salt and pepper. Toss with the pasta.

Anchovy sauce For 1 lb/500 g spaghetti or *linguine*. To olive oil and garlic sauce (above), add 4 chopped anchovy fillets at the same time as the garlic.

Egg and bacon (*carbonara*) For 1 lb/500 g spaghetti or thin string-shapes. Sauté 6 oz/180 g chopped *pancetta* or bacon, 1 small, sliced onion and 1 chopped garlic clove in 2 tbsp butter until the onion is soft. Add ¼ cup/60 ml white wine and simmer until it reduces to 1 tbsp. Boil the pasta and drain. In a serving bowl, beat 3 eggs with ⅓ cup/40 g grated Parmesan cheese until mixed. Add the bacon mixture and hot pasta and toss – pasta must still be hot so egg thickens slightly. Sprinkle with 2 tbsp chopped parsley and serve.

Butter and sage (*burro e salvia*) For 1 lb/500 g egg pasta and filled pasta. Melt ½ cup/125 g butter in a saucepan. Add 16 fresh sage leaves and cook until crisp. Strain the sauce and toss with the hot pasta.

Egg and anchovy For 1 lb/500 g pasta such as *bavette*. In a serving bowl, combine 4 chopped anchovy fillets, 3 egg yolks and 4 oz/125 g chopped mozzarella. Toss with 1 lb/500 g cooked hot pasta and ⅓ cup/75 g butter, cut in pieces.

Gorgonzola For 1 lb/500 g *fettuccine* or filled pasta. Heat 4 oz/125 g crumbled Gorgonzola, ½ cup/125 ml heavy cream and 2 tbsp/30 g butter over low heat, stirring until smooth. Toss with cooked hot pasta and add ¼ cup/30 g grated Parmesan.

Alfredo For 1 lb/500 g *fettuccine*. Melt ¼ cup/60 g butter in 1 cup/250 ml heavy cream. Boil pasta, and drain. Return it to the pan with ½ cup/60 g grated Parmesan cheese and toss, off the heat, ½ minute until just melted. Pour over the melted butter and cream and toss over the heat for 1-2 minutes. Season to taste.

Primavera For 1 lb/500 g *fettuccine*. Following recipe for Alfredo, add 2 cups/500 g cooked chopped vegetables to cooked pasta before adding melted butter and cream.

Seafood (*tutto mare*) For 1 lb/500 g spaghetti. Heat ¼ cup/60 ml olive oil and sauté 1 onion and 1 carrot, chopped, until soft. Add 4 oz/125 g sliced mushrooms, 2 chopped garlic cloves, salt and pepper and toss. Lower heat and cook until liquid evaporates, 2-3 minutes. Add ¼ cup/60 ml white wine and reduce for 4-5 minutes.

Add 2 peeled, seeded and chopped plum tomatoes and simmer 5-7 minutes. Add 1 lb/500 g raw peeled shrimp and simmer 1-2 minutes. Stir in 2 lb/1 kg mussels or clams, steamed open and shucked (p.170), with 1 cup/250 ml of their liquid and ½ cup/45 g chopped parsley. Season to taste.

White clam sauce (*salsa bianca alle vongole*) For 1 lb/500 g *fettuccine* or spaghetti. Makes 2½ cups/625 ml sauce. In a heavy frying pan, brown 2 chopped garlic cloves in 1 cup/250 ml olive oil. Add 1½ lb/750 g steamed clams (p.170) with their juice, 2 tbsp chopped parsley and season. Bring just to a boil and serve.

Red clam sauce (*salsa rossa alle vongole*) For thin pasta such as *linguine*. Makes about 1 qt/1 L sauce. Using recipe for white clam sauce, add 2 lb/1 kg peeled, seeded and chopped tomatoes, or 1 lb/500 g canned crushed tomatoes to sautéed garlic.

Italian meat sauce (*ragù bolognese*) For fresh, dried and filled pasta. Sauté 2 tbsp each finely chopped onion, carrot and celery in 3 tbsp/45 ml olive oil and 3 tbsp/45 g butter until soft. Stir in 1 lb/500 g ground beef and cook, stirring, for about 5 minutes or just until the meat has lost its pink color. Add 1 cup/250 ml white

wine and cook over medium heat until wine has evaporated. Pour in ½ cup/125 ml milk with a pinch of nutmeg and cook again until liquid evaporates. Stir in 1½ lb/750 g fresh or canned peeled plum tomatoes, seeded and coarsely chopped with their juice. Simmer 3-4 hours, stirring occasionally. If the sauce starts to stick, add a little veal or chicken stock or water. Before serving season the sauce with salt and pepper.

Matching sauce and shape of pasta

Each pasta family is suited to a particular type of sauce. Most spaghetti goes well with butter and cream-based sauces, or tomato sauces, while the thinner string shapes like *vermicelli* and *linguine* are best with seafood, or sauces based on olive oil. Both thin and thick string shapes go well with strongly flavored tomato sauces containing garlic, anchovy or chili pepper.

Shorter dried pastas are good with meat sauce, in particular hollow tubes like *ziti* and *rigatoni,* and shapes like *conchiglie*, that catch plenty of sauce. Particularly well-suited are Italian meat sauce and fresh egg ribbon pasta.

Stuffed pastas call for subtle sauces, since the main seasoning is in the filling. Good accompanying sauces include tomato (with or without cream), reduced cream, or melted butter and herbs.

DESSERT PASTA

Dessert pasta, currently in fashion, has an international background. Poppy seed lasagne is an Austrian favorite also found in northern Italy, which is served with plenty of melted butter and sugar. Other sweet Italian pasta mixtures often contain chocolate or sweet chocolate powder, golden raisins, candied peel, cinnamon and even breadcrumbs. In both northern and central Europe, hot buttered pasta is sometimes tossed with nuts and sugar, and perhaps lemon peel. Sweet noodle turnover "dumplings" appear in Russia, while some Italian dessert tarts are filled with buttered noodles, sugar and sweet liqueur. Contemporary creations include fruit-filled chocolate pasta, cream or ricotta-filled sweet ravioli with chocolate or fruit sauce, *fettuccine* in fruit purée, and fruit and nut lasagne.

DUMPLINGS

Dumplings are small pieces of dough, often leavened, that are usually poached in simmering liquid. Like pasta, most dumplings are made from a paste-like mixture but with a wider range of ingredients. Some are baked in the oven, some pan-fried after poaching, and others steamed for dessert. They can be plain or filled and are served in soups, or tossed in butter or a sauce to accompany meats, poultry or vegetables.

The key to good dumplings is to keep them light while at the same time ensuring that they are firm enough to keep their shape when poached. Lightness is provided by the basic ingredient, by eggs or by a leavening agent (p.359).

There are also starchy potato dumplings such as Czechoslovakian *bramborové knedlíky*, bound with a little flour and egg, and Italian *gnocchi di patate* made with floury potatoes, egg, butter, garlic and Parmesan cheese. These are formed by a special technique in which the dough is flicked against the tines of a fork, resulting in a dumpling that is hollow, with a ridged exterior perfect for trapping a rich sauce such as *pesto* or simply melted butter. The dough can also be rolled into a long sausage and cut into pieces before poaching.

Wheat-based and flour dumplings include Jewish matzoh balls or *kneydlach*, traditionally cooked and stirred in chicken soup. A base of breadcrumbs is also popular, particularly in central Europe, for meat and vegetable variations and for well-known German liver dumplings (*leberknödeln*). Grains such as semolina and cornmeal can be used with equal success. One example is *gnocchi alla romana*, which are made with semolina bound with eggs and cheese, cooked on top of the stove and then baked in the oven with butter or more cheese.

German or Alsatian *spätzle* are batter dumplings made with eggs or breadcrumbs. They are so fragile that they must be cut into small pieces or pushed through a sieve or *spätzle* press directly into gently simmering liquid.

Fruit dumplings, topped with crisp fried breadcrumbs, or a spoonful of custard, can be the best of all. In central Europe, noodle, potato, yeast or sour cream dough is wrapped around fruits such as plums, apricots and cherries and poached or deep-fried. English apple pastry dumplings are even more delicious.

USEFUL INFORMATION

Portion Dough made with 2 cups/250 g flour makes 18-20 walnut-sized dumplings to serve 4-6.

Problems Dry dumplings are heavy; soft dumplings break up during cooking; test one dumpling in simmering liquid and add more egg or binding agent as necessary.

Cooking methods Depends on recipe. *Large plain:* simmer 10-15 minutes. *Small plain:* simmer 7-10 minutes. *Large or small filled:* simmer 12-18 minutes.

When done *Plain dumplings:* float to surface. *Filled:* tender.

Processed forms Packaged mix; frozen.

Storage *Uncooked:* refrigerate 12 hours; freeze 1 month. *Cooked:* refrigerate 2 days, with meat or fish 1 day; freeze 3 months.

Typical dishes *Topfenknödeln* (cottage cheese dumplings, Austria); *dampfknödeln* (steamed sweet dumplings, Germany); *speckknödeln* (bacon dumplings, Germany); *gnocchi alla genovese* (with *pesto* sauce, Italy); matzoh balls (with matzoh meal, Jewish); *csipetke* (small dumplings for soup, Hungary); *kødboller* (meat dumplings, Denmark); *kreplach* (three-cornered dumplings filled with meat, Jewish); *pelmeni* (yeast envelopes filled with ground beef and onion, Russia); *spätzle mit schinken* (with ham, Germany); *griessklosser gnocchi di patate* (potato dumplings, Italy); *knedle z wiśniami* (dumplings stuffed with cherries, Poland); cloutie dumpling (with dried fruit, apples and treacle, Scotland).

MAKING DUMPLINGS

The shape and cooking method for dumplings depend on the type of dough used. The proportions for a soft dough are: 1 cup/125 g flour, 1½ tsp baking powder, and ½ tsp salt to 2 tbsp/30 g butter, combined as for pie pastry (p.372). Mix in ⅓ cup/75 ml milk; a beaten egg may also be added.

For softer dumplings, drop spoonfuls of dough straight on to the top of a nearly-cooked stew, cover and simmer for 10 minutes, or until a skewer inserted into the dough comes out clean. For a firmer type of dumpling, such as *gnocchi*, add extra flour to the basic dough and drop

spoonfuls on to a floured baking sheet. Flour your hand and, with three fingers, shape a three-sided pyramid (left). Alternatively, shape the mixture into balls between your hands. Chill them for 20 minutes before poaching, covered, in simmering broth for about 15 minutes.

Dumpling recipes

Bayerische semmelknödeln (Bavarian bread dumplings). To accompany meat and poultry stews. Makes 16-18 dumplings. Discard the crusts from a 1 lb/500 g sliced loaf and cut it in large cubes. Pour over ½ cup/125 ml milk and leave for 5 minutes until soaked. Stir to break up the bread. Fry 1 finely chopped onion in 2 tbsp/30 g butter until soft but not brown and stir into the bread, together with 2 tbsp chopped parsley. Season to taste and stir in two beaten eggs to bind the mixture. Using two tablespoons, shape balls of the mixture and drop them into a pan of salted boiling water, or into soup or broth. Poach for 10-15 minutes or until the dumplings are well done (see previous page).

Matzoh balls To serve in chicken soup. Makes 16-20 balls. In a bowl whisk 4 eggs with 4 tbsp/60 g chicken fat until thoroughly mixed. Stir in 1 cup/125 g matzoh meal and 2 tbsp salt, followed by ¼ cup/60 g chicken soup or water. Cover and leave for 30 minutes to allow the matzoh meal to swell. Shape the mixture into balls, adding a little more liquid if it is too dry. Poach, covered, in soup or salted water for 12-15 minutes or until done (see previous page). **Note** Covering the pot while the balls are cooking helps to make them lighter in texture.

MAKING SPATZLE

The flour dumplings may be tossed with melted butter for serving, or sautéed in plenty of butter or oil until brown. The name *spätzle* means "little sparrows" in German.

Serves 6-8	For serving
3½ cups/440 g flour (more if needed)	½ cup/125 ml melted butter
1 tsp salt	*spätzle press (optional)*
2 eggs, beaten to mix	
1 cup/250 ml water (more if needed)	

1 Sift the flour, with the salt, on to a board. Make a well in the center and add the eggs and water. Stir, gradually drawing in more and more flour from the edges until all the ingredients are well combined and form a smooth, soft dough. Add a little more flour or water if necessary to achieve the right consistency. **Note** The softer the dough, the lighter the *spätzle* will be. If using a *spätzle* press (p.511), add more water so that the dough falls easily through the holes.

2 Bring a large pan of salted water to a boil. Divide the dough into two or three pieces. Press each piece with the heel of your hand on a floured surface until it is about ¼ in/6 mm thick.

3 With a wet knife (to prevent sticking), cut the dough into slivers. Using the knife, push the *spätzle* into boiling water. If using a *spätzle* press, squeeze out the dough while moving the press in a circular motion over the pan.

4 Simmer the *spätzle* until they rise to the surface of the water and are tender, 5-7 minutes. Remove with a slotted spoon and cook the remainder. Either toss with butter or sauté in the butter until brown. Season with salt and pepper and serve immediately.

4

page

FLOUR, BREADS & BATTERS
342

PASTRY & COOKIES
370

CAKES & ICINGS
390

SUGAR & CHOCOLATE
411

COLD DESSERTS & ICE CREAMS
430

FRUIT & NUTS
446

FLOUR, BREADS & BATTERS

IN ALMOST every culture, flour and yeast are full of symbolism. Not for nothing is bread extolled as the staff of life. No part of the repertoire of cooking is as infused with history as the harvesting of grain, the milling of flour, the fermentation of dough and the raising of bread.

Flour may be made from finely ground dried grains, from other seeds, or occasionally from roots or tubers. Wheat flour is by far the most common, while there are strong regional preferences for such flours as rye and buckwheat. This chapter looks at the great variety of breads, some raised with yeast, others with baking powder or soda, some with no leavening at all. Then the multitude of dishes which depend on flour or bread is explored, for example fried breads and fritters, bread puddings, pancakes and waffles, crêpes, batter puddings and bread stuffings.

FLOUR

The production of flour from grain is a complex process. During milling, the grain is "reduced", or broken down and sieved into specific parts called fractions. For some types of flour, notably whole wheat, the whole grain is milled; for others, the outer layers of bran and the germ (embryo), which is rich in protein, vitamins and oil, are removed. The endosperm that remains makes up 85 percent of the grain and is the part that supplies the starch. This is the part used in milling white flour. Flours milled from grains other than wheat – for example, rye – are milled from the whole grain. Coarsely ground flour is often called meal, as in cornmeal.

Storing flour
Flour should be stored in a cool, dark, dry place in an airtight container. Over a period of time the moisture and fat content, and sometimes the weight, alter; eventually the flour turns rancid. Refined white wheat flour, semolina flour, white rice flour, and starches like potato starch, keep longest – for three to six months. When refrigerated, white flour keeps well for at least a year. Whole grain flour or meals that contain the oily germ should be used within two months if possible, though they do not deteriorate seriously. It is a good idea to keep these flours separate from any plain white flours to avoid any problems of contamination. Refrigeration doubles their storage time, and they freeze well for six months. Wheat germ must be refrigerated and used within a month. Improperly stored flours and meals can become infested with small harmless beetles called weevils.

WHEAT FLOUR

There are thousands of varieties of wheat in the *Triticum* genus, each with distinctive cooking properties. As with all grains, a wheat kernel (berry) consists of three parts: the bran, the germ, and the endosperm (Grains and Legumes, p.314). Whole wheat flour is ground from the entire kernel, but for refined white flour, both germ and bran are removed. This is done because the oil in the germ can turn rancid and greatly reduce the shelf-life of flour.

The first step in making white flour is milling and bolting (sifting): the wheat kernels are ground to a fine powder between grooved rollers or millstones, then sifted through fine sieves to remove the germ and the bran, leaving flour that is made up mainly of starch and protein. Stones grind the kernels less finely, but produce less heat than metal, leaving a fuller flavor and greater nutritional value. White flour is bleached with chlorine dioxide to eliminate yellowing and speed up maturation. (Aging or maturing flour develops better baking qualities). Unbleached flour is aged naturally; it whitens to some extent, but has a more creamy color. For household baking, the two flours are interchangeable. Both are usually fortified with thiamine, riboflavin and iron to replenish some of the nutrients removed with the germ and bran.

For the cook, the most important characteristic of flour is its protein content. As the string-like proteins in the flour are kneaded with water, gluten develops and gives dough its elasticity, enabling it to be molded and to form a mesh fine enough to retain the gas bubbles generated by yeast. A hard flour contains a relatively high proportion of protein to starch, and therefore develops the strong gluten ideal for breadmaking and pasta. Soft flour is the reverse, with a high amount of starch and less gluten-forming protein, better suited to the production of light cakes and pastries.

In general, hard wheats are found in Canada and the northern United States, while soft wheats are found in more temperate regions such as western Europe and the southern United States. All-purpose flour (English plain flour and French *farine de gruau, type 45*) is a blend of hard and soft wheat flours but in general North American flours contain

Wheat flour

Instant flour

Wheat bran

Wheat germ

Unbleached flour

Sieved cake flour

a higher proportion of hard wheat than their European counterparts. American bread flour (usually chemically treated to improve the gluten's elasticity), English plain bread flour, and French *farine panifiable, type 55* (which is fortified with hard wheat and used by commercial bakers), are harder flours best for bread and pasta.

The hardest flour is made from durum wheat. It is often blended with other flours because some bakers maintain that if durum wheat flour is used alone, the dough develops too much gluten and becomes too elastic. Semolina flour (not to be confused with semolina (p.319), is milled only from the heart, or endosperm, of durum wheat and is favored for use in pasta; it is not normally used in bread doughs.

Gluten flour is manufactured from wheat flour from which most of the starch has been removed, leaving 70 percent protein. It is primarily intended for special high-protein diets, and produces a dry, fine-grained bread.

Soft wheat flours, like American cake and pastry flours, are best suited to pastry and airy cakes such as Angel food cake (p.397). Regular French flour, *farine ménagère, type 45*, is also quite soft. Approximate protein levels (which indicate gluten) are often indicated on the packaging of commercial flours. Typically, cake flour – the softest of all – contains six percent protein, soft pastry flour has seven to nine percent, all-purpose about 10 percent, and hard flour up to 12 percent.

Whole wheat flour (UK wholemeal) retains all the natural flavor and nutrients of the whole wheat grain. Particularly when stone-ground, whole wheat flour can vary greatly from mill to mill and even year to year. In Britain, a distinction is made between wholemeal flour, which is stone-ground and contains only the wheat berry, and "brown" flour, which has some of the coarsest bran removed and may contain additives. In the United States, finely milled whole wheat flour is sometimes called graham flour, (named for Sylvester Graham, the nineteenth-century Boston reformer), but strictly speaking this flour is made by extracting and finely grinding the bran and the germ, then returning some or all of it to the flour. Its composition varies from brand to brand.

Whole wheat flour is of prime importance in adding character and an agreeably chewy texture to plain yeast breads. However, even with a high proportion of protein, whole wheat flour is more difficult to use for bread, as its bran content reduces the effectiveness of the gluten and inhibits rising. Whole wheat flour is also the base of some yeastless breads such as Irish soda bread and spice muffins. However, it should not be used in pastries and cakes known for their lightness.

Self-rising (UK self-raising) flour is all-purpose flour with baking powder and salt added. It is used occasionally in yeastless breads (p.359) and in some puddings. However, many cooks prefer to vary the quantities of raising agents themselves, since those contained in self-rising flour can deteriorate over time, especially in a damp atmosphere. Instant flour is a free-pouring product that was developed as a convenient thickener for soups and sauces and is not intended for baking.

Both wheat bran and wheat germ are also available in various forms, used to give body to breads. Other wheat products, including bulghur, cracked wheat, sprouted wheat, and couscous are covered in the Grains and Legumes chapter (p.314). **Note** Each type of flour type has so many individual properties that substitutions are seldom successful, particularly in baking.

Reducing gluten

The amount of protein in a dough, and thus the amount of gluten that develops, determines baking potential and is important in making all breads and pastries. In general, high protein is beneficial to yeast bread doughs, but it can be a problem in puff pastry and folded breads such as Danish pastries or croissants (p.357), making them difficult to roll.

Hard flour mixtures, whether bread or all-purpose flour, feel drier and grittier in the hand than soft flour, but the only reliable way to test the protein content of a flour is by using it. Hard flour can be softened by adding one part of a low- or gluten-free flour such as pastry flour for every four parts of hard flour. Alternatively, gluten development can be impeded simply by adding less flour to the dough. A scant cup/110 g of hard wheat flour has the same gluten strength as one full cup/125 g pastry flour. Another solution is to work the dough as little as possible, keeping it well chilled and adding a minimum of water. Leaving dough to rest in the refrigerator also relaxes the gluten and reduces its elasticity.

Note Acid and fat have a tenderizing effect on gluten: adding one teaspoon of lemon juice or vinegar or two tablespoons of oil for every cup/125 g of hard flour, reduces elasticity and makes folded breads and pastries easier to roll.

NON-WHEAT FLOURS

Non-wheat flours and starches are made from a number of dried grains, other seeds, nuts, and even from roots and tubers such as cassava, arrowroot and potato. Their uses are quite specific, as they tend to have strong earthy flavors that do not adapt easily. Historically, in areas where wheat was scarce, they gave rise to regional dishes like Scottish oatcakes and Breton *galettes*. Only rye flour contains an adequate proportion of protein for breadmaking, although even this is better mixed with wheat flour. Some non-wheat flours can be used with chemical raising agents (p.359).

Potato flour

Buckwheat flour

Semolina

Barley flour

Corn is perhaps the most useful grain in baking other than wheat. It is frequently milled into meal. Cornmeal is best made into batter and non-yeast breads, as it contains no gluten proteins. It has a pleasantly gritty texture; the best being stone-ground flour from the whole kernel. ("Water-ground" implies the use of a water mill to grind the flour.) Cornmeal that has been "degerminated" has had the nutritious germ removed. Although it stores better than ordinary cornmeal, it loses a good deal of body and flavor in the process. "Bolted" cornmeal has been sifted to remove some of the bran layer, but it does include the germ.

Cornmeal appears in many American breads, usually leavened with baking soda or baking powder. It is the main ingredient in spoon bread – a baked pudding of cornmeal, milk and eggs – and of deep-fried cornmeal balls called hush puppies. Mexican *masa harina* is a finer corn flour that is treated with lime and used for making tortillas and other flatbreads (p.363).

Rye flour is a coarse flour milled from the husked grain. Popular in central and northern Europe, rye breads have a distinctive, sour tang and are often topped with caraway or aniseed. Triticale flour, made from a North American hybrid grain (p.321), has the sweetness of wheat flour. However, it is low in protein and must be handled gently. Nutritious triticale flakes may be added to breads for texture.

Oats are ground to meal in several degrees of coarseness, while rolled oats are made by steaming and then flattening the whole grain. Barley flour is tan-gray in color, with a pleasantly malty taste and soft, cake-like texture. Adding lightly toasted barley flour to bread dough produces a particularly tasty loaf.

Rice flour is sold brown or white; the brown variety, milled from the whole grain, bakes to be dark and dense, while white rice flour gives a dry, fine-grained crumb. It is used mainly as a thickener. A thin, edible paper made with white rice flour is used for baking very sticky confections such as macaroons. Buckwheat flour, milled from the seed of a plant related to rhubarb, is dark with a nutty flavor. It is an ingredient essential for traditional Breton crêpes and Russian *blinis*.

Other foods occasionally milled to make flour include the carob bean, which has a flavor similar to chocolate, and chickpeas, milled into *besan* flour to make savory fritters (*pakoras*) and breads. Jerusalem artichoke flour was developed in the 1920s as a nutritious alternative to whole wheat flour, and it is still used in the production of pasta and specialty breads. Soy flour, finely ground from raw soybeans, is high in protein, giving a dark crust and a slightly sweet flavor if used in bread. Breads that have some soy flour included keep well. Soya flour is made from roasted soy beans and has more body and a better taste. Millet flour produces a nutty, sweet loaf with a chewy crust and fine-grained crumb.

In those areas of the world where grains were once scarce, nuts often provide the basis for flour. Typical is sweet chestnut flour, used in Italy to make *pisticcini* bread, flavored with rosemary, pine nuts and raisins. A tablespoon or two of ground almonds, walnuts or hazelnuts, may be added to breads for additional moisture and richness without changing the balance of a dough.

STARCHES

Starch is a primary component of flour, left when the protein is separated from the rest of a grain or other plant. It is familiar to the cook as a fine white powder used for thickening sauces, fruit pies and puddings, and has the advantage of being shiny and translucent when cooked, with a light texture. Starch is a more effective thickener than flour; up to twice the volume of flour is required for the same effect.

Grains, notably corn, and roots or tubers such as arrowroot, potato and cassava (p.303) are the two main sources of starch for thickenings. Cornstarch is used for sweet sauces, puddings and Asian dishes. Arrowroot is often used to thicken fruit glazes, savory brown sauces or dessert mixes. However, if arrowroot is cooked for too long, it loses its thickening property. Potato starch has similar uses. Tapioca (finely ground from the cassava root) and sago (extracted from an Indian palm) are also used as thickeners for sauces, puddings and fruit pies. Root starches have a slightly lighter thickening effect than grain starches.

BREAD

The bread family is best divided into two parts: breads made with yeast and those made without it. Yeast breads range from the basic white loaf and crusty French and whole wheat breads, to rich specialty breads such as brioche. Yeastless breads include quick breads and batter breads such as English scones and American cornbread. They use baking powder and other chemical raising agents, and are quicker to make than yeast breads; indeed, the more rapidly they are mixed and baked, the better they are.

Breadmaking can never be an exact process. Much depends on the flour, which may absorb more or less liquid according to the type of grain, where and when the wheat was gathered, how it was milled and stored, and the quality and quantity of gluten proteins. For yeast breads, rising time varies considerably with room temperature, while kneading time depends on the flour. High altitude can also affect the way bread rises and bakes; some adjustments for this are suggested in the Cakes chapter (p.395).

Baking and cooling bread

An even circulation of oven heat is important so that breads rise and brown evenly. The oven shelves should be set one-third up from the oven floor. Baking pans should be set directly on the shelf, or on a baking sheet, leaving plenty of space for the bread to rise without touching a higher shelf or the top of the oven. To avoid the danger of collapse, do not open the oven until the dough has risen completely and has started to brown, when the pans or baking sheet may be turned around so the dough colors evenly. After baking, breads should be transferred to a rack to cool, allowing the steam to escape, and leaving a crisp crust on the bread. However, delicate yeast breads like *babas* have a soft crust that may crumble if turned out when hot.

Storing bread

All but the richest of yeastless breads – gingerbread, honey-sweetened and fruit breads – are best eaten within a few hours of baking, while some breads, such as pizza and scones, should be eaten while still warm. Yeast breads reheat successfully in a low oven, particularly if they are only a day or two old. On keeping, plain breads can turn moldy in a humid atmosphere, but more commonly they become so firm that after a few days they are unpalatably dry. French bread, with its open texture and lack of fat, becomes stale within a few hours. **Note** Dry bread is good for breadcrumbs and croûtes (p.352).

Richer yeast or yeastless breads containing a high proportion of fat, eggs or dried fruits have a longer shelf-life but soon lose some of their texture and taste. Storage time for quick breads depends very much on their richness: plain biscuits and scones are best eaten at once, while still warm. However, breads with good quantities of eggs, sugar (or honey) and, most importantly, fat, fruit or nuts, can be kept in an airtight container for a week or more. All baked breads freeze well if properly wrapped (p.496).

Glazes and toppings for bread

Almost all breads have some kind of finish added before or after baking. To flavor the crust, the bread may be shaped on a board sprinkled with rolled oats, cornmeal, chopped nuts, or simply with generous amounts of flour. Baking pans may be similarly coated. Egg glaze gives bread a shiny, golden-brown surface; for extra sheen the dough can be glazed, left to dry, then given a second coating of the glaze.

Savory toppings baked with the bread include seeds such as sesame or poppy, coarse salt crystals, and chopped or flaked nuts such as almonds (the bread is first brushed with egg white to make them stick). For a sweet baked topping, the dough may be brushed with water, milk, or lightly whisked egg white and sprinkled with sugar – coarse sugar adds a pleasant texture. Some sweet buns and coffeecakes are baked with a sticky topping. After baking, a sweet glaze made with sugar, milk, butter and honey, for example, may be poured over the bread while it is still hot (To shape sticky buns, p.356), or a soft icing may be spread on top when the bread is cold. In French *babas* and *savarin*, the baked bread is soaked in sugar syrup, often flavored with rum, so that it expands and is lusciously moist.

unglazed	water	milk	flour
butter	sugar	sugar syrup	confectioners' sugar
whole egg	egg yolk	egg white	

YEAST BREADS

The most basic yeast dough contains four primary ingredients: flour, yeast, water and salt. From such simple doughs come white bread, French bread, rye bread, whole wheat bread, country-style loaves, rolls and Middle Eastern pita bread. (In Tuscany the salt is left out of bread so that it will keep for longer, since salt absorbs moisture.) Simple doughs are often enriched with cheese, fruit or vegetables and sweet ingredients like chocolate or molasses. Other simple yeast doughs include sourdough, a specialty of San Francisco, and British crumpets, rounds of thin pancake-like honeycombed bread toasted on a griddle.

Richer yeast breads are almost always based on white flour, together with small or large amounts of butter, eggs, cream, sweeteners, fruits, nuts, herbs, and/or fillings. Many traditional rich yeast breads are associated with festivals, for example the Jewish bread, *challah*, enriched with egg and sometimes saffron, which is eaten on the Sabbath, and *panettone*, the Italian Easter bread enriched with butter and candied fruit. The dough for French brioche is so rich in eggs and butter that hardly any liquid is used in the dough at all. In rich yeast breads, the butter is layered into the dough to give a flaky, multi-leaved effect, as in croissants and Danish pastries. Many fried breads, such as crispy, puffed doughnuts, are also based on yeast.

Making yeast bread may seem complicated, but in fact the procedure is simple enough, designed to give a fine texture to the dough, and permit the nutty flavor of the yeast to develop. The breadmaking process begins with dissolving the yeast, mixing the dough, and kneading it to develop the gluten. Then the dough is left to rise. After knocking out the gas produced during rising, the dough is shaped, glazed, scored, and left to rise again until light. Finally it is baked. The method is much the same for almost all yeast breads, although individual steps may vary according to different recipes. Just occasionally, however, whole wheat bread is made like baking powder bread (p.359), and no kneading is required (a British wholemeal scone loaf is an example). The result is a crumbly rather than a resilient bread, with a soft crust.

INGREDIENTS FOR BREADS

Besides flour and raising agents, certain other ingredients bring individuality to breads.

Buttermilk and sour cream The acidity of buttermilk or sour cream releases carbon dioxide gas in baking powder and baking soda breads.

Eggs Eggs are often added for richness and to give lightness and color, particularly in quick breads.

Fats Butter is the preferred fat for breads because of its flavor; it may be added in generous quantities in croissants and brioche. Margarine is a possible substitute, while shortening gives a light texture to some coffeecakes and muffins. Oil is sometimes used in yeastless breads, making them moist and dense. A few tablespoons of oil softens the texture of yeast doughs, particularly pizza. Lard or bacon fat is used in some regional recipes. Some breads, such as French bread and Mexican tortillas, contain no fat at all.

Milk and milk solids Milk gives a softer, whiter bread than water. Dry milk has a similar effect without adding liquid.

Salt Salt is almost indispensable for adding flavor; standard proportions for plain white bread are ½ tbsp/10 g salt to 1 lb/500 g flour. Salt slows down the fermentation of yeast and is best if mixed with the flour before adding the yeast. It also affects the rising time – the more salt, the longer the rising time.

Sugar In plain breads, small quantities of sugar help to develop flavor, particularly of whole wheat and non-wheat breads. A tablespoon of brown sugar or honey is often added to the dough, while caramel is used commercially to sweeten and darken rye bread. In yeast breads the sugar is converted into carbon dioxide and alcohol during fermentation. The alcohol is driven off during baking. When fresh or compressed yeast is mixed with sugar it softens to a paste in a few minutes, but dry yeast must first be moistened before mixing with sugar. However, if the recipe calls for a large amount of sugar, which would stimulate the yeast too much, it is usually mixed with the flour so that fermentation starts slowly. For extra sweetness in rich yeast breads, sugar fillings or toppings may be added to them before or after baking.

Using yeast

Yeast is a living, single-celled organism. Scientists have identified over 400 species, but it is a specific strain that is used for making bread. Yeast leavens bread by transforming the natural sugars in the flour into tiny bubbles of carbon dioxide that become trapped in the dough. During baking, the bubbles expand to give bread its characteristic texture, lightness and taste. Yeast can only be effective in thick high-gluten doughs that are strong enough to hold in the bubbles. The way in which yeast reacts depends also on the temperature of the dough. The ideal level for fermentation is 85°F/30°C; low temperatures slow yeast activity, and at a temperature above 130°F/54°C, yeast is killed. Yeast is relatively more active in a large quantity of dough, so when doubling a recipe it is not always necessary to double the quantity of yeast.

There are two types of yeast: compressed and dry (the latter may be regular or fast-acting). Compressed yeast, also called fresh yeast, contains about 70 percent moisture and is generally sold by weight. It may be refrigerated up to two weeks or frozen up to two months. As compressed yeast ages, it turns brown and loses its potency. Dry yeast, sold in dated envelopes or jars, has a much longer shelf-life and may be stored at cool room temperature, 1 tbsp/7 g of dry yeast is the equivalent of ½ oz/15 g of compressed yeast.

There is little to choose between these two yeasts, though some cooks think compressed yeast gives a slightly better flavor. Both compressed and dry yeast are activated by dissolving in warm water (or sometimes milk), at an optimum temperature of 100°F/38°C. Dry yeast does not dissolve well in milk, however, so dissolve it in water first, then add any milk called for in the recipe. Freshness may be tested by dissolving yeast in warm water then adding a teaspoon of sugar; active yeast will bubble and froth slightly within 5-10 minutes. You can use the tested yeast for baking, or test it separately if there is no sugar in your recipe.

Fast-acting or rapid-rise yeast is a special variant of dry yeast with a fine grain that raises bread in as little as half the normal time and gives a good flavor. It does not need dissolving in water, but instead is mixed directly with the other dry ingredients. All the liquid ingredients, including any fat in the recipe, are then heated to 125°F/53°C before being added to the dough.

Selecting and preparing bread pans

Simple breads made from firm dough that holds its shape may be baked directly on a baking sheet. Always use a thick, heavy sheet that will not buckle in the high heat needed for baking. However, many breads rely on a specific pan for shape and character. Most common is the standard rectangular loaf pan. Sandwich bread is baked in a pullman pan with a lid, and French-bread pans (not used by bakers in France) are shaped like a pipe that is split horizontally. Yeast breads, particularly if the dough is rich, rise best in a narrow pan such as a *kugelhopf*, brioche or charlotte pan, with high sides to support the dough; metal molds are best for a toasted golden crust. Many doughs stick easily so greasing the mold is important. Nonstick pans can be helpful, or a nonstick lecithin spray (p.102) can be used. Black steel pans reduce baking time and encourage browning. For rich baking powder breads, the mold may be lined with paper (Cakes and Icings, p.391).

Note The pan has an important effect on the way bread bakes, and on baking time, so keep to the specified shape and size.

DISSOLVING YEAST & MAKING A SPONGE

Bread made with a sponge has a better texture. As a preliminary step in yeast breads, a sponge can be made with the yeast and some of the flour. Dissolve the yeast in warm water, allowing 3-4 tbsp/45-60 ml water per ½ oz/15 g fresh or 1 tbsp/7 g dry yeast.

1 Mix the yeast with water, warmed to the temperature recommended for the yeast (left). Leave until dissolved to a smooth paste, about 5 minutes.

2 **To make a sponge:** mix the dissolved yeast to a soft paste with a few handfuls of flour. Leave it to ferment in a warm place for an hour or more until it is spongy.

MIXING BREAD DOUGH

Since yeast rises best when warm, the mixing bowl and ingredients should be warmed. The warmth of your hand is ideal for stirring, though a wooden spoon may be used.

1 Sift the flour on to the work surface with salt and sugar. Make a large well in the center. Pour in the dissolved yeast (Step 1, above) with the other liquids. Alternatively, add the "sponge". Start mixing in the flour with your fingertips.

2 Gradually draw in all the flour, mixing with both hands or using a pastry scraper. If the dough is very sticky, add more flour.

3 The dough should be soft and slightly sticky. Scrape up crumbs from the work surface with a pastry scraper or spatula.

KNEADING BREAD DOUGH

Kneading is the most important operation in making bread. It develops the gluten-induced elasticity of the dough and distributes the gas bubbles produced by the yeast so that the bread develops a close, even texture, becoming supple and smooth. Kneading is easier and more effective if you develop a regular, rhythmic action for pushing, peeling back and turning the dough.

There are two methods of kneading, one for firm doughs such as whole wheat or rye, the other for soft doughs such as brioche. Rich doughs, containing more eggs and butter than simple doughs, take longer to knead because the sugar and fat they contain appreciably slow down the development of gluten. The larger the batch of dough, the longer it will take to knead it to the right consistency.

1 **For firm doughs:** Holding one end of the dough with one hand, press firmly down into the dough with the heel of your other hand, pushing it away from you.

2 Peel the dough back from the work surface in one piece, shape it into a loose ball and give it a quarter turn. Continue kneading in this way for 5-8 minutes, pushing the dough away from you and then gathering it up into a ball.

3 At the end of kneading, the dough should be smooth and very elastic.
Note If the dough sticks during kneading, work in a little more flour.

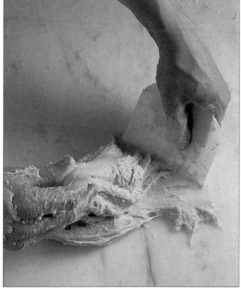

1 **For soft doughs:** gather up the dough with one hand or with the help of a scraper, then slap it down on the work surface.

2 Continue to knead the dough, throwing with one hand and then the other, for 5-8 minutes, or longer if necessary.

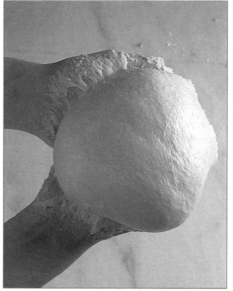

3 At the end of kneading, the dough should be very even-textured and elastic, and should feel soft and satiny smooth.

Mixing and kneading yeast dough by machine

Bread dough, whether firm or soft, may be mixed in a food processor or mixer.

If using a food processor: the machine must have a heavy duty motor, and be fitted with a short, stubby plastic kneading blade or a standard metal chopping blade. Dissolve the yeast. Add the dry ingredients to the bowl and process briefly. With the machine running, add the dissolved yeast and liquid ingredients, with just enough liquid to bring the dough together. Process the dough for 45 seconds just to start the kneading, then turn the dough on to a work surface and finish kneading by hand.

If using a mixer: choose a heavy duty machine fitted with a dough hook. Dissolve the yeast in the mixing bowl. Add the liquid ingredients and mix at low speed for a few seconds. Add most of the flour, and run the machine until these ingredients are mixed. Knead the dough at low speed for a few seconds, adding more flour if it is too sticky. The dough should be smooth, shiny and resilient. Stop the machine if necessary to scrape off any dough that is clinging to the dough hook.

Note If the dough slackens and loses its elasticity, it has been overkneaded. As a precaution, turn the dough on to a work surface and finish kneading by hand for one or two minutes.

LEAVING DOUGH TO RISE

Dough rises or "proofs" best in a warm, humid, draft-free place at an optimum temperature of 85°F/30°C, for example in a bowl inside an oven heated only by a pilot light, or on a rack over a pan of gently steaming water. At a lower temperature fermentation takes longer. At higher temperatures gas will be produced more quickly, but the bread will have a sour taste.

To improve its texture and flavor, dough is sometimes given a second rising after punching down (see below), particularly if it is made with high protein flour. This rising usually takes half as long as the first rising. If dough is left too long, air bubbles develop on the surface; when these burst the dough collapses. Very rich, delicate doughs such as brioche are sometimes left to rise in the refrigerator; this slows down the rising so that a close and even texture develops.

1 Shape the dough into a ball. To prevent it sticking, put it in an oiled bowl and turn it around so the surface is oiled also. Alternatively, the surface of the dough may be floured generously. Cover the bowl with a damp cloth and leave the dough to rise.

2 When the dough is risen completely and the gluten is stretched to its maximum elasticity, it will have almost doubled in volume. To test if the dough has risen sufficiently, press it, gently but firmly, with your fingertip. The impression should not spring back.

PUNCHING DOWN DOUGH

Before shaping, dough is punched down to knock out the air bubbles that have developed during rising. Work lightly so the dough does not become elastic.

Tip the dough out on to a lightly floured work surface. Knead lightly with your fist for ½-1 minute until the dough returns to its original volume.

SHAPING LOAVES

After punching down, dough is divided and shaped into loaves or rolls. Work on a floured board, handling the dough gently, stretching rather than tearing it. **Note** Use as little flour as possible so as not to change the proportions of the dough.

1 To form a round loaf: shape the dough into a loose ball. Fold the sides over to the center, turning to make a tight round ball.

2 Flip the ball over so that the smoothly rounded, unseamed side is upwards. If it is then slashed with a cross, this kind of a loaf is traditionally called a Coburg.

1 To form a crown loaf: shape the dough into a cylinder (French *baguette*, opposite). Curve it to form a ring. Wrap one end of the dough over the other, pinching it with your fingertips to seal it.

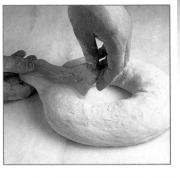

2 Transfer the ring to a greased baking sheet and let the dough rise until it has almost doubled in volume, about 45 minutes. With scissors, snip around the top surface of the ring in a zig-zag design. Bake before the dough rises further.

Crown loaf

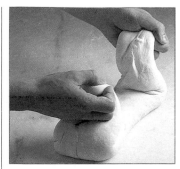

1 **To form a bread pan loaf:** pat the dough into an oval the length of the pan. Roll the oval into a cylinder. Seam side up, fold over the ends to the length of the loaf pan.

2 Flip the dough with both hands so that the folded ends are underneath, and drop it into the greased pan.

1 **To shape a French *baguette*:** pat the dough into a rectangle and roll it into a cylinder. Flatten it with your palms, stretch it into a rectangle, then roll into a cylinder.

2 Using the palms of your hands, roll the cylinder on the work surface, stretching it into a long stick shape. Transfer the loaf to a greased baking sheet.

To shape a cottage loaf: shape a third of the dough into a small, round ball. Shape the remaining dough into a round loaf and set it on a greased baking sheet. Flatten it slightly and set the smaller ball on top. Holding your forefinger vertically, press the center of the two loaves, down to the baking sheet, to hold them together.

To keep the shape of French *baguettes*: during rising, arrange them on a floured cloth, pleating it between each loaf.

1 **To form a braided loaf:** cut the dough into three even strips. Roll each strip under the palm of your hand to form a long strand, stretching and tapering each end. Line the strands up next to each other. Starting at the center and working toward one end, overlap the strands to form a braid.

2 Stretch the strands as you move toward the end to accentuate the taper, so that the loaf is fatter in the center. Turn the dough and braid the other half. Pinch the ends and tuck them under the braid.

Braided loaf

Cottage loaf

French *baguette*

SHAPING ROLLS

Rolls may be made of many different plain doughs, and they provide an excellent and attractive opportunity for displaying the flavor of whole wheat or other flours.

When shaping the dough, use only a small amount of flour on your hands and on the work surface; too much will change the consistency, making the dough too dry and stiff.

1 On a lightly floured work surface, shape the dough into a cylinder, then cut it crosswise into even pieces. Gently punch down each piece of dough to knock out the air before shaping the rolls.

2 **For a round roll:** under the cupped palm of each hand, roll a piece of dough in a circular motion to form a smooth ball. To make an oval roll, shape each ball into a broad cigar by rolling it back and forth with your fingers.

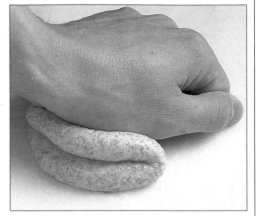

3 **For a Parker House roll:** shape a piece of dough into a ball and pat it out to a round ⅜ in/ 1 cm thick. Brush the round with butter, then fold it in half like a turnover and press down firmly with the heel of your hand.

4 **For a twist:** roll a piece of dough into a long rope, fold it in half and twist the ends one over the other. On a baking sheet, press down the ends so they do not unravel.

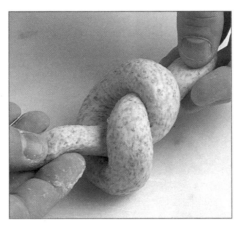

5 **For a bow knot:** roll a piece of dough into a long rope and tie a single knot, pulling the ends through.

6 **For a snail:** roll a piece of dough into a long rope and wind it round in a spiral, tucking the end underneath.

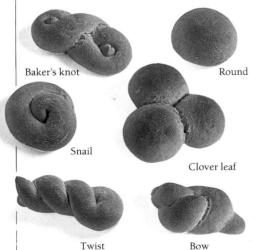

Baker's knot

Round

Snail

Clover leaf

Twist

Bow

7 **For a baker's knot:** roll a piece of dough into a long rope. Shape it into a figure eight and tuck the ends through the holes to keep them in place.

8 **For a clover leaf:** divide a piece of dough into three and shape each one into a small ball. Push them close together so that they are touching. If you like, bake the clover leaf in a muffin tin (p.509).

SHAPING PIZZA DOUGH

For pizza, use the bread dough recipe (p.353) with 2 tablespoons olive oil. The topping here is 1 can plum tomatoes, drained and chopped, 2 tablespoons olive oil, salt, 1 tablespoon tomato paste.

1 Shape the dough into a ball and flatten it into a round with a rolling pin. On a work surface, pull and slap the dough to a round ⅜ in/1 cm thick.

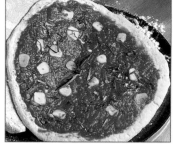

2 Transfer the dough to a heavily floured pizza paddle (p.511) or baking sheet and press the edge of the dough with your fingertips to form a shallow rim to contain the topping. Add the topping, leaving a ¾ in/2 cm border. Leave the dough to rise 10-15 minutes.

3 With a sharp jerking movement, slide the pizza on to a preheated stone, griddle or baking sheet. (If it sticks, chill for 5 minutes in the freezer.) Bake in a 450°F/230°C oven until browned, 10-15 minutes depending on the size of the pizza and thickness of the topping.

The second rising

After shaping, yeast dough is left to rise again so it almost doubles in bulk, becoming plump and puffy. The rising can take place on the work surface or on a greased baking sheet. For a crisp bottom crust, the surface may be dusted with cornmeal. If pans are used, they should be filled almost to the brim, so that the dough puffs in the oven to form a crust. This second rising can be achieved at a slightly higher temperature, around 90°F/32°C. Drafts must be avoided during rising, but often the bread cannot be covered as a cloth would stick to it. The yeast works faster in the second rising, requiring about half the time of the first.

SCORING BREAD

After brushing with glaze (p.345) and before baking, loaves or rolls are often scored with a sharp blade – diagonally (for a long loaf) or in a lattice (for a round loaf). Scoring allows the dough to expand without cracking, enhancing the appearance of the baked loaf; the deeper the cuts, the more the bread will open. Loaves can also be snipped with scissors in a "zigzag" or "hedgehog" cut.

Using a very sharp knife, scalpel or razor, slash the top of the loaf with a firm stroke, cutting about ½ in/ 1.25 cm deep.

Hedgehog roll

BAKING BREAD

Yeast bread is sensitive to the environment in which it is baked. Brick ovens are said to produce the best bread: bread stones (p.511) can be used in a domestic oven to achieve a similar effect at home. The shaped loaves are slid on to the stone from a paddle or baking sheet that has been dusted with flour or cornmeal to prevent sticking. A steamy heat develops the best crust, achieved by placing a shallow pan of boiling water in the oven with the bread. (To create a blanket of steam, drop a heated object, like a pot lid, into the water the moment you place the bread in the oven.) Alternatively, once it has started to brown, the loaf can be sprayed with water from an atomizer, or a handful of ice cubes can be tossed on the floor of the oven. (Commercial baking ovens are equipped with steam jets.)

Bread is baked at a high temperature so the yeast is killed and its action halted. As it bakes, the dough goes through three stages. During the first, called "oven spring", the gas bubbles in the dough expand and it rises rapidly. During the second stage, the dough solidifies and is transformed into bread. Finally, in the third stage, the exterior browns to a crisp or soft crust. Plain loaves should be baked at 400-425°F/200-220°C, a heat high enough to kill the yeast quite rapidly and give a good "spring" to the dough. Then, if bread browns too quickly, the oven should be turned down to finish the baking. Rolls may need a higher heat, while breads that are rich with eggs or sugar should be baked more slowly.

The crust formed by bread depends partly on the dough itself – egg or milk doughs give a soft, golden crust, while plain water-based doughs, such as French bread, bake so that they are crisp. A glaze (p.345) of egg, or brushing with water during baking crisps the crust, while milk, cream or butter glaze softens it. Steam in the oven during baking helps crisp the crust; so does the circulating air of a convection oven. Bread may be covered with a cloth as it cools, to retain steam and soften the crust.

TESTING WHEN BREAD IS DONE

The standard test for yeast bread is to take the loaf from the pan and tap the bottom. If it sounds hollow, it is cooked. As for the color, it should be well-browned on the bottom, sides and top.

Remove the loaf from the pan. Turn it upside down and tap the bottom with your knuckles. The bread should sound hollow. Press the sides, which should feel crisp and firm.

SIMPLE YEAST BREADS

Simple yeast breads depend on flour for their character. The lightest are made with white all-purpose wheat flour, the foundation of household bread, sandwich bread, French bread and pizza dough. Many rolls are also made with white flour, the crust varying from crunchy to soft and golden. More varied simple yeast breads are made with whole wheat, or one of the many flours made from other grains (p.343). An addition of sprouted or cracked wheat, rye or wheat flakes, as well as finely processed oats, can transform plain white bread into a hearty loaf. The dense texture and rich flavor of German pumpernickel bread, for example, comes from rye flour, often with molasses or un-sweetened chocolate added. Cornmeal can add a pleasant gritty texture: American anadama bread is a delicious example.

Whatever the flour used, it is the taste of the grain itself that should be highlighted in these simple breads, so other ingredients such as buttermilk, butter, sugar, honey and eggs should be added with a light hand. Savory additions such as herbs, spices and seeds can enliven bread, but if used excessively, heavy ingredients such as grated cheese will stop the dough from rising. Italian bakers are particularly imaginative, adding herbs, chopped olives and puréed pumpkin to their flat *focaccia* breads (p.363). Many central European and Scandinavian

Wheatear loaf

Round loaf

Pan loaf

breads are perfumed with dill seed, aniseed and caraway seed. An example is Swedish *limpa*, which combines these flavorings with orange peel. Cooked spicy sausage or fried diced bacon give a salty flavor, while saffron adds a golden color to any bread.

Slow, steady rising is important in developing an even texture and mature flavor for simple breads. With low protein flours, the first rising may take as long as four to five hours, though two hours is average. The dough for simple yeast breads may be shaped in many different ways (p.348), although some shapes are traditional for particular breads. A cylinder is characteristic of French bread, for example, and two rounds for a cottage loaf.

USEFUL INFORMATION

Portion Dough made with 3 cups/ 375 g flour makes a large 9 × 5 × 4 in/23 × 12 × 10 cm loaf to serve 3-4.
Typical pan Loaf pan; Pullman sandwich loaf pan.
Preparation of pan Greased.
Cooking methods *White loaves*: bake at 425°F/220°C, 15 minutes, then at 375°F/190°C, 20-30 minutes. *Dark loaves*: bake at 425°F/220°C, 15 minutes, then at 375°/190°C, 25-30 minutes. *Rolls*: bake at 450°F/230°C, 12-15 minutes. *English muffins, crumpets*: bake at medium heat on griddle, 5-7 minutes each side.
When done *Loaves*: brown, crisp crust; bottom sounds hollow when tapped; *English muffins, crumpets*: golden brown.
Problems See p.354.
Processed forms *Baked*: frozen. *Unbaked*: frozen, package mix.
Storage Best if freshly baked, or stored 2 days in an airtight container; freeze 6 months.
Glazes/toppings Egg glaze; milk, water; egg white; sesame seeds; poppy seeds; caraway seeds; rolled oats; cornmeal.
Typical simple breads Cottage (UK); buttermilk (USA); *weissbrot mit kümmel* (wheat with caraway, Germany); cracked wheat (USA); *pusstabrot* (wheat with fennel, Hungary); *pan de pueblo* (plain white, Spain); *zeppelin* (hearth-baked long loaf, Austria); *pane all'olio* (olive oil white, Italy); *pain de campagne* (peasant, France); Parker House rolls (USA); pumpernickel (Germany); *pan gallego de centeno* (Galician rye, Spain); anadama (molasses, cornmeal, USA); *bauernbrot* (buckwheat peasant, Austria); oatmeal (Scotland); English muffins (USA); crumpets (UK); *pane al latto* (milk bread, Italy).

CROUTES, CROUTONS & TOAST

The terms croûte and croûton tend to be interchangeable, referring to shapes of bread that are toasted or fried as a garnish for other foods. A croûte is usually larger than a croûton, sometimes shaped as a case by hollowing out the center of a thick slice. It makes a pleasantly crispy container for moist foods such as scrambled eggs. A croûton may be more narrowly defined as a slice of bread cut in squares, triangles, rounds – even in hearts or teardrops. Both croûtes and croûtons are added to salads, particularly of mixed greens. Fried croûtons are used to garnish dishes with a sauce or as a crispy base for foods like steak and poached egg; toasted croûtons often accompany soups and fish stews. Cubed croûtons, whether fried or toasted, are popular with cream and puréed soups. Melba toast, wafer-thin slices of bread that curl in the oven, makes a light alternative to bread rolls. (Commercially made Melba toast is flat.)

For toasted croûtes and croûtons Cut white bread in ⅜ in/1 cm slices, then trim it into the shape you want. For country dishes, crusty rolls or loaves of French bread may be sliced without trimming. Bake the bread at 350°F/175°C until crisp and lightly browned, 10-15 minutes. For garlic croûtes, rub the bread with a cut clove of garlic. Toasted croûtes and croûtons keep well for two weeks in an airtight container.

For fried croûtes and croûtons Cut white bread in ¼ in/6 mm thick slices, then cut into shape or dice it, discarding crusts. In a frying pan heat enough oil, or a combination of oil and butter, to form a ¼ in/6 mm layer. Add the bread and brown on both sides over medium heat. Stir fried croûtons constantly so that they brown evenly. Drain them on paper towels. To store for a day, wrap them in aluminum foil and reheat in the foil. Croûtes and croûtons may also be fried in clarified butter (p.99).

For toasted cubed croûtons Toast sliced bread, and while still warm, brush both sides with melted butter. Cut the toast in cubes and discard the crusts.

For Melba toast Bake the thinnest possible slices of plain white bread in a 350°F/175°C oven until curled, crisp, and unevenly brown, 8-12 minutes. Alternatively, toast sliced bread of medium thickness, discard the crusts and split the slice horizontally, placing your palm flat on the slice as you cut. Bake the slices in the oven until crisp.

Plain white bread

For a crisp crust, white bread should be baked in a steamy oven with a shallow pan of water placed on the bottom of the oven.

Makes 2 large loaves or 16-20 small rolls

½ oz/15 g compressed yeast or 1 tbsp/7 g dry yeast	1 tbsp salt
2 cups/500 ml lukewarm water	**For the glaze**
6 cups/750 g bread flour (p.343) or all-purpose flour (more if needed)	1 egg beaten to mix with ½ tsp salt

1 Dissolve the yeast in 3-4 tbsp/50 ml of the warm water in a small bowl. Sift the flour with the salt into a large warm bowl, make a well in the center and add the remaining water with the yeast. Mix with your hand, drawing in enough flour to make a thick batter. Sprinkle more of the flour on top, cover and leave in a warm place until bubbles break the surface, 15-20 minutes.
2 Mix in the remaining flour to make a smooth dough. If it is sticky, work in more flour. Knead the dough as for firm doughs (p.347) and leave it to rise, 1-1½ hours.
3 Punch the air out of the dough. Divide it in half and shape into loaves (p.348). Leave to rise ¾ hour. Brush the loaves with glaze, score the tops (p.351), and bake at 425°F/220°C for 15 minutes. Lower the heat to 375°F/190°C and continue baking 20-30 minutes longer, or until loaves sound hollow when tapped on the bottom.

Variation

White rolls Makes 16-20 small rolls. With your hands, roll the plain white bread dough into a cylinder and cut it in 16-20 pieces. Shape each piece into a roll (p.350). Leave to rise on a greased baking sheet, 15-20 minutes. Brush with glaze and bake at 425°F/220°C, 12-18 minutes, or until they sound hollow when tapped.

Simple yeast bread recipes

Whole wheat bread Makes three round loaves. Dissolve ½ oz/5 g compressed yeast or 1 tbsp/7 g dry yeast in 3-4 tbsp/50 ml lukewarm water. Stir in 1 tbsp honey. Put 4 cups/500 g stone-ground whole wheat flour, 2 cups/250 g all-purpose flour and 1 tbsp salt on a work surface and make a well in the center. Add the dissolved yeast with 2 cups/500 ml more warm water. Mix in the flour to make a smooth dough, working in more flour if it is sticky. Knead the dough as for firm doughs (p.347) and leave it to rise 2-3 hours. Punch the air out of the dough, divide it into three portions and shape each to a round loaf (p.348). Set loaves on a floured baking sheet, or in greased 6-in/15-cm round cake pans and generously flour the tops. Leave to rise again 30-45 minutes. Score the loaves (p.351), then bake 15 minutes at 425°F/220°C. Lower the oven heat to 375°F/190°C and continue baking 30-40 minutes or until the bread sounds hollow when tapped.

Whole wheat fruit and nut bread To whole wheat recipe above, add 2 tsp ground cinnamon with the flour. Knead in 7 oz/200 g chopped walnuts and 8 oz/200 g raisins before shaping the loaves.

Rye bread Makes two long loaves. Dissolve ½ oz/15 g compressed yeast or 1 tbsp/7 g dry yeast in ½ cup/125 ml lukewarm water. Put 4 cups/500 g rye flour, 4 cups/500 g whole wheat flour and 1 tbsp salt on a work surface and make a well in the center. Add 2½ cups/625 ml lukewarm milk, the yeast mixture, 3 tbsp honey and 3 tbsp oil. Mix with your hand, gradually drawing in the flour to make a smooth soft dough; work in more whole wheat flour if the dough is sticky. Knead the dough as for firm doughs (p.347). Leave it to rise until doubled in bulk, about 2 hours. Punch the air out of the dough, divide it in half and shape two French *baguettes* (p.349). Set them on a baking sheet, cover and leave to rise again, about 30 minutes. Bake at 375°F/190°C until the loaves sound hollow when tapped, 50-60 minutes.

FRENCH BREAD & SOURDOUGH

French bread is much imitated but rarely with complete success. A large number of factors contribute to its unique quality, including relatively soft flour (rather than the hard flour used for many white breads), slow rising with temperature and humidity carefully controlled, and the use of a steam oven. The bread is allowed to rise three times: the first time until tripled in bulk, the second time until doubled and the third time after being formed into long slender loaves. A *baguette*, literally "wand", is the standard size, with thinner *flûtes* and even more slender *ficelles* often sliced for *croûtes*. Larger family loaves are called simply *pains* or "bread". None of these breads has a shelf-life extending beyond a few hours. Traditional French bread is made with a cultured yeast and bacteria "starter" or leaven (Fr. *levain*), which may be a piece of dough saved from the previous batch, or a mixture of flour, water and yeast freshly mixed to make a sponge (p.346).

Sourdough bread gets its name from the agreeably tangy flavor produced by a starter of flour and water (or milk) that is activated by wild yeasts and left to ferment before being added to the dough. Historically, sourdough was made in areas where fresh yeast was scarce, and where wild, airborne spores would do the same job by feeding and multiplying in the starter mixture. Sourdough is especially successful in certain microclimates such as San Francisco, where the sourdough bread is justly famous; when moved to other regions, the starter often changes character. To make sourdough bread, a portion of the starter is combined with the remaining ingredients and the bread is finished like any other. The remaining starter is replenished with flour and water and kept to leaven subsequent batches of dough. The dough is sometimes enriched with flours such as rye or whole wheat.

Making a sourdough starter

Dissolve 2 tbsp/15 g fresh yeast or 1 tbsp/7 g active dry yeast in ¼ cup/60 ml water and 1 tsp sugar. Stir in 2 cups/500 ml warm water and about 2 cups/250 g unbleached all-purpose flour – enough to obtain a thick but pourable batter. Cover the starter with a damp cloth and set it in a warm, draft-free place. Let it ferment at room temperature for three to five days before using. Commercial sourdough starters are also available.

To use a sourdough starter, add about ½ cup/125 ml starter for every 2 tbsp/15 g of yeast called for in the recipe. (For reliable results, replace only half, not all, the fresh yeast.) Whenever you use a starter, reserve at least 1 cup/250 ml and replenish it with as much flour and water (in equal amounts) as you have taken out. Sourdough starters should be nourished every four to five days by adding ¼ cup/30 g flour and ¼ cup/60 ml water.

BREADCRUMBS

Breadcrumbs have many uses. Fresh breadcrumbs are used to bind stuffings, thicken sauces and coat food to be sautéed in butter. The soaked breadcrumb paste used to bind stuffings and dumplings, and the flour paste that is the basis of choux pastry (p.376) are both what the French call a *panade*. Dry white breadcrumbs are needed when coating food to be deep-fried. Dry brown breadcrumbs may be sprinkled on gratins and other baked dishes for color and crunch. For bread stuffings, see p. 364.

For fresh white breadcrumbs: discard crusts from fairly dry white bread and cut it in large cubes. Grind the crumbs in a food processor or blender, or work it with your hands through a drum sieve (p.506). Use within two days.

For dry white breadcrumbs: discard crusts from white bread and dry it in a warm place or very low oven until crisp. Purée in a food processor or blender, or crush with a rolling pin and work through a coarse sieve. Alternatively, dry fresh breadcrumbs in a very low oven so they do not brown. Store for one month in an airtight container.

For dry brown breadcrumbs: make as for dry white bread-crumbs, first toasting the bread in the oven at 350°F/175°C until golden brown, 10-15 minutes. Store the breadcrumbs for three months in an airtight container.

PROBLEMS WITH YEAST BREADS

Dough has risen poorly or not at all
1 Yeast was stale. See Using yeast (p.346).
2 Liquid for dissolving yeast was too hot.
3 Dough had too much soft flour, sugar, salt, fat or eggs.
4 Yeast came in contact with salt or too much sugar during mixing.
5 Dough was under- or over-kneaded.
6 Oven temperature was too low.

Heavy bread (Often the crust is dark and the loaves are misshapen.)
1 Dough had too much liquid.
2 Dough rose too much during first rising.
3 Dough did not rise enough before baking (second rising).

Soft, puffy bread (Often the crust is pale, the loaves flat and the crumb loose with open holes.)
1 Dough had too much yeast.
2 Dough rose at too high a temperature.
3 Dough rose too much before baking (second rising).
4 Oven temperature was too low.

Yeasty or sour taste
1 Dough had too much yeast, or rose too much.
2 Dough rose too fast during first rising.
3 Dough rose too slowly.

RICH YEAST BREADS

Almost all rich yeast breads are based on white flour. The interaction between all the ingredients is complex: eggs help the loaf rise higher and the fat-rich yolks lengthen shelf-life. However, during baking the egg whites tend to dry out the dough, which is one reason why butter is added in compensation. Substantial amounts of butter impede the initial activity of gluten, so many rich doughs are made in separate stages. First a basic dough is mixed and left to rise, then the butter is incorporated. Heavy ingredients such as dried fruits are kneaded in just before shaping because they can also hinder the rising of an even-textured dough. Many rich yeast doughs include a tablespoon or two of sugar to feed the yeast. An example is Vienna bread, a simple milk- and egg-based dough that is often shaped in a braid.

The richest of all breads is brioche, with a very high proportion of butter and eggs. The dough is shaped in a characteristic fluted mold, with a round "head" crowning its stubby body. As well as being shaped into small and large loaves, brioche dough may be used to make coffeecakes and raisin buns, and as a wrapping for game pâté (p.245), beef Wellington, sausages in brioche and salmon *coulibiac*. Brioche *mousseline* is usually baked in a tall cylindrical shape; traditionally it accompanies foie gras.

Most other rich yeast doughs are sweetened with more sugar, then mixed with dried fruits or nuts to make sweet rolls, buns or coffeecakes. Many are of eastern European, German or Scandina-vian origin. An Easter crown (p.356) is typical. In one French version, dough that has risen to its maximum is baked and soaked in sugar syrup as a ring-shaped *savarin*, or as tub-shaped *babas* flavored with rum. Such doughs are delicate, so maintaining the right temperature for each stage of work is important.

Ornamental shapes are characteristic of rich yeast breads as the dough is often too soft to hold its shape on a baking sheet and is usually baked in a mold. Alsatian *kugelhopf*, flavored with raisins, is baked in a fluted ring mold of the same name; *kulich*, a Russian Easter bread, is shaped in the same tall cylinder as brioche *mousseline*. Rich doughs need room to rise, so fill the molds no more than a third-to-half full, and let the dough rise to the top.

USEFUL INFORMATION

Portion Dough made with 1½ cups/175 g flour makes a 9 × 5 × 4 in/23 × 12 × 10 cm loaf to serve 4-5.

Typical mold *Brioche*: fluted. *Kugelhopf*: fluted ring. *Savarin*: plain ring. *Kulich*: cylindrical. *Baba*: small tub.

Preparation of mold Greased; for very rich doughs, grease mold, chill and grease again.

Cooking methods *Loaves*: bake at 425°F/220°C, 15 minutes, then at 375°F/190°C, 10-30 minutes longer. *Coffeecake*: bake at 400°F/200°C, 25-35 minutes. *Buns*: bake at 425°F/220°C, 15-20 minutes.

When done Crust deep golden; bottom sounds hollow when tapped and a skewer inserted in the center comes out clean.

Problems See box, above.

Storage Best if freshly baked, or store in an airtight container 3 days; freeze 6 months.

Processed forms *Baked*: frozen.

Glaze/icings Coarse and colored sugars; egg glaze; milk; egg white and sugar; honey glaze; soft icing; sugar glaze.

Typical rich breads *Choerec* (sweet, flavored with black sesame seeds and/or ground black cherry pits, Armenia); *lambropsomo* (Easter bread garnished with dyed hard-boiled eggs, Greece); sticky buns (spiral sweet rolls with cinnamon and pecans, soaked in syrup, USA); *panettone* (Easter bread enriched with butter and candied fruit, Italy); Sally Lunn (teacake enriched with butter, eggs and cream, UK); Lenten buns (milk toast with almond paste and whipped cream, UK); *veneziana* (sweet holiday bread with whole almonds, Italy); *schnecken* ("snails", small sweet breads, Germany); *barm brack* (fruit and candied peel egg loaf, Ireland); *vanocka* (braided sweet egg bread with fruit and nuts, Czechoslovakia); *pan dulce chileno* (sweet, frosted egg bread, Chile); *striezel* (large, braided holiday loaf with sultanas and lemon, Austria); hot cross buns (UK); *potica* (egg and sour cream loaf with raisins and nuts, Yugoslavia); *challah* (with egg and saffron, Jewish).

MAKING BRIOCHE

Shaping the head of a brioche loaf so that it does not sink or slip off during cooking is a sign of a skilled baker.

Makes 2 large loaves

½ oz/15 g compressed yeast or 1 tbsp/7 g dry yeast	5-6 eggs
2 tbsp lukewarm water	¾ cup/175 g cold, unsalted butter
3 cups/375 g flour (more if needed)	1 egg, beaten to mix with ½ tsp salt (for glaze)
1½ tsp salt	**Two 7-8 in/18-20 cm brioche molds**
2 tsp sugar	

1 Dissolve the yeast in the warm water (p.346). Sift the flour on to a work surface and make a large well. Add the salt and sugar in a pile on the side and separate them with a wall of flour. Drop 5 of the eggs into the well.

2 Add the yeast mixture to the well and mix it into the eggs with your fingertips, gradually drawing in the flour, salt and sugar. The dough should be soft and sloppy. If it seems dry, whisk the last egg until mixed and add as much of it as is needed to bring the dough to the correct consistency.

3 Knead the dough by hand as for soft doughs (p.347) until soft and even-textured, or use a mixer or food processor to knead it. Put the dough in an oiled bowl and leave to rise for 1½-2 hours.

4 Flatten the cold butter with a rolling pin, fold it in half, then pound and roll it until soft and pliable. Put the butter on the dough and pinch the two together repeatedly to combine.

5 Pass the dough from one hand to the other, scooping it up from the board and squeezing until the butter is completely incorporated, 3-5 minutes. Knead the dough for 1 minute more.

6 Re-oil the bowl, replace the dough, cover and let it rise again overnight in the refrigerator. **Note** When chilled, the dough is easier to form into whichever brioche shape you wish.

SHAPING BRIOCHE

For large and tall brioches, divide the dough in two. For small brioches, roll dough into a cylinder and cut into 10 pieces. Butter the molds and knead the dough lightly to punch out the air.

1 **Shaping large brioches** Pinch off one third of the dough for the "top". Shape both portions into a ball. With your fingertips, press the center of the large ball. Transfer to a large buttered brioche mold.

2 Set the small ball on top. With your fingers, push down to the base of the mold, underneath the small ball, so that the small ball is firmly attached to the large one and will not sink or slip.

Shaping small brioches Roll a piece of dough into a round, then roll it with the side of your hand to form the "top". Pinching the top between your fingers, press the dough into the mold until you can feel the base.

Shaping tall brioches Shape the dough into a ball. Elongate it slightly and drop into a buttered 1 lb/500 g coffee can lined with buttered parchment paper that extends above the rim to form a collar.

3 Let the dough rise until almost doubled in bulk and the molds are nearly full, 20-30 minutes. Heat the oven to 425°F/220°C. Brush the dough with egg glaze and bake in the oven until the bread sounds hollow when tapped. For large and tall brioches, bake at 425°F/220°C for 15 minutes, then lower the heat to 375°F/190°C and continue baking 20-30 minutes longer. For small brioches, bake at 425°F/220°C, 15-25 minutes.

Brioche *mousseline*

Large brioche   Small brioches

Coffeecake

This rich yeast dough can be shaped into a variety of plain and ornamental breads, called coffeecakes in the United States. Sticky buns are made from the same dough.

Makes 1 large coffeecake or 9 sticky buns

½ cup/125 ml milk	**For the filling**
¼ cup/60 g unsalted butter	¼ cup/60 g currants
½ oz/15 g compressed yeast or 1 tbsp/7 g dry yeast	¼ cup/60 g golden raisins
¼ cup/60 ml lukewarm water	2 tbsp chopped mixed candied peel
3 cups/375 g flour (more if needed)	¼ cup/50 g brown sugar
¾ tsp salt	½ tsp ground cinnamon
¼ cup/50 g sugar	¼ tsp ground nutmeg
1 egg, beaten to mix	grated zest of 1 lemon

1 Heat the milk and the butter until the butter has melted. Let the liquid cool to lukewarm. Dissolve the yeast in the warm water (p.346). Sift the flour into a warm bowl, add the salt and sugar and make a well in the center. Add the yeast mixture, milk and egg. Mix with your hand, gradually drawing in the flour to form a smooth dough. If the dough is sticky, work in more flour.
2 Knead the dough as for firm doughs (p.347). Leave it to rise ¾ to 1 hour. Shape and fill it (below) and leave it to rise again for ½-¾ hour. Heat the oven to 400°F/200°C.
3 Bake the bread until deep golden brown and a skewer comes out clean, 25-35 minutes. Transfer to a rack to cool.
Note: Coffeecakes can be glazed before baking, if you wish (To shape sticky buns, step 2), or iced after baking (To shape Easter crown, step 4).

Variations

Vienna bread Makes 1 loaf. In the coffeecake dough, reduce the sugar to 1 tbsp. Shape the dough into a braid (p.349) on a greased baking sheet and leave to rise. Brush with egg glaze and bake as for coffeecake until bread sounds hollow when tapped.
Streuselkuchen For streusel topping, mix 1 cup/200 g dark brown sugar, ¼ cup/30 g flour, 4 tsp ground cinnamon and stir in 6 tsp/90 g melted butter. On a floured board, roll coffeecake dough to a 8 × 12 in/20 × 30 cm rectangle. Transfer it to a greased baking sheet and spread the dough with the topping, leaving a ¾ in/2 cm border. Fold over 2 in/5 cm of the short sides, then the long sides. Leave to rise, then bake as for coffeecake.

SHAPING COFFEECAKES

The spiral design of rolled coffeecake dough shows clearly in the techniques for shaping an Easter crown and for sticky buns.

1 **To shape Easter crown:** on a floured board, roll out the dough to a 9 × 16 in/23 × 40 cm rectangle. Mix together ingredients for coffeecake filling (see recipe) and sprinkle over dough, leaving a ¾ in/2 cm border. With a rolling pin, press the filling lightly into the dough. Roll the rectangle into a cylinder, pressing the seam to seal it.

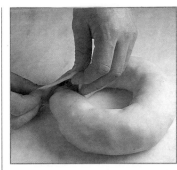

2 Curve the roll into a circle, overlapping and sealing the ends. Transfer the circle to a greased baking sheet.

3 Make a series of deep cuts around the circle with a sharp knife, without cutting right through the circle. Pull the slices apart slightly and twist them over so they lie flat, revealing the spiral design.

4 Let the dough rise and bake it (see recipe). While still hot, brush with soft icing made with ½ cup/65 g confectioners' sugar mixed with 2-3 tbsp water.

1 **To shape sticky buns:** shape a cylinder with filling as for Easter crown (step 1, left). Cut the cylinder into 9 even slices.

2 Pack the slices, cut side upward, in a greased 8 in/20 cm square pan and leave to rise (see recipe). Make a honey glaze by boiling together ½ cup/100 g sugar, ¼ cup/60 ml milk, ¼ cup/60 g butter and ¼ cup/60 g honey. Pour the glaze over the buns and bake immediately (see recipe).

3 Leave to cool for 15 minutes in the pan, then unmold, leaving the pan on top for 1-2 minutes so that the glaze drips down the sides.

FOLDED BREADS

Folded breads are rich yeast breads taken one step further: the dough is layered with butter so that the richness of brioche is combined with the flaky lightness of puff pastry. The most famous examples of folded breads are croissants and Danish pastries.

To make folded breads, the dough is sandwiched with butter and repeatedly rolled and folded in three, so that it is "turned" in the manner of puff pastry (p.378). This process distributes the butter throughout the dough in dozens, sometimes hundreds, of paper-thin layers, depending on the number of rollings. During baking, the moisture in the butter is trapped between the layers of dough and thus converts to steam, causing the dough to puff up. As baking continues, the dough dries and is transformed into flaky layers. Folded doughs are unsurpassed in their delicacy, lightness, and rich, buttery flavor.

Flaky croissants are the quintessential French breakfast bread, now enjoyed all over the world for sandwiches and snacks as well. On both sides of the Atlantic, versions are available with a variety of sweet fillings, including fruit croissants (filled with jam or fruit compote), almond croissants (filled with almond paste), and *pain au chocolat*, a rectangular roll filled with chocolate. Savory croissants may have fillings such as ham, cheese, spinach, even luxuries such as sun-dried tomatoes.

Danish pastry (the Danish term is *Wienerbrod*, "Vienna bread", reflecting its true origin) is made in the same way as croissant dough, but the pastry always has a sweet filling and is often topped with a soft icing. Popular fillings include pastry cream, poppyseeds, raisins and soft fresh cheese, as well as fruits and almond paste. Danish pastries can be made in a variety of shapes, from pinwheels to snails, envelopes and crescents.

USEFUL INFORMATION

Portion Dough made with 4 cups/500 g flour makes 12-16 croissants or pastries.
Typical pan Baking sheet.
Preparation of baking sheet Greased.
Storage Best freshly baked or 2 days in airtight container; freeze 6 months.
Cooking methods *Croissants*: bake at 425°F/220°C, 5 minutes, then at 375°F/190°C, 10-12 minutes longer. *Danish pastries*: bake at 400°F/200°C, 10 minutes, then at 350°F/175°C about 10 minutes longer.
When done Crisp and deep golden brown.
Problems If gluten in flour develops too much, dough shrinks and rises poorly; to reduce the gluten of flour, see p.343; to avoid over-developing the gluten, keep the dough thoroughly chilled, handle it as little as possible, and refrigerate 20-30 minutes between turns.
Processed forms *Baked and unbaked*: packaged; frozen.
Glazes/icings Egg white and sugar; soft icing.
Typical folded breads Apple turnovers (USA); *canoe salate* (savory canoes, Italy); *gipfelteig* (crescents, Switzerland); bearclaws (Danish pastry with nut filling, USA); *kolache* (sweet fruit-filled breads, Czechoslovakia); *sörkifli* (salted crescents, Hungary); Danish pastry with lemon curd (Denmark); *gatah* (squares or rectangles, Armenia); ham and cheese croissants (USA); *fazzoletti salati* (savory turnovers, Italy).

MAKING CROISSANTS

Croissants are rolled and folded to form layers following the method for puff pastry (p.378).

Makes 12-16 croissants

4 cups/500 g flour (more if needed)	¾ cup/175 ml lukewarm water
1½ tsp/10 g salt	½ cup/125 ml lukewarm milk
3 tbsp/45 g sugar	1 cup/250 g butter
½ oz/15 g compressed yeast or 1 tbsp/7 g dry yeast	1 egg, beaten to mix with ½ tsp salt (for glaze)

1 Sift the flour with the salt and sugar on to a board and make a well in the center. Crumble or sprinkle the yeast over half the warm water in a bowl and leave until dissolved (p.346).

2 Pour the yeast mixture into the well with the milk and remaining water and mix gradually, drawing in the flour with a spatula or pastry scraper to make a smooth dough. Work just until the dough is mixed, adding more flour if it is very sticky. Shape it into a ball and let rest in the refrigerator 15 minutes.

3 Sprinkle the butter with flour and, with a rolling pin, pound it until flat. Fold it and continue pounding and folding until it is pliable. Shape the butter into an 8 in/20 cm square. Roll the dough into a 16 in/40 cm square, put the butter in the center, and fold the dough to enclose it, pinching the edges to seal the package.

4 Flatten the package of dough and butter slightly with the rolling pin and turn it over. Roll out the package to a 24 in/60 cm × 8 in/20 cm rectangle.

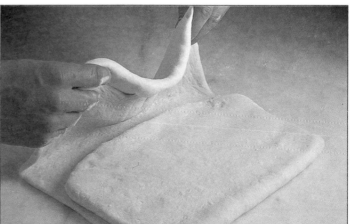

5 Fold over one of the short sides of the dough, then the other, so that the rectangle is folded in three layers, like a business letter, and forms a square. Press the open ends lightly with the rolling pin to seal them.

6 Give the dough two turns (p.378). Wrap it and let it rest in the refrigerator 20-30 minutes until firm. Give it two more turns; rest again 20-30 minutes.

SHAPING CROISSANTS

If you like, you can add a filling – chopped ham, diced cheese, or a spoonful of jam – to the croissants before rolling them into shape. Alternatively wait until the baked croissants are completely cool before splitting them horizontally and adding a filling. Filled sweet croissants can be iced with glacé icing (p.406).

1 Roll the dough to a 15 × 25 in/ 38 × 62 cm rectangle and cut it into 3 strips 5 in/13 cm wide. Cut each strip diagonally into a series of even-sized triangles.

2 Roll each triangle, starting at the long edge and ending with the point. Tuck the point underneath; this prevents the croissant from unravelling as it bakes.

3 Transfer the rolls to a greased baking sheet and shape into crescents. Cover and leave to rise until almost doubled in size. Brush the croissants with egg glaze.

4 Bake the croissants at 425°F/ 220°C until brown and crisp, 15-20 minutes. Transfer the croissants to a rack to cool.

Danish pastry

Danish pastry dough is made with more milk than croissant dough, so that it browns more easily.

Makes 12 pastries

3½ cups/400 g flour (more if needed)	¼ cup/60 ml lukewarm water
	1 tsp vanilla extract
1 tsp salt	1 cup/250 g unsalted butter
3 tbsp/45 g sugar	1 egg, beaten to mix with ½ tsp salt (for glaze)
½ oz/15 g compressed yeast or 1 tbsp/7 g dry yeast	
¾ cup/175 ml lukewarm milk	glacé icing, p.406 (optional).

1 Make dough as for croissants (p.357), adding the vanilla with the yeast mixture and milk. Roll the dough as for croissants.
2 Roll and shape the pastries (right) and set them on a greased baking sheet. Let them rise, 30-40 minutes.
3 Heat the oven to 400°F/200°C. Brush the pastries with egg glaze and bake for 10 minutes. Lower the heat to 350°F/175°C and continue baking until browned and crisp, about 10 minutes longer. Transfer the pastries to a rack and, if you like, brush with glacé icing while still warm.

SHAPING DANISH PASTRIES

Popular fillings for Danish pastries include jam, vanilla pastry cream, chopped apples or fresh cheese sweetened with sugar.

1 Roll the dough to ¼ in/6 mm thickness and cut into twelve 4 in/10 cm squares Brush the edges of each square with egg glaze.

2 **For envelopes:** add the filling to the center of the square and fold the corners into the center.

3 Press the corners firmly together with your fingertips to form a four-cornered package.

4 **For pinwheels:** add the filling. Cut diagonally from each corner to within ¾ in/2 cm of the center.

5 Fold the four alternate points to the center, pressing them down lightly to hold them in place.

6 **For Danish crescents:** Cut the dough into triangles, as for croissants. Add a filling and shape like croissants.

Crescent

Pinwheel

YEASTLESS BREADS

Yeast doughs are only half of the bread picture. A wide variety of breads, called "quick breads" in the United States, are leavened with chemical raising agents such as baking powder or baking soda, and sometimes a combination of baking powder and soda. In contrast to yeast breads, which should have the even, chewy texture produced by kneading, quick breads are soft and crumbly, particularly when the bread is sweet. As soon as liquid is added to the dough, chemical raising agents start to release carbon dioxide, so mixing must be completed within 10 minutes. Always stir gently to avoid dissipating the gas and developing the gluten in the flour. The finished dough should be soft and sticky, even pourable in some cases, with a rough appearance. Once in the oven, the carbon dioxide is released rapidly, and the dough doubles in volume before it has time to cook and set. **Note** Electric machines overwork the dough and are a drawback when making quick breads.

Yeastless breads tend to fall into two categories: simple quick breads that contain little sugar and are made with a soft dough, and batter breads, usually sweetened, made with a pourable batter. Some soft doughs are stiff enough to roll lightly or shape into a free-form loaf, but batter breads always require a loaf pan or cake pan. The batter will rise considerably in the oven, so do not fill the mold more than two-thirds full. For all these breads, toppings are simple, at most a brushing of egg glaze before baking or, for sweet breads, a soft sugar icing added after the bread has been baked. Some quick breads are best served warm.

BAKING SODA, BAKING POWDER & CREAM OF TARTAR

Baking soda and baking powder have been in common use only since the mid-nineteenth century, and feature prominently in northern European and North American recipes. They are well-suited to thin doughs, such as pancake batter, which lack sufficient gluten to contain the carbon dioxide generated by yeast. These chemical raising agents are also used with low-gluten flours that cannot be raised with yeast. They must be measured with care, and can discolor doughs containing chocolate or blueberries.

Baking soda is the common name for sodium bicarbonate. When combined with acid ingredients such as buttermilk, lemon juice or vinegar, baking soda generates carbon dioxide bubbles, thus raising the dough. The right balance of leavening agent and acid in a dough is important. For every half-teaspoon of baking soda, use 1 cup/250 ml sour milk, buttermilk or yogurt, or 1 tablespoon of lemon juice or vinegar. Baking soda can also be activated by combining it with cream of tartar (an acid in powder form) in a ratio of 2:2½, then adding milk or water.

Baking powder is a ready-prepared combination of soda and acid (usually cream of tartar), designed to give consistent results. It generates carbon dioxide on contact with water. "Double-acting" baking powder contains two acids, one activated when liquid is added at room temperature, the other activated at oven heat. As a rule, 1½ teaspoons of baking powder are needed to leaven 1 cup/125 g of flour.

SIMPLE QUICK BREADS

American biscuits and British scones are the quintessential plain quick breads. They are both made with a simple dough – based on flour and milk or buttermilk raised with baking powder or baking soda – and flavored with little else except salt and a few tablespoons of butter. For scones, the dough is lightly patted out with a fist on a floured surface to about ¾ in/2 cm thickness, then stamped in rounds. The crust of scones is pleasantly floury and the flavor slightly acid. Numerous variations may be made with dark flours and dried fruits, but the texture should always be soft and light. Scones are a British teatime treat, split and spread with butter, or served in the Cornish style with clotted cream and strawberry jam. They are best while still warm.

The classic American biscuit is very similar, being a small round cake usually eaten hot with butter and honey, or plain to accompany a meal. These biscuits may also be flavored with herbs, cheese or cracklings. Biscuits that are split while still hot and filled with whipped cream and sweetened strawberries become strawberry shortcake. They may also be split to sandwich country ham or smoked turkey, or smothered in gravy for a traditional hearty Southern breakfast. The dough can be patted out like scones, or rolled to ¼ in/6 mm thickness for crustiness. Drop biscuits are spooned directly on to the baking sheet.

Another famous American quick bread is cornbread, which may be baked southern-style in a hot skillet greased with bacon fat, or perhaps as slender corn sticks (p.360) in special iron molds. Other cornbreads may be flavored with bacon or hot pepper, or corn kernels may be added for extra texture.

Another type of quick bread is typified by the famous Irish soda bread, made with the local low-gluten whole wheat flour, and scored with a cross for even baking. In the classic version no solid fat is used at all, but only flour, buttermilk, salt and baking soda, so that the full flavor of the flour is appreciated. Like all whole wheat breads, the taste and texture of Irish soda bread varies with the flour used.

USEFUL INFORMATION

Portion Dough made with 2 cups/250 g flour makes 6-8 scones or biscuits or a loaf to serve 3-4.
Preparation of baking sheet Greased. *Scones:* greased and floured.
Cooking methods *Loaves:* bake at 400°F/200°C, 25-35 minutes. *Scones, biscuits:* oven-bake at 425°F/220°C, 12-18 minutes; griddle-bake 4-7 minutes each side.
When done *Loaves:* crust browned; bottom sounds hollow when tapped. *Scones, biscuits:* crust browned and skewer inserted in center is clean when withdrawn.
Problems Bread is heavy if dough overmixed or too dry; flavor sour if too much raising agent or acid used.
Processed forms *Baked:* frozen; packaged. *Unbaked dough:* frozen and refrigerated.
Storage Best if freshly baked, or store in an airtight container 3-4 hours; freeze 3 months.
Glazes/icings Egg glaze.
Typical simple quick breads Currant bread (UK); Irish sweet bread (raisins, egg and lemon zest, Ireland); *gatah* (sprinkled with sesame seeds, Armenia); hominy sticks (USA); oatbread (Scotland); North Riding bread (fruit bread flavored with almond, UK); sour milk "cake" (UK); *Blitzkuchen* (quick coffee cake, Germany); whole wheat cheese scones (UK); white buttermilk bread (UK); shooting cake (raisin bread with lemon, UK); sweet potato biscuits (USA); Isle of Man barley bread (UK); Creole rice bread (USA); Cornish brown oatmeal bread (UK); Jamaican banana bread (Caribbean); carrot corn bread (USA).

Currant scones

Scones may be baked in the oven or on a griddle (p.511). They are best served still warm, split to spread with butter, or cream and jam.

Makes 6-8 scones

2 cups/250 g flour	¾ cup/175 ml buttermilk and 1 tsp cream of tartar *or* ¾ cup/ 175 ml fresh milk and 2 tsp cream of tartar (more liquid if needed)
2 tsp sugar	
1 tsp baking soda	
½ tsp salt	
¼ cup/60 g shortening	
2 tbsp/30 g currants	*2½ in/6 cm pastry cutter*

1 Heat the oven to 425°F/ 220°C and grease and flour a baking sheet. Sift the flour into a bowl with the sugar, baking soda and salt. With your fingers or two knives, work in the shortening until the mixture resembles coarse crumbs. Stir in the currants and make a well in the center of the mixture. Stir the cream of tartar into the buttermilk or milk and add to the well. Stir lightly, just until the dough clings together. It should be soft and sticky, so add more liquid if necessary.
2 On a floured board knead the dough lightly for 1 minute. Pat it to 1 in/2.5 cm thickness. Stamp out rounds with a pastry cutter (above). Transfer the rounds to the baking sheet and bake in the preheated oven for about 15 minutes, until lightly browned and a skewer inserted in the center comes out clean.

Simple quick bread recipes

Irish soda bread Makes 1 large loaf. Mix 4 cups/500 g whole wheat flour, 1½ tsp salt and 1½ tsp baking soda in a bowl and make a well in the center. Add 2 cups/500 ml buttermilk and stir, quickly drawing in the flour to make a slightly rough dough. Add more buttermilk during mixing if necessary so the dough is sticky. On a well-floured board, shape the dough to a round loaf (p.348). Set it on a greased baking sheet, flatten to about 2 in/5 cm thickness and score in a deep cross. Bake at 400°F/200°C until done, 30-35 minutes.

Cornbread sticks Makes 16-18 sticks. In a mixing bowl sift together 1 cup/125 g flour, 1 cup/140 g cornmeal, 2 tsp sugar, 4 tsp baking powder and 1½ tsp salt. Make a well in the center and add 2 slightly beaten eggs, 1 cup/250 ml milk and ¼ cup/ 60 g melted butter. Grease 16-18 cast iron cornstick pans (p.509) or medium muffin tins and heat in a 425°F/220°C oven until very hot. Spoon in the batter to half fill the pans; it should sizzle. Bake until golden brown, 10-12 minutes.

Baking powder biscuits Makes 6-8 biscuits. In the currant scone recipe (above), omit the sugar, currants and cream of tartar and add 1 tbsp baking powder. Mix the dough as for scones, adding more buttermilk if necessary to get a soft consistency. On a floured board, knead the dough lightly, pat it to ¾ in/2 cm thickness and stamp into 2 in/5 cm rounds with a pastry cutter. Transfer the biscuits to a greased baking sheet and chill them for 30 minutes. Brush the biscuits with melted butter and bake 8-10 minutes. Serve while still hot, or at room temperature.

SWEET BATTER BREADS

American muffins, made with a thick batter rather than a dough, are the best-known of sweet batter breads. A profusion of flavorings – dark sugar, honey, spices and dried fruit can be added to the roughly blended batter. Although American recipes dominate the field with breads and muffins flavored with fruit, vegetables or nuts, gingerbreads and spice breads – the nearest equivalent – are popular in Europe. They range from the Finnish *pepperkaka* (p.401) to the French honey-laden *pain d'épices*, often flavored with candied orange peel. The English are famous for buns, some of them yeast-raised, but many, such as rock cakes, are made with sweetened baking powder mixtures. These are stiff enough to hold a craggy shape on the baking sheet. The Jewish honey cake, *Lekach* (p.413), fragrant with cinnamon and orange, also belongs to the sweet batter bread family.

USEFUL INFORMATION

Portion Batter made with 2 cups/ 250 g flour makes a 9 × 5 × 4 in/ 23 × 12 × 10 cm loaf to serve 4, or 8-10 muffins.
Typical pan Loaf; square cake; muffin.
Preparation of pan Greased, occasionally lined with paper.
Cooking methods *Loaves*: bake at 375°F/190°C, 45-60 minutes. *Muffins*: bake at 425°F/220°C, 15-20 minutes.
When done Browned, cracked, and shrinks slightly; a skewer inserted in center comes out clean.
Problems If chewy or coarse-textured and tunnelled with holes, too much raising agent was used or batter was overmixed; if dry, batter was overbaked; if top is flat, oven was too low. *Fruit*: fruit falls easily to bottom of dough, so dry it thoroughly and toss to coat with a little of the flour.
Processed forms *Baked*: frozen, packaged. *Unbaked dough*: packaged mix.
Storage Best if freshly baked; or store in an airtight container 2 days; freeze 3 months.
Glazes/icings Soft icing (p.406); streusel topping (p.356); egg white and sugar; egg glaze.
Typical sweet batter breads *Breads*: Rice-flour (USA); zucchini (USA); barley-orange (UK); raisin-walnut (USA); *yaourpita* (yogurt, Greece); blueberry-orange (USA); cranberry-cheese (USA); lemon tea (USA); apricot-prune (USA); molasses (USA); currant tea (UK); pumpkin (USA). *Muffins*: maple syrup (USA); applesauce (USA); pearl (with vanilla, USA); orange-pecan (USA); elderberry (UK); bran (USA); rhubarb oat (USA).

BAGELS & PRETZELS

A bagel is a traditional ring-shaped Jewish bread, unusual in being cooked twice: first by boiling for about 15 seconds, then by baking. Bagels are usually brushed with an egg glaze so that they are golden brown when cooked. They come in a variety of flavors, among the most popular are egg, pumpernickel and cinnamon-raisin. Plain bagels can be enlivened with toppings of dried garlic, onion flakes and poppy or sesame seeds. A split bagel with cream cheese and lox (salted salmon, p.126) is a New York delicatessen classic. A *bialy* – named for the Polish city of Białystok – is made of the same dough but is not boiled, and has only a slight indentation instead of a hole.

Yeast dough can be rolled into a cylindrical strip, shaped in a characteristic knot and baked into hard pretzels, the familiar dry, crunchy snack sprinkled with coarse salt. Alternatively, the dough can be tied into knots and, like bagels, boiled before baking to make soft pretzels which are chewy on the outside and soft inside. These are sprinkled with salt, like hard pretzels, and often eaten warm with American yellow mustard.

Date nut bread

Date bread is delicious with butter for breakfast, or served with cheese.

Makes 1 medium loaf

1 cup/250 ml milk
½ cup/100 g sugar
¼ cup/60 g butter
1 cup/170 g chopped, pitted dates
1 cup/125 g all-purpose flour
1 cup/125 g whole wheat flour
1½ tsp baking powder
½ tsp salt
1 egg, beaten to mix
½ cup/60 g walnuts, chopped
8½ × 4½ × 2½ in/22 × 11 × 7 cm loaf pan

1 Heat the oven to 350°F/175°C; grease the loaf pan and line it with wax paper. Heat the milk, sugar and butter until melted, stir in the dates and leave until cooled to lukewarm. **2** In a bowl, mix both types of flour, baking powder and salt. Make a well in the center and add the milk mixture, egg and walnuts. Stir until just mixed.

3 Pour the batter into the prepared pan and bake until a skewer inserted in the center of the bread comes out clean, 35-45 minutes. Leave to cool in the pan before slicing.

Sweet batter bread recipes

Banana nut bread Makes 1 large loaf. Sift 2½ cups/310 g flour, 2 tsp baking powder and ½ tsp salt into a bowl. In a separate bowl, beat 1 cup/250 g shortening, 2 cups/400 g sugar, 2 cups/500 g mashed bananas, 4 eggs and 1 cup/120 g chopped walnuts until mixed. Add the flour mixture and stir just until blended. Pour into a greased 9 × 5 × 4 in/23 × 13 × 10 cm loaf pan and bake at 350°F/175°C, 50-60 minutes until a skewer inserted in the center comes out clean.

Fruit muffins Makes 12 muffins. Sift 1¼ cups/150 g flour, 1 tbsp baking powder, 6 tbsp/90 g sugar, ¼ tsp cinnamon, ¼ tsp nutmeg and ½ tsp salt into a bowl and make a well in the center. Beat 1 egg, ½ cup/125 g melted butter and ¾ cup/175 ml milk and pour into the well. Stir with a spatula or wooden spoon until mixed, then stir in 1 cup/150 g blueberries, raspberries or diced strawberries. Do not overmix. Drop the mixture into 12 greased medium muffin tins and bake at 425°F/220°C, 15-20 minutes, until a skewer inserted in the center comes out clean.

FRUIT, VEGETABLE & NUT BREADS

Dried fruits (p.473), especially currants and raisins, are commonly paired with candied peel (p.475), essential in breads such as Welsh *bara brith* (speckled bread) or Irish *barm brack* (freckled bread). Fresh fruits such as banana, berries or citrus fruits are particularly popular in North American sweet batter breads and muffins, often served with butter or a spread such as fresh cream cheese or lemon curd. *Birnenbrot*, made with pears and walnuts and flavored with kirsch and black pepper, is celebrated in Switzerland, while coconut is a popular Caribbean ingredient for breads such as *boija*.

A great variety of vegetables may also be added to bread doughs. Potato breads feature in the cuisine of so many northern countries. Popular examples include Finnish *perunarieska* and Norwegian *lefse*. Sweet flavorings such as orange and chocolate pair especially well with the moist richness of potato breads. Carrots, onions, zucchini and pumpkin are also familiar ingredients, but other vegetables such as fennel, beet and celery root are excellent alternatives. Chopped onions may be added to a bread dough for texture and flavor, and onion flakes are also used as a tasty topping, added a few minutes before the bread is done. Many vegetable breads are enlivened with sweet spices such as cinnamon, allspice and nutmeg, while fresh or dried herbs, and even a dash of hot pepper sauce, are more likely to be paired with savory breads. Seeded fresh tomatoes, tomato sauce or a tablespoon of tomato paste may be added directly to bread dough, and the flavor may be heightened by oregano, rosemary and other complementary herbs. Olive breads with both olive oil and chopped ripe olives in the dough are a specialty of several countries bordering the Mediterranean.

Nuts add moisture and texture as well as an imitable aroma to both sweet and savory breads; for best flavor, buy whole nuts, then blanch and grind them at home. Chopped nuts are a favorite ingredient for sweet batter breads, especially banana, cranberry, date or pumpkin breads.

FRIED BREAD & FRITTERS

The most famous deep-fried breads are doughnuts, some raised with yeast, others with baking powder (cake doughnuts). Doughnuts may be eaten warm or cold, and simply sprinkled with sugar, glazed with sugar syrup or chocolate, or rolled in shredded coconut. Some are shaped as buns instead of rings, holding a surprise filling of jam or pastry cream. Richest of all are doughnuts of brioche dough. There are many others, such as Mexican *buñuelos* flavored with sugar, anise and cinnamon, and Dutch *oliebollen*, flavored with citrus peel, currants and apples.

At least one type of Chinese *dim sum* dumpling, the *bao*, filled with barbecued pork or sweet bean paste, is deep-fried rather than steamed or baked. *Dal puri* are savory fried breads enjoyed in India. They are usually stuffed with cooked split peas or lentils and flavored with spices such as cumin.

When the dough is fried until crisp, the bread is often called a fritter. Typical are American crullers, made of yeast or baking powder dough, twisted to an elongated wand and fried until crisp outside with an airy center. American corn pones are robust little balls of cornmeal dough flavored with bacon fat and deep-fried, and hush puppies (p.343) are similar. One popular fritter, the French *beignet*, consists simply of deep-fried choux pastry (p.376), which puffs to a luscious hollow ball and is served warm, sprinkled with confectioners' sugar.

Yeast breads are not difficult to deep-fry, but both the dough and the fat must be at the correct temperature. The fat should be at 360°F/180°C; if it is too hot, the dough tends to scorch, and if it is too cool, the dough soaks up too much fat. The proper temperature for the dough itself when frying is around 75°F/24°C, or cool room temperature for baking powder or unleavened doughs. Thick shapes should brown on the outside but remain soft in the center, while flatter shapes should be crisp right through. Crullers and fancy shapes should be stirred lightly in the hot fat so they brown evenly, but doughnuts are turned only once.

Most fried breads and fritters are best served hot, with a dusting of confectioners' sugar or a topping of honey or jam for sweet breads.

USEFUL INFORMATION

Portion Dough made with 2 cups/ 250 g flour makes 18-20 doughnuts or large fritters.
Cooking methods Fry at 360°F/ 180°C, 3-4 minutes.
When done Golden brown. *Fritters:* crisp.
Problems Soggy if fried too slowly; scorch if fried too fast.
Processed forms *Doughnuts:* frozen; packaged.
Storage *Doughnuts:* best served warm, or store 12 hours in airtight container. *Fritters:* best served warm or store in an airtight container, 2-3 hours.
Glazes/icings Confectioners' sugar; sugar glaze; chocolate *Sachertorte* icing (p.406); soft icing (p.406); jam sauce (p.66); honey.
Typical deep-fried breads and fritters *Calas* (New Orleans fried dough, USA); *loukmades* (honey doughnuts, Greece); *bugnes d'Arles* (crullers, France); *churros* (fluted sugar fritters, Spain); *beignets* (deep-fried choux puffs, France); *Fastnachtkuchen* (jelly doughnuts, Germany); *Polsterzipfel* (cinnamon-flavored turnovers, Germany); *oliebollen* (doughnuts with currants, citrus peel, apple, Netherlands); fried saucers (fried baking powder bread layered with jam, USA); *malsadas* (raised, fried dough, Portugal); *croquignolles* (crunchy, deep fried sweet baking powder dough, France); *aebleskiver* (raised light doughnuts with cardamom, Denmark); *tippaleipa* (thin yeast batter drizzled in hot oil, Finland); *Strauben* (fried puff-pastry strips with sugar, Germany); cinnamon twists (USA); *buñuelos* (doughnuts with sugar, anise and cinnamon, Mexico).

MAKING DOUGHNUTS

To make six to eight doughnuts, use the lightly sweetened dough for coffeecakes (p.356) or the brioche dough (p.355.)

1 Roll out the dough to about 1 in/ 2.5 cm thickness and, with a cutter, stamp out 3 in/7.5 cm rounds. With a smaller cutter, stamp a round in the center of each one and discard it, leaving six to eight dougnut rings.

2 Transfer the prepared rings to a baking sheet or tray and leave them to rise, 20-30 minutes, until doubled in bulk.

3 LEFT Heat a pan of fat for deep-frying to 360°F/180°C. Gently lower the doughnuts into the fat, cooking just a few at a time.

4 Fry the doughnuts until browned on one side, then turn and brown them on the other side, 3-4 minutes.

5 LEFT Lift the doughnuts out of the pan and drain them on absorbent paper towels. Sprinkle the doughnuts with confectioners' sugar for serving.

FLATBREADS

Flatbreads are among the world's oldest and most traditional breads, similar to the yeastless breads baked on heated stones in Neolithic times. Some are chewy, some crisp and almost all are shaped into rounds varying in diameter from 6-12 in/15-30 cm. They are based on a variety of flours, some with leavening agents.

Middle Eastern pita bread, made with wheat flour and raised with yeast, is a flat round of dough baked in the oven until puffed and speckled with brown. The crusts can be pulled apart easily to form a convenient pocket for stuffing: popular fillings are Middle Eastern *falafel* (chickpea or fava bean patties) or *hummus* (chickpea purée). Traditional Jewish matzohs use unbleached wheat flour (variations may include egg or whole wheat flour). Religious laws prohibit fermentation of dough, so the bread is completely flat, resembling a cracker. Scandinavian flatbread, often made with rye or whole wheat, is also baked until crisp. There are many other regional flatbreads based on the local grain: Scottish oatcakes and Finnish *perunarieska*, made with barley flour and potato respectively, are just two examples.

A variety of flatbreads come from India. *Chappati*, for example, are made from whole wheat flour, ghee, salt and water, and cooked in two stages: first the dough is browned in a pan, then it is toasted directly over the flame, so the steam forms moist puffed pockets in the center. *Paratha* are brushed with oil, then folded and rolled so that the dough separates into flaky layers when cooked on a griddle. *Nan* is a leavened flatbread baked in a traditional *tandoor* oven.

Mexican tortillas, made from corn *masa harina* p.343, or from wheat flour, water and salt, enjoy widespread popularity in Latin America. Shaped with a special press, a tortilla is quickly baked on a griddle so it stays flat, raising at most a blister. Tortillas are the basis for many Mexican dishes, such as enchiladas (corn tortillas softened in oil or sauce, then rolled and stuffed with chicken, meat or beans, and topped with cheese and hot sauce), or tacos, which are tortillas folded and fried until crisp then stuffed. *Tostadas* are deep-fried flat tortillas, often topped with avocado and cheese. Corn chips are corn tortillas cut into pieces and deep-fried to serve as snacks with piquant tomato *salsa* (p.65). Flour tortillas may be stuffed to make *burritos*, folded, stuffed and fried as *quesadillas*, or stuffed and deep-fried as *chimichangas*.

Injera is East African, a large, fermented pancake made from millet flour leavened with yeast, with a slightly sour taste. It serves simultaneously as the bread accompaniment to a meal and the dish on which it is served. Pieces are torn off and used to scoop up dishes of legumes, or stews. Peking pancakes are made from flour and water. They are softened by steaming and are usually served with *moo shu* pork and Peking duck.

Paratha

Pita

Corn tortilla

Nan

Flour tortilla

Savory Italian flatbread

Focaccia

Flat, soft-crumbed *focaccia* is brushed with oil and sprinkled with flavorings such as herbs or nuts. The extra dose of yeast in the recipe gives the bread a particularly zesty lightness.

Makes two 10 in/25 cm flatbreads to serve 8-10

2 lb/1 kg flour (more if needed)	1½ oz/45 g fresh yeast or
2 tsp pepper	¾ oz/22 g dry yeast
1¼ pt/750 ml lukewarm water	flavoring (see right)
3 tbsp/45 ml olive oil	

1 Sift the flour with the pepper on to a work surface and make a well in the center. Add the water and oil to the well, sprinkle the yeast over and leave for 5 minutes or until dissolved. With the fingers of one hand, gradually mix the flour into the yeast mixture to make a paste. With a pastry scraper or metal spatula, work in the remaining flour and gather the dough into a ball. It should be soft but not sticky; if necessary, work in more flour.
2 Flour the work surface and knead the dough until smooth and elastic, 5-7 minutes. Alternatively, knead it in an electric mixer (p.347). Transfer the dough to an oiled bowl and turn it over so that all the sides are oiled. Cover with a damp cloth and leave in a warm place until doubled in bulk, 1-1½ hours. Prepare two baking sheets by brushing them with olive oil.
3 Knead the dough lightly to knock out the air and divide it in half. Flavor and roll each portion of dough (below). Place the dough on the baking sheets, cover it with a damp cloth and leave to rise in a warm place until almost doubled in bulk, ¾-1 hour. The bread can be refrigerated for up to 6 hours before baking.
4 Heat the oven to 400°F/200°C. Bake the breads one at a time until brown, 20 minutes. Serve them warm, as soon as possible after baking.

Variations

Sage bread (*Focaccia alla salvia*) Knead 2 oz/60 g coarsely chopped fresh sage into each portion of dough. Roll the dough to a 10 in/25 cm round and brush with olive oil. Sprinkle with 1 tbsp coarse salt just before baking.
Sausage bread (*Focaccia alla salsiccia*) Knead 5 oz/50 g coarsely chopped peperoni sausage and 1 tsp salt into each portion of *focaccia* dough. Roll to a 10 in/25 cm round, brush with olive oil, and, if you like, sprinkle with 2 tsp dried red pepper flakes.
Walnut bread (*Focaccia ai noci*) Divide the dough in half and roll one portion to a 10 in/25 cm round. Transfer to a baking sheet, brush with walnut oil or olive oil and sprinkle with 3 oz/90 g walnut pieces and 1 tsp coarse salt. Roll out the remaining dough to another round the same size, set it on top of the walnuts and seal the edges. Brush the top with walnut oil or olive oil.

BREAD STUFFINGS

Stuffings, also called dressings or forcemeats, and occasionally by their French name *farce*, are designed to highlight other, usually more luxurious, ingredients. Breadcrumbs provide a particularly versatile base for stuffings, binding lightly but firmly, and blending with almost any ingredient. Rice and other grains add their own character; they hold ingredients together only lightly, so are often bound with egg. A wide range of stuffings include ground meat, with pork a particular favorite as it is so rich. Veal makes a delicate stuffing, and its high gelatin content adds richness and makes it a good binding agent.

The seasoning for a stuffing is crucial, for it should complement the flavor of the main ingredient without overwhelming it. Salty or piquant ingredients like ham, anchovy, olives, chili peppers and lemon zest are favorites, while tart fruits like apple or prunes add contrast as well as providing a foil for rich meats. Herbs and spices, onion, garlic and shallot are good in moderation. Stuffing that is too strong can be overpowering; bake extra stuffing in a separate dish. The cavity of a roast bird or hollow vegetables make good containers for stuffing, as does the pocket left when meat and fish are boned.

Note Bacteria grow rapidly in raw meat, poultry and fish, so never add warm stuffing to raw meat. Food should not be stuffed more than a few minutes before cooking, and stuffings should not be prepared too far in advance. Cavities in poultry should be stuffed loosely to allow sufficient heat to penetrate the bird.

Bread stuffing recipes

Sage and onion To stuff poultry, especially goose. Makes about 3 cups/750 ml. Gently fry 4 chopped, medium yellow onions with salt and pepper in 3 tbsp/45 g butter until soft but not browned, 10-15 minutes. Let cool, then stir in 1½ cups/100 g fresh white breadcrumbs (p.354), 3 tbsp coarsely chopped fresh sage or 1½ tbsp crumbled dried sage. Moisten with 1 lightly beaten egg and ½ cup/125 ml stock and season to taste.

Apple and onion To stuff duck, goose, pork and ham. Makes about 3 cups/750 ml. In sage and onion stuffing, omit 2 of the onions and the sage. Add 2 peeled, cored and coarsely chopped tart apples and 2 tbsp chopped parsley with the breadcrumbs.

Sausage and chestnut To stuff turkey, goose and pork. Makes 5 cups/1.25 L. Peel and boil 2 lb/1 kg fresh chestnuts (p.481), or drain a 1 lb/500 g can whole chestnuts in water. Coarsely crumble them. Fry 2 chopped onions in 2 tbsp/30 g butter until soft but not brown. Stir in 1 lb/500 g sausagemeat and fry, stirring constantly, until crumbly and brown, 5-8 minutes. Stir into the chestnuts with 2 cups/125 g fresh white breadcrumbs (p.354) and ½ tsp each ground allspice and nutmeg. Season to taste.

Eggplant, spinach and roasted pepper For lamb, pork, veal and vegetables. Makes 1 qt/1 L. Cut one eggplant (½ lb/250 g) in ½ in/1.25 cm cubes, sprinkle with salt and leave 15 minutes to release juices. Rinse and drain thoroughly. Sauté in 2 tbsp olive oil until lightly browned, 2-3 minutes. Stir in ½ lb/250 g cooked spinach, squeezed dry (p.273) and chopped, and 2 peeled, cored, and seeded green or red bell peppers, cut in ½ in/1.25 cm cubes. In a frying pan, fry 2 chopped medium onions in 2 tbsp more oil until browned and stir into the vegetable mixture with 2 cups/125 g fresh white breadcrumbs (p.354), 2 chopped cloves of garlic and the grated zest of 1 lemon. Season to taste.

BREAD PUDDINGS

Some of the best-loved of all desserts are based on bread. After languishing in the nursery for decades, bread and butter pudding (devised as a way to use stale bread) now appears on the smartest tables, enriched with chocolate, sweetened with raisins, spiced with nutmeg or cinnamon, even served with a whiskey sauce. In New Orleans, bread pudding is a traditional dessert and every chef has his own secret recipe. The bread should be quite dry and hard so that the finished pudding has a slightly chewy texture. Bread puddings may be served warm or chilled, sometimes accompanied by a sauce such as custard, or a rich ice cream. A similar dish is the American breakfast or brunch favorite, French toast (opposite), which is dry bread soaked in egg custard, then toasted or fried in butter; the French call it *pain perdu* or "lost bread". It is usually topped with a sweet syrup and accompanied by fresh fruit or jam. More elaborate bread puddings include savory variations such as ham and cheese pudding, and sweet versions such as apple charlotte, made in a mold with slices of buttered bread and a tart filling of puréed apple, baked until crisp and golden. For British Summer pudding (p.463), slices of bread are molded in a deep bowl and covered with fresh or poached fruit, particularly berries in season.

Many of the international family of soufflé puddings are based on bread, or sometimes a grain like semolina, lightened with whipped egg whites so they puff in the oven. More compact than a true soufflé, a soufflé pudding can be unmolded to serve hot or cold with a sauce. Typical is the French *pouding soufflé aux cerises* or German *Kaffeeauflauf* (opposite), coffee pudding darkened with rye breadcrumbs. Steamed puddings are a British specialty, often enriched with suet. Fresh breadcrumbs are often included to lighten the dough; a baking powder batter is also popular. A steamed pudding can be cooked in a water bath in the oven, but usually it is done in a stovetop steamer, in a pudding bowl covered with a cloth. The pudding is always unmolded to serve, often with a sauce, and the texture is agreeably moist. Cooking can take several hours – up to six hours for Christmas pudding, the richest steamed pudding of them all.

USEFUL INFORMATION

Portion 1 qt/1 L pudding serves 4.
Typical mold Charlotte, soufflé dish, pudding bowl or mold.
Preparation of mold Greased.
When done Skewer inserted in center is hot when withdrawn.
Problems *Steamed pudding*: water leaks in if pudding is not tightly covered.
Storage Best served still warm, or refrigerate 2-3 days, but will be heavy when reheated. *Steamed fruit puddings*: tightly wrapped in cool place 1 month to mellow before reheating.
Accompaniments Custard, sabayon, caramel sauce, English hard sauce, red jam sauce (see Sauces chapter pp.66-67); vanilla ice cream (p.443).
Typical bread puddings Apple brown betty (USA); queen of puddings (with custard, jam and meringue, UK); *torta nicoletta* (with raisins, citron and cinnamon, Germany); *capirotada* (with banana, apple, peanuts and cheese, Mexico); *pouding à la reine* (with lemon, cream and apricot, France); chocolate bread pudding (USA); *schwabischer ofenschlupfer* (with raisins and plums, Germany); *torta di pere e pan giallo* (cornbread with pears, wine and cinnamon, Italy); summer pudding (UK); poor knight's pudding (with raspberries, cinnamon and cream, UK); *maglyarakas* (with sour cherries, walnuts and apples, Hungary); Chester steamed pudding (black currant pudding with black currant sauce, UK); *eish es seray* ("Palace Bread": bread soaked in honey and rosewater syrup, spread with cream, Middle East).

Bread pudding recipes

Bread and butter pudding Serves 4. Lay two thin slices of buttered white bread, cut in fingers without crusts, in a buttered baking dish. Sprinkle with ⅓ cup/45 g currants or dark raisins and cover with two more slices of buttered bread. Whisk together 3 eggs, ½ cup/100 ml sugar, grated zest 1 lemon, ¼ tsp nutmeg and 3 cups/750 ml milk. Pour this custard over the bread and leave to soak 15 minutes. Bake at 325°F/160°C until browned and set, 40-45 minutes.

Coffee soufflé pudding (*Kaffeeauflauf*) Serves 6. Cream ¼ cup/60 g butter with ¼ cup/50 g sugar until soft and light. Gradually beat in 6 egg yolks, reserving the whites. Fold in 1 cup/125 g ground almonds. Soak ⅔ cup/50 g fresh rye breadcrumbs in ½ cup/125 ml strong black coffee and 1 tbsp instant coffee, and stir into the butter mixture. Stiffly whip 6 egg whites. Add ¼ cup/50 g sugar and continue beating 30 seconds until glossy. Fold the egg whites into the coffee mixture and spoon into a buttered 1½ qt/1½ L charlotte mold. Set in a water bath (p.510) and bring to a boil on top of the stove. Bake at 350°F/175°C until the pudding is puffed and a skewer inserted in the center comes out clean, about 1¼-1½ hours. Remove the mold from the water bath and let cool for 5-10 minutes; the pudding will puff, then sink, so the sides should be pushed back inside the mold as it shrinks. Unmold the pudding on to a shallow dish and serve hot with sabayon sauce, or cold with vanilla custard (p.67).

French toast Serves 4. In a shallow dish whisk 2 eggs, 3-4 cups/850 ml milk, ½ tsp vanilla extract, 1 tsp sugar and ½ teaspoon salt. Quickly dip in eight slices of stale bread so they are only lightly soaked. Pan-fry the bread in 3-4 tbsp of butter, or bake on a hot griddle until brown on both sides. Sprinkle with cinnamon and sugar and serve with maple syrup or a fruit preserve.

WRAPPING A PUDDING FOR STEAMING

Traditionally, steamed puddings are cooked in a deep bowl covered with pleated paper and cloth to allow for expansion. The bowl should be set on a rack so it does not touch the water.

1 Fill a heatproof bowl three-quarters full with batter. Grease a sheet of parchment paper, pleat it in the center and lay it over the bowl.

2 Lay a pleated napkin on the paper and tie it under the lip of the bowl with string. Knot the ends of the napkin so it does not trail in the water.

3 Lift the bowl, using the knotted napkin as a handle, and lower it into the steamer. Cover the steamer and cook for the required time, replenishing the water as necessary.

Steamed ginger pudding

The honey or golden syrup at the bottom of the bowl soaks the pudding and forms a syrupy layer on top when it is unmolded.

Serves 8

3 cups/175 g fresh white breadcrumbs	1 tbsp ground ginger
½ cup/125 ml milk	½ cup/125 ml honey or golden syrup
1 cup/200 g ground beef suet	
3 eggs	
1 cup/200 g sugar	*1qt/1 l heatproof bowl*

1 Grease the bowl and prepare a steamer or deep pan with plenty of boiling water. Soak the breadcrumbs in the milk. Stir in the beef suet. Beat together the eggs, the sugar and the ginger and stir into the crumbs. Pour the honey or golden syrup into the pudding bowl, then add the crumb mixture.
2 Cover the bowl (left) and steam it for 2 hours, replenishing the boiling water regularly. **Note** The water must boil continuously.
3 To test the pudding, untie the cloth. Insert a skewer in the pudding; it should be hot to the touch when withdrawn. Unmold the pudding on to a serving dish and serve with extra honey or golden syrup.

Variations

Steamed date pudding Serves 8. In the steamed ginger pudding recipe, omit the ginger and honey or golden syrup. Stir 1 cup/250 g chopped, pitted dates and ½ cup/75 g chopped almonds into the breadcrumb mixture. Steam 2½-3 hours. Serve with sabayon sauce or vanilla custard (p.67).

BATTERS

At its simplest, a batter is a mixture based on flour, or some other starch, that is soft enough to pour. Eggs contribute richness and help it rise; some batters also include baking powder or soda. Water makes a batter light, while milk makes it smoother and helps it to brown more quickly. A few spoonfuls of oil or melted butter enriches batters and helps prevent them from sticking. Seasoning is usually confined to salt, with sugar and liqueurs for sweet batters. Sometimes chili pepper, garlic, brandy or other pungent flavors are included in a savory batter.

Most batters should be stirred only to combine the ingredients. However, a few batters are yeast-raised, and they should be beaten vigorously to develop gluten, following the same principle as for kneading dough. Batters of both types are usually left to stand so that the starch grains soften and expand in the liquid, making the finished dish lighter. Yeast doughs should rise until bubbly. Wheat flour batter will thicken slightly on standing, as the starch in the flour expands, and it may need thinning with extra liquid before use. From a simple batter a wide range of sweet and savory dishes can be made, including crêpes, pancakes, waffles and a variety of traditional puddings.

MIXING BATTERS

Non-yeast batters should be stirred with a whisk until smooth, but too much beating develops the gluten in the flour, making the batter elastic and tough when cooked.

1 Sift the flour into a bowl with salt (and sugar, if using) and make a well in the center. Break the eggs into the well and whisk them until they are thoroughly mixed.

2 Add half the liquid in a steady stream and whisk, gradually drawing in the flour to make a smooth paste. If too much liquid is added at this point, the batter will become lumpy.

3 Thin the paste to the desired consistency with more liquid: a thick cream is needed for many pancakes, fritters and for binding ingredients, and a thinner cream is required for crêpes.

CREPES

The most famous of all batter preparations must be crêpes, whether served by themselves or as wafer-thin wrappers for a wide variety of foods. Savory crêpes lend themselves to fillings – from grated cheese, cream cheese and scrambled egg to sumptuous sweetbreads moistened with a sauce, or caviar and sour cream. Sweet ideas range from a sprinkling of sugar and liqueur or a filling of jam or chocolate – often rolled into a "cigarette" crêpe to be eaten with the fingers – to fresh fruit mixtures. Crêpes can be piled one on top of the other, sandwiched with filling, then cut in wedges like a multi-layered cake.

For flaming, crêpes may first be sautéed with butter and sugar to heat and caramelize them, as in *Crêpes Suzette* (p.367), then folded in triangles or rolled. When the filling is more substantial, the crêpe is usually rolled loosely with the ends turned in to form a bundle, called a *pannequet* in France. For added richness and to prevent them drying out in the oven, crêpes are frequently coated with sauce. **Note** Avoid coating with emulsified sauces (p.60), egg custards (p.94), and sauces with an egg yolk and cream thickener, as they will separate when reheated.

USEFUL INFORMATION

Portion Batter with 1 cup/125 g flour makes 14-16 crêpes to serve 4-6.
Typical pan Crêpe pan.
Preparation of pan Greased.
Cooking methods Pan-fry 1-2 minutes each side.
Problems Heavy if too thick; fall apart if too thin; scorch over high heat; tough if cooked too slowly.
Storage *Unfilled crêpes:* layer with wax paper and refrigerate 3 days; freeze 2 months. *Filled crêpes:* refrigerate 2 days; freeze 2 months.
Typical dishes *Pannequets à la muscovite* (with caviar, France); with *ratatouille* (USA); with curried chicken (UK); with ice cream, bananas and caramel sauce (USA); *crespelle di farina dolce* (chestnut-flour crêpes with ricotta and rum, Italy); *crêpes soufflées* (with sweet soufflé filling, France); *Apfelpfannkuchen* (with apple filling, Germany); *blintz* (with fresh cheese and lemon filling, Jewish); *tunna pannkakor* (served with fruit purée, Scandinavia); *blinis* (buckwheat, served with sweet or savory fillings, Russia); *Palatschinken* (filled with vegetables or chicken, Germany); *flensjes* (with yogurt, filled with cheese, Netherlands).

Plain crêpes

A tablespoon of sugar may be added to the batter for sweet crêpes, but with more they tend to scorch.

Makes 14-16 crêpes

1 cup/125 g all-purpose flour	2 tbsp/30 g melted butter
pinch of salt	¼ cup/60 g clarified butter (p.99), for frying
3 eggs	
1 cup/250 ml milk (more if needed)	
	7 in/18 cm crêpe pan (p.510)

1 Mix the batter (left), stirring in enough milk to give the consistency of thin cream. Let it stand 30 minutes.
2 Fry the crêpes (right). If storing, layer them with wax paper and wrap tightly so they do not dry out.

Variations

Whole wheat crêpes Substitute ½ cup/60 g whole wheat flour for half the all-purpose flour.

Breton buckwheat galettes Substitute ½ cup/60 g buckwheat flour for half the all-purpose flour and omit one of the eggs.

FRYING CREPES

The ideal wafer-thin crêpe depends on the consistency of the batter and the pan in which it is cooked (p.510). For frying crêpes, there is no substitute for butter. Oil or margarine can be used but neither gives the golden color or rich flavor; to lessen scorching, use clarified butter (p.99). During cooking, add more butter to the pan only when the crêpes start to stick; if too much is used they will be greasy. The side of the crêpe that is fried first looks more attractive and should be on the outside for serving. Turn crepes either with your hands or by tossing.

1 Assemble the batter, a ladle, a metal spatula, a plate and a small bowl. Heat 2-3 tablespoons of clarified butter in the pan, and pour the excess into the bowl. Reheat the pan, add a drop of batter and wait until it spatters briskly before adding the rest.

2 Quickly add a small ladle of batter, rotating and shaking the pan with a turn of the wrist so the base is completely coated. With too much batter, the crêpe will be thick; with too little it will have holes.

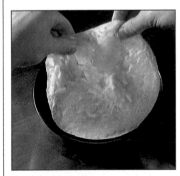

3 Fry the crêpe quickly over medium high heat until it is set on top and brown underneath. Loosen it with a spatula and turn it quickly using both hands.

4 ALTERNATIVELY, toss the crêpe with a quick flip of the wrist (left). Continue cooking for ½-1 minute until brown on the other side. Pile the cooked crêpes on a plate, one on top of the other to keep them moist.

Savory and sweet crêpe recipes

Chicken and mushroom crêpes Serves 6. Make 3 cups/750 ml thick velouté sauce (p.55) with chicken stock. Stir 1½ cups/275 g diced cooked chicken and 4 oz/125 g diced mushrooms, sautéed in 1 tbsp butter, into half the sauce. Season the filling to taste with lemon juice, salt and pepper and fill into 14-16 crêpes, folding them in *pannequets* (below). Pack them in a buttered baking dish. Stir 1 cup/250 ml light cream into the remaining sauce, taste and spoon over the crêpes to coat them. Sprinkle the crêpes with 3 tbsp/1 oz grated Gruyère cheese. Bake in a 350°F/175°C oven until bubbling and browned, 20-30 minutes.

Seafood crêpes In the recipe for chicken and mushroom crêpes, substitute cooked seafood such as shrimp, lobster, crabmeat and cooked flaked white fish for the chicken; make velouté sauce with fish instead of chicken stock, and omit the cheese topping.

***Crêpes suisses* (ham and cheese)** Serves 6. Make 3 cups medium béchamel (p.54) and add ½ cup/25 g grated Gruyère cheese until it melts. Season the sauce with 1 tsp Dijon mustard and salt and pepper. Add ½ cup/25 g diced cooked ham to half the sauce and fill 14-16 crêpes, rolling each into a cigarette. Pack into a buttered baking dish, coat with the remaining sauce and sprinkle with ½ cup/25 g grated Gruyère cheese. Broil the rolled pancakes until bubbling and browned.

Broccoli crêpes In *crepes suisses*, substitute ½ lb/250 g broccoli for the ham. Cook the chopped broccoli stems and whole florets in boiling water, 4-5 minutes. Drain and refresh and add to the white sauce. Bake as in *crepes suisses*.

Crêpes Suzette Serves 4-6. Make orange butter (p.99). Spread the butter on 14-16 crêpes. Fry the crêpes, butter side down, 1-2 minutes until hot, fold them in triangles and pile at the side of the pan. Continue frying; the sugar will start to caramelize and coat the crêpes. When all are fried, spread them evenly in the pan. Flame them (p.38) with 3 tbsp/45 ml brandy and 3 tbsp/45 ml Grand Marnier, basting until the flame dies. Serve warm.

Apple crêpes Serves 4-6. Fry 3 sliced apples in 3 tbsp/45 g butter, sprinkling them with 3 tbsp/45 g sugar and turning them so they caramelize. Fill 14-16 crêpes with the apples, then roll them and pack in a shallow buttered baking dish. Heat the crêpes in a 400°F/200°C oven for 8-10 minutes. Flame them (p.38) with ¼ cup/60 ml Calvados or brandy. Spoon 3-4 tbsp/45-60 ml cream over the crêpes and serve.

Poached fruit crêpes Serves 4-6. In the *crepes Suzette* recipe, add warm poached fruit (p.448) such as peaches, cherries or pears to each crêpe before folding them into triangles. Finish by flaming as described for *crêpes Suzette*.

Cigarette · Triangle · Roll with filling · Pannequet

PANCAKES & BATTER PUDDINGS

Pancakes (known in Britain as drop scones or Scotch pancakes) are no more than flat cakes fried in a frying pan or baked on a griddle. Thicker than crêpes, most are based on a simple batter leavened with baking powder or baking soda, or sometimes with yeast, often lightly sweetened and enriched with an egg or two. Variety is added with different flours – cornmeal and buckwheat work particularly well – or by basing the pancakes on a starchy ingredient like potatoes or rice, combined with a small amount of wheat flour. A fairly thick batter is best for small pancakes, and a thinner one for large pancakes occupying the whole pan. When frying, butter gives the best flavor, and medium heat ensures the batter will rise well. The pancake is ready to turn when tiny bubbles appear on the surface.

Pancakes may be savory or sweet. Examples of savory pancakes are the large American breakfast pancake, and potato *galettes*, a French term meaning simply a round cake. The *Salzburger nockerl* is a fluffy soufflé-like pancake, a specialty of Salzburg.

Waffles are made with a similar batter, but are cooked in a hinged, heated iron with a patterned grid (opposite). They range from a simple crispy rectangle with a topping of jam or whipped cream, to mixtures that include some rye flour, cornmeal, potato or nuts. Thin waffles, suitable for serving with ice cream, include the delicious heart-shaped Belgian *gaufrettes*, Italian *brigidini* and Swedish *krumkakor*. Similar to waffles, but deep-fried rather than baked, are little flower-shaped Swedish *sockerstruvor*, made with a special iron that is heated in fat, dipped in batter, then returned to the hot fat to cook the batter to a crisp case.

There is also a small family of sweet and savory batter puddings that are baked in the oven. Yorkshire pudding is part of a roast beef meal, traditionally served as a first course with gravy. Its American cousin, the popover, goes well with savory and sweet dishes. They are both made from a simple egg batter baked in a deep mold in a very hot oven so it rises to form a crisp brown cup. The batter may be flavored with herbs or baked with meats such as ham and sausage. Alternatively, vanilla or fresh fruits such as apple or prunes may be added for sweet puddings. French *clafoutis* baked with tart fresh cherries and Armagnac is an excellent example. Batter can also be formed into a "tree" cake (Ger. *Baumkuchen*). The batter is dripped on to a revolving spit and, as it bakes, forms uneven peaks that resemble a pine tree.

USEFUL INFORMATION

Portion Batter with 2 cups/250 g flour makes about 12×4-in/10-cm pancakes, 6 large waffles, or a pudding to serve 4-6.
Typical pan Griddle; crêpe pan; waffle iron; muffin tin; shallow baking dish.
Preparation of pan Greased.
Cooking methods *Pancake:* fry 3-5 minutes on each side. *Waffle:* toast 3-6 minutes. *Pudding:* bake at 400°F/200°C, 25-40 minutes, depending on size.
When done *Pancake:* when bubbles appear on the top, flip and cook on other side until lightly browned. *Waffle:* brown and starting to shrink.
Problems *Pancakes, waffles:* heavy if batter is too thick, fall apart if too thin (fry a test pancake before thinning the batter); batter sticks if pan too thin, if heat is too low, or if batter has too much sugar. *Pudding:* does not rise if cooked too slowly; falls if underdone.
Processed forms *Baked pancake; waffle:* frozen. *Unbaked batter:* package mix.
Storage *Pancake:* serve immediately. *Waffle:* serve within 1-2 hours. *Pudding:* serve warm.

Accompaniments Sugar; confectioners' sugar; honey; maple syrup; vanilla ice cream; melted butter; sour cream; whipped cream; jam; fresh or poached fruit; fruit purées; bacon; soft cheese.
Typical pancakes, waffles and batter puddings *Pancakes:* plätter (with fruit preserves, Sweden); *rahm dalken* (sour cream layered with prune butter, Austria); *tattoriblinit* (buckwheat, Finland); rolled with crayfish and cheese, (Sweden); cornmeal hotcakes (USA); *Kaiserschmarren* ("Emperor's pancake" with raisins, rum, vanilla, Austria); *syrniki* (cheese, Russia); with chopped nuts and cinnamon (Middle East). *Waffles:* goràn goro (rectangular with brandy, Norway); buttermilk (USA); *äggvåffla* (egg waffles for Lady Mary Day, 24 March, Scandinavia); *gaufrettes bruxelloises* (made with beer, Belgium); cornmeal (USA); *pizelle* (thin waffle cones or tulips with cream or ice cream, Italy). *Puddings:* drochona (with caviar or fruit, Russia); *appelpannkaka* (with apples, Scandinavia); toad-in-the-hole (baked with sausage, UK); Botham (with candied peel, UK); Charleston pudding (with apples and pecans, USA); *flashpannkake* (with ham, Scandinavia).

Spiced waffles

The honeycomb surface of a waffle is designed to catch a topping of whipped cream, honey, maple syrup, jam or ice cream.

Makes 6 large waffles

2 cups/250 g all-purpose flour	2 tsp sugar
2 tsp baking powder	2 eggs
½ tsp salt	6 tbsp/90 g melted butter
1 tsp baking soda	2 cups/500 ml buttermilk (more if needed)
1 tsp ground ginger	
½ tsp ground cinnamon	
½ tsp ground allspice	**Waffle iron (p.511)**

1 Mix the batter (p.366), adding the baking powder, baking soda, ginger, cinnamon and allspice to the flour with the salt. Let the mixture stand for 30 minutes.
2 Cook the waffles (Making waffles, right) and serve warm with a topping of your choice.

Batter recipes

Popovers Makes about 10 popovers. Mix a batter (p.366) with 1 cup/125 g flour, ½ tsp salt, 2 eggs and 1 cup/250 ml milk and let it stand 30 minutes. Pour the batter into 9-10 greased deep muffin or popover pans. Bake at 450°F/230°C, for 15 minutes. Lower the heat to 350°F/175°C and continue baking until the popovers are brown and crisp, 15-20 minutes.

Yorkshire pudding Makes 10-12 puddings. Mix a batter (p.366) with 1 cup/125 g flour, 2 eggs, salt and pepper and 1¼ cups/300 ml milk and let stand 30 minutes. Pour 2 tsp melted meat dripping or lard into each of 10-12 muffin or Yorkshire pudding pans. In a 425°F/220°C oven, heat the pans until the fat smokes. Pour in the batter and bake 25-30 minutes until crisp on top.

Cherry batter pudding (*clafoutis limousin*) Serves 4-6. Spread 1 lb/500 g tart cherries in a buttered baking dish (traditionally, the cherry pits are left in). Mix a batter (p.366) with ¼ cup/30 g flour, ⅓ cup/60 g sugar, a pinch of salt, 4 eggs, 2 egg yolks and 2½ cups/625 ml milk. Strain the batter over the cherries and leave to stand 30 minutes. Bake at 375°F/190°C, 40-45 minutes or until the pudding is puffed and brown. Let it cool until just warm; it will sink slightly. Spoon over 2-3 tbsp brandy and sprinkle with confectioners' sugar.

MAKING WAFFLES

To test the consistency of the batter, bake and test a waffle. If it is heavy, add more liquid.

1 Heat the waffle iron. Pour the batter on to cover about two-thirds of the iron, close it and wipe off any excess batter.

2 Cook the batter for 3-4 minutes, turning the iron over during cooking. The waffle is ready when it stops steaming. If the waffle iron does not open easily, cook for another ½ to 1 minute.

Baking on a griddle

Many baking powder and baking soda breads are traditionally baked on a cast-iron griddle. Scones, American biscuits and pancakes are suited to griddle baking, as are Scottish griddle (or girdle) cakes made with buttermilk. A griddle produces a crisp brown crust and, if cooked over an open fire, a slightly smoky flavor. A peat fire is perfect for making Irish soda bread. Extra flavor may be added with a tasty fat like lard to grease the griddle.

Some yeast doughs are cooked on a griddle, notably Britain's crumpets and America's "English" muffins. A crumpet ("pikelet" in some parts of England) is a small, round flat bread with holes on the surface. The dough is quite soft, and is molded and baked in metal rings directly on the griddle. Traditionally, crumpets are toasted and spread with butter and honey that drips down into the holes. English muffins have a similar honeycombed texture and are griddle-baked on both sides. They are split with a fork and toasted before serving. They bear no relation to sweet muffins, which are raised with baking powder or soda (p.359). To test the heat of a griddle, sprinkle it with a few drops of water: it should spatter. Pour out enough batter to make one large or several small rounds. Bake over medium heat 5-7 minutes until firm and browned on the bottom, then turn and brown the other side.

Buttermilk pancakes

Pancakes are traditionally served for breakfast in a stack, with butter, maple syrup or honey, and crisp bacon.

Makes about 12 × 4 in/10 cm pancakes to serve 4

1 cup/125 g all-purpose flour	2 tbsp/30 g melted butter
½ tsp sugar	1 cup/250 ml buttermilk (more if needed)
½ tsp salt	
1 tsp baking powder	2-3 tbsp/30-45 g melted butter (for frying)
¾ tsp baking soda	
1 egg	***Large skillet or griddle (p.510)***

1 Mix the batter (p.366), adding the baking powder and baking soda to the flour with the salt. Leave to stand at least 30 minutes. It should pour easily; if it is thick, add more buttermilk.
2 Heat the skillet or griddle, brush it with butter and pour on two or three 4 in/10 cm pancakes using a pitcher or ladle. Cook over medium heat until bubbles appear on the surface and the underside is brown, 3-5 minutes. Turn with a metal spatula and brown the other side, 2-3 minutes.
3 Fry the remaining pancakes in the same way, piling them one on top of the other to keep them warm. Serve at once.

Variations

Blueberry pancakes Add 1 cup/200 g fresh blueberries to the batter just before frying. Serve with maple syrup.
Whole wheat pancakes Substitute 1 cup/125 g whole wheat flour for 1 cup flour. Serve with maple syrup and crispy bacon.

PASTRY & COOKIES

FLOUR IS THE main ingredient in both bread and pastry, but how they differ! Bread dough is kneaded until elastic to develop the gluten, but the opposite effect is sought when making pastry. Great care is taken in mixing and baking to achieve a pastry that is rich yet light, with a crumbly or flaky texture. Some doughs are folded into dozens or, in the case of puff pastry, into hundreds of layers.

Three doughs dominate the classic pastry field – plain, puff and choux. English shortcrust and American pie pastry are prime examples of plain pastry dough; French *pâte brisée* and its cousin *pâte sucrée* are similar in composition but are mixed differently to give a more pliable texture. Puff pastry, which challenges even the accomplished cook, is in fact only one of several leaved pastry doughs, which include phyllo and strudel (p.382). The "odd man out" is choux pastry, which depends on eggs for its lightness.

Cookies are included in this chapter since so many of the techniques overlap with pastry. Rolled and molded cookies are little more than sweet pastry dough, rolled and cut into amusing shapes, while softer, richer doughs are often shaped or piped. Drop cookies are softer still and tend to spread generously on the baking sheet, while the texture of bar cookies, baked in a pan to slice in bars, is closer to a cake. Since by no means all cookies are sweet, dry crackers are also included.

Mixing pastry dough

A light, crisp finish is the goal for pastry. The high fat content of most pastry doughs has a beneficial "shortening" effect, separating starch granules and gluten strands within the dough itself. Mixing must be done quickly. Otherwise the gluten that develops will make the dough too elastic, and thus difficult to roll, more inclined to shrink during cooking and tougher when cooked.

Making pastry by machine

Doughs can be prepared in an electric mixer or in small batches in a food processor, but be careful not to overwork the dough. An electric mixer does a good job of cutting the butter into the flour. It helps also to get round the problem of handling the mixture too much, thus making the butter soft and the dough oily. As soon as the dough begins to form a clump, it should be taken out of the work bowl and kneaded with the heel of the hand (p.373) until it is pliable. Never let the dough form a ball when working it by machine. Any dough made in a machine, especially a food processor, will need to rest thoroughly to "relax" the gluten.

Chilling pastry dough

For puff pastry, chilling the dough in between "turns" (Rolling and folding, p.379) is critical. Chilling is also important for pie pastry. In effect, the gluten and fat in the dough are separated, ensuring a light texture when baked. Cold also helps to "relax" the gluten and set the fat, making the dough firmer, more manageable and less likely to shrink. It must be wrapped tightly in plastic wrap or wax paper (otherwise the edges may dry and crack when it is rolled) and chilled for at least 30 minutes. By working on a marble slab and using chilled ingredients and utensils from the start, the process should be trouble-free. **Note** Chilling cannot cure problems caused by overworking the dough.

INGREDIENTS FOR PASTRY

The exact proportions of water or egg required for a perfect pastry dough depend on the dryness of the flour used, which varies according to age, country and even season. The proper measure of flour and sugar is more accurately gauged by weight than by volume. (See also the chapters on Flour, Breads and Batters, and Sugar and Chocolate.)

Flour Fairly soft wheat flour (p.342) is best for pastry as it develops less gluten, a protein that gives dough its elasticity and is developed by kneading flour with liquid. Hard flours develop a strong gluten, making pastry difficult to roll and shape. Tasty but heavy, whole wheat flour can be used in pie pastry and ground nuts may be substituted for part of the flour. Special pastry flour, made from soft wheat, is high in starch and easier to roll.

Fat Butter gives outstanding flavor to pastry, while vegetable shortening lightens it. Block margarine is an alternative to both, and special firm margarine is available for puff pastry. Viewed with caution because of its high cholesterol content, lard produces a particularly flaky crust that is excellent for meat pies. Some specialty doughs may call for sour cream, or oil, which yields a less flaky crust. The fat used for preparing your baking sheet or mold should be the same as that used in the dough.

Egg As well as making the dough crumbly and rich, egg yolks provide color. Whole eggs bind the dough and make it more pliable; in choux pastry, eggs make it rise like a cake.

Water As well as moistening dough, water helps pie pastry expand and turn crumbly, and produces steam so that choux and puff pastry will rise in the oven. In some doughs, milk can be substituted for water, producing a softer dough that browns well.

Salt An important ingredient for adding flavor.

Sugar Granulated sugar is commonly added to dessert pastries. Confectioners' sugar gives a fine grain, and brown sugar adds color and gives sweetness. Pastry with a high proportion of sugar will scorch easily.

Raising agents Baking powder is occasionally added to lighten pastry dough. (See also Flour, Breads and Batters, p.359.)

Vanilla This is the usual flavoring for sweet doughs, though grated lemon zest and spices like cinnamon are good alternatives.

Storing pastry

All uncooked pastry doughs, except choux, can be refrigerated for two to three days; unbaked choux can be refrigerated for up to 12 hours. Dough freezes so well that puff pastry dough and shells of pie pastry are often sold commercially. Plain and puff pastry doughs also freeze well after being rolled and shaped, ready for baking. They can be transferred directly from the freezer to the oven, but will need a few minutes extra baking time.

For cooked pastries, storage time depends very much on the filling. Richer pastries without filling freeze and reheat well, while *pâte sucrée* should be treated like cookies (p.386). Baked choux puffs tend to dry and crumble in the freezer; they may be stored in an airtight container for two to three days.

Rolling pastry dough

To roll properly, pastry dough must be of the right consistency. If the dough is too soft, chill it to set the fat; if too firm, strike it with the rolling pin (p.507) until the butter starts to soften and is pliable. A cold surface, such as marble, is ideal for rolling pastry; failing that, the smoothness of formica is preferable to wood. Dust the surface lightly with flour to prevent the dough sticking to it. Dough may also be rolled between two layers of plastic wrap or wax paper, or on a well-floured pastry cloth.

Fillings for pies and tarts

It is the filling, rather than the type of pastry dough, that makes a pie or tart distinctive, and it is here that imagination counts. Apples may appear sliced, chopped or puréed; most berries look best in an open tart with a shiny glaze. Fruits that tend to discolor, such as pears and peaches, are poached (p.448) before being arranged in a baked pastry shell and glazed with the poaching syrup. Often a layer of pastry cream (p.384) is hidden beneath the fruit. Other fruit pies may be baked with a double crust, the trick being to brown the top evenly while thoroughly cooking the base. A preheated baking sheet helps here, and the fruit may be mixed with cornstarch, in American style, to absorb the juice. Deep-dish pies with a top crust are a British specialty, baked in an oval dish with a support in the center to hold up the crust.

Fillings for pies are by no means limited to fruit: other possibilities include a vast selection of nut fillings, as in the Italian *torta di pignoli*, a tart of pine nuts with custard, the almond *frangipane* (p.384) and pear pies of France, and American pecan pie, dark with molasses. On festive occasions, the British favor mincemeat pies, while the Swiss add a filling of eggs, cinnamon and sugar. Americans are particularly creative with their cream pies with custard filling, fluffy chiffon pies set with gelatin and meringue or whipped cream. Soft cheese is an internationally popular filling, ranging from English curd tarts to Italian ricotta-based tarts, not to mention the many American cheesecakes.

Many molded pâtés (p.243) also rely on pie pastry or *pâte brisée*. There are as many savory fillings for pastry as there are sweet ones. The classic quiche Lorraine, which originated in France, is now popular on tables all over the world. Often the tart shell is partially baked blind (p.375) before the filling is added.

Other savory pie or tart fillings are made from cooked vegetables, fish, meat mixed with béchamel or velouté sauce or just a little egg or cheese, before being cooked again in the oven, either in a pastry shell or under a crust.

PIE PASTRY, PATE BRISEE & PATE SUCREE

Pie pastry is the easiest and most versatile of all doughs. The ingredients are mixed as quickly as possible in a bowl, the fat lightly rubbed into the flour with the fingertips. Water is added, with egg yolk for a richer dough that should be soft but not sticky. Pie pastry can be given a flaky texture by rolling for one or two "turns" (Rolling and folding, p.379).

Pâte brisée is the French version of pie pastry, made in traditional European style directly on the work surface with the dry ingredients spread in a well or "fountain" to enclose the fat (usually butter), egg yolks and water. The name means broken dough, because the ingredients are "broken" into each other after mixing, then kneaded until they are as pliable as putty. *Pâte brisée* is rolled more thinly than pie pastry, to about ⅛ in / 3 mm thick.

The French like their *pâte brisée* to be thin yet sturdy, with none of the flaky texture that is the pride of British and American cooks. Like pie pastry, it is principally used to line pie pans, but there are national differences: European tarts are generally open, while the British prefer deep and shallow pies with a top crust, and many American pies have a top and bottom (double) crust.

The most popular variant of *pâte brisée* is *pâte sucrée*, a sweet pastry that is made with sugar. When a high proportion of sugar is added to *pâte sucrée*, the character of the dough is changed and it becomes as crumbly as a cookie, hence its other name *pâte sablée* or "sandy pastry". The Italian version, *pasta frolla*, is usually flavored with lemon, while German *mürbeteig* is often enhanced by the addition of brandy, rum or white wine. Ground nuts may be substituted for half the flour in *pâte sucrée* and spices may also be added. The sweetness of these doughs makes them favorites for fruit tarts, particularly for tartlets filled with berries.

USEFUL INFORMATION

Portion Pie dough with 2 cups/ 250 g flour or *pâte brisée* or *sucrée* with 1⅔ cups/200 g flour makes a 10 in/25 cm pie for 6-8 or 6 × 3½ in/9 cm tartlets.

Typical pan Round pie pan (USA); oval pie dish (UK); tart pan with removable base (France); tart ring; tartlet molds; barquette molds.

Preparation of pan Greased.

Cooking methods *Unfilled*: bake large shell at 425°F/220°C, 10 minutes, lower heat to 375°F/ 190°C and bake 10-15 minutes longer; bake tartlet shells at 425°F/ 220°C, 14-18 minutes. *Filled*: depends on recipe.

When done Crisp and light brown in color.

Problems If poorly wrapped, dough may dry and crack at edges when rolled; if elastic, flour is too hard or dough is overworked, so leave it to rest; if dry, add more water before pressing crumbs together; if sticky, chill and then work in more flour; if dough shrinks in oven, it was overworked; if it collapses in oven,

it was not sufficiently chilled. Sugar and nut doughs scorch easily in hot oven.

Storage *Raw dough*: wrap well and refrigerate 2 days or freeze 3 months. *Baked unfilled*: 2-3 days in airtight container, or freeze 3 months. *Baked filled*: depends on recipe.

Reheat In low oven to serve warm or hot.

Glazes Egg; apricot jam; red currant jelly; sugar.

Typical pastries *Tarte Tatin* (upside-down caramelized apple pie, France); shoofly pie (with caramel filling and crumb topping, USA); Bakewell tart (filled with jam and almonds, UK); *Linzertorte* (with cinnamon and almond crust and raspberry filling, Austria); ricotta cheese pie (Italy); fresh apricot torte (Austria); *tarta pasiega* (Easter tart with cheese and rose water, Spain); cherry meringue tart (Germany); treacle tart (UK); deep-dish apple pie (USA); *tartelettes aux fruits* (with fresh fruit and glaze, France).

MAKING PIE PASTRY

When making pie pastry, it is important that the fat is chilled so that it remains firm during mixing.

Makes a 10 in/25 cm tart shell

2 cups/250 g flour	⅓ cup/75 g shortening or lard
1 tsp salt	1 egg yolk (optional)
2 tsp sugar (for sweet pies)	¼ cup/60 ml cold water (more if needed)
⅓ cup/75 g cold unsalted butter	

1 Sift the flour with the salt, and sugar if using, into a bowl. Add the butter and shortening and cut into small pieces with a pastry cutter or two knives, using one in each hand. Rub with your fingertips until the mixture forms fine crumbs, lifting and crumbling to help aerate it.

2 Make a well in the center of the mixture, add egg yolk if using, and water. Mix quickly with a knife to form crumbs. If they are dry, mix in 1-2 tablespoons more water. Press the dough together with your fingers. It should be soft but not sticky.

3 Work the dough lightly with your hand for a few seconds to form a rough ball. Wrap it tightly in plastic wrap and chill in the refrigerator for 30 minutes or until it is firm. Knead and roll as for *pâte brisée*.

Baking pie pastry, *pâte brisée* and *pâte sucrée*

The initial oven temperature for pie pastry is high so that the dough keeps its shape; it is then lowered to complete cooking. To prevent dough becoming soggy in pies and tarts with a moist filling, a shell may be baked ahead that is, baked blind (p.375), then filled and baked again. It helps to preheat the baking sheet and to bake the pie on a low shelf.

Richer doughs like *pâte sucrée* are often baked completely and the filling added shortly before serving so that the pastry remains crisp. To prevent moisture soaking a pre-baked shell, sprinkle the base of the shell with breadcrumbs, brush the sides with egg white and bake again for a few minutes. Brush the pastry with jam glaze (p.385) after baking. If filling with juicy fruits, spread with a layer of pastry cream first.

CRUMB CRUSTS

Quick bottom crusts for sweet tarts, cheesecakes, gelatin pies such as lemon chiffon, and ice-cream cakes can be made from crumbled cookies. Chocolate cookies, graham crackers, ginger cookies and macaroons, or cereals like cornflakes, are all popular. The standard proportions are 2 cups/225 g crumbs to ½ cup/125 g melted butter and ¼ cup/60 g sugar. For small, even pieces, crush the cookies with a rolling pin between two sheets of paper, or work a few at a time in a food processor or blender. Add sugar, perhaps a little spice, and melted butter to bind the mixture. Press the mixture into the pan, then chill or bake it before filling.

MAKING PATE BRISEE

A plastic or metal pastry scraper is useful for mixing the dough. If the dough is dry when mixed, add 1-2 tablespoons more water.

Makes a 10 in/25 cm tart shell

1⅔ cups/200 g flour	½ tsp salt
6½ tbsp/100 g cold unsalted butter, cut into pieces	2 tsp sugar (for sweet tarts)
1 egg yolk	3 tbsp/45 ml water (more if needed)

1 Sift the flour on to a work surface and make a well in the center. Pound the butter and add with the egg yolk, salt, sugar if using, and water.

2 With your fingertips, mix together the ingredients in the well. Gradually draw in the flour from the sides.

3 With your fingers, work the flour into the other ingredients until coarse crumbs are formed.

4 Using a pastry scraper, gather the dough into a neat ball and knead it (see Kneading and rolling, opposite page).

KNEADING & ROLLING PATE BRISEE & PATE SUCREE

The dough must be kneaded first to prepare it for rolling; the French term for this technique is *fraiser*.

1 Lightly flour the work surface. Blend the dough by pushing it away from you with the heel of your hand.

2 Gather it up with a pastry scraper or metal spatula and continue to knead it. After 1-2 minutes, the dough will be as smooth as putty and will peel easily from the work surface in one piece.

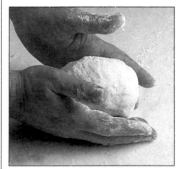

3 Shape the dough into a ball, wrap it in plastic wrap and chill for 30 minutes or until firm.

4 On a floured surface, roll the dough to the required shape, working briskly so that it does not soften too much.

5 Keep the dough moving loosely on the board as you roll so that it does not stick. Every three or four strokes with the rolling pin, lift the dough and sprinkle the work surface with a little flour. **Note** If too much flour is worked in, it will alter the proportions of the dough.

Pâte brisée variations

Pâte à pâté (savory pie pastry dough) For meat pâtés and raised pies. Substitute 3 tbsp/45 g lard for half the butter, and one egg for the yolk. Use 1-2 tbsp water.

Sour cream pastry dough For *coulibiac* (p.132), *piroshki* (p.374), and meat pâtés. Substitute 2-3 tbsp/30-45 ml sour cream for water.

Pâte sucrée

Pâte sucrée is made and kneaded in much the same way as *pâte brisée*. It can be flavored with one to two tablespoons of kirsch or brandy instead of vanilla.

Makes a 10 in/25 cm tart shell

1 2/3 cups/200 g flour	4 egg yolks
6 1/2 tbsp/100 g cold, unsalted butter	1/2 tsp salt
1/2 cup/100 g sugar	1/2 tsp vanilla extract

1 Sift the flour on to a work surface and make a well in the center. With your fist, pound the butter to soften it slightly. Add the butter and the rest of the ingredients to the flour and mix with your fingertips.
2 Using a pastry scraper or metal spatula draw in the flour and work until coarse crumbs are formed. Press the dough into a ball; if it is sticky, work in 2-3 tbsp/30-45 g more flour.
3 Knead the dough until it is smooth, wrap it tightly and chill in the refrigerator for at least 30 minutes.

Pâte sucrée variations

Pâte sucrée with nuts For fruit tarts and cookies. Substitute 3/4 cup/90 g ground blanched almonds, ground walnuts or toasted ground hazelnuts for half the flour; omit two of the egg yolks.
Italian *pasta frolla* For *frangipane* and cheese tarts. Add grated zest of one lemon with the vanilla.

MAKING A PASTRY ROSE

Firm dough such as hot water dough (p.244), puff or quick puff dough is best. Pastry roses top many savory pork and game pies.

1 Roll pastry trimmings to 3 in/7.5 cm wide by 1/4 in/6 mm thick. Flour and cut into four squares.

2 Stack the squares, pull the corners together and squeeze the layers to make a ball.

3 With a knife, cut a deep cross in the ball of dough.

4 Open the layers out to form the petals; discard dough from base.

Savory pies and turnovers

The words from the nursery rhyme "Sing a song of sixpence, a pocket full of rye/Four and twenty blackbirds, baked in a pie," are not just poetic license. Such joke pies filled with birds, live frogs, even the court jester, were often the star at medieval banquets. One rather disconcerting survival is Cornish stargazey pie in which whole herrings poke their heads from a blanket of dough as if trying to escape.

A favorite in Britain is steak and kidney pie, dark and mellow, with one Victorian variant calling for an enrichment of oysters, but quick puff pastry crust may also cover game fillings such as pheasant or grouse with mushrooms, jugged hare, or venison with juniper berries. Pastry makes a convenient portable picnic case too, hence the pasties made in Cornwall for workers in the local tin mines. A traditional Cornish pasty, made from a circle of dough folded in half and joined along the top, is a complete and nourishing meal of meat, potato and vegetables, sometimes with a dessert of apples packed into one end.

Most countries make savory turnovers – in France they are called *chaussons*, while Latin American *empanadas* are semicircles of lard dough enclosing ingredients such as fish, meat, poultry and vegetables. Often they are deep-fried instead of baked. The Russian version is *piroshki* – little beef-, cabbage-, or mushroom-filled turnovers served with soup, or dessert *piroshki* filled with poppy seeds, walnuts, honey and apples. *Pirogi* are larger pies, often square or rectangular.

LINING TARTLET MOLDS

Tartlet molds, whether round or boat-shaped (p.508) can be lined individually using a pastry cutter of corresponding shape. Alternatively, line several molds at once, as follows. Push the dough above the rim of the molds to allow for the filling.

1 Grease the molds and arrange them close together on a baking sheet. Roll out the dough to about 1/8 in/3 mm thickness and wrap it around the rolling pin. Unroll it gently over the molds, taking care not to stretch it.

2 Press the dough into the molds with a floured ball of dough.

3 Roll the pin over the tops of the molds to trim the dough.

4 Using your forefinger and thumb, press the dough up the sides of each mold to increase the height of the rim. Neaten the edges.

5 Prick the bottoms of the shells thoroughly to prevent air bubbles forming during baking. Chill the shells for 10-15 minutes or until firm, before baking.

BAKING TARTLETS BLIND

A pastry shell is baked blind when fillings that do not need cooking are added, or it may be partially baked blind to help it stay crisp when a moist filling is added. Line the molds with dough and chill them. Heat the oven to 425°F/220°C.

1 Fold a piece of wax or parchment paper into four to make a square about 1 in/2.5 cm larger than one mold. Trim the square to the shape of the mold, leaving a 1/2 in/1.25 cm border. This gives four paper liners. Press a paper liner into the dough in each mold.

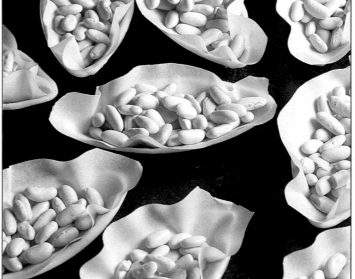

2 Fill the paper with dried beans or rice. Alternatively, set a second mold on top of the dough to hold it in shape for baking blind.

3 Cook the tartlets in the oven for 8-10 minutes until firm, then remove the paper and beans (or rice). If baking completely, cook for 8-12 minutes longer until browned. Let the shells cool slightly, unmold them and transfer to a rack to cool. Tartlet shells are fragile and break easily, so they are often replaced in the molds for filling.

LINING A TART PAN

If possible use a tart pan with a removable base so that the finished tart can be unmolded easily. For baking blind (right) the dough can also be molded on an upturned tart pan or an attractively shaped baking dish.

1 Grease the pan. On a lightly floured surface, roll the dough to a round about 2 in/5 cm larger than the diameter of the pan.

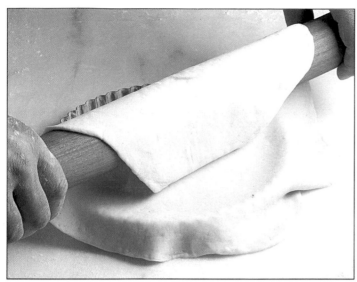

2 ABOVE Wrap the dough around the rolling pin, lift it and unroll it gently over the pan, taking care not to stretch it. Let the dough rest over the edge, overlapping the sides.

3 Gently lift the edges of the dough with one hand and press it well into the bottom of the pan with the other hand.

4 Roll the pin over the top of the pan, pressing down to cut off the excess dough.

5 LEFT With your forefinger and thumb, press the dough evenly up the sides, from the bottom, to increase the height of the rim.

6 Neaten the rim with your finger and thumb and flute it if you like. Do not let the dough overhang the edge of the pan.

7 Prick the base of the shell to prevent air bubbles forming during cooking. Chill for at least 15 minutes, or until firm.

BAKING A TART SHELL BLIND

Line the pan with dough and chill it until firm. Heat the oven to 425°F/220°C. Prick the base of the dough.

1 Fold a large square of parchment paper to form a narrow triangle. Trim the triangle to make a round 2 in/5 cm larger than the diameter of the pan or mold. Open out the paper and put it on top of the dough, pressing it into the edge of the pan.

2 RIGHT Fill the paper three-quarters full with dried beans or dry rice to weight the dough.

3 To bake the shell: cook in the oven for 10 minutes. Lower the heat to 375°F/190°C and continue baking until the pastry is lightly browned, about 5 minutes. Remove the paper and beans.

4 If cooking the shell completely, bake it for 8-12 minutes longer until browned. Let it cool slightly in the pan, unmold and transfer to a rack.

FINISHES FOR PASTRY

Open-faced savory pies can be left plain, or decorated simply. For sweet pies, more elaborate fluted edges are appropriate.

Pinch with pastry pincers.

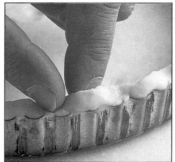

Flute pastry with the fingers.

Seal top and bottom with a fork.

Scallop puff pastry with a knife.

CHOUX PASTRY

Choux or cream puff pastry (Fr. *pâte à choux*) is unlike any other since it is cooked twice – its original name was *pâte à chaud*, meaning heated pastry. First, butter is melted in water and brought to a boil, then flour is beaten in off the heat. The warmth of the butter and water mixture cooks the flour to a ball of dough, which is usually dried over the heat for half a minute. Next, eggs are beaten, one by one, into the dough, which should be warm enough to cook them slightly.

Gauging the amount of egg is the only tricky aspect of making choux pastry. At first the dough thickens, then it starts to thin and look glossy. At this point lightly beaten egg is added gradually until the dough falls easily from the spoon. Quantities vary depending on the size of the eggs, dryness of the flour, amount of water that evaporates as it comes to a boil, and on how much the dough was dried. Choux pastry is too soft to be rolled and is always piped or spooned onto the baking sheet (p.507).

Savory choux puffs may be made with a hot filling, such as cubes of ham in cheese sauce, and cold puffs are often stuffed with a mayonnaise-based mixture. In modern cooking, choux puffs may be filled with smoked salmon mousse or poached eggs and served on a bed of spinach or sorrel purée. Choux flavored with diced or grated cheese become *gougères*, while tiny plain or cheese choux puffs are a good accompaniment to soup.

More versatile than other doughs, choux can be deep-fried as fritters (*beignets soufflés*), or poached as dumplings (*gnocchi alla pangina*). Choux mixed with a double quantity of mashed potato is deep-fried for crisp brown *pommes dauphines* (p.105). Choux also acts as a binding agent in mixtures such as *quenelles* (p.146).

Baking choux pastry

Choux pastry puffs up as it bakes, but it must cook further to become dry and crisp. To help it rise evenly, score the dough with a fork before cooking and leave plenty of space for it to expand on the baking sheet. The dough produces a good deal of steam; in a standard electric oven, the door should be propped open slightly after 10 minutes cooking, but do not open the door completely as partly cooked choux is liable to deflate in a cold draft.

Note Choux puffs often appear done before they are crisp.

USEFUL INFORMATION

Portion Dough with 3 eggs makes 20-25 medium puffs to serve 6.
Preparation of baking sheet Greased.
Cooking methods *Medium puffs:* bake at 400°F/200°C, 20-25 minutes. *Beignets:* deep-fry at 375°F/190°C, 3-5 minutes. *Small gnocchi:* poach 8-10 minutes.
When done *Baked:* golden color, crisp; cracks formed during rising are brown, not pale. *Deep-fried:* crisp and golden. *Gnocchi:* firm.
Problems If boiled before butter melts, water evaporates and changes dough proportions; if too little egg, dough rises poorly; if too much egg, dough cannot be shaped; if underdone, puffs fall so test by removing one from oven.
Reheat If soft, dry in a low oven.

Storage *Raw dough:* refrigerate 12 hours; do not freeze. *Baked unfilled:* 3 days in airtight container; freeze 1 month. *Baked filled:* 3-4 hours. *Deep-fried:* serve at once. *Gnocchi in sauce:* refrigerate 1 day; freeze 3 months.
Glaze Egg.
Typical pastries Cocktail (small puffs with savory filling or sauce); profiteroles (medium puffs with Chantilly cream, pastry cream or ice-cream filling and sauce); *salambôs* (oval puffs with pastry cream and caramel glaze); *Paris Brest* (large ring with cream or pastry cream); Chantilly swans (swan-shaped puffs filled with Chantilly cream); *croquembouche* (caramel coated puffs in a mound): all from France.

MAKING CHOUX PASTRY

Common fillings for choux puffs are vanilla, coffee or chocolate pastry cream (p.384). In France, a savory ham filling is popular.

Makes 20-25 medium puffs	Makes 30-35 medium puffs
¾ cup + 2 tbsp/110 g flour	1¼ cups/150 g flour
¾ cup/175 ml water	1 cup/250 ml water
½ tsp salt	¾ tsp salt
⅓ cup/75 g butter, cut in pieces	6½ tbsp/100 g butter, cut in pieces
3-4 eggs	4-5 eggs

1 Sift the flour on to a piece of paper. In a saucepan heat the water, salt and butter until the butter has melted. Bring just to a boil and take from the heat. Add all the flour at once and beat vigorously with a wooden spoon.

2 Beat until the mixture is smooth and pulls away from sides of pan to form a ball, about 20 seconds. Return the pan to the stove and beat for half a minute over very low heat. Remove from the heat and let cool slightly.

3 Beat in two eggs. Add the remaining eggs one at a time, beating well after each addition. Beat the last egg with a fork in a small bowl and add it little by little (you may not need all of it).

4 When enough egg has been added, the dough will be shiny, and soft enough to fall from the spoon.

Choux variation

Gougères Make choux pastry with 3-4 eggs and beat in ½ cup/ 50 g diced or grated Gruyère cheese. Drop the mixture in rough mounds on to the baking sheet, top with grated cheese and bake.

PIPING CHOUX PASTRY

A pastry bag and plain tube (⅜-½ in/1-1.25 cm) is used for piping choux pastries such as profiteroles, cream puffs and éclairs. For how to fill a pastry bag, see p.406.

1 Pressing the pastry bag evenly, let the dough fall from the tube on to the greased baking sheet so that it is well-rounded. Shown here, from left to right are: éclairs, profiteroles, *salambôs* and smaller profiteroles.

2 After brushing the dough with egg glaze press down lightly with a fork to smooth the top. **Note** Don't let any glaze fall on the baking sheet; it makes the dough stick and prevents it from rising evenly.

Profiteroles with Melba sauce

A fresh raspberry sauce makes a lighter and less rich coating than the more usual chocolate sauce.

Serves 6-8	For the filling
choux pastry made with 3-4 eggs (recipe, p.376)	vanilla pastry cream (p.384)
¾ cup/75 ml water, ½ tsp salt, ⅓ cup/75 g butter, cut in pieces	1 cup/250 ml heavy cream, lightly whipped
3-4 eggs	2 cups/500 ml Melba sauce (p.66)
For glaze	
1 egg, beaten to mix with ½ tsp salt	*Pastry bag and ⅜ in/1 cm plain tube*

1 Heat the oven to 400°F/200°C and grease two baking sheets. Make the choux pastry (previous page). Using the pastry bag, pipe 1 in/2.5 cm mounds, well apart on the prepared baking sheets. Brush the pastry with beaten eggs and score lightly with the tines of a fork. Bake in the heated oven until the puffs are firm and brown, 20-25 minutes. Transfer to a rack and split each puff horizontally to release steam.
2 Make the pastry cream and let it cool, then make the Melba sauce. Fold the whipped cream into the pastry cream to make light pastry cream and spoon the mixture into the choux puffs, filling them generously. Pile the puffs onto individual plates or into a shallow bowl.
3 Just before serving, gently reheat the Melba sauce. Pour it over the puffs and serve at once.

Variations

Ice-cream chocolate profiteroles Substitute 1 qt/1 L vanilla ice cream (p.443) for light pastry cream, and chocolate sauce for Melba sauce.

Butterscotch profiteroles Substitute 2 cups/500 ml butterscotch sauce (p.67) for the chocolate sauce in ice-cream chocolate profiteroles (above).

PUFF PASTRY

Puff pastry (Fr. *pâte feuilleté*) is raised by literally hundreds of layers of butter that are interspersed with a flour and water dough. In the oven, the butter melts, detaching the dough layers, while the water turns to steam, lifting the pastry to three or four times its original thickness. There are quicker versions of puff pastry, such as British flaky and American quick puff (p.381), but none so light and rich as puff pastry, and none so challenging to the cook.

Exact proportions for puff pastry are fixed by weighing the dough, or *détrempe,* after mixing, then adding half its weight in butter. The *détrempe* is made European-style by sifting flour on to a work surface, adding water, salt, and a tablespoon or two of butter (sometimes more), and perhaps a teaspoon of lemon juice to help cut the gluten (p.343). Elasticity is the bane of puff pastry and is accelerated by repeated rollings. Therefore, when a hard wheat flour is used, as in the United States, cake flour may be substituted for up to a quarter of the volume of regular flour in order to counter the flour's gluten. The ingredients are mixed to form a soft, slightly sticky dough. This is wrapped around the additional butter, which has been pounded with a rolling pin so that it is pliable, making the two easy to roll together.

The most crucial stage of puff pastry making is rolling and folding the dough (each roll and fold called a "turn", ensures that the dough is rolled in one direction and then the other). The practice of resting the dough between every second turn is also important. If the dough is to be stored, only four turns are made, the last two when it is shaped to bake.

Every step in puff pastry is geared to producing a dough that is stacked in even layers so it rises straight and tall. For shaping, the dough is rolled very thin, to no more than ¼ in/6 mm, so it does not weigh itself down. It is then turned over before cutting so that the unstretched side faces down. The edge must be trimmed before baking, or it will rise unevenly. Be sure the knife or cutter is sharp, so that the layers of dough are not torn. After cutting, the dough is pressed onto a damp baking sheet to hold its shape in the oven. Steam from the sheet also helps the dough to rise.

In the oven the surface of the puff pastry will dry and crack. To counter this, the top is scored with a knife so that it splits in an even pattern. A finish of egg glaze is sufficient, with a sprinkling of sugar lightly baked until it caramelizes for sweet pastries, or a topping of fondant (p.417) after baking.

Puff pastry makes the perfect light and airy container for shellfish, creamed chicken, or ham and mushrooms, and for more modern mixtures like spinach and crayfish or asparagus with chervil butter. Puff pastry also forms the most luxurious of wrappings for beef Wellington or *pâté en croûte* (see p.244). Sweet puff pastries range from *millefeuilles* ("a thousand leaves"), also called Napoleons, to confections like *gâteau Pithiviers* filled with *frangipane* (p.384). Croissants and Danish pastries are made in a similar way but contain yeast.

Pastry trimmings are invaluable: layer them side by side so that they are not squashed then roll to use for turnovers, cocktail appetizers, *fleurons* (decorative crescents and other shapes), and other tidbits for which the richness of the dough is more important than the lightness. *Palmiers* (p.381) are particularly popular. Pastry trimmings may also make a tart shell or top crust for meat and fruit pies. Trimmings from quick puff pastry can be used in the same way.

USEFUL INFORMATION

Portion Dough with 2 cups/250 g flour makes six to eight 4 in/10 cm *feuilletés* or one 8 in/20 cm vol-au-vent (p.380).

Preparation of baking sheet Sprinkle with water.

Cooking methods *Feuilleté:* bake at 425°F/220°C, 8-12 minutes, then at 375°F/190°C, 12-15 minutes. *Vol-au-vent:* bake at 425°F/220°C, 20-25 minutes.

When done Crisp and golden.

Problems If dough sticks during rolling, flour generously and chill until firm; if dough shrinks or rises unevenly, it was overworked; if dough melts in oven, it was not sufficiently chilled or the oven was too low.

Storage *Raw dough:* wrap well and refrigerate 2 days; freeze 3 months. *Baked unfilled:* 2-3 days in airtight container; freeze 3 months. *Baked filled:* depends on recipe.

Glazes Egg; sugar.

Typical puff pastries Cocktail ham or cheese crescents (USA); cream horns (UK); *chaussons* (turnovers filled with pastry cream or fruit, France); *sacristains* (straws with sugar or cheese topping, France); *palmiers* (trimmings shaped into palm leaves sprinkled with sugar or cheese, France); thousand layer torte (Germany); apricot windmills (small pastries with apricot filling, Germany); *canutillos* (custard horns with cinnamon, Spain); *millefeuilles* (layers filled with pastry cream, sprinkled with powdered sugar, France); ricotta tart with candied fruit (Italy); *gateâu Pithiviers* (with almond cream, France); *canoe di mele* (canoe-shaped pastry boats with rum pastry cream and glazed apples, Italy); maids of honour (with almond filling, UK).

MAKING PUFF PASTRY

Six turns are needed for puff pastry, as described below, with the last two given just before shaping the dough.

Makes 6-8 feuilletés or an 8 in/20 cm vol-au-vent

2 cups/250 g flour	1 tsp lemon juice
1 cup/250 g cold unsalted butter	½ cup/125 ml cold water (more if needed)
1 tsp salt	

1 To make the *détrempe:* sift the flour on to a chilled marble slab or a work surface and make a well in the center.

2 Add 2-3 tablespoons of butter, cut in pieces, with the salt, lemon juice and water and mix quickly with your fingertips.

3 Gradually draw in the flour, working the ingredients together with the fingertips of both hands to form coarse crumbs. If the crumbs seem dry add more water to the dough mixture.

4 Cut the dough several times and turn with the pastry scraper to form a rough, slightly moist ball of dough. At this stage, try to handle the dough as little as possible.

5 RIGHT Score the dough to prevent shrinkage, wrap in plastic or wax paper and chill for 15 minutes.

6 Weigh the dough and measure half its weight in butter. Lightly flour the butter and pound with a rolling pin until pliable. Shape it into a 6 in/15 cm square.

7 Roll out the *détrempe* to double the size, forming a 12 in/30 cm square that is slightly thicker in the center than at the sides.

8 Place the butter in the center and wrap the dough like a parcel, pinching the edges of the dough together to seal it.

9 Set the parcel, seam-side down, on a floured surface and flatten it with a rolling pin. Roll and fold the dough twice (two turns, see opposite). Wrap and chill it for 15 minutes, then repeat two more turns. If storing the dough, wrap and chill it at this stage. Just before using, give the dough two more turns, wrap and chill it for 15 minutes.

ROLLING & FOLDING PUFF PASTRY

Each roll and fold of puff pastry is called a "turn". Usually two turns are done at once, then the dough is chilled. Quick puff pastry is also turned, but fewer times than puff. The dough must be kept cool if its layers are not to stick during rolling. A marble slab is ideal, but any work surface can be chilled by setting a roasting pan filled with ice on the surface.

1 Roll out the dough to a rectangle 6 in/15 cm wide and 18 in/45 cm long, keeping the corners square. Work briskly, rolling away from you and keeping the dough moving on the floured surface.

2 Fold the pastry rectangle in three like a business letter so that it forms a square.

3 Turn the dough 90 degrees to bring the seam side to your left. Gently press the seams with the rolling pin to seal them. This completes the first turn.

4 Repeat a second turn before wrapping the dough in plastic wrap or wax paper. Mark the number of turns by pressing your fingertips into one corner.

Baking puff pastry

A quick blast of heat is the ideal way to begin baking puff pastry, so as to melt the butter layers and at the same time convert the water in the dough to steam, making it rise in the oven. Once the dough has risen, the heat can be lowered to cook it thoroughly inside. Puff pastry should be well browned since toasting adds flavor as well as crispness. However, the relatively high heat maintained throughout cooking means the base is inclined to scorch. To prevent this happening put a cold baking sheet under the hot one halfway through cooking. If the pastry browns too much on top, cover it loosely with foil. After baking, scoop out and discard any uncooked dough from hollow shells, such as vol-au-vents. Puff pastry cases are frequently baked blind (p.375), for maximum crispness, before a filling is added. Prick the base before baking if you don't want it to rise too much.

SHAPING A VOL-AU-VENT

A vol-au-vent or "puff of wind" is a deep round container of puff pastry measuring 6-8 in/15-20 cm in diameter. It is usually filled with savory shellfish, poultry or meat mixtures in a cream sauce.

SHAPING BOUCHEES

Small puff pastries or *bouchées* ("mouthfuls") may be cocktail-sized, or larger (3 in/7.5 cm) as a main course. They are filled like vol-au-vents with a filling that should be highly seasoned.

1 Roll the dough to ¼ in/6 mm thickness. Cut a circle, using a vol-au-vent cutter or pan lid.

2 Using a smaller cutter or lid cut a concentric circle to make a ring about 1 in/2.5 cm wide.

1 Roll the dough to ⅛ in/3 mm thickness and stamp out rounds with a pastry cutter. (*Bouchées* will shrink in the oven.)

2 With a smaller pastry cutter, stamp a circle in the centers of half the rounds so that there are an equal number of rounds and rings. Small circles are used as trimmings.

3 Remove the ring by folding one half over the other and set aside. Roll the remaining pastry to the same diameter as the ring, then trim it.

4 Set the round on a damp baking sheet, brush with egg glaze and prick the center so that it rises evenly. Set the ring on top of the round and press gently.

3 Transfer the rounds to a damp baking sheet and brush with egg glaze. Set the rings on the rounds and gently press the rings so they stick. Scallop the sides. Brush the tops with egg glaze and mark them in a lattice.

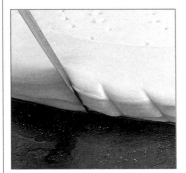

5 Scallop the sides of the dough to help it rise.

6 Glaze the ring. Mark it in a "V" pattern with the back of a knife.

7 Score the center in a lattice pattern. After baking, the center of the vol-au-vent will have risen to form a lid. Lift it off and scoop out the uncooked dough from under the lid and inside the case. Dry out the vol-au-vent case for a few minutes in a low oven.

4 After baking, the centers of the *bouchées* will have risen to form lids. Remove them and scoop out any uncooked dough.

SHAPING FEUILLETES

Diamond-shaped *feuilletés* are an easy alternative to *bouchées* and use the dough more economically.

1 Roll the dough to a sheet ⅛ in/ 3 mm thick. Cut 4 in/10 cm diamonds and brush with egg glaze.

2 Trace a line inside each diamond to make a lid, cutting halfway through the dough.

3 Mark a design, such as a fish, less deeply, on each *feuilleté* and scallop the edges (p.375) to help rising.

4 After baking, cut the lids from the *feuilletés* and scoop out any uncooked dough from under the lids and inside the cases. Fill as required.

SHAPING PALMIERS

Heart-shaped *palmiers* may be made from puff pastry trimmings. Sprinkle the dough and work surface with confectioners' sugar before starting. The *palmiers* should caramelize in the oven until golden brown. Watch them carefully as they color quickly.

 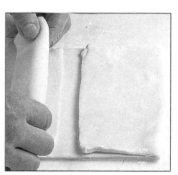

1 Roll the dough ⅛ in/3 mm thick in a rectangle 12 in/30 cm wide. Trim and sprinkle with more sugar.

2 Fold each long side over to meet in the center. Sprinkle with sugar and repeat to make four layers.

3 Fold one folded section of the dough on top of the other so that you have eight layers.

4 Cut the roll into thin slices. Open them out a little as you place them on the baking sheet.

MAKING QUICK PUFF PASTRY

With only two turns, quick puff pastry is a shorter version of classic puff pastry. It is particularly good as a crust for rich tarts and pies, baking to a golden flaky finish. Roll the dough on a floured work surface; if lightly handled so that the gluten does not develop, it needs only a short rest between each rolling.

Makes 10–12 pastries

2 cups/250 g flour	¼ cup/60 g shortening (or butter)
1 tsp salt	⅔ cup/150 ml water
½ cup/125 g butter, cut in pieces	

1 Sift the flour and salt into a bowl. Add half the butter and with a pastry cutter or two knives, cut it into the flour to form coarse crumbs then rub with your fingertips to form fine crumbs. Make a well in the center, add the water and mix with a knife. If the dough is dry, add a little more water; it should be soft but not sticky.

2 Roll out the dough to a rectangle 6 in/15 cm wide by 18 in/45 cm long. Put the remaining butter and shortening over two-thirds of the dough. Fold the unbuttered dough over half the buttered portion.

3 Fold the dough again so the butter is completely enclosed in layers and press the edges with the rolling pin to seal. Wrap and chill the dough for 15 minutes.

4 Roll the dough as for puff pastry giving it two turns (p.379). Wrap and chill it for 15 minutes before using.

Note Quick puff pastry is a useful alternative to puff pastry trimmings for making palmiers, cheese straws and other pastries. The dough freezes well and should be given one more turn after thawing.

STRUDEL & LEAVED PASTRIES

All leaved pastries, except puff, are made in the same way – by rolling and pulling pliable dough into a sheet so thin that it is said you can read your love-letters through it! In Austria, Germany and eastern Europe, flaky strudel dough vies with puff pastry for popularity, while half a dozen leaved pastries are found in Mediterranean countries, the most familiar being Greek phyllo.

Gluten is the enemy of most pastry doughs. However, for leaved doughs it is developed quite deliberately by kneading – as with pasta and bread doughs – to make it very pliable. The dough needs lengthy resting before it is rolled, pulled to a sheet and brushed with fat, which is usually melted butter, except in Mediterranean countries where they tend to use oil.

In Morocco, wafer-thin pastry is made by gently pressing a ball of dough on to a hot griddle. The pastry for Chinese spring rolls follows a similar method. Strudel dough, although thicker than phyllo pastry, is softer, while spring roll skins (made with starch) are quite tough. All three types are difficult to make, but are readily available commercially, usually frozen, and they will keep frozen for up to three months. It is important, particularly with phyllo pastry and strudel dough, to defrost thoroughly and at room temperature to prevent crumbling. Cover unwrapped dough with a damp dish cloth as it soon dries out and becomes brittle.

Before baking, the dough is cut into sheets to layer in a pan, or it may be rolled in triangles, individual rolls, or in one large roll, the method typical for strudel. Fillings range from dried or fresh fruit (popular in Europe), nuts and honey (Greek *baklava*), meat (Turkish *borek*), to cheese and spinach. The dishes can be served as an accompaniment to a meal, as an appetizer, or as a dessert.

USEFUL INFORMATION

Portion *Strudel*: dough made with 2 cups/250 g flour serves 6-8 when filled. *Phyllo*: 1 lb/500 g dough makes about 20 × 2 in/5 cm pastries.

Preparation of baking sheet Greased.

Cooking methods *Small pastries*: bake at 375°F/190°C, 20-30 minutes. *Large pastries*: bake at 375°F/190°C, 30-40 minutes.

When done Crisp and brown, hot in center.

Problems If stiff or not rested sufficiently, dough breaks when pulled; dough dries rapidly so when stretching, work quickly and when storing, keep covered as much as possible.

Storage *After shaping*: refrigerate dough 24 hours; freeze 1 month. *After baking*: store in airtight container 3 days; freeze 3 months.

Processed forms Fresh and frozen dough sheets.

Typical pastries *Apfelstrudel* (with apple and sultanas, Austria); strudel with cream and raisin filling (Italy); nut *rétes* (with walnuts and jam, Hungary); wine strudel (with white wine and breadcrumb filling, Hungary); *brik* (deep-fried pastries with egg, fish, or vegetable filling, Tunisia); *b'stilla* (pigeon, pine nuts and cinnamon, Morocco); *tiropita* (cheese pastries, Middle East).

Shaping leaved pastries

Brush the dough with melted butter, goose fat, or oil. For purses, cut the dough into 4 in/10 cm squares. Pile three squares on top of each other and add a tablespoon of filling. Gather up the corners to enclose the filling and twist to seal. For triangles, cut the dough into 2-3 in/5-7 cm strips. Put a tablespoon of filling near one end and fold one corner of the strip over the filling to make a triangle. Continue folding the strip to form a neat triangular parcel. For crescents, cut the dough into 6 in/15 cm squares. Spread a tablespoon of filling along one edge and roll up. Curve the ends of the roll to form a crescent and pinch them to seal.

Baklava

When cut into small diamond shapes, these rich Greek honey and nut pastries are delicious with coffee. Larger portions make a good dessert.

Makes 20-25 pastries

1 lb/500 g package phyllo pastry	¼ cup/50 g sugar
1 cup/250 g melted butter	1 tsp ground cinnamon
20-25 whole cloves	*For the syrup*
For the filling	1 cup/200 g sugar
1½ cups/250 g finely chopped pistachio nuts	1 cup/250 ml water
	1 cup/400 g honey
1½ cups/250 g finely chopped almonds	grated zest and juice of 1 lemon
	9 × 13 in/23 × 32 cm baking dish

1 Heat the oven to 350°F/175°C. **To make the filling:** mix the pistachio nuts, almonds, sugar and cinnamon.
2 Brush the baking dish with melted butter, then line the pan with a third of the phyllo sheets. Brush each sheet with butter, and press the dough into the corners and sides of the dish. Top with half of the nut filling. Repeat this process. Use the remaining phyllo dough to cover the top, pressing it into the corners and sides of the dish and trimming the excess with a sharp knife.
3 Brush the phyllo with melted butter and score it ½ in/1.25 cm deep in diagonal lines to form 2 in/6 cm diamonds. Pierce the center of each diamond with a clove. Bake in the oven until the top is golden brown, 1¼-1½ hours.
4 **To make the syrup:** heat the sugar with the water until dissolved. Add the honey and boil until the syrup reaches the soft ball stage (p.415), 239°F/115°C on a sugar thermometer. Let it cool, then stir in the grated lemon zest and juice.
5 Pour the syrup over the *baklava* as soon as it comes out of the oven. Run a sharp knife through the nuts to allow the syrup to penetrate the bottom layers. Cool and store the *baklava* in the pan. The flavor mellows with time and the pastries may be kept for up to 2 weeks. Cut through the diamond shapes completely to serve.

Blue Brie and prawn parcels

Savory phyllo parcels are usually served hot as an appetizer with a salad garnish. They can be filled with a variety of ingredients – for example, chicken and asparagus, spinach and cheese, or seafood. In this recipe the dill and lemon zest add an unusual fragrance.

Makes 6 parcels

8 oz/250 g cooked prawns	6 sheets phyllo pastry
2 tbsp chopped fresh dill	sesame seeds
½ tsp grated lemon zest	*For the garnish*
10 oz/300 g blue Brie	lettuce leaves, sprigs of dill, prawns and lemon slices
salt and black pepper	

1 Heat the oven to 400°F/200°C. Mix together the prawns, dill and lemon zest. Remove the rind from the cheese, then cut it into small pieces. Stir into the prawn mixture and season.
2 To make each phyllo parcel, brush a pastry sheet with melted butter. Add the filling as directed for shaping leaved pastries, left.
3 Place seam-side down on a lightly greased baking sheet. Brush the tops of the parcels with melted butter and sprinkle with sesame seeds. Bake in the pre-heated oven for 25 minutes or until golden brown. Serve warm with the lettuce, dill, prawns and lemon slices.

MAKING STRUDEL

Thorough kneading of strudel dough is essential to develop the gluten and make it easier to stretch out.

Serves 6-8

2 cups/250 g all-purpose unbleached flour	confectioners' sugar (for sprinkling)
1 egg	**For the filling**
¾ cup/175 ml lukewarm water	1 lb/500 g cherries, pitted
½ tsp lemon juice	½ cup/100 g brown sugar
pinch of salt	½ cup/70 g chopped walnuts
½ cup/125 g melted butter	1 tsp ground cinnamon (optional)
	grated zest of 1 lemon

1 Sift the flour on to a board and make a well in the center. Add the egg, water, lemon juice and salt to the well and work with your fingertips until thoroughly mixed. Quickly work in the flour with your fingertips to form coarse crumbs. If the crumbs seem dry, add a little more water. Press the dough into a ball; it should be quite soft.

2 Flour the work surface and knead the dough for 5-7 minutes, picking it up and throwing it down until it is shiny and smooth. Alternatively, work it in a mixer with the dough hook. Cover the dough with an upturned bowl so that it does not dry out and leave to rest for at least 30 minutes. Meanwhile, heat the oven to 375°F/190°C and grease a baking sheet.

3 **To roll the dough:** cover the table with a sheet, lightly flour it and roll the dough to as large a square as possible. Cover it with a damp towel and leave to rest for 15 minutes.

4 Flour your hands and place them under the dough. Starting at the center and working outward, carefully stretch the dough with both hands. Do not worry about any small holes that appear; they will not show when the dough is rolled up.

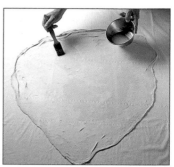

5 Continue to work outward as the dough gets thinner, gently lifting and flopping it on the surface. it should be about 1 yd/1 m square.

6 Brush the dough with melted butter. **Note** Use stretched strudel dough at once as it dries quickly and will become brittle.

7 Sprinkle with the cherries, sugar and walnuts, cinnamon if using, and lemon zest.

8 **To shape the strudel:** trim the thick edge of the dough. Roll it up with the help of the sheet.

9 Transfer the roll to the prepared baking sheet and shape it into a crescent. Brush with butter and bake in the preheated oven until crisp and light brown, 30-40 minutes.

10 The strudel is cooked when a skewer inserted in the center is hot when withdrawn. Serve hot, sprinkled with confectioners' sugar.

Strudel variations

Cream cheese strudel Omit the cherries, walnuts and cinnamon. Beat 5-6 tbsp/75-90 ml light cream into 1½ cups/375 g cream cheese. Beat in sugar. Stir in 1 egg, ½ cup/70 g raisins and lemon.

Apple strudel Substitute 2 lb/1 kg tart apples, peeled, cored and thinly sliced for the cherries, and add ½ cup/70 g raisins.

SWEET FILLINGS FOR PASTRY

As its name implies, pastry cream (Fr. *crème patissière*) is designed specifically for pastry. It is a custard mixture thickened with enough flour (or sometimes cornstarch), to hold its shape without making the pastry soggy. This also means that pastry cream can be refrigerated a day or two and that it will blend with a wide variety of flavorings from chocolate and coffee to liqueurs, even a stiff fruit purée. It also forms the basis of hot sweet soufflés (p.92).

Pastry cream can be heavy, so it is often lightened with an equal quantity of butter cream, Italian meringue (to make *crème Chibouste*), or whipped cream (to make light pastry cream). Light butter cream keeps well, but *crème Chibouste* and light pastry cream hold up for only a few hours. Chantilly cream (p.70), which is whipped cream with a flavoring of sugar and vanilla or brandy, is a light quick filling. However, it is delicate and will separate within an hour or two, making pastry unpleasantly soft. Other fillings for pastry include cold mousse and soufflé mixtures set with gelatin (p.431), and the wide variety of American pie fillings, many of which are topped with meringue.

A contrast to these creamy fillings is *frangipane*, a mixture of eggs, sugar and ground almonds that is cooked in the pastry shell until firm. Fruit such as apple or pear can be embedded in it before cooking, or fruits may be arranged on top after baking.

USEFUL INFORMATION

Portion 3-4 tbsp/45-60 ml.
Problems Heavy consistency if too thick; soaks pastry if too thin; cloying if too sweet.
Storage *Frangipane:* 2-3 days in airtight container. *Pastry cream:* refrigerate 1-2 days. *Fillings with whipped cream:* refrigerate 1-2 hours.
Used for Pie pastry; *pâte brisée; pâte sucrée;* puff pastry; quick puff pastry; choux pastry .

MAKING PASTRY CREAM

To prevent a skin from forming on the pastry cream, rub a lump of butter over the surface as it cools.

Makes 2½ cups/625 ml pastry cream

2 cups/500 ml milk	½ cup/100 g sugar
1 vanilla bean, split or 1 tsp vanilla extract	3 tbsp/20 g flour
6 egg yolks	*Small heavy saucepan*

3 Return the mixture to the pan and heat. Bring to a boil, whisking constantly. If lumps form as it thickens, take it from the heat at once and whisk until the cream is smooth.

4 Cook the cream gently, whisking constantly until it softens slightly, indicating that the flour is completely cooked, about 2 minutes. (If the cream is undercooked it will taste floury.) Take the pan from the heat, transfer the pastry cream to a bowl and, if using vanilla extract, add it now. Cover the bowl and let the cream cool.

1 Bring the milk just to a boil. If using a vanilla bean, add it, cover the pan and leave over low heat to infuse for 10-15 minutes. Meanwhile, whisk the egg yolks with the sugar until thick and light, about 2 minutes, then whisk in the flour.

2 Strain the milk into the egg yolk mixture, reserving the vanilla bean to use again. Stir to mix with a whisk, until the cream is smooth and there are no lumps.

Pastry cream variations

Chocolate or coffee pastry cream Used for choux pastry, especially éclairs. For chocolate, melt 6 oz/150 g chocolate on a heatproof plate over a pan of hot water and beat into the pastry cream. For coffee, dissolve 2 tbsp dry instant coffee in the milk.

Light pastry cream Used for pastry tarts, puff pastry desserts, cream puffs. Fold whipped cream made with 1 cup/250 ml heavy cream into any flavor of pastry cream.

Crème Chibouste Used for light pastries, especially puff. Fold Italian meringue (p.437) made with 2 egg whites, ½ cup/100 g sugar and 2 tbsp water into any flavor of pastry cream.

GLAZES FOR PASTRY

The prime function of a pastry glaze is to add shine and color to pastry. One type is added before baking, the other after the pastry or cookie has been baked. A glaze also acts as a protective layer when moist fillings are added.

Glazes for dough

The most useful glaze for raw dough is egg glaze, made by whisking a whole egg with a large pinch of salt. The salt breaks down albumen in the egg white, making the glaze easier to brush smoothly. A glaze of egg yolk, salt and a tablespoon of water, gives a less shiny, more golden, finish.

Egg glaze also helps stick the dough together, and is useful for sealing the edges of leaved doughs and the lids of pies. However, if egg glaze drips down the sides of the dough, it will act as glue and prevent the dough from rising. This is especially true of puff pastry. When scoring dough in a pattern with a knife or other tool, glaze the dough first so the egg does not drip into the cracks.

Other glazes to be baked include sugar syrup, or water sprinkled with sugar, both of which cook to a crisp finish. For a golden color, use lightly beaten egg white or milk in place of water. Thin royal icing (p.408) can also be spread on cooked pastry and baked again for one to two minutes to set. Richer glazes with honey or nuts are more commonly used for breads and cakes. Since sugar glazes caramelize and burn easily, they are often added toward the end of cooking.

USEFUL INFORMATION

Portion Glaze made with 1 egg covers 1-2 lb/500 g-1 kg dough.
Problems If applied too generously, glaze drips or soaks dough.

Used for *Egg*: pie pastry; *pâte brisée*; *pâte sucrée*; puff pastry; choux pastry; raised pies; cookies. *Sugar icing*: pie pastry; *pâte sucrée*; puff pastry, cookies.

Glazes for finished pastry

Many glazes added after cooking are fruit-based. Red currant jelly glaze is used for tarts filled with berries and red fruits such as plums. All other fruits – green, gold or white – should be coated with apricot jam glaze or a glaze of a similar color such as orange marmalade. When fruits are poached in syrup, a fruit syrup glaze can be made by reducing the poaching liquid, then thickening it with cornstarch or arrowroot. If brushed on a cooked pastry shell,

fruit glaze protects the pastry and helps prevent the juice of ripe fruit from saturating it. Other possibilities, particularly for puff and choux pastry, include sugar icings like *glacé* (p.406), fondant (p.417), and melted chocolate. Hot caramel (p.418), another good insulator, sets to a thin brittle sheet.

USEFUL INFORMATION

Portion 2-3 tbsp jelly or jam glaze per tartlet.
Problems If too thick, glaze looks lumpy; if too thin, the pastry becomes soaked.

Used for *Fruit*: pie pastry; *pâte brisée*; *pâte sucrée*; puff pastry; cookies. *Sugar icing*: *pâte sucrée*; puff pastry; choux pastry; cookies.

Apricot jam glaze

Citrus marmalade, or a jam that matches the fruit, may be used instead of apricot jam. The glaze should be used while still warm.

Makes 1½ cups/375 ml glaze

1½ cups/375 g apricot jam	3 tbsp/45 ml water (more if needed)
juice of ½ lemon	

Heat the jam, lemon juice and water gently, stirring until melted. Work the glaze through a sieve. Melt the glaze before using and, if necessary, thin it with more water.

Poached fruit glaze

A glaze for pears, plums, cherries, peaches or apricots and any fruit that has been poached.

Makes 1½ cups/375 ml glaze

2 cups/500 ml syrup from poaching fruit (p.448)	1 tbsp cornstarch or 2 tbsp arrowroot, mixed to a paste with ¼ cup/60 ml water
¼ cup/60 g red currant jelly (for red fruits) or apricot jam (for green or yellow fruits)	1 tbsp kirsch (optional)

Boil the syrup until reduced to 1 cup/250 ml. Add the red currant jelly or apricot jam and heat, stirring, until smooth. Whisk in the cornstarch or arrowroot paste, which will thicken the glaze. Take from the heat and stir in the kirsch if using. Use warm.

Red currant jelly glaze

Substitute red currant jelly for the jam in apricot jam glaze above. Gently whisk the jelly over low heat until melted and use while warm to glaze strawberries or other berries in a fruit tart.

COOKIES

The American word "cookie" is of Dutch origin, from *koekje* meaning little cake, while the British word "biscuit" comes straight from the French *bis cuit* meaning twice cooked. The original biscuits were cooked twice, to preserve them on long sea voyages, and even today many crisp cookies look as if they have been in the oven twice. Some cookies are a version of pie pastry (p.371), with the fat rubbed into the flour, then liberally sweetened and often flavored with nuts. Others follow the mixing method for creamed (p.398) or melted cakes, though results differ as cookie mixtures are compact rather than fluffy, designed for baking in a thin layer rather than rising.

Ingredients for cookies

Unlike cakes, which often rely on fillings and icings, cookie doughs have their own character. Much is made of nuts, grains such as oatmeal, and dried fruits such as raisins and dates. Butter is the key flavoring ingredient in plain cookies, while honey, molasses and brown sugar provide color and sweetness. Many cookies would be dull without chocolate, coffee, spices like ginger, cinnamon or nutmeg, or seeds like sesame or caraway. Occasionally baking soda or powder is used, which makes the cookie more crumbly.

PREPARING A BAKING SHEET FOR COOKIES

Heavy baking sheets (p.507) that do not buckle in the heat are important for cookies so that they do not slide together in the oven. Delicate mixtures can be protected by lining the sheet with parchment paper (grease the sheet so the paper sticks to it). Foil is less effective, conducting the heat too well to provide much insulation, but it will allow the cookies to slide more easily off the sheet in one batch. Depending on the recipe, the baking sheet or paper may be greased with butter or shortening and coated with flour. Non-stick baking sheets are particularly useful for rich cookies and wafers, and they need no preparation.

1 Brush the baking sheet with melted butter or shortening, and chill. Sprinkle flour on to one end.

2 Shake the sheet to coat it evenly. Rap it to remove excess flour.

Making cookie batter by machine

Electric machines are invaluable for making cookies. Stiff doughs that require kneading do well in a food processor or mixer with a dough hook, while softer doughs can be beaten in a food processor or with an electric beater. However, do not overwork the dough as this will make the cookies tough. Chopped ingredients should be mixed in by hand to give a more even distribution in the dough.

Baking cookies

Given the high oven temperature and the common use of ingredients that scorch easily like sugar and nuts, achieving a batch of even-sized, perfectly browned cookies requires more skill than one might think. Always allow 10-15 minutes for the oven to reach the correct temperature before baking cookies. In general, the best position for the baking sheet is on a shelf in the center of the oven, although this depends to some extent on where the source of heat is and whether it is evenly distributed, as in a convection oven. The main thing is to make sure the heat can circulate freely around the edges of the sheet. If the dough browns too much on the bottom, the use of two baking sheets, one on top of the other, may help. Baking two shelves of cookies at once is inadvisable: bake one sheet in the oven while you prepare another and transfer a third to a rack to cool.

Cookies rarely cook evenly and those at the edges and back of the sheet are likely to brown first. Therefore, the sheet should be turned around about two-thirds of the way through baking. Once cookies start to brown, watch them closely as they burn fast. Some cookies may need to be removed before the others are done.

Decorating cookies

Many cookies are a decoration in themselves. Take, for example, the studded surface of a chocolate chip cookie, the almond crescents of Hungary, or elegant cigarette- and tile-shaped wafers (p.388). Rolled cookies can be cut in amusing shapes such as gingerbread men, and decorated with chocolate or whole nuts. Rich doughs may be formed into decorative shapes using a pastry bag or a metal cookie press. Plain cookies may be sandwiched together and topped with a melted frosting before being sliced.

When baked, cookies can be coated with cake icings, particularly fondant (p.417), and glazes based on sugar (p.406) or chocolate. A sprinkling of nuts, grated chocolate and colored sugar (p.412), or icing or melted chocolate piped with a paper cone (p.407), may also be added. To coat the cookie, spread a spoonful of icing with a metal spatula in a swift circular motion.

Storing cookies

When stored, crisp cookies tend to go soft, and soft ones harden and dry out. Some cookies – for example, French *croquants* and Italian *cantucci* – are deliberately baked very dry so that they can be dipped in beverages. Except for wafers, limp cookies can be revived by drying briefly in the oven. Rich cookies keep well if layered with wax paper in an airtight container, while bar cookies can be stored in the pan, tightly wrapped. Cookies such as German *pfeffernusse* (peppery nuts), and others that contain honey, nuts and spices, mellow when stored and can be kept for months. Before or after baking, most cookies freeze well, although spicy flavors tend to fade and wafers will disintegrate.

COOLING COOKIES

Cookies should be removed from the baking sheet as soon as possible, partly to stop them cooking further, and partly because they remain soft while still warm and will not break so easily. If they stick as they cool, warm them briefly in the oven to release them. Slide the paper off the baking sheet, peel the cookies from it and leave them on a rack to cool. Loosen cookies baked on the sheet with a sharp flexible knife. For sticky cookies (above), pour a little water under the paper, onto the hot baking sheet; the steam will loosen the cookies so that they can be lifted off the baking sheet easily.

ROLLED & MOLDED COOKIES

A single characteristic unites rolled and molded cookies: the dough must not spread on the baking sheet. Within this simple definition there are soft and crisp cookies, thin and chewy ones, made following any of the methods for cakes as well as pastry. Doughs that are stiff enough to roll may be cut with a knife into squares or triangles, or stamped into rounds or fancy shapes. Doughs that are too rich to roll out can be shaped by hand or with a pastry bag and large tube, often in a star or ribbon shape (Icings, p.405). For very stiff doughs, a metal cookie press (p.507) which forces the dough through a serrated blade, may be used. For refrigerator cookies, it is shaped into a rectangle or cylinder, wrapped and chilled and then sliced and baked as needed.

Rolled and molded cookies are popular throughout Europe: there are butter-flavored "sand" cookies (Fr. *sablés*) made like *pâte sucrée* (p.373), festive cookies to hang on the Christmas tree, or molded cookies, such as macaroons. Ingredients include nuts, spices and grated citrus zest, while typical coatings are royal icing for rolled cookies and sugar glaze for molded ones.

USEFUL INFORMATION

Portion 1 lb/500 g dough makes about 30-40 × 2 in/5 cm cookies.
Preparation of baking sheet *Rolled:* greased. *Molded:* greased and floured.
Cooking methods Shape may affect baking times. *Rolled:* bake at 375°F/190°C, 8-15 minutes. *Molded:* bake at 325°F/160°C, 10-15 minutes.
When done *Rolled:* firm and lightly browned. *Molded:* brown edges, slight depression left if pressed with the fingertips.
Problems Tough if dough is overworked; dry if too much flour used during rolling. If dough

spreads, add more flour; if too soft, chill dough thoroughly.
Storage 2-5 days in airtight container; freeze 6 months.
Icings and glazes (p.405) Fondant; glacé; egg white and sugar; egg.
Typical cookies *Rolled:* gingersnaps (UK); *sablés* (butter cookies, France); *friedenstauben* (Viennese); Shrewsbury (shortbread with currants, UK); *Molded:* cardamom butter (Denmark); caraway crisps (Scotland); Neapolitans (pine nuts, chocolate, Italy), *wienerstube* (black pepper, chocolate, Austria).

ROLLING COOKIE DOUGH

Principles are the same as for rolling pastry dough, except that cookie dough tends to crumble and stick. After mixing, knead it lightly so it holds together, then chill for at least an hour until firm. If stiff enough, roll the dough as for *pâte brisée* (p.373).

1 Generously sprinkle the dough with flour or sugar and place it between two sheets of wax paper or plastic wrap.

2 Tap the dough with a rolling pin to flatten it, then gently roll the dough between the papers to the required thickness.

3 Peel off the top layer of paper. Cut out shapes with a cutter or knife dipped in flour. Press the dough trimmings together and roll again.

MOLDING COOKIE DOUGH

First try molding the dough without chilling. If it is too sticky, chill it until firm. Some recipes call for moistening your hands with water, others for flouring them, before handling the dough.

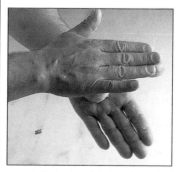

1 Roll the dough into walnut-sized balls, and roll these in confectioners' sugar. Set them well apart on a prepared baking sheet.

2 Flatten the balls with a fork dipped in water, or with the base of a tumbler dusted with confectioners' sugar.

DROP & WAFER COOKIES

Drop cookies are the simplest of all, shaped by piping or dropping spoonfuls of dough on to a baking sheet. Sometimes the dough must be spread with a fork or teaspoon, but often this is unnecessary since it melts and spreads during baking. Allow enough space on the baking sheet for the cookies to expand.

Mixing methods for the batter are equally simple, with liquid ingredients stirred into dry ones in a bowl, following the melted method for cakes (p.401). When baked, drop cookies vary in texture, a prime example being American chocolate chip cookies. These are so popular that both crisp and soft types are touted commercially, each with their own devotees.

By their nature, drop cookies invite the use of coarse-textured oatmeal or cornmeal, chopped nuts and candied fruits – ingredients that could cause rolled or molded cookies to break up. A sprinkling of chopped nuts or coarse sugar tends to be the only topping because the cookies' surface is too rough for an icing or glaze. The exception is the French *florentine*, which is spread on the underside with melted chocolate.

Wafers are the most delicate of all drop cookies, and pose the greatest challenge for the cook. The batter is particularly thin, scarcely thicker than for crêpes (p.366), and a tablespoon more or less of flour or liquid can make the difference between success and failure. The batter may be sugary, flavored only with vanilla, but often orange, ginger or ground almonds add interest. Some wafers are baked in a special hinged iron, but many are cooked directly on the baking sheet, then molded while still warm into characteristic shapes: *cigarettes* are rolled around a wooden spoon handle, lacy *tuiles* are bent over a rolling pin to the shape of Provençal roof tiles, and *tulipes* are molded into crisp cups for filling with mousse, ice cream or sorbet. Although many wafers are left plain, British rolled brandysnaps may be filled with whipped cream, sweetened if desired.

USEFUL INFORMATION

Portion 2 cups/500 ml makes 25-30 × 2 in/5 cm cookies or 60 wafers.

Preparation of baking sheet Greased.

Cooking method Drop: bake at 350°F/175°C, 12-15 minutes. Wafer: bake at 375°F/190°C, 5-8 minutes.

When done Crisp drop: evenly browned. Soft drop: brown around edges and slight depression left when pressed with the fingertips. Wafer: brown around edges.

Problems Drop: if dough spreads too much, add a little more flour; if it does not spread, flatten it with a fork, or add 1-2 tbsp liquid. Wafer: use a non-stick baking sheet to prevent sticking; if dough too stiff,

wafer will not curl; if overbaked, wafer will break; if too thin, wafer will disintegrate.

Storage Drop: 3-5 days in airtight container; freeze 6 months. Wafer: 24 hours in airtight container.

Toppings Drop: chopped nuts, coarse sugar; melted chocolate.

Typical cookies Drop: anise caps (Germany); caraway drops (UK); cornmeal drops (Italy); *galettes aux raisins secs* (France); hermits (honey, nutmeg, USA); oatmeal and raisin (USA); poppyseed (Austria). Wafers: suspiros (Spain); maple pecan lace crisps (USA); pralines (pecan, brown sugar, USA); *mohr* (poppyseed, raisins, nutmeg, Hungary); anise, coriander and coffee (Mexico).

Wafer batter

Set the oven at very hot, 450°F/230°C. Whisk 4 egg whites in a bowl just until mixed. Sift in 1¼ cups/150 g flour and 1 cup/200 g confectioners' sugar until combined. Add 5 tbsp/75 g butter, melted and cooled, and 2 tbsp heavy cream.

BAKING & SHAPING WAFERS

Test consistency by baking a single wafer first before shaping a full batch of *tulipe* or *cigarette russe* batter.

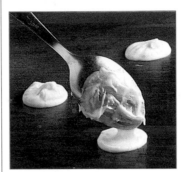

1 Grease the baking sheet, then add spoonfuls of batter.

2 Spread it as thinly as possible with the back of a spoon.

3 Bake the wafers just until brown around the edges. With a sharp flexible knife or metal spatula, lift the wafers off the baking sheet while still hot. If they stick, warm them briefly in the oven.

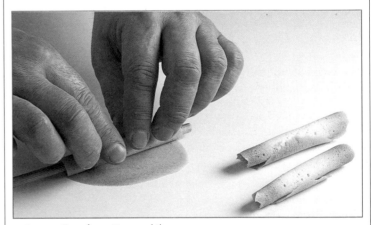

4 ABOVE **For *cigarettes*:** curl the hot wafers at once around a wooden spoon handle. If they harden while shaping, return them to the oven briefly until they soften.

5 RIGHT **For *tulipes*:** Lift the hot wafers from the tray and place on upturned glass tumblers.

6 Press a ramekin over each wafer and leave to cool on the glasses. The finished *tulipes* can be filled just before serving.

Old-fashioned chocolate chip cookies

For superior flavor, use coarsely chopped dessert chocolate instead of commercial chocolate chips.

Makes about 24 × 3 in/7.5 cm cookies

1¼ cups/150 g flour	½ tsp vanilla extract
½ tsp salt	1 egg
½ cup/125 g unsalted butter, softened	½ tsp baking soda
	1 tsp hot water
6 tbsp/75 g granulated sugar	1 cup/125 g walnut pieces
6 tbsp/75 g light brown sugar	1 cup/175 g chocolate chips

1 Heat the oven to 375°F/190°C. Line two baking sheets with aluminum foil and butter the foil. Sift the flour with the salt.
2 Cream the butter, add both sugars and beat until soft and light (Cakes and Icings, p.398). Beat in the vanilla, add the egg and beat for one minute. Mix the baking soda with water until dissolved and stir it into the mixture. With a spoon, stir in the flour in two to three batches. Stir in the walnut pieces and chocolate chips.
3 Using two teaspoons, drop small mounds of mixture on to the baking sheets, leaving at least 3 in/7.5 cm between each. Flatten the mounds slightly with the back of a wet teaspoon. Bake the cookies in the oven until lightly but evenly browned, 10-12 minutes. **Note** Do not underbake the cookies as they should be crisp. While still warm, transfer the cookies to a rack to cool.

BAR COOKIES

Bar cookies are baked in rectangular or square pans. Flavors are bold, with generous measures of chocolate, nuts, lemon and other citrus fruits. The batter is often soft enough to pour or spread with a spatula, though it can also be so crumbly that it must be pressed in an even layer. A pastry base may be added to hold a rich filling, as with Austrian hazelnut Linzer bars.

The texture of finished cookies varies, from moist American date-nut bars, to chewy British oatmeal flapjacks. Generally, the thinner the layer of batter the crisper the cookie will be, so it is important to use the pan size specified. Bar cookies may be baked in multi-colored layers, marbled, or sandwiched like small cakes and coated with glaze, icing or butter cream.

USEFUL INFORMATION
Portion 10½ × 15½ in/ 27 × 40 cm pan makes 12 bars.
Typical pan Jelly roll, shallow square.
Preparation of pan Greased, lined with wax paper.
Cooking method Bake at 375°F/ 190°C, 12-15 minutes, depending on type.
When done Firm; skewer inserted in the center comes out clean.
Problems If underbaked, central bars are too soft; slice when warm or bars may crack.
Storage 3-5 days tightly wrapped in the pan; freeze 6 months.
Frostings and icings (p.405) Butter cream; whipped; ganache; fondant; glacé.
Glazes and toppings (p.385) Chopped nuts; coarse sugar; colored sugar; sugar glaze; honey glaze; egg white and sugar.
Typical cookies Almond cinnamon shortbread (Switzerland); lemon squares (USA); *petits trianons* (chocolate fudge bars, France); rocky roads (chocolate, pecans, marshmallow, USA); walnut bars (Hungary); crunchy chocolate bars (oatmeal and coconut, Australia); *lebkuchen* (Christmas bars with honey, nuts and spices, Germany); macaroon-meringue bars (Switzerland); *mazurkas* (wedding cookies with hard-boiled egg and almonds, Poland); cinnamon-almond bars (UK); lemon and caraway bars (Italy); marzipan bars (Austria); flapjacks (oatmeal and demerara sugar, UK); *zimt-pitte* (almond and cinnamon bars, Switzerland); chocolate walnut (Austria).

CRACKERS

Freshly baked crackers are a rarity today, yet they are easy to make. The stiff, pliable dough made from flour, salt and water, should be rolled as thinly as possible. Lifted in one piece on to the baking sheet, the dough is scored in squares, pricked to prevent rising, then baked in the oven. It may also be baked in large or small rounds on a griddle (p.511), although this is harder to control as the dough tends to buckle and rise from the hot surface.

Wheat flour crackers often have butter rubbed into the flour before water is added, but if whole wheat, cornmeal, or oatmeal flour is used, the dough is usually plain, perhaps with a little sugar or honey for flavor. These more robust crackers are often called flat breads. Some wheat flour must be included to hold the mixture together. Rye flour adds a sharp taste, oats and millet a nutty one; flavorings include strong cheese such as Parmesan, coarse salt, caraway, celery and sesame seeds, and spices. American soda crackers are particularly crisp, a result of the dough being rolled and folded until smooth.

USEFUL INFORMATION
Portion 1 lb/500 g dough makes 90-100 × 2 in/5 cm crackers.
Preparation of baking sheet or griddle Ungreased.
Cooking methods Bake at 425°F/ 220°C, 5-8 minutes; cook on griddle 3-4 minutes each side.
When done Edges of dough lightly browned, surface blistered.
Problems Dough lifts off baking sheet if not pressed down firmly before baking; if underbaked, crackers are not crisp.
Storage 1-2 months in airtight container; if no longer crisp, warm crackers in low oven.
Typical crackers *Knackbröd* (whole wheat with buttermilk, Scandinavia); Vermont common crackers (USA); water biscuits (UK); rye biscuits (Sweden); Melba (UK); soda crackers (USA); cream crackers (Ireland); cheese crackers (USA); oatcakes (Scotland); *flattbröd* (whole wheat and rye flour flatcakes, Norway); Bath olivers (UK); graham crackers (USA); matzohs (Jewish); *matthi* (with yogurt and lovage seeds, India); *sajtos izelitö* (hot cheese crackers, Hungary); sesame seed crackers (USA).

CAKES & ICINGS

THE GREAT French chef of the early nineteenth century, Antonin Carême, proclaimed: "The fine arts are five in number – painting, sculpture, poetry, music, and architecture, whose main branch is confectionery". It is still true to say that cakes have an architectural element, with the cake as the structure, the filling as the mortar, and the icing – the tiles and woodwork – embellishing the whole.

The basic ingredients for a cake – eggs, sugar, flour, and often some kind of fat – are few, but variations are achieved by changing flavors, texture and shape. Consider the many types of English sponge, rich French *génoises*, and the American layer cakes, all of which use these basic ingredients.

There are three standard mixing methods for making a cake, the distinction between them reflected in the types of cake they produce: whisked (sponge) cakes including *génoise, biscuit* and angel food cakes; creamed cakes including pound cakes and many fruit cakes, and melted cakes, such as gingerbread, which generally need a leavening agent to help them rise. All three can be made into layer cakes. Some cake recipes are a blend of two methods – for example, creamed cakes often have whisked egg whites added as in a whisked cake – but the same principles apply to both. This chapter also covers flourless cakes and meringue cakes, rich cheesecakes, small cakes and *petits fours*.

Filling, icing and decoration form an important part of cakemaking, and it is worth taking extra time for a perfect finish. Icing must be absolutely smooth, nuts used for coating should be evenly browned, and butter cream rosettes should be of a uniform size.

Selecting cake pans

The type of pan in which a cake is baked radically affects the baking time and also gives character to the finished cake. It is important to use the shape and size of pan stated in the recipe. A springform pan or one with a removable bottom is useful for fragile cakes that need careful unmolding. In general, dense, long-cooking cake mixtures need thicker pans to prevent scorching. See also Cake and baking pans (p.509).

Preparing and greasing cake pans

Cake pans are coated with fat, flour or both to give a smooth golden surface to the cake. To make the cake easy to unmold and to protect the batter from oven heat, the pan is usually lined with wax paper or baking parchment. For some cakes, notably those made with egg whites, the pan is not greased as the batter is supposed to cling. Non-stick pans are particularly helpful for moist batters and do not need greasing unless a coating is needed (above right), or a protective paper lining is used.

Greasing a pan helps loosen a cake so it is easy to unmold after baking. The fat used for greasing should be the same as that used in the batter. Melt or soften the fat and, using a pastry brush, apply a thin, even coating, taking care to brush the corners and rim.

COATING A CAKE PAN

Some cake recipes need an additional coating of flour after greasing the pan. Sugar, breadcrumbs and chopped or sliced nuts may also be used. **Note** A sugar coating will scorch if overcooked.

For a flour, sugar or breadcrumb coating: sprinkle the greased pan generously with coating, making sure it reaches the edges. Turn and shake the pan to coat the surface evenly. Tap it upside down on the work surface to remove excess flour. **For a nut coating:** sprinkle the greased pan with nuts, shake it and press the nuts on to the sides.

LINING THE BASE OF A ROUND CAKE PAN

For whisked cakes, and some creamed and melted cakes that are inclined to stick, the base of the pan is lined with paper.

Method 1
Set the cake pan upside down with a square of paper on top. Press the paper down with your hand, and with the back of a heavy knife press against the pan in a stroking motion, cutting the paper into a circle. Brush the pan with fat and press the paper into the base. Grease the paper.

Method 2 Follow steps for lining a springform pan (opposite).

Preparing your oven for baking

Most ovens take 10-15 minutes to reach the correct temperature and should therefore be heated in advance. Precision is important, so check the temperature of the oven with a thermometer beforehand. Position the shelf so that the cake will fit in the center of the oven or slightly lower. Deep cakes should be placed lower in the oven than shallow ones. If baking more than one cake at a time, stagger the pans so that one is not directly above another. If the oven temperature is uneven, rearrange the pans when the cakes start to brown. So that the heat circulates freely, the edges of a baking sheet should never be less than 1 in/2.5 cm from the sides of the oven. Trays of cakes often need turning front to back during cooking so that they brown evenly. However, do not open the oven door until a cake is set and lightly browned.

LINING A SPRINGFORM PAN

For rich cakes that need long cooking, both the base and sides of a pan should be lined. When cooking time is more than two hours, the pan may be lined with extra thicknesses of paper.

1 Fold a square of paper in quarters, then in triangular eighths or sixteenths depending on the size. Set the point of the paper in the center of the upturned pan. Cut the paper level with the edge.

2 Cut a second circle in the same way. Grease the pan, open one circle of paper and place it in the base of the pan. Grease the paper.

3 Cut a strip of paper a little longer and deeper than the circumference of the pan. Fold one long edge and cut slits along it.

4 Press the strip around the sides of the pan so the folded cut edge overlaps the base. Set the second round of paper in the base of the pan to hold the overlap in place, then grease the paper.

LINING A LOAF PAN

Loaf pans can be lined by cutting a rectangle of paper to fit the base and sides. The same method is appropriate for lining shallow, square, or rectangular pans. A loaf pan can also be lined quickly using two strips of paper (see Method 2). Whichever method you use, grease the pan before lining it with paper.

Method 1

1 Cut a piece of paper as wide as the base and sides of the pan. Fold the paper so that it fits the base.

2 Unfold the paper and cut the corners along the folds so that it fits the pan. Grease the pan. Press the paper into the pan and grease it.

Method 2

1 Grease the pan. Cut a strip of paper the same width as the pan and 6 in/ 15 cm more than the length. Press the strip lengthwise into the pan, so the ends overlap the edge. Grease the paper.

2 Cut a second strip of paper as wide as the pan's length and 6 in/15 cm longer than the width. Press the paper crosswise into the base of the pan and grease it also.

MIXING CAKES

In cake recipes there are several common terms for mixing:

To stir or combine means to mix ingredients thoroughly in a circular, scooping motion. Often a wooden spoon or spatula is used, but for large quantities your cupped hand is more effective.

To cream fat and sugar is to combine until smooth (p.398).

To fold is the lightest way of combining ingredients (p.392).

To blend usually implies beating, though it may simply mean to combine ingredients. (When an electric blender is needed, this is stated.) The belief that a cake should be beaten clockwise or counterclockwise, never both, is a fallacy.

To whisk means to incorporate air, usually in eggs. A balloon whisk, whether hand or electric, is often used, although an electric mixer or egg beater can be substituted.

To whisk to the ribbon is to combine eggs and sugar to form a light mousse (p.394).

To beat means to work ingredients so thoroughly that a physical change takes place, for example beating egg yolks and sugar to the ribbon. Often, air is incorporated at the same time. An electric mixer or wooden spoon is used, with a wire balloon whisk for softer mixtures.

To knead, commonly applied to bread dough (p.347), means to work thoroughly, often by pressing and pounding with the hands.

INGREDIENTS FOR CAKES

For all cakes, success depends on following a recipe precisely. Ingredients should be measured accurately and instructions followed to the letter. Doubling or reducing quantities of a batter is risky and results are not always reliable, particularly if the cake is made with whisked eggs. Do not substitute, for example, whole wheat flour for all-purpose flour or corn syrup for honey. When following a recipe never substitute one fat for another.

Eggs Most recipes assume an egg weighs 2 oz/60 g, graded in France by weight, in the United States as "large", and in Britain as size 3. Eggs should be at room temperature before mixing. See also Milk, Cheese and Eggs (p.80).

Sugar Granulated sugar is most commonly used in cakes. Coarser sugar blends less well and gives cakes a spotted surface. Brown sugars give color and heavier texture; confectioners' sugar adds lightness, but as it often contains starch to keep it dry, it should be used only when specified. See also Sugar (p.412).

Salt A pinch of salt develops the flavor of any sweet mixture.

Flour Most cake recipes use all-purpose flour. American cake flour, highly refined and milled from soft wheat, gives a very light texture, while whole wheat, semolina, rye and other flours each have a characteristic effect. Cornstarch, potato starch, arrowroot and rice flour are often used for lightness. Self-rising flour contains raising agents and must not be substituted for all-purpose flour. Flour is most accurately measured by weight, but if measuring by volume, sift the flour after measuring unless otherwise specified. Sifting is particularly important for lightness in whisked cakes. See also Flour, Breads and Batters (p.342).

Fats Butter adds incomparable flavor to a wide variety of delicate cakes. Recipes should indicate use of salted or unsalted butter; extra salt is noticeable. Firm margarine may be substituted for butter, but it lacks flavor. Shortening gives a light cake, but no flavor, while animal fats such as lard are appropriate to certain regional cakes. Oil is a lighter alternative, called for in instances such as chiffon cakes and Greek olive oil cakes. Some eastern European and Scandinavian cakes rely on heavy or sour cream.

Note Fat improves the shelf life of cakes, keeping them moist longer. See Fats and Oils (p.96).

Mixing cakes by machine

An electric mixer is invaluable for cake-making: for whisking whole eggs or egg whites, for beating egg yolks and sugar and for creaming butter. Models vary according to power and speed, so be sure to use the speed and attachment recommended by the manufacturer for specific tasks. You may need to stop the motor and scrape the sides of the bowl from time to time during beating. Modern mixers often come with pouring shields that help to direct ingredients to the center of the bowl as they are added. A mixer can help to distribute ingredients such as nuts and dried fruit evenly in heavier or richer cakes. A food processor can be used for creamed cakes, if care is taken. All liquid ingredients should be combined before dry ones are added. Heavy ingredients should always be chopped first, added toward the end of the mixing process and combined at low speed or using the pulse button on the machine. For lighter batters, it is better to fold in last-minute ingredients by hand so the mixture is not overworked.

FOLDING CAKE BATTER

Folding is the lightest way to combine two mixtures, particularly when incorporating egg whites. Ingredients such as nuts and vanilla extract are added first to a batter, followed by flour and egg whites. In whisked cakes, melted butter is added last.

1 To fold the flour into the batter, first tip it into a sieve or sifter. Sift about one-third of the flour over the batter and fold the two together. When almost blended, sift half the remaining flour over the batter, and continue folding.

2 Sift the remaining flour over the batter and fold it in until the batter is smooth. Scrape the insides of the bowl while folding, as flour tends to cling to it. If folding egg whites into the batter, add them one-third at a time, with the flour.

3 If adding clarified butter, fold it in as quickly as possible just after the last batch of flour has been added.

Note To make folding easier, a few spoonfuls of batter may be mixed with the butter, then this can be folded into the main batter.

Filling cake pans with batter

Soft batters can be poured into the pan and will spread flat. Rap the pan on the table once or twice to knock out any large air bubbles. Firmer batters must be spooned into the pan and spread evenly into the corners. Spread the batter level with a spatula or, for slow-baking cakes, leave a slight dip in the center because the batter may rise more here. For light batters that rise, the pan should be half to two-thirds full, for others three-quarters full.

UNMOLDING A CAKE

Leave all cakes to stand for a few moments before unmolding them. Whisked cakes, and more delicate cream cakes, should be unmolded after two to three minutes so that steam can escape. Angel food cakes, chiffon cakes, and cheesecakes are left to cool in the pan so they do not shrink or collapse, and rich fruit cakes are also cooled in the pan to keep moist. The base of a springform pan may be left under a fragile cake to hold it together.

1 Run a knife around the edge of the cake, holding the blade against the edge of the pan so that the cake is not cut.

2 Unmold the cake on to a wire rack. Peel off the lining paper so steam can escape. Paper is often left on rich cakes for storage.

3 To avoid grill marks on light cakes, tip the cake on to a round of paper and set it, with the paper, on the rack.

Testing when a cake is done

All cakes shrink slightly from the sides of the pan when done. For whisked cakes, test by pressing the center of the cake with your fingertip. The cake should spring back if it is done. For creamed and melted cakes, insert a wooden toothpick or skewer into the center of the cake; if it comes out clean, the cake is ready.

Storing cakes

Once cooled, cakes should be stored, lightly covered in plastic wrap, in an airtight container. Cakes with icing, filling, or fancy decoration keep better in the refrigerator without a wrapping. The fat content of a cake helps moisten it, and extends its keeping time. Cakes that contain fresh or dried fruits, nuts, chocolate, spice mixtures or honey mellow on standing, as do those with fillings such as butter cream. Elaborate decorations are best added shortly before serving as they crush easily. Cakes and butter cream freeze well, but sugar fillings and icings will crystallize.

Slicing cakes

Cakes are most easily sliced with a sharp serrated knife, using a gentle sawing motion to prevent the cake from crumbling. For rich cakes filled with butter cream and for cheesecakes, the knife can be dipped in hot water first. Special comb-like cutters and cake-cutting wires are available for cutting angel food and other light cakes; wires also help to cut a cake into even layers.

Note To slice a loaf cake, hold the slice upright with your hand while cutting so that it does not break.

SLICING A CAKE INTO HORIZONTAL LAYERS

To make handling a cake easier, set it on a piece of cardboard before you start.

1 With a serrated knife, trim the crusty edges from the cake. With scissors, trim the cardboard level with the edge of the cake.

2 With the point of a knife make a small cut in the side of the cake. This makes sliced layers easy to line up when reassembling the cake.

3 Cut the cake in horizontal layers, holding your hand firmly on top of the cake to guide the knife.

PROBLEMS WHEN MAKING CAKES

No matter what method is used for mixing cake batter, baking problems usually have a common cause.

Sunken center
1 Too much sugar, shown by very brown crust and sticky center.
2 Too much baking powder or other raising agent.
3 Too much liquid, shown by a sticky layer forming above the bottom crust.
4 Oven temperature too low.
5 Batter exposed to a draft before it has set.
6 Undercooking, shown by a sticky central layer.

Peaked top
1 Too much gluten developed in mixture, caused either by using too hard a flour (p.343) or by overbeating.
2 Oven temperature too high.

Tough, close-textured cake
1 Batter insufficiently beaten or whipped.
2 Not enough raising agent.
3 Not enough sugar.
4 Batter overmixed.

WHISKED CAKES

The charm of a whisked cake lies in its simplicity – a plain sponge can be whisked in five minutes with the aid of a mixer, and there are numerous possibilities for fillings and icings. Whisked cakes have an open, airy texture (as their other name, sponge cake, implies) and they rely on eggs and sifted flour for lightness.

According to French pastry chefs, whisked cakes fall into two main categories: for whole-egg cakes such as *génoise*, the eggs are whisked together, while in *biscuit*, the egg yolk and white are whisked separately. The pure white batter for American angel food cake (p.397) is raised only with egg whites.

To avoid losing air from the batter, flavorings for whisked cakes are confined usually to vanilla, grated citrus zest, spices or orange flower water, but after baking the cake may be moistened with a liqueur and light sugar syrup (p.414). For lightness, cornstarch or arrowroot is sometimes substituted for some of the flour, or powdered cocoa in the case of a chocolate sponge cake.

Though served on their own, plain whisked cakes are a good accompaniment to fruit compote or ice cream. They are often used for layer cakes (p.400) and are the foundation of many charlottes, whether shaped as ladyfingers (p.396) or thinly layered with red jam and cut in cheerful striped slices. Thin layers of sponge are also used as a base for bavarian creams.

Decoration for a whisked sponge cake can be merely a sprinkling of confectioners' sugar or a thin coating of glacé icing. The cake may be filled with jam or frosting and covered with more frosting, or a smoother melted icing. Simple decorations include toasted nuts, shredded coconut, colored sprinkles and chocolate curls. In many parts of Europe the decoration of whisked sponges has been raised to a fine art. Hundreds of classic gâteaux exist, with decorations which may be as plain as a lattice pattern of confectioners' sugar, or as elaborate as pulled sugar roses, caramel cages (p.418), or rosettes and whirls of butter cream.

USEFUL INFORMATION

Portion Depends on filling and icing; plain 3-egg cake serves 4.
Typical pan *Génoise and biscuit:* round with straight or sloping sides; deep square or rectangle. *Angel food:* tube pan.
Preparation of pan Greased paper; coated with flour, and sugar (optional).
Cooking times *3-egg cake:* bake at 350°F/175°C, 20-30 minutes in 8 in/20 cm pan. *4-egg cake:* bake at 350°F/175°C, 30-40 minutes in 9-10 in/23-25 cm pan.
When done Shrinks from sides of pan; springs back when pressed.

Problems Scorches in too high heat; dry if overcooked.
Storage All freeze well except if iced. *Plain:* best eaten on day of baking. *With butter in batter:* 2-3 days in airtight container. *With filling and icing:* 4-5 days in airtight container.
Fillings Butter cream; pastry butter cream; Chantilly cream; chocolate mousse; ganache; jam or jelly; pastry cream.
Frostings and icings Almond paste; butter cream; pastry cream; butter icing; fondant; ganache; glacé; glaze; whipped frosting.

Adding butter to whisked cakes

Butter may or may not be called for in *génoise* and *biscuit* cakes; if not added carefully, it quickly knocks the air from the beaten eggs. Some cooks like the butter to be pourable but still creamy, others melt it completely or flavor it by cooking it until it is nut brown. In any case, the butter must be cool before it is folded into the batter with the last portion of flour (p.366). Sometimes a small portion of batter is added to the butter, mixed and folded back into the remaining batter.

WHISKING TO THE RIBBON

Whole eggs and egg yolks are whisked with sugar to form a light, close-textured mousse that is the basis of Sabayon sauce (p.67) and cold dessert mousses, as well as cakes.

Whole eggs Whisk eggs and sugar in a large bowl – preferably of stainless steel – with a balloon whisk (p.503) until just mixed. If using an electric beater with a whisk attachment, continue whisking at medium-high speed 5-7 minutes, until the mixture holds a ribbon trail for 8-10 seconds when the whisk is lifted. If whisking by hand, set the bowl over a pan of hot, but not boiling, water and whisk with a balloon whisk or egg beater until the mixture holds a trail for 4-5 seconds (it will thicken further on cooling). Take the bowl from the heat and continue whisking until the mousse is cool.

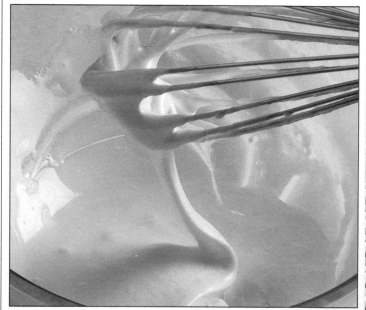

Egg yolks Beat yolks and sugar in a bowl with an electric beater, balloon whisk or egg beater for 3-5 minutes until thick, light-colored and a trail is left for 8-10 seconds when the whisk is lifted. The mousse will be closer-textured than with whole eggs.

Génoise whisked cakes

Moist and light, *génoise* is the most common whisked cake both for serving alone and for filling and icing. For *génoise* whisked cakes, whole eggs and sugar are whisked to the ribbon. Flour is folded in, with standard ingredients being 2 tbsp/30 g sugar and ¼ cup/30 g flour to each egg. The addition of butter for richness is optional – one tablespoon per egg is the maximum. To conserve as much air as possible in the batter, it should be baked at once; advance preparation is therefore important.

USEFUL INFORMATION

Typical cakes Handsome tipsy (*génoise* drenched with brandy and covered with jam and custard, Australia); almond *génoise* (Scandinavia); *latt sockerkaka* (light *génoise*, flavored with vanilla, almond, or orange, Sweden); *pasta Maddalena* (plain *génoise*, Italy); *torta Margherita* (layered with meringue, fresh fruit and whipped cream, Italy); fruit-filled cake frosted with jellied fruit purée (Finland); yule cake with prune or plum filling (Finland); chocolate caraque cake (France); *gâteau moka* (with coffee butter cream, France); *gâteau d'Isigny* (with butter cream, raspberry jam and fondant icing, France), *gâteau aux groseilles* (with red currant jelly filling, white fondant icing and frosted red currants, France); *cendrillon* (coffee butter cream, hazelnuts and almonds, France); *praliné* (with praline butter cream and crushed praline decoration, France); caramel (lemon *génoise* with Chantilly cream and caramel icing, France); *gâteau physalis* (filled with Cape gooseberries in fondant, France); *rosace à l'orange* (orange pastry cream and candied orange slices, France); *Régence* (chocolate *génoise*, chocolate mousse filling, France); *bûche de Noël aux marrons* (yule log with chestnut cream, France); *Wiener orangetorte* (with curaçao butter cream, Austria).

Biscuit whisked cakes

Biscuit whisked cakes, in which egg yolks and whites are whisked separately, closely resemble *génoise*, but have a slightly drier, firmer texture. Common examples are jelly rolls and ladyfingers (p.396). The batter is more robust than that of *génoise*, but it should nonetheless be baked at once.

For *biscuit* whisked cakes, the eggs are separated. The yolks are beaten with sugar until thick and light, while the egg whites are whisked separately, then beaten with a little sugar to make a light meringue. The meringue is then folded into the egg yolk mixture in three batches with the flour, and possibly a final addition of butter. In one variation, the egg yolks are folded straight into the meringue without being beaten with sugar, but the resulting batter is very similar.

USEFUL INFORMATION

Typical cakes *Pan di Spagna* (honey and rum sponge, Italy); *baumstamm* (chocolate log, Germany); *pan de pessic* (Catalan sponge cake, Spain); *pastel Sant Jordi*/St George's cake (with chocolate butter cream, Barcelona, Spain); *haselnusstorte* (hazelnut torte, Germany); *sahnetorte* (whipped cream cake, Germany); *dobostorte* (thin cake layers with chocolate butter cream and caramel topping, Hungary); *biscuit de Savoie* (with currants, France); sponge with cherries (Austria); *rehrücken* (spice cake with chocolate glaze, Germany); *Joconde* (almond sponge, France); sunshine cake (lemon sponge, USA); *torta del cielo* (almond sponge, Mexico); *brazo de gitano* (roll with rum cream, Spain); *Schwarzwalder kirschtorte*/Black Forest torte (chocolate sponge, whipped cream, cherries and chocolate shavings, Germany); *torta delizia* (apricot filling, covered with almond paste, Italy); hazelnut roll with whipped cream (USA); *hallonrulltarta* (raspberry roll, with whipped cream, Sweden); sponge with raspberries (France).

Génoise

For a chocolate batter, substitute unsweetened cocoa powder for 20 percent of the flour and add 1½ tbsp/25 g more sugar.

Makes an 8 in/20 cm cake	*Makes a 9 in/23 cm cake*
⅔ cup/90 g flour	1 cup/125 g flour
pinch of salt	pinch of salt
3 tbsp/45 g unsalted butter	¼ cup/60 g unsalted butter
3 eggs	4 eggs
7 tbsp/90 g sugar	⅔ cup/135 g sugar
¾–1 tsp vanilla extract *or* 1-2 tsp orange flower water *or* grated zest 1 orange or 1 lemon	¾-1 tsp vanilla extract *or* 1-2 tsp orange flower water *or* grated zest of 1 orange or 1 lemon
8 in/20 cm round cake pan	*9 in/23 cm round cake pan*

1 Grease and flour the pan. Heat the oven to 350°F/175°C. Sift the flour and salt. Clarify the butter if using (p.99) and cool.
2 Whisk the eggs and sugar to the ribbon. Whisk in the flavoring. Sift the flour over the batter in three batches and fold together as lightly as possible. Add the butter with the last batch, leaving the sediment at the bottom of the saucepan.
3 Pour the batter into the prepared pan and bake for 20-30 minutes for a 3-egg cake or 30-40 minutes for a 4-egg cake. Allow to cool in the pan then transfer it to a rack. Ice with butter icing, for example coffee butter cream (p.405) as shown here.

HIGH-ALTITUDE BAKING

It should be noted that at altitudes above 3,000 feet the air pressure reduces and baking cakes becomes more difficult. Creamed and melted cakes adapt better than whisked sponges. Special recipes are available for high-altitude baking. The following corrections should help:
1 Refrigerate eggs before using; underbeat eggs somewhat.
2 Reduce quantity of raising agents.
3 Add an extra 1-2 tablespoons liquid per cup of flour.
4 Reduce sugar by 1-2 tablespoons per cup.
5 Raise oven temperature slightly.

MAKING LADYFINGERS

When ladyfingers (Fr. *biscuits à la cuiller*) are lightly mixed, they bake so that "pearls" of confectioners' sugar form on top. **Note** If you are using an electric oven with no ventilation, prop the door open slightly during baking.

Makes 24 ladyfingers

¾ cup/100 g flour	1 tsp vanilla extract
pinch of salt	confectioners' sugar (for sprinkling)
4 eggs, separated	
½ cup/100 g sugar	***Pastry bag with ¾ in/2 cm plain tube***

1 Grease and flour two baking sheets. Mark parallel lines in the flour across the width of the tray about 4 in/10 cm apart. Heat the oven to 350°F/175°C. Sift the flour and salt together.

2 Whisk the egg yolks with two-thirds of the sugar to the ribbon (p.394). Whisk in the vanilla. Stiffly whip the egg whites, add the remaining sugar and continue whisking about 30 seconds until the mixture is glossy and makes a light meringue.

3 Using a spatula, fold the flour and meringue into the egg yolk mousse in three alternate batches. Spoon the mixture into a pastry bag (p.406), handling it as lightly as possible.

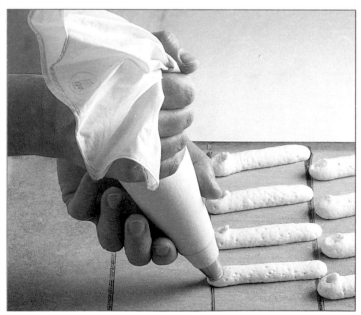

4 Pipe fingers about 4½ in/11 cm in length on to prepared baking sheets using the lines as a guide. Dust the tops with confectioners' sugar and gently blow off the excess.

5 Bake the ladyfingers in the preheated oven until just firm on the outside, but still soft in the center, 15-18 minutes. Cool on a rack.

Jelly roll

It is no wonder that every country has a favorite rolled cake – the American jelly roll, the British Swiss roll, the French *biscuit roulé*, the custard-filled gypsy rolls of Spain – for rolled cakes are eminently satisfying, offering a pretty presentation in return for just a little expertise. They most often grace the tea table but, with a luscious filling, are also grand enough to serve as dessert.

Rolled cakes are based on a thin sheet of *génoise* or *biscuit* batter (p.395), spread with filling and rolled to enclose it. To emphasize their spiral form, the filling should be of contrasting taste and color: light Chantilly cream (p.70) or perhaps a pink raspberry butter cream (p.405) in a rich chocolate roll, sweet red jam in a basic white roll. The French really go to town with their traditional yule log (*bûche de Noël*) of chocolate cake with ganache filling, lavishly decorated on the outside as well. The "grain" of the log is simulated in coffee or chocolate butter cream traced with a flat ridged piping tube or the tines of a fork. Marzipan holly, meringue mushrooms, a sprinkling of confectioners' sugar snow and spun sugar all complete the festive picture.

Jelly roll pans (p.509) are useful for thin layers of cake that may be used in elaborate charlottes or elegant layer cakes as well as for rolling into a log. However a special pan is not necessary; the batter may be spread into a wide, shallow pan of the appropriate size (a 10 × 15 in/25 × 37 cm rectangle is useful for a 4-egg batter) or onto a baking sheet lined with greased and floured wax paper or baking parchment. The batter should be thick enough to hold its shape. The cake is baked in the oven until springy to the touch and with firm edges, 8-10 minutes. As it cools, cover it with a damp cloth or roll and unroll it until cool enough to spread. Thick jam fillings may be warmed before spreading, but cream fillings should be soft enough to spread.

ROLLING A JELLY ROLL

The key to rolling a cake without cracking it is not to overbake it. Unmold on to wax paper sprinkled with confectioners' sugar.

1 Peel off cooking paper. Roll and unroll the cake in the wax paper several times.

2 When cool, spread the unrolled cake with an even layer of buttercream filling using a spatula.

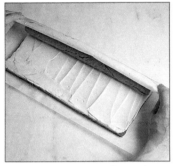

3 Using the paper underneath to help you, carefully roll the filled cake as tightly as possible.

4 To serve, cut the ends of the roll on the diagonal.

Angel food cake

The classic American angel food cake, which is snowy white, is based on egg whites with no egg yolks or fat. Because it is so delicate, a mystique surrounds its preparation, but in fact the principles are the same as for other whisked cakes.

Cake flour must be used, as its low gluten content gives a particularly light, moist texture. Some cooks also like to use confectioners' sugar for lightness. The beating of the egg whites is especially important (p.82): when they start to foam, a pinch of cream of tartar is added to stiffen them. As soon as they form stiff peaks, a portion of sugar is added to make a light meringue. Careful folding of the mixture is essential as the eggs must not be overbeaten and dry: this would make them difficult to incorporate into the other ingredients. The cake should be baked as soon as possible after mixing and must be protected from drafts during and after baking. For this reason, angel food cake is always left to cool inside the upturned pan. Some angel food cake pans have legs that hold the inverted pan up, helping it to cool.

A favorite topping is boiled frosting (p.410) as white as the cake itself. Alternatively, angel food cake may be left plain or sprinkled with confectioners' sugar. Plain angel food cake batter can be varied with chocolate, cherries, pecan nuts and almonds, but some cooks feel these ingredients detract from the purity of the cake. Popular accompaniments include a spoonful of whipped cream and fresh or macerated fruits.

USEFUL INFORMATION/ANGEL FOOD CAKE

Portion 12-egg white cake serves 8-10 people.
Preparation of pan None.
Cooking times *12-egg white cake:* bake at 350°F/175°C, 40-50 minutes.
When done Shrinks from sides of pan; springs back when pressed.
Problems Rises poorly if egg whites under- or over-beaten.
Storage *Plain:* 2-3 days in airtight container; freeze 2 months. *Frosted:* 1-2 days in airtight container.

Frostings Glacé; ganache; white mountain frosting.
Typical cakes Angel cake (with fondant or glacé icing, UK); angel food custard cake (USA); white mountain cake (with white mountain frosting p.410, USA); marble angel food cake (with swirled chocolate and vanilla batters, USA); "bits of gold" angel food cake (with orange extract and peel, USA).

Angel food cake

Angel food cake is made in a special tube pan which is not greased so that the light, airy batter clings to the sides as it rises.

Serves 8-10

1 cup/110 g cake flour	1 tsp vanilla extract
1½ cups/300 g sugar	confectioners' sugar or white mountain frosting (for coating)
1½ cups/375 ml (about 12) egg whites	
1½ tsp cream of tartar	
pinch of salt	*10 in/25 cm angel food cake tube pan, with removable base (p.509)*

1 Heat the oven to 350°F/175°C. Sift the flour. Add about one-third of the sugar and sift the mixture twice again.
2 Whip the egg whites until foaming. Add the cream of tartar and salt and continue beating until the egg whites are stiff. Whip the remaining sugar into the egg white a tablespoon at a time, taking 30-60 seconds. Continue whisking for 30-60 seconds until the mixture is glossy and holds peaks. Beat in the vanilla.
3 Fold in the flour in three batches. Transfer the batter to a pan that is not greased and floured. Bake for 40-45 minutes or until the cake is done (p.393). Leave the cake to cool upside down in the pan so it does not shrink. (Rest the inverted pan on a jar so the air reaches the surface of the cake.)
4 Shortly before serving, sprinkle the cake with confectioners' sugar or coat with frosting.

CREAMED CAKES

The key to successful creamed cakes is lengthy beating of the batter made with whole eggs or egg yolks. The more you beat the batter, the better the cake will be. Preparation starts with creamed fat that is beaten with sugar (see below), providing a robust base for flour and heavy ingredients such as ground nuts and dried fruits. Sometimes the eggs are added whole, sometimes the yolks only, with the whites whisked and folded in at the last moment. The batter is more robust than that for sponge cakes, but flour and heavy ingredients should still be folded or stirred in with care. Even simpler is the all-in-one method, whereby all the ingredients are combined at once.

Proportions for creamed cakes vary from recipe to recipe, but many are similar to the standard proportions for a classic pound cake, made with equal weights of butter, sugar, eggs and flour. Baking powder or baking soda is needed to help many creamed cakes rise and liquid such as milk may soften the batter.

Creamed cakes demand simpler fillings and icings than whisked sponges. Pound cakes can be dusted with confectioners' sugar, or topped with a thin layer of sugar glaze (p.345). Fruit cakes may be plain or decorated as a wedding or Christmas cake.

CREAMING FAT & SUGAR

After prolonged beating, granulated or brown sugar softens and dissolves in fat (usually butter) to form a fluffy, light mixture, the basis of creamed cakes and hard sauces (p.67).

1 Let the butter soften at room temperature. Beat it for 1-2 minutes with a balloon whisk, wooden spoon or electric beater until creamy.

2 Gradually beat in the sugar and continue beating vigorously for 3-5 minutes; the mixture will become creamy and fluffy and almost double in volume.

3 When sufficiently creamed, the mixture will lighten perceptibly in color, and be soft enough to fall easily from the whisk or spoon.

Pound cake

In old-fashioned recipes for pound cake, the eggs were used as weights on one side of the scale and balanced with equal weights of butter, sugar and flour. The most familiar version is flavored simply with vanilla, orange flower water, or grated orange or lemon zest. Rich but light, with outstanding flavor when butter is used, pound cake is popular in many countries. In France you will find *quatre quarts*, in Germany *sandkuchen*, in Finland *murokakku*, and in Britain Madeira cake (which does not contain Madeira but is intended as an accompaniment to it).

Variations of pound cake mixtures include spiced cakes such as caraway seed cake, American antebellum cake with allspice and cloves, and Whitby nun's cake with rose water and spices.

USEFUL INFORMATION

Portion 4-egg cake serves 6-8.
Typical pan Springform, loaf.
Preparation of pan Greased and lined (p.390).
Cooking times Bake at 350°F/ 175°C, 40-50 minutes in 9-10 in/ 23-25 cm pan or 30-40 minutes in 8 × 4 × 3 in/20 × 10 × 7.5 cm loaf pan.
When done Cake shrinks from sides of pan; a skewer inserted in center comes out clean.
Problems When egg is added, batter curdles if too cold or if fat and sugar are not creamed enough; can be smoothed by warming bowl and beating thoroughly.
Storage 1 week in airtight container; freeze 2 months.

Icings Glacé; glaze; confectioners' sugar.
Typical cakes Hunter cake (almond, lemon, raspberry jam and almond icing, USA); oatmeal cake (with spices and rolled oats, USA); *Frankfurter kranz* (flavored with rum and decorated with crushed praline, Germany); princess cake (lightened with meringue, USA); seed cake (with caraway, Australia); lemon pound cake (Finland); Venetian almond cake (Italy); chocolate and amaretti cake (Italy); *sachertorte* (chocolate cake with apricot preserves and chocolate glaze, Austria); Victoria sponge (with raspberry jam and whipped cream filling, UK).

Pound cake

A French variation of pound cake includes fresh fruit such as strawberries or pitted cherries; the cake will need a few more minutes' baking time.

Makes a 9-10 in/23-25 cm cake	For the topping
2 cups/250 g flour	confectioners' sugar *or* sugar glaze (p.345) made with ½ cup/ 100 g confectioners' sugar and 5-6 tbsp/75-90 ml water, lemon or orange juice
1 tbsp baking powder	
pinch of salt	
1 cup/250 g unsalted butter	
1¼ cups/250 g sugar	
4 eggs	
1 tsp vanilla extract *or* grated zest of 1 lemon or 1 orange	9-10 in/23-25 cm round or springform pan

1 Grease the pan and line the base with paper. Grease the paper and coat it with flour and sugar (p.390). Heat the oven to 350°F/ 175°C. Sift the flour with the baking powder and salt.
2 Cream the butter and sugar (left). Beat the eggs one by one, beating thoroughly after each addition. Beat in the flavoring. Fold the flour into the batter in three batches (p.392), then spoon the batter into the prepared pan.
3 Bake the cake in the preheated oven for 40-50 minutes or until the cake tests done (p.393). Transfer the cake to a rack to cool.
4 Shortly before serving, sprinkle the cake with confectioners' sugar or top it with sugar glaze.

Fruit cakes

The creaming method is followed for many fruit cakes, particularly rich mixtures for festive occasions (for example a wedding or Christmas cake) in which the batter is no longer open-textured, but acts more as a binder for the other ingredients. Brown sugar, liquor and spices color many fruit cakes, but one variation has a white batter, golden raisins and candied pineapple.

Careful baking is important. Rich fruit cakes can take two hours or more to cook and the oven temperature must be kept low and steady. To avoid a dry crust, the pan may be lined with several layers of paper. If the cake starts to brown too quickly, it may be covered loosely with foil to deflect the heat. Testing when a fruit cake is done can be difficult: no batter should be visible when a skewer is drawn out of the center, but moist fruit may still leave a sticky film. For reliability, therefore, always insert the skewer at several different points.

The longer a rich fruit cake is kept, the more succulent it will be, particularly when coated with a layer of almond paste (p.409). For festive decorations, see p.408.

USEFUL INFORMATION

Portion Depends on fruit content; rich 3-egg cake serves 8-10.
Typical pan Deep round; springform; loaf.
Preparation of pan One or two layers of paper in base and sides of greased pan, then greased (p.390).
Cooking times Time varies according to the richness of the mixture; bake at 325°F/160°C, 1¼-2 hours.
When done Shrinks from sides of pan; a skewer inserted in center of cake comes out clean.
Problems During baking, fruit and nuts fall to the bottom of the cake if they are not sufficiently dried, if batter has too much raising agent, or if cake is baked too slowly.
Icings Almond paste; fondant; royal; whipped frosting.
Typical cakes Twelfth night cake (currants, candied peel, almonds, brandy, UK); Dundee cake (almonds, currants, sultanas, candied peel, raisins, Scotland); black bun (shortcrust dough filled with currants, raisins, almonds, candied peel, spices, black pepper, brandy, Scotland); Wimbledon tennis cake (white cake with mixed peel, cinnamon, glacé cherries, Maraschino liqueur, covered with almond paste and glacé icing, UK); Welsh funeral cake (rich cake with raisins, currants and candied peel, Wales); *pestringolo* (rich fruit cake with figs and honey, Italy); Kentucky bourbon (bourbon, nutmeg, raisins and pecans, USA); raisin cake (lemon peel and raisins, Sweden); bishop's cake (candied cherries, pineapple, dates, walnuts, chocolate pieces, Germany); white fruit cake (pineapple, almonds, lemon, USA); Simnel cake (currants, candied peel, covered with almond paste, UK); Irish whiskey cake (lemon peel, orange peel, whiskey; raisins, caraway seed, pecans (USA); Vermont scripture cake (USA).

Preparing dried and candied fruits for cakes

For raisins and currants: pick over the fruit, discarding any stems. Cover with boiling water, leave until tepid and drain.
For candied fruits: use whole fruit pieces (they have the best flavor), soak them in boiling water to soften them and dissolve the crystallized sugar coating, then drain. Coarsely chop the fruit in ⅛ in/3 mm dice. If the fruits are already chopped, soak them in boiling water for a few minutes to dissolve the excess sugar and drain them. Dry all fruits thoroughly on paper towels, then toss them until coated with a little of the flour already measured for the recipe. Candied green angelica leaves are used for decorating cakes but their flavor is too perfumed to add to the cake batter.

Storing fruit cake

Rich fruit cakes should be aged at least a month to allow the flavor to mature and may be stored for a year or more. Wrap the cake in cheesecloth moistened with alcohol such as sherry, Madeira or brandy, set it in an airtight container, with a halved apple for moisture, and cover tightly. Baste the cake from time to time with a few more spoonfuls of alcohol.

Rich fruit cake

Topped with marzipan and royal icing, this becomes a traditional British Christmas cake. Store it for at least one month (p.393).

Makes a 9 in/23 cm cake

3⅓ cups/500 g raisins	½ tsp ground allspice
3⅓ cups/500 g dried currants	1½ cups/375 g unsalted butter, softened
1 cup/250 g chopped candied orange peel	1¾ cups/375 g brown sugar
1 cup/250 g chopped candied citrus peel	6 eggs
3 cups/375 g flour	3 tbsp/45 ml brandy
½ tsp salt	
½ tsp grated nutmeg	**9 in/23 cm round cake pan or springform pan**

1 Grease the pan and line with a double layer of paper, then grease the paper. Heat the oven to 300°F/150°C. Prepare the fruit see above. Sift the flour with salt, nutmeg and allspice.
2 Cream the butter and sugar (p.398). Add the eggs one by one, beating well after each addition. Stir in the flour in two or three batches, followed by the brandy and dried fruits.
3 Spoon the batter into a prepared pan and smooth the top, hollowing the center slightly. Bake for 2½-3 hours until the cake tests done (p.393). If it browns too much, cover loosely with foil.
4 Leave to cool in the pan, then unmold and peel off the paper.

LAYER CAKES

Layer cakes can be made with whisked sponge cakes, creamed cakes or nut mixtures. A typical American white layer cake may have only egg whites, while yellow layer cake includes the yolks, and gold layer cake has no whites at all and is raised with baking powder. The Germans and Scandinavians enjoy large layer cakes filled with jam, seasonal fruits and whipped cream.

Layer cakes may be simple or grand; many are made with very thin layers of *génoise* or sponge moistened with liqueur and filled with preserves; the Italians might coat them with decorative almond paste, and the French with fondant (p.417).

It is vital to assemble these cakes in even layers of cake and filling. Layers may be formed by baking as many as four separate cakes and trimming each, or by slicing a single thick cake horizontally into two or three layers (p.393).

USEFUL INFORMATION

Portion Depending on filling, 3-egg cake serves 6-8.
Typical pan Shallow round, rectangle or square; springform.
Preparation of pan Greased and lined (p.390).
Cooking times Bake at 350°F/175°C, 20-25 minutes in an 8-9in/20-23 cm pan.
When done Shrinks from sides of pan; a skewer inserted in the center comes out clean.
Problems See whisked cakes and pound cakes; layers bake unevenly if too many pans are in the oven at once.
Storage Refrigerate in airtight container. *Plain:* 1 week. *Filled or frosted:* 2-3 days.
Fillings Butter cream; pastry butter cream; Chantilly or whipped cream; jam or jelly; lemon or orange curd.
Frostings and icings Butter cream; pastry butter cream; butter icing; fondant; soft icing; whipped frosting; fresh fruit and whipped heavy cream.

Typical layer cakes *Algarvia* (almond, Portugal); Othello (vanilla custard, macaroons and cocoa icing, Denmark); Lady Baltimore (filled with macaroons, pecans, almonds and cherries, topped with seven-minute frosting, USA); *marjolaine* (nut cake layered with chocolate, vanilla and praline butter cream, decorated with chocolate shavings and confectioners' sugar, France); *opéra* (chocolate nut cake layered with coffee cream and chocolate cream, topped with chocolate glaze, France); Queen of May cake (with pineapple filling and white frosting, USA); cardamom cake with prune filling (Iceland); *vert-vert* (pistachio cake layered with pistachio pastry cream, France); Chichester chocolate cake (with honey, UK); *Habsburgertorte* (hazelnut layers, pistachio and chocolate butter cream, Austria); chocolate torte layered with pastry cream and hazelnuts and covered with praline (Germany).

FLOURLESS CAKES

By no means all cakes are based on wheat flour. Arrowroot and cornstarch make light, rather dry cakes, while flours such as rye are full-flavored but heavy. Breadcrumb cakes are soft and crumbly, whether or not the breadcrumbs used are dried or fresh. Richest of all are cakes based on ground nuts or chocolate, sometimes in combination; these are particularly popular in Austrian and German baking. Few of these ingredients can be substituted for one another, although ground almonds can take the place of hazelnuts and potato starch that of arrowroot. However, when wheat flour is entirely replaced in a cake a dense yet crumbling texture results. In the United States, the name "torte" is often given to such flourless cakes. The original German word has the more general sense of "gâteau" and extends also to rich pastry desserts.

Chocolate walnut cake

The texture of this flourless cake varies depending on whether the walnuts are coarsely or finely ground.

Makes a 9 in/23 cm cake

1⅔ cups/250 g walnut pieces	4 eggs, separated
7 oz/220 g unsweetened chocolate	*For topping*
1 cup/250 g unsalted butter	1-2 tbsp confectioners' sugar
1 cup/200 g sugar	1-2 tbsp powdered cocoa
	9 in/23 cm springform pan

1 Grease the pan, line the base with paper and grease the paper. Heat the oven to 300°F/150°C.
2 Grind the walnuts with the chocolate in two batches in a food processor or a few at a time in a blender. Alternatively, grind them with a rotary cheese grater.
3 Cream the butter with three-quarters of the sugar (p.398). Beat in the egg yolks, one by one, then stir in the chocolate mixture. Stiffly whip the egg whites, add the remaining sugar and continue whipping for about 30 seconds to make a light meringue. Fold the meringue into the chocolate mixture in three batches.
4 Spoon the batter into the prepared pan and smooth the top. Bake for 45-55 minutes until the cake shrinks slightly from the sides of the pan and a skewer inserted in the center comes out clean. Let the cake cool in the oven 5-10 minutes as it is delicate. Let it cool completely in the pan before unmolding it.
5 Shortly before serving, mix the confectioners' sugar and cocoa and sprinkle the mixture over the cake.

MELTED CAKES

As most melted cakes contain little butter or eggs, a liquid such as milk, sour cream, corn syrup or water is needed to moisten the batter. The batter is made by stirring or melting together the liquid ingredients with sugar – hence the name. Such mixtures rely on chemical raising agents (p.359) for lightness, often with the help of an egg or two. A well is made in the dry ingredients, the cooled liquid is added, and the mixture is stirred until smooth. There are many variations on this theme – for example the egg whites may be whisked to add separately, or fat may be rubbed into the flour as for pastry, but the basic method is always the same. Melted cakes closely resemble quick breads (Flour, Breads and Batters, p.359) with a crumbly cake-like texture. Like quick breads, they are often enlivened with spices, or with dried fruits and nuts. Brown sugar, honey, golden syrup or molasses may be used to give color and taste.

Recipes for melted cakes range from simple, everyday British gingerbreads and parkins, hearty with oatmeal, to Scandinavian spice cakes with buttermilk or sour cream, and the French *pain d'épices*. Flat layers of gingerbread are the basis of festive gingerbread houses, glued together with royal icing and adorned with icicles, candy windows and tiles of chocolate. Spices for such cakes vary from country to country and region to region, with a base of cinnamon, ginger, nutmeg or cloves. The French might add a touch of anise to the mixture, and the Americans a spoonful or two of whiskey.

Other cakes made by the melted method include German fruit-filled cakes with sour cream, moist American chocolate mayonnaise cakes, and delectably rich Italian cakes like *panforte*, laden with fruit and honey. The odd men out are American chiffon cakes. These follow the standard melted method but are fluffy and rich; oil is included and the cakes are lightened with generous amounts of whipped egg white.

Most melted cakes are decorated with a simple butter or glacé icing (p.406), except chiffon cakes which may be topped with the full range of boiled frostings (p.410).

USEFUL INFORMATION

Portion Cake made with 2 cups/250 g flour serves 8-10. *Chiffon:* 6-egg-white cake serves 10-12.
Typical pan Springform; loaf; deep square or rectangle. *Chiffon:* tube pan.
Preparation of pan Greased and lined (p.390). *Chiffon:* none.
Cooking times Depends on the richness of the cake batter. *For plain cakes:* bake at 350°F/175°C, 35-40 minutes in 8 × 4 × 3 in/20 × 10 × 7.5 cm loaf pan or 25-35 minutes in 8 in/20 cm square pan. *Chiffon:* bake at 325°F/160°C, 60-70 minutes in 10 in/25 cm tube pan.
When done Shrinks from sides of pan; skewer inserted in center comes out clean.
Problems Tough if overmixed; dry if overcooked.
Storage 1-2 weeks in airtight container; freeze 3 months.

Frosting and icings Glacé; glaze; whipped. *Chiffon:* butter cream; butter icing; whipped.
Typical cakes Tuscan chestnut cake with pine nuts (Italy); *frustenga* (cornmeal fruit cake, Italy); marbled tea cake (chocolate and vanilla ring cake, USA); devil's food cake (with sour milk and cocoa, USA); lemon chiffon cake (with fresh lemon juice, USA); *piimäkakku* (buttermilk spice cake, Finland); passion fruit chiffon cake (passion fruit icing, Australia); *chokladkaka* (rich chocolate cake, Sweden); chocolate cake with cinnamon (Chile); porter cake (with currants, spices and stout, UK); apple orange coffeecake (USA); banana chiffon cake (with banana purée, USA); heather honey cake (Scotland); Mount Vernon gingerbread (with buttermilk, USA).

Finnish gingerbread

This gingerbread (called *mjuk pepperkaka* in Finland) is excellent served warm with whipped cream, or cold, sliced and spread with butter. The moist ingredients in the cake ensure that it can be stored for longer than other cakes.

Makes 16 2 in/5 cm squares

6 tbsp/90 g butter	2 tsp ground ginger
¼ cup/60 ml milk	1 tsp ground cinnamon
½ cup/125 ml sour cream	½ tsp ground cloves
1 egg	½ tsp ground cardamom
1 cup/200 g brown sugar	¼ cup/30 g chopped almonds
1½ cups/175 g flour	
1 tsp baking soda	***8 in/20 cm square cake pan***

1 Grease the pan, line the base with paper and grease it also (p.390). Heat the oven to 350°F/175°C.
2 Heat the butter with the milk until melted and let it cool to tepid. Stir in the sour cream. With a whisk, stir in the egg and brown sugar until smooth.
3 Sift together the flour, baking soda, ginger, cinnamon, cloves and cardamom. Stir in the chopped almonds.
4 Make a well in the center of the flour mixture. Pour in the liquid and stir together until smooth.
5 Spoon into the prepared pan and smooth the top. Bake until the cake tests done with a skewer, 25-35 minutes. Transfer it to a rack to cool. Serve warm or cold according to taste.

MERINGUE CAKES

A few important classic cakes are based on meringue (Cold Desserts and Ice Creams, p.435). The batter is either plain or mixed with finely chopped nuts such as almonds, hazelnuts or pistachios. The mixture is baked in rounds which are mounted in layers with butter cream or a whipped cream filling. After a few days, the meringue and filling soften and mellow to a lusciously rich cake. Classically, the name of the type of cake is piped across the top against a background of chopped nuts, butter cream rosettes or sugar roses.

USEFUL INFORMATION

Portion 4-egg white meringue cake serves 6-8.
Typical pan Baking sheet.
Preparation of pan Greased and floured or lined with parchment paper (p.390).
Cooking times Bake at 250°F/120°C about 1 hour, then turn off heat and leave to dry.
When done Firm and lightly colored, crisp when cool.
Problems Meringue separates and sticks to the baking sheet if under-beaten; browns if heat is too high.
Storage At least 1 day and up to 5 days in airtight container; freeze 3 months.
Fillings Butter cream; pastry butter cream.

Typical cakes *Dacquoise* (plain or almond meringue, coffee or orange butter cream, France); *japonais* (almond meringue, vanilla butter cream, white praline coating, France); *progrès* (almond or almond and hazelnut meringue, praline or other butter cream, fondant icing, France); *schneetorte* (plain meringue, chocolate whipped cream, Austria); *turquoise* (browned almond meringue, chocolate mousse, cocoa and grated chocolate topping, France); *Spanische windtorte* (ornate meringue cake filled with fruit and cream, Austria).

PIPING MERINGUE ROUNDS

For an even result, meringue rounds should be piped in a spiral; however, they can also be shaped with a spatula.

1 Butter and flour the baking sheet and mark 3 × 8 in/20 cm circles. Using a pastry bag and a ⅝ in/1.5 cm plain tube, pipe rounds of mixture using the circles as a guide.

2 RIGHT After baking, transfer the rounds to a rack to cool. They should be a light cream color and will become crisp when cool.

Gâteau succès

This cake tastes better if it is assembled a day before serving. It can also be kept, refrigerated, for up to one week, depending on the freshness of the butter cream.

Serves 6-8

1½ cups/150 g ground blanched almonds	butter cream (p.405)
2 tbsp/15 g potato starch or cornstarch	confectioners' sugar (to sprinkle)
1½ cups/300 g sugar	2 oz/60 g chopped toasted almonds (p.478)
6 egg whites	*Pastry bag with ⅝ in/1.5 cm plain tube*

1 Heat the oven to 250°F/120°C.
2 **To make the almond meringue:** mix together ground almonds, potato starch or cornstarch, and all but 6 tablespoons of the sugar. Stiffly whip the egg whites, add the remaining sugar and continue whipping for 30 seconds or until the mixture forms a glossy meringue that holds peaks. Fold in the almond mixture in 3 batches (p.392).
3 Pipe 3 meringue rounds following the instructions opposite. Bake in the preheated oven until crisp and dry, 40-50 minutes. While meringue is still warm, trim rounds neatly with a sharp knife. Transfer them to a rack to cool. Make butter cream and flavor it with praline or coffee.
4 **To assemble the cake:** spread about one quarter of the butter cream on a meringue layer. Add the second layer, spread with more butter cream and top with the remaining meringue layer. Spread remaining butter cream over the top and sides, reserving 2-3 tablespoons.
5 Sprinkle the top thickly with confectioners' sugar and press chopped almonds around the edge of the cake. Make a paper piping cone (p.407), fill it with the reserved butter cream and pipe the word *"succès"* across the top.

CHEESECAKES

The term cheesecake is something of a contradiction in terms, for cakes containing any quantity of cheese totally lack the crumbly texture of a cake. Textures vary from the fluffy smoothness of some Italian and German cakes to the dense richness of American cheesecake, but all are soft and moist. Cheese is so heavy that when eggs are added to the batter, they set in the oven's heat, rather than making the cake rise. A few cheesecakes are set with gelatin and chilled rather than baked.

So that the flavor of the cheese does not conflict with that of the sugar, a light fresh cheese such as cream cheese, curd cheese, ricotta or even yogurt is used as the basic ingredient. There are, however, many types of fresh cheese to choose from, each with a different moisture and butterfat content, not to mention flavor, and it is essential to use the type specified. (For example, some American recipes will not work in Europe without the stabilizers used in American commercial cream cheese.)

Many cheesecakes are a type of tart, sometimes with a top as well as a bottom crust. Because the filling is moist, the crust is often baked ahead, or a dry biscuit or cracker crust may be used (Pastry, p.372). Raisins are a popular addition to cheesecake mixtures, while the classic American cheesecake is often topped with fruit such as strawberries or blueberries, or with a sour cream icing. For most cheesecakes, however, a dusting of confectioners' sugar is sufficient decoration.

USEFUL INFORMATION

Portion Cake made with 1 lb/ 500 g cheese serves 10-12.
Typical pan Springform; tart pan with removable base.
Preparation of pan Greased and lined with wax paper (p.390).
Cooking times Vary with recipe.
When done Skewer inserted in center comes out clean.
Problems Dry heat and drafts can cause cracks during baking; cake sinks in the middle if cooked too fast or cooled too rapidly.
Storage Refrigerate 2-3 days in airtight container; add topping just before serving.

Typical cakes New York cheesecake (dense cream cheese filling, baked in graham cracker crust, USA); *tourteau fromager* (with goat cheese, France); *crostata di ricotta* (with raisins and Marsala, Italy); cottage cheese torte with raisins and almonds (Austria); cheesecake lightened with beaten egg whites (Austria); *käsekuchen* (with cottage cheese and sour cream, Germany); curd tart (curd cheese and raisins in shortcrust pastry, UK); *pastiera* (Neapolitan Easter ricotta cake with wheat berries, Italy).

FRUIT & VEGETABLE CAKES

Many fruits and vegetables are valuable ingredients in cakes. Chopped apple or apple sauce, puréed prunes, mashed bananas, fresh berries, or ground orange or lemon peel are just a few of the fruit possibilities. Among vegetables, puréed pumpkin and shredded zucchini are old American favorites, while in central Europe, notably Germany, many cakes are made with grated carrot. Other variations include Swedish mashed potato cake and American apple spice cake, tomato cake made with tomato soup, banana nut cake, and apple-dapple cake – an apple coffee cake.

A sturdy batter, often made by the melting method, is needed to support such moist ingredients. The crisp, golden crust is usually coated with a thin apricot glaze or a layer of soft icing. In the United States, whipped frosting made with cream cheese is popular for carrot cake.

German cheesecake

This cheesecake has a rich filling of cream cheese enlivened with sour cream, lemon zest and raisins. Like many cheesecakes, this recipe is excellent topped with fresh fruit, such as strawberries or sliced peaches macerated in red wine.

Makes a 9 in/23 cm cake

4 eggs, separated	2 tsp grated lemon zest
1 cup/200 g sugar	1 tbsp lemon juice
2 cups/500 g fresh cream cheese, at room temperature	¾ cup/80 g raisins
2 cups/500 g sour cream	*pâte sucrée* made with 1⅔ cups/ 200 g flour (p.373)
3 tbsp/20 g cornstarch	
2 tsp vanilla extract	*9 in/23 cm springform pan*

1 Grease the pan. Line it with *pâte sucrée* and chill. Heat the oven to 400°F/200 °C.
2 Beat the egg yolks in a bowl until smooth. Gradually beat in the sugar and continue beating until light and fluffy. Add the cream cheese little by little, beating until smooth. Mix in the sour cream, cornstarch, vanilla extract, lemon zest and juice. Finally, stir in the raisins.
3 Beat the egg whites until stiff. Gently fold them (p.392) into the cheese mixture.
4 Pour the cheese mixture into the pastry-lined pan; it should reach the top of the pastry dough. Bake until lightly brown and almost set, about 1 hour. **Note** Filling rises while baking; it will sink and become firm as it cools. If top browns too quickly, cover it loosely with aluminum foil.
5 Allow the cheesecake to cool thoroughly in the pan, at room temperature. Chill for 4-6 hours before unmolding and serving.

SMALL CAKES

Small cakes have a personality of their own: no American regards a brownie simply as chocolate batter with a few nuts, or cupcakes as mere sponge cake baked in a paper case. One secret of success is a distinctive shape. Consider the charm of an English butterfly cake, the top hollowed out for frosting and the lid split to form wings, or a Spanish *bizcochos borrachos* – a small sponge cake soaked in wine and sprinkled with cinnamon. Often the shape of the cake is its own decoration, as with British rock cakes, or French shell-shaped madeleines; both are served plain.

The flavor and texture of a small cake must be pronounced – rich chocolate slices, crisp or chewy nut cakes, feather-light cupcakes, and airy meringue shells. However, even the most delicate of small cakes should not fall apart in the hand. The basic methods and techniques of baking are the same as for larger cakes, although higher temperatures and shorter cooking times are often necessary. Design and decoration for small cakes should be effective, yet simple enough not to detract from their essential charm. French *printaniers* topped with colored butter cream, or small sponge rounds sandwiched with butter cream and covered with chocolate icing are just two possibilities. Simpler still is a layer of soft icing, topped with colored sprinkles.

MAKING MADELEINES

Madeleines are baked in a hot oven so that they form a characteristic peak on top with a shell-shaped underside.

Makes 25-30 medium madeleines

1 cup/125 g flour	1 tsp orange flower water *or* grated zest of 1 orange or 1 lemon
1 tsp baking powder	
4 eggs	½ cup/125 g butter, melted
⅔ cup/135 g granulated sugar	*25-30 medium madeleine molds*

1 Sift the flour with the baking powder. Whisk the eggs and sugar to the ribbon (p.394). Beat in the orange flower water or grated zest. Fold in the flour in three batches (p.392), adding the butter with the last batch. Chill for 20-30 minutes until the butter hardens slightly and the dough stiffens.

2 Heat the oven to 450°F/230°C. Grease and flour the molds. With a large spoon, pour the batter into the molds, so that they are two-thirds full.

3 Bake the madeleines for 5 minutes. Reduce heat to 400°F/200°C and continue baking until golden brown, 5-7 minutes; a peak in the center of the cakes is characteristic. Transfer the madeleines to a rack to cool.

PETITS FOURS

Elegant, frivolous, more confection than cake, *petits fours* are the exhibitionists of the pastry world. The color must be vivid and the taste emphatic, with only the best ingredients used – smooth chocolate, crunchy nuts and rich caramel – to produce an eye-catching display for a grand reception or after a splendid dinner.

Petits fours cover a range of small cookies, from amusing contrivances such as wafer-thin tiles (Fr. *tuiles*) or cat's tongues (Fr. *langues de chat*) to miniature *génoise* cakes (see *génoise* recipe p.395) cloaked in fondant. Many *petits fours* are not baked at all, despite their name (French for "little ovens") and belong more to the world of confectionery than to patisserie. Fruits glazed with fondant or caramel, almond paste bonbons, chocolate truffles and *colettes* – chocolate cups or boxes filled with ganache – are just as much *petits fours* as miniature cookies and cakes. (For details of these see the section on candies in Sugar and Chocolate, p.426, and Cookies, p.388.)

Inevitably making *petits fours* is time-consuming and those that are baked need to be watched carefully during their short spell in the oven. They scorch easily, so it helps to line the baking sheet with paper and turn the sheet during cooking. *Petits fours* should be bite-sized and uniform, calling for close attention to detail. A pastry bag may be necessary for shaping and decorating.

Petits fours invite decoration, with coatings of chocolate and nuts, toppings of candied cherries, butter cream rosettes and scrolls of royal icing, all meticulously executed in miniature. For serving, frilled paper cups or foil cases lend a professional touch.

Almond petits fours

Care must be taken not to overbake almond *petits fours* as they are supposed to be soft in the center. To make macaroons, the same almond mixture is used, piped with a large plain tube into 2 in/5 cm rounds, and baked 15-20 minutes.

Makes about 50 petits fours

6½ oz/200 g blanched, ground almonds	*For the glaze*
	1 tbsp confectioners' sugar
¾ cup/150 g sugar	2 tbsp milk
2 egg whites	
½ tsp vanilla extract	*Pastry bag and large star tube;*
candied cherries (for decoration)	*paper cases (optional)*

1 Grease a baking sheet with melted butter or margarine using a pastry brush and line it with wax paper. Heat the oven to 350°F/175°C. Stir together the ground almonds and sugar.
2 Beat the egg whites until frothy, then beat them into the almond mixture, adding enough to make a stiff paste that is just soft enough to pipe. Beat in the vanilla. Using the pastry bag, pipe 1 in/2.5 cm rosettes, S-shapes, hearts or teardrops on to the baking sheet. Top with tiny pieces of cherry. (For macaroons pipe 2 in/5 cm rounds and top with almonds.)
3 Bake in the oven until just beginning to brown, 10-12 minutes (15-20 minutes for macaroons). Take the baking sheet from the oven and pour a little water under the paper: the heat from the baking sheet produces steam which loosens the *petits fours*.
4 **For the glaze:** gently heat the sugar with the milk and brush the mixture over the *petits fours* while still hot. Transfer them to a rack to cool. Serve in paper cases.

CAKE FILLINGS, ICINGS & FROSTINGS

Fillings and toppings complement cakes. Butter cream is rich, appearing as the filling, coating and decoration of many European cakes. Soft icings are more classical, notably fondant (p.417), which offers a mirror-smooth background for decorations of nuts, sugared or almond paste flowers, or a piped message. Alternatives are an almond paste or spectacular royal icing coating.

Simple whipped frostings are more frivolous and may also double as fillings. Others include pastry cream (p.384), thick custard, ricotta and cream cheese. With the exception of whipped or Chantilly cream (p.70), fillings, icings and frostings are usually added ahead so flavors mellow.

The function of a filling or topping is to highlight the cake itself. Flavors should be lively, otherwise a finished cake can taste unpleasantly sweet and rich. Coloring should be added with a light hand for soft pastel shades. Nuts, shredded coconut or chocolate shavings may provide a final decorative touch.

BUTTER CREAM

The most common butter cream is made with egg yolks beaten with hot sugar syrup (p.414) to a light mousse, then mixed with creamed butter. A lighter version uses egg whites. Flavorings vary from coffee and chocolate to liqueurs and fruit purées. Use unsalted butter and beat thoroughly for lightness. It may also be lightened by folding in an equal volume of pastry cream to make pastry butter cream (Fr. *crème mousseline*).

USEFUL INFORMATION

Portion 2 cups/375 g fills and coats a two-layer 8-9 in/20-23 cm cake.
Problems If egg mousse is added warm, butter melts; curdles if too cold but can be reconstituted if

warmed and beaten; may melt if too warm, so keep cake chilled.
Storage Refrigerate 1 week; freeze 3 months.
Used for *biscuit; génoise;* layer; meringue cakes.

Butter cream

Makes 2 cups/375 g butter cream

½ cup/100 g sugar	1 cup/250 g unsalted butter
6 tbsp/90 ml water	½ tsp vanilla extract
4 egg yolks	

1 In a small saucepan, heat the sugar with the water until dissolved, then boil until the syrup reaches the soft ball stage, 239°F/115°C on a candy thermometer (p.503).
2 Meanwhile, beat the egg yolks just until mixed. Gradually pour in the hot syrup, beating constantly. Beat as fast as possible until the mixture is cool and forms a thick mousse, about 5 minutes.
3 Cream the butter and gradually beat it into the cool yolk mixture. Beat in the vanilla.

Butter cream variations

White butter cream Makes 2 cups/375 g butter cream. Following the recipe for butter cream, substitute Italian meringue (p.437) made with 2 egg whites, ½ cup/100 g sugar, and ¼ cup/60 ml water, for egg yolk mousse. Cream the butter and gradually beat in the cooled meringue.
Chocolate or coffee butter cream Melt 6 oz/180 g chopped semisweet chocolate or dissolve 2 tbsp instant coffee in 2 tbsp hot water, cool slightly and beat into 2 cups/375 g butter cream.
Orange or lemon butter cream Beat grated zest of 2 oranges or lemons, ¼ cup/60 ml orange or lemon juice and 3 tbsp/45 ml Grand Marnier into 2 cups/375 g butter cream.
Praline butter cream Beat praline (p.419) made with 3 oz/90 g whole unblanched almonds and 7 tbsp/90 g sugar into 2 cups/375 g butter cream.
Raspberry butter cream Purée 1 pt/250 g fresh or thawed, frozen raspberries, strain and beat into 2 cups/375 g butter cream.

Butter icing

This is a domestic version of butter cream, consisting simply of equal weights of creamed butter and sugar thoroughly beaten together. Confectioners' sugar gives a smooth filling, granulated sugar adds crunch, while brown sugar has more taste. Flavorings are the same as for butter cream. For fruit and vegetable cakes, cream cheese may be substituted for the butter.

ADDING FILLING TO CAKES

Filling (here, butter cream) should be soft enough to spread without tearing crumbs from the cake. If it is too thick to spread, warm over a water bath or dilute slightly. The cake will be easier to handle while adding filling if placed on a round of cardboard.

1 Slice the cake into horizontal layers (p.393). To moisten the cake, brush the cut surface with sugar syrup (p.414) or liqueur.

2 Spread the filling evenly almost to the edge of the cake with a metal spatula. The thickness depends on the richness of the filling.

3 Set the next layer on top with the help of a cardboard round to move it. Press gently with the flat of your hand to squeeze the filling out just to the edge of the cake.

FILLING A PASTRY BAG

A variety of tubes (below) can be used with a pastry bag, some plain for shaping meringue and choux pastry, others cut in shapes for piping decorations of whipped cream and butter cream (here).

1 Drop a tube into the bag and twist, tucking the bag into the tube. This will prevent any filling from leaking out at the bottom.

2 Fold the top of the bag over your hand to form a collar and add the filling, scraping the spatula against your hand.

3 When the bag is full, twist the top until there is no air left in it.

4 Holding the twisted end of the bag taut in one hand, with the other gently press the filling at the top of the bag to start it flowing.

SOFT ICINGS

Soft icings vary in complexity from a simple glaze of confectioners' sugar and water to the shimmering density of fondant (p.417), the favorite of European pastry chefs. The aim is a thin sugar coating, smooth enough to shine and soft enough to slice easily. Maintaining the correct temperature, so that coarse crystals do not form, is the key to smoothness, assisted by stabilizers such as glucose, corn syrup, cream of tartar and lemon juice. A glaze is thinner than icing, giving a semi-transparent coating; it may be added after baking or baked with the batter, as for some coffee cakes.

USEFUL INFORMATION

Portion 1 cup/250 ml icing or ¾ cup/175 ml glaze coats top and sides of 9 in/23 cm cake.
Problems If overheated, icing is dull and crystalline; once set, icing cracks if cake is carelessly handled.

Storage Varies with icing, 1-2 days in airtight container; do not refrigerate as sugar icing will dissolve and chocolate lose gloss.
Used for *biscuit*; *génoise*; pound; fruit; layer; melted cakes.

Types of soft icing

Glacé icing Makes 1 cup/250 ml icing. Sift 1½ cups/200 g confectioners' sugar into a bowl. Stir in 6-7 tbsp/90-105 ml water with ½ tsp vanilla extract, adding enough water to make a soft paste. Lemon or orange juice may be substituted for water.
Honey glaze Makes 1 cup/250 ml glaze. In a saucepan mix ½ cup/100 g sugar, ¼ cup/60 ml milk, ¼ cup/60 g butter and ¼ cup/60 g honey. Heat gently, stirring until melted, and bring just to a boil. Spread on batter or dough for baking.
Chocolate *sachertorte* icing For a 9 in/23 cm cake. In a heavy saucepan combine 1¼ cups/250 g sugar and ½ cup/125 ml water. Bring just to a boil and leave to cool. Melt 6 oz/180 g chopped semisweet chocolate and gradually stir into the sugar syrup. Cook in a water bath over low heat, stirring, for 5 minutes. Take from the heat, stir in ½ tsp vegetable oil and let cool, stirring gently until just warm and of coating consistency.

BUTTER CREAM DECORATIONS

Plain tube

Basket or ribbon

Leaf tube

6-point star tube

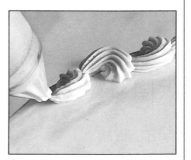

Alternate scroll border, using 6-point star tube

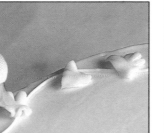

Basket work, using basket and plain tubes

Leaves, using leaf tube

Large rosettes, using 6-point open star tube

Shell border, using 6-point star tube

COATING WITH SOFT ICING

Soft icings and glazes are used while warm so that they set on contact with the cool cake. A cake with sloping sides is easier to coat than one with straight sides.

1 Set the cake on a rack with a tray underneath to catch the drips. Brush the cake with apricot glaze (Pastry and Cookies, p.385) so that crumbs are not picked up by the icing. Leave until cool, about 5 minutes.

2 Warm the icing in a water bath until tepid and just thick enough to coat a spoon. If too thin, beat in sifted confectioners' sugar (or more stiff fondant if using). If too thick, add a little water (or sugar syrup for fondant).

3 Pour the icing over the cake so that it drips down the sides.

4 At once spread the top smooth with a metal spatula.

5 Smooth the sides, if necessary patching gaps with more icing. Bumps can be smoothed with a metal spatula dipped in hot water.

MARBLING WITH SOFT ICING

An attractive marbled effect can be created by piping chocolate or contrasting icing on to the background icing using a small cone.

1 Coat the cake with icing. At once pipe a spiral of contrasting icing (starting at the center).

2 Mark the cake into 8 with the point of a knife working from the center to the edge. Divide each segment again, this time working from the edge to the center to give a "spider's web" effect.

3 When the last line has been drawn, swirl the icing at the center with the tip of the knife.

ALTERNATIVELY, for a square cake, pipe parallel lines in contrasting icing and mark crosswise lines to marble it.

MAKING A PAPER PIPING CONE

Disposable paper cones are useful when several piping tubes or different colors of icing are being employed at once. The cone can also be used without a piping tube for plain writing.

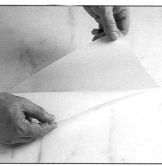

1 Fold an 8 × 14 in/20 × 35 cm rectangle in half diagonally and cut along the fold.

2 Fold the short side of one triangle over to the right-angled corner to form a cone.

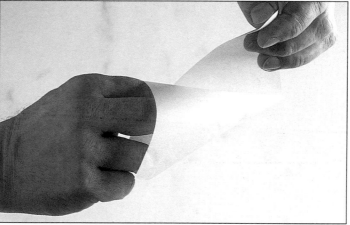

3 Holding the cone together with one hand, wrap the long point of the triangle around the paper cone.

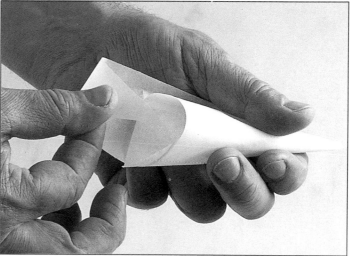

4 Tuck the point of paper inside the cone to secure it. (Repeat with the second triangle for a second cone.)

For writing: fill the cone with 2-3 tbsp/30-45 ml icing and fold over the top. Snip the tip and press the cone to form a thin ribbon of icing.
For a piping tube: snip a larger opening and drop in a piping tube.

ROYAL ICING

Royal icing is made of confectioners' sugar beaten to a smooth paste with egg white and a little lemon juice for whiteness. It holds a crisp, stiff shape that makes it above all a decorator's tool, the medium for virtuoso displays of ribbons, roses, lattice, basket and geometric designs. They may be white or delicately tinted to show clearly against a plain white background of royal icing. A wide range of special small piping tubes (below) is used, and complicated designs are composed in stages to allow the icing to dry. Royal icing is also handy for writing on soft coatings.

USEFUL INFORMATION

Portion 2 cups/500 ml icing coats top and sides of a 9 in/23 cm cake. (For decoration allow at least 1 cup/250 ml.)
Problems If too soft, beat in more confectioners' sugar; if too stiff, dilute with a few drops water; icing dries quickly so keep bowl covered with a wet cloth.
Storage 12 hours in a bowl covered with a wet cloth.
Used for whisked; fruit cakes.

Royal icing

Makes 2 cups/500 ml icing

3½ cups/500 g confectioners' sugar	1 tsp lemon juice
2 egg whites	

Sift the confectioners' sugar. Beat the egg whites until frothy and beat in the sugar a tablespoon at a time. Beat in the lemon juice and continue beating at least 8 minutes until the mixture forms soft peaks. **Note** Lengthy beating makes the icing more flexible. If keeping the icing, beat again before using.

Chocolate royal icing Add 1¼ cups/125 g cocoa powder to the confectioners' sugar before adding three egg whites.
Cookie icing Sift the confectioners' sugar and add 1 tsp lemon juice and enough egg white to make icing with a thin consistency for dipping.

ROYAL ICING DECORATIONS

Use a 6-point star tube to pipe a chain of rosettes and to make small stars.

Use an 8-point star tube to pipe a lattice in a long-tailed shell design.

Use a 6-point star tube to pipe a row of shells and a fine writing nozzle for lines.

Use a 6-point star tube to make swirls and a fine nozzle for dots and lines.

Use an 8-point star tube to pipe a row of double-sided shells

8-point star tube

Ribbon/petal tube

6-point star tube

Fine writing tube

Use a petal tube for the roses and leaves and a fine nozzle to link them.

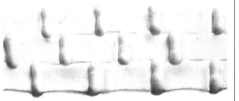

Use a ribbon tube to make a series of strips and a fine nozzle to join them.

Use a 6-point star tube to pipe a series of scrolls and small rosettes.

Use a fine writing tube to make a chain of bows, loops and tiny dots.

ALMOND PASTE

Almond paste, often called marzipan, is a versatile, durable alternative to soft icings and butter cream for many classic whisked cakes. Soft, pliable and colored in pretty pastel shades, the paste can be rolled and molded to a thin smooth coating.

Almond paste is made with ground almonds and sugar bound with egg white, but proportions vary enormously. Commercial almond paste has a good malleable texture that cannot be reproduced at home.

A coating of almond paste is usually left a few hours until firm. A top coat of fondant or chocolate icing is then added, or the paste may be broiled to brown it lightly (take care as it scorches easily).

USEFUL INFORMATION

Portion 1½ lb/750 g covers 9-10 in/23-25 cm cake with enough for decorations.
Problems If stiff, sprinkle with water and knead until pliable.
Storage 1 week in airtight container.
Used for *biscuit*; *génoise*; fruit cakes.

ALMOND PASTE DECORATIONS

To make decorative shapes with almond paste, knead a small amount of paste until it is soft and pliable. Then roll or mold it with your hands to form shapes. For detailed work special tools (right) can be used. To color the paste sprinkle a few drops of coloring on to it and knead until the paste is evenly coated. Alternatively, paint the shapes with a brush when finished.

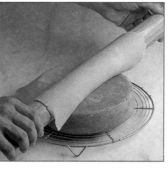

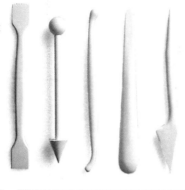

Roses Small balls of paste are shaped into thin flat ovals and molded to resemble petals.

Fruits Almond paste is molded to shape by hand, and tools are used for detail.

COVERING A CAKE WITH ALMOND PASTE

Before being covered with almond paste, a cake must be brushed with melted apricot jam glaze (p.385) or coated with a thin layer of butter cream and thoroughly chilled. To color the paste, spread it on a work surface, sprinkle with a few drops of color and knead it until it is evenly tinted.

1 Set the cake on a round of cardboard on a rack and brush it with apricot glaze. Sprinkle the work surface lightly with confectioners' sugar and roll the paste to a thin round with a heavy rolling pin. Brush excess confectioners' sugar from the surface.

2 Gently wrap the paste loosely around the rolling pin, lift the rolling pin and unroll the paste over the cake leaving enough overlap to cover the sides.

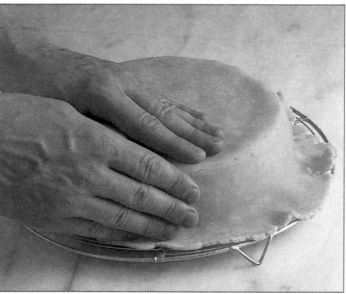

3 Press the paste against the sides and rim of the cake, molding it to shape with your hands. Trim any excess paste around the base.

4 For a smooth finish, rub the paste with a cardboard disk.

5 Turn the cake over and rub round the sides.

WHIPPED FROSTINGS

Frosting is an apt name for these light toppings. The most common whipped frosting is Italian meringue (p.437), made by adding hot sugar syrup (p.414) to whipped egg whites. This stabilizes the egg whites so the frosting can be kept for two to three days. Americans are particularly fond of whipped frostings, such as boiled fudge frosting made by boiling chocolate with sugar and milk, or seven-minute frosting, beaten until thick in a double boiler. Frostings set on standing so they must be spread in free-form swirls and peaks while still warm.

Vanilla is commonly used as a flavoring, though chopped nuts or raisins may be folded into the frosting just before spreading. Whipped frosting can be used as both filling and topping.

USEFUL INFORMATION

Portion 2 cups/500 ml fills and coats two-layer 9 in/23 cm cake.
Cooking times Boil syrup to a hard ball, 248°F/120°C on candy thermometer (p.503); brown in oven at 250°F/120°C for 10-15 minutes (White frosting only).
When done Cool, fluffy and holds a stiff peak.
Problems If syrup is underboiled, frosting will be thin; whisk frosting in a bowl over a pan of hot water until stiff; if syrup is overboiled, frosting sets too fast; add 1-2 tsp boiling water.
Storage After spreading, 2-3 days in airtight container.
Used for *biscuit*; chiffon; *génoise*; layer; angel food cakes.

FESTIVE CAKES

National allegiances come more clearly to the fore in festive cakes than in any other dish. Typically British are the dense, spirit-soaked fruit cakes covered in almond paste and coated in a lacy trellis of snow-white royal icing; these are traditionally tiered and used as wedding cakes. In the United States, tiered wedding cakes are of a lighter construction – layers of sponge sandwiched with delicious fillings of butter cream, lemon curd with strawberries or chocolate cream with raspberries.

For Christmas, the cake is usually a single layer. *Panforte*, a thin, rich cake filled with honey, pepper, nuts and sweet candied fruits, can be found in Italian delicatessens the world over at Christmas time. Christmas is also the season for a festive yule log, whether constructed in the French style as a rolled sponge with butter cream, almond paste holly and meringue mushrooms, or a rolled yeast dough laden with fruits, like the German *stollen*, which is traditionally tied with red ribbon and presented as a gift.

Easter brings further inspiration with Italian *cassata*, a cheese-cake made of sponge layered with ricotta cheese, candied fruit and chocolate pieces, wrapped in almond paste and decorated with candied oranges and citron curls. In Spain, the Easter cheesecake is *tarta pasiega* which is flavored with rose water and honey.

In many countries birthdays are celebrated with a special cake finished with decorative piping and candles. Lesser occasions offer possibilities for confections such as the French *gâteau St. Honoré*, a crown of caramel-coated choux puffs filled with light pastry cream and named after the patron saint of pastry cooks. Other festive cakes include the eastern European yeast crown filled with candies, the Russian "mother-in-law" cake of crisp walnut layers filled with butter cream and draped in chocolate glaze, and the Dutch *Haarlem* celebration cake of lemon sponge filled with butter cream and covered in whipped cream.

COATING WITH WHIPPED FROSTING

Shredded coconut is often pressed into the surface of a smooth coat of whipped frosting. In Italy, a favorite practice is to pipe the frosting in rosettes then brown it quickly in the oven.

1 Coat the sides and top of the cake generously with icing.

2 With a metal spatula, swirl the icing so that it forms soft peaks.

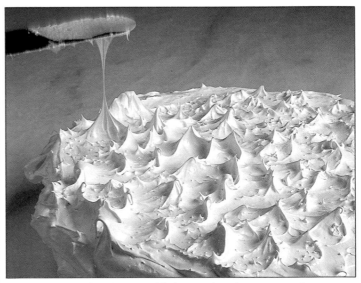

3 Continue swirling the icing with the spatula to form an attractive even decoration of soft peaks across the top of the cake and then repeat around the sides until the desired effect is achieved.

Whipped frostings

White mountain frosting Add 1 tbsp corn syrup when making sugar syrup in Italian meringue (p.437) and 1 tsp vanilla extract just before using.

Raisin or nut frosting Fold ½ cup/75 g golden raisins or chopped or slivered nuts into Italian meringue (p.437) before using.

American fudge boiled frosting In a heavy saucepan, combine 2 oz/60 g chopped unsweetened chocolate with 1½ cups/300 g sugar, ½ cup/125 ml milk, ¼ cup/60 g butter, 1 tbsp corn syrup and a pinch of salt. Boil 1 minute, stirring constantly. Cool, add 1 tsp vanilla extract and beat until thick.

Seven-minute frosting In the top of a double boiler, mix ¾ cup/150 g sugar, 2 tbsp water, 1 tbsp light corn syrup, pinch of salt and 1 egg white. Beat by hand for 1 minute, set over boiling water and beat until stiff peaks form, about 6 minutes. Remove from the heat and continue beating until thick enough to spread. Can be flavored with vanilla, coffee, shredded coconut or chopped nuts.

SUGAR &
CHOCOLATE

SUGAR AND CHOCOLATE feature prominently in our diet – not surprisingly, for we are born with a taste for sugar. They are the primary ingredients in confectionery and are of great importance in cake-making and desserts. When dissolved as syrup, sugar is the foundation of many preparations, including poached and candied fruits, crisp sugar coatings, pulled and blown sugar, and fondant. Caramel, the product of sugar boiled at high temperatures, is both a candy and the basis for the flavorings praline and nougatine. Boiled sugar syrup candies demonstrate the versatility of sugar in such familiar favorites as toffee, fudge, taffy, caramels and pralines.

Sugar has other roles besides that of a sweetener. It helps to preserve foods, especially fruit, it can give baked foods a rich, brown color and helps to tenderize cakes, pastry and bread. Sugar prevents batters and doughs from setting too quickly, so cakes rise better. It also retains moisture, prolonging the shelf-life of cakes and other baked goods.

Chocolate is the favorite sweet flavoring, as epitomized by ganache filling, rich fudge and other dessert sauces. The malleable texture of chocolate makes it suitable for shaping decorations, such as curls, cigarettes and leaves and for coating cakes, *petits fours* and a multitude of candies.

SUGAR

The earliest known sweeteners were honey, sweet fruits, and syrups concentrated from fruit. These are still popular, but nowadays, the most common sweetener is white table sugar, refined from sugar cane or sugar beet. Cane and beet sugar have the same taste and cooking properties. Sugar can also be obtained from certain palm trees and maple trees, as well as from grains such as sorghum and barley.

Due to differences in refining techniques and marketing terminology, sugars vary from country to country. For cane sugar, the juice is extracted and boiled until it crystallizes. The resulting liquid is then passed through a centrifuge to separate the raw sugar crystals from the liquid molasses. The crystals are redissolved and carbon dioxide is added to purify and whiten them. Finally, the sugar is recrystallized into the forms we recognize in our supermarkets. The liquids siphoned off during processing may be made into brown sugars and syrups. For beet sugar, the root, rather than the stem, provides the juice.

In general, brown sugar can be substituted for white, although a very dark brown sugar or one that contains a high proportion of molasses, will darken color and give a more bitter flavor. Changes are inadvisable in any recipe in which the sugar content is substantial. It is particularly important not to alter the type of sugar specified when baking, as the difference in moisture content between brown and white sugar can impair the success of a recipe. Syrups can be used more or less interchangeably, though the straight substitution of syrup for dry sugar is risky, as the liquid content in a recipe must also be adjusted.

Structure of sugar

White sugar is 99.8 percent sucrose, which is a simple carbohydrate produced by all plants during photosynthesis. Sucrose is composed of two sugars in equal amounts: glucose (also called dextrose, corn or grape sugar) and fructose (also called levulose or fruit sugar). In white sugar, glucose and fructose naturally cling together in a uniform pattern to form sugar crystals. In honey and syrups, glucose and fructose exist in unequal proportions, which inhibits crystallization. Therefore, adding any sugar other than sucrose (for example corn syrup, liquid glucose or honey) to a white sugar (sucrose) syrup interrupts the uniform pattern and helps to prevent the formation of crystals. Similarly, the addition of acid ingredients such as lemon juice or cream of tartar will discourage crystallization by causing the sucrose to break down into glucose and fructose – a process called inversion. Commercially-produced inverted sugar can be bought in the form of a white paste, sold at specialty baking shops. (It cannot be substituted directly for white sugar.)

Fructose and glucose are available individually and can be used to prevent crystallization. Glucose is sold as a thick, colorless syrup. Less sweet than white sugar, it is similar to corn syrup, which has a high glucose content. Fructose, found naturally in sweet fruits and honey, is the sweetest sugar and is sold as fine crystals, liquid and tablets. Some diet-conscious cooks like to use fructose because it is sweeter than white sugar and can therefore be used in smaller quantities. Heat destroys some of its sweetness, however, so it is not so effective as ordinary sugar when substituted for it in cooked food, particularly in cakes and pastries. Typically, it is used in sauces, bottled sodas and in syrups for canned fruits.

Two other types of sugar are worth mentioning although they are of little direct interest to the cook: maltose, or malt sugar, the primary sugar contained in malted barley, and lactose, also called milk sugar, which is the natural sugar found in milk and used mainly by the pharmaceutical industry.

WHITE SUGAR

Granulated sugar is the most common type of white sugar. It is crystalline, highly refined and pours easily. British granulated sugar is coarser than American granulated, and is used for making syrups and other heated mixtures. In Britain there is also caster sugar, which closely resembles American granulated but is slightly finer, very like French *sucre en poudre*, used in desserts and baking.

In North America, superfine sugar (also known as extra-fine, berry or bar sugar) is marketed. Its consistency lies mid-way between American granulated and confectioners' sugar. Since it dissolves quickly, it is good for making drinks and is often used for cakes and frostings.

Confectioners' sugar, or powdered sugar, is white sugar ground to a fine powder and mixed with cornstarch to prevent it from caking. It is used for icings, to sweeten uncooked foods that should not be grainy, particularly cream, and for dusting cakes and candies.

The large crystals of preserving sugar dissolve easily and are therefore less likely to burn when making jams (p.490). Cube sugar, also called loaf or lump sugar, is made by molding moist sugar into blocks; it is popular for hot drinks.

USEFUL INFORMATION
Nutritive value per 3½ oz/100 g: 385 calories; no protein; no fat; 100 g carbohydrates; 2.5 mg sodium; no cholesterol.
Problems *Confectioners' sugar*: forms lumps when damp and must be sifted.
Storage Indefinitely in airtight container.

white sugar cubes

granulated   preserving

superfine

confectioners'

colored crystals

brownulated

dark brown

light brown

glucose syrup

coffee crystals   Demerara

BROWN SUGAR

Brown sugar, produced only from cane sugar, was once a less-refined form of white sugar containing some molasses left over from the refining process. Today, it is usually made by recombining white sugar with molasses, giving it flavor, moisture and color. Brown sugar is available light or dark; in most recipes they are used interchangeably, the latter being softer with a slightly stronger taste. Sand sugar, soft sugar, "pieces" and "yellows" are all regional names for light brown sugars.

Brown sugar is often used in baking. It is usually combined with sweet spices such as cinnamon. Since brown sugar traps air, it should always be packed down before being measured by volume.

American "brownulated sugar" is a dry free-pouring sugar that consists of brown sugar combined with caramel coloring. It should not be used in baking as it behaves differently when heated.

Barbados and Demerara sugars are refined, moist crystalline brown sugars from the Caribbean. Barbados sugar is the darker of the two.

In many countries, completely raw sugars are forbidden because of potential contamination. One relatively unrefined sugar that is available is *muscovado* (Portuguese for "unrefined"), in which most or all of the molasses remains; another is *turbinado*, which has honey-brown crystals and pours easily. In the United States, a similar product is labeled "sugar in the raw". Coarse brown palm sugar is available in cakes or lumps made by boiling the sap of various palms, and is popular in India and Southeast Asia. Moist dark brown sugar can be substituted. Jaggery is used in Indian desserts and is a brown unrefined lump sugar made from cane sugar or palm sap. Date sugar, resembling raw brown sugar and made from ground dates, can be used for sprinkling but not for cooking as it does not fully dissolve.

USEFUL INFORMATION
Nutritive value per 3½ oz/100 g. *Light or dark brown:* 375 calories; no protein; no fat; 96 g carbohydrates, 48 mg sodium, no cholesterol.
Problems Dries quickly to a block when exposed to air; keep soft by placing in a closed container with a damp cloth or a piece of apple or lemon; if already hard, warm the sugar in a low oven.
Storage Indefinitely in airtight container in cool, dry place.

ORNAMENTAL SUGARS

Ornamental sugars are used to decorate breads and cakes, and some are served to sweeten hot drinks, for example candy crystals – light brown, irregular crystals, often called coffee crystals. Colored or confetti sugar is white sugar that has been dyed with food coloring, and is popular as a dessert decoration. White or colored crystal sugar, also called coarse or pearl sugar, remains crunchy even after baking and is sprinkled on sweet bread and pastry doughs such as English Bath buns.

HONEY

Honey is the original sweetener, popular long before cane sugar became common. Some of the most valued honeys come from orange blossom, buckwheat, sage blossom, heather, rosemary, lavender, acacia and eucalyptus. The color varies with the flower. Usually, the paler the honey, the milder its flavor. Plain, or extracted, honey is often pasteurized to prevent crystallization. Chunk honey containing bits of honeycomb is not processed, neither is comb honey, which comes straight from the beehive.

Honey not only adds distinctive flavor to baked goods, it makes them dense and moist, so that they keep longer. It is the characteristic sweetener in many pastries and cakes like spice bread or Greek *Baklava* (p.382). Many caramels, candies, and liqueurs such as Benedictine, are also flavored with honey.

USEFUL INFORMATION
Nutritive value per 3½ oz/100 g: 304 calories; no protein; no fat; 82 g carbohydrates; 5 mg sodium; no cholesterol.
Problems If honey crystallizes, put jar in a pan of warm water until liquified.
Storage Indefinitely in airtight container in cool, dry place; if refrigerated, becomes grainy.

clear   thick   light

dark   honey-comb

Jewish honey cake

This cake (Hebrew *lekach*), is traditionally served at the festival of Rosh Hashana in the hope of a sweet New Year.

Makes one large loaf

2¼ cups/275 g flour	3 tbsp/45 g melted butter or margarine
2 tsp ground cinnamon	
1 tsp baking powder	¾ cup/300 g dark honey
½ tsp baking soda	2 tbsp instant coffee, dissolved in ¾ cup/175 ml tepid water
½ tsp salt	
3½ oz/100 g walnuts, coarsely chopped	2 tbsp grated orange zest
3 eggs	***9 × 5 × 3 in/23 × 13 × 7.5 cm loaf pan***
¾ cup/150 g dark brown sugar	

1 Heat the oven to 350°F/175°C. Grease the pan and line the sides and bottom with wax paper (p.391). Sift together the flour, cinnamon, baking powder, baking soda and salt, removing one tablespoon to toss with the walnuts in a small bowl. Set aside.
2 Lightly beat the eggs and sugar in a large bowl until just mixed. Stir in the melted butter or margarine, and honey. Stir the dry ingredients into the honey mixture in three batches, adding them alternately with the coffee. Stir until smooth, then add the grated orange zest and the floured walnuts.
3 Pour the batter into the prepared pan. Set the pan low down in the oven and bake for 1–1¼ hours or until a skewer inserted in the center comes out clean. If the cake browns too much during baking, cover it loosely with aluminum foil.
4 Let the cake cool in the pan. Remove and wrap it tightly, leaving the paper on. Store in an airtight container for at least two days and up to two weeks so that the flavor mellows.

COMMERCIAL SYRUPS

Syrups available from supermarkets such as molasses, maple syrup, golden syrup and others, may have characteristic flavors but are basically all sugar in liquid form. All are popular as toppings for dishes such as pancakes or oatmeal, with the exception of molasses, which is too strong and bitter. Syrups are also popular in icings and desserts. The mild varieties – golden and corn syrup – can usually be substituted for one another.

Molasses is the syrup left after sugar has been crystallized from cane sap. "First" or light molasses is the sweetest and most refined, "second" molasses is less so. "Final" or "blackstrap" molasses (in Britain, black treacle) is very heavy and dark, with a harsh flavor. "Premium" table molasses is made by blending cane syrup with "first" molasses. Molasses lends a strong characteristic taste to food and is used most typically in cookies, gingerbread, spicy fruit cakes and some candies; it also features in barbecue sauces and Boston baked beans and some Asian savory preparations.

Cane syrup tastes like molasses and is made commercially by simmering sugar cane juice until thick and golden-brown. Pale yellow golden syrup, also made from sugarcane sap, is milder, with a thick honey-like consistency. Corn syrup or honey are the nearest substitutes.

Corn syrup is a sweet, thick liquid derived from corn kernels, used in baking, desserts, candies and snack foods. Light corn syrup tastes like liquid sugar but dark corn syrup is mixed with molasses for added color and flavor. North American pancake syrup is corn syrup mixed with a small amount of maple syrup.

Maple syrup, made from the sap of the sugar maple tree, is the most highly prized of all syrups. It has a very sweet, distinctive flavor and auburn color; although there is a grading system to indicate quality, imitations are common. Maple sugar, crystallized from the sap, is available granulated or in candies.

Sorghum or molasses syrup is extracted from the stalks of the sorghum plant. Golden and tart, it is quite common in the American South. Barley malt syrup (barley malt or malt extract) has a delicate flavor and is high in vitamins and iron.

USEFUL INFORMATION

Nutritive value per 3½ oz/100 g.
All: no protein; no fat; no cholesterol. *Molasses:* 215 calories; 55 g carbohydrates; 95 mg sodium. *Cane:* 265 calories; 70 g carbohydrates; 95 mg sodium. *Golden:* 300 calories; 80 g carbohydrates; 279 mg sodium. *Corn:* 285 calories; 75 g carbohydrates; 150 mg sodium.
Maple: 250 calories; 65 g carbohydrates; 15 mg sodium. *Sorghum:* 260 calories; 65 g carbohydrates; 20 mg sodium. **Problems** If syrup crystallizes, set in a warm water bath to liquefy; if mold forms, skim it off. **Storage** Indefinitely in bottles at room temperature. *Maple:* refrigerate indefinitely.

SUGAR SUBSTITUTES

There are two widely used low-calorie alternatives to sugar for people on low-calorie diets. Saccharine is derived from coal tar and is much sweeter than sugar. Usually available as a liquid or powder, it can be used in some recipes calling for sugar, but not for syrups. (**Note** In high quantities, it may be unsafe.) Aspartame, also called by the brand name Nutrasweet, is 200 times sweeter than sugar and so used in much smaller quantities. It cannot be heated, but it can be used to sweeten cold desserts and drinks.

SUGAR SYRUP

Refined white sugar and water, brought briefly to a boil, yields a simple syrup that can range in concentration from light to saturated (in which the maximum sugar has been dissolved). As a syrup boils, water evaporates, changing the concentration. If boiled beyond saturation point the syrup becomes a boiled sugar syrup, the properties of which change dramatically as evaporation continues (see opposite page).

SIMPLE SUGAR SYRUP

Simple sugar syrups are used to moisten cakes and fruit salads, and to glaze certain pastries. They are essential for poaching and glazing fruits and as the base of sorbets. Flavorings of vanilla or liqueur may be added. The density of the syrup is usually specified in recipes and will vary according to the type of cooking for which it is required. (See chart, right.) If more ingredients are added to a sugar syrup, its density must be retested.

USEFUL INFORMATION

Problems Sugar crystals form easily, so dissolve sugar completely before boiling the syrup.

Storage *Light*: refrigerate 2-3 days. *Medium*: refrigerate 8-10 days. *Heavy*: refrigerate 2 weeks.

Making simple sugar syrup

Heat water and granulated (not confectioners') sugar in a saucepan over low heat and stir gently. The sugar must be completely dissolved before the syrup comes to a boil. If crystals remain, they may burn, making the syrup cloudy and inclined to crystallize. Once the sugar has dissolved, stop stirring and bring the syrup to a boil. When it is sparkling clear – usually in less than a minute – it is ready. If a specific density of syrup is required, test it with a saccharometer (p.503). If the density tests low, add a little concentrated syrup; if high, add more water.

DENSITIES OF SIMPLE SUGAR SYRUPS

Simple syrups are often defined according to their density, that is, the concentration of sugar relative to water. Density is measured on a scale of 1,000 to 1,400, using a saccharometer.

proportion	density measure	use
2 lb/1 kg sugar to 2 qt/ 2 L	1,140	soaking *babas*
2 lb/1 kg sugar to 1 qt/ 1 L	1,200	moistening *génoise*; making candied fruit
2 lb/1 kg sugar to 3 cups/750 ml water	1,260	basic syrup for sorbets

BOILED SUGAR SYRUP

When sugar syrup is boiled, water evaporates until the syrup reaches its saturation point and the temperature starts to rise. The higher the temperature, the more concentrated the syrup and the less moisture it contains; therefore the harder it will set when cooled. Stages are tested either with a candy thermometer or by hand, and even a degree or two of temperature can make the difference between a sugar syrup that is malleable when set and can be used to make a light, smooth butter cream for example, and one that is too stiff to use. (The various stages are shown opposite.) The final stage is caramel, when the sugar changes rapidly from translucent gold to deep brown. Caramel is too hot to test by hand and, rather than rely on a thermometer, it is usually better to judge it by its color (p.418). Boiled sugar syrups that contain additional ingredients, such as cream or butter, will reach each stage at a lower temperature than plain boiled sugar syrup. When a temperature is specified in a recipe, it should be followed precisely.

The main difficulty when boiling sugar syrup is that it tends to crystallize. Adding an acid such as lemon juice, or a sweetener such as honey, corn syrup or liquid glucose, will help arrest this. The precautions taken when making simple sugar syrup are even more important here; do not stir the syrup once it has come to a boil; be sure that the sugar is completely dissolved before boiling begins; and clean the sides of the pan with a damp pastry brush during boiling to dissolve any sugar crystals.

USEFUL INFORMATION

Problems Boiling sugar syrup crystallizes if stirred, if crystals are not washed from the sides of the pan, or if sugar contains impurities; if sugar syrup is allowed to boil to too high a temperature, add a little cold water; however, if sugar starts to caramelize, it cannot be reversed. **Storage** 1-6 hours, depending on type. Hardened sugars soften rapidly in a humid atmosphere.

MAKING BOILED SUGAR SYRUP

A special unlined copper pan (Fr. *poêlon*, p.510) is used for heating sugar. It should be cleaned with vinegar and salt, then rinsed with water. (Do not use a tin-lined copper pan as the lining may melt.) A heavy-bottomed stainless steel saucepan can be substituted. Prepare a bowl of cold water in which to dip the hot saucepan to stop the sugar cooking once the desired stage has been reached. Rest a candy thermometer in a bowl of hot water. Add sugar to the saucepan with enough water to cover the sugar; the initial proportion is not important.

Heat the sugar and water over low heat, stirring occasionally at the beginning to help dissolve the sugar. Skim off any gray foam. When the sugar has dissolved, increase the heat to boil the sugar rapidly. Put the thermometer in the pan after the sugar comes to a boil. Boil the sugar, without stirring, until it reaches the desired temperature (see opposite). During the last few minutes, temperatures rise quickly so reduce the heat slightly.

1 During boiling, clean the sides of the pan with a brush dipped in water to remove crystals; these can burn, discoloring the syrup and causing it to crystallize.

2 As soon as the correct temperature is reached, dip the base of the hot pan into a bowl of cold water to stop cooking.

Note Sugar reaches very high temperatures. If you are burned, immediately plunge the burn in cold water, and wash off the syrup. Always exercise great care and never leave a pan of hot syrup within the reach of children.

TESTING BOILED SUGAR SYRUP BY HAND

The easiest and most reliable way to check the temperature of boiled sugar syrup is to use a candy or sugar thermometer (p.503). However, professionals often test by hand, particularly for small amounts of syrup for which a thermometer may not be accurate. Boiling sugar syrup can be tested by hand until the hard-crack stage is reached. Beyond this point, at the caramel stage (p.418), a hand test would be too dangerous.

1 Dip your finger and thumb into a bowl of iced water. Quickly dip them in the boiling syrup to catch a small ball, and immediately in the iced water again. Knead the syrup between your fingers to test the consistency. ALTERNATIVELY, dip a teaspoon into the boiling syrup, take a little of the syrup on the spoon and dip it in the iced water. Knead as above.

Stage Thread.
Temperature 230°F/110°C.
Test Forms a fine thread.
Use Fruit paste; candies.

Stage Soft-ball.
Temperature 239°F/115°C.
Test Forms a soft ball.
Use Fondant; butter cream; fudge.

Stage Hard-ball.
Temperature 248°F/120°C.
Test Forms a firm, pliable ball.
Use Italian meringue; almond paste.

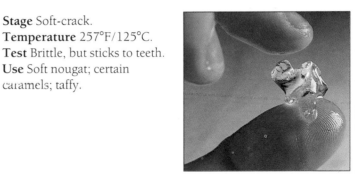

Stage Soft-crack.
Temperature 257°F/125°C.
Test Brittle, but sticks to teeth.
Use Soft nougat; certain caramels; taffy.

Stage Hard-crack.
Temperature 295°F/146°C.
Test Very brittle and does not stick to teeth.
Use Pulled sugar; spun sugar; glazed fruits; candies.

Color testing The caramel stage occurs at such high temperatures, it is tested not by hand, but by the color (p.418).

PULLED & BLOWN SUGAR

Pulled and blown sugars are sometimes called "artistic sugars" and are a high point of culinary competitions and exhibitions. An experienced confectioner can pull sugar into slender ribbons, shape it into flower petals, or blow it like a glass-blower.

For pulled sugar, sugar syrup is boiled to the hard-crack stage, sometimes colored with food coloring, and then poured on to a lightly oiled marble slab. While still very hot, it is folded and pulled repeatedly by hand until it becomes shiny and pliable enough to be shaped into ribbons or flower petals. For blown sugar, the sugar syrup is boiled in the same way and worked briefly until smooth. Then a tube is inserted in the mass of sugar and air is blown in. As the sugar expands, it is molded into fruits, animals or other shapes. Gum paste (Fr. *pastillage*) is another decorative sugar substance, most often used by professional chefs for modelling. The ingredients include confectioners' sugar, cornstarch, gum tragacanth and water. It is not edible.

DIPPING IN BOILED SUGAR SYRUP OR CARAMEL

Sugar boiled to the hard-crack stage (p.415) or to a light caramel (p.418) makes an attractive simple topping for candies such as dates stuffed with almond paste, for small choux puffs, and for fruits such as cherries, grapes, orange segments and strawberries. However, they can be kept for only 3-4 hours. Work quickly, letting excess syrup drain back into the pan so the candy does not form a "foot" when left to harden on a sheet of parchment or wax paper. If the caramel in the pan starts to cool and harden, return it to the heat but do not let it reboil.

Dipping candies Make a boiled sugar syrup (p.414). Heat the boiled sugar syrup to the hard-crack or light caramel stage (p.418). Pierce the base of the candy or other item with a skewer to hold it. Dip the candy in the syrup, then lift it out, twisting the skewer quickly so the coating is even. Push the candy on to a lightly oiled sheet or wire rack with the point of a knife, not with your fingers. Leave the candy on the sheet or rack to cool and keep in a dry place. When cool, remove the candies with a palette knife and serve in paper cases.

MAKING SPUN SUGAR FROM BOILED SUGAR SYRUP

Spun sugar, or angel's hair, is an ethereal sugar decoration made with sugar syrup boiled to a light caramel. The temperature of the sugar is important, so for best results, it is advisable to use a sugar thermometer. Spun sugar can be used for garnishing ice creams, desserts, festive cakes, and French choux confections such as *croquembouche*. It breaks very easily, and so it is shaped into loose nets or circles. It will keep only an hour or two because it quickly dissolves in moist air, so make it at the last possible moment.

1 Lay plenty of sheets of newspaper on the floor for easy cleaning. Boil sugar syrup to the light caramel stage (p.418) and dip the base of the pan briefly in cold water to stop the syrup cooking further. Let it stand for 1 minute so it thickens slightly. Hold a rolling pin in one hand and a trimmed wire whisk (p.503) or two forks back to back, in the other. Dip the whisk in the caramel and flick it to and fro over the rolling pin so that threads of sugar are formed. (Alternatively, balance two wooden dowels or broom handles on a table and flick the sugar over them.) Repeat until enough spun sugar is made.

2 RIGHT Gently lift the spun sugar from the rolling pin between your finger and thumb. Handle the spun sugar as quickly and lightly as possible to stop it becoming sticky.

Note Making successful spun sugar requires practice. For a first attempt it is advisable to allow the caramel to cool for about 5 minutes before using. Do not leave it longer than 10 minutes, otherwise it will start to set and make strands of spun sugar that are too thick.

3 Loosely wrap the spun sugar into a circle or lift it as a veil over a dessert or pastry.

FONDANT

Fondant is popular as a center and coating for candies and, when softened, as a sweet, shiny icing for cakes and pastries such as eclairs. It can be purchased commercially or made at home.

Fondant is made by boiling sugar syrup to the soft-ball stage, then cooling it and working it by hand to keep the sugar crystals very fine, until it becomes white and creamy. The consistency of finished fondant can vary from stiff but pliable to hard.

For use as an icing, fondant is softened over gentle heat and slightly diluted until it reaches the correct consistency (see below). The fondant should never be heated beyond 100°F/37°C or it will lose its gloss. Flavorings such as peppermint extract and sometimes colorings can be added to the finished fondant icing just before use. For chocolate fondant, melted semisweet chocolate is added when softening the fondant.

USEFUL INFORMATION

Problems If fondant does not set, sugar syrup was not boiled to the soft-ball stage, it was worked when temperature was still too high, or the atmosphere was too humid; if it is granular, it was cooked for too long; if it will not work to a paste,
it was left to cool too long before being worked; if fondant becomes hard and impossible to work to a paste, cover it with a bowl 1-2 hours until pliable.
Storage Refrigerate indefinitely in airtight container.

MAKING FONDANT

For a flavored or colored coating or center, add a few drops of flavoring essence or extract or food coloring when working the fondant, after it has stiffened.

1 Heat 2 cups/400 g sugar and 1 cup/250 ml water in a heavy pan until the sugar has dissolved. Stir in 2 tbsp corn syrup or liquid glucose dissolved in 2 tbsp water. Boil to the soft-ball stage (p.415).

2 Holding the pan about 1 ft/ 30 cm above a dampened marble slab or tray, pour out the syrup. Sprinkle it with a little water to prevent a crust forming and leave to cool for 2-3 minutes.

3 Using a triangular scraper, work the sugar syrup, scraping it from the slab and turning the sides to the center. ALTERNATIVELY, work the fondant in an electric mixer with a dough hook.

4 Work vigorously, particularly when the fondant starts to thicken and become creamy. After 3-5 minutes it will suddenly become stiff.

5 Break off one piece of fondant at a time and work it by pinching it hard in your fingers until pliable and smooth. Press all the pieces of pliable fondant together and knead in any flavoring or coloring. Pack into an airtight container and leave in the refrigerator or a cool place at least 1 hour, preferably 1 day, to mellow.

USING FONDANT AS AN ICING

Heat the finished fondant gently with a little simple sugar syrup or fruit juice in a water bath (p.510) or over very low heat, stirring with a wooden spatula. Heat only the minimum amount of fondant needed and test it by lifting the spatula, holding it flat. It should be lightly but thoroughly coated. If the fondant is too thick, thin it by adding more liquid. If it is too thin, add more fondant. For icing, the ideal temperature is tepid, about 100°F/ 37°C; if the fondant is heated further, it will become dull. To glaze the top of small items such as candies and choux puffs, spear them on a dipping fork or hold them in your fingers. Dip the top in warm fondant, and set right side up to cool.

Coating small cakes or candies with fondant

If coating fragile items, or those with a crumbling surface such as *génoise*, set the item on a metal spatula. Hold the spatula over the pan and use a spoon to apply the icing. If the item is very crumbly in texture, do not let the excess fondant drip back into the pan as the crumbs will ruin the texture.

CARAMEL

Caramel is formed during the last stage of cooking sugar, when all the moisture has evaporated and the melted sugar colors to a golden brown. Caramel is liquid when hot but sets when cool to become crisp and brittle. Light caramel, at around 320°F/160°C, has little flavor and is used much like sugar syrup boiled to the hard crack stage (p.415) for coating candies or fruits (p.416), rings of meringue, or French *croquembouche*, a cone-shaped tower of choux pastry puffs. Light caramel is also used for spun sugar (p.416) and for making a caramel cage (right).

Medium caramel, which is a medium to dark golden brown color (at 330°-350°F (165°-175°C) is valued mainly for its nutty, sweet flavor, which becomes increasingly bitter as the temperature rises and the color darkens. It is used to line molds for desserts such as *Crème caramel* (p.95). If the caramel sets too quickly, warm it gently in the pan until it melts, taking care not to cook it further. When dissolved in water, it forms a simple sauce that can be served with ice cream and a variety of desserts.

USEFUL INFORMATION
Problems Overcooks rapidly and becomes very bitter.
Storage *Crisp caramel:* 1 week in airtight container; softens rapidly in humid atmosphere. *Sauce:* refrigerate 1 week.

MAKING CARAMEL

Caramel can be made in two ways: by heating plain sugar or by heating a sugar syrup. The latter method is the more successful as syrup is less likely to burn and the color will be more even.

1 **To caramelize sugar syrup:** boil syrup rapidly until it starts to brown around the edge of the pan. Lower the heat and continue cooking, swirling the pan once or twice so the syrup colors evenly.

2 Tip the pan sideways during cooking to check the color of the caramel as it runs off the bottom of the pan. Here, light caramel is shown.

3 For dark caramel, continue cooking, watching the syrup closely. When smoke starts to rise, the caramel is done.

4 To stop caramel from cooking further in the heat of the pan, plunge the base of the pan in a bowl of cool water.

Caramelizing sugar

Spread the sugar in the base of a heavy unlined frying pan. Cook over medium heat until the sugar starts to melt. Stir very gently so that the sugar melts evenly, then let it cook to the desired color (steps 2–4 above).

Note If the heat is too high, the sugar will burn at the edges before the sugar in the center has melted.

MAKING A CARAMEL CAGE

A caramel cage makes a shiny, delicate decoration in which to serve ice cream, poached fruit or creamy desserts. It softens in 1-2 hours, so make it at the last possible moment.

1 Oil the outside of a round-bottomed bowl or ladle. Boil sugar syrup to the light caramel stage (step 2, left) and dip the base of the pan briefly in cold water to stop cooking. Let the caramel stand 1-2 minutes so that it thickens slightly, enough for it to be dripped in long threads.

2 With a tablespoon, trail thin threads of caramel back and forth across the oiled surface of the ladle in a criss-cross pattern.

3 Continue until the cage is complete. Seal the edge of the cage by trailing a ring of caramel around the edge of the ladle. Let the cage cool until it is crisp.

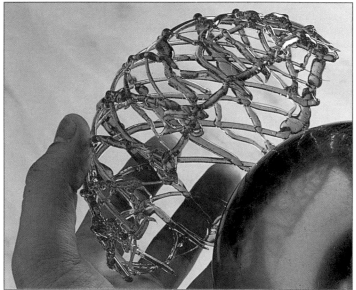

4 Gently loosen the caramel cage from the mold, by pushing it up and off the ladle with your fingers. Remove it from the mold and set it on an oiled tray. Keep in a dry, cool place until ready to serve.

Caramel sauce

Caramel sauce is made by dissolving medium or dark caramel in water. To make 1 cup/250 ml sauce, make a sugar syrup with 1 cup/200 g sugar and ½ cup/125 ml water. Boil the syrup until caramelized, then take the pan from the heat and let the bubbles subside. Add ½ cup/125 ml water to the caramel, standing back as it will spatter. Reheat, stirring until the caramel dissolves. If necessary, boil until syrupy. For a creamy sauce, dissolve the caramel in cream instead of water. To make *gastrique*, for sweet and sour sauces, use vinegar instead of water.

PRALINE & NOUGATINE

The praline and nougatine used by the pastry cook should not be confused with the candies of the same name, although like the candies, both are based on a mixture of caramel and nuts. Praline is made with whole almonds or hazelnuts and has a wonderfully fragrant taste. It is a favorite dessert flavoring for mousses, pastry cream and ice cream. It can be bought ready-made from specialty baking shops as a compact brown paste, or made at home (see below). Nougatine (right) is cut into decorative shapes or used as a base for *gâteaux* and to line molds.

The weight of nuts used in praline and nougatine varies from half to equal the weight of the sugar. The caramel base for both can be made with either a boiled sugar syrup or by caramelizing the sugar directly with no added water (see methods for making caramel, previous page). Liquid glucose (p.411) can be added to nougatine to prevent crystallization. For praline, the whole nuts are often toasted with the caramel to add to the flavor. For nougatine, they are added at the end of cooking so the whiteness of the nuts contrasts with the golden caramel.

USEFUL INFORMATION

Problems *Praline*: nuts will taste burnt if caramel is overcooked. *Nougatine*: cools and hardens quickly; if necessary warm and soften it in the oven.

Storage *Praline*: several weeks in airtight container at room temperature; freeze 1 year. *Nougatine*: after rolling, keeps several weeks in airtight container.

MAKING PRALINE

Praline is usually made by caramelizing sugar with whole almonds directly over the heat. The nuts should be thoroughly toasted to develop their flavor. Use equal weights of nuts and sugar; the quantity depends on the amount of praline required.

1 Combine whole unblanched almonds or hazelnuts and sugar in a copper sugar pan (p.510) or heavy saucepan. Heat gently until the sugar melts, stirring often. Continue cooking over fairly low heat to the medium caramel stage (330°F/165°C), stirring lightly, until the sugar turns deep golden brown and the almonds make a popping sound, showing they are toasted.

2 Remove the pan from the heat immediately and pour the sugar mixture on to a lightly oiled marble slab or oiled baking sheet, taking great care as the mixture is very hot.

3 Spread the praline out with a wooden spatula and leave it until it is cool and crisp.

4 Crack the praline in pieces and grind to a powder in a food processor, blender, or rotary grater. **Note** If overworked in a food processor, the praline becomes a paste.

Making nougatine

Nougatine is usually made with equal weights of sugar and chopped or sliced almonds (these should be warmed first so they do not make the sugar crystallize).

Heat granulated sugar gently in a copper sugar pan (p.510) or a heavy saucepan, adding ¼ cup/60 g glucose or 2 tablespoons of lemon juice for each cup/200 g of sugar, stirring occasionally until the sugar melts. Boil the sugar, stirring gently, to the medium caramel stage (p.418). Stir in a half-to-equal weight of chopped or sliced blanched almonds, previously warmed in the oven. Return the nougatine to high heat for ½-1 minute so that it boils and detaches from the sides of the pan. Pour immediately on to a lightly oiled baking sheet and then shape the nougatine (below).

SHAPING NOUGATINE

Nougatine becomes brittle and unworkable when cold, so it must be worked quickly and kept warm. Work near the oven if possible and warm the work surface by placing a roasting pan of hot water on it. Make sure the surface is dry, then oil it; all utensils should be lightly oiled. Any nougatine scraps can be reused.

1 With a metal spatula, keep folding and spreading the prepared nougatine. Repeat several times while it is still warm to keep it pliable and speed cooling.

2 While still pliable, roll the nougatine out very thinly. (A metal rolling pin is best but a wooden one may be used.) If the nougatine becomes too brittle, warm it on a baking sheet in a low oven.

3 With a heavy knife, cut the nougatine into strips and then into shapes. If you find that the nougatine is very difficult to cut, use a wooden rolling pin as a mallet to help force the knife through the nougatine.

CHOCOLATE

One of the greatest discoveries made on the American continent was the bean of the cacao tree – the source of chocolate. Smooth in texture, rich in taste, chocolate is loved by almost everyone – even the gods, as its scientific name *Theobroma cacao* attests (*theobroma* means "food of the gods" in Greek). Today, much of the world's cocoa crop comes from Africa and Brazil.

Through a process of drying, roasting and grinding, cocoa beans are converted into a thick paste called chocolate liquor, composed of cocoa solids and a light yellow fat called cocoa butter. When the paste hardens, it is subjected to "conching", in which a heavy roller compresses the chocolate, giving it a smooth texture and mellow flavor. The blend of beans, the method of roasting and conching, and the proportion of cocoa butter are all important factors affecting the final flavor of chocolate.

Cocoa powder is pure chocolate liquor from which much of the cocoa butter has been extracted; content varies from eight percent to over 20 percent. Sweetened cocoa, often called powdered chocolate, is used for drinks. In Britain it is also blended with powdered milk and sold as "drinking chocolate". Unsweetened cocoa powder is most commonly used for baking and preparing desserts. Dutch-process or alkalized cocoa, reputed to be the best, is darker and milder than other cocoas, and is easier to dissolve. Use Dutch-process cocoa when you are not adding a sweetener, such as when rolling chocolate truffles in cocoa.

The finest quality block chocolate always contains a high proportion of cocoa butter; on average 35 percent, but sometimes as much as 50 percent. In inferior types, palm or vegetable oils and shortenings are substituted.

Types of block chocolate can be divided into five general categories: first, chocolate may be unsweetened; often called bitter or baking chocolate, it is approximately 50 percent cocoa butter and may be flavored with vanilla or vanillin. It is used primarily in baking. Bittersweet, plain, or semisweet chocolate contains enough sugar to make it palatable to eat alone. The many types of chocolate in this category contain varying amounts of cocoa butter (the average is around 27 percent), but in recipes they are generally interchangeable. A third type of chocolate includes sweet or eating chocolate (mainly candy bars), milk chocolate, and bittersweet chocolate with cream, all of which are rarely used in cooking. White chocolate has a creamy, opaque color because it contains cocoa butter (the exact quantity varies considerably depending on the brand), but no cocoa solids. Marketed as chocolate in Europe, the same product must be labeled as "white coating" in the United States. Despite its paler appearance, white chocolate is similar in texture to regular chocolate. However, when substituting white for regular chocolate in recipes, remember that white chocolate sets less firmly. This must be compensated for, either by adding extra butter or more white chocolate. Some inferior brands of white chocolate contain vegetable oil rather than cocoa butter and lack the taste of true chocolate.

Couverture, often called "dipping chocolate" or "coating chocolate", has a high cocoa butter content (usually 35 percent and sometimes as much as 50 percent), and is available in bittersweet, semisweet, white and milk chocolate varieties. This is the chef's chocolate, ideal for dipping because the high proportion of cocoa butter means that it melts easily and smoothly. It is also used for chocolate decorations, and candies in which the chocolate is the main ingredient, because both need a good quality chocolate. The best *couverture* comes from Belgium, Switzerland and France.

Other forms of chocolate include chocolate chips, an ever-popular ingredient in cookies and available in several sizes in semisweet, bittersweet, milk and white chocolate flavors, and "jimmies" or sprinkles, shiny little chocolate sticks used for decoration. So-called Mexican chocolate contains ground almonds and cinnamon as well as sugar and is less smooth than other types.

Cocoa butter, the most valuable component of the original bean, is occasionally called for in candy recipes to inhibit crystallization. It can be purchased at specialty baking shops, or in small quantities at the pharmacy.

Although most commonly used as a sweet flavoring, chocolate is also added to a small number of savory dishes such as Mexican *mole poblano* – turkey baked in a sauce made with chocolate, nuts, chili peppers and other spices. French cooks occasionally use a touch of chocolate to balance their red wine sauces; Paul Bocuse created *poulet au cacao*, chicken with cocoa-flavored sauce. In Italy, cocoa-flavored pasta is sometimes served with chocolate-flavored sweet-and-sour sauce, and there is a Sicilian rabbit stew with chocolate. A few Spanish dishes, including one with calf's tongue and another with spiny lobster, also contain chocolate.

In the kitchen, chocolate plays a variety of roles besides flavoring. The stark contrast of dark chocolate adds allure to dishes like the ever-popular chocolate profiteroles – little choux puffs (p.377) filled with cream or ice cream and topped with chocolate sauce. Dark and white chocolate terrines are a happy inspiration, striped in layers and adorned with one of the many chocolate decorations that are so rewarding to make, such as cigarettes, squares and curls (p.423). More elaborate chocolate decorations are best made with tempered chocolate (p.422) – chocolate that is heated and worked so the cocoa butter crystals are broken down and the chocolate is extra smooth and glossy.

Finally, chocolate acts as a binder for other ingredients. For example, chocolate soufflé is one of the few soufflés not requiring any flour as the chocolate holds the mixture together.

cocoa powder

jimmies or sprinkles

white

semisweet chocolate chips

milk chocolate chips

cocoa butter

couverture

semisweet

plain

milk

USEFUL INFORMATION

How to choose Chocolate with a high cocoa butter content will be richer and smoother in taste; the sweetness will vary according to brand; the best test is to taste it.

Nutritive value per 3½ oz/100 g. *Cocoa:* 410 calories; 28 g protein; 14 g fat; 46 g carbohydrates; 21 mg sodium; no cholesterol. *Unsweetened:* 507 calories; 10 g protein; 52 g fat; 28 g carbohydrates; 3.5 mg sodium; no cholesterol. *Bittersweet:* 507 calories; 10 g protein; 52 g fat; 28 g carbohydrates; 3.5 mg sodium; no cholesterol. *Semisweet:* 500 calories; 3 g protein; 35 g fat; 56 g carbohydrates; 14 mg sodium; no cholesterol. *Sweet:* 525 calories; 3 g protein; 35 g fat; 56 g carbohydrates; 17 mg sodium; no cholesterol. *Milk:* 507 calories; 7 g protein; 31 g fat; 56 g carbohydrates; 80 mg sodium; 21 mg cholesterol. *White (US coating):* 532 calories; 7 g protein; 31 g fat; 59 g carbohydrates; 87 mg sodium; cholesterol content varies according to type.

Problems Small amounts of water or steam make melted chocolate "seize" or tighten; if overheated, white or milk chocolate develops lumps easily.

Used in Drinks, desserts (cocoa); baking (unsweetened chocolate); desserts, dipping, decorations, ganache, drinks, savory dishes (semisweet, bittersweet, sweet, milk, white).

Storing chocolate

Chocolate should be stored at a temperature of about 60°F/16°C in a dry, airy place. Chocolate decorations can be refrigerated or frozen. Wrap opened chocolate in plastic wrap or aluminum foil, and store it away from ingredients with strong odors. Dark chocolate and cocoa keep better than white and milk chocolates that contain a high proportion of milk solids.

If stored in less than ideal conditions, the cocoa butter in chocolate may rise to the surface and leave a whitish film or "fat bloom". "Sugar bloom", a similar discoloration, occurs when water condenses on the surface of chocolate, dissolving some of the sugar content and leaving a white crust when the moisture evaporates. This often affects refrigerated chocolate candies that are too loosely wrapped. Chocolate with sugar or fat bloom can still be melted, but it is unsuitable for grating.

Grating and chopping chocolate

Chocolate is grated as a sweet garnish and to add to desserts or cake batters. On a warm day, chill chocolate briefly before grating and, if using bulk chocolate, first break it into large pieces and then hold it in wax paper so that it will not melt in your hand.

For chopping chocolate, it is important to use a dry board and a large chopping knife. Chocolate can also be chopped in a food processor, but on a warm day, take care to chill the chocolate and blade first. Cut the chocolate in small chunks and chop it with the pulse button of the processor. If overworked, the chocolate may melt or stick together.

Melting chocolate

Chocolate should be melted very gradually as it will scorch if overheated; milk and white chocolate can develop lumps. Some cooks melt chocolate in a very low oven, or in a microwave oven, but the most common method is to use a water bath or double boiler. Be sure the container in which the chocolate is placed is uncovered and completely dry, unless the recipe specifies that a liquid should be added. To melt the chocolate, set it in a heatproof bowl inside a saucepan of hot, but not simmering, water, or in a container resting over the mouth of the pan. In a double boiler, the water may be allowed to surround the bowl. Heat the saucepan or double boiler gently to maintain the temperature, or replace the hot water occasionally as it cools. Once the chocolate starts to melt, stir it frequently. For making a sauce, the chocolate may be melted directly over a low heat with plenty of liquid, but must be stirred frequently.

"Seized" chocolate

If the chocolate is in contact with water or steam, it "seizes"; that is, the chocolate tightens and becomes a thick rough mass that will not melt. This can be corrected by stirring in one of the following ingredients: cocoa butter, vegetable shortening, clarified unsalted butter (p.99), or vegetable oil; any one of these should be added a teaspoon at a time, until the chocolate becomes smooth again. **Note** Adding any of these ingredients may affect the proportions and texture of the final recipe.

Combining melted chocolate with other ingredients

Chocolate is usually combined with other ingredients while it is still warm and easy to pour. If it is to be combined with another liquid, both of them should be at a similar temperature. Adding a liquid that is hotter than the melted chocolate may cause the cocoa butter to separate, while adding a colder liquid may make the chocolate lumpy.

Chocolate mousse

For best results, use the finest chocolate and leave the mousse to chill for at least six hours before serving so that flavors mellow.

Serves 4

6 oz/175 g semisweet chocolate, chopped	3 tbsp/45 g sugar
¼ cup/60 ml strong black coffee, or water	*For decoration*
4 eggs, separated	Chantilly cream (p.70) made with ½ cup/125 ml heavy cream, 2 tsp sugar, ½ tsp vanilla extract
1 tbsp/15 g butter	4 chocolate cigarettes (p.423)
1 tbsp/15 ml rum or ½ tsp vanilla extract	*Pastry bag and medium star tube*

1 Heat the chocolate in the coffee or water, stirring until melted. Simmer until slightly thickened but still falling easily from the spoon. Remove from the heat and beat the egg yolks one by one into the hot mixture so they thicken slightly. Beat in the butter and rum or vanilla. Let the mixture cool until tepid.
2 Stiffly whip the egg whites. Add sugar and continue whipping for 30 seconds to make a light meringue. Fold into the tepid chocolate mixture. Pour into pots or glasses and chill.
3 Using a pastry bag and star tube, top each mousse with a large rosette of Chantilly cream, not more than 2 hours before serving. Add a chocolate cigarette to each one.

Variations

Iced chocolate mousse Fold ½ cup/125 ml cream, whipped until it holds a soft shape, into the chocolate and meringue mixture. Pour it into ramekins and freeze. Serve the mousse with chocolate cigarettes or Dutch butter cookies (p.100).

Orange chocolate mousse Substitute ½ cup/125 ml fresh orange juice for the coffee in original recipe, and Grand Marnier or other orange liqueur for the rum. Before serving, garnish with rosettes of whipped cream and a strip of candied orange zest.

CHOCOLATE SUBSTITUTES

Compound chocolate, also called chocolate coating, is designed to replace *couverture* chocolate for coating and has the advantage of not needing to be tempered. Made from a vegetable oil base with sugar, milk solids and flavoring, compound chocolate contains cocoa powder, but no cocoa butter. Its flavor is inferior to *couverture*, but it sets faster in hot weather, so it is the choice of many cooks for candymaking in summer, and is also used for chocolate decorations. For dipping, compound chocolate is melted exactly like other chocolate.

Carob, also called locust bean and St. John's bread, is the fleshy pod of a tree native to the Middle East and the Mediterranean. It is often substituted for chocolate for nutritional reasons, since it has a lower fat content and contains no caffeine. The pod's sweet pulp is available as a raw powder, as blocks and chips, or roasted like coffee beans. The whole pod can be eaten fresh or dried as a candy. Dishes in which carob has been substituted for chocolate differ in appearance from those made with real chocolate: they lack the shine of correctly tempered real chocolate. They also have a coarse, waxy texture compared with the rich, smooth taste of chocolate. In baking, carob powder can be used as a substitute for cocoa powder, though it does not taste the same and is much sweeter.

TEMPERING CHOCOLATE

Tempering makes chocolate more malleable and glossy. *Couverture* chocolate (p.420) is most often tempered because it has a high cocoa butter content and may form different kinds of crystals as it cools. If the crystals are stable, the chocolate will be firm and shiny, but unstable crystals make it sticky and streaked. Tempering encourages the formation of the right kind of crystal. After tempering, the chocolate is heated to the ideal temperature for dipping and coating (p.427). Tempered chocolate can be molded more easily into shapes.

The first of the following methods for tempering chocolate is classic, but the others are quicker and may be used for smaller amounts. It is important to work in a cool room, preferably no warmer than 70°F/21°C. Test chocolate with an instant-read thermometer (p.503).

1 Melt chopped chocolate in a water bath until it reaches 115°F/45°C, stirring gently with a spatula until it is very smooth. Take care not to allow any steam or drops of water to reach the chocolate, or it will "seize" (p.421) and become unworkable.

2 Pour two-thirds of the chocolate on to a marble slab or work surface (make sure that the surface is completely dry). With a metal spatula, work the chocolate by spreading it back and forth across the work surface for at least three minutes until it is thick and on the point of setting (at about 80°F/25°C).

3 With a scraper, quickly transfer the chocolate from the marble to the reserved chocolate. Reheat it in the water bath, stirring constantly to 88-90°F/30-32°C for bittersweet or semisweet chocolate, or 84-85°F/29°C for milk or white chocolate. The chocolate is now tempered and ready to use.

Alternative method 1 Melt the chocolate in a bowl, then set it in a bowl of cold (not ice) water. Stir the chocolate often until it cools to 80°F/25°C, then set it again above hot water and heat to 88-90°F/30-32°C for bittersweet or semisweet chocolate, or 84-85°F/29°C for milk or white chocolate.

Alternative method 2 Coarsely chop all but one-tenth of the chocolate then melt it in a water bath. Remove it and stir in the reserved chunk of chocolate. Continue stirring until the chocolate cools to the desired temperature (see method 1). If part of the chunk remains unmelted, remove it.

Alternative method 3 Coarsely chop all but one-quarter of the chocolate, then melt it in a water bath. Remove it and grate the reserved chunk of chocolate into it until the melted chocolate cools to the desired temperature (see method 1).

Testing tempered chocolate

After tempering, remove a small amount of chocolate and spread it on a marble slab or cooled plate. Let it harden, while keeping the remaining chocolate at the right temperature and stirring it often. If the test chocolate sets smooth and glossy, it is ready. If there are gray streaks in it, temper again.

MAKING CURLS & SHAVINGS

Decorative curls are made from chocolate that is at room temperature; for shavings, it should be chilled.

1 With a vegetable peeler, shave the sides of the chocolate.

2 Curls or shavings will fall from the block, depending on the temperature of the chocolate.

CHOCOLATE CIGARETTES

Chocolate cigarettes are favorite decorations on festive cakes and creamy mousses.

1 Pour tempered or cooled, melted chocolate on to a cool marble slab or work surface. Spread the chocolate as smoothly as possible using a flexible metal spatula, in a layer 1/16 in/1.5 mm thick without leaving any holes. If the chocolate is too thick, it will not roll.

2 When the chocolate is cooled to the point of setting, mark it in parallel lines the width of a metal pastry scraper. Hold the scraper at an angle of 45°, pressing the blade firmly against the marble. Push the scraper slowly away from you to roll the chocolate into a neat cylinder.

3 Continue to make cigarettes. If the chocolate is too warm, it will stick to the scraper. If it is allowed to cool too much it will merely make shavings. It should be reheated in a water bath (p.510) and the process repeated.

MAKING CHOCOLATE TRIANGLES & OTHER SHAPES

These are usually made from melted chocolate, marked in shapes and left to harden. Geometric shapes are simple to make, yet they add a professional look to special cakes and desserts. They can be stored in a refrigerator for several weeks and used as required.

1 Cut a sheet of wax paper in a 2 in/5 cm strip. Brush it with tempered or cooled melted chocolate and spread it to an even layer 1/16 in/1.5 mm thick. Leave to cool until on the point of setting.

2 Lightly cut into shapes. For curved shapes, lift the paper on to a rolling pin. Leave to set. **Note** Do not refrigerate as the chocolate will shrink away from the paper.

3 When the chocolate has set, lift the paper from the rolling pin.

4 Carefully peel the shapes away from the paper.

5 Store shapes in a refrigerator between layers of wax paper so they do not stick together. Here curved and flat chocolate triangles are shown.

423

MAKING CHOCOLATE LEAVES

Use stiff, fresh leaves such as rose, lemon, or ficus (here) that are non-poisonous and have raised veins on their undersides. Keep enough stem on each leaf to hold it. Wash and dry the leaves. Use tempered or cooled, melted chocolate.

1 Using a small brush, spread chocolate on the shiny top side of a leaf in an even layer. Leave a little of the stem exposed so it will be easy to remove the chocolate. Wipe the edge and underside of the leaf between finger and thumb to ensure there is no overlap of chocolate on it.

2 Set the leaves on a tray or plate and leave them at cool room temperature, refrigerate them, or freeze until the chocolate is completely set.

3 With the tips of your fingers, peel the leaf away from the chocolate, handling it as little as possible because fingerprints can spoil the shiny surface. Turn it over to display the veined markings.

4 Leaves have an attractive shape and can be used singly on individual desserts or cakes or arranged in a spray on larger ones. If not using all the leaves at once, they can be stored between layers of wax paper in an airtight container in a cool place or the refrigerator.

PIPING CHOCOLATE DECORATIONS

Chocolate can be piped into ornamental shapes for decorating desserts and cakes. Once you are experienced you can pipe chocolate free-hand directly on to cakes and desserts, but for a first attempt it is advisable to pipe over traced outlines, as shown here. When piping directly onto a cake or dessert, always point the cone upward between words or shapes so the chocolate does not leak out and spoil the decoration.

1 Trace a simple drawing on to a piece of thin paper. Tape a sheet of wax paper or parchment to the work surface in two places so it will be steady, then slide the drawing under the sheet of paper.

2 Make two or more paper piping cones (p.407). Fill one with tempered or cooled, melted chocolate and fold the top to seal. Keep the rest of the chocolate warm, so that when the first cone is finished you will be able to fill the second cone and continue.

3 Using light pressure, pipe melted chocolate on to the paper following the outline of the drawing, letting the chocolate fall evenly from the tip without forcing it. Leave it to set at cool room temperature, or refrigerate.

4 Once set, remove the decorations carefully with a metal spatula, handling them as little as possible so the chocolate does not melt or become dull.

GANACHE

Ganache is a creamy chocolate mixture that is used as an icing or filling for cakes, and as a center for chocolate candies. It is sometimes compared to fudge, but is smoother and less sweet. Ganache is usually made of two ingredients – cream and chocolate (whether dark, milk, or white) – although other flavoring ingredients such as coffee or liqueurs can be added. The chocolate used will determine the texture of the ganache; the higher the proportion of cocoa butter, the firmer the ganache. A high proportion of chocolate also produces a firm ganache, while relatively more cream makes it more soft and moist. Ganache may be whipped so that it becomes light and pale, and butter may be added to make an easy butter cream.

USEFUL INFORMATION

Typical uses Filling for chocolate mousse cake (USA); *délices aux clementines* (orange tartlets, France); *caraques* (filled butter cookies covered with fondant, France); black and white cake (chocolate cake layered with white chocolate ganache, USA); *Saint-Eloi* (chocolate *génoise* layered with coffee ganache, France).

Chocolate ganache Put 6 oz/175 g good quality chopped chocolate in a bowl. Bring ⅓ cup/75 ml heavy cream with 1 tablespoon butter to a boil and pour over the chocolate. Stir until smooth, if necessary warming over low heat. Chill the ganache, without stirring, until firm. Ganache can be refrigerated 1 week, or frozen up to 3 months. Soften it in a tepid water bath before using.
Light ganache Whip cooled ganache until fluffy, 3-5 minutes.

CHOCOLATE SAUCES

Given its thickening capacities, chocolate is easily made into sauce, the simplest version being chocolate melted in water to serve hot or at room temperature. Often a little butter and vanilla or liqueur are added for flavor, while richer sauces are based on cream or milk instead of water. Chocolate sauces that contain a generous amount of sugar are sometimes called fudge sauces, though the term is not precise. A chocolate sauce should be tailored to the dish it accompanies. For example, chocolate fudge sauce for ice cream should be made with bitter chocolate and be thick enough to set on contact with the cold dessert, while sauces for puddings and mousses should be thinner and sweeter.

USEFUL INFORMATION

Typical uses Hot fudge sundae (vanilla ice cream, chopped nuts, whipped cream, USA); *poires belle Hélène* (poached pears, France); *copa el galeon* (poundcake with cream filling, filberts, Spain); Weimar pudding (cocoa custard, Germany); walnut fudge pie (USA); blancmange (almond and milk gelatin dessert, UK); vanilla cream (Israel); *roulade marquise* (chocolate roulade, France).

Chocolate sauce Makes 1 cup/250 ml sauce. Over low heat, melt 6 oz/175 g chopped semisweet chocolate in 6 tbsp/90 ml water, stirring. Boil for 1 minute or until slightly thickened. Off the heat, add 1 tsp rum or brandy. Serve cold with mousses and creams.
Chocolate fudge sauce Makes 1 cup/250 ml sauce. Heat ¾ cup/175 ml heavy cream, 3 tbsp light corn syrup, 1 cup/200 g sugar and a pinch of salt, stirring until the sugar dissolves. Add 3 oz/90 g of chopped unsweetened chocolate and simmer, stirring often, until the sauce thickens, 20 minutes. Off the heat, stir in 2 tbsp of butter, cut in pieces, and ½ tsp vanilla extract. Serve hot with ice cream.

Chocolate chestnut pavé

Chestnut *pavé* is molded in a block shape like the paving stones that once lined the streets of Paris. For serving, it is sliced thinly and topped with whipped cream.

Serves 8

3 lb/1.4 kg fresh chestnuts or 1½ lb/750 g canned, unsweetened chestnuts, drained	1 cup/200 g sugar
	2 tbsp brandy
1 vanilla bean or 1 tsp vanilla extract	***For serving***
	Chantilly cream (p.70)
¾ lb semisweet chocolate, chopped	
½ cup/125 ml water	***9 × 5 × 3 in/23 × 13 × 7.5 cm loaf pan***
6 oz/175 g butter	***Pastry bag and medium star tube***

1 Lightly grease the loaf pan, line the base with wax paper, and grease the paper. If using fresh chestnuts, peel them (p.481), and put them in a saucepan with the vanilla bean, if using. Add enough water to cover, cover the pan and simmer until the nuts are tender, 25-30 minutes. **Note** Canned nuts need not be cooked. Remove the vanilla bean and drain the nuts. Purée fresh or canned nuts in a food processor or work through a food mill.
2 Melt the chocolate in the ½ cup/125 ml water over low heat, stirring until smooth. Let it cool to tepid. Beat butter and sugar until soft and light. Stir in the cooled chocolate and then the chestnut purée, brandy and vanilla extract, if using. Mix until smooth. Pack the mixture into the prepared pan, cover and chill at least 12 hours or up to a week.
3 To serve, unmold the *pavé* and discard the paper. Cut the *pavé* in thin slices with a knife dipped in hot water. Set the slices on individual plates and decorate with rosettes of Chantilly cream, using a pastry bag and star tube. Top the rosettes with chocolate decorations and chill until ready to serve.

CANDIES & CHOCOLATES

Glossy lollipops, barley sugar, rich fudge and soft marshmallow, are based on boiled sugar syrup. Other candies are luscious filled and dipped chocolates, melting in the mouth with fondant (p.417), crisp with nuts, or sweet with liqueurs. A candied fruit, or nuts, whole or chopped and held together with ganache, and nut pastes are other alternative centers. Almond paste can be molded into centers in an array of shapes and colors, served as a candy on its own or used to fill dried fruits such as dates.

Chocolate is by far the most popular coating for candy (see the instructions on the opposite page.) However, fondant is an alternative and fresh fruits dipped in fondant are agreeably tart. Less long-lasting but temptingly crisp are fruits, nuts and almond paste candies glazed in boiled sugar syrup. The coating can be clear and shiny if the syrup is boiled to the hard-crack stage, or it can be golden if boiled to a light caramel color. Full instructions for dipping candies in boiled sugar syrups are given on p.416.

BOILED SUGAR CANDIES

All the cook's skill and precision is called into play when making boiled sugar syrup candies, as exactly the right stage of boiled sugar syrup (p.414) is crucial. The degree to which the sugar syrup is cooked and the method by which crystallization is controlled during cooling have a marked effect on texture. Weather is an important factor. In a humid atmosphere, sugar syrup absorbs moisture from the air as it cools and can make the final candy too soft. In these conditions, the sugar must be cooked to the upper end of the desired temperature range. Crystallization must also be watched very closely. Occasionally, it is deliberately sought, as in making sugared almonds, or in the case of fudge and fondant, but when used as a coating for candies, boiled sugar syrup should never be crystallized.

Boiled sugar syrup is enriched with cream or butter to make fudge. It is cooked to the soft-ball stage (p.415), then cooled and beaten to disperse air and minute sugar crystals throughout the mixture. Favorite flavors include chocolate, coffee and vanilla.

Like fudge, toffee is made by adding butter to a boiled sugar mixture. The mixture is boiled to the soft- or hard-crack stage but is not beaten when cool. The richest version, with the highest proportion of butter, is called butter toffee or butterscotch. The flavor of caramels comes from the caramelization of lactose in cream, which is boiled with sugar to the hard-ball stage. As the mixture is beaten during cooking, it remains moist and chewy. For taffy, a sugar solution, usually containing corn syrup and butter, is boiled to the soft-crack stage (p.415), then poured on to a work surface, stretched into ropes and cut up.

Other candies rely on the inclusion of egg whites for their character. Divinity is made of sugar cooked to the soft-crack stage, then beaten into whipped egg whites, with nuts and dried or candied fruits. Marshmallow consists simply of boiled sugar syrup or simple syrup combined with egg whites and/or gelatin. Turkish delight is closely related, often flavored with rosewater, cardamom or peppermint and spiked with pistachios. Nougat is totally different from decorative nougatine (p.419). Like marshmallow, it is made of syrup and egg whites, cooked until dense rather than fluffy. Flavorings include honey, almonds and candied fruits.

The name praline refers to two different types of candy. In Europe, pralines are toasted almonds, individually coated several times with sugar syrup boiled to the soft-crack stage. In the United States, pralines are made of boiled sugar syrup, combined with nuts, often containing cream or butter. Nut brittle resembles praline but is made of light caramel with nuts and butter. The mixture is then poured on to a baking sheet, spread thinly, and broken into pieces after it has set.

Almond paste with dates and nuts in a coating of sugar syrup.

USEFUL INFORMATION

Problems Method and temperature instructions must be followed very precisely or sugar will not crystallize as required.
Storage *Fondant, fudge, nut brittle:* layered between sheets of wax paper in an airtight container.

Nougat, toffee, hard candies: individually wrapped in wax paper in an airtight container. *Caramels:* refrigerate individually wrapped in plastic wrap or wax paper. *Divinity, marshmallow:* in airtight container lined with wax paper or parchment.

Penuche

Pistachios or toasted hazelnuts can be added to the brown sugar fudge before it is left to set.

Makes 2 lb/1 kg

4 cups/800 g light brown sugar	1 tsp vanilla extract
2 cups/500 ml heavy cream	
pinch of salt	8 in/20 cm square pan

1 Grease the pan and line the sides and bottom with wax paper. Put the sugar, cream and salt in a saucepan. Cook over medium heat, stirring with a wooden spoon until the sugar melts completely. Bring to a boil and continue cooking over medium heat without stirring to the soft-ball stage (239°F/115°C). If crystals form on the sides of the pan, wash them down with a pastry brush dipped in warm water.
2 Let the mixture cool to 100°F/38°C; the texture should be glossy and smooth. Transfer it to a bowl and add the vanilla extract. With a wooden spoon, beat until the fudge is thick and creamy, about 5 minutes.
3 Pour the fudge into the prepared pan and leave it for at least 2 hours or until set. Cut it in 1 in/2.5 cm squares and store it in an airtight container, layered between sheets of waxed paper.

DIPPED & FILLED CHOCOLATES

One of the world's greatest treats must be a box of fresh chocolates. Centers for dipped chocolates are often based on chocolate pastes like ganache, which is the filling for truffles, or Italian *gianduja*, a paste of chocolate or cocoa butter and ground toasted nuts.

For liqueur centers, a special technique is required. A mold is prepared by marking shapes in a smooth layer of very dry cornstarch, then a light, liqueur-flavored syrup is poured into the mold. The filling is covered with more cornstarch, left overnight to set, and then dusted off. The cornstarch helps the outer surfaces of syrup to crystallize and form a shell with a liquid center. The liqueur shell is then dipped in chocolate.

Sheets of gold or silver foil may be applied to dipped and filled chocolates to give them a shining allure and to highlight their rich chocolate color. Although their appearance is luxurious, there is such a small quantity of metal in the tissue-thin leaf that the chocolates are entirely edible. (Gold and silver leaf is also used for lacquered decorations, particularly on poultry and sophisticated desserts.) For easy attractive candies or decorations for cakes, whole almonds, pecans, walnuts and brazil nuts can be half-dipped in chocolate, as may fruits such as cherries or strawberries.

USEFUL INFORMATION

Problems Tiny white spots on coating are caused by excess humidity in the room during dipping or while in storage, or because the chocolate was overheated; dull coating is result of lack of tempering, or dipping in a room that was too hot, too cold, or too humid; if coating cracks, the center was too cold; if the coating is dull in spots, center was too hot for dipping; if coating is wet and sticky, the chocolate was too hot.

Storage *Hard centers:* 1 week in cool dry place (65-68°F/18-20°C). *Soft centers:* wrap in tightly sealed bag or between layers of wax paper and refrigerate 1 week; freeze 1 month and defrost in refrigerator then in a cool place.

MAKING DIPPED CHOCOLATES

Work in a dry, cool room, about 60-65°F/16-18°C. For soft centers, the temperature may be higher, about 70°F/21°C. Soft centers should be cool or cold so they do not melt when combined with warm chocolate, but if too cold, they cause streaks in the coating. Some cooks like to dip soft centers twice: the first time to protect the soft center; the second time for a glossy finish.

Temper enough chocolate (p.422) to submerge the candies easily and keep it warm in a water bath. The chocolate must be thin enough for a delicate coating but thick enough not to run off the item being coated. The ideal temperature varies with the type of chocolate (p.420). Leftover chocolate can be saved and remelted for use in desserts, but should not be reused for dipping because it will contain impurities.

Professionals recommend a straight-pronged dipping fork (p.503) for dipping, but a standard four-prong fork may be used, or candies may be dipped with your fingers. All utensils for stirring and dipping should be completely dry. From time to time, stir the chocolate well.

2 Use the fork to lift the candy center out of the chocolate without piercing it. Lightly tap the fork against the side of the bowl to stop excess chocolate forming a pool or "foot" on the candy.

3 Carefully tip the candy on to the work surface or parchment by turning the fork upside down. If you like, while the chocolate is still soft, decorate the top of the candy by touching it with the fork to mark it with three parallel lines. Alternatively, add an almond or any other nut for decoration.

4 Let the dipped candies set without touching them. Chocolate is shinier if allowed to cool at room temperature; only refrigerate the candies if chocolate has not set after 15 minutes. When set, put candies in paper candy cups. **Note** Be careful not to smudge the chocolate with your fingers.

1 **Dipping with a fork** Test the chocolate for consistency (p.422). Using a fork, lower the candy center into the melted, tempered chocolate. Gently draw chocolate over the exposed surface.

Dipping by hand Follow the procedure for dipping with a fork, using two fingers of one hand. This method is suitable for chocolates that should have a rough finish.

MAKING FILLED CHOCOLATES

Filled chocolates are made in special molds, usually shaped as cubes, ovals or rounds. Tempered chocolate gives the best results, yielding a firm chocolate with an attractive gloss. A variety of soft fillings may be added such as nut pastes and softened fondant. Here, ganache (p.425) is used.

3 Add filling to the molds, using a pastry bag or small spoon and filling them nearly to the top. Smooth the surface. Chill until the filling is firm, at least 30 minutes.

1 Wipe the molds so they are perfectly clean and dry. Brush each hollow with a thin layer of melted, tempered chocolate (p.422). Using a ladle, fill the molds generously with more chocolate. Tap the sheet of molds on the work surface to eliminate all of the air bubbles.

4 Ladle a thin layer of melted, tempered chocolate over the filling to seal the chocolates. Tap the mold lightly to remove air bubbles. Scrape excess chocolate back into the bowl.

5 Cool or chill the filled chocolates. When firm, turn the molds over and tap gently to release the chocolates. They should come out quite easily, because chocolate shrinks as it cools.

Presenting filled chocolates The color and gloss of home-made chocolates are enhanced by a simple, plain white background such as a china plate or paper doily. When packaging chocolates to present them in a gift box, set them in small paper cases so they do not stick together or chip.

2 After ½–1 minute, turn the molds upside down over the bowl of chocolate. Leave to set, 10-15 minutes, then run a spatula across the molds to scrape off excess chocolate.

MAKING HOLLOW CHOCOLATE SHAPES

If using *couverture* chocolate (p.420), a cold room (not more than 60°F/16°C) is essential. All utensils must be clean, dry and at room temperature. Here, a rabbit mold is shown.

1 Carefully clean a hollow chocolate mold with a soft, dry cloth. With another cloth, polish the interior with melted cocoa butter.

2 Holding the mold by its edge, brush a ¼-⅜ in/6-10 mm layer of melted, tempered chocolate into the mold. Repeat with the second half of the mold. Wipe the rims of the molds clean in order to prevent the two halves of the mold sticking when they are put together.

3 Clip the two halves together and allow the chocolate to harden, 5-10 minutes.

4 Completely fill the mold with chocolate. Tap the edge with a spatula to eliminate air bubbles.

5 Turn the mold upside down over the bowl of chocolate so that the excess chocolate pours out into the bowl. Tap the mold lightly with a spatula or wooden spoon so the layer of chocolate is even and to eliminate air bubbles. Leave the mold upright on a rack to set.

6 Let the mold set completely in a cool, airy place, at 55-60°F/12-16°C. Cooling can take from 30 minutes to several hours, depending on the thickness of the chocolate layer and the humidity of the room. When the chocolate pulls away from the bottom of the mold slightly, it is set. Press the chocolate lightly with your finger to make sure. Carefully pull the two halves of the mold away from the chocolate.

7 Dip a small, sharp knife in hot water and run it along the surface of the chocolate at the seam where the two halves are joined. The chocolate will melt slightly on contact with the hot knife, leaving a smooth finish.

Chocolate truffles

These coated chocolate candies are dusted with cocoa to give them the earthy appearance of real truffles.

Makes about 24

1 portion ganache (p.425)	¼ cup/30 g unsweetened cocoa or sweetened powdered chocolate
For the coating	
4 oz/125 g semisweet chocolate (more if needed)	

1 With two teaspoons, scoop pieces of chilled ganache and set them on wax paper. Roll into balls with your palms and chill.
2 **For the coating**: melt the chocolate for dipping (p.427). Spread cocoa on a sheet of wax paper. With your fingers or a dipping fork, dip balls of ganache in the melted chocolate, and transfer to the cocoa. Using two forks, roll the balls in the cocoa until covered, then transfer to a sheet of wax paper. Leave to harden for at least one hour at room temperature, or refrigerate. Store the truffles in an airtight container, between layers of wax paper.

Coconut fruit truffles Add 3 tbsp chopped dried fruit, soaked in brandy and drained, to the ganache. Substitute toasted, shredded coconut for cocoa powder.

COLD DESSERTS & ICE CREAMS

DESSERTS, APPEARING as they do at the end of a meal, must carry a clear message – subtle or simple, rich or light, as the case may be. Flavors should be pure: the sweet acidity of fruit or the intensity of chocolate. Above all, the eye must be caught by the appeal of colors and shapes, so the dessert forms a memorable finale.

First in this chapter come molded desserts – fruit gelatins, bavarian creams, charlottes, mousses and cold soufflés. Meringue follows, the inspiration of grand creations like *vacherin* – layered meringue with Chantilly cream – ice-cream and meringue coupes, as well as the famous snow eggs (Fr. *oeufs à la neige*). Frozen desserts include lush fruit sorbets, satin-smooth ice creams and fantasies such as parfaits, bombes, sundaes and the legendary baked Alaska. Still more ideas appear in the Pastry and Cookies chapter, and many of the *gâteaux* to be found in Cakes and Icings could double as desserts. Soufflé omelets and baked custards appear in Milk, Cheese and Eggs, while for a richer dessert, Sugar and Chocolate should be explored.

Dessert-making draws on many cooking techniques that are covered elsewhere in this book. For example, the Flour, Breads and Batters chapter covers the whole family of waffles, pancakes, crêpes and bread puddings, while the Fruit and Nuts chapter contains myriad fruit desserts. For sweet sauces to accompany desserts, see the Sauces chapter.

MOLDED GELATIN DESSERTS

Many of our favorite desserts are given form and body by an addition of gelatin. Gelatin traps air within whipped eggs and cream, thus sustaining their lightness. If too little gelatin is added, or it is incorrectly mixed, a gelatin dessert will not set firmly enough to hold its shape when unmolded. Yet adding excess gelatin as a preventative measure may produce a rubbery texture.

Gelatin desserts are set in molds, as plain or fancy as mood and mixture dictate. Soft foamy mixtures are best when set in shallow, simple shapes, but creams and mousses can be relied upon to set firmly in tall peaked molds and patterned ring molds like *kugelhopf* (p.509). The more complicated the design of the mold, the more likely a gelatin mixture is to stick during unmolding. Most gelatin desserts are enhanced by a ruff of whipped cream or a ring of contrasting sauce around the base; tall molds are emphasized when crowned with rosettes of cream studded with fresh berries or toasted nuts.

USEFUL INFORMATION

Portion 1 cup/250 ml, somewhat more for soufflés.
Typical mold *Cream, mousse*: peaked, springform, steel ring, *kugelhopf, moule à manqué*. *Charlotte*: charlotte, deep bowl. *Soufflé*: soufflé dish, ramekin.
Preparation of mold Rinse with water. *Soufflé*: add paper collar.
Storage Refrigerate 2 days. *Fruit gelatins*: refrigerate 3 days. *All*: do not freeze.
Problems If not carefully stirred, mixture forms strings or separates; with too much gelatin, mixture is rubbery; with too little, does not set firmly; in warm temperatures, may collapse; if overchilled, will crystallize.
Accompaniments Fruit *coulis* (p.450); macerated fresh fruit; poached fruit; fruit sauces (p.66); caramel sauce (p.67); butterscotch sauce (p.67); chocolate sauce (p.425); Chantilly (p.70) or whipped cream.

UNMOLDING GELATINS

Once set, molded gelatin desserts need to be loosened from the mold and inverted on to a plate for serving. The same technique is used for all gelatin molds, whether or not they are foamy with eggs and cream.

1 Lower the mold into hand-hot water so it almost reaches the rim. Leave 2-3 seconds for metal molds, 5-8 seconds for ceramic ones. Lift out the mold and dry the base.

2 Tip the mold sideways and gently pull the mixture away from the edge with your fingertips to break the air lock.

3 Rinse the serving plate with water so that if the mold does not land centrally, it can be pushed into place. Set the plate upside down on the mold; quickly turn over both together, holding them firmly.

4 Give a quick forceful shake sideways and down, and the dessert will fall on to the plate. If it sticks, give several shakes. If it still sticks, put a hot, wet cloth over the mold for 10-20 seconds.

GELATIN

For the cook, there are two kinds of gelatin: natural gelatin, which is extracted from bones and skin, and commercial gelatin. Natural gelatin is found chiefly in the knuckle bones of calves, and is extracted by simmering in liquid for up to eight hours. Pigs' feet also yield a good deal, as do fish bones and chicken carcasses.

Commercial gelatin is available as a powder or in brittle sheets. Both are almost tasteless and easy to use. Powdered gelatin can be weighed or measured by the spoon; one tablespoon weighs ¼ oz/7 g. In the United States, it is sold in sachets in pre-measured weights of ¼ oz/7 g; in the UK it is sold in larger sachets of ⅓ oz/11 g, reflecting the larger British pint and quart liquid measures. Sheet gelatin must be weighed before use as individual sheets vary – seven sheets weigh about ½ oz/15 g.

Gelatin is important for consommé or aspic (p.253) as well as for setting molded desserts. The amount required is determined by the recipe and, for savory dishes, by the amount of natural gelatin already present. Maintaining the proper temperature is also critical – gelatin sets to a firm gel at 68°F/20°C. To gel 2 cups/500 ml clear liquid such as fruit juice, 1 tbsp/7 g of gelatin is needed. Soft, fluffy mixtures need less, while heavy, creamy ones may need more. **Note** A few fruits, notably raw pineapple, contain an enzyme that inhibits gelatin from setting.

Gelatin should be softened in cold liquid, usually water, then melted in a water bath (p.510). The mixture to which melted gelatin is added must be warm enough to prevent the gelatin from setting immediately. Thorough stirring is important so that the gelatin is evenly distributed. As it cools, gelatin will separate from a fluffy mixture such as a mousse, and must be stirred gently but frequently while cooling so that it does not fall to the bottom.

To chill a gelatin mixture, the bowl (preferably metal) is set over ice. Once cold, gelatin will set quite rapidly. As soon as it starts to thicken, remove the bowl from the ice and fold in any whipped ingredients such as cream or egg whites, then pour the mixture into the mold. Clear aspics and molds that have set before being poured into the mold can be melted over very low heat, but those that contain egg will curdle; whipped cream will melt.

Once set, a gelatin mixture should be left at least two hours in the refrigerator to become firm. **Note** Gelatin crystallizes and separates easily in a freezer, so quick chilling is not advisable. Many gelatin dishes keep well for two to three days but they stiffen with age. After 12 hours or more, they should be left at room temperature to soften for half an hour before serving.

Two gelatin substitutes based on seaweed are occasionally used. Carragheen moss (p.283) adds a mildly perceptible flavor to recipes like blancmange, while agar-agar sets much more firmly than gelatin. Both are still found in pharmacies. Isinglass, extracted from fish, was an early form of commercial gelatin, now used only in winemaking.

One traditional dessert that has been all but ousted by commercial substitutes is the homemade fruit gelatin mold. In the old days, sweet gelatins were made by clarifying fruit juice with egg whites to make a transparent glistening mold, as for aspic. Today only a few cooks still go to the trouble of setting fresh fruit juice with gelatin, sometimes whisking it into an opaque foam just before it sets.

SOFTENING & MELTING GELATIN

Both sheet and powdered gelatin must be softened in cold liquid before use. The gelatin may then be melted in a water bath over low heat, or stirred directly into a hot mixture.

1 **To soften sheet gelatin:** cover it with cold water and leave to soak 5 minutes or until very soft. Remove it with your hand, squeeze out excess water, and put the gelatin in a small pan.

2 **To soften powdered gelatin:** sprinkle it over a small quantity of cold liquid in a small pan, allowing 3-4 tbsp liquid per 1 tbsp/7 g of gelatin. Leave the gelatin for 5 minutes without stirring, until it swells to a spongy consistency.

3 **To melt sheet or powdered gelatin:** put the pan in a water bath (p.510) and heat until melted, shaking the gelatin gently without stirring.

Note If the gelatin is stirred, it may form strings. To check that all the crystals have dissolved fully, lift a little of the gelatin in a spoon – there should be no unmelted crystals.

CHARLOTTES & CREAMS

Perhaps the most famous molded dessert is the charlotte, traditionally set in a tall, bucket-shaped mold. Charlottes are rich, based on egg custard, egg mousse or fruit purée, lavishly lightened with cream. Favorite flavorings include chocolate, praline and acid fruits such as raspberry, orange and lemon, or exotic fruits like passion fruit and mango. A dash of kirsch or fruit liqueur is invariably included to heighten flavor. In a class by itself is charlotte Malakoff, made with equal parts of butter, sugar, whipped cream and ground almonds. Such richness needs a contrast, and charlotte molds are invariably lined with ladyfingers. For lateral support, the cream mixture may be layered between ladyfingers or cake soaked in sugar syrup and liqueur. Occasionally, fresh or candied fruits are included, but only in moderation as they destabilize the mold. Dessert charlottes may also be set in a shallow steel ring and the sides covered with trimmed ladyfingers, or with slices of jelly roll or spongecake layered with jam. In yet another presentation, called royale, a deep bowl is lined with slices of jelly roll and filled with charlotte mixture. The texture of a charlotte mixture is important: it should be firm enough to hold its shape, yet retain lightness.

Although most charlottes are cold desserts, others are made to serve hot, including the famous apple charlotte, baked with a crispy crust of overlapping slices of browned buttered bread. The traditional charlotte mold (Cooking Equipment, p.508) is also used for all sorts of other mixtures, including soufflé bread puddings (p.364), and berry-filled Summer pudding (p.463). Another example is the celebrated *Chartreuse*, traditionally a molded vegetable dish named for *La Grande Chartreuse*, the Carthusian monastery where Chartreuse liqueur originated.

The term "cream" is an even broader category than the charlotte, referring to almost any mixture with a soft, satiny texture that melts on the tongue. In creams, basic flavors such as vanilla, coffee and chocolate may be varied with fruits like raspberry, nuts such as pistachio, and liqueurs like Cointreau. Most famous are bavarian creams (Fr. *bavarois*) made of egg custard, in which a modicum of whipped cream adds richness without disturbing the smoothness. Traditional bavarian creams are set in a peaked mold with layers of different flavors, each displaying its soft pastel color. Recently, however, both they and fruit mousses have taken on a new look, molded like modern charlottes in a shallow 2 in/5 cm layer in a special steel ring or a springform pan (p.509). A thin base of sponge cake may support creams, while the preferred topping is a shiny glaze of fresh fruit jelly, a single perfect fruit or cluster of chocolate leaves being the only decoration.

Other gelatin creams may be spiked with sherry or flavored with crunchy crumbled macaroons. The blancmange (p.36), dating from medieval times, is a molded cream made with egg-white custard and sometimes thickened with ground almonds and cornstarch instead of gelatin. A *marquise* is usually a bavarian cream enriched with extra cream, the name invoking the luxurious quality of the dessert rather than its shape. However, chocolate *marquise* is a super-rich combination of butter, sugar and the finest chocolate, embellished with liqueur.

USEFUL INFORMATION

Typical dishes *Charlotte: à la Parisienne* (custard, pistachios, cream, France); strawberry custard (France); coffee custard with caramel sauce (France); *Mexicaine* (mocha custard, Chantilly cream, France). *Cream*: coffee (France); bavarian with chestnuts and apricot sauce (France); *Nesselrode* (macaroons, almonds, custard, Germany); *diplomate* (génoise, custard, macerated fruit, apricot sauce, France); *bavarois rubané* (chocolate, vanilla and coffee layers, France); brown bread (UK); *beau rivage* (custard with orange, red currant jelly, France); *marquise Alioe* (macaroons, praline, custard, Chantilly cream, France); *crema de Jerez* (sherry custard, Spain).

LINING A CHARLOTTE MOLD

A charlotte mold is designed for stability, and its wide top offers scope for decoration. To prepare the mold, line the base with wax paper. Butter the sides so the ladyfingers or jelly roll will stick.

Lining a mold with ladyfingers

1 Take 4-6 ladyfingers. Trim them into long triangles to resemble "flower-petals". Arrange them in a flower shape, rounded sides down, in the base of the mold. Use as many as will fit comfortably, without overlapping.

2 Trim the sides of another 12-15 ladyfingers and set them upright, rounded sides out, round the sides of the mold, packing them close together.

3 After the mold has been filled and the dessert has set (see charlotte recipe), trim the tops of the ladyfingers level with the mixture, using a sharp knife. **Note** To make ladyfingers, see Cakes and Icings (p.396).

Charlotte russe

This recipe is typical of the French dishes popular at the Russian court in the nineteenth century.

Serves 6-8

⅓ cup/75 ml maraschino liqueur or kirsch
½ cup/65 g chopped mixed candied fruit
20-24 ladyfingers (p.396)
1½ tbsp/10 g gelatin
4-5 tbsp/60-75 ml water
2 cups/500 ml vanilla custard (p.67)
½ cup/125 ml heavy cream, lightly whipped

For decoration

Chantilly cream (p.70)
small leaves cut from angelica (optional)
4-5 candied cherries, quartered (optional)
Melba sauce or apricot jam sauce (p.66), for serving

1½ qt/1.5 L charlotte mold; pastry bag and medium star tube

1 Mix half the maraschino liqueur or kirsch with the candied fruit and leave to macerate for ½-1 hour. Line the mold with ladyfingers (previous page). Cut the remaining ladyfingers in pieces and sprinkle with the remaining maraschino. Make the custard. Soften the gelatin in the water (p.431) and stir it into the hot vanilla custard until completely melted. Leave until quite cool, stirring occasionally.

2 Stir the macerated fruit into the custard, set the bowl over ice, and stir until it starts to set. Take from the ice and at once fold in the lightly whipped cream. Spoon about half the mixture into the lined mold, top with the ladyfingers in a layer, and add the remaining mixture. **Note** If the mixture is too liquid, it will soak between the ladyfingers lining the mold. Cover and chill until firmly set, at least 3 hours.

3 Unmold the charlotte on to a flat plate. Make the Chantilly cream, put it into a pastry bag with a star tube and pipe vertical lines of cream up the sides of the charlotte, between the ladyfingers, and rosettes around the base. If you like, decorate the rosettes with angelica leaves and small pieces of candied cherry. Chill until ready to serve. Serve the charlotte with Melba sauce or apricot jam sauce.

Lining with jelly roll

1 Use a shallow steel ring or the sides of a springform pan and a baking sheet or tart pan base. Make a jelly roll (p.397) with a contrasting filling. Cut the roll into ¼ in/6 mm slices.

2 RIGHT Pack the slices flat in the base of the mold to cover it.

3 Line the sides of the mold with remaining slices, packing them tightly without overlapping them.

4 Fill the mold with charlotte mixture and leave to set. To unmold, invert and lift off ring.

Charlotte and cream recipes

Fruit charlotte Serves 8. Line the base of a 9 in/23 cm steel circle and baking sheet or springform pan with a thin layer of *génoise* (p.395). Sprinkle with 2-3 tbsp sugar syrup and 2-3 tbsp kirsch. Line the sides with thin slices of *biscuit* jelly roll. Follow the charlotte russe recipe, omitting the candied fruits and maraschino and increasing the gelatin to 2 tbsp/15 g. Flavor the custard with 2 cups/500 ml fruit purée and 2-3 tbsp kirsch. Spoon into the mold and chill until set. Top with ½ cup/125 ml commercial fruit gelatin, or with rosettes of whipped cream and fresh fruits.

Chocolate charlotte royale Serves 8. Line a 1½ qt/1.5 L charlotte mold or bowl with chocolate jelly roll (p.396). Melt 4 oz/125 g chocolate with the milk when making the custard for the charlotte russe recipe, and flavor it with ½ tbsp brandy or rum. Omit the candied fruits; increase the whipped cream to 1 cup/250 ml. Mold and chill until set. Serve plain or with a ruff of whipped cream around the base, with sabayon sauce (p.67).

Pistachio bavarian cream Serves 6-8. Make vanilla custard, first infusing the milk with 3½ oz/100 g ground pistachios. Strain out the nuts. Soften 1½ tbsp/10 g gelatin in ½ cup/125 ml water, and add to the warm custard. Set over ice, whisking until almost set. Whip 1 cup/250 ml heavy cream and fold into the custard. Pour into a 1 qt/1 L mold and chill until set. Unmold and coat the sides with chopped pistachios.

COLD MOUSSES & SOUFFLES

Departing from the satiny texture of a cream, a mousse is light and frothy. With a base of custard sauce, eggs (either whole or separated) beaten with sugar, or simply puréed fruit, a mousse acquires its volume from a generous amount of whipped cream and/or egg whites. Flavorings for a mousse must be forceful enough to cut through the richness of the cream and eggs; good choices are citrus fruits or tart berries – perhaps fortified with a splash of liqueur such as kirsch.

Cold soufflés are closely allied to mousses, the only difference being that soufflés are lightened with egg whites. Their preparation is a playful culinary illusion: to give the appearance of having risen in the oven like a hot soufflé, the mixture is set in the customary straight-sided soufflé mold fitted with a paper collar so that the mixture may be poured high above the rim of the mold.

When the soufflé has set and the collar is removed, the top looks as though it simply puffed up in the oven. A cold soufflé may be embellished with fruit and whipped cream, but overloading a cold soufflé with heavy decorations courts the risk of collapse, much like its oven-baked look-alike. To avoid too much weight on top of the soufflé, the sides above the dish may be decorated with finely chopped browned almonds or pistachios, or with shredded coconut. For frozen soufflés, see p.444.

USEFUL INFORMATION

Typical dishes *Mousse*: apricot (France); honey hazelnut (USA); raspberry (France); white chocolate (USA); pumpkin with rum sabayon (UK); pineapple mousse filled with pineapple, *amaretti*, kirsch (France). *Soufflé*: strawberry (France); *Milanese* (fruit purée, cream, France); rhubarb (USA); *Nantaise* (orange custard, cream, macaroons, France); pear with brandy (UK).

Lemon mousse with caramel sauce

The sweetness of the caramel sauce complements the tart lemon flavor of this mousse. Nuts and cream are the perfect finish.

Serves 6-8

1½ tbsp/10 g gelatin	
½ cup/125 ml cold water	
3 eggs	
2 egg yolks	
½ cup/100 g sugar	
½ cup/125 ml lemon juice	
grated zest of 2 lemons	
1 cup/250 ml heavy cream, lightly whipped	
caramel sauce (p.67)	

For decoration

Chantilly cream (p.70) made with ¾ cup/175 ml heavy cream, 1 tbsp sugar and ½ tsp vanilla extract

1-2 tbsp chopped blanched pistachios

1 qt/1 L jelly mold (p.508); pastry bag and medium star tube

1 Dampen the mold. Soften the gelatin in the water. In a bowl, combine the eggs and egg yolks and gradually beat in the sugar, lemon juice and zest. Set the bowl over a pan of simmering water and beat until the mixture is light and thick enough to leave a ribbon trail (p.394), 5-8 minutes. Take from the heat and beat until cool. Melt the gelatin; whisk into the lemon mixture.
2 Set the bowl over ice and stir gently until the mixture starts to set. At once take from the ice and fold in the lightly whipped cream. Pour the mousse into the prepared mold, cover and chill until set, at least 2 hours. Make the caramel sauce.
3 Unmold the mousse and spoon caramel sauce around it. Make the Chantilly cream, fill it into the pastry bag and pipe rosettes on the mousse, topping them with chopped pistachios.

Variations

Orange mousse Substitute orange juice and zest for lemon, and add 2 tbsp Grand Marnier with the cream. Serve with strawberries macerated in Grand Marnier.

Coffee mousse Substitute 3 tbsp instant coffee dissolved in ⅓ cup/75 ml hot water for the lemon juice and zest. Add 2-3 tbsp brandy with the cream. Serve with chocolate sauce (p.425).

Cold mousse and soufflé recipes

Prune mousse Serves 4. Simmer ½ lb/250 g pitted prunes in 2 cups/500 ml strong tea and the juice and pared zest of 1 lemon until tender, 15-20 minutes. Drain them, reserving the liquid, and purée in a food processor or blender (with a little liquid), or work through a food mill. Stir in ¾ cup/150 g sugar, or to taste. Soften and melt 1½ tbsp/10 g gelatin in ½ cup/125 ml of the prune juice. Stir gelatin into the prune purée with 1 tbsp rum. When cool, fold in ½ cup/125 ml heavy cream, lightly whipped, and 2 stiffly whipped egg whites. Spoon into a bowl and chill.

Cold coconut soufflé Serves 6-8. Make vanilla custard (p.67), omitting the vanilla and using 4 egg yolks, ¾ cup/150 g sugar, and 2 cups/500 ml coconut milk (p.477). While still hot, stir in 2 tbsp/15 g gelatin, dissolved in ½ cup/125 ml water. Cool over ice, whisking frequently. Beat 4 egg whites until stiff. Add ¼ cup/50 g sugar and beat until glossy. When the mixture reaches the point of setting, fold in the egg whites. Then fold in 1½ cups/375 ml lightly whipped heavy cream, ¾ cup/75 g toasted, grated coconut, 1 tbsp dark rum and 1 tbsp lemon juice. Wrap a paper collar around a 1 qt/1 L soufflé dish, and pour in the mixture. Smooth the top and chill until set.

USING A PAPER COLLAR

Cold soufflés look impressive when they are molded above the rim of the dish with the help of a collar of aluminum foil or wax paper, giving the impression of having risen like a hot soufflé.

1 Cut a piece of aluminum foil or wax paper about 2 in/5 cm longer than the circumference of the soufflé dish; fold it lengthways to double it. Wrap it around the soufflé dish; it should extend about 2 in/ 5 cm higher than the rim. Secure the foil or paper with adhesive tape. Pour in the soufflé mixture and leave to set in the refrigerator.

2 When ready to decorate, cut the collar level with the top of the soufflé, and add a decoration such as the sprinkling of cocoa and confectioners' sugar shown here.

3 Just before serving, remove the aluminum foil or paper collar, easing it away carefully with a knife. Wipe the soufflé dish clean of any mixture that has leaked.

MERINGUE

Meringue is made with whipped egg whites and sugar, and three types can be clearly identified. Simple meringue, sometimes called Swiss meringue, is made by folding granulated sugar into whipped egg whites. Italian meringue is more stable, as hot sugar syrup is beaten into whipped egg whites so that they are partially cooked, holding their shape longer. Cooked meringue is the most robust of all, made by beating egg whites with sugar over heat. To some extent, all three types are interchangeable, but simple meringue is lighter and more fragile.

The proportion of sugar in simple and Italian meringue – ¼ cup/50 g to each egg white – may seem high, but is necessary for crispness. Cooked meringue uses sugar in almost the same proportions. As always when whisking egg whites, a copper bowl produces the lightest, finest texture and is particularly useful for cooked meringue. **Note** After it is beaten, meringue must not be left more than a few minutes in the copper bowl as it will discolor. A pinch of salt or cream of tartar also helps stiffen the whites. Meringue is stiff enough to pipe or spread directly on a baking sheet, so no molds are needed.

Meringue is baked (dried is perhaps a more accurate term) at a very low heat. It should remain white or acquire only very slight color – if necessary, the oven temperature should be lowered during baking. For any baked meringue, the ideal texture is crunchy, yet soft enough to collapse at the pressure of a fork. A touch of marshmallow stickiness at the center is permissible, but the "chalkiness" of commercial meringues containing starch is not.

Crisp meringue invites a contrasting filling, be it whipped cream, ice cream or fruit. A layer of meringue set inside a mousse or iced dessert adds a pleasing contrast. Once mixed with other ingredients, however, meringue will soften within an hour or two.

USEFUL INFORMATION

Portion Meringue made with 3-4 egg whites serves 3-4.
Preparation of baking sheet Lined with parchment paper, or greased and floured.
Storage *Simple, unbaked*: use within 15 minutes; *baked as topping*: 3-4 hours. *Italian, unbaked*: refrigerate 2 days; *baked as topping*: 1 day. *Cooked, unbaked*: refrigerate 1 week; *baked as topping*: 1 day. *All: baked until crisp*: 3 weeks in airtight container; freeze 6 months.
Cooking times *Topping*: brown at 350°F/175°C, 10-15 minutes. *Rounds or 3 in/7.5 cm mounds*: bake at 250°F/120°C, ¾-1 hour.

When done *Baked as topping*: tips are brown. *Baked until crisp*: firm and very pale beige; becomes crisp only when cool.
Problems *Simple*: separates in the bowl if overwhisked; weeps sugar syrup during baking if baked too fast or for too short a time; separates if left too long before cooking. *Italian*: egg whites may solidify on sides of bowl, so pour hot sugar syrup into center. *Cooked*: use very low heat so meringue does not stiffen before air has been incorporated. *Topping*: browns easily so keep oven temperature very low. *Rounds, mounds*: may stick to baking sheet, so use parchment paper if possible; soften in humid atmosphere but can be crisped in a low oven.
Accompaniments Chantilly cream (p.70); fruit sauces (p.66); chocolate sauce (p.425); fresh fruits, especially berries; butter cream (p.405); ice cream.

SIMPLE MERINGUE

To make simple meringue, egg whites are very stiffly whipped, then a tablespoon of sugar for every egg white is beaten in so that the whites turn glossy, forming characteristic short peaks. Then more sugar is folded in lightly. The first batch of sugar stabilizes the egg-white foam, but if the second, larger batch is overmixed, the egg whites will lose their volume and turn to syrup. Finally, a flavoring is added.

Simple meringue may be baked and sandwiched with cream to make *meringues Chantilly*, spread on a tart as a topping, as in lemon meringue pie, or spread to cloak ice cream as in baked Alaska. Mixed with ground almonds or hazelnuts, it forms the basis of delicious cakes (p.402). Most famous of all is *vacherin*, a pinnacled castle of meringue constructed in two stages. A pavlova is the intriguing New Zealand and Australian version; the meringue is softened with vinegar and cornstarch so that it bakes to resemble a marshmallow. Meringue may also be poached in water or milk, as for the popular snow eggs in which spoonfuls of it are floated in vanilla custard and topped with caramel trails; alternatively, the meringue is baked as one puff for Floating Island.

USEFUL INFORMATION

Typical dishes Lemon meringue pie (USA); with vanilla ice cream and hot chocolate sauce, (USA); *mont blanc* (with chestnut purée, whipped cream, France); *délice aux framboises* (with raspberries, butter cream, chocolate, Grand Marnier, France); *Schaumtorte* (lime custard topped with whipped cream, Germany); chocolate angel pie (chocolate pastry cream, whipped cream, grated chocolate, USA).

MAKING SIMPLE MERINGUE

A sprinkling of sugar added before baking gives a sparkle and extra crispness to simple meringue.

Makes about 2½ cups/625 ml

4 egg whites, at room temperature	1 cup/200 g sugar
	1 tsp vanilla extract

1 With a balloon whisk, beat the egg whites until stiff. Add 4 tbsp of the sugar, one at a time.

2 Continue beating until the egg whites are glossy, about 30 seconds. The meringue should form short peaks when the whisk is lifted.

3 With a spatula, fold in the remaining sugar, a few tablespoons at a time. Fold in the vanilla with the last of the sugar and continue folding for ½-1 minute until the meringue forms long peaks.

Simple meringue recipes

Baked meringues A 4-egg white quantity makes 6-8 meringues. Using a pastry bag and large star tube, pipe 3 in/7.5 cm mounds of meringue on to a greased and floured baking sheet, or shape mounds with two tablespoons. Sprinkle with sugar and bake at 250°F/120°C until firm and pale beige, ¾-1 hour. If the meringues are to be filled with whipped cream or ice cream, turn them over when almost cooked, crack the center of the base to hollow the shell and continue baking until dry.

Snow eggs (*oeufs à la neige*) Serves 4-6. Make vanilla custard (p.67) and leave to cool. Make simple meringue. With two tablespoons, shape ovals of meringue and drop them into a large pan of simmering water. Poach them until firm, 2-3 minutes, turning them once. Drain them on paper towels. Pour the custard into a shallow bowl and pile the meringue "eggs" in the center. Make caramel (p.418) with ½ cup/100 g sugar and ¼ cup/60 ml water. While still hot, trail it in an uneven lattice over the meringue eggs. Chill until ready to serve.

COOKED AND ITALIAN MERINGUE

Italian meringue is made by beating hot sugar syrup, boiled to the hard ball stage (p.415), into stiffly whipped egg whites. The egg whites are cooked by the heat of the syrup so that they hold up well for as much as two days without further cooking. Close-textured and shiny, Italian meringue bakes to be more melting, less crisp and frothy than simple meringue. Cooked meringue is even stiffer. It is made by whisking unbeaten egg whites with sugar over a pan of steaming water, until a smooth fluffy paste is formed. Cooked meringue is hard work to whisk by hand, but has the advantage that it can be stored for a week or more.

Cooked and Italian meringues have similar uses. They are the basis of a multitude of small cakes and *petits fours*, often enriched with nuts. When baking, a portion of meringue may be set aside and flavored to use as a soft filling. Both meringues form sharp contours when piped, ideal for whimsical shapes like mushrooms, or baskets to fill with fruit.

Pastry chefs often keep a supply of cooked or Italian meringue on hand, for not only do they hold well, but they also maintain their volume when mixed with other ingredients. Italian meringue may be mixed with butter to make a version of butter cream (p.405), or added to sweeten whipped cream or to lighten sorbets. Combined with whipped cream, it is frozen as a light bombe filling. When mixed with fruit purée, it may be cooked as a simple hot dessert soufflé.

USEFUL INFORMATION

Typical dishes *Saint Cyr* (baked, with frozen chocolate mousse, France); raspberry soufflé (USA); *rochers de neige* (almond cookies, France); *brioche polonaise* (brioche, meringue, almonds, France); *gâteau napolitain* (layered with *génoise* and pineapple, France); *windtorte* (meringue with chocolate almond filling, Spain); *bombe Victoria* (filled with chocolate ice cream, kirsch, raspberries, and broiled, UK); baskets with fruit and whipped cream (USA).

MAKING COOKED MERINGUE

A metal bowl is best for cooked meringue so that the heat of the water is transferred quickly. The meringue can be whisked by hand with a balloon whisk, or with a hand-held electric beater.

Makes about 2½ cups/625 ml

4 egg whites	1 tsp vanilla extract
1 cup/200 g sugar, sifted	

1 BELOW Put the egg whites, sugar and vanilla in the bowl and whisk with a balloon whisk or electric whisk until they are well mixed.

2 Set the bowl over a pan of simmering water and whisk until the mixture forms a stiff peak when the whisk is lifted, 10-15 minutes. Take from the heat and continue whisking until the meringue is cool.

MAKING ITALIAN MERINGUE

Italian meringue is easily made in an electric mixer. Start beating slowly, then more quickly as the eggs stiffen.

Makes about 2½ cups/625 ml

1 cup/200 g sugar	4 egg whites
½ cup/125 ml water	1 tsp vanilla extract

1 Heat the sugar and water over low heat until dissolved. Bring to a boil and boil without stirring to the hard ball stage (248°F/120°C) on a candy thermometer (p.503).

2 RIGHT Meanwhile, stiffly whisk the egg whites, preferably using an electric mixer. Gradually pour in the hot syrup, whisking constantly.

3 Continue whisking until the meringue is completely cool, about 5 minutes; it will be very stiff. Beat in the vanilla. **Note** When adding syrup, pour it directly into the egg whites or it will stick to the sides of the bowl.

MAKING A VACHERIN

The oven heat must be carefully watched when making *vacherin* so that the twice-baked meringue does not brown. Other fruits such as raspberries or kiwi fruit may be substituted for the strawberries.

Serves 6-8

2½ cups/625 ml simple meringue (previous page)	1 qt/500 g strawberries
sugar (for sprinkling)	**For decoration:** raspberries and mint sprigs
2½ cups/625 ml Italian meringue	
Chantilly cream made with 2 cups/ 500 ml heavy cream, 3–4 tbsp sugar and 2 tsp vanilla extract	*Pastry bag with ½ in/1.25 cm plain and medium star tubes*

1 Grease and flour a baking sheet or line it with non-stick parchment paper. Mark an 8 in/20 cm circle. Heat the oven to 250°F/120°C. Make the simple meringue and put it into the pastry bag fitted with the plain tube. Pipe an 8 in/20 cm round on the marked circle, and 12-14 fingers 4 in/10 cm long, patching any gaps in the round so it has no air bubbles. Sprinkle with sugar and bake until crisp and dry, 40-50 minutes. While the meringue is still warm, trim the round neatly with a knife. Leave to cool on the baking sheet.

2 Set the meringue fingers on a cloth so they do not splinter and, using a small knife, cut a small piece from one end of each to square it. Make the Italian meringue and fill into a pastry bag filled with a medium star tube.

3 RIGHT Set the meringue round on a parchment paper-lined baking sheet. Pipe a strip of Italian meringue round the rim and press meringue fingers side by side upright into it (level ends down and rounded sides outward). On the outside, pipe a decorative line of meringue down each finger, and add another next to it. Continue piping to conceal the seams between each pair of fingers.

4 Bake the case in the heated oven until dry, about 1 hour. Transfer it to a rack and leave to cool.

5 **To finish:** not more than 3 hours before serving, make the Chantilly cream (p.70). Pile half into the prepared meringue case and spread it with the strawberries (or other fruit of your choice), reserving 8-10 for decoration. Fill the remaining cream into a pastry bag with a medium star tube. Cover the strawberries with rosettes of cream and top with the reserved strawberries, raspberries and sprigs of mint. Refrigerate the finished *vacherin* until ready to serve.

OTHER COLD DESSERTS

Many of our favorite cold desserts are centuries old. Typical are puddings of egg custard thickened slightly with flour, cornstarch or arrowroot so the mixture just holds the mark of the spoon. Chocolate, coffee or vanilla remain the most popular flavors. A few desserts, notably those with chocolate and cheese, set firmly enough to be unmolded. Chocolate mixtures with a high proportion of nuts, particularly chestnuts, set satisfactorily to simple rounds or loaf shapes, as in the French *pavé*, or paving stone, of puréed chestnuts and chocolate (p.425).

The British contribute desserts such as fool, made of fruit purée folded into whipped cream, or thickened custard and whipped cream. Syllabub is even lighter, made by whipping cream with sugar and wine (or tart fruit juice). A simple mousse can be created with a purée of fruit, such as prune or apple, beaten with whipped egg whites until fluffy and slightly thickened, served piled in a bowl. Lightest of all is Italian *zabaglione* made of whipped egg yolks, sugar and Marsala.

USEFUL INFORMATION

Typical dishes Apricot whip (puréed apricots with whipped egg whites and cream, UK); *ovos moles de papaia* (papaya and egg yolk pudding, Mozambique); gooseberry fool (UK); butterscotch pudding (USA); *crème Celesta* (egg-thickened raspberry purée with Chantilly cream, France); apple huff (puréed apples, sugar syrup, and whipped egg white, UK); *kisel iz klubniki* (strawberry purée with cream, Russia); *weinschaum* (wine custard, Germany); grape custard, walnuts (Bulgaria); *zuppa inglese* (egg custard, ladyfingers, Italy).

Cold dessert recipes

Fruit fool Serves 6. Work 2 cups/500 ml fruit purée through a sieve and flavor to taste with sugar, lemon juice and kirsch. Fold in 1 cup/250 ml heavy cream, lightly whipped, and continue stirring 30 seconds until thoroughly mixed and slightly thickened, about 30 seconds. Pile the fool into 4-6 stemmed glasses and chill. Just before serving, top with a piece of fruit or a mint sprig.

Trifle Serves 6-8. Cut a 1 lb/500 g sponge or pound cake lengthwise in three layers and spread each layer with 2-3 tbsp raspberry jam. Restack the cake into its original shape and cut it in 1 in/2.5 cm squares. Put these in a large glass bowl, sprinkle with ½ cup/125 ml sherry, mix well, and press down lightly. Add 2 cups/500 g drained, sliced, poached peaches or pears. Make vanilla custard (p.67) with 3 cups/750 ml milk, a vanilla bean, 6 egg yolks, ¾ cup/150 g sugar and 2 tbsp cornstarch, adding the cornstarch to the egg yolk and sugar mixture and boiling the custard just until thickened. Let the custard cool slightly, then pour over the fruit. Leave to cool, then cover and chill at least 12, and up to 24 hours, for flavor to mature. Shortly before serving, pipe a lattice of Chantilly cream (p.70) across the top of the custard and decorate the edge with rosettes of cream, each one topped with a toasted whole almond.

Zabaglione For each serving, combine 1 egg yolk, 1 tbsp sugar and 2 tbsp Marsala in a bowl, preferably of copper. Set over a pan of hot but not boiling water, or over very low direct heat, and whisk steadily until the mixture is very light and almost thick enough to leave a ribbon trail when the whisk is lifted. **Note** If the *zabaglione* is cooked too long, it will separate. Take from the heat and continue whisking 1 minute. Pour into glasses and serve. (After 5-10 minutes, it will start to separate.)

Sherry syllabub

Port or a sweet white wine such as Sauternes may be substituted for the sherry in this recipe.

Serves 4-6

½ cup/125 ml dry sherry	½ cup/100 g sugar
¼ cup/60 ml brandy	1½ cups/375 ml heavy cream
¼ cup/60 ml lemon juice	ground nutmeg (for decoration)

1 In a large bowl, mix the sherry, brandy, lemon juice and sugar until the sugar is dissolved. Stir in the cream, set the bowl over ice, and beat until thick enough to hold a soft peak, 4-5 minutes.
2 Spoon the syllabub into stemmed glasses and chill for at least 2 hours and up to 2 days. Sprinkle with ground nutmeg just before serving. **Note** On standing, syllabub separates slightly, forming a thick cream that has a few spoons of clear sauce at the bottom.

Variation

Strawberry syllabub Substitute 1 cup/250 ml fresh strawberry purée for the sherry and use only 2 tbsp each of brandy and lemon juice to balance the amount of liquid.

SORBETS, ICE CREAMS & FROZEN DESSERTS

A wide range of desserts are created simply by freezing. They fall into two main categories: sorbets made of simple combinations of fruit juice or purée, wine or liqueur, plus sugar and various flavorings, and richer mixtures based on eggs, milk or cream. Of the latter, the most common are custard-based ice creams made of milk and thickened with egg, but some even richer mixtures are used for parfaits, frozen soufflés, bombes and other frozen creations of *grande cuisine*.

The key to good sorbet and ice cream is smoothness; the ice crystals that form naturally during freezing must be forestalled. This is accomplished by stirring the mixture constantly, usually by machine (p.509). The higher the proportion of water, the more easily ice crystals form, and therefore the more thoroughly it must be stirred. This is why sorbets, particularly those based on wine or on fruit juices rather than fruit purées, are quite hard to make. On the other hand, very rich mixtures such as parfaits and bombes with a high proportion of eggs and cream, freeze smoothly with no stirring at all. Good sorbets and ice creams should also be light from the air absorbed during churning; sorbets may be lightened further by adding whipped egg white or meringue halfway through freezing, while parfaits and bombes are lightened with whipped eggs and cream. One commercial ruse is to increase bulk by adding air, as can be shown by weighing equal volumes of commercial and homemade ice cream.

When making any mixture to be frozen, bear in mind that taste is blunted by cold, so flavors must be concentrated, with a bite of acid lemon or alcohol as well as plenty of sugar. Fruits are excellent in sorbets and ice cream, especially acid fruits such as passion fruit, citrus fruits and berries. For ice cream, the straightforward tastes of vanilla, coffee and chocolate are still preferred, together with crushed nut mixtures such as praline, or candied fruits macerated in liqueur. Ice cream may also be tinted with food coloring, but with discretion. Mint and pistachio ice creams, for example, are appealing when tinted the palest green, and some fruits may need picking up with pale pink.

INGREDIENTS FOR SORBETS, ICE CREAMS & FROZEN DESSERTS

Each type of ingredient used in a frozen mixture has a specific effect. Every sorbet or ice cream contains some of those listed.

Sugar Often dissolved in water as syrup, white or brown sugar adds smoothness by hindering the formation of ice crystals. However, sugar also lowers the freezing point of a mixture, so it takes longer to stiffen. With too little sugar, a mixture may be grainy; with too much sugar, it may scarcely stiffen at all.

Honey, maple syrup and other sweeteners These act like sugar syrup when frozen, though the flavor may be more cloying. Artificial sweeteners lack sugar's capacity to produce a smooth mixture. (See also the chapter on Sugar and Chocolate, p.411.)

Glucose A natural sugar, glucose is less sweet than regular sugar. Professional chefs often use small quantities of glucose, or invert sugar, to give a smoother texture to sorbets without making them too sweet.

Cream and milk The butterfat content, that is, the proportion of cream in frozen mixtures, has an important effect on their consistency: the higher the butterfat, the smoother the ice cream. However, cream with a high fat content (whether it is whipped first or not) may curdle or form granules of fat. Therefore milk is the usual base for ice-cream custards, often with some cream added halfway through churning. Evaporated or condensed milk is an inexpensive alternative to cream, but adds a tell-tale flavor. (See also the chapter on Milk, Cheese and Eggs, p.68.)

Crème fraîche, soft cheese and yogurt *Crème fraîche* adds a pleasant bite to ice creams and frozen desserts, and fresh cream cheeses like French *fromage frais* and Italian ricotta give body. Yogurt retains its characteristic flavor when frozen and may be used alone or with milk as the basis of a wide variety of mixtures. More imaginative mixtures may include ingredients such as bean curd (tofu). (See also the chapter on Milk, Cheese and Eggs, p.68.)

Liqueur and wine Many traditional sorbets are based on wines; and frozen desserts may be flavored with liqueurs. However alcohol sharply lowers the freezing point of a mixture, so strong liqueurs or spirits must be used in moderation. (See also the chapter on Herbs, Spices and Flavorings, p.38.)

Fruit Purées of fruit are often used for sorbet and to flavor ice cream. Fruit juices, particularly lemon, are important in sorbets in adding acid to balance sugar and heighten flavor. Some fruits, particularly berries, can be puréed to use raw, but the flavor of many fruits, including peaches, plums and pears is developed by first poaching in syrup. Fruits such as pineapple and kiwi must also be poached to destroy certain enzymes that inhibit freezing. A few pulpy fruits such as figs or gooseberries are mealy when frozen, even after poaching.

Nuts Chopped walnuts, pecans or almonds offer a contrasting crunch and are classic in ice cream with praline or caramel. They are also a traditional topping, sprinkled on American banana splits and other ice-cream desserts. In the United States, walnuts soaked in maple syrup are another ice-cream parlor favorite. (See also the chapter on Fruit and Nuts, p.476.)

Cornstarch, potato starch and other thickeners Thickeners make ice cream heavy, sacrificing quality for economy. (See also the chapter on Flour, Breads and Batters, p.344.)

Eggs Whole eggs and egg yolks are indispensable for thickening custard ice creams and bombe mixtures. Often whole egg or egg yolk is whisked with sugar to the ribbon. In sorbets, egg white may be added for lightness.

Note Raw egg yolk can harbor bacteria that are not killed by freezing. Therefore, in any frozen mixture that is to be stored, the egg yolk must be cooked, either as a custard or by whisking with sugar over heat.

FREEZING SORBET & ICE CREAM

Sorbets, and all but very rich ice creams, have the smoothest texture when churned in a hand or electric machine (p.509). First chill the mixture to reduce churning time, so freezing is complete before the ice melts or the churn gets too warm.

1 Fill the container not more than two-thirds full as the mixture will expand when frozen. Churning time required until a mixture begins to stiffen

depends on the quantity, ingredients and temperature. If churned in less than 7-8 minutes, the texture is likely to be grainy.

If mixture has not frozen in 30 minutes: **for container with coolant** (used here), remove the mixture and refreeze the container; **for churn**, add more salt to the ice; **for sorbetiere,** lower the freezer temperature.

2 Add whipped egg white (to sorbet) or flavorings like chocolate chips (to ice cream) when the mixture starts to stiffen. Continue churning until stiff – many electric machines stop automatically. Remove the paddle (right). Pack down the mixture, or transfer it to a chilled container or mold, and store it in the freezer until needed (see below).

ALTERNATIVELY, freeze ice cream or sorbet directly in the freezer by the stirring method: pour the mixture into ice trays, preferably of metal to conduct the cold. Freeze it until half-frozen, then turn it into a chilled bowl and whisk until smooth. Return the mixture to the trays and continue freezing, whisking once or twice more, until the mixture is stiff. This is the method used for making a *granita*.

Storing sorbet and ice cream

Sorbet and ice cream should always be kept an hour or two after churning to let the flavor mellow. The richer the mixture, the longer it can be stored before ice crystals start to form. Sugar inhibits crystallization, as do stabilizers such as gelatin and gum, often used in commercial preparations. Homemade frozen yogurt mixtures keep up to a week; plain ice creams can be frozen a month or more, while rich mixtures such as parfaits can be stored three months; light sorbets are best eaten within two to three hours, though they can be frozen up to two weeks with little change. However, a *granita*, with its slightly crunchy texture, must be served at once or it will start to solidify.

Frozen mixtures must be tightly sealed as they easily pick up other flavors. A fresh-frozen mixture thaws quickly, so handle it as little as possible and chill any equipment, such as spoons. Before serving, transfer ice cream or sorbet that has been frozen for more than 12 hours to the refrigerator for half an hour or until it softens slightly. The texture should be soft enough to scoop easily.

Presenting sorbets, ice creams, and frozen desserts

For a simple presentation, ice cream may be set into a square or round mold with an indented design, then easily unmolded on to a chilled serving dish. Even plainer is the tall, rounded mold intended for rich bombe mixtures. Sorbets can be served in stemmed glasses, in crisp "tulip" wafers (p.388), or in the gilded paper cups often used by caterers. Hollowed-out shells of lemons and other citrus fruits offer handy containers that may be frozen; just before serving, add a decorative green leaf.

To serve more than one flavor at once, ice cream and sorbet may be formed into balls with a scoop and piled in a coupe glass or shaped into ovals with two spoons and set in a star shape on a cold flat plate against a background of brightly colored sauce or fruit *coulis* (p.450). Sliced fruits may be added as garnish, with a sprig of mint, frosted fresh fruit (p.474) or a candied violet as decoration. Many pretty frozen desserts – such as the multi-colored slices of a bombe, or a frozen soufflé – need no additional decoration.

A layer of powdered sugar or cocoa sprinkled thickly on top of parfaits and frozen desserts adds a simple finishing touch. A sprinkling of browned chopped nuts or crushed caramel may be preferred, contributing texture as well as color; alternatives include shredded coconut, candied citrus peel (p.475), chopped crystallized fruits, grated chocolate or ornamental chocolate leaves (p.424). Decorative rosettes of whipped cream must be added just before serving as when frozen, they acquire the texture of butter. Grandest finish of all for frozen desserts is a cloud of spun sugar (p.416) or a cage of caramel (p.418) that must be cracked to reach the dessert itself.

Accompaniments are equally traditional. The intense flavor of a sorbet demands at most a spoonful or two of liqueur, but the rounder flavors of ice cream invite a bevy of sweet sauces from fruit to butterscotch to chocolate. Richer frozen desserts, however, are often complete in themselves, needing only the crispy rolled cigarette, macaroon, or fan wafer; an accompaniment that is also appreciated with ice cream.

PROBLEMS WHEN MAKING SORBETS & ICE CREAMS

Lumps

1 Mixture (particularly fruit purée) was not smooth before being frozen.
2 Paddle did not scrape sides of container during churning.

Granular texture

1 Too much water or alcohol in mixture.
2 Amount of sugar or fat too low.
3 Mixture was insufficiently churned, or churned too slowly.
4 Freezing done too quickly at too low a temperature.
5 Cream curdled during churning.
6 Container was too full.
7 Finished dessert was stored too long.

Poor flavor

1 Too little sugar.
2 In a sorbet, too little acid such as lemon juice was used.

SORBET

Sorbet, sometimes called ice or water ice, consists of sugar or sugar syrup and flavoring, but there are countless variations on this simple theme. First come fruit sorbets, whether of single fruits or a mixture, the taste accented with a liqueur or kirsch. Chopped herbs such as mint, or spices such as cinnamon, may be added to the fruit juice. Thyme, rosemary, and other infused herb sorbets are even more unusual. Recent additions to the repertoire are savory sorbets to serve as refreshing first courses or interludes to clear the palate. Flavors range from avocado to olive, or more adventurous mixtures like mullet roe (*tarama*) and garlic, or smoked salmon and caviar.

When a sorbet is based on a spirit such as Calvados or *marc*, difficult ingredients that drastically lower the freezing point of a mixture, a sharp fruit flavor such as apple or unripe grape is often included. Wine sorbets are best with the sweetness of aperitifs like port and vermouth, or wines such as Sauternes. Most famous of all is Champagne sorbet, though an inexpensive sparkling wine can well be substituted, since the bubbles can hardly be appreciated. Often a few spoons of the wine are poured over the sorbet when it is served. An intense, satin-smooth sorbet is well able to stand on its own; at most a decoration of frosted fruits, or perhaps a few spoons of macerated berries or fruit compote may be added.

Finding just the right balance of flavor and sweetness in a sorbet and its cousins is a matter of tasting and adjusting ingredients until the combination is just right. The proportion of sugar is critical; it can vary so much for every batch of fruit that chefs often measure the density of a sorbet mixture with a hydrometer (p.503) – a fruit mixture should measure 18, and wine mixtures slightly less. Sweetness should be determined according to a sorbet's role: when served between courses to clear the palate, it should be crisp and acidic, whereas for dessert, it may be soothingly sweet.

The texture of a sorbet may be lightened by adding lightly whipped egg whites or Italian meringue (p.437) halfway through churning – even a teaspoon or two perceptibly smooths texture and increases volume. When more meringue is used, a sorbet changes so much that it is given another name, "spoom". However, egg white can mask the pure flavor of sorbet and nowadays many cooks prefer to lighten the texture by substituting glucose or invert sugar for up to a quarter of the regular sugar in a recipe.

Sorbet is not the only frozen dessert based on sugar syrup. The same basic mixture may also be put directly in the freezer and frozen into an Italian *granita* by the stirring method, rather than with a churn. A *granita*, which has the texture of coarse snow and some of the same frosty appearance, should be consumed within the hour or it will solidify. If frozen too fast, the ice crystals in the *granita* will divide; the heavier, more flavorful ones move to the bottom, while the watery, bland ones stay on top. The old-fashioned preparation called a shrub is very similar to a *granita*, made by pouring sour fruit juices, sometimes acidified with vinegar, over shaved ice. A sherbet is yet another variation, often confused with a sorbet. (The same name is also sometimes given to a summer drink.) To make sherbet, milk is substituted for the water in a sorbet usually flavored with citrus or other tart fruits. Sherbets are pleasant, but lack the richness of ice cream and the bite of a true sorbet.

USEFUL INFORMATION

Portion 1 qt/1 L serves 4-6.
Storage *Sorbet, sherbet*: freeze 2 weeks. *Granita*: freeze 15 minutes.
Toppings *All*: few spoons of liqueur or champagne. *Sorbet*: frosted berries (p.474); chocolate decorations (p.423); candied citrus zest (p.475); mint sprigs; candied violets.

Accompaniments *Sorbet, sherbet*: macerated fresh fruit, especially berries; compote of fresh or dried fruit; tulip and cigarette wafers (p.388).
Typical dishes *Sorbet: mandarines givrées* (sorbet-filled tangerines, France); black raspberry (USA); *punch à la romaine* (with champagne, France); juniper with *genièvre* liqueur (Belgium); tea with lime (UK); red currant water-ice (UK); with Sauternes wine, (France); watermelon ice (USA); rose petal water-ice (UK); lemon (France); melon and champagne (France); green apple sorbet (USA); pineapple water-ice (UK); blackberry water-ice (UK). *Granita*: lemon (Italy); black grape (UK); coffee (Italy); with red wine and cinnamon (France); *di fragole* (strawberry, Italy); passion fruit (France); coffee with Bourbon (USA). *Sherbet*: orange milk (USA); mint (UK); bitter chocolate with coffee granita (France).

SHAPING SORBET & ICE CREAM OVALS

Ovals are best displayed in a fan or star shape against a background of brightly-colored sauce, fruit *coulis* (p.450) or a plate of contrasting color. Serving spoons are used for shaping larger ovals, or tablespoons for smaller ones.

LEFT Dip the spoons in cold water. Use one to scoop a generous spoonful of ice cream or sorbet, scraping off the excess against the bowl. Use the second spoon to shape an oval, then to detach it, letting it fall on to a chilled plate.

RIGHT A finished presentation of sorbet and ice cream ovals.

Raspberry sorbet

All sorts of changes can be made in the following basic sorbet recipes by varying the ingredients, or the garnish.

Makes 1 qt/1 L to serve 6-8

1 pt/500 g raspberries	1 cup/200 g sugar (more if needed)
juice of 1 lemon or 1 tbsp kirsch (more to taste)	**For decoration**
1 cup/250 ml water	fresh raspberries, sprigs of mint, or chocolate leaves (p.424).
For the sugar syrup	
1 cup/250 ml water	**Ice cream churn or freezer (p.509)**

1 For the sugar syrup: heat the water and the sugar in a saucepan until dissolved. Bring to a boil, simmer 2 minutes and leave to cool. Purée the raspberries and work them through a sieve to remove the seeds; there should be 1 cup/250 ml of purée. Stir the sugar syrup, lemon juice or kirsch, and water into the purée and taste, adding sugar or lemon juice if needed. Chill the mixture and taste again.
2 Freeze the mixture in an ice cream churn or freezer, and store in the freezer. Serve in stemmed glasses decorated with fresh raspberries, mint sprigs or chocolate leaves.

Variations

Lemon sorbet Substitute ¾ cup/175 ml lemon juice and the finely grated zest of 3 lemons for raspberry purée. After freezing, pack into chilled hollowed lemon shells and top with the lid.
Orange or tangerine sorbet Substitute 2 cups/500 ml fresh orange or tangerine juice for raspberry purée and water. After freezing, pack into chilled fruit shells as for lemon sorbet.
Black currant sorbet Substitute black currants for raspberries. Simmer them with the sugar syrup until very soft, 15-20 minutes, then purée and sieve them. Serve in stemmed glasses, topped with a spoonful of cassis liqueur and frosted black currants (p.474).
Champagne or wine sorbet Substitute 1 bottle (3 cups/750 ml) Champagne or wine for raspberries and water. Pour a few spoonfuls of Champagne or wine over sorbet when serving and top with candied lemon or orange zest (p.475).

ICE CREAM

The classic ice cream made with egg custard is incomparable. The standard proportions are 2 cups/500 ml milk, ⅔ cup/135 g sugar and 6-8 egg yolks, plus 1 cup/250 ml cream, but there are many variations. Opinion is divided as to whether the cream should be cooked with the milk as custard, or should be whipped and stirred in for lightness. For richness, cream may replace some or all of the milk. To make so-called French ice cream, more egg yolks are added to the standard custard.

Ice cream based only on milk or light cream, or even a mixture of both, is common in Italy and in the United States, where it is often called Philadelphia ice cream. Sweetened with sugar, it can support the full gamut of flavors, but must rely on top-quality basic ingredients for success. Unlike custard-based ice creams, this mixture need not be cooked before freezing, but the cream is often boiled to reduce and enrich it.

In mixtures such as frozen yogurt or ice creams with soft cheese, the egg-yolk custard may also be dropped; its thickening power is not needed. Mixtures made with fruit purée may be thickened with gelatin. **Note** When tart fruit purée or juice is used, or a sweet ingredient (like chocolate), is added to the basic mixture, proportions of sugar may need to be adjusted.

Flavorings for ice cream are legion – commercial varieties range from traditional chocolate chip, butter pecan and rum raisin to the picturesque rocky road (chocolate with nuts and marshmallow) and even more unusual flavors such as bubble gum. Preferences vary from nation to nation – the French enjoy pistachio and praline; Italians are fond of hazelnut, while chocolate ripple is favored by the British.

Fruit ice creams such as strawberry should be flavored with a purée that is thick and concentrated so the custard is not thinned. As in sorbet, fresh raw fruit must be at its peak of ripeness for its aroma to survive the chilling process, otherwise it is better to poach the fruit in syrup before using. **Note** Fruits with too much acid may curdle an egg custard; for example, the zest of orange and lemon is used in ice cream, with little or no juice, and fruits such as plums must be cooked before they are puréed and added to the mixture.

A vast range of sauces, toppings and accompaniments transform plain ice cream into the coupe of *grande cuisine* and the sundae of the American ice cream parlor. Escoffier's Peach Melba with its vanilla ice cream, poached peach halves, and fresh raspberry purée is known around the world, as are his *poires Belle Hélène* (pears, chocolate sauce, and vanilla ice cream). A "banana split" is just one of the other possibilities — a halved banana with scoops of ice cream, served with a hot fudge sauce and topped with whipped cream.

USEFUL INFORMATION

Portion 1 qt/1 L serves 4-6.
Storage *Ice cream*: freeze 1 month; let ice cream soften slightly in refrigerator ½ hour before serving. *Frozen yogurt*: freeze 3-4 days.
Toppings Crushed praline (p.419), *nougatine* (p.419), caramel or toffee (p.418); toasted flaked or shredded almonds; toasted chopped hazelnuts; shredded coconut; grated chocolate or sprinkles; chocolate decorations (p.423); Chantilly cream (p.70).
Accompaniments macerated fresh fruit; poached fruit; *tulipe* wafer cookies (p.388); *tuile* cookies; *amaretti*; macaroons; ladyfingers (p.396); hot chocolate fudge sauce (p.425); butterscotch sauce (p.67); caramel sauce (p.67); Melba sauce (p.66).

Ice cream dessert recipes

Peach Melba For each serving, put a scoop of vanilla ice cream in a coupe glass and set two poached peach halves on each side. Top with ¼ cup/60 ml Melba sauce (p.66), and sprinkle with toasted, shredded almonds.

Banana split For each serving, cut a peeled banana in half and set in a sundae dish on each side of two scoops of vanilla ice cream. Add ¼ cup/60 ml hot fudge sauce (p.425) and a rosette of Chantilly cream. Sprinkle with chopped toasted almonds and top with a maraschino cherry.

Coupe Chateaubriand For each serving, layer one scoop each of vanilla and peach ice cream in a parfait glass, with ½ cup/125 ml sliced fresh strawberries and 2 tbsp/30 ml brandy. Top with a rosette of Chantilly cream and a fresh strawberry.

Dusty road For each serving, put one scoop each chocolate and coffee ice cream in a sundae dish. Add ¼ cup/60 ml each chocolate and butterscotch sauces (p.67). Top with a rosette of Chantilly cream, chopped, toasted almonds and cocoa powder.

Oranges en surprise Serves 4. Cut off the top and scoop the flesh from 4 large navel oranges. Half-fill with 1 cup/125 g mixed fruit macerated in 1-2 tbsp kirsch. Fill the oranges with 1 cup/250 ml vanilla or strawberry ice cream. Seal the top with rosettes of Italian meringue made with ½ cup/100 g sugar, 6 tbsp water and 2 egg whites (p.437). Brown in a 450°F/230°C oven, 4-5 minutes.

Vanilla ice cream

This is the classic ice cream, flavored with the pure sweet taste of vanilla. Chocolate sauce or fudge sauce (p.425) is a perfect rich accompaniment.

Makes 1 qt/1 L to serve 6

vanilla custard made with 2 cups/500 ml milk, vanilla bean or 1 tsp vanilla extract, 6-8 egg yolks and ⅔ cup/135 g sugar	1 cup/250 ml heavy cream, lightly whipped
	Ice cream churn or freezer

1 Make the custard (p.67) and chill it until very cold. Freeze it in an ice cream churn or freezer until slushy. Add the whipped cream, making sure to combine it thoroughly, and continue freezing until the mixture is firm.
2 Lift out the paddle. Pack down the ice cream in the churn, or pack it into a chilled container, cover tightly and store in the freezer. If chilling for more than 12 hours, let ice cream soften in refrigerator 30 minutes before serving.

Variations

Banana ice cream Makes 1½ qt/1.5 L. Peel and purée 3 bananas with the juice of 1 orange. Sweeten to taste with confectioners' sugar and stir into the chilled vanilla custard.

Coffee ice cream Makes 1 qt/1 L. Omit the vanilla in the custard and stir 3 tbsp instant coffee into the custard while still hot.

Praline ice cream Strain vanilla custard and stir in praline (p.419) made with 1 cup/150 g unblanched almonds and ¾ cup/150 g sugar.

Strawberry ice cream Makes 1½ qt/1.5 L. Purée 1 qt/500 g fresh strawberries to make 1½ cups/375 ml and stir into the chilled vanilla custard with 1-2 tbsp kirsch or lemon juice. Sweeten the mixture to taste.

Peach or plum ice cream Makes 2 qts/2 L. Halve 3 lb/1.4 kg peaches or plums and poach in sugar syrup (p.414) made with 1 qt/1 L water and 1½ cups/300 g sugar. Drain the fruit, purée it, and work it through a sieve. There should be 1 qt/1 L of purée. Stir the purée into the chilled vanilla custard with a few drops of almond extract for peaches, or 1-2 tbsp kirsch for plums.

Chocolate chip ice cream Add 1 cup/250 g (or to taste) chopped chocolate chips to vanilla ice ceam with the whipped cream.

Peppermint ice cream Omit the vanilla and add 1 tbsp peppermint extract (or to taste), and a few drops of green coloring to the cooled custard. Chocolate chips can also be added (as for chocolate chip ice cream).

Pears Belle Hélène

This dessert dates from the nineteenth century and Offenbach's opera, *La Belle Hélène*.

Serves 4

3 cups/750 ml vanilla ice cream	sugar syrup (p.414) made with water, sugar and vanilla bean or ½ tsp vanilla extract
4 whole pears	
chocolate sauce (p.425)	

1 Make the vanilla ice cream and freeze. Peel and core the pears, leaving the stems. Make the sugar syrup in a small deep pan and add the pears. Poach them until tender and transparent, 15-20 minutes. Leave to cool in the syrup, then drain them.
2 Make the chocolate sauce. Set the pears on chilled plates and add 1-2 scoops ice cream. Coat each pear with chocolate sauce and serve at once.

BOMBES, PARFAITS & FROZEN SOUFFLES

Even richer than ice cream are the frozen desserts that need no churning to be smooth when frozen. Simple to make, they take several hours to set firmly in the freezer. Most common are bombes, made with a mousse of egg yolks (or whole eggs) and sugar mixed with an equal quantity of whipped cream. For a pure white color, Italian meringue may be substituted for the egg yolk mousse. To balance such richness, forceful flavors such as brandy, kirsch, fruit purée, even anise, are added, often with nuts and candied fruits for texture.

When making a bombe, the mixture is usually set in a smooth domed mold. First the mold is lined with one or two layers of contrasting ice cream, or occasionally sorbet, then the bombe mixture itself is added and chilled. When cut in wedges, colorful striped slices emerge. Typical combinations are French *bombe tutti-frutti*, with the inside of the mold lined with strawberry ice cream, then filled with vanilla bombe mixture flavored with candied fruits macerated in maraschino liqueur, or *bombe Nesselrode* in which vanilla ice cream lines the mold and surrounds a mixture of glacé chestnuts flavored with raisins and kirsch.

A parfait is based on essentially the same mixture as a bombe. It may be frozen on its own in a parfait glass (a stemmed glass thick enough to withstand freezing) or layered with macerated fruits, crushed macaroon crumbs and other fillings. The traditional flavor for a parfait is coffee, but popular alternatives include chocolate, praline, maple, liqueurs and fruit purées.

Frozen soufflés are an alternative bombe presentation, piled high above the rim of one large or several individual soufflé dishes within a paper collar that is removed before serving. Often whipped egg white or Italian meringue is folded into the basic mixture to give a hint of the lightness of a hot soufflé.

The bombe family of desserts is so rich that they need little decoration. After unmolding, a bombe may be given a ruff of whipped cream around the base, with a rosette for parfaits or miniature soufflés. A large frozen soufflé may be simply dusted with powdered cocoa or finely crushed macaroons. Toppings such as fresh berries or chocolate leaves should be minimal, but a contrasting tart fruit sauce is a welcome accompaniment.

USEFUL INFORMATION

Portion 1 qt/1 L serves 4-6.
Storage Freeze 3 months. *Bombe with ice cream:* freeze 1 month.
Toppings Chantilly cream rosettes (p.70); frosted berries (p.474); chocolate decorations (p.423); candied citrus zest (p.474); crushed praline or macaroon crumbs; chopped nuts; mint sprigs.
Accompaniments Macerated fresh fruit; brandied fruits; Melba sauce (p.66); chocolate sauce (p.425); coffee custard sauce (p.67); caramel sauce (p.67).
Typical dishes *Bombe: Grimaldi* (vanilla ice cream, mousse flavored with kummel, candied violets and pistachio nuts, France); *aux marrons* (chocolate ice cream, rum, chestnut purée, France); *boule de neige* (chocolate ice cream, orange, curaçao, France); *à l'abricot* (vanilla ice cream, apricot purée, France); *Harlem* (chocolate and vanilla ice cream, rum, raisins, France); *pralinée aux noix caramel* (vanilla ice cream, caramelized walnuts, France); *de la passion* (chocolate ice cream, passion fruit, whipped cream, France). *Parfait:* chocolate, strawberry and vanilla (USA); almond-cherry (UK); praline (France). *Soufflé: au Cointreau* (orange, France); chocolate mint (USA); with prunes, brandy (France); caramel (France); with rum, bananas (France).

CLASSIC FROZEN DESSERTS

Semifreddo An Italian frozen dessert, similar to ice cream but with a high cream or sugar content that prevents hard freezing, thus creating the illusion that it is less cold than ice cream. The name of the dessert in Italian means "half cold".

Spumoni A molded dessert with an outer layer of ice cream and interior of *semifreddo*. It resembles a bombe, but is not made in a hemispherical mold.

Cassata The typical Italian version of bombe; a mixture of Italian meringue, whipped cream and candied fruit, surrounded by layers of ice cream.

Biscuit glacé A variation of bombe mixture that uses Italian meringue in addition to the usual mousse and whipped cream. A *biscuit glacé* is molded in a square or round mold to resemble a cake. The basic mixture can also be used to make frozen soufflés.

Baked Alaska (Fr. *omelette à la norvégienne*) Ice cream set on a layer of cake, encased in meringue and baked to serve with a warm coating of browned meringue. Italian meringue is preferred so that the dessert can be assembled long in advance and frozen; it is then browned in the oven just before serving.

Biscuit tortoni An Italian mixture of whipped cream and confectioners' sugar combined with *amaretti* macaroons and sweet sherry, frozen in small molds or to form a block. Crushed *amaretti* are usually sprinkled on top just before serving. Apricot sauce is a popular accompaniment.

Ice cream layer cake Alternating layers of ice cream and sponge cake frozen to resemble a layer cake and cut in wedges to serve, often with a hot fudge sauce (p.425). Popular flavor combinations are chocolate sponge with mint chocolate chip ice cream, or vanilla sponge with coffee or praline ice cream.

Zucotto A dome-shaped Italian ice-cream cake with whipped cream and chocolate, soaked in liqueur.

Christmas ice pudding A frozen version of Christmas pudding containing rum-soaked dried fruits mixed into a chocolate- and chestnut-flavored egg custard, lightened with whipped cream. The mixture is frozen in a lined pudding basin and unmolded before serving to resemble a traditional Christmas pudding.

Bombe mixture

A wide variety of flavorings such as fruit purée, chocolate or coffee, praline, nuts and spirits or liqueurs, may be added to this basic vanilla bombe mixture.

Makes 2 cups/500 ml

1 cup/200 g sugar	½ cup/125 ml heavy cream, lightly whipped
½ cup/125 ml water	
4 egg yolks	1 tsp vanilla extract

1 In a small saucepan, heat the sugar with the water until dissolved, then boil until the syrup reaches the soft ball stage (p.415), 239°F/115°C on a sugar thermometer. Meanwhile beat the egg yolks until just mixed. Gradually pour in the hot syrup, beating constantly. Beat as fast as possible for 5 minutes, then continue beating at low speed until the mixture is cool and forms a thick mousse, about 10 minutes.
2 Fold in the lightly whipped cream with the vanilla. **Note** The mousse mixture must be cool or the cream will lose its lightness.

FILLING & UNMOLDING A BOMBE

A charlotte mold or deep metal bowl may be used instead of the traditional bombe mold. (p.508).

1 Chill the mold over ice or in the freezer. The vanilla ice cream should be soft enough to shape. If necessary, let it stand in the refrigerator.

2 Line the ice cream over the base and sides of the mold in a 1-2 in/2.5-4 cm layer, smoothing a central hollow with the back of a spoon or a metal spatula. Freeze it until firm, 2-3 hours.

3 Fill the mold with contrasting bombe mixture (below) and smooth the top level with a metal spatula. Cover with wax paper and the lid and freeze until very firm, at least 8 hours.

4 Dip the mold in cool water for 30-60 seconds. Lift it out, wipe it dry, and run the point of a knife round the edge of the mixture.

5 Set a chilled serving plate on top of the bombe, turn upside down and lift off the mold. If the bombe sticks, hold a hot damp cloth against the mold for a few moments. Cut the bombe in wedges for serving, adding a sauce if you like.

Bombe recipes

Bombe Alhambra Serves 6-8. Line a 1½ qt/1.5 L bombe mold with 1 pt/500 ml vanilla ice cream. Purée 2 cups/250 g strawberries with the juice of half a lemon and sugar to taste. Fold the purée into 2 cups/500 ml bombe mixture with 2 tbsp kirsch. Fill into the bombe and freeze. Unmold and decorate with a ruff of Chantilly cream and fresh whole strawberries. Serve with a purée of fresh strawberries.

Bombe Francillon Serves 6-8. Line a 1 qt/1 L bombe mold with 1 pt/500 ml coffee ice cream. Fold 4 oz/125 g grated semisweet chocolate and 2 tbsp brandy into 2 cups/500 ml bombe mixture. Fill into the bombe and freeze. Unmold and decorate with a ruff of Chantilly cream and chocolate decorations (p.423).

Bombe Monselet Serves 6-8. Line a 1 qt/1 L bombe mold with 1 pt/500 ml tangerine sorbet. Fold ½ cup/65 g finely chopped, candied orange peel macerated in 3-4 tbsp Port wine into 2 cups/ 500 ml bombe mixture. Fill into the mold and freeze. Unmold and decorate the top with rosettes of whipped cream, crowning them with candied orange julienne (p.474).

Parfait recipes

Coffee parfait Serves 4. When making bombe mixture, add to the cooled egg mousse 1½ tbsp instant coffee dissolved in 3 tbsp hot water. Layer the mixture in parfait glasses with ¾ cup/125 g crushed macaroons soaked in 2-3 tbsp Amaretto or Cointreau liqueur. Just before serving, top each dessert with a rosette of whipped cream and a mint sprig or a whole fresh strawberry. Serve whole macaroons as an accompaniment.

Chocolate hazelnut parfait Serves 4. When making bombe mixture, substitute 3 egg whites for the egg yolks. Fold 5 oz/150 g chopped chocolate, melted on a plate over hot water, into the egg white mixture, followed by ½ cup/75 g coarsely chopped toasted hazelnuts. Finally fold in the whipped cream. Freeze the mixture in a bombe mold. Unmold and decorate the base with a ruff of whipped cream and chocolate decorations (p.423).

Frozen soufflé and dessert recipes

Frozen praline soufflé Serves 6. When making bombe mixture, add praline (p.419) made with 1 cup/150 g whole, unblanched almonds and ¾ cup/150 g sugar to the cooled egg mousse. With the whipped cream, fold in 3 egg whites, stiffly whipped and folded with 2 tbsp sugar to a light meringue. Freeze in 6 individual soufflé dishes fitted with paper collars. For serving, sprinkle with powdered cocoa and discard the collars.

Frozen raspberry soufflé Serves 6-8. When making bombe mixture, substitute 2 egg whites for the egg yolks. Purée 1½ cups/ 375 g raspberries, sieving to remove seeds. Stir the purée into the egg white mixture before folding in the cream. Freeze in 6-8 individual soufflé dishes fitted with paper collars and top each soufflé with a raspberry and a sprig of mint.

Semifreddo al cioccolato Serves 6-8. Beat 2 cups/500 ml heavy cream until soft peaks form. Beat in ¾ cups/150 g sugar until stiff peaks form. Fold in 4 oz/125 g grated semisweet chocolate followed by 6 egg whites stiffly beaten with 2 tbsp/25 g sugar. Pour into a 2-2½ qt/2.5 L mold and freeze until firm, about 6 hours. Unmould as for a bombe and slice for serving.

FRUIT & NUTS

N O FRESH FOOD has been subjected to more technological changes in modern times than fruit. Disease-resistant varieties of familiar fruits are being developed constantly, to give a high yield over a long season, to withstand transportation and to keep well. Many of these new fruits are hybrids, crossbred from cultivated or natural parent plants, while others, called cultivars (meaning cultivated varieties), are developed under controlled conditions in greenhouses or on farms.

Today, fruit growth can be managed so that an entire crop reaches the same size and maturity at a given moment. Modern storage methods allow most fruit to be held in more or less static condition until the ripening process is "switched on", often through the stimulus of ethylene gas, which is already produced by fruit under natural ripening conditions. In theory, fruit should reach the market in a perfectly ripe condition, despite, in some cases, having been separated from the tree or vine long before.

Nonetheless, home-grown fruit that ripens before being picked tastes especially good, and with greater or lesser effort (depending on location and climate) the amateur gardener can outperform the commercial grower, at least for a brief season in the year. Small farmers' markets often carry produce that is exceptional because it is locally picked and tree-ripened. Rarer varieties of fruit can be found that are not viable on a large commercial scale. Moreover, a single variety may vary greatly from place to place, as well as from season to season.

Such wealth of choice is a luxury that has no place in mass markets. The only way fruit supplies can be stabilized year-round at low cost is by careful control of cultivation and ripening. It is tempting to condemn the changes modern technology has brought regarding fruit, but these are counter-balanced by huge benefits. Thanks to rapid refrigerated transport, many fruits are now available all year, the result of careful timing of supplies between temperate and tropical regions. Exotic fruits have also arrived in many markets. Only a few generations ago, fruit was a seasonal treat, spoilage was a recurring problem and all but native fruits were scarce and expensive. Nowadays, supermarket shelves contain a wide choice of fruits from around the world.

Choosing fruit

Maturity and ripeness are two different stages in the development of a fruit. For the commercial grower, maturity is all-important, as this marks the point at which metabolic changes are complete and most fruit is poised to ripen, if necessary, by artificial means, after picking from the tree or vine. It is during ripening that a fruit acquires its characteristic flavor and texture. A fruit that has been picked before it is mature will not ripen properly although its skin may be richly colored. This is why fruits that look tempting on the market shelf are frequently disappointing when eaten.

Generally, the heavier a piece of fruit is in the hand, the juicier and better tasting it will be. It should be fragrant and soft enough to yield to gentle pressure from the fingers. Avoid fruit that is bruised or beginning to turn moldy. Overripe fruit smells musty and often has soft or dark patches; the flesh inside is likely to be dark or rotten. Once ripe, fruit cannot be stored very long, so buy only as much as you need.

Storing fruit

The degree of ripeness of fruit when you buy it determines how long it can be kept. Some fruits ripen relatively slowly after they mature – apples, pears and oranges, for example. Others, such as grapes and berries, are ripe or overripe within a few days of maturity and thus cannot be stored for long.

Fully ripened fruit should be refrigerated immediately, first discarding any overripe or moldy pieces – berries are particularly susceptible to mold. Handle fruit gently, as bruising or crushing encourages rot, and wrap it loosely in a brown paper or plastic bag punctured with holes.

If a fruit needs to ripen further at home, it should be left at room temperature. It will ripen more quickly if wrapped, so store the fruit in a brown paper bag punctured with holes. If the fruit is extremely hard, the process can be accelerated by adding a very ripe piece of fruit to the bag. Note, however, that some fruits such as apples, nectarines, berries and pears will rot if left with their skins touching, so if ripening them for more than a day, spread them out separately, individually wrapped in paper if you wish. For ways to preserve fruits for longer storage, see individual fruits and also Preserving and Freezing (p.484).

Cleaning fruit

Fruits that are eaten with their skins may be washed gently in cold or warm water but should never be left to soak. Water encourages rotting in soft fruits, so avoid washing delicate fruits like berries (unless they are very sandy). Some fruits, such as apples and citrus fruits, are preserved with an edible wax that can usually be removed by scrubbing the fruit under running water.

Note Most modern pesticides used on fruit cannot be eliminated by washing. However, peeling fruit usually reduces contamination.

Preventing discoloration

When exposed to air, certain tannins and enzymes in fruits such as apples, peaches and pears react, turning the cut fruit brown. Acid helps prevent this: rub the cut surfaces of the fruit with a halved lemon or lime, or immerse it in acidulated water (water to which lemon or lime juice has been added). Poaching fruit in sugar syrup (p.148) immediately after cutting also preserves its color. Always peel or cut fruit with a stainless steel knife as other metals may encourage discoloration. Adding ascorbic acid (vitamin C) to fruits that are to be frozen may also help. Fruits that discolor should be prepared as quickly as possible, just before they are needed.

Cooking with fruit

Fruit provides inspiration for innumerable desserts and may also be served alone, with cheese, or as an accompaniment to poultry and meat dishes. It provides the basic flavoring in creams, mousses and charlottes, not to mention ice creams and sorbets, all discussed in the Cold Desserts and Ice Creams chapter (p.430). Pastry is another natural partner for fruit. America is famous for its apple pie, France for pear *feuilletés* and Austria for *strudel*. Many fruit desserts such as soufflés, batter puddings and crêpes, also use dairy products and eggs.

Sugar and lemon are to fruit as salt and pepper are to meat; a sprinkling of either enlivens uncooked fruit and develops the sweet flavor of cooked preparations, especially when paired with spices such as ginger and cinnamon for compotes and pie fillings. Lime juice also develops the taste of fruit, particularly of melon, mango and papaya. A dash of white wine complements the heavy perfume of mellow fruits such as peaches, pears and sweet berries, while peaches soaked in brandy, cherries in kirsch and apricots in Amaretto are just a few of the many ideas for using fruit with liqueurs and *eaux de vie*.

Baking fruit

A simple way of cooking fruit is to bake it. Many larger fruits act as edible baking containers for sweet and savory fillings. Baked apples are the most obvious example, but peaches and pears are other candidates for stuffing. Quinces are a more unusual choice, and may be filled with a savory stuffing such as lamb and chestnut. The cavity left by coring or pitting invites fillings such as one or two tablespoons of raisins mixed with chopped walnuts, crushed macaroons, or cottage cheese mixed with chopped, dried apricots. The fruit itself may be studded with cloves or slivered almonds for extra flavor.

Apples are cored and baked with their skins, which must be scored around the diameter to allow room for the apple pulp to expand as it cooks, without bursting the skin. Bananas are usually peeled, although green bananas can be baked in their skins. Other fruits may also be peeled, as well as cored and pitted. To preserve the color of peeled fruit for baking, the flesh is often rubbed with lemon juice.

Fruit mixtures also bake successfully. Good combinations include an assortment of berries as well as red or black currants for sharpness; blackberries with apple; cranberries with orange; apples with plums, or with figs, perhaps baked under a topping. Baked fruits are often served as a side dish with meats such as pork or game, or as part of a braise of rich meats and poultry. Plums, for instance, pair well with pork and ham, bananas with chicken, and apricots with lamb.

To bake fruit, set it in a shallow baking dish and bake at 350°F/175°C, basting with a mixture of butter, honey, white or brown sugar, wine and other fruit juices or spices. A tablespoon each of butter, sugar and liquid per serving is an average proportion. For cooking times, see individual fruits.

Many baked fruit desserts are only slightly more complicated than plain baked fruit. They include fruit crumble or crisp – a flour, sugar and butter topping that is spread on the fruit to bake. A British dessert, Eve's pudding, consists of apple with cake batter poured on top and baked. In Italy, fruits are often layered with a sweet breadcrumb mixture, while in a number of countries baked batter puddings are often filled with fruit, such as the French *clafoutis* (Cherry batter pudding, p.368). In the United States, regional baked fruit specialties abound: a "buckle" has layers of cake, blueberries and crumble, while a "cobbler", "slump" or "grunt" consists of fruit topped with either a dumpling or a biscuit dough, or a shortcrust pastry lattice.

A novel way to bake fruit is *en papillote* – in a parchment paper case that puffs up in the oven to a brown balloon (p.121). A minimum amount of liquid is added, since the fruit will exude juice during baking. Fruits such as peaches, plums, strawberries, bananas and kiwi fruit are well-suited to this method; they may be sautéed lightly in butter before wrapping.

PEELING FRUIT

Many fresh fruits need little preparation apart from washing. Some may need to be peeled and cored or seeded. The peel of firm fruits such as apples and pears may be removed in strips with a knife or peeler, while the tougher, loose skins of citrus may be pulled off in pieces. To avoid bruising, treat softer fruits such as mango, or very ripe fruits with extra care. Soft-skinned fruit such as peaches may be blanched so the skin can be peeled off easily, while fruits consisting of soft pulp or seeds, such as passion fruit, are cut in half and the flesh and seeds scooped out with a spoon.

To peel loose-skinned fruit: hold the fruit in one hand. With a vegetable knife, slit the skin lengthwise in 4 or 5 places. Grasp each piece of skin between your thumb and the knife and gently pull the skin away from the fruit.

To peel firm fruit: hold the fruit in one hand and use a vegetable knife or peeler to peel the skin from the fruit in strips.
Note For round fruit such as apples, the skin can be removed by peeling around the fruit in one long spiral.

To peel soft-skinned fruit: immerse the whole fruit in boiling water. Leave for 10-30 seconds, depending on the ripeness of the fruit, then transfer to iced water. With a knife, loosen the skin at the stem end and gently peel the skin from the flesh.

POACHING FRUIT

Poached fruit, often called fruit compote or stewed fruit, is one of the simplest preparations and may be served hot or cold. For poaching, choose juicy but firm fruit that is not too ripe. Peel, core or stone the fruit, leaving it whole, or cutting it in halves or smaller pieces (see individual fruits). Stems may be left on whole fruits for decoration or to help lift the fruit out of a hot syrup.

Fruit is poached in a simple sugar syrup (p.414) until just soft enough to be cut with a spoon, but not enough to fall apart. The proportion of sugar to water in the syrup is important: with less sugar, the syrup penetrates the fruit more easily, cooking it evenly to the center. In a concentrated syrup, fruit takes longer to become tender and has less tendency to break up. Therefore whole fruits such as pears need a light syrup, while soft berries or very ripe fruits are best poached in a heavier syrup so that they keep their shape for as long as possible.

The syrup for poaching may be flavored with vanilla (preferably a whole bean), lemon juice or wine, and spices such as cinnamon and cloves. Whole peppercorns, a modern favorite with poached pears in red wine, add an intriguing bite. Often a few spoonfuls of brandy or liqueur are added to the syrup at the end of poaching.

Poached fruit may be served alone as a dessert, topped with plain or whipped cream, *crème fraîche* or vanilla custard (p.67). It is used to fill sweet tarts, stuff crêpes and flavor baking powder breads (pp.359-61), and is puréed for creams, mousses and ice creams (p.430). Compotes of tart fruits such as sour cherries or cranberries often accompany meats, poultry or game.

1 Add prepared fruit to the hot syrup and press a piece of paper on top to immerse it.

2 Poach gently, with the syrup scarcely bubbling, so the fruit holds its shape. A vanilla bean can be added for flavor.

3 To test if the fruit is cooked, lift it out of the poaching liquid with a slotted spoon and pierce the flesh with the point of a knife. The cooking time will depend on the type of fruit as well as ripeness. When done, poached fruit is translucent and just tender.

Broiling fruit

Broiled fruit is a refreshing alternative to baked fruit, particularly in summer when an outdoor barbecue grill may be used. Fruits suitable for the intense heat of broiling are bananas, pineapple, apples, pears, figs and peaches. Under very high heat, grapefruit, plums and apricots also respond well. The fruit may be cut in slices or chunks, one attractive idea being to string mixed fruits on skewers and cook them as kebabs. Otherwise the fruit must be set on an oiled close-meshed barbecue grill, or on an oiled baking sheet if you are using an overhead broiler. A knob of butter or a topping of sugar, honey, maple syrup or fruit liqueur supplies richness to the fruit to be broiled, while lemon or lime juice enlivens the flavor without being overpowering. Sweet spices such as cinnamon and ginger may be included, but in moderation, as they scorch easily. Fruit softens according to type but usually takes three to five minutes on each side. Broiled fruit is delicious served with ice cream, vanilla custard or sabayon sauce (p.105), and as an accompaniment to meats.

Sautéing and caramelizing fruit

To give fruit a rich syrupy flavor, it can be sautéed in butter. Cherries, apples, pears, peaches, pineapple and bananas are good candidates as they keep their shape well. The fruit should be peeled, cored or seeded if necessary, then cut into pieces of equal size that cook evenly. Apples are sliced into rings, pears and peaches cut in wedges, pineapple into chunks, and bananas into diagonal slices or long halves. Plums and apricots should be halved and pitted before sautéing, while small fruits such as cherries may only need pitting and stemming.

Sugar-dipped cherries being added to hot butter.

If the fruit is to be served with meat, onion may be added first for flavor, or the fruit may be cooked in bacon fat instead of butter, allowing about one tablespoon of fat per serving. Do not crowd the pan with fruit, and cook it briskly so it does not soften too much and stew in its own juices. If you like, add a sprinkling of sugar and season the fruit with salt and pepper. Cook it until just tender, five to eight minutes depending on the type of fruit and its stage of ripeness. Sautéed apples or apricots are delicious with pork, peaches with chicken, or bananas with spicy sausages and curries. A version of the celebrated dish from Normandy, Pork with apples and cream (p.228), uses caramelized sautéed apples, together with Calvados apple brandy.

When it is to be eaten as a dessert, sautéed fruit is caramelized by adding extra sugar (one to two tablespoons for each serving). This may be done either by dipping the fruit in sugar before frying, or by sprinkling sugar over the fruit when it is already in the pan, then turning the fruit sugar-side down. As the fruit cooks, so the sugar caramelizes to form a delicious golden glaze. Baste the fruit with the syrup that forms as it cooks in the butter, taking care that it does not stick to the pan and scorch.

FLAMBEING FRUIT

For a festive dessert, fruit is often flambéed, or flamed, after being sautéed, by adding a spirit such as brandy, rum or kirsch, or any liqueur. Brandy and rum blend with almost any fruit, while kirsch, the cherry-based *eau de vie*, suits stone fruits like plums, peaches, and of course, cherries themselves. A fruit-based liqueur may be added to intensify the flavor of the fruit, or to change its color. As well as looking spectacular, flambéed fruit tastes delicious; it can be served alone with ladyfingers or *petits fours*, but is best of all spooned on top of crêpes or ice cream.

1 RIGHT To flambé fruit, sauté it in butter and sugar until it is tender and caramelized, basting it with the syrup produced by the fruit juices.

2 Pour in the alcohol, allowing 1-2 tablespoons per serving – do not add too much alcohol at a time as the flames can be fierce.

3 Hold a lighted match to the side of the pan, or carefully tilt the edge of the pan over a gas flame so that the flame just catches the alcohol. Baste the fruit with the flaming alcohol until the flame is almost extinguished. Transfer the fruit and liquid to hot serving plates and serve at once.

Note Keep your face and hair away from the pan while flambéing fruit.

Deep-frying fruit

Only a few fruits are suited to this delectable treatment, as they must withstand intense heat. Apples, pears, bananas, apricots and pineapple are the most successful, but strawberries or well-drained peaches also have lusciously soft centers when deep-fried. Fruit that is too soft will fall apart in the hot oil.

The fruit should be cut into even slices or chunks, and dried before being dipped in a simple batter (p.105). If the fruit is too moist, the batter will not stick. For extra flavor, fruit may be marinated first in brandy, rum or liqueur, but should then be drained and sprinkled with confectioners' sugar before being coated with batter. Wine or liqueur may be added to the batter for extra flavor. Deep-fried pieces take three to four minutes in oil at 375°F/190°C. Like all deep-fried foods, they must be drained on absorbent paper when cooked and should be served as soon as possible while still crisp, with a sprinkling of confectioners' sugar (see Fruit fritters in beer batter, p.106). Banana fritters may also be served as an accompaniment to chicken or ham.

Fruit purées and sauces

Fruit purées, either raw or cooked, are important as the basis of sorbets, dessert gelatins and refreshing fruit soups as well as fruit paste candies. They flavor soufflés, mousses and ice creams (Cold Desserts and Ice Creams, p.430). Simple purées are made from a single fruit: apple sauce (p.66) for instance, is nothing more than cooked, flavored and puréed apple, and Melba sauce (p.66) is simply sweetened raspberry purée. In fact many fresh or thawed frozen fruits may be puréed to create a delicate sauce to spoon underneath or on top of desserts. Other purées are made from a combination of two fruits, as in the popular American rhubarb and strawberry sauce. Some fruit sauces are made especially for serving with savory dishes. Gooseberries make a pleasantly sharp sauce for serving with smoked mackerel, while plum sauce is delicious with ham or gammon, as well as being popular in Chinese cuisine.

Coulis is the French term for a purée that is just thin enough to pour easily (couler means "to run"). Traditionally, a coulis is strained of seeds and skin and has some texture, but the term has come to apply to any fruit sauce, regardless of its consistency. Kissel, a fruit dessert found in eastern Europe, is made with berries or fruit juice thickened with cornstarch, arrowroot or gelatin and served chilled with heavy clotted or whipped cream. Soft kissel is also served warm as a sauce for savory dishes. In Germany, a similar dish is called rote Grütze or "red pudding".

Fruit soups

Cold fruit soups have long been popular in Scandinavia and Hungary and appear more and more frequently in modern menus as a refreshing end to a meal. A few cold soups are based on thinly puréed fresh fruits such as melon or peaches, which have plenty of perfumed juice. However, most are made by simmering fruit with a little sugar until soft, then working it through a sieve. The purée should be thin and piquant, and is often enriched with sweet wine. Choose tart fruits such as sour cherries and cranberries, especially when the recipe calls for an enrichment of heavy cream or crème fraîche, adding a sprinkling of spice such as cinnamon or nutmeg. Fruit may be used to make hot soups too. These are usually served at the start of a meal.

Other cooking methods for fruit

Whole fruits wrapped in dumplings are common in some European countries, served with vanilla custard or sour cream. If puff pastry is used and the fruit is baked in the oven, dumplings are particularly delicious. In Asia, fried fruits are dipped in boiling sugar syrup at the hard crack stage, then cooled immediately in water to give a crunchy coating to the soft fruit.

For fruit fondue, pieces of fresh fruit are dipped in melted chocolate (p.421) or butterscotch sauce (p.67). Often served as part of a petits fours platter are pieces of fruit dipped in sugar syrup (p.416) or partly dipped in chocolate or fondant.

PUREEING FRUIT

Soft fruits can be puréed raw, but firmer fruits like cherries or red currants, and fruits that discolor easily like pears and peaches, must be cooked first. Only a few fruits are puréed either raw or cooked; pineapple is one example. To develop flavor, the fruit is often sweetened, either during cooking or after puréeing. Fruit liqueurs such as Grand Marnier, eaux de vie like framboise, or extracts of fruit or nuts may also be added. Fruit for puréeing should be peeled, hulled or cored if necessary, and any stones or pits removed. Small seeds will be strained out during puréeing.

The consistency of the finished purée can be important. A fool, for example, is improved if the fruit has texture, while a sorbet should be made with a smooth purée.

1 **To cook fruit before puréeing:** poach (p.448) and drain, reserving the syrup. Alternatively, bake the fruit (p.447), or cut it in pieces and simmer it until tender in 1 in/2.5 cm of water, adding a little sugar if it tastes very sour.

2 **For a rough purée:** mash raw or cooked fruit with a potato masher, or work it in a food processor. Cooked rhubarb, apples or gooseberries, and raw strawberries or pineapple are suited to working in a food processor. (**Note** Food processors or blenders do not remove fibers, seeds or skin.)

3 **For a medium purée:** work raw or cooked fruit a little at a time in a blender or purée it thoroughly in a food processor. Alternatively, work it through the coarse grid of a food mill.

4 **For a fine purée:** push raw or cooked fruit a little at a time through a drum sieve, pressing it through with a pestle or a plastic scraper, or work it through a food mill (p.506) fitted with the fine disk. Alternatively, purée it in a blender or food processor, then strain it through a fine sieve to obtain the smoothest possible texture.

5 Flavor the purée to taste with granulated or confectioners' sugar, and liqueur if you like. If the purée is too stiff, it may be thinned with the syrup from poaching, or with water.

Hungarian cherry soup

Sour cherry soup is usually served chilled in spring and summer –
the cherry season – but it is just as good served hot to open an
autumn dinner of game.

Serves 8

1 bottle (750 ml) dry white wine	3 cups/750 ml *crème fraîche* (p.70) or heavy cream
½ cup/100 g sugar (or to taste)	
1 lb/500 g sour cherries, pitted	2 tbsp kirsch
juice of 2 lemons	ground cinnamon (for sprinkling)

1 Heat the wine and sugar until the sugar is dissolved. Bring to a
boil, add the pitted cherries (p.457) and simmer 3-5 minutes.
2 Purée the soup in a food processor or blender or work it
through a food mill. Add the lemon juice and let it cool. Stir in
two-thirds of the *crème fraîche* or cream and the kirsch and taste,
adding more sugar if necessary. Cover and chill thoroughly.
3 To finish: spoon the soup into bowls. To each one, add a
spoonful of the remaining *crème fraîche* or cream, stir to marble it
and sprinkle with cinnamon.

Variation

Strawberry soup: substitute strawberries for the cherries, cooking
the strawberries only 1-2 minutes. Decorate the bowls with mint
sprigs instead of cinnamon.

Macerating fruit

Macerating is marinating as applied to fruits and occasionally to
vegetables. Quite simply, it means to steep fruit in sugar or sugar
syrup and/or some kind of alcohol, so that it softens while
absorbing the flavorings. At the same time, juice is drawn into the
macerating liquid. Soft-fleshed fruits such as melon, peach and
mango, and particularly soft berries, are the most suitable.

Several fresh fruits may be combined, macerated and chilled
for a fresh fruit salad, or a single fruit may be macerated in white
or red wine or liqueur to accompany ice cream or other cold
desserts. For a pretty effect, pile macerated fruits into a natural
fruit container, such as a scooped-out melon or pineapple (p.468),
or into a glass bowl that shows off the colors of the fruit. Fruits
may also be macerated in wine or liqueur, then combined with
whipped cream, as in strawberries *Romanoff*. The acid from the
macerating liquid thickens the cream slightly. For a refreshing
summer salad to accompany fish, poultry or spicy meats, macerate
fruits with wine and fresh herbs, or in a light citrus marinade.

Presenting raw fruit and fruit salads

Unlike most ingredients, fresh fruit needs little preparation, and
when ripe it should overflow with flavor and aroma. A mixture of
top-quality whole fruits may be presented for each diner to choose
from, or may be cut up for a salad. Fruit salads should include a
seasonal selection of fairly firm, ripe fruits of contrasting color,
texture and flavor. Choose at least four different fruits that
complement each other: good combinations include peaches,
pears, plums and grapes, different types of melon or berries, or a
mixture of citrus fruits. Fruits such as melon should not be paired
with tart ones like citrus, as the sharp flavor of the citrus would
overwhelm the milder fruit. The fruit should be peeled, if
appropriate, and cut into uniform pieces so that it is easy to eat.

Toss fruits that discolor such as peaches, apples and pears in
lemon juice as soon as they are cut. Attractive color combinations
can be achieved by choosing all green, or all red fruits.

Classic dressings for fruit salads include mixtures of sugar,
wine and liqueurs, or a light sugar syrup flavored with lemon and
vanilla. In Germany honey is often added, in the United States
yogurt and sweetened sour cream are favorite toppings, while in
Britain fresh sweet cream often accompanies fruit salad. Savory
dressings include classic vinaigrette, fruit vinaigrette and mayonnaise. Garnishes should be simple – a few chopped nuts, raisins,
chopped dates or a sprinkling of coconut.

Traditionally, fruit salads are spooned into glass or porcelain
stemmed bowls for serving, but modern chefs favor a careful
arrangement of fresh fruit pieces, with the dressing on one side of
the plate. Alternatively, hollowed-out half fruit shells, chilled, can
make attractive containers for fruit salads. Pineapple or large
melon shells can hold several servings, while half a small melon
makes an individual serving container.

Raw fruits are often combined with cooked ingredients such as
poultry, shellfish, rice and other grains. Typical examples include
Avocado and grapefruit with smoked salmon (p.470), shrimp
with rice and grapes, and figs with duck. Onions, olives, celery
and other vegetables may be included, with herbs such as mint
and parsley. Such salads are usually presented on a bed of crisp
chilled lettuce or arranged in a fan on the serving plate. Savory
salad combinations for serving with meat, poultry and fish include
Middle Eastern apricot, yogurt and tarragon, or Moroccan oranges
and radishes dressed with a fruity olive oil or vinaigrette.

Fruit is also complemented by cheese, forming a natural part of
a cheese tray (p.75); apples are traditional with Cheddar, pears
with blue cheese, and grapes with fresh cheeses such as ricotta and
goat cheeses.

Apple, pear, crab apple & quince

In the days when fruit was a luxury, apples and pears were the only fruits that could be stored for more than a week or two, which meant that they were available for more than half the year. Today there are numerous apple and pear varieties, some developed by accident and others by careful crossbreeding, and many dating back to the eighteenth or nineteenth century. However of these, barely a hundred are exploited commercially and far fewer are grown as a common crop.

For the cook, apples and pears divide simply into dessert fruits (sweet and fragrant when raw), and cooking fruits (tart and high in acidic tannin). Some types are good for eating raw but are still acid enough to poach or to give bite to a sauce. Varieties that remain firm when heated are good for sautéing, poaching or baking in a tart; those that cook quickly to a fluffy purée are best for plain baking or reducing to a sauce. For poaching or sautéing, the fruit should be firm, even slightly underripe, but for baking or puréeing it may be softer. Both apples and pears discolor when peeled or sliced, but new varieties that turn brown less quickly are being developed.

Ripe apples vary in color from green to yellow to deep red, though they are consistent within their variety. Whether an apple is crisp, soft, tart or sweet depends not only on type, but also on the season and handling during storage. The world's leading dessert apple is the crimson, slightly pointed Red Delicious, with bland, sweet flesh. Its relative, the Golden Delicious, is not far behind, acceptable for both cooking and eating. Australia's Granny Smith (now grown worldwide) is probably the most popular cooking apple in the United States, with crisp flesh that is good raw and also stands up well to long cooking.

Raw apple makes a crunchy addition to salads such as chicken salad or creamy Waldorf with celery and walnuts. Apple blends as easily with strong savory flavors like bacon or watercress as with other fruits. It is a natural partner for cheese such as a tangy Cheddar or a more delicate Camembert. Raw apples may be grated to add to salads, breads, cakes and pancakes (they will discolor without lemon juice). Apple pie and tart fillings range from chunks to rings, slices and purée. Nothing is as American as apple pie, spiced with cinnamon in a double crust, but the same claim could be made by the French for *Tarte Tatin* (p.455), by the British for apple pie baked with blackberries, or by the Danish for apple cake. When cooked down to a sauce, apples are often flavored with cinnamon or cloves. Sautéed apple rings or slices may be flamed in apple brandy to serve with pork or duck, while deep-fried apple fritters (p.106) are a family favorite. Apples may also be preserved as apple butter, or spiced in vinegar.

Like apples, pears can be divided into dessert and cooking varieties, with some being suitable for both uses. Most pears in the West are of European origin, although some modern pears have been developed by crossing European and Chinese varieties, the latter being more resistant to disease. Many fine dessert pears have the name *beurré*, meaning "buttered", to describe their soft and rich flesh; they are best eaten raw. In France, the stems of the finest Comice variety may be sealed with red wax to prevent evaporation during storage. A half-dozen varieties of pear are generally considered good for cooking, including the British

Starking

Star Crimson

Crab apple

Red Delicious

McIntosh

Sturmer Pippin

Granny Smith

Golden Delicious

Russet

Cox's Orange Pippin

Conference and the American Bosc. The small hard Seckel variety is best for traditional preserves such as pear butter (p.493).

A perfectly ripe pear may be served with a soft or blue cheese. Peeled and cored pears are transformed by poaching in a wine- and vanilla-flavored sugar syrup; they may also be baked, basted with honey or wine syrup and stuffed with raisins. If sautéed quickly in butter they are excellent with duck or venison, or as a dessert, or a filling for soufflé omelet.

Two elderly relatives of apples and pears, the wild crab apple and the quince, are usually cooked to mellow their sour flesh. Crab apples, which came originally from southeastern Europe and southwest Asia, are probably the ancestor of the modern apple. Today the trees are often planted to be ornamental. The fruit is too tart to be eaten raw, but because of its high pectin content, it is often preserved – either on its own or added to other fruits, particularly in jelly (p.490). When baked whole with sugar or pickled with sweet spices, crab apples make a handsome accompaniment to game, pork and poultry.

A quince resembles a craggy apple or pear in appearance, depending on the variety. The flesh is sour, but cooking releases its rich, slightly gritty sweetness. Now a rarity, for centuries quince was a staple of European kitchens. It is another fruit high in pectin, excellent for pastes and jellies, as well as for making a purée to accompany meats or to serve with custard. It is still popular in the Middle East, Latin America and parts of Europe.

Bramley

Quince

Williams

Beurré Hardy

Conference

Bosc

Packham

Washington Red

Comice

Anjou

Seckel

CIDER APPLES & PERRY PEARS

Bittersweet cider apples and perry pears are closely related to our standard sweet varieties, though they are too acid to eat raw. The juice is fermented into hard apple cider or into perry, an alcoholic drink made from pears. These apples and pears are celebrated in areas where they are grown, notably Normandy, the west of England, northern Spain and cooler regions of the United States. Examples of the colorful nicknames given to some varieties, are "slack-my-girdle" and "brown snout" apples.

To make cider or perry, the fruit is reduced to a pulp (called the pomace), then the juice is pressed out and fermented in barrels or tanks. Sweet cider is filtered before all the sugar has fermented, while for hard or "champagne" cider, the juice is left to ferment until quite alcoholic. Some varietal ciders are still made, but most are processed from a blend of different apples. Sparkling cider is simply carbonated juice. Perry, however, is not blended but made from a single variety. For cooking with cider, see p.39.

USEFUL INFORMATION

Common apple varieties *Dessert*: Red Delicious (midwest USA); Golden Delicious (mid-Atlantic USA, France); Cortland (northeast USA); James Grieve (Scotland); Starking (UK); Sturmer Pippin (UK); Cox's Orange Pippin (UK); McIntosh (Canada); Blenheim Orange (UK); Jonathan (northeast USA); Rome (midwest USA); Reine des Reinettes (France); Gala (New Zealand); Belle de Boskoop (France); Russet (UK); Stayman (midwest USA); Reinette Franche (France); Winesap (USA). *Cooking*: Granny Smith (Australia); Bramley (UK); Gravenstein (Germany); Golden Grimes (USA); Calville (France); Grenadier (UK).

Common pear varieties *Dessert*: Doyenné du Comice (France); Bartlett (USA); Williams (UK); Beurré Hardy (France); Clapp's Favorite (USA); Magness (USA); Durondeau (France); Packham's Triumph (Australia). *Cooking/ Dessert*: Anjou (France); Seckel (USA); Bosc (USA); Conference (UK); Kieffer (USA); Grieser Wildeman (Netherlands).

Peak season Depends on variety. *Apple, pear*: early summer to late autumn. *Crab apple, quince*: autumn to early winter.

How to choose *Apple, crab apple*: bright, even background color; firm, no bruises or soft patches; "russeting" or brown patches do not indicate poor quality. *Pear*: stem still attached; firm but yielding slightly at stem end. *Quince*: plump, bright yellow-orange (hard, even when ripe).

How to clean *Apple, pear*: core with apple corer. *Quince, crab apple*: quarter and core with knife. Remove peel if you like (apples are often waxed).

Nutritive value per 3½ oz/100 g (raw). *Apple, pear*: no protein, no fat, no sodium, no cholesterol. *Apple*: 59 calories; 15 g carbohydrates. *Pear*: 59 calories; 15 g carbohydrates. *Crab apple*: 76 calories; no protein; no fat; 20 g carbohydrates; 1 mg sodium; no cholesterol. *Quince*: 57 calories; no protein; no fat; 15 g carbohydrates; 4 mg sodium; no cholesterol.

Cooking methods Times vary with variety and ripeness. *Apple, whole*: bake at 425°F/220°C, 15-25 minutes; *halves*: poach 10-15 minutes; simmer for purée 10-20 minutes; *slices*: bake at 425°F/ 220°C, 10-15 minutes; broil 5-8 minutes; deep-fry 3-4 minutes; poach 5-8 minutes; sauté 5-7 minutes. *Pear, whole*: bake at 375°F/190°C, 20-30 minutes; poach 15-25 minutes; *quarters*: bake at 375°F/190°C, 15-20 minutes; poach 8-12 minutes; *slices*: broil 5-8 minutes; macerate 2-3 hours; sauté 3-5 minutes. *Quince, whole, stuffed*: bake at 375°F/190°C, until tender, 1½-2 hours; *halves*: poach 15-20 minutes; *slices*: poach 10-15 minutes; simmer for purée 20-40 minutes.

When done Translucent, tender but holding shape; soft for purée.

Problems *All*: discolor when cut, so coat with lemon juice or store in acidulated water (p.446); flesh can be mealy if improperly stored, too large or overripe. *Pear, quince*: can rot from inside.

Processed forms *Apple*: canned rings or slices in juice; canned fried or pickled; pie filling; dried; bottled juice; frozen concentrated juice; bottled applesauce; apple butter; jelly. *Pear*: canned halves or slices in juice or sweetened syrup; bottled/canned nectar; jelly; preserves. *Crab apple*: jelly, pickle. *Quince*: paste; jelly; preserves.

Storage *Apple, crab apple*: small apples store best; refrigerate 3 weeks; add lemon juice and dry-pack or toss in sugar or pack in sugar/honey syrup to freeze 1 year. *Sauce*: freeze 9 months. *Pear*: refrigerate 10 days; add lemon juice, toss in sugar or pack in sugar/honey syrup to freeze 1 year. *Quince*: refrigerate in plastic bag 2 weeks; blanch and peel, then dry-pack to freeze 1 year.

Typical dishes *Apple*: snow (cold mousse, UK); pandowdy (pie with molasses and spices, USA); hot charlotte (France); applesauce cake (USA); *apfeltorte* (with meringue and raisins, Germany); soufflé (Hungary); scalloped (USA); curried soup (UK); pancakes (Germany); brown Betty (bread pudding, USA); with red cabbage (Hungary); soup (Scandinavia); *crêpes Normande* (with Calvados and cream, France); sauce with roast pork (UK). *Pear*: *poires à l'Angevine* (in red wine, France); poached in white wine (Germany); with duck (Spain); *piquenchagne* (pie with walnuts, France); caramelized (Italy); in crabmeat salad (USA). *Quince*: poached, filled with cream (eastern Europe); baked in honey (UK); soup with cinnamon (Brazil); in tomato jam (Australia); *hirino me kydonia* (with pork, Greece); jelly (UK); *dulce de membrillo* (fruit paste, Spain).

PREPARING APPLES, PEARS & QUINCES

Apples, pears and quinces may be cored whole for baking, poaching or slicing into rings. All three fruits should be rubbed with lemon juice as soon as they are cut so they do not discolor.

Coring a whole apple: wash the apple, leaving on the skin if you like. Push the apple corer (p.505) into the apple, down to the base. Push out the cylinder containing the core and seeds. If you like, more pips and membrane can be scooped out from inside the apple with a teaspoon.

Coring a whole pear: working from the bottom of the pear, scoop out the pips and membrane with a teaspoon or a melon baller (p.505) without breaking open the pear. Peel the pear, leaving the stem intact.

Coring apple, pear or quince halves: before the core can be removed from halved apples, pears and quinces, the flower and stem ends must be removed. With the tip of a small knife, cut out the flower and stem end of the apple. Cut the fruit in half. For pear and quince, twist the stem end to remove it and scoop out the flower end, then cut the fruit in half.

1 With the point of a knife, cut around the core to loosen it.

2 Scoop out the seeds and membrane, leaving the flesh.

Coring apple, pear and quince quarters: prepare and halve the fruit as above. Cut the halves in two and cut out the core with a knife, removing any fibrous stem. Leave the quarters as they are or slice them thinly, if you like.

SLICING APPLES, PEARS & QUINCES

Apples, pears and quinces may be sliced in one of two ways, depending on whether you want even crescents, or slices of exactly the same thickness.

For crescents: cut the fruit in quarters. With a small, sharp knife, cut each quarter lengthwise in even crescents. Cut toward you, following the shape of the crescent.

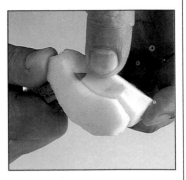

1 **For slices:** halve and core the fruit (left). Set the fruit cut-side down on a board. Cut in even vertical thick or thin slices.

2 The fruit half should hold together neatly after slicing. If you wish, flatten it to form a decoration of overlapping slices.

CUTTING PEAR FANS

Pear halves can be cut attractively into the shape of a fan to decorate salads or pastries.

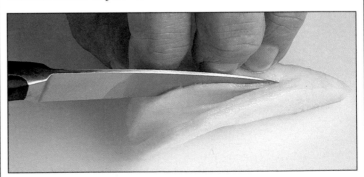

1 ABOVE Peel, quarter and core the pear. Slice it finely and evenly, cutting almost, but not quite, through the stem end.

2 RIGHT With the flat of your hand, fan out the slices so that they remain attached at the stem end.

Tarte Tatin

This upside-down apple pie is known around the world as *la tarte des Demoiselles Tatin*, after two sisters from the small town of Lamotte Beuvron, who invented it. The sisters ran the Hôtel de la Gare, where it is still possible to see their cooking stove and eat *tarte Tatin*. Sugar caramelizes on the bottom of the pan to form a rich topping when the tart is unmolded, with the succulent apples lying underneath, and the pastry on the base.

Serves 8-10

pâte brisée made with 1⅔ cups/ 200 g flour (p.372)	*crème fraîche* or Chantilly cream (p.70), for serving
¾ cup/175 g unsalted butter	
2 cups/400 g sugar	*12-14 in/30-36 cm heavy ovenproof non-stick frying pan or skillet*
6 lb/2.8 kg firm apples, peeled, halved and cored	

1 Make the *pâte brisée* and chill it. Melt the butter in the pan and sprinkle with the sugar. Arrange the apple halves, cored side up, in concentric circles on top of the sugar: they should fill the pan completely and be tightly packed. Cook the apples on top of the stove until a deep golden caramel is formed, 15-20 minutes. **Note** The apples will produce juice that must evaporate before the fruit will caramelize.
2 Let the apples cool slightly. Heat the oven to 425°F/220°C. Roll out the *pâte brisée* to a circle slightly larger than the diameter of the pan. Set the pastry on top of the apples so that they are completely covered, tucking it in at the edges. Work fast so that the dough is not softened by the heat of the apples.
3 Bake until the pastry is crisp and golden brown, 20-25 minutes. Let the tart cool in the pan for 5-10 minutes. Unmold the tart on to a large tray or plate, as any juice that is left may splash. If any apple sticks to the bottom of the pan, transfer it to the top of the tart with a spatula. Serve the tart warm, with *crème fraîche* or Chantilly cream handed separately.

RHUBARB

Botanically a vegetable, pink-stalked rhubarb (sometimes called pie plant) is treated by cooks as a fruit, appearing in sweet pies, tarts and all manner of cold desserts. The umbrella-like green leaves are poisonous and so are usually removed before sale. Rhubarb flourishes almost untended in cold and temperate climates alike, but it can be forced so that it is available in markets of northern countries as early as January. The thin, bright stems of the forced varieties are generally tender, but the large stems of some tougher outdoor varieties may need peeling like celery (p.299), with a vegetable peeler.

Rhubarb is never eaten raw and must be baked or stewed with plenty of sugar before it is palatable; an alternative is to sweeten it with strawberry or raspberry jam. Rhubarb is excellent in pies, but since it produces a great deal of juice during cooking it is best covered with a top crust only, or cooked separately and added to a baked tart shell. Once cooked, the crisp rhubarb stalks become soft and easy to purée (to remove strings, the rhubarb must be worked through a food mill or drum sieve). Rhubarb is excellent in creamy desserts such as mousses and fools. Citrus fruits and sweet spices like cinnamon also complement it well, and rhubarb and candied ginger jam is delicious. In the Middle East, rhubarb is often cooked like sour cherries to produce a sharp sauce for serving with meat, particularly beef. Rhubarb also makes an unusual sauce to accompany fish, and in Denmark, a rhubarb sauce is sometimes served with pork.

USEFUL INFORMATION

Peak season Early spring to mid-summer.
How to choose Crisp, firm stalks, deep color, not too large.
Preparation Trim root end and remove any leaves; wash thoroughly; cut stem in lengths.
Portion 1 lb/500 g makes 2 cups/ 500 ml cooked purée to serve 3-4.
Nutritive value per 3½ oz/100 g (raw): 21 calories; 1 g protein; no fat; 5 g carbohydrates; 4 mg sodium; no cholesterol.
Cooking methods Time depends on size: bake at 350°F/175°C, 10-20 minutes; poach 10-20 minutes.
Problems Wilts rapidly if stored at room temperature; too tart to cook without sugar; falls apart as soon as cooked.
Processed forms Canned in syrup; frozen; jam.
Storage Refrigerate in plastic bag 5 days; peel, dry-pack or blanch and put pieces, or cooked purée, in honey syrup to freeze 1 year.
Typical dishes Fool (UK); *rebarbarakompot* (compote with sour cream, Hungary); *rabarberkage* (with macaroons and sherry, Denmark); jellied with strawberries (USA); stewed with orange and ginger (UK); *khoresh* (stewed with meat, Middle East); pie with strawberry (USA); crumble (UK); custard (UK);

rhubarb and peach cobbler with lattice biscuit topping (USA); *granita* (puréed and served cold on crushed ice flavored with wine or liqueur, Italy); puréed with beets and sour cream (Poland); jam with ginger (UK); jam with orange (USA); sauce with baked chicken (USA); *khoresh* (with beef stew, Middle East).

STONE FRUITS
PEACH, NECTARINE, APRICOT, PLUM, CHERRY

Most fruits of the *Prunus* genus can be identified by a central woody stone or pit, soft pulpy flesh and a thin skin. They are all delicious raw, play a lead role in innumerable desserts, and are excellent additions to meat, game and poultry dishes, for example pork with plums and apricots or duck with cherries or peaches. Stone fruits dry well (Preserving, pp.484-485) and are often distilled into fruit liqueurs and brandies, or macerated in kirsch or brandy. They need careful handling, as they are easily bruised when ripe. Occasionally the almond-flavored kernels extracted from apricots are used in cooking, but the kernels of other stone fruits can contain poisonous acid and should be avoided.

All peach varieties have juicy flesh. Yellow is the most common color, though white-fleshed peaches are traditionally held to have the finest flavor. A red blush does not indicate ripeness. The two major peach types are the clingstone – whose flesh adheres closely to the stone – and the more modern freestone, whose stone separates easily from the flesh. Clingstone peaches hold their shape well when cooked, so they are often canned, while freestone peaches are more commonly sold fresh. The skin of a ripe peach can be peeled by blanching (p.447). If the fuzzy skin is left on and removed after cooking, its color will transfer to the flesh beneath. Underripe peaches will soften as they cook – poaching and baking are favorite methods – and slices can be softened by steeping in hot sugar syrup. The raw fruit is popular in mixed fruit salads and in savory salads with chicken or shellfish.

The nectarine is closely related to the peach, with a richer flavor when raw and very juicy flesh. Nectarines may be clingstone or freestone, but unlike peaches they do not stand up well to long cooking and are better suited to cold desserts, fruit salads and fresh fruit tarts. The skin is smooth and thin so nectarines are not usually peeled.

The apricot – cultivated in China as long ago as 2,000 BC – resembles the peach in flavor, but when it is cooked, dried or preserved, its tart, tangy taste surpasses that of peaches or nectarines. The musk variety of apricot, a specialty of the Loire valley in France, is particularly fine. Cooked apricots feature in Middle Eastern dishes; the dried fruit is used extensively in savory dishes, particularly with pork, duck and chicken. Fresh apricots are good poached or baked whole, or puréed for a sauce, ice cream or sorbet. For the pastry chef, apricot jam is a staple for glazing fruits and it gives tartness to sweet cakes, particularly those made with chocolate.

There are more varieties of plum than of any other stone fruit. They range in color from pale gold to green to deep purple. The British purple damson is so sour it is used only for cooking in compotes or pies, or for making preserves or damson cheese (a thick purée with sugar). The green- or golden-gage varieties are small and sweet with tender flesh. They are worth looking for and make excellent eating as well as being popular for poaching. The mirabelle plum is a particularly sweet and fragrant golden gage, used extensively for canning and preserving, distilling, homemade liqueurs and splendid tarts.

The standard European or purple plum is sweet with rather dry

Sour cherry

Burlat cherry

Black cherry

Golden-gage

Montmorency

Duke cherry

Greengage

Damson

flesh. So-called Japanese plums are large with softer, juicier flesh that may be tart near the stone. They are usually red, orange, yellow or pink, but never blue or purple. The small wild sloe plum is inedible fresh, so is processed into jelly or used to flavor sloe gin. The bullace plum is a European plum, the forerunner of the cultivated damson. Although small, it is not as bitter as the sloe. The beach plum, found along the American shoreline, is similar but much sweeter. When fully ripe, plums can also be eaten raw. They may be poached in syrup or cooked with meat in a stew or roast, and their tartness and juiciness can be used to enrich baked goods such as coffeecakes, quick breads and batter puddings. Plums broil and bake well, featuring in the fruit tarts of Alsace.

Cherries may be divided into three groups: black (actually dark red or purple, as with the popular Bing variety), white (usually pale yellow) and sour. Black cherries may be sweet or tart, while white ones, such as the Queen Anne variety, are almost always sweet. Sweet cherries are best eaten raw, as once cooked, they lose their fragrant flavor. The sour cherry, on the other hand, is often inedible when raw, but delicious when poached, canned, or cooked in jam. Most familiar are the red-fleshed European Morello, the yellow-fleshed Amarello and the sweeter French Montmorency. Sour cherries feature in American cherry pie, and in soup (p.451), and are well suited to poultry or meat dishes. Hybrid varieties such as Duke or Royale combine the shape and color of sweet cherries with the hardiness and taste of sour types. For most purposes, cherries should be pitted; however, removing the cherry pit releases the juice, so they must be left whole for frosting or coating with fondant or chocolate. In country dishes like *clafoutis* batter pudding (p.368) the cherries are often left unpitted. Cherries may be candied for cakes, dried as a substitute for raisins, or macerated in brandy. Pickled cherries are served with cold meats and game, while maraschino cherries, colored and preserved in sweet syrup with almond oil, are still popular as a colorful garnish.

Purple plum

Japanese plum

Mirabelle

Peach Nectarine Apricot

USEFUL INFORMATION

Peak season *Peach, nectarine*: early to late summer. *Apricot, plum, sour cherry*: summer. *Cherry*: late spring to late summer.

How to choose *Peach, nectarine*: yellow or cream background color, firm but not hard, well-shaped with a distinct "seam" along one side; avoid those with green tinge, bruised, wrinkled or shrivelled skin; brown patches signal decay. Nectarine is softer along the seam when ripe. *Apricot*: soft, velvet skin; no green tinge; flesh should give when pressed. *Plum*: uniform color; slightly soft flesh; smooth skin. *Cherry*: plump, shiny well-colored fruit with green, not dark or dry stem.

Preparation Rinse, discard stem.
Portion *Peach, nectarine, apricot, plum*: 1 lb/500 g yields 2 cups/500 ml sliced or halved to serve 2-3. *Cherry*: 1 lb/500 g yields 1½ cups/375 ml pitted.

Nutritive value per 3½ oz/100 g (raw). *All*: no protein; no fat; no sodium; no cholesterol. *Peach, nectarine, apricot*: 43 calories; 11 g carbohydrates. *Plum*: 55 calories; 13 g carbohydrates. *Cherry*: 72 calories; 17 g carbohydrates.

Cooking methods *Peach, nectarine, halves*: bake at 350°F/175°C, 15-20 minutes; broil 8-10 minutes; poach 10-15 minutes; *slices*: deep-fry in batter 2-3 minutes; marinate 3-6 hours; sauté 5-7 minutes. *Apricot, plum, whole*: poach 8-15 minutes; *halves*: bake at 350°F/175°C, 10-15 minutes; broil 6-8 minutes; macerate 3-5 hours; poach 8-15 minutes. *Cherry*: macerate 6-12 hours; poach 5-10 minutes; sauté 4-7 minutes.

Greengage tart

When done Tender.
Problems *Peach, nectarine*: cut flesh discolors (p.446); if poorly ripened, flesh can be woolly and dry. *Apricot, plum*: can be soft and tasteless or sour. *Cherry*: can be sour-tasting.

Processed forms *Peach*: canned; pie filling; dried; preserves; jam. *Apricot*: canned; dried; preserves; jam; nectar. *Plum*: canned; juice from dried; preserves; jam. *Prune (dried plum)*: whole dried (pitted or unpitted); canned in syrup. *Cherry*: pie filling; dried; candied; in syrup; jam; liqueur; extract.

Storage Ripen at room temperature; refrigerate in plastic bag 2-7 days. *Peach, nectarine, apricot*: peel, toss in sugar with lemon juice, or pack in sugar/honey syrup to freeze 1 year. *Plum*: peel, dry-pack, or toss in sugar or pack in sugar/honey syrup to freeze 1 year. *Cherry*: add lemon juice, dry-pack or remove stones and pack in sugar/honey syrup to freeze 1 year.

Typical dishes *Peach, nectarine*: poached (Germany); sour cream pie (USA); *pêches cardinal* (with raspberry, kirsch and almonds, France); stuffed with macaroons (Italy). *Apricot*: *Weiner Marillenknödel* (dumplings, Austria); poached with cloves and cinnamon (UK); tart with almonds (Sweden); cold soup with cinnamon (Sweden). *Plum*: jellied pudding (Australia); *porc à la vosgienne* (with pork, France); *tzimmes* (braised with beef and apricots, Jewish); sauce for game (Netherlands); sweet soup with toast (Brazil); cake (Germany); damson cheese (reduced sweetened pulp, UK); *karcho* (soup with beef, Russia). *Cherry*: jubilee (flamed with liqueur, ice cream, USA); *canard Montmorency* (with duck, France); pie (USA); in port wine sauce (UK); *lahma bil karaz* (with meatballs, Middle East); *cerises au vinaigre* (pickled, France); *Schwarzwaldkirschtorte* (Black Forest cake, Germany); *gâteau Bigarreau* (spongecake with praline filling, France).

PITTING CHERRIES

Cherries are usually pitted with a convenient tool (p.505), which pokes a hole right through the cherry, extracting the pit. A neater result may be obtained with the tip of a vegetable peeler, so that less juice will leak from cherries cooked in a pie.

1 Remove the stem from the cherry and put it in the cherry pitting tool, with the indentation left by the stem pointing upward.

2 Squeeze the handles of the tool together to extract the pit. (Olives may be pitted in the same way using the same tool.)

HALVING PEACHES, PLUMS, NECTARINES & APRICOTS

All of these fruits can be halved to slice or broil, bake in a pie, or stuff and bake. When peeling peaches or apricots, blanch and drain them (p.447), but halve them before removing the skin.

1 With a small sharp knife, cut the fruit in half, using the indentation on one side as a guide.

2 Using both hands, give a quick sharp twist to each half to loosen it from the stone. If the flesh clings, loosen it with a knife.

3 Lift or scoop out the stone with a knife and discard it. If peeling the fruit, do it at this stage. To prevent discoloration, rub cut surfaces of peaches and nectarines with lemon, or immerse them in acidulated water (p.446).

CITRUS FRUITS
LEMON, LIME, ORANGE, GRAPEFRUIT, EXOTIC CITRUS

Members of the large citrus group include the lemon, lime, orange, tangerine and grapefruit as well as more exotic fruits such as the ugli fruit, shaddock, citron and kumquat, and hybrids such as the clementine, tangelo, ortanique and limequat. With their aromatic acidity, citrus fruits are used in soups, savory stews and salads, and often form the main flavor in desserts such as soufflés and mousses. Invaluable as decoration (p.474), their vivid colors complement almost all foods.

Citrus fruits are covered in a thick rind, mainly white pith (properly called the albedo), which has a thin colorful outer layer of zest or rind, where citrus oil and most of the vitamins are concentrated. Tropical yellow and orange citrus varieties usually remain green even when ripe, turning bright yellow or orange when treated with ethylene gas. In cooler climates some varieties may change color while on the tree. Almost all citrus on the market have been treated with wax to prevent loss of moisture.

The most versatile member of the citrus family must be the lemon, whose cultivation goes back at least 2,000 years. It is grown extensively in the United States and Italy, and other large producers include Greece, Spain, Argentina and Chile. There are two main types of lemon. The common or acid lemon seen in most markets has relatively few seeds and may be small with a smooth thin skin, and valued for juice, or large with a thicker, rough skin preferred for its peel. The other type, the sweet lemon, is grown mostly as a novelty. A good lemon is heavy for its size with a perceptible smell. The juice is more easily extracted if the fruit is first rolled on a hard surface with the palm of your hand.

Lemons have many uses in cooking: a squeeze of fresh lemon juice enlivens many savory dishes, and particularly sweet dishes, such as American lemon meringue or lemon chiffon pie, French lemon mousse (p.434), British lemon jelly, or Italian *torta di limone* (lemon tart). In Britain, bread or scones are often served with lemon curd, a thick paste of lemon, butter, sugar and egg yolks. In savory dishes, lemon juice suits light ingredients – shellfish and fish, chicken and vegetables – and provides depth in stews, sauces and soups. It often takes the place of vinegar in vinaigrette and marinades, and can "cook" thinly sliced raw meat or fish, as in Latin American *seviche* (p.125). Lemons may also be preserved in salt or pickled to serve as a condiment, while their sourness is a useful substitute for salt in special diets. Lemon is also used in cooking to prevent the flesh of fruit or vegetables from discoloring. A cut lemon can be rubbed over the peeled fruit or vegetables, or they can be dropped into acidulated water (water to which lemon juice has been added).

Bright green limes are also full of sour juice and are prepared and treated in the same way as lemons. Tahitian varieties have a thick skin and juicy pulp, while sour Mexican varieties are smaller with a thin, smooth skin and yellowish color. In the United States, Florida's "key" lime is the most celebrated Mexican variety. Americans enliven their melon with lime, while in the tropics a squeeze of lime is mandatory with papaya and guava, and in Asia fresh lime juice is often added to curries, pairing well with hot pepper. In Mexico, limes are often used in place of lemon with cold seafood and fruit salads, as well as in *guacamole* (avocado dip). Lime juice is used extensively in desserts, especially those with cream.

Through the centuries, orange trees have been symbols of opulence, and their fruit has become one of the most important of all fruit crops. The bitter orange, also called the sour, Bigarade or Seville orange, is believed to be the common ancestor, and was the standard orange until the early nineteenth century. Too sour for eating out of hand, its tart aromatic flavor is superior in marmalade and other preserves as well as in candying and liqueurs.

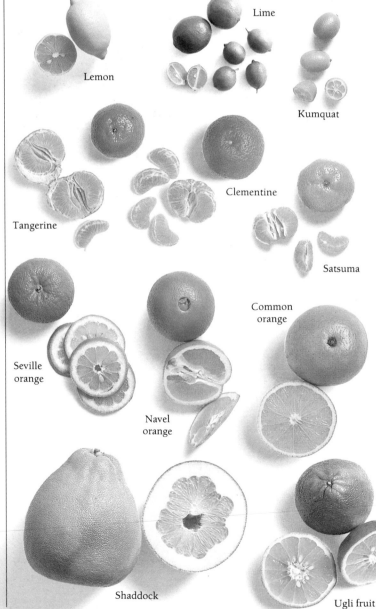

Lime

Lemon

Kumquat

Clementine

Tangerine

Satsuma

Common orange

Seville orange

Navel orange

Shaddock

Ugli fruit

Pink grapefruit

White grapefruit

Sweet oranges can be divided into three types. The common orange, used for juice, is a medium-sized heavy fruit, with a fine-grained skin. It is often known by varietal names such as Jaffa, from Israel, and Valencia, which is grown in Florida, California, Latin America, South Africa, Europe and Australia but not, paradoxically, in Valencia, Spain. The navel orange, which has the growth of a tiny second orange at the flower end, contains less juice but peels more easily. Navel oranges have no seeds and are ideal for slicing and cutting in segments. Less common, but prized for its pink-red seedless flesh, is the blood, or pigmented, orange that is an essential ingredient in the French *sauce Maltaise* (p.60). Mainly grown in Italy, it has a particularly rich flavor, reminiscent of berries. Another variety, the aromatic pineapple orange, is chock-full of seeds and is used commercially for juice.

Mandarins are small, slightly flat, loose-skinned oranges with a sweet taste. The segments are widely available in cans and are popular in fruit cups and for decorating pastries. Perhaps the best known mandarin is the tangerine. The Japanese satsuma is a seedless mandarin with a green-tinged skin, while the Algerian clementine (a bitter orange and tangerine cross) is bright orange-red with a pebbled skin and tangy sweet flavor.

One of the largest citrus is the grapefruit, with a diameter of up to 6 in/15 cm. Grapefruit are either white-fleshed with a yellow rind or pink-fleshed with a pinkish blush to the rind. The two differ little in taste, which depends more on the presence of seeds than on color. Seedy fruits have a pronounced flavor and are grown for canning, while the milder, seedless varieties are usually eaten fresh or in salads. Grapefruit juice can be added to fruit jellies and sorbets, and the flesh suits bitter greens, avocado and fresh cheese. Grapefruit halves may be broiled with honey or sugar. Like other citrus fruits, grapefruit makes good marmalade and candied peel. The ugli fruit resembles a squashed grapefruit with a mottled greenish skin but its flesh is surprisingly sweet and juicy, despite its discouraging name. Usually eaten raw, in the Caribbean it is baked in its skin then eaten hot with sugar.

The shaddock (also called pummelo or pomelo) is the largest citrus, resembling a large grapefruit with coarse, bittersweet dry flesh with a greenish, yellow or pinkish skin. It was brought from southeast Asia to the New World by a Captain Shaddock in 1696. Also rarely seen in markets is the citron, cultivated for its thick aromatic rind. Never eaten fresh, it is often used in marmalade, and candied for use in cakes. Candied citron appears in markets for Christmas – it should be moist and sticky with a fresh flavor.

The smallest citrus is the tiny, orange oval kumquat, which originated in the East but is now grown mainly in Brazil. The fruit has a distinctive sour-sweet flavor; the sweetness is especially evident in the rind and kumquats are usually eaten unpeeled. They are delicious fresh (rub them around in your palm to encourage the aroma) but may also be candied (p.475), preserved in syrup or pickled. When blanched to soften, they add a palatable bittersweet taste to meat and fish salads. For a pretty garnish, look for kumquats with the stem and small leaves still attached.

The citrus family embraces a high number of hybrids developed from existing fruits for color, flavor or to be seedless. Notable are the tangelo (tangerine/grapefruit), the citrange (sweet orange/trifoliate orange), the West Indian ortanique (sweet orange/tangerine), the limequat (lime/kumquat) and the citrangequat (citrange/kumquat).

USEFUL INFORMATION

Peak season *Lemon*: summer. *Lime*: year-round. *Bitter orange, mandarin*: winter. *Blood orange, ugli fruit, kumquat, sweet orange*: winter to spring. *Grapefruit*: autumn to early summer.

How to choose *All*: should feel heavy with juice. *Lemon, lime*: uniform color; no shrivelled skin. *Orange, kumquat*: firm, no blemishes. *Mandarin*: deep orange color; loose skin. *Grapefruit*: resilient, no soft patches. *Ugli fruit*: loose, spongy skin.

Preparation For peel, scrub under hot water to remove wax.

Portion *Lemon*: 1 medium yields 3-4 tbsp juice. *Lime*: 1 yields 2-3 tbsp juice. *Orange*: 1-2 per person; 1 medium yields ⅓-½ cup/75-125 ml juice. *Mandarin*: 1 yields ⅓ cup/75 ml juice. *Grapefruit, ugli fruit*: 1 per person; 1 fruit yields ½-¾ cup/125-175 ml juice.

Nutritive value per 3½ oz/100 g (raw). *All*: 1 g protein; no fat; no cholesterol. *Lemon*: 20 calories; 11 g carbohydrates; 3 mg sodium. *Lime*: 30 calories; 11 g carbohydrates; 3 mg sodium. *Orange*: 47 calories; 12 g carbohydrates; no sodium. *Grapefruit*: 32 calories; 8 g carbohydrates; no sodium. *Kumquat*: 63 calories; 16 g carbohydrates; 6 mg sodium.

Cooking methods *All*: candy peel and slices (pp.474-75); macerate segments 2-3 hours. *Grapefruit, ugli fruit*: broil or bake at 450°F/230°C, 4-6 minutes. *Kumquat*: poach 15-20 minutes.

Problems Sour if underripe; dry if stored too long; older fruits may have many seeds.

Processed forms *Lemon, lime* (*juice*): frozen concentrate; unsweetened reconstituted; in syrup. *Lemon, lime*: candied and dried peel; extract; marmalade; jelly. *Orange, tangerine, grapefruit* (*juice*): fresh; pasteurized; concentrate. *Orange*: candied and dried peel; extract; marmalade; flower water. *Grapefruit, mandarin*: canned segments. *Kumquat*: preserves.

Storage *Lemon*: refrigerate 1 month. *Lime*: refrigerate 1 week. *Orange*: store at room temperature 1 week; refrigerate 1 month. *Mandarin*: refrigerate 2-3 weeks. *Grapefruit, ugli fruit, citron*: store at room temperature 1 week, refrigerate in bag 2-3 weeks. *Kumquat*: store at room temperature 2 days; refrigerate 2-3 weeks. *All*: peel, remove membrane, dry-pack or toss in sugar or pack in sugar/honey syrup, to freeze 1 year; to use for juice, dry-pack and freeze 3 months.

Typical dishes *Lemon*: avgolemono (soup with egg and rice, Greece); meringue pie (USA); tart (France); curd (UK); butter (USA). *Lime*: Key-lime pie (USA); seviche (marinated fish, South America); butter with ginger (USA). *Orange*: caramelized (Italy); duck in orange sauce (France); cake with ginger (UK); sauce with chicken (Mexico); iced (France). *Grapefruit, ugli fruit*: broiled with sugar (USA); stuffed with fennel (USA). *Citron*: riz à l'impératrice (rice pudding with candied fruit, France). *Kumquat*: preserved in brandy (Australia). *Also good with* mint, shellfish, parsley, chicken, fish (lemon); chili pepper, tequila, avocado (lime); soft cheese, mint, rosemary, beef, chocolate (orange); hearty greens, bananas, avocado (grapefruit, ugli fruit).

PEELING CITRUS FRUITS

The zest and pith pull away easily from most citrus fruits, leaving segments covered in skin. However, when cutting segments or slicing for salads, zest, pith and skin should be cut away together.

For large citrus (right): with a serrated knife, cut a slice from top and bottom of the fruit through to the flesh. Cut away the zest, pith and skin, working from top to bottom, and following the curve of the fruit.

For smaller citrus: cut zest, pith and skin off in one piece, in a spiral as when peeling an apple.

SECTIONING CITRUS

The flesh of citrus fruit is often cut out in segments for salads and to garnish savory dishes. If possible, use seedless fruit.

1 RIGHT Cut away the zest, pith and skin (p.459). Slide the knife down one side of a segment, cutting it from the skin. Cut down the other side and pull out the section.

2 Repeat with the remaining segments, turning back the flaps of skin like the pages of a book.

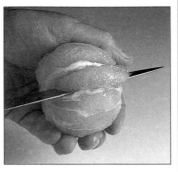

GRATING CITRUS ZEST

The zest of citrus fruit, containing the aromatic oil, is often used with the juice, adding a mellow, perfumed flavor.

If using a flat grater: rub the surface of the fruit backwards and forwards on the fine grid 2-3 times to remove the zest without any of the bitter white pith.

If using a zester tool (right): scrape it against the surface of the fruit to remove the zest.

Note Citrus oil can also be extracted by rubbing the fruit with sugar cubes to soak up the oil. (The sugar should then be crushed or dissolved to be used as a flavoring.)

CUTTING CITRUS ZEST & JULIENNE STRIPS

Strips of citrus zest are simmered to flavor sugar syrup and some savory recipes such as beef cooked *en daube*. Citrus julienne is an attractive garnish for desserts and savory dishes that are flavored with juice from the fruit, and they can also be candied for desserts (p.474). To soften the strips and remove bitter flavor, they should be blanched in boiling water for a couple of minutes and drained.

1 With a vegetable peeler, cut strips of zest from the rind, leaving the bitter pith behind.

2 Stack several strips and with a large knife cut them into very thin julienne.

Fresh orange soufflé

This hot fruit soufflé includes fresh orange segments, layered within the Grand Marnier soufflé mixture. Berries and bananas are other fruits suitable for hot soufflés, which are often made with puréed, instead of sliced fruit. See also Soufflés (p.92).

Serves 4-6

thick pastry cream (p.384), made with 1 cup/250 ml milk, 3 egg yolks, ½ cup/100 g sugar, and ¼ cup/30 g flour	5 egg whites
	2 tbsp/30 g granulated sugar
	confectioners' sugar (for sprinkling)
2 oranges	
⅓ cup/75 ml Grand Marnier	**6 cup/1.5 L soufflé dish**

1 Make the pastry cream. Grate the zest of one orange and stir it into the cream with 3 tbsp/45 ml Grand Marnier. Peel and section both oranges (see Sectioning citrus, above left). Sprinkle the orange segments with the remaining Grand Marnier and set them aside.
2 Heat the oven to 425°F/220°C. Generously butter the soufflé dish. Heat the pastry cream over low heat until it is hot to the touch. Beat the egg whites until stiff. Add the granulated sugar and beat until glossy to make a light meringue, about 30 seconds.
3 Stir about a quarter of the meringue into the pastry cream (the heat of the pastry cream will lightly cook the meringue). Gently fold this mixture into the remaining meringue.
4 Transfer half the soufflé mixture to the prepared dish. Set the orange segments on top. Add the remaining mixture and smooth the surface with a metal spatula. Run your thumb around the edge of the dish so the soufflé rises in a hat shape. Bake the soufflé until puffed and brown, 12-15 minutes. Sprinkle the top with confectioners' sugar and serve at once.

GRAPES

Grapes are one of the oldest and most widely traded fruits in the world. Most are made into wine, or squeezed for juice, or dried into raisins and currants (p.473). Most grapes are descended from a single ancient species, *Vitis vinifera*, with some dozen varieties, sold as black (red) or white table grapes. Black grapes shade from dark pink to deep purple. Any surface bloom (a dusty look) on the skin is produced by yeasts and is a sign of recent harvesting. Ranging in color from amber yellow to pale green, white grapes are usually blander than black ones, with a thinner skin and firm musky flesh; the muscatel is notable for its perfume. It is the skin of grapes that contains the color and most of the flavor. Most table grapes contain seeds, but the American Thompson variety is conveniently seedless. Slip-skin varieties, named for skin that slides easily from the flesh, include the American Concord and Catawba. They are often used for juice, jelly and to make regional wines. In Europe a much wider variety of table grapes is available.

Grapes complement many foods, including other fruits, fish, shellfish, and light meats such as chicken and veal, particularly in a white wine and cream sauce. One traditional combination is quail wrapped in vine leaves, garnished with grapes and served in wine sauce. Grapes are a natural partner to high-fat cheeses and soft cheeses such as Brie. In fruit tarts, often made with nut pastry, whole seeded or seedless grapes are packed in concentric circles on a layer of pastry cream. Fresh grapes frosted with sugar (p.474) make a fine dessert decoration, while black and red grapes add color to salads, like cold chicken salad with melon. For serving hot, grapes are seeded and often peeled.

Muscat

Ribier Black

Sweet Italian Rosy

California Seedless

Concord Slip-skin

Biendonné White

USEFUL INFORMATION

Common table grapes *Black, red*: Alphonse Lavalle (Europe, Israel, S. Africa); Red River (USA); Barlinka (S. Africa); Black Beauty (USA); Cardinal (USA, S. America, Europe, S. Africa); Frankenthaler (Belgium, Netherlands); Red Flame Seedless (USA); Gros Maroc (UK); Emperor (USA, S. America, S. Africa); Fredonia (USA); Ribier (USA). *White*: Muscat (France); Almeria Ohanes (Europe); Champion (UK, Netherlands); Biendonné (Europe); Muscatel (Mediterranean); Italia (Europe); Thompson Seedless (USA); Rosaki/ Regina Bianca (Europe); New Cross (S. Africa); Himrod Seedless (USA). *Slip-skin (all USA): black*. Concord; Van Buren; Sheridan; Catawba; Pierce. *White*: Niagara.
Peak season *Black, red*: late summer to winter. *White*: summer to autumn.
How to choose Plump, unblemished fruit of uniform color firmly attached to stems; good aroma. *Black, red*: should not have green tinge.
Preparation Rinse with water.
Portion 1 lb/500 g serves 3-4.
Nutritive value per 3½ oz/100 g (raw): 67 calories; 1 g protein; no

fat; 18 g carbohydrates; 2 mg sodium; no cholesterol.
Cooking methods Blanch 5-10 seconds; macerate 3-6 hours; poach or simmer in sauce 3-5 minutes.
Problems Acidic if underripe; mold quickly if overripe or kept at high temperature; overcook easily.
Processed forms Dried as raisins and currants; bottled juice; frozen concentrated juice; preserves; jam; jelly.
Storage Refrigerate in a plastic bag 2 weeks; remove seeds and dry-pack or pack in sugar/honey syrup, to freeze 1 year.
Typical dishes *Weintraub in olivensalat* (salad with olives, Germany); *sopa de uvas blancas malagreña* (cold soup, Spain); with brown sugar and sour cream (USA); *fazan po kavkazki* (with guinea fowl, Russia); *canard à la vigneronne* ("vineyard style" duck with grapes, carrot and onion, France); *pollo con uvas* (with chicken, olives and wine, Latin America); *bavaroise aux raisins* (Bavarian cream, France); with duck livers (France). *Also good with* berries, avocado, cheese, veal, poultry, fish, walnuts, almonds.

PEELING & SEEDING GRAPES

To serve in sweet or savory dishes, grapes should be seeded. Thick skin should also be removed, if the grapes are to be served hot as a garnish, or in a sauce. Halved grapes are easy to seed, but many recipes call for grapes to be left whole and seeded.

To peel grapes: starting at the stem end, pull away the skin with a knife. If the grapes are hard to peel, blanch them in boiling water for 5-10 seconds and try again.

To seed grapes: sterilize a metal bobby pin by holding it for a few seconds in an open flame. Pull the grapes from the stems. Insert the bobby pin at the stem end of the grape and twist to pull out the seeds. Alternatively, poke out the seeds with the tip of a vegetable peeler.

BERRIES
STRAWBERRY, RASPBERRY, BLUEBERRY, CRANBERRY

In the kitchen, berries can be divided into soft types, such as strawberries and raspberries, and firm ones like currants, gooseberries and cranberries. Soft berries are best raw but are extremely perishable. They should be washed only when sandy, as washing softens them and rinses away some of their perfume. Firm berries are almost always cooked, and are often puréed and mixed with other ingredients for incorporating in desserts and preserves. Many berries grow best in cool, northern climates.

Nowadays we take strawberries for granted, but they are a fairly recent development, resulting from careful crossbreeding of a small wild American strawberry with a juicy specimen from Chile. Wild strawberries (Fr. *fraises des bois*), also called alpine or wood strawberries, are now cultivated as well. They are valued for their fragrance, and when choosing all strawberries, an intense perfume is the best indication of

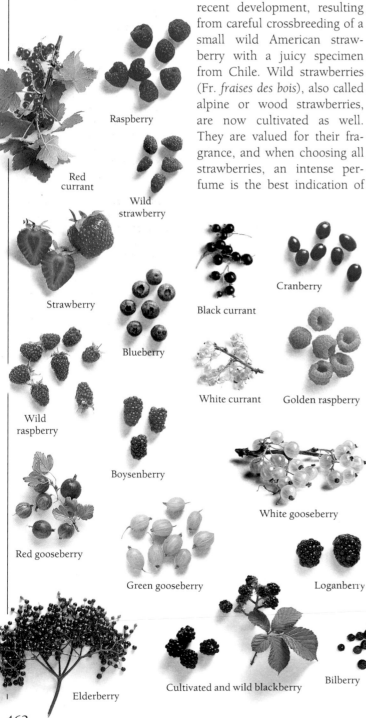

Raspberry

Red currant

Wild strawberry

Strawberry

Blueberry

Black currant

Cranberry

White currant

Golden raspberry

Wild raspberry

Boysenberry

White gooseberry

Red gooseberry

Green gooseberry

Loganberry

Elderberry

Cultivated and wild blackberry

Bilberry

Cape gooseberry

quality. Both wild and domestic strawberries should have their hulls (short leafy green stem) intact. Usually these are removed for serving, but they may be left as decoration, or for dipping the fruit in chocolate or cream.

Strawberries are often puréed for cold sauce or soup, or as a flavoring. The seeds are so small that the purée need not be strained. In the United States, strawberries partner rhubarb in pies, in France they fill puff pastry *feuilletés* and in Britain they are served with clotted cream. Strawberries may also be macerated in champagne, orange juice, red wine or liqueur. They are best cooked only lightly, for instance in a soufflé or fruit gratin.

Raspberries and blackberries are technically multiple fruits, since each tiny segment hides a hard seed. The classic raspberry is deep-red, but black, purple and even golden-amber varieties are also grown. Black raspberries differ from blackberries in that the flesh of the berry detaches easily from the core. Raspberries are surely at their best with a light sprinkling of sugar and a spoonful of cream. However, they can be used in fruit tarts and are popular as a filling and decoration for desserts such as Austrian *Linzertorte* (a nut pastry). They are also puréed to make Melba sauce (p.66), and to flavor mousses, soufflés, ice creams and sorbets. Like strawberries they are rarely cooked, except in preserves. Most blackberries, on the other hand, improve on cooking, since this intensifies their flavor and softens their seedy texture. They combine well with apple, in pies and puddings, and make very good preserves. The same goes for the mulberry, which is a rarer berry; the black kind is best for cooking.

Blackberries and raspberries have many look-alike cousins: the dewberry is a juicy trailing variety of blackberry; the American loganberry is often considered too tart to eat fresh, the youngberry (a dewberry/loganberry hybrid), is bred for sweetness, as is the northwestern Pacific olallieberry. The large red, juicy boysenberry is yet another hybrid. It has few seeds and a bittersweet flesh. The Scandinavian cloudberry resembles a blush-pink raspberry with a honey-sweet taste; unfortunately it is fragile and rarely cultivated. Similar is the North American thimbleberry.

Blueberries, bilberries and cranberries are members of the same genus of plants found on both sides of the Atlantic. The plump, cultivated blueberry and the wild huckleberry are still largely North American fruits, as is the Juneberry or serviceberry. The tiny European bilberry is known by a host of colorful names such as blaeberry, whortleberry and hurtleberry. Bilberries are rarely seen in American markets, but to confuse matters, Canadians often refer to blueberries as bilberries. Blueberries may be bland when raw and are best in sauces, pies, muffins (p.361) and cobblers. Bilberries are tart, often used to make liqueur, or puréed as a sauce for game. Both are good in preserves and cold soups.

The cranberry is found all over Europe and Asia, but only the native American cranberry is important commercially. This small, acid fruit, cultivated for over 200 years, was a staple of the American Indians. It may have appeared at the first Thanksgiving dinner, as it still invariably does every November. The fruit is much too sour and hard to eat raw, but is transformed when cooked with sugar or fruit juice, making an excellent sauce to serve with turkey, duck and game. Cranberry juice is refreshing, while chopped cranberries are popular in quick breads and muffins. The Scandinavian lingonberry, also called a mountain cranberry, is a relative that is similar in taste, popular for use in compotes, soups and sweet sauces.

The purple or red elderberry looks like a bilberry; it is considered among the most healthy of wild fruits because of its high vitamin C content. Bitter or woody when raw, it is often made into preserves or homemade wine.

The most common edible currants are the black and red currant, with white currants a variation on the red. ("Currant" also refers to a seedless dried raisin.) As a garnish, red currants add just the right touch of color, but they are tart when raw unless almost overripe. Usually they need a good sprinkling of sugar, and they are particularly good frosted with sugar (p.474). When removed from the stem, red currants may be sprinkled over desserts as well as savory dishes of meat or poultry, to give a sharp touch, especially welcome for rich meats and game as well as creamy desserts. (White currants can be used in the same way.) Red currant jelly is, with apricot jam, a staple for the pastry chef, acting as a glaze for red fruits (p.385), and a filling for cakes.

Black currants lack the gleam and taste of the red, with a sour bite that dissipates when the fruit is cooked. Black currants can be made into preserves (they are especially rich in pectin), into syrups like the British Ribena drink, and into liqueurs like the celebrated *cassis* from Dijon. They go well in pies and puddings, offering plenty of vitamins as well as a rich berry flavor. Black currants are rare in America but are common in Europe.

Closely related to the black currant, the gooseberry is a translucent oval, whose color is dependent on the variety. It grows well in Britain, where it is used in desserts such as fruit fool and pie; the French call it the "mackerel currant" and turn its sour taste to advantage with smoked meats and oily fish. Northern Europeans enjoy spiced gooseberries as a condiment and in soups.

The Cape gooseberry, also called *physalis* and golden berry, is in fact related to the tomatillo (p.303) and the ground cherry, having a similar papery husk. It is one of the prettiest fruits, especially when frosted with fondant or used to top an elegant gâteau. The smooth shiny berry is bright orange when ripe.

USEFUL INFORMATION

Peak season *Strawberry*: late spring to early summer. *Cranberry*: autumn. *All others*: summmer.

How to choose Pick small containers, as berries in large containers may be crushed by their own weight. *Strawberry*: uniform color, moist green hull. *Other soft berries*: plump, brilliant-to-deep color, no mold or rot. *Firm berries*: plump, shiny, deep color. *Cape gooseberry*: undamaged husks.

Portion *Strawberry*: 1 qt/1 L weighs 1⅓ lb/650 g, makes 2 cups/500 ml purée. *Raspberry*: 1 qt/1 L weighs 2 lb/1 kg, makes 2 cups/500 ml purée. *Blueberry*: 1 qt/ 1 L weighs about 2 lb/1 kg, cooks to 3 cups/750 ml. *Firm berries*: 1 qt/1 L weighs 1 lb/500 g, cooks to 3 cups/750 ml.

How to clean *All*: discard damaged, moldy or green berries; if dusty rinse lightly in water just before using. *Strawberry*: hull. *Other berries*: remove stems and tops. *Cape gooseberry*: fold back husk as decoration.

Nutritive value per 3½ oz/100 g (raw). *All*: 1 g protein; 1 g fat; no cholesterol. *Strawberry*: 30 calories; 7 g carbohydrates, 1 mg sodium. *Raspberry, blackberry*: 49 calories; 12 g carbohydrates; no sodium. *Blueberry*: 56 calories; 14 g carbohydrates; 6 mg sodium. *Currant*: 60 calories; 15 g carbohydrates; 2 mg sodium. *Gooseberry*: 44 calories; 10 g carbohydrates; 1 mg sodium. *Cranberry*: 49 calories; 13 g carbohydrates; 1 mg sodium.

Cooking methods *Soft berries*: macerate 1-3 hours. *Blackberry, blueberry*: bake at 350°F/175°C, 10-15 minutes; poach 5-8 minutes. *Firm berries*: bake at 350°F/175°C, 8-15 minutes, depending on type; poach 5-15 minutes depending on type.

When done *All*: just tender. *Cranberries*: pop and soften.

Problems *All*: hard and acidic when underripe; juice stains. *Soft berries*: lose fragrance when refrigerated or frozen.

Processed forms Frozen whole; canned in sweetened syrup; concentrated juice; sweetened syrup; preserves; pie filling; jam; relish; dried.

Storage *All*: discard damaged or moldy fruit. *Soft berries*: refrigerate loosely wrapped 1-3 days. *Firm berries*: refrigerate in perforated plastic bag 3-5 days, up to 2 weeks for cranberry. *All*: dry-pack or toss in sugar/honey, or pack in sugar/ honey syrup to freeze 1 year.

Typical recipes Strawberry shortcake (USA); strawberries *Romanoff* (with orange juice, orange liqueur and whipped cream, Russia); *rodgrod* (cold berry soup, Scandinavia); *tarte à la cannelle* (blueberry-cinnamon flan, France); blueberry buckle (USA); black currant ice cream (Norway); red currant jelly (UK); cloudberry preserve with venison (Denmark); blackberries with whiskey and bacon (Scotland); gooseberry fool (UK); gooseberry and elderflower jelly (UK); blueberry pancakes (USA); red currant tarte (Austria); gooseberry sauce (UK); cranberry and orange relish (USA); *noisettes d'agneau aux myrtilles* (lamb with bilberries and hazelnuts, France).

Summer pudding

Any berries may be used to make this juicy cold pudding.

Serves 6

1½ lb/750 g mixed berries	½ lb/250 g stale sliced white bread, crusts removed
6 tbsp/75 g sugar (more to taste)	
	1½ qt/1.5 L pudding bowl

1 Pick over the berries and rinse with water. Combine the wet fruit and the sugar in a saucepan and simmer, stirring, until the fruit softens and releases juice, 5-10 minutes depending on the berry. Let the fruit cool and add sugar to taste.

2 Line the bowl with the bread slices, trimming so that they fit tightly. Reserve several to cover the pudding. Add the fruit and enough juice to moisten the bread thoroughly, reserving the remaining juice. Cover with the rest of the bread. Set a plate and 1 lb/500 g weight on top and refrigerate for at least one day and up to two days.

3 Shortly before serving, unmold the pudding. Baste any white patches with the reserved juice. Serve with heavy cream.

MELONS

There are two kinds of melon – the dessert melon and the watermelon. Dessert melons have tan, green or yellow rind and dense, fragrant flesh. Depending on their variety, the skin is either netted (covered with brown, fibrous net-like markings) or furrowed. The watermelon has thick, dark green skin flecked with yellow, which surrounds red, pink or yellow watery flesh.

Perhaps the most familiar dessert melon is the cantaloupe. In the United States the name is given to a round netted melon with a tan-colored rind, while the European cantaloupe is more craggy and furrowed in appearance. Both have salmon-orange, highly-scented flesh that is quite firm and exceptionally sweet. Similar to the cantaloupe, but smaller, is the French Charentais. The ridged Ogen and the larger Galia both have green flesh. The pink-fleshed Persian melon is oval, while the particularly sweet honeyball is yet another common variety; both have lightly netted yellowish skin.

Other dessert melons, often called winter melons, resemble winter squashes, with smooth, furrowed skin. They store better than other types. Most common of these is the honeydew, which turns from pale green to yellow when fully ripe. The lavan resembles a round honeydew, but with even sweeter flesh. Casaba melons are large and white-fleshed, with deep-ridged, golden-yellow skin. The Santa Claus melon, named for its Christmas peak season, looks like a yellow-flecked watermelon with sweet flesh. The newly popular Crenshaw is a hybrid Persian Casaba, with golden-green skin, shallow ribs and bright salmon-orange flesh; it can weigh as much as 9 lb/4 kg.

Watermelon is an international fruit and belongs to a different genus. Three general types are now cultivated: small, round "icebox" melons, bred to fit neatly into the refrigerator; a large round type with smooth skin, and a large striped oval melon.

Most have red or pink flesh, but newer varieties may be white, pale yellow or even bright orange inside.

For sweetness, it is essential that a melon be fully mature and ripe. It is usually served plain, chilled to accentuate its succulence, and with the seeds removed from the center. Watermelon seeds, which are embedded in the flesh, may be lightly scraped away with a spoon before the melon is served, sliced into wedges. The flesh may be scooped into balls with a melon baller (p.505). Melon is a good foil for smoked or cured meats, notably Italian prosciutto ham. Melon makes a refreshing soup, and for dessert it may be offered with a sprinkling of liqueur or port. In the United States, it is often served with a dash of salt, or a squeeze of lemon or lime juice, while the British favor ground ginger as a seasoning.

USEFUL INFORMATION

Peak season *Dessert melon*: summer to winter. *Watermelon*: summer to early autumn.

How to choose *Dessert melon*: size no indication of quality though usually the bigger the better; look for heady aroma with no rotting undertones; should be heavy for its size, firm with no soft patches, cracks or mold; soft-skinned types should give a little when pressed at the stem end. *Watermelon*: look for deep-green, matt, velvety skin (white or yellow patches may form where the melon has rested on the ground); shake small watermelon as loose seeds indicate ripeness; when cut, flesh should be juicy with dark shiny seeds and no white streaks.

Preparation When cut, scrape out seeds and any strings.

Portion *Dessert melon*: 1½ lb/ 750 g yields 2 cups/500 ml chunks; ½-¾ lb/250-375 g per person of large melon; small whole melon or half medium melon serves one. *Watermelon*: 1-1½ lb/ 500-750 g per person.

Nutritive value per 3½ oz/100 g. *Dessert melon*: 35 calories; 1 g protein; no fat; 8 g carbohydrates; 9 mg sodium; no cholesterol. *Watermelon*: 32 calories; 1 g protein; no fat; 7 g carbohydrates; 2 mg sodium; no cholesterol.

Cooking methods Macerate 1-2 hours; pickle (p.490), preserve.

Problems Woolly with little juice if picked when underripe;

ferments if it is overripe.

Processed forms Frozen (with other fruits); bottled in syrup; pickled or candied rind.

Storage *Dessert melon, whole*: room temperature 1-2 days; *halves, slices*: refrigerate 3 days; *pieces*: peel, dry-pack, or pack in sugar/honey syrup to freeze 1 year. *Watermelon, whole*: room temperature 2-3 days; *halves, slices*: refrigerate 1 week; do not freeze.

Typical dishes With prosciutto (Italy); with salt and pepper (USA); in liqueur (France); stuffed with mangoes and grapes (Middle East); soaked in vodka (USA); stuffed with peaches and bananas (Spain); salad with cumin and chili pepper (southern USA); soup (Russia); tart (France); fritters with strawberry sauce (France). *Also good with* honey, *crème fraîche*, wild strawberries, raspberries, salad greens, soft cheese, chicken, crunchy vegetables, ham, duck.

Casaba

Santa Claus

Charentais

Ogen

Cantaloupe

Honeydew

Crenshaw

Canary

Galia

Watermelon

BANANAS

The most common banana in the West is the dessert banana, the same few varieties being sold under various names. Picked when still green, bananas ripen well off the tree. The texture of the flesh changes from starchy and bland to soft and sweet and the skin turns yellow. Lesser-known varieties include the small delicate apple and peach bananas, which have thin skin and much sweeter flesh.

Less familiar in Western cuisine, but commonplace in Africa and the Caribbean, is the plantain or cooking banana, with green skin flecked or scarred with patches of brown. The skin is difficult to peel and turns from light green to black when the banana is fully ripe. They are usually sold singly and are never eaten raw. Now appearing in the West are red dessert and cooking bananas, with deep red or pink skin and creamy pink flesh.

Plantains and some varieties of red banana are best for cooking; green dessert bananas can also be used, although they tend to lose their shape in high heat. Baked or sautéed bananas are a popular alternative to potatoes with all manner of baked, broiled or stewed meats, fish or poultry. In Caribbean style, they may be sprinkled with lemon, lime or hot spices, perhaps mixed with beans, bacon or ham. They may also be poached, enlivened with chili sauce, or mellowed with coconut. Banana leaves, which are large enough to wrap most foods, provide protection for barbecued, steamed or baked fish and poultry.

As a dessert, bananas may be topped with brown sugar and orange juice, baked, then flambéed with rum (p.449). Ripe bananas are mashed to add to cakes and breads, used as a base for drinks, savory or sweet stuffings, or added to dumplings for soups and stews. Both desert and cooking bananas can be deep-fried to make chips, or coated and deep-fried as fritters.

Finger banana

Red banana

Dessert banana

Ripe and unripe plantain

USEFUL INFORMATION

Peak season Year-round.
How to choose *Dessert:* yellow skin, possibly with brown spots but no black patches. *Plantain:* plump fruit (blemishes on skin rarely penetrate to fruit).
Preparation Peel to use at once.
Portion 2 medium ripe bananas yield 1 cup/250 g.
Nutritive value per 3½ oz/100 g (raw). *Dessert:* 92 calories; 1 g protein; no fat; 7 g carbohydrates; 2 mg sodium; no cholesterol. *Plantain:* 122 calories; 1 g protein; no fat; 23 g carbohydrates; 4 mg sodium; no cholesterol.
Cooking methods *Dessert:* times depend on ripeness; bake at 375°F/190°C, 15-20 minutes; sauté 5-10 minutes. *Plantain:* bake peeled or in skin at 375°F/190°C, 40-50 minutes; poach 30 minutes.
When done Tender but still holding shape.
Problems Discolor when cut.
Processed forms Chips, dried, extract.
Storage Ripen at room temperature; refrigerate 1-2 days

(dessert banana skin blackens but does not affect flesh); dry-pack unpeeled or peeled to freeze 1 year; purée, add lemon juice, freeze 1 year.
Typical dishes *Dessert:* chicken Maryland (USA); with cream and sugar (France); honeyed chips (sweetened and fried, Australia); purée (France); sliced with whipped cream, rum and almonds (Brazil); with Dover sole (France); *céleste* (baked with cream cheese, brown sugar and cinnamon, Caribbean); *bananes Baronnet* (sliced with lemon juice, cream and kirsch, France). *Plantain:* *platanos fritos* (pan-fried, Mexico); chips (deep-fried and salted, USA), savory cake (Mexico); soup (Puerto Rico); baked in pastry (Guatemala); tortilla (Cuba). *Also good with* bacon, onions, liqueurs, rum, yogurt (dessert); red bell pepper, ginger, chili pepper, sour cream (plantain).

Bananas Foster

This is a favorite dish in New Orleans, named after a local personality of the 1950s. For tableside presentation, a chafing dish and table burner can be used.

Serves 4

¼ cup/40 g raisins	¼ tsp ground cinnamon
⅓ cup/75 ml light or dark rum	1 qt/1 L vanilla ice cream
¼ cup/60 g unsalted butter	¼ cup/25 g slivered almonds, toasted (p.477)
¼ cup/50 g brown sugar	
4 ripe bananas, peeled and sliced lengthwise	

1 Soak the raisins in the rum to plumpen them. Melt the butter in a frying pan. Add the brown sugar and heat gently, stirring until the sugar has melted, about 2 minutes. Add the bananas and cook until tender, 3-5 minutes, turning once with a spatula. Sprinkle the bananas with cinnamon.
2 Pour the rum and raisins over the bananas and flambé them (p.449), basting the fruit with the sauce until the flames subside.
3 Transfer the banana slices to four plates. Top with the vanilla ice cream, spoon over the rum and raisin sauce, sprinkle with almonds and serve at once.

TROPICAL FRUITS
PINEAPPLE, MANGO, PAPAYA, KIWI FRUIT, PASSION FRUIT, GUAVA

Most tropical fruits are treated alike, being ideal candidates for salads, whether of fruit or combined with shellfish, fish or poultry. Often special techniques are needed for peeling and extracting the flesh of tropical fruits. However, all purée well for sauce and make a rich base for sorbets and ice creams. When they are green and unripe, mango and papaya may even be cooked like a vegetable.

The best-known tropical fruit is the pineapple. When it was first seen by travellers to the New World, the British thought it resembled a pine cone, while the French named it *ananas* from the original Carib words *nana memi*, meaning "exquisite fruit". The pineapple was first cultivated in Britain in the seventeenth century and in France in the eighteenth century. It was a luxury, since it needed to be ripened on the plant. Modern techniques of transport and storage have ensured that pineapples (and many other tropical fruits) are more available and may be eaten worldwide. Varieties differ slightly in size and color; some are greenish yellow, others a deep orange.

All pineapples have "eyes" that should be removed before slicing and removing the woody central core. Alternatively, the fruit may be halved or cut in wedges, and the flesh scooped out in one piece, then cored and cut in chunks. A fresh ripe pineapple needs only a sprinkling of sugar, rum or kirsch, but the fruit also stands up to sautéing or broiling with brown sugar. It is an excellent accompaniment to dishes based on chicken, pork or ham. Easter ham, adorned with pineapple rings and bright red cherries, is a popular American dish.

The mango is nicknamed "apple of the tropics", southern India being the largest producer of mangoes. There are many varieties in a wide range of colors, but all have a mellow, deep orange flesh that is sometimes unpleasantly fibrous. Sizes of mango vary, but they can weigh as much as 3 lb/1.4 kg. Ripe mango is a perfect foil for smoked meats, chicken and turkey, a welcome addition to a vegetable salad and the basis of many desserts, when the flesh is strained to make a purée. Another traditional role for mangoes is in fresh chutney, made from the unripe green fruit. **Note** Like poison ivy, which belongs to the same family, mangoes may cause an allergic skin reaction in certain people.

The papaya, also called pawpaw (the wild American pawpaw is no relation), is usually shaped like a large pear, with pale green to deep orange skin. Its apricot-colored flesh surrounds a cavity of shiny black seeds which, although edible, are usually discarded. Ripe papaya is good when eaten completely plain, like melon, with just a sprinkling of lime. It may also be paired with coconut and lime, and when unripe (green), cooked in chutneys and preserves. Papaya and its leaves contain an enzyme often used to tenderize meat.

The kiwi fruit, once called the Chinese gooseberry, came into fashion as a pretty accompaniment to the dishes of modern cuisine. There are two varieties, both shaped like an elongated egg with fuzzy thin skin. Tasting rather like a grape, kiwi fruit is usually eaten raw, peeled and halved or sliced to show the seeds. Since they do not discolor, kiwis are often used in open fruit tarts and salads, and to accompany cheese. As a dessert fruit, kiwi fruit is probably best known in meringue Pavlova, an Australian and New Zealand specialty, created to commemorate the visit of the famous Russian ballerina Anna Pavlova.

The egg-shaped passion fruit, or grenadilla, is native to Brazil. The name "passion fruit" derives from the fact that the Spanish Jesuit missionaries who found the fruit in South America distinguished the signs of the Passion in the flower of the plant. The complex blooms displayed the Three Nails, the Five Wounds, the Crown of Thorns, and the Apostles. The other name, grenadilla, means "little pomegranate" and is used because of the host of seeds inside the sour-sweet yellow pulp. The fruit is purple on the outside and, when ripe, has a tough wrinkled skin. Both pulp and seeds may be eaten with a teaspoon, or the seeds may be scattered over a salad. More often the fruit is puréed for sauce or as a dessert base. This is one of the most fragrant and distinctive-tasting of all tropical fruits, so it often flavors cocktails and punches. The yellow passion fruit, a Malaysian variety, is slightly larger with a more acidic taste and smoother skin.

The guava, formerly associated with Latin America, is now grown around the world in tropical areas; its availability is largely restricted to the growing regions. There are two main types: the tropical or common guava, and the smaller, redder, more fruity strawberry variety. Another fruit, the feijoa (p.472), is sometimes mistaken for it. Tropical guava is slightly larger than an egg with a similar shape; the fruit is usually yellow when ripe, and inside the flesh ranges from white to dark pink. Some guavas have a great many seeds, making them gritty, others are smooth on the palate. Rather bland when raw, guava is often cooked and puréed for sauce, or added to savory dishes with ground meat, fresh cheese or yams. In South America, it is made into jelly or paste and served as a dessert candy.

Yellow passion fruit

Purple passion fruit

Common guava

Papaya

Kiwi fruit

Pineapple

Mango

USEFUL INFORMATION

Peak season *Pineapple*: spring. *Mango*: autumn to late winter. *Papaya*: spring and autumn. *Kiwi fruit*: year-round, especially winter. *Passion fruit*: spring to autumn. *Guava*: year-round.

How to choose *Pineapple*: large, heavy with sweet aroma; central leaves can be pulled from top; good color; skin yields slightly but with no soft patches. *Mango*: sweet smell, taut skin with no soft spots. *Papaya*: deep color and small size. *Kiwi fruit*: flesh yields slightly, with no soft spots. *Passion fruit*: shrivelled skin, heavy for its size. *Guava*: firm with no dark blemishes.

Preparation *Pineapple*: (see right). *Mango*: (see p.468). *Papaya*: peel skin with fingers or cut away skin, depending on ripeness; discard seeds. *Kiwi fruit*: peel skin with fingers. *Passion fruit*: cut off top and scoop pulp with a spoon. *Guava*: discard blossom end, cut away peel and slice fresh.

Portion *Pineapple*: 2 lb/1 kg serves 5-6. *Mango*: serves 1-2. *Papaya*: serves 1-2 depending on size. *Kiwi fruit*: serves 1. *Passion fruit*: 1-2 serves 1 and makes ½ cup/125 ml purée. *Guava*: serves 1.

Nutritive value per 3½ oz/100 g. *All*: no fat; no cholesterol. *Pineapple*: 49 calories; no protein; 12 g carbohydrates; 1 mg sodium. *Mango*: 65 calories; 1 g protein; 17 g carbohydrates; 2 mg sodium. *Papaya*: 39 calories; 1 g protein; 10 g carbohydrates; 3 mg sodium. *Kiwi fruit*: 61 calories; 1 g protein; 15 g carbohydrates; 5 mg sodium. *Passion fruit*: 97 calories; 2 g protein; 23 g carbohydrates; 28 mg sodium. *Guava*: 51 calories; 1 g protein; 12 g carbohydrates; 3 mg sodium.

Cooking methods *Pineapple*: broil 5-7 minutes; candy (p.475); deep-fry as fritters 3-4 minutes; macerate 4-6 hours; poach 5-8 minutes; sauté 3-5 minutes. *Mango, papaya (ripe)*: macerate 1-2 hours. *Mango (unripe)*: bake in skin at 375°F/190°C, 30 minutes; poach 15-20 minutes. *Papaya (unripe halves)*: bake at 375°F/190°C, 25-30 minutes; simmer 15-35 minutes; sauté 5-10 minutes. *Guava*: bake at 375°F/190°C, 25-30 minutes; poach 15-20 minutes.

When done *All*: tender but holds shape. *Guava*: very soft.

Problems *Pineapple, kiwi fruit*: bruise easily; must be cooked to use with gelatin (p.431). *Guava*: despite high pectin and acid content, jelly often does not set.

Processed forms *Pineapple*: canned rings, chunks, or crushed in juice; pie filling; dried slices; fresh and pasteurized juice; bottled juice; frozen concentrated juice; nectar; preserves; extract. *Mango*: nectar; pickled pieces; chutney; preserves. *Papaya*: pieces in syrup; nectar. *Kiwi fruit*: slices in syrup. *Passion fruit*: in syrup. *Guava*: nectar; paste; sauce; jelly; preserves.

Storage Ripen at room temperature. *Pineapple*: refrigerate in plastic bag 3-4 days (chunks keep better than whole fruit); toss peeled chunks in sugar or pack in own juice or sugar/honey syrup to freeze 1 year. *Mango, papaya, kiwi fruit, guava*: refrigerate 1-2 weeks; peel and dry-pack pieces or purée in sugar/honey syrup to freeze 1 year. *Passion fruit*: refrigerate 2-3 days; dry-pack or purée to freeze 1 year.

Typical dishes *Pineapple*: jellied salad with cherries (Scandinavia); sorbet (France); *ananaskraut* (with sauerkraut, Germany); upside-down cake (USA); shish kebab (grilled with beef and green pepper, USA); with chicken and lentils (Dominican Republic); bread stuffing (for meats, Caribbean); *anaskrem* (dessert cream, Norway); ambrosia (dessert salad with banana, coconut and mandarin oranges, USA). *Mango*: with cream (India); sauce (Caribbean); salad with lime and onion (Caribbean); braised with beef (Hawaii); sweet pastries (Central America); sautéed with chicken and almonds (USA). *Papaya*: stuffed with seafood (Caribbean); salad with avocado (Caribbean); with veal chops (USA); baked with chicken (North Africa). *Kiwi fruit*: Pavlova (New Zealand); sautéed with beef (Australia); *crème brûlée aux kiwis* (in custard, France). *Passion fruit*: in marrow jam (Australia); soufflé (France); *passievrucht salade* (salad with strawberries, Scandinavia); tea cake (Australia). *Guava*: cold salad with fish (Philippines); with cream cheese (USA); *goyabada* (paste, Latin America). *Also good with* sweet potatoes, pork, chocolate, chicken, almonds, ham (pineapple); sour cream, maple syrup, honey, liqueurs, chocolate, berries, citrus fruits (mango, papaya, kiwi fruit); raspberries, honey, banana, coconut (passion fruit); cream, sweet potatoes, pork, duck, ham (guava).

PEELING PINEAPPLE

The eyes of pineapple should be removed at the same time as the peel. The first method is to simply cut away the peel; the second is to remove the peel diagonally, producing an attractive spiral design. First of all, cut away the plume and base of the pineapple.

Method 1

Hold the pineapple firmly, resting it on the cut base. With a long knife, cut away the peel in strips, working from top to bottom and cutting deep enough to remove the eyes with the pineapple skin.

Method 2

1 With a small pointed knife, trace the lines of eyes that twist around the pineapple; cut round, following the lines and slanting the knife inwards at a 45 degree angle.

2 Cut along the other side of the same line of eyes, slanting the knife in the opposite direction. The cuts should meet in the middle, under the eyes. Lift out and discard the strip of peel. Continue cutting along the other lines until all of the peel has been removed.

CUTTING PINEAPPLE IN RINGS

Pineapple rings are particularly suitable for flambéing (p.449) and as a salad garnish. First peel the pineapple, as shown above.

1 With a long, thin-bladed knife, cut the peeled pineapple into even slices.

2 Core each slice with a small cookie cutter, pressing down hard and lifting out the center.

HOLLOWING OUT A WHOLE PINEAPPLE

A hollowed-out pineapple makes an attractive container for fruit salad: fill it very full, then set the plume on top as a lid.

1 Cut a slice from the top of the pineapple, including the plume. Reserve this as a lid for the hollowed-out container.

2 Using a knife with a long thin blade, cut around the edge of the pineapple. Cut into the flesh, about ½ in/1.25 cm inside the skin, without cutting through the bottom.

3 Turn the pineapple round. Insert the point of a knife near the cut plume end and move the knife from side to side to loosen the flesh inside, all the way down to the base.

4 LEFT Turn the pineapple upside down, and release the flesh in one cylindrical piece.

5 With a long knife, core the pineapple, cut the cylinder in rings or chunks and replace in the shell for serving. Add the plumed lid for decoration.

HOLLOWING OUT A HALVED PINEAPPLE

A small half pineapple shell makes a container for one serving.

1 Cut the pineapple in half lengthwise, leaving the plume. Cut a thin slice from the bottom of each half so it sits flat for serving.

2 With a small sharp knife, cut the core from the center of the halved pineapple.

3 With a serrated grapefruit knife, cut out the flesh. Cut into strips, then chunks, and replace for serving.

PEELING & STONING A MANGO

With its soft, pulpy flesh that is full of juice and clings so tightly to the flat stone, mango is one of the most difficult fruits to cut neatly. In method one, the mango is halved and then cut in cubes from the peel. In method two, the mango is peeled, then the flesh is sliced from the stone.

Method 1

1 Holding the mango horizontally, cut it in two lengthwise, slightly off-center, so the knife just misses the stone.

2 Repeat on the other side so a thin layer of flesh remains around the stone.

3 Slash the mango flesh in a lattice, cutting down to but not through the peel. Repeat with the other half of the mango.

4 Holding the mango flesh upwards, carefully push the center of the peel with your thumbs to turn it inside out, opening the cuts in the flesh. Cut the mango cubes from the peel.

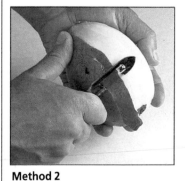 

Method 2

1 Cut away the mango peel with a vegetable peeler.

2 Slice the mango flesh until the central stone is reached.

3 Continue slicing on the other side of the stone, then cut away, in chunks, any flesh that remains on the stone.

Pineapple en surprise

Any combination of tropical fruits may be hidden under the ice cream and meringue topping in this recipe. The technique of hollowing out a halved pineapple (previous page) is used here.

Serves 4

2 small pineapples, halved, flesh removed and cut in pieces	2-3 tbsp/30-45 ml rum
1 mango or papaya, peeled, seeded and sliced (opposite)	1 qt/1 L vanilla ice cream
1 carambola, sliced	Italian meringue (p.437), made with 6 egg whites, 1½ cups/300 g sugar, ¾ cup/175 ml water and 1 tsp vanilla extract
4-6 kumquats, sliced *or* 2 kiwi fruits, peeled and sliced	
2-3 tbsp/30-45 g sugar	**Pastry bag and large star tube**

1 To make the fruit salad: mix the pineapple pieces, mango or papaya, carambola, kumquats or kiwi fruit, sugar and rum in a bowl. Cover and leave to macerate in the refrigerator for 1-2 hours. Pile the fruit salad into the pineapple halves and chill.
2 Make the Italian meringue. Heat the oven to 375°F/190°C. Cover the fruit in each pineapple shell with ice cream, then spread a layer of meringue over the top, sealing it carefully at the sides. Fill a pastry bag and star tube with the remaining meringue and pipe rosettes on top of the meringue layer on each pineapple half to cover it completely. Bake the pineapples in the pre-heated oven until browned, 8-12 minutes. Serve at once.

AVOCADO

Botanically a fruit, the avocado pear can be eaten as a fruit or a vegetable. The skin is inedible but the rich creamy flesh goes well with citrus and other fruits such as pineapple, and with salty foods like ham and anchovy. It is also good peeled and sliced in salads.

Three types of avocado are common. Most familiar is the alligator type, which has a rough leathery skin and pronounced taste – it is picked while still hard and green but ripens to be almost black. The West Indian avocado is rounder with smoother skin and a more neutral taste. The Mexican avocado (also widely cultivated in Florida) is larger than the others, with a sweet milky flesh and smooth green skin, even when ripe. Tiny seedless avocados from Israel, often called pickle or cocktail avocados, are a treat if you can find them. Mature avocados do not ripen until they are picked. They should be rock hard when transported to the stores; once they soften deterioration is rapid, so it is best to buy them hard and ripen them at home.

The avocado is a highly nutritious fruit, rich in natural oils as well as vitamins and minerals. Although the nutty flavor is agreeable, the great attraction of the avocado is its smooth, plump flesh. Mashed or puréed, avocado is excellent in cold soups (p.51), gelatin molds and dips such as Mexican *guacamole* flavored with onion, chili pepper and lime juice. Avocado is also good served plain with vinaigrette dressing, and it adds a contrasting texture and subtle flavor to green salads. Both shellfish and chicken are popular fillings that can be piled into a pitted avocado half. When cooked lightly, avocado adds a note of richness to soups and baked dishes. If avocado is to be cooked, however, it should be treated with care, as it quickly loses its flavor if heated for too long.

Cocktail avocado

Rough-skinned avocado

Smooth-skinned avocado

USEFUL INFORMATION

Peak season Year-round.
How to choose Full-necked (showing it has matured on the tree); yields slightly when pressed; if very soft, avocado is overripe; skin color varies with variety, not ripeness.
Preparation Remove peel and slice; cut in half and remove stone to serve plain with dressing.
Portion Half to one per person.
Nutritive value per 3½ oz/100 g (raw): 161 calories; 2 g protein; 15 g fat; 7 g carbohydrates; 10 mg sodium; no cholesterol.
Cooking methods Bake at 350°F/175°C, 10-15 minutes; simmer 5 minutes.
Problems Dark and streaked if overripe or bruised; sometimes bitter; discolors quickly when cut so must be rubbed with lemon juice.

Storage Ripen at room temperature 2-3 days; refrigerate if ripe, 2-3 days; purée: add lemon juice, freeze 1 year.
Typical dishes Stuffed with crabmeat (USA); *guacamole* (puréed with lime juice, chilis, garlic, Mexico); *crema de abacate* (sieved with lime juice and sugar, Brazil); with scallops and mint (USA); chilled soup with sour cream (USA); avocado ice cream (UK); stuffed with tomato sauce (Peru); diced with kirsch (Austria); with strawberry sauce (UK); sauce for cold poached fish (Cuba). *Also good with* guava, feijoa, citrus fruits, cheese, ham, fresh coriander, lime, eggs, chicken, bitter greens, salad greens, red bell pepper, carambola, cucumber, Cape gooseberries.

PITTING AVOCADO

To serve with dressing, to fill with a salad, or for peeling and slicing, avocado is cut in half and the pit is removed.

1 LEFT Cut lengthwise around the avocado, through to the pit. Twist with both hands to loosen the pear halves and pull them apart.

2 BELOW With a chopping movement, embed the blade of a heavy knife in the pit and lift it free of the avocado. Alternatively, scoop out the pit with a spoon.

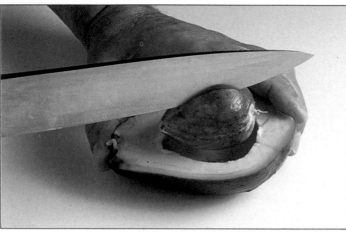

PEELING & SLICING AVOCADO

A halved avocado may be peeled and sliced to serve in a salad, or as garnish. Use a stainless steel knife as avocado tends to discolor.

1 LEFT To peel the avocado, strip off the skin with your fingers; if it is ripe it will peel easily.

2 BELOW With a stainless steel knife, evenly slice the peeled avocado crosswise. Fan out the slices on a serving plate and immediately sprinkle them with lemon juice to prevent browning.

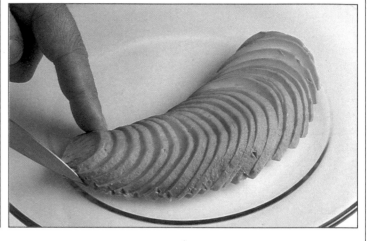

Avocado and grapefruit salad with smoked salmon

Any type of grapefruit may be used in this salad, but the pink variety lends color. Serve as an appetizer or light main course.

Serves 4

2 pink grapefruit

3 oz/90 g arugula or other bitter salad greens

½ cup/125 ml vinaigrette dressing (p.64) made with lime juice instead of vinegar or lemon juice

4 oz/125 g smoked salmon, thinly sliced

2 avocados, peeled and sliced lengthwise

1 Pare the zest from one of the grapefruit and cut it in julienne strips (p.460). Blanch the strips of zest in boiling water for 2 minutes and then drain. Cut segments from both of the grapefruit (p.460). Wash and dry the salad greens and cut them in a chiffonade (p.259). Make the dressing.
2 Spread the greens on four plates. Cut the salmon slices into strips and arrange on the greens, overlapping them with the avocado and grapefruit. Spoon over the dressing, sprinkle with grapefruit julienne and serve.

POMEGRANATE & PERSIMMON

Persimmon

Pomegranate

With the autumn come two bright fruits for the holiday table. The blushed pomegranate, also called the Chinese apple, is an ancient symbol of fertility, while the persimmon, the national fruit of Japan, stays on the tree long after the leaves have fallen.

Pomegranates are round with a brownish blossom end (calyx) and leathery pink or yellow skin. Inside, tough cell cavities contain a multitude of seeds, each encased in juicy red kernels. Both membrane and seeds can be very bitter, containing a good deal of tannin. Pomegranates may be cut open and the kernels scooped from the membrane (the seeds are edible though crunchy), or the whole fruit may be rolled in your palm until the seeds and pulp are loosened, then a hole poked in the fruit to extract the juice.

Whole pomegranate kernels make a pretty decoration for both hot and cold dishes, especially mousses, ice creams and fruit salads. In the Middle East, pomegranate juice is used in soup and the kernels are mixed with mint for a refreshing salad. Pomegranate juice is used as a flavoring in the same way as lemon juice, although it has more perfume. Originally, it was used to flavor the French grenadine syrup.

Even more eye-catching, the persimmon resembles a large orange with a papery blossom end. When unripe, the flesh of the persimmon is cottony and extremely astringent, but it ripens to a musky, sweet and slightly gelatinous pulp. The hundreds of varieties of persimmon fall into two groups: the Asian persimmon, called *kaki* in Asia (where it has been cultivated for over 1,000 years) and Europe, and the wild American persimmon, which is not raised commercially. The most common Asian persimmon, the *hichiya*, is shaped like an acorn and has sweet, tender flesh. Other Asian varieties such as the *fuyu* contain no tannin; their flesh is crisp and may be eaten when unripe and quite hard. One *fuyu*-type of persimmon, much cultivated in Israel, is called the Sharon fruit. Sweet enough to eat when still firm, it sports a glistening star pattern when cut open.

Ripe persimmon pulp may be eaten plain, and can be added to mousses, custards and puddings and used to top other fruits or ice cream. Like melon and figs, persimmon is an excellent accompaniment to fresh cheese or smoked meat. The unripe fruit may be enlivened with lemon, and added to fruit and poultry salads.

USEFUL INFORMATION

Peak season Autumn to winter.
How to choose *Pomegranate*: large, bright pink or yellow, heavy in the hand with clean skin. *Persimmon*: bright orange when ripe, stem attached, with thin skin and soft, yielding pulp.

Preparation *Pomegranate*: see right. *Persimmon*: slice off blossom end; scoop out pulp; slice if firm.
Portion *Pomegranate*; 1 per person. *Persimmon*; 1-2 per person.
Nutritive value per 3½ oz/100 g.

All: no fat, no cholesterol. *Pomegranate*: 68 calories; 1 g protein; 17 g carbohydrates; 3 mg sodium. *Persimmon*: 70 calories; 1 g protein; 19 g carbohydrates; 1 mg sodium.
Problems *Pomegranate*: juice may be bitter if membrane extracted with it. *Persimmon*: many varieties are bitter when unripe.
Processed forms *Pomegranate*: juice.
Storage *Pomegranate*, *whole*: refrigerate 3 weeks; *kernels*:

refrigerate 1 week, freeze 1 year. *Persimmon*: refrigerate 2 days; *peeled or unpeeled*: dry-pack or add lemon juice and toss in sugar to freeze 1 year; *purée*: add lemon juice, freeze 1 year.
Typical dishes *Pomegranate*: salad with mint (Lebanon); *faisinjan* (juice with poultry and walnuts, India); soup with lentils, onions, spinach (Egypt). *Persimmon*: ginger cream (Australia); cookies (USA); pork with persimmon dressing (Japan); broiled with sugar (USA).

PREPARING POMEGRANATE

The sweet kernels of pomegranate must be detached from their tough, bitter membrane cavities. To extract the juice from the kernels, they should be crushed in a strainer.

1 Using the point of a sharp knife, cut around the blossom end of the fruit to remove it.

2 With the tip of the sharp knife, score the skin in quarters, taking care not to puncture any of the juicy kernels inside.

3 ABOVE With your hands, follow the score lines and break the fruit in half. Break each half in quarters. **Note** Cutting the fruit at this stage would puncture the kernels, causing juice to leak.

4 RIGHT Peel the hard skin back from each quarter and release the kernels into a bowl. Discard any stray membrane.

EXOTIC FRUITS

An increasing number of unusual fruits (some tropical) can regularly be found in Western markets. Most have a short shelf-life, which is probably the reason why they have previously been rare outside their growing region.

The feijoa, or pineapple guava, is a small oval fruit native to southern Brazil but now grown in New Zealand, California and Australia. Slightly gritty in texture like the guava, the feijoa is green and shiny, with heavily scented flesh surrounding a seed cavity. It is good plain, sliced for salads or puréed as a base for desserts. The peel should be removed as it can be bitter.

The tamarillo, originally from Peru and now cultivated in New Zealand, is sometimes called the tree tomato because its flavor resembles that of the tomato. A member of the same family as such important food plants as the tomato, potato, aubergine and pepino, the tamarillo has satiny, blood-red or bright-yellow skin and an elegant long stem, which is usually left on for the market. The dark yellow flesh, studded with black seeds when ripe, is soft and can be skinned by blanching. A ripe tamarillo can be eaten raw with a generous sprinkling of sugar or treated like a vegetable and added to meat and poultry stews. The pepino, or melon pear, has a smooth green skin streaked with purple when fully ripe, and the flesh ranges from pale greenish-yellow to dark orange. The pepino tastes like an acidic but perfumed melon, and is often eaten in the same way as melon, or sautéed lightly as an accompaniment to fish and meat.

The custard apple is a generic name given to a tropical family (*annona*) of some 60 fruits. All are heart-shaped, with thick, green, scaly skin enclosing compartments, each with a large seed. Custard apples vary in sweetness, but when ripe have a juicy, slightly granular flesh that is particularly refreshing chilled. They may be cut open and the flesh scooped out with a spoon to eat plain, or puréed to make ice cream.

The tamarind, or Indian date, comes from an East Indian tree, now cultivated in most parts of the tropics. The leaves and flowers are eaten in India, while the fruit or pod is used in preserves. The seeds are ground to a meal and baked into cakes.

Originally native to the American Southwest is the prickly pear, also called cactus pear, Indian or Barbary fig. The pulp is bland, but may be simmered with sugar and strained to make a gorgeous orange-red purée for custards, ices, jams, pastes and candies. The prickly pear also produces *nopales* (edible cactus paddles, p.303).

The tropical sapodilla, cultivated in Asia, the West Indies and the southeastern United States, is the source of chicle sap, used for chewing gum. The flesh of the fruit, sometimes called the naseberry, is honey-brown and soft when ripe, and studded with shiny black seeds. It may be sliced to serve with cream or fruit salad, or scooped out to use in mousses and other cold desserts.

The white sapote (unrelated to the sapodilla), is a grapefruit-sized fruit with thin green or yellow skin and soft, sweet flesh. It may be eaten plain, or puréed for cold desserts. The mamey sapote is no relation to the white, though it should be treated similarly. It has ugly brown skin and when ripe, a soft, salmon-colored flesh.

From Asia come a number of fruits that are still unfamiliar in the West. The oval and winged carambola (or star fruit as it is commonly known) is perhaps the prettiest. Its waxy skin is quite thick, but contains juicy flesh that may be crunchy and tart, or soft and sweet when ripe. When sliced crosswise, it gives attractive star-shaped slices for use in fruit salads or as a garnish. An autumn fruit, the carambola is good with poultry and shellfish or pickled, as in India. The bilimbi is similar in shape, but less sweet.

One related group of fruits – of which the lychee is the most common in Western markets – has a characteristic tough skin, juicy translucent flesh and a smooth central seed. The lychee, originally from China but now cultivated in other parts of the world including the United States, has bumpy, pink to brownish skin that is easy to peel, revealing white, perfumed flesh. These small fruits are good plain or with cream or ice cream. The longan is similar, with orange skin that turns brown after picking. The rambutan is covered in soft brown spines, with yellow flesh that is exceptionally fragrant.

The unprepossessing mangosteen, with four brittle petals and a crusty exterior, is one of the most succulent of Asian tropical fruits. Best eaten fresh and quite plain – it needs no sugar – the mangosteen is still a rarity, though it can be found pickled in jars. The prickly durian is an extraordinarily large Asian fruit (sometimes weighing up to 6 lb/3 kg), best known for its repulsive odor when ripe and a creamy, rather spicy flesh.

A couple of fruits have become rare from neglect. The medlar tree, still found in old-fashioned gardens, has a dark brown fruit with an open-petalled cavity. The spicy flesh of the fruit is hard, even when ripe, so medlars are "bletted" or left to rot slightly before being used for jelly and jam. The yellow or orange loquat has juicy orange flesh that can be used in preserves.

Longan

Prickly pear

Custard apple

Loquat

Lychee

Sapodilla

Carambola/
Star fruit

Pepino

Feijoa

Mangosteen

Tamarillo

Rambutan

FIGS & DATES

Originally from Asia Minor, figs and dates are ancient fruits now cultivated worldwide in warm climates. Both are perishable and something of a luxury when fresh. The most celebrated variety of fig is still the amber Turkish Smyrna, pollinated by a single species of wasp. Other common varieties include the Calimyrna (a Smyrna hybrid), the dark purple mission, often used for drying, and the yellow-green Greek kadota, popular for canning. Figs are often dried, making them sweet and chewy.

With their fragile skin, fresh figs are damaged easily. When ripe they are succulent, full of tiny edible seeds and sweet, deep red flesh. Raw figs may be eaten whole, or peeled by simply pulling off the skin. They taste good plain, sprinkled with a little lemon juice and sugar, or eaten with fresh goat cheese. In Italy, figs may take the place of melon as an accompaniment to prosciutto ham, while figs and cream are the perfect partners for a summer breakfast. Always serve figs at room temperature, as chilling masks their sweetness. Fresh figs may be sliced for an open tart or macerated for fruit salad. Lengthy cooking destroys their delicate flavor, so light poaching or baking with a touch of liqueur is the best approach, particularly for underripe fruit. Prick the figs before cooking so that the syrup or basting liquid penetrates.

Today, Israel is the largest producer of dates, the fruit of the handsome date palm. Most date varieties that appear in markets are large and moist, like the Halaway and the celebrated Deglet Noor (Arabic for "date of the light"). Sweetness is the measure of their quality. Other, drier varieties are still a staple food in North Africa and the Middle East, and are sometimes found in Western markets in blocks. For winter festivals, dates are often stuffed with soft cheese or almond paste to serve as a sweetmeat. When their skin is peeled, the sticky flesh may also be rolled in coconut or in toasted chopped nuts. Chopped dates lend sweetness to nut breads, to cookies, and to chutney. In the Middle East, they are often softened in cream or yogurt, then served with fresh fruits.

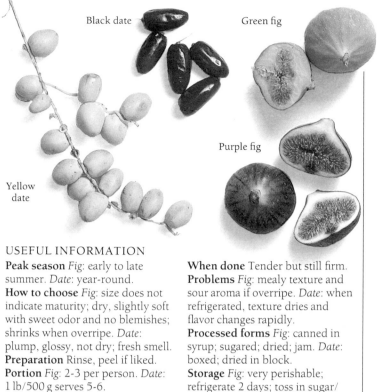

Black date

Green fig

Yellow date

Purple fig

USEFUL INFORMATION

Peak season *Fig*: early to late summer. *Date*: year-round.
How to choose *Fig*: size does not indicate maturity; dry, slightly soft with sweet odor and no blemishes; shrinks when overripe. *Date*: plump, glossy, not dry; fresh smell.
Preparation Rinse, peel if liked.
Portion *Fig*: 2-3 per person. *Date*: 1 lb/500 g serves 5-6.
Nutritive value per 3½ oz/100 g (raw). *Both*: no fat, no cholesterol. *Fig*: 74 calories; 1 g protein; 19 g carbohydrates; 1 mg sodium. *Date*: 275 calories; 2 g protein; 74 g carbohydrates; 3 mg sodium.
Cooking methods *Fig*: bake at 350°F/175°C, 15-20 minutes; poach 10-12 minutes. *Date*: bake at 350°F/175°C, 10-15 minutes; poach 15-20 minutes; sauté 3-5 minutes.

When done Tender but still firm.
Problems *Fig*: mealy texture and sour aroma if overripe. *Date*: when refrigerated, texture dries and flavor changes rapidly.
Processed forms *Fig*: canned in syrup; sugared; dried; jam. *Date*: boxed; dried in block.
Storage *Fig*: very perishable; refrigerate 2 days; toss in sugar/honey to freeze 1 year. *Date*: refrigerate 2 weeks; dry-pack to freeze 1 year.
Typical dishes *Fig*: hot soufflé (France); with raspberries and cream (UK); stuffed with chocolate (Italy); with duck in port wine (USA); in rum syrup (Italy). *Date*: fried (India); compote (France). *Also good with* veal, apple, citrus fruit (fig); walnuts, dried fruit, bacon, orange (date).

DRIED FRUITS

Drying has always been an important way of preserving fruit. Today, dried fruits are one of the principal flavoring ingredients of much European and American baking, as well as in stuffings and salads of Middle Eastern origin.

Common dried fruits include black and white raisins from several varieties of grape, notably the succulent Muscat; currants from small seedless grapes, and prunes from pitted or unpitted plums. Dried apples, peaches, pears, figs and apricots (especially the tiny Hunza variety) are good poached to serve with ice cream or custard, or as a side dish for rich meats. Dried apricots and prunes are used frequently in Middle Eastern and Persian lamb dishes. In the United States, dried cherries and blueberries are a recent innovation.

Many dried fruits are graded according to size, color and juiciness: look for intensely colored fruit that is still soft and springy. If raisins or currants seem dry, add boiling water and leave them to soak for 10-15 minutes, draining and drying them before use. They may also be macerated in liqueur or brandy. Other fruits may need to be soaked in warm water or tea. When poaching dried fruit, add any sugar at the end of cooking as it inhibits the fruit from absorbing moisture.

USEFUL INFORMATION

Typical dishes *Far Breton* (raisins, prunes and batter, France); rabbit and prunes (France); *Birnenbrot* (bread with dried pears, Switzerland); Christmas pudding (plum pudding, UK); stewed in white wine (Germany); Christmas Eve compote (red wine (Spain); fig and almond torte (Portugal); mince pies (UK).

Prune

Banana

Fig

Apricot

Peach

Date

Apple

Fruit garnishes

The colors and shapes of fruit provide a host of possible garnishes for the imaginative cook. Simple slices of citrus fruit, kiwi and tamarillo may be used to decorate a wide variety of dishes. The garnish should match the dish: for example, lime slices suit rich soups, while spiced apple rings pair well with robust meats like pork. Thin slices of strawberry make a simple and elegant garnish for cakes and desserts.

Citrus fruit slices are particularly versatile and make a pretty garnish when fluted with a channel knife (p.505). They can be twisted or halved, or quartered and cut into a butterfly shape for decorating individual dishes or the border of a serving dish. Lemon and lime wedges or halves for squeezing may accompany poached and fried fish, vegetable dishes, light meats such as veal, and salads. The wedges may be cut in a zigzag pattern to make a garnish called wolves' teeth, or a thin strip of zest may be cut from one edge to tie in a knot. For desserts, a garnish of orange, cut in similar shapes to those mentioned above, is more popular. All citrus fruits can be hollowed out as cups and filled with sorbet or chilled fruits. Citrus fruit cut into baskets can be filled with soufflé mixture or with small vegetables or cold sauces. A hollowed-out melon, particularly a water-melon, makes an attractive container for fruit salads (p.464). The rind can be etched with a knife in a decorative pattern.

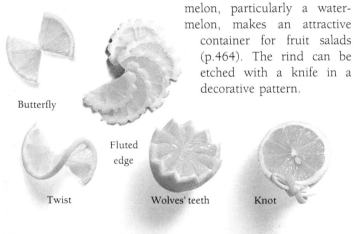

Butterfly

Fluted edge

Twist

Wolves' teeth

Knot

CANDYING CITRUS JULIENNE

Candied citrus julienne makes an attractive garnish for poached fruits, mousses and sorbets. Orange, lemon, lime and grapefruit are all successful. After cutting the zest into julienne strips (p.460), blanch for two minutes in boiling water and then drain.

1 In a small pan gently heat 2 tbsp/ 30 g sugar and 2 tbsp water until the sugar is dissolved. Add blanched julienne of 2 lemons or 1 orange.

2 Simmer until all the water has evaporated and the julienne is transparent, 8-10 minutes. Lift the julienne out with a slotted spoon; it can be stored in an airtight container for 2 days before using.

FROSTING FRUITS

Frosted, or sugared, fruits make pretty decorations for cold desserts or *petits fours* (p.404), while sugared flowers, rose petals or mint leaves enhance small cakes and pastries. Small bunches of grapes or fresh currants are particularly attractive when frosted in sugar. Cape gooseberries and strawberries may also be sugared. Frosted fruits should be used on the day they are made.

1 Separate the fruit or keep in small bunches; divide the leaves or flowers. Rinse the fruit, leaves or flowers and dry them on paper towels. Lightly whisk 2 egg whites.

2 Dip each piece for frosting into the egg white and lift to drain slightly.

3 Transfer fruit, leaves or flowers to a tray of sugar. Turn to coat them and sprinkle a little sugar on top.

4 Transfer the fruit pieces to a rack and leave for 1-2 hours in a dry place to harden. Store in an airtight container for up to 12 hours.

Candied fruit

Fruits are often candied by cooking them in concentrated sugar syrup until they become translucent. The technique, which is tricky as the concentration of the syrup must be carefully controlled, varies according to the ripeness of the fruit and the speed at which it simmers. The candying of whole fruits such as plums or kumquats, or of chestnuts (Fr. *marrons glacés*), requires skill, and several days of successive cooking in ever more concentrated syrups. The syrup must penetrate to the center, so that the fruit can be kept for several weeks at room temperature. Boxes of these fruits – with a glistening coating of sugar glaze – are traditional at Christmas.

Simpler candied fruits, particularly citrus peel and slices, can be made at home. Strips of lemon, orange and grapefruit make a tangy garnish for cakes and cold desserts, and may be dipped in chocolate as a candy (Sugar and Chocolate, p.427). Finely cut citrus julienne, when candied, can make a feathery topping for mousses, cold soufflés and sorbets, as well as for grander desserts or festive cakes. Thick slices of orange or lemon (including the peel) candy well, as do small fruits such as cherries, cranberries and kumquats or pineapple chunks. These fruits are good with meats such as pork and game, as well as with desserts, and they make a pleasant diversion on a plate of *petits fours*. If used in a dessert, candied fruits may be steeped in alcohol such as kirsch or orange liqueur for additional flavor.

Commercially candied fruits are much used in baking. Orange, lemon and citron peel provide flavor, while red and green cherries and angelica are valued for their color. Candied fruits should be tender but not wet. Always buy whole fruits if possible, as pre-cut fruits are more likely to be soapy-flavored or dry and tasteless. If the fruit is dry or encrusted with sugar, soak it in warm water before chopping. Rinse off any syrup in warm water.

CANDYING FRUIT

Sliced fruits or julienne of citrus peel can be candied to eat alone, as a garnish, or to dip in chocolate. Small whole fruits such as cherries can be candied in the same manner. This is a simpler method than for larger whole fruits, such as *marrons glacés*.

1 Cut about 1 lb/500 g fruit such as oranges, grapefruit or limes in ⅜ in/1 cm slices. (Cut pineapple in half slices or chunks.) Heat 2 lb/1 kg sugar with 1 qt/1 L water in a shallow pan until dissolved. Bring the syrup just to a boil.

2 ABOVE Arrange the pieces of fruit or small whole fruits loosely overlapping on a rack and lower it into the pan. Press a round of wax paper on top of the fruit so it is completely immersed in the hot syrup.

3 LEFT Bring the syrup slowly to a simmer, and simmer 10-15 minutes. Do not let it boil. Take the pan from the heat and let the fruit cool. Leave it in the syrup, covered, for 24 hours at room temperature. During this time, leave the fruit undisturbed.

4 ABOVE Carefully lift out the fruit on the rack and leave it to drain for ½-1 hour. Transfer the pieces of fruit to paper towels and leave until dry, 3-5 hours. Store, layered in wax paper, in an airtight container for up to 3 days. The surface of the fruit should be completely dry and hard.

NUTS

Nuts are difficult to define botanically. Technically, they are one-celled fruits with a dry shell, but only hazelnuts, chestnuts, cashews and acorns fall within this narrow scientific definition. Other nuts we eat are in fact edible kernels from which the fruit wall has been removed (almonds, walnuts, coconuts and macadamia nuts); some are seeds (Brazil, pistachio and pine nuts); or legumes (peanuts). Nuts are highly nutritious and full of flavor. Except for peanuts, their cost makes them a relative luxury, but even in small quantities, nuts are a valuable cooking ingredient.

The flavor of individual nuts varies a great deal. Almonds are delicate and are widely used in cooking, while the more strongly flavored walnut is usually restricted to robust dishes, or paired with another strong flavor such as blue cheese or chocolate. Peanuts and cashews have a distinctive flavor that blends well with many ingredients, but their main use in cooking is to add crunch to savory dishes. The mild pistachio lends a pale green color to both savory dishes and sweet fillings or sauces.

All nuts contain oil, but walnuts, hazelnuts and almonds are especially rich and must be carefully ground and handled when mixing with other ingredients so that the oil does not separate and make the mixture heavy. Most nuts can be substituted for one another in a dish when they are intended only to accent flavor or add a contrasting crunch. However, in doughs and cake batters, oily nuts should be interchanged with caution. Chestnuts are the least adaptable, as their texture is quite different.

Choosing nuts

Nuts are processed for the market in a number of ways. The freshest nuts are still in the shell. These are abundant in markets during the winter holiday season and are best for long storage. In general, the larger the nut the better the taste, though small wild nuts can have a wonderfully earthy flavor. Nuts in the shell should be heavy for their size, and intact with no cracks or holes. Scarring can betray age and dryness. Any nut with visible mold should be avoided. Unshelled nuts are often sold in bulk, while shelled nuts are usually packaged, and may be raw or roasted, left whole, slivered, sliced, chopped, broken into larger pieces, or finely ground. All these forms have specific uses in the kitchen. Packaged whole, shelled nuts should be plump and have a uniform color; in bulk they should smell fresh.

Packaged nuts may be processed with preservatives and dyes, and are often heavily seasoned with salt. Dry-roasted nuts are cooked without additional fat, but many other nuts are roasted in different types of fat, or even tossed with honey. Spiced nuts, nuts dipped in chocolate or carob, and sugared or yogurt-coated nuts are also available.

Storing nuts

Because most nuts contain substantial amounts of oil, they easily turn rancid. Exposure to light, moisture or heat will reduce their shelf-life, so they are best kept in their original package or in an airtight container in the refrigerator or freezer. For short-term storage, an airtight container in a dark, cool place will suffice. Nuts in the shell keep longer than shelled ones, and shelled whole nuts last longer than those that are chopped or ground. Nuts sealed in cans may be stored at room temperature until they are opened, and then kept in the refrigerator. Nuts that have become stale or soft may be partially restored by roasting them in the oven. For information on storing individual nuts, see the storage sections on the following pages.

Cooking with nuts

Ground nuts, especially almonds, form the base of many cookies and cakes, pairing well with chocolate, coffee and other flavorings; they are also a natural thickener for sauces. In health food stores, ground nuts are often referred to as "meals" for adding to vegetable pancakes and cereals, or to use as a crunchy topping for gratins, bean dishes, tarts and ice cream desserts. Whole nuts, whether toasted or left plain, decorate cakes and pastries, while chopped nuts may be added to cake batters, meringue mixtures and bread doughs, sprinkled in salads, or mixed with sautéed vegetables. Nut oils (p.103) are popular in salad dressings.

SHELLING & SKINNING NUTS

Soft nuts such as peanuts can be shelled by hand, but tougher types like walnuts need to be cracked first with a nutcracker. Chestnuts are shelled differently (p.481).

Some nuts, such as almonds, are blanched in boiling water to loosen their papery outer skin, but others, such as hazelnuts, are best toasted. The crinkled surface of walnuts and pecans is extremely difficult to peel, so the skin is usually left intact.

1 **To blanch and skin almonds and pistachios:** cover the nuts with boiling water and let them stand for 2-3 minutes. Drain the nuts and let them cool slightly before removing the skin.

2 For almonds, pinch the nut between your thumb and index finger; the nut should slip right out of the skin. If they do not do so easily, return to the hot water for another minute. For pistachios, rub off the skin with your fingers while still warm.

1 **To skin hazelnuts:** roast or toast the hazelnuts (opposite). Wrap the warm nuts in a coarse-textured cloth.

2 Rub the nuts briskly in the cloth to loosen as much skin as possible. Some skin may still adhere and must be removed.

ROASTING OR TOASTING NUTS

Many recipes call for browning nuts in the oven or under the broiler to bring out their rich flavor, deepen their color and increase their crunchiness.

To oven-roast shelled whole or chopped nuts (right): spread the nuts in a single layer on a shallow pan or baking sheet with edges. Bake at 350°F/175°C, shaking the sheet occasionally until the nuts are golden, 7-12 minutes, depending on size. Leave them to cool.

To toast nuts: spread the nuts in a single layer on a shallow pan or baking sheet with edges and broil them about 6 in/15 cm from the heat. Turn the nuts frequently until they are golden, 3-5 minutes. **Note** Nuts scorch very quickly, so keep a careful eye on them while roasting or toasting.

MAKING NUT MILK

Coconut and almonds are the most popular nuts for nut milks, used to flavor stews, sauces, creams, ice creams and summer drinks.

Makes ¾ cup/175 ml nut milk

1 cup/250 ml hot water *or* milk *or* coconut liquid (for coconut milk)

1 cup/100 g unsweetened, shredded coconut *or* ground almonds

1 In a small saucepan, pour the liquid over the nuts. Cover and leave over low heat, 30 minutes. Strain the milk into a bowl through a piece of cheesecloth.

2 ABOVE Gather the ends of the cheesecloth together and squeeze the cloth tightly with your fist to extract as much liquid as possible from the nuts.

Chopping and grinding nuts

The consistency of nuts, whether chopped or ground to a powder, is important to the success of a recipe. Nuts are best chopped by hand so the finished texture can be controlled; it may be coarse or quite fine and will always be uneven. A food processor, coffee grinder or nut mill may also be used for chopping and grinding. It will give a more even consistency, but can very quickly overwork the nuts, forming a paste (see below).

To chop by hand: using a large chopping knife or a curved mincing knife (p.504) in a wooden bowl, chop about ½ cup/50 g nuts at a time until they are broken into pieces of desired size.

To chop in a food processor: using the pulse button, chop about ½ cup/50 g nuts at a time, turning the button on and off until the nuts are broken into the desired size. **Note** Do not overwork them – the machine breaks down the nuts very quickly.

To grind nuts: use a special nut mill, a clean coffee grinder, or a food processor. Work a small amount of nuts at a time so that as little oil as possible is released. If overworked, the nuts will turn into a paste. In a processor, if a recipe uses sugar or flour, add some to the nuts to avoid overworking.

MAKING NUT BUTTERS

Nut butters are simply pastes made from ground nuts, popular as spreads and as flavorings for sauces, soups and stews. Peanuts are the most common, but almonds, hazelnuts and cashews all work well, especially for sweet dishes. All-purpose oil helps the emulsification without adding another flavor.

1 Purée 1 cup/70 g nuts in a food processor or blender until they are ground to a very fine consistency.

2 Pour in 1-2 tablespoons all-purpose oil and continue to process to a paste, 1-2 minutes.

3 The paste may be quite crunchy, or smooth and creamy, as you like. The volume of nuts will be reduced by half.

Making sweetened nut paste

All nuts may be combined with sugar to make a sweetened paste. (This is a good way of using nuts that have been overworked in a food processor or nut mill.) One type of paste is a simple mixture made from grinding nuts to a fine powder with sugar added in equal proportions by weight. In France, this mixture is called *tant pour tant*, denoting equal quantities. It results in a very fine, fluffy paste, used as a delicious flavoring for pastry doughs, cake batters, or fillings such as butter cream. Almonds are traditional, but other nuts such as walnuts and hazelnuts may be substituted.

The second type of paste always contains almonds and is perhaps more familiar as marzipan (Fr. *pâte d'amandes*), which is used to mold into playful shapes, fill elegant chocolates, or coat festive fruit cakes such as wedding or Christmas cakes. Marzipan is slightly more complicated to make than *tant pour tant*, being made with cooked sugar. Different proportions of nuts to sugar may be used depending on the desired texture: a greater proportion of almonds will produce a softer paste that is easier to work and thus ideal for filling or molding, while a greater proportion of sugar will produce a paste that is best for use as a topping. Homemade almond paste almost always has a coarser texture than the commercial type (which is kneaded through mechanical rollers to a highly malleable texture) and should only be used as a topping or coating. To make almond paste, see p.478.

ALMONDS

There are two types of almond: bitter and sweet. Bitter almonds are used to make oil, extract and liqueurs such as Amaretto. Sweet almonds are the most versatile of all nuts. In some cakes and pastries, they may take the place of flour to produce a rich, moist texture and fragrant taste. Almond-based meringues, pastry dough and *petits fours* are staples of French *pâtisserie*; in Italy, almonds provide texture for popular sponge cakes such as *panforte*. Combined with caramel, almonds are the basis of praline and decorative nougatine (p.419).

Sweet almonds also appear in many savory dishes. Whether left whole, sliced or ground, they have an affinity for fish and chicken, appearing in dishes such as the Spanish *suquet* (fish stew) and Indian royal chicken with almond sauce. The French term *amandine* refers to a garnish of sliced or slivered almonds, sautéed in butter until golden brown and sprinkled over fish fillets, chicken breasts or vegetables. Finely ground almonds flavor German soup and Austrian pancakes, served hot with sugar and lemon.

Sweet almond

USEFUL INFORMATION

Portion 2 lb/1 kg unshelled yields 3 cups/500 g shelled; 1 cup/70 g whole yields 1-1¼ cups shredded or ground.
Nutritive value per 3½ oz/100 g (raw): 598 calories; 19 g protein; 54 g fat; 20 g carbohydrates; no cholesterol; 4 mg sodium.
Problems May be dry and tasteless if bought pre-ground.
Processed forms *Shelled*: roasted; blanched; unblanched; whole; halved; slivered; shredded; chopped; ground; salted; unsalted; smoked; sugared; candy-coated; chocolate-coated; extract; butter; oil; flour (meal); unsweetened and sweetened paste (marzipan).
Storage In airtight container. *Unshelled*: in a cool, dry place 1 year. *Shelled*: refrigerate 6 months; freeze 1 year.
Typical dishes Baked Brie with toasted almonds (USA); with spiny lobster, chicken and tomato (Spain); with veal escalopes (Germany); stuffed in chicken (Hungary); shortbread (UK); biscuits (Russia); pudding (Middle East); Bakewell tart (with raspberry jam, almond cream, UK); chicken in egg, almond, and sherry sauce (Spain); macaroons (Italy); soufflé (Germany); flummery (custard, UK); saffron pudding with almonds (India); tart (Portugal); with chocolate and cinnamon for sweet pasta (Italy).

Almond paste

Almond paste, or marzipan, is used as a cake topping; it may be easily molded into cake decorations, and is a popular filling for candies and chocolates (p.428).

Makes 2 cups/500 g

1½ cups/300 g sugar	1¾ cups/175 g ground almonds
¾ cup/175 ml water (plus 2 tbsp)	

1 Make a sugar syrup with the sugar and water, and cook it to the hard-ball stage (p.415), 248°F/120°C on a sugar thermometer.
2 Meanwhile, put the ground nuts in a mixer with a dough hook, or in a mortar and pestle and stir in 2 tbsp water. Let the bubbles subside in the hot syrup, then pour it on to the ground almonds, with the mixer turning, or pound constantly in a mortar. Continue working until the paste clings together.
3 With your fingers, knead small portions of the paste until smooth. Pack it into an airtight container and store up to 2 weeks.

WALNUTS & PECANS

Walnuts and pecans are closely related and share the same type of irregular nutmeat that is hard to peel. With the exception of fresh "wet" walnuts, the skin is left on for eating raw and cooking.

The most common species of walnut is the European, English or Persian walnut; the same species is known in the United States as the California walnut. Native only to America is the black walnut, a dark brown nut surrounding a rather astringent kernel; the texture is somewhat oily, good in cookies, cakes and ice cream. The milder white American butternut is also rich in oil, and it is used in cooking like the common walnut.

Walnuts are particularly useful in baking, where they add rich flavor to hearty breads and cakes, sometimes combined with fruit such as bananas. Broken walnuts add crunch to salads such as Toasted walnut and Roquefort salad (p.102), while ground walnuts form the base of sauces like Turkish *tarator* and Italian walnut sauce for pasta (p.66). Walnut oil is expensive and often used to dress salads in the south of France.

Native to the United States and a particular specialty of the American South, pecans are a type of hickory nut. They are famous paired with molasses in pecan pie, and in butter pecan ice cream, and also feature in vegetable dishes and stuffings, especially for festive turkey and goose. Other less common, regional hickory nuts, such as the aromatic shagbark nut and shellbark nut, may be treated like pecans.

USEFUL INFORMATION

Portion 2 lb/1 kg unshelled yields 5 cups/500 g shelled.
Nutritive value per 3½ oz/100 g (raw). *Common walnut*: 651 calories; 15 g protein; 64 g fat; 16 g carbohydrates; 2 mg sodium. *Pecan*: 687 calories; 9 g protein; 71 g fat; 15 g carbohydrates; trace sodium.
Problems Can be very oily, so taste before grinding and reduce fat in recipe accordingly, some varieties can be bitter. *Pecan*: shells very hard, so buy pre-shelled.
Processed forms *Walnut, unshelled*: pickled; *shelled*: halves; pieces; chopped; ground; oil; jam; jelly; ketchup. *Pecan, shelled*: roasted halves; pieces; chopped; ground.
Storage In airtight container. *Unshelled*: in a cool, dry place 2-3 months. *Shelled*: refrigerate 6 months; freeze 1 year.
Typical dishes *Walnut*: cold trout in walnut sauce (Russia); sweet turnovers (Spain); cake (USA); green walnut preserve (Middle East); pickled green walnuts (UK, France); pastries (Greece); *gâteau aux noix* (cake, France); biscuits (Balkans), raisin and walnut pie (USA); peppers in walnut sauce (Mexico); cake with candied peel (Italy); beet and walnut salad (USA); soup (with cream and chicken stock, Mexico). *Pecan*: with chicken (USA); sandies (cookies, USA); pie (USA); meat loaf with pecan stuffing (USA).

European walnut   **Butternut**

Pecan

HAZELNUTS

Hazelnuts (also known as cobnuts, and commercially as filberts) contribute a wonderful aromatic flavor to all types of baked goods. When ground, they may replace some of the flour and fat in cakes and cookies. Hazelnuts make an excellent butter and are often used to flavor ice cream, especially in Italy. Most hazelnuts are cultivated in Europe and North America. They grow in clusters, each nut surrounded by a fuzzy husk that opens when the nut is ripe. The skin is so hard to remove from the kernel that the nuts must be toasted (p.477) and then rubbed with a towel. Handle ground hazelnuts with special care so that the oil does not separate in a batter, making it heavy.

Although chiefly prized in cakes and pastries, hazelnuts also suit savory ingredients such as chicken and game. When chopped, they may be combined with melted butter to scatter on fish and shellfish such as trout or lobster or used plain to sprinkle over soups, salads and summer fruit dishes. They pair well with mushrooms and green vegetables such as Brussels sprouts.

USEFUL INFORMATION

Portion 2 lb/1 kg unshelled yields 4½ cups/500 g shelled.
Nutritive value per 3½ oz/100 g (raw): 634 calories; 13 g protein; 62 g fat; 17 g carbohydrates; no cholesterol; 2 mg sodium.
Problems Quickly turn rancid at room temperature.
Processed forms *Shelled:* whole; pieces; raw; roasted; blanched; unblanched; salted; unsalted; candied; butter; oil.
Storage In airtight container. *Unshelled*: in a cool, dry place 1 month. *Shelled*: refrigerate 3-4 months; freeze 1 year.
Typical dishes Ham steaks with hazelnut butter (Germany); torte (Hungary); biscuits (Spain); apple pudding (Austria); *pavé aux noisettes* (gâteau with chocolate,

France); *haselnüssbogen* (crescent cookies, Austria); rum Linzertorte (Austria); omelet (Germany); *noisettines* (pastries, France); in caramel (USA); cake with chocolate filling (Middle East); *croquets aux noisettes* (hazelnut cookies, France); hazelnut jelly roll (*biscuit* with whipped cream filling, USA); in meringue layer cake with raspberries and cream (UK); hazelnut and cherry salad (USA).

ALL-PURPOSE NUTS

Some nuts we think of primarily as snacks. They are sold toasted and salted, sometimes even sweetened with honey or sugar. However, for the cook, plain, untreated nuts are the most useful.

The most popular of all snacks must be the peanut, also called groundnut and earth nut. Originally from South America, the peanut is actually the seed of a tropical legume. Two types are important commercially: the small Spanish, and the longer Virginian peanut; both are similar in flavor. Smaller varieties are important for oil (p.102). Peanuts appear in curries, vegetable stews and sauces, notably in West African cooking.

The pistachio is valued for its pale green color, and is used whole in pâtés and terrines, as a topping for cakes and candies, or puréed in dessert sauces and ice cream. Native to central Asia and the Middle East, the pistachio has a beige shell that splits open when roasted. For cooking, avoid pistachio shells that have been dyed bright red.

Kidney-shaped cashews, exported from India, East Africa, and South America, are rare in Western cuisine, although they appear extensively in both sweet and savory Asian dishes. The nut grows under an edible fleshy fruit, the cashew apple, and is surrounded by two shells that contain a caustic oil so irritating to the skin that cashews are always sold shelled. During cooking they may become soggy so they should be added just before serving.

The culinary uses of brazil nuts and macadamias are similar. Both are high in calories and fat, well-suited to stuffings, cakes and cookies, although they are more often eaten as a snack. The Brazil nut is the fruit of a huge tropical tree that bears pods containing up to two dozen nuts. It is native to the Amazon. Macadamia nuts were first developed in Australia but nowadays the largest commercial crop is in Hawaii.

USEFUL INFORMATION

Portion *Peanut, cashew*: 2 lb/1 kg unshelled yields 6½ cups/750 g shelled. *Pistachio*: 2 lb/1 kg unshelled yields 3 cups/540 g shelled. *Brazil, macadamia*: 2 lb/1 kg unshelled yields 4½ cups/500 g shelled.
Nutritive value per 3½ oz/100 g (raw). *Peanut*: 564 calories; 26 g protein; 48 g fat; 19 g carbohydrates; no cholesterol; 5 mg sodium. *Pistachio*: 594 calories; 19 g protein; 54 g fat; 19 g carbohydrates; no cholesterol; 7 mg sodium. *Cashew*: 561 calories; 17 g protein; 46 g fat; 29 g carbohydrates; no cholesterol; 200 mg sodium. *Brazil*: 654 calories; 14 g protein; 67 g fat; 11 g carbohydrates; no cholesterol; 1 mg sodium. *Macadamia*: 691 calories; 8 g protein; 72 g fat; 16 g carbohydrates; no cholesterol; 7 mg sodium.
Problems Can become soft if overcooked. *Pistachio*: can be oversalted. *Brazil, macadamia*: hard to shell without crushing kernel.
Processed forms *Peanut, shelled*: raw; roasted; whole; pieces; blanched; unblanched; salted; unsalted; dry-roasted; honey-roasted; chocolate-covered; brittle;

butter; oil. *Pistachio, shelled*: roasted; salted; unsalted. *Cashew, shelled*: whole; pieces; raw; roasted; dry-roasted; salted; unsalted; butter. *Brazil, shelled*: roasted whole; chopped. *Macadamia, shelled*: roasted in coconut oil; dry-roasted; salted; unsalted.
Storage In airtight container. *Peanut, unshelled*: refrigerate 9 months; *shelled*: refrigerate 3 months; freeze 6 months. *Pistachio, unshelled*: refrigerate 3 months; freeze 1 year; *shelled*: refrigerate 3 months; do not freeze. *Cashew*: refrigerate 6 months; freeze 1 year. *Brazil, unshelled*: in a cool, dry place 2 months; *shelled*: refrigerate 6 months; freeze 9 months. *Macadamia, shelled*: refrigerate 2 months; do not freeze.
Typical dishes *Peanut*: butter cookies (USA); soup with sherry (Caribbean); peanut-colored rice (Mexico); chicken with shrimp in sauce (Brazil); peppery soup (Africa); groundnut chop (beef stew with tomatoes, Africa); chutney (with ginger, yogurt, coriander, India); sauce for aubergines (China); sauce with coconut for turnip greens and spinach (Asia). *Pistachio*: ice cream (USA); rice salad with currants and chopped vegetables (USA); cake (France); pudding with cardamom (India); pastries (Middle East). *Cashew*: nut mousse (Brazil); nut fudge (India); with chicken in Hoisin sauce (China). *Brazil*: cake (Brazil); dipped in chocolate (UK); in salad with watercress and orange (USA). *Macadamia*: pie (Hawaii); with chicken (Hawaii).

Macadamia

Brazil nut

Pistachio

Peanut

COCONUT

Coconuts are much larger and fleshier than other nuts, often the size of a football, with a shaggy coat that is usually removed before sale to make matting. Coconut liquid, from inside the nut, is not to be confused with the coconut milk that is made by infusing grated coconut in milk or water (p.477). In tropical Asia and Africa where the coconut is cultivated, the nut is often gathered still green and immature, when the jelly-like meat is soft and the liquid clear. In the West, coconuts reach the markets fully ripened, with a brown skin and solid meat surrounding the milky liquid. When choosing a coconut, shake it to listen for the splash of liquid; stale coconuts contain little liquid.

Coconut meat is usually grated to use as a topping or to add to a variety of cookies, cakes and puddings. In Asia, it is often used in savory curries or combined with other ingredients for a refreshing condiment. Shredded, dried (desiccated) coconut is popular as a topping or it may be mixed with butter cream for a frosting. Fresh coconut milk flavors summer drinks such as piña colada. Some canned coconut cream may be heavily sweetened and should not be substituted for canned unsweetened or freshly made coconut milk.

USEFUL INFORMATION

Portion 1 coconut yields about 2½ cups/225 g grated meat.
Nutritive value per 3½ oz/100 g. *Fresh*: 346 calories; 4 g protein; 35 g fat; 9 g carbohydrates; no cholesterol; 23 mg sodium. *Dried unsweetened*: 660 calories; 7 g protein; 64 g fat; 23 g carbohydrates; no cholesterol; 39 mg sodium. *Dried sweetened*: 443 calories; 4 g protein; 32 g fat; 53 g carbohydrates; no cholesterol; 20 mg sodium.
Problems Fresh coconut meat is difficult to extract.
Processed forms Shredded; grated; flaked; dry; moist; cream; sweetened; unsweetened; toasted; extract; canned milk; syrup; honey; oil.
Storage *Unopened*: at room temperature 2-4 months. *Opened*: refrigerate 1 week; freeze 9 months.
Typical dishes *Flan de coco* (custard, Spain); coconut cream pie (USA); pudding (Hawaii); soup with chicken and nutmeg (Brazil); *cocada* (custard with sherry, Mexico); cake with ginger (Africa); chicken in coconut milk (Caribbean); jam (Middle East).

Shrimp in coconut sauce

Hot boiled rice is the perfect foil to this spicy dish, *Sambal goreng udang*, which is Indonesian in origin.

Serves 4

1 lb/500 g raw jumbo shrimp	½ in/1.25 cm piece of fresh ginger, peeled and chopped
2 fresh hot chili peppers, stemmed, seeded and chopped	1 cup/250 ml water
1 large onion, chopped	1 cup/250 ml coconut milk (p.477)
zest of 1 lemon	2 tsp fresh lemon juice
4-5 fresh basil leaves	1 tsp salt
1 tsp ground turmeric	1 scallion, cut in julienne

1 Shell the shrimp (p.160). Rinse and dry them on paper towels.
2 Purée the chili peppers, onion, and lemon zest in a food processor or blender. Transfer to a heavy saucepan; stir in the basil, turmeric, ginger and water. Bring to a boil, reduce heat, and simmer until the water has almost evaporated, 6-8 minutes.
3 Add the coconut milk and shrimp. Cook gently, stirring frequently, until the shrimp are firm and pink, 4-5 minutes. (Do not boil the sauce hard or it will curdle.) Remove the pan from the heat, stir in the lemon juice and salt, and taste for seasoning. Sprinkle the julienne of scallion on top; serve immediately.

PREPARING FRESH COCONUT

Coconuts must be cracked open and the juice drained before the meat can be removed.

1 Using an awl or small screwdriver, pierce each of the three weak spots, found at the stem end, called "eyes".

2 Drain the liquid through the holes. **Note** If using the liquid for coconut milk or drinks, strain through a coffee filter.

3 Set the coconut on a cloth. With a hammer, the back of a cleaver, or a heavy knife, tap the coconut about one-third down from the eyes while turning the nut slowly. When you hear a faint cracking sound, you will have reached the nut's natural fault line. Continue tapping until the coconut separates into two pieces (this may not happen at once, but persist until it does). Break the coconut into pieces with the hammer.

4 With a knife, pry out the white meat from the shell and trim off the brown skin.

PINE NUTS

Pine nuts (also called pignolia nuts or by their Spanish name, *piñons*) are the seeds obtained from the cones of certain pine trees such as the European stone pine and the pinon pine of the southwestern United States and Mexico.

The soft edible kernel is white, oval, and very small with a sweet aroma. Much appreciated in the Mediterranean and the Middle East, pine nuts are often added to stuffings for poultry and vine leaves (p.265), and to meat, game and vegetable stews and soups, as well as to desserts. They are the foundation of Italian *pesto* sauce (p.17) and may be sprinkled on custard-filled tarts and pastries and included in salads.

Pine nuts are usually sold already blanched. After toasting, which improves their sweet flavor, they may be ground for adding to savory dishes, or left whole and sprinkled on meats and salads, especially those with cheese. The natural oil in pine nuts turns rancid very quickly, so they should be refrigerated for no more than one month or frozen for two to three months.

EXOTIC NUTS

A number of exotic nuts are native to Africa; most familiar is probably the cola (or kola) nut, which contains the stimulants theobromine, kolanine and caffeine, minute amounts of which may be found in sparkling drinks such as Coca-Cola. The cola nut is rather bitter; few Westerners have found a place for it in their cuisine, though the French sometimes use small amounts in desserts. Another African nut is the dika, of much less importance and used only when ground into an oily paste, called dika "bread".

The cohune nut, similar in structure and appearance to the coconut, is native to central America and is valued exclusively for its oil, used for making margarine. Another oily nut, the Asian candlenut (so-named because it is said to burn just like a candle), is ground to use in sauces, soups and curries. When young and raw, the candlenut is quite poisonous, so it is roasted before eating.

The beechnut, little used today, was formerly ground into flour and crushed to make oil. The castanopsis nut looks like a chestnut and is a name given to a large family of fruits, including native American chinquapins, the tonkin chestnut, and Asian chestnuts. The fruits are boiled or roasted before eating. Water chestnuts (p.303) are not a fruit, but a corm, or tuber.

Grating fresh coconut

Fresh coconut must be grated or shredded before it is used in sweet or savory dishes. A food processor or blender may be used to shred the coconut finely; grating by hand produces a coarser flake. Freshly grated coconut gives the best results when making coconut milk – indispensable to many Indian and Indonesian dishes. Dried, or desiccated coconut, available coarsely or finely shredded, is better suited to desserts and confectionery.

To grate coconut by hand: pare off any brown skin still attached to the meat. Grate the coconut using the coarse side of the grater.
To grate coconut by machine: put the coconut and a little water into the work bowl of a food processor or in a blender and turn the machine on and off until you reach the desired texture.

CHESTNUT

The edible chestnut (not to be confused with the horse chestnut) is particularly sweet and starchy. Wild chestnuts (Fr *châtaigne*), contain two or three smaller nuts with flat sides within their outer prickly husk, while common chestnuts (Fr. *marrons*) have a single large nut. To increase their sweetness, freshly gathered chestnuts are often "cured" by storing for a few days so that some of their starch is converted into sugar.

The French and Italians like to treat chestnuts as a vegetable, glazing and mixing them whole with Brussels sprouts or red cabbage, or puréeing them for a classic accompaniment to meat and in stuffings for poultry, often with sausagemeat, onion or celery. Celebrated desserts include *mont blanc*, a meringue topped with sweetened chestnut purée and whipped cream, and chestnuts with chocolate in a pavé (p.425). Dried chestnuts are an Italian specialty for simmering in soup, or making light cakes.

Fresh chestnuts must be skinned of both peel and papery skin (below). Peeled, vacuum-packed chestnuts most nearly approach the fresh. Whole, unsweetened canned chestnuts are a substitute for cooked fresh ones, though they are dense and weigh the same as a fresh nut with its peel. Canned, sweetened chestnut purée is more widely available but is heavy and extraordinarily rich.

USEFUL INFORMATION

Portion 2 lb/1 kg unpeeled yields 1½ cups/375 g peeled.
Nutritive value per 3½ oz/100 g (raw): 194 calories; 3 g protein; 2 g fat; 42 g carbohydrates; no cholesterol; 6 mg sodium.
Cooking methods *Unpeeled*: blanch 1 minute before peeling; broil or roast at 400°F/200°C, 15-20 minutes. *Peeled*: braise at 350°F/175°C, ¾-1 hour; simmer ½-¾ hour.
When done Very tender.
Problems Fragile, easily break into pieces when cooked; moist, so they mold quickly at room temperature.

Processed forms *Whole, peeled*: canned in water and syrup; candied, dried; flour. *Purée*: canned sweetened, unsweetened.
Storage In airtight container. *Fresh, unpeeled*: at room temperature 1 week; refrigerate in perforated plastic bag 1 month; freeze 6 months. *Dried*: in a cool, dry place 2 months; freeze 6 months.
Typical dishes Glazed (Germany); stuffing with wild rice and sherry (USA); soup with ham and bacon (Spain); *gâteau Lyonnais* (chocolate cake, France).

PREPARING CHESTNUTS

Chestnuts may be peeled in three different ways; each method is time-consuming as the peel clings tightly.

Method 1 Cut all the shell and skin from the nuts with a very sharp knife. This method is best if you do not wish to cook the chestnuts.

Method 2 Pierce nuts once with the point of a knife, then broil until the shells split. When cool, peel. With this method, the nut is partially cooked but dry.

Method 3 RIGHT: Bring nuts to a boil in water. Drain a few at a time and peel while still hot. If they start to cool and are difficult to peel, reheat.

page

5

PRESERVING & FREEZING

484

MICROWAVE COOKING

497

COOKING EQUIPMENT

502

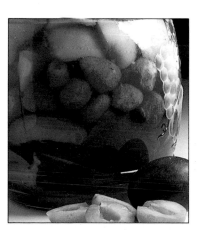

PRESERVING & FREEZING

THE PROCESS OF preserving food was developed out of necessity as one of the first culinary skills of the human race, to ensure survival through the winter months. The natural preserving agents were sun, sand, salt, smoke and wind. Fruit and vegetables were laid in the sun or buried in the sand to dry; meat and fish were rubbed with salt or packed in brine, or hung in the smoke from peat fires; salted fish and meat could also be dried in the wind.

Modern technology has made food preserving one of the world's most important industries, but many of the traditional techniques developed over the centuries are still useful in the home kitchen. There is great satisfaction to be had out of turning a surplus of home-grown produce into jams and pickles, freezing young vegetables, or smoking a freshly caught trout. Home preserving is economical, and the flavor is incomparable.

Preventing food spoilage

To preserve food, by whatever means, is to arrest the development of decay. Unless food is consumed when fresh or preserved, bacteria, molds and yeasts will grow and feed on it, making it rot. Bacteria spread rapidly in warm, moist conditions and cause food poisoning that can sometimes be fatal. Salmonella is the best known of the harmful bacteria, especially prone to develop in meat that has been standing in a warm place, or which has not been thoroughly cooked. Mold is easy to spot, and is usually blueish-green or white. Some types of mold, such as that in blue cheese, are benign; others taste extremely bitter and can be harmful. Yeast causes fermentation and grows on the skins of fruit. In wine and bread, fermentation is cultivated deliberately, but most fermented foods develop a sharp, unpleasant taste. Tiny bubbles also betray fermentation.

Most living organisms can be destroyed by heat and cold, and their action can be inhibited by preserving agents such as alcohol, vinegar, salt and sugar. Removing all moisture from food is another way of inactivating bacteria; hence the efficacy of drying and smoking. Commercially, food can also be freeze-dried. Botulism, the most deadly form of food poisoning, can survive without oxygen and can only be killed at extremely high temperatures. Botulism is a serious, if rare, hazard of canning.

DRYING

Drying is the oldest form of food preservation, and dried foods, including rice, nuts, and legumes, still form a vital part of the modern diet. Traditional drying techniques depend on the forces of nature – sunlight and shade, air temperature and humidity – and require considerable skill. If food dries too slowly, micro-organisms can grow; if it dries too fast, moisture can be trapped inside, spoiling the food.

Drying can be done in the open air, under glass or indoors. The food is stacked on racks with enough space between to allow air to circulate. A light netting or cheesecloth cover can be employed to protect food against bugs and debris, but it should not touch the food. Most commercially dried fruits are sun-dried in hot, dry climates. The process is particularly suited to fruits high in acid and sugar, like apples, apricots, citrus peel, plums, figs and dates.

Most fruits and vegetables may be dried easily in a home oven. A convection oven is excellent because of the built-in fan, but the most important requirement is that the oven should be able to maintain a temperature of 120-140°F/49-60°C. Drying heat should never exceed 140°F/60°C or the fruits and vegetables will become tough and lose their nutrients. If the temperature is too low, it will allow mold and bacteria to develop. The food is arranged on racks narrow enough to let air circulate around the sides, and with no less than 3 in/7.5 cm between each tray. For conventional ovens, the door should be propped open and a fan positioned to blow air into the oven; the kitchen itself must be well ventilated during the process. From time to time, rotate the racks top to bottom and back to front. Turn over the food once or twice but not until all visible juices appear to have dried.

Oven drying can be successful, but if you are drying foods regularly, a commercial dehydrator, which allows the control of temperature and humidity, is more efficient and effective. Fruit and vegetables can be dried successfully, but drying meat, poultry and fish at home is not recommended. For the best method of drying herbs, see p.14.

Fruit and vegetables

Select fruit that is firm and just ripe. Melons and citrus fruit, whose fragrant flesh consists mostly of water, are not good candidates for drying as the finished product is too bland; blackberries and raspberries tend to be too seedy to be palatable when dried.

Peel the fruit if necessary (berries may be left whole) and cut it into fairly thin pieces. The more cut surface exposed to the air, the more moisture can evaporate. Cut away any bruised patches. To prevent pale fruit from darkening by oxidation, soak it in a solution of ascorbic acid and water, allowing 1½ tsp acid to 1 cup/250 ml water for apples, or half that amount for peaches, nectarines and pears. A sweet sugar and honey solution may be used instead: dissolve 1 cup/200 g sugar in 3 cups/750 ml water, then add 1 cup/250 ml honey. Fruit dried with honey produces a candied effect. Do not soak fruit for more than one hour as it will absorb too much moisture and resist drying.

For extra sweetness, fruits may be cooked for a few minutes in a heavy sugar syrup (p.414), drained and then dried. Spread the fruit in a single layer on a drying tray and, if air-drying, cover it with netting to protect it against insects. When done, the dried fruit should feel leathery and pliable. Successfully dried fruit can be stored for six to eight months in a cool place.

The fruit, root and tuber vegetables generally dry better than leaves or stems, but the key to successful drying and rehydration is always to use fresh produce that is mature but not woody or overripe. Prepare vegetables for drying by cutting them into thin, even slices. Most vegetables should be blanched first, though this is not necessary with tomatoes, bell peppers, mushrooms, okra, beet and onions.

Depending on the structure of their flesh, vegetables will range in texture from leathery to crisp and brittle when dried. Drying time varies according to the texture of the food and how thickly or thinly it has been sliced. Slices about ¼ in/6 mm thick take about two hours to dry; ½ in/1.25 cm slices would take about eight hours. The longer the drying process and storage time, the less tender and flavorsome the vegetable will be when it is finally rehydrated, so thinner slices that require a shorter drying time give the best results.

Storage and rehydration

Dried food must be packed immediately, so it does not absorb moisture from the air. Pack the food loosely in a glass or plastic container and store in a cool, dry place.

Vegetables rehydrate more slowly than fruits because they lose more of their moisture content when drying. Immerse the dried food in water and let it soak long enough to plump out by reabsorbing moisture, which may be any time from 15 minutes to two hours. Use alone or in dishes as desired. Cook rehydrated fruits and vegetables immediately, and simmer rather than boil them so that they retain their shape.

Drying tomatoes

Split plum tomatoes lengthwise and arrange cut-side up on racks so that the slices are not touching each other. Sprinkle lightly with salt and dry in an oven at 120°F/49°C until they are leathery, about 24 hours. Pack the tomatoes in sterilized jars with a peeled garlic clove and fresh rosemary or basil. Cover with good quality olive oil and store in a cool, dry place. These tomatoes are best eaten after they have mellowed for a week or two and do not need rehydrating.

PRESERVING IN ALCOHOL

Alcohol is an excellent preservative, particularly of fruit. Fruit steeped in alcohol will keep almost indefinitely and in any case should be allowed to mature for several weeks before eating. Small portions can be served with some of the syrup as an after-dinner liqueur, or spooned over ice cream or sponge cake.

Distilled spirits like rum, brandy, *eau de vie* or vodka, which are at least 80 proof (containing 40 percent alcohol) may be used for flavor. Pure ethyl alcohol, generally sold in strengths up to 95 proof, is a cheaper alternative. As high proof alcohol tends to shrink the fruit and some sweetening is desirable, it is generally mixed with a sugar-and-water syrup before use. For each 1 lb/ 500 g fruit, you will need 2 cups/500 ml alcohol and a syrup made with ½ cup/100 g sugar and ¼ cup/60 ml water.

To preserve whole fruits, pack the washed fruit in jars leaving ½ in/1.25 cm headroom. Pour the sweetened alcohol over the fruit; store in a tightly closed jar in a cool, dark place.

Note Soft fruits lose their texture if stored for too long; discoloration is a sign the fruits may have started to ferment.

Making a *rumtopf*

A crock of spirits to which layers of stemmed, pitted and cut-up fruit are added as they come into season is called a *rumtopf* (German for rum pot), tutti frutti, or brandy pot. Most ripe, perfect fruit can be used, but strawberries, sour cherries, apricots, peaches, plums, pears and pineapple are best, being both juicy and reasonably firm. As each variety becomes available, prepare about 1 lb/500 g fruit, sprinkle with ½ cup/100 g sugar and leave to stand overnight. Then add the fruit to the crock, being careful not to disturb the layer beneath, and pour on rum or brandy to cover. Replace the lid and store in a cool, dry place. Before eating, leave to mature for a few weeks after the last addition.

Rumtopf made with a variety of soft fruits of contrasting colors.

Making mincemeat

Preserving meat by steeping it in alcohol has been practised since the fifteenth century. One recipe calls for "a hare, a pheasant, two partridges, two pigeons and conies [rabbits] strongly spiced and cooked". But not until the seventeenth century did the traditional Christmas fruit preserve with raisins, sugar and citrus peel begin to evolve. Nowadays many mincemeat recipes use only suet (see Animal fats, p.97) or even no meat at all, but the real product should contain meat. Beef tongue, brisket or rump are traditional and survive as ingredients particularly in many American recipes for mincemeat. The meat and other ingredients mature agreeably without spoiling with the addition of a hearty dose of alcohol, and the sugar also acts as a preservative.

Mincemeat

Brandy or sherry is the preferred alcohol for mincemeat. In similar versions to this one, the meat can be omitted, and less alcohol will be needed for the suet. Mincemeat is normally baked in a double crust pie and served hot with whipped cream or hard sauce.

Makes 8-10 cups/2-2.5 kg

6 oz/175 g rump steak (optional)	3 cups/600 g sugar
3 cups/375 g ground suet (p.97)	½ tsp each ground cinnamon, nutmeg, allspice and cloves
3 cups/375 g raisins	
3 cups/375 g currants	salt and pepper
3 cups/375 g candied mixed peel	¾ cup/175 ml brandy
3 cups/375 g tart green apples, peeled, cored and chopped	juice and grated zest of 2 lemons

1 Broil the steak until well done. Allow it to cool, discarding the juice, then grind it or chop it finely.
2 Mix all the ingredients together in a bowl, cover and leave to stand for several hours.
3 Pack the mincemeat into sterilized jars, seal tightly and store in a cool, dry place for up to six weeks.

PRESERVING WITH FAT

A time-honored way of protecting meat, fish and shellfish from air, and thus from some of the micro-organisms that cause spoilage, is to seal it in fat. The method best suits pork, goose and duck, which all render quantities of tasty fat during cooking. Long, slow cooking reduces the moisture content of the meat and eliminates bacteria, as well as making the meat fork-tender. However, because fat turns rancid, fat-sealing is a relatively short-term means of preservation: four months in the refrigerator is the recommended maximum.

Techniques

The *confits*, or conserves, of southwestern France are made with portions of duck, goose, pork or poultry giblets. The meat is first salted (p.488) to pickle it lightly and draw out the moisture, then it is gently cooked in fat until it falls off the bone. Lastly it is sealed in its own cooking fat. *Confits* are indispensable to bean *cassoulets*, soups such as *garbure*, and other winter dishes with lentils and beans. *Confit* needs several weeks to mellow. When consuming a jar of *confit* little by little, keep the remaining pieces of meat covered with more melted fat.

Rillettes (p.243) are a type of coarse-textured pâté. Pork, goose or rabbit is gently cooked in fat as for *confit*. Then the fat is strained off, the meat shredded, packed in sterilized crocks and covered with a layer of fat. *Rillettes* may be kept in the refrigerator for two months but once the seal is broken they should be eaten within the week.

In Britain, a technique known as potting, where meat, fish and shellfish are preserved in fat in little jars, is an ancient practice. The principle is the same as for *rillettes* – long, slow cooking and sealing with fat – but the meat or fish is often spiced and puréed before potting. Potted shrimp are often left whole, preserved in butter and flavored with allspice and cayenne. Potted cheese is also a delicacy. The cheese is not cooked, but pounded with butter and sometimes a spirit such as Armagnac.

Confit of duck

The pieces of duck should be immersed completely in fat so that they do not come into contact with the air. A piece of *confit* is an essential ingredient of bean *cassoulet* and *garbure* soup, both specialties of southwest France. The *confit* is added after the main ingredients are cooked, to add flavor. Serving portions of goose, pork or turkey can be prepared in the same way.

Serves 4

4 lb/1.8 kg duck	2 lb/1 kg melted lard or goose fat (more if needed)
2-3 tbsp/30-45 g coarse salt	
pepper	
2-3 bay leaves	**Large terrine or earthenware crock**
2-3 sprigs thyme	

1 Cut the duck into eight pieces (p.176), removing the backbone and trimming the neck and wings. Rub the pieces with salt and put in a crock or terrine. Season with pepper, crumble on the bay leaves and add the thyme; cover and leave in a cool place for 6-12 hours (the longer you leave it, the stronger it will be) turning the pieces occasionally.
2 When ready to cook, wipe off the excess salt and put the duck pieces skin side down in a flameproof dish. Bake at 300°F/150°C until the fat runs and the duck begins to brown, 15-20 minutes. Add melted lard or goose fat just to cover the duck pieces, cover the pan and continue cooking until the duck is very tender and has rendered all its fat, about two hours.
3 Remove the duck from the pan. Strain the fat and separate it from the gravy. Pour a layer of the rendered fat in the base of a terrine and leave until set. Lay the duck pieces on top and cover completely with melted fat, adding more melted fat if necessary. Cover the terrine and refrigerate for at least a week for the flavors to mellow.
4 To serve *confit* as a main course, lift out the pieces of duck, brushing off as much fat as possible. Bake at 350°F/175°C until very hot and the skin is browned, 15-20 minutes. Use the remaining fat for deep-frying potatoes with garlic to serve as an accompaniment to the duck.

Potted shrimp

Serve the shrimp with toast or buttered wholewheat bread, as an appetizer or tasty snack.

Serves 8

2 lb/1 kg tiny or medium-sized shrimp, cooked	salt and pepper
¼ tsp ground allspice	1½ cups/375 g clarified butter (p.99)
¼ tsp ground nutmeg	
pinch cayenne	**Earthenware crock**

1 Peel the shrimp. In a heatproof dish, combine the shrimp with the allspice, nutmeg, cayenne, salt and pepper. Pour over three-quarters of the clarified butter, cover the dish and bake at 300°F/150°C for one hour.
2 Let cool slightly, then coarsely chop medium-sized shrimp in a food processor. Leave tiny shrimp whole. Taste for seasoning. Pack the shrimp into a sterilized crock, smooth the top and pour over the remaining butter to seal them. The shrimp will keep for two weeks in the refrigerator.

SMOKING

Smoking has long been used to preserve foods; today it is valued chiefly for the distinctive flavor it gives to fish, meat, and even cheese. Traditionally, meat, poultry, game and fish are salted before being smoked; in the past smoking and salting processes for fish often resulted in such a strong taste that the fish had to be soaked in water before being prepared for the table; modern techniques allow a lighter hand.

Home smoking has developed into a well-documented hobby, particularly popular with hunters and fishermen who experiment with different processes. They vary smoking times, temperatures and fuel to achieve subtle differences in taste, and often build ingenious cold-smokers from converted sheds or oil drums.

Characteristic flavors can be imparted to food by building fires of aromatic woods. Pieces of hardwood, corn cobs, maple, hickory, birch or mesquite are best, while fruit woods such as apple and cherry, and grapevine cuttings also smoke well. However, woods like pine, cypress, and balsam contain resins that interfere with both flavor and preservation.

Cold- and hot-smoking techniques

There are two kinds of smoking: cold-smoking, which is a true preserving technique, and hot-smoking, which partially preserves the food. In cold-smoking, food is exposed to cold (50-85°F/10-29°C) smoldering smoke, so it dries rather than cooks. Chemicals in the smoke kill any toxic micro-organisms, thus preventing the fats in the food from turning rancid. Smoke also gives flavor and a rich amber color. Commercially cold-smoked foods include poultry, salmon, kippers, ham and bacon.

Shellfish such as mussels, clams and oysters need several processes. First they should be shucked and steamed briefly to firm up the flesh. Then they are dry-salted or brined, quickly cold-smoked and finally hot-smoked, each process lasting only about 20 minutes. Many nuts, eggs and cheeses can also be cold-smoked for a distinctive flavor.

The approximate storage time for cold-smoked products is: two weeks after 24 hours' smoking, four weeks after two days' smoking, two months after three days' smoking, one year after a week's smoking and three years after two weeks' smoking. However, for the home cook, successful cold-smoking of shellfish, fish and meat is tricky because factors such as the quality and quantity of the oil content in the food are crucial and are difficult to assess at home.

Hot-smoking cooks the food in smoke at temperatures between 200-250°F/93-121°C. Since the food is only partially preserved, it should be eaten within a few days. Some hot-smokers have a chamber for liquids such as water, beer, wine or fruit juice, which will impart flavor to the food as it smokes. Food that has been hot-smoked too long has a shriveled appearance, an uneven color and a sour smell.

Technically, barbecuing is also a method of hot-smoking as the food is cooked by the heat of the charcoal, and flavored slightly in the smoke from aromatic wood chips. However, barbecued dishes are best eaten at once.

Fish

Whether you are smoking fish by the traditional method – in a chimney – or using a smoker, fish for hot-smoking should be scaled, cleaned and gutted when it is fresh, then dry-salted or brined (p.488). This draws out moisture from the flesh and also acts as a short-term preservative to keep the fish from spoiling during smoking. After salting, hang the fish on a hook for about three hours until it has dried out and formed a thin hard skin called a pellicule, which helps the smoke penetrate evenly.

Hot-smoke fish at a temperature no higher than 180°F/82°C for up to two hours; above this temperature it may disintegrate. To make sure any harmful organisms are killed off during the smoking, this temperature must be maintained for at least 30 minutes. Fattier fish such as salmon, trout, tuna, bluefish, mackerel, herring and whitefish smoke the best. Baste the fish with oil during smoking so they do not dry out.

Meat and poultry

The maximum temperature for hot-smoking meat and poultry is 250°F/121°C. Higher temperatures dry out the meat and cook the outer surface prematurely, leaving the inside underdone. Tough cuts of meat will be more tender if dry-salted or brined (p.488) before smoking. The length of smoking time will vary according to weight and whether the meat has been previously salted. The best way to time the smoking period is to insert a thermometer into the food and cook to the same temperature as you would in a conventional oven. For temperature see Poultry, p.180, and Meat, p.199. Birds weighing 3½ lb/1.5 kg or more are best for smoking. Fatter birds are more tender and taste better, while game and other lean birds, like Rock Cornish hens, may be barded (see Roasting poultry, p.188) with bacon or fat for smoking.

Cut the bird in half (p.175) to make sure it smokes evenly, and put it on a rack, skin-side down. Hot-smoked poultry may be eaten hot from the smoker, or cooled, wrapped and stored in the refrigerator for use within a few days. Commercially cold-smoked poultry is cured in smoke no hotter than 90°F/32°C until it is a rich golden brown or mahogany color. For a stronger flavor of smoke, cold-smoke the meat for several hours before hot-smoking.

SALTING & BRINING

There are two basic methods of preserving food with salt: dry-salting and brining.

Dry-salting

For this method, salt is rubbed into the food to draw out the juices, which produce a brine. Dry salting is most suitable for use in the home kitchen with thin pieces of food that absorb salt quickly, such as sliced vegetables, fish roe, or small fish, especially anchovies and herrings. Larger pieces of food obviously take longer to cure, but the slowness of the process can be advantageous – for example a classic dry-cured ham. Fish takes about a week to dry-salt; ham, bacon and pork take two to three days for every 1 lb/500 g. Signs of poor salting include salt crystals on the food, discoloration, and soft or dry, stringy texture.

MAKING GRAVAD LAX

This lightly dry-salted salmon flavored with dill is a Swedish specialty. For serving, slice the salmon in very thin diagonal slices and serve with Scandinavian mustard sauce (p.63).

1 Sprinkle 3 tbsp/45 g coarse salt, 2 tbsp/30 g sugar and 12 crushed black peppercorns on the cut side of a thick salmon fillet (about 12 oz/375 g). Cover with sprigs of dill (use a large bunch).

2 Lay another piece of salmon of the same size on the top, cut side down and head to tail so the fish is an even thickness.

3 Set a heavy board or a weighted plate on top of the salmon. Cover loosely and refrigerate two days, turning the salmon over every 12 hours. Baste with the juice drawn out by the salt. Drain the fish and discard the seasonings and dill. The salmon will keep 1-2 days.

Sauerkraut

For every 5 lb/2.3 kg firm white cabbage, allow about ¼ cup/65 g coarse salt and a tablespoon of spices. Trim the cabbage of its outer leaves, and shred it, discarding the core. Toss it in a large bowl with kosher or pickling salt and flavorings such as caraway seed, juniper berries or black peppercorns. Let the cabbage, salt and spices stand about five minutes, then pack into a large sterilized crock, tamping the cabbage down with a pestle, and leaving about 3 in/7.5 cm at the top. Weight the cabbage with a plate, cover the crock with a cloth and store in a cool place (below 70°F/20°C). After one week, uncover it and skim off any scum on the cabbage or on the rim of the crock. Repeat daily for at least a month until no more scum appears, which means the fermentation has stopped and the sauerkraut is ready. Pack into smaller jars and refrigerate. To store sauerkraut more than a few months, process it in a boiling water bath (p.494), after which it will keep for about one year.

Brining

Brining is the wet-cure equivalent of dry-salting, but the process takes less time. The food is steeped in a salt solution until thoroughly permeated. As in dry-salting, the best results are obtained with fresh food, chilled before preparation. The brine must be strong enough to extract the juices from the food, and this is achieved with a 20 percent salt solution. The salinity can be tested with a salometer (p.503), but the traditional method is to add salt to water until a fresh egg can float on the solution.

Brine should be made with pure water; tap water may be treated with chemicals that would interfere with the curing, so use bottled water instead. Allow 8 lb/3.5 kg salt for every 4 qt/4 L water, and add sugar equal to a quarter of the weight of salt.

The best containers for brining are stoneware crocks. Plastic and glass can also be used, but wooden or metal containers may affect the flavor of the food.

Brining fish Make a brine solution as above, and immerse the chilled (35°F/20°C) whole fish or pieces in it. They should be soaked for 30 minutes if under 3½ oz/100 g; or for an hour if between 8 oz/250 g and 1 lb/500 g. Add one hour of brining for each extra 1 lb/500 g weight, and add an extra 25 percent of the time calculated if the fish are oily.

Brining can be carried out at room temperature in cool climates, but in hot weather cool the solution by putting a bag of ice cubes in the crock. During the process check that the fish remain completely immersed in brine, and move them around from time to time to make sure the solution reaches every part of each fish. This is called overhauling.

After brining, soak the fish in cold water for 30 minutes to remove surface salt, and hang them up to dry for at least eight hours or overnight. This will prevent the flesh from streaking if it is to be subsequently smoked. Brined fish will keep for two years in a cool, dry place such as a pantry.

Brining meat Meat is cured by being immersed in brine for several days in the refrigerator. Because of the risk of spoiling, it is safest to follow individual recipes, such as the one for corned beef (above, right). One way of speeding up brining in meat cuts is to inject the solution into the meat, particularly close to the bone where the meat spoils first. The equipment must be sterilized and no pockets of air should be left trapped in the meat to spoil it.

Corned beef

Once cut, corned beef can be stored in the refrigerator, covered, for one to two days; uncut it will keep for two to three weeks.

Serves 8

4-5 lb/2 kg beef brisket	2 tsp whole allspice berries
4 qt/4 L water	2 bay leaves
2 cups/520 g coarse salt	4 garlic cloves, peeled
2 cups/440 g dark brown sugar	
1 tbsp juniper berries	Stoneware crock

1 Wipe the piece of beef brisket with a damp cloth and pierce it all over with a two-pronged fork. Put it in a deep container.
2 For the brine, stir together the water, salt, sugar, juniper berries, whole allspice berries, bay leaves and garlic cloves, until the sugar and salt are dissolved. Pour over the meat.
3 Weight the meat to submerge it at least 2 in/5 cm under the surface of the brine, cover and refrigerate it. After about 10 days, discard the brine, rinse the beef, and put it in a kettle with cold water. Bring to a boil, reduce the heat and simmer for an hour.
4 Pour off the water, add more and repeat the cooking process until the beef is very tender when pierced with a two-pronged fork. Serve hot with braised cabbage or sauerkraut (opposite), or cold with potato salad and chutney (below).

PICKLES & CHUTNEYS

Pickles and chutneys are preparations of fruits and vegetables, alone or in combination, preserved in spiced vinegar. They range in flavor from sour to sweet; darker, spicier chutneys tend to be more concentrated. Pickles are usually eaten alone or as a condiment with dishes of cheese, meat and fish. Coarse-textured chutney, (lime or mango), often accompanies curry. A vinegar-pickled combination of chopped vegetables and fruit is often called a relish, for example, British piccalilli.

Fruit and vegetables for pickling should be firm and young; small varieties are best for pickling whole. Cauliflower florets, baby onions, beets, cucumbers and gherkins and shredded cabbage all make good pickles.

The essential ingredient of a pickle is vinegar, as it preserves the ingredients against spoilage by micro-organisms. To enable it to do this, vinegar must have an acetic acid content of at least five percent. For light-colored pickles use distilled white vinegar. Cider and malt vinegar impart a stronger flavor and a darker color to the food. Specially prepared spiced pickling vinegar is also available, and its high acetic acid content (eight percent) speeds up the pickling process. **Note** Some "pickles", such as dill pickles, are merely salted and contain no vinegar.

Ingredients for pickles are usually prepared by being first brined or dry-salted. The salt draws the moisture from the vegetable, making it more receptive to the vinegar and making a firmer, crunchier pickle. Pure or kosher salt is best for any type of pickling. Iodized salt will impart an iodine flavor and table salt will cloud the pickle because of the additives it contains.

Use whole spices when pickling, as ground ones cloud the liquid. They can be added directly to the vinegar or tied in a muslin bag and removed after the pickling. Traditional pickling spices are allspice, cloves, black peppercorns, mustard seeds and coriander seeds. Use white sugar unless otherwise specified. Dark brown sugar and molasses may be called for in dark chutneys. Hard water tends to shrivel pickles, so use bottled water.

Pickling techniques

Select and prepare the vegetables, wash and drain thoroughly. Make a brine with ¼ cup/50 g salt to 2 cups/500 ml cold water for each 1 lb/500 g vegetables. This is suitable for firm vegetables, which should be weighted down under the brine for 24 hours. Vegetables with a high water content, such as gherkin cucumbers, can be layered with dry salt for the same period. Rinse and drain the vegetables thoroughly, then pack into sterilized jars. Fill the jars with spiced vinegar, making sure it covers the vegetables.

For preserving, use glass jars with metal screw-tops, and paraffin for sealing (p.491). Unlacquered metal will corrode if exposed to vinegar. Label the jars with contents and date and store in a cool, dark place. Pickles should be left to mellow for a month if high-strength vinegar has been used; allow three months for ordinary pickling vinegar. All pickles and chutneys that are to be preserved for more than a few weeks should be processed by the water bath method (p.494). Consume within a year.

PROBLEMS WHEN MAKING PICKLES

1 Soft or slippery pickles The vinegar was too weak, or the food was not properly immersed.
2 Shriveled pickles The solution is too salty, too acid or too sweet.
3 Dark discoloration Too much iron in the water that was used.
4 Hollow pickles float The ingredients were left too long after picking before they were pickled.

Apple and tomato chutney

Chutneys often include vegetables such as the tomatoes and onions in this recipe.

Makes 2 qt/2 L

4 lb/1.8 kg tart apples, peeled, cored and sliced	5 cups/1.25 L cider vinegar
	2 cups/440 g dark brown sugar
4 lb/1.8 kg ripe tomatoes, peeled, seeded and coarsely chopped	2 tbsp salt
	1 tbsp ground ginger
4 onions, sliced	2 tsp whole peppercorns

1 Combine all the ingredients in a large preserving pan. Heat until the sugar is dissolved, then bring to a boil, reduce the heat and simmer, stirring frequently, until the mixture is thick and pulpy, about 1½ hours.
2 Let the mixture cool, pour into sterilized jars, and seal.

Watermelon pickle

Makes 2 qt/2 L

1 large watermelon	2 cups/400 g sugar
½ cup/100 g salt	2 tsp whole cloves
2½ cups/625 ml cider vinegar	1 stick cinnamon, cut into pieces

1 Cut the rind from the watermelon into strips about 2 in/5 cm long and 1 in/2.5 cm wide, discarding the green outer skin and any pulp. The rind should measure about 2 qt/2 L. Put it in a large pan, cover with water and boil for 5 minutes. Drain and rinse with cold water.
2 Mix the salt with 1½ qt/1.5 L cold water and pour over the rind. Let this stand at room temperature for six hours. Drain, cover with cold water and drain again. Repeat three times. Cover with water and boil until tender, about 45 minutes, then drain.
3 In a preserving pan, combine the cider vinegar and sugar with 1 cup/250 ml water, and add the cloves and cinnamon tied in a cheesecloth bag. Heat without boiling until the sugar is dissolved. Add the rind and simmer until translucent, 40-45 minutes.
4 Pack the melon rind in sterilized jars and cover with the hot cooking liquid. Let cool and seal. Store for 4 weeks before using.

Corn, pepper and mustard seed relish

Makes 1 qt/1 L

8-12 ears of fresh corn or 3 cups/750 ml canned kernels	¾ cup/150 g sugar
1 each red and green bell pepper, cored, seeded and diced	1 cup/250 ml cider vinegar
	1 cup/250 ml water
1 carrot, finely chopped	2 tbsp yellow mustard seed
2 onions, finely chopped	1 tsp dry mustard
	½ tsp celery seed

1 If using fresh corn, boil in salted water until barely tender, 6-10 minutes. Drain, let the ears cool and cut off the kernels (p.286) to make about 3 cups/750 ml.
2 Combine all the ingredients in a saucepan. Cover and simmer until the corn and vegetables are just tender, 40-45 minutes.
3 Pack the relish in sterilized jars, let cool and seal. Store for 4 weeks before using.

Sour gherkins in vinegar

Makes 2 qt/2 L

2 lb/1 kg (about 1¾ pt/1.75 L) small pickling cucumbers	6 sprigs fresh thyme
	2 bay leaves
1 cup/260 g coarse salt	4 sprigs fresh tarragon
½ cup/120 g pearl onions, peeled	6 whole cloves
6 dried hot chili peppers	white wine vinegar

1 Rub the pickling cucumbers to remove any spines. Mix them with the coarse salt in a bowl and leave for 24 hours.
2 Drain the cucumbers and put them in a bowl with water to cover. Soak for 5 minutes and drain again.
3 Wipe the cucumbers dry and put them in two sterilized 1 quart/1 liter glass jars or crocks. Divide the pearl onions, dried hot chilies, thyme, bay leaves, tarragon and cloves equally between the two jars.
4 Fill the jars with white wine vinegar, seal and refrigerate. Let the gherkins mellow 3-4 weeks before eating. Store in the refrigerator for up to 3 months.

JAMS, JELLIES & MARMALADES

Jams, jellies and marmalades all consist of fruit boiled with sugar to jell point (p.492). Fruit contains acid and the natural setting agent pectin as well as its own sugar. The acid, pectin and sugar must be in the right proportions for the preserve to set. Jam, or conserve is made with whole or cut fruit, marmalade with citrus fruit, and jelly with strained fruit juice boiled with sugar.

Acid fruits make the best preserves, and barely ripe fruit is to be preferred because at this stage the pectin content is highest. Tart apples, red currants, black currants and plums are all good choices. Bitter Seville oranges make the best marmalade, and crab apples are a natural choice for jelly.

The setting agent pectin is found mostly in the skin, seeds and core of fruit. It is destroyed by long cooking, which is why jams and jellies are made in small, rapidly cooked batches. Low pectin fruits include sweet cherries, peaches, strawberries, and pears. If the fruit is not acid enough or is low in pectin (see test opposite), you will need to add lemon juice; the juice of one lemon (2 tablespoons) per 3 lb/1.5 kg fruit. Alternatives are commercial pectin, in liquid or powdered form, or the strained reduced juice of sour apples.

Preserves should have a minimum of 60 percent sugar content to prevent mold. Special preserving sugar has easily soluble crystals, but ordinary white sugar can be used. Substitute up to a quarter of the sugar with brown sugar or molasses for a dark rich taste, especially in marmalade. In Europe, a sugar is sold for preserving, which includes pectin. However, this means that the quantity of pectin cannot be varied according to the ripeness of the fruit.

Equipment for preserving

You will need a shallow wide preserving pan with a capacity of about 2.5 gal/9 L. A sugar thermometer (p.503) will tell you when the preserve reaches 105°C/220°F: the jell point. Keep it to hand in a bowl of very hot water and do not rest the bulb on the bottom of the pan when testing. A funnel with a wide tube (4-5 in/10-13 cm diameter) is useful for filling jars with jam or jelly. Without a funnel, jam-making can be messy and burns are more likely. A tightly woven conical cloth sack, called a jelly bag (Extracting juice for jelly, opposite), is used for draining the puréed fruit for clear jellies. The bag is suspended over a bowl and the juice is allowed to drip through. A thick dish towel can be substituted.

Sterilizing and sealing jars

Containers for storing preserved foods must be sterilized to kill micro-organisms – only heatproof containers may be used. Wash glass jars in detergent and water, then boil them in water for 10 minutes. Dry them upside-down in a warm oven. The rubber gaskets for clamped jars should be covered in simmering rather than boiling water. They may be used once only. Alternatively, cover the jar with a screw top (dome lid and metal cap). Fill jars to within ⅛ in/3 mm of the top. Jars without lids need ½ in/1.25 cm headroom for sealing with paraffin (opposite).

Paraffin sealing

Break the paraffin wax into small pieces, or use white, unscented household candles. Melt the paraffin wax over a very low heat or in a water bath (p.510). Pour a thin layer of tepid paraffin over the hot preserve; if the paraffin itself is too hot, it will shrink away

from the sides of the jars when it cools. Prick any air bubbles that appear in the paraffin before they have time to set and burst the seal. When the first layer has hardened, repeat the process until the seal is ⅛in/ 3 mm thick. As the paraffin seal cools, it sets hard, becoming opaque and slightly sunken in the center.

TESTING PECTIN

In a bowl, mix one tablespoon of cooked unsweetened fruit juice with one tablespoon of 70 percent rubbing alcohol.

Swirl the liquid on a plate for a couple of minutes until it starts to clot. Push your finger into the solution; a large clot indicates high pectin, while small lumps indicate a low pectin level. **Note** Always discard the mixture as the alcohol is poisonous.

Making jams, jellies and marmalades

To prepare the fruit, wash it and remove peel, pith, any damaged flesh, stalks and stones. Cut up the fruit, or leave small berries whole. For a coarse marmalade, the fruit may be cooked whole, and then chopped and seeded. For a finer textured marmalade, the zest may be cut into a julienne (p.460) and added with the fruit. Tie the seeds in a cheesecloth bag, to be included in the pan, so that the pectin is extracted by cooking. Put the fruit in a preserving pan with the correct amount of water and cook until pulpy. Test for pectin. For jelly, strain the fruit into a bowl through a scalded jelly bag (right). To keep the jelly clear, do not squeeze the bag. Test the combined juices for pectin.

Add the sugar to the fruit, and lemon juice if needed. Stir to dissolve, then bring to a boil. Maintain at a full rolling boil until the jell point (p.492) is reached. Take the pan off the heat and test with a sugar thermometer (p.503) or by placing a spot of preserve on a cold saucer. If it is ready, a skin will form on the surface as it cools. It will wrinkle if you push it with your finger.

Skim the preserve to remove any scum, and leave to cool for 10 minutes (this prevents the juice from rising to the top of each jar). Pour into hot sterilized jars, using a ladle and a wide-mouthed funnel. Fill the jars, wipe the rims and seal them, leaving the appropriate amount of headroom (left). Label them and store in a cool, dark, dry place for up to a year. Preserves will crystallize if stored in the refrigerator.

EXTRACTING JUICE FOR JELLY

Fruit for making jelly must first be cooked and then the juice is extracted. Soft fruits, such as red currants, will need very little cooking before they give up their juice and will need only enough water to moisten them. Harder fruits, such as apples, will need more water and longer cooking before the juice is extracted.

1 Cut the fruit in large chunks or leave berries or other small fruit whole. Skins and cores may be left on apples and pears to add flavor and pectin. Add water to the pan to thoroughly moisten the fruit, and simmer, stirring occasionally, until very soft.

2 Let the fruit cool slightly, then spoon it into a jelly bag (p.506) suspended over a large bowl. Leave to drain. **Note** Do not press the bag or the jelly will be cloudy.

3 Leave the bag in place overnight to allow the juice to drip slowly into the bowl.

TESTING FOR JELL POINT

Preserves should be boiled over a high heat so that they cook as quickly as possible. The cooked fruit, when tender, is tested to see if it has set (jelled) sufficiently.

1 During boiling skim off scum that rises to the surface of the mixture with a ladle; this ensures that the preserve will be clear and shining.

2 The jell point is reached at 220°F/105°C, which can be measured on a sugar thermometer. At this temperature, the preserve falls from a spatula in a characteristic "sheet" of drips.

3 Alternatively, take the pan from the heat, pour a few drops of preserve on a cold saucer and wait for a moment to see if the drops begin to set. Push with your finger – if setting point has been reached, the surface of the preserve will wrinkle.

PROBLEMS WHEN MAKING PRESERVES

1 **Fruit discolors**. The preserve was cooked for too long. To shorten cooking time, warm the sugar in the oven first.
2 **Whole fruit has risen to top of the jar**. Syrup was too liquid and needed longer boiling. Cooked jam did not rest in the pan before being bottled.
3 **Jam crystallizes, ferments, forms a mold**. Equipment was not properly sterilized (p.490).
4 **Jam ferments or goes fizzy**. Cooking time was too short or pectin, acid and sugar were not in the right proportion. Use the wrinkle test (see Testing for jell point, left).
5 **Jam crystallizes in the refrigerator**. Preserves are best kept in a cool place, such as a pantry or dark shelf.

Mango and ginger jam

Makes 1 qt/1 L jam

5 cups/1 kg mango, peeled and cubed (p.468)	1 oz/30 g candied ginger, finely chopped
¼ cup/60 ml lemon juice	5 cups/1 kg sugar
1 tsp grated orange zest	

1 Combine the mango, lemon juice, orange zest and ginger in a preserving pan and simmer for 12-15 minutes to a thick purée. Add ½ cup/125 ml water if necessary to prevent sticking. Heat the sugar in a very low oven.
2 Stir in the hot sugar and boil to the jell point (left), stirring frequently. Cool slightly, pour into sterilized jars (p.490) and seal.

Lime and orange marmalade

Makes 1½ qt/1.5 L

4 limes	3 qt/3 L water
2 oranges	5 cups/1 kg sugar

1 Wash the limes and the oranges, cut off and discard the ends. Peel the fruit and discard the pith. Cut the peel into fine shreds. Remove the seeds and tie in a cheesecloth bag. Slice the fruit and put it in a preserving pan with the peel and seeds. Add the water, bring to a boil and simmer 1 hour.
2 Heat the sugar in a very low oven. Stir it into the fruit and boil as fast as possible to the jell point (left), stirring often. Let the mixture cool slightly, discard the bag of seeds, pour the marmalade into sterilized jars (p.490) and seal.

Making apple jelly

Use well-flavored apples or crab apples and add the juice of one lemon for every 3 lb/1.4 kg fruit. Scrub the apples, especially at the blossom ends, and discard the stalks. Cut the apples into quarters and put in a pan with just enough water to cover. Simmer until tender, then strain and measure the juice. Bring the mixture to a boil and stir in 1 lb/500 g warmed sugar for each 1 pt/500 ml juice. Boil until the jell point is reached (left). Let the jelly cool slightly, before pouring into sterilized jars (p.490). Seal the jars.
Note Herbs or spices can be added to the apples during cooking.

FRUIT BUTTERS, CHEESES & CURDS

These preserves were a highlight of Victorian and Edwardian tea tables in Britain, where they were spread on bread or used as fillings in trifles and cakes. Both fruit butters and cheeses are made by cooking fruit to a purée and adding sugar. Fruit cheeses, as the name suggests, are the more solid of the two, being made with extra sugar; they can be sliced and eaten with coffee after a meal, and team well with dairy cheeses. Fruit butters and cheeses are often spiced: typical combinations are apple with cinnamon or pears with cloves.

Large fruits should be washed and cut up, but they need not be peeled, stemmed, pitted or cored. Place the fruit in a preserving pan with just enough water to cover and add lemon juice for fruit low in pectin (p.491). Simmer the fruit to a purée, then rub it through a fine sieve. Weigh the sieved pulp and return it to a clean pan. If making a fruit cheese, the pulp should be thick, so reduce it by fast boiling if necessary. For fruit cheese allow equal weights of fruit and sugar; for fruit butter allow half to three-quarters as much sugar as pulp. Stir over medium heat until the sugar dissolves, then simmer for about an hour, stirring constantly.

Fruit butter is ready when all the liquid has evaporated and the surface is creamy. Fruit cheese is ready when you can draw a clean line over the base of the pan with a wooden spoon. Ladle fruit butters into warm sterilized jars (p.490). They should not be stored for more than a few weeks and should be consumed within three or four days of opening. Fruit cheeses can be stored in molds or small canning jars from which they may be unmolded. Warm the molds and brush the inside with vegetable oil before sealing.

Fruit curds are rich preserves containing eggs and butter. Lemon is the traditional flavor, but oranges, limes and passion fruit, or mixtures of different fruits, also make delicious curds. To make lemon curd, put the juice and grated zest of four lemons in a water bath (p.510) over low heat and cook gently with ½ cup/125 g butter and 1¼ cups/250 g sugar. Stir constantly until the ingredients have melted and combined. Add four beaten eggs and continue to cook, stirring, until the mixture thickens enough to coat the back of a spoon. Pour the hot curd into sterilized jars (p.490) and seal. Store in a cool, dark place for one month or in the refrigerator for up to three months. For orange curd, use three oranges and one lemon.

Apple butter

Windfall apples from the garden make excellent butter.

6 lb/3 kg crab or cooking apples	sugar
4 cups/1 L water	1 tsp each ground cloves and ginger
4 cups/1 L cider or apple juice	

1 Wash the apples and chop roughly, leaving the cores and peel. Simmer gently, covered, with the water and cider until soft.
2 Work through a sieve or food mill and weigh the pulp. Allow 1½ cups/375 g sugar for each 4 cups/500 g pulp and heat it in a very low oven.
3 Simmer the pulp until reduced by a third. Stir in the hot sugar and spices and simmer, stirring constantly, until creamy. Pour the butter into sterilized pots (p.490) while still hot, and seal them.

CANNING FRUIT

Canning or bottling is the process by which food is treated at high temperatures and hermetically sealed to preserve it. In Britain "canning" refers to the commercial process of sealing foods in a metal can, and "bottling" is the term for the domestic activity of sealing fruit in glass jars. In the United States "canning" covers both processes. For high acid food, such as fruit and tomatoes, that are relatively hostile to bacteria, the boiling water method (p.494) is used. Raw or cooked food is packed into jars (see below) which are heated in boiling water until the contents reach 212°F/100°C. **Note** This temperature is not high enough to kill *botulinum* toxins that may develop in low-acid foods such as meat, fish, poultry and most vegetables. The canning of low-acid foods at home is not recommended therefore, as it must be done under carefully controlled conditions.

Preparing the jars

Use only special canning jars with metal or glass tops (check for any cracks or misshapen lids). Some jars have rubber seals that may be used once only and should be replaced each year. Wash jars and seals and rinse in scalding water: they will be sterilized during the canning process. Keep jars in a low oven or submerged in hot water until you are ready to fill them. Do not use jars with more than 1 qt/1 L capacity, as the contents may not process fully.

Preparing the fruit

Fruit retains the best color, flavor and texture when processed by the boiling water method (p.494). For canning it should be firm and just ripe, but not overripe. Wash and prepare fruit as directed in individual recipes, cutting away any bruised spots that might spoil a whole batch. The stalks, 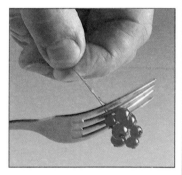 and any other green matter, should be removed from small fruit such as blueberries, black and red currants (above), damsons, and gooseberries and the fruit may be left whole. It is best to halve and stone large fruit such as peaches and apricots, removing any inner fibers that may toughen over time. Pack quickly to avoid discoloration. Peel apricots, peaches and nectarines by blanching (p.447) and peel, core and slice apples and pears. Both apples and pears should be left to stand in acidulated water (water with lemon juice added to it) until you are ready to pack them, to prevent discoloration. As pears are comparatively low in acid, it is advisable to add two teaspoons of lemon juice to each 1 pt/500 ml fruit before processing.

Fruit may be canned raw, cooked or as a purée, depending on the type. The raw-pack (or cold-pack) method is best for delicate fruits like berries or tomatoes, as well as plums, cherries, currants and peaches. Pack the fruit tightly into the jars, filling them a third at a time and adding sugar syrup to the level of the fruit as you go. Allow ½ cup/125 ml syrup for each 1 pt/500 ml fruit. Fruit may be packed in water alone, but generally some sugar is added. Not only does a syrup preserve the color and texture of the fruit, it also makes a delicious accompaniment for serving. The sweetness of the syrup is a matter of taste. Two parts water to one part sugar will make a medium syrup, while one to one will make a heavy syrup. Light corn syrup or mild honey may replace half the sugar to make a slightly richer syrup. Fruit juice or wine may be substituted for the water, and flavorings such as cloves and other spices, *eau de vie*, rum or finely grated citrus zest may be added as well.

Firm and fibrous fruits benefit from preliminary cooking in sugar syrup as this makes them easier to pack into jars, and provides an opportunity for adding flavor by infusing them with spices during cooking. To prevent the fruit darkening during simmering, rub peeled apples, pears, peaches, nectarines and apricots with lemon juice. Alternatively, soak them in a solution of 1 tsp crystalline ascorbic acid (vitamin C) per 1 cup/250 ml water. Do not soak the fruit for more than 20 minutes or its nutrients will begin to leach out.

Processing the fruit

Use the water bath method for canning fruit (including tomatoes). Jams, pickles or relishes may also be processed in a water bath to extend their shelf-life. The processing time depends on the type of fruit, the size of the container and the density with which it is filled. You will need either a canning kettle or a saucepan large enough to hold the jars without crowding, and deep enough for the water to cover them with at least 1 in/2.5 cm of water. Insert the rack into the kettle and arrange the jars so they do not touch. Alternatively, put a cloth on the bottom of the saucepan, arrange the jars on it and wedge more cloths between them to prevent rattling and possible cracking. Tightly close the jars, then loosen the screw a quarter of a turn. Pour on hot water to cover the jars, bring to a boil and boil for the specified time.

Testing the seal

Remove the jars from the water bath and set to cool on a folded cloth or board. Let them stand for 24 hours before testing the seal. The lids of screw-top jars should pull down and make a seal as they cool; the lid will appear slightly concave. If the lid remains flat, press it with a finger – if it pops up, the jar is not sealed. Alternatively unscrew the lid and remove the screw band. Lift the jar by the lid. If you can do this, a vacuum has formed and the seal is secure. To test clamp-on jars, tilt the jar to press the food against the lid; bubbles indicate a poor seal. If the jar is not correctly sealed, reprocess it immediately or refrigerate the food and consume it within a few days. Wash correctly sealed jars, label them and store in a cool, dark place for up to a year. Wash and store the screw rings separately for future use. Repeat the seal test before consuming the contents of the jars.

Note If you find that the seal of your canned food has been ruptured or pops up, discard it immediately and make sure that neither people nor animals eat it: it may harbor dangerous toxins.

USEFUL INFORMATION

Typical canning times (for 1 qt/ 1 L jars). *Berries, currants, rhubarb*: boiling water bath, 15 minutes. *Peaches*: boiling water bath, 30 minutes. *Pears*: boiling water bath, 20 minutes. *Tomatoes*: boiling water bath, 45 minutes.
Storage Sealed jars, up to 1 year in

a cool dark place.
Problems Overcooking while processing; improper sealing.
Signs of poor canning Loose seal; leakage from jars, bulging lids; moving bubbles; murky liquid; fermentation; mold; discoloration.

FREEZING

In cold climates, ice and snow have always been used to preserve food; modern refrigeration and freezing techniques make this a method that can now be employed all year round at home. Freezing is the most natural method of preserving as it does not involve altering the structure of the food. It can, however, alter the balance of flavoring so thawed, cooked dishes may need seasoning before being served.

Cold arrests the growth of living organisms: at 40°F/4°C food can be kept for a few days in good condition. At 18°F/–8°C micro-organisms become dormant and at 0°F/–18°C all food spoilage ceases. Most home freezers do not reach levels below this and constant opening of the door can mean the temperature is more likely to be around 15°F/–9°C. Enzyme activity will not have stopped completely, but at this level deterioration is very minor and foods remain safe for up to a year.

Always equip your freezer with a thermometer (p.503), and to keep the temperature down make sure it is at least three-quarters full. As a general rule, avoid freezing more than 2lb/ 1 kg of food per cubic foot/30 cc freezer space within a 24-hour period. Larger quantities should be frozen at fast-freeze or lower than normal temperature. If your freezer constantly registers above 10°F/–12°C, food should be eaten within two months.

Food should be frozen as quickly as possible so that the ice crystals that form are small, and hold the juices in the cells of the food. Slow freezing makes large ice crystals – these rupture the food cells and cause the moisture, and the flavor, to run out.

When frozen at peak flavor and in perfect condition, fresh fruit and vegetables, meat and fish, emerge from the home freezer in good condition. To avoid disappointment, guard against freezing plainly roasted meats and poultry unless in a sauce, as they tend to dry out. Potatoes and legumes are not ideal candidates for freezing, as their texture may become mealy. Aspics and other gelatin preparations cannot be successfully frozen as they crystallize. If in doubt, check freezing instructions under individual foods. **Note** Never refreeze foods.

Packing food for the freezer

Cold air is very drying, so all foods should be packed in moisture-proof materials. Use rigid containers with tight lids wherever possible – plastic boxes and foil containers from commercially frozen foods are both suitable and reusable. When filling the containers, leave headroom for the expansion of liquids during freezing. Freezer bags made of heavy transparent polythene are useful for vegetables, meat and irregular shaped foods. Squeeze out as much air as possible when wrapping and seal packages with twist ties or special freezer tape. Ordinary tapes are not suitable for the freezer as they quickly lose their grip. Make sure everything is labeled with contents, weight and date – use a freezer pen so that the writing will not come off.

Fruit

There are many ways of freezing fresh fruit depending on the type and what you intend to use it for. As freezing will soften fruit, choose very firm pieces for anything other than a purée.

Tray freezing is excellent for small fruits such as blueberries or raspberries that keep their shape well. Strawberries tend to collapse: sprinkle them with sugar to keep them firm. Arrange the fruits on a tray so they do not touch each other and freeze until firm, two to four hours. Put them in freezer bags or rigid containers, eliminating as much air as possible, and freeze again.

When fruit is dry-packed and frozen without the addition of sugar it freezes in a solid block, which suits cranberries, blueberries, gooseberries, figs, currants and rhubarb. More fragile fruits yield their juices as they freeze, but softening can be mitigated if the fruit is packed with sugar equaling a fifth of the weight of the fruit. As the fruit freezes, the juices combine with the sugar to produce a light syrup that helps firm up the fruit. This works well with juicy fruits such as strawberries and pineapples.

Fruits that discolor easily (for example, apples and pears) should be frozen in sugar or honey syrup. For 1 qt/1 L fruit, bring to a boil 3 cups/600 g sugar and 1 qt/1 L water (or 1 cup/250 ml mild honey in 3 cups/750 ml water). The syrup may be acidulated by adding either one teaspoon of lemon juice or a half teaspoon of ascorbic acid to each quart/liter of syrup. Let the syrup cool and then slice in the fruit directly so it is completely immersed. Press a crumpled piece of wax or parchment paper on top. Use unsweetened liquids such as water or apple juice instead of sugar or honey if you prefer.

Puréed fruit can be frozen, with or without sugar, depending on its final use. For specific times see individual fruits in the chapter on Fruit and Nuts.

Vegetables

Most vegetables (unlike fruit) are low in acid and deteriorate as a result of enzyme activity, unless they are blanched or cooked before freezing. Three exceptions are leeks, onions and green peppers. Delicate vegetables such as spinach and other greens, asparagus tips, cauliflower and broccoli florets should be steam-blanched rather than cooked in water. Hardier types such as green beans, carrots, okra and corn can be blanched in water. (For specific times see individual vegetables, in the Vegetables chapter). Watery vegetables like summer squash become too limp if blanched. Instead they can be lightly sautéed to firm them before freezing, as can most other vegetables.

After blanching, plunge the vegetables immediately into ice-cold water to refresh them, then dry thoroughly before packing in plastic freezer bags or rigid containers. Vegetables can also be tray-frozen like berries (above). Boiled and puréed vegetables freeze well, but add seasonings and enrichments after thawing. Most defrosted vegetables are best cooked in a small amount of water while still solid, but corn ears must be fully thawed or the center cob will still be frozen when the kernels are cooked.

Mushrooms freeze well and retain much of their aroma. Firm varieties like truffles, boletes and chanterelles do best, while the common mushroom and other moist varieties tend to soften when thawed. All mushrooms should be trimmed and frozen whole without washing. They may also be cleaned and sautéed or cooked *à blanc* (p.308) first.

Pasta and rice

Fresh pasta dough freezes well after shaping. Let the pasta dry for two to three hours, then freeze in bags, removing as much air as possible. Frozen pasta, including filled varieties like ravioli, should be cooked straight from the freezer, and pasta in prepared dishes also freezes well. Grain foods such as rice dishes freeze well and do not need defrosting before reheating.

Meat

Frozen meat varies in quality depending on how quickly it is frozen and how much fat it contains. As quick freezing causes less damage to the texture and juiciness of meat, smaller pieces freeze more successfully than large cuts. Fat gradually turns rancid, even in the coldest temperatures, so a lean piece of beef will keep better than a well-marbled rib roast. The high fat content of sausages makes them poor candidates for freezing, while the salt in many cured meats like bacon and ham often hastens deterioration in the freezer. Careful wrapping is vital, not only to prevent freezer burn, but also because oxygen accelerates rancidity.

For convenience, meat is best frozen ready to use as individual chops, chunks for stew, or patties of ground meat. Individual portions can be divided with freezer wrap. Very thin slices of meat tend to dry out, so they should be cut after thawing.

Beef, lamb and venison can be frozen up to a year depending on the cuts, while veal and pork lose quality rapidly after eight months. Rabbit and hare should be treated like poultry. **Note** Always defrost frozen meat in the refrigerator, loosely wrapped; large cuts may need up to five hours per 1 lb/500 g.

Poultry and game birds

The texture of poultry and game birds is not changed much by freezing, but the more fat the shorter the storage life of the frozen cut. Lean birds like quail freeze better than fatty birds like goose. **Note** Stuffed poultry should not be frozen at home; the stuffing will not freeze enough to prevent bacteria.

To freeze a whole bird, remove the fat from the vent end and take out and wrap giblets separately. Trussing a whole fowl with string helps it keep its shape ready for cooking. Put the bird in a plastic freezer bag and overwrap with heavy-duty aluminum foil. Poultry can be frozen in recipe-sized portions, and wings, backbones and other trimmings can be frozen separately for stock. Ideally, raw poultry, should be thoroughly defrosted in the refrigerator – allow two hours per 1 lb/500 g. Game birds can be frozen with or without the feathers, as for poultry, though never freeze a bird that has not been drawn (p.174) and cleaned.

Dairy products

Many dairy products freeze adequately, though with a slight alteration of taste and texture. Butter keeps very well, particularly when unsalted. Cream that contains more than 40 percent fat can be frozen, although it may separate when thawed and its whipping ability will be impaired. Lighter creams and milk do not freeze well. Sour cream, yogurt and buttermilk may separate if frozen.

Flavor tends to fade and texture change when cheese is frozen. Hard, aged cheese fares best, and grated hard cheese may be frozen. Soft and semi-soft cheeses will lose their creamy texture, but once thawed may be used in cooking. Fresh and unpasteurized cheeses are disappointing, losing much of their flavor.

Eggs

Eggs can be frozen out of their shells (which would burst in the freezer), but the yolks turn thick and gelatinous unless a little salt or sugar is added. For every six whole eggs, allow ½ teaspoon salt or one tablespoon of sugar, or for every six egg yolks, allow ½ teaspoon salt or ½ teaspoon sugar. Use the eggs in savory or sweet dishes, adjusting seasoning if necessary. Egg whites can be frozen without sugar or salt for up to three months; some cooks maintain that egg whites whip better after freezing and thawing. Do not freeze hard-boiled eggs because the whites turn rubbery. **Note** Eggs in cooked dishes – like custards – may become grainy when thawed.

Stocks and soups

Any stock, be it poultry, beef or fish, freezes perfectly without significant change in taste or consistency, provided it is cooled and skimmed of fat before freezing. Some cooks freeze concentrated stock or glaze in ice cube trays, then put the cubes in a plastic freezer bag for handy use. Thin soups that are similar to plain stock or *bouillon* (p.44) freeze best, since the texture of chunky or puréed vegetables and meats is altered by freezing. However, a thawed puréed soup will improve in texture if worked in a food processor or blender. Soups that are bound or enriched with egg yolks or cream will separate if frozen, so enrichments should be added only after defrosting. Herbs and other flavorings are also best added afterwards.

Sauces

Emulsified sauces such as hollandaise and mayonnaise separate if frozen, as do sauces with a large amount of cream, milk or cheese. Only sauces bound with waxy corn or rice flours are consistently stable when frozen. Tomato sauces freeze well.

Pastry, cakes and bread

Baked pastries, cakes, and especially breads, may be frozen with little loss of quality, but they should be well wrapped so as not to lose moisture or absorb odors from other food in the freezer. Some frostings and fillings can also be frozen, though fondant and *glacé* icings will crack, fillings made with whipped cream may separate and frostings with high egg-white content such as royal icing will dry out. To freeze a frosted pastry or cake without crushing the decoration, freeze it unwrapped for a short time until very firm, then wrap and freeze again.

Raw pastry doughs such as *pâte brisée* or puff pastry may be shaped before freezing, then baked while still frozen. Dough may be frozen in a block, but let it thaw completely before rolling, otherwise the edges will crack. Avoid freezing uncooked doughs containing yeast as cold temperatures may kill some of the yeast and interfere with the leavening process. Raw batters containing other leavening agents are too fragile to freeze; but pancakes of all kinds freeze well.

Nuts and seeds

Freeze nuts in their shells or shelled whole, chopped or ground. Seeds such as sesame also freeze well. Untoasted nuts or seeds last slightly longer than toasted ones, but salt or spice shortens storage time. In most recipes, nuts may be used directly from the freezer. Chestnuts are best cooked and puréed and then frozen.

Herbs

Freezing renders herb leaves too limp to be used as decoration, but it is an excellent way of preserving the flavor of fresh herbs, especially fragrant ones such as basil and tarragon that do not stand up well to drying. To freeze herbs chopped or whole, rinse them, pat dry and wrap in plastic freezer bags, pressing out the air. Alternatively, cram herb sprigs into small plastic cartons, pressing on the lids. You can grate what you need from the frozen wedge. This method is particularly good for parsley. Herb butters (p.99) and sauces such as *pesto* (p.17) also freeze well.

Fish and shellfish

Fish destined to be frozen must be absolutely fresh, as it is one of the most perishable foods. Whole fish should be scaled, gutted and rinsed to remove any traces of blood that will discolor the flesh. Steaks and fillets may also be frozen. A 30-second dip in a brine solution of 1 cup/260 g salt to 1 gal/4 L water will help firm the flesh and ensure a good texture when the fish is thawed.

For freezing, mollusks should be shucked raw or steamed open and shucked, and packed in their own juice, with added brine if necessary. Whole crabs and lobsters should be cooked and frozen shelled or unshelled. Shrimp may be frozen raw or cooked. Fish and shellfish will keep up to a year in the freezer; frozen fish should be thawed in the refrigerator.

GLAZING FISH

Fish flesh must be protected from the cold and dryness of the freezer, so wrap it carefully and, because it is delicate, freeze it for the shortest possible time. For longer storage, fish can be sealed by "glazing" in a thin coating of ice.

First tray freeze (see Fruit, p.495) a scaled, gutted and rinsed fish until solid, then ladle iced water over it, and allow to dry for a few seconds until a thin film of ice forms. Repeat until a solid coating forms. Wrap the iced fish carefully; small fish or fillets can be sealed in rigid containers with water. Frozen fish may need up to eight hours per 1 lb/500 g to thaw in the refrigerator.

MICROWAVE COOKING

T HE TECHNOLOGY for microwave cooking has been with us since World War II and ovens have been available for a good twenty years, but it is only recently that microwave cooking – not just defrosting or the reheating of coffee – has begun to come into its own. Why bother with a microwave oven? All of us are busy, but at the same time we have become more sophisticated in our food tastes in terms of both nutrition and flavor. The microwave oven is uniquely suited to our new lifestyles and tastes. Soon it will be a standard piece of equipment and we will have our own repertoire of microwave recipes.

Consumers were initially wary of the microwave oven and microwave cooking, often confusing the energy with atomic energy, to which it bears no relation. In terms of radiation, microwave ovens are very much safer than television sets. Since the late 1970s, there have been high international standards controlling the amount of microwave energy that can be emitted by ovens. The doors have two seals and, when opened, the oven automatically switches off.

Note Since the doors open from the right, you should place your oven where you can open it easily.

Safety precautions

No one, including children who may be fascinated by its resemblance to a television screen, should stare at a microwave oven in operation any more than they should stare at a light bulb. The eye cannot cool itself and may be damaged. Today's pacemakers are generally shielded so that they cannot be disturbed by any microwaves – including those from radio transmitters. Wearers can check with their doctors that their pacemakers are protected.

It is important to have your microwave oven checked by a service center or the manufacturer if it has been dropped, or if the door doesn't seem to close properly.

Used correctly, microwave ovens seem to be perfectly safe for ordinary cooking. Please see the various sections below for the safety concerns that have to do with culinary hazards rather than those that relate to the equipment itself.

The possibilities of microwave cooking

It is important to understand how a microwave oven works, and its virtues and limitations, before trying to cook with it. Although many cooking methods are best left to other appliances, the microwave oven is a good appliance for what it does well. Of course the microwave oven does not obviate preparation of ingredients, but it does shorten cooking time. In any case, a meal has many parts and it is inefficient to do everything in a microwave oven. The hardest part for someone who already cooks is the necessity to relearn certain techniques. This has happened in the past, to the advantage of the cook, with the advent of patent stoves, refrigerators, freezers and food processors. The same adaptation will take place with the microwave oven as we work with it and discover its basic rules. A comprehensive list of timings will, however, still have to come from specialist cookbooks.

Let us dispose first of those things the microwave oven does inefficiently or badly, so that we can get on to the fun part. A microwave oven does not roast well, so put whole chickens, rib roasts, legs of lamb, and geese in your regular oven or grill them out of doors for good results. It is possible to speed the cooking of such cuts by blanching, partially cooking, or defrosting a frozen roast in the microwave oven first. The microwave oven is also inefficient at broiling or sautéing.

The microwave oven is at its least attractive with breads – other than those that are steamed – even though some people feel that they get satisfactory results by wrapping breads for reheating in paper towels and cooking very briefly (see Covering dishes, p.500). The problem lies in the way flour, particularly high-gluten flour, quickly absorbs liquid and becomes gluey. This is also a problem for cakes and other baked goods. It is best to confine baking to cakes without flour, or to cakes where cake flour (low-gluten) and another starch such as corn starch, potato flour, rice flour, or water chestnut flour can be substituted.

The microwave oven tends to set protein very quickly, which creates problems with some egg dishes such as soufflés and custards. Soufflés can be made more or less to work at lower powers, but I never find them as sumptuous as oven-baked soufflés and as there is no time saving I would relegate them to the regular oven. Custards can be made to work very successfully by cooking at 50 percent power (p.498).

One additional cautionary note about eggs. They should not be cooked in their shells in a microwave oven, since the pressure that builds up inside the shell may burst it. Even when shelled, the yolks of eggs are surrounded by a membrane that needs to be pierced before cooking in order to eliminate a similar problem. This is simple to accomplish. Place your raw egg where you want it or break it on to a plate ready to be slipped into place. Take the tip of a very sharp knife or skewer and with two quick light jabs prick the membrane over the yolk in order to make an invisible hole in it. Oddly enough, the yolk will not run, but will stay in place for baking or poaching.

What, you may ask, is left for the microwave oven when all these foods have been eliminated from its purview? Let us begin with vegetables. Never have they been cooked so quickly, so evenly, so well, with brilliant color, maximum retention of vitamins and such intensity of flavor that they rarely need salt.

Then, fish is perfect in a microwave oven. Those who have tasted or cooked fish in a microwave will never cook it in any other way, except out of doors. If you follow a few simple rules (see Cooking in a microwave oven, opposite), the fish stays moist and cooks through absolutely evenly: no more overcooked surface or fish raw at the bone; no more unwieldy pots of water.

Stews are rapid and succulent in the microwave oven, particularly chicken, veal and pork stews. Fruit desserts, as well as preserves, chutneys and relishes are also excellent. Stocks will cook in 20 to 40 minutes and taste just as good as those simmered for six to eight hours.

Components of other dishes, such as caramel and mushroom *duxelles*, are quickly made and, more importantly, controllable – there is no risk of scorching. Polenta and risotto dishes become convenient staples instead of dishes that require long stirring.

Classic steamed puddings, which can take hours to make by conventional cooking methods, take a scant six minutes in the microwave oven with no water bath. Water baths are also unnecessary for custards and pâtés.

From a health angle, it should be noted that fat is rarely needed for microwave cooking because food does not stick to the dishes in which it is cooked. When fat is used, for example butter or olive oil, it should generally be viewed as a seasoning with the quality maximized and the quantity minimized.

From the point of view of efficiency and economy, it becomes reasonable to make dishes such as *coq au vin* or *osso buco* for one. These are not dishes that have to be saved for a crowd. With a microwave oven, both time and quantity become manageable. Such dishes and many others can be cooked on the plates from which they are to be eaten. When cooking for one or two, it is often feasible to cook vegetables on the same plate as the main dish.

Vegetarians will find that dried beans still require more cooking time than other foods, but even so the time is roughly a quarter of that required for conventional cooking. While plain boiled rice – white or brown – is just as easily cooked on top of the stove, rice dishes such as pilafs and risottos are splendid in the microwave oven. Similarly, pasta is best cooked on top of the stove, but pasta sauces cook quickly and are successful in the microwave oven.

It is important to get into the habit of boiling water for these starchy foods cooked on top of the stove well in advance, so that they are cooked by the time the microwave-cooked accompaniment is done. It was not until I began cooking in a microwave oven that I realized how much time was concealed in the conventional recipe's "bring the water to a boil". This time is included in all microwave recipes.

Now, I hope you are convinced that learning to cook in a microwave oven is worth your while even though there are many things you need to know. These can only be outlined in this chapter, but if you consult good microwave cookbooks, you will find recipes similar to those you wish to make. Then, by using the material in this chapter you can use them as models for adapting recipes and creating new ones.

Choosing and using a microwave oven

First, it is important to understand your oven, whether you already have one or are planning to buy one. The most important thing to know about a microwave oven is how much power it emits. This is measured in watts. A 650–700 watt oven is a full power machine. A 500–650 watt machine is medium power; a 400–500 watt oven is low power. It will take approximately one and a half times as long to cook in a low power oven as it takes to cook in a full power oven. However, this simple mathematical formula is not precise and it is a good idea to consult a good cookbook. A medium power oven is harder to judge; but the timing will fall somewhere between the other two. You may well find that a low power oven will not cook large amounts of food efficiently. Wherever possible buy a full power oven.

Ovens are designed to run on either 110 volts or 220 volts. In the United States, most of us have a 110-volt power supply. In the United Kingdom, 220 volts is standard. In 110 volt areas I would recommend avoiding dual usage machines (convection and microwave cooking in one oven) unless the oven is a very small one intended mainly for toasting and defrosting. An all-microwave oven draws very little power and stays cool. A convection-microwave draws much more power and gets hotter. On a 110 outlet, unless a separate electric line is available for that outlet, a combination oven may well blow out your circuit. Additionally, 110 volts is not enough power to permit both forms of cooking to go on at the same time and so the machines alternate one sort of cooking with the other. Therefore it is very hard to know exactly what you are doing.

Even in a 220 volt oven which has none of these problems, there are difficulties with combined cooking. While the convection element will brown your food, it cooks it as well and in a different way than the microwaves do. Consequently, it is still more complicated than either form of cooking on its own. While some people like such ovens very much, I feel that you already have other kitchen appliances to do what the microwave does not and that you will find that there are so many uses for microwave cooking that your oven will be fully employed in that capacity.

While all microwave ovens have metal walls to retain the microwave energy in the oven, some walls are exposed while others are coated with plastic. All combination ovens have exposed metal walls which act as reflectors. This does not matter much except when you are melting a small amount of chocolate or butter or making a small amount of caramel. In such cases, you will need to cut the cooking time by 30 seconds to one minute (the time varies with quantity and the size of the oven).

Whatever the oven – unless it is the small toaster kind mentioned above – you want one with variable power. This means that it can cook at 100 percent power (the default setting), which is most often used, or at 50 percent power, which you use for custard, or at 30 percent power to defrost meat. Remember that a low power oven is already only operating at 60 percent power. You may have trouble working out which power is which on your oven. The highest setting is 100 percent. Medium (or 5) is usually 50 percent. Defrost, low-medium (or 3) is usually 30 percent. You also need to know the interior capacity of your oven. A large oven should have a 1½ ft³/45 cm³ interior capacity.

Ovens may have manual or digital controls. Digital are preferable because they are more exact at the lower end of the time scale. Remember that you are setting minutes and seconds just like a clock. Three and one half minutes is set as 3.30, three minutes as 3:00. You will have to consult the oven manual to find out how to open and close the door, set the time, set the controls and start the machine running. There are just too many variations between manufacturers to give guidelines here.

Some microwave ovens come with extras, none of which are essential. These include a revolving dish in the bottom of the oven called a carrousel, pre-programmed computer cooking options, which are expensive and useless, and built-in temperature probes, which can actually distort cooking. Temperatures can be ascertained in the easy way given on p.501.

Once you begin to use your microwave oven, you may find that the cooking smells linger in the oven despite the built-in exhaust fans. It is easy to remove such odors. Simply slice a cucumber, spread it out on a plate and cook it in the microwave oven at 100 percent power for five minutes. The cooked cucumber may then be puréed for soup.

If there are spills or spatters, the ordinary cleaning of the oven is easy, since the food will generally not bake on. Most ovens come with a removable glass pan at the bottom (this can be used as a baking sheet). Ovens with a carrousel will have the pan on the carrousel mechanism. These pans can be removed and washed in the sink with warm soapy water. Remember to handle them gently, since they are glass and can chip. The walls of the oven can be cleaned with a damp sponge. If you find that you need detergent, make sure to rinse it all off with clear water, so that the smell of detergent does not taint your food.

Cooking in a microwave oven

Microwave cooking is determined by the amount of microwave energy (measured in wattage), the length of time the food is in the oven, and by the quantity, bulk, and type of food (protein, fat, water, sugar). While these factors are important in conventional cooking, with the microwave oven their interaction is more complex and exaggerated.

The microwaves pass through the surface of the food and produce heat among the molecules in its interior. This is the reason that food browns so badly. These waves run out of energy very quickly and only penetrate about 1½ in/3.8 cm into the food, although the energy comes from all sides. This means that the ideal piece of food for microwave cooking is roughly 3 in/7.5 cm in every dimension. However, a large whole fish that is about 3-4 in/7.5-10 cm thick will cook perfectly. Remember to keep the pieces of food separated by a small space; the microwave oven will treat touching pieces as if they were one piece.

Additionally, microwave energy acts on food in liquid – a stew for instance – as if it were one mass. Water and thin liquids heat relatively slowly in a microwave oven and many foods, vegetables particularly, cook better with very little liquid added. When making a soup, stew or sauce, it is often most efficient to cook solid ingredients separately with little or no liquid and then add the rest of the liquid when the solids are almost entirely cooked, leaving enough time to bring the liquid to the boil.

The microwave energy also regards an empty space in the food as an object to be heated. This is another reason, in addition to the lack of browning, why it is not a good idea to cook a whole bird in the microwave oven. Instead, cut the bird into several serving pieces before cooking.

Microwave energy cooks food from the outside of the dish and proceeds toward the center. Think of this as the way in which a cake layer cooks in a regular oven, becoming firm at the edges first. It is the opposite of the way your food cooks on top of the stove, where the center of the pan is the hottest place. Since many of the foods that are cooked in the microwave oven are those normally cooked on top of the stove, it is important to keep this difference in mind when using a microwave oven.

As already mentioned, the microwave oven is an exaggerator: the difference in cooking time from the edge to the center of a dish is much more pronounced than it is in a conventional oven. When cooking foods that are equal – the same food in pieces of uniform size (salmon medallions, for instance) – it is best to arrange them in a ring, without touching, toward the edge of the cooking dish.

When cooking different foods at the same time in the same dish, you can obtain results that are unexpected, and superior to those produced by other forms of cooking. Place the slower cooking food (for example the dark meat of chicken or shellfish, and carrots or other dense vegetables) toward the edge of the dish and the quicker cooking foods (for example the white meat of chicken, fish, and non-dense vegetables such as mushrooms and peppers) toward the center of the dish. This will give you food that is deliciously succulent and evenly cooked, with no over- or under-done parts.

This variation in the cooking time is important enough to emphasize with more examples. When cooking a breast of chicken, whether boned or not, it is best to divide it in half along the breast bone and to reverse the anatomic position of the two halves so that the thin, rib edges are facing each other and the thicker, breast bone edges are toward the side of the plate. The difference is so marked that, when cooking several fish fillets at once, it is best to arrange them pinwheel fashion, with the thin tips toward the center of a circular dish. The thick outside ends should be doubled over to fit into the dish. This apparently exaggerated disparity in thickness will assure even cooking.

Assorted vegetables for dishes such as *pasta primavera*, which uses cooked chopped vegetables in a cream sauce (p.337), can be cooked all at once by following the principles above and arranging the vegetables in concentric rings, starting with the longest cooking vegetable at the outer edge. Conversely, a single fillet of fish should be centered on the cooking dish with its thin end tucked under so that it conforms as far as possible to the ideal, single-piece shape described above.

It should be noted that I keep referring to circles of food, in the shape of the piece of food or in concentric arrangements. Obviously, not all foods can or should be made to conform, but it is a good principle to keep in mind. This is particularly true when picking dishes for use in the microwave oven.

Microwave cookware

Circular or oval dishes are much better than those with corners, which can create pockets of microwave energy that will burn the food. There are a few special dishes that you may want to buy for use in your microwave oven, especially if you have a large oven and want to cook in quantity. You will, however, be pleasantly surprised by how many dishes you already have in your kitchen that are appropriate for microwave cooking. All oven-proof and stove-top glass containers such as pie plates, loaf pans, lasagne dishes, casseroles and even measuring cups can be used. Ceramic casseroles, soufflé dishes, quiche pans, paella pans and other baking dishes – even those that you hesitate to use in your regular oven or on top of the stove – may be used for microwave cooking.

There are only a few precautions. Do not use enameled pots that are really metal at the core. Avoid any pot with gold, silver or platinum decoration; it will discolor. Avoid those pots with an all-over metallic glaze such as cobalt blue, or the bright orange-red that results from iron-based glazes. You should obviously avoid lead glaze, which is poisonous no matter where it is used.

You will note the avoidance of metal containers in a microwave oven. Metal blocks the passage of the microwaves and thus inhibits cooking. Additionally, there are special parameters for the construction of metal pans for use in microwave ovens to avoid the unpleasant show of sparks called "arcing". There are some metal pans specially manufactured for microwave ovens that are useful if you want to brown food on top of the stove and then transfer it directly to the microwave oven. A special ceramic browning dish can be used to brown small amounts of food in the oven. The dish is preheated, and a little fat is used (with the caution this demands). For the use of aluminum foil, see the section on covering dishes (right). A few words of warning: even though a microwave oven does not heat the cooking dishes directly, they are heated by the food. Pot holders should be used when removing dishes from the oven. Do not use chipped, repaired or crazed dishes any more than you would in conventional cooking, and do not place hot glass or ceramic dishes on a wet counter or cold marble slab. When adding a liquid to a hot mixture, make sure the liquid is at room temperature and add it slowly – particularly if there is fat or sugar-rich food in the hot container.

The special dishes that I recommend purchasing, especially by cooks with full-size ovens, are an 11 × 14 × 2 in/28 × 36 × 5 cm rectangular glass-ceramic dish with rounded corners. It is very useful for accommodating two cut-up chickens and is the largest size that will fit on a carrousel. A somewhat smaller and more readily available dish that will also fit in smaller ovens is a 9 × 13 × 2 in/23 × 33 × 5 cm oval made of oven-proof glass. If you can find a glass ring mold, it can be useful for such foods as meatloaf, to prevent the center portion of the loaf from under-cooking. It can be employed also when arranging small fruits for cooking in a circle. It will, for example, keep figs in place, and accommodate their cooking liquid. An oven-glass casserole that holds 5 qt/5 L, with a lid, is useful for large quantities.

Most plates and platters (as long as they fit in the oven) can be used in microwave ovens, which saves on cleaning-up when cooking for one or two. Mugs, small crocks and glass jars are also suitable cooking containers, but they should not be filled too full. When heating a product that comes in a microwavable container, such as a sauce or baby food, remove some of the food before heating to avoid spills. Be sure to stir the heated food thoroughly after removing it from the oven to disperse the heat evenly, and test the temperature if the food is to be given to a baby or pet.

Many containers made of plastic can be used in the microwave oven, but take care to select only those items that are sold as suitable for microwave cooking. You need to be particularly careful with plastic storage containers that do not state that they can be used in the microwave. These may soften with the heat of microwave cooking and adversely affect the food. They will also be unsafe to handle, as the hot food tends to spill out once they have softened. Always check that the lids, even of those plastic containers sold for microwave use, are not labeled (often in nearly invisible letters) "for storage only" or "not for microwave oven use". This means that you will have to use another covering for the food instead (see Covering dishes, below).

Generally, I do not like plastics, because they tend to discolor when used with strongly colored or oily foods – even fish stock. In any case, be careful with plastics unless they are marked as suitable for heating to temperatures of 400°F/200°C. They are not suitable for foods that get very hot, for example fats and sugars such as caramel. Dishwasher-safe rigid plastic containers can be used for reheating food.

It is important to use pans that are as near as possible to the size and shape called for in the recipes you are using. The analogy here is cake baking. You would not make a cake layer that was supposed to go into an 8 in/20 cm cake pan in a 10 in/25 cm or 6 in/15 cm pan and expect it to turn out correctly. When deep containers are called for, shallow ones should not be substituted because of the likelihood of contents boiling over. Also, foods that are intended for use in a casserole will cook differently in a shallow pan that is large enough to hold them. As I have already stressed, the arrangement of food and the amount of covering liquid are important factors in the way food cooks and how long it takes to cook in the microwave oven.

Covering dishes

All containers need to be covered for cooking in the microwave oven unless, as in risotto, you wish to stir the food to promote evaporation. This is particularly important as it relates to two aspects of microwave oven exaggeration. We are all familiar with hot spots in our conventional ovens and pots, and with the drying out of food due to evaporation. In the microwave oven, the combination of hot spots and accelerated evaporation can create problems. When cooking on top of the stove, it is relatively easy to spot these things and to correct them by stirring or by adding more liquid. However, it is hard to see in the enclosed cavity of the microwave oven where cooking is rapid, and as a great deal of manipulation is undesirable, it is best to take steps to avoid problems before they occur. Covering the food helps to remedy the problems in part. If your dishes have tight-fitting covers they can be used. However, I find that microwavable plastic film (cling wrap) is better. There are different formulations of plastic film: some are quite rigid and will not expand, while others are more flexible and may expand in the oven.

There is some argument about how plates or other cooking dishes should be covered with plastic wrap for microwaving. The conventional method is to almost seal the dish with an overlap of film around the edge, but with a small steam vent made by leaving a small corner of the wrap unattached and turned back. After much testing, I believe that it is better to make a complete seal: that is, to have the wrap adhere to the plate or cooking vessel all around the perimeter with a significant overlap of at least 1 in/2.5 cm cling wrap. Flexible cling wrap can be drawn tight; less flexible wrap should be eased carefully as it is put over the dish (like making darts in a dress) to allow steam to escape. I prefer the tight sealing method and deal with the steam problem by telling people to prick the plastic wrap with the tip of a sharp knife at the end of the cooking time to make a vent and release the steam. This is a similar precaution to removing the lid from a pot of boiling water away from your face, or averting your head when opening the door of a steamy oven.

Whatever method you choose for applying the wrap, it is important to remove it carefully because of the risk of scalding from escaping steam. If you have vented the wrap, do not start to remove it from the loose, vented corner. Remember that all the steam will rush toward it. Take a piece of wrap that is hanging down and pull it sideways away from the cooking dish, either with it held between your thumb and a knife, or with tongs. Pull it up to release the remaining steam and then carefully remove it. You will notice that when the food gets hot, tightly sealed wrap will form a bubble pushed up by steam. This is not dangerous in any way. It is your assurance that a tight seal has been made. After you have pricked it, the bubble will collapse.

If you have followed my method and wrapped the dish tightly, it is relatively easy to stir food such as stews during cooking without entirely removing the cling wrap or even taking the dish out of the oven. Slit the top of the plastic with the tip of a sharp knife. Insert a wooden spoon into the slit and stir. Remove the spoon and patch the plastic by laying a small piece of wrap over the slit. It will adhere to form an airtight patch. Continue cooking and you will see the bubbles re-form.

It is easy to test the temperature of foods such as pork if you are using this method Simply stick the tip of an instant-read thermometer through the wrap right into the meat in the center of the dish, or in several places, to get a temperature reading. If the meat is not sufficiently cooked, patch the plastic and continue to cook. Similarly, the tip of a sharp knife can be inserted through the wrap into a vegetable to see if it is done to your liking.

In addition to the container covers and special plastic wrap, there are two other coverings that you will find helpful: paper towels and aluminum foil. Paper towels should only be bought if they are labeled "microwavable" or "microwave safe". This will mean that they contain no dyes, plastic or metal filaments. The latter is often found in recycled paper due to the use of metallic inks in the type. Paper towels are primarily useful for loosely covering dishes containing a fat and a liquid mixture, such as butter sauces. These tend to spit, just as they do on top of the stove. Do not be alarmed by the spitting, but do use the loose covering method to avoid messing the oven. Paper towels are also layered under and on top of greasy foods such as bacon to drain them as they cook. Always be careful when removing a paper towel that has been exposed to food. If it has absorbed moisture, this may well be in the form of steam, which is very hot.

Aluminum foil can be used in limited quantities in a microwave oven even though I have suggested avoiding metal pots and glazes. The rule is not to let the foil touch any other metal surface such as the wall of the oven or a metal rack. Foil is used to avoid overcooking the thinner parts of food, such as the tail of a fish, or even the shank end of a leg of lamb when defrosting it. This is called shielding. Normally, the foil is loosely applied so that it can be removed easily part-way through cooking.

Adapting recipes for the microwave oven

To create new recipes or to adapt favorite recipes for microwave cooking, it is a good idea to find a recipe in a microwave cookbook that has given you good results. Follow it for weights (try to get into the habit of weighing ingredients, since weight is such an important determinant of cooking time), measures, pan size, proportion of liquids to solids, and timing.

If you were adapting a chicken stew recipe for the microwave oven, for example, you would adjust the ingredients so that you have the amount of liquid and vegetables called for in the prototype recipe from the microwave cookbook. Your recipe might tell you that you could remove the chicken skin and eliminate the preliminary sautéing of the chicken, since fat is not needed in microwave cooking. If your recipe calls for thickening the sauce either at the start of cooking with flour or at the end in some manner, note that you can thicken at the end with cornstarch, or look at another recipe book for thickening with eggs and cream.

You will note that some recipes call for standing time. This is exactly like the standing time allowed for a roast after removing it from the oven. The food continues to cook from retained heat and in certain dishes, such as risotto and steamed puddings, liquid continues to be absorbed. I prefer to serve fish dishes directly they are made and to time them accordingly so that they don't get cold.

Remember, when deciding on a timing, it is better to undercook than overcook. You can always cook for longer if necessary, but you cannot reclaim overcooked foods.

Seasoning food for the microwave oven

There are other factors that you should be aware of when adapting your recipe for microwave cooking, mostly to do with the flavor changes that occur in microwave cooking.

Alcohol-based flavors such as red wine and sherry, and vanilla and other extracts become evanescent very rapidly in the microwave oven. When using a wine or liquor, the percentage in relation to other liquids will need to be increased. A whole vanilla bean should be substituted for vanilla extract where feasible.

Many seasonings that develop their flavor in water act like tea infusions and become strong too rapidly in the microwave oven. These seasonings, including black pepper and dried herbs, need to be sharply reduced in microwave cooking.

Salt can often be decreased as well, since the natural flavor of the food – vegetables in particular – will be accented in any case. When possible, add salt at the end of the cooking. Fresh herbs should be added toward the end of cooking, otherwise the normal quantity must be increased by half again.

A final word on seasoning applies to garlic. Garlic cooks quickly – in about six minutes – to the soft, gentle stage which is achieved in conventional cooking only by long simmering. This means that the cook can make dishes like the Spanish *sopa de ajo* (garlic soup) quickly, but for more conventional recipes the amount of garlic needs to be increased, or it should only be added for the last few minutes of cooking. Otherwise, it will simply become a background taste.

BARBARA KAFKA

COOKING EQUIPMENT

DIFFERENT PIECES of cooking equipment exist for every purpose. There are pots and pans to suit each method of cooking and utensils for every technique, many of them versatile enough to fulfill several functions. Quality is the key when buying kitchen equipment – a few well-made and highly practical tools will more than pay for themselves. This chapter lists the most common and useful equipment, most of which is demonstrated elsewhere in the book.

Materials for cookware

Metal is the most important material for cooking equipment, although glass and plastic are also common. Of prime importance is the ability of the material to conduct heat quickly to the food or to retain it for slow cooking. Weight, ease of handling and cleaning, and cost are also important. See also Pots and pans (p.510).

Copper This is the best conductor of heat. It is used for saucepans, sauté pans and sugar boiling pans and for gratin dishes, casseroles and other cook-and-serve dishes. The best copper pans are heavy and lined with nickel, tin or stainless steel. Copper sugar pans are left unlined, however, because none of the metals used for lining can withstand the temperatures reached in sugar boiling. They must not be used for acidic ingredients, which may react with the copper to form toxic substances.

Aluminum This is lightweight and a good heat conductor; it is used for saucepans, casseroles, sauté pans, frying pans and stockpots. Aluminum is often coated with stainless steel, nickel or nonstick plastic as it reacts to foods containing acid and may give them a metallic taste. Aluminum alloys have been developed in which other metals are included to reduce acid reaction.

Cast iron Used for Dutch ovens, griddles, frying pans and skillets. Ideal for long, slow cooking methods such as braising and baking, cast iron cookware needs seasoning (p.89). It is very heavy and sturdy, but can crack if dropped.

Enameled cast iron Used for casseroles, saucepans, gratin dishes, terrines and frying pans. A thin layer of glass covers the cast iron to prevent it from rusting or reacting to acid. These pots are best for slow cooking.

Steel Used for frying pans, omelet and crêpe pans, deep-fryers and woks; all need seasoning (p.89). Tinned steel is used for a wide range of baking pans and molds. Steel is popular in Europe for fast cooking. It is tough, durable, and does not warp over high heat, although it can rust.

Stainless steel Used for saucepans, casseroles, frying pans, pans for boiling, roasting pans and many kitchen bowls and utensils. It does not rust like plain steel and requires no seasoning. Stainless steel is non-reactive even when it is used with pure acids, but it is an inferior heat conductor. Pans must be thick enough to avoid hot spots: some cookware has layers of copper or aluminum to improve heat conduction.

Enamelware Enamel on thin steel is inexpensive, but it chips easily and is a poor conductor. The pans are often so thin that food scorches; they are recommended only for boiling and poaching.

Earthenware, ceramic and glass These materials are not good conductors of heat, but once hot they retain heat well and therefore are suitable for long simmering and braising. Traditionally used on top of the stove, they are now widely used in the oven. Flameproof glass and ceramics can be used over a low direct flame, but earthenware is best set on a heat diffusing mat. For all these materials, oven temperatures should be 25°F/14°C lower than for metal dishes. Stoneware is a less porous alternative to earthenware and can withstand higher temperatures.

Nonstick plastic Known by proprietary names such as "Teflon" or "Tefal", this is a coating of polytetrafluoroethylene (PTFE) that prevents food from sticking. Nonstick pans are easy to clean, but the coating eventually wears off, so non-abrasive cleaners and utensils should be used.

WEIGHING & MEASURING

Accurate measurement by weight or volume is essential in cooking, particularly for cakes and pastry. In North America, volume measurements are standard for both liquid and dry ingredients, while elsewhere liquid is usually measured by volume and dry ingredients by weight – a more accurate system.

Measuring cups and spoons The standard measures in North America are the eight fluid ounce cup (so called because the water it holds weighs eight ounces). This is divided into 16 tablespoons. For dry ingredients, cup and spoon measures that hold only the desired quantity are recommended because level measurement is more accurate. Liquids are less likely to overflow if the measure has headroom.

Scales There are two types of kitchen scales: spring and balance. Spring scales operate by tension and they will, of course, wear out in time. Balance scales work in several ways: they may have a fixed counter-balance and an indicator that moves along the scale as weight is added, a balance bar along which weights are moved to set the desired weight, or a beam balance in which weights are set on one tray and the ingredients to be weighed on the other. Beam balance scales are the most accurate and durable, and are available in a wide range of sizes. For domestic use, they should measure increments of 1 oz/30 g or smaller, up to at least 4 lb/1.8 kg.

Beam balance
scales and weights

THERMOMETERS

Meat thermometer Two types of thermometer are used to measure the internal temperature of meats and poultry during roasting. Dial thermometers are inserted into the food and left until the desired internal temperature is reached. The disadvantages are that they may cause juices to run out, and that their metal shaft can distort cooking times by conducting additional heat to the center of the food.

Instant-read thermometer This is more accurate, inserted for one or two minutes while the food is in the oven. It can also be used to test doughs and liquids. Most register 200°F/95°C maximum.

Oven thermometer This must be able to withstand oven temperatures up to 500°F/260°C; dial thermometers are more robust but less accurate than mercury thermometers.

Fat thermometer Used for deep-frying. The best fat thermometer uses mercury and has a scale large enough to be read at a distance. A candy thermometer that registers to 400°F/200°C or more can be substituted for a fat thermometer.

Dairy thermometer Used to accurately check the temperature of milk when making yogurt or cheese. The temperature range is 10-230°F/−12-110°C.

Candy/sugar thermometer As accuracy is vital for making candy, test the thermometer each time to ensure it registers 212°F/100°C in boiling water. For use, see Making boiled sugar syrup, p.414.

Freezer thermometer Both mercury and dial types are used for freezing. Thermometers that register up to 40°F/5°C can also be used for refrigerators.

Density thermometer or hydrometer Used to test pickling brines and sugar syrups. They have hollow glass rods that are weighted so they sink to specific points in liquids of different densities when cold. A salometer is used for brines, a saccharometer for sugar syrups.

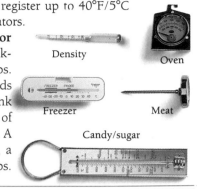

Density

Oven

Freezer

Meat

Candy/sugar

SPOONS, SPATULAS, WHISKS & PIERCING TOOLS

Metal spoons The best metal spoons are oval with a pointed end. Some basting spoons have a handle attached at the side to make pouring easy.

Wooden spoons A flat surface with little or no "bowl" (often called a wooden spatula) is easiest to use. Wood does not conduct heat, so wooden spoons can be used for lengthy stirring over heat.

Spatula A flexible metal blade set in a handle, used for spreading ingredients like icing and cream (p.405). A Chinese metal spatula is used for moving food around in the wok when stir-frying. Plastic spatulas are useful for non-heat-related tasks.

Pancake flipper A short, wide blade with a long handle. Used for turning pancakes and for transferring them.

Ladle Used for pouring liquid, skimming stocks (p.42), and sauces, ladles come in many sizes. Small ones are also used for pushing sauces through a conical mesh sieve. Choose one with a hooked or pierced handle for easy storage.

Skimmer A shallow perforated metal spoon used for skimming stock and lifting food from a pot, leaving the liquid behind.

Ice cream scoop This can be a spoon-shaped flat shovel, or it may have a hemispherical bowl, often with a spring blade to loosen the ice cream from the scoop. Some metal scoops contain anti-freezing liquid to prevent sticking.

Whisks The classic whisk for sauces is made entirely of metal, with a plump handle that is easy to grip. Handy lengths range from 8 in/20 cm to 12 in/30 cm. Balloon whisks for egg whites are mounted on wooden handles and are more rounded, often with thinner wires, so they can incorporate more air. A rotary whisk has two handles, and two beaters suspended in a wire frame. Rotary whisks are used for beating eggs and are particularly good for handling heavy mixtures.

Trimmed whisk A home-crafted tool for spun sugar made by cutting the wires of a whisk so that only a few inches remain attached to the handle.

Two-pronged fork Commonly used in the kitchen to test if foods are cooked. A carving fork has two prongs with a hand guard.

Dipping fork A specialist tool used to immerse ingredients to be coated in chocolate or sugar. Dipping forks have long thin tines. Small circles of wire mounted on a shaft can be used instead.

Skewer This is a sharp, thin rod of metal or wood used to spear kebabs and other foods for broiling or frying. Small skewers can be used to close poultry or meat cavities after stuffing. Wooden skewers are used to test whether cakes are done, while metal skewers perform the same function for roasts and terrines. Thinner bamboo skewers are used in Asian cooking.

Trussing needle Available in different sizes. A large needle used to truss poultry and to sew up stuffed meat.

Larding needle Two types of larding needle exist. One has a sharp point, a channeled shaft about 18 in/45 cm long and a wooden handle, and is used to thread strips of fat or ham deep inside meat. The other, a piqué needle, is smaller, with a slotted end to stitch small strips of fat into the surface of meat. See p.196.

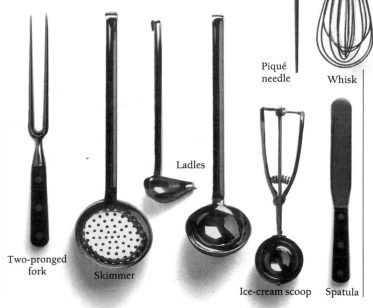

Piqué needle

Whisk

Two-pronged fork

Ladles

Skimmer

Ice-cream scoop

Spatula

CUTTING TOOLS

Cutting tools for peeling, trimming and shaping ingredients are so important that professional chefs carry a personal portfolio of knives. Sharpness is critical, so also is matching the correct tool to a specific job. Handles made of heat-resistant plastic, or coated with it, are the easiest to maintain as they do not split or warp after washing. Avoid knives with a space between the handle and the blade, as bacteria may collect there.

Knives

Knife blades of carbon steel can be sharpened at home to a much finer edge than those of stainless steel. Unlike stainless steel, they discolor on contact with acid and should be dried thoroughly after washing to prevent rusting. More expensive knives made from high carbon stainless steel combine the best of both materials; unaffected by acid and moisture, they can be hand-sharpened to give a razor-like edge. When choosing knives, look for sturdy construction, with the tang (handle end) of the blade running inside the handle and solidly attached with rivets. The best knives have a "heel" at the wide end of the blade to protect the fingers and reinforce the blade.

Good knives should be looked after carefully. Store them in a rack on the wall so the blades do not get damaged and keep them sharp. Electric knife sharpeners are easy to use, but eventually they wear down blades. The traditional knife sharpener, a textured rod made of hardened steel – and now also of ceramic – set into a handle, will prolong the life of the blade.

A traditional wooden cutting board also protects the blade, which can be damaged or dulled on a tiled or marble work top. End-grain hardwood is sturdy enough to withstand heavy chopping, and a board 1½ in/4 cm thick will not warp with washing. Some cooks prefer lighter cutting boards made of plastic, which can be cleaned by bleaching.

Paring knife A small knife for trimming and peeling vege-tables. The blade may be from 2 in/5 cm to 4 in/10 cm long; some are curved, but most are straight.

Chopping, or chef's, knife This has a heavy, wide blade ideal for chopping vegetables, herbs and other ingredients. The blade length ranges from 6 in/15 cm to 12 in/30 cm, but an 8 in/20 cm blade is often the most useful and easiest to handle. The side of the blade can also be used to flatten thinly sliced meats, to crush garlic (p.15), ginger (p.31) and scallions, and to transfer ingredients from the cutting board to the pan.

Meat carver The long, slender blade of a carving knife is used to cut even slices from cooked meat. Knives with a beveled edge are used for ham; others are more rounded to add strength to the length of the blade.

Boning knife Two types of boning knife are common: French chefs use a rigid blade about 6 in/15 cm long held in the fist like a dagger; the other type has a longer, thinner blade that can be rigid or flexible. In both cases, only the tip of the blade is used, so a fine point is essential.

Filleting knife Used to bone fish, the pointed, flexible blade easily follows the contours of delicate bones. It can also be used to slice vegetables and fruit thinly.

Butcher's scimitar The extra long blade of this knife, often curved, is used to slice raw meats into even-sized steaks or chops.

Serrated knife A large serrated knife is best for slicing breads, cakes and pastries as the edge cuts through the crumb without tearing (p.393). Smaller serrated knives are best for slicing tomatoes and citrus fruits. The edge must be sharpened professionally but lasts almost indefinitely. A long serrated blade may be used to create a ripple design on butter, cream or cream cheese coatings.

Mincing knife Often called by its Italian name *mezzaluna* (half moon), this knife has a curved blade with handles at each end. It is used with a rocking motion to chop large quantities of ingredients like nuts and herbs. Some mincing knives have multiple parallel blades. For how to use, see p.13.

Cleaver The cleaver is the heaviest knife and is used for hacking through bone. Roughly rectangular in shape, it is unbalanced so the wide, heavy blade adds to the momentum of the stroke. Cleavers come in various sizes; the largest are used by butchers. Meat saws (hacksaws) can also be used to sever bones.

Chinese cleaver This has a broad rectangular blade that comes in varying weights and sizes. Chinese chefs use a cleaver for almost everything – from trimming meat to slicing ginger. A medium weight is the most versatile.

Cutlet bat This is used to flatten fish and meat, especially escalopes, to an even thickness. Two forms are common: a flat, heavy, shovel-shaped bat; and a heavy metal disc mounted on a perpendicular handle. The flat side of a cleaver blade can also be used as a cutlet bat.

Sharpening steel A textured rod, usually made of hardened steel, but also of ceramic. Other types of knife sharpener, including electric ones, may be easier to use, but they tend to wear away the knife blades more quickly. See also Knife sharpening (p.207).

Chefs   Filleting   Boning   Paring

Cleaver   Chinese cleaver   Serrated   Meat carver   Cutlet bat

Specialty knives and cutters

A wide variety of specialty knives and cutting tools exist for specific purposes. The best of these tools are made of rustproof, easy-to-clean stainless steel.

Channel knife/stripping tool A short, flat blade with a small U-shaped indentation, which cuts thin strips of citrus fruit rind or the peel of vegetables (p.283) to create a decorative pattern.

Oyster knife Used to force open the shells of shellfish, especially oysters or clams (p.166), this knife has a short, fat, pointed blade, often with a guard to protect the hand. The hand holding the shellfish should be protected with a towel or glove.

Grapefruit knife A small knife with a double-edged serrated blade. For preparing grapefruit (p.459), or hollowing out small fruits or vegetables.

Kitchen scissors/shears These must be strong enough to cut through fish fins or poultry bones. Stout shears are traditional, with straight blades for fish and curved blades for poultry. Asian scissors with large handles and short blades are becoming popular since they are as strong as the heavier Western models. Some kitchen scissors can be taken apart for cleaning.

Grater Two types of grater are used in the kitchen. One has a flat or convex surface of perforated, abrasive metal. A miniature grater of this kind is available for nutmeg. Sometimes four grating surfaces are joined to form a box grater. The other type is a rotary grater in which the food for grating is held in a hopper and the grater is rotated by a handle. Rotary graters can be used for anything that fits inside them; they require less strength to use.

Mandoline A flat wooden or metal frame with adjustable cutting blades for slicing vegetables. Most mandolines have fixed different blades: smooth for cutting French fries, matchstick and shoestring potatoes and fluted for waffle potatoes. A more expensive version has a protective holder in which to put the vegetables. For use, see p.296.

Vegetable peeler The blade of this knife has two sharp slits and is used to strip peel from vegetables and fruit as thinly as possible. Peelers are available with a fixed or rotary blade.

Melon baller Scoop-shaped cutter that comes in several sizes, with round or oval, smooth or fluted blades. These are most commonly used for making melon or cucumber balls. Small ballers are useful for removing seeds from halved apples or pears.

Corer A short, sharp-ended cylinder set on a shaft with a handle. It is used to core whole apples or pears, or to hollow squash for stuffing. Some corers cut fruit into wedges.

Pitter This is used to remove stones from cherries or olives. It works like a pair of scissors, with a ring-shaped holder for the fruit

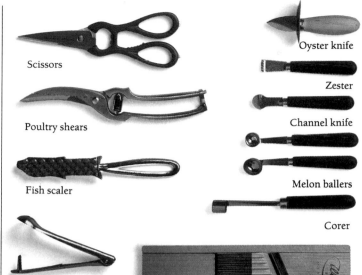

Scissors

Poultry shears

Fish scaler

Pitter

Oyster knife

Zester

Channel knife

Melon ballers

Corer

Wooden mandoline

Rotary grater

and a solid shaft which extracts the pit. See p.457 for use.

Zester The short, flat blade has a blunt, beveled end and five small holes. When drawn over the skin of an orange or lemon, the tool scrapes away thin strips of the colored zest, leaving the white pith behind (p.460).

Egg slicer This has very thin, parallel wires that are pulled down through a hard-boiled egg to slice it evenly. One version cuts an egg into wedges.

Fish scaler This is equipped with rows of teeth that scrape the scales off fish without tearing the skin (p.112). Large scalers are heart-shaped and have a sturdy wooden handle. The back of a strong knife can be used in place of a scaler.

Truffle and aspic cutters These small metal cutters in geometric shapes are used for cutting sliced truffle, hard-boiled egg white, tomato skin and other ingredients into elaborate decorative designs. Aspic cutters for sliced aspic are similar but larger. Truffles may also be cut in thin shavings using a miniature mandoline.

BOWLS

Bowls come in many sizes and a variety of materials. As well as those used for mixing ingredients, there are bowls for storing them and for serving. Deep bowls can be used to protect yeast doughs from drafts while they are rising. Bowls made of glass or ceramic are heavy enough to sit firmly on the counter and, if heatproof, can be used in a water bath or in the freezer. Stainless steel bowls are increasingly common; as well as being durable, they are good conductors of heat and cold.

Mixing bowls These should be wide enough to allow for vigorous whisking or gentle folding. A traditional glazed ceramic mixing bowl has a gripstand – a flat area that allows the bowl to rest at an angle for beating. Also available are unbreakable melamine bowls with a rubber ring on the bottom that keeps the bowl steady.

Copper bowls A round-bottomed bowl of unlined copper is best

for whipping egg whites, which interact harmlessly with the copper to produce a dense texture and maximum volume. The size of the bowls vary: for 6-8 egg whites, a diameter of 12 in/30 cm with a 16 in/40 cm whisk is appropriate. To prepare a copper bowl for use, see Whipping egg whites, p.82. A good tip for keeping the bowl steady on the work surface is to put a folded towel under the bowl.

Wooden bowls These are mainly used for tossing and serving salads. They should be wiped out with a wet cloth rather than washed with soap. The bowl can be rubbed with garlic to give the salad extra flavor; garlic may impart a flavor to the wood.

Copper bowl

DRAINERS, GRINDERS & PURÉEING TOOLS

Each of these tools has a particular function in separating solid ingredients from liquid, or in grinding ingredients or making purées.

Colander The best colanders are made of sturdy metal with solid legs so that heavy foods do not unbalance them. They should have many holes for even draining.

Conical sieve Made of perforated metal (Fr. *chinois*) or fine wire mesh (Fr. *chinois fin*). The former is used for draining, much like a colander, but has the advantage that liquid flows through in a steady stream. The mesh strainer, sometimes called a tammy, gives smoother results and is normally used for straining and puréeing stocks and soups (p.46) and sauces (p.53). Stainless steel requires less maintenance than tin-coated metal versions.

Jelly bag A tightly woven cloth sack used for draining puréed fruit to make clear jellies. The bag is suspended over a bowl, and the juice is allowed to drip through slowly. For use, see p.491.

Cheesecloth A thin, loosely woven cotton cloth originally designed to drain curds for making cheese (p.77), it is often used today to line a sieve (p.46), or to wrap a bouquet garni.

Drum sieve and pounder Called a *tamis* in French, this is the traditional implement for puréeing. It is a flat mesh set in a wooden ring. The mesh may be fine or coarse and made of tinned wire, horsehair or nylon. It is usually used with a mushroom-shaped wooden pestle to pound the ingredients through the mesh (p.266). Soft ingredients like berries can be worked through with a pastry scraper or a wooden spoon.

Food mill (Fr. *mouli*) Used for simultaneous puréeing and straining of ingredients. Food is forced through the perforated metal disks by an angled metal scraper turned by a handle (p.266). Most models have three disks of varying degrees of coarseness.

Spice mill Similar to a mincing machine with a clamp to fix it to the work surface. A coffee grinder, kept specifically for grinding spices, is a good and less cumbersome alternative.

Pestle and mortar The traditional tool for making purées, crushing shellfish shells for butter, for grinding herbs for sauces such as *pesto* (p.17), and spices (p.23). Marble is the best material for the bowl-shaped mortar as it does not absorb flavor. Other mortars may be ceramic or wood. All pestles should be heavy so their weight does some of the work.

Meat grinder A classic grinder operates with a screw-shaped cutting blade turned by a handle. Disks with different sized holes can be used to grind meat, poultry and fish coarsely or finely. Electric models are available. Meat grinders cut across tough fibers, thus making meat more tender. In many domestic kitchens the grinder has been supplanted by the food processor, which tends to pound rather than grind.

Drum sieve and pounder

Food mill

PASTA TOOLS

A few special tools of Italian origin simplify pasta making.

Pasta rolling pin A long, narrow wooden pin. The extra length allows even rolling of a large sheet of pasta, while its narrow diameter makes thin sheets easier to roll.

Ravioli mold A mold in the form of a metal tray with fluted-edged indentations ensures uniform size for ravioli. These often come with a tiny rolling pin for pressing out the shapes.

Pasta rack A wooden rack used to dry pasta for storing. The rack is usually small enough to sit on a chair.

Pasta machine The best pasta machine has hand-turned rollers (p.332).

Pasta machine

These knead and thin the mixed pasta dough; a cutting attachment forms very thin, narrow noodles. An electric machine mixes and extrudes spaghetti and other pasta through disks. However, the pasta lacks the resilience of hand-worked dough.

WRAPPERS

Wrappers are used to protect and preserve food, to prevent it sticking to dishes and molds and to present candies and cakes.

Wax paper A thin paper with a waterproof wax coating on both sides, used to line cake pans and baking sheets. It withstands only gentle oven heat.

Silicone paper Paper coated with silicone to make a nonstick surface for lining baking pans and sheets and making baking cases. It withstands higher temperatures than wax paper.

Parchment paper A nonstick paper for lining cake pans and for cooking *en papillote* (p.121).

Foil Made of aluminum, this is easily molded to shape and conducts heat well. It is used to enclose ingredients for baking, to cover dishes in the oven and to line baking sheets. Its resistance to heat makes it ideal for enclosing foods on an outdoor grill. Foil must be greased to prevent food sticking to it.

Plastic wrap or cling film Used more for storage than cooking, but some brands may be used in the microwave oven (pp.500-501).

Roasting bags These are made of paper or plastic for roasting meats such as fowl. Tightly sealed, they prevent juices escaping and keep the meat moist, often at the expense of a browned surface.

Paper cases The smallest are used for presenting candies and the largest to line pans for muffins and cupcakes. They can be made of parchment paper or of sturdier foil for sorbets and ice creams.

PASTRY TOOLS

Pastry tools made of metal, particularly baking sheets, should be washed as little as possible. With use, their surface acquires a patina and foods are less likely to stick.

Baking sheet Often called a cookie sheet, this is made in a variety of metals; the best are heavy and will not warp at high temperatures. The sheet should be at least 1 in/2.5 cm smaller than the oven on all four sides to allow air and heat to circulate. Heavy aluminum baking sheets, particularly those with a nonstick finish, are gaining in popularity. Sheets with little or no rim make baked goods easy to remove. A bar cookie pan is somewhat deeper, intended for cookies to be cut into squares.

Pastry slab This is made of marble or granite; both are well suited to pastry making because they are smooth and cool. To chill before rolling, set a roasting pan full of ice on the surface for 15 minutes. Wipe the slab completely dry before use.

Rolling pin A long hardwood cylinder 2-3 in/5-7 cm in diameter, with or without handles. A heavy pin helps in rolling large quantities of dough, as does a pin which revolves on shafts (best of all with ball bearings) for even operation. A hollow glass rolling pin filled with ice or iced water is convenient for puff pastry except in hot conditions, when condensation is a problem.

Cooling rack A wire grill on which pastries, cakes or breads are set to cool. It should have legs to allow air to circulate underneath.

Pastry blender This consists of steel wires bent to an oval and set into a handle; it is used to cut fat into dry ingredients for pastry. Large blending forks perform the same purpose, but are less common. A knife held in each hand can be used for the same task.

Pastry scraper (Fr. *corne*) A flexible plastic scraper used to cut dough, scrape the sides of bowls and scoop up dough from the work surface (p. 379).

Dough scraper A metal scraper with a wooden handle, similar to a paint scraper. It is used for cutting dough into portions and loosening baked goods from the pan. It is also used for kneading fondant and tempering chocolate, as well as for forming chocolate ruffles and curls (p.423).

Sifter This sifts and removes lumps from dry ingredients such as flour and aerates them for better mixing. A simple bowl-shaped wire strainer is quite adequate, but models with a spring mechanism to agitate the ingredients are also used.

Dredger A can with a perforated screw-on top used to sprinkle confectioners' sugar or cocoa lightly over pastries and cakes.

Pastry brush Used for applying egg glaze, melted butter, fruit glaze, or aspic. Brushes of various widths with natural or synthetic bristles are available.

Pastry pincher Used to flute the edge of pastry before baking. A variety of shapes are available; the most common is tweezer-shaped, with serrated edges.

Pastry wheel A straight or scalloped wheel with a handle. It speeds the cutting of pastry or pasta shapes (p.336). A larger pizza cutter is used for dividing cooked pizza into portions.

Pastry cutters Available in round, oval and barquette shapes, as well as animals and numbers. The edges may be smooth or fluted and should be sharp and absolutely even so the pastry cuts cleanly. To cut clean shapes, press the cutter quickly and forcefully through the dough.

Vol-au-vent circles A set of concentric domed metal disks with a finger hole in the center. The disks are used to guide the cutting of circles of varying sizes in dough. For use, see p.380.

Croissant cutter A short wooden or plastic cylinder with blades set diagonally in it. As the roller passes over the dough, the blades cut out elongated triangles.

Pastry bag Available in various sizes in nylon and plain or plastic-lined canvas. The best bags are waterproof and easily pliable. They are used with tubes for piping decorations and filling pastries and pasta. For instructions on filling a pastry bag, see p.406.

Piping tube A conical nozzle that shapes whipped cream, choux pastry dough and icing, as it is forced through. Piping tubes of tinned steel or plastic come in a wide range of decorative shapes and sizes. For clean-cut patterns, the nozzle must be incisively sharp. A great variety of small tubes are used for cake decorations, particularly of royal icing. Some slot into metal piping guns, or they may simply be dropped into a paper piping cone (p.407) or pastry bag. Common piping tubes are illustrated on pp.406, 408.

Cookie press Used for soft doughs, this is a cylindrical mold with a series of disks for different designs.

Pastry scraper

Pastry wheel

Pastry brush

Pastry pincher

Pastry cutters

Pastry bag

Piping tubes

Pastry blender

Rolling pin

Sifter

Dredger

Pizza cutter

Vol-au-vent circles

MOLDS & BAKING PANS

Molds are used for many jobs in the kitchen and are made of various materials suited to different tasks. For example, ice cream and gelatin dishes require metal molds that allow the food to be released when heat is applied. Molded chocolate, however, which is pushed out of the mold and must not be heated, is often set in flexible plastic or rubber molds. Dishes that are served directly from their mold, especially those requiring long cooking such as rice pudding, can be made in earthenware or glass.

The specific shape of a mold or pan is important. Yeast breads, for instance, rise less well in a shallow pan. Pastry, on the other hand, cooks best in a shallow, even layer.

Ice cream molds

Metal molds are best for ices as they chill quickly and can be warmed for unmolding. All ice cream molds should be equipped with tight lids to prevent the formation of crystals during storage. Smooth sides guarantee that rich mixtures will unmold easily. For unmolding iced desserts, see p.445. Ice cream molds may be round, square or brick-shaped. Often the bottom is embossed, leaving a raised design on the ice cream block when it is unmolded. Animal-shaped molds are also popular for ice cream.

Bombe mold Traditionally, this is a spherical metal mold with a lid. A bombe can also be cylindrical or square with a rounded top.

Ice cream mold

Bombe mold

Dessert and gelatin molds

Designed to display desserts and jellies to best advantage, these molds pose special problems for the cook. Ornate molds with scalloped edges and geometric indentations are impressive but hard to unmold neatly. Mixtures for tall molds must be more firmly set than for shallow ones as they are more likely to collapse; the less firm the mixture, the plainer and lower the mold should be. Dessert molds need not be very heavy as they are rarely heated, but remember that thin molds tend to dent and warp.

Charlotte mold This is bucket-shaped, with gently sloping sides and flat handles near the top to make unmolding easy. A charlotte mold may also be used for soufflés and puddings, or for aspic molds (p.254).

Jelly molds Used for aspics, fruit gelatins or Bavarian creams, these are typically made from thin metal and are quite ornate, with intricate peaks. For unmolding gelatin desserts, see p.430.

Dariole mold A smaller version of a *baba* mold, it is used for making small *mousselines*, aspics and mousses.

Pudding molds These are used for steamed puddings. Lidded metal molds come in a wide variety of forms from simple rounds to fantasy shapes like a melon. They can also be used for molding aspics and Bavarian creams.

***Coeur à la crème* mold** This is a heart-shaped perforated ceramic mold for making *coeur à la crème* (p.76): excess liquid drains through the holes. It may be large or small.

Aspic egg molds These are oval with a smooth bottom, just large enough to contain a poached or *mollet* egg enrobed in aspic.

Dariole mold   Jelly mold   Charlotte mold

Pastry molds

To prevent food sticking, metal molds or pans should not be washed, but wiped clean immediately after use while still warm. Pans with a black finish are available, and give the pastry a particularly crisp brown crust.

Tart pan A shallow pan, usually made of metal, and often with a removable base. It may be round or rectangular.

Pie plate or pan This may be round, square or rectangular and has shallow sloping sides and a flat rim to hold the pastry top. British pie dishes are deeper and are usually oval.

Tart ring A metal ring ¾ in/2 cm high that is placed on a baking sheet and lined with dough for baking tarts and quiches.

Tart pan This is made of porcelain or metal and often has fluted edges. Porcelain looks attractive, but pastry does not brown as

well as it would in a metal pan and may be hard to unmold.

Tartlet molds These are miniature tart pans with a solid or removable bottom. They come in many shapes and sizes: round, square, diamond and barquette (oval with pointed ends). They are used for baking small hors d'oeuvres and dessert pastries. Miniature pans are used for candies and petits fours.

Pâté or raised pie mold A hinged metal mold, usually oval or rectangular, with elaborate fluted designs pressed into the side. The mold often has no bottom, so is placed directly on the baking sheet. Once the pâté or pie is cooked, the hinge is unfastened to loosen the mold, revealing an ornate pastry crust.

Horn mold or cornet This narrow metal cone is used to shape puff pastry horns. Wider pointed molds are designed to be lined with ham or lettuce leaves and then stuffed.

Tart ring   Pâté or raised pie mold   Tart pan   Horn molds or cornets   Tartlet molds

Cake and baking pans

The most versatile cake and baking pans are made of tinned steel or aluminum. Glass or ceramic pans should only be used for foods that brown easily.

Cake pans For sponge and creamed cakes, pans have relatively low, gently sloping sides. Shallow pans with straight sides are intended for layer cakes. Extra deep pans with straight sides make tall cakes for slicing into layers. The French *moule à manqué* has sloping sides so that icing runs down the sides of the finished cake.

Jelly roll pan This is rectangular, with sides about ¾ in/2 cm deep. It is used for sheets of cake to be filled and rolled. A baking sheet lined with parchment paper may be used instead.

Springform pan A deep metal ring equipped with a spring release and a base that is clamped on. It is used for deep cakes and desserts that are not to be inverted (fruitcakes, mousse cakes). A similar deep steel ring is used for charlottes and other desserts.

Loaf pan A brick-shaped pan with slightly sloping sides, available in a wide range of sizes. It is used for bread, fruitcakes, pound cakes and other rich cakes. A variation is the Pullman loaf pan, with a sliding lid and straight sides.

Ring mold A round pan with curved sides and a hollow center. The ring is usually as wide as it is deep. It is used for *savarin* cakes, vegetable and fish turbans and aspics.

Tube pan Deeper than a ring mold, with a narrower center, a kugelhopf pan has fluted sides and is traditionally made of earthenware. An angel food cake pan has feet attached to the top to raise the pan from the table when it is inverted to cool the cake. A bundt pan has broad fluting and a wide center tube. It is used for traditional pound cake.

Muffin tin A sheet of cup-shaped hollows for cupcakes and muffins, the size and number of cups vary per sheet.

Madeleine tin A sheet of elongated shell-shaped depressions for baking madeleine cakes.

Baba mold A bucket-shaped mold 3-4 in/7.5-10 cm high and usually made of tinned steel. It is used for baking rum *babas* and molding fish *mousselines*, pâtés and vegetable timbales.

Brioche mold Made of tinned steel with a flat bottom and fluted, sloping sides, this is used for brioches, custards and gelatin desserts.

Cast-iron molds Heavy molds used for batter breads. They come in a variety of shapes, including corn-shaped sticks (cornstick molds) and houses for gingerbread.

Baba mold

Brioche mold

Kugelhopf pan

Madeleine tin

Angel food cake pan

ELECTRIC MACHINES

Electric machines are labor saving, and mixtures can be worked rapidly with little fear of spoilage through heat transfer.

Mixer Hand-held mixers are useful for small quantities and for stirring ingredients over heat. The best stationary models have a fixed bowl with a beater that moves across the bottom. Heavy-duty motors are required for yeast doughs and thick batters; some machines have a meat-grinding attachment.

Blender Used to purée and liquify. It has a tall, narrow beaker with cutting blades at the bottom; some liquid must be combined with the solids at the start. It makes the smoothest purées, and has an emulsifying effect on some mixtures.

Food processor A fixed bowl with removable cutting and kneading blades and cutting and shredding disks. Although it is very versatile, it does not purée as finely as a blender. To avoid overworking, use the pulse switch. Choose a machine that has a circuit breaker to prevent it overheating or burning out.

Deep-fryer This maintains the proper temperature of the fat by means of a thermostat, which should register a wide temperature range. Models with a safety feature are recommended.

Pressure cooker A hermetically sealed stovetop or electric pot in which steam pressure builds up so that foods cook quickly at temperatures above boiling point. A safety valve releases excess steam. A pressure cooker is particularly useful for dishes that require lengthy cooking.

Crockpot This simmers food slowly for extended periods and can be left unattended with little danger of scorching.

ICE CREAM MACHINES

A machine for making sorbet and ice cream must stir the mixture at the same time as freezing it to well below 32°F/0°C.

Hand churn freezer A cylindrical tub equipped with a paddle. The tub is surrounded by ice and coarse rock salt in the proportion of 1 qt/1 L of ice to ½ cup/100 g salt. This lowers the melting point of the ice, thus chilling the mixture in the churn to below the freezing point of water. The paddle is turned by hand for 10-20 minutes until the mixture sets. This machine gives excellent results, but too much salt added to the ice will make the mixture set too quickly and become grainy.

Manual freezer This innovation consists of a hand-operated paddle in a sealed metal container of chemical refrigerant that is frozen ahead of time. No ice or salt is required. The freezer is available in several sizes; the most useful is the model with two metal containers – one for storing, one for using. The freezer is quick to use and results are satisfactory, but only small amounts of mixture can be frozen at one time and it can be grainy.

Electric churns The traditional model resembles a hand churn but uses a motor to drive the paddle. Another version is a small compact unit, often called a *sorbetière*, which fits into the freezer compartment of a refrigerator. The motor turns the mixture until it is stiff, when the paddle automatically lifts. Some *sorbetières* have two compartments, for making two flavours at once.

Free-standing machines These have an automatic stirring and cooling mechanism. They are expensive, but invaluable for making ice cream and sorbet in larger quantities.

POTS & PANS

Weight is the key to quality for all stovetop cookware. Thin skillets and saucepans scorch quickly, and lightweight braising pots and casseroles do not maintain a constant temperature. Cookware with a large cooking surface is best for sautéing and other quick cooking, while a tall, slim pot guards against over-evaporation during long cooking. A pot or pan should be the right size for the job. If too little food is cooked in a large pot, it may scorch; if the pot is too small, food may overflow.

Stockpot This should be taller than it is wide, with two sturdy handles. The high sides ensure gradual evaporation of the stock, while a comparatively narrow base means that heat spreads easily to the edges. A capacity of 12 qt/12 L leaves plenty of room for cumbersome bones, yet is still quite easy to lift.

Saucepan The best pan for sauces is the classic lined copper pan that ensures the contents do not scorch during long cooking. Many sizes are available. A special sloping-sided copper saucepan is indispensable for delicate butter sauces, since a whisk can reach every part of the pot. Stainless steel is the next best choice.

Double boiler This may be made of a variety of metals and also of glass; the latter allows the cook to monitor the water level in the bottom half of the saucepan. It is used for delicate sauces, melting chocolate, reheating and keeping foods warm.

Water bath (Fr. *bain marie*) A pan of simmering water, for example a roasting pan large enough to accommodate smaller pans or baking dishes. It is used to control cooking of delicate mixtures like custards and to keep sauces and soups warm.

Frying pan or skillet For best results, the base of the pan should be thick so that heat spreads evenly. Copper and cast iron pans are preferred because they are good heat conductors. The traditional American skillet is made of heavy cast iron. Enamel coatings often chip after repeated exposure to high heat. Nonstick frying pans allow frying with a minimum of fat, but they scratch easily.

Fish frying pan A large oval pan with low sides to accommodate small whole fish or fillets.

Omelet pan Made of aluminum, cast iron or steel, it should have a thick base to distribute the heat evenly and curved, gently sloping sides. The handle should be angled to make transferring the omelet to the plate easier (p.90). A steel omelet pan must be seasoned (p.89) to prevent sticking and should not be washed.

Crêpe pan Traditionally made of steel, but a nonstick surface is also good. The sides should be shallow so that the pan is light and crêpes are easy to flip or turn (p.367). Steel crêpe pans must be seasoned (p.89) when new and should not be washed.

Flambé pan Usually made of lined copper, this is used for tableside cooking, especially for foods flambéed with alcohol.

Sauté pan Made of lined copper or stainless steel, with a wide, heavy base and low sides to allow steam to escape. A heatproof handle means that the pan is ovenproof.

Deep-fryer The traditional fryer is made of steel, with two handles and a basket for lowering and removing foods from the fat (p.105). It should be wide enough to hold a good quantity of food and deep enough for 2-3 in/5-7 cm fat to bubble without overflowing. Electric models are available (p.509).

Nest basket Used for making deep-fried potato nests or baskets (p.297). It consists of a set of two bowl-shaped wire baskets, one of which fits inside the other.

Fish poacher (p.118) A long, narrow pan as deep as it is wide, so the minimum of liquid covers a whole fish. The fish can be lifted out by means of a two-handled rack that fits into the base. Fish poachers may be made of copper, tinned metal or stainless steel.

Steamer A perforated container that fits over a pan of boiling water and holds ingredients to be steamed. Oriental stacking steamers of bamboo or metal can be set on top of one another to hold a variety of foods. For small quantities, a folding basket that fits within a saucepan can be used.

Wok A large bowl-shaped steel pan with a rounded bottom. It comes with a domed lid, metal ring and sometimes a steaming rack. In the West, woks are most commonly used with a metal scoop for stir-frying. In Asia, they double as pans for steaming, boiling, braising and deep-frying. Electric models are available.

Sugar pan A copper saucepan (Fr. *poêlon*) with straight sides, a pouring spout and a hollow copper handle. It is unlined because a lining would melt at high temperatures. For sugar and caramel only.

Griddle A heavy, flat – usually cast iron – griddle used for crêpes, pancakes, griddle cakes and unleavened breads. It has a small rim and a handle that can be laid flat.

Ridged griddle A cast iron pan with ridges, and a spout for pouring off juices.

Fish poacher

Fish frying pan

Sugar pan

Frying pan

Double boiler

Griddle

Sauté pan

SPECIAL-PURPOSE TOOLS

Waffle iron A hinged mold for cooking waffle and wafer batter. It is usually made of cast iron coated with nonstick plastic. Both stovetop and electric models are available. For how to use a waffle iron, see p.369.

Spätzle press For making spätzle dumplings. There are several versions of this machine: one is similar to a vegetable grater, another is a large perforated cone with a lever that forces the dough through the holes. The third kind is like a food mill with revolving blades; this machine comes with a board (with a hole in the center), which rests the machine on the pan.

Tongue press A hinged metal plate and bowl for pressing tongue. It keeps the meat steady as it cools.

Pizza paddle A flat wooden or metal shovel with a long handle, used to transfer pizza to the oven or table.

Pizza or bread stone A ceramic round, used instead of a baking sheet, for bread or pizza. A modern version is a set of tiles in a metal tray. The stone or tiles are used because they give bread or pizza a crisp bottom.

Bagna cauda pot A tall glazed earthenware pot for bagna cauda (p.101). Sometimes the pot is sold as a set with the burner.

Couscous pot or couscousière A special double pot, made of aluminum or earthenware, for cooking the North African specialty grain dish, couscous (p.320). The meat and vegetables are cooked in the bottom half, while the couscous is steamed in the perforated steamer that fits into it and rests on top.

Asparagus pan A tall, narrow aluminum pan with an inner basket, for cooking asparagus upright so that the tips are steamed.

OVEN COOKWARE

Many ovenproof dishes have no lids as they are designed for browning. Exceptions are casseroles that can be used in the oven or on top of the stove, and various clay cookers designed for slow oven cooking. Ceramic ovenware is often used for baking and gratin dishes as the food can be served directly from the dish; enameled cast iron cookware is more durable and almost as attractive.

Casserole Modern casseroles are heavy and deep with a tight fitting lid, the successor to the traditional stewpot, which was set in the hearth and covered with embers so the food was surrounded by heat. Designed for braising and pot roasting, a casserole retains the moisture generated during cooking. Heavy earthenware casseroles such as the Provençal *daubière* are still made, but they are very fragile and must only be used over direct heat with great care.

Marmite A traditional French earthenware pot – round or tall with straight sides – used for stews, cassoulet or *pot-au-feu*.

Dutch oven A deep roaster with a lid, popular in North America and used mainly for pot roasts or braises. Heavy cast iron spreads the heat better than lightweight (often enameled) metal.

Oven or turkey roaster For large birds, an alternative to the roasting pan is the oven roaster – a deep, oval pan with a domed lid. The oven roaster can double as a braising pan.

Chicken brick An unglazed earthenware pot with a lid, shaped to fit a chicken. For moisture the brick is submerged in water for about 30 minutes before the bird is placed in it for baking.

Roasting pan This is rectangular, made of metal, with sides low enough for direct heat to reach the sides of a roast but deep enough to contain the rendered fat and juices. A roasting pan should be heavy enough not to scorch when making gravy on the stove top. Stainless steel or aluminum is the best material. A roasting rack in the base of the pan lifts the meat away from its juices so that it browns on all sides.

Gratin dish A round or oval two-handled dish with a flat bottom and straight low sides that enable the food to brown well. It may be made of glass, china, earthenware or enameled cast iron and is used for dishes such as layered pasta, puddings and shallow soufflés. Plain glass baking dishes can be substituted.

Egg dish A small, round dish with shallow sides for making baked eggs; it is usually made of china or earthenware.

Pot de crème A small, ceramic pot with a lid in which individual rich custards are baked and served. The pots may also be used for mousses and other hot or cold desserts.

Soufflé dish This is round with high straight sides so the soufflé mixture rises vertically as it expands. Size varies considerably and is measured by volume not diameter. White glazed porcelain fluted on the outside to resemble a pleated paper case, is traditional. The underside of the dish should be unglazed so that the heat can penetrate quickly. Alternatives are glass and earthenware. A straight-sided mold, such as a charlotte mold, may be substituted for baking soufflés.

Ramekin A miniature soufflé dish, usually made of porcelain. It is used for baking individual portions (Eggs *en cocotte*, p.87), particularly in a sauce, and for molding hot and cold dishes.

Custard cups Small pots, common in the United States for baked custards and some puddings. They are similar to ramekins, but more rounded and often decorated.

Terrine A straight-sided mold with a lid, made from earthenware, porcelain or enameled cast iron thick enough to diffuse oven heat. Some terrine lids have a small hole for steam to escape, and to allow the insertion of a skewer to test cooking. Shape varies from a long narrow rectangle to a deep oval. Long terrines provide a neat loaf shape for slicing, but their use is more limited than oval dishes, which double as casseroles for stews and braises. Popular are pastry-colored porcelain terrines with fluted edges to give the illusion of a cooked *pâté en croute*, often crowned with the head of a game bird.

Timbale mold A small, round, metal or ceramic dish similar to a ramekin.

Pot de crème

Soufflé dish and ramekins

Gratin dish

Terrine

Glossary of culinary terms

The cooking terms defined here occur throughout the book, and appear on many restaurant menus.

Acidulated water Water with added acid, such as lemon juice or vinegar, which prevents discoloration of ingredients, particularly fruit or vegetables. The proportion of acid to water is 1 tsp per 1¼ cups/300 ml.

Al dente Italian cooking term for ingredients that are cooked until tender but still firm to the bite; often applied to pasta.

Américaine (à l') Method of serving seafood – usually lobster and monkfish – in a sauce flavored with olive oil, aromatic herbs, tomatoes, white wine, fish stock, brandy and tarragon.

Anglaise (à l') A cooking style for simple cooked dishes such as boiled vegetables. *Assiette anglaise* is a plate of cold cooked meats.

Antipasto Italian for "before the meal", it denotes an assortment of cold meats, vegetables and cheeses, often marinated, served as a first course. A typical *antipasto* might include salami, prosciutto, marinated artichoke hearts, anchovy fillets, olives, tuna fish and Provolone cheese.

Barbecue To cook over or in front of glowing coals, often of charcoal; woods such as mesquite, hickory or apple chips may be added for flavor. The fire should glow without flaming so the food toasts but does not scorch. As when broiling, heat is controlled by placing the food closer to or further from the fire. Barbecued food is often basted during cooking.

Baste To moisten food with melted fat or a highly-flavored sauce, usually during roasting, barbecuing or broiling.

Bind To add egg, roux or melted fat to dry ingredients in order to combine them. A sauce may be bound to thicken it also (p.59).

Bird See *paupiette*.

Blanquette A white stew of lamb, veal or chicken, bound with egg yolks and cream and accompanied by onions and mushrooms.

Blanch To put food in cold unsalted water, bring to a boil, skim, simmer a few minutes and drain. However, some vegetables are blanched in boiling water (p.260) so that they cook further. Meaning literally "to whiten", the term is appropriate, as blanching also effectively "tones down" the flavor by removing salt and other strong flavors from foods, notably bacon, and firm meats such as sweetbreads. Blanching sets the brilliant color of green vegetables and herbs, loosens the skins of tomatoes and nuts (such as almonds), and rids rice and potatoes of excess starch. Vegetables are often blanched before freezing to destroy the enzymes that can cause them to deteriorate.

Bollito misto An Italian dish of boiled meats such as *cotechino*, *zampone*, beef, veal, chicken and tongue.

Bonne femme Dishes cooked in the traditional French "housewife" style. Chicken and pork *bonne femme* are garnished with bacon, potatoes and baby onions, fish *bonne femme* with mushrooms in a white wine sauce.

Bordelaise (à la) Denotes dishes made with Bordeaux wine, usually with shallots. Typical is *entrecôte bordelaise*. Ceps are often cooked in this manner too.

Bourguignonne (à la) Dishes cooked in red Burgundy wine with glazed pearl onions, mushrooms and bacon. Snails cooked in this style (*escargots à la bourguignonne*) are served in garlic herb butter.

Braise To cook whole or large pieces of poultry, game, fish, meat or vegetables in a small amount of wine, stock or other liquid in a closed pot, usually with a *mirepoix* (p.263) of vegetables. Often the main ingredient is first browned in fat and then cooked in a low oven or very slowly on top of the stove. Braising suits tough meats and older birds and produces a mellow, rich sauce.

Butterfly To slit a piece of food in half horizontally, cutting it almost through so that when opened it resembles butterfly wings. Chops, large shrimp and thick fish fillets are often butterflied so that they cook more quickly.

Cacciatora (alla) Literally, hunter-style. Italian dishes of meat, game or poultry with mushrooms, tomatoes and wine.

Caramelize To cook sugar syrup or sugar to the caramel stage (p.418). The term is also used when broiling a sugar topping until brown, when glazing food in butter with sugar and when cooking meat juices to a dark glaze.

Carpaccio A traditional peasant dish from the Val d'Aosta, made fashionable in 1961 in Harry's Bar in Venice. It consists of thinly sliced raw fillet of beef served with a cream sauce. The name is also applied to a similar dish with the meat marinated in olive oil and lemon juice.

Chasseur (hunter) A French cooking style in which meat and chicken dishes are cooked with mushrooms, shallots, white wine, and often tomato. See also *cacciatora*.

Clarify To clear a liquid of impurities. Stock is clarified by simmering with egg white to make consommé and aspic, while butter is clarified by melting and skimming.

Cocido A grand and hearty Spanish soup, also called *olla-podrida*. Ingredients include chickpeas, various meats, poultry, sausages, vegetables, potato, garlic and seasonings.

Concasser To chop coarsely, usually tomatoes.

Confit From the French verb *confire*, meaning to preserve. Food that is made into a preserve by cooking very slowly and thoroughly until tender. In the case of meat, such as duck or goose, it is cooked in its own fat, and covered with it so that it does not come into contact with the air. Vegetables such as onions are also good in *confit*.

Coulis A thin purée, usually of fresh or cooked fruit or vegetables, which is soft enough to pour (*couler* means to run). A *coulis* may be rough-textured or very smooth.

Crudités Raw vegetables, whether cut in slices or sticks to nibble plain or with a dipping sauce, or shredded and tossed as salad with a simple dressing.

Curdle To cause milk or sauce to separate into solid and liquid. The term is loosely applied to any mixture that separates, for example, overcooked egg mixtures.

Decoration The ornamenting of food for presentation; unlike a garnish, a decoration does not form an integral part of the dish. Correctly, a decoration such as sprigs of herbs or pieces of fruit should echo flavors in the food itself.

Deglaze To dissolve congealed cooking juices or glaze on the bottom of a pan by adding liquid, scraping and stirring vigorously, while bringing the liquid to a boil. The juices may be used to make gravy or to add to sauce.

Degrease To skim grease from the surface of liquid. If possible the liquid should be chilled so the fat solidifies. If not, skim off most of the fat with a large metal spoon, then trail strips of paper towel on the surface of the liquid to remove any remaining globules.

Deviled A dish or sauce that is highly seasoned with a hot ingredient such as mustard, Worcestershire sauce or cayenne pepper.

Dredge To sprinkle the surface of food thickly, usually with flour or confectioners' sugar.

Empanada A popular South American pastry turnover stuffed with a mixture of chopped meat, onions, hard-boiled eggs, dried fruits and olives, usually served as a first course.

Emulsion A mixture of two liquids that are not mutually soluble – for example, oil and water.

Entrée In Europe, the "entry" or appetizer; in North America entrée means the main course.

Eye meat An oval, eye-shaped section of meat, usually lean and close-textured, as in eye of loin or round of beef. Also present in lamb noisettes.

Fermentation Effervescence, usually caused by the action of enzymes. This may be deliberate, as when yeast is used to raise bread, or accidental, as in preserves that ferment when incorrectly prepared.

Flake To pull cooked food apart, particularly fish, so it falls into natural divisions; two forks are often used.

Florentine (à la) A dish made with or garnished with spinach.

Frangipane A sweet almond and egg filling that is cooked inside pastry. *Frangipane* is also a thickening *panade* (right).

Fricassée A dish in which poultry, fish or vegetables are bound together with a white or velouté sauce. In Britain and the United States, the name applies to an old-fashioned dish of chicken in a creamy sauce.

Galette Any sweet or savory mixture that is shaped in a flat round.

Garnish In classic cooking, garnish refers to one or more subsidiary ingredients appearing with the main ingredient in a dish and giving it special character. The apple, Calvados and cream added to pork or chicken *normande* is an example. A decoration, by contrast, is added when a dish is complete. However, the word garnish is sometimes used for decorations such as bunches of watercress or stuffed tomatoes.

Gastrique Caramelized sugar deglazed with vinegar and used in fruit-flavored savory sauces, in such dishes as duck with orange.

Genovese, alla Literally "in the style of Genoa", this is an Italian dish made with olive oil, herbs and often garlic.

Glaze A mixture that is brushed or sprinkled on the surface of food for color and gloss. Many glazes are used for bread, pastry and cakes. Foods (for example, vegetables) may be cooked with butter and sugar to glaze them. Glaze also refers to the concentrated syrupy liquid produced by boiling down meat, poultry or fish stock.

Gluten A protein in flour that is developed when dough is kneaded, making it elastic.

Gratin A dish cooked in the oven or under the broiler so that it develops a brown crust. Breadcrumbs or cheese may be sprinkled on top first. Shallow gratin dishes ensure a maximum area of crust.

Infuse To immerse herbs, spices or other flavorings in hot liquid to flavor it. Infusion takes from two to 15 minutes depending on the flavoring. The liquid should be very hot but not boiling.

Jardinière (à la) A garnish of garden (Fr. *jardin*) vegetables, typically carrots, pearl onions, green beans and turnips.

Lights Lungs of an animal, used in various meat preparations such as pâtés and faggots.

Lyonnaise (à la) A dish garnished with onions.

Macerate To soak food in liquid to soften it.

Magret A boned breast of duck.

Marengo Veal or chicken cooked in olive oil, tomatoes and garlic and garnished with deep-fried eggs, crayfish and croûtons.

Marinara, alla Italian "sailor's style" cooking that does not apply to any particular combination of ingredients. Marinara tomato sauce for pasta is the most familiar example.

Marinière (à la) French "sailor's style" cooking for seafood, usually mussels, using white wine, shallots, garlic and herbs.

Milanese, alla (Italy) or milanaise, à la (France) A method of cooking "in the style of Milan". In Italy, the name does not apply to a specific cooking method. In France, the name is given to dishes with a garnish of pasta, cheese, tomatoes and mushrooms.

Mole A Mexican chili sauce, from the Aztec word *molli*. It is also used in the names of dishes, for example *mole poblano* (p.420), made with three kinds of chili, other spices, almonds and chocolate.

Niçoise (à la) A garnish of tomatoes, garlic and black olives; *salade niçoise* with anchovy, tuna and green beans, is typical.

Noisette Small "nut" of lamb cut from boned loin or rack that is rolled, tied and cut in neat slices. Noisette also means flavored with hazelnuts or butter cooked to a nut-brown color.

Normande (à la) A cooking style for fish, with a garnish of shrimp, mussels and mushrooms in a white wine cream sauce; for poultry and meat, a sauce with cream, Calvados and apple.

Oyster meat In poultry, two succulent ovals of meat along either side of the backbone, level with the thigh.

Panade A mixture for binding stuffings and dumplings, notably *quenelles*, often of choux pastry or simply breadcrumbs (Fr. *pain*). A *panade* may also be made of *frangipane*, puréed potatoes or rice.

Papillote (en) To cook food in oiled or buttered parchment paper or aluminum foil. Also a decorative frill to cover bone ends of chops and poultry drumsticks (US cutlet frill).

Paprikàs Hungarian stew with a thick pink sauce of paprika and sour cream.

Parboil To boil or simmer until partially cooked (i.e. cooked further than when blanching).

Parmigiana, alla An Italian dish containing Parmesan cheese and sometimes prosciutto ham. The term may also be used for dishes baked with mozzarella cheese and tomato sauce.

Paupiette A thin slice of meat, poultry or fish spread with a savory stuffing and rolled. In the United States, this is also called a "bird" and in Britain, an "olive".

Périgueux or Périgourdine (à la) A dish containing truffles, and often foie gras as well. Périgord is the primary truffle-growing region of France.

Piroshki, pirogi Russian pies or patties, usually of pastry filled with sweet or savory ingredients. *Piroshki* are small, *pirogi* are larger.

Poach To cook in liquid, usually water, just below simmering so the liquid shivers in one or two places rather than bubbling. Delicate foods that break up easily, such as fish and fruits, should be poached. Also, dishes such as *pot au feu* are poached to cook them slowly and develop maximum flavor.

Pot-roast A method that resembles braising, but is applied more widely to any large piece of meat or poultry cooked in a covered pot with flavorings and a little liquid.

Pressure cooking A method whereby food is cooked, in a pressure cooker, at specific levels of pressure. The higher the pressure, the higher the temperature at which water boils. By cooking food with liquid in this way, the steam created by the liquid is sealed in under increasing pressure, thereby cooking the food in less time than conventional methods of steaming.

Provençale (à la) A cooking style using olive oil, garlic and sometimes tomato and fresh herbs. Frogs' legs and chicken are often cooked in this way.

Ragout Traditionally a well-seasoned, rich stew containing meat, vegetables and wine. Nowadays, a term applied to any stewed mixture.

Refresh To cool hot food quickly, either under running water or by plunging it into iced water, to stop it cooking. Used particularly for vegetables and occasionally, shellfish.

Roulade A piece of meat, usually pork or veal, that is spread with stuffing, then rolled and often braised or poached. A roulade may also be a sweet or savory mixture that is baked in a jelly roll pan or paper case, filled with a contrasting filling, and rolled.

Salsa (Italy, Mexico) A juice derived from the main ingredient being cooked or a sauce added to a dish to enhance its flavor. In Italy, the term is often used for pasta sauces; in Mexico the name usually applies to uncooked sauces served as an accompaniment, especially to corn chips.

Sauté To cook small pieces of food over high heat, in fat, butter or oil, shaking the pan so that the food "jumps".

Sauté A dish in which food is sautéed in fat until partly cooked, then finished with a small amount of wine, stock, vegetables and flavorings to make a concentrated sauce. Ingredients steam in their own juices, so they should be relatively tender.

Savory Highly seasoned last course of traditional English dinner. Typical savories are devils on horseback (prunes wrapped in bacon), angels on horseback (oysters wrapped in bacon) and Scotch woodcock (scrambled eggs with anchovy).

Sear To seal the surface of meat by cooking over strong heat.

Scald To bring just to boiling point, usually for milk. Also to rinse with boiling water.

Score To mark shallow or deep cuts in a decorative pattern with the point of a knife. Food such as a whole fish is often scored so that it will cook evenly.

Sift To shake a dry, powdered substance through a sieve or sifter to remove any lumps and give lightness.

Simmer To cook food gently in liquid that bubbles steadily just below boiling point so that the food cooks in even heat without breaking up.

Singe To quickly flame poultry to remove all traces of feathers after plucking.

Skim To remove a surface layer (often of impurities and scum) from a liquid with a metal spoon or small ladle.

Smörgåsbord Swedish buffet meal featuring a wide variety of hot and cold meats, smoked and pickled fish, salads, vegetables, cheese, condiments and desserts.

Sous vide See Vacuum-packing (below).

Souse To cover food, particularly fish, in wine vinegar and spices and cook slowly; the food is cooled in the same liquid. Sousing gives food a pickled flavor.

Steep To soak in warm or cold liquid in order to soften food and draw out strong flavors or impurities.

Stew To simmer gently and steadily in liquid with a variety of vegetables and flavorings. The liquid should cover the ingredients. Stewing suits tough foods with plenty of flavor, such as mature poultry and less expensive cuts of beef.

Stir-fry To cook small pieces of food rapidly in very little fat, tossing constantly over high heat, usually in a wok.

Sugo An Italian sauce made from the liquid or juice extracted from fruit or meat during cooking.

Sweat To cook sliced or chopped food, usually vegetables, in a little fat and no liquid over very low heat. Parchment paper or aluminum foil is pressed on top so that the food steams in its own juices, usually before being added to other dishes.

Tempura Japanese style of deep-frying pieces of fish, meat, poultry or vegetables in a light batter; individual bowls of a soy-flavored sauce are served for dipping.

Vacuum-packing As most micro-organisms require oxygen, cooked or uncooked food can be kept longer by vacuum-sealing (and sometimes freezing) in plastic bags to exclude almost all the air. In a more complicated process called cook-chill or *sous vide* (Fr. "under vacuum"), food is vacuum-sealed and then cooked with very rapid heating and cooking so that much of the flavor, moisture, color and aroma of fresh ingredients are retained. However in many countries *sous vide* processing is prohibited because of the risk of fatal poisoning.

Zakouski Russian for appetizers – a collection of hot and cold canapés that can include pickled mushrooms, radishes in sour cream, salted and pickled herring and stuffed peppers. The most famous *zakouski* are *blini* (buckwheat pancakes served with melted butter, sour cream and caviar).

Zest Thin outer layer of citrus fruits containing the aromatic citrus oil. It is usually thinly pared with a vegetable peeler, or grated with a zester or on a grater to separate it from the bitter white pith underneath.

Index

Bold *text indicates a complete Recipe. Page numbers in* Bold *type are used for major or particularly significant references to a subject. Page numbers in Italic indicate illustrated ingredients.*

A

abalone, *163*, 163, **164**
acorn squash, 265, 287, **287**
adzuki (aduki), 323, 327
agar-agar, 283, 431
Aigo saou, **48**
Aïoli (Garlic Mayonnaise), **63**
air-dried food, 484
alcohol, 38-9, 105, 449, 450, 451, 475, **485-6**; flambéing food, esp. fruit, 38, **449**, 452, 464
alewife, 147
alfalfa sprouts, 327
alliums, *see* onion family
allspice, **25**, 27
almond extract, 36
almond oil, 96, 103
almond paste (marzipan), 405, **409**, 415, 426, 477; **Recipe, 478**
almonds, 321, 419, 439, 477, **478**; milk, 477; Steamed date pudding, 365. *See also* praline
almonds, ground, 36, 384, 400, 432, 435; **Almond** *petits fours,* **404; Scented blancmange, 36;** flour, 344; *frangipane,* 371, 384, 513
Alsatian onion quiche, 94
amaranth, *321,* 321
amaretti macaroons, 444
amberjack, **140-1**
American fudge boiled frosting, **410**
ancho, 28, *28;* Romesco sauce, **29**
anchovies, **147-9**, 150; *anchoiade,* 101; Anchovy butter, **99;** anchovy paste, **33; Anchovy sauce for pasta, 337;** Egg and anchovy pasta sauce, **337;** Green goddess dressing, **63; Olive oil, anchovy and garlic dip, 101;** preserving, 110, 126, 488; *Tapenade,* **34**
andouille, 246, *247*
andouillettes, 246, *246,* 247
angel food cake, 393, 394, **397;** pan, *509;* **Recipe, 397**
angelica, 22, **22,** 475
angel's hair, **416**
anglerfish, *see* monkfish
angostura bitters, **39**
animal fats, **96,** 97, 104, 392
anise chervil (sweet cicely), 22, 24
anise-flavored spices, e.g. licorice, 24, *24*
anise-pepper, 30
aniseed, *see* cumin
annatto seed, 25, *25*
applemint, *16,* 17
apples, 38, 40, 181, 438, 446, 447, 448, 449, 452-3, **452-5,** 505; apple butter, 493; **Recipe, 493;** apple charlotte, 364, 432; **Apple crêpes, 367; Apple jelly, 492-3;**

apple pastry dumplings, 338; apple rings, 452, 474; Apple sauce, 66; **Apple strudel, 383; Apple and tomato chutney, 489;** in Cornish pasties, 374; **Mincemeat, 486;** pies and tarts, 371, 452, *Tarte tatin,* **455;** preserving, 473, 484, 490, 493; stuffings 364, **Apple and onion stuffing, 364**
apricots, 447, 448, 449, **456-7,** *457;* **Apricot jam glaze, 385;** Apricot jam sauce, 66; preserving (dried etc.), 473, 484, 485, 493
arm roast (picnic ham), 206-7, 226, 250
arrowroot, **59,** 343, 344, 400
artichoke, Chinese (Japanese), 303
artichokes (globe, French artichokes) 39, 261, 263, 265, *300,* **300-3; Artichokes and pine nuts, 302; Poached eggs Clamart, 85; Ragout of lamb, artichokes and fava beans, 326.** *See also* Jerusalem artichokes
arugula, 269, **269-71; Avocado and grapefruit salad with smoked salmon, 470**
asparagus, 37, 39, 262, 267, *298,* **298-300,** 495; **Asparagus with breadcrumb sauce, 300; Vinaigrette salad, 268**
asparagus chicory, 269-71
asparagus pea, 284-6
aspartame, 413
aspic, 44, 119, **253-5,** 267, 431, 494; equipment, 505, 507, 508; **Poached salmon in aspic, 144**
attar of roses, 36
Avgolemono, **55**
avocado, *469,* 469-70; **Avocado and grapefruit salad with smoked salmon, 470; Chilled spinach and avocado soup, 51; Shrimp and avocado omelet, 91**

B

babas, 354, 414; mold, *509,* 509
bacon, 227, 241, *249,* **249,** 263, 487, 488, 495, 512; **Baked beans with red wine, 324;** Cheddar and bacon omelet, **91;** Egg and bacon sauce, **337;** Peasant omelet, **91; Raised veal and ham pie, 244;** smoked bacon, 249
bacon fat, 262, 345
bacon lardons, **249**
bagels, 360
Bagna cauda, **101,** 511
Baked Alaska, **444**
baked beans, 322; **Baked beans with red wine, 324**

Baking powder biscuits, **360**
baking soda and powder, breads, 369; cookies, 386
Baklava, **382**
ballotines, 241, **255**
Balmain bugs, **162**
balsam pear, **288**
bamboo shoots, *303,* **303**
bananas, 447, 448, 449, *465,* **465;** **Bananas Foster, 464;** Banana ice cream, **443; Banana nut bread, 361;** Banana split, **443; Fresh orange soufflé, 460;** leaves, 464
bananas, dried, *473*
bantam egg, *80*
bar cookies, **389**
bara brith, 361
Barbary fig (prickly pear), *303,* 472
barbecue, 264, 512; sauce (table sauce), **35;** sauces, **65**
barbecued foods, 198, 201-7, **228,** 264, 285, 448, 487; **Barbecued quail with pepper marinade, 192**
barley, 315, *321,* 321, 411
barley flour, 342, 343, 344, 363
barley malt syrup (or barley malt, malt extract), 413
barley sugar, 426
barm brack, 361
barnacle, 173
baron of lamb, 208, 219
basil, 12, 13, *16,* **17,** 21, 496; *Pesto,* **17**
bass, **137-8,** *138;* calico and rock, 145; sea, 124, 125, 134, **137-8;** striped, 138, 142
batter, 39, 119, **366-9,** 496, 509; deep-frying, 104, **105-6,** 449; **Fruit fritters in beer batter, 106**
batter breads, sweet, 360-1
batter dumplings *(spätzle),* 43, 338, 511; **Recipe, 339**
batter puddings and pancakes, **368-9,** 456; Yorkshire pudding, **368;** Cherry batter pudding, **368**
battuto, 263, 337
Bavarian bread dumplings, 339
bavarian creams, 432; Pistachio bavarian cream, **433**
bay leaf, 12, 14, *18,* **18,** 181
Bayerische semmelknödeln, **339**
bean curd, 322
bean paste (bean sauce), 33
bean sprouts, 324, 327
beans, Asian black, 323
beans, black-eyed (black-eyed pea) 284-6, *285,* 322, *323,* 323, 327
beans, Boston (or navy bean, pearl haricot, pea bean) 323; Boston baked beans, **324**
beans, butter, *284,* **284**
beans, cannellini, *323,* 323
beans, dried, 266, 284, **314, 322-4,** *323,* 327, 498

beans, fava, 284, **284-6,** 326, 327; **Ragout of lamb, artichokes and fava beans, 326**
beans, *flageolet,* 284, *285,* 323, *323*
beans, French *(haricot vert),* 284-6, *285*
beans, green (snap, string), 266, 267, 268, **284-6,** 495; **Cold vegetable terrine, 267;** *Macédoine* of cooked vegetables (Russian salad), **268; Vinaigrette salad, 268**
beans, Jamaican red, 322
beans, kidney, *323,* **323-4,** 326; black, 33, *323,* 323; **Black bean soup, 50;** red, 323; **Baked beans with red wine, 324;** white, 314, red, *323,* 323; white bean soup, **50;** *Minestrone di verdura,* **45;** White beans with port wine, **324**
beans, lima, *284,* **284-6,** 326, **326**
beans, pinto, *323,* 323; **Mexican bean salad, 327**
beans, runner, 284, *285*
beans, wax, 284
beans, winged, 284-6
béarnaise sauce, **60-1; Recipe, 61**
béchamel sauces, 52, **54,** 264, 265; **Recipes, 54;** roux, 56
beechnut, 481; oil, 481
beef, 194, 195, **197-8,** 199, **200-1,** 209-13, 232, 252, 254, 455, 495; **Beef consommé, 46;** brisket, **197-8,** *200,* **200-1,** 209, **213,** 252, **488;** US and French cuts, 200-1; cooking methods for beef cuts, 201; nutritive values, 200; flank, *200,* **200-1,** 209, **213; Hungarian beef stew, 212;** leg, **200-1,** *209;* leg round, **200-1, 212-13;** loin, 197-8, **200-1,** *209,* **212;** London broil, 212, **213;** plate, skirt, *200,* **200-1,** *209,* **213;** ribs, **200-1,** *209,* 209, *211,* 211, 495; roast, 195, 199, **200-1,** 210, **211,** 495; sausages, 246, 247, 354; shank, *200,* **200-1,** *209,* 212, **213,** 254; shoulder, **200-1,** *209,* 209, **211;** sirloin, *200,* **200,** 208; steaks, 200, 212; tenderloin (fillet), 197, 199, *200,* **200-1,** *209,* 210, *210,* 212, (hanging) **213,** (dried) 252, 512; variety meats, **229-35**
beef, corned, 213, *252,* 252; **Recipe, 488**
beef, ground, 46, 201, 211, 213, **214,** 253, 335; Italian meat sauce, 338. *See also* meat, ground
beef bones, 235
beef fat, 96, *97,* 97, for frying 104; unrendered (suet), 96, 97, 364
beef jerky, 252, *252*
beef liver, **230**

beef stock, 42, 43, **44**
beer, 38, **39**, 487
beer batter, 105; **Fruit fritters in beer batter, 106**
beets, 25, 266, 271, **292-4**, *293*, 361, 485, 489; beet greens, 272-3, *273*; preserving, 485
beignets, 362
Belgian endive (chicory, *endive*) 263, 264, *269*, 269-71
berries, 371, 439, 446, 447, 448, 451, *462*, **462-3**, 484, 490-1; **Fresh orange soufflé, 460; Summer pudding, 463**. *See also* strawberries, etc
Beurre fondu, **62**
beurre manié, **59**
beurre noir, see black butter
beurre noisette, see brown butter
Beurre rouge, **62**
bierwurst, 247, *248*
bilberries, *462*, 462
biltong, 252, *252*
biscuit cakes, 394
Biscuit glacé, **444**
Biscuit tortoni, **444**
biscuits, 72, **359**, 369; **Baking powder biscuits, 360**
bisques, 49, 153; **Shrimp bisque, 49**
Bistecca cacciatora, 209
bitter melon (balsam pear, bitter gourd), **288**
bivalves, 152, 163, **165-70**
Black bean soup, 50
black butter (*beurre noir*), 98, *98*
black currants, 447, 462, 463, 490, 493; **Black currant sorbet, 442**
black pudding, 246, 247
blackberries, 447, 462, *462*, 484
blanching food, 497, 512
Blancmange, Scented, 36
blood, to thicken sauces, **59**
blood pudding (blood sausage, *Blutwurst*), 246, 247
blowfish, 142
blown sugar, **415**
Blue brie and prawn parcels, 382
blueberries, 403, 447, 462, **462-3**, 473, 493, 495; Blueberry pancakes, **369**
bluefish, 126, 134, 136, **147-9**, *148*, 487; **Panaché of steamed fish with dill butter sauce, 130**
blutwurst, 246, 247
boar, wild, 236, **238**
bockwurst, 246, 247
boiled dressing, **64**
bok choy, **298-9**
boletes, 304, 306, *311*, **311**, 495
bologna, 246, 247
bombes, **439**, **444-5**; **Bombe mixture, 444; Recipes, 445**
bones, 42, **235**, 504, 505, 510, 512
bonito, 133, 148
borage, *16*, **17**, 21
borscht, 45
bottling fruit, *see* canning fruit

bouchees, **380**
boudin blanc, 246, *246*
boudin noir, 246, *246*
bouillabaisse, 48, 142
bouquet garni, 14
boysenberry, *462*, 462
brains, 229, 230, *233*, **233**, 512
Braised stuffed veal breast, 215
bran, 314
brandy, 38, 449; **Sherry syllabub, 438**
brandysnaps, 388
bratwurst, 247, *247*
brawn, 254
brazil nuts, *479*, 479
bread, **342-69**; baking, 351, 511 (at high altitude) 344; with cheese tray, 75; dough, **94**, **348-51**, 370, 507, flour, 343; folded, **357-8**; fried, 362 (croûtes and croûtons) 43, 271, **352**; glazes and toppings, 345; ingredients, 69, 345; pans 346; **Plain white bread, 353**; quick breads, 359-61, 456, 463; rolls, *350*, 350; **Plain white bread rolls, 353**; shapes *348-9*, (rolls) *350*, 352; sweet batter breads, 360-1; yeast breads, 344, **352-8**, 362, 496; yeastless breads, 68, 344, **359-61**, 511
bread: used in, bread stuffings, **364**; club sandwiches (poultry), 183; **Hot salad of chicken livers** (fried cubes), 271; bread puddings, **364-5**; Apple charlotte, 432, bread and butter pudding, 364, **Recipe, 365; Summer pudding, 463**; thickening sauces, **64**; thickening soups, 43, **47**; toasted, 43, **352**
breadcrumbs, **354**; for coating, **104**, **105-6**, 107, 119, 263; used, 179, 265, 364, 365, 400, 447; **Asparagus with breadcrumb sauce, 300**
breadfruit, *303*, 303
bream, 110, **112**, 117, 119, **125**, **140-1; Mediterranean baked bream, 141; Pompano *en papillote*, 121**; sea, 134, **140-1**
bresaola (dried beef tenderloin), *252*, 252
Brie, 73, 74, 77; **Blue brie and prawn parcels, 382**
brill, *129*, **129-30; Panaché of steamed fish with dill butter sauce, 130**
brining food, 484, **488-9**
brioche, 354, **355-6**; *mousseline*, 354, 355; in recipe, **122**
broccoli, 261, 262, 263, 277, **277**, 495; **Broccoli crêpes, 367; Stir-fried vegetables, 262**
broth-based soups, 42, 43, **45**, 51
brown butter, 98, *98*; **Brown butter hollandaise, 61**
brown sauce (table sauce), **35**

brown sauces, 52, 53, **57-8**; Basic brown sauce, 58; **Recipe, 58; Recipe** (chaudfroid), 56; roux, 56
brown stew, 197
brown stock, 43, **44**; Brown veal stock (two recipes), **44**
brown trout (salmon trout), 113, **143-4**
Brussels sprouts, 275, **275**
bubble and squeak, 262
buckling, 126
buckwheat, 314, *320*, **320**; flour, 328, *343*, 343, 344; Breton buckwheat galettes, **366**; pasta, 328, **331**
buffalo (European bison), 236, 238; cured (*biltong*), 252. *See also* water buffalo
buffalo milk, mozzarella cheese, 334
bulghur (bulgur, burghul), 204, *319*, 319, 320
buns, 354, **356**; for hamburgers, 213
burdock, *303*, 303
butifarra, 247
butter, 50, 96, *98*, **98-9**, 181, 264, 495, 498; in cakes etc, 345, 370, 386, 392, **394**; **Dutch butter cookies, 100**; for frying and sautéing, 106, 119, 262
butter, kneaded (*beurre manié*), **59**
butter, shellfish, **155**
butter cream, **405**, 405, *406*, **406**, 415, 436, 503; **Recipe, 405**
butter icing, **405**
butter sauces, 53, 53, **510**; Butter and sage pasta sauce, 337; emulsified (hollandaise and béarnaise), **60-3**, 496; **Red butter sauce, 62**; Softened butter sauce, 62; white butter sauce, 52; **Recipe, 62**
butter toffee (butterscotch), 426
butterfish (a pomfret), 141
buttermilk, 70, **71-2**, 345, 495; **Buttermilk pancakes, 369**
Butternut, 478, 478
Butternut squash, 287, *287*
Butterscotch profiteroles, 377
Butterscotch sauce, 67

C

cabbage, 44, 260, 262, 263, 267, 268, **274-6**; stuffing, 265, **276**, *275*; Chinese, 274-5, *275*; European green, *275*; Nappa, 274-5, *275*; red, 263, 274-5, *275*, 489; **Red cabbage rolls, 276**; round, *275*; Savoy, 274-5, *275*; white, (Dutch) 263, 275, **276**, 489; **Coleslaw, 268**; sauerkraut, **488**; white-stemmed, **298-9**
cactus pear (prickly pear), *303*, 472
Caesar's mushroom, 313
cake decorations, 405, 427

cake pans, **390-1**, 393, 397, **509**
cakes, **390-410**, 432, 447, **496**, 503; baking at high altitude, 395; cheesecakes, 403, **German cheesecake, 403; Coffee walnut spice cake, 37**; common problems, 393; creamed, 393, **398-9**, 400, **Pound cake, 398; Rich fruit cake, 399**; festive, 396, **410**, Easter crown, 354, **356**; fillings, icings and frostings, 404, **405-10**; flourless, 400, **Chocolate walnut cake, 400**; ingredients, 68, 99, 343, **392**, 456, 463; **Jewish honey cake, 413**; layer, 400; Madeira cake, 398; melted, **401**, Finnish gingerbread, **401**; meringue, 402, *Gâteau Succès*, **402**; mixing, 391, 392, 393, **394**; *vermicelli*, 338; whisked, 393, **394-7**, 400, **Angel food cake, 397**, *Génoise*, 395, jelly roll, 396, **Ladyfingers, 396**
cakes, small cakes, *petits fours* etc, 360, **404**, 474, 475; **Almond petits fours, 404; Madeleines, 404**
calendulas, 25, 268
calf: variety meats, 173, *229*, 229, 230, **230**, 231, **231**, 232, 232, **234**, 254
calico bass, 145
Camembert, 73, 77; **Camembert croquettes, 107**
candies, 404, 415, 417, 418, 421, **426**, **426-9**, *427*, 503
candlenut, 481
candy bars, chocolate, 420
cane sugar, 411; syrup, 411
cannelloni, 183, *329*, 333, 334, 335
canning fruit, **493-4**
cantaloupe, **464**
Cape gooseberries, 462, *463*, 474
capers, **34**
capons, 180, *184*, 184
capsicum family, *see* chili peppers, *and* peppers, sweet
carambola, *472*, 472
caramel, 385, 404, 411, **418-9**, 426, 439, 498, 510, 512, 513; caramel cage, 418; caramel custard, 95, **Recipe, 95**; dipping in, **416**; sauce, 67, 418, **Lemon mousse with caramel sauce, 434**, Snow eggs (*oeufs à la neige*), **436**
caraway seeds, 24, **24**
cardamom, 26, **26**, 27
cardoon, 263, **298**, **298-9**
carob, 344, 422
carp, 131, *145*, **145-6**
carragheen moss, 283, 431
carrots, 25, 258, 260, 261, 262, 263, 266, 267, 268, 283, *292*, **292-4**, 361, 495, 499; **Cold vegetable terrine, 267; Coleslaw, 268; Ragout of lamb,**

artichokes and fava beans, 326; *Macédoine* of cooked vegetables, 268; in stock, 43, 44
cashews, 476, 477, 479
Cassata, 410; **Recipe, 444**
cassava (yuca root), 303, 343, 344
cassia, *26, 26*
cassoulet, 322
castanopsis nut, 481
catfish, 110, 115, *145*, **145-6**
catsup, 35
caul fat, *235*, 235, 241, 246
cauliflower, 261, 262, 277, **277-8**, 489, 495; **Stir-fried vegetables, 262**
caviar, **131,** 134
cayenne pepper, 27, 28, **29**
celeriac, *see* celery root
celery, 14, 22, **22,** 43, 263, **298-9,** *299,* 451
celery cabbage, 274-5
celery root, 260, 261, 262, 267, 268, 292, *293,* 297, 361
cep, 311
cervelat, 246, 246, 248
chamomile, 21
Champagne sorbet, **442**
chana dal, 325
chanterelles, 304, *312,* **312,** 495
Chantilly cream, **70,** 384, 405; **Lemon mousse with caramel sauce, 434; Trifle, 438;** *Vacherin,* **437**
Chantilly mayonnaise, **63**
chappatis, 363
charcuterie, **194-208, 241-55**
charlottes and creams, **432-3;** *Charlotte russe,* **433**
chartreuse, 432
Châteaubriand, **210,** *210*
chayote, 287, *287*
Cheddar, 73, 74, 75, 79, *79*; **Cheddar and bacon omelet, 91**
cheeks of meat, 226, 229
cheese, **68, 73-9,** 91, 263, 265, 271, 438, 461, 495, 503; fresh, 75, **76-7;** hard, 73, 74, 78, **79,** 495; high-fat, **79;** with pasta, **334,** 337, 338; potted, 486; processed, 73; smoked, 73, 487; soft, 73, 74, **77;** in frozen desserts, 439
cheese, kinds of: Asiago de Allevo, 334; Bel Paese, 74, 77, 334; Bleu d'Auvergne, 78; Bleu de Bresse, 78; blue, 73, 74, 75, **78;** blue-veined, 334; Brie, 73, 74, 77; Brillat-Savarin, 73, 79; Caciocavallo, 79, 334; Caerphilly, 74; Camembert, 73, 77; Cantal, 79; Cheddar, 73, 74, 75, 79; cottage, 76; Coulommiers, 77, cream, 76, 403, 405; Creole, 76; curd, 403; Danish Blue, 78; Double Gloucester, 79; Edam, 79; Emmenthal, 73, 79; Explorateur, 79; farmer, 76; feta, 74, 75;

Fontina, 77, 334; goat, 73, 74, **75,** Gorgonzola, 74, 78, 334; Gouda, 73, 79; Gruyère, 73, 74, 79; 377; Jarlsberg, 79; Lanark Blue, 75; Limburger, 73; Limeswold, 77; Livarot, 77; Mascarpone, 76; Maytag, 77, 78; Monterey Jack, 77; mozzarella, 74, 75, 77, 334, 337, 514; Munster, 73; Parmesan, 73, 74, 79, 334, 337, 514; Pecorino Romano, 74, 79, 334; Petit Suisse, 76; Pont l'Evêque, 73, 77; Port Salut, 77; Provolone, 75, 79; Quark, 76; raclette, 77; ricotta, 74, 76, **77,** 334, 335, 403, 405, 410; in pasta desserts, 338; Roncal, 79; Roquefort, 73, 75, 78; Saint Paulin, 74; Samsoe, 73; soy, 322; Stilton, 73, 75, 78; Wensleydale, 78, 79
cheese recipes **Blue brie and prawn parcels, 382; Camembert croquettes, 107, Cheesecake, German (cream) 403;** *Coeur à la crème* **(curd, farmer), 76; Cold vegetable terrine (Gruyère), 267; Cream cheese strudel, 383; Crêpes suisses, 367;** *flamiche,* **94;** *Gougères* **(Gruyère), 377;** Monterey omelet, **91;** *Pesto* (Parmesan), **17;** Ricotta cheese, **77;** sauce, **54; Shrimp ravioli with goat cheese, 336; Soufflé, 93; Spinach and feta pie, 94; Spinach and ricotta lasagne, 334; Toasted walnut and Roquefort salad, 102; Veal escalopes with Stilton, 78**
cheese sauce, 74, 264, 376; **Recipe, 54**
cheese tray, **75,** 77, 78, 451
cheesecakes, 371, 393, **403,** 410; **German cheesecake, 403**
Chef's salad, 271
cherries, 38, 447, 448, 449, 450, *456,* **456-7,** 473, 474, 475, 485, 490, 495; **Cherry batter pudding, 368; Hungarian cherry soup, 451;** pitter, *505;* **Poached fruit crêpes, 367; Strudel, 383**
chervil, 12, 14, **16,** 496
chestnut flour, 344
chestnut stuffings, 179
chestnuts, 266, 438, 475, 476, *481,* **481,** 496; **Chocolate chestnut** *pavé,* **425; Sausage and chestnut stuffing, 364**
chicken, 41, **174-83,** *174, 183, 184,* **184-5,** 190, 214, 241, 255, 265; *bonne femme,* 512, **Broiled chicken in yogurt, 72; Chicken and mushroom crêpes, 367;** consommé, 46; **Recipe, 46;** with fruit, 447, 449, 456, 466; in microwave oven, 498, 499;

Poule au pot, **182;** in sausages, 246, 247
chicken brick, 511
chicken fat, 96, 97, 189
chicken glaze, 57
chicken livers, **Country terrine, 241; Game pâté en croûte, 245; Hot salad of chicken livers, 271;** Omelet Waldorf, **91**
chicken stock, 42, **43,** 44
chicken of the woods (mushrooms), 304, *312,* **312**
chickpeas, 322, *325,* **325,** 344
chicory family, **269-71; Hot salad of chicken livers, 271**
chiffon cakes, 393, 401
chiffonade, 13, **259**
chili oil (hot oil, red pepper oil, hot chili oil), 103
chili peppers (chilies, hot peppers), 27, 28, **28-9,** 35, 262, 268, 279
chili powder (spice mix), 27, 28. *See also* cayenne pepper
chili sauces, 35; **Red chili pepper sauce, 63**
Chinese apple (pomegranate), 25, **471**
Chinese artichoke, 303
Chinese cabbage, 274-5
Chinese five spice, 27, *27*
Chinese long bean, *284,* 284-6
chips, 296
chives, 14, *15,* **15,** 268, *496*
chocolate, 39, 338, 361, 385, **411,** *420,* **420-9,** 438, 439; Bombe Francillon, **445; Bombe mixture, 444;** chips, *420, 420;* couverture, *420,* 420, 422; equipment, 503, 507, 510; *Semifreddo al cioccolato,* **445;** white, *420,* 420
Chocolate butter cream, **405**
Chocolate cakes, 396, 400;
Chocolate walnut cake, 400
Chocolate charlotte royale, **433**
Chocolate chestnut *pavé,* **425**
Chocolate chip cookies, 388; **Old-fashioned chocolate chip cookies, 389**
Chocolate chip ice cream, **443**
Chocolate custard, **67**
chocolate decorations, 420, 421, 423-4, 507
chocolate fondant, **417**
Chocolate hazelnut parfait, **445**
Chocolate mousse, 421
Chocolate pastry cream, **384**
chocolate profiteroles, 420
Chocolate royal icing, **408**
Chocolate *sachertorte* icing, **406**
chocolate sauces, **425; Recipes, 425**
chocolate substitutes, **422**
chocolates and candies, 404, 421, **426-9; Chocolate truffles, 404, 429;** dipped and filled, **427-8;** hollow shapes, **429**
chops, 194, 208; butterfly, 219;

224-5, 227, 512. *See also* beef chops *etc.*
chorizo, 247, *247, 248;* **Seafood paella, 317**
choux pastry, *see* pastry, choux
chowder, 48
Christmas ice pudding, **444**
Christmas pudding, 364
chutney, **489-90,** 498; **Apple and tomato chutney, 489**
cider, 38, **39, 453**
cigarettes (cookies), 388
cinnamon, 21, *26,* **26,** 27, 36
citrons, *458, 459*
citrus fruit, 446, 451, 455, *458,* **458-60,** *474,* 474, 475, 484. *See also* grapefruit, lemons, etc
citrus julienne, candied, **474,** 475
citrus peel, 475, 484, **486**
clafoutis, 368; *Clafoutis Limousin,* **368**
clams, 125, 153, *163,* 165, *168,* **168-9,** 170, 487, 505; pasta sauces, **337, 338; Seafood paella, 317**
clementines, *458, 459*
cling film (plastic wrap), 500, 506
cloudberry, 462
cloves, 21, *26,* **26,** 27, 36
coalfish, **138-9**
cobnuts, *see* hazelnuts
cockles, *163,* **164,** *168,* **168-9**
coco beans, 284-6
cocoa butter, *420, 420*
cocoa powder, *420,* 420
coconut milk, 68, 477; **Shrimp in coconut sauce, 480**
coconut oil, 96, 100
coconuts, 361, 476, *480,* **480-1; Cold coconut soufflé, 434**
cod, 110, 111, **117,** 124, 126, 134, **138-40,** *139;* **Cod, shrimp and samphire pie, 140; Seafood paella, 317**
cod roe, 131, 139
Coeur à la crème, **76**
coffee, 37, 67, 269, 384, 405, 456; cold desserts, **434,** 438, 444, **445; Coffee soufflé pudding, 365**
Coffee ice cream, 439, **443; Bombes, 444, 445**
Coffee walnut spice cake, 37
coffeecakes, 354; **Recipe, 356**
Cold vegetable terrine, 267
Coleslaw, 268
coley, **138-9**
collard greens, 272-3, *273*
colocassi, **303**
colorings, food, 25
colza, 96, 102
comfrey, *20, 20*
conch, *163, 163,* **164**
confectionery, *see* candies and chocolates
confits, 486, *512; Confit* of duck, **486**
consommé, 42, 43, 44, **46-7**

cookie crust, for cheesecakes, 403
Cookie icing, **408**
cookie sheets (baking sheets), 386, 499, 507, 511
cookies, 75, 99, **372**, **386-9**; **Dutch butter cookies, 100; Flemish spiced cookies, 27; Old-fashioned chocolate chip cookies, 389**
coral, 152, **154**, 173
cordials, 38, **39**
coriander, 12, 22, **22**, 27; **Baked fennel with lamb and coriander, 23**
corn, 262, 265, 267, **319-20**, 327, 495; **Corn, pepper and mustard seed relish, 490**
corn, sweet, 264, **284-6**, *285*, 319
corn chips, 363
corn oil, 96, 97, *102*, 102, 104, 106
corn sugar (glucose), 411, 412, 439
corn syrup, 401, 411, 413, 493
cornbread, 359; **Cornbread sticks, 360**
cornmeal, 119, 263, 314, *319*, 319, 320, 342, 343; mush (polenta), 319, 320, 498
cornstarch, 59, 319, 344, 400, 439
costmary, *20*, 20
cotechino, 247, 247
cottonseed oil, 96, 100
coulibiac, 132, 354
coulis, 65, 450, 512
Coupe Châteaubriand, **443**
court bouillon, 119, 152; **Recipes, 44**
couscous, 315, *320*, **320**
cowpea, 284-6, 322, 323, 327
crab, 48, 120, 152, 153, **158-9**, *159*, 496; Eggs New Orleans, **85**; **Pompano** *en papillote*, **121**
crab apples, **452-4**, 490; **Apple butter, 493; Apple jelly, 492-3**
cracked grains, 314, 319, 320, 321
crackers, 43, 75, **389**
cranberries, 447, 448, 450, *462*, **462-3**, 475, 495; Cranberry sauce, **66**
crayfish, 152, 153, *161*, **161-2**
crayfish sauce (Nantua sauce), 147; **Recipe, 55**
cream, 50, **68, 69-71**, 266, 267, 451, 495, 503; **Cream sauce, 54; Crème brûlée, 71;** in frozen desserts, **439-43**; non-dairy substitutes, 68; **Sherry syllabub, 438.** See also sour cream
cream cheese, 76, 76, 403, 405; Cream cheese strudel, **383**; **German cheesecake, 403**
cream puddings, grain puddings, **315**
cream, whipped, **69**, 70; for fillings, 405, 435, 436
creams and charlottes, **432-3**
Crème anglaise, see Vanilla custard
Crème brûlée, 71
Crème caramel, see Caramel custard

Crème Chibouste, **384**, 384
crème fraîche **69, 70**, 71, 439
***Crème patissière*, 384**
Cremini mushroom, 306
crêpes, 183, **366-7**, 510, 511; **Recipes, 366-7**
crépinettes, 246, 247, *247*
cresses, *269*, **270**
croaker, **137-8**
Croissants, 357-8
croquettes, 104, 125, 183, 263; **Camembert croquettes, 107**
croûtes and croûtons, 43, **352**
crown roasts, 216, 222, **223**, 227
crudités, 268, 512
crullers, 362
crumb crusts, **372**
crumpets, 369
crustaceans, **152-62**
cucumbers, 258, 282, **282-3**, 489, 499, 505; **Sour gherkins in vinegar, 490**
cucumbers, pickling (Kirby), *282*, 282
Cumberland sausage, 247, *247*
cumin, 24, **24**, 27
curd cheese, 403; *Coeur à la crème*, **76**
curdling milk or cream, 68, 442
currants, 462, 463, 495; **Currant and pistachio pilaf, 315; Currant scones, 360; Mincement, 486.** See also black currants, red currants
curry, 26, 449; **Curry sauce, 54; Eggs mimosa with curry mayonnaise, 84**
custard apples, 472, *472*
custards, **67**, 81, **384**, 405, 434, 439, 498; **Recipes, 67**
custards, baked, 80, **94-5**, 510, 511
cuttlefish, *170*, **170-3**

D
dab, 110, 127
Daikon radish, *293*, 293-4
dairy products, freezing, **495**
dal lentils, 322, 324, 325, 362
damsons, *456*, 456; canning, 493
dandelions, 268, 271, 272, 272-3
dangers in cooking, 36, 96, 104, 105, 194, 413, 499; allergic reactions, 33, 148, 284; canned foods, 484, 494; eggs, 80, 439; fava beans, 284, 326; fish and shellfish, 133, 134, 142, 145, 163, 169; microwave cooking, 497, 499-501, microwave ovens, 497; plants and flowers, 20, 37, 268, *303*, 327, 446, 455, 456; mushrooms (inedible), 304, 311, 313; pork, 226, 246; poultry, 174, 179, 364; raw fish and meat, 125, 364; wild game, 236, 240
Danish pastries, 357; **Recipe, 358**
dates, **321**, 416, 473, **473**, 484;

Date nut bread, 361; Steamed date pudding, **365**
decorations, for cakes, 405, **406, 408, 409**; candied rose petals and violets, 268; from vegetables, 283
deep-frying, **104-6**, 503; equipment, 509, 510. See also meat, deep-fried, etc.
defrosting, in microwave oven, 497
demi-glace sauce, 52; **Recipe, 58**
Demidoff, 298
dende oil (palm oil), 96, 100, 102
desserts, cold and frozen, **430-45**
desserts, other recipes
    Apple crêpes, 367; *Baklava*, 382; **Bananas Foster, 465; Bread and butter pudding, 365; Caramel custard, 95; Cherry batter pudding, 368; Chocolate chestnut pavé, 425; Chocolate mousse, 421;** *Coeur à la crème*, **76; Coffee soufflé pudding, 365;** *Crème brûlée*, **71;** *Crêpes Suzette*, **367; Fresh orange soufflé, 460; Fruit fritters in beer batter, 106;** *Gâteau succès*, **402; German cheesecake, 403; Indian creamed rice, 318; Pineapple** *en surprise*, **469; Poached fruit crêpes, 367; Profiteroles with Melba sauce, 377; Rosemary and lemon sorbet, 19; Scented blancmange, 36; Steamed ginger pudding, 365; Strudel, 383; Summer pudding, 463;** sweet soufflé omelets, **91;** *Tarte Tatin*, **455**
détrempe, 378. See also puff pastry
dewberries, 462
dextrose (glucose), 411, 412, 439
dill, 22, **22**, 139, 282, 496
dimbala, 284-6
discoloration of vegetables, **261**
divinity (a candy), 426
dodines (ballotines), 241, **255**
dogfish, *132*, 132
dolphin fish (dorado), **136**
doner kebab, 204
dough: equipment, *507*, 507
dough, hot water, **244**; sour cream, 245, **373.** See also bread
doughnuts, 362; **Recipe, 362**
Dover sole, *127*, 127; **Fillets of sole with mushrooms and tomatoes, 128**
dressings, 268, 271, 364
drum (a fish), **137-8**, *138*
dry-frying, **106**, 262
dry-salting food, **488**
drying foods, **484-5**
duck, 41, **174-83**, *188*, **188-9**, 190, *191*, 364, 486; breasts (*magrets*), 183, 188, 271; *Confit* of duck, **486; Duck ragout with pears and orange, 189;** with particular fruits, 451, 452, 456, 462-3

duck, wild, **174-83**, 174, *191*
duck eggs, 80, 84, 86
duck fat, 96, 97
duck liver, 189, **190**
dumplings, 43, 183, 268, **338-9**, 450, 511
durian, *472*
durum wheat, 319, 343; pasta (couscous), 315, **320**
Dusty road, 443
Dutch butter cookies, 100
duxelles, 306, 498

E
Easter crown (cake), 354, **356**
eddo, 303
eel, 115, 124, 125, 126, 134, *150*, **150-1; Broiled marinated eel or mackerel, 151**
eel, rock, 132
egg plant, 260, 262, 263, 264, 265, 266, **278-81**, *279*; **Eggplant, spinach and roasted pepper stuffing, 364**
eggs, 68, **80-95**, 345, 370, 392, 395, **496**, 497; baked, 80, 81, 87; baked egg dish, 511; boiled, 80, 81, **83-4**, *83*, 496, 505; **Eggs mimosa with curry mayonnaise, 84;** Eggs mimosa with herb mayonnaise, **84;** Eggs mimosa with *orzo* pasta salad, **84;** coddled, 83; cured or pickled, **86**, 487; custards 432, 438, Christmas ice pudding, **444;** Egg and anchovy pasta sauce, **337;** Egg and bacon sauce, **337;** egg glaze, 385; **Egg and lemon sauce, 55;** egg rolls, spring rolls and wontons, 107, 328, 333, 335, 382; *en cocotte*, 80, 81, **87**, 87; fried, 80, **88-9;** in frozen desserts, **439-43**, **444;** microwave cooking, 497; *mollet*, 83, *83*; poached, 80, 81, 83, **85**, 376; Eggs Benedict, **85;** Eggs New Orleans, **85;** Eggs Sardou, **85; Poached eggs Clamart, 85;** scrambled, 80, 81, **86;** in soups, 45, 46, 50; separating, **81;** smoked, 86; *sur le plat*, 80, 87; whipping, **82**, 503; whites only, 80, 92-3, 266, 435-7, 438, 441, 496; folding, **83;** whipping, **82;** whisking, 80, 81; yolks only, 80, **59**, 81, 439. See also breadcrumbs, coating, mousses, omelets, soufflés
eggs, exotic, **84**
elderberry, *462*, 463
elderflower, 21
electric machines, **392, 509**
elephant garlic, 14, *15*
enchiladas, 363
endive, Belgian (chicory, *endive*), 263, 264, *269*, 269-71
endive, curly, 269, 269-71, 270;

Hot salad of chicken livers, 271
enokitake (mushrooms), 309, **309**
entrecôte (rib, rib steaks, rib eye), 211, 200-7
equipment, **13**, 102, **499-501, 502-11**; for preserving, 490-1
Escabèche (Marinated red snapper), **137**
escalopes, 504. *See also* veal escalopes, etc
Escalopes of monkfish with lime and ginger, 135
escarole, 269-71; **Hot salad of chicken livers, 271**
espagnole sauce, **57**; **Recipe, 57**
essences, 36
Eve's pudding, 447
extracts (flavoring), **36**

F

falafel in pita bread, 363
farmer cheese, 76; *Coeur à la crème*, **76**
fats, 42, **96-107**, 264, 343, 498, 503; for bread, cakes, etc, 101, 345, 370, 386, 392; in frozen meat, 495; as preserving agent, **486-7**; removing from stocks and broths, 42, 513; rendering, **97**; saturation values, **96**; for sautéing and pan-frying, 119, 262
fats, chicken, 96, 97, **97**, 189
feet of animals, 214, 229, 254; pig's trotters, 206-7, 226, 229, 247, 254
feijoa, 466, 472, **472**
fennel, 22, 263, 361; **Baked fennel with lamb and coriander, 23; Baked tuna with fennel and mushrooms, 134**
fennel seed (seed of fennel bulb), 24, **24**
fennel, sweet or Florence, **298-9**, 299
fenugreek, 22, **22**, 27, 327
feta cheese, 74, 75, **75**; **Spinach and feta pie, 94**
fettuccine, 330, 333, 337, 338
feuilletés, **381**
fiddleheads, **303**
figs, 417, 448, 451, 473, **473**, 484, 495, 500; frozen, 439, 495; granola, **321**
filberts, *see* hazelnuts
filet mignon steaks, 210, 219, 227
Fillets of sole with mushrooms and tomatoes, 128
fines herbes, 14
Finnish gingerbread, 401
Finocchiona, 248
fish, **110-51**, 246, 265, 371, 374, 455, 498, 499, 512; available forms, **111**; baked, 112, 117, **120-2**, 126; barbecued, **120**; braised, 125; broiled, 112, 117, **120**, 126; Cajun "blackened

fish", 125; coating, 119; cooked whole, 112, 114, 117, **118**, 119, 120, 122, 126; dried, salted and smoked, **126**, 488; fried, 104, 105, **119**, 125, 510; frozen, 110, 111, **494**, 496; glaze, 57; marinated, **125**; poached, **116**, 117, **118**, 118, **119-20**, 126, 510; potted, 486; preparing, **111-17, 149**, 504, 505; puréed, **122-4**; raw dishes, **125**, 125, 133, **134**, **146-7**, 364; salads, 120, **125**; salted, **126**, 488; sauces, 33, 119, 120, 139; sautéed, **119**; smoked, **126**, 487; soufflés, 92, **Recipe, 93**; steamed, 112, **116**, 117, **120**, **Panaché of steamed fish with dill butter sauce, 130**; stewed, 125; stuffed, 120. *See also* shellfish
fish eggs, **131**, 488; coral, 152, **154**, 173
fish soups, 46, 48, 50, 142; *Aigo saou*, 48
fish stock, 42, **44**, 115; **Recipe, 44**
fish terrines, 241
flageolets, 284-6, 285
flambéing (flaming) food, esp. fruit, 38, **449**, 452, 464, 510
flamiches, **94**
flatbreads, **363**; **Savory Italian flatbread (*foccacia*), 363**
flavorings, **12**, **32-41**
Flemish spiced cookies, 27
Floating Island, **435**
Florence fennel, 298-9
"florentine", 272, 513
flounder, 120, 126, **127-8**, 134; **Fillets of sole with mushrooms and tomatoes, 128**
flour, 119, **328**, 342, **342-4**, 370, 393, 497; in breads and batters, **342-69**; in cakes, 392; for pasta, 328; in pastry, 370; in sauces, **56**, 59; in soups, 51; starches, **344**
flourless cakes, **400**; **Chocolate walnut cake, 400**
flower waters, 36; **Scented blancmange, 36**
flowers, 21, 22, 34, 268, **268**, 287
Focaccia, 363
foie gras, **59**, 183, 188, **190**, 514
foil, aluminum, 120, **181**, 183, 264, 386, **435**, 500, 501, 506
foil, gold and silver, on chocolates, 427
folded breads, **357-8**
fondant, 385, 404, 405, **417**, 496, 507
forcemeat, **199**, 214, **241**, 354, **364**
frangipane, 371, 384, 513
freezing foods, 111, **494-6**, 503
French bread, **353**
French fries, 104, **296**, 505
French onion soup, 47
French toast, 364; **Recipe, 365**

Fresh egg pasta, 331
Fresh orange soufflé, 460
fricassées, 181, 513
fried bread, **362**
fries (testicles) as food, 229
frisée de ruffée, 269-71
fritters, 104, **107**, 263, **362**, 376, 452; **Fruit fritters in beer batter, 106**
frogs, **172**; legs, 172, 172
fromage blanc, 76
fromage frais, 76, 76; *Coeur à la crème*, 76
frosted fruits, **474**
frostings, icings and fillings for cakes, **405-10**, 496
Frozen praline soufflé, 445
Frozen raspberry soufflé, 445
fruit, 328, 338, 364, 439, 440, **446-75**, 498, 500; baked, **447**; broiled, **448**; candied, 399, 414, 426, 444, **474**, **475**; caramelized, 418, **449**; deep-fried, **449**; dried, **353**, 354, 360, 361, **399**, **473**, **473**, **484-5**; frosted and sugared, 416, 449, **474**; **Fruit fool, 438**; **Fruit fritters in beer batter, 106**; glazed, 344, 404, 415; macerating, **451**; with meat and poultry, 179, 181, 447, 449; poached (fruit compote, stewed fruit), **448-9**; **Poached fruit crêpes, 367**; **Poached fruit glaze, 385**; preserved, **484-94**; sautéed, **449**
fruit brandies, 38, 39
fruit breads, cakes, etc, 371, 382, 403, 435, 461; fruit breads, 354, **361**; fruit cakes, **399**, **403**, 410; **Rich fruit cake, 399**; **Fruit muffins, 361**
fruit butters and cheeses, **493**
fruit charlotte, **433**
fruit curds, **493**
fruit gelatin molds, 431
fruit ice creams, 442
fruit purée, 432, 434, 436, 438, 439, **450**, 495; **Bombe mixture, 444**
fruit salads, **451**
fruit sauces, **66**, 450
fruit soups, 42, **450**; **Hungarian cherry soup, 451**
fruit syrups, as sweeteners, 411
fruit vegetables, **278-81**, 485
Fruit vinaigrette, **64**
frying, *see* deep-frying; dry-frying; pan-frying; sautéed foods
fudge, 415, 426; **Penuche, 426**

G

galantines, 241, **255**
gambas (jumbo shrimp or jumbo prawns), 160
game, 179, 183, 195, 199, 241, 252; and fruits, 447, 462-3; pâtés and terrines, 241, 354, **Game**

pâté en croûte, **245**; pies, 243, 374; soups, 49, 50; stock, 43, **44**
game, birds **174-93** (esp. 179, 183, **191-3**), 265. *See* poultry and game birds for full entry
game, furred, 195, 199, **236**, 236, **237-40**, 447; exotic, **238**, 240
gammon (UK), 249, 250, 450
ganache, **425**, 428
garam masala, 27, **27**
garfish, **150-1**
garlic, **14-15**, 14, **15**, 261, 262, 263, 268, 271, 364, 504; **Garlic mayonnaise, 63**; **Garlic sauce, 14**; in microwave cooking, 501; **Olive oil, anchovy and garlic dip, 101**; *Pesto* (pine nut, garlic and basil sauce) **17**; in stock, 43, 44; *Tapenade*, **34**
Gâteau succès, **402**
gazpacho, 51, 282
gelatin, 43, 46, **235**, 267, **431**, 494; desserts, **430-3**, 450; molds, 508
génoise whisked cakes, 394, **395**, 404, 414; **Recipe, 395**
German cheesecake, 403
ghee, 96, 282, 489
gherkins, 282, 282, 489; **Sour gherkins in vinegar, 490**
giblets, poultry, 175, 189, 486
ginger, 14, 21, 27, **30**, **30-1**, 262, 504; **Mango and ginger jam, 493**; **Steamed ginger pudding, 365**
gingerbreads, 360, 401, 509; **Finnish gingerbread, 401**; Gingerbread men, 27
Glacé icing, **406**, 496
glasswort, *see* marsh samphire
glazed fruits, 415
glazes, **57**, 263, 344, **345**, 385, 507, 513
glucose, 411, 412, 439
gluten, **343**, 370, 497
gnocchi alla romana, 338
gnocchi, useful information, 376
goat cheese, 73, 74, **75**, 75; **Shrimp ravioli with goat cheese, 336**
goat meat, 208
goat milk, 69; butter, 98; yogurt, 71
goatfish, **137-8**
golden berry (Cape gooseberry), 462, 463
golden syrup, 413
goose, 43, **174-83**, *190*, **190**, 364, 486, 495
goose *confit*, 190, 486
goose eggs, 80, 84
goose fat, 96, 97, 97, 189, 190
goose livers, 189, 190; foie gras, **190**
goose, wild, **174-83**, 174, 191
gooseberries, 439, 450, 462, 463, 493, 495
Gorgonzola, 74, 78, 78, 334; Gorgonzola pasta sauce, **337**
Gougères, **377**
goujonettes, 127

goujons, 119
gourds, 287, **288**
gourmet powder, 33
graham flour, 343
grain sprouts, **327**
grains, **314-27**, 364, **372**; boiling, **314**; puddings, **315**; simmering, **315**; steaming, **314**; unusual, **321**. *See also* individual grains
granita, 441
granola, **321**
grape sugar (glucose), 411, 412, 439
grapefruit, 448, 451, 458, **459**, 505; **Avocado and grapefruit salad with smoked salmon, 470**; candied citrus julienne, **474**
grapes, 40, 446, 451, *461*, **461**, 473, 474
grapeseed oil, 96, 103
grapevine leaves, **265**
gratin dishes, 264, *511*, 511
gravad lax, 125, **488**
gravy, **57**
gray mullet, 131, *137*, **137-8**
green goddess dressing, **63**; **Lobster salad green goddess, 157**
green mayonnaise, **63**
green salad, **271**
green tomato, *see* tomatillo
greens, 25, 258, 260, 261, 262, 265, **272-4**
grenadilla (passion fruit), 447, **466-9**
grenadine, 25
grenadins, 216
griddle, 119, **369**, *510*, 510
ground cherry, 303
ground meat, *see* meat, ground, *also* beef, ground, etc
ground tomato, *see* tomatillo
groundnuts, *see* peanuts
grouper, 124, 125, *136*, **136**
grouse, **174-83**, *174*, *191*, 191, 374; red, 191
Gruyère, 73, 74, *79*, 79; **Cold vegetable terrine, 267**; *Crêpes suisses*, **367**; *Gougères*, **377**
guard of honor, 222, **223**
guava, **466-9**
guinea fowl, **174-83**, *174*, *184*, 184
Gulyàs (Hungarian beef stew), **212**
gum paste (*pastillage*), 415
gumbos, **49**
gurnard, *142*, **142**

H

haddock, 124, 126, **138-9**, *139*; **Seafood paella, 317**
haggis, *246*
hake, 110, 126, **138-9**, *139*
halibut, 115, *129*, **129-30**; *Panaché* of steamed fish with dill butter sauce, **130**

ham, *179*, *206-7*, *228*, **228**, 241, *250-1*, **250-2**, 253, 254, 271, 364, 487, 488, 495; bones, **235**; **Country terrine, 241**; *Crêpes suisses*, **367**; with fruit, 447, 449, 450, 466; **Game *pâté en croûte*, 245**; ham and cheese pudding, 364; picnic (shoulder), 206-7, 226, 250; **Raised veal and ham pie, 244; Seafood paella, 317**; smoked ham, 250-2
Hamburg parsley, 303
hamburgers, **213**, 487
hare, 236, *239*, **239-40**, 374
haricot vert, 284-6
harissa, 35, 320
hazelnuts, 419, 435, 476, 477, **479**; butter, 98; Chocolate hazelnut parfait, **445**; flour, 344; oil, 96, 103; *Penuche* (fudge), **426**; Turkish tarator sauce, **66**
heads of animals, in cooking, 173, 229, 238, 254
heart, 230, *233*, **233-4**, 246
hen of the woods (mushroom), **312**
hen's egg, 80
herb bennet, *20*, 20
herb butters, 496; *Beurre aux fines herbes*, **99**; sauce (*Beurre blanc aux herbes*), **62**
Herb vinaigrette, **64**
herb-flavored vinegar, **41**
herbes de Provence, 14
herbs, **12-22**, 43, 263, 271, 364, 441, 501, 504; in breads, 361; in cheeses, 73; drying, **14**; Eggs mimosa with herb mayonnaise, **84**; freezing, **496**; infused oils, **103; Salad of mixed herbs, 20**. *See also* individual herbs
herring, 110, 125, **147-9**, *148*, 150, 374, 496; preserved, 124, 126, 487, 488; **Pickled fried herring, 149**; roes, 131
hickory nuts, 478
hock of pork, 226, 249, 250
hollandaise, **60-1**, 496; **Recipe, 60-1**
hominy, *319*, 319, 320
honey, 345, 360, 411, *412*, **412-13**, 439, 485; *Baklava*, **382**; with fruit, 451, 493, 495; Honey butter, **99**; Honey glaze, **406**; **Jewish honey cake, 413**
honey mushrooms, *313*, 313
hops (vegetable), 303
horse mackerel, *140*, **140-1**
horse mushrooms, 304, 310
horsemeat, 208
horseradish, 28, *30*, **31**; sauce, **29**
huckleberries, 462
hummus bi tahina, 322, 325, 363
Hungarian beef stew, 212
Hungarian cherry soup, 451
hurtleberry, 462
hush puppies, 343, 362
husk tomato (ground cherry), 303

I

ice cream, 435, 436, **439-43**; equipment, *503*, 503, *508*, **508**, 509; Ice cream chocolate profiteroles, **377**; Ice cream layer cake, **444; Recipes, 442-3**
Iced chocolate mousse, 421
ices, *see* sorbets
icings, frostings and fillings for cakes, 385, **405-10**, 496, 503
icings, fondant, 385, 405, **417**, 496
icings, royal, 385, 404, 405, **408**, 496, 507; **Recipe, 408**
icings, soft, **406-7**
Indian creamed rice, 318
Indian date, 472
Indian fig (prickly pear), 303, 472
infused teas, **21**
injera, 363
ink cap (mushroom), 311
instant flour, *342*, 343
intestines, as sausage casings, 235, 248; pig's, 246
Irish moss (carragheen), *283*, 431
Irish soda bread, 359; **Recipe, 360**
isinglass, 431

J

jack (fish), **140-1**
jaggery, 412
jam soufflé omelet, **91**
jams, 268, 412, 432, 455, **490-3**; apricot jam glaze, 456; **Recipe, 385; Mango and ginger jam, 493**; sauces, 66
Japanese artichoke, 303
jellies, **253-5**, 268, **490-3**; **Apple jelly, 492-3**; equipment, 506, 508
jelly roll, **396-7**, in charlottes, 432-3, **433**; pan, 509
Jerusalem artichokes (root artichokes, sunchokes), 260, 292, *293*, 293, **326**; flour, 344
jewfish, 136
Jewish honey cake, 413
Jew's ear mushroom, 309
jicama (yam bean), *292*, 293
Job's tears, 321
John Dory, *129*, **129-30**; *Panaché* of steamed fish with dill butter sauce, **130**
julienne strips, fruit, **460**; vegetable, *259*, 283, **307**
Juneberry, 462
juniper berry, 26, **26**, 38

K

kale, *272*, 272 3
kaszanka, *246*, 247
kasha, *320*, 320
kebabs, 204, 208, 503; **Vietnamese shrimp kebabs, 33**
ketchup, **35**
Kheer (Indian creamed rice), 318
Kibbeh, 204

kidneys, 208, 219, 229, 230, *231*, **231; Kidneys with Madeira, 230**
kielbasa, *246*, 247
kingfish (king mackerel), 148
kingfish (species of drum), **137-8**
kippered herring, 124, 126, 487
Kirby cucumber (pickling cucumber), 282
kirsch, 38, 49, 432
kissel, 450
kiwi fruit (formerly Chinese gooseberry), 66, **437**, 439, 447, *466*, **466-9**, 474
knackwurst, *246*, 246, 247
kneydlach (matzoh balls), 338, 363; **Recipe, 339**
knife sharpening, 207
knuckle bones, 213, **235**
kofta, 204
kohlrabi, 265, *293*, 293
kumquats, *458*, *459*, 475; **Pineapple *en surprise*, 469**

L

lactose, 68, 98, 411
Ladyfingers, 396; in charlottes, **432-3**
lake herring, 145
lake whitefish, 126, 145
lamb, 194, **195**, **204-5**, **218-25**, 364, 447, 495; breast, *204*, **204-5**, *218*, *220*, **220; Ragout of lamb, artichokes and fava beans, 326**; chops, **204-5**, 219, 222, **224-5**, *227*; leg, *204*, **204-5**, *218*, 224, **224-5**; loin, *204*, **204-5**, *218*, 219; US and French cuts, **204-5**; cooking methods for lamb cuts, 204; Middle eastern dishes, 204; nutritive values, 205; kidneys, **231; Kidneys with Madeira, 230**, 204; neck, **204-5**, *218*, **222**, best end (rack of lamb), *204*, **204-5**, *218*, **222-3**; noisettes (medallions), 198, *204*, **204-5**, 219, *220*, 513; roast, baron of lamb, 208, 219; crown roast (guard of honor), 222; **(Stuffed crown roast of lamb), 223**; suckling, 208; roasting times, 199; saddle, *204*, **204-5**, **219**; shank, **204-5**, *218*, **221; Ragout of lamb, artichokes and fava beans, 326**; shoulder, *218*, *221*, **221**; sirloin, **204-5**, *218*, **219**; variety meats, **229-34**, 246
lamb, ground, 204, **214**, 279; **Baked fennel with lamb and coriander, 23**. *See also* meat, ground
lamb bones, **235**
lamb fat, 97
lamb stock, 43
lamb's lettuce, *269*, **269-71**
lamprey, **150-1**
langouste, 153

lard, 95, *97*, 97, 119, 262, 263; in bread, etc, 345, 370, 392
larding meat, **196**, 503
lardons, **249**
lardy cakes, 97
lasagne, 328, *329*, *330*, 330, 333, 334; desserts, 338; Lasagne Bolognese, **334**; **Spinach and ricotta lasagne, 334**
laver, 283
layer cakes, **400**
leaf mustard, 272-3
leaved pastries, 97, **383-3**
leeks, 14, 263, 268, **289-90**, *290*, 495; **Cold vegetable terrine, 267**; *flamiche*, **94**; in stock, 43, 44; **Vinaigrette salad, 268**
legume sprouts, 327
legumes, 314, **322-7**, 494. *See also* beans, lentils, peas
lemon sole, 127; **Sole with mushrooms and tomatoes, 128**
lemon-flavored herbs, *21*, **21**
lemons, 14, 68, 343, 370, 447, *458*, **458-60**, 474, 505; candied citrus julienne, *474*, **475**; Lemon butter cream, **405**; **Lemon curd, 493**; **Lemon mousse with caramel sauce, 434**; lemon oil, 36; **Lemon and parsley sauce, 55**; Lemon sorbet, **442**; for raw fish dishes, 125; **Rosemary and lemon sorbet, 19**
lentils, 50, *322*, *325*, **325-6**, 327; soup, **50**; **Spiced lentil purée, 325**. *See also* legumes
lettuce, 258, 260, 263, 264, 266, 267, **269-71**, *270*
licorice, *see* anise
lights (lungs), 235, 246, 247, 513
lime tea (dried lime leaves), 21
limequat, 458, 459
limes, 447, *458*, **458-60**, 474; candied citrus julienne, **474**; **Lime and orange marmalade, 493**
limpets, 163
lingonberry, 463
linguica, 247
liqueurs, 38, *39*, **39**, 105, 432, 439, 449, 501; cold and frozen desserts, 439, 440, 444; Liqueur custard, **67**; with fruit, 447, 449
liver, **59**, 229, *230*, **230**, 246, 247; dumplings (*leberknödeln*), 338; pâtés, 243; sausage, 246, 247
livers, poultry, 189
lobster, 135, 152, *153*, **153-7**, 496, 512; **Lobster salad green goddess, 157**; spiny (rock lobster), 153
lobster coral, *154*; **Sauce cardinale, 55**
lobster mushroom, 313
loganberries, *462*, 462
longan, *472*, 472
loquat, *472*, 472
lotus root, *303*, 303

Louis dressing, 63
lovage, *22*, **22**
lox, 126
luganeghe, 247
lumpfish, 142; hard roe, 131
lungs (lights), 235, 246, 247, 513
lychees (litchis), *472*, 472

M

macadamia nuts, 476, *479*, 479
macaroni, 331, 334
macaroons, 404, 444, **445**
mace, *26*, **26**, 27
Macédoine of cooked vegetables (Russian salad), 268
macerating fruit, **451**
mackerel, 44, 110, 111, **113**, 124, **140-1**, **147-9**, *148*, **Broiled marinated eel or mackerel, 151**; preserved 134, 450, 487, 496; **Pickled fried herring, 149**
Madeleines, 404; tin, 509
mahi mahi, **136**
Maître d'hôtel (parsley) butter, **99**
mallard, *191*
maltose, 411
mamey sapote, 472
mandarins, 459
mandoline, **296**, 505
mangetout (snow peas), 262, 284-6
mango, 447, 451, *466*, **466-9**; **Mango and ginger jam, 493**
mangosteen, *472*, 472
manioc (yuca root), 303, 343, 344
mantis shrimp, **162**
maple syrup, 319, 413, 439
maple tree sugar, 411
mare's milk, 69, 72
margarine, 96, *99*, **99**, 100, 106; in bread, etc, 345, 370, 392
marigolds, 25, 34, 268
marinades, 41, 101, 183, **188**, **195**; fruit (macerated), **451**; vegetables, 27, 101, 264, 268
Marinated red snapper, 137
marjoram, *18*, 18, **19**, 21
marlin, **133-4**
marmalade, **385**, 459, **490-3**; **Lime and orange marmalade, 493**
marrow bones, 202, **235**, 512; **Red wine, shallot and bone marrow sauce, 58**
Marsala, **39**; *Zabaglione*, **438**
marsh samphire, *283*, 283
marshmallow, 426, 435
marzipan, *see* almond paste
Matchstick potatoes, **296**, 505
matsutake, 306, **312**
matzoh balls, 338, 363; **Recipe, 339**
mayonnaise, 52, **60**, **62-3**, 268, 496; **Recipes, 63**; **Eggs mimosa with curry mayonnaise, 84**
meagre fish, **137-8**
meat and charcuterie, **194-255**, 447, 494, 495, 503, 504, 505. *See also* beef, lamb, pork and veal

meat, in aspic, **253-4**; barbecueing, **197-8**; barding and tying, **196**; blanching, **196**; "boiled", 197; boned, **196**; boned, stuffed and rolled, 241, **255**; braised, 194, **199**, 268; broiled, 194, 195, **197-8**, 208; cold dishes, 208, **215**, **253-4**, **255**; cuts, 200-7; deep-fried, 104, 208; festive, **208**; glossary, 208, **512-14**; larding, **196**; marinating, **195**; mincemeat, **486**; pies and tarts, **243-4**, 371, 374; poaching, **197**; pot-roast, **199**, 208; potted, 241, **243**, 486; preserved, 241, **249-51**, 252, 486, **487**, **488-9**, 495; raw dishes, 208, 364, 512; roast, 194, 195, **198-9**, 208, 494, 503, 511; sautéed, 195, **198**; smoked, 252, **487**; stewed, 194, 195, **197**, 268, 320, 498, 499, 514; stir-fried, 208; stocks and soups, 43, 45, 50; tenderizing, **195**; trimming and cutting, **195**; variety meats, 194, **229-35**
meat, ground, 194, 208, **214**, 364, 506. *See also* beef, ground, etc
meat *coulis*, **57**
meat cuts, *200-7*
meat extracts, 33
meat glaze, 57
meatballs, 214
meatloaf, **215**, 500
Mediterranean baked bream, 141
medlar, 472
Melba toast, 352
melilot, *20*, 20
melon pear, 472
melons, 447, 450, 451, *464*, **464**, 474, 484, 505
melt (spleen), 235
meringue, 83, 418, **435**, **435-7**, **436**; **Baked meringues, 436**
meringue, cooked, 435, **436**
meringue, Italian, 415, **435**, **436-7**, 441; **Pineapple *en surprise*, 469**; *Vacherin*, **437**
meringue, Swiss (simple), **435-6**
meringue cakes, **402**; *Gâteau succès*, **402**
Mexican bean salad, **327**
Mexican chocolate, 420
Mexican green tomato, **303**
Mexican oregano (Mexican sage), 19
microwave cooking, **497-501**
milk, esp. cow's milk, **68-72**, 370, 401, 495, 503
milk, non-dairy substitutes, 68; preserved, 69; souring, 68
milk desserts, frozen, **439-43**, 439; grain puddings, 315
milk sugar (lactose), 68, 98, 411
millet, *320*, **320**, 344
Mincemeat, 371, *486*, **486**
minestrone, 50; *Minestrone alla fiorentina*, **45**; *Minestrone di verdura*, **45**

mint, 12, *16*, **17**, 21, 496
mirepoix, **263**, 263
miso, 33
molasses, 411, 413, 489
molded gelatin desserts, **430-5**, 450
molds and pans, **508**, *509*, 511
mollusks, 152, **163-72**, 496
monkfish, 115, 120, 125, *135*, **135**, 512; **Escalopes of monkfish with lime and ginger, 135**
Monterey omelet, **91**
moonfish, **140-1**, 145
Morcilla, 246, 247
morels, 304, 306, *310*, **310**; **Morels with cream, 310**
mortadella, 246, *248*
mountain oysters, 229
mountain spinach, 272-3
moussaka, 279
mousselines, 122, **123**, 127, 183, 241, 243
mousses, dessert, **434-5**, 438, **Chocolate mousse, 421**, Lemon mousse with caramel sauce, **434**; fish, 122, **124**; vegetable, 267
muffins, 360, 361, 369, 463; **Fruit muffins, 361**; equipment, 509
mulberries, 462
mullet, **137-8**; freshwater, 145; gray, 131, *137*, **137-8**; *Panaché of steamed fish with dill butter sauce, 130*; red, 120, **121**, 126, **137-8**, 142
mung beans, 324, 327, 328
mushrooms, 105, 263, 264, 265, 268, **304-13**, *306*, 306, 485, 495, 498, 499; **Baked tuna with fennel and mushrooms, 134**; **Chicken and mushroom crêpes, 367**; **Cold vegetable terrine, 267**; **Creole omelet, 91**; dried, 306; **Mushroom brown rice pilaf, 315**; mushroom julienne, 307; mushroom ketchup, 35; **Mushroom sauce, 54**; **Mushroom sauce (*sauce allemande*), 55**; Mushroom soufflé, **93**; **Mushroom, white wine and tomato sauce (*sauce chasseur*), 58**; **Mushrooms à la grecque, 307**; Omelet Waldorf, **91**; raw, 304, 306; *sauce suprême*, **55**
mushrooms, Chinese winter, 306, 308
mushrooms, common, 304, 305, **306-8**, 495
Mushrooms, cultivated, 304, **308-9**; cloud ear, 306, *309*, **309**; enokitake, *309*, **309**; oyster, 304, *309*, **308-9**; shiitake, *308*, **308**
mushrooms, wild, 304, **310-313**; beefsteak, *313*, **313**; bolete (cep), *311*, **311**; Caesar's, **313**; chanterelle, *312*, **312**; chicken of the woods, *312*, **312**; field, *310*; fairy ring, *313*, **313**; hedgehog,

Mushrooms, wild, *continued*
304, *311*, **311**; hen of the woods,
312; honey, *313*, **313**; lobster,
313; matsutake (pine), 306, **312**;
morel, *310*, **310**; parasol, *311*,
311; puffball, **312**, *313*; saffron
milk cap, *313*, **313**; shaggy mane,
311, **311**; truffles, 58, *313*, **313**,
495, **514**; wood blewit, *312*, **312**
mussels, 48, 125, *163*, 165, *169*,
169-70, 487; **Seafood paella,
317**; Seafood sauce for spaghetti,
337
mustard, 28, *31*, **31**; Mustard
barbecue sauce, **65**; Mustard
butter, **99**; **Mustard
hollandaise, 61**; **Mustard,
vinegar and onion sauce, 58**;
Scandinavian mustard sauce, **63**
mustard and cress, **270**
mustard greens, 272-3, *273*
mustard seeds, 27, 28; **Corn,
pepper and mustard seed
relish, 490**; sprouts, 327
mutton, 194, 195, **204-5**, 218, 246,
252; **Ragout of lamb, artichokes
and fava beans, 326**

N

nam pla, **33**
nan (bread), *363*, 363
Nantua sauce, 55; *Quenelles
sauce Nantua*, **147**
Nappa cabbage, 274-5
naseberry, 472
nasturtiums, 34, *268*, 268
nectarines, 446, **456-7**, *457*, 484,
493
nettle, stinging, **303**
nonstick cookware, 346, 502, 510
noodles, 43, 328, 330, 338
nopale, **303**
Northampton pork sausage, *247*
nougat, 415, 426
nougatine, **419**
nuoc nam, 33
nut brittle, 426
nut butters, 477
nut flour, 344
nut milks, **477**
nut oils, 96, 97, 100, 103, 104,
271, 476, 478
nut paste, **477**
nut sauces, **66**
nutmeg, 21, *26*, **26**, 27, 266
nuts, 261, 371, 404, **476-81**, 487,
496, 504; *Baklava*, **382**; in
breads, 354, **361**; **Banana nut
bread, 361**; **Date nut bread,
361**; Whole wheat fruit and nut
bread, **353**; for cakes, 390, 400;
Nut frosting, **410**; candied, 426;
in cold desserts, 438, 439;
dipped in chocolate, 427, 503;
exotic, **481**; nougatine, **419**;
praline, **419**, 426; roasting or
toasting, **477**

O

oatcakes, 321, 363
oatmeal, 119, *321*, 321, 342, 344,
401
oats, 321, **321**, 344
octopus, **170**, *171*, **172**
Oeufs à la neige (**Snow eggs**), **436**
oils, **96-107**, *96-7*, **100-3**, 113,
262, 264, 343; in bread, etc, 345,
370, 392, 401; exotic, **103**;
infused, **103**; nut, 96, 97, 100,
103, 104, 271, 476, 478;
saturation values, **96**; smoking
point, 104. *See also* olive oil
okra, 263, *283*, **283**, 485, 495;
gumbos, 49
**Old-fashioned chocolate chip
cookies, 389**
olive oil, 96, **100-1**, *101*, 104, 119,
262, 263, 264, 498; for cakes,
392; **Olive oil, anchovy and
garlic dip, 101**, Olive oil and
garlic pasta sauce, **337**; for pasta
sauces, 337, 338
olives, *34*, **34**, 451, 505; *Tapenade*,
34; olive breads, 361
omelets, 80, 81, 83, **89-91**, 510;
Recipes, 91
onion family (alliums), as herbs,
14; as vegetables, **289-91**
onions, 14, 96, 258, 260, 263, 268,
289, **289-91**, 495; Alsatian onion
quiche, **94**; **Apple and onion
stuffing, 364**; **Apple and
tomato chutney, 489**; in breads,
361; **French onion soup, 47**;
with fruit, 451; **Onion confit
with raisins, 291**; Onion rings,
105; **Onion sauce, 54**; peel, for
colouring, 25; for pickles, 489;
preserving, 485; Spanish omelet,
91; in stock, 43, 44; stuffed, 265;
in stuffings, 364; **Sage and onion
stuffing, 364**
onions, green (scallions), 14, 262,
268, 283, *289*, **289-90**, 504
opah, **140-1**; sea-water (moonfish),
140-1, 145
orache, 272-3
orange flower water, **Scented
blancmange, 36**
orange roughy, **136**
oranges, 14, 361, 446, 447, *458*,
458, 505; **Bitter orange sauce,
58**; candied, **474**, 475; **Fresh
orange soufflé, 460**;
marmalades, 490, 491; **Lime and
orange marmalade, 493**;
Orange butter, **99**, *Crêpes
Suzette*, **367**; Orange butter
cream, **405**; orange curd, **493**;
Orange custard, **67**; Orange
hollandaise (*Sauce maltaise*), 298,
Recipe, 60; orange mousse, **434**;
Orange chocolate mousse, **421**;
Orange sorbet, **442**; *Oranges en
surprise*, **443**

oregano, 14, *18*, **19**, 27
ormer, 163, **164**
ortanique, 458, 459
orzo, **329**, Eggs mimosa with *orzo*
pasta salad, **84**
osso buco, 202, 235
oven, preparing for baking, 390,
393, 395
oven equipment, 498-9, 499-500,
503, **511**
ovens, microwave, **497-501**
ox meat, 194, 229, **234**
oxtail, *229*, 229
ox tongue, *234*, **234**
oyster meat, 176, 185, 513
oysters, 48, *163*, 165, *166*, **166-7**,
487, 505; oyster sauce, 33;
Recipe, 54; **Oysters in
champagne sauce, 167**

P

paella, **Seafood paella, 317**
pain perdu, 364; **Recipe, 365**
palm oil, 96, 100, 102
palm sugar, 411, 412
palm tree: hearts of palm, **303**
palmiers, 381
palometa, **140-1**
pan-broiling, **106**, 262
pan-frying, **106**, 198, 208, 510
panachés, 120; **Panaché of steamed
fish with dill butter sauce, 130**
panada, 354
panade, 513
pancakes and batter puddings, 72,
368-9, 503, 511; **Buttermilk
pancakes, 369**
panisse, 325
pans, 261, 502, 508, 509, **510-11**;
nonstick, 346, 502
papaya (pawpaw), 41, 447, *466*,
466-9
paper, for cooking, 386, 506
paper, collars for soufflés, **435**;
edible rice paper, 344
paper-wrapped cooking, **121**, 181,
183, 447; **Pompano *en
papillote*, 121**
paprika, **29**; oil, 103
parathas, 363, 363
parboiling, 260, 513
parfaits, **439**, **444-5**
parkins, 401
Parma ham, 250, *251*, 251
Parmesan, 73, 74, 79, **79**, 334, 337,
514; *Pesto*, **17**; **Spinach and
ricotta lasagne, 334**
parsley, 12, 13, 14, *16*, **16**
parsley butter, **99**
parsley, Hamburg, 303
parsnips, 44, 263, 267, **292-4**, *293*
partridge, **174-83**, *174*, *191*, 191
partridge eggs, 84
passion fruit, 447, *466*, **466-9**
pasta, 45, **328-38**, 495, 498, 499;
baked, **334**; boiled, **333**, 337;
and cheese, **334**; couscous, 315;

320; equipment, **506**, 511; fried,
333; salads, **331**; Eggs mimosa
with *orzo* pasta salad, **84**; *pastine*,
374; sauces, **337-8**; stuffed, **335**,
335-6, 338
pasta, dessert, 328, **338**
pasta, egg, 328, **330-1**; **Fresh egg
pasta, 331**
pasta, eggless, 328, **329-30**; **Basic
eggless pasta, 330**
pasta, shapes: eggless, *328*, *329*;
egg, *330*; stuffed, *335*
pastrami, 252, *252*
pastry, and pastries, 43, 99, 101,
268, 343, **370-85**; 456, **496**,
513, 514; baked blind, 371, **374**,
375; deep-fried, 107, 324, 328,
333, 335, 382; dough, **370-1**; *en
croûte*, **122**, 183; *pâtés en croûte*,
241, 243, **244-5**; and fruit, 371,
382, 447, 450, 452, 455, 461;
glazes, **385**, 463, 513. *See also
pâté*, pies, quiches, tarts
pastry, choux, **146-7**, 362, 370,
371, **376-7**; choux puffs, 43,
371, 376, 410, 416, 417, 418,
420; **Profiteroles with Melba
sauce, 377**; *Pommes
dauphines*, **105**
pastry, flaky, **378**
pastry, hot water dough, 244;
Raised veal and ham pie, 244
pastry, leaved, 97, **382-3**
pastry, phyllo, 382; **Blue brie and
prawn parcels, 382**
pastry, puff, 244, 370, 371,
378-81, 385, 496; **Cod, shrimp
and samphire pie, 140**;
trimmings, 378
pastry, quick puff, **381**
pastry, sour cream dough, 245,
373; **Game pâté en croûte, 245**
pastry, strudel, **382-4**, 447; Apple
strudel, **383**; Cream cheese
strudel, **383**
pastry bags, for piping, **406**
pastry cream, **384**; **Recipes, 384**
pastry rose, 373
pastry tools, 507, **507**, **508**
pâte (Fr. for "pastry"), 241; *pâte à
pâté*, 243, 244; **Recipe, 373**
pâte brisée, **371-3**, 496; **Recipe,
373**; *Tarte tatin*, **455**; *pâte
sablée*, 371; *pâte sucrée* **371-3**,
371; Recipe, 373
pâtés, 122, **124**, 208, **241**, **243-5**,
243, **244-5**, 486, 498
pâtés en croûte, 241, 243, **244-5**
paupiettes, **124**, 127
pavlovas, 435
peaches, 371, 439, 446, 447, 448,
449, 450, 451, **456-7**, *457*; Peach
ice cream, **443**; Peach Melba,
443; **Poached fruit crêpes, 367**;
dried, *473*; preserved (jams, etc),
473, 484, 485, 490, 493; **Trifle,
438**
peanut oil, 96, **102**, *102*, 104, 262

peanuts, 476, 477, 479, 479; Asian peanut sauce (*Bumbu satay*), **66**
pearl onions, **289-91**; Onion *confit* with raisins, **291**
pears, 38, 371, 439, 446, 447, 448, 449, 450, 451, **452-4**, *453*, 505; in *Birnenbrot*, 361; pear butters, 493; **Pears Belle Hélène, 443**; **Poached fruit crêpes, 367**; preserving (jams, etc), 473, 484, 485, 490, 493; **Trifle, 438**
peas, 261, 266, **284-6**, *285*; **Macédoine of cooked vegetables, 268; Seafood paella, 317**. See also legumes
peas, asparagus, 284-6
peas, black-eyed, 284-6, 322, 323, 327
peas, dried, 284, 314, **322**, **325-6**
peas, green, 265, 284-6, *285*; **Poached eggs Clamart, 85**
peas, marrowfat, 325
peas, snow (*mangetout*), 262, 284, 284-6
peas, split, 322, *325*, 325; split pea soup, 322; **Recipe, 50**
pecan oil, 103
pecans, 439, 476, *478*, **478**
pectin, 490, **491**
pennyroyal, *16*, 17
Penuche, 426
pepperoni, 246, 247
pepino, 472, *472*
pepper, and peppercorns, 27, 12, 28, *30*, **30**, 42; black, 14, 27, 501; **Black pepper, red currant and cream sauce, 58**; white, *24*; cayenne (ground red chili), 27, **29**; red (or hot red pepper flakes), 28. See also seasoning
peppermint, *16*, 17; Peppermint ice cream, **443**
peppers, sweet, 28, 268, **278-81**, *279*, 499
peppers, bell (green, red, yellow), 264, *279*, 485, 495; **Cold vegetable terrine** (red), **267**; **Corn, pepper and mustard seed relish** (green and red), **490**; Creole omelet (green), **91**; **Eggplant, spinach and roasted pepper stuffing** (green or red), **364**; **Mediterranean baked bream, 141**; Spanish omelet (green or red), **91**; stuffed, 265, **281**; **Wild rice pilaf** (red), **316**
peppers, hot, *see* chili peppers
perch (freshwater), *145*, **145-6**
perch, Atlantic ocean (rockfish), 136, 142
perch, Pacific ocean (rockfish), 142
perch, silver, **137-8**
permit, **140-1**
perry, **453**
persillade, 14
persimmon, 66, *471*, **471**
perunarieska, 361, **363**
Pesto, 17

petits fours, **404**, 474, 475; **Almond petits fours, 404**
petits pois, 284-6
pheasant, **174-83**, *174*, *191*, 191, 374; **Game pâté en croûte, 245**
pheasant eggs, 84
phyllo pastry, 382; **Blue brie and prawn parcels, 382**; *Baklava*, 382
Pickled fried herring, 149
"pickled" meats, 252
pickles, **489-90**, 503; pickled onions, *289*, **289-90**; **Vinegar and pickle sauce, 58**; **Watermelon pickle, 490**
pickling salt, 32
pickling spice mixtures, 27
picnic ham (arm roast), 206-7, 226, 250
pies, **94**, 183, **243-4**, *243*, *371*, *374*, 374, **375** 508; baked blind, 371, **374**, **375**; **Cod, shrimp and samphire pie, 140**; fruit, 371, 382, 452, 455, 461; pie pastry, **371-3**; **Recipe, 372**; **Raised veal and ham pie, 244**; **Spinach and feta pie, 94**. See also pastry
pig meat: variety meats, 229, **230**, **231**, 233, **234**, 235, 246, 247, 254; trotters, 206-7, 226, *229*, 229, 247, 254. See also pork
pigeon, **174-83**, *174*, *191*, 191
pigeon eggs, 84
pike, 122, 125, *145*, **145-6**
pilaf, **315**, 498; **Currant and pistachio pilaf, 315; Mushroom brown rice pilaf, 315; Wild rice pilaf, 316**
pilchards, **147-9**
pimiento (pimento), 279
pine nuts, 371; *481*, **481**; **Artichokes and pine nuts, 302**; **Pesto, 17**; pine nut oil, 481
pineapple guava, 466, *472*
pineapples, 439, 448, 449, 450, 451, *466*, **466-9**, 475, 485, 495; **Pineapple en surprise, 469**
piping cake decorations, 406, 408
piquant mayonnaise, **63**
piquant sauces, 29
pistachios, 476, *479*, 479; **Currant and pistachio pilaf, 315**; **Penuche, 426**; Pistachio bavarian cream, **433**
pistou, see pesto
pita bread, *363*, 363
pizza, **351**, 507, 511
plaice, 110, *127*, **127-8**
plantains, *465*, **465**
plastic wrap (cling film), 500, 506
plastics, for microwave cooking, 500
plums, 38, 439, 447, 448, 449, 450, *456-7*, **456-7**; Plum ice cream, **443**; Plum sauce, **66**; preserved, (jams etc) 490, 475, 484, 485, 493. See also prunes

polenta, 319, 320, 498
pollack, **138-9**
pomegranate, 25, *471*, **471**
pomelo, 458, 459
pomfret, *140*, 141
Pommes Dauphine, 376; **Recipe, 105**
pompano, *140*, **140-1**; **Escalopes of monkfish with lime and ginger, 135; Panaché of steamed fish with dill butter sauce, 130; Pompano en papillote, 121**
popcorn, *319*, 319
popovers, 368; **Recipe, 368**
poppy seeds, *24*, **24**; oil, 103; Poppy seed lasagne, 338
pork, 179, 194, 195, **226-8**, 249, 486, 488, 495; belly, *206*, **206-7**, *226*, **227**, 249; chops, 197-8, **206-7**, *226*, **227**, 227, 249; **Pork chops with apple and cream, 228; Country terrine, 241**; US and French cuts, 206-7; cooking methods for pork cuts, 206; nutritive values, 206; feet/trotters, *226*; and fruits, 447, 449, 452, 455, 456, 466; **Game pâté en croûte, 245**; leg, *206*, **206-7**, *226*, **228**, 249, **250-2**; loin, *206*, **206-7**, *226*, **227**, 249; neck end (Boston butt), *206*, **206-7**, *226*; roast, crown roast, 227; roast suckling pig, 208; roasting times, 199; sausages, 246, 247, 247, *see also* Spanish spiced sausages; shank (knuckle), *206*, 288; shoulder, **206-7**, *226*, **226**; sirloin, *206*, **206-7**, *226*, **227**; spareribs, *206*, **206-7**, *226*, 227, **228**, 228; stuffings, 364; tenderloin, 198, *206*, 206-7, 218, 227; variety meats, **229-35**. See also bacon *and* ham
pork, ground, **214**; in stuffed white cabbage, **276**; for stuffings, 364. *See also* meat, ground
pork, salt, **249**; **Baked beans with red wine, 324**
pork bones, 235
pork charcuterie, 241
pork fat, 96, *97*, 97; unrendered, *see* lard
pork stock, 43
porridge, 319, 320, 498
pot marigold, *25*, 25, 34, 268
pot-au-feu, 208
Potage Saint-Germain (split pea soup), **50**
potato breads, 361
potato flour, *343*, 497; flatbreads, 363
potato starch, **59**, 344, 400, 439, 512
potatoes, 38, 50, 96, 97, 216, 268, **294-7**, *295*, 494, 512; *au gratin*, 264, 295; barbecueing and

broiling, 264; fried, 262, 263, **296**, 510; French fries, 104, *296*, **296**, 505; Matchstick potatoes, *296*, **296**, 505; *gulettes*, 368; Peasant omelet, **91; Peruvian mashed potatoes, 297**; Potato baskets, nests, 297, 510; puréed, 266, 268, 292, **296**; *Pommes Dauphine*, 376; **Recipe, 105**, Straight-cut potatoes, *296*, **296**; Straw potatoes, *296*, **296**; stuffing, 265; in vegetable croquettes, 263; in vegetable molds, 267; **Vinaigrette salad, 268; Waffled potatoes**, *296*, **296**
pot de crème, 511, **511**
pots and pans, **499-500**, **510-11**
potted cheese, 486
potted fish and shellfish, 486; shrimps, 486; **Recipe, 487**
potted meats, 241, *243*, 486
Poule au pot, **182**
poulet au sang, 181
poultry, and game birds, **174-93**, 241, 253, 447, **495**, 497, 499, 513; braised, **181**, 183; broiling or barbecuing, **183**; cooked and leftover, 183; fried, sautéed, 104, **182**, **183**, 83, **185**; giblets and other trimmings, 175, **189**, 486; pies, 183, 374; plucking, **193**; poaching, **182**; pot-roast, **181**, 183; removing sinews, **190**; roast, **180**, **181**, 183, 494, 503, 511; seasoning, 14; smoked, **487**, 487; soups, 49, 50; spit-roast, **181**; steamed, 183; stew, **181**; stir-fried, **183**; stuffings, 179, 182, 364, 503. *See also* individual birds.
poultry livers, 183, 189; foie gras, **190**
poultry *mousselines*, 183
pound cake, **398; Recipe, 398; Trifle, 438**
poussin, 180, *184*
praline, **419**; Frozen praline soufflé, **445**; Praline butter cream, **405**; candies, 426; Praline ice cream, 439, **Recipe, 443**
prawns, 152, 153, *160*, **160-1; Blue brie and prawn parcels, 382**
pressure cookers, 509, 514
pretzels, 360
prickly pear, *303*, *472*, 472
Primavera sausage, *248*
Profiteroles with Melba sauce, 377
prunes, 364, 438, *473*, 473; **Prune mousse, 434**
puddings, bread, **364-5**; Apple charlotte, 432; Bread and butter pudding, **365; Summer pudding**, 463. *See also* steamed puddings.
puff pastry, 244, 370, 371, **378-81**, 385, 496; **Cod, shrimp and samphire pie, 140**

puff pastry, quick, **381**
puffball, **312-13**, *313*
pulled sugar, *415*
pummelo, 458, 459
pumpkin seed sprouts, 327
pumpkins, 264, *287*, **287-8**, 335, 361
pumpkinseed (fish), 145
purées, puréeing, fish, 122-4; fruit, 432, 434, 436, 438, 439, **450**, 495; **Bombe mixture**, 444; soups, 43, **50**, 51; tools, **506**; vegetables, 266-7, 268, 292, **296**, 495
puri, 362
purslane, *20*, 20

Q

quahog, *168*
quail, **174-83**, *174*, *179*, *191*, 191, 461, 495; **Barbecued quail with pepper marinade, 192**
quail eggs, *80*, 84
Quark, 76
quatre épices, 27
quenelles, 46, 127, 183, **146-7**; **Quenelles sauce Nantua, 147**
quiches, **94**; Alsatian onion quiche, **94**; Quiche Lorraine, **94**, 371
quick breads, **359-61**, 456, 463
quinces, 447, **452-4**, *453*, 490
quinoa, *321*, 321

R

rabbit, 198, 236, *239*, **239-40**, 247, 486; **Rabbit with prunes, 239**
radicchio, 269-71
radish, white, 262, *292*, 292-4
radishes, 283, *292*, **292-4**
Ragout of lamb, artichokes and fava beans, 326
rainbow trout, *143*, **143-4**
raised meat pies, **243-4**; **Raised veal and ham pie, 244**
raising agents, 343; in breads, 345-6, 359; in cakes, 343, 392, 393, 395, 401; in pastry, 370
raisins, *321*, 463, 473; **Mincemeat, 486**; raisin buns, 354; Raisin frosting, **410**; Whole wheat fruit and nut bread, **353**
rambutan, *472*, 472
rapeseed oil (colza), 96, 102
rascasse, black, 142; red, **142**, 142
raspberries, 38, *462*, **462-3**, 484, 493, 495; Frozen raspberry soufflé, **445**; Melba sauce, **66**; Raspberry butter cream, **405**; **Raspberry sorbet, 442**; *Vacherin*, **437**
ratatouille, 279
ravioli, 183, 328, *330*, 330, 333, *335*, 335, 495; **Shrimp ravioli with goat cheese, 336**; sweet, 338; tools, **506**
ray, *131*, **131**
Ray's bream, 141

red currants, 447, 450, *462*, 463, 490, 491, 493; **Black pepper, red currant and cream sauce, 58**; Cumberland sauce, **66**; Red currant jelly glaze, **385**
red drum, **137-8**
red mullet, 120, **121**, 126, *137*, **137-8**, 142
red peppers, hot, 28, 35, 279. *See also* chili oil
red snapper, 120, 126, *136*, 136; **Marinated red snapper, 137**; **Panaché of steamed fish with dill butter sauce, 130**
Red wine marinade, 41
Red wine, shallot and bone marrow sauce, 58
redbreast (fish), 145
redfish, **137-8**
rémoulade, see mayonnaise
rhubarb, 66, *455*, **455**, 495
ribs, 197-8, 200-7, 209, 487; **Rib roast braised in red wine, 209**
rice, 134, 314, 315, **317-18**, *318*, 451, 495, 498; **Currant and pistachio pilaf, 315**; hopping John, 322; **Indian creamed rice, 318**; **Mushroom brown rice pilaf, 315**; **Rice salad, 84**; **Seafood paella, 317**; in soups, 43, 45, 49, 50; for stuffings, 179, 364. *See also* wild rice
rice flour, 328, 344, 497
rice paper, 344
rice sticks, 328
Rich fruit cake, 399
ricotta, 74, 76, 334, 335, 403, 405, 410; in pasta desserts, 338; **Recipe, 77**; **Spinach and ricotta lasagne, 334**
rigani, 19
rillettes, *124*, 241, **243**, 486
rock cakes, 360, 494
Rock Cornish hen, **174-83**, *174*, 184, **487**
rock lobster, 153
rock salmon, 132
rock samphire (sea fennel), 283
rocket, *see* arugula
rockfish, 136, *142*, **142**
rockfish (striped bass), 138, 142
rockling, *139*, 139
roe, **131**, 134, 147, 488
rolled cakes, **396-7**
rolled grains, 314, 319, **321**, 321
rollmops, 126
rolls, *see* bread rolls
root celery, 260, 261, 267, 268, 292, 297, 361
root vegetables, and tubers **292-7**, 258, 260, 261, 262, 263, 264, 265, 268, **303**, 485; **Vinaigrette salad, 268**. *See also* carrots, etc
Roquefort, 73, 75, *78*, 78; **Toasted walnut and Roquefort salad, 102**
rosemary, 13, 14, *18*, **19**, 21; **Rosemary and lemon sorbet, 19**

rosemary vinegar, 40
roses, and rosehips, 21, 38; rose vinegars, 40; rose water, 36
rotolo di pasta, 335
roulades, 92-3
roux, **56**
royal icing, 385, 404, 405, *408*, **408**, 496, 507; **Recipe, 408**
royale garnish, for consommé, 47
rue, 20
rum, 38, 447, 449, 464; **Bananas Foster, 464**
rumtopf, **485**
runner (fish), **140-1**
Russian dressing, **63**
Russian salad (*Macédoine* of cooked vegetables, 268
rutabaga, *292*, 292-4
rye, *321*, **321**, 321; sprouts, 327
rye flour, 328, 342, 343-4, 363, 400; rye breads, 321, 344, 345, **353**, 363

S

sabayon, 52, 53, **67**
safety, *see* dangers in cooking
safflower, 25; oil, 96, 102, 103, 104, 106
saffron crocus, *25*, 25
saffron milk-cap, *313*, 313
sage, 13, *18*, **19**, 21; Butter and sage sauce, **337**; Sage bread, **363**; Sage and onion stuffing, **364**
sago, as thickener, 344
sailfish, **133-4**
saithe, **139**
salad burnet, *16*, **17**
salad cream, **64**
salad dressings, thickened, **64**. *See also* mayonnaise
salad greens, **269-71**
salade Niçoise, 125
salads, 74, 76, 254, **268**, **271**, 303, **327**, **331**; **Avocado and grapefruit salad with smoked salmon, 470**; fish and shellfish, 120, **125**, 153; **Lobster salad green goddess, 157**; fruit, **451**; **Hot salad of chicken livers, 271**; *Macédoine* of cooked vegetables (Russian salad), 268; Rice salad for **Eggs mimosa with curry mayonnaise, 84**; **Salad of mixed herbs, 20**; **Toasted walnut and Roquefort salad, 102**
salami sausages, 246, 247
salciccie, 247
salmon, 110, 111, **114**, **116**, **117**, **118**, 119, 120, **122**, 122, 126, 132, 134, *143*, **143-4**, 496; in aspic, 119, 253; *coulibiac*, 132, 354; *gravad lax*, 488; *paupiettes*, 124; **Poached salmon in aspic, 144**; raw dishes, 125; raw fish salad, **125**; rilletes and terrines, 124; salted, 126, **488**

salmon, smoked, 126, 376, 451, 487; **Avocado and grapefruit salad with smoked salmon, 470**; Smoked salmon omelet, **91**
salmon, rock (dogfish), 132
salmon roe (caviar), 131, 134
salmon trout, **113**, **143-4**
salmonella, 80, 484
salsify, 261, **292-4**
salt, 32, **32**, 42, **261**, 345, 370, 392, 501, 512; and eggs, 81, 435; for preserving, 183, 484, 487, **488**, 489, 494, 495. *See also* seasoning
sambals, 35
samosas, 107, 324
samphire, *283*, 283; **Cod, shrimp and samphire pie, 140**
sand sole, 127
sand-dab, 110, 127
sand-eel, 150
sapodilla, *472*, 472
sapote, mamey, *472*; white, 472
sardines, 110, 111, **147-9**, *148*
sashimi, 125, 133, **134**
satsumas, *458*, 459
sauces, **52-67**, 71, 442, **496**, 499; equipment, 501, 503, 510; with fish, **33**, 119, 120, 139; *Aglio e olio*, **337**; **Aïoli**, **63**; Alfredo sauce, **337**; Anchovy sauces, **337**; Apple sauce, **66**; Apricot jam sauce, **66**; Asian peanut sauce, **66**; *Avgolemono*, **55**; barbecue sauce (table sauce), **35**; barbecue sauces, **65**; Béarnaise sauce, **60-1**, Recipe, **61**; béchamel, 52, **54**, 56, 264, 265, **Recipes, 54**; *Beurre blanc*, 62; *Beurre blanc aux herbes*, 62; *Beurre fondu*, 62; *Beurre rouge*, 62; **Bitter orange sauce, 58**; **Black pepper, red currant and cream sauce, 58**; Boiled dressing, **64**; bread-thickened sauces, **64**; **Brown butter hollandaise, 61**; brown sauce (table sauce), 35; brown sauces, 52, 53, **57-8**, Basic brown sauce, **58**, Recipe, 58, (Chaudfroid) sauce, **56**; *Bumbu satay*, **66**; *Burro e salvia*, **337**; Butter and sage sauce, **337**; butter sauce, white, 62; butter sauces, 52, 53, **53**; butter sauces, emulsified, **60-3**, 496; Butterscotch sauce, **67**; **Caramel sauce, 67, 418**; *Carbonara*, **337**; Caribbean hot pepper sauce, **29**; **Chantilly hollandaise, 60-1**; Chaudfroid sauce, **56**; Cheese sauce, 74, 264, 376, **Recipe, 54**; chocolate sauces, **425**, **Chocolate fudge sauce, 425**, Chocolate sauce, **425**; coating sauces, 52, **53**; Cranberry sauce, **66**; Crayfish sauce, **147**, **Recipe, 55**; **Cream sauce, 54**; Cumberland sauce,

66; **Curry sauce**, 54; Demi-glace sauce, 52, **Recipe**, 58; **Devil sauce**, 58; Egg and anchovy sauce, 337; **Egg and bacon sauce**, 337; **Egg and lemon sauce**, 55; emulsified butter sauces, 60-3, 496; English bread sauce, **64**; English hard sauce, **67**; *Espagnole* **sauce**, 57; French tomato sauce, 65; Fresh tomato *coulis*, 65; fruit sauces, 66, **450**; Fruit vinaigrette, **64**; Garlic mayonnaise, **63**; glazes, 57; Gorgonzola sauce, **337**; gravy, **57**; Green goddess dressing, **63**; Green mayonnaise, **63**; Herb butter sauce, **62**; Herb vinaigrette, **64**; Hollandaise, **60-1**, 496, **Recipe**, **60-1**; Horseradish sauce, **29**; hot (chili) sauces, 35, **63**; Italian green sauce, **64**; Italian meat sauce, 337, **338**; Italian tomato sauce, **65**; Italian tomato sauce, 65; jam sauces, **66**; ketchup, **35**; **Lemon and parsley sauce**, 55; Louis dressing, 63; **Madeira sauce**, 58; meat coulis, **57**; Melba sauce, **66**; Meurette, **56**; **Mock hollandaise**, **61**; mushroom ketchup, 35; **Mushroom sauces**, **54, 55**; **Mushroom, white wine and tomato sauce**, 58; Mustard barbecue sauce, **65**; **Mustard hollandaise**, **61**; **Mustard, vinegar and onion sauce**, 58; nut sauces, **66**; Olive oil and garlic sauce, **337**; **Onion sauce**, **54**; Orange custard, **67**; Orange hollandaise, 298; **Recipe**, 60; Oyster sauce, 33, **Recipe**, **54**; pasta sauces, 337-8; *Pesto* (pine nut, garlic and basil sauce), **17**; piquant sauces, **29**; Plum sauce, **66**; Primavera sauce, **337**; *Ragù Bolognese*, 337, **338**; Red butter sauce, **62**; Red chili pepper sauce, **63**; Red clam sauce, **338**; **Red wine, shallot and bone marrow sauce**, 58; rich white sauces, 53; Romesco sauce, **29**; rouille, **63**; Russian dressing, 63; Sabayon, 52, 53, **67**; Salad cream, **64**; salad dressings, thickened, **64**; *Salsa cruda*, 65; *Salsa Napoletana*, 65; *Salsa rossa e vongole*, **338**; *Salsa sugo fresco di pomodoro*, 65; *Salsa verde*, **64**; **Sauce allemande**, 55; *Sauce aurore* (béchamel), **54**; *Sauce aurore* (velouté), **55**; *Sauce bâtarde*, **61**; *Sauce bigarrade*, **58**; *Sauce bordelaise*, 58; *Sauce bretonne*, 58; *Sauce cardinale*, 55; *Sauce charcutière*, **58**; *Sauce chasseur*, 58; *Sauce diable*, **58**; *Sauce Escoffier*, 33, **54**; *Sauce gribiche*, **63**; *Sauce*

indienne, 54; *Sauce maltaise*, 298, **Recipe**, 60; *Sauce mousseline*, **60-1**; *Sauce moutarde*, **61**; *Sauce noisette*, 61; *Sauce Périgueux*, 58; *Sauce poivrade*, **58**; *Sauce poulette*, **55**; *Sauce ravigote*, 64; *Sauce rémoulade*, 63; *Sauce Robert*, **58**; *Sauce rouille*, **63**; *Sauce smitane*, 71; *Sauce Soubise*, **54**; *Sauce suprême*, **55**; Scandinavian mustard sauce, **63**; **Seafood sauce**, **337**; Softened butter sauce, 62; Soy barbecue sauce, 65; *Sugo di vongole bianco*, **338**; Tabasco, 28, 35; table sauces, 35; Tartare sauce, **63**; Thousand Island dressing, 63; **Tomato barbecue sauce**, 65; **Tomato béarnaise**, **61**; **Tomato brown sauce**, 58; **Tomato chaudfroid sauce**, 56; tomato ketchup, 35; tomato sauce, 65; **Tomato sauce** (béchamel), **54**; **Tomato sauce** (velouté), **55**; Tomato sauce, Mexican, 65; **Truffle sauce**, 58; Turkish tarator sauce, 66; *Tutto mare*, **337**; veloutés, 52, 53, **55**, **56**, **Recipe**, 55; Vinaigrette dressing, **64**, 68, **Recipe**, 64; **Vinegar and pickle sauce**, 58; White butter sauce, 52, 62, **Recipe**, 62; **White chaudfroid sauce**, 56; White clam sauce, **338**; white sauce, 53, **54**; **55**; roux, 56; White wine butter sauce, **62**; Worcestershire sauce, 35. *See also* custards, mayonnaise sauger, 145
sauerkraut, 274, *488*
Sausage bread (*Focaccia alla salsiccia*), 363
Sausage and chestnut stuffing, **364**
sausages, 183, 241, *246-8*, **246-8**, 449, 495; casings, 235, **248**; **Spanish spiced sausages**, 248
sautéed, and shallow-fried foods, **106**, 200-7, 497, 510; **Sautéed sweetbreads with vegetables**, 232
savarin, 354
saveloy, 246
savory, 14, *18*, **18**, 21
Savory Italian flatbread (focaccia), 363
savory, summer, 12, *18*, **18**
scabbardfish, 150
scad, **140-1**
scales, kitchen, *502*, **502**
scallions, 14, 262, 268, 283, *289*, **289-90**, 504
scallops, 48, *163*, 164, 165, *167*, **167-8**; **Shrimp and scallop brochettes**, 161
scampi, 152, 153, *160*, **160-1**
schmaltz (chicken fat), 96, 97, 189

scones, 359, 369; **Currant scones**, 360
scorpion fish, *142*, **142**
scorzonera, *293*, 293-4
sea anemones, 173
sea bass, 124, 125, 134, **137-8**
sea bream, 134, **140-1**, *141*
sea cucumber, 173
sea fennel, 283
sea trout (Atlantic spotted, speckled or gray trout), **137-8**
sea trout (salmon trout), 113, *143*, **143-4**; (species of croaker), 143
sea urchins, 173
sea vegetables, **283**, 431
Seafood crêpes, **367**
Seafood paella, **317**
seafood, *see* fish, shellfish
seakale, **298-9**; beet, **298-9**
seasoning, 12, 42, 51, 52, 241, 364, 501. *See also* salt, pepper
seaweed, 283, 431
seed sprouts, **327**
seeds, **22, 24**, 319, **496**
Semifreddo, **444**
Semifreddo al cioccolato, **445**
semolina, 36, 319, 364
semolina flour, 328, *343*, 343
serviceberry, 462
sesame oil, 96, 103, 262, 264
sesame seeds, 24, **24, 321**, 496
seviche, 125
shad, 110, **147-9**, *148*, 496
shad roe, 131, 147
shaddock, *458*, 459
shagbark nut, 478
shaggy mane (mushroom), *311*, **311**
shallots, 14, *15*, **15**, 44, 268, **289-91**, 364; **Red wine, shallot and bone marrow sauce**, 58
shank bones, **235**
shark, 110, 125, *132*, **132**
sheep cheeses, 75
sheep meat, 194, 246. *See also* lamb, mutton
sheep's milk, 69, 71, 98
sheepshead (bream), 141
sheepshead, freshwater, 145
sheepshead (wrasse), 142
shellbark nut, 478
shellfish, 121, **125**, 152-73, 246, 487, **496**, 499, 505; with pasta, 337, 337, 338, potted, 486; soups, 48-9. *See also* individual species
shellfish butter, **155**
sherbets, 441
sherry, 38, 39, 501; **Sherry syllabub**, 438
shiitake, 306, *308*, **308**; **Stuffed shiitake**, 309
shish kebab, 204
shoots and stalks (asparagus, etc), *298-9*, **298-302**
shortening, **100**, 345, 392
shoulder ham (picnic ham), 226, 250
shoyu, 32

shrimps, 105, 121, 125, 126, 134, 152, 153, *160*, **160-1**, 451, 496; **Cod, shrimp and samphire pie**, 140; **Pompano en papillote**, 121; potted, 486, **Recipe**, 487; **Seafood paella**, 317; Seafood sauce for spaghetti, 337; **Shrimp and scallop brochettes**, 161; Shrimp and avocado omelet, 91; **Shrimp bisque**, 49; **Shrimp in coconut sauce**, 480; **Shrimp ravioli with goat cheese**, 336; Shrimp tempura, **105**; **Vietnamese shrimp kebabs**, 33
shrimps, mantis, **162**
shrub, 441
Sichuan pepper, 27, 30, *30*
silk snapper, 136
silver perch, **137-8**
silverside, 212, 216
sirloin, 200-7, **212**; broiling and barbecueing, **197-8**
skate, **131**
skipjack, 133, 148
skipper, 150
Skordalia (Garlic sauce), **14**
sloe plums, 456
smelts, 119, **147-9**, 150, 496
"smoking point" of fats and oils, 104
smoking to preserve foods, 484, **487**. *See also* specific foods
snail butter, **165**
snails, 163, **164-5**, *165*, 512; eggs, 164
snapper, *136*, **136-7**. *See also* red snapper
snapper (yellowtail), 136
snips, **174-83**, 174
Snow eggs (*Oeufs à la neige*), 436
snow peas (*mangetout*), *284*, 284-6, 262
soba (buckwheat noodles), 328
soda breads, 72; Irish, 359; **Recipe**, 360
soffrito, 263
sole, 110, **114**, 115, 115, **116**, 117, 120, 122, *127*, **127-8**, 150; **Escalopes of monkfish with lime and ginger**, 135; **Fillets of sole with mushrooms and tomatoes**, 128; *sole à la Colbert*, 127; *sole bonne femme*, 127; *sole meunière*, 106, 127; *sole Véronique*, 127; sole Walewska, 127
somen (wheat noodles), 328
sorbetières, 509
sorbets, 414, **439-43**, 441, 444, 450, 474; common problems, **440**; **Raspberry sorbet**, 442; **Rosemary and lemon sorbet**, 19
sorghum, 320, 327, 411, 413
sorrel, 21, 272, *272-3*
soufflé omelets, 89, 91; Jam soufflé omelet, **91**; Soufflé omelet normande, **91**
soufflé potatoes, 296

soufflés, 80, 81, **92-3**, 497, 508, 511; **Fish soufflé, 93**; **Smoked haddock soufflé, 93**; dessert, 92, 93, 364, **434-5**, **439**, **444-5**; **Coffee soufflé pudding, 365**; **Cold coconut soufflé, 434**; **Fresh orange soufflé, 460**
soups, and stocks, 42-51, 71, 153, 322, **496**, 498, 499, 512; accompaniments, 43; *Aigo saou*, 48; **Black bean soup, 50**; bread-thickened, **47**; broth-based, **45**; **Chilled spinach and avocado soup, 51**;cold, 42, 43, 47, **51**; **Consommé, 46**; cream, 43, 50, **51**, 51; enrichments, **50**; fish and shellfish, **48-9**; **French onion soup, 47**; fruit soups, **450**, **Hungarian cherry soup, 451**; Lentil soup, **50**; *Minestrone di verdura*, 45; puréed, 43, **50**, 51; **Shrimp bisque, 49**; Split pea soup, **50**; White bean soup, **50**
sour cream, 68, 70, **71-2**, 345, 451, 495; half-and-half, 71; for pastry and cakes, 370, 392, 401; **German cheesecake, 403**; Sour cream pastry dough, 245, **373**
Sour gherkins in vinegar, 490
sourdough bread, **353**
soybeans, 68, 322, **322**, 323; Soy barbecue sauce, **65**; soy cheese, 322; soy flour, 344; soy oil, 96, 102; soy sauce, **32**; sprouts, 327
spaghetti, 328, *329*, 329, 333, 337, 338. *See also* pasta
spaghetti squash, 287, **287-8**
Spanish omelet, **91**
Spanish spiced sausages (*chorizo*), 247; **Recipe, 248**; **Seafood paella, 317**
spareribs, *see* pork, spareribs
spatchcocking a bird, **180**
spätzle, (batter dumplings), 43, 338, 511; **Recipe, 339**
spearfish (marlin), **133-4**
spearmint, *16*, 17, 36
Speculaas (Flemish spiced cookies), **27**
Spiced lentil purée, 325
Spiced waffles, 368
spices, **12**, 21, **23-31**, *24*, *25*, 103, 266, 364, 506; fragrant, *26*, 26-7; hot, *28*, 28; in breads, etc, 360, 361, 370, 401; for pickling, 27, 489; spice mixtures, 27, **27**
spinach, 25, 262, 263, 264, 266, 267, 268, *272*, **272-4**, 335, 495; **Chilled spinach and avocado soup, 51**; **Eggplant, spinach and roasted pepper stuffing, 364**; with eggs, 83, Eggs Sardou, 85; **Spinach and feta pie, 94**; **Spinach and ricotta lasagne, 334**; **Spinach timbales, 274**; stuffed and rolled, **276**
spirits, **38-9**, 441
spit roasting, 199, 208

sponge (bread making), 346
sponge cakes, 410, **444**; whisked, 393, **394-7**, 400
spot (a drum fish), **137-8**
sprats, **147-9**, **150**
spray oils, 102
spring greens, 272, 273
spring ham (picnic ham), 206-7, 226, 250
spring rolls, egg rolls and wontons, 107, 328, 333, 335, 382
sprouts (of seed, grain, legumes), 319, **327**
sprue asparagus, *298*, **298-9**
Spumoni, **444**
spun sugar, **416**, 503
squab, 179, 191
squash flowers, *268*, 268
squashes, 258, 262, 264, 265, *287*, **287-8**, 335, 495
squid, 25, 48, 134, **170-3**, *171*, **Seafood paella, 317**; **Stuffed squid in its ink, 173**
stalks and shoots, *298-9*, **298-302**
star anise, *24*, 24, 27
star fruit, *472*, 472
steak and kidney pie, 374
steaks, 400-7, **486**; broiling and barbecueing, **197-8**, **209**, 487; presenting, 208; storing, 194; Steak with tomato, fennel and Marsala, **209**; porterhouse, 194, 197-8, 212; T-bone, 197-8, 212
steamed puddings, **364-5**, 498; Steamed date pudding, **365**; **Steamed ginger pudding, 365**
steelhead (rainbow trout), **143-4**
stews, *see* meat, stewed
sticky buns, 354, **356**
Stilton, 73, 75, 78; **Veal escalopes with Stilton, 78**
stinging nettle, **303**
stockfish, 126
stocks, **42-51**, **496**, 498, 503, 510; stock cubes, 42
stollen, 410
stomach parts, 229, 235, 246, 248; tripe, 45, 229, *235*, **235**, 247, 252
stone fruits, *456-7*, **456-7**. *See also* apricots etc
strawberries, 38, 447, 449, 451, *462*, **462-3**, 474, 485, 490, 495; Bombe Alhambra, **445**; Strawberry ice cream, **443**; Strawberry soup, **451**; Strawberry syllabub, **458**; **Vacherin, 437**
Streuselkuchen, **356**
striped bass, *138*, 138, 142
strudel pastries, **382-3**, 447; **Recipes, 383**
stuffing, breadcrumbs in, 354; **Recipes, 264**; for meat, **199**; for pâtés and terrines, **241**; for poultry, **179**; for vegetables, 214, **265**
sturgeon, 126, **132**; roe, **131**

sucrose, 411
suet, 96, *97*, 97, 364
sugar, 105, 263, 345, 370, **411-19**, *412*, 439, 447, 484; in cakes, 392, 393, 395; dipping fork, 503; frosted and sugared fruits, 416, 449, **474**; glazes, 263, 385; jams, jellies and marmalades, 490
sugar, confectioners', **412**, 440
sugar, preserving, *412*, 412, 490
sugar, spun, **416**, 503
sugar snap peas, 284-6
sugar substitutes, **413**, 439
sugar syrup, 385, 411, **414-16**, 436, **448-9**, 485, 503; candies, **426**; commercial, **413**; for fruits, **448-9**, **451**, 495; for sorbets, 441, **442**
summer pudding, 364; **Recipe, 463**
summer savory, 12, *18*, **18**
sunchoke, *see* Jerusalem artichoke
sunfish, **140-1**, **145**; North American, 145
sunflower oil, 96, 97, *102*, 102, 103, 104
sushi, 125, 133, **134**
sweet cicely, 22, *24*, 24
sweet clove, 20
sweet corn, 264, **284-6**, *285*, 319
sweet cumin (anise), *24*, 24
sweet licorice root, *24*, 24
sweet potatoes, 263, 266, 267, 268, *295*, **295**; **Peruvian mashed potatoes, 297**
sweet woodruff, *20*, 20
sweetbreads, 229, 230, *232*, **232-3**, 271, 512; **Sautéed sweetbreads with vegetables, 232**
sweeteners (incl. artificial), **413**, 439. *See also* sugar.
Swiss chard, *276*, *298*, **298-9**
Swiss meringue, **435-6**
swordfish, 110, **133-4**
syllabub, 438; **Sherry syllabub, 438**

T

tabasco, *28*, 35
tabbouleh, 319
tacos, 363
taffy, 415, 426
tagine, 320
tagliatelle, *330*, 334. *See also* pasta
tamarillo, *472*, 472, 474
tamarind, 472
tangelo, 458, 459
tangerines, *458*, 459; Tangerine sorbet, **442**; Bombe Monselet, **445**
Tapenade, **34**, 34
tapioca, 303, 344
taramasalata, 131
taro, *303*, **303**
tarragon, 14, *16*, **16**, 496
Tarte tatin, **455**
tartlets, **374**
tarts, **94**, **371**, **375**, 508

tea eggs, 86
tea as flavoring, **37**
teas, herbal, **21**
tempeh, 322
tempura, 119; Shrimp tempura, **105**
tenderloin, *see* beef, pork
terrines, 122, **124**, 183, 208, **241-2**, 420; **Cold vegetable terrine, 267**; **Country terrine, 241**; equipment for, 511
thermometers, *503*, **503**; for deep-frying, 104; in microwave ovens, 501; for preserving, 490; for roasting meat, 199; for sugar syrup, 414-5; for tempering chocolate, 422; for yogurt, 72
thickeners, **59**, 343, 344, 354, 439, 501
thyme, 12, 13, 14, *18*, **18**, 21
tilefish, **137-8**, *138*
timbales, **Spinach timbales, 274**
toast, **352**
toast, French (*pain perdu*), 364
Toasted walnut and Roquefort salad, 102
toffee, 426
tofu, 322
tomatillo, *303*, **303**
tomatoes, 258, 260, 262, 263, 264, 265, 266, 267, 268, 271, **278-81**, *280*, 327, 361; **Apple and tomato chutney, 489**; Creole omelet, **91**; dried, **485-6**; green (under-ripe), 278, *280*; Monterey omelet, **91**; **Mushroom, white wine and tomato sauce, 58**; preserving, **485-6**; sauces, **65**, 337, 338, 496; table sauce (ketchup), **35**, **Tomato barbecue sauce, 65**; **Tomato béarnaise, 61**; Tomato brown sauce, **58**; **Tomato chaudfroid sauce, 56**; Tomato mayonnaise, **63**; **Tomato sauce (*Sauce aurore*) (béchamel), 54**, **Tomato sauce (*Sauce aurore*) (velouté), 55**; **Seafood paella, 317**; in stock, 43, 44
tomatoes, ground (Mexican green tomatoes), **303**
tomatoes, husk (ground cherry), 303
tongue, 229, 230, *234*, **234**, 254, 511
Torbay sole, 110, 127
tortillas, 183, *363*, 363
tostadas, 363
tournedos (filet mignon steak), *210*, 210, 219, 227
tree onions, **289-90**
tree tomato (tamarillo), *472*, 472, 474
Treviso chicory, 269-71
trichinosis, 226, 246
Trifle, 438
tripe, 45, 229, *235*, **235**, 247, 252
triticale, 321; flour, 344
trotters, pigs', 226, 229, *229*, 247, 254

trout, 110, 119, 120, 124, 126, *143*, **143-4**, 487
trout, salmon (sea trout, brown trout), **113**, *143*, **143-4**
trout, sea (Atlantic spotted, speckled or gray trout), **137-8**
trout, sea (species of croaker), 143
Truffles, Chocolate (candies), **429**
truffles (mushrooms), *313*, **313**, 495, 514; **Truffle sauce (sauce Périgueux)**, 58
tubers (vegetables), **292-7**, 303, 485. *See also* individual species
tulipes (cookies), 388
tuna, 110, 125, *133*, **133-5**, 134, 487, 496; **Baked tuna with fennel and mushrooms, 134**; roe, 131; skipjack, 133, 148
turbot, 110, **115**, **116**, 120, *129*, **129-30**; **Panaché of steamed fish with dill butter sauce, 130**
turkey, 174-83, 179, *186*, **186-7**, 190, 241, 247, 271, 364, 462-3, 466; *galantines*, 255; **Recipe, 255**; **Turkey escalopes with julienne of vegetables, 187**
turkey, wild, 191
Turkish delight, 426
turmeric, *25*, 25, 27
turnip greens, 272, **272-3**
turnips, 260, 261, 263, 265, 266, 267, 268, *292*, **Macédoine of cooked vegetables, 268**

U

udder as meat, 229
udon (wheat noodles), 328
ugli fruit, *458*, 459
univalves, *163*, 163
urd, 324

V

Vacherin, **437**
vanilla, 36, *37*, 370, 438, 439, 501; **Vanilla custard, 67**; **Snow eggs (Oeufs à la neige), 436**; **Trifle, 438**; **Vanilla ice cream, 443**
variety meats, 246-8. *See also* sausages
veal, 41, 194, 195, **202-3**, **214-18**, 495; breast, *202*, **202-3**, 214, **217**, **Braised stuffed veal breast, 215**; chops, **202-3**, *214*, **215**; cutlets, broiling and barbecuing, 197-8; US and French cuts, 202-3; cooking methods for veal cuts, 202; nutritive values, 203; osso buco, **202**; escalopes, 194, 198, *202*, **202-3**, **218**; **Veal escalopes with Stilton, 78**; eye round, **202-3**, 216; flank, *202*, **202-3**, *214*, **217**; leg, *214*, **217**; loin, *202*, **202-3**, *214*, 216; neck, *202*, **202-3**, *214*, 216, best end (center rib), 216; scrag end, 216; ribs, *202*, **202-3**, *214*, **218**; roast, crown roast, 216; roasting times, 199; rump (rump sirloin, fillet), *202*, **202-3**, *214*, **216**; saddle, 216; sausages, 246, 247; shank, *202*, **202-3**, *214*, **218**; shoulder, *202*, **202-3**, *214*, **215**, **Raised veal and ham pie, 244**; shoulder chops, *214*, **215**; stocks, 42, *43*, 214, **235**, **White veal stock, 44**; stuffings, 179, 364; tenderloin, 216, medallions, *202*, 216; top round, *202*, **202-3**, 216; variety meats, 202-3, **229-35**
veal, ground, **214**; **Country terrine, 241**; for stuffed pasta, 335. *See also* meat, ground
veal bones, **235**
veal charcuterie, 241
vegetable marrow, 265, 287, **287**
vegetables, 92, *106*, 181, **258-313**, **361**, 371, 374, **403**, 497-8, 499, 512; in aspic, 253, 254; "baby" vegetables, 258; baked, **264**; baked *au gratin*, **264**, 295; blanched, 260, 268, 512; boiled, **261**, 495; braised, **263**; broiled, **264**; cutting, **258-60**, 504-5, as decorations, **283**; with mandoline, **296**, roll-cut, 260, 262, turning, **260**; deep-fried, 104, 105, 260, 262, **263**; discoloration, **261**, 263, 512; exotic, *303*, **303**, freezing, **494-5**; glazed, **263**; grown hydroponically, 258; julienne strips, **259**, 283, **307**; left-over, 262; mixed, 262, **263**, 263; molds, **267**; mousse, 266, **267**; pan-fried, **262**; parboiled, **260**; peeling, 258, 504, 505; presentation, **268**; preserved, 484, 485; puréed, **266-7**, 268, 292, 296, 495; refreshed, **261**; salads, **268**, salt to draw out bitter juices, **261**; sautéed, **262**; soups, 42, 49, **Minestrone di verdura, 45**; steamed, **261**; stir-fried, **262**, Recipe, **262**; stock, 42, **44**; stuffing, 265, 364; sweating, **262**; terrines, 241, **267**
veloutés, 52, 53, **55**, **56**; **Recipe, 55**
venison, **236-8**, 247, 374, 452; cured (*biltong*), 252; sausage, 247; **Game paté en croûte, 245**; **Venison with wild mushrooms (haunch or saddle), 237**
vermicelli, 328, *329*, 338
Vienna bread, **356**
Vietnamese shrimp kebabs, 33
vinaigrette dressing, *64*, 68; **Recipe, 64**
Vinaigrette salad, 268
vine leaves, **265**
vinegar, *40*, **40**, 343, 484, 489; **Vinegar and pickle sauce, 58**
vodka, **38**
vol-au-vents, 380

W

Wafer cookies, 388
Waffled potatoes, *296*, **296**
waffles, 368, 511; **Recipe, 369**; **Spiced waffles, 368**
wahoo, 148
walnut oil, 96, 97, 103, 104, 271, 478
walnuts, 271, 439, 476, 477, *478*, **478**; breads, etc, 361, 410; **Banana nut bread, 361**; **Chocolate walnut cake, 400**; **Coffee walnut spice cake, 37**; **Date nut bread, 361**; flour, 344; **Jewish honey cake, 413**; **Strudel, 383**; **Walnut bread, 363**; **Whole wheat fruit and nut bread, 353**; **Toasted walnut and Roquefort salad, 102**; Turkish tarator sauce, **66**
wapiti, 236, 238
wasabi, 31
water, 370, 401, 489
water, acidulated, 261, 512
water bath, 498, 510
water buffalo, meat, 238; milk, etc, 69, **75**, 77, 98
water chestnuts, *303*, **303**, 481, 497
water ices, *see* sorbets
watercress, **269**, **270**
watermelons, 464, **464**, 474; **Watermelon pickle, 490**
waterzooi, 45
wax bean, *284*, 284
weakfish, 134, **137-8**, *138*
wedding cakes, 410
weever (fish), 142
weisswurst, 247
wheat, *319*, **319-20**, bran, 319, *342*, 343; granola, **321**; flour, 342, **342-3**; germ, 319, 320, *342*, 342, 343; sprouts, 327
whelks, *163*, 163, **164**
whipped frostings, 405, **410**
whiskey, 38
white butter cream **405**
white (or Dutch) cabbage, **274-5**, *275*
white horehound, 20, *20*
White mountain frosting, **410**
white radish, 262, *292*, **292-4**
white sapote, *472*
white sauces, 52, 53; preventing skin, **54**; roux, **56**. *See also* béchamel and velouté
white stew, 197
white stock, 43; **White veal stock, 44**
white sucker, 145
whitebait, 119, **150**, 150
whitefish, 125, **145-6**, 487
whiting, 110, 111, **112**, 122, **123**, *139*, 139; **Panaché of steamed fish with dill butter sauce, 130**
whole wheat bread, **353**; flatbreads, 363; Whole wheat fruit and nut bread, **353**
whole wheat flour (wholemeal), 342, 343
whole wheat pancakes, **369**
whole wheat pasta flour, 328
whortleberry, 462
wiener, 246
wild boar, 236, **238**. *See also* venison
wild rice, *316*, **316**; **Wild rice pilaf, 316**
wine, **38-9**, 439, 447, 449, 487, 493, 501; **Mushroom, white wine and tomato sauce, 58**; **Red wine marinade, 41**; **Red wine, shallot and bone marrow sauce, 58**; sorbets, 441, 442; **White wine butter sauce, 62**
winged bean, 284-6
winkles, *163*, 163, **164**
winter flounder, **127-8**
winter melon, **288**
witch flounder, 127
woks, 503, 510
wontons, egg rolls and spring rolls, 107, 328, 333, 335, 382
wood blewit (mushroom), *312*, **312**
woodcock, **174-83**, 174, *191*, 191
Worcestershire sauce, **35**
wrapped foods, edible seaweeds, 283. *See also* paper-wrapped cooking
wrappers for cooking, **506**
wrasse, 142

Y

yak milk butter, 98
yam bean, 292, 293
yams, *295*, **295**
yeast, **346**. *See also* bread
yeast extracts, **33**
yellowtail, 134
yellowtail (jack), **140-1**
yellowtail (snapper), 136
yellowtail (sole), 127
yobe, 321
yogurt, 41, 70, **71-2**, 403, 439, 451, 495, 503; **Broiled chicken in yogurt, 72**
Yorkshire pudding, 368; **Recipe, 368**
youngberries, 462
yuca root, *303*, 303, 343, 344
yucca plant, 303
yule log cakes, 396, 410

Z

Zabaglione, 438
zampone, 247, *247*
zander, 145
zatar, 18
zesters, *505*, 505
ziti, *329*, 334, 338
zucchini, 260, 262, 263, *268*, **287-8**, 361
zucchini flowers, *268*, 268, 287
Zucotto, **444**

Bibliography

Several hundred books have been used for researching this book, most of them originally published in France, the USA or UK. Current major sources on the cooking and ingredients of these countries include books by James Beard, Simone Beck, Julia Child, Craig Claiborne, Elizabeth David, Alan Davidson, Jane Grigson, Rosemary Hume, Prue Leith, Raymond Oliver, Richard Olney, Jacques Pepin, Waverly Root and Tom Stobart. Classical reference books include those by Auguste Escoffier, Fannie Farmer, Prosper Montagné, and Henri-Paul Pellaprat as well as works like *Larousse Gastronomique* and *The Joy of Cooking*. The La Varenne recipe archives and books by Anne Willan have also been an important source, as well as multi-volume series such as *Foods of the World* and *The Good Cook* (Time-Life Books), and *Woman's Day Encyclopedia*. Included below are some additional titles on these subjects as well as a selection of books on cuisines other than American, British or French.

INGREDIENTS AND TECHNIQUES

ANDROUET, Pierre. *French Cheese*. New York: Harper's Magazine Press, 1973.

ASQUITH, Pamela. *Truffles and Other Chocolate Confections*. New York: Holt, Rinehart & Winston, 1984.

ATLAS, Nava. *The Wholefood Catalog*. New York: Ballantine Books, 1988.

BAILEY, Janet. *Keeping Food Fresh*. New York: Doubleday, 1985.

CLAYTON, Bernard Jr. *The Breads of France and How to Bake Them in Your Own Kitchen*. New York: Macmillan, 1985.

DELPLANQUE, A & CLOTEAUX, S. *Les Bases de la Charcuterie*. Paris: J. Lanore, 1982.

DOWELL, Phillip & BAILEY, Adrian. *The Book of Ingredients*. London: Dorling Kindersley, 1980.

FLETCHER, Janet. *Grain Gastronomy*. California: Aris Books, 1988.

FRIEDMAN, Sara Ann. *Celebrating the Wild Mushroom*. New York: Dodd, Mead & Co., 1986.

HANNEMAN, H. J. *Patisserie*. London: L. J. Hanneman, 1971.

HARRISON, S. G, MASEFIELD G. B. & WALLIS, Michael. *The Oxford Book of Food Plants*. London: Peerage Books, 1980.

HEALY, Bruce & BUGAT, Paul. *Mastering the Art of French Pastry*. New York: Barron's, 1984.

HEATH, Ambrose. *The Wine and Food Society's Guide to Meat*. London: The Wine and Food Society, 1968.

HUPPING, Carol. *Stocking Up*. Pennsylvania: Rodale Press, 1986.

JONES, Evan. *The Book of Cheese*. New York: Alfred A. Knopf, 1980.

KAFKA, Barbara. *Microwave Gourmet*. New York: William Morrow, 1987.

KOWALCHICK, Claire & HYLTON, William H., (Eds.). *Rodale's Illustrated Encyclopedia of Herbs*. Pennsylvania: Rodale Press, 1987.

LEVY, Faye. *Chocolate Sensations*. Arizona: HP Books, 1986.

LOBEL, Evan & LEON, Stanley. *All About Meat*. New York: Harcourt Brace Jovanovich, 1975.

McCLANE, A. J. *The Encyclopedia of Fish Cookery*. New York: Holt, Rinehart & Winston, 1977.

McGEE, Harold. *On Food and Cooking: The Science and Lore of the Kitchen*. New York: Charles Scribner's Sons, 1984.

MORASH, Marian. *The Victory Garden Cookbook*. New York: Alfred A. Knopf, 1982.

OWEN, Millie. *A Cook's Guide to Growing Herbs, Greens, and Aromatics*. New York: Alfred A. Knopf, 1978.

OECD. *Multilingual Dictionary of Fish and Fish Products*. Farnham, Surrey: Fishing News Books, 1977.

PAULI, Eugen. *Classical Cooking the Modern Way*. Boston: CBI Publishing, 1979.

PECK, Paula. *The Art of Fine Baking*. New York: Simon & Schuster, 1961.

PLAGEMANN, Catherine. *Fine Preserving: M.F.K. Fisher's Annotated Edition of Catherine Plagemann's Cookbook*. California: Aris Books, 1986.

PLOTKIN, Fred. *The Authentic Pasta Book*. New York: Simon & Schuster, 1985.

ROBERTSON, Laurel, FLINDERS, Carol & GODFREY, Bronwen. *Laurel's Kitchen: A Handbook for Vegetarian Cookery and Nutrition*. California: Nilgiri Press, 1976.

ROMER, Elizabeth. *Italian Pizza and Hearth Breads*. New York: (C. N. Potter Books) Crown, 1987.

SCHNEIDER, Elizabeth. *Uncommon Fruits and Vegetables: A Commonsense Guide*. New York: Harper & Row, 1986.

SYLVESTRE, J & PLANCHE, J. *Les Bases de la Cuisine*. Paris: J. Lanore, 1982.

UBALDI, Jack & CROSSMAN, Elizabeth. *Jack Ubaldi's Meat Book*. New York: Macmillan, 1987.

WILSON, C. Anne. *The Book of Marmalade*. London: Constable, 1985.

NATIONAL CUISINES

ALBERINI, Massimo & MISTRETTA, Giorgio. *Guida all'Italia Gastronomica*. Milan: Touring Club Italiano, 1984.

ANDERSON, Jean. *The Food of Portugal*. New York: William Morrow, 1986.

BENGHIAT, Suzy. *Middle Eastern Cookery*. London: Weidenfeld and Nicholson, 1984.

BRIZOVA, Joza. *The Czechoslovak Cookbook*. New York: Crown, 1965.

BONI, Ada. *Il Talismano della Felicità*. Rome: Colombo, 1965.

BRENNAN, Jennifer. *The Original Thai Cookbook*. New York: Coward, McCann & Geoghegan, 1981.

BUGIALLI, Guiliano. *The Fine Art of Italian Cooking*. New York: Quadrangle Books, 1977.

CASAS, Penelope. *The Foods and Wines of Spain*. New York: Alfred A. Knopf, 1983.

CRAIG, Elizabeth. *Scandinavian Cooking*. London: André Deutsch, 1958.

CREWE, Quentin. *International Pocket Food Book*. London: Mitchell Beazley, 1980.

DE ANDRADE, Maragette. *Brazilian Cookery: Traditional and Modern*. Vermont: Charles E. Tuttle Co., 1965.

DEVI, Yamuna. *Lord Krishna's Cuisine: The Art of Indian Vegetarian Cooking*. New York: Bala Books, 1987.

ELLISON, J. Audrey. *The Great Scandinavian Cook Book*. New York: Crown, 1967.

GOLDSTEIN, Darra. *A Taste of Russia*. London: Robert Hale, 1983.

HAZAN, Marcella. *More Classic Italian Cooking*. New York: Alfred A. Knopf, 1983.

HAZELTON, Nika. *Classic Scandinavian Cooking*. London: André Deutsch, 1958.

JAFFREY, Madhur. *A Taste of India*. London: Pavilion Books, 1985.

KENNEDY, Diana. *The Cuisines of Mexico*. New York: Harper & Row, 1972.

KUO, Irene. *The Key to Chinese Cooking*. New York: Alfred A. Knopf, 1978.

LANG, George. *The Cuisine of Hungary*. New York: Atheneum, 1971.

LANGSETH-CHRISTIANSEN, Lillian. *Gourmet's Old Vienna Cookbook*. New York: Gourmet, 1964.

MIRODAN, Vladimir. *The Balkan Cookbook*. Lennard Publishing Ltd, 1987.

OCHOROWICZ-MONATOWA, Marja. *Polish Cookery*. New York: Crown, 1958.

OJAKANGAS, Beatrice A. *The Finnish Cookbook*. New York: Crown, 1977.

ORTIZ, Elisabeth Lambert. *The Book of Latin American Cooking*. New York: Alfred A. Knopf, 1979.

ORTIZ, Elisabeth Lambert. *The Complete Book of Caribbean Cooking*. New York: Ballantine Books, 1986.

OWEB, Sri. *Indonesian Food and Cooking*. London: Prospect Books, 1980.

RODEN, Claudia. *A Book of Middle Eastern Food*. London: Thomas Nelson & Sons, 1968.

SAHNI, Julie. *Classic Indian Cooking*. New York: William Morrow, 1980.

SIMONDS, Nina. *Classic Chinese Cuisine*. Boston: Houghton Mifflin, 1982.

TSUJI, Shizuo. *Japanese Cooking: A simple art*. Tokyo: Kondasha International, 1980.

WILSON, Anne. *A West African Cookbook*. New York: M. Evans & Co., 1971.

WOLFERT, Paula. *Couscous and Other Good Food from Morocco*. New York: Harper and Row, 1973.

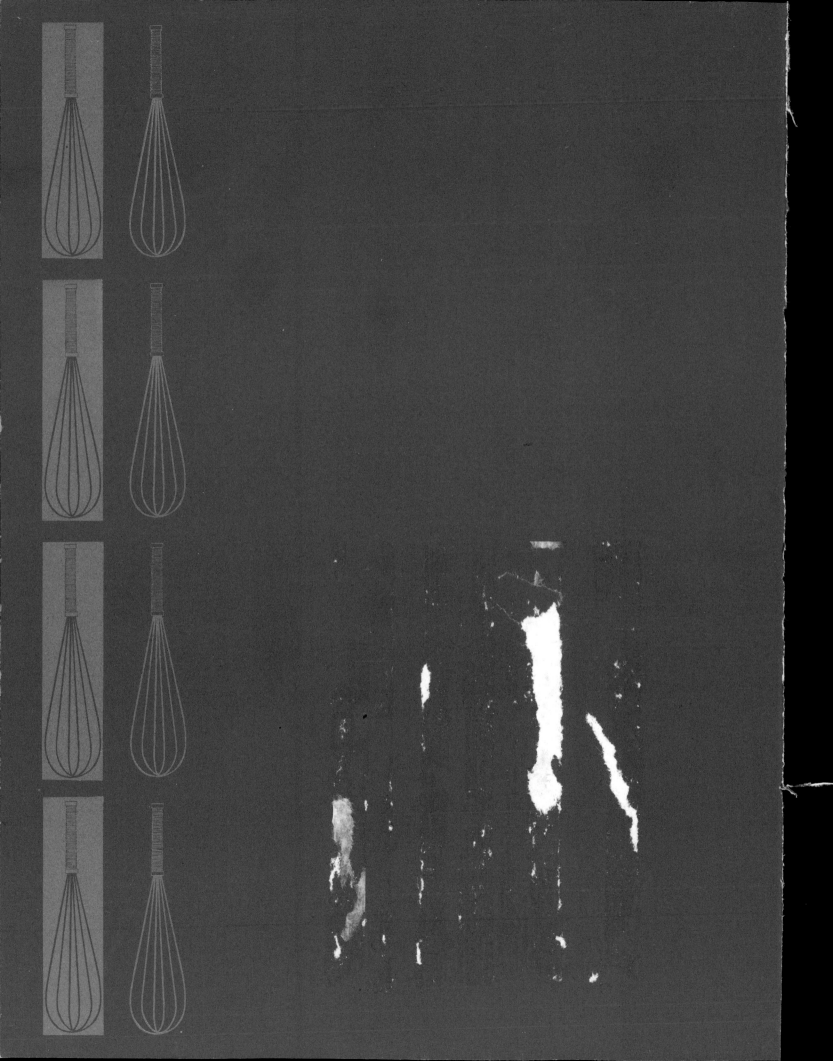